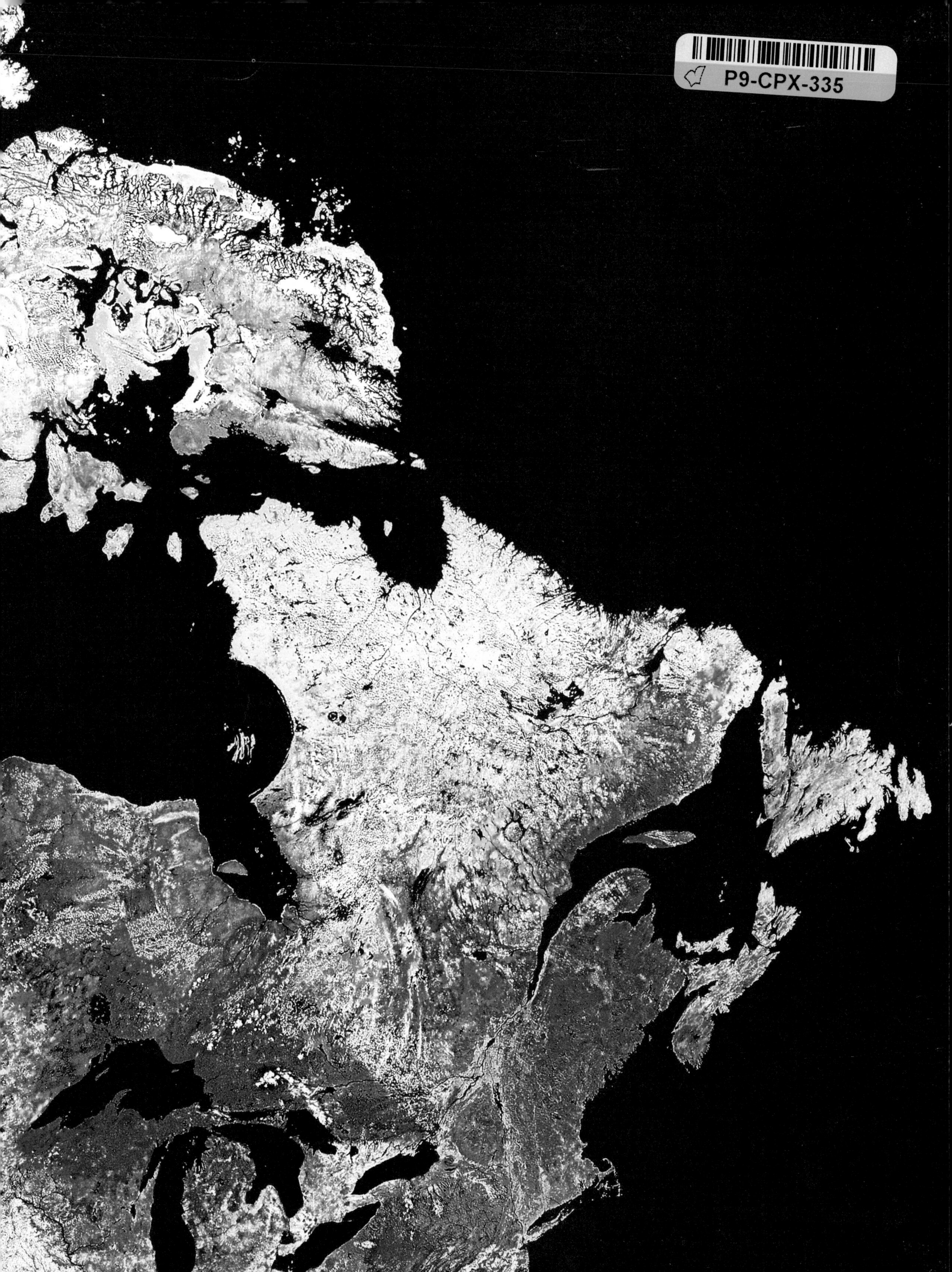

CANADIAN OXFORD SCHOOL ATLAS

6TH EDITION

Edited by Quentin H. Stanford

Toronto **OXFORD UNIVERSITY PRESS**

2 Contents

Canada, satellite images 4·5
Latitude and longitude 6
Map projections 7
Understanding topographic maps 8·9

Canada Thematic

Canada 10·11
Pleistocene glaciation 10
Geology 12
Glacial effect on landforms 12
Landforms 13
Climate: Isotherms 14
Temperature range 14
Mean annual precipitation 15
Mean annual snowfall 15
Thunderstorms and
tornadoes 15
Air masses and winds 15
January wind chill 16
Growing season 16
Sunshine 16
Climate regions 17
Natural vegetation, forestry 18
Ecozones 19
Fishing: Pacific Coast 19
Atlantic Coast 19
Soils 20
Agriculture 20
Agricultural lands 21
Wheat production and export 21
Endangered lands and species 22
Water resources, electrical power 23
Great Lakes pollution 23

Electricity trade 23
Nonfuel minerals 24
Fuel minerals 25
Production and consumption 25
Manufacturing: Value added by
manufacturing 26·27
Southern Ontario 26
Southern Québec 27
Population distribution, 1991 28
Population distribution, 1901 28
Native peoples 29
First language/ethnic origin 29
Immigrant population 29

Canada Topographic (Physical/Political)

Atlantic Provinces 30·31
Nova Scotia and Prince Edward
Island 31
Québec 32·33
Ontario 34·35
Central Canada 36·37
Central Ontario 38
Manitoba 39
Saskatchewan 40
Alberta 41
British Columbia 42·43
Southwestern BC 42
Northern Canada 44·45

North America Urban Land Use

Vancouver, Toronto 46
Montréal, Ottawa, Halifax 47
Edmonton, Calgary, Winnipeg 48
San Francisco 49
New York 50
Los Angeles 51
Boston, Detroit 52
Chicago, Pittsburgh 53

North and South America

Relief 54·55
Minerals, build 55
Climate 56·57
Land use: Agriculture 58·59
Natural vegetation 59
Population and communications 60·61
Political 61
U.S.A. 62·63
Northeastern U.S.A. 64·65
Mexico, Central America and
the Caribbean 66·67
Trinidad 66
Barbados 66
Panama Canal 67
Jamaica 67
South America 68·69
Rio de Janeiro (urban land use) 69

Europe

Relief 70
European economic organizations 70
Climate 71
Land use 72
Population and communications 73
Europe 74·75
Western Europe 76·77
Ruhr (urban land use) 76
British Isles 78
Scandinavia and Iceland 79
Eastern Europe 80·81
London (urban land use) 82
Paris, Berlin (urban land use) 83

Asia

Relief 84
Climate 85
Land use 86

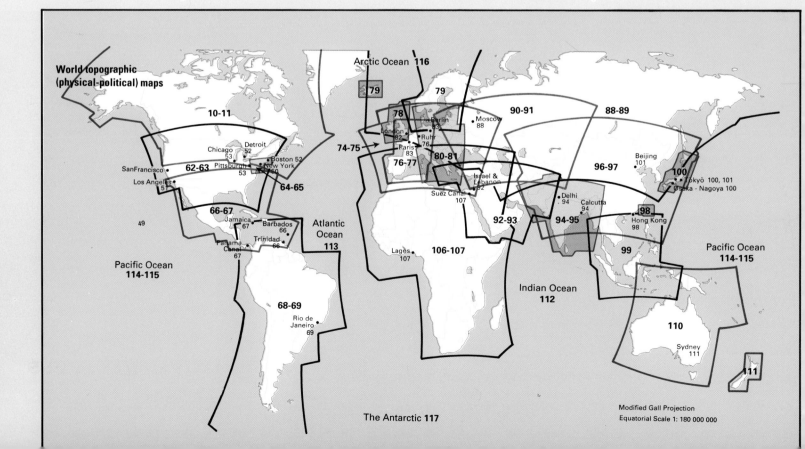

World topographic
(physical-political) maps

Arctic Ocean **116**

10-11

79   **79**

78   Berlin   Moscow **88**   **90-91**   **88-89**

74-75 → London **82**   Ruhr **76**   Paris **83**

Chicago **53**   Detroit **52**   **62-63** Pittsburgh **53**   Boston **52**   New York **50**   **76-77**   **80-81**   Beijing **101**

SanFrancisco **49**   Los Angeles **51**   **64-65**   Israel & Lebanon **82**   **96-97**   **100** Tōkyō 100, 101   Ōsaka - Nagoya 100

66-67   Suez Canal **107**   Delhi **94**   Calcutta **94**   **98**

Jamaica **67**   Barbados **66**   Atlantic Ocean **113**   **92-93**   **94-95**   Hong Kong **98**

Panama Canal **67**   Trinidad **66**   Lagos **107**   **106-107**   **99**

Pacific Ocean **114-115**   Rio de Janeiro **69**   Indian Ocean **112**   Pacific Ocean **114-115**

68-69   **110**   Sydney **111**

The Antarctic **117**   **111**

Modified Gall Projection
Equatorial Scale 1: 180 000 000

Contents 3

Population and communications 87
Northern Eurasia 88·89
Moscow (urban land use) 88
Central Eurasia 90·91
Middle East 92·93
Israel and Lebanon 92
Southern Asia 94·95
Delhi, Calcutta (urban land use) 94
China 96·97
Taiwan, Hong Kong 98
South East Asia 99
Japan 100
Ōsaka - Nagoya area 100
Tōkyō area 100
Tōkyō, Beijing (urban land use) 101

Africa
Relief 102
Political 102
Climate 103
Land use 104
Tsetse fly 104
Population and communications 105
Africa 106·107
Suez Canal 107
Lagos (urban land use) 107

Australasia
Climate 108
Land use, population and
 communications 109
Australasia 110
Sydney (urban land use) 111
New Zealand 111

Oceans
Indian Ocean 112
Rainfall during the summer
 monsoon 112

Atlantic Ocean 113
Pacific Ocean 114·115
Fiji 114
Subregions of Oceania 114
Hawaiian Islands 115

Poles
The Arctic 116
The Antarctic 117

World
Political 118·119
Physical 120·121
Plate tectonics 120
The moving continents 120·121
Climate: Rainfall 122·123
 Temperature, ocean
  currents 122·123
 Pressure and winds 122·123
 Tropical revolving storms 123
 Air masses 123
Climate regions 124
Water 124
Natural vegetation 125
Soils 125
Natural hazards: Storms and
  floods 126
 Earthquakes and
  volcanoes 126
Environmental damage:
 Drought, fire and pests 127
 Tropical deforestation 127
Global warming 128
Atmospheric pollutants 129
Fresh water 130
Protected areas and
 endangered species 130
Nuclear 131
Military expenditure 131
Population 132·133

Quality of life: Life expectancy at birth 134
 Medical care 134
 Education 135
 Radios and TVs 135
Agriculture: Agriculture 136
 Percentage of labour
  force in agriculture 136
 Nutrition 137
 Cropland 137
 Irrigated land 137
Pacific Rim countries, trade with
 Canada 138·139
Standard Time 138
Economic development:
 Gross Domestic Product 140
 Industrialization 140
 Employment 141
 Givers and receivers of aid 141
Energy: Oil 142
 Gas 142
 Coal 143
 Electricity 143
Energy consumption 144

Gazetteer
How to use the gazetteer 145
Gazetteer of Canada 146·156
Gazetteer of the World 157·184
Glossary 216

Canada   Statistics
Land 185
Population 185·190
Agriculture 190·193
Forestry and fishing 194·195
Mining 196
Energy 197·199
Manufacturing 199·200
Transportation 200·202
Trade 202
The economy 203
Conservation and pollution 204·205
Climate 206·207

World   Statistics
Trade 208·209
Demographics 210·214
Acknowledgements, credits 215
Notes to countries and regions
 of the world statistical data 216

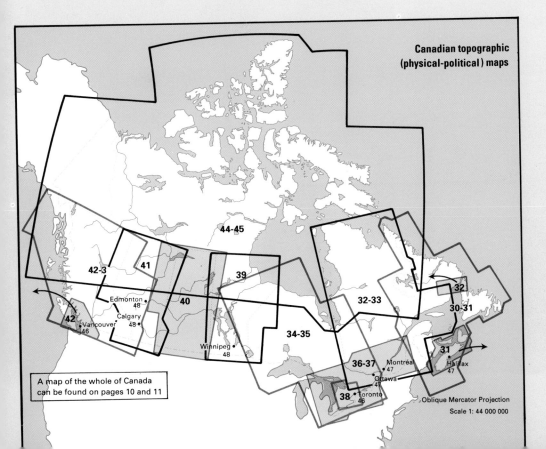

Canadian topographic
(physical-political) maps

A map of the whole of Canada
can be found on pages 10 and 11

Oblique Mercator Projection
Scale 1: 44 000 000

These images were produced by Landsat satellites which orbit the earth 14.5 times each day at an altitude of approximately 900 km. Each image covers approximately 34 000 km²; in order to be visible, objects on the earth must be at least 30 m² in size.

The satellite does not take a photograph in the normal sense. Rather, sensors record the reflected light, heat, and radio waves from the microwave portion of the electromagnetic spectrum, through the infra-red and visible light sections, to the near ultra-violet sections. This information is digitized and sent back to earth, where it is stored on computer tapes. It is then transformed into images such as the ones shown here.

Since every object on the surface absorbs and reflects radiation differently, different surfaces such as trees, rocks, concrete, and crops can be easily recognized. For the most part, however, the colours we see on the images are "false" colours. This is because each surface reflects one part of the electromagnetic spectrum better than another. For example, green vegetation appears in various red tones since it reflects infra-red radiation more strongly; urban areas show up in blue and grey; and bare ground is seen from black to blue to white depending on the moisture and organic content of the soil. On some images, notably the one of Toronto on page 9, colours of the features have been changed to normal ones. Thus on this image vegetation is shown in green.

Scale 1:1 000 000

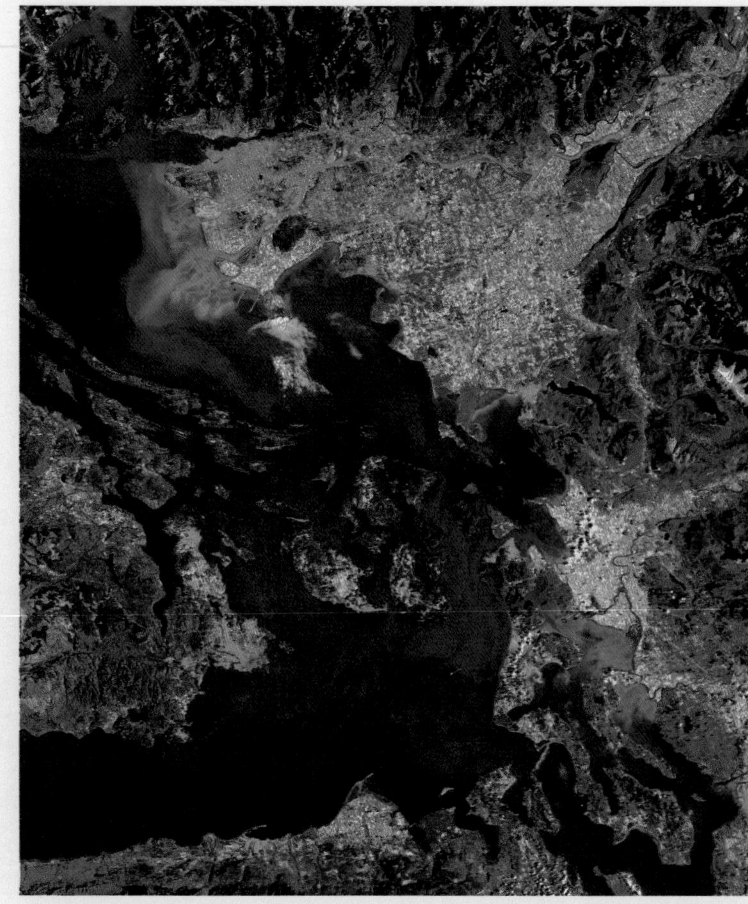

Southwestern British Columbia, including the cities of Vancouver and Victoria.

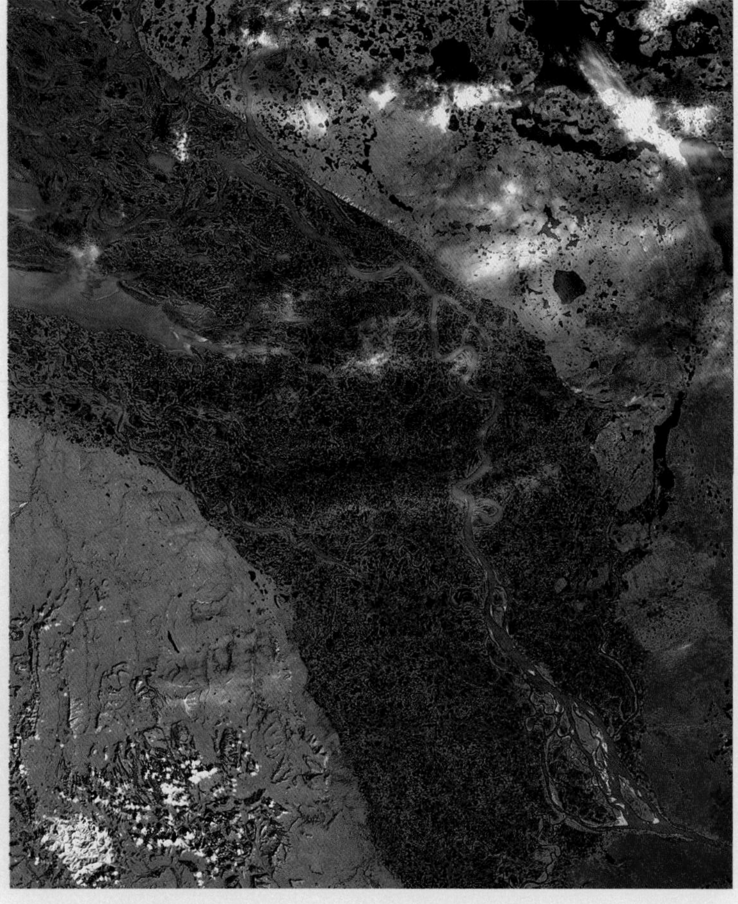

The Mackenzie River delta, with the town of Inuvik in the centre.

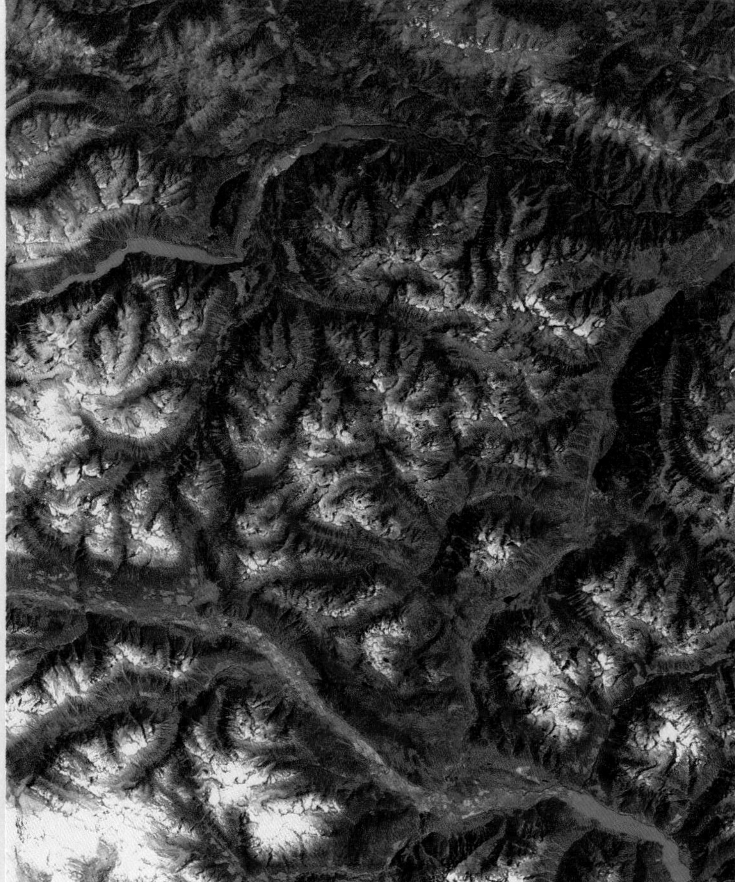

The Fraser River near Lillooet, British Columbia.

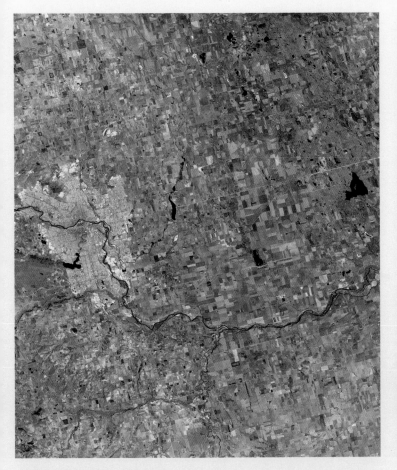

Calgary, Alberta, on the Bow River.

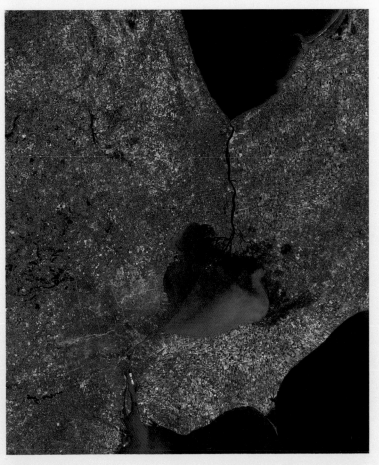

Lake Huron, Detroit-Windsor, and western Lake Erie.

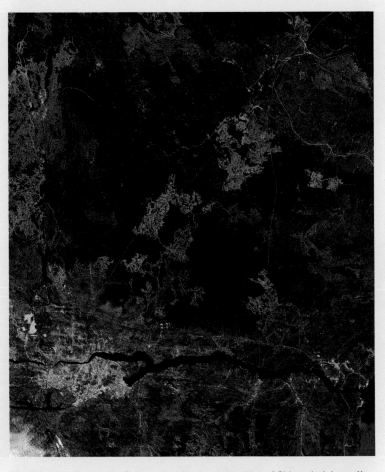

The Canadian Shield, the Saguenay valley, and the cities of Chicoutimi-Jonquière.

Southern Nova Scotia, including the Annapolis Valley and Halifax-Dartmouth.

6 Latitude and Longitude

The earth is a small, blue planet.
Seen from space it has no right way up.

An imaginary grid is used to pinpoint the position of any place on earth.
This grid consists of two sets of lines. Those running east and west are called parallels of latitude, and those extending north and south are called meridians of longitude. Both are measured in degrees.

Latitude
Parallels of latitude are concentric circles that diminish in diameter from the equator to the poles. They are used to determine locations either north or south in relation to the equator. North of the equator parallels are designated north (N), while those south of the equator are labelled south (S). The equator is at latitude 0°. The poles are at latitudes 90°N and 90°S.

Longitude
Meridians of longitude pass through both poles intersecting all parallels of latitude at right angles. The meridian through Greenwich, England was chosen in 1884 as the Prime Meridian and given the value 0°. Meridians determine locations east (E) or west (W) of the Prime Meridian. The 180° meridian of longitude was designated the International Date Line and has a special role in the operation of Standard Time.

The equator divides the earth into halves: the Northern Hemisphere and the Southern Hemisphere. The Prime Meridian and the 180° meridian together also divide the earth into halves: the Western Hemisphere and the Eastern Hemisphere.

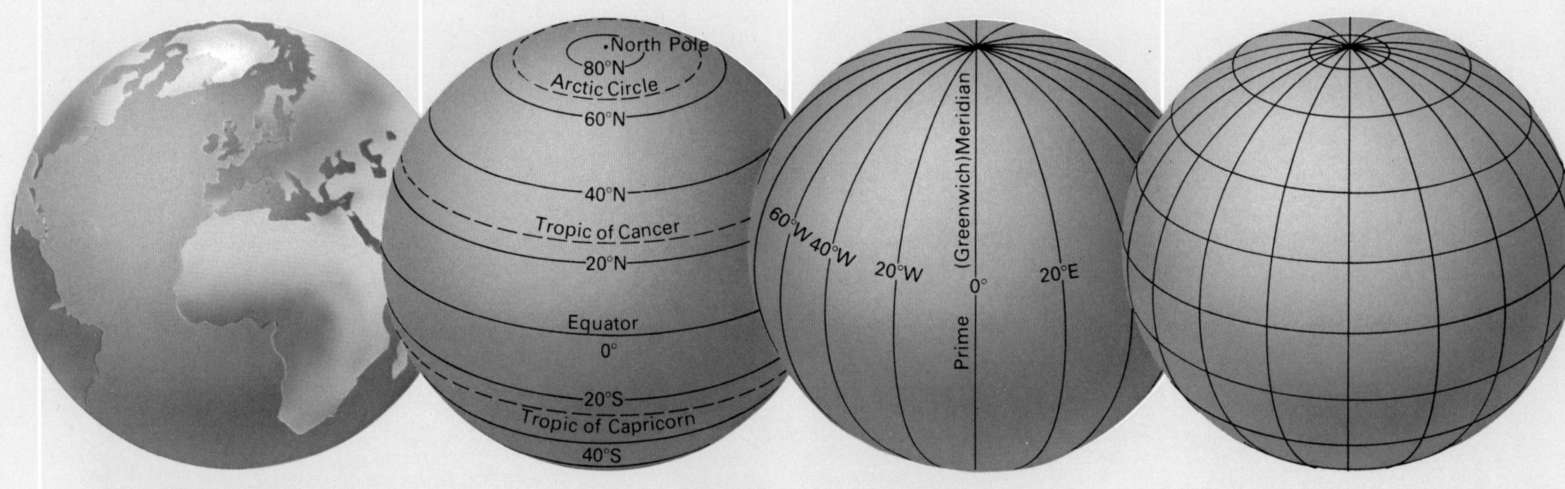

When used together, lines of latitude and longitude form a grid. The position of places on the surface of the earth can be located accurately using this grid.

To locate places really accurately, each degree of latitude and longitude can be divided into 60 minutes and each minute into 60 seconds. A location specified in degrees, minutes, and seconds (for example, 44° 25' 14" N, 80° 45' 36" W) will describe a location accurately to within a few metres.

Extract from a Meteosat view of Europe, 35 790 km above the equator.
(This is an enlargement of the image of the earth shown at the top of the page.)

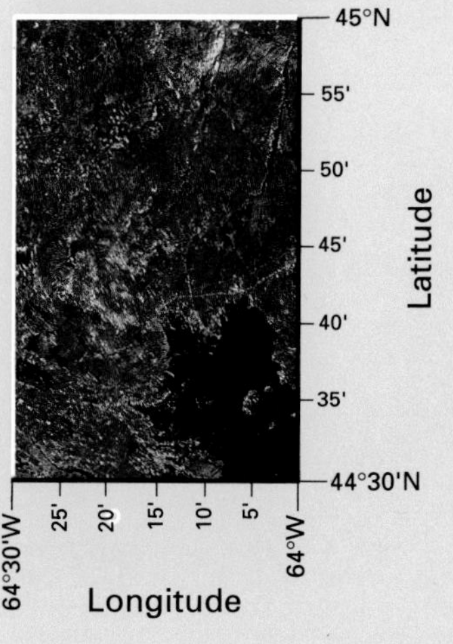

Extract from the Landsat view of Southern Nova Scotia shown on page 5.
Scale 1: 1 000 000.

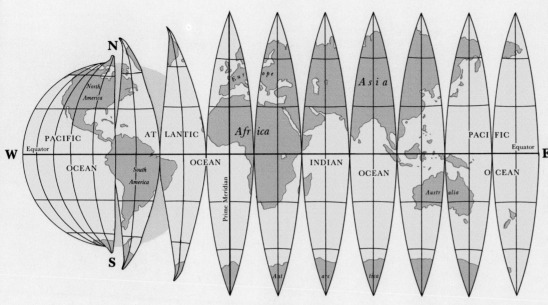

The most accurate way of looking at the earth's land and sea areas is to use a globe. For obvious reasons maps are more convenient to use than globes. One method of changing the surface of the globe into a map is to unpeel strips or gores from the globe's surface, but such a method has obvious drawbacks. Since it is impossible to flatten the curved surface of the earth without stretching or cutting part of it, it is necessary to employ other methods in order to produce an orderly system of parallels and meridians on which a map can be drawn. Such systems are referred to as **map projections**.

There are two main types of projections: **equal area projections,** where the area of any territory is shown in correct size proportion to other areas, and **conformal projections,** where the emphasis is on showing shape correctly. No map can be both equal area and conformal, though some projections are designed to minimize distortions in both area and shape.

The **Oblique Aitoff projection** is equal area. The arrangement of the land masses allows a good view of routes in the northern hemisphere. The position of North America and Asia on either side of the Arctic is shown clearly.

Mercator's projection is a conformal projection and was initially designed (1569) to be used for navigation. Any straight line on the map is a line of constant compass bearing. Straight lines are not the shortest routes, however. Shape is accurate on a Mercator projection but the size of the land masses is distorted. Land is shown larger the further away it is from the equator. (For example, Alaska is shown four times larger than its actual size.)

——— Line of constant compass bearing

- - - - Shortest route

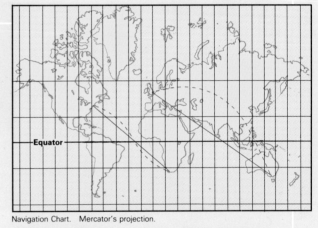

Navigation Chart. Mercator's projection.

Peters' projection is an equal area projection. The land masses are the correct size in relation to each other, but there is considerable distortion in shape. This projection has been used to emphasize the size of the poor countries of the South compared with the rich countries of the North.

——— Brandt Line

[ ] Rich North.

[ ] Poor South.

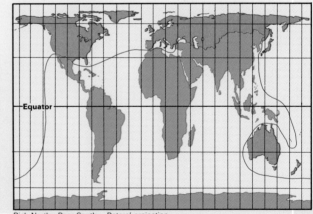

Rich North—Poor South. Peters' projection.

Gall's projection compromises between equal area and conformal. A modified version is used in this atlas as a general world map. This map shows states which have gained their independence since 1945.

[ ] States independent since 1945.

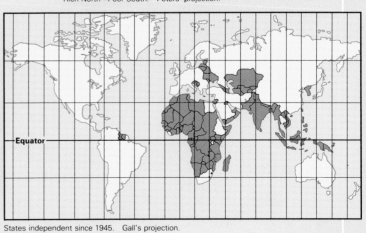

States independent since 1945. Gall's projection.

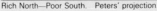

Major air routes. Oblique Aitoff projection.

Understanding Topographic Maps

Topographic maps (physical-political) show the main features of the physical and human landscape. There are small differences in the symbols and colours used for the maps of Canada and those for the rest of the World.

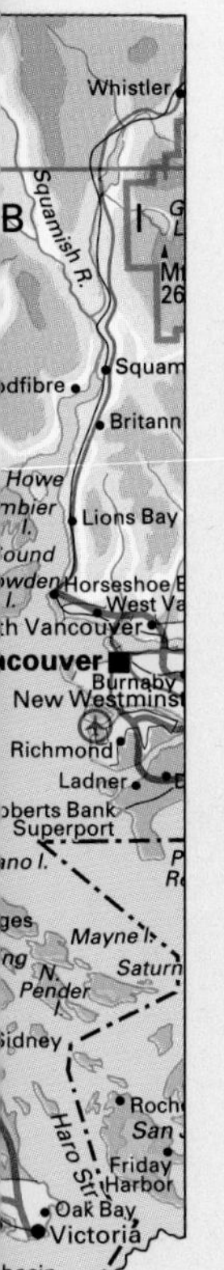

Canadian Maps

Boundaries

international

province, territory

region, county, district, regional municipality

national park/ provincial park

Communications

expressway/other multilane highway

other highway

winter road

railway

canal

⊕ major airport

✦ other airport

Cities and towns

◇ built-up areas

■ over 1 million inhabitants

● more than 100 000 inhabitants

• smaller urban places

Physical features

marsh

ice cap

Scale 1:5 000 000

0   50   100 km

Scale is shown by a representative fraction and a scale line.

Non-Canadian maps

Boundaries

international

disputed

internal

national park

Communications

expressway

other major road

track

railway

canal

✈ major airport

Cities and towns

◇ built-up areas

■ over 1 million inhabitants

● more than 100 000 inhabitants

• smaller towns

+ historic sites

Physical features

seasonal river/lake

marsh

salt pan

ice cap

sand dunes

coral reef

Place names
Local spellings are used. Anglicised and other common spellings are shown in brackets.

e.g. **Roma** (Rome)

This atlas has been designed for English speaking readers and so all places have been named using the Roman alphabet. Compare this extract of the map of Southern Asia with the same map printed in Bengali.

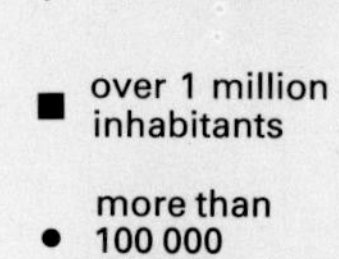

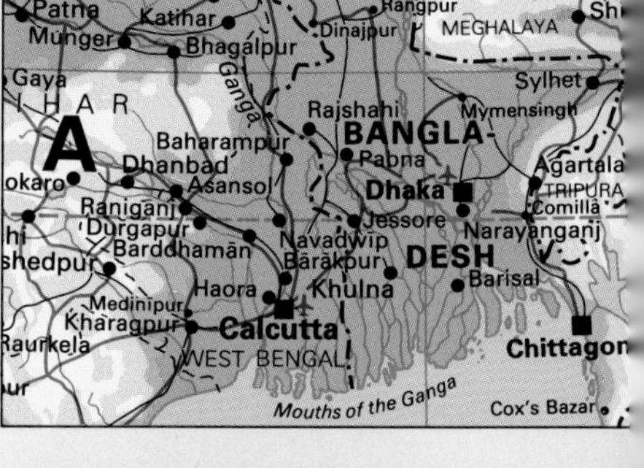

Type style
Contrasting type styles are used to show the difference between physical features, settlements, and administrative areas. Physical features (except for peaks) are shown in italics.

e.g. *Hautes Fagnes*   *Maas*

Peaks are shown in condensed type.

e.g. Hohe Acht 746

Settlement names are shown in upper and lower case.

e.g. Valkenswaard

Administrative areas are shown in capital letters.

e.g. LIÈGE

The importance of places is shown by the size of the type and whether the type face is **bold**, medium or light.

e.g. Malmédy   Bergheim   Duisburg

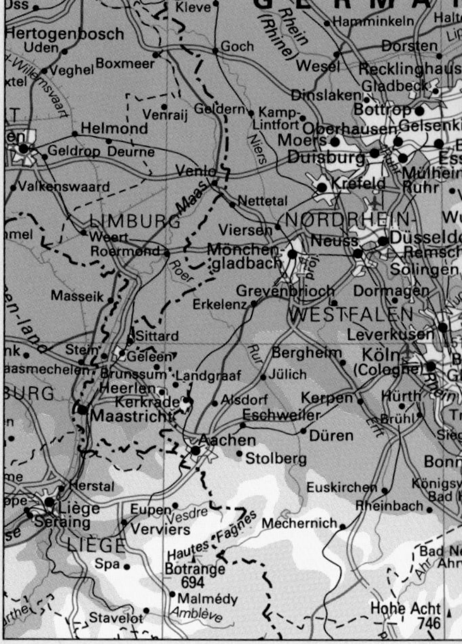

Land height
Colours on topographic maps refer only to the height of the land. They do not give information about land use or other aspects of the environment.

Sea ice
White stipple patterns over the sea colour show the seasonal extent of sea ice.

Sea Ice

unnavigable

pack ice - average fall minimum

pack ice - average spring max.

Sea depth

metres below sea level

200
3000
4000
5000
6000

sea depths shown as minus numbers

Land height

metres

5000
3000
2000
1000
500
300
200
100

sea level
land below sea level

▲ spot height in metres

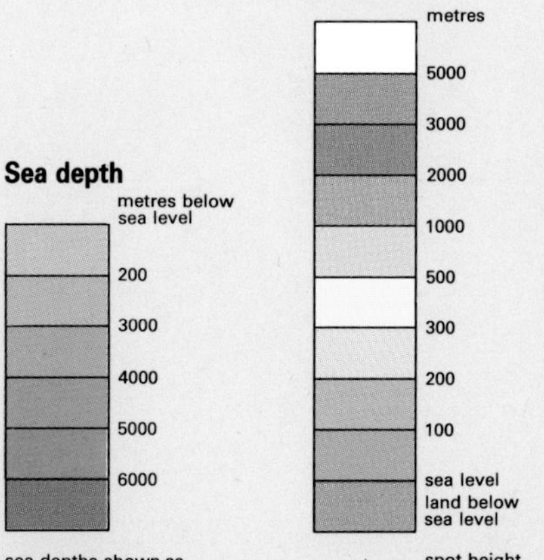

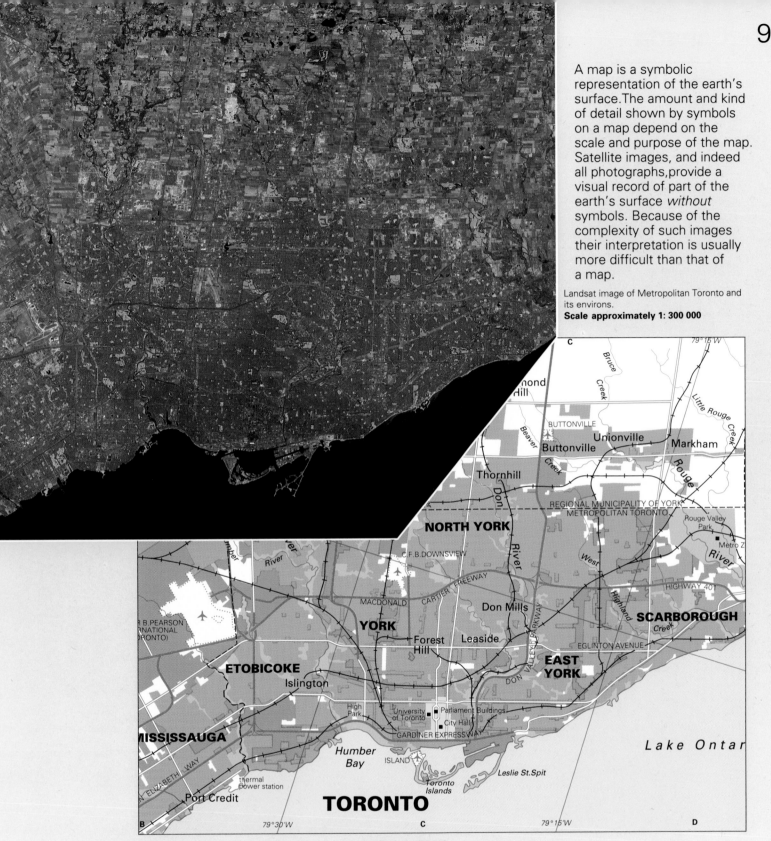

A map is a symbolic representation of the earth's surface. The amount and kind of detail shown by symbols on a map depend on the scale and purpose of the map. Satellite images, and indeed all photographs, provide a visual record of part of the earth's surface *without* symbols. Because of the complexity of such images their interpretation is usually more difficult than that of a map.

Landsat image of Metropolitan Toronto and its environs.
Scale approximately 1: 300 000

Extract from the urban land use map of Toronto, page 46. **Scale 1: 300 000**

Extract from the topographic map of Central Ontario, page 38.
Scale 1: 1 250 000

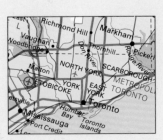

Extract from the topographic map of Ontario, page 35.
Scale 1: 5 000 000

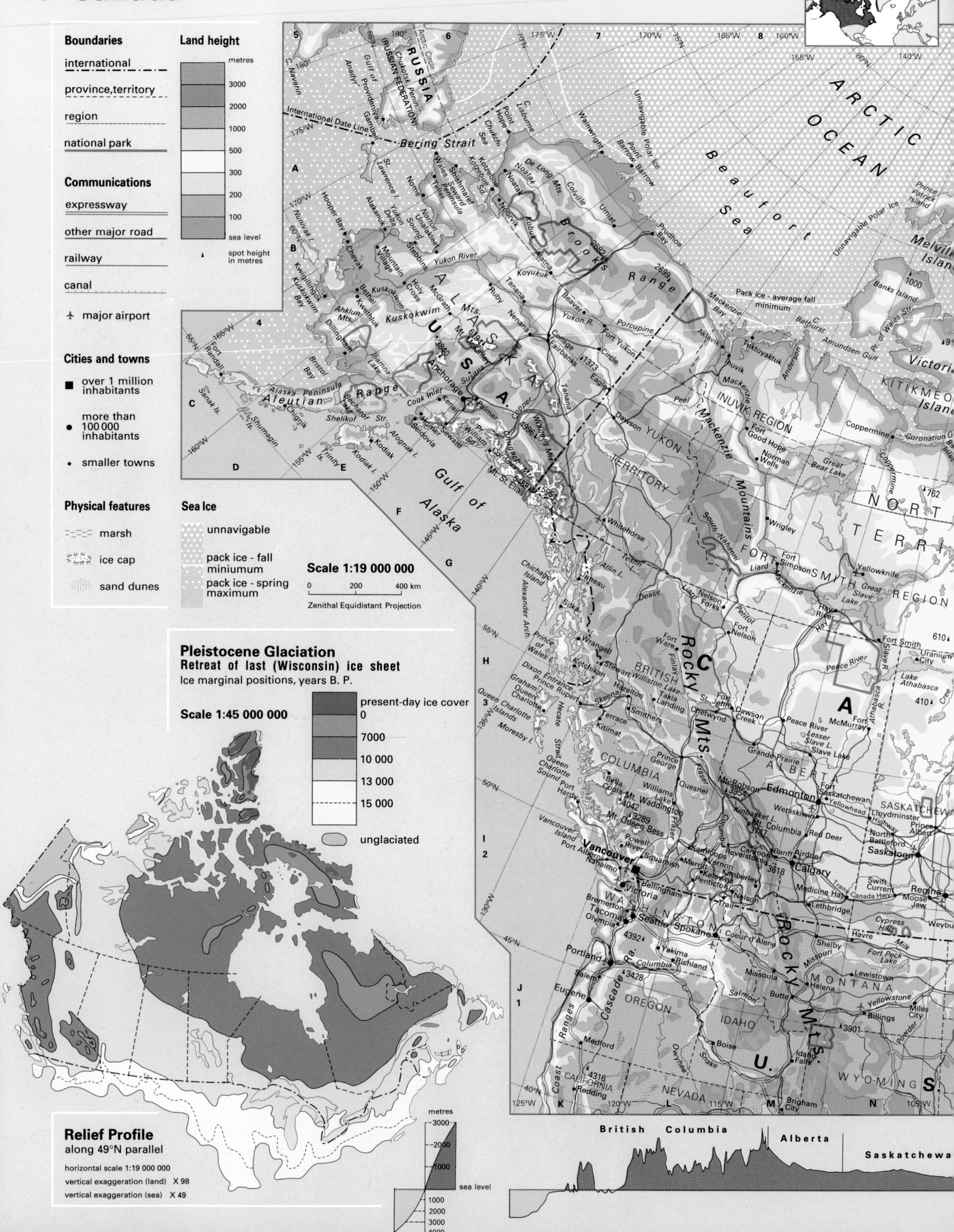

Boundaries

international

province, territory

region

national park

Land height

metres

3000
2000
1000
500
300
200
100
sea level

▲ spot height in metres

Communications

expressway

other major road

railway

canal

✈ major airport

Cities and towns

■ over 1 million inhabitants

● more than 100 000 inhabitants

• smaller towns

Physical features

marsh

ice cap

sand dunes

Sea Ice

unnavigable

pack ice - fall miniumum

pack ice - spring maximum

Scale 1:19 000 000

0   200   400 km

Zenithal Equidistant Projection

Pleistocene Glaciation
Retreat of last (Wisconsin) ice sheet
Ice marginal positions, years B. P.

Scale 1:45 000 000

present-day ice cover

0
7000
10 000
13 000
15 000

unglaciated

Relief Profile
along 49°N parallel

horizontal scale 1:19 000 000
vertical exaggeration (land) X 98
vertical exaggeration (sea) X 49

Distance chart

official highway distances, in kilometres

Calgary	Charlottetown	Edmonton	Fredericton	Halifax	Montréal	Ottawa	Québec	Regina	St. John's	Saskatoon	Thunder Bay	Toronto	Vancouver	Victoria	Whitehorse	Winnipeg	Yellowknife	
•	4917	299	4558	5042	3743	3553	4014	764	6183	620	2050	3434	1057	1123	2385	1336	1811	Calgary
	•	4949	359	232	1184	1374	945	4163	1294	4421	2878	1724	5985	6051	7034	3592	6460	Charlottetown
		•	4598	5082	3764	3574	4035	785	6212	528	2071	3455	1244	1310	2086	1357	1511	Edmonton
			•	346	834	1024	586	3813	1622	4070	2527	1373	5634	5700	6684	3241	6109	Fredericton
				•	1318	1508	912	4297	1349	4554	3011	1857	6119	6185	7168	3726	6593	Halifax
					•	190	270	2979	2448	3236	1693	539	4801	4867	5850	2408	5275	Montréal
						•	460	2789	2638	3046	1503	399	4611	4677	5660	2218	5086	Ottawa
							•	3249	2208	3507	1963	810	5071	5137	6120	2678	5546	Québec
								•	5427	257	1286	2670	1822	1888	2871	571	2297	Regina
									•	5684	4141	2987	7248	7314	8298	4855	7723	St. John's
										•	1543	2927	1677	1743	2614	829	2039	Saskatoon
											•	1384	3108	3174	4157	715	3582	Thunder Bay
												•	4492	4558	5528	2099	4966	Toronto
													•	66	2697	2232	2411	Vancouver
														•	2763	2298	2477	Victoria
															•	3524	2704	Whitehorse
																•	2868	Winnipeg
																	•	Yellowknife

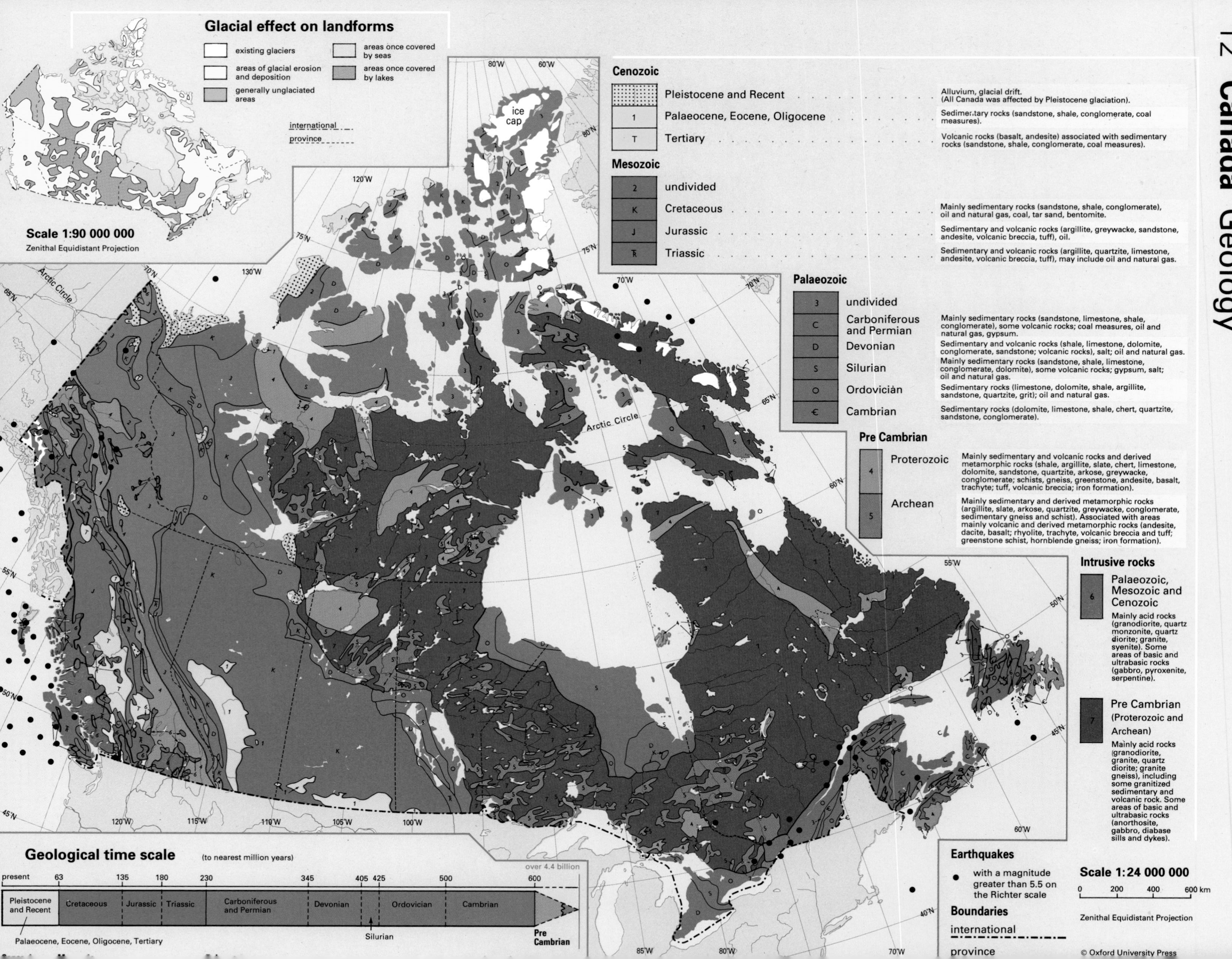

Glacial effect on landforms

existing glaciers		areas once covered by seas
areas of glacial erosion and deposition		areas once covered by lakes
generally unglaciated areas		

international --------
province --------

Scale 1:90 000 000

Zenithal Equidistant Projection

ice cap

Arctic Circle

Cenozoic

1	Pleistocene and Recent
	Palaeocene, Eocene, Oligocene
T	Tertiary

Mesozoic

2	undivided
K	Cretaceous
J	Jurassic
℞	Triassic

Palaeozoic

3	undivided
C	Carboniferous and Permian
D	Devonian
S	Silurian
O	Ordovician
€	Cambrian

Pre Cambrian

4	Proterozoic
5	Archean

Alluvium, glacial drift.
(All Canada was affected by Pleistocene glaciation).

Sedimentary rocks (sandstone, shale, conglomerate, coal measures).

Volcanic rocks (basalt, andesite) associated with sedimentary rocks (sandstone, shale, conglomerate, coal measures).

Mainly sedimentary rocks (sandstone, shale, conglomerate), oil and natural gas, coal, tar sand, bentomite.

Sedimentary and volcanic rocks (argillite, greywacke, sandstone, andesite, volcanic breccia, tuff), oil.

Sedimentary and volcanic rocks (argillite, quartzite, limestone, andesite, volcanic breccia, tuff), may include oil and natural gas.

Mainly sedimentary rocks (sandstone, limestone, shale, conglomerate), some volcanic rocks; coal measures, oil and natural gas, gypsum.

Sedimentary and volcanic rocks (shale, limestone, dolomite, conglomerate, sandstone; volcanic rocks), salt; oil and natural gas.

Mainly sedimentary rocks (sandstone, shale, limestone, conglomerate, dolomite), some volcanic rocks; gypsum, salt; oil and natural gas.

Sedimentary rocks (limestone, dolomite, shale, argillite, sandstone, quartzite, grit); oil and natural gas.

Sedimentary rocks (dolomite, limestone, shale, chert, quartzite, sandstone, conglomerate).

Mainly sedimentary and volcanic rocks and derived metamorphic rocks (shale, argillite, slate, chert, limestone, dolomite, sandstone, quartzite, arkose, greywacke, conglomerate; schists, gneiss, greenstone, andesite, basalt, trachyte; tuff, volcanic breccia; iron formation).

Mainly sedimentary and derived metamorphic rocks (argillite, slate, arkose, quartzite, greywacke, conglomerate, sedimentary gneiss and schist). Associated with areas mainly volcanic and derived metamorphic rocks (andesite, dacite, basalt; rhyolite, trachyte, volcanic breccia and tuff; greenstone schist, hornblende gneiss; iron formation).

Intrusive rocks

6	Palaeozoic, Mesozoic and Cenozoic
7	Pre Cambrian (Proterozoic and Archean)

Mainly acid rocks (granodiorite, quartz monzonite, quartz diorite; granite, syenite). Some areas of basic and ultrabasic rocks (gabbro, pyroxenite, serpentine).

Mainly acid rocks (granodiorite, granite, quartz diorite; granite gneiss), including some granitized sedimentary and volcanic rock. Some areas of basic and ultrabasic rocks (anorthosite, gabbro, diabase sills and dykes).

Earthquakes

• with a magnitude greater than 5.5 on the Richter scale

Boundaries

international --------·--------
province --------

Scale 1:24 000 000

| 0 | 200 | 400 | 600 km |

Zenithal Equidistant Projection

© Oxford University Press

Geological time scale

(to nearest million years)

present	63	135	180	230	345	405 425	500	600	over 4.4 billion
Pleistocene and Recent	Cretaceous	Jurassic	Triassic	Carboniferous and Permian	Devonian	Silurian / Ordovician	Cambrian	Pre Cambrian	

Palaeocene, Eocene, Oligocene, Tertiary

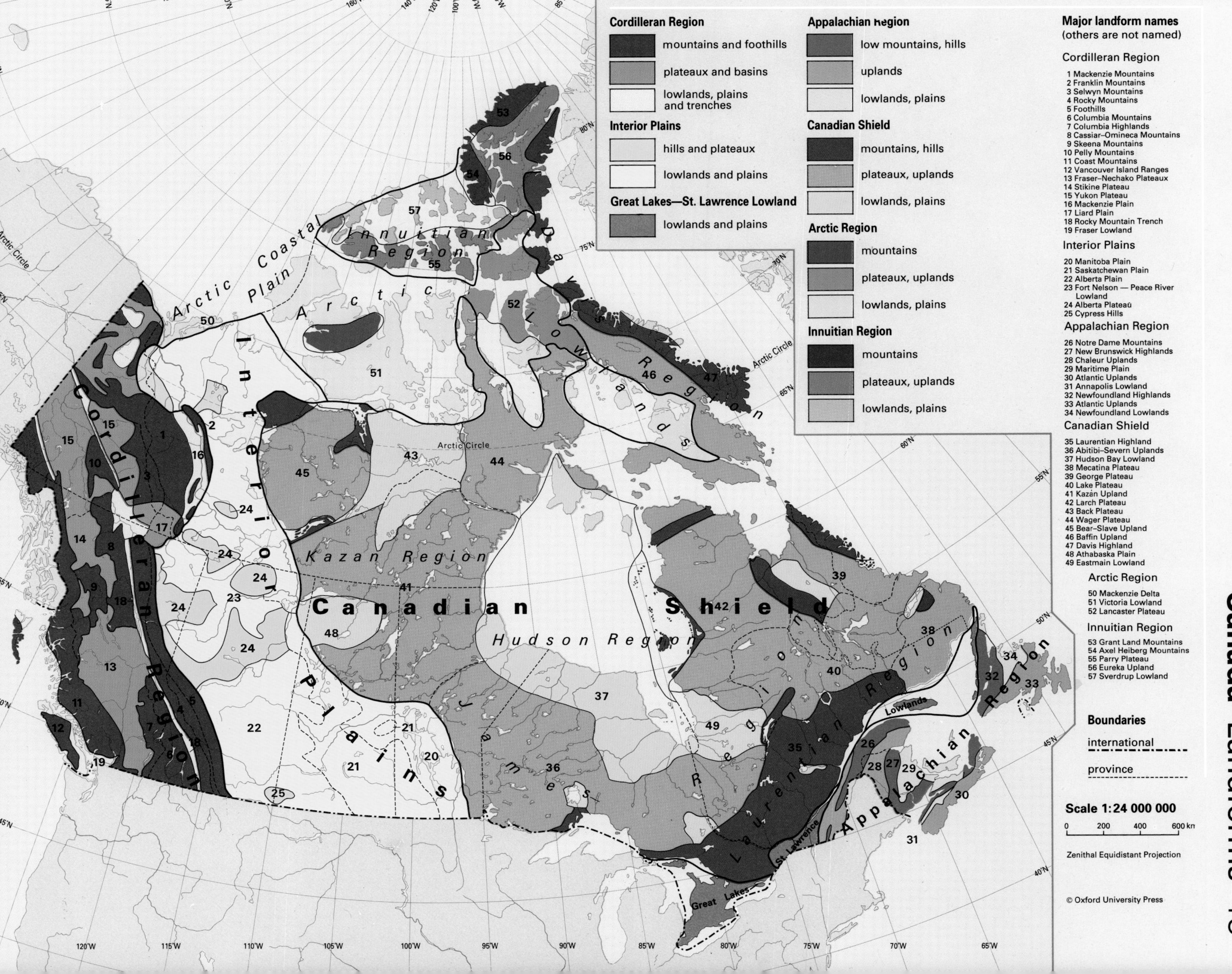

Major landform names
(others are not named)

Cordilleran Region
1 Mackenzie Mountains
2 Franklin Mountains
3 Selwyn Mountains
4 Rocky Mountains
5 Foothills
6 Columbia Mountains
7 Columbia Highlands
8 Cassiar–Omineca Mountains
9 Skeena Mountains
10 Pelly Mountains
11 Coast Mountains
12 Vancouver Island Ranges
13 Fraser–Nechako Plateaux
14 Stikine Plateau
15 Yukon Plateau
16 Mackenzie Plain
17 Liard Plain
18 Rocky Mountain Trench
19 Fraser Lowland

Interior Plains
20 Manitoba Plain
21 Saskatchewan Plain
22 Alberta Plain
23 Fort Nelson — Peace River
   Lowland
24 Alberta Plateau
25 Cypress Hills

Appalachian Region
26 Notre Dame Mountains
27 New Brunswick Highlands
28 Chaleur Uplands
29 Maritime Plain
30 Atlantic Uplands
31 Annapolis Lowland
32 Newfoundland Highlands
33 Atlantic Uplands
34 Newfoundland Lowlands

Canadian Shield
35 Laurentian Highland
36 Abitibi–Severn Uplands
37 Hudson Bay Lowland
38 Mecatina Plateau
39 George Plateau
40 Lake Plateau
41 Kazan Upland
42 Larch Plateau
43 Back Plateau
44 Wager Plateau
45 Bear–Slave Upland
46 Baffin Upland
47 Davis Highland
48 Athabaska Plain
49 Eastmain Lowland

Arctic Region
50 Mackenzie Delta
51 Victoria Lowland
52 Lancaster Plateau

Innuitian Region
53 Grant Land Mountains
54 Axel Heiberg Mountains
55 Parry Plateau
56 Eureka Upland
57 Sverdrup Lowland

Boundaries
international
province

Scale 1:24 000 000

0 200 400 600 km

Zenithal Equidistant Projection

© Oxford University Press

Cordilleran Region
mountains and foothills
plateaux and basins
lowlands, plains
and trenches

Interior Plains
hills and plateaux
lowlands and plains

Great Lakes—St. Lawrence Lowland
lowlands and plains

Appalachian region
low mountains, hills
uplands
lowlands, plains

Canadian Shield
mountains, hills
plateaux, uplands
lowlands, plains

Arctic Region
mountains
plateaux, uplands
lowlands, plains

Innuitian Region
mountains
plateaux, uplands
lowlands, plains

Heating the Earth
The Greenhouse Effect

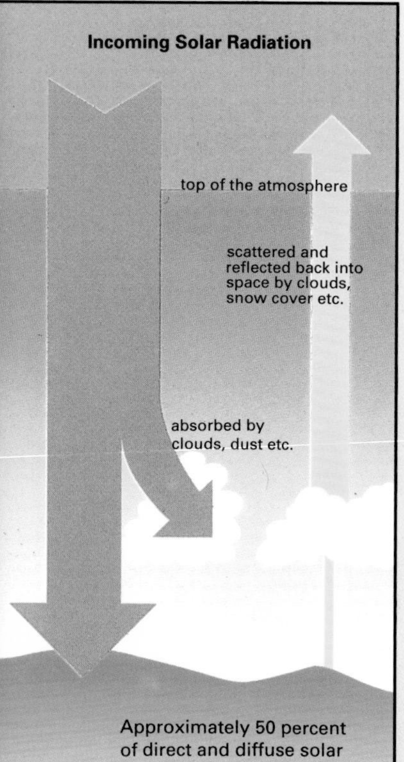

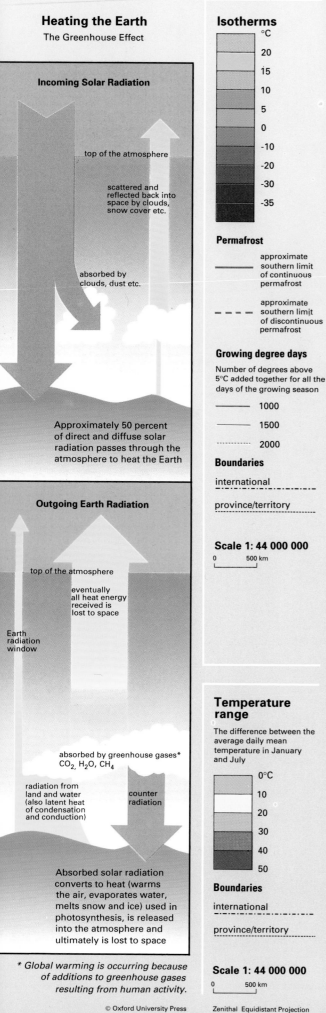

Incoming Solar Radiation

top of the atmosphere

scattered and reflected back into space by clouds, snow cover etc.

absorbed by clouds, dust etc.

Approximately 50 percent of direct and diffuse solar radiation passes through the atmosphere to heat the Earth

Outgoing Earth Radiation

top of the atmosphere

eventually all heat energy received is lost to space

Earth radiation window

absorbed by greenhouse gases* CO_2, H_2O, CH_4

radiation from land and water (also latent heat of condensation and conduction)

counter radiation

Absorbed solar radiation converts to heat (warms the air, evaporates water, melts snow and ice) used in photosynthesis, is released into the atmosphere and ultimately is lost to space

Global warming is occurring because of additions to greenhouse gases resulting from human activity.

© Oxford University Press

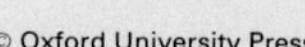

Isotherms
°C

20
15
10
5
0
-10
-20
-30
-35

Permafrost

—— approximate southern limit of continuous permafrost

- - - approximate southern limit of discontinuous permafrost

Growing degree days

Number of degrees above 5°C added together for all the days of the growing season

—— 1000
—— 1500
······ 2000

Boundaries

—— international

- - - province/territory

Scale 1: 44 000 000

0   500 km

Temperature range

The difference between the average daily mean temperature in January and July

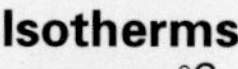

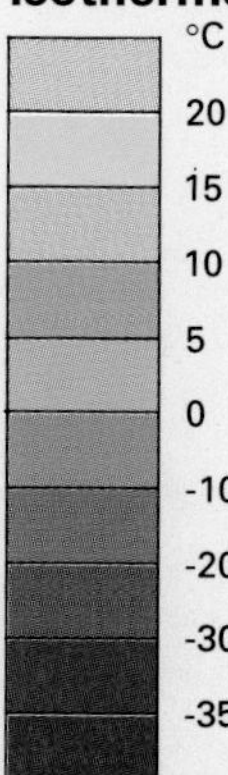

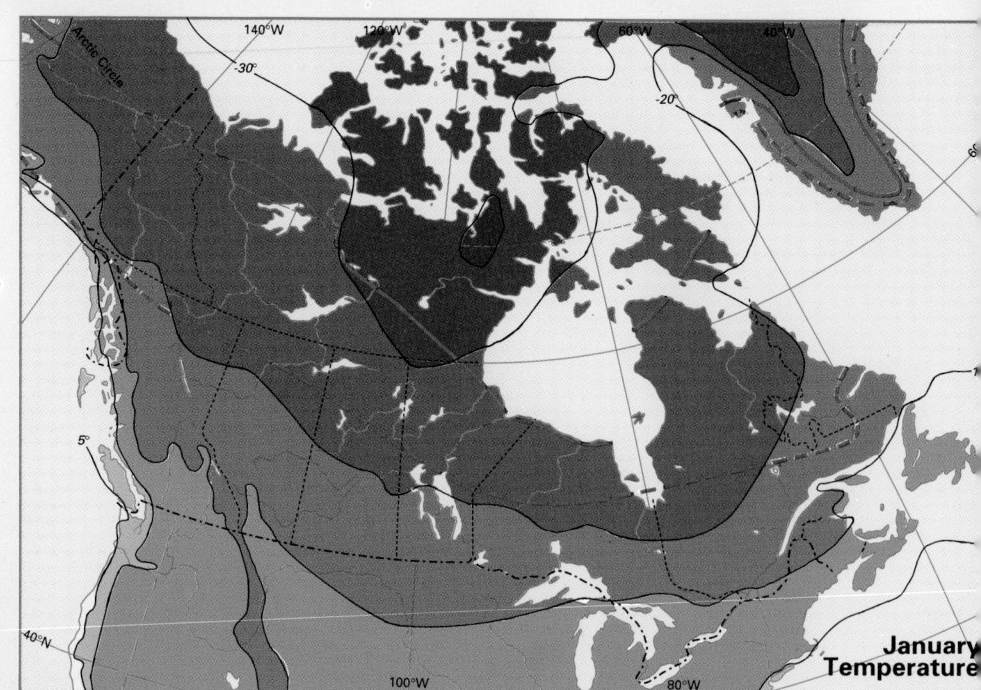

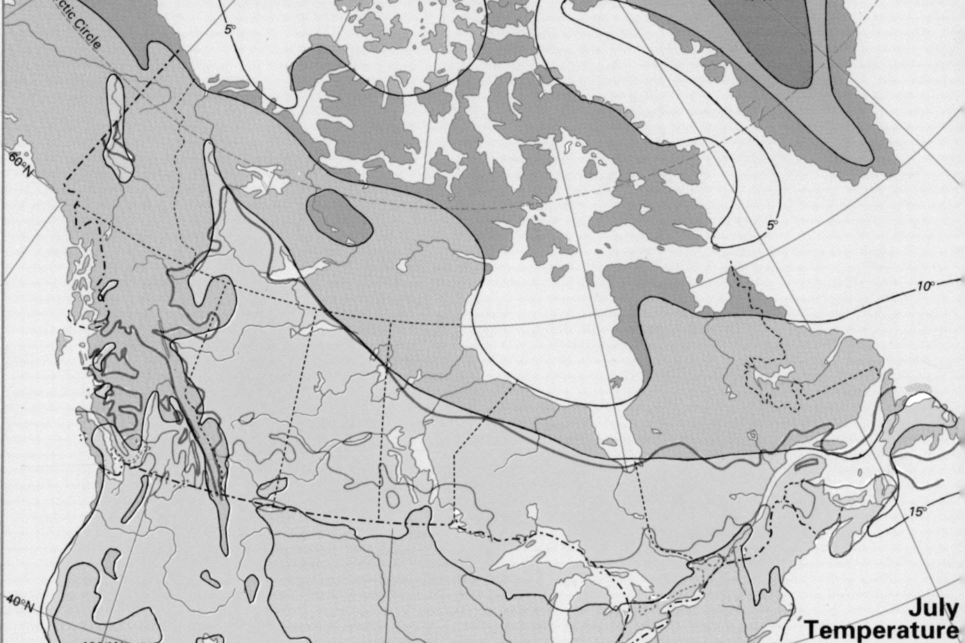

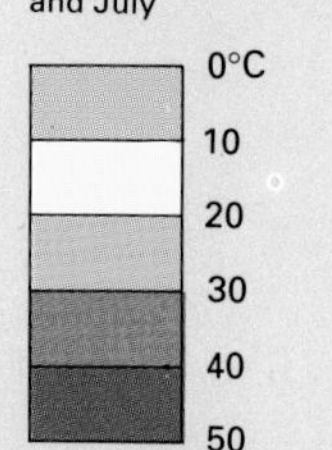

0°C
10
20
30
40
50

Boundaries

—— international

- - - province/territory

Scale 1: 44 000 000

0   500 km

Zenithal Equidistant Projection

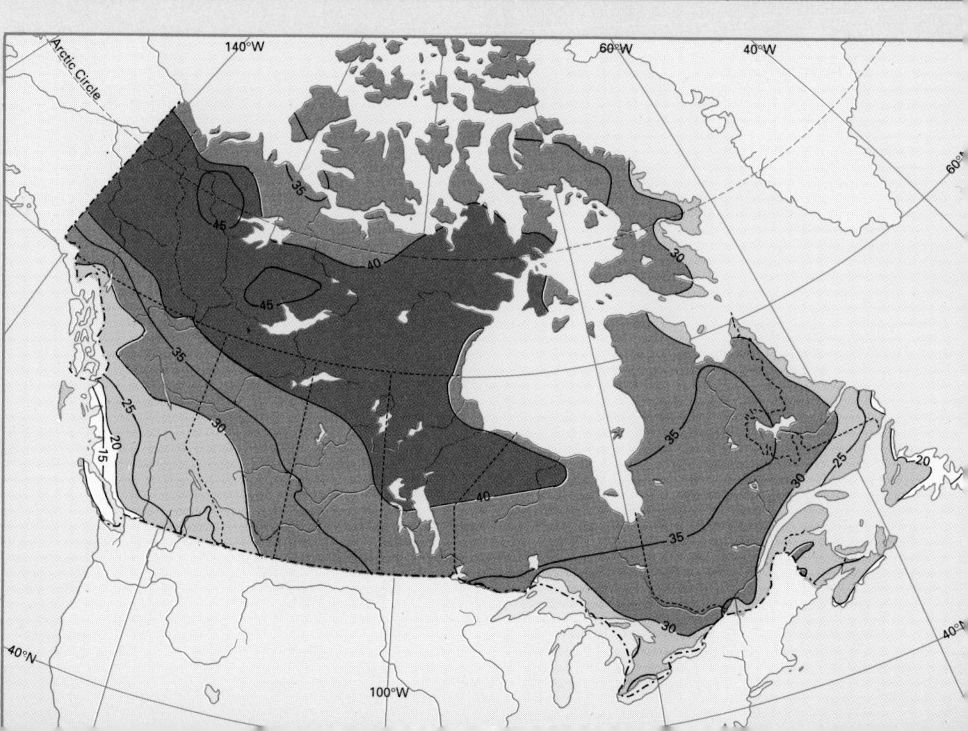

January Temperature

July Temperature

Mean annual precipitation

mm

- over 2000
- 1000-2000
- 600-1000
- 400-600
- 200-400
- under 200

Boundaries

international

province/
territory

Scale 1: 44 000 000

0   500 km

(map labels) 200 mm, 400 mm, 400 mm, 600 mm, 1000 mm, Arctic Circle, 140°W, 60°W, 40°W, 60°N, 100°W, 40°N

Winter

- maritime arctic
- Aleutian Low **L**
- maritime arctic
- maritime polar
- continental arctic
- Icelandic Low **L**
- maritime polar
- **H** North Pacific High
- maritime tropical
- maritime tropical
- **H** Azores-Bermuda High

Mean annual snowfall

cm

- more than 400
- 300-400
- 200-300
- 100-200
- less than 100

Boundaries

international

province/
territory

Scale 1: 44 000 000

0   500 km

(map labels) Arctic Circle, 140°W, 60°W, 40°W, 60°N, 120°W, 100°W, 80°W, 40°N

Summer

- maritime polar
- maritime arctic
- North Pacific High **H**
- maritime tropical
- maritime tropical
- **H**
- Azores-Bermuda High

Air masses and winds

→ prevailing winds

▸▸ polar jet stream

H high ⎫ semi-permanent
L low ⎬ pressure

Scale 1: 108 000 000
Oblique Mercator Projection

Thunderstorms

Average annual number of days with thunderstorms

- 5
- 10
- 20

(map labels) 0 days, 1 day, Arctic Circle, 140°W, 60°W, 40°W, 60°N, 40°N

Tornadoes

Average annual frequency of tornadoes per 10 000 km²

- more than 2.0
- 1.2-2.0
- 0.8-1.2

Scale 1: 44 000 000

0   500 km

Zenithal Equidistant Projection

(map labels) 25, 15, 25, 15, 25, 30, 100°W, 80°W

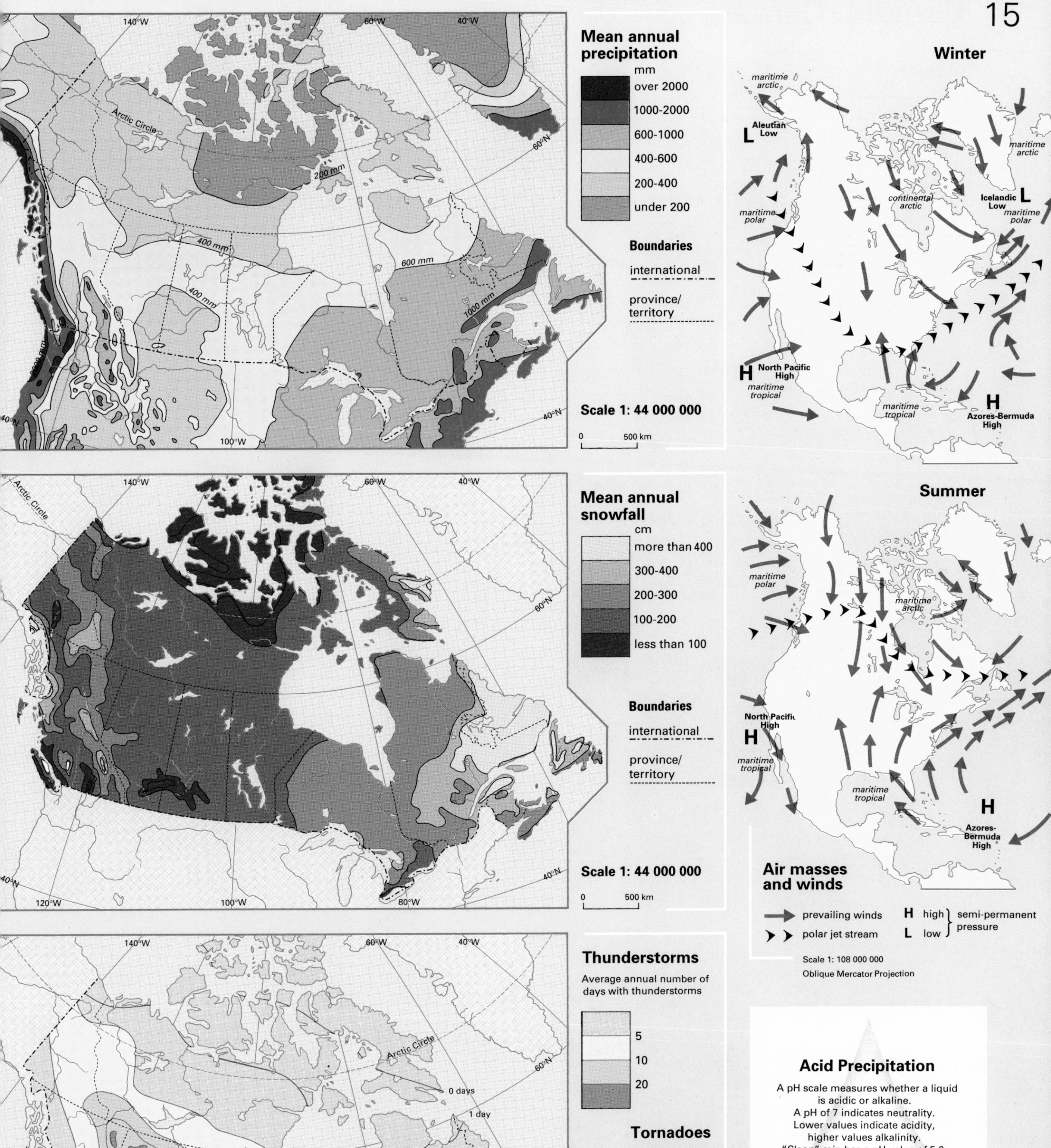

Acid Precipitation

A pH scale measures whether a liquid is acidic or alkaline.
A pH of 7 indicates neutrality.
Lower values indicate acidity, higher values alkalinity.
"Clean" rain has a pH value of 5.6.

For a map of annual mean values of pH in precipitation in North America see page 129.

Wind Chill

a measure of the wind's cooling effect, as felt on exposed flesh, expressed either as the **wind chill equivalent temperature** (in °C) or as **heat loss** (in watts/m²)

Wind chill equivalent temperature

referenced to a base wind speed of 8 km per hour

Temperature (°C)	wind speed in km per hour					
	10	**20**	**30**	**40**	**50**	**60**
5	4	-2	-5	-7	-8	-9
0	-2	-8	-11	-14	-16	-17
-5	-7	-14	-18	-21	-23	-24
-10	-12	-20	-25	-28	-30	-32
-15	-18	-26	-32	-35	-38	-39
-20	-23	-32	-38	-42	-45	-47
-25	-28	-39	-45	-49	-52	-54
-30	-33	-45	-52	-56	-60	-62
-35	-39	-51	-59	-64	-67	-69
-40	-44	-57	-65	-71	-74	-77

January wind chill

The values on the map indicate the maximum wind chill; there is a 5% chance of having a wind chill value worse than the value shown

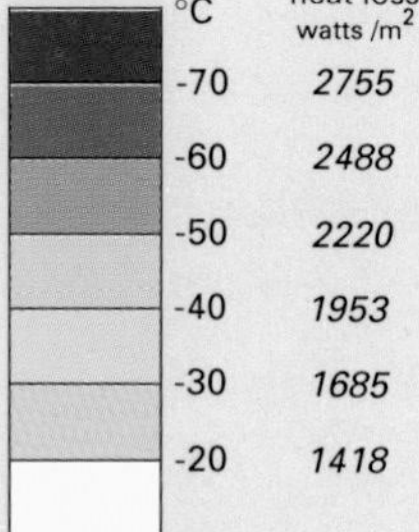

Wind chill equivalent temperature

	°C	heat loss watts /m²
	-70	2755
	-60	2488
	-50	2220
	-40	1953
	-30	1685
	-20	1418

Boundaries

international

province/territory

Scale 1: 44 000 000

0   500   1000 km

Humidex

an index showing temperature measures that allow for the added stress that results from high humidities - referred to as **effective temperature**

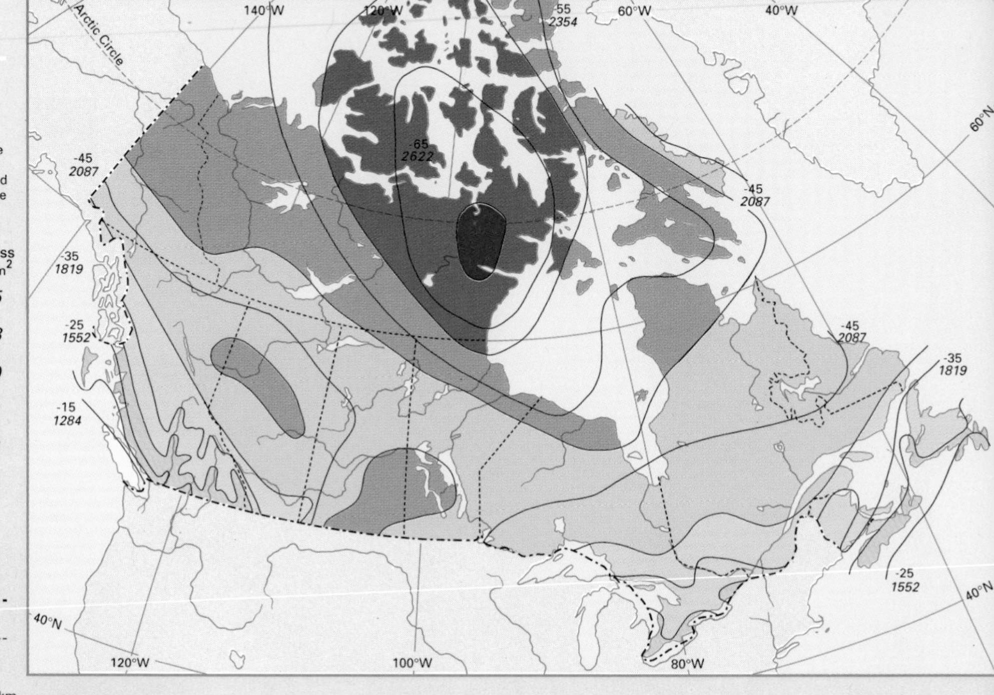

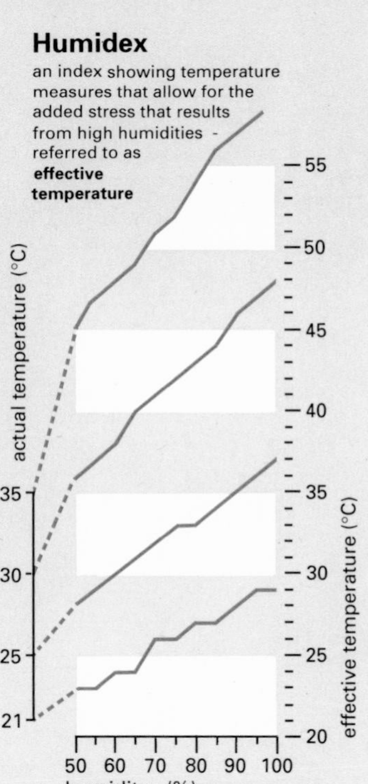

Growing season

Average number of days with an average temperature over 5 °C

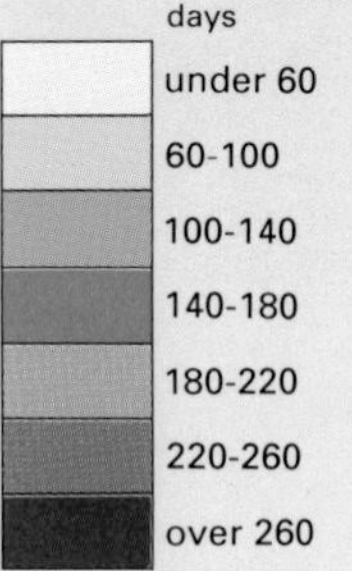

days

under 60
60-100
100-140
140-180
180-220
220-260
over 260

Boundaries

international

province/territory

Scale 1: 44 000 000

0   500   1000 km

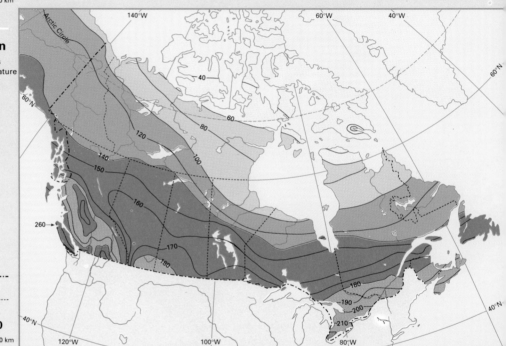

Canadian weather records

highest air temperature	45°C Midale and Yellow Grass, Sask. July 5, 1937
lowest air temperature	-63°C Snag, Y.T. February 3, 1947
coldest month	-47.9°C Eureka, N.W.T February, 1979
highest sea-level pressure	107.96 kPa Dawson, Y.T. February 2, 1989
lowest sea-level pressure	94.02 kPa St.Anthony, New foundland January 20, 1977
greatest precipitation in 24 hours	489.2 mm Ucluelet Brynnor Mines, B.C. October 6, 1967
greatest precipitation in one month	2235.5 mm Swanson Bay, B.C. November 1917
greatest precipitation in one year	8122.6 mm Henderson Lake, B.C. 1931
greatest average annual precipitation	6655 mm Henderson Lake, B.C.
least annual precipitation	12,7 mm Arctic Bay, N.W.T 1949
highest average annual number of thunderstorm days	34 days London, Ontario

Sunshine

Average annual hours

1200
1600
2000

253 number of days with some sun

Boundaries

international

province/territory

Scale 1: 44 000 000

0   500   1000 km

Zenithal Equidistant Projection

© Oxford University Press

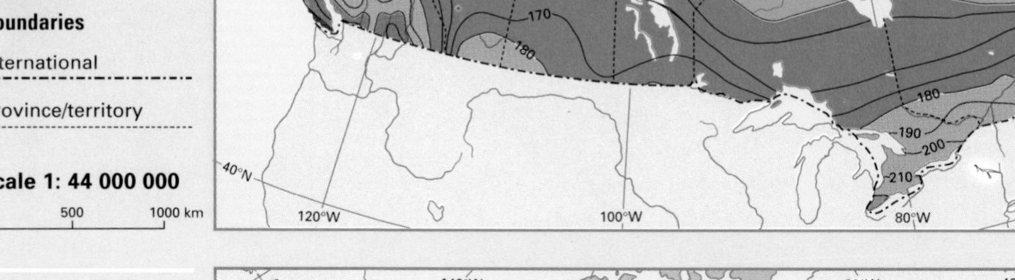

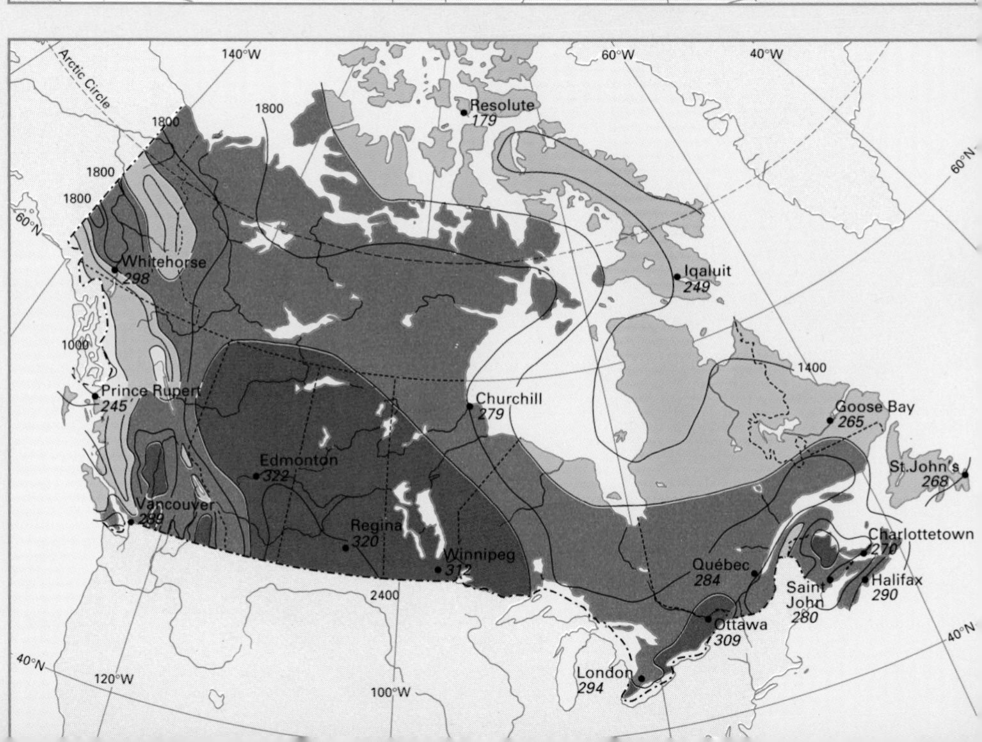

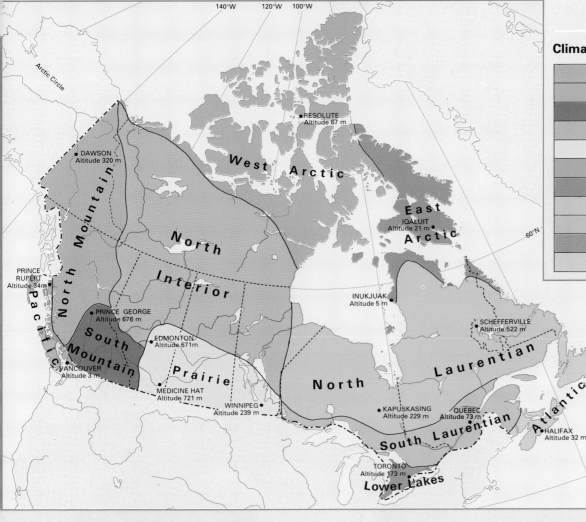

Climate regions

- mild wet winter and warm summer
- cold winter and cool summer; warmer in valleys.
- cold winter and warm summer
- cold winter; precipitation decreasing northwards
- cold winter and hot summer; very dry in the south
- cold and dry throughout the year
- cold throughout the year; light precipitation
- long cold winter and short warm summer
- cold winter and hot summer
- cold winter with heavy snowfalls; hot humid summer
- cold stormy winter with heavy rain and snow; warm summer

Boundaries

international

province/territory

Scale 1: 35 000 000

0   500   1000 km

Climate graphs

for selected stations (1951-80 averages)

PRINCE RUPERT

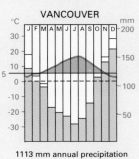
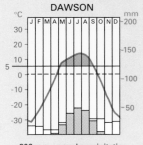
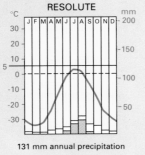
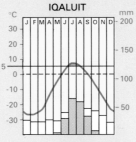
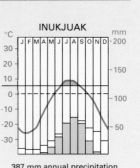

DAWSON — 306 mm annual precipitation
RESOLUTE — 131 mm annual precipitation
IQALUIT — 433 mm annual precipitation
INUKJUAK — 387 mm annual precipitation
PRINCE RUPERT — 2523 mm annual precipitation

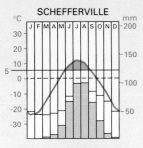
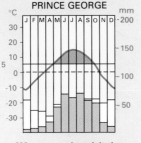
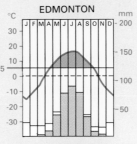
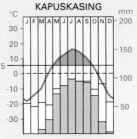
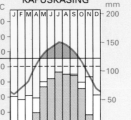

SCHEFFERVILLE — 769 mm annual precipitation
PRINCE GEORGE — 628 mm annual precipitation
EDMONTON — 466 mm annual precipitation
KAPUSKASING — 872 mm annual precipitation
QUÉBEC — 1174 mm annual precipitation

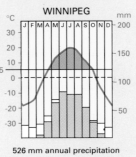
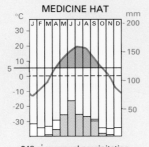
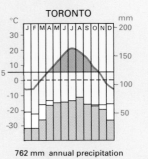
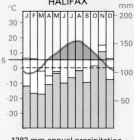
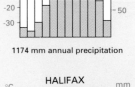

VANCOUVER — 1113 mm annual precipitation
MEDICINE HAT — 348 mm annual precipitation
WINNIPEG — 526 mm annual precipitation
TORONTO — 762 mm annual precipitation
HALIFAX — 1282 mm annual precipitation

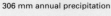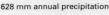

average daily temperature — growing season (that part of the year when average daily temperature remains above 5°C) — average snowfall — average rainfall — 10 mm of snowfall is the water equivalent of 1 mm of rainfall

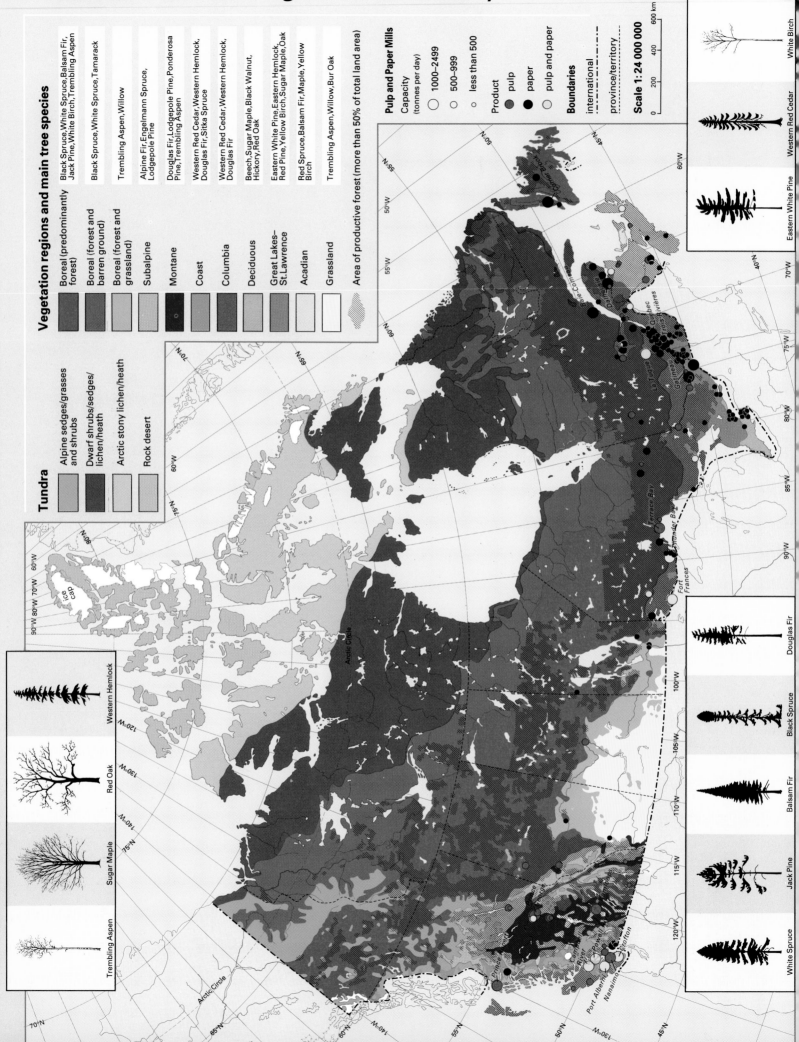

Vegetation regions and main tree species

Boreal (predominantly forest)
Black Spruce, White Spruce, Balsam Fir, Jack Pine, White Birch, Trembling Aspen

Boreal (forest and barren ground)
Black Spruce, White Spruce, Tamarack

Boreal (forest and grassland)
Trembling Aspen, Willow

Subalpine
Alpine Fir, Engelmann Spruce, Lodgepole Pine

Montane
Douglas Fir, Lodgepole Pine, Ponderosa Pine, Trembling Aspen

Coast
Western Red Cedar, Western Hemlock, Douglas Fir, Sitka Spruce

Columbia
Western Red Cedar, Western Hemlock, Douglas Fir

Deciduous
Beech, Sugar Maple, Black Walnut, Hickory, Red Oak

Great Lakes–St.Lawrence
Eastern White Pine, Eastern Hemlock, Red Pine, Yellow Birch, Sugar Maple, Oak

Acadian
Red Spruce, Balsam Fir, Maple, Yellow Birch

Grassland
Trembling Aspen, Willow, Bur Oak

Area of productive forest (more than 50% of total land area)

Tundra

Alpine sedges/grasses and shrubs

Dwarf shrubs/sedges/lichen/heath

Arctic stony lichen/heath

Rock desert

Pulp and Paper Mills

Capacity (tonnes per day)
○ 1000–2499
○ 500–999
○ less than 500

Product
● pulp
● paper
● pulp and paper

Boundaries
— · · — international
— · — province/territory

Scale 1:24 000 000
0 200 400 600 km

White Birch

Western Red Cedar

Eastern White Pine

Douglas Fir

Black Spruce

Balsam Fir

Jack Pine

White Spruce

Western Hemlock

Red Oak

Sugar Maple

Trembling Aspen

Zenithal Equidistant Projection

© Oxford University Press

Atlantic Coast Fishing

Hamilton Bank
Tooker Bank
Flemish Cap
Grand Bank
The Grand Banks of Newfoundland
St.Pierre Bank
Burgeo Bank
Green Bank
Banquereau
Middle Bank
Sable Island Bank
Bradelle Bank
Emerald Bank
Browns Bank
George Bank
200 mile fishing limit

Fishing

Pelagic and estuarial
fish usually found in shoals near the surface, e.g. herring,sardine,swordfish, salmon.

Groundfish
fish that live at depths below 50 m as well as on the sea bottom, e.g. cod,haddock, pollock,flounder,sole.

Molluscs and crustaceans
hard-shelled invertebrates found in shallow waters, e.g. lobster, scallops, oysters,clams.

Sea depth

sea level to 500 m

more than 500 m

international boundary

Scale 1:16 000 000

0   250   500 km

Conical Orthomorphic Projection

Pacific Coast Fishing

125°W
130°W
135°W
55°N
50°N
200 mile fishing limit

Ecozones

Boundaries

international

province/territory

A table describing the biophysical characteristics of each ecozone is found on page 204.

Arctic Cordillera
Northern Arctic
Southern Arctic
Hudson Bay Plain
Taiga Shield
Taiga Plain
Tundra Cordillera
Boreal Cordillera
Pacific Maritime
Montane Cordillera
Boreal Plain
Prairie
Boreal Shield
Mixed-Wood Plain
Atlantic Maritime

Scale 1:35 000 000

0   500   1000 km

Zenithal Equidistant Projection

© Oxford University Press

Ecozones

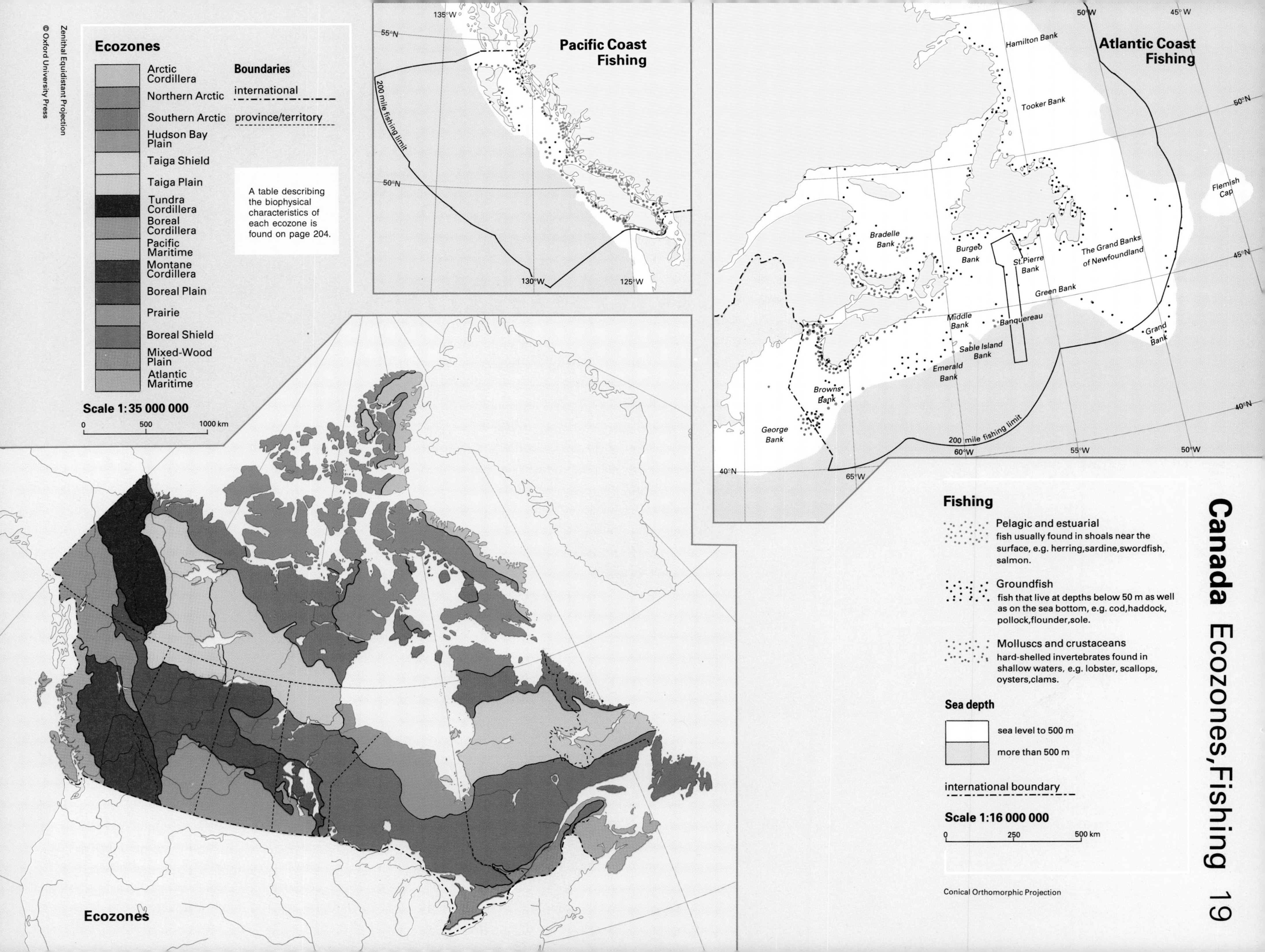

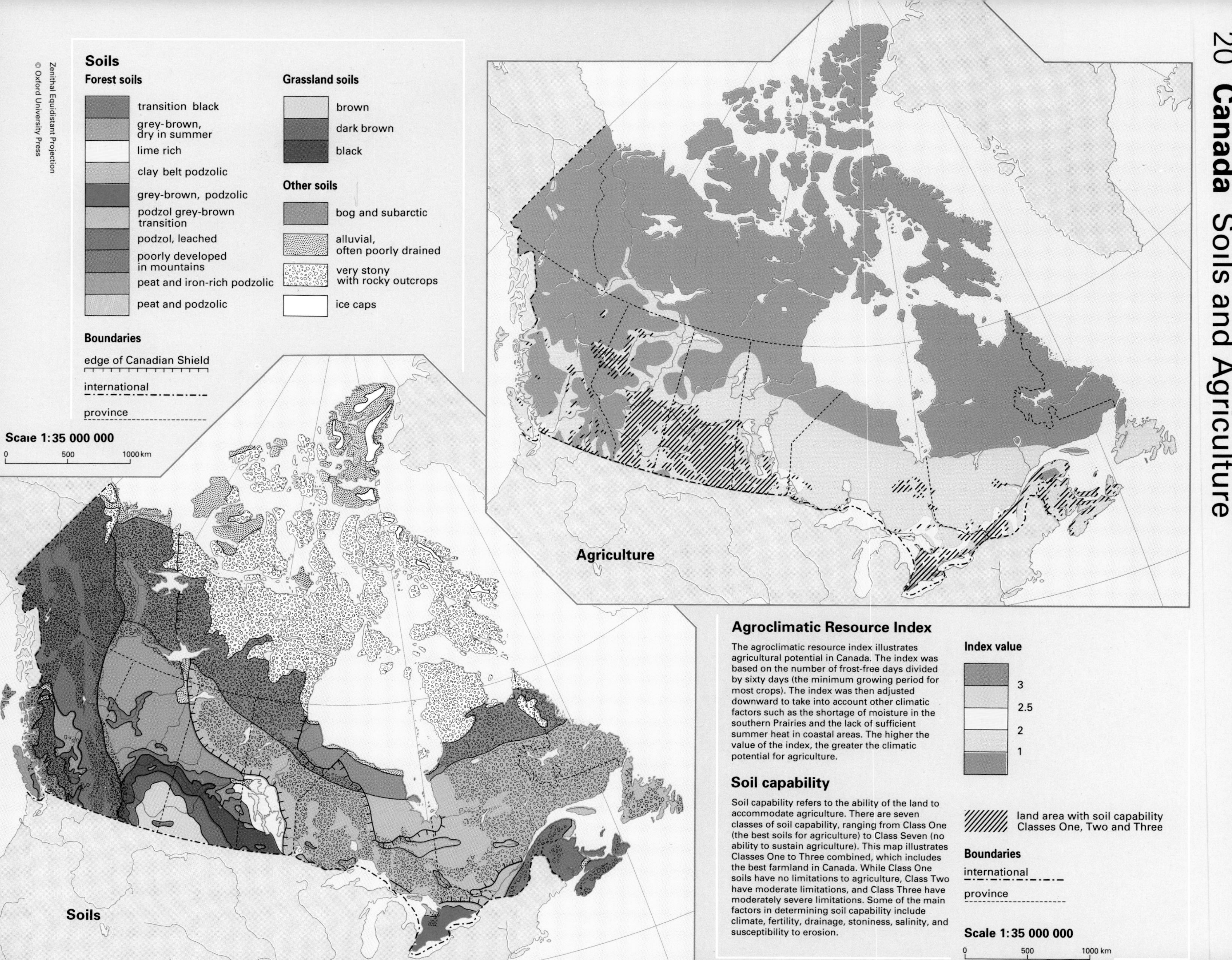

Agriculture

Agroclimatic Resource Index

The agroclimatic resource index illustrates agricultural potential in Canada. The index was based on the number of frost-free days divided by sixty days (the minimum growing period for most crops). The index was then adjusted downward to take into account other climatic factors such as the shortage of moisture in the southern Prairies and the lack of sufficient summer heat in coastal areas. The higher the value of the index, the greater the climatic potential for agriculture.

Soil capability

Soil capability refers to the ability of the land to accommodate agriculture. There are seven classes of soil capability, ranging from Class One (the best soils for agriculture) to Class Seven (no ability to sustain agriculture). This map illustrates Classes One to Three combined, which includes the best farmland in Canada. While Class One soils have no limitations to agriculture, Class Two have moderate limitations, and Class Three have moderately severe limitations. Some of the main factors in determining soil capability include climate, fertility, drainage, stoniness, salinity, and susceptibility to erosion.

Index value

3
2.5
2
1

land area with soil capability
Classes One, Two and Three

Boundaries

international
province

Scale 1:35 000 000

0   500   1000 km

Soils

Soils

Forest soils

transition black
grey-brown,
dry in summer
lime rich
clay belt podzolic
grey-brown, podzolic
podzol grey-brown
transition
podzol, leached
poorly developed
in mountains
peat and iron-rich podzolic
peat and podzolic

Grassland soils

brown
dark brown
black

Other soils

bog and subarctic
alluvial,
often poorly drained
very stony
with rocky outcrops
ice caps

Boundaries

edge of Canadian Shield
international
province

Scale 1:35 000 000

0   500   1000 km

Zenithal Equidistant Projection

© Oxford University Press

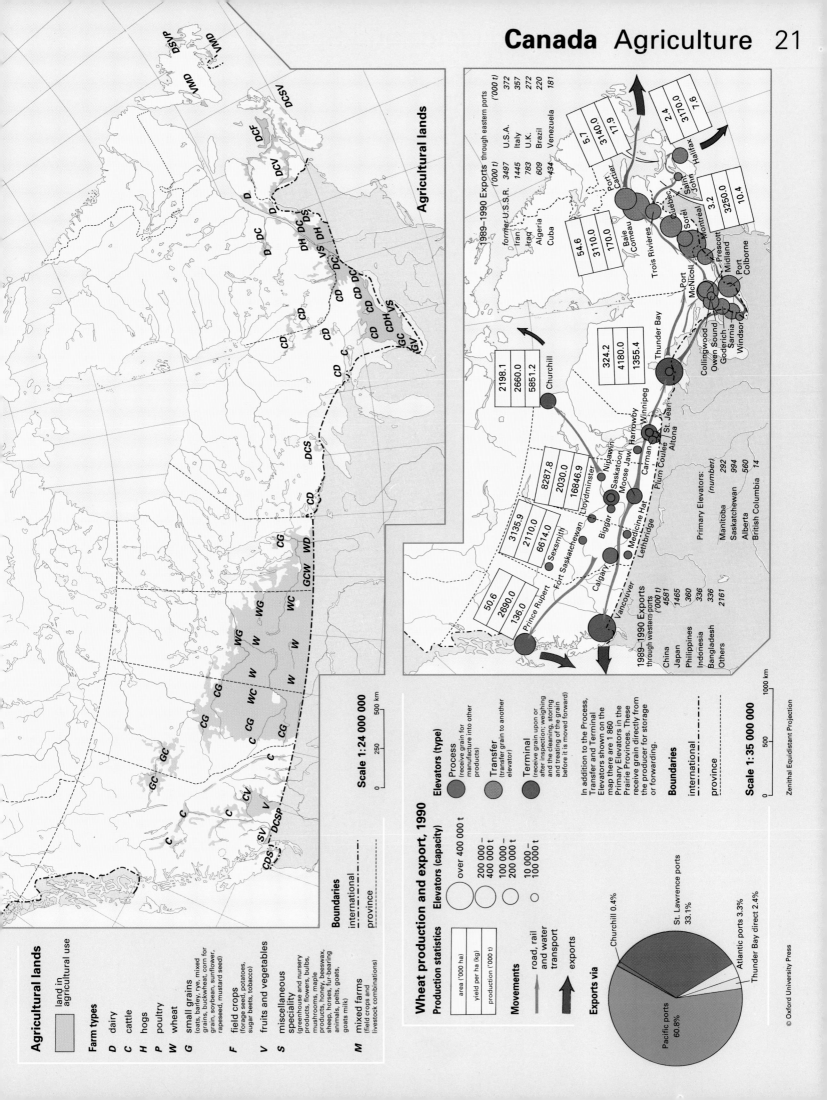

Agricultural lands

land in agricultural use

Farm types

D dairy
C cattle
H hogs
P poultry
W wheat
G small grains
(oats, barley, rye, mixed grains, buckwheat, corn for grain, soybean, sunflower, rapeseed, mustard seed)
F field crops
(forage seed, potatoes, sugar beets, tobacco)
V fruits and vegetables
S miscellaneous speciality
(greenhouse and nursery products, flowers, bulbs, mushrooms, maple products, honey, beeswax, sheep, horses, fur-bearing animals, pelts, goats, goats milk)
M mixed farms
(field crops and livestock combinations)

Boundaries
international
province

Scale 1:24 000 000

0   250   500 km

Wheat production and export, 1990

Production statistics

area ('000 ha)		
yield per ha (kg)		
production ('000 t)		

Elevators (capacity)

○ over 400 000 t
○ 200 000 – 400 000 t
○ 100 000 – 200 000 t
○ 10 000 – 100 000 t

Elevators (type)

Process (receive grain for manufacture into other products)

Transfer (transfer grain to another elevator)

Terminal (receive grain upon or after inspection; weighing and the cleaning, storing and treating of the grain before it is moved forward)

In addition to the Process, Transfer and Terminal Elevators shown on the map there are 1 860 Primary Elevators in the Prairie Provinces. These receive grain directly from the producer for storage or forwarding.

Movements
→ road, rail and water transport
⬆ exports

Exports via

Boundaries
international
province

Scale 1:35 000 000

0   500   1000 km

Zenithal Equidistant Projection

Agricultural lands (map 1:24 000 000)

DSVP
VMD
VMD
DCSV
DCF
DCV
D
D DC
DC
DH DCV
DS DS
VS DH
DC
CD
CD
CD
CD DC
CDH VS
GC
GV
CD
C
CD
CD
CD
CD
DCS
CD
CG
GCW WD
WG
WC
WG
W
WG WC
W
W
W
WC
GC GC
C CG
CG
CG
C CG
V CG
C
CV
CV
C
C C
SV
CDS DCSP

Wheat production and export map (1:35 000 000)

1989–1990 Exports through eastern ports ('000 t)

former U.S.S.R.	3497	U.S.A.	372
Iran	1445	Italy	357
Iraq	783	U.K.	272
Algeria	609	Brazil	220
Cuba	434	Venezuela	181

Port Cartier: 5.7 / 3140.0 / 17.9
Halifax: 2.4 / 3170.0 / 7.6
Saint John: 3.2 / 3250.0 / 10.4
Québec
Sorel
Montréal
Baie Comeau: 54.6 / 3110.0 / 170.0
Trois Rivières
Port McNicoll
Prescott
Midland
Port Colborne
Collingwood
Owen Sound
Goderich
Sarnia
Windsor

Thunder Bay: 324.2 / 4180.0 / 1355.4

Churchill: 2198.1 / 2660.0 / 5851.2

Winnipeg
Harrowby
St. Jean
Altona
Carman
Plum Coulee
Nipawin
Saskatoon
Moose Jaw
Medicine Hat
Lethbridge
Biggar
Lloydminster: 8287.8 / 2030.0 / 16846.9
Sexsmith: 3135.9 / 2110.0 / 6614.0
Fort Saskatchewan
Calgary
Vancouver
Prince Rupert: 50.6 / 2690.0 / 136.0

Primary Elevators: (number)

Manitoba	292
Saskatchewan	994
Alberta	560
British Columbia	14

1989–1990 Exports through western ports ('000 t)

China	4581
Japan	1465
Philippines	360
Indonesia	336
Bangladesh	2161
Others	

Exports via (pie chart)
Pacific ports 60.8%
St. Lawrence ports 33.1%
Churchill 0.4%
Atlantic ports 3.3%
Thunder Bay direct 2.4%

© Oxford University Press

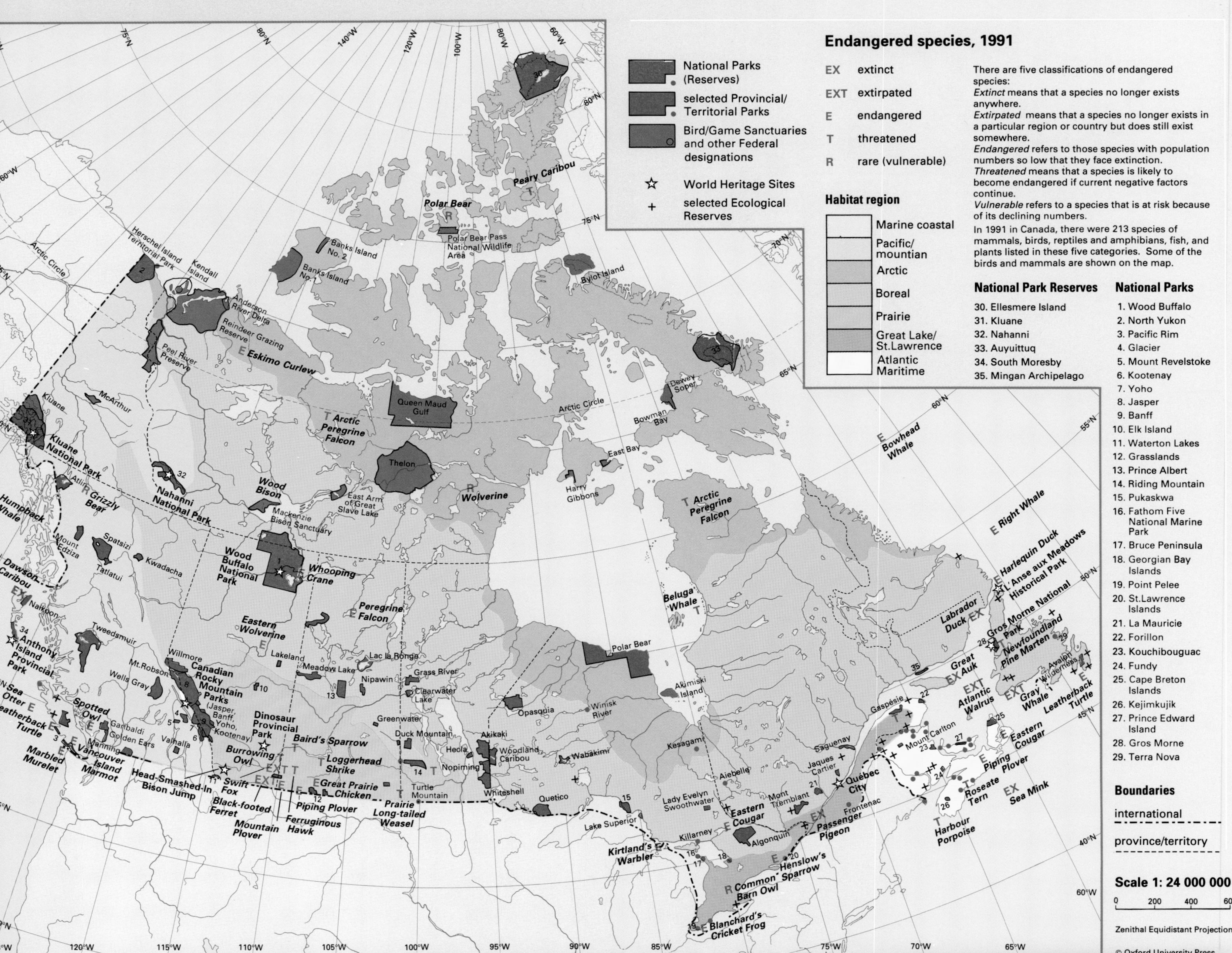

Endangered species, 1991

EX extinct
EXT extirpated
E   endangered
T   threatened
R   rare (vulnerable)

There are five classifications of endangered species:
Extinct means that a species no longer exists anywhere.
Extirpated means that a species no longer exists in a particular region or country but does still exist somewhere.
Endangered refers to those species with population numbers so low that they face extinction.
Threatened means that a species is likely to become endangered if current negative factors continue.
Vulnerable refers to a species that is at risk because of its declining numbers.

In 1991 in Canada, there were 213 species of mammals, birds, reptiles and amphibians, fish, and plants listed in these five categories. Some of the birds and mammals are shown on the map.

National Parks
1. Wood Buffalo
2. North Yukon
3. Pacific Rim
4. Glacier
5. Mount Revelstoke
6. Kootenay
7. Yoho
8. Jasper
9. Banff
10. Elk Island
11. Waterton Lakes
12. Grasslands
13. Prince Albert
14. Riding Mountain
15. Pukaskwa
16. Fathom Five National Marine Park
17. Bruce Peninsula
18. Georgian Bay Islands
19. Point Pelee
20. St. Lawrence Islands
21. La Mauricie
22. Forillon
23. Kouchibouguac
24. Fundy
25. Cape Breton Islands
26. Kejimkujik
27. Prince Edward Island
28. Gros Morne
29. Terra Nova

National Park Reserves
30. Ellesmere Island
31. Kluane
32. Nahanni
33. Auyuittuq
34. South Moresby
35. Mingan Archipelago

Habitat region
Marine coastal
Pacific/mountain
Arctic
Boreal
Prairie
Great Lake/St.Lawrence
Atlantic Maritime

National Parks (Reserves)
selected Provincial/Territorial Parks
Bird/Game Sanctuaries and other Federal designations
☆ World Heritage Sites
+ selected Ecological Reserves

Boundaries
international
province/territory

Scale 1: 24 000 000

0   200   400   600 km

Zenithal Equidistant Projection

© Oxford University Press

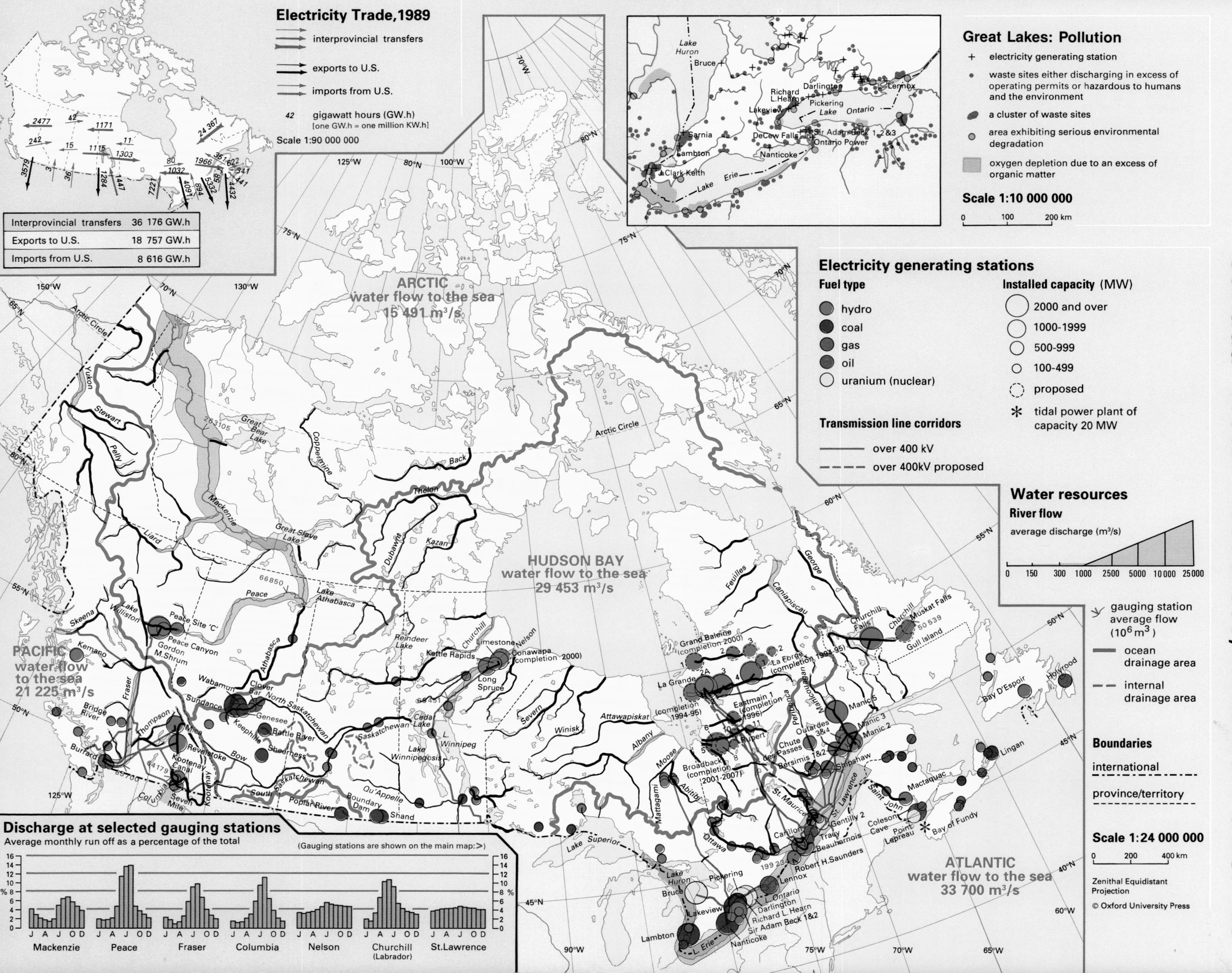

Great Lakes: Pollution

+ electricity generating station

  waste sites either discharging in excess of
  operating permits or hazardous to humans
  and the environment

● a cluster of waste sites

● area exhibiting serious environmental
  degradation

  oxygen depletion due to an excess of
  organic matter

Scale 1:10 000 000

0   100   200 km

Electricity generating stations

Installed capacity (MW)

○ 2000 and over
○ 1000-1999
○ 500-999
○ 100-499
○ proposed

✳ tidal power plant of
  capacity 20 MW

Fuel type

● hydro
● coal
● gas
● oil
○ uranium (nuclear)

Transmission line corridors

—— over 400 kV
---- over 400kV proposed

Water resources

River flow

average discharge (m³/s)

25000
10000
5000
2500
1000
300
150

0

→ gauging station
  average flow
  (10⁶ m³)

—— ocean
  drainage area

---- internal
  drainage area

Boundaries

—·—·— international

--·-- province/territory

Scale 1:24 000 000

0   200   400 km

Zenithal Equidistant
Projection

Electricity Trade, 1989

  interprovincial transfers

↑ exports to U.S.

↑ imports from U.S.

42 gigawatt hours (GW.h)
    [one GW.h = one million KW.h]

Scale 1:90 000 000

Interprovincial transfers	36 176 GW.h
Exports to U.S.	18 757 GW.h
Imports from U.S.	8 616 GW.h

Discharge at selected gauging stations

Average monthly run off as a percentage of the total

(Gauging stations are shown on the main map)

16
14
12
10
8 %
6
4
2

Mackenzie   Peace   Fraser   Columbia   Nelson   Churchill (Labrador)   St.Lawrence

J A J O D (repeated under each)

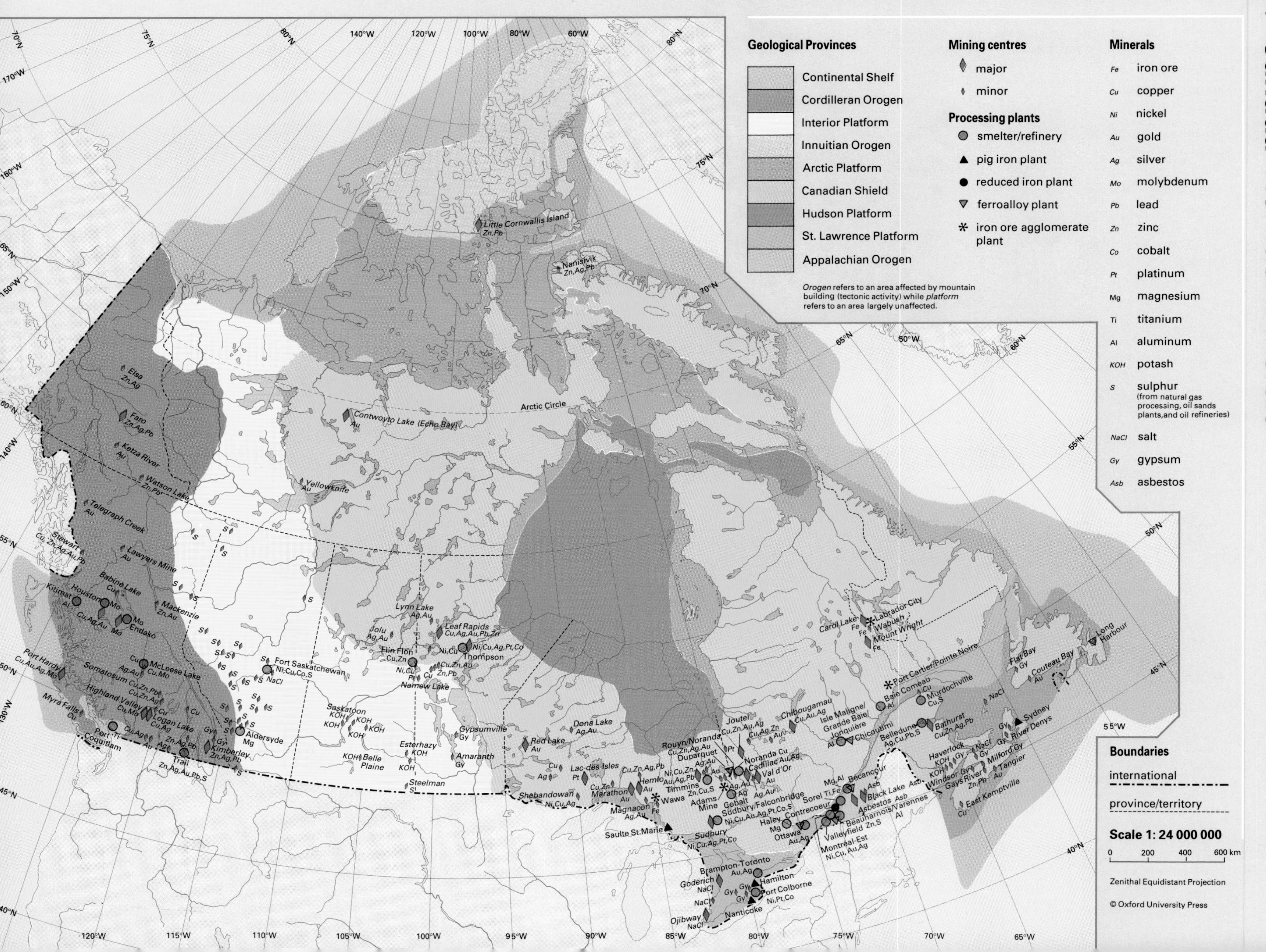

Minerals

Fe	iron ore
Cu	copper
Ni	nickel
Au	gold
Ag	silver
Mo	molybdenum
Pb	lead
Zn	zinc
Co	cobalt
Pt	platinum
Mg	magnesium
Ti	titanium
Al	aluminum
KOH	potash
S	sulphur (from natural gas processing, oil sands plants, and oil refineries)
NaCl	salt
Gy	gypsum
Asb	asbestos

Mining centres
◆ major
◆ minor

Processing plants
● smelter/refinery
▲ pig iron plant
● reduced iron plant
▽ ferroalloy plant
* iron ore agglomerate plant

Geological Provinces

Continental Shelf
Cordilleran Orogen
Interior Platform
Innuitian Orogen
Arctic Platform
Canadian Shield
Hudson Platform
St. Lawrence Platform
Appalachian Orogen

Orogen refers to an area affected by mountain building (tectonic activity) while *platform* refers to an area largely unaffected.

Boundaries

international
province/territory

Scale 1 : 24 000 000

0   200   400   600 km

Zenithal Equidistant Projection

© Oxford University Press

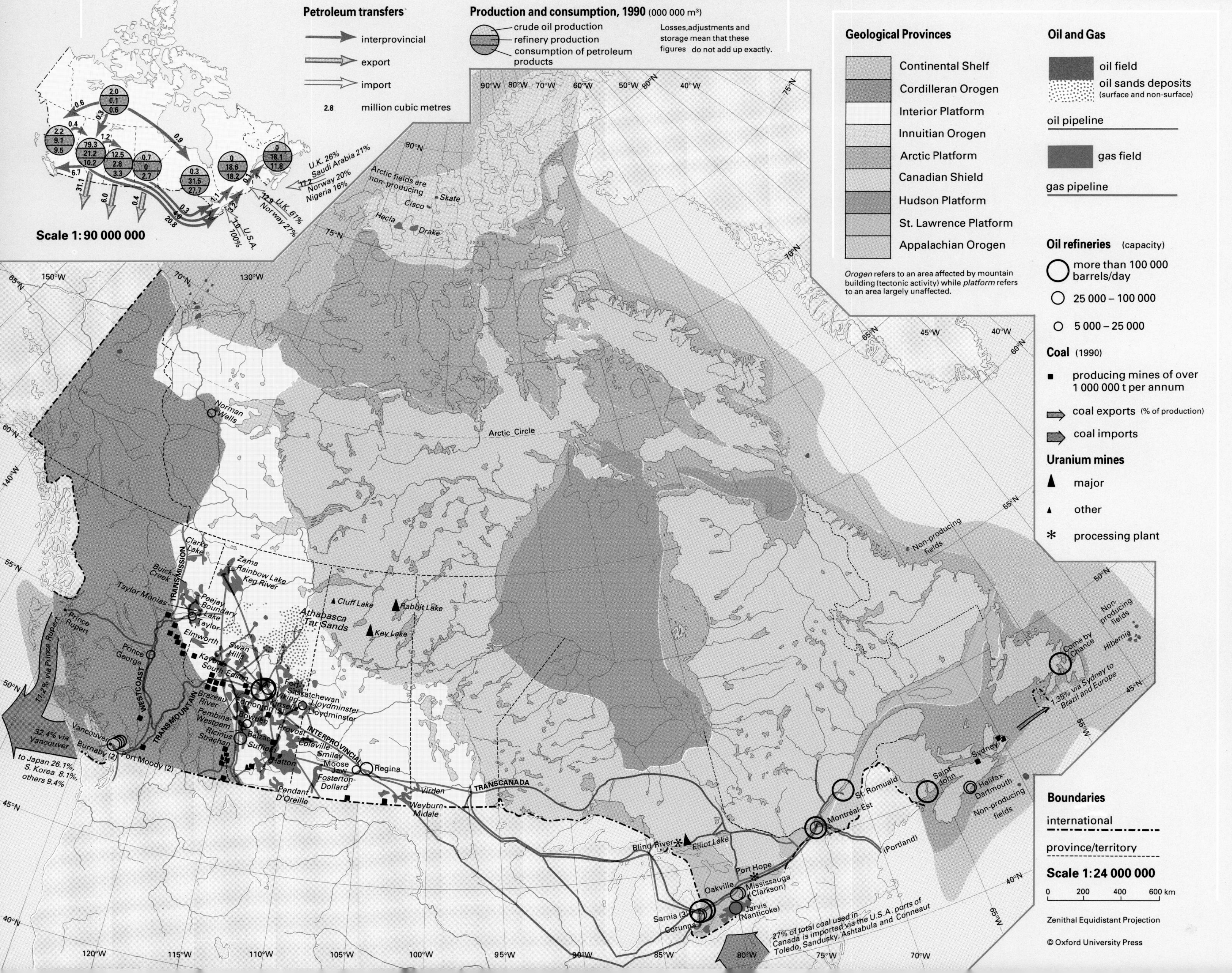

Oil and Gas

- oil field
- oil sands deposits (surface and non-surface)
- oil pipeline
- gas field
- gas pipeline

Geological Provinces

- Continental Shelf
- Cordilleran Orogen
- Interior Platform
- Innuitian Orogen
- Arctic Platform
- Canadian Shield
- Hudson Platform
- St. Lawrence Platform
- Appalachian Orogen

Orogen refers to an area affected by mountain building (tectonic activity) while platform refers to an area largely unaffected.

Oil refineries (capacity)

- more than 100 000 barrels/day
- 25 000 – 100 000
- 5 000 – 25 000

Coal (1990)

- producing mines of over 1 000 000 t per annum
- coal exports (% of production)
- coal imports

Uranium mines

- major
- other
- * processing plant

Boundaries

- international
- province/territory

Scale 1:24 000 000

0   200   400   600 km

Zenithal Equidistant Projection

© Oxford University Press

Production and consumption, 1990 (000 000 m³)

- crude oil production
- refinery production
- consumption of petroleum products

Losses, adjustments and storage mean that these figures do not add up exactly.

Petroleum transfers

- interprovincial
- export
- import

2.8 million cubic metres

Scale 1:90 000 000

Arctic fields are non-producing

Skate
Cisco
Hecla
Drake

Norman Wells

Zama
Rainbow Lake
Keg River
Clarke Lake
Peejay
Boundary
Taylor
Kaybob
Elmworth
Brazeau River
Pembina
Westerose
Strachan
Ricinus

Buick Creek
Taylor Moraes
Prince George
Prince Rupert

TRANSMISSION
WESTCOAST
TRANSMOUNTAIN

Vancouver
Burnaby (2)
Port Moody (2)

to Japan 26.1%
S. Korea 8.1%
others 9.4%
32.4% via Vancouver
11.2% via Prince Rupert

Athabasca Tar Sands
Cluff Lake
Key Lake
Rabbit Lake

Zama
Swan Hills
South Edson

Fort Saskatchewan
Edmonton
Hardisty
Lloydminster

Kinsella
Bodo
Provost
Coleville
Pendant
D'Oreille

Suffield
Medicine Hat
Dollard
Foster
Smiley

INTERPROVINCIAL

Regina
Moose Jaw
Weyburn
Midale
Vidor

TRANSCANADA

Elliot Lake
Blind River *

Sarnia (3)
Corunna
Nanticoke
Jarvis
Oakville
Mississauga (Clarkson)
Port Hope

Montréal Est
St. Romuald

Saint John
Sydney
Halifax
Dartmouth

Come by Chance to Brazil

Non-producing fields

Hibernia

Non producing fields

27% of total coal used in Canada is imported via the U.S.A. ports of Conneaut, Toledo, Sandusky, Ashtabula and Conneaut

U.K. 26% Saudi Arabia 27%
Norway 20% Nigeria 6%
U.K. 61% Norway 27%
U.S.A. 100%

18.1   11.8
0
18.6   18.2
0
0.3   31.5
27.1
0.3   20.8
2.0   0.1
9.1
0.7   0
2.7
12.5   2.8
3.3
0.9
79.3   21.2
0.2
2.2   9.5
0.4
0.6
6.0
31.1
6.7

Manufacturing centres

Value added by manufacturing
($ 000 000)

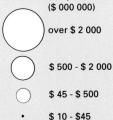

○ over $ 2 000

○ $ 500 - $ 2 000

○ $ 45 - $ 500

· $ 10 - $45

Manufacturing centres include Census Metropolitan Areas (CMAs), Specified Census Agglomerations and selected Municipalities [see *Statistics Canada* publication 31-209 (1986)]. Manufacturing outside CMA's, towns and cities is not shown.

Toronto and Montréal are shown separately

390 value added by manufacturing ($ 000 000)
(The value of manufactured goods shipped less the cost of materials and supplies used, including fuel and electricity.)

531 / 25 574 manufacturing establishments/number employed
(data only for those centres with a value-added figure of over $45 000 000)

Manufacturing

For CMAs and Specified Census Agglomerations, the colour indicates the major industrial group and the numbers indicate the principal types of manufacture in each group.

- food and beverages
- textiles and clothing
- wood
  - 1 wood products
  - 2 furniture
- paper
  - 3 paper products
  - 4 printing
- metals
  - 5 primary metals
  - 6 fabricated metals
- machinery
  - 7 machinery
  - 8 transport equipment
  - 9 electrical and electronic products
- non-metallic minerals
  - 10 cement and concrete
- chemicals
  - 11 petroleum products
  - 12 chemicals
- others
  including the above industrial groups where the value added is less than 5% of the total

Boundaries

international ▬ · ▬ · ▬

province/territory ▬ ▬ ▬

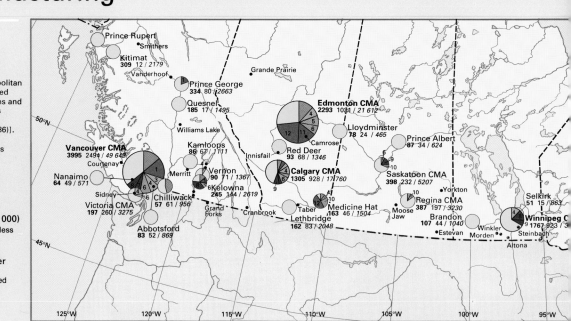

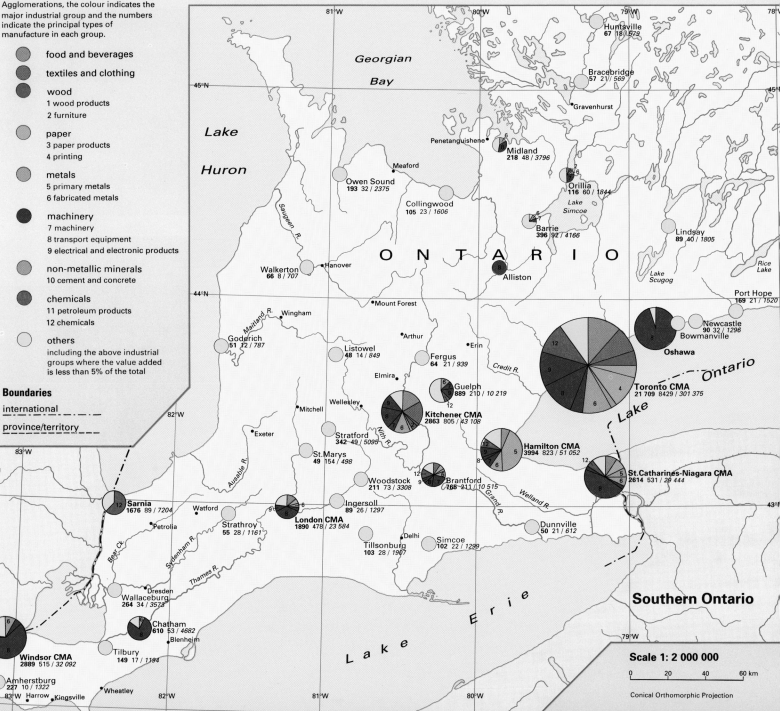

Southern Ontario

Scale 1: 2 000 000

0   20   40   60 km

Conical Orthomorphic Projection

Value added by manufacturing, 1987

($ 000 000)

Canada	118 290
Ontario	62 453
Québec	30 288
British Columbia	10 709
Alberta	5 539
Manitoba	2 910
New Brunswick	2 092
Nova Scotia	1 978
Saskatchewan	1 371
Newfoundland	786
Prince Edward Island	138
Yukon & Northwest Territories	26

Scale 1: 19 000 000

0   200   400 km

Zenithal Equidistant Projection

© Oxford University Press

Southern Québec

Scale 1: 2 000 000

0   20   40   60 km

Conical Orthomorphic Projection

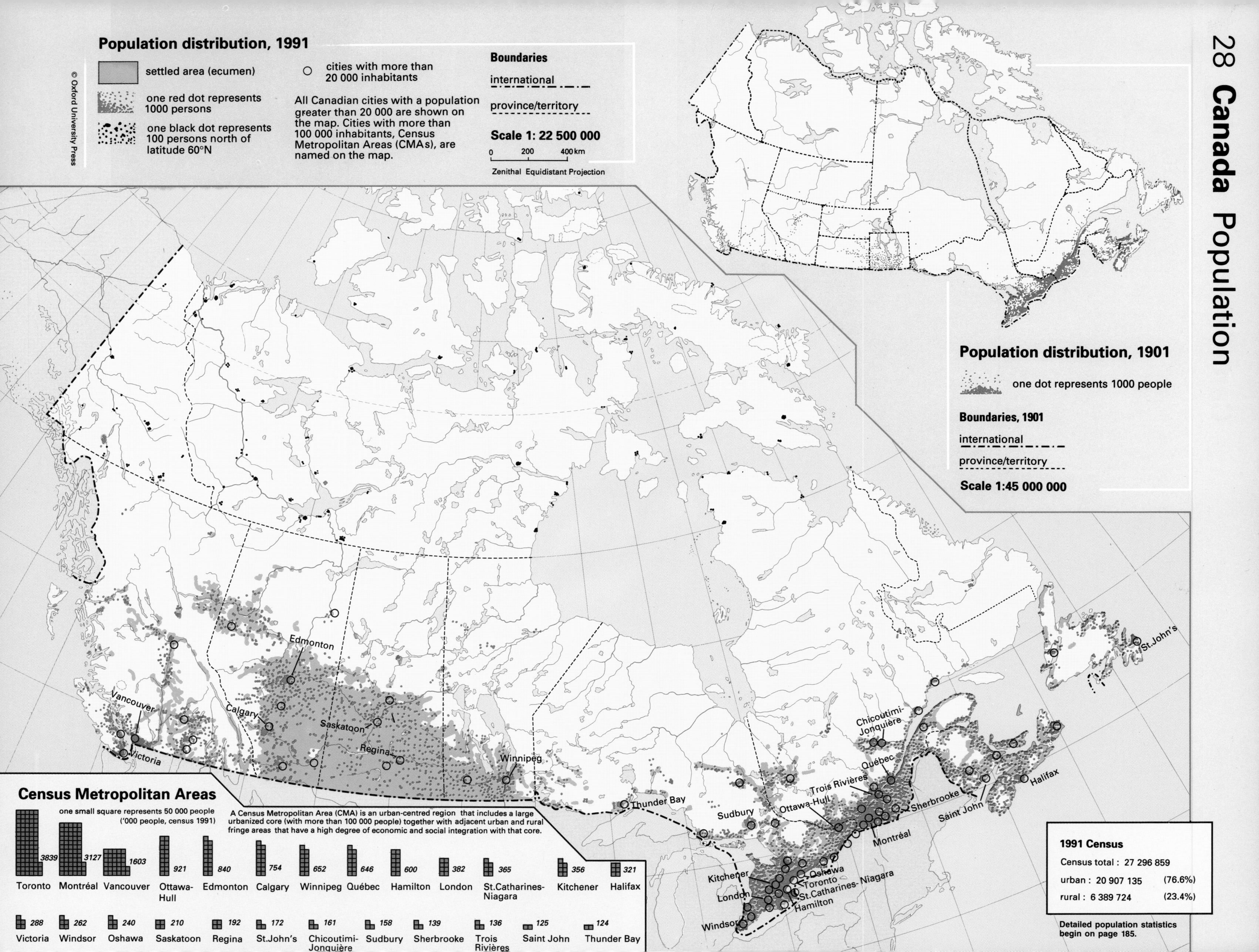

Population distribution, 1991

- settled area (ecumen)
- one red dot represents 1000 persons
- one black dot represents 100 persons north of latitude 60°N

○ cities with more than 20 000 inhabitants

All Canadian cities with a population greater than 20 000 are shown on the map. Cities with more than 100 000 inhabitants, Census Metropolitan Areas (CMAs), are named on the map.

Boundaries

international — ·· — ·· —
province/territory — · — · —

Scale 1: 22 500 000

0   200   400 km

Zenithal Equidistant Projection

© Oxford University Press

Population distribution, 1901

· one dot represents 1000 people

Boundaries, 1901

international — ·· — ·· —
province/territory — · — · —

Scale 1:45 000 000

1991 Census

Census total : 27 296 859
urban: 20 907 135   (76.6%)
rural : 6 389 724   (23.4%)

Detailed population statistics begin on page 185.

Census Metropolitan Areas

one small square represents 50 000 people
('000 people, census 1991)

A Census Metropolitan Area (CMA) is an urban-centred region that includes a large urbanized core (with more than 100 000 people) together with adjacent urban and rural fringe areas that have a high degree of economic and social integration with that core.

3839 Toronto	3127 Montréal	1603 Vancouver
921 Ottawa-Hull	840 Edmonton	754 Calgary	652 Winnipeg	646 Québec	600 Hamilton	382 London	365 St.Catharines-Niagara	356 Kitchener	321 Halifax
288 Victoria	262 Windsor	240 Oshawa	210 Saskatoon	192 Regina	172 St.John's	161 Chicoutimi-Jonquière	158 Sudbury	139 Sherbrooke	136 Trois Rivières	125 Saint John	124 Thunder Bay

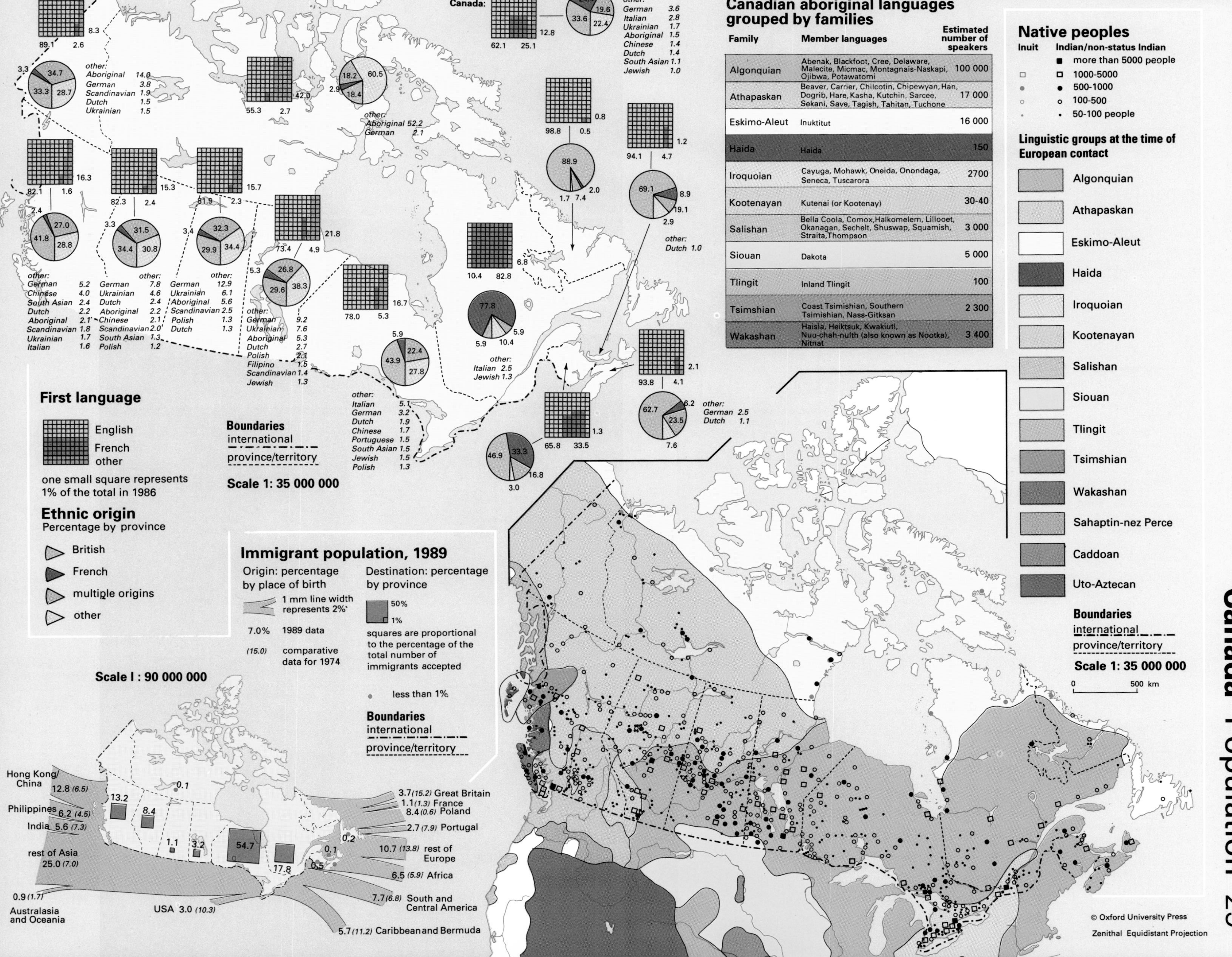

© Oxford University Press
Zenithal Equidistant Projection

Native peoples

Inuit
- □ more than 5000 people
- ■ 1000-5000
- ● 500-1000
- ○ 100-500
- ∘ 50-100 people

Indian/non-status Indian
(same symbol scale)

Linguistic groups at the time of European contact
- Algonquian
- Athapaskan
- Eskimo-Aleut
- Haida
- Iroquoian
- Kootenayan
- Salishan
- Siouan
- Tlingit
- Tsimshian
- Wakashan
- Sahaptin-nez Perce
- Caddoan
- Uto-Aztecan

Boundaries
- international
- province/territory

Scale 1 : 35 000 000

0   500 km

Canadian aboriginal languages grouped by families

Family	Member languages	Estimated number of speakers
Algonquian	Abenak, Blackfoot, Cree, Delaware, Malecite, Micmac, Montagnais-Naskapi, Ojibwa, Potawatomi	100 000
Athapaskan	Beaver, Carrier, Chilcotin, Chipewyan, Han, Dogrib, Hare, Kasha, Kutchin, Sarcee, Sekani, Save, Tagish, Tahitan, Tuchone	17 000
Eskimo-Aleut	Inuktitut	16 000
Haida	Haida	150
Iroquoian	Cayuga, Mohawk, Oneida, Onondaga, Seneca, Tuscarora	2700
Kootenayan	Kutenai (or Kootenay)	30-40
Salishan	Bella Coola, Comox, Halkomelem, Lillooet, Okanagan, Sechelt, Shuswap, Squamish, Straita, Thompson	3 000
Siouan	Dakota	5 000
Tlingit	Inland Tlingit	100
Tsimshian	Coast Tsimshian, Southern Tsimshian, Nass-Gitksan	2 300
Wakashan	Haisla, Heiktsuk, Kwakiutl, Nuu-chah-nulth (also known as Nootka), Nitinat	3 400

First language

- English
- French
- other

one small square represents 1% of the total in 1986

Ethnic origin
Percentage by province

- △ British
- ▲ French
- △ multiple origins
- △ other

Boundaries
- international
- province/territory

Scale 1 : 35 000 000

Immigrant population, 1989

Origin: percentage by place of birth

7.0% 1989 data
(15.0) comparative data for 1974

1 mm line width represents 2%

Destination: percentage by province

- 50%
- 1%

squares are proportional to the percentage of the total number of immigrants accepted

- less than 1%

Boundaries
- international
- province/territory

Scale 1 : 90 000 000

Hong Kong/China 12.8 (6.5)
Philippines 6.2 (4.5)
India 5.6 (7.3)
rest of Asia 25.0 (7.0)
Australasia and Oceania 0.9 (1.7)
USA 3.0 (10.3)
South and Central America 7.7 (6.8)
Africa 6.5 (5.9)
rest of Europe 10.7 (13.8)
Portugal 2.7 (7.9)
Poland 8.4 (0.6)
France 1.1 (1.3)
Great Britain 3.7 (15.2)
Caribbean and Bermuda 5.7 (11.2)

Canada:

Boundaries

- international
- province, territory
- county
- national park / provincial park

Communications

- expressway/other multilane highway
- other highway
- railway
- canal
- ferry
- ⊕ major airport
- ✈ other airport

Cities and towns

- built-up areas
- ● more than 100 000 inhabitants
- ● smaller urban places
- • smaller urban places

Physical features

- marsh

Sea Ice

- pack ice spring max.

Land height

metres	
	1000
	500
	300
	200
	100
	sea level

▲ spot height in metres

Scale 1:5 000 000

0 ———— 100 km

Newfoundland

Land Area: 371 690 km²
Total Area: 405 720 km² (4.1% of Canada)

Census Population

1871	152 500
1891	202 040
1911	242 619
1931	281 500
1951	361 416
1971	522 105
1991	568 474

of which, Farm	0.3%
Rural non-farm	40.8%
and Urban	58.9%

†Newfoundland became a province of Canada in 1949.

Census Metropolitan Areas, 1991

St. John's (capital)	171 859

Other important urban centres, 1991

Corner Brook	33 790
Happy Valley–	
Goose Bay (Labrador)	8 610

Gross Domestic Product (1986 $5.5 billion)

	%
goods producing	
Agriculture	0.5
Forestry	1.0
Fishing & Trapping	2.5
Mining	8.7
Manufacturing	9.2
Construction	8.2
Utilities	5.3
service producing	
Transportation	9.8
Wholesale & Retail	10.5
Finance	8.7
Services	21.9
Government Services (including defence)	13.8

Nova Scotia

Land Area: 52 840 km²
Total Area: 55 490 km² (0.6% of Canada)

Census Population

1871	387 800
1891	450 396
1911	492 338
1931	512 846
1951	642 584
1971	788 960
1991	899 942

of which, Farm	1.6%
Rural non-farm	44.4%
and Urban	54.0%

Census Metropolitan Areas, 1991

Halifax (capital)	320 501

Other important urban centres, 1991

Sydney	116 100
Glace Bay	19 501
Truro	44 003

Gross Domestic Product (1986 $10.8 billion)

	%
goods producing	
Agriculture	1.6
Forestry	0.4
Fishing & Trapping	2.0
Mining	1.5
Manufacturing	11.4
Construction	7.4
Utilities	2.9
service producing	
Transportation	8.1
Wholesale & Retail	12.4
Finance	15.8
Services	22.6
Government Services (including defence)	13.9

New Brunswick

Land Area: 72 090 km²
Total Area: 73 440 km² (0.7% of Canada)

Census Population

1871	285 594
1891	321 236
1911	351 889
1931	408 219
1951	515 697
1971	634 556
1991	723 900

of which, Farm	1.7%
Rural non-farm	48.9%
and Urban	49.4%

Census Metropolitan Areas, 1991

Saint John	124 981

Other important urban areas, 1991

Fredericton (capital)	71 869
Moncton	106 503

Gross Domestic Product (1986 $8.1 billion)

	%
goods producing	
Agriculture	1.5
Forestry	2.1
Fishing & Trapping	0.5
Mining	3.1
Manufacturing	13.9
Construction	7.3
Utilities	4.4
service producing	
Transportation	10.6
Wholesale & Retail	11.0
Finance	13.0
Services	21.8
Government Services (including defence)	10.7

Prince Edward Island

Land Area: 5 660 km²
Total Area: 5 660 km² (0.05% of Canada)

Census Population

1871	94 621
1891	109 078
1911	93 728
1931	88 038
1951	98 429
1971	110 640
1991	129 765

of which, Farm	8.1%
Rural non-farm	53.8%
and Urban	38.1%

Important urban centres, 1991

Charlottetown (capital)	57 472
Summerside	15 237

Gross Domestic Product (1986 $1.4 billion)

	%
goods producing	
Agriculture	9.4
Forestry	0.0
Fishing & Trapping	2.2
Mining	0.1
Manufacturing	7.2
Construction	5.7
Utilities	1.9
service producing	
Transportation	6.8
Wholesale & Retail	11.6
Finance	10.3
Services	21.1
Government Services (including defence)	23.7

Pack ice - average spring maximum

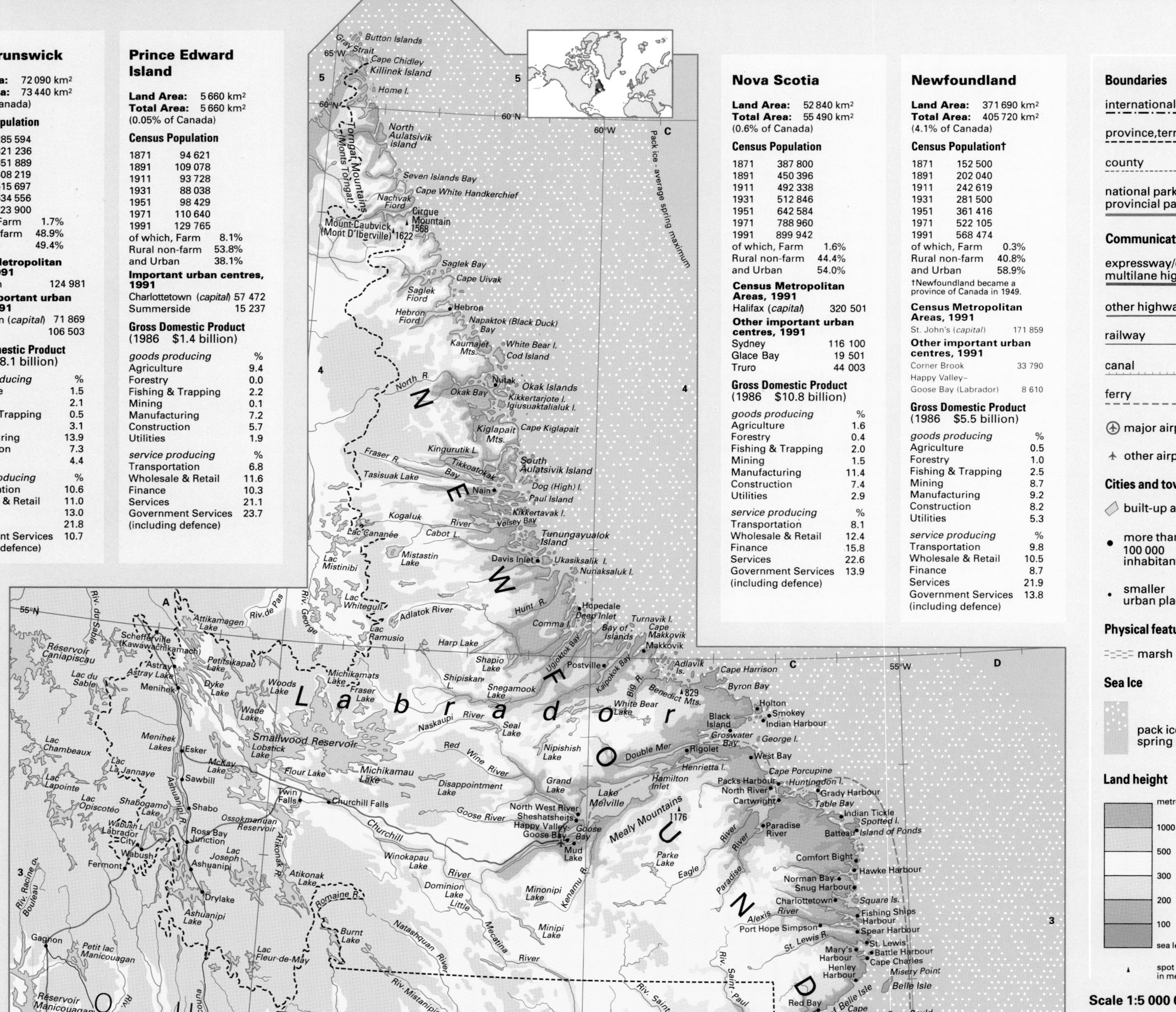

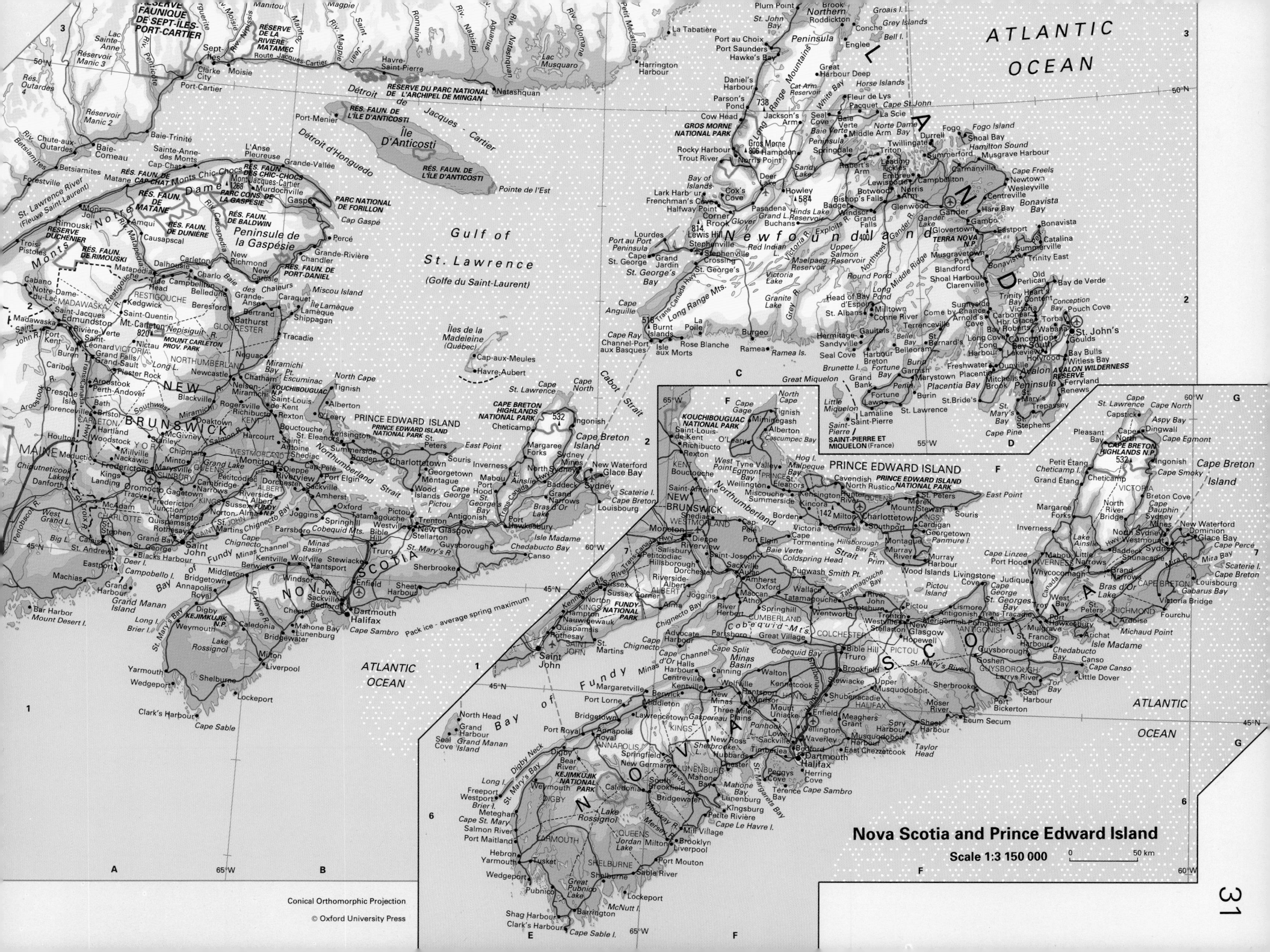

Nova Scotia and Prince Edward Island

Scale 1:3 150 000

© Oxford University Press

Conical Orthomorphic Projection

Boundaries

international

province

national park/ provincial park

Communications

expressway/other multilane highway

other highway

railway

major airport

other airport

Cities and towns

built-up areas

over 1 million inhabitants

more than 100 000 inhabitants

smaller urban places

Physical features

marsh

Sea Ice

pack ice spring max.

Land height

metres

1000

500

300

200

100

sea level

spot height in metres

Scale 1:5 000 000

0 50 100 km

Détroit d'Hudson

Baffin Island

Edgell I.

Resolution Island

Button Is.

Port Burwell

Gray Strait

Cape Chidley

Home I.

Labrador Sea

North Aulatsivik I.

Seven Sisters Bay

Nachvak Fiord

Torngat Mountains

Monts Torngat

1622 Mont D'Iberville (Mt. Caubvick)

Saglek Bay

Saglek Fiord

Hebron Fiord

NEWFOUNDLAND

North R.

Fraser R.

Tasisuak Lake

Lac Cananée

Mistastin Lake

Lac Whitegull

Lac Mistinibi

Lac Ramusio

Lac de la Hutte Sauvage

Lac Résolution

Riv. de Pas

Lac Tudor

George

Rivière

Abloviak Fiord

Riv. Koroc

Riv. Ford

Lac Jeannin

Lac Champdoré

Kangiqsualujjuaq

Riv. Mucaliq

Rivière à la Baleine

Riv. Wheeler

Lac Wakuach

Lac le Moyne

Lac Otelnuk

Lac Chaconipau

Lac Nichicapau

Riv. False

Akpotak Island

Baie d'Ungava

Gyrfalcon Is.

Kuujjuaq

Riv. Koksoak

Rivière Caniapiscau

Lac Cambrien

Riv. Pons

Riv. Sérigny

Rivière Caniapiscau

Riv. du Sable

Schefferville (Kawawachikamach)

Astray Lake

Attikamagen Lake

Petitsikapau Lake

Menihek

Menihek Lakes

Esker

Labrador

McKay Lake

Shabo

Shabogamo

Lobstick Lake

Smallwood Reservoir

Twin Falls

Ossokmanuan

Lac du Sable

Réservoir Caniapiscau

Lac Chambeaux

Lac Bermen

Cap Hopes Advance

Quaqtaq

Payne Bay

Hopes Advance Bay

Aupaluk

Tasiujaq

Lac Bérard

Kangirsuk

Lac Roberts

Lac Tasiaalujjuak

Lac Faribault

Lac Tasiataq

Riv. Delay

Mélèzes

Rivière aux Mélèzes

Riv. du Gué

Lac Potherie

Rivière aux Feuilles

Rivière Arnaud

Rivière Vachon

Cap Prince-de-Galles

Kangiqsujuaq

Cap de Nouvelle-France

Purtuniq

Déception

Salluit

Monts Povungnituk

Rivière de Povungnituk

Lac Nantais

Lac Lesdiguières

Lac Klotz

Péninsule d'Ungava

Lac Châtelain

Lac Bécard

Lac Pélican

Lac Payne

Lac Tassialouc

Lac Bacqueville

Lac Minto

Lac des Loups Marins

Petit lac des Loups Marins

Lac D'Iberville

Lac Saindon

Lac Bienville

Lac à l'Eau Claire

Nastapoca

Lac Bourdel

Rivière

Lac Guillaume-Delisle

Petite rivière de la Baleine

Grande rivière de la Baleine

Réservoir Laforge 2

Réservoir Laforge I

Réservoir de La Grande 4

Réservoir de La Grande 3

La Grande 4

Kanaaupscow

Rivière Kanaaupscow

Lac Anuc

Lac Tasiat

Lac le Roy

Lac Chavigny

Lac Couture

Riv. Kogaluc

Riv. Mariet

Lac Qilalugalik

Riv. Innuksuac

Ivujivik

Riv. Kovik

Riv. Chukotat

Kovik Bay

Kettlestone Bay

Akulivik

Smith I.

Cape Smith

Povungnituk

Kogaluc Bay

Inukjuak

Hopewell Islands

Cap Dufferin

Baie d'Hudson

Mansel Island

Cape Acadia

Sleeper Islands

King George Islands

North Belcher Is.

Belcher Islands

Nastapoka Islands

Umiujaq

Riv. Coats

Kuujjuarapik (Poste-de-la-Baleine) (Whapmagoostui)

Long I.

Pointe Louis-XIV

Lac Burton

Red Bay

L'Anse au Loup

Eddies Cove

Main Brook

Forteau

Blanc-Sablon

Détroit de Belle Isle

St. Barbe

Plum Point

Northern Peninsula

St. John Bay

Hawke's Bay

Port au Choix

Port Saunders

NEWFOUNDLAND

Harbour Deep

Riv. Saint-Paul

Vieux-Fort

Riv. Saint-Augustin

La Tabatière

Mécatina

Rivière du Petit Mécatina

Riv. Olomane

60°N

65°W

70°W

75°W

55°N

A

B

C

D

E

3

4

5

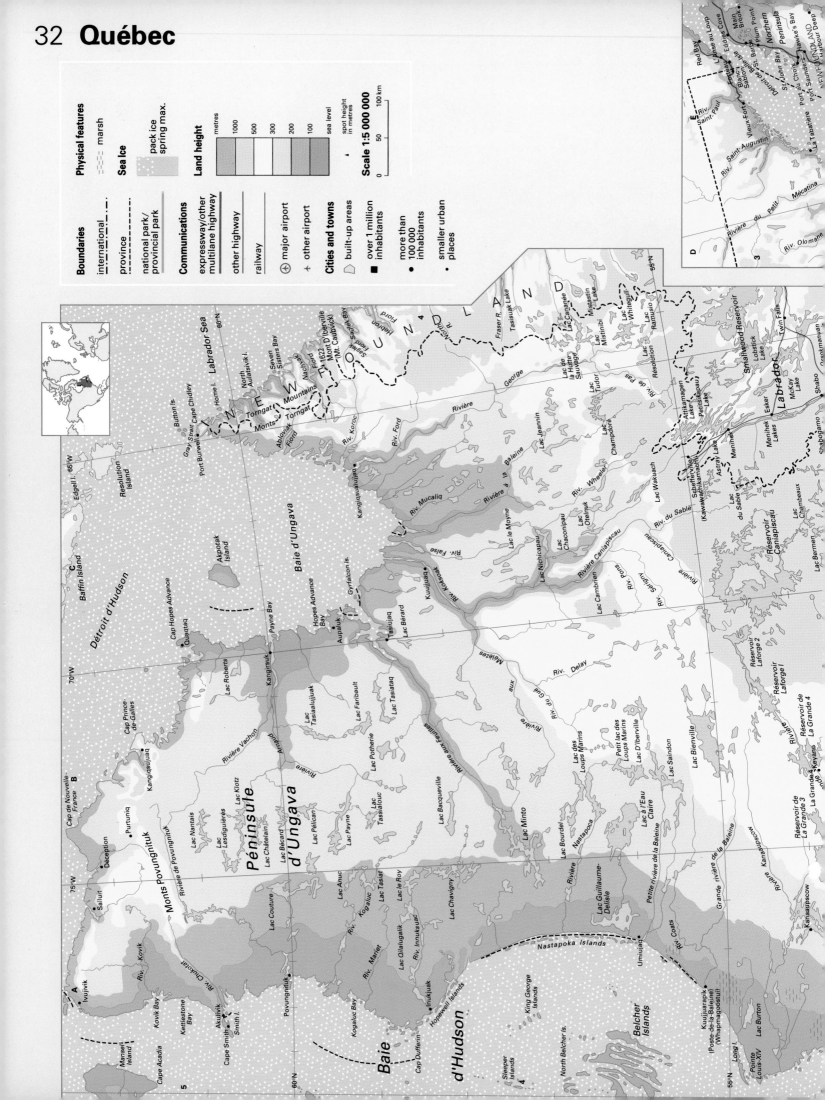

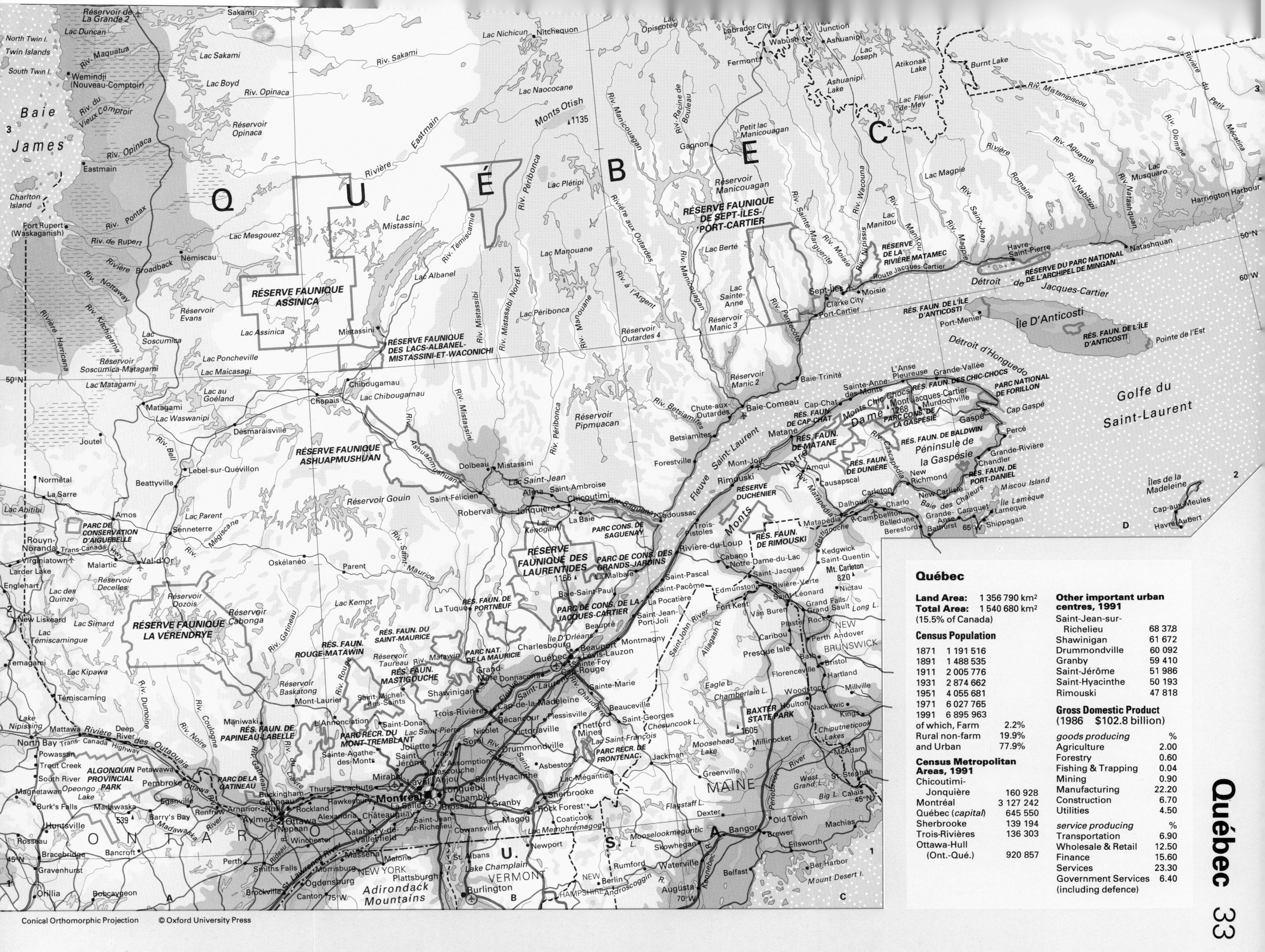

Québec

Land Area: 1 356 790 km²
Total Area: 1 540 680 km²
(15.5% of Canada)

Census Population

Year	Population
1871	1 191 516
1891	1 488 535
1911	2 005 776
1931	2 874 662
1951	4 055 681
1971	6 027 765
1991	6 895 963
of which, Farm	2.2%
Rural non-farm	19.9%
and Urban	77.9%

Census Metropolitan Areas, 1991

Chicoutimi-Jonquière	160 928
Montréal	3 127 242
Québec (capital)	645 550
Sherbrooke	139 194
Trois-Rivières	136 303
Ottawa-Hull (Ont.-Qué.)	920 857

Other important urban centres, 1991

Saint-Jean-sur-Richelieu	68 378
Shawinigan	61 672
Drummondville	60 092
Granby	59 410
Saint-Jérôme	51 986
Saint-Hyacinthe	50 193
Rimouski	47 818

Gross Domestic Product
(1986 $102.8 billion)

goods producing	%
Agriculture	2.00
Forestry	0.60
Fishing & Trapping	0.04
Mining	0.90
Manufacturing	22.20
Construction	6.70
Utilities	4.50

service producing	%
Transportation	6.90
Wholesale & Retail	12.50
Finance	15.60
Services	23.30
Government Services (including defence)	6.40

Conical Orthomorphic Projection

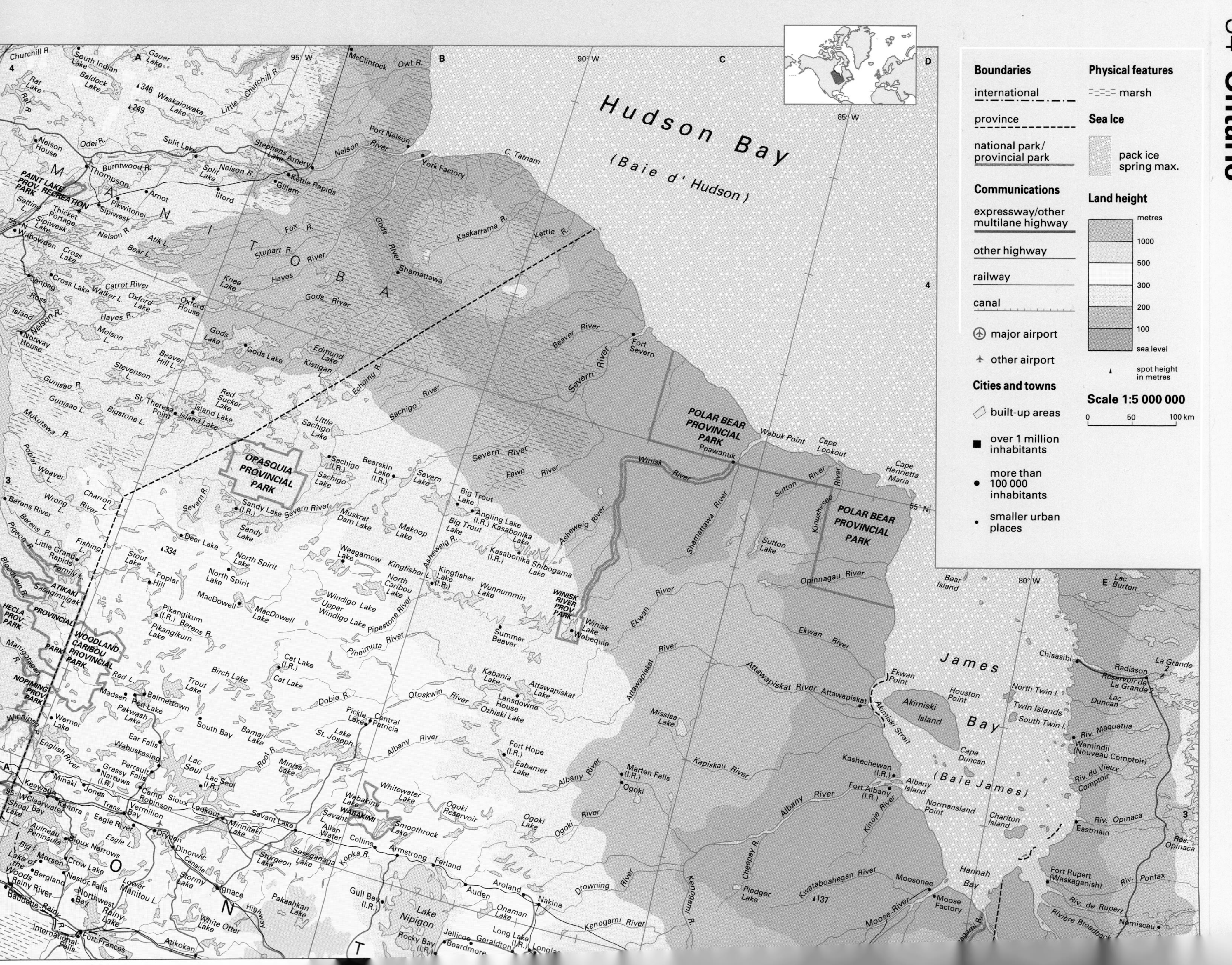
Boundaries
international
province
national park/ provincial park
Communications
expressway/other multilane highway
other highway
railway
canal
major airport
other airport
Cities and towns
built-up areas
over 1 million inhabitants
more than 100 000 inhabitants
smaller urban places
Physical features
marsh
Sea Ice
pack ice spring max.
Land height
metres
1000
500
300
200
100
sea level
spot height in metres
Scale 1:5 000 000
0
50
100 km
Hudson Bay
(Baie d' Hudson)
James Bay
(Baie James)
POLAR BEAR PROVINCIAL PARK
WINISK RIVER PROV. PARK
OPASQUIA PROVINCIAL PARK
WOODLAND CARIBOU PROVINCIAL PARK
ATIKAKI PROVINCIAL
NOPIMING PROV. PARK
HECLA PROV. PARK
PAINT LAKE PROV. RECREATION PARK
WABAKIMI
MANITOBA
ONTARIO
Akimiski Island
Akimiski Strait
Cape Henrietta Maria
Moosonee
Moose Factory
Fort Severn
Peawanuk
Attawapiskat
Fort Albany
Kashechewan
Big Trout Lake
Sandy Lake
Red Lake
Sioux Lookout
Dryden
Kenora
Fort Frances
Lake Nipigon
Lac Seul
Geraldton
Nakina
Thompson
Gillam
York Factory
Port Nelson
Churchill R.
Nelson River
Hayes River
Gods Lake
Severn River
Winisk River
Ekwan River
Attawapiskat River
Albany River
Kenogami R.
Moose River
85° W
90° W
95° W
80° W
55° N

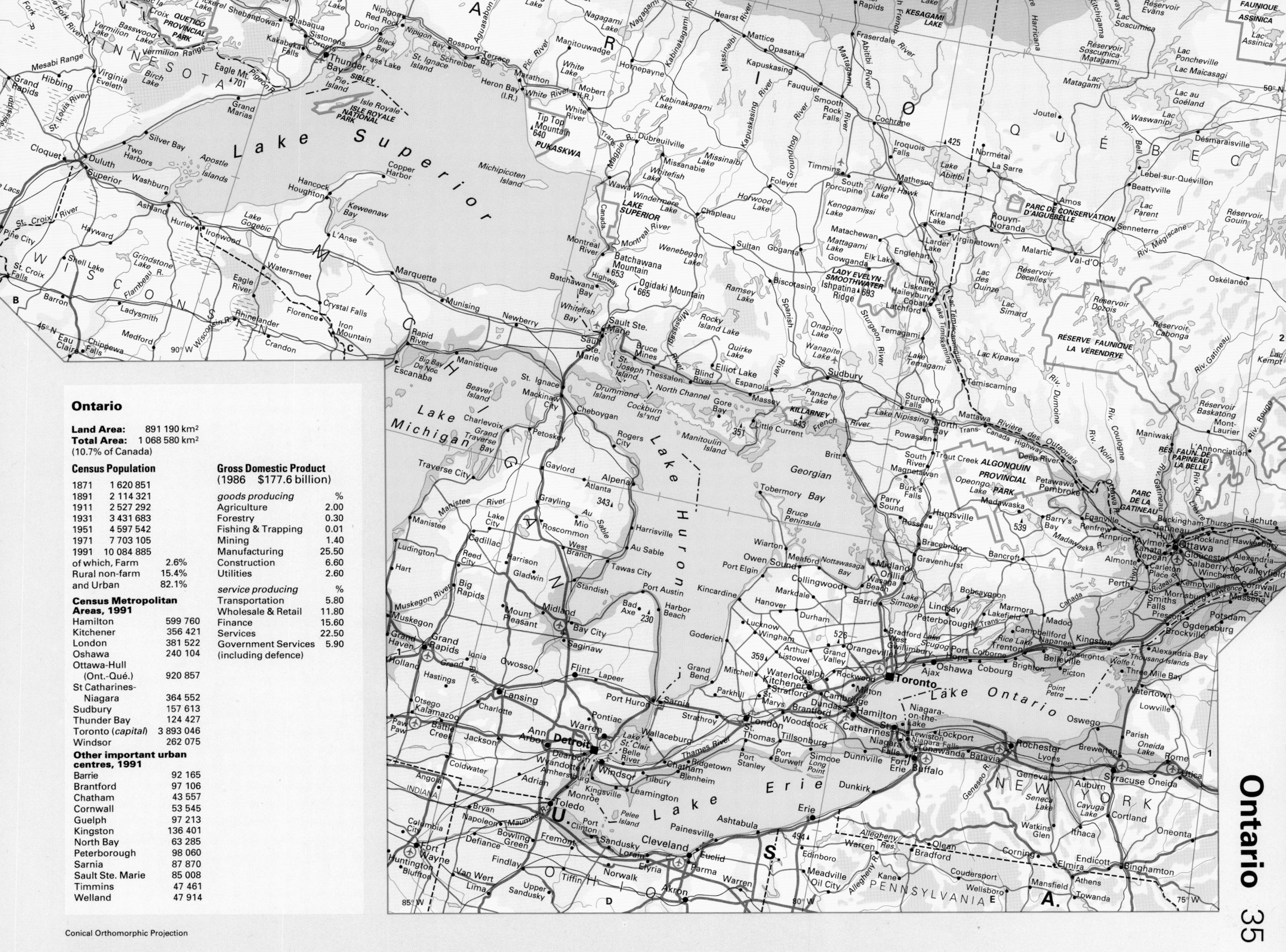

Ontario

Land Area: 891 190 km²
Total Area: 1 068 580 km²
(10.7% of Canada)

Census Population

1871	1 620 851
1891	2 114 321
1911	2 527 292
1931	3 431 683
1951	4 597 542
1971	7 703 105
1991	10 084 885
of which, Farm	2.6%
Rural non-farm	15.4%
and Urban	82.1%

Census Metropolitan Areas, 1991

Hamilton	599 760
Kitchener	356 421
London	381 522
Oshawa	240 104
Ottawa-Hull (Ont.-Qué.)	920 857
St Catharines-Niagara	364 552
Sudbury	157 613
Thunder Bay	124 427
Toronto (capital)	3 893 046
Windsor	262 075

Other important urban centres, 1991

Barrie	92 165
Brantford	97 106
Chatham	43 557
Cornwall	53 545
Guelph	97 213
Kingston	136 401
North Bay	63 285
Peterborough	98 060
Sarnia	87 870
Sault Ste. Marie	85 008
Timmins	47 461
Welland	47 914

Gross Domestic Product (1986 $177.6 billion)

	%
goods producing	
Agriculture	2.00
Forestry	0.30
Fishing & Trapping	0.01
Mining	1.40
Manufacturing	25.50
Construction	6.60
Utilities	2.60
service producing	%
Transportation	5.80
Wholesale & Retail	11.80
Finance	15.60
Services	22.50
Government Services (including defence)	5.90

Conical Orthomorphic Projection

© Oxford University Press

Boundaries

international

province

regional municipality/ district/ county

national/provincial park

Cities and towns

built-up areas

■ over 1 million inhabitants

● more than 100 000 inhabitants

• smaller urban places

Communications

expressway/other multilane highway

other highway

railway

canal

✈ major airport

✈ other airport

Physical features

marsh

Sea Ice

pack ice spring max.

Land height

metres
1000
500
300
200
100
sea level

▲ spot height in metres

Scale 1:3 150 000

0   50   100 km

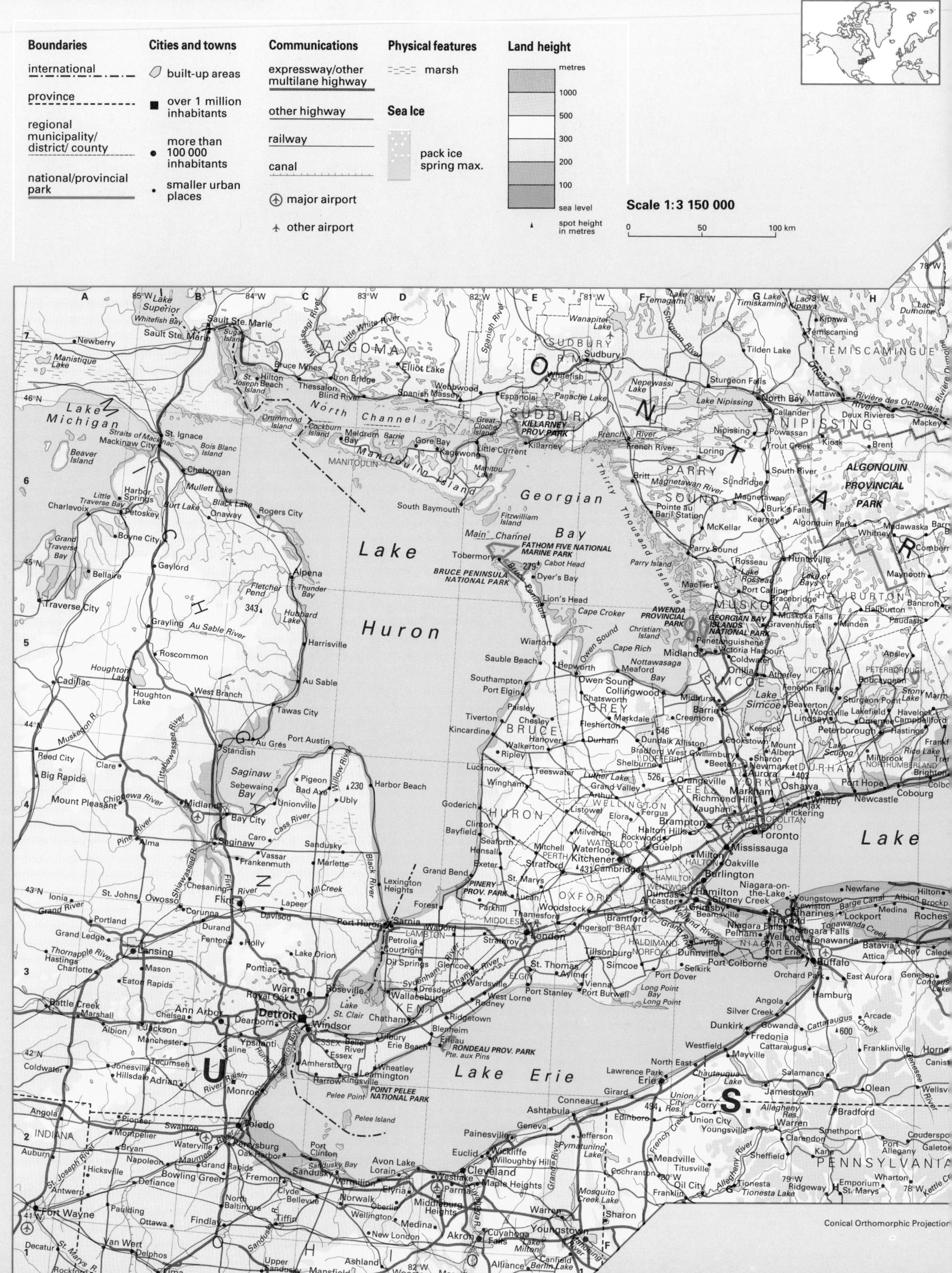

Conical Orthomorphic Projection

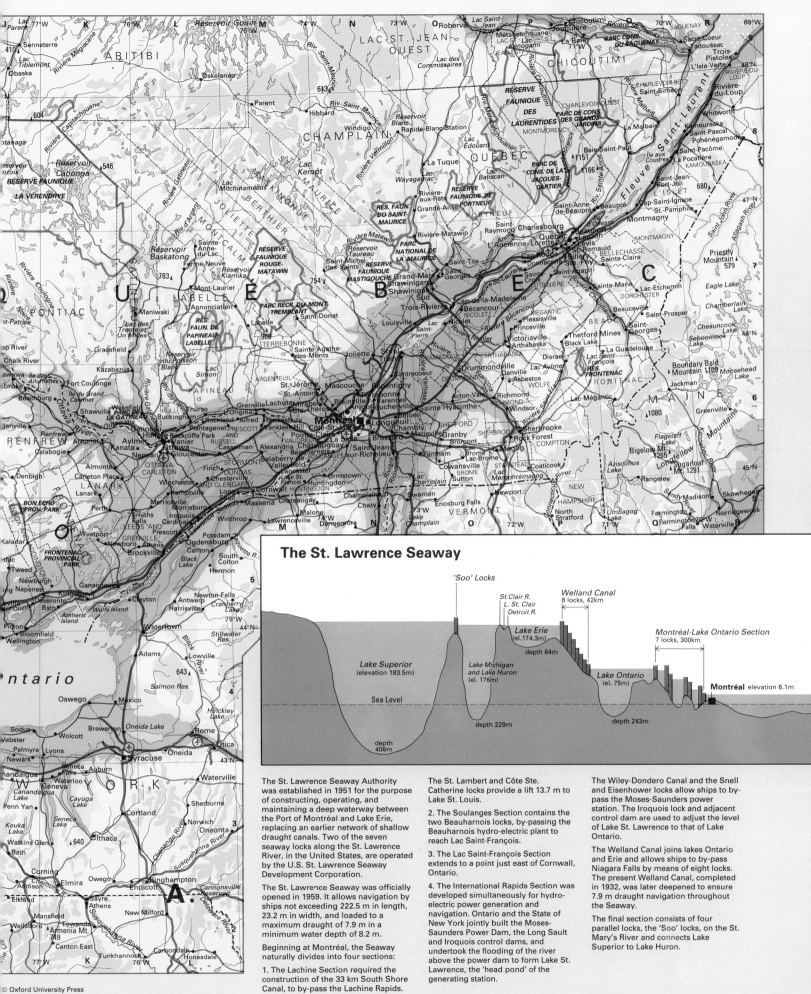

The St. Lawrence Seaway

'Soo' Locks

St.Clair R.
L. St. Clair
Detroit R.

Welland Canal
8 locks, 42km

Lake Erie
(el. 174.3m)

depth 64m

Montréal-Lake Ontario Section
7 locks, 300km

Lake Superior
(elevation 183.5m)

Lake Michigan
and Lake Huron
(el. 176m)

Lake Ontario
(el. 75m)

Montréal elevation 6.1m

Sea Level

depth 229m

depth 243m

depth 406m

The St. Lawrence Seaway Authority was established in 1951 for the purpose of constructing, operating, and maintaining a deep waterway between the Port of Montréal and Lake Erie, replacing an earlier network of shallow draught canals. Two of the seven seaway locks along the St. Lawrence River, in the United States, are operated by the U.S. St. Lawrence Seaway Development Corporation.

The St. Lawrence Seaway was officially opened in 1959. It allows navigation by ships not exceeding 222.5 m in length, 23.2 m in width, and loaded to a maximum draught of 7.9 m in a minimum water depth of 8.2 m.

Beginning at Montréal, the Seaway naturally divides into four sections:

1. The Lachine Section required the construction of the 33 km South Shore Canal, to by-pass the Lachine Rapids.

The St. Lambert and Côte Ste. Catherine locks provide a lift 13.7 m to Lake St. Louis.

2. The Soulanges Section contains the two Beauharnois locks, by-passing the Beauharnois hydro-electric plant to reach Lac Saint-François.

3. The Lac Saint-François Section extends to a point just east of Cornwall, Ontario.

4. The International Rapids Section was developed simultaneously for hydro-electric power generation and navigation. Ontario and the State of New York jointly built the Moses-Saunders Power Dam, the Long Sault and Iroquois control dams, and undertook the flooding of the river above the power dam to form Lake St. Lawrence, the 'head pond' of the generating station.

The Wiley-Dondero Canal and the Snell and Eisenhower locks allow ships to by-pass the Moses-Saunders power station. The Iroquois lock and adjacent control dam are used to adjust the level of Lake St. Lawrence to that of Lake Ontario.

The Welland Canal joins lakes Ontario and Erie and allows ships to by-pass Niagara Falls by means of eight locks. The present Welland Canal, completed in 1932, was later deepened to ensure 7.9 m draught navigation throughout the Seaway.

The final section consists of four parallel locks, the 'Soo' locks, on the St. Mary's River and connects Lake Superior to Lake Huron.

Conical Orthomorphic Projec
© Oxford University P

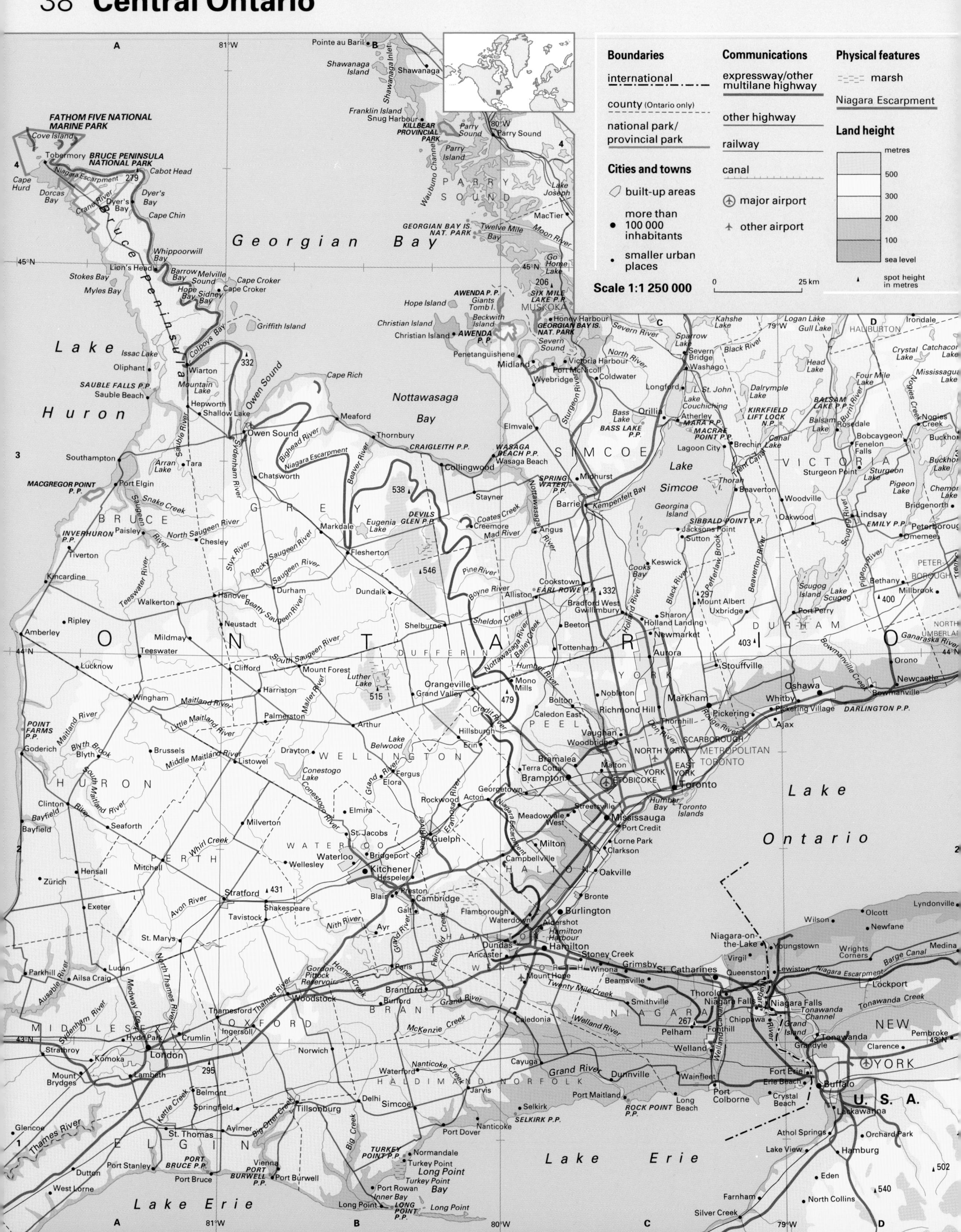

Boundaries

international

county (Ontario only)

national park/
provincial park

Cities and towns

built-up areas

more than
100 000
inhabitants

smaller urban
places

Communications

expressway/other
multilane highway

other highway

railway

canal

major airport

other airport

Physical features

marsh

Niagara Escarpment

Land height

metres
500
300
200
100
sea level

spot height
in metres

Scale 1:1 250 000

0   25 km

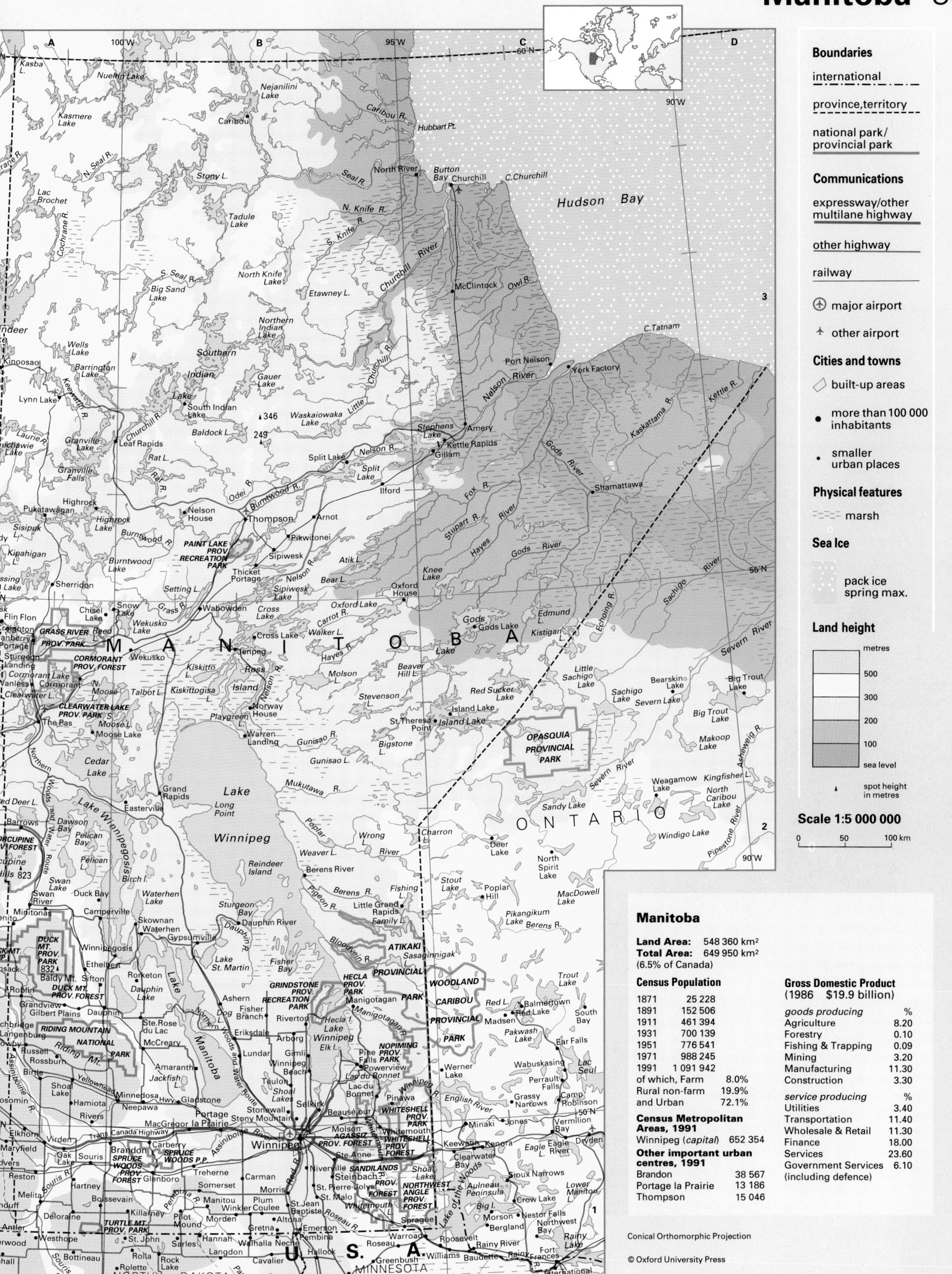

Boundaries

international

province, territory

national park/
provincial park

Communications

expressway/other
multilane highway

other highway

railway

✈ major airport

✦ other airport

Cities and towns

▱ built-up areas

● more than 100 000
inhabitants

• smaller
urban places

Physical features

marsh

Sea Ice

pack ice
spring max.

Land height

metres
500
300
200
100
sea level

▲ spot height
in metres

Scale 1:5 000 000

0   50   100 km

Manitoba

Land Area: 548 360 km²
Total Area: 649 950 km²
(6.5% of Canada)

Census Population

1871	25 228
1891	152 506
1911	461 394
1931	700 139
1951	776 541
1971	988 245
1991	1 091 942
of which, Farm	8.0%
Rural non-farm	19.9%
and Urban	72.1%

**Census Metropolitan
Areas, 1991**

Winnipeg (*capital*) 652 354

**Other important urban
centres, 1991**

Brandon	38 567
Portage la Prairie	13 186
Thompson	15 046

Gross Domestic Product
(1986 $19.9 billion)

goods producing	%
Agriculture	8.20
Forestry	0.10
Fishing & Trapping	0.09
Mining	3.20
Manufacturing	11.30
Construction	3.30
service producing	%
Utilities	3.40
Transportation	11.40
Wholesale & Retail	11.30
Finance	18.00
Services	23.60
Government Services
(including defence)	6.10

Conical Orthomorphic Projection

40 Saskatchewan

Boundaries

international

province, territory

national park/
provincial park

Communications

expressway/other
multilane highway

other highway

railway

✈ major airport

✈ other airport

Cities and towns

▱ built-up areas

● more than 100 000
inhabitants

• smaller
urban places

Physical features

===== marsh

Land height

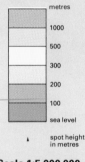

metres

1000
500
300
200
100
sea level

▲ spot height
in metres

Scale 1:5 000 000

0   50   100 km

Saskatchewan

Land Area: 570 700 km²
Total Area: 652 330 km²
(6.5% of Canada)

Census Population

1871	included in
1891	NWT
1911	492 432
1931	921 785
1951	831 728
1971	926 240
1991	988 928
of which, Farm	16.0%
Rural non-farm	22.6%
and Urban	61.4%

Census Metropolitan
Areas, 1991

Regina (*capital*)   191 692
Saskatoon   210 023

Other important urban
areas, 1991

Lloydminster   17 283
Moose Jaw   35 552
Prince Albert   41 257
Swift Current   14 815
Yorkton   18 023

Gross Domestic Product
(1986 $17.4 billion)

goods producing	%
Agriculture	12.4
Forestry	0.2
Fishing & Trapping	0.0
Mining	12.5
Manufacturing	5.7
Construction	4.3
Utilities	2.7
service producing	%
Transportation	7.7
Wholesale & Retail	9.7
Finance	17.0
Services	17.8
Government Services	10.0
(including defence)	

© Oxford University Press

Conical Orthomorphic Projection

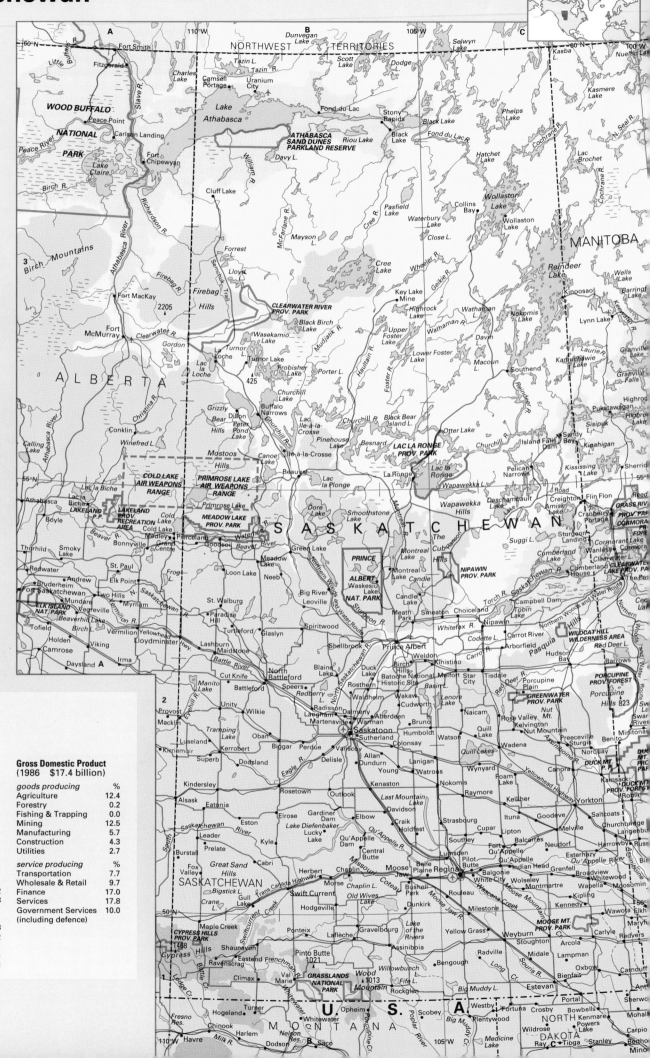

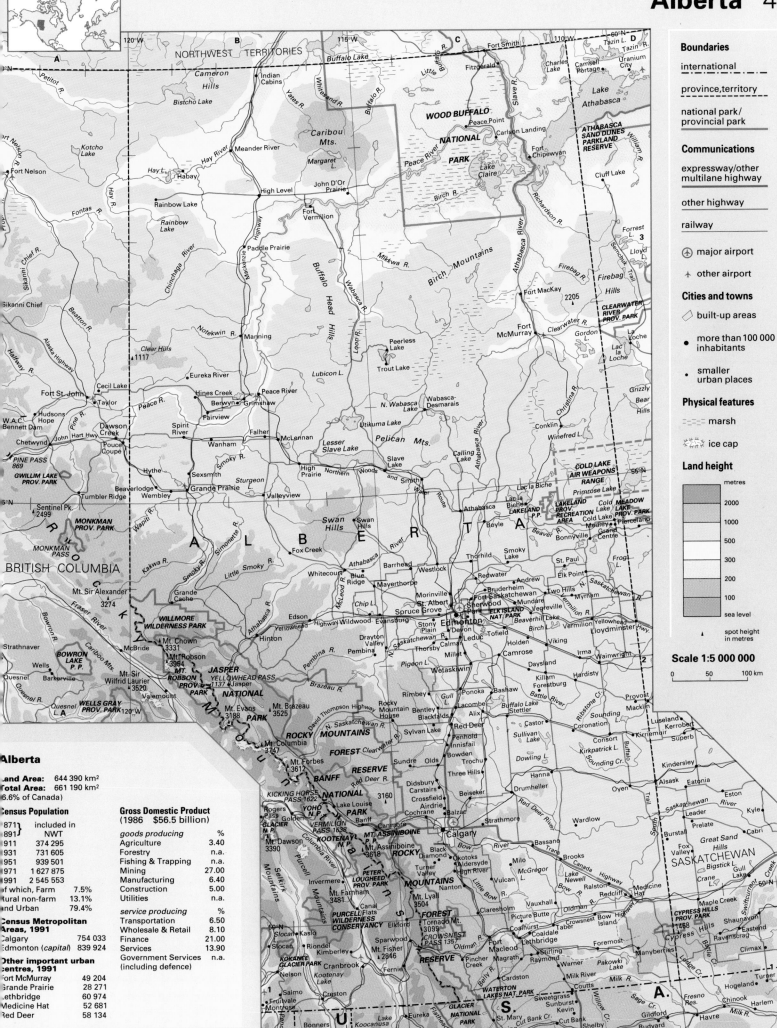

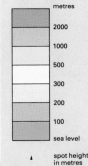

Boundaries
international
province, territory
national park/ provincial park

Communications
expressway/other multilane highway
other highway
railway
⊕ major airport
✈ other airport

Cities and towns
built-up areas
● more than 100 000 inhabitants
• smaller urban places

Physical features
- - - marsh
ice cap

Land height

metres
2000
1000
500
300
200
100
sea level

▲ spot height in metres

Scale 1:5 000 000
0   50   100 km

Alberta

Land Area: 644 390 km²
Total Area: 661 190 km² (6.6% of Canada)

Census Population

1871	included in
1891	NWT
1911	374 295
1931	731 605
1951	939 501
1971	1 627 875
1991	2 545 553
of which, Farm	7.5%
Rural non-farm	13.1%
and Urban	79.4%

Census Metropolitan Areas, 1991

Calgary	754 033
Edmonton (capital)	839 924

Other important urban centres, 1991

Fort McMurray	49 204
Grande Prairie	28 271
Lethbridge	60 974
Medicine Hat	52 681
Red Deer	58 134

Gross Domestic Product (1986 $56.5 billion)

goods producing	%
Agriculture	3.40
Forestry	n.a.
Fishing & Trapping	n.a.
Mining	27.00
Manufacturing	6.40
Construction	5.00
Utilities	n.a.

service producing	%
Transportation	6.50
Wholesale & Retail	8.10
Finance	21.00
Services	13.90
Government Services (including defence)	n.a.

© Oxford University Press

Conical Orthomorphic Projection

Boundaries

international

province, territory

national park/
provincial park

Communications

multilane highway

other highway

railway

✈ major airport

✈ other airport

Cities and towns

built-up areas

■ over 1 million
inhabitants

● more than
100 000
inhabitants

• smaller urban
places

Physical features

marsh

ice cap

Land height

metres
2000
1000
500
300
200
100
sea level

▲ spot height
in metres

Scale 1:5 000 000

0   50   100 km

Conical Orthomorphic Projection
© Oxford University Press

Southwestern BC

Scale 1:2 000 000

0   25   50 km

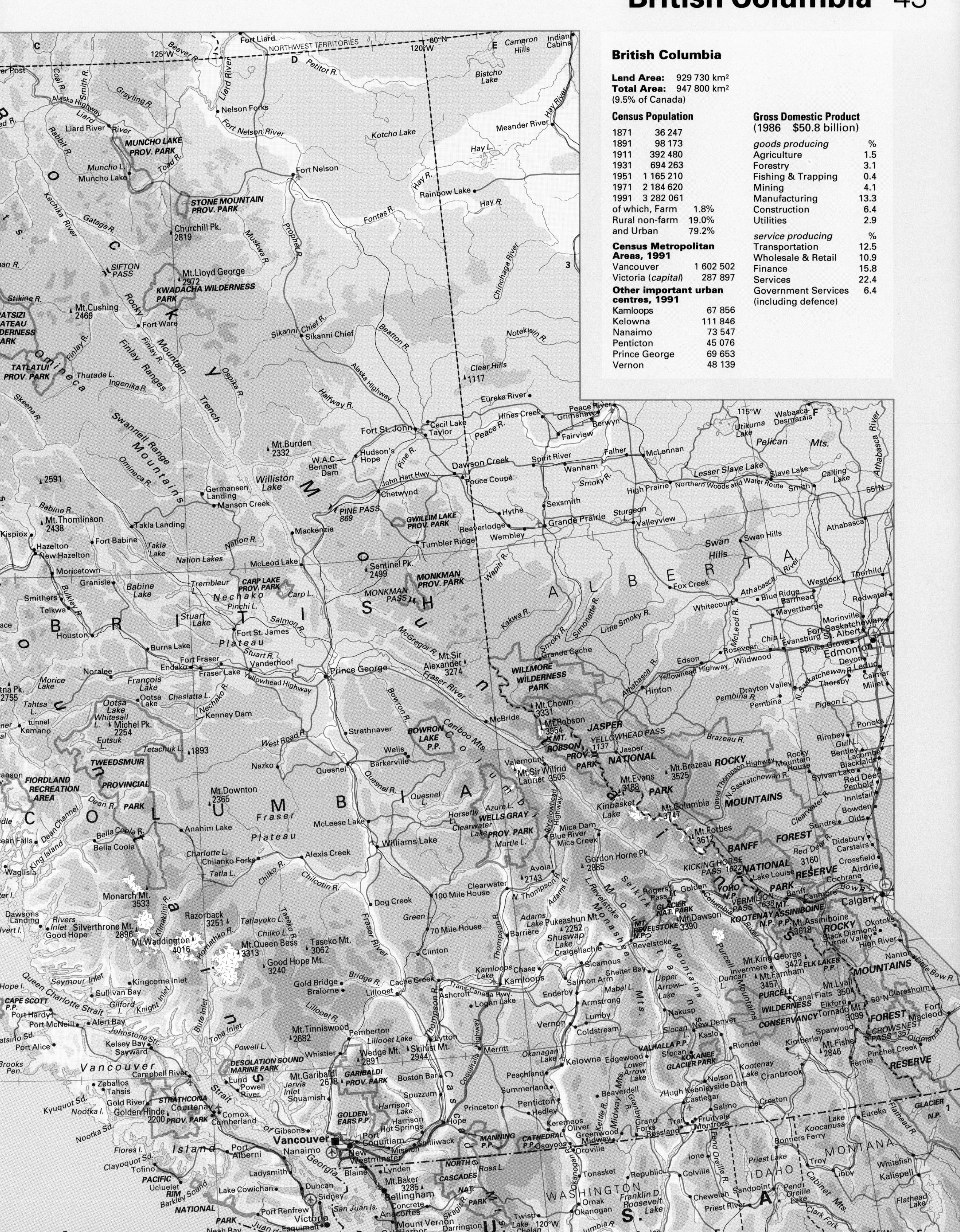

British Columbia

Land Area: 929 730 km²
Total Area: 947 800 km²
(9.5% of Canada)

Census Population

1871	36 247	
1891	98 173	
1911	392 480	
1931	694 263	
1951	1 165 210	
1971	2 184 620	
1991	3 282 061	
of which, Farm	1.8%	
Rural non-farm	19.0%	
and Urban	79.2%	

Census Metropolitan Areas, 1991

Vancouver	1 602 502
Victoria (*capital*)	287 897

Other important urban centres, 1991

Kamloops	67 856
Kelowna	111 846
Nanaimo	73 547
Penticton	45 076
Prince George	69 653
Vernon	48 139

Gross Domestic Product
(1986 $50.8 billion)

goods producing	%
Agriculture	1.5
Forestry	3.1
Fishing & Trapping	0.4
Mining	4.1
Manufacturing	13.3
Construction	6.4
Utilities	2.9

service producing	%
Transportation	12.5
Wholesale & Retail	10.9
Finance	15.8
Services	22.4
Government Services (including defence)	6.4

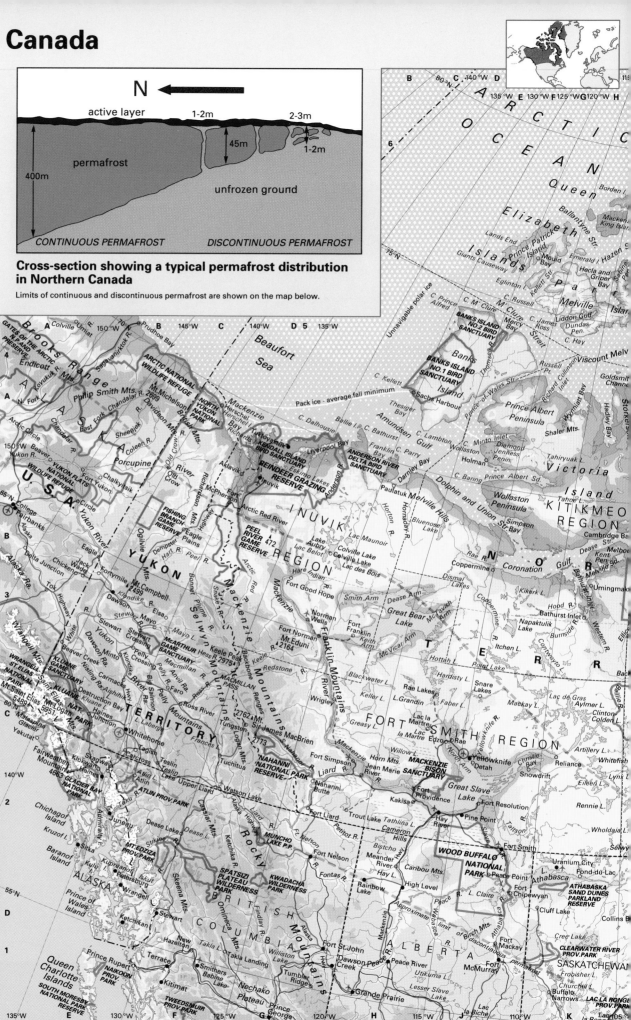

Conical Orthomorphic Projection

© Oxford University Press

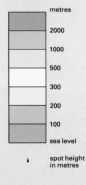

Boundaries

international

province, territory

region

national/provincial
park/sanctuary

Communications

other road

winter road

railway

⊕ major airport

✈ other airport

Towns

● more than 1000 inhabitants

○ less than 1000 inhabitants

Physical features

marsh

ice cap

Sea Ice

unnavigable

pack ice fall minimum

pack ice spring max.

Land height

metres

2000

1000

500

300

200

100

sea level

▲ spot height in metres

Scale 1:12 000 000

0   200km

Cross-section showing a typical permafrost distribution in Northern Canada

Limits of continuous and discontinuous permafrost are shown on the map below.

N

active layer

1-2m   2-3m

45m

1-2m

permafrost

400m

unfrozen ground

CONTINUOUS PERMAFROST   DISCONTINUOUS PERMAFROST

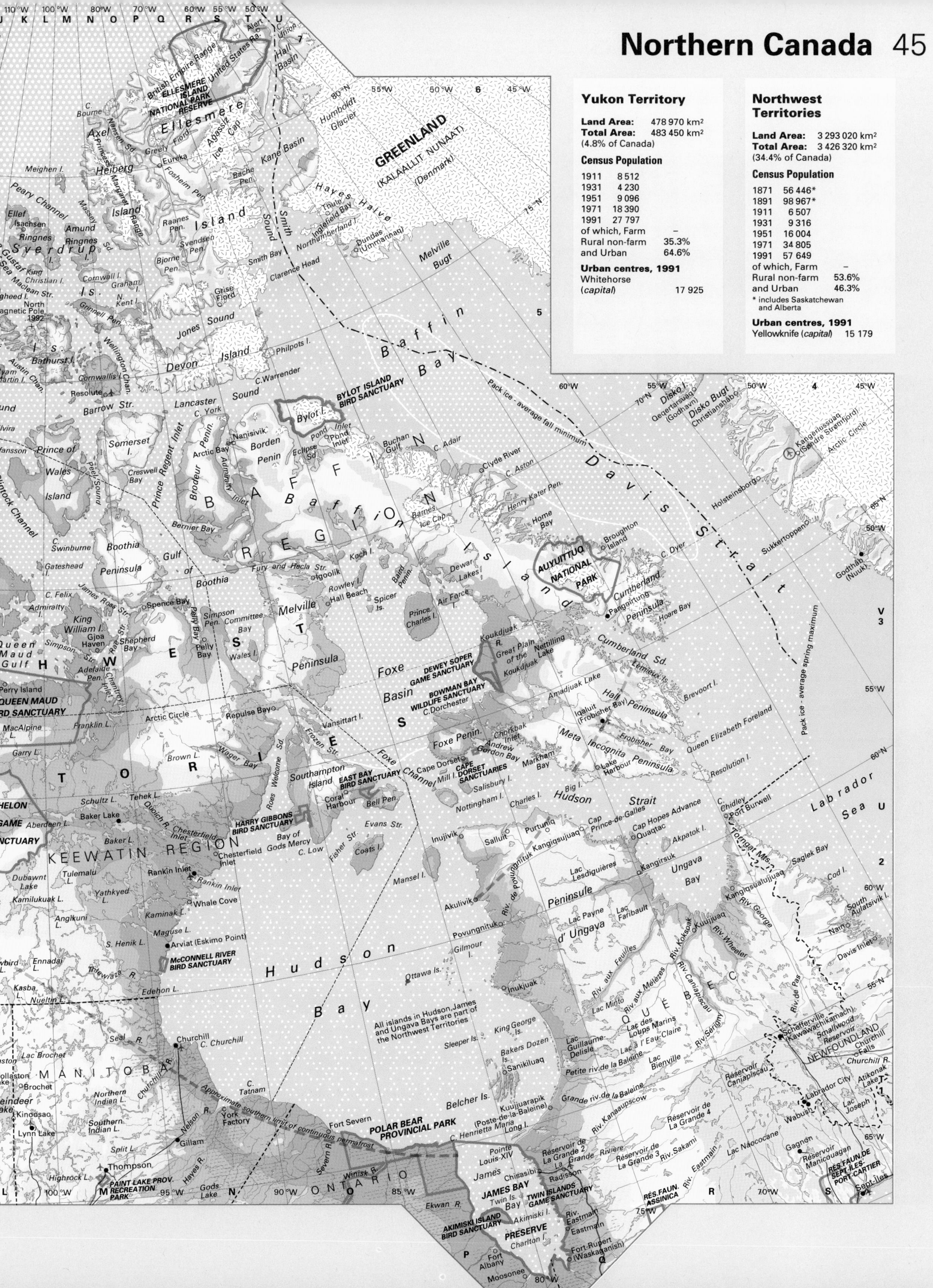

Yukon Territory

Land Area: 478 970 km²
Total Area: 483 450 km²
(4.8% of Canada)

Census Population

Year	Population
1911	8 512
1931	4 230
1951	9 096
1971	18 390
1991	27 797
of which, Farm	–
Rural non-farm	35.3%
and Urban	64.6%

Urban centres, 1991

Whitehorse
(*capital*)   17 925

Northwest Territories

Land Area: 3 293 020 km²
Total Area: 3 426 320 km²
(34.4% of Canada)

Census Population

Year	Population
1871	56 446*
1891	98 967*
1911	6 507
1931	9 316
1951	16 004
1971	34 805
1991	57 649
of which, Farm	–
Rural non-farm	53.6%
and Urban	46.3%

* includes Saskatchewan and Alberta

Urban centres, 1991

Yellowknife (*capital*)   15 179

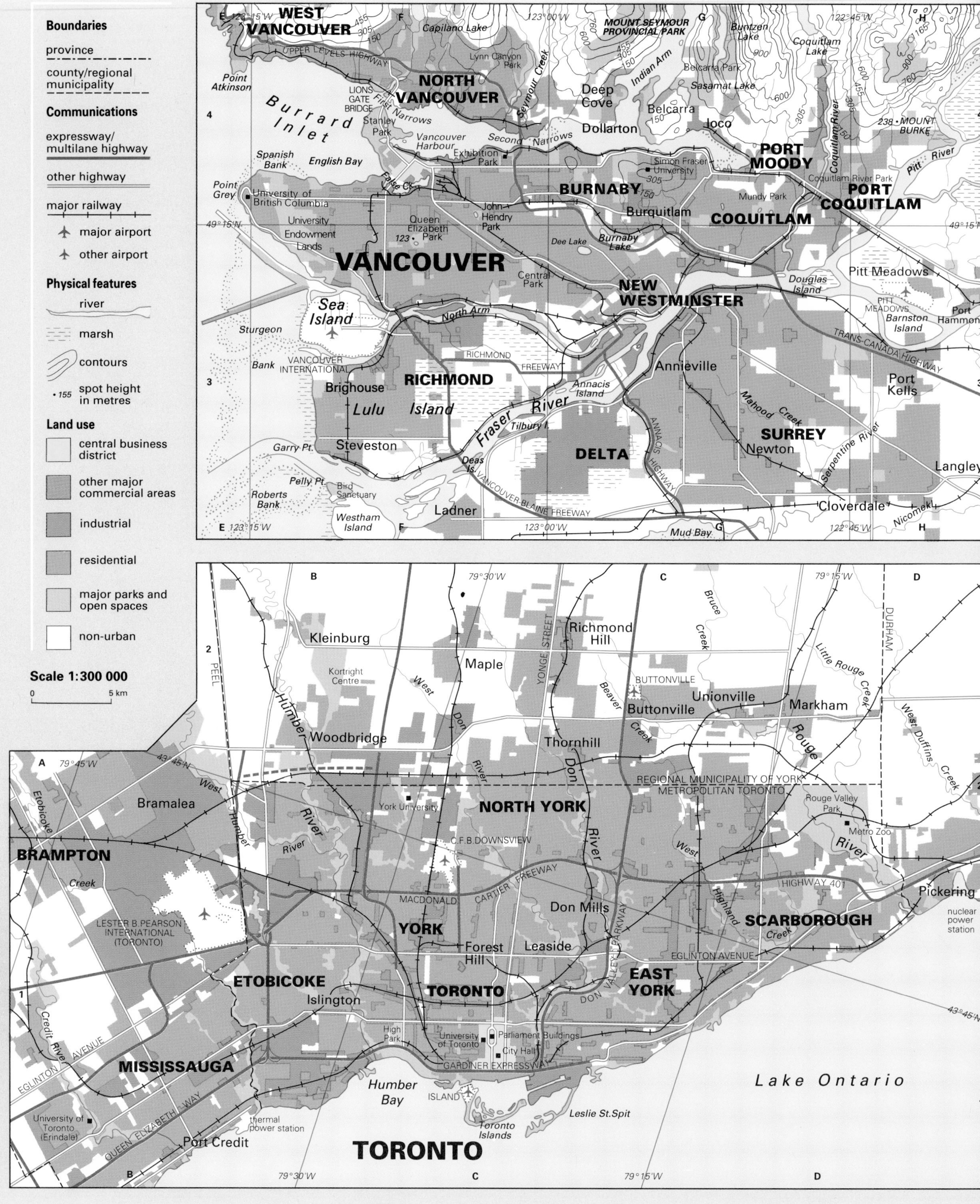

Boundaries

province

county/regional
municipality

Communications

expressway/
multilane highway

other highway

major railway

✈ major airport

✈ other airport

Physical features

river

marsh

contours

·155 spot height
in metres

Land use

central business
district

other major
commercial areas

industrial

residential

major parks and
open spaces

non-urban

Scale 1:300 000

0   5 km

VANCOUVER map

WEST VANCOUVER

NORTH VANCOUVER

Point Atkinson

Capilano Lake

Lynn Canyon Park

MOUNT SEYMOUR PROVINCIAL PARK

Buntzen Lake

Coquitlam Lake

Indian Arm

Deep Cove

Belcarra Park

Sasamat Lake

Belcarra

Dollarton

Ioco

·238 MOUNT BURKE

Burrard Inlet

LIONS GATE BRIDGE

Stanley Park

First Narrows

Vancouver Harbour

Second Narrows

Exhibition Park

Simon Fraser University

PORT MOODY

Coquitlam River Park

Coquitlam River

Pitt River

Spanish Bank

English Bay

Point Grey

University of British Columbia

University Endowment Lands

False Ck.

John Hendry Park

BURNABY

Burquitlam

Mundy Park

PORT COQUITLAM

Queen Elizabeth Park

123

Dee Lake

Burnaby Lake

COQUITLAM

Pitt Meadows

VANCOUVER

Central Park

NEW WESTMINSTER

Douglas Island

PITT MEADOWS

Barnston Island

Port Hammond

Sea Island

North Arm

Annieville

TRANS-CANADA HIGHWAY

VANCOUVER INTERNATIONAL

RICHMOND FREEWAY

RICHMOND

Brighouse

Lulu Island

Annacis Island

Fraser River

Mahood Creek

Port Kells

Sturgeon Bank

Tilbury I.

SURREY

Steveston

Garry Pt.

Deas Is.

DELTA

Newton

Serpentine River

Langley

Pelly Pt.

Roberts Bank

Bird Sanctuary

VANCOUVER-BLAINE FREEWAY

ANNACIS HIGHWAY

Cloverdale

Nicomekl

Westham Island

Ladner

Mud Bay

TORONTO map

Kleinburg

Kortright Centre

PEEL

Maple

YONGE STREET

Richmond Hill

Bruce Creek

BUTTONVILLE

Buttonville

Unionville

Markham

DURHAM

West Duffins Creek

Humber River

West

Don River

Thornhill

Beaver Creek

Rouge

Little Rouge Creek

Woodbridge

Bramalea

West Humber River

York University

REGIONAL MUNICIPALITY OF YORK

METROPOLITAN TORONTO

Rouge Valley Park

Metro Zoo

BRAMPTON

NORTH YORK

C.F.B. DOWNSVIEW

Don River

West Rouge River

Etobicoke Creek

Creek

MACDONALD CARTER FREEWAY

Don Mills

HIGHWAY 401

Pickering

LESTER B. PEARSON INTERNATIONAL (TORONTO)

YORK

Forest Hill

Leaside

DON VALLEY PARKWAY

SCARBOROUGH

nuclear power station

ETOBICOKE

Islington

TORONTO

EAST YORK

EGLINTON AVENUE

Highland Creek

MISSISSAUGA

University of Toronto (Erindale)

Credit River

EGLINTON AVENUE

QUEEN ELIZABETH WAY

High Park

University of Toronto

Parliament Buildings

City Hall

GARDINER EXPRESSWAY

Humber Bay

ISLAND

Toronto Islands

Leslie St.Spit

Lake Ontario

thermal power station

Port Credit

TORONTO

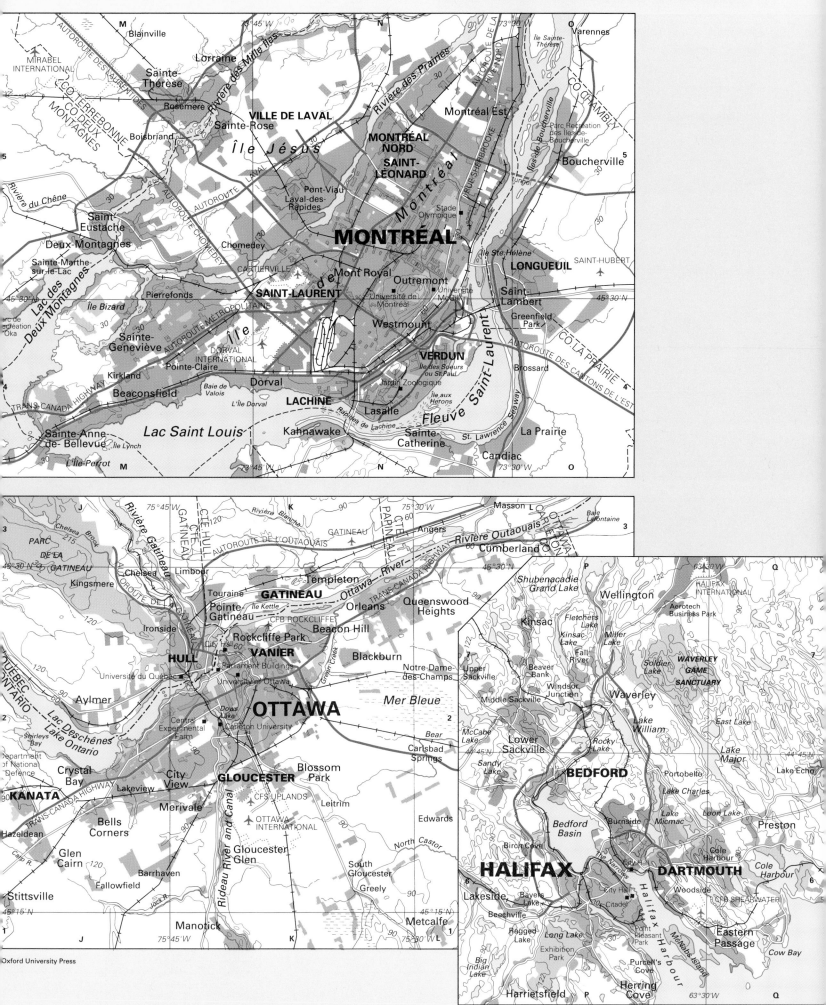
MONTRÉAL
Blainville
MIRABEL INTERNATIONAL
Lorraine
Sainte-Thérèse
Rosemère
VILLE DE LAVAL
Sainte-Rose
Boisbriand
Île Jésus
MONTRÉAL NORD
SAINT-LÉONARD
Montréal Est
Varennes
Boucherville
Pont-Viau
Laval-des-Rapides
Stade Olympique
Saint-Eustache
Deux-Montagnes
Sainte-Marthe-sur-le-Lac
Chomedey
CARTIERVILLE
Mont Royal
Outremont
SAINT-LAURENT
Université de Montréal
Université McGill
LONGUEUIL
SAINT-HUBERT
Saint-Lambert
Greenfield Park
Pierrefonds
Île Bizard
Sainte-Geneviève
DORVAL INTERNATIONAL
Westmount
VERDUN
Pointe-Claire
Kirkland
Beaconsfield
Dorval
LACHINE
Jardin Zoologique
Brossard
Lasalle
Lac Saint Louis
Kahnawake
Sainte-Catherine
La Prairie
Candiac
Sainte-Anne-de-Bellevue
L'Île-Perrot
Fleuve Saint-Laurent
St. Lawrence Seaway
Lac des Deux Montagnes
Rivière des Mille Îles
Rivière des Prairies
OTTAWA
Masson
Angers
Cumberland
Rivière Outaouais
Ottawa River
Chelsea
Kingsmere
Limbour
Templeton
Touraine
GATINEAU
Pointe-Gatineau
CFB ROCKCLIFFE
Orleans
Queenswood Heights
Ironside
Rockcliffe Park
Beacon Hill
HULL
VANIER
Blackburn
Parliament Buildings
University of Ottawa
Université du Québec
Notre-Dame-des-Champs
Aylmer
OTTAWA
Mer Bleue
Lac Deschênes
Lake Ontario
Central Experimental Farm
Carleton University
Crystal Bay
City View
GLOUCESTER
Blossom Park
Carlsbad Springs
KANATA
Lakeview
Merivale
CFS UPLANDS
Leitrim
OTTAWA INTERNATIONAL
Edwards
Bells Corners
Hazeldean
Glen Cairn
Gloucester Glen
South Gloucester
Barrhaven
Fallowfield
Greely
Stittsville
Rideau River and Canal
Manotick
Metcalfe
HALIFAX
Shubenacadie Grand Lake
Wellington
HALIFAX INTERNATIONAL
Aerotech Business Park
Kinsac
Fletchers Lake
Miller Lake
Fall River
Upper Sackville
Beaver Bank
Windsor Junction
WAVERLEY GAME SANCTUARY
Middle Sackville
Waverley
Lake William
Lower Sackville
Rocky Lake
Lake Major
BEDFORD
Portobello
Lake Echo
Lake Charles
Bedford Basin
Burnside
Lake Micmac
Preston
Birch Cove
HALIFAX
DARTMOUTH
Cole Harbour
Lakeside
Bayers Lake
Citadel
Woodside
CFB SHEARWATER
Beechville
Long Lake
Point Pleasant Park
Eastern Passage
Exhibition Park
Halifax Harbour
McNabs Island
Cow Bay
Purcell's Cove
Herring Cove
Harrietsfield
Big Indian Lake

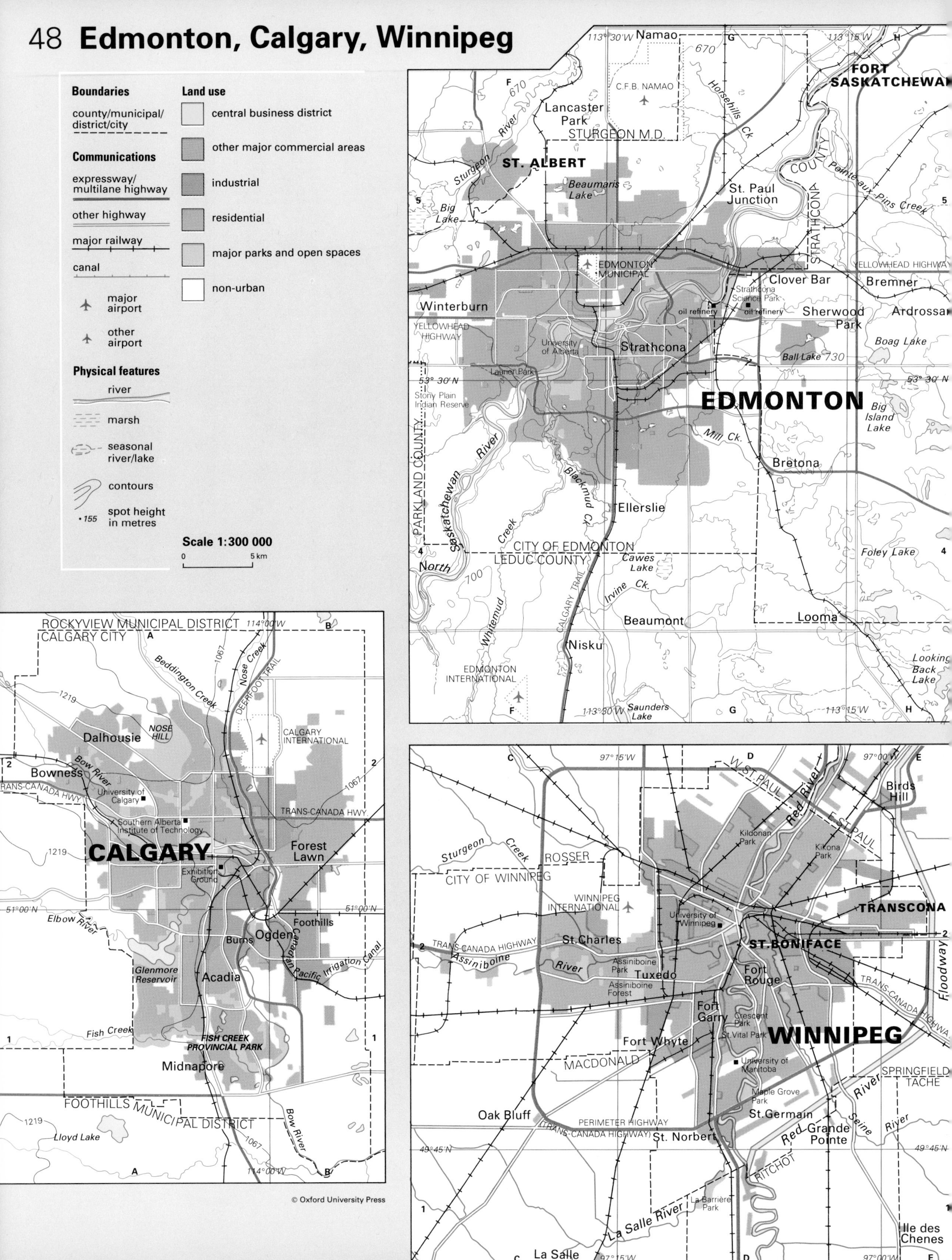

Boundaries

county/municipal/
district/city ·-·-·-

Communications

expressway/
multilane highway

other highway

major railway

canal

✈ major airport

✈ other airport

Physical features

river

marsh

seasonal river/lake

contours

•155 spot height in metres

Land use

central business district

other major commercial areas

industrial

residential

major parks and open spaces

non-urban

Scale 1:300 000

0   5 km

EDMONTON

Namao
C.F.B. NAMAO
FORT SASKATCHEWAN
Lancaster Park
STURGEON M.D.
ST. ALBERT
Beaumaris Lake
Big Lake
St. Paul Junction
STRATHCONA COUNTY
Pointe aux Pins Creek
Horsehills Ck.
YELLOWHEAD HIGHWAY
EDMONTON MUNICIPAL
Clover Bar
Bremner
Strathcona Science Park
oil refinery
oil refinery
Winterburn
Sherwood Park
Ardrossan
YELLOWHEAD HIGHWAY
University of Alberta
Strathcona
Boag Lake
Ball Lake 730
53° 30' N
Laurier Park
Mill Ck.
Big Island Lake
Stony Plain Indian Reserve
Bretona
North Saskatchewan River
Blackmud Creek
Whitemud Ck.
Cawes Lake
Foley Lake
CITY OF EDMONTON
LEDUC COUNTY
Irvine Ck.
Looma
700
Ellerslie
Beaumont
Looking Back Lake
Nisku
EDMONTON INTERNATIONAL
Saunders Lake
113° 30' W
113° 15' W
PARKLAND COUNTY

CALGARY

ROCKYVIEW MUNICIPAL DISTRICT
CALGARY CITY
114° 00' W
Beddington Creek
Nose Creek
DEERFOOT TRAIL
1067
1219
NOSE HILL
Dalhousie
CALGARY INTERNATIONAL
Bowness
Bow River
University of Calgary
TRANS-CANADA HWY.
1067
Southern Alberta Institute of Technology
TRANS-CANADA HWY.
CALGARY
Forest Lawn
1219
51° 00' N
Exhibition Ground
Elbow River
Foothills
Burns
Ogden
Canadian Pacific Railway
Irrigation Canal
Glenmore Reservoir
Acadia
Fish Creek
FISH CREEK PROVINCIAL PARK
Midnapore
FOOTHILLS MUNICIPAL DISTRICT
1219
Lloyd Lake
Bow River
1067
114° 00' W

WINNIPEG

97° 15' W
97° 00' W
W. ST. PAUL
Red River
E. ST. PAUL
Birds Hill
Sturgeon Creek
Kildonan Park
Kildona Park
ROSSER
CITY OF WINNIPEG
WINNIPEG INTERNATIONAL
University of Winnipeg
TRANSCONA
TRANS-CANADA HIGHWAY
St. Charles
Assiniboine River
Assiniboine Park
Tuxedo
ST. BONIFACE
Floodway
Assiniboine Forest
Fort Rouge
TRANS-CANADA HIGHWAY
Fort Garry
Crescent Park
St. Vital Park
Fort Whyte
WINNIPEG
MACDONALD
University of Manitoba
SPRINGFIELD
TACHE
Maple Grove Park
Oak Bluff
PERIMETER HIGHWAY
St. Germain
Red
Grande Pointe
Seine River
49° 45' N
TRANS-CANADA HIGHWAY
St. Norbert
RITCHOT
La Salle River
La Barrière Park
Ile des Chenes
La Salle
97° 15' W
97° 00' W

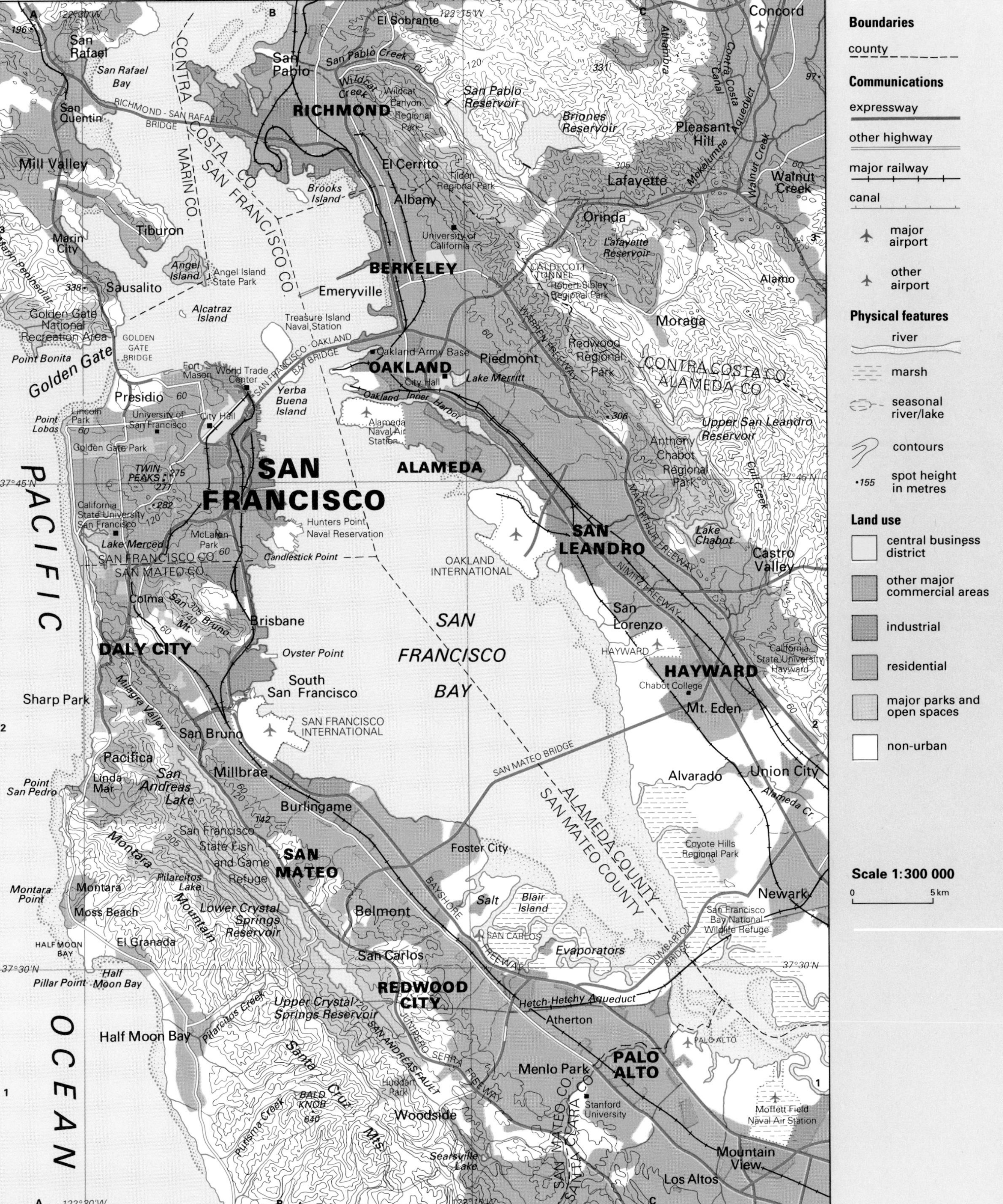

Boundaries

county

Communications

expressway

other highway

major railway

canal

✈ major airport

✈ other airport

Physical features

river

marsh

seasonal river/lake

contours

·155 spot height in metres

Land use

central business district

other major commercial areas

industrial

residential

major parks and open spaces

non-urban

Scale 1:300 000

0   5 km

Map labels

PACIFIC OCEAN

San Rafael
San Rafael Bay
San Quentin
CONTRA COSTA CO.
MARIN CO.
SAN FRANCISCO CO.
El Sobrante
San Pablo
San Pablo Creek
RICHMOND
RICHMOND - SAN RAFAEL BRIDGE
Wildcat Creek
San Pablo Reservoir
Briones Reservoir
Concord
Pleasant Hill
Walnut Creek
Lafayette
Mill Valley
Marin City
Tiburon
Sausalito
Angel Island
Angel Island State Park
Alcatraz Island
Brooks Island
El Cerrito
Albany
Tilden Regional Park
University of California
BERKELEY
Emeryville
Wildcat Canyon Regional Park
Orinda
Lafayette Reservoir
Alamo
Moraga
Golden Gate National Recreation Area
Point Bonita
Golden Gate
GOLDEN GATE BRIDGE
Fort Mason
Presidio
World Trade Center
Treasure Island Naval Station
Yerba Buena Island
SAN FRANCISCO - OAKLAND BAY BRIDGE
Oakland Army Base
OAKLAND
City Hall
Piedmont
Lake Merritt
CALDECOTT TUNNEL
Robert Sibley Regional Park
Redwood Regional Park
CONTRA COSTA CO.
ALAMEDA CO.
Point Lobos
Lincoln Park
University of San Francisco
City Hall
Golden Gate Park
SAN FRANCISCO
TWIN PEAKS
California State University San Francisco
Lake Merced
McLaren Park
SAN FRANCISCO CO.
SAN MATEO CO.
Hunters Point Naval Reservation
Candlestick Point
Alameda Naval Air Station
ALAMEDA
Oakland Inner Harbor
Upper San Leandro Reservoir
Anthony Chabot Regional Park
Lake Chabot
SAN LEANDRO
Castro Valley
OAKLAND INTERNATIONAL
San Lorenzo
Colma
San Bruno Mt.
Brisbane
Oyster Point
South San Francisco
SAN FRANCISCO BAY
DALY CITY
Sharp Park
Milagra Valley
Pacifica
Linda Mar
San Andreas Lake
Millbrae
San Bruno
SAN FRANCISCO INTERNATIONAL
Burlingame
HAYWARD
Chabot College
Mt. Eden
California State University Hayward
Point San Pedro
Montara Mountain
Pilarcitos Lake
San Francisco State Fish and Game Refuge
SAN MATEO
Foster City
ALAMEDA COUNTY
SAN MATEO COUNTY
Coyote Hills Regional Park
Alvarado
Union City
Alameda Cr.
Montara Point
Montara
Moss Beach
El Granada
Lower Crystal Springs Reservoir
Belmont
Salt
Blair Island
SAN CARLOS
Evaporators
Newark
San Francisco Bay National Wildlife Refuge
HALF MOON BAY
Pillar Point
Half Moon Bay
Pilarcitos Creek
Upper Crystal Springs Reservoir
San Carlos
SAN ANDREAS FAULT
BAYSHORE FREEWAY
REDWOOD CITY
Atherton
Hetch-Hetchy Aqueduct
DUMBARTON BRIDGE
Purisima Creek
Santa Cruz Mts.
BALD KNOB
Woodside
Huddart Park
Menlo Park
PALO ALTO
Stanford University
Moffett Field Naval Air Station
Searsville Lake
Mountain View
Los Altos
SAN MATEO CO.
SANTA CLARA CO.
JUNIPERO SERRA FREEWAY
NIMITZ FREEWAY
MACARTHUR FREEWAY
WARREN FREEWAY
Contra Costa Canal
Mokelumne Aqueduct
SAN MATEO BRIDGE

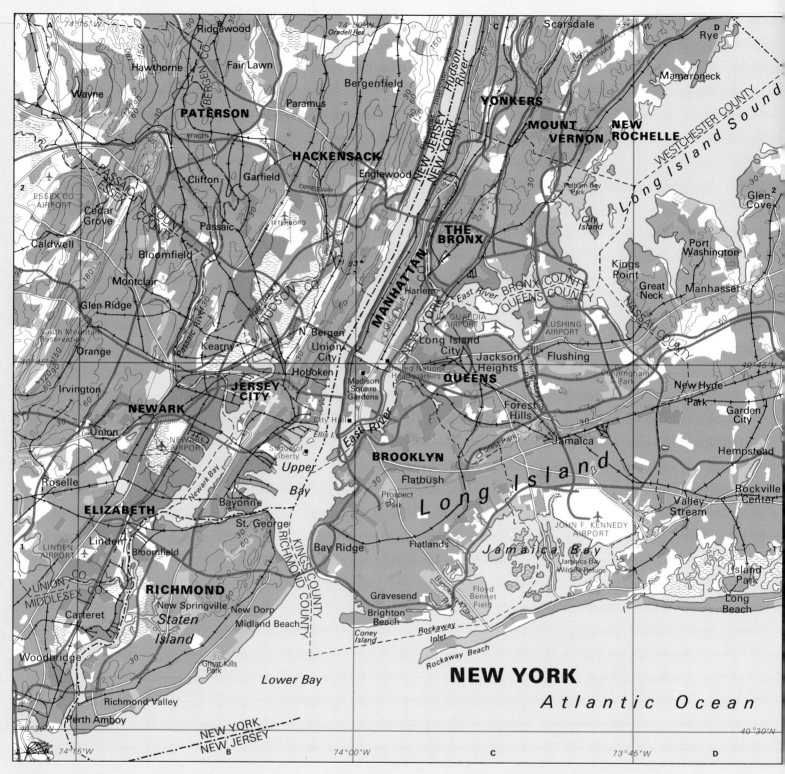

NEW YORK

Atlantic Ocean

Boundaries
state
county

Physical features
river
marsh
contours
• 155   spot height in metres

Communications
expressway
other major road
major railway
canal
✈ major airport
✈ other airport

Land use
central business district
other major commercial areas
industrial
residential
major parks and open spaces
non-urban

Scale 1 : 300 000

0   5 km

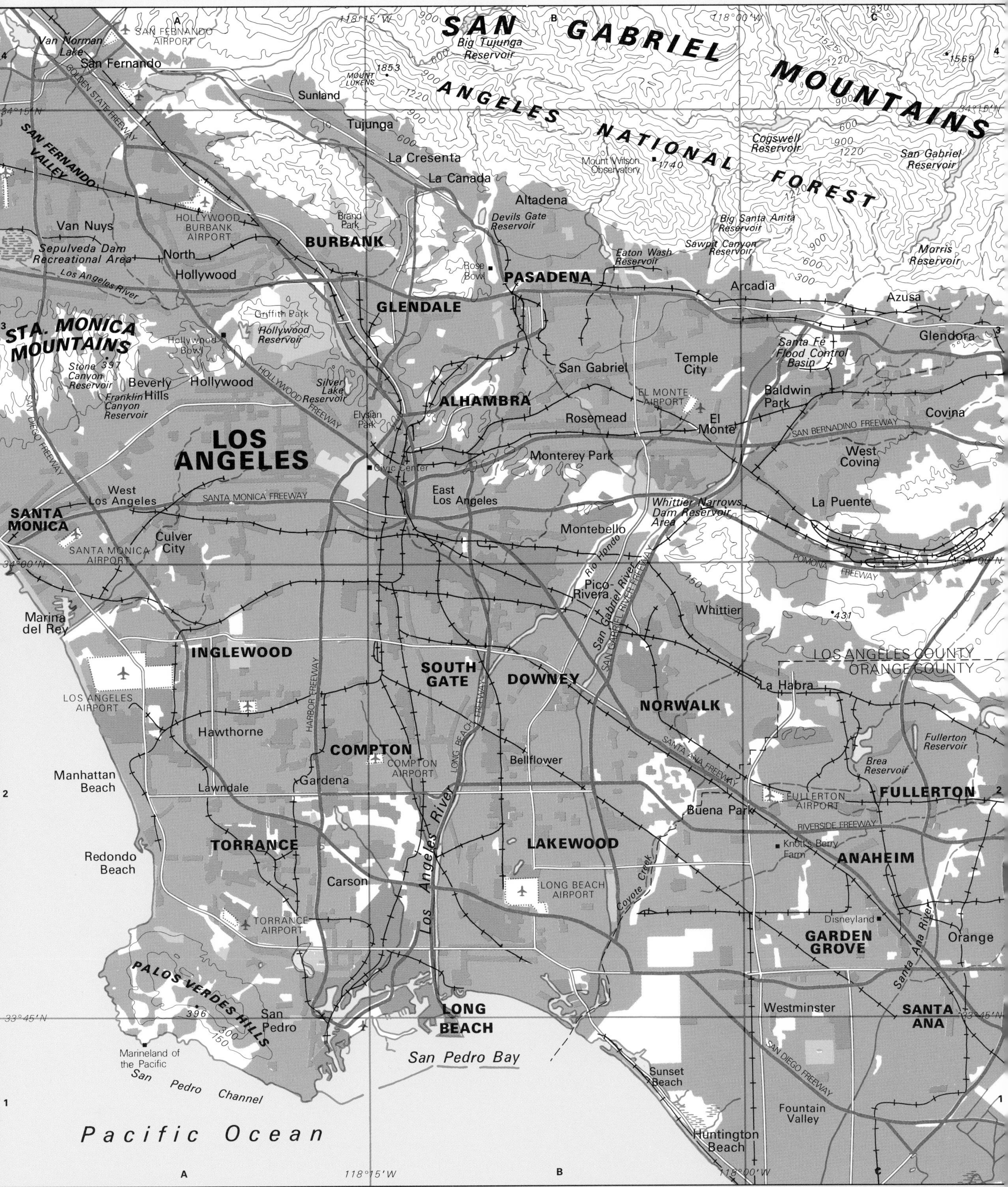

SAN GABRIEL MOUNTAINS

SAN GABRIEL

ANGELES

MOUNTAINS

NATIONAL

FOREST

118°15'W

118°00'W

Van Norman Lake

San Fernando

San Fernando Airport

Big Tujunga Reservoir

Big Tujunga Reservoir

1853

Cogswell Reservoir

San Gabriel Reservoir

1569

SAN FERNANDO VALLEY

Sunland

MOUNT LUKENS

Tujunga

La Cresenta

La Canada

Altadena

Mount Wilson Observatory

1740

Big Santa Anita Reservoir

Sawpit Canyon Reservoir

Morris Reservoir

GOLDEN STATE FREEWAY

Van Nuys

North Hollywood

HOLLYWOOD BURBANK AIRPORT

BURBANK

Brand Park

Devils Gate Reservoir

Eaton Wash Reservoir

Sepulveda Dam Recreational Area

Los Angeles River

Griffith Park

GLENDALE

Rose Bowl

PASADENA

Arcadia

Azusa

STA. MONICA MOUNTAINS

Hollywood Bowl

Hollywood Reservoir

Silver Lake Reservoir

San Gabriel

Temple City

Santa Fe Flood Control Basin

Glendora

Stone 397 Canyon Reservoir

Beverly Hills

Hollywood

ALHAMBRA

Rosemead

EL MONTE AIRPORT

Baldwin Park

Covina

Franklin Canyon Reservoir

Elysian Park

Monterey Park

El Monte

SAN BERNADINO FREEWAY

LOS ANGELES

West Los Angeles

SANTA MONICA FREEWAY

Civic Center

East Los Angeles

West Covina

SANTA MONICA

Santa Monica Airport

Culver City

Montebello

Whittier Narrows Dam Reservoir Area

La Puente

La Puente

POMONA FREEWAY

Marina del Rey

Pico-Rivera

Rio Hondo

San Gabriel River

Whittier

431

INGLEWOOD

LOS ANGELES AIRPORT

SOUTH GATE

DOWNEY

LOS ANGELES COUNTY ORANGE COUNTY

La Habra

Hawthorne

NORWALK

HARBOR FREEWAY

SANTA ANA FREEWAY

Fullerton Reservoir

COMPTON

Bellflower

Manhattan Beach

Lawndale

COMPTON AIRPORT

Gardena

LONG BEACH FREEWAY

Brea Reservoir

FULLERTON

FULLERTON AIRPORT

TORRANCE

LAKEWOOD

Knott's Berry Farm

RIVERSIDE FREEWAY

ANAHEIM

Redondo Beach

Carson

LONG BEACH AIRPORT

Buena Park

Los Angeles River

Coyote Creek

TORRANCE AIRPORT

Disneyland

Orange

PALOS VERDES HILLS

GARDEN GROVE

396

San Pedro

SAN DIEGO FREEWAY

Marineland of the Pacific

LONG BEACH

Westminster

SANTA ANA

San

Pedro

Channel

San Pedro Bay

Sunset Beach

Fountain Valley

Huntington Beach

Pacific Ocean

118°15'W

118°00'W

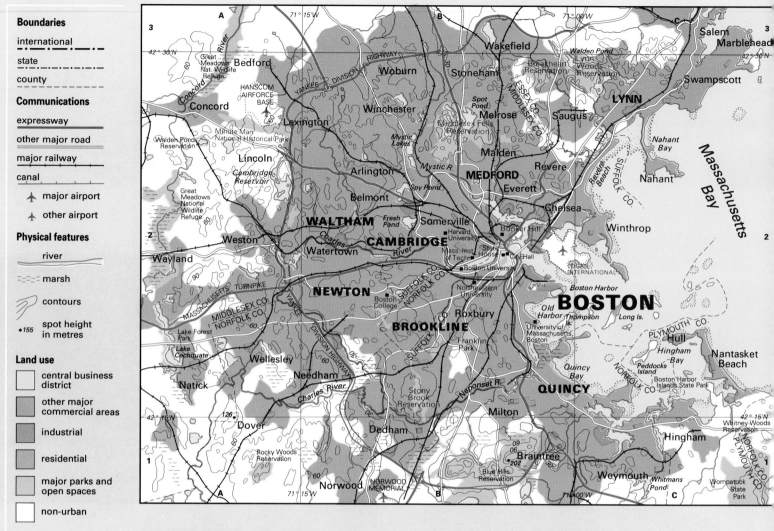

Boundaries

international
state
county

Communications

expressway
other major road
major railway
canal
✈ major airport
✈ other airport

Physical features

river
marsh
contours
•155 spot height in metres

Land use

central business district
other major commercial areas
industrial
residential
major parks and open spaces
non-urban

Scale 1 : 300 000

0   5 km

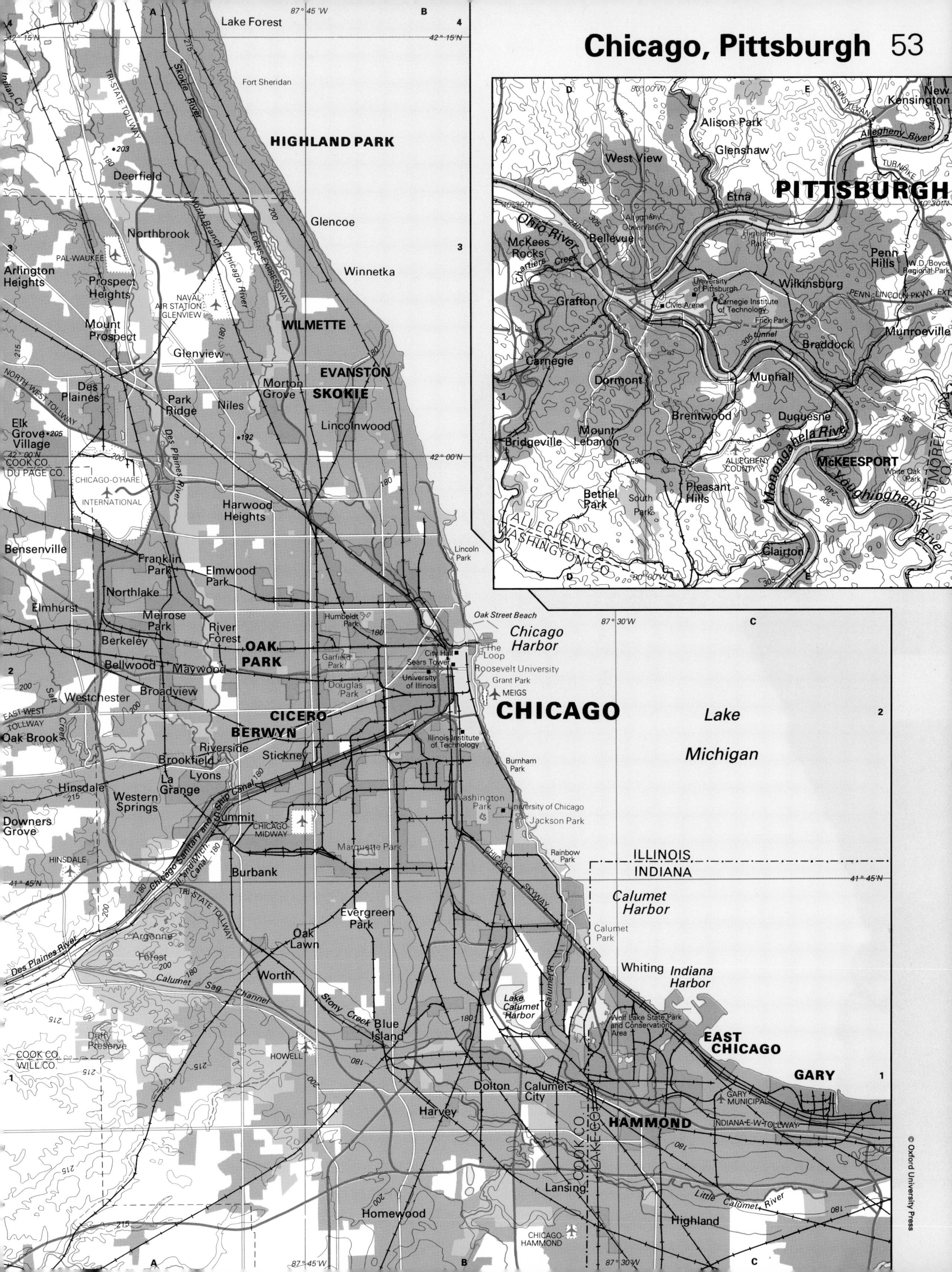

PITTSBURGH

New Kensington
Allegheny River
Alison Park
Glenshaw
West View
Etna
TURNPIKE
Ohio River
Bellevue
Allegheny Observatory
Highland Park
Penn Hills
McKees Rocks
Chartiers Creek
W.D. Boyce Regional Park
University of Pittsburgh
Civic Arena
Carnegie Institute of Technology
Wilkinsburg
PENN-LINCOLN PKWY EXT
Grafton
Frick Park
Munroeville
tunnel
Carnegie
Braddock
Dormont
Munhall
Mount Lebanon
Brentwood
Duquesne
Bridgeville
Monongahela River
ALLEGHENY COUNTY
Bethel Park
South Park
Pleasant Hills
Youghiogheny River
McKEESPORT
White Oak Park
ALLEGHENY CO.
WASHINGTON CO.
Clairton

Lake Forest
Fort Sheridan
87° 45' W
42° 15' N

HIGHLAND PARK

Indian Cr.
TRI-STATE TOLLWAY
Skokie River
Deerfield
• 203
180
Glencoe
200
North Branch Chicago River
EDENS EXPRESSWAY
Northbrook
PAL-WAUKEE
Winnetka
Arlington Heights
Prospect Heights
WILMETTE
Mount Prospect
NAVAL AIR STATION GLENVIEW
Des Plaines
Glenview
EVANSTON
Morton Grove
SKOKIE
Park Ridge
Niles
Lincolnwood
Elk Grove Village
• 205
• 192
COOK CO.
DU PAGE CO.
42° 00' N
NORTH WEST TOLLWAY
CHICAGO-O'HARE INTERNATIONAL
180
Harwood Heights
Bensenville
200
Lincoln Park
Franklin Park
Elmwood Park
Oak Street Beach
Northlake
River Forest
Humboldt Park
180
Chicago Harbor
Elmhurst
Melrose Park
Berkeley
OAK PARK
Garfield Park
City Hall
Sears Tower
The Loop
Roosevelt University
Bellwood
Maywood
Douglas Park
University of Illinois
Grant Park
Westchester
Broadview
MEIGS
Oak Brook
EAST-WEST TOLLWAY
Salt Creek
CICERO
BERWYN
Illinois Institute of Technology
CHICAGO
Lake
87° 30' W
Riverside
Stickney
Burnham Park
Michigan
Brookfield
Lyons
Washington Park
Hinsdale
La Grange
University of Chicago
Jackson Park
Downers Grove
Western Springs
Summit
Chicago Sanitary and Ship Canal
CHICAGO MIDWAY
Rainbow Park
HINSDALE
Burbank
Marquette Park
ILLINOIS
INDIANA
41° 45' N
TRI-STATE TOLLWAY
Argonne
Evergreen Park
CHICAGO SKYWAY
Calumet Harbor
Des Plaines River
Oak Forest
Oak Lawn
Calumet Park
200
Calumet Sag Channel
180
Worth
Stony Creek
Whiting
Indiana Harbor
Daily Preserve
HOWELL
Blue Island
Lake Calumet Harbor
Calumet R.
Wolf Lake State Park and Conservation Area
COOK CO.
WILL CO.
215
EAST CHICAGO
Harvey
Dolton
Calumet City
GARY MUNICIPAL
GARY
COOK CO.
LAKE CO.
HAMMOND
INDIANA-E-W TOLLWAY
Lansing
CHICAGO-HAMMOND
Homewood
Highland
Little Calumet River
87° 45' W
87° 30' W

© Oxford University Press

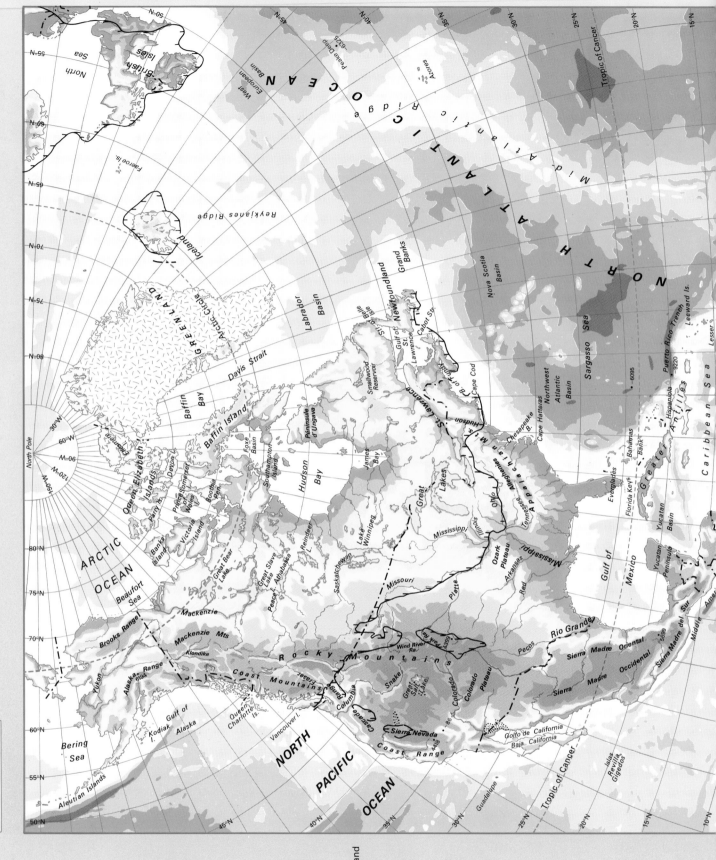

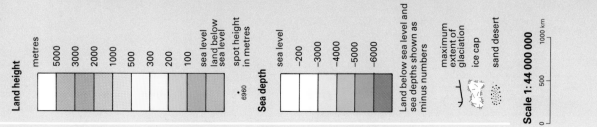

Land height

metres

5000
3000
2000
1000
500
300
200
100

sea level
land below
sea level

spot height
in metres

6960

Sea depth

sea level

-200
-3000
-4000
-5000
-6000

Land below sea level and
sea depths shown as
minus numbers

maximum
extent of
glaciation

ice cap

sand desert

Scale 1:44 000 000

1000 km

500

Oblique Mercator Projection

© Oxford University Pres

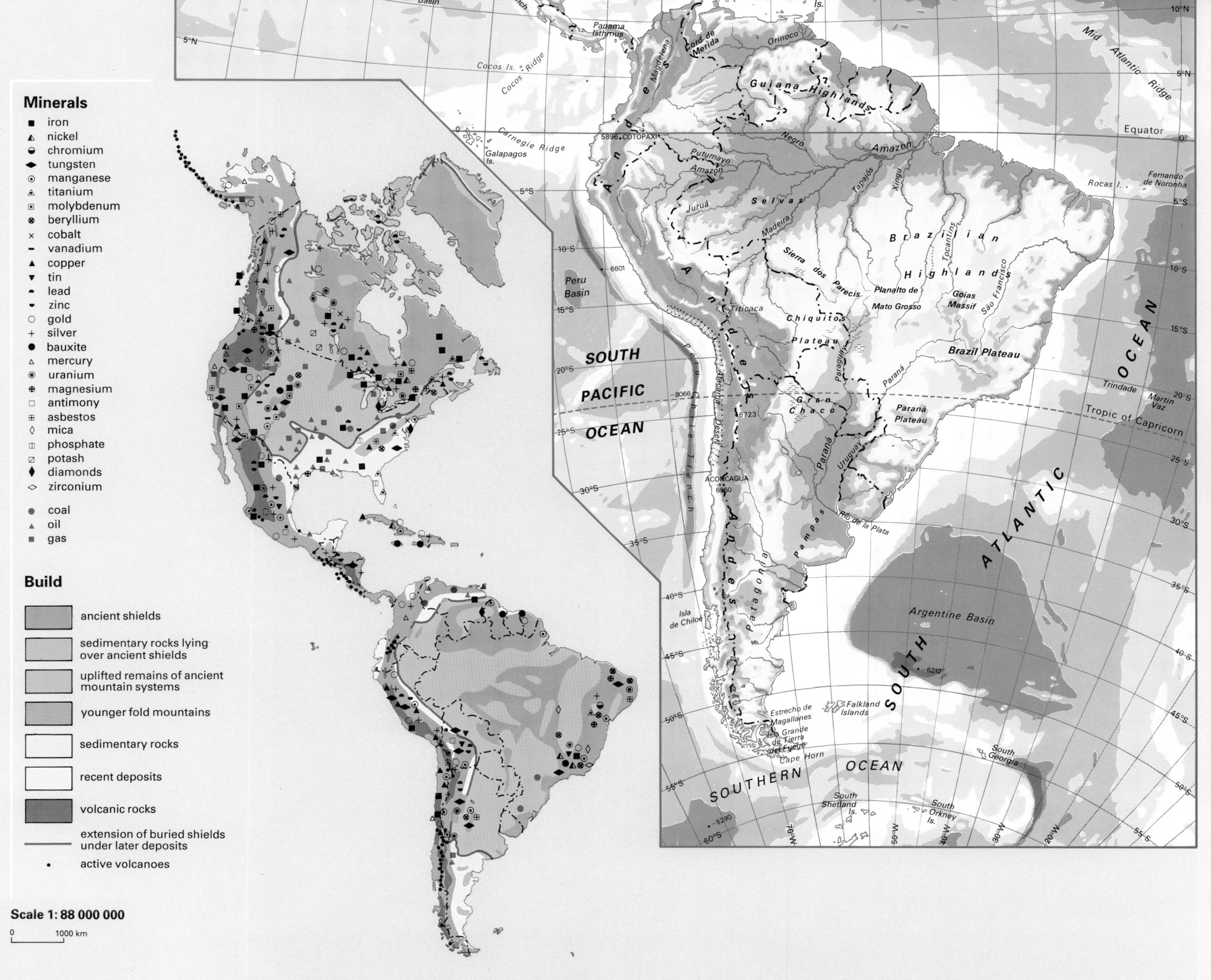

Minerals

- ■ iron
- ▲ nickel
- ◐ chromium
- ◆ tungsten
- ⊙ manganese
- ▲ titanium
- ⊗ molybdenum
- ⊗ beryllium
- ✕ cobalt
- ∣ vanadium
- ◀ copper
- ◣ tin
- ◀ lead
- ● zinc
- ○ gold
- + silver
- ● bauxite
- ◁ mercury
- ▲ uranium
- ⊕ magnesium
- ▢ antimony
- ⊞ asbestos
- ⊡ mica
- ▨ phosphate
- ◆ potash
- ◆ diamonds
- ◇ zirconium
- ● coal
- ◀ oil
- ■ gas

Build

- ancient shields
- sedimentary rocks lying over ancient shields
- uplifted remains of ancient mountain systems
- younger fold mountains
- sedimentary rocks
- recent deposits
- volcanic rocks
- extension of buried shields under later deposits
- • active volcanoes

Scale 1 : 88 000 000

0 ____ 1000 km

Mid Atlantic Ridge
Equator
Fernando de Noronha
Rocas I.
Trindade
Martin Vaz
Tropic of Capricorn

OCEAN

SOUTH ATLANTIC

Brazilian Highlands
São Francisco
Goiás Massif
Brazil Plateau
Planalto de Mato Grosso
Paraná Plateau
Paraná

Guiana Highlands
Orinoco
Negro
Amazon
Tapajós
Xingu
Tocantins
Selvas
Madeira
Sierra dos Parecis
Chiquitos
Plateau
Gran Chaco
Paraguay
Paraná
Uruguay
Río de la Plata

Argentine Basin
South Georgia
South Orkney Is.
South Shetland Is.
Falkland Islands

SOUTHERN OCEAN

Cordillera de Mérida
Magdalena
Putumayo
Amazon
Juruá
Titicaca
Andes
COTOPAXI
5896
ACONCAGUA
6723
6601
6601
Atacama Desert
Peru-Chile Trench
8066
8016
Patagonia
Estrecho de Magallanes
Isla Grande de Tierra del Fuego
Cape Horn
Isla de Chiloé

SOUTH PACIFIC OCEAN

Peru Basin
Cocos Is.
Carnegie Ridge
Galapagos Is.
Panama Isthmus
Trench
Basin

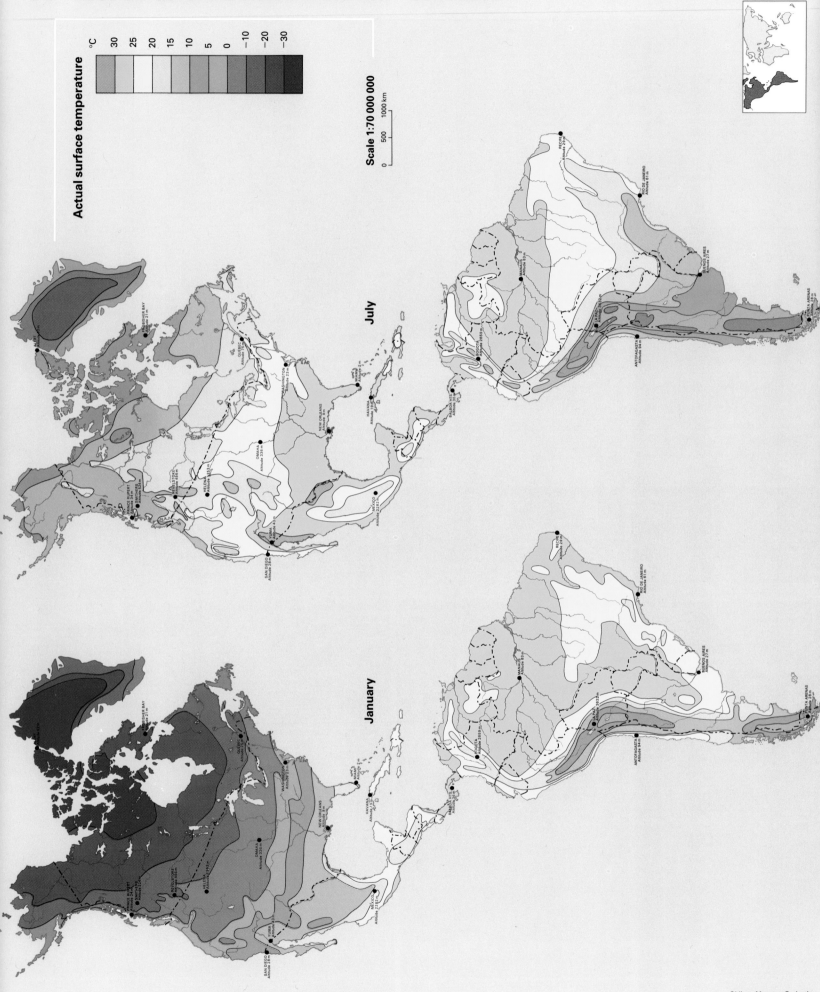

°C
30
25
20
15
10
5
0
−10
−20
−30

Actual surface temperature

Scale 1:70 000 000

0   500   1000 km

July

January

Oblique Mercator Projection

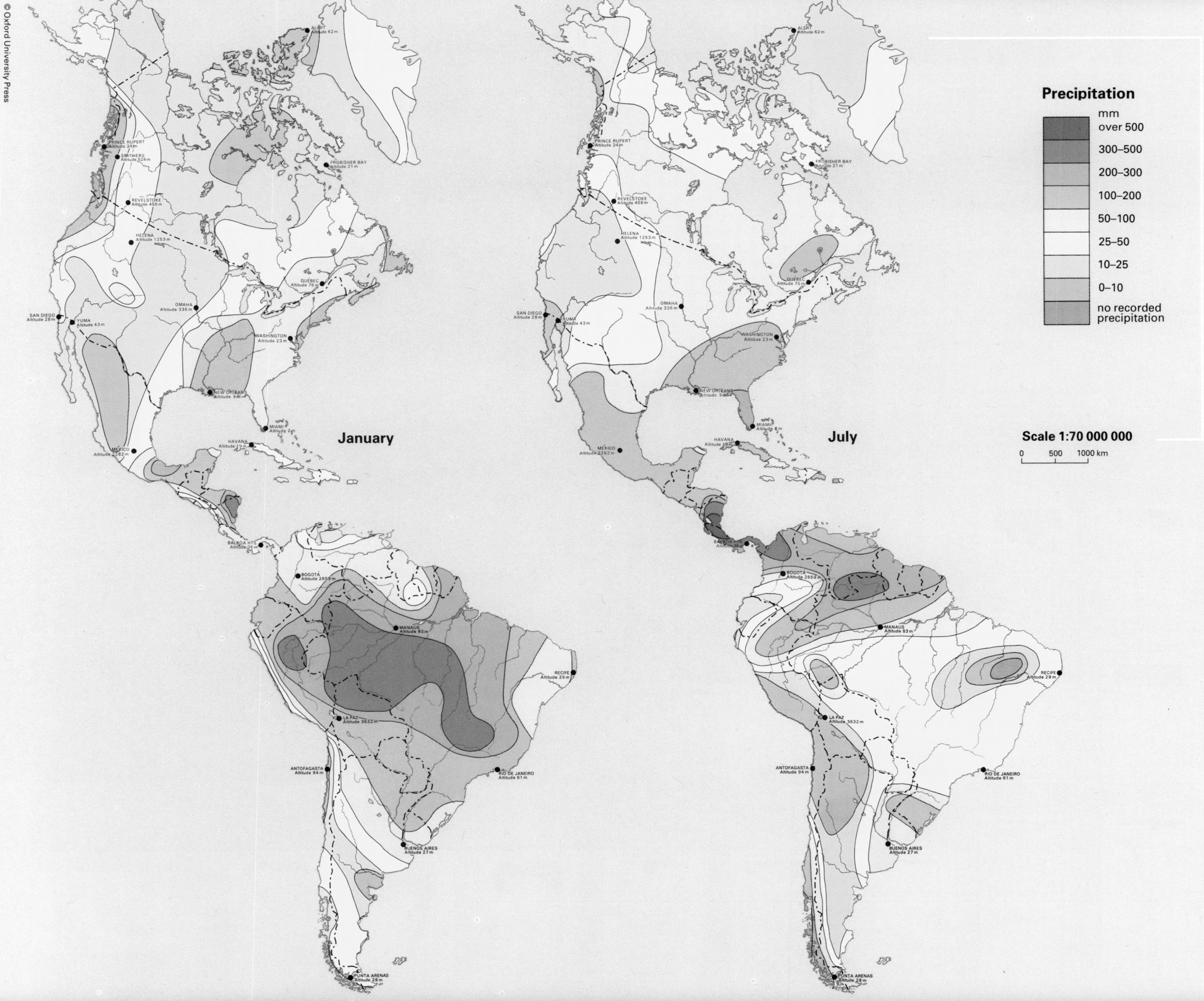

Precipitation

mm
over 500
300–500
200–300
100–200
50–100
25–50
10–25
0–10
no recorded
precipitation

Scale 1:70 000 000

0   500   1000 km

July

January

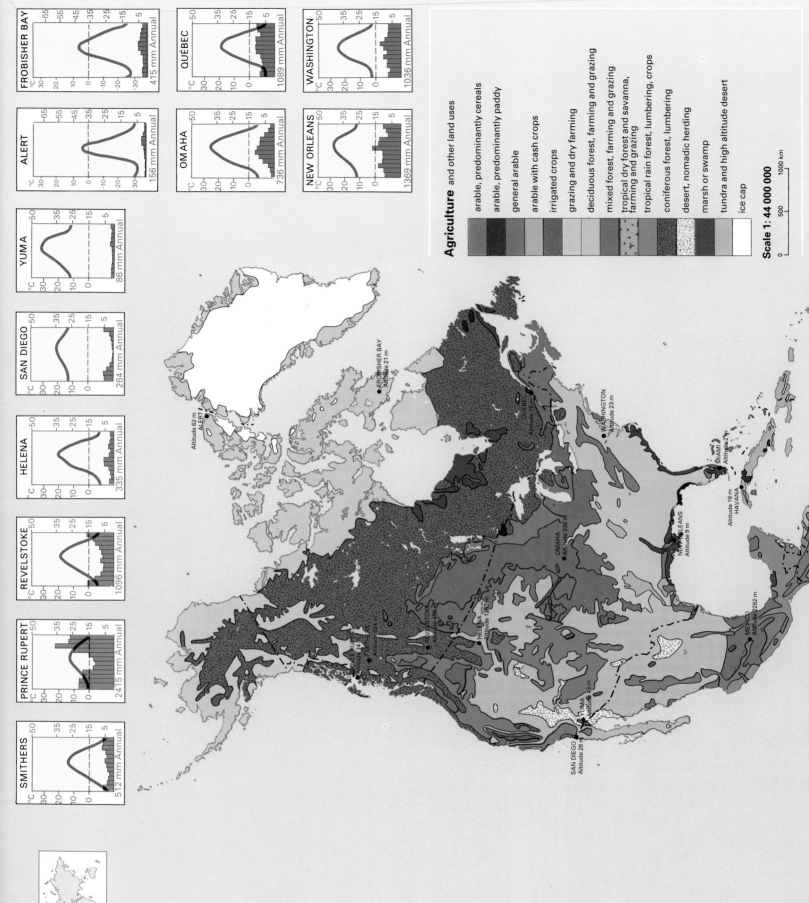

Agriculture and other land uses

arable, predominantly cereals
arable, predominantly paddy
general arable
arable with cash crops
irrigated crops
grazing and dry farming
deciduous forest, farming and grazing
mixed forest, farming and grazing
tropical dry forest and savanna, farming and grazing
tropical rain forest, lumbering, crops
coniferous forest, lumbering
desert, nomadic herding
marsh or swamp
tundra and high altitude desert
ice cap

Scale 1: 44 000 000

500   1000 km

FROBISHER BAY   415 mm Annual
QUÉBEC   1089 mm Annual
WASHINGTON   1036 mm Annual
ALERT   156 mm Annual
OMAHA   736 mm Annual
NEW ORLEANS   1369 mm Annual
YUMA   86 mm Annual
SAN DIEGO   264 mm Annual
HELENA   335 mm Annual
REVELSTOKE   1096 mm Annual
PRINCE RUPERT   2415 mm Annual
SMITHERS   512 mm Annual

Oblique Mercator Projection

North and South America Land Use 59

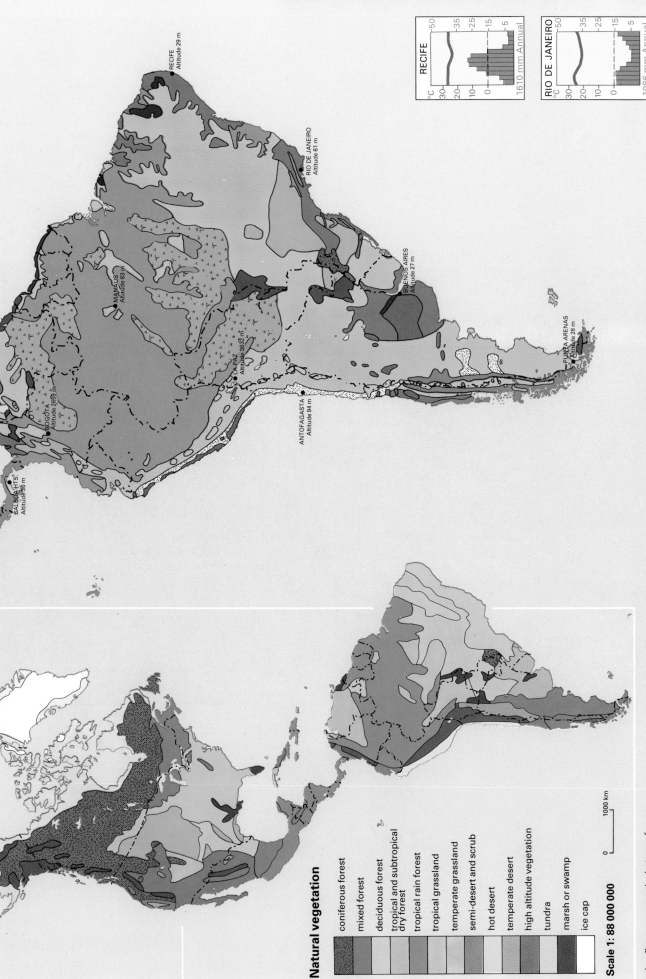

Natural vegetation

- coniferous forest
- mixed forest
- deciduous forest
- tropical and subtropical dry forest
- tropical rain forest
- tropical grassland
- temperate grassland
- semi-desert and scrub
- hot desert
- temperate desert
- high altitude vegetation
- tundra
- marsh or swamp
- ice cap

Scale 1:88 000 000

0   1000 km

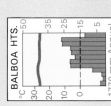

RECIFE
Altitude 29 m
1610 mm Annual

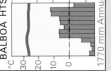

RIO DE JANEIRO
Altitude 61 m
1086 mm Annual

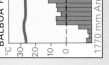

BUENOS AIRES
Altitude 27 m
1027 mm Annual

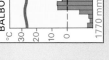

PUNTA ARENAS
Altitude 28 m
366 mm Annual

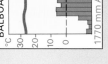

ANTOFAGASTA
Altitude 94 m
13 mm Annual

LA PAZ
Altitude 3632 m
47 mm Annual

MANAUS
Altitude 83 m
1811 mm Annual

BOGOTÁ
Altitude 2669 m
1059 mm Annual

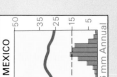

BALBOA HTS.
Altitude 36 m
1770 mm Annual

MEXICO
726 mm Annual

HAVANA
1224 mm Annual

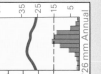

MIAMI
1518 mm Annual

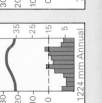

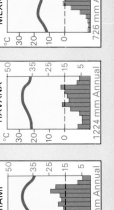

Precipitation figures on graphs in tens of millimetres except for annual totals

© Oxford University Press

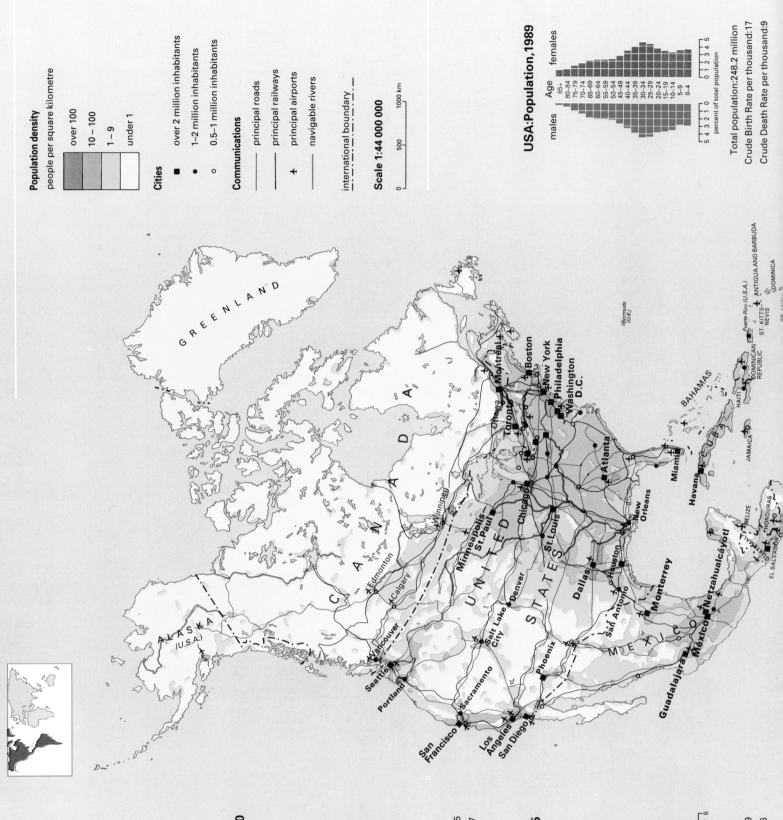

Population density

people per square kilometre

- over 100
- 10 – 100
- 1 – 9
- under 1

Cities

- ■ over 2 million inhabitants
- ● 1–2 million inhabitants
- ○ 0.5–1 million inhabitants

Communications

- principal roads
- principal railways
- ✈ principal airports
- navigable rivers
- – · – international boundary

Scale 1:44 000 000

1000 km
500
0

USA:Population,1989

males   Age   females

85+
80–84
75–79
70–74
65–69
60–64
55–59
50–54
45–49
40–44
35–39
30–34
25–29
20–24
15–19
10–14
5–9
0–4

5 4 3 2 1 0   0 1 2 3 4 5

percent of total population

Total population:248.2 million
Crude Birth Rate per thousand:17
Crude Death Rate per thousand:9

GREENLAND

C A N A D A

Edmonton
Calgary

ALASKA
(U.S.A.)

Vancouver
Seattle
Portland
Sacramento
San Francisco
Los Angeles
San Diego
Phoenix
Salt Lake City
Denver
San Antonio

U N I T E D   S T A T E S

Winnipeg
Minneapolis St.Paul
Chicago
St.Louis
Houston
Dallas

Ottawa
Toronto
Montréal
Boston
New York
Philadelphia
Washington D.C.
Atlanta
New Orleans
Miami

M E X I C O

Monterrey
Guadalajara
México
Netzahualcáyotl

Havana   CUBA
BAHAMAS
HAITI
JAMAICA
BELIZE
GUATEMALA
EL SALVADOR
HONDURAS

®Bermuda
(U.K.)
Puerto Rico (U.S.A.)
ANTIGUA AND BARBUDA
ST. KITTS-
NEVIS
DOMINICAN
REPUBLIC
DOMINICA

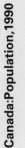

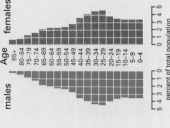

Canada:Population,1990

males   Age   females

85+
80–84
75–79
70–74
65–69
60–64
55–59
50–54
45–49
40–44
35–39
30–34
25–29
20–24
15–19
10–14
5–9
0–4

5 4 3 2 1 0   0 1 2 3 4 5

percent of total population

Total population:26.6 million
Crude Birth Rate per thousand:15
Crude Death Rate per thousand:7

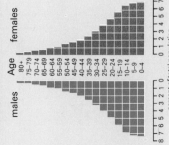

Mexico:Population,1985

males   Age   females

80+
75–79
70–74
65–69
60–64
55–59
50–54
45–49
40–44
35–39
30–34
25–29
20–24
15–19
10–14
5–9
0–4

8 7 6 5 4 3 2 1 0   0 1 2 3 4 5 6 7 8

percent of total population

Total population:78.5 million
Crude Birth Rate per thousand:29
Crude Death Rate per thousand:6

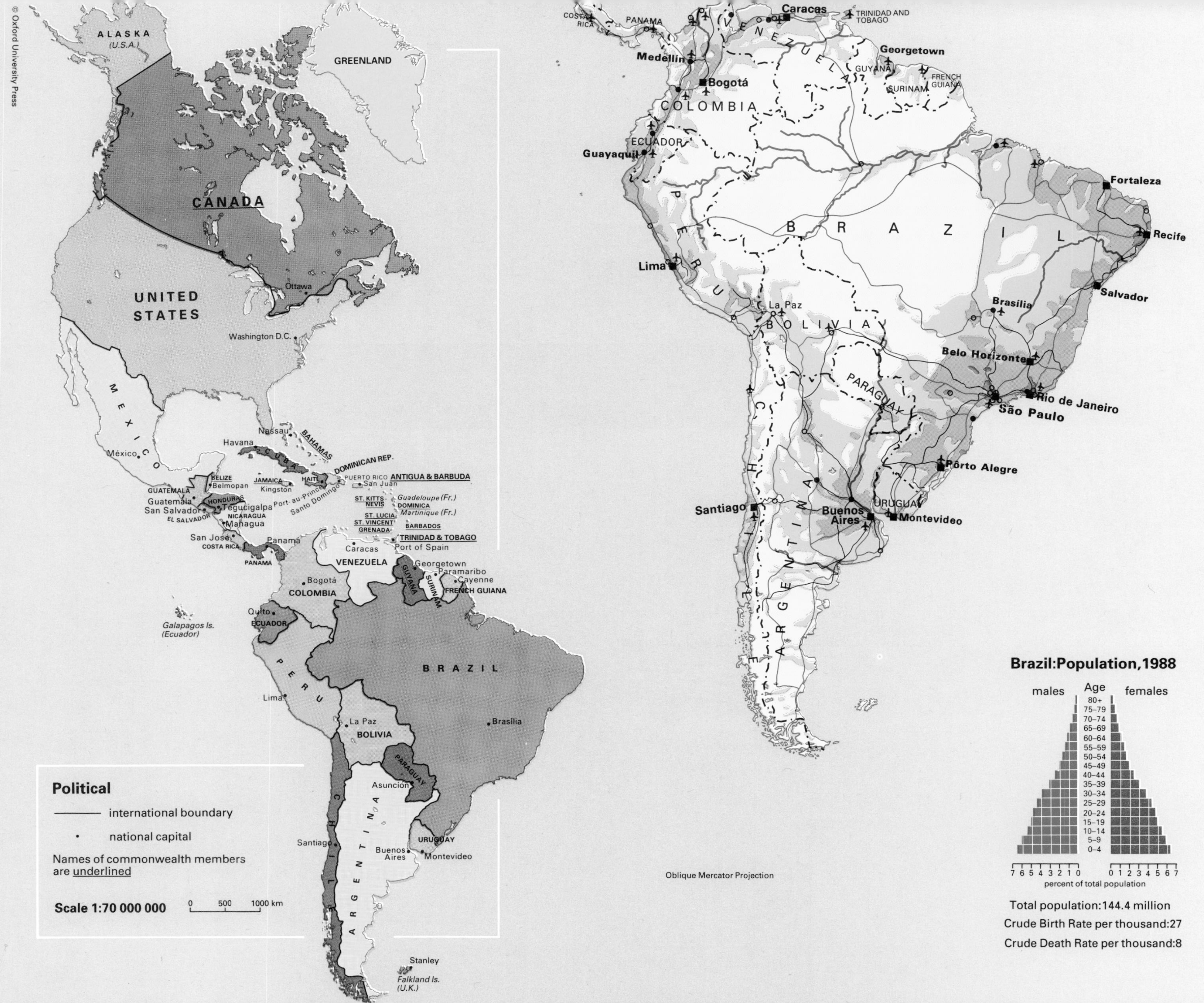

Brazil:Population,1988

males   females

Age
80+
75-79
70-74
65-69
60-64
55-59
50-54
45-49
40-44
35-39
30-34
25-29
20-24
15-19
10-14
5-9
0-4

7 6 5 4 3 2 1 0   0 1 2 3 4 5 6 7

percent of total population

Total population:144.4 million
Crude Birth Rate per thousand:27
Crude Death Rate per thousand:8

Oblique Mercator Projection

GREENLAND

CANADA

ALASKA
(U.S.A.)

UNITED
STATES

Ottawa

Washington D.C.

M E X I C O

México

Havana

Nassau

BAHAMAS

CUBA

JAMAICA
Kingston

HAITI
Port-au-Prince

DOMINICAN REP.
Santo Domingo

PUERTO RICO
San Juan

ANTIGUA & BARBUDA
ST. KITTS-
NEVIS
DOMINICA

Guadeloupe (Fr.)
Martinique (Fr.)
ST. LUCIA
ST. VINCENT
GRENADA
BARBADOS
TRINIDAD & TOBAGO
Port of Spain

BELIZE
Belmopan
GUATEMALA
Guatemala
San Salvador
EL SALVADOR
HONDURAS
Tegucigalpa
NICARAGUA
Managua
San José
COSTA RICA
Panama
PANAMA

VENEZUELA
Caracas

COLOMBIA
Bogotá

Quito
ECUADOR

Galapagos Is.
(Ecuador)

GUYANA
Georgetown
SURINAM
Paramaribo
Cayenne
FRENCH GUIANA

P E R U
Lima

B R A Z I L
Brasília

BOLIVIA
La Paz

PARAGUAY
Asunción

URUGUAY
Montevideo

A R G E N T I N A
Buenos
Aires

C H I L E
Santiago

Stanley
Falkland Is.
(U.K.)

Political

— international boundary
• national capital

Names of commonwealth members
are underlined

Scale 1:70 000 000

0   500   1000 km

© Oxford University Press

Caracas
TRINIDAD AND
TOBAGO
Georgetown
FRENCH
GUIANA
SURINAM
GUYANA

V E N E Z U E L A

PANAMA

COSTA
RICA

Medellín
Bogotá
COLOMBIA

ECUADOR
Guayaquil

P E R U

Lima

B R A Z I L

La Paz
BOLIVIA

Brasília

PARAGUAY

Fortaleza
Recife
Salvador

Belo Horizonte
Rio de Janeiro
São Paulo

Pôrto Alegre

URUGUAY
Montevideo

Buenos
Aires

A R G E N T I N A

C H I L E

Santiago

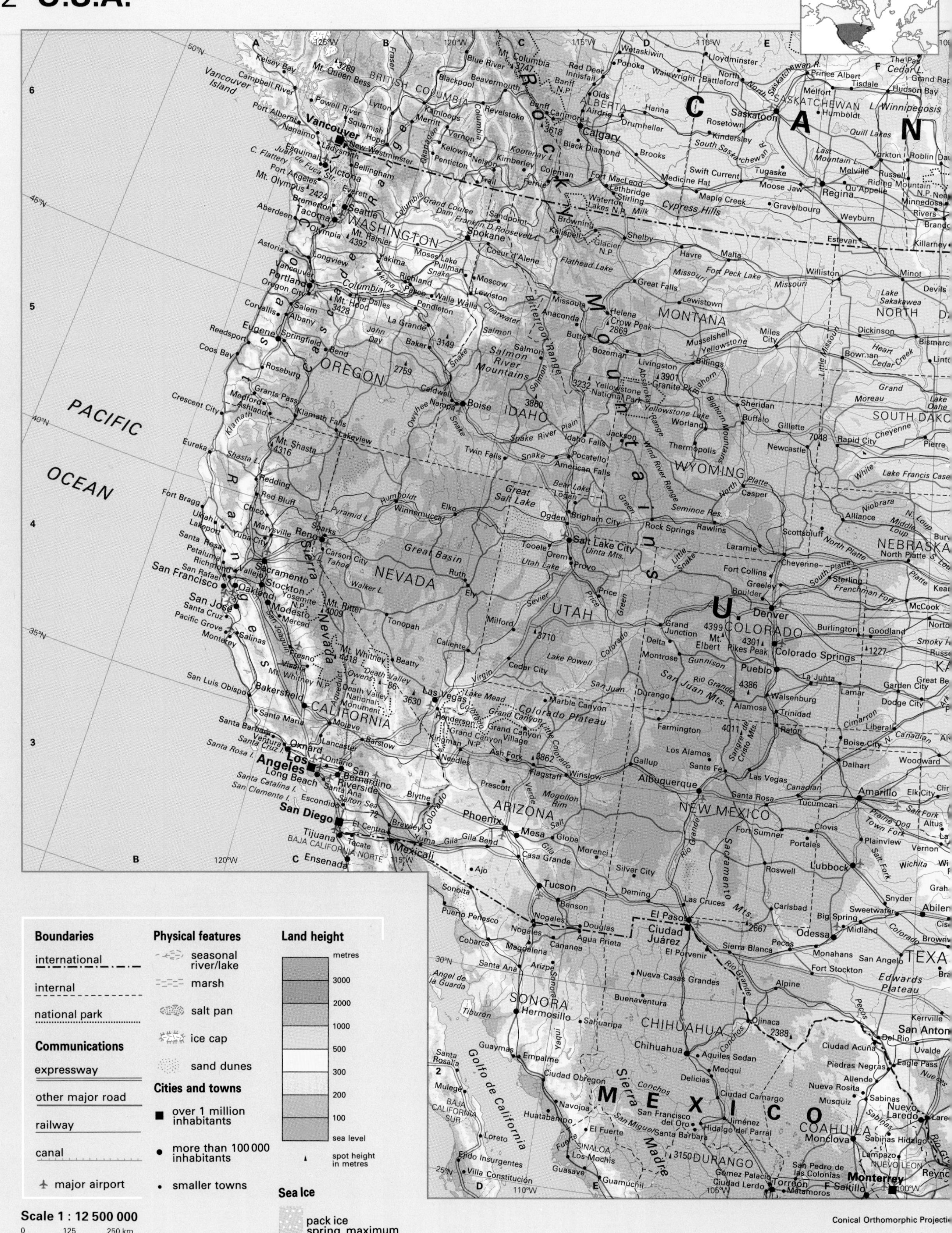

Boundaries

international

internal

national park

Communications

expressway

other major road

railway

canal

✈ major airport

Physical features

〰 seasonal river/lake

marsh

salt pan

ice cap

sand dunes

Cities and towns

■ over 1 million inhabitants

● more than 100 000 inhabitants

• smaller towns

▲ spot height in metres

Land height

metres

3000
2000
1000
500
300
200
100
sea level

Sea Ice

pack ice
spring maximum

Scale 1 : 12 500 000

0   125   250 km

Conical Orthomorphic Projection

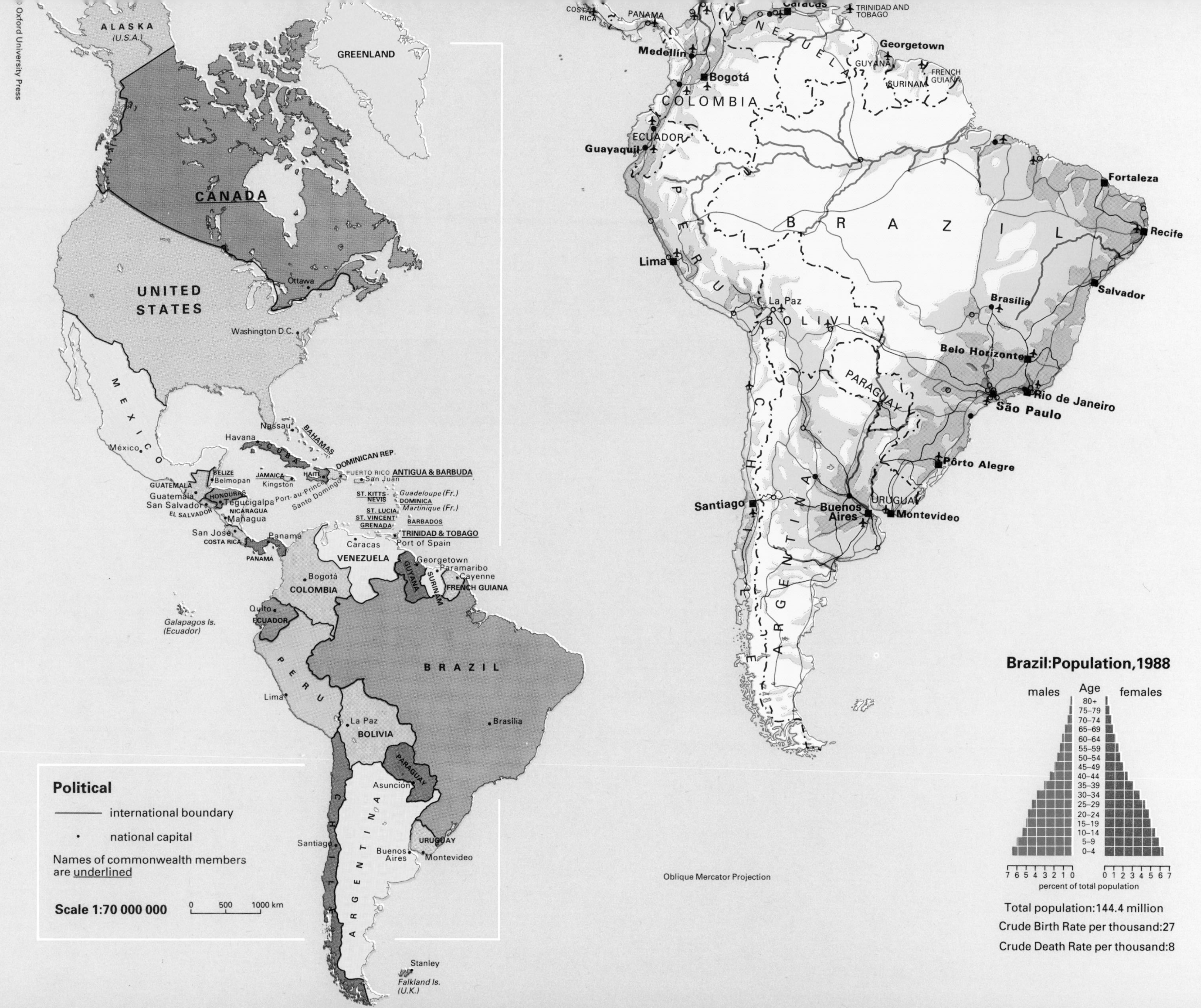
ALASKA
(U.S.A.)
GREENLAND
CANADA
Ottawa
UNITED STATES
Washington D.C.
MEXICO
México
Havana
Nassau
BAHAMAS
DOMINICAN REP.
PUERTO RICO
San Juan
ANTIGUA & BARBUDA
BELIZE
Belmopan
JAMAICA
Kingston
HAITI
Port-au-Prince
Santo Domingo
GUATEMALA
Guatemala
HONDURAS
Tegucigalpa
San Salvador
EL SALVADOR
NICARAGUA
Managua
San José
COSTA RICA
Panama
PANAMA
ST. KITTS-NEVIS
Guadeloupe (Fr.)
DOMINICA
ST. LUCIA
Martinique (Fr.)
ST. VINCENT
GRENADA
BARBADOS
TRINIDAD & TOBAGO
Port of Spain
Caracas
VENEZUELA
Georgetown
GUYANA
Paramaribo
SURINAM
Cayenne
FRENCH GUIANA
Bogotá
COLOMBIA
Quito
ECUADOR
Galapagos Is.
(Ecuador)
PERU
Lima
BRAZIL
Brasilia
La Paz
BOLIVIA
PARAGUAY
Asunción
CHILE
Santiago
ARGENTINA
Buenos Aires
URUGUAY
Montevideo
Stanley
Falkland Is.
(U.K.)
Political
international boundary
national capital
Names of commonwealth members are underlined
Scale 1:70 000 000
0
500
1000 km
COSTA RICA
PANAMA
Caracas
TRINIDAD AND TOBAGO
Medellín
Georgetown
GUYANA
FRENCH GUIANA
SURINAM
Bogotá
COLOMBIA
ECUADOR
Guayaquil
PERU
Lima
BRAZIL
Fortaleza
Recife
Salvador
Brasília
La Paz
BOLIVIA
Belo Horizonte
PARAGUAY
Rio de Janeiro
São Paulo
Pôrto Alegre
URUGUAY
Montevideo
Buenos Aires
Santiago
CHILE
ARGENTINA
Oblique Mercator Projection
Brazil:Population,1988
males
Age
females
80+
75–79
70–74
65–69
60–64
55–59
50–54
45–49
40–44
35–39
30–34
25–29
20–24
15–19
10–14
5–9
0–4
7 6 5 4 3 2 1 0
0 1 2 3 4 5 6 7
percent of total population
Total population:144.4 million
Crude Birth Rate per thousand:27
Crude Death Rate per thousand:8

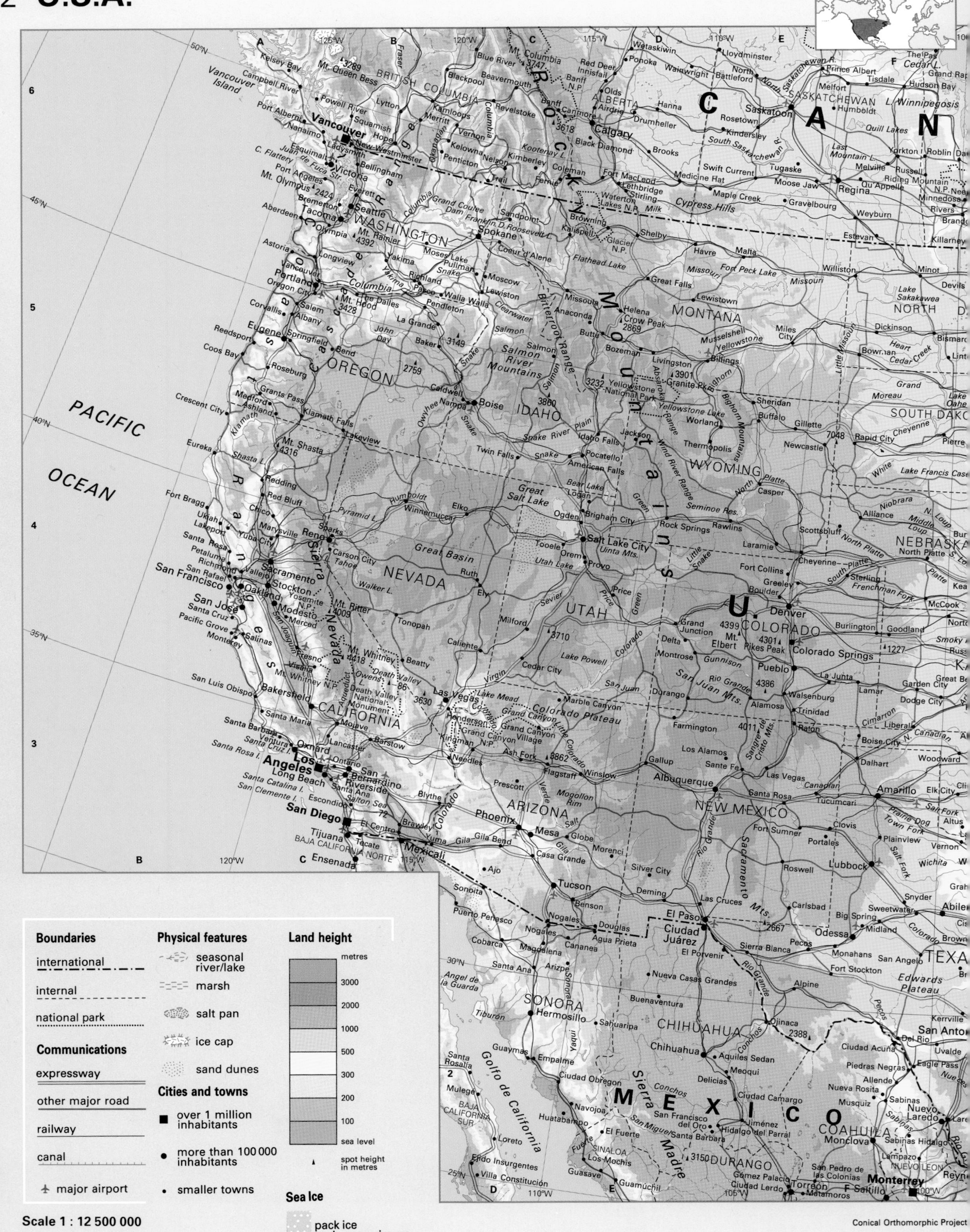

PACIFIC

OCEAN

BRITISH COLUMBIA

CANADA

ALBERTA

SASKATCHEWAN

WASHINGTON

OREGON

IDAHO

MONTANA

NORTH D

SOUTH DAKOTA

WYOMING

NEBRASKA

NEVADA

UTAH

COLORADO

U.

CALIFORNIA

ARIZONA

NEW MEXICO

KA

TEXA

BAJA CALIFORNIA NORTE

SONORA

CHIHUAHUA

COAHUILA

BAJA CALIFORNIA SUR

SINALOA

DURANGO

MEXICO

NUEVO LEON

Golfo de California

Sierra Madre

Boundaries

international

internal

national park

Communications

expressway

other major road

railway

canal

✈ major airport

Physical features

🌿 seasonal river/lake

🌾 marsh

🥚 salt pan

❄ ice cap

⋯ sand dunes

Cities and towns

■ over 1 million inhabitants

● more than 100 000 inhabitants

• smaller towns

Land height

metres
3000
2000
1000
500
300
200
100
sea level

▲ spot height in metres

Sea Ice

pack ice
spring maximum

Scale 1 : 12 500 000

0   125   250 km

Conical Orthomorphic Project

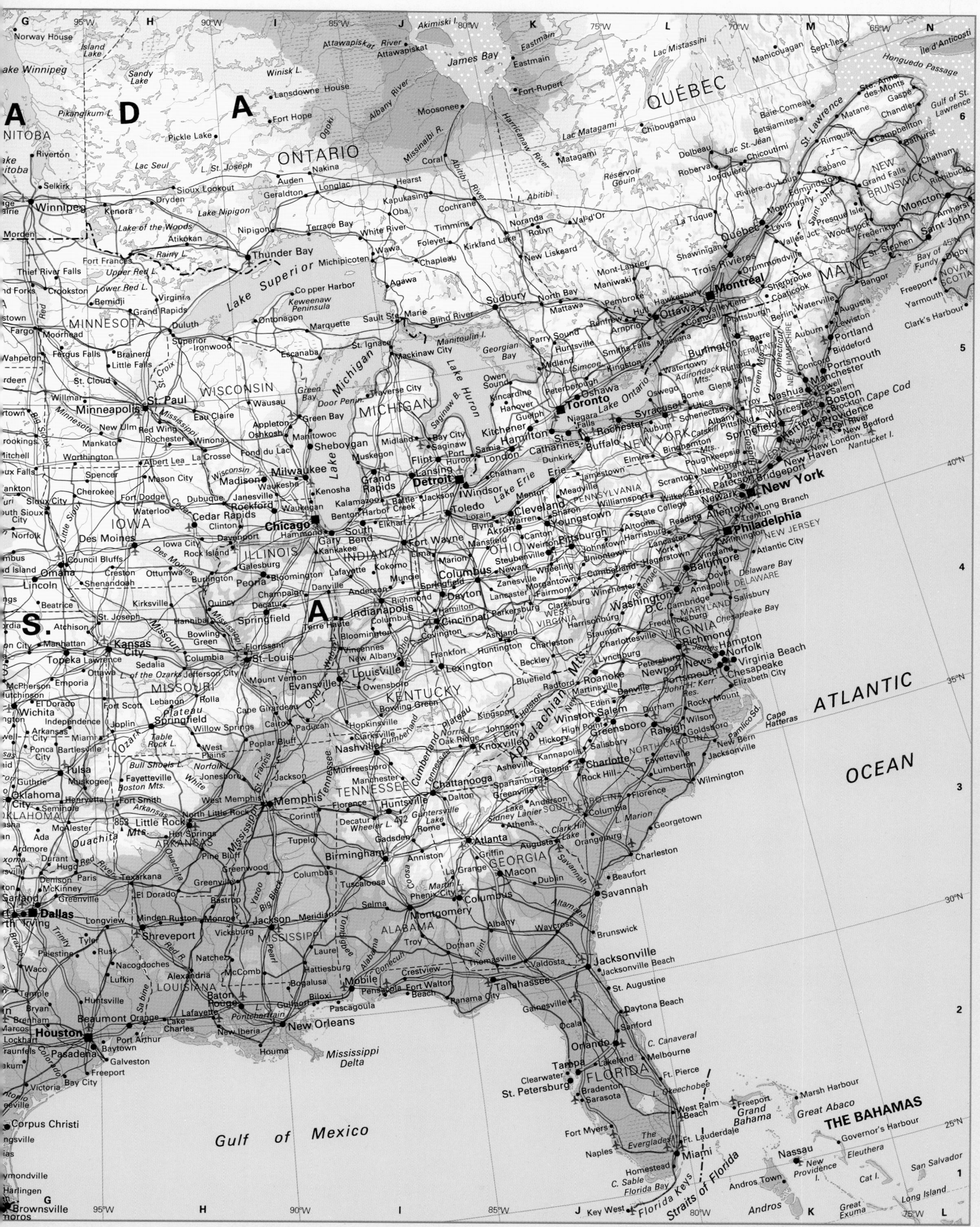
CANADA
U.S.A.
QUÉBEC
ONTARIO
NEW BRUNSWICK
NOVA SCOTIA
MAINE
VERMONT
NEW HAMPSHIRE
MINNESOTA
WISCONSIN
MICHIGAN
IOWA
ILLINOIS
INDIANA
OHIO
PENNSYLVANIA
NEW YORK
NEW JERSEY
DELAWARE
MARYLAND
WEST VIRGINIA
VIRGINIA
KENTUCKY
MISSOURI
TENNESSEE
NORTH CAROLINA
SOUTH CAROLINA
GEORGIA
ALABAMA
MISSISSIPPI
ARKANSAS
LOUISIANA
FLORIDA
THE BAHAMAS
ATLANTIC
OCEAN
Gulf of Mexico
Straits of Florida
James Bay
Lake Superior
Lake Michigan
Lake Huron
Lake Erie
Lake Ontario
Appalachian Mts.
Mississippi Delta
Cape Hatteras
Chicago
Detroit
Toronto
Montreal
Ottawa
Québec
New York
Philadelphia
Boston
Baltimore
Washington D.C.
Pittsburgh
Cleveland
Columbus
Indianapolis
Cincinnati
Louisville
St. Louis
Kansas City
Minneapolis
St. Paul
Milwaukee
Nashville
Memphis
Atlanta
Charlotte
Jacksonville
Tampa
Miami
New Orleans
Houston
Dallas
Oklahoma City
Birmingham
Montgomery
Nassau
95°W
90°W
85°W
80°W
75°W
70°W
65°W
40°N
35°N
30°N
25°N

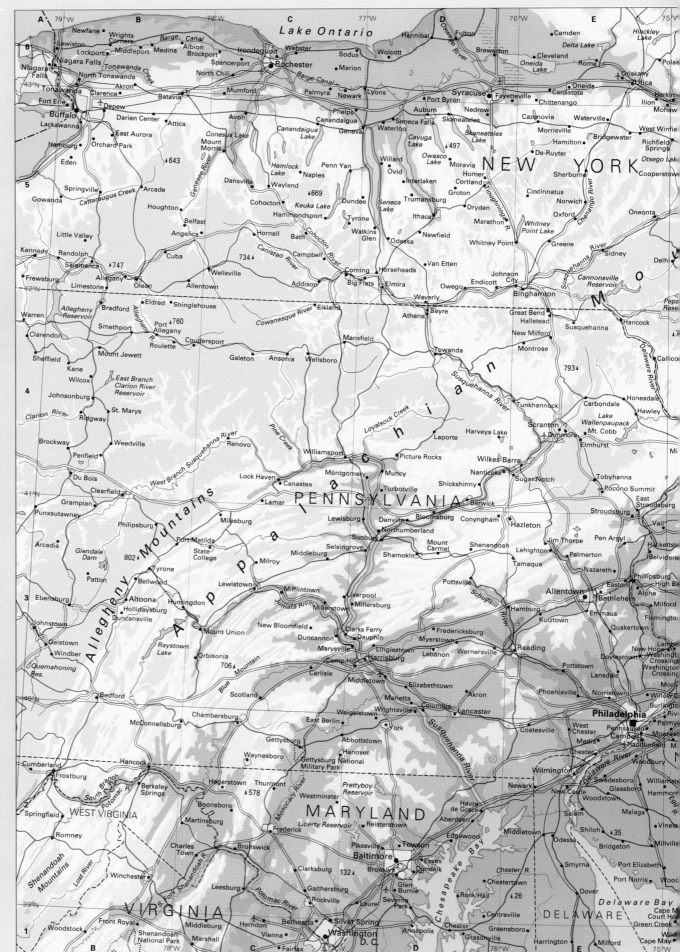

Boundaries

international

internal

national park

Communications

expressway

other major road

railway

canal

✈ major airport

Cities and towns

◹ built-up areas

■ over 1 million
inhabitants

● more than 100 000
inhabitants

• smaller towns

Physical features

‡‡‡‡‡ marsh

Land height

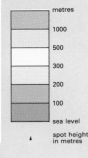

metres
1000
500
300
200
100
sea level

▲ spot height
in metres

Scale 1: 2 000 000

0   25   50 km

Conical Orthomorphic Projection

© Oxford University Press

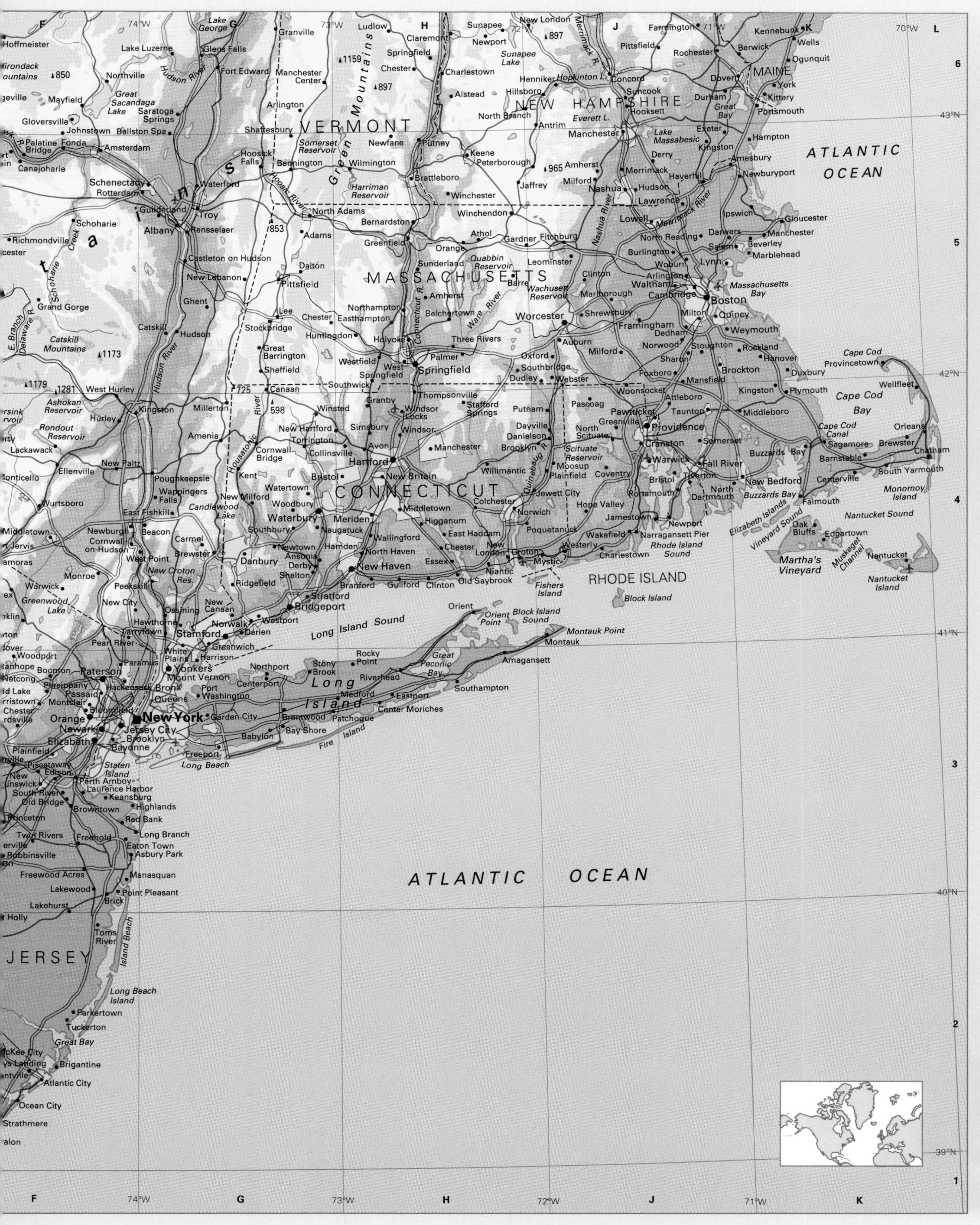
VERMONT
NEW HAMPSHIRE
MAINE
MASSACHUSETTS
CONNECTICUT
RHODE ISLAND
JERSEY
ATLANTIC OCEAN
ATLANTIC OCEAN
Long Island Sound
Long Island
Block Island Sound
Rhode Island Sound
Nantucket Sound
Vineyard Sound
Buzzards Bay
Cape Cod Bay
Massachusetts Bay
Cape Cod
Cape Cod Canal
Martha's Vineyard
Nantucket Island
Muskeget Channel
Elizabeth Islands
Block Island
Fishers Island
Fire Island
Staten Island
Long Beach Island
Island Beach
Great Bay
Montauk Point
Orient Point
Green Mountains
Catskill Mountains
Hudson River
Connecticut R.
Merrimack R.
Merrimack River
Nashua River
Housatonic River
Hoosic River
Ware River
Quinebaug R.
Schoharie Creek
E. Branch Delaware R.
Quabbin Reservoir
Wachusett Reservoir
Scituate Reservoir
Ashokan Reservoir
Rondout Reservoir
Harriman Reservoir
Somerset Reservoir
New Croton Res.
Candlewood Lake
Great Sacandaga Lake
Lake Luzerne
Lake George
Sunapee Lake
Lake Massabesic
Greenwood Lake
Great Bay
Everett L.
Hopkinton L.
New York
Boston
Providence
Hartford
Springfield
Worcester
New Haven
Bridgeport
Stamford
Albany
Schenectady
Troy
Concord
Manchester
Nashua
Lowell
Lawrence
Cambridge
Quincy
Brockton
Fall River
New Bedford
Pawtucket
Cranston
Warwick
Newport
Waterbury
Danbury
Norwalk
New London
Yonkers
Paterson
Newark
Jersey City
Elizabeth
Atlantic City
Ocean City
Portsmouth
Dover
Kennebunk
Plymouth
Provincetown
Chatham
Hyannis
Falmouth
Nantucket
Edgartown
Montauk
Southampton
Riverhead
Kingston
Poughkeepsie
Newburgh
Pittsfield
Northampton
Holyoke
Fitchburg
Keene
Brattleboro
Bennington
Middletown
Meriden
New Britain
Norwich
Westerly
74°W
73°W
72°W
71°W
70°W
43°N
42°N
41°N
40°N
39°N
F
G
H
J
K
L
6
5
4
3
2
1

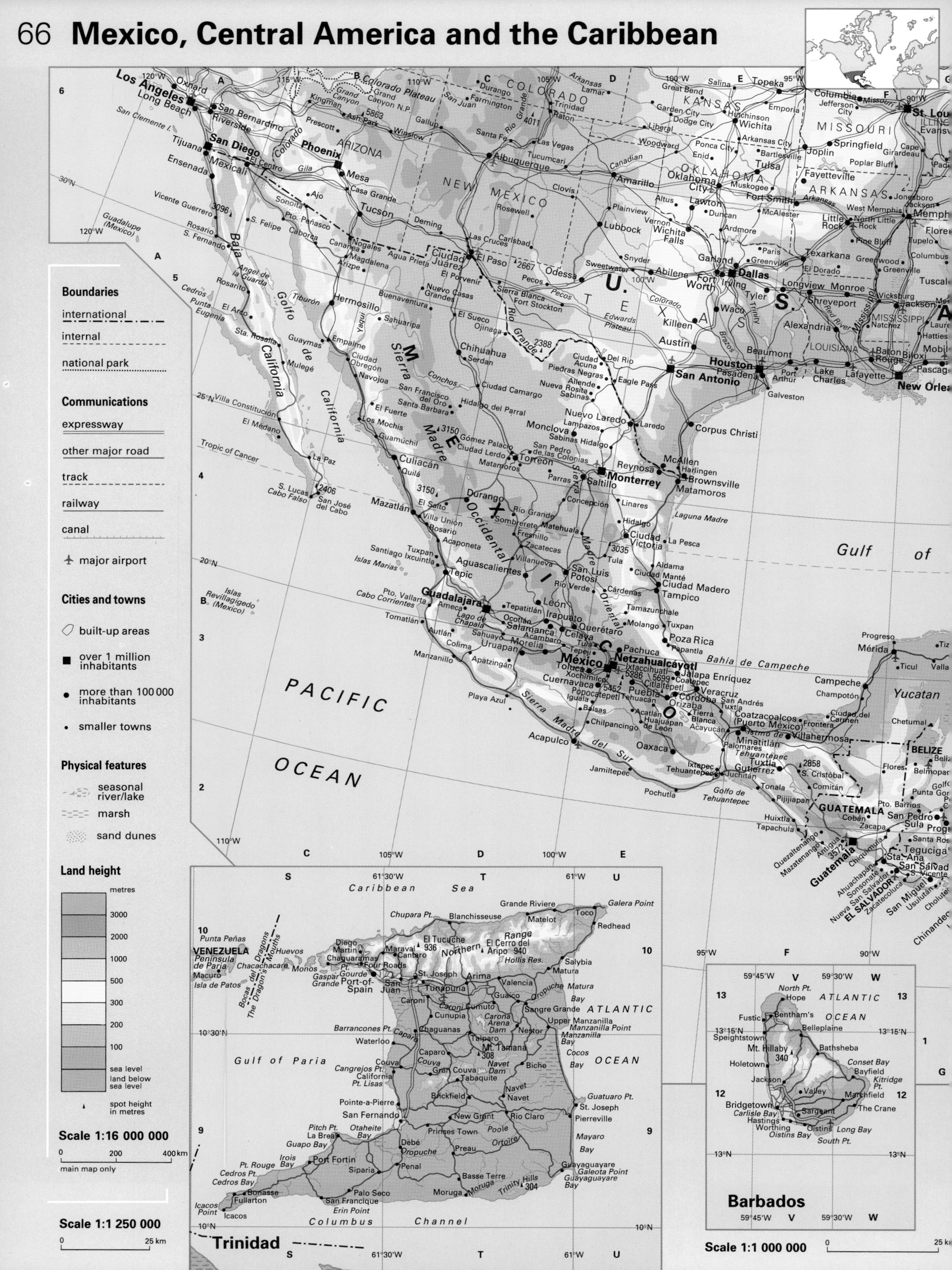
Boundaries
international
internal
national park
Communications
expressway
other major road
track
railway
canal
major airport
Cities and towns
built-up areas
over 1 million inhabitants
more than 100 000 inhabitants
smaller towns
Physical features
seasonal river/lake
marsh
sand dunes
Land height
metres
3000
2000
1000
500
300
200
100
sea level
land below sea level
spot height in metres
Scale 1:16 000 000
0 200 400 km
main map only
Scale 1:1 250 000
0 25 km
Trinidad
Barbados
Scale 1:1 000 000
PACIFIC
OCEAN
Gulf of
Caribbean Sea
Gulf of Paria
ATLANTIC OCEAN
Columbus Channel
Bahía de Campeche
Golfo de California
Golfo de Tehuantepec
MEXICO
U. S. A.
GUATEMALA
BELIZE
EL SALVADOR
VENEZUELA
Los Angeles
San Diego
Phoenix
Dallas
Houston
San Antonio
Monterrey
Guadalajara
México
Netzahualcóyotl
Guatemala
Port-of-Spain
Bridgetown

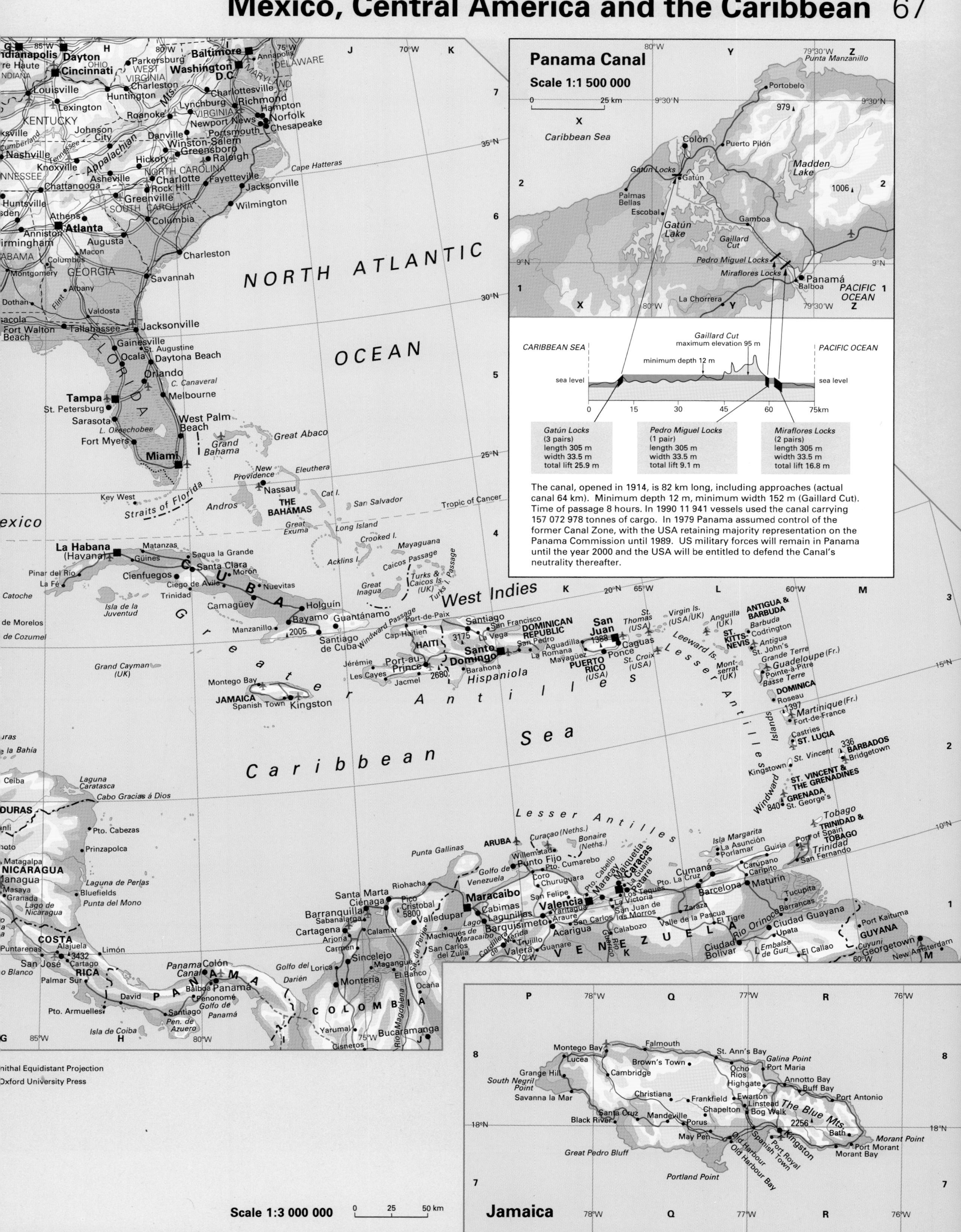
Panama Canal
Scale 1:1 500 000
Caribbean Sea
Colón
Puerto Pilón
Portobelo
Madden Lake
Gatún Locks
Gatún
Palmas Bellas
Escobal
Gatún Lake
Gamboa
Gaillard Cut
Pedro Miguel Locks
Miraflores Locks
Panamá
Balboa
PACIFIC OCEAN
La Chorrera
CARIBBEAN SEA
Gaillard Cut
maximum elevation 95 m
minimum depth 12 m
PACIFIC OCEAN
sea level
sea level
0 15 30 45 60 75km
Gatún Locks
(3 pairs)
length 305 m
width 33.5 m
total lift 25.9 m
Pedro Miguel Locks
(1 pair)
length 305 m
width 33.5 m
total lift 9.1 m
Miraflores Locks
(2 pairs)
length 305 m
width 33.5 m
total lift 16.8 m
The canal, opened in 1914, is 82 km long, including approaches (actual canal 64 km). Minimum depth 12 m, minimum width 152 m (Gaillard Cut). Time of passage 8 hours. In 1990 11 941 vessels used the canal carrying 157 072 978 tonnes of cargo. In 1979 Panama assumed control of the former Canal Zone, with the USA retaining majority representation on the Panama Commission until 1989. US military forces will remain in Panama until the year 2000 and the USA will be entitled to defend the Canal's neutrality thereafter.
NORTH ATLANTIC OCEAN
West Indies
Greater Antilles
Lesser Antilles
Caribbean Sea
Leeward Is.
Windward Islands
THE BAHAMAS
CUBA
La Habana (Havana)
HAITI
DOMINICAN REPUBLIC
Santo Domingo
Port-au-Prince
Hispaniola
JAMAICA
Kingston
PUERTO RICO (USA)
San Juan
ANTIGUA & BARBUDA
DOMINICA
ST. LUCIA
BARBADOS
ST. VINCENT & THE GRENADINES
GRENADA
TRINIDAD & TOBAGO
VENEZUELA
Caracas
Maracaibo
COLOMBIA
PANAMA
COSTA RICA
NICARAGUA
GUYANA
Georgetown
FLORIDA
GEORGIA
Miami
Atlanta
Washington D.C.
Tropic of Cancer
Straits of Florida
Azimuthal Equidistant Projection
Oxford University Press
Scale 1:3 000 000
0 25 50 km
Jamaica
Montego Bay
Falmouth
St. Ann's Bay
Ocho Rios
Spanish Town
Kingston
The Blue Mts.
Port Antonio
Mandeville
May Pen
Morant Point
Portland Point
Great Pedro Bluff

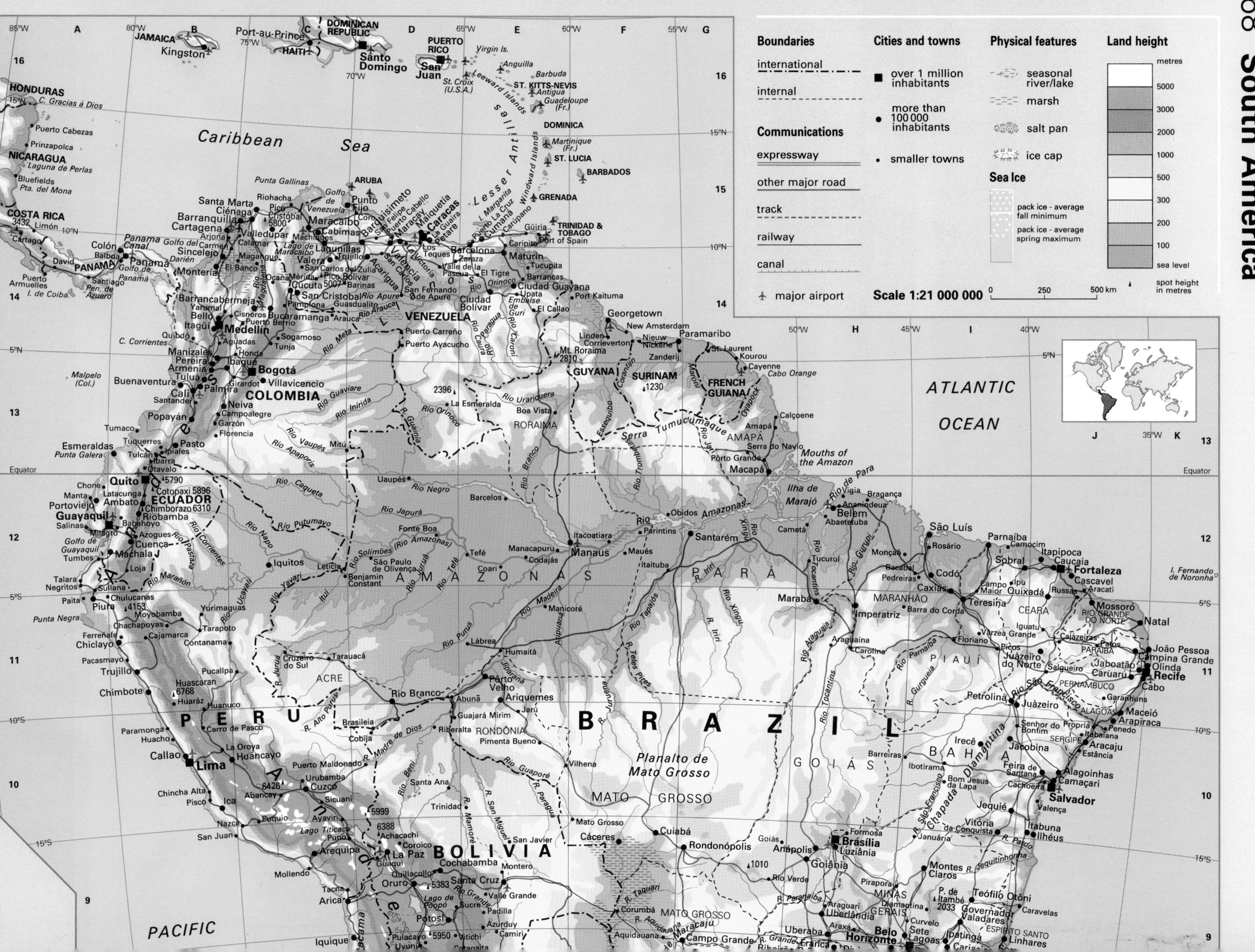

Land height

metres	
5000	
3000	
2000	
1000	
500	
300	
200	
100	
sea level	

spot height in metres

Physical features

- seasonal river/lake
- marsh
- salt pan
- ice cap

Sea ice

- pack ice - average fall minimum
- pack ice - average spring maximum

Cities and towns

- ■ over 1 million inhabitants
- ● more than 100 000 inhabitants
- ● smaller towns

Boundaries

- international
- internal

Communications

- expressway
- other major road
- track
- railway
- canal
- ✈ major airport

Scale 1:21 000 000

0   250   500 km

ATLANTIC OCEAN

PACIFIC

Caribbean Sea

JAMAICA
HONDURAS
NICARAGUA
COSTA RICA
PANAMA
DOMINICAN REPUBLIC
HAITI
PUERTO RICO (U.S.A.)
ST. KITTS-NEVIS
DOMINICA
ST. LUCIA
BARBADOS
GRENADA
TRINIDAD & TOBAGO

COLOMBIA
VENEZUELA
GUYANA
SURINAM
FRENCH GUIANA
ECUADOR
PERU
BRAZIL
BOLIVIA

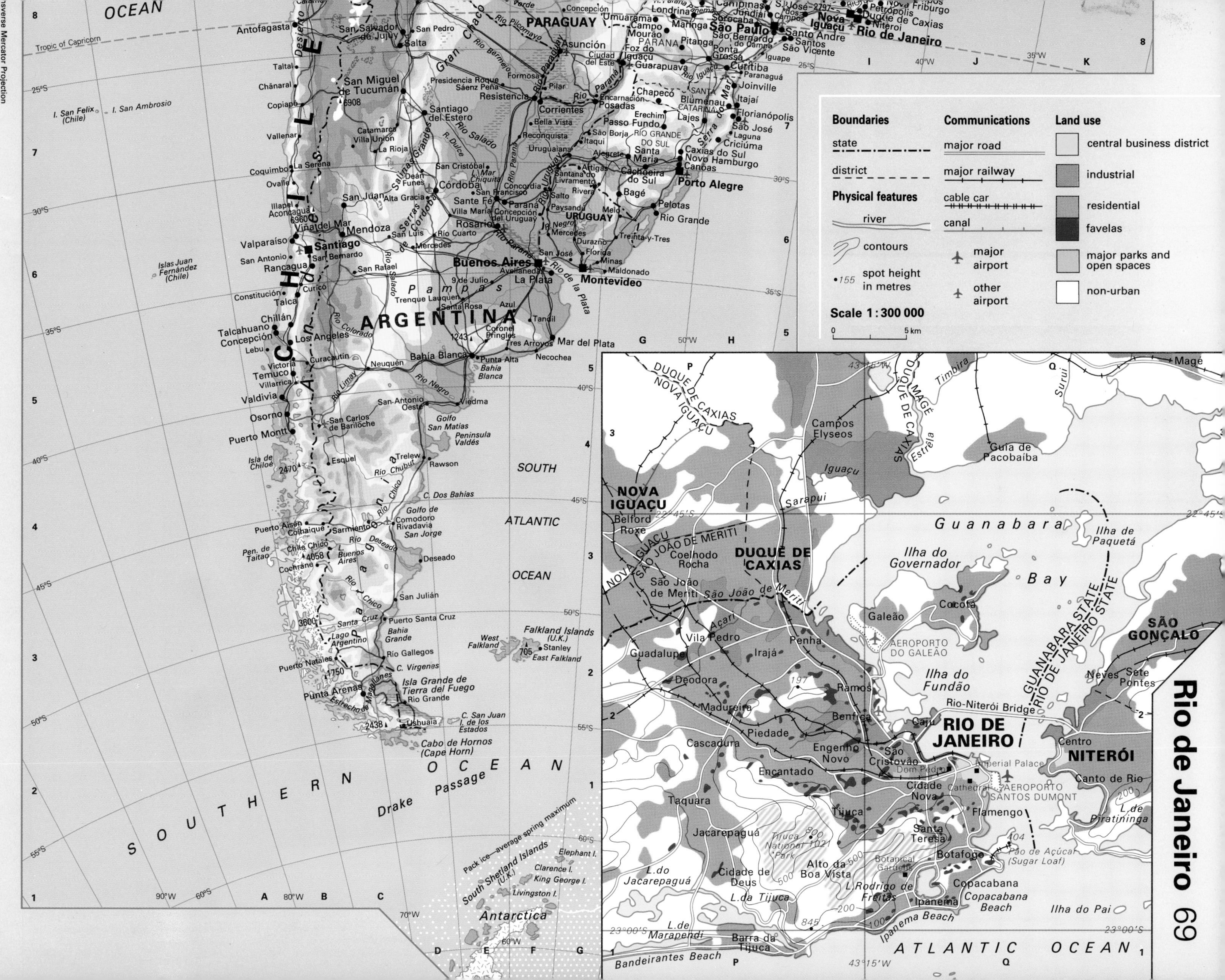

Land use

- central business district
- industrial
- residential
- favelas
- major parks and open spaces
- non-urban

Communications

- major road
- major railway
- cable car
- canal
- + major airport
- + other airport

Boundaries

- state
- district

Physical features

- river
- contours
- •155 spot height in metres

Scale 1:300 000

0   5 km

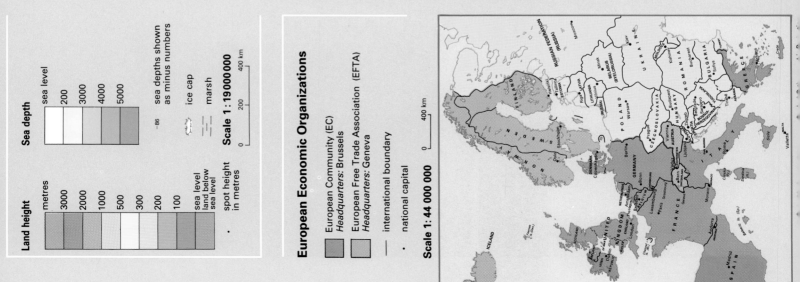

Sea depth

	sea level
	200
	3000
	4000
	5000

-86   sea depths shown as minus numbers

ice cap

marsh

Scale 1:19 000 000

0   200   400 km

Land height

metres	
3000	
2000	
1000	
500	
300	
200	
100	
	sea level land below sea level

· spot height in metres

European Economic Organizations

European Community (EC)
Headquarters: Brussels

European Free Trade Association (EFTA)
Headquarters: Geneva

— international boundary

· national capital

Scale 1: 44 000 000

0   400 km

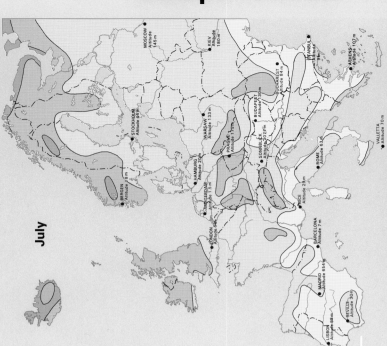

January

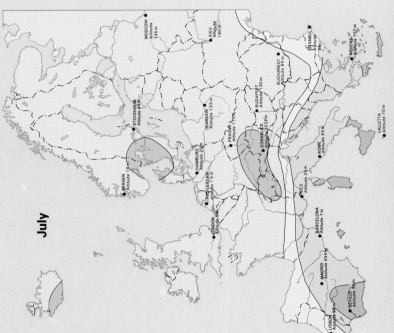

July

Actual surface temperature

°C
25
20
15
10
5
0
-5
-10
-15

Scale 1: 40 000 000

0   200   400 km

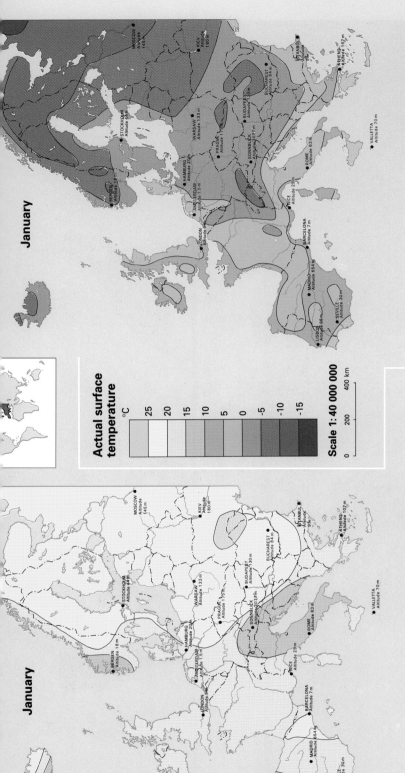

January

July

Rainfall
and other forms
of precipitation

mm
over 100
50-100
25-50
10-25
0-10

Scale 1: 40 000 000

0   200   400 km

Conical Orthomorphic Projection

© Oxford University Press

Rainfall figures on graphs in tens of
millimetres except for annual totals

STOCKHOLM   1958 mm Annual
555 mm Annual

MOSCOW
575 mm Annual

NICE
862 mm Annual

ROME
749 mm Annual

BARCELONA
598 mm Annual

ATHENS
402 mm Annual

BERGEN
1958 mm Annual

WARSAW
471 mm Annual

LONDON
594 mm Annual

SONNBLICK
1495 mm Annual

LISBON
708 mm Annual

BUCHAREST
578 mm Annual

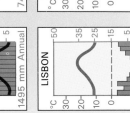
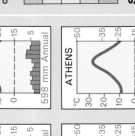
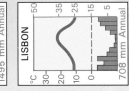
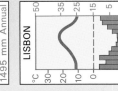
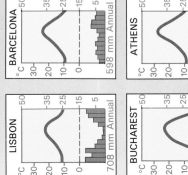
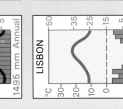
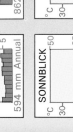

See page 72 for other climate graphs relating
to climate stations shown on the maps.

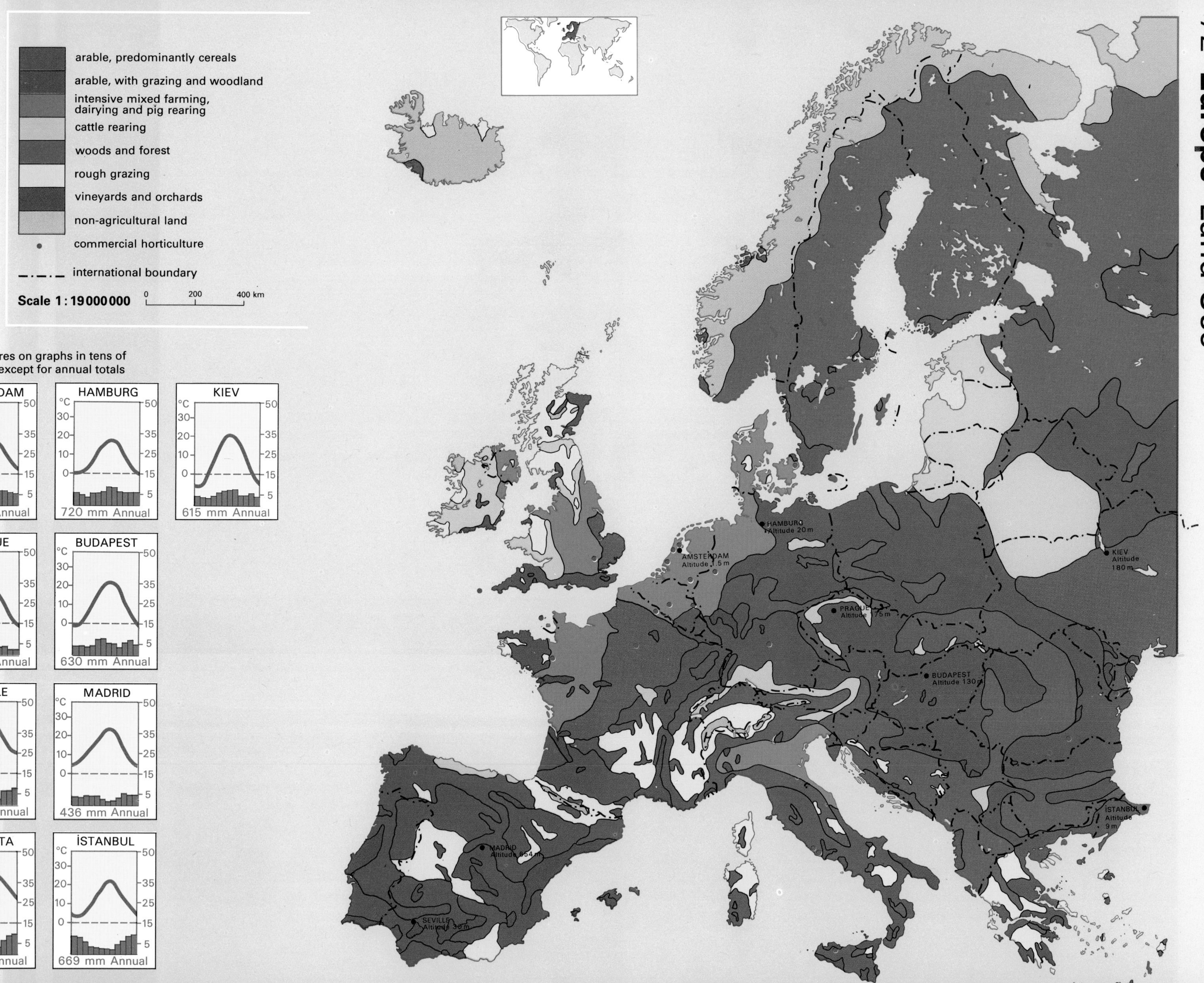

Scale 1:19 000 000

Legend:
- arable, predominantly cereals
- arable, with grazing and woodland
- intensive mixed farming, dairying and pig rearing
- cattle rearing
- woods and forest
- rough grazing
- vineyards and orchards
- non-agricultural land
- commercial horticulture
- international boundary
- ●

0   200   400 km

Conical Orthomorphic Projection

© Oxford University Press

Rainfall figures on graphs in tens of millimetres except for annual totals

KIEV 615 mm Annual

HAMBURG 720 mm Annual

BUDAPEST 630 mm Annual

MADRID 436 mm Annual

İSTANBUL 669 mm Annual

AMSTERDAM 787 mm Annual

PRAGUE 508 mm Annual

SEVILLE 559 mm Annual

VALLETTA 516 mm Annual

See page 71 for climate graphs for other

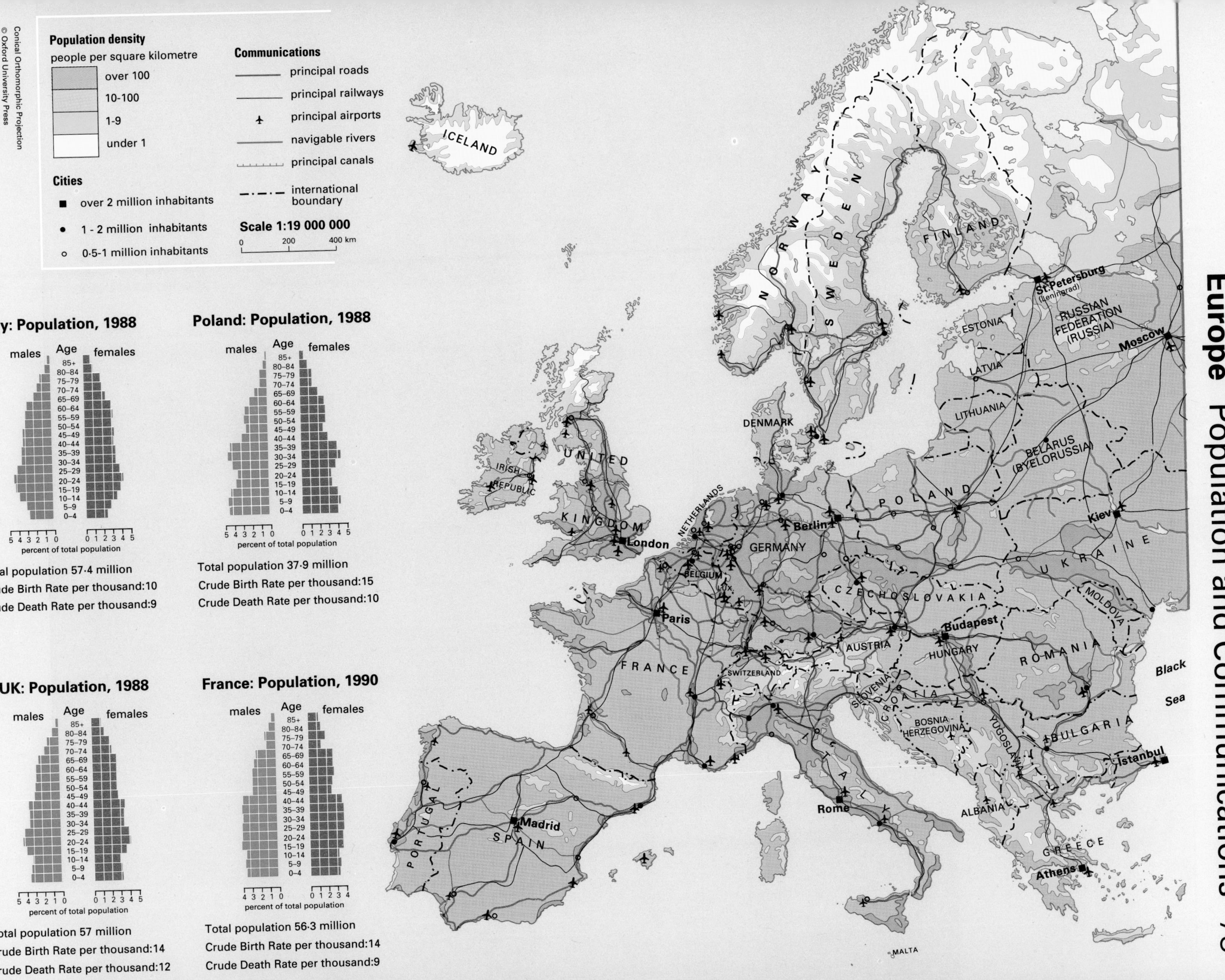

Population density

people per square kilometre

- over 100
- 10–100
- 1–9
- under 1

Cities

- ■ over 2 million inhabitants
- ● 1 – 2 million inhabitants
- ○ 0·5–1 million inhabitants

Communications

- principal roads
- principal railways
- ✈ principal airports
- navigable rivers
- principal canals
- international boundary

Scale 1:19 000 000

0   200   400 km

Conical Orthomorphic Projection

© Oxford University Press

Italy: Population, 1988

males   Age   females

85+
80–84
75–79
70–74
65–69
60–64
55–59
50–54
45–49
40–44
35–39
30–34
25–29
20–24
15–19
10–14
5–9
0–4

5 4 3 2 1 0   0 1 2 3 4 5
percent of total population

Total population 57.4 million
Crude Birth Rate per thousand:10
Crude Death Rate per thousand:9

UK: Population, 1988

males   Age   females

85+
80–84
75–79
70–74
65–69
60–64
55–59
50–54
45–49
40–44
35–39
30–34
25–29
20–24
15–19
10–14
5–9
0–4

5 4 3 2 1 0   0 1 2 3 4 5
percent of total population

Total population 57 million
Crude Birth Rate per thousand:14
Crude Death Rate per thousand:12

Poland: Population, 1988

males   Age   females

85+
80–84
75–79
70–74
65–69
60–64
55–59
50–54
45–49
40–44
35–39
30–34
25–29
20–24
15–19
10–14
5–9
0–4

5 4 3 2 1 0   0 1 2 3 4 5
percent of total population

Total population 37.9 million
Crude Birth Rate per thousand:15
Crude Death Rate per thousand:10

France: Population, 1990

males   Age   females

85+
80–84
75–79
70–74
65–69
60–64
55–59
50–54
45–49
40–44
35–39
30–34
25–29
20–24
15–19
10–14
5–9
0–4

4 3 2 1 0   0 1 2 3 4
percent of total population

Total population 56.3 million
Crude Birth Rate per thousand:14
Crude Death Rate per thousand:9

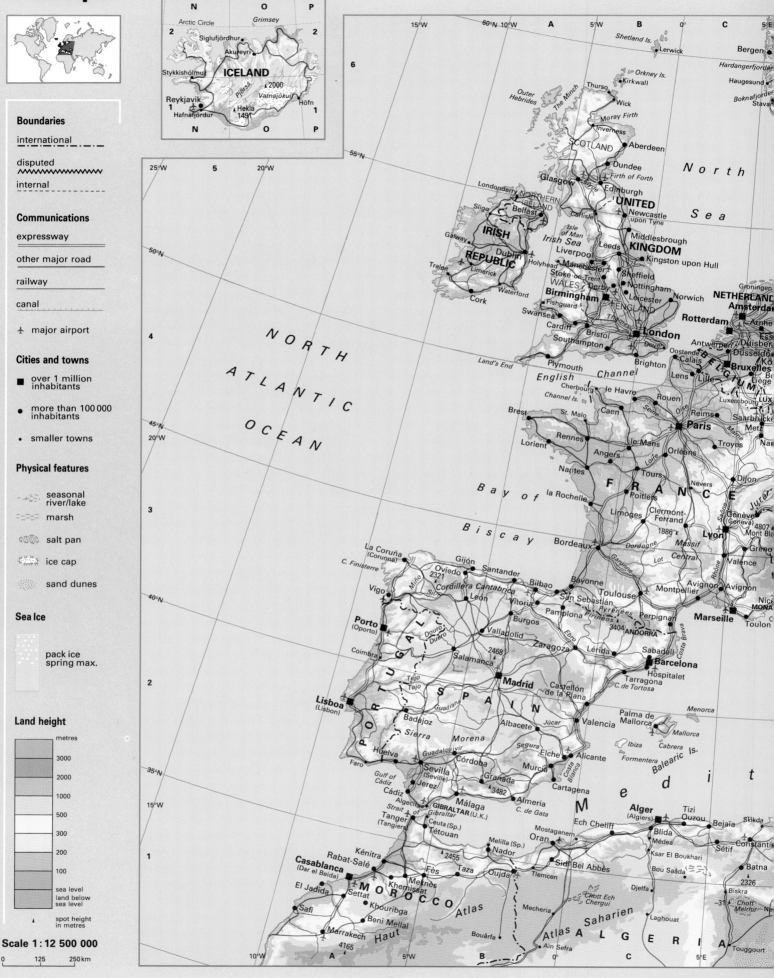

Boundaries

international

disputed
〰〰〰〰〰〰〰〰〰

internal
– – – – – – – –

Communications

expressway

other major road

railway

canal

✈ major airport

Cities and towns

■ over 1 million
  inhabitants

● more than 100 000
  inhabitants

• smaller towns

Physical features

seasonal
river/lake

marsh

salt pan

ice cap

sand dunes

Sea Ice

pack ice
spring max.

Land height

metres
3000
2000
1000
500
300
200
100
sea level
land below
sea level

▲ spot height
  in metres

Scale 1 : 12 500 000

0   125   250 km

ICELAND inset:

N   O   P

Arctic Circle   *Grimsey*

Siglufjördhur
Akureyri

Stykkishólmur

ICELAND

▲2000

Pjórsá   *Vatnajökul*

Reykjavik   Hekla ▲Höfn
Hafnafjördur   1491

N   O   P

N O R T H   A T L A N T I C   O C E A N

Bay of

Biscay

North Sea

Shetland Is.
Lerwick

Orkney Is.
Kirkwall
Thurso   Wick
Outer
Hebrides   The Minch
Moray Firth
Inverness
SCOTLAND   Aberdeen
Dundee
Glasgow   Firth of Forth
Edinburgh
Londonderry   NORTHERN   UNITED   Newcastle
                IRELAND   upon Tyne
Sligo   Belfast   Carlisle
IRISH   Isle   Middlesbrough
         of Man
Galway   Irish Sea   KINGDOM
         Liverpool   Leeds   Kingston upon Hull
REPUBLIC   Dublin   Holyhead   Manchester   Norwich
Tralee   Stoke-on-Trent   Sheffield
Limerick   WALES   Nottingham
         Birmingham   Leicester
Waterford   Fishguard   ENGLAND
Cork   Swansea   Thames
         Cardiff   Bristol   London
         Swansea   Southampton   Dover
Land's End   Plymouth   Brighton
English   Channel
         Cherbourg   Le Havre   Rouen
Channel Is.   Caen   Seine
Brest   St. Malo
Rennes   Le Mans   Orleans
Lorient   Angers   Tours
Nantes   F R A N C E   Loire
         la Rochelle   Poitiers
         Limoges   Clermont-
                Ferrand   1886▲
Bordeaux   Dordogne   Massif
         Garonne   Central
Bayonne   Toulouse
San Sebastián   Pyrénées   Montpellier
C. Finisterre   Pireneos
La Coruña   Gijón   Santander   Bilbao   3404 ANDORRA
(Corunna)   Oviedo   Vitoria   Pamplona   Perpignan
Vigo   2321▲   Cordillera Cantabrica   Lérida
         Leon   Burgos   Zaragoza
Porto   Miño   Valladolid   Ebro   Sabadell
(Oporto)   Sil   Duero   2468▲   Barcelona
         Douro   Salamanca   Tarragona   Hospitalet
Coimbra   Duero   C. de Tortosa
P O R T U G A L   Madrid   Castellón
         Tejo   S P A I N   de la Plana
Lisboa   Tajo   Palma de
(Lisbon)   Guadiana   Albacete   Mallorca   Menorca
Badajoz   Júcar   Valencia
         Sierra   Segura   Mallorca
Huelva   Morena   Ibiza   Cabrera   Balearic Is.
         Guadalquivir   Elche   Formentera
Faro   Córdoba   Murcia
Sevilla   Granada   Alicante
(Seville)   Jerez   3482▲   Almería   Costa
         Cádiz   Málaga   Blanca
Gulf of   Algeciras   GIBRALTAR   C. de Gata
Cádiz   Strait of   (U.K.)
Tanger   Gibraltar   Alger   Tizi
(Tangiers)   Ceuta (Sp.)   (Algiers)   Ouzou
Rabat-Salé   Tétouan   Ech Cheliff   Blida   Bejaïa
Kénitra   Melilla (Sp.)   Mostaganem   Médéa   Skikda
Casablanca   Nador   Oran   Sétif   Constantine
(Dar el Beida)   Fès   Sidi Bel Abbès   Ksar El Boukhari
El Jadida   Taza   Oujda   Tlemcen   Bou Saâda
Settat   Meknès   Djelfa   Batna
Safi   Khemissat   2326▲
M O R O C C O   Tlemcen   A L G E R I A
Khouribga   Laghouat
Beni Mellal   Atlas   Chott Ech   -31
Marrakech   Atlas   Chergui   Chott
         Haut   Mecheria   Atlas Saharien   Melrhir
4165▲   Bouârfa   Ain Sefra   Biskra
         Touggourt

North America / World inset (top left): small world map

Bergen
Hardangerfjorden
Haugesund
Boknafjorden
Stavanger

Groningen
NETHERLAND
Amsterdam
Arnhe
Rotterdam   Duisber
Antwerpen   Düsseldo
Oostende   BELGIUM   Kö
Calais   Bruxelles
Lens   Lille   Liège
         Luxembourg   LUX
Reims   Saarbrücke
Paris   Marne   Metz
Troyes
Dijon   Jura
Nevers   4807▲
         Genève   Mont Bla
Lyon   (Geneva)
Massif   Greno
Lyon   Rhône   Valence
         Avignon   Nice
Avignon   MONA
Marseille   Toulon

M e d i t

Conical Orthomorphic Projection

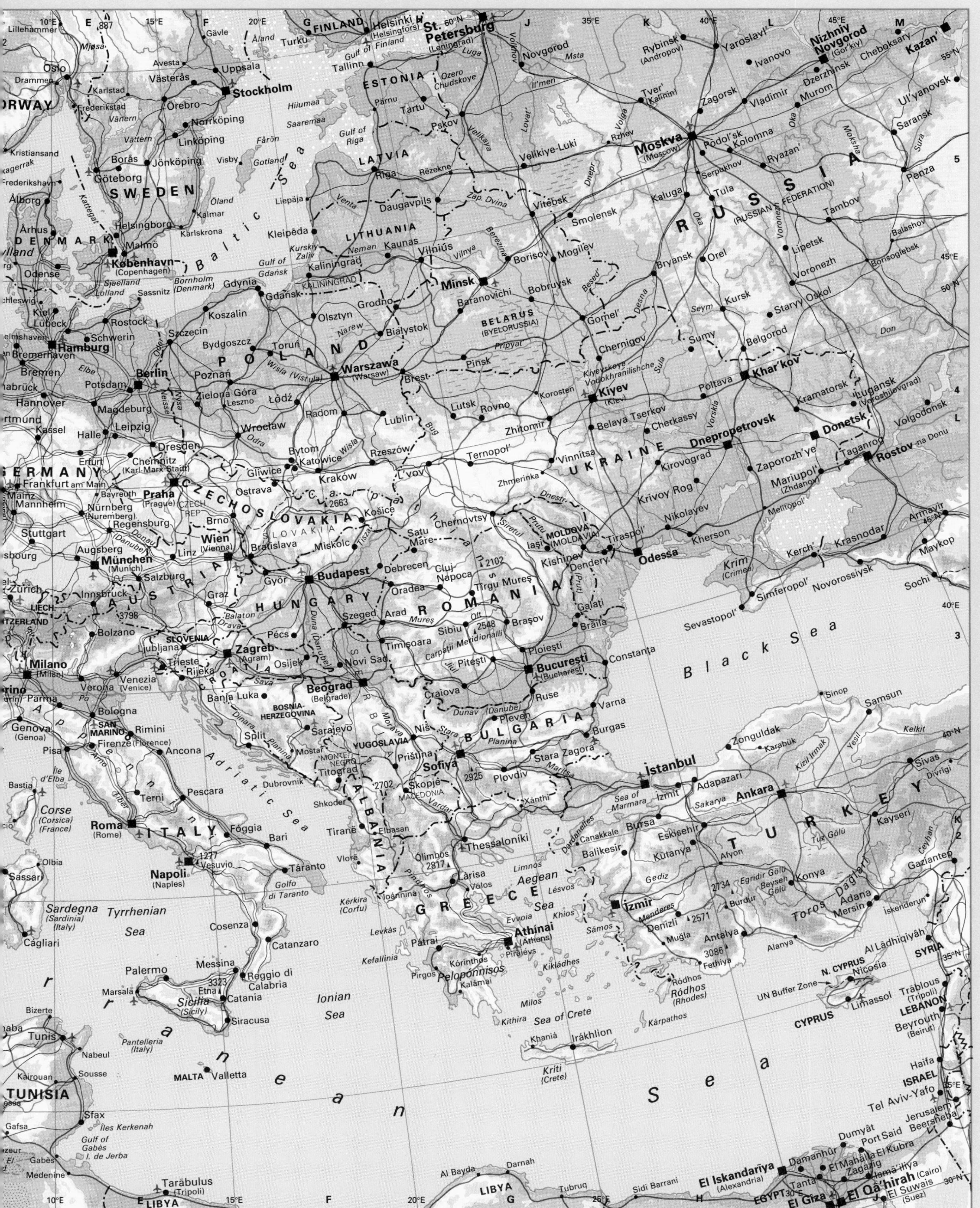
FINLAND
Helsinki
(Helsingfors)
St. Petersburg
(Leningrad)
Gulf of Finland
Tallinn
ESTONIA
Stockholm
Uppsala
Gävle
Åland
Turku
Avesta
Västerås
Örebro
Norrköping
Linköping
Oslo
Drammen
Karlstad
Frederikstad
Vänern
Vättern
Mjøsa
Lillehammer
Kristiansand
Frederikshavn
Ålborg
Århus
Borås
Jönköping
Göteborg
SWEDEN
Kattegat
Helsingborg
Malmö
København
(Copenhagen)
Odense
Sjælland
Lolland
Kalmar
Karlskrona
Öland
Visby
Gotland
Fårön
Hiiumaa
Saaremaa
Gulf of Riga
Pärnu
Tartu
Pskov
Ozero
Chudskoye
Luga
Novgorod
Msta
Il'men
Volkhov
Velikaya
Lovat'
LATVIA
Riga
Rezekne
Liepāja
Daugavpils
Venta
Zap. Dvina
LITHUANIA
Klaipėda
Kaunas
Vilnius
Neman
Kurskiy Zaliv
Gulf of Gdańsk
Kaliningrad
KALININGRAD
Baltic Sea
Bornholm
(Denmark)
Gdynia
Gdańsk
Sassnitz
Kiel
Lübeck
Rostock
Schwerin
Hamburg
Bremerhaven
Bremen
Elbe
Koszalin
Szczecin
Oder
Bydgoszcz
Toruń
Olsztyn
Grodno
Narew
Białystok
POLAND
Wisła (Vistula)
Warszawa
(Warsaw)
Poznań
Berlin
Potsdam
Hannover
Magdeburg
Zielona Góra
Leszno
Łódź
Radom
Lublin
Brest
Kassel
Halle
Leipzig
Wrocław
Odra
Dresden
Bytom
Katowice
Gliwice
Kraków
Rzeszów
GERMANY
Erfurt
Chemnitz
(Karl-Marx-Stadt)
Frankfurt am Main
Mainz
Mannheim
Bayreuth
Praha
(Prague)
CZECH REP.
CZECHOSLOVAKIA
SLOVAKIA
Ostrava
Brno
Nürnberg
(Nuremberg)
Regensburg
Donau
(Danube)
Stuttgart
Augsberg
München
(Munich)
Linz
Wien
(Vienna)
Bratislava
Košice
Miskolc
Tisza
Salzburg
Zürich
LIECH.
Innsbruck
AUSTRIA
Graz
Győr
Budapest
HUNGARY
Balaton
Drava
Bolzano
Pécs
Szeged
Debrecen
Satu Mare
Cluj-Napoca
Oradea
Arad
Mureş
Tirgu Mureş
ROMANIA
Sibiu
Olt
Braşov
Timişoara
Carpaţii Meridionali
SLOVENIA
Ljubljana
Zagreb
(Agram)
Trieste
Rijeka
CROATIA
Osijek
Sava
Novi Sad
Milano
(Milan)
Venezia
(Venice)
Verona
Po
Parma
Bologna
SAN MARINO
Rimini
Genova
(Genoa)
Firenze (Florence)
Ancona
Pisa
Arno
Banja Luka
BOSNIA-HERZEGOVINA
Sarajevo
Split
Beograd
(Belgrade)
Morava
YUGOSLAVIA
Mostar
MONTENEGRO
Titograd
Dubrovnik
Niš
Priština
Sofiya
Skopje
MACEDONIA
Vardar
Shkoder
Tirane
ALBANIA
Elbasan
Vlorë
Adriatic Sea
Pescara
Terni
Tiber
Roma
(Rome)
ITALY
Foggia
Bari
Napoli
(Naples)
Vesuvio
Taranto
Golfo di Taranto
Île d'Elba
Bastia
Corse
(Corsica)
(France)
Olbia
Sassari
Sardegna
(Sardinia)
(Italy)
Cagliari
Tyrrhenian Sea
Cosenza
Catanzaro
Palermo
Messina
Reggio di Calabria
Marsala
Etna
Catania
Sicilia
(Sicily)
Siracusa
Ionian Sea
Bizerte
Tunis
Nabeul
Sousse
Kairouan
TUNISIA
Pantelleria
(Italy)
MALTA
Valletta
Sfax
Îles Kerkenah
Gafsa
Gulf of Gabès
Gabès
I. de Jerba
Medenine
Tarābulus
(Tripoli)
LIBYA
Al Bayda
Darnah
Tubruq
Sidi Barrani
El Iskandarîya
(Alexandria)
EGYPT
El Gîza
El Qâ'hirah (Cairo)
El Suwais
(Suez)
Tanta
Damanhûr
Zagazig
Dumyât
Port Said
Mediterranean Sea
Kérkira
(Corfu)
Ioánnina
Pindhos
GREECE
Olimbos
Lárisa
Vólos
Thessaloníki
Pátrai
Kefallinía
Levkás
Athínai
(Athens)
Piraiévs
Kórinthos
Pelopónnisos
Pírgos
Kalámai
Kíthira
Mílos
Kikládhes
Sea of Crete
Khaniá
Irákhlion
Kríti
(Crete)
Aegean Sea
Límnos
Lésvos
Khíos
Evvoia
Sámos
Ródhos
(Rhodes)
Kárpathos
Stara Planina
BULGARIA
Plovdiv
Pleven
Stara Zagora
Maritsa
Xánthi
Burgas
Varna
Ruse
Craiova
Piteşti
Ploieşti
Bucureşti
(Bucharest)
Dunav (Danube)
Constanţa
Brăila
Galaţi
Iaşi
Prut
Siretul
Chernovtsy
L'vov
Ternopol'
Vinnitsa
Zhmerinka
MOLDOVA
(MOLDAVIA)
Kishinev
Tiraspol'
Dnestr
Odessa
Black Sea
Sevastopol'
Simferopol'
Krim
(Crimea)
Kerch'
Novorossiysk
Krasnodar
Sochi
Maykop
Armavir
Rostov-na Donu
Taganrog
Mariupol'
(Zhdanov)
Melitopol'
Zaporozh'ye
Donetsk
Luhansk
(Voroshilovgrad)
Kramatorsk
Volgodonsk
Dnepropetrovsk
Krivoy Rog
Kirovograd
Nikolayev
Kherson
UKRAINE
Belaya Tserkov
Cherkassy
Kiyev
(Kiev)
Kiyevskoye Vodokhranilishche
Zhitomir
Korosten
Rovno
Lutsk
Pinsk
Pripyat
BELARUS
(BYELORUSSIA)
Minsk
Baranovichi
Bobruysk
Borisov
Berezina
Mogilev
Gomel'
Chernigov
Desna
Sumy
Poltava
Vorskla
Khar'kov
Belgorod
Kursk
Seym
Staryy Oskol
Voronezh
Don
Orel
Bryansk
Smolensk
Vitebsk
Velikiye-Luki
Dnepr
Rzhev
Tver'
(Kalinin)
Volga
Moskva
(Moscow)
Zagorsk
Vladimir
Ivanovo
Yaroslavl'
Rybinsk
(Andropov)
Nizhniy Novgorod
(Gor'kiy)
Dzerzhinsk
Murom
Cheboksary
Kazan'
Ul'yanovsk
Saransk
Moksha
Sura
Penza
Podol'sk
Kolomna
Oka
Ryazan'
Serpukhov
Tula
Kaluga
RUSSIA
(RUSSIAN FEDERATION)
Tambov
Lipetsk
Voronezh
Balashov
Borisoglebsk
İstanbul
Sea of Marmara
İzmit
Adapazari
Sakarya
Ankara
Zonguldak
Karabük
Kizil Irmak
Sinop
Samsun
Yeşil
Kelkit
Sivas
Divriği
Kayseri
TURKEY
Tuz Gölü
Bursa
Eskişehir
Kütahya
Afyon
Çanakkale
Dardanelles
Balikesir
Gediz
İzmir
Menderes
Denizli
Muğla
Burdur
Eğridir Gölü
Beyşehir Gölü
Konya
Toros Dağlari
Adana
Mersin
İskenderun
Gaziantep
Ceyhan
Antalya
Alanya
Fethiye
Al Lādhiqīyah
SYRIA
N. CYPRUS
Nicosia
UN Buffer Zone
CYPRUS
Limassol
Trāblous
(Tripoli)
LEBANON
Beyrouth
(Beirut)
Haifa
ISRAEL
Tel Aviv-Yafo
Jerusalem
Beersheba

Ruhr, Western Europe

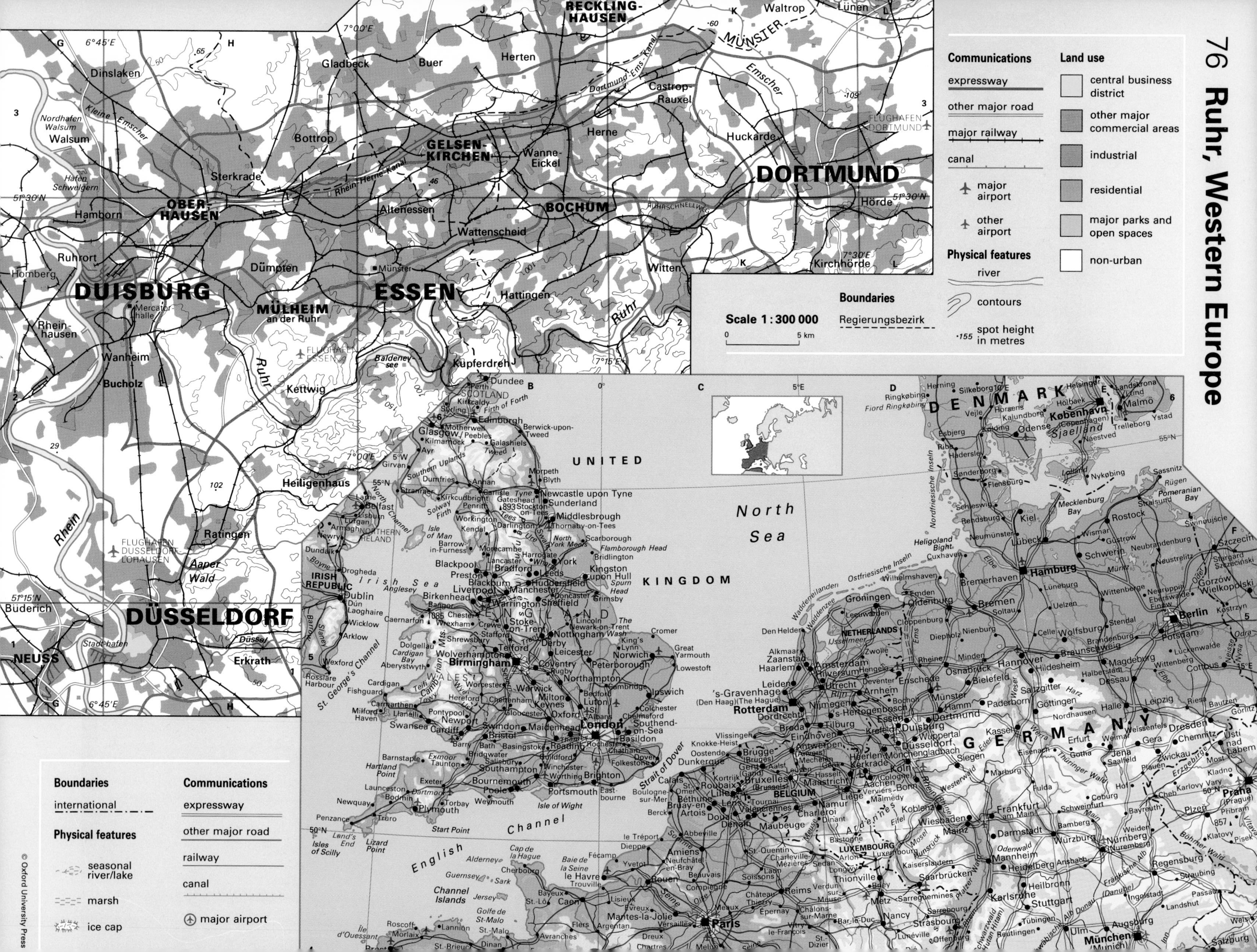

Communications
expressway
other major road
major railway
canal
major airport
other airport
Physical features
river
contours
spot height in metres
Land use
central business district
other major commercial areas
industrial
residential
major parks and open spaces
non-urban
Boundaries
Regierungsbezirk
Scale 1 : 300 000
5 km
DORTMUND
ESSEN
BOCHUM
DUISBURG
DÜSSELDORF
GELSEN-KIRCHEN
OBER-HAUSEN
MÜLHEIM an der Ruhr
RECKLING-HAUSEN
NEUSS
Ruhr
Rhein
Emscher
North Sea
English Channel
UNITED KINGDOM
DENMARK
GERMANY
NETHERLANDS
BELGIUM
LUXEMBOURG
IRISH REPUBLIC
Boundaries
international
Physical features
seasonal river/lake
marsh
ice cap
Communications
expressway
other major road
railway
canal
major airport

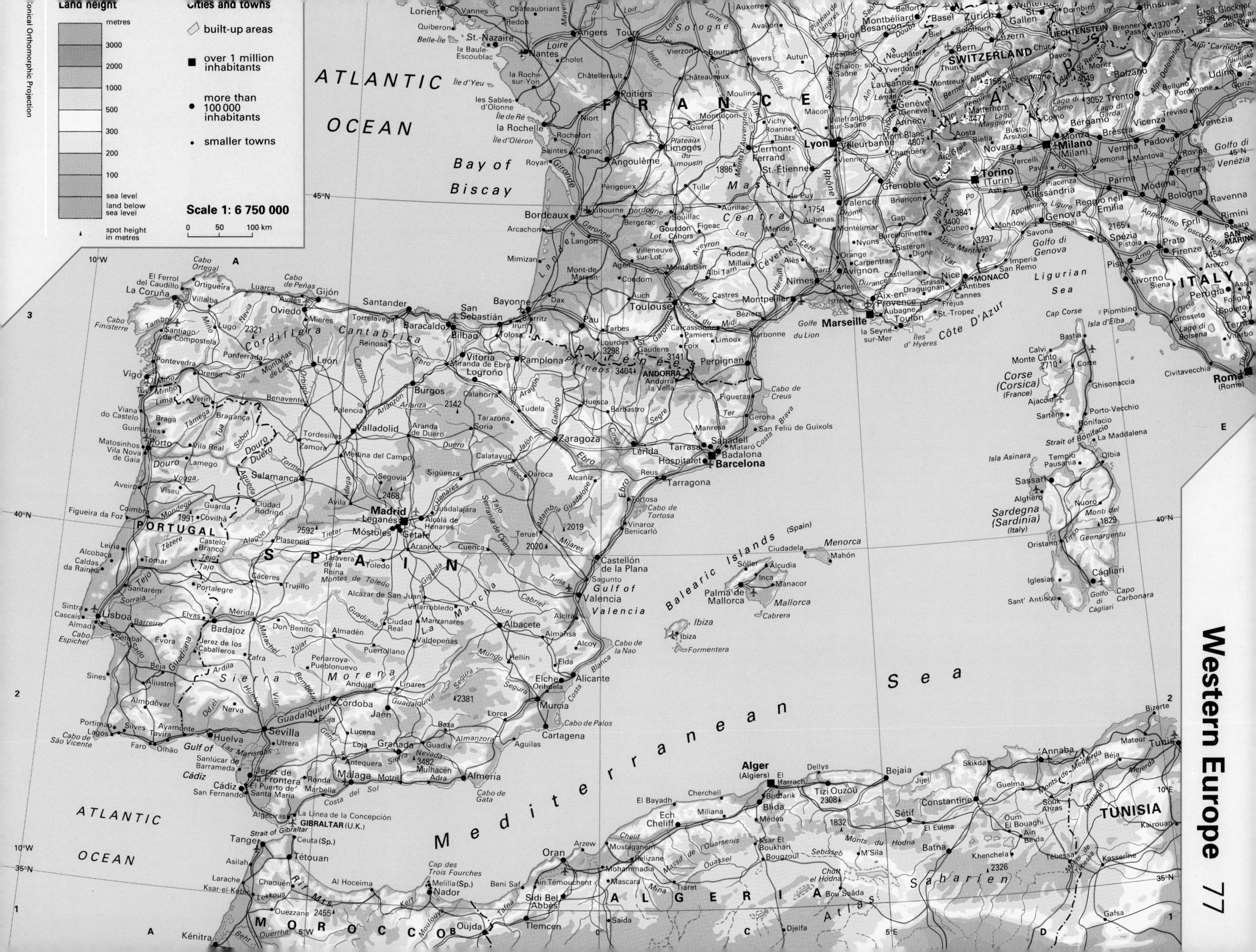

Cities and towns
- built-up areas
- over 1 million inhabitants
- more than 100 000 inhabitants
- smaller towns

Scale 1: 6 750 000

0   50   100 km

Land height

metres
3000
2000
1000
500
300
200
100
sea level
land below sea level

spot height in metres

Conical Orthomorphic Projection

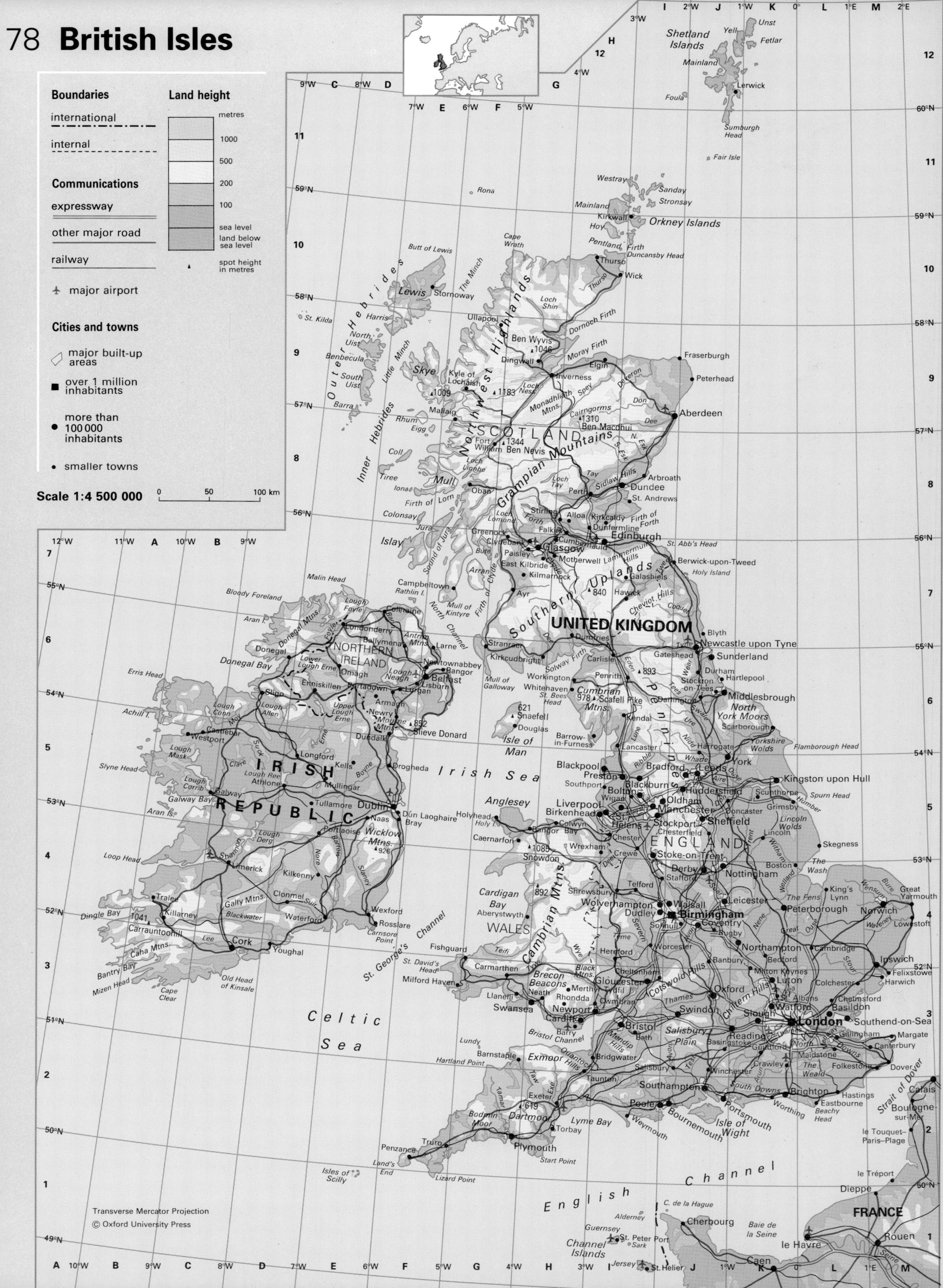

Boundaries

international

internal

Communications

expressway

other major road

railway

✈ major airport

Cities and towns

major built-up areas

■ over 1 million inhabitants

● more than 100 000 inhabitants

· smaller towns

Land height

metres

1000

500

200

100

sea level

land below sea level

▲ spot height in metres

Scale 1:4 500 000

0   50   100 km

Transverse Mercator Projection

© Oxford University Press

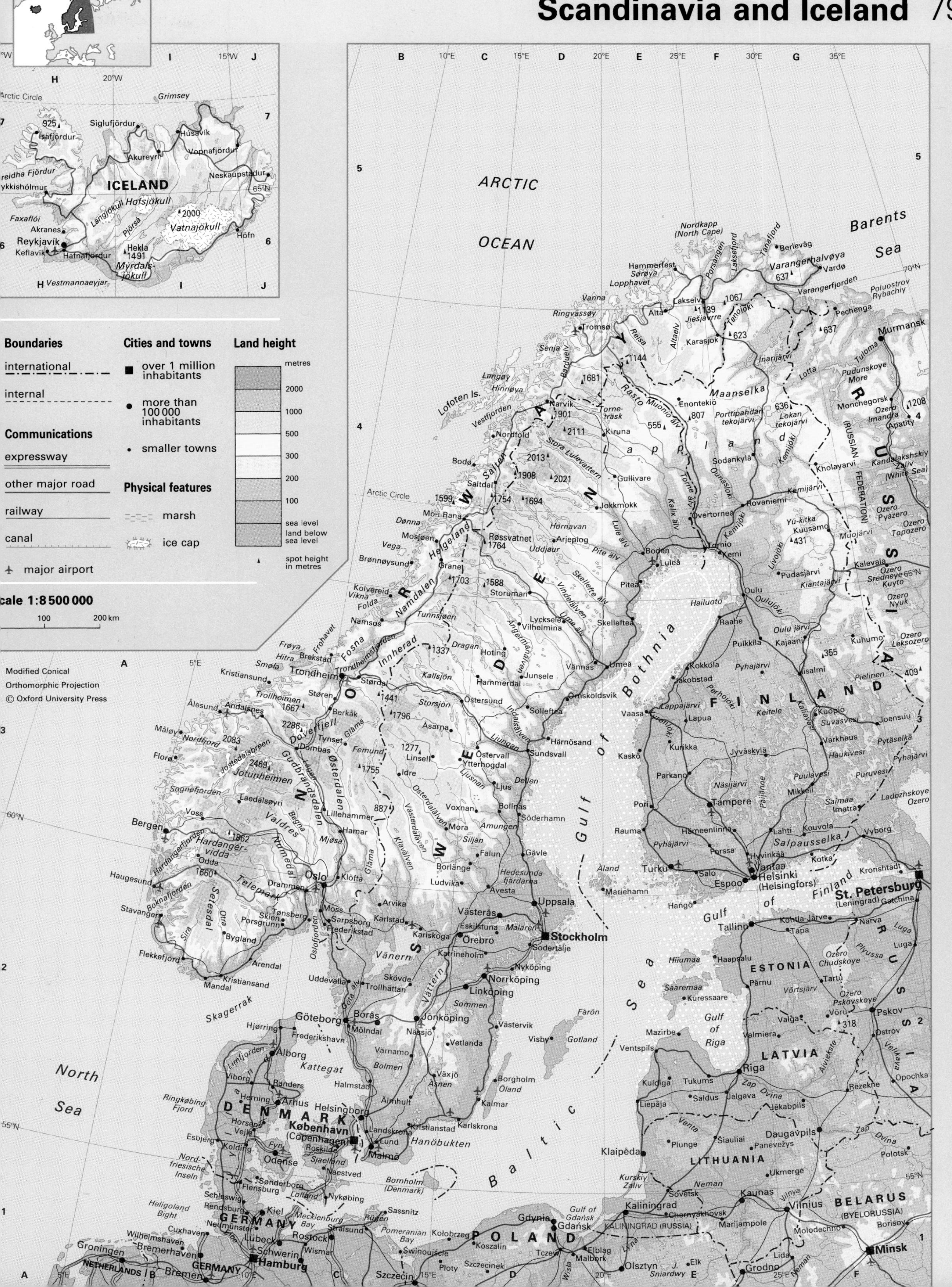

ICELAND

Boundaries

international

internal

Communications

expressway

other major road

railway

canal

✈ major airport

Scale 1:8 500 000

100   200 km

Modified Conical
Orthomorphic Projection
© Oxford University Press

Cities and towns

■ over 1 million inhabitants

● more than 100 000 inhabitants

• smaller towns

Physical features

marsh

ice cap

▲ spot height in metres

Land height

metres

2000
1000
500
300
200
100

sea level
land below sea level

Eastern Europe

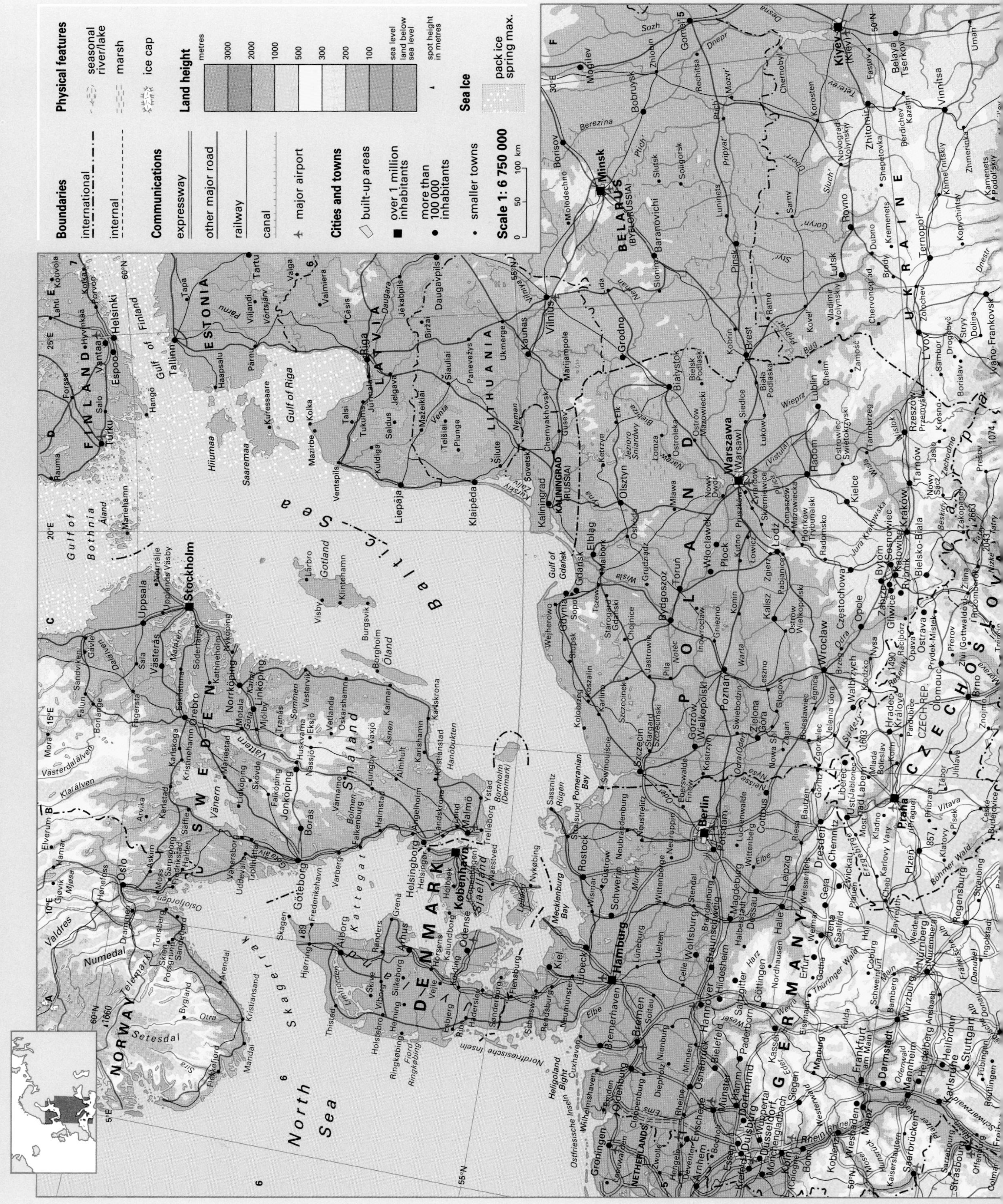

Boundaries
international
internal
Communications
expressway
other major road
railway
canal
major airport
Cities and towns
built-up areas
over 1 million inhabitants
more than 100 000 inhabitants
smaller towns
Scale 1: 6 750 000
0 50 100 km
Physical features
seasonal river/lake
marsh
ice cap
Land height
metres
3000
2000
1000
500
300
200
100
sea level
land below sea level
spot height in metres
Sea Ice
pack ice spring max.
FINLAND
ESTONIA
LATVIA
LITHUANIA
BELARUS (BYELORUSSIA)
UKRAINE
POLAND
SWEDEN
NORWAY
DENMARK
GERMANY
NETHERLANDS
CZECH REP.
KALININGRAD (RUSSIA)
Baltic Sea
North Sea
Skagerrak
Kattegat
Gulf of Bothnia
Gulf of Finland
Gulf of Riga
Stockholm
Oslo
København (Copenhagen)
Helsinki
Tallinn
Riga
Vilnius
Minsk
Kiyev (Kiev)
Warszawa (Warsaw)
Berlin
Hamburg
Praha (Prague)

Conical Orthomorphic Proje

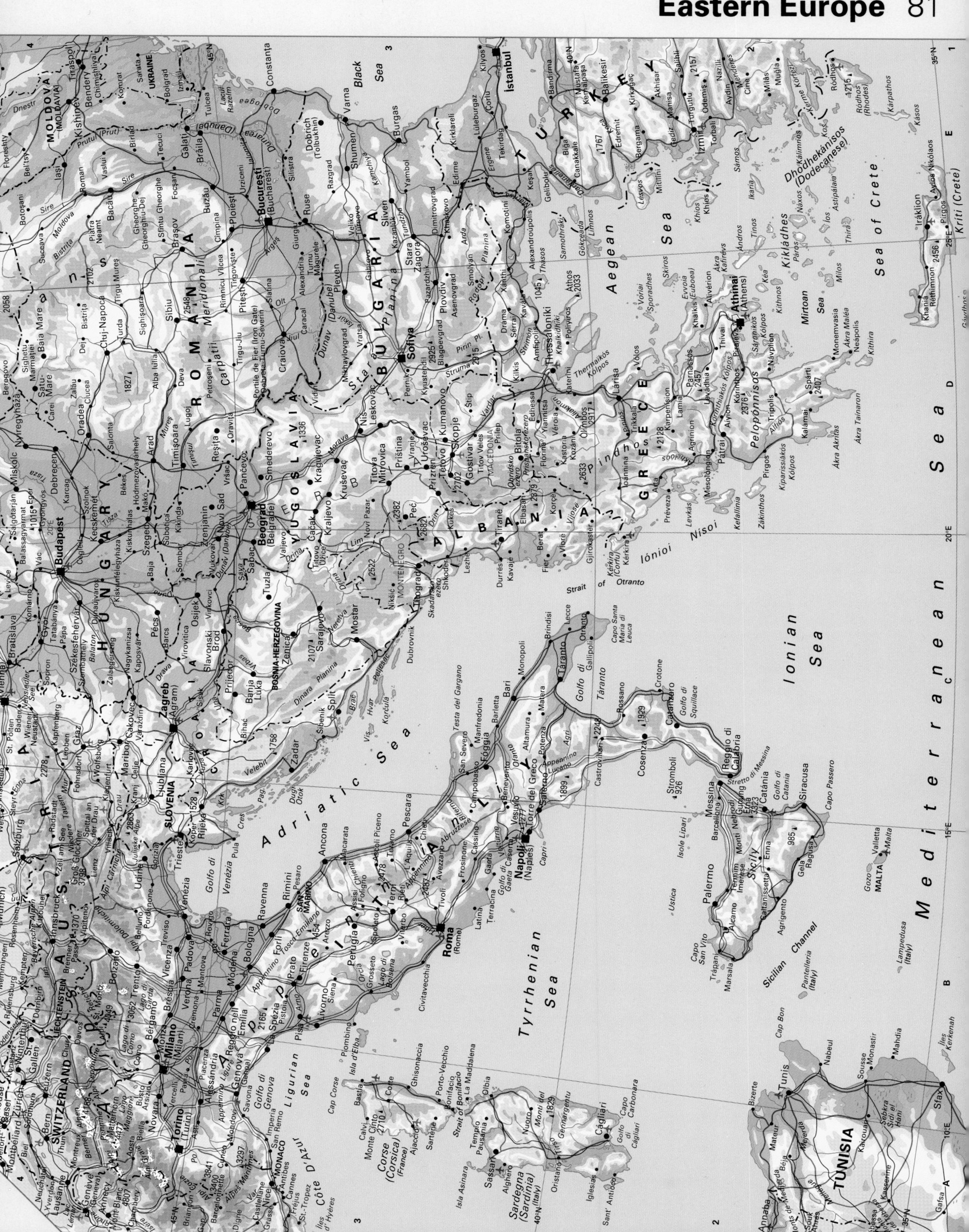
MOLDOVA
UKRAINE
ROMANIA
BULGARIA
TURKEY
GREECE
ALBANIA
YUGOSLAVIA
MONTENEGRO
MACEDONIA
BOSNIA-HERZEGOVINA
CROATIA
SLOVENIA
HUNGARY
AUSTRIA
SWITZERLAND
LIECHTENSTEIN
ITALY
SAN MARINO
MONACO
TUNISIA
MALTA
Black Sea
Aegean Sea
Sea of Crete
Mirtoan Sea
Ionian Sea
Adriatic Sea
Tyrrhenian Sea
Ligurian Sea
Mediterranean Sea
Strait of Otranto
Sicilian Channel
Sicily
Corse (Corsica) (France)
Sardegna (Sardinia) (Italy)
Kriti (Crete)
Pelopónnisos
Kikládhes
Dhodhekánisos (Dodecanese)
Karpatii Meridionali
Bucureşti (Bucharest)
Sofiya
Istanbul
Athinai (Athens)
Beograd (Belgrade)
Budapest
Zagreb (Agram)
Roma (Rome)
Napoli (Naples)
Milano (Milan)
Torino (Turin)
Genova (Genoa)
Wien (Vienna)
Tunis

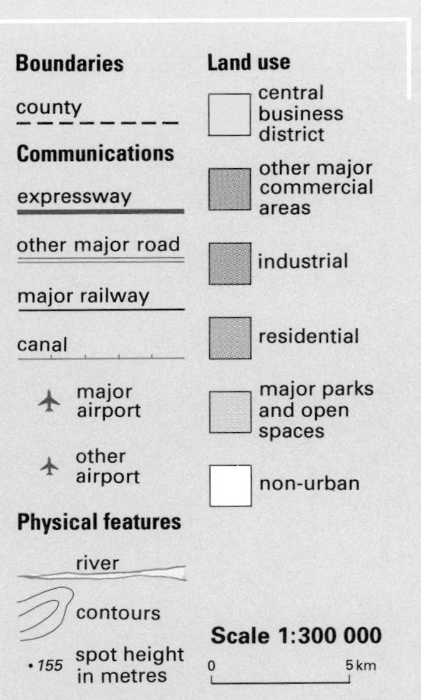

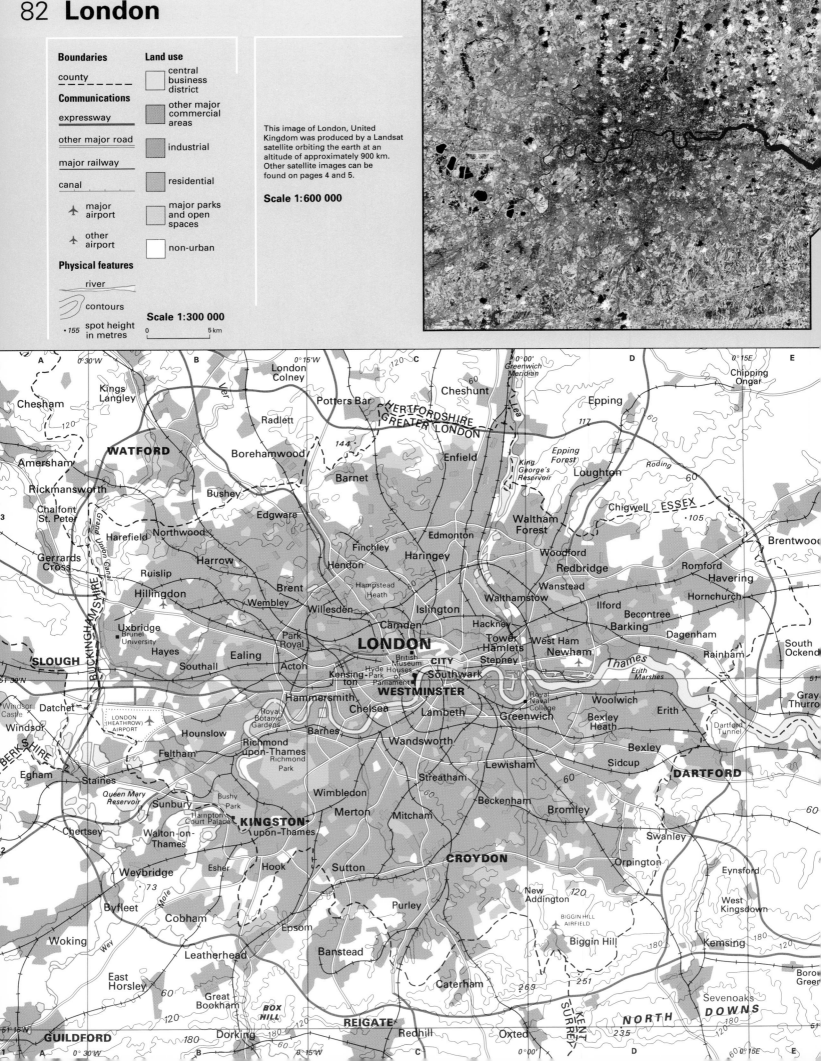

Boundaries
county — · — · —

Communications
expressway
other major road
major railway
canal
✈ major airport
✈ other airport

Physical features
river
contours
· 155 spot height in metres

Land use
central business district
other major commercial areas
industrial
residential
major parks and open spaces
non-urban

Scale 1:300 000
0   5 km

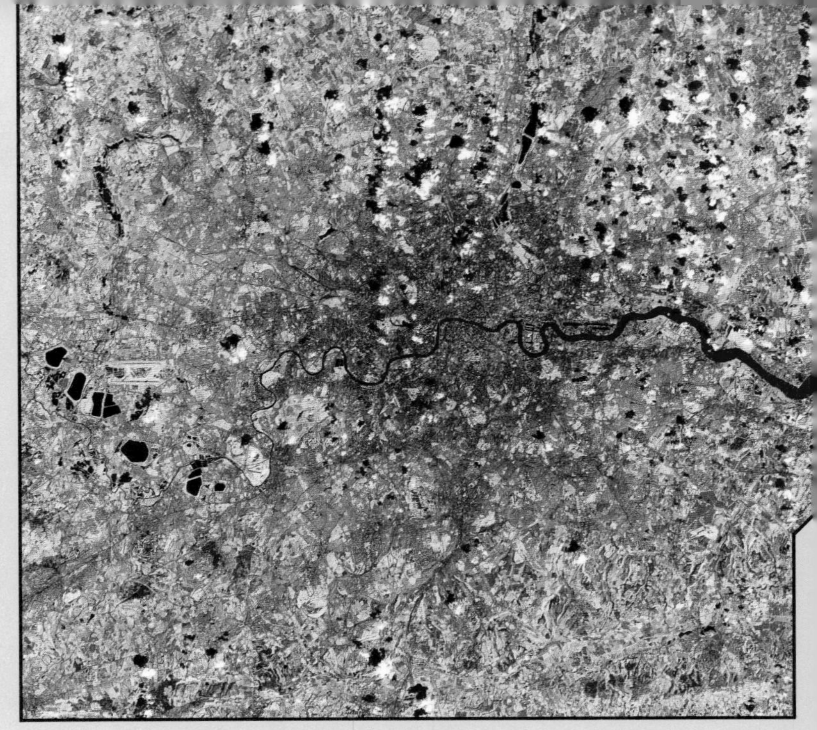

This image of London, United Kingdom was produced by a Landsat satellite orbiting the earth at an altitude of approximately 900 km. Other satellite images can be found on pages 4 and 5.

Scale 1:600 000

Boundaries

département (Paris)

regierungsbezirk (Berlin)

Communications

expressway

other major road

major railway

canal

major airport

other airport

Physical features

river

contours

• 155 spot height in metres

Land use

central business district

other major commercial areas

industrial

residential

major parks and open spaces

non-urban

Scale 1:300 000

0 5 km

PARIS

Taverny
Forêt de Montmorency
Écouen
Goussainville
Conflans Ste-Honorine
Beauchamp
Autoroute du Nord
Lille
AÉROPORT CHARLES DE GAULLE
Herblay
Montmorency
Sarcelles
Gonesse
Andrésy
Forêt
MAISONS-LAFFITTE
de
Cormeilles-en-Parisis
Enghien
AÉROPORT DU BOURGET
Mitry-Mory
Argenteuil
ST-DENIS
le Blanc-Mesnil
Aulnay-sous-Bois
Villeparisis
POISSY
St. Germain
Sartrouville
Gennevilliers
Drancy
Canal de l'Ourcq
Colombes
Asnières
Aubervilliers
Bobigny
Les Coudreaux
Faculté de Nanterre
Clichy
Pantin
le Raincy
SEINE-ST-DENIS
ST-GERMAIN-en-Laye
Chatou
Nanterre
la Défense
Neuilly
Sacré Coeur
Nord
Est
Noisy-le-Sec
Chelles
St-Lazare
Opéra
Rouen
Marly-le-Roi
Rueil-Malmaison
Bois de Boulogne
Arc de Triomphe
PARIS
Marne
Autoroute de Normandie
Louvre
Notre Dame
Vincennes
Neuilly Plaisance
Champs-s-Marne
Eiffel Tower
Invalides
Sorbonne
Montparnasse
Lyon
Vaucresson
St-Cloud
Austerlitz
BOULOGNE-BILLANCOURT
Parc de St. Cloud
Boulevard Périphérique
St-Mandé
Nogent
Metz & Nancy
Bois de Vincennes
Autoroute de l'Est
VERSAILLES
Sèvres
Vanves
Montrouge
Champigny
MARNE-LA-VALLÉE
Forêt de Meudon
Meudon
Ivry-s-Seine
St Maur
Château de Versailles
Vitry-s-Seine
Créteil
St. Cyr-l'École
Villejuif
Choisy-le-Roi
ST. QUENTIN-EN-YVELINES
AÉRODROME DE VILLACOUBLAY
Sceaux
Forêt de Notre Dame
Sucy-en-Brie
Bièvres
HAUTS-DE-SEINE
VAL-DE-MARNE
SEINE-ET-MARNE
Rungis
Thiais
Orly
Verrières
Centre d'études nucléaires
Saclay
Massy
AÉROPORT D'ORLY
Villeneuve-St. Georges
Chevreuse
Palaiseau
St. Rémy
Orsay
Autoroute Aquitaine
Autoroute du Soleil
Brunoy
Brie-Comte-Robert
YVELINES
ESSONNE
Chartres & Orléans
Juvisy-sur-Orge
Montgeron
les Ulis
Lyon
Draveil

BERLIN

Borgsdorf
Basdorf
Velten
POTSDAM
FRANKFURT
Birkenwerder
Schönwalde
Bernau
Marwitz
Havel
Bötzow
Zepernick
Frohnau
Schildow
Schwanebeck
Pausin
Glienicke
HENNINGSDORF
Berliner
Hermsdorf
Buchholz
Panke
Havelkanal
Forst
Karow
Schönwalde
Lindenberg
Blumberg
Brieselang
Tegel
Reinickendorf
Blankenburg
Berliner Forst Spandau
Tegeler See
FLUGHAFEN BERLIN-TEGEL (OTTO LILIENTHAL)
Pankow
Altlandsberg
Ahrensfelde
Falkensee
Jungfernheide
Weissensee
BERLIN
SPANDAU
Wedding
Dallgow
Siemensstadt
Prenzlauer Berg
Staaken
Reichstag
Dom
Friedrichshain
Hellersdorf
Fredersdorf
Charlottenburg
Brandenburger Tor
Lichtenberg
Neuenhagen
Tiergarten
Olympiastadion
Kreuzberg
Schöneberg
Treptow
Kaulsdorf
CENTRAL FLUGHAFEN BERLIN-TEMPELHOF
FLUGHAFEN BERLIN-GATOW
Berliner
Wilmersdorf
AVUS
Neukölln
Karlshorst
Forst
Berliner Stadtforst
Schöneiche
Grunewald
Tempelhof
Kladow
Königsheide
Friedrichshagen
Havel
Steglitz
Spree
Zehlendorf
KÖPENICK
Grosser Müggelsee
Rahnsdorf
Teltowkanal
Buckow
Erkner
Berliner Stadtforst Köpenick
Wannsee
Berliner Forst Düppel
Kleinmachnow
Müggelheim
Grosser Zernsee
POTSDAM
Babelsberg
Teltowkanal
TELTOW
Rudow
Langer See
Bohnsdorf
Seddin-See
Lichtenrade
Stahnsdorf
Eichwalde
Werder
Templiner See
Drewitz
Nuthe
FLUGHAFEN BERLIN-SCHÖNEFELD
Mahlow
Schulzendorf
Zeuthener See
Oder-Spree-Kanal
Schwielowsee
Grossbeeren
Blankenfelde
Dahlewitz
Wildau
BERLINER RING
Königs Wusterhausen
Zernsdorf
Rangsdorf
Ludwigsfelde

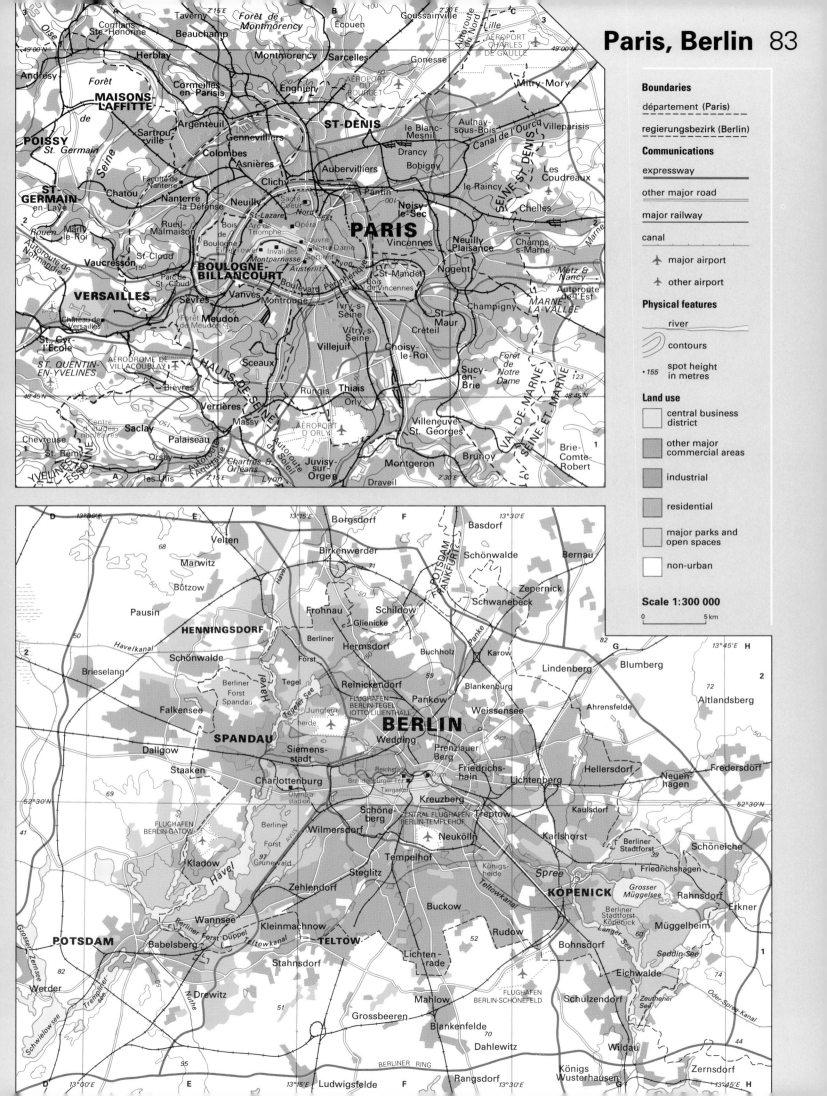

Asia Relief

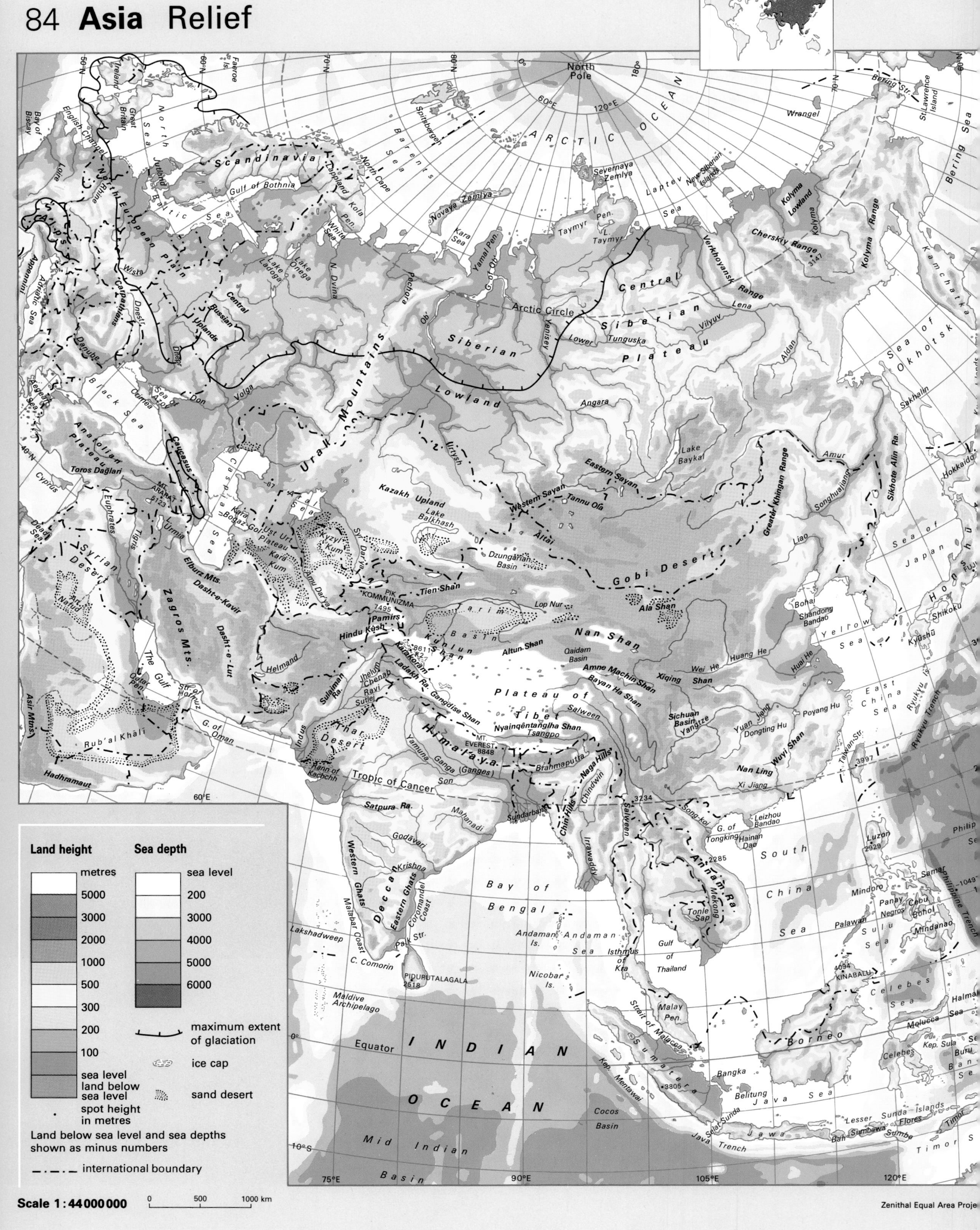

North Pole
ARCTIC OCEAN
Bering Str.
St. Lawrence Island
Wrangel
Bering Sea
Faeroe Is.
Ireland
Great Britain
North Sea
Bay of Biscay
English Channel
Loire
Rhine
Alps
Apennini
Adriatic Sea
Jutland
Scandinavia
Gulf of Bothnia
Baltic Sea
Lapland
North Cape
Kola Pen.
White Sea
Spitsbergen
Barents Sea
Novaya Zemlya
Kara Sea
Yamal Pen.
G. of Ob'
Severnaya Zemlya
New Siberian Islands
Laptev Sea
Taymyr Pen.
L. Taymyr
Kolyma Lowland
Kolyma
Cherskiy Range
3147
Kolyma Range
Kamchatka
Verkhoyansk Range
Lena
Vilyuy
Aldan
Sea of Okhotsk
Sakhalin
North European Plain
Wisła
Carpathians
Dnestr
Danube
Dnepr
Central Russian Uplands
Lake Ladoga
Lake Onega
N. Dvina
Pechora
Ob'
Arctic Circle
West Siberian Lowland
Yenisey
Central Siberian Plateau
Lower Tunguska
Angara
Lake Baykal
Ural Mountains
Volga
Don
Sea of Azov
Crimea
Black Sea
Aegean Sea
Anatolian Plateau
Toros Dağlari
Cyprus
Caucasus
MT. ARARAT 5123
Caspian Sea
Kara Bogaz Gol
Ust Urt Plateau
Aral Sea
Kyzyl Kum
Kara Kum
Syr Darya
Amu Darya
Kazakh Upland
Lake Balkhash
Irtysh
Dzungarian Basin
Altai
Western Sayan
Eastern Sayan
Tannu Ola
Gobi Desert
Greater Khingan Range
Amur
Songhuajiang
Sikhote Alin Ra.
Hokkaido
Sea of Japan
Honshu
Shikoku
Kyūshū
Liao
Bohai
Shandong Bandao
Yellow Sea
Euphrates
Tigris
Urmia
Dead Sea
Syrian Desert
An Nafud
Elburz Mts.
Dasht-e-Kavir
Dasht-e-Lut
Zagros Mts.
The Gulf
Qatar Pen.
Str. of Hormuz
G. of Oman
Rub' al Khālī
Asir Mts.
Hadhramaut
Tien Shan
PIK KOMMUNIZMA 7495
Pamirs
Hindu Kush
Tarim Basin
Lop Nur
Ala Shan
Nan Shan
Kunlun Shan
8611 K2
Altun Shan
Qaidam Basin
Amne Machin Shan
Bayan Har Shan
Xiqing Shan
Wei He
Huang He
Huai He
Helmand
Sulaiman Ra.
Karakoram
Ladakh Ra.
Jhelum
Chenab
Ravi
Sutlej
Indus
Thar Desert
Rann of Kachchh
Plateau of Tibet
Gangdise Shan
Nyainqêntanglha Shan
Tsangpo
Salween
Sichuan Basin
Yangtze
Yuan Jiang
Dongting Hu
Poyang Hu
East China Sea
Ryukyu Is.
Ryukyu Trench
Himalaya
MT. EVEREST 8848
Yamuna
Ganga (Ganges)
Brahmaputra
Naga Hills
Tropic of Cancer
Son
Satpura Ra.
Mahanadi
Sundarbans
Chin Hills
Chindwin
Irrawaddy
Salween
3234
Wuyi Shan
Nan Ling
Xi Jiang
Taiwan Str.
3997
Song-koi
G. of Tongking
Leizhou Bandao
Hainan Dao
Luzon
2929
South China Sea
Godavari
Krishna
Western Ghats
Deccan
Eastern Ghats
Coromandel Coast
Malabar Coast
Bay of Bengal
Annam Ra.
2285
Mekong
Tonle Sap
Mindoro
Samar
Panay
Negros
Cebu
Bohol
Palawan
Sulu Sea
Mindanao
Philippine Trench
-1049
Lakshadweep
Palk Str.
C. Comorin
PIDURUTALAGALA 2518
Andaman Is.
Andaman Sea
Nicobar Is.
Isthmus of Kra
Gulf of Thailand
Malay Pen.
Strait of Malacca
4094 KINABALU
Celebes Sea
Halmahera
Molucca Sea
Borneo
Celebes
Kep. Sula
Buru
Banda Sea
Maldive Archipelago
Equator
INDIAN OCEAN
Kep. Mentawai
Sumatera
3805
Bangka
Belitung
Java Sea
Selat Sunda
Jawa
Java Trench
Lesser Sunda Islands
Bali
Sumbawa
Flores
Sumba
Timor
Timor Sea
Cocos Basin
Mid Indian Basin
50°N
60°N
70°N
80°N
0°
60°E
120°E
180°
40°N
60°E
75°E
90°E
105°E
120°E
10°S
Land height
metres
5000
3000
2000
1000
500
300
200
100
sea level
land below sea level
Sea depth
sea level
200
3000
4000
5000
6000
maximum extent of glaciation
ice cap
sand desert
spot height in metres
Land below sea level and sea depths shown as minus numbers
international boundary
Scale 1:44 000 000
0
500
1000 km
Zenithal Equal Area Proje

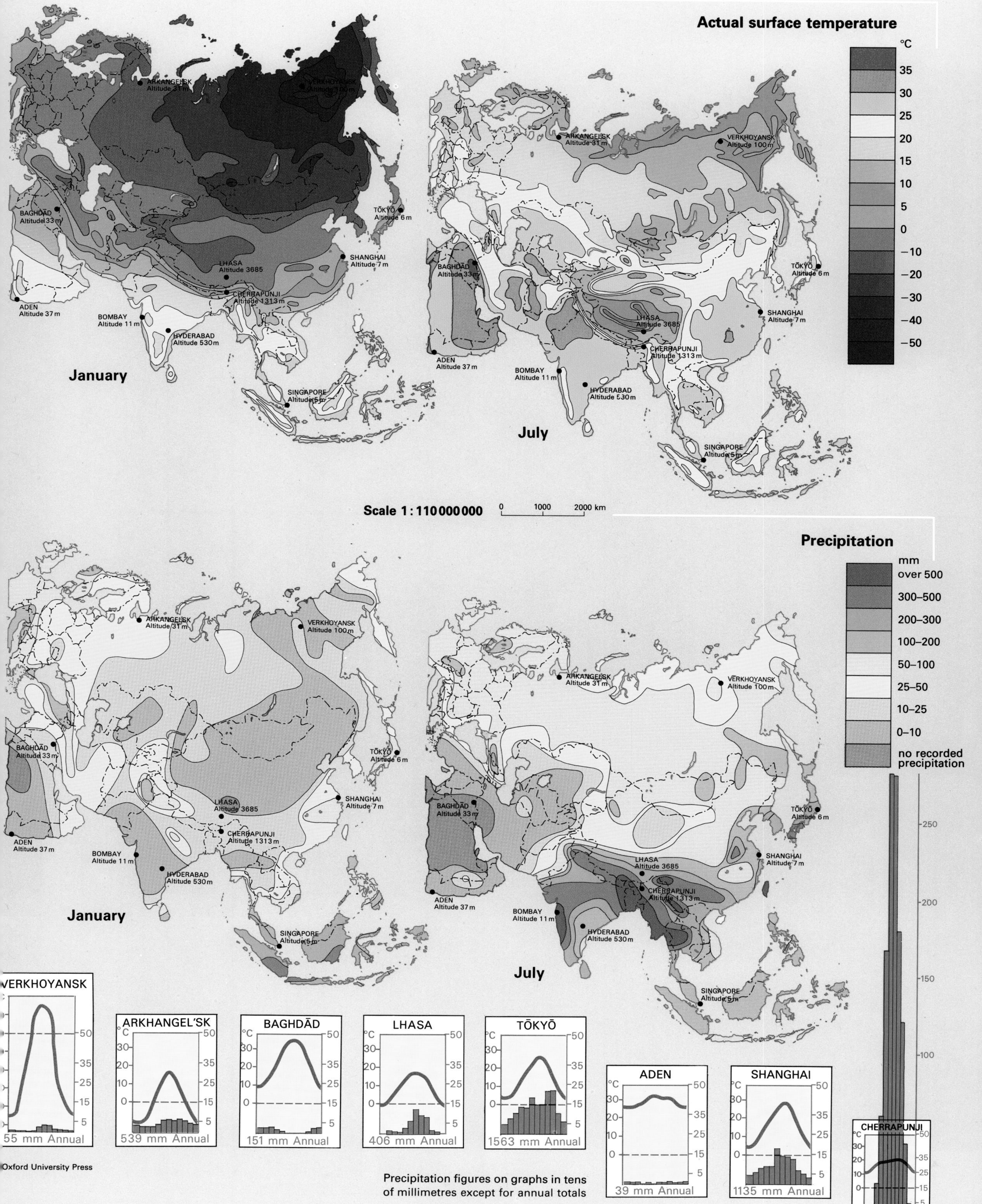

Actual surface temperature

°C
35
30
25
20
15
10
5
0
−10
−20
−30
−40
−50

January

July

Scale 1:110 000 000   0   1000   2000 km

Precipitation

mm
over 500
300–500
200–300
100–200
50–100
25–50
10–25
0–10
no recorded precipitation

January

July

VERKHOYANSK
55 mm Annual

ARKHANGEL'SK
539 mm Annual

BAGHDĀD
151 mm Annual

LHASA
406 mm Annual

TŌKYŌ
1563 mm Annual

ADEN
39 mm Annual

SHANGHAI
1135 mm Annual

CHERRAPUNJI
11437 mm Annual

Precipitation figures on graphs in tens of millimetres except for annual totals

Oxford University Press

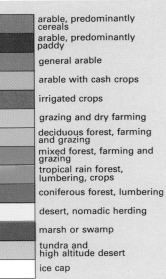

arable, predominantly cereals

arable, predominantly paddy

general arable

arable with cash crops

irrigated crops

grazing and dry farming

deciduous forest, farming and grazing

mixed forest, farming and grazing

tropical rain forest, lumbering, crops

coniferous forest, lumbering

desert, nomadic herding

marsh or swamp

tundra and high altitude desert

ice cap

Scale 1 : 44 000 000

0   500   1000 km

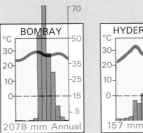

BOMBAY

2078 mm Annual

HYDERABAD

157 mm Annual

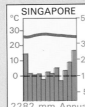

SINGAPORE

2282 mm Annual

Precipitation figures on graphs in tens of millimetres except for annual totals

Zenithal Equal Area Projec

© Oxford University Pr

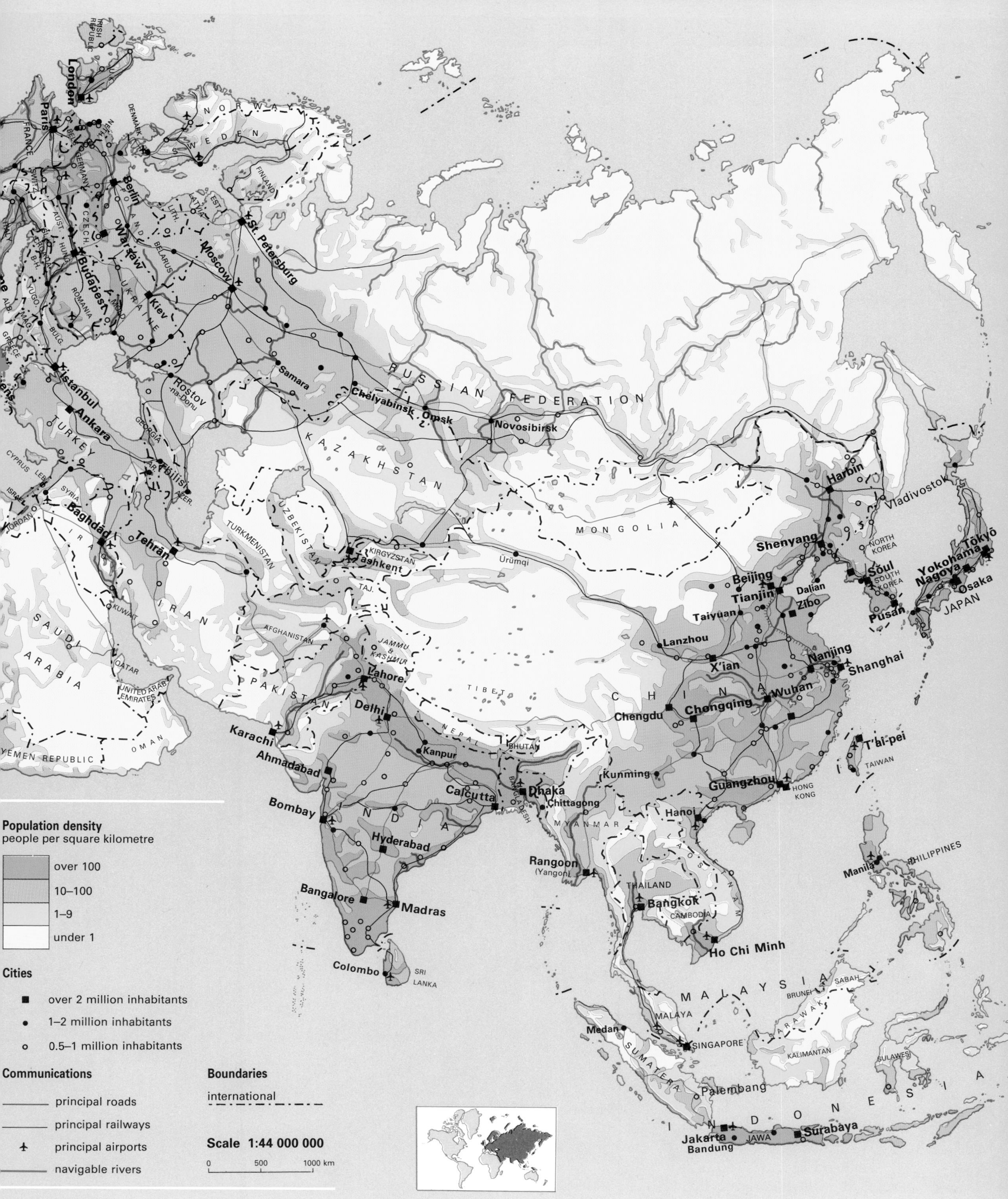

Population density
people per square kilometre

- over 100
- 10–100
- 1–9
- under 1

Cities

- ■ over 2 million inhabitants
- ● 1–2 million inhabitants
- ○ 0.5–1 million inhabitants

Communications

- —— principal roads
- —— principal railways
- ✈ principal airports
- —— navigable rivers

Boundaries

- —— international

Scale 1:44 000 000

0   500   1000 km

Zenithal Equal Area Projection
Oxford University Press

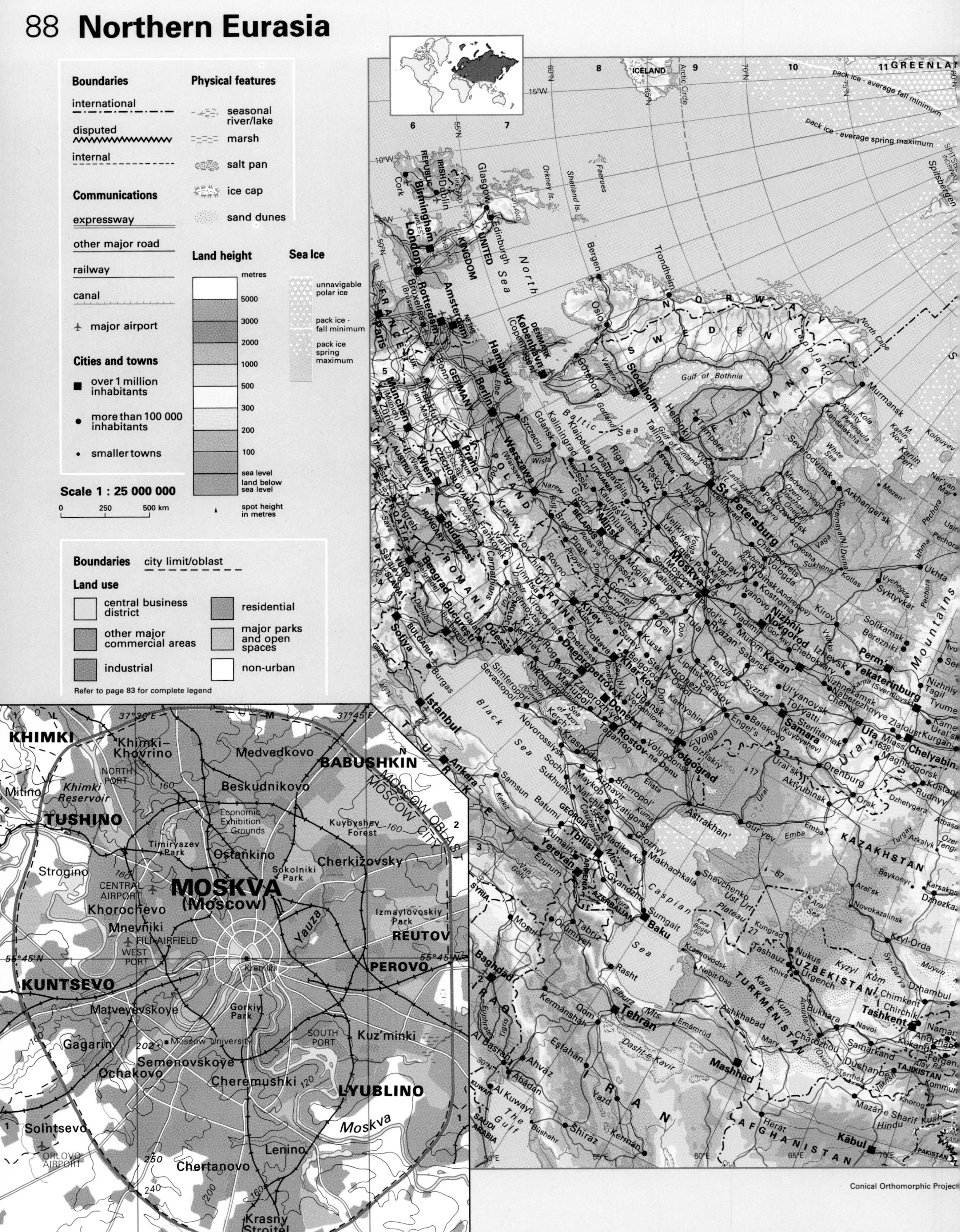
Boundaries
international
disputed
internal
Communications
expressway
other major road
railway
canal
major airport
Cities and towns
over 1 million inhabitants
more than 100 000 inhabitants
smaller towns
Physical features
seasonal river/lake
marsh
salt pan
ice cap
sand dunes
Land height
metres
5000
3000
2000
1000
500
300
200
100
sea level
land below sea level
spot height in metres
Sea Ice
unnavigable polar ice
pack ice - fall minimum
pack ice spring maximum
Scale 1 : 25 000 000
0
250
500 km
Boundaries
city limit/oblast
Land use
central business district
other major commercial areas
industrial
residential
major parks and open spaces
non-urban
Refer to page 83 for complete legend
pack ice - average fall minimum
pack ice - average spring maximum
ICELAND
GREENLAND
Arctic Circle
North Sea
Baltic Sea
Gulf of Bothnia
Black Sea
Caspian Sea
Moskva
St. Petersburg
Stockholm
London
Paris
Berlin
Warszawa
Kiyev
Bucureşti
İstanbul
Ankara
Tbilisi
Yerevan
Baku
Tehran
Baghdad
Tashkent
Kābul
Mashhad
Volgograd
Samara
Kazan'
Nizhniy Novgorod
Yekaterinburg
Perm'
Ufa
Chelyabinsk
KAZAKHSTAN
UZBEKISTAN
TURKMENISTAN
AFGHANISTAN
IRAN
IRAQ
UKRAINE
POLAND
ROMANIA
FINLAND
SWEDEN
NORWAY
Ural Mountains
Conical Orthomorphic Projection
MOSKVA (Moscow)
KHIMKI
Khimki-Khovrino
Medvedkovo
BABUSHKIN
Beskudnikovo
Khimki Reservoir
NORTH PORT
Mitino
TUSHINO
Economic Exhibition Grounds
Kuybyshev Forest
Timiryazev Park
Ostankino
Sokolniki Park
Cherkizovsky
Strogino
CENTRAL AIRPORT
Khoroshevo
Mnevniki
FILI-AIRFIELD
WEST PORT
Izmaylovskiy Park
REUTOV
Yauza
Kremlin
PEROVO
KUNTSEVO
Matveyevskoye
Gorkiy Park
Moscow University
SOUTH PORT
Kuz'minki
Gagarin
Semenovskoye
Ochakovo
Cheremushki
LYUBLINO
Solntsevo
Moskva
ORLOVO AIRPORT
Lenino
Chertanovo
Krasny Stroitel
Butovo
MOSCOW OBLAST
MOSCOW CITY
37°30'E
37°45'E
55°45'N

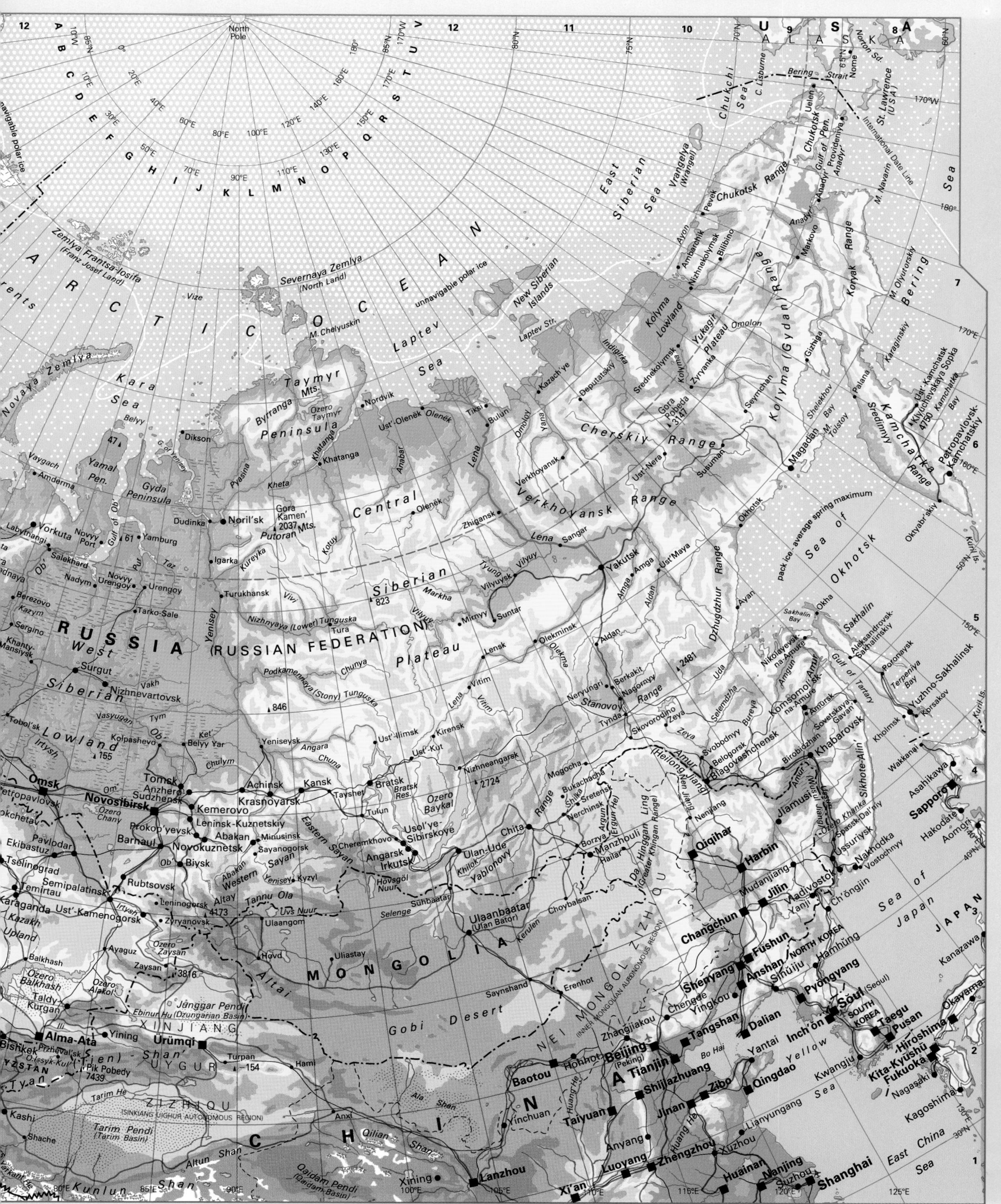
ARCTIC OCEAN
RUSSIA
(RUSSIAN FEDERATION)
MONGOLIA
CHINA
NORTH KOREA
SOUTH KOREA
JAPAN
Sea of Okhotsk
Sea of Japan
Bering Sea
East Siberian Sea
Laptev Sea
Kara Sea
Central Siberian Plateau
West Siberian Lowland
Gobi Desert
Moscow

Boundaries

international

disputed

Communications

expressway

other major road

railway

canal

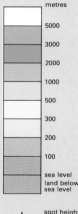

✈ major airport

Cities and towns

■ over 1 million
inhabitants

● more than 100 000
inhabitants

● smaller towns

Physical features

seasonal
river/lake

marsh

salt pan

ice cap

sand dunes

salt lake

Sea Ice

pack ice
spring max.

Land height

metres

5000

3000

2000

1000

500

300

200

100

sea level
land below
sea level

▲ spot height
in metres

Scale 1: 12 500 000

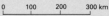

0   100   200   300 km

Conical Orthomorphic Projection

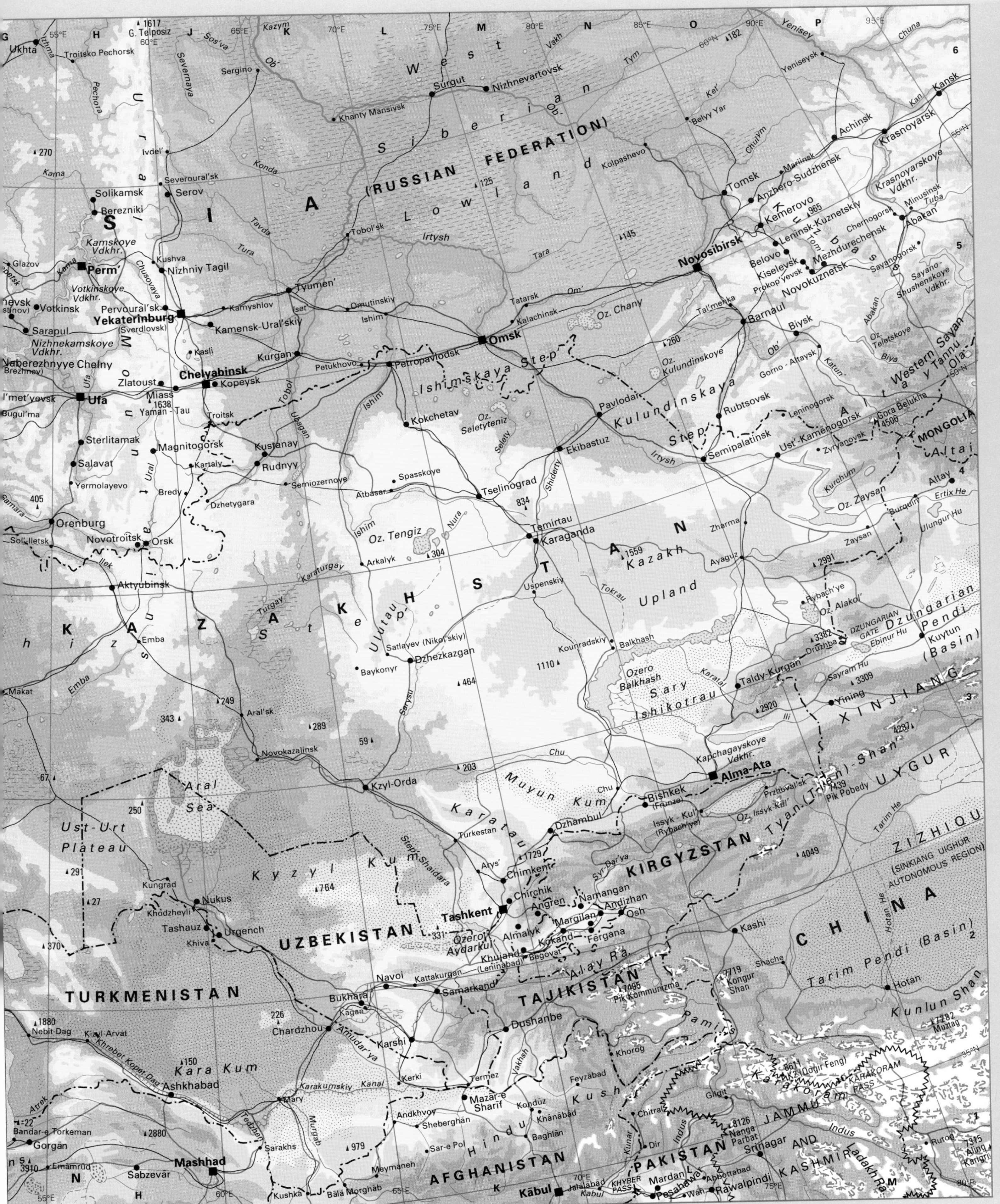

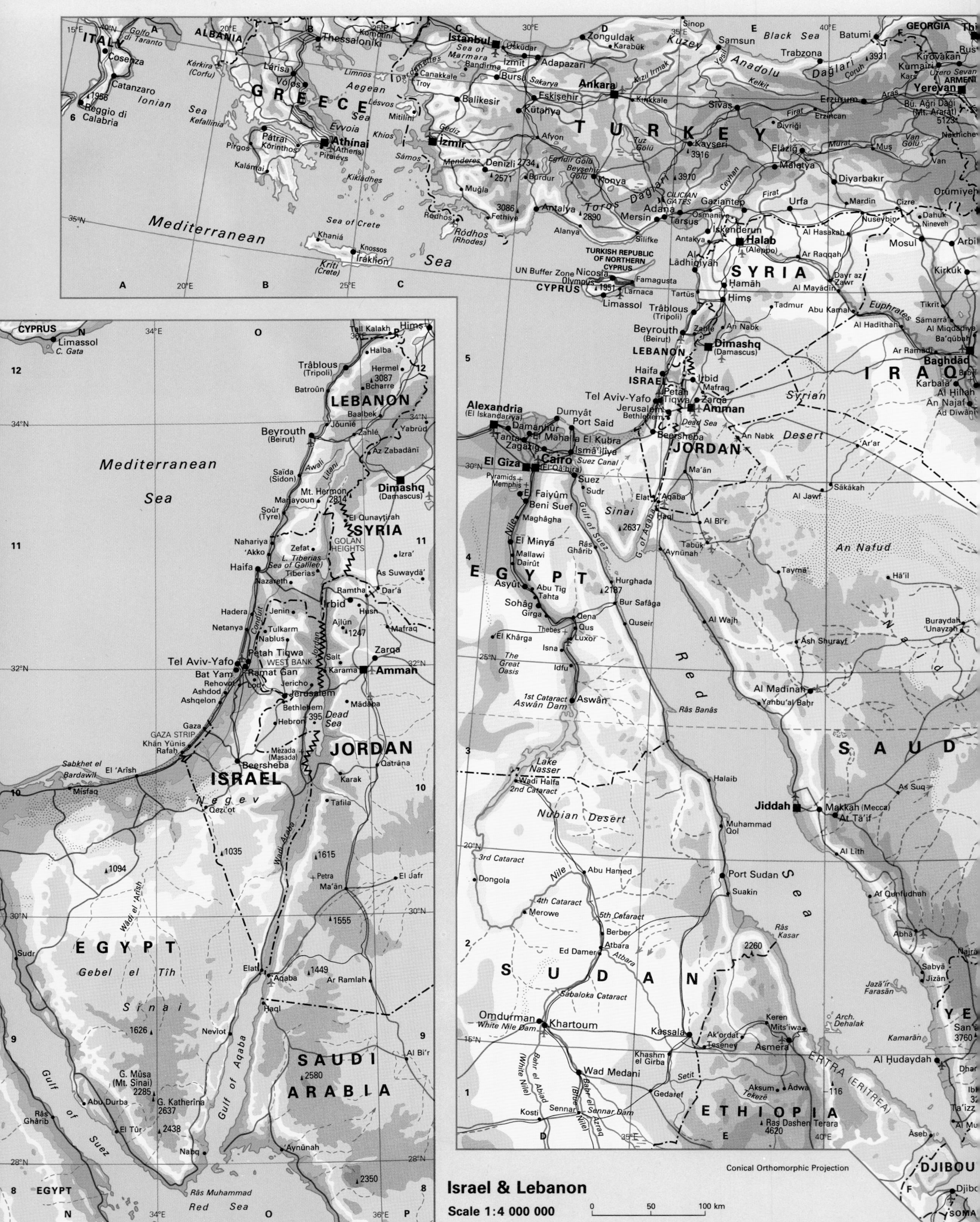

Israel & Lebanon

Scale 1:4 000 000

Conical Orthomorphic Projection

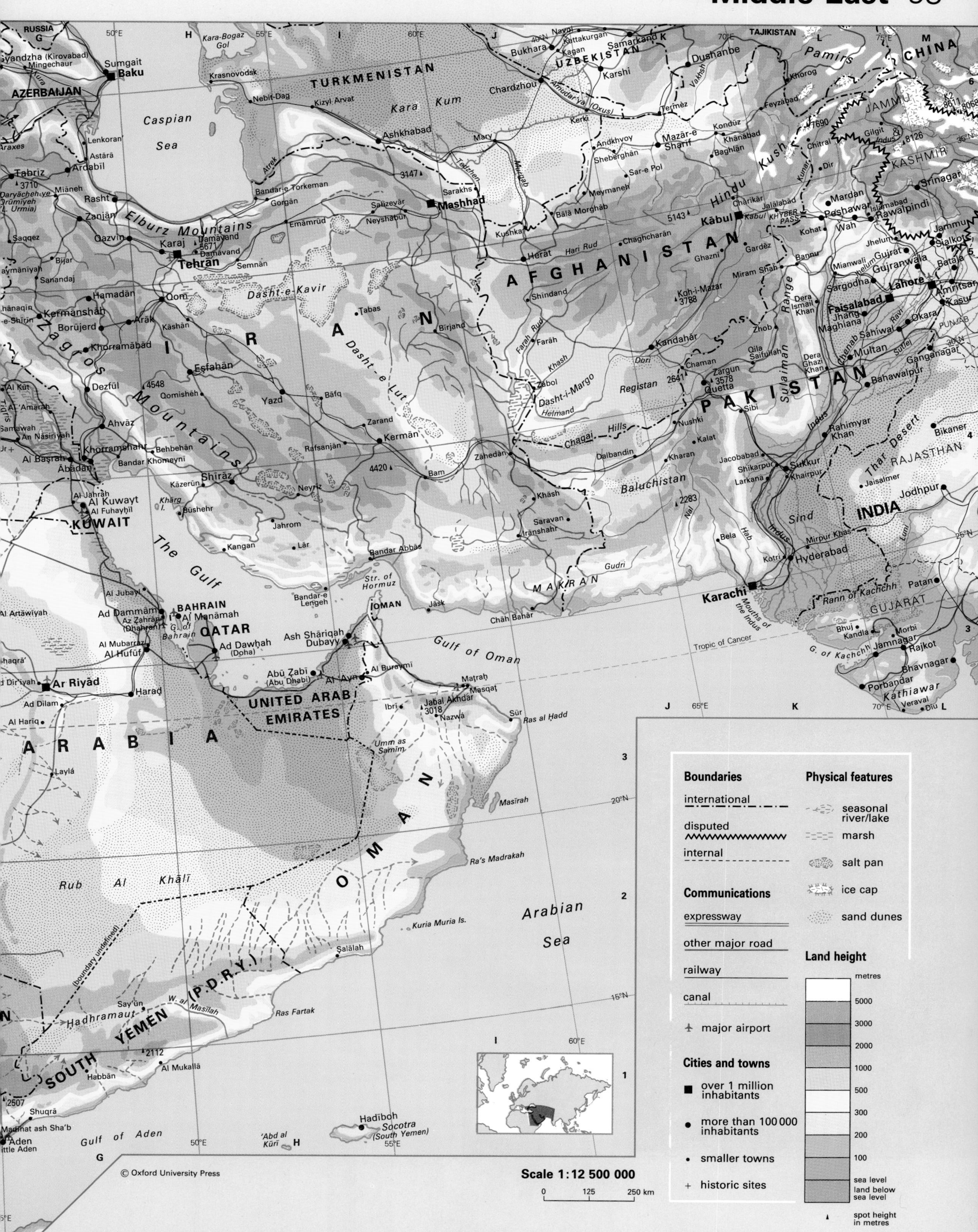

RUSSIA
G
50°E
H
Kara-Bogaz Gol
55°E
I
60°E
J
40°N
Nava
TAJIKISTAN
L
70°E
M

yandzha (Kirovabad)
Mingechaur
Sumgait
Baku
AZERBAIJAN
Kura
Araxes
Caspian Sea
Krasnovodsk
TURKMENISTAN
Kara Kum
Bukhara
Kagan
Karshi
UZBEKISTAN
Chardzhou
Kattakurgan
Samarkand
K
Dushanbe
Pamirs
CHINA
6

Nebit-Dag
Kizyl Arvat
Amu dar'ya (Oxus)
Kerki
Khorog
K2
8611
8068

Tabriz
3710
Astārā
Ardabīl
Lenkoran
Rasht
Elburz Mountains
Ashkhabad
Atrek
Bandar-e Torkeman
Gorgān
Mary
Andkhvoy
Sar-e Pol
Mazar-e Sharif
Khānābād
Baghlān
Gilgit
18126
JAMMU
Chitral
7690
Feyzabad

Daryācheh-ye Ūrūmīyeh
(L. Urmia)
Miāneh
Zanjān
Qazvīn
Karaj
Damāvand 5671
Tehrān
Semnān
Emāmrūd
Neyshābūr
Sabzevār
Mashhad
3147
Sarakhs
Meymaneh
Bālā Morghāb
Chaghcharān
5143
Kabul
Charikar
Jalālābād
KHYBER PASS
Mardan
Peshawar
Rawalpindi
Islamabad
Hindu Kush
KASHMIR
Srinagar

hānaqīn
aymāniyah
Sanandaj
Hamadān
Qom
Dasht-e Kavir
Herāt
Hari Rud
Ghaznī
Gardēz
Koh-i-Mazar 3788
Miram Shah
Kohat
Wah
Jammu
Sialkot
5

Zagros Mountains
Kermānshāh
Borūjerd
Arāk
Kāshān
Tabas
Shindand
Farāh Rud
AFGHANISTAN
Dera Ismail Khan
Zhob
Bannu
Mianwali
Jhelum Gujrat
Gujranwala
Lahore
Amritsar
Kasur

Al Kut
Dezfūl
4548
Esfahān
Qomishēh
Birjand
Khash
Farāh
Kandahār
Chaman
Zargun 3578
Quetta
Sibi
Qila Saifullah
Dera Ghazi Khan
Multan
Chenab Sahiwal
PUNJAB
Faisalabad
Jhang Maghiana
Sargodha
Sutlej

Al 'Amārah
Samawah
An Nāsirīyah
Ahvāz
Khorramābād
Yazd
Bāfq
Dasht-e Lut
Zābol
Dasht-i-Margo
Helmand
Registan
2641
Dori
Nushki
Kalat
Bahawalpur
Ganganagar
40°N
4

Jr+
Khorramshahr
Al Başrah
Ābādān
Bandar Khomeynī
Shiraz
Kāzerūn
Rafsanjān
Zarand
Kermān
4420
Bam
Zāhedān
Khāsh
Chagai Hills
Dalbandin
Kharan
Jacobabad
Shikarpur
Sukkur
Khairpur
Rahimyar Khan
Bikaner
Thar Desert
RAJASTHAN

KUWAIT
Al Kuwayt
Al Fuhayhil
Kharg I.
Būshehr
Jahrom
Neyriz
Saravan
Arānshahr
2283
Nal
Baluchistan
Larkana
Bela
Mirpur Khas
Jaisalmer
Jodhpur

Al Jahrah
Behbahān
Kangan
Lār
Bandar Abbās
Jāsk
MAKRAN
Hab
Indus
Sind
Hyderabad
INDIA
25°N
3

Al Artāwīyah
Ad Dammām
Az Zahrān (Dhahran)
BAHRAIN
Al Manāmah
G. of Bahrain
Bandar-e Lengeh
Str. of Hormuz
Gudri
Kotri
Rann of Kachchh
Patan
GUJARAT

shaqrā'
Al Mubarraz
Al Hufūf
QATAR
Ad Dawhah (Doha)
OMAN
Chāh Bahār
Karachi
Mouths of the Indus
Bhuj
Kandla
Jamnagar
Morbi
Rajkot

Ad Dilam
Ar Riyād
Haraq
Abū Zabī (Abu Dhabi)
Al 'Ayn
Al Buraymī
Matrah
Masqat
Tropic of Cancer
J
65°E
K
70°E
L
Bhavnagar
Porbandar
Kathiawar
Veraval
Diu

Al Hariq
UNITED ARAB EMIRATES
Ash Shāriqah
Dubayy
Ibrī
Jabal Akhdar 3018
Nazwā
Sūr
Ras al Hadd

ARABIA
Laylā
OMAN
Umm as Samīm
Ibrī

© Oxford University Press

Boundaries
international
disputed
internal

Communications
expressway
other major road
railway
canal
✈ major airport

Cities and towns
■ over 1 million inhabitants
● more than 100 000 inhabitants
• smaller towns
+ historic sites

Physical features
seasonal river/lake
marsh
salt pan
ice cap
sand dunes

Land height
	metres
	5000
	3000
	2000
	1000
	500
	300
	200
	100
	sea level
	land below sea level

▲ spot height in metres

ARABIA
Rub' Al Khālī
(boundary undefined)
Masīrah
Ra's Madrakah
Arabian Sea
Kuria Muria Is.
3
2

SOUTH YEMEN (P.D.R.)
Hadhramaut
Say'ūn
W. al Masilah
Ras Fartak
Salālah
2112
Al Mukallā
Habbān
Shuqrā
2507
Madinat ash Sha'b
Aden
ittle Aden
Gulf of Aden
50°E
Hadiboh
Socotra (South Yemen)
55°E
'Abd al Kūrī
15°N
1

Scale 1:12 500 000

0   125   250 km

India:Population,1989

males Age females
70+
65-69
60-64
55-59
50-54
45-49
40-44
35-39
30-34
25-29
20-24
15-19
10-14
5-9
0-4

7 6 5 4 3 2 1 0   0 1 2 3 4 5 6 7
percent of total population

Total population 811.8 million
Crude Birth Rate per thousand:31
Crude Death Rate per thousand:10

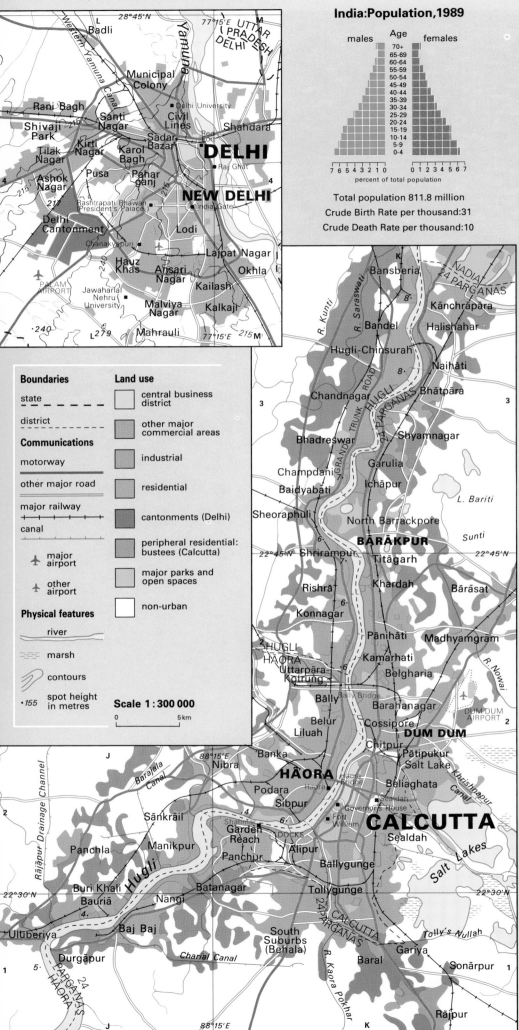

DELHI
Badli, 28°45'N, 77°15'E, UTTAR PRADESH, DELHI, Municipal Colony, Rani Bagh, Santi Nagar, Civil Lines, Shahdara, Shivaji Park, Kirti Nagar, Sadar Bazar, Delhi University, Red Fort, Tilak Nagar, Karol Bagh, Pahar ganj, Pusa, Ashok Nagar, Hauz Khas, Ansari Nagar, Okhla, Kailash, Rashtrapati Bhawan President's Palace, India Gate, Lodi, PALAM AIRPORT, Delhi Cantonment, Chanakyapuri, Jawaharlal Nehru University, Malviya Nagar, Kalkaji, Lajpat Nagar, NEW DELHI, Mahrauli

CALCUTTA area
Bansberia, NADIA, 24 PARGANAS, Kanchrapara, Halishahar, Bandel, Hugli-Chinsurah, Naihati, Chandnagar, Bhatpara, Bhadreswar, Shyamnagar, Garulia, Champdani, Ichapur, Baidyabati, Sheoraphuli, North Barrackpore, BARAKPUR, Shrirampur, Titagarh, Rishra, Khardah, Barasat, Konnagar, Panihati, Madhyamgram, HUGLI, HAORA, Kamarhati, Uttarpara-Kotrung, Belgharia, Bally, Barahanagar, Belur, Liluah, Cossipore, DUM DUM, Chitpur, Patipukur, Salt Lake, Banka, Nibra, HAORA, Beliaghata, Podara, Sibpur, Garden Reach, Alipur, CALCUTTA, Sealdah, Sankrail, Manikpur, Panchla, Panchur, Ballygunge, Tollygunge, Batanagar, Buri Khali, Nangi, Bauria, Baj Baj, Durgapur, Uluberiya, South Suburbs (Behala), Gariya, Baral, Sonarpur, Rajpur, L. Bariti, Sunti

Regional map
AFGHANISTAN, Herat, Shindand, Ghazni, Farah, Khash, Koh-i-Mazar 3798, Zabol, Kandahar, Chaman, Dasht-i-Margo, Registan, Zargun 2641, 3578 Quetta, IRAN, Saravan, Chagai Hills, Nushki, PAKISTAN, Dalbandin, Kalat, Sibi, Jacobabad, Shikarpur, Larkana 2283, Sukkur, Kharan, Bela, Karachi, Hyderabad, Kotri, Mirpur, Arabian Sea, Porbandar, Junagadh, Rann of Kach, Bhuj, Mandvi, G. of Kachchh, Tropic of Cancer, Mouths of the Indus

Legend

Boundaries
state
district

Communications
motorway
other major road
major railway
canal
major airport
other airport

Physical features
river
marsh
contours
·155 spot height in metres

Land use
central business district
other major commercial areas
industrial
residential
cantonments (Delhi)
peripheral residential: bustees (Calcutta)
major parks and open spaces
non-urban

Scale 1:300 000
0 5km

Boundaries
international
disputed
internal

Communications
major road
railway
canal
major airport

Cities and towns
over 1 million inhabitants
more than 100 000 inhabitants
smaller towns

Physical features
marsh
salt pan
ice cap
sand dunes

Land height
metres
5000
3000
2000
1000
500
300
200
100
sea level
spot height in metres

Scale 1:12 500 000
0 200 400 km

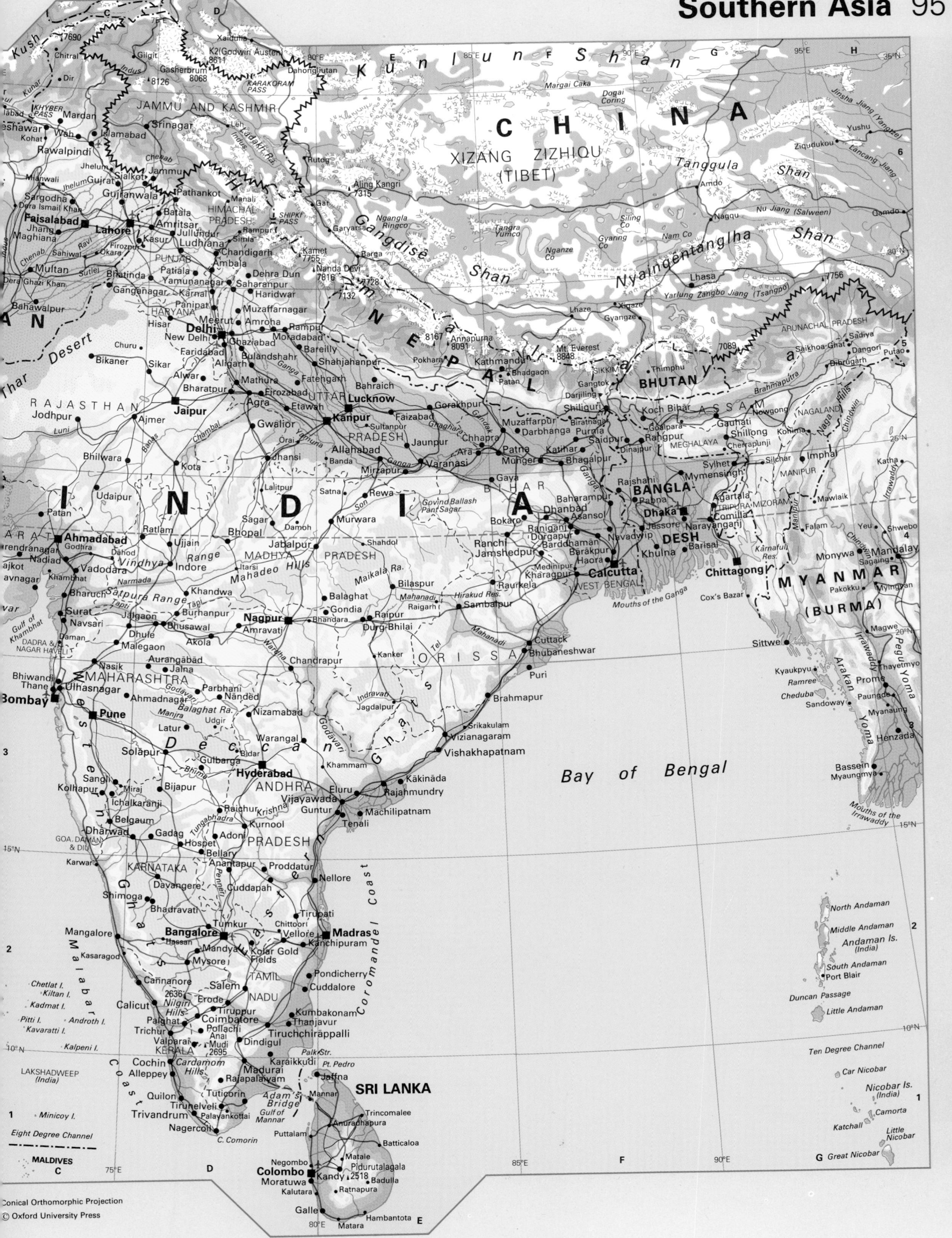
Kunlun Shan
CHINA
XIZANG ZIZHIQU (TIBET)
Tanggula Shan
Nyainqentanglha Shan
Gangdisê Shan
Margai Caka
Dogai Coring
Jinsha Jiang (Yangtze)
Yushu
Zaqudukou
Lancang Jiang
Amdo
Nagqu
Nu Jiang (Salween)
Qamdo
Siling Co
Nam Co
Tangra Yumco
Gyaring Co
Ngangla Ringco
Nganze Co
Aling Kangri 7315
Lhasa
Yarlung Zangbo Jiang (Tsangpo)
Xigazê
Gyangzê
Lhazê
Garyarsa
Barga
Gar
Rutog
Xaidulla
K2 (Godwin Austen) 8611
Gasherbrum 8068
8126
KARAKORAM PASS
Dahongliutan
Kush
Chitral
Dir
Gilgit
17690
Kunar
KHYBER PASS
Mardan
Peshawar
Kohat
Wah
Islamabad
Rawalpindi
JAMMU AND KASHMIR
Srinagar
Leh
Indus
Ladakh Ra.
Jhelum
Chenab
Jammu
Mianwali
Gujrat
Sialkot
Sargodha
Gujranwala
Pathankot
Dera Ismail Khan
Faisalabad
Lahore
Jhang Maghiana
Amritsar
Batala
Jullundur
Kasur
Firozpur
Ludhiana
Okara
Sahiwal
Ravi
Multan
Sutlej
Dera Ghazi Khan
Bahawalpur
Manali
HIMACHAL PRADESH
SHIPKI PASS
Rampur
Simla
Chandigarh
Ambala
PUNJAB
Patiala
Bhatinda
Yamunanagar
Ganganagar
Kamet 7755
Nanda Devi 7816
7728
7132
Dehra Dun
Saharanpur
Haridwar
Karnal
Panipat
HARYANA
Muzaffarnagar
Meerut
Amroha
Hisar
Delhi
New Delhi
Ghaziabad
Rampur
Moradabad
Bareilly
Faridabad
Bulandshahr
Aligarh
Churu
Bikaner
Sikar
Thar Desert
Shahjahanpur
Ganga
Mathura
Fatehgarh
Alwar
Bharatpur
Firozabad
Agra
Etawah
Bahraich
Lucknow
UTTAR PRADESH
Kanpur
Faizabad
Gorakhpur
RAJASTHAN
Jodhpur
Jaipur
Ajmer
Luni
Gwalior
Chambal
Banas
Orai
Jhansi
Allahabad
Banda
Yamuna
Jaunpur
Varanasi
Mirzapur
Bhilwara
Kota
Lalitpur
Satna
Rewa
Son
Govind Ballash Pant Sagar
Udaipur
INDIA
Patan
Ahmadabad
Godhra
Dahod
Ratlam
Ujjain
Bhopal
Sagar
Damoh
Murwara
Shahdol
Jabalpur
MADHYA PRADESH
Vindhya Range
Indore
Itarsi
Mahadeo Hills
Maikala Ra.
Bilaspur
Narmada
Vadodara
Khambhat
Nadiad
Bharuch
Satpura Range
Khandwa
Tapti
Gulf of Khambhat
Surat
Navsari
Daman
Jalgaon
Burhanpur
Bhusawal
Dhule
Nagpur
Amravati
Akola
Balaghat
Gondia
Bhandara
Raipur
Durg-Bhilai
Mahanadi
Raigarh
Hirakud Res.
Sambalpur
Malegaon
DADRA & NAGAR HAVELI
Nasik
Aurangabad
Jalna
Wardha
Chandrapur
Kanker
ORISSA
Tel
Cuttack
Bhubaneshwar
Puri
Bhiwandi
Thane
Bombay
Ulhasnagar
MAHARASHTRA
Parbhani
Nanded
Godavari
Ahmadnagar
Balaghat Ra.
Manjra
Udgir
Pune
Nizamabad
Indravati
Jagdalpur
Brahmapur
Srikakulam
Vizianagaram
Vishakhapatnam
Latur
Deccan
Warangal
Bidar
Solapur
Gulbarga
Hyderabad
Khammam
Eastern Ghats
Western Ghats
Bhima
Sangli
Miraj
Kolhapur
Bijapur
Ichalkaranji
ANDHRA PRADESH
Krishna
Vijayawada
Eluru
Kakinada
Rajahmundry
Machilipatnam
Guntur
Tenali
Raichur
Belgaum
Tungabhadra
Kurnool
Dharwad
Gadag
Hospet
Adoni
GOA, DAMAN & DIU
Bellary
Anantapur
Proddatur
Karwar
KARNATAKA
Pennar
Nellore
Davangere
Cuddapah
Shimoga
Bhadravati
Tirupati
Chittoor
Vellore
Madras
Kanchipuram
Tumkur
Bangalore
Hassan
Mangalore
Kasaragod
Mysore
Mandya
Kolar Gold Fields
Malabar Coast
Coromandel Coast
Pondicherry
Cuddalore
TAMIL NADU
Salem
Cannanore
2636
Nilgiri Hills
Erode
Calicut
Tiruppur
Coimbatore
Kumbakonam
Thanjavur
Palghat
Pollachi
Trichur
Tiruchchirappalli
Anai Mudi 2695
Valparai
KERALA
Dindigul
Cochin
Cardamom Hills
Madurai
Karaikkudi
Alleppey
Rajapalaiyam
Palk Str.
Pt. Pedro
Jaffna
Quilon
Tuticorin
Tirunelveli
Palayankottai
Adam's Bridge
Gulf of Mannar
Mannar
Trivandrum
Nagercoil
C. Comorin
Chetlat I.
Kiltan I.
Kadmat I.
Pitti I.
Androth I.
Kavaratti I.
Kalpeni I.
LAKSHADWEEP (India)
Minicoy I.
Eight Degree Channel
MALDIVES
SRI LANKA
Trincomalee
Anuradhapura
Puttalam
Batticaloa
Negombo
Matale
Colombo
Kandy
Pidurutalagala 2518
Badulla
Moratuwa
Kalutara
Ratnapura
Galle
Hambantota
Matara
NEPAL
Annapurna 8091
8167
Pokhara
Kathmandu
Bhadgaon
Patan
Mt. Everest 8848
Himalaya
SIKKIM
Gangtok
Darjiling
Thimphu
BHUTAN
7089
ARUNACHAL PRADESH
Sadiya
Saikhoa Ghat
Dangori
Putao
Dibrugarh
Brahmaputra
ASSAM
Nowgong
NAGALAND
Naga Hills
Chindwin
Koch Bihar
Gauhati
Shiliguri
Goalpara
Shillong
Kohima
Rangpur
MEGHALAYA
Cherrapunji
Dinajpur
Saidpur
Biratnagar
Purnia
Muzaffarpur
Darbhanga
Gandak
Ghaghara
Chhapra
Ara
Patna
Munger
Katihar
Bhagalpur
Gaya
BIHAR
Sylhet
Silchar
Imphal
MANIPUR
Mymensingh
Katha
Irrawaddy
Rajshahi
Pabna
BANGLADESH
Baharampur
Dhanbad
Asansol
Agartala
TRIPURA
MIZORAM
Mawlaik
Comilla
Dhaka
Narayanganj
Jessore
Navadwip
Khulna
Barisal
Bokaro
Raniganj
Durgapur
Barddhaman
Ranchi
Jamshedpur
Barakpur
Haora
Calcutta
Medinipur
Kharagpur
WEST BENGAL
Raurkela
Mouths of the Ganga
Chittagong
Karnafuli Res.
Cox's Bazar
Falam
Yeu
Shwebo
Monywa
Mandalay
Sagaing
MYANMAR (BURMA)
Pakokku
Myingyan
Magwe
Sittwe
Kyaukpyu
Ramree
Cheduba
Sandoway
Arakan Yoma
Pegu Yoma
Thayetmyo
Prome
Paungde
Myanaung
Henzada
Bassein
Myaungmya
Mouths of the Irrawaddy
Bay of Bengal
North Andaman
Middle Andaman
Andaman Is. (India)
South Andaman
Port Blair
Duncan Passage
Little Andaman
Ten Degree Channel
Car Nicobar
Nicobar Is. (India)
Camorta
Katchall
Little Nicobar
Great Nicobar
7756
35°N
30°N
25°N
20°N
15°N
10°N
75°E
80°E
85°E
90°E
95°E
C
D
E
F
G
H
1
2
3
4
5
6

Conical Orthomorphic Projection

Boundaries

international

disputed

internal

Communications

expressway

other major road

railway

canal

✈ major airport

Cities and towns

■ over 1 million inhabitants

● more than 100 000 inhabitants

• smaller towns

Physical features

seasonal river/lake

marsh

salt pan

ice cap

sand dunes

Land height

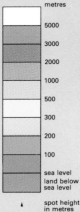

metres

5000

3000

2000

1000

500

300

200

100

sea level

land below sea level

▲ spot height in metres

Scale 1:19 000 000

0   200   400 km

Conical Orthomorphic Project

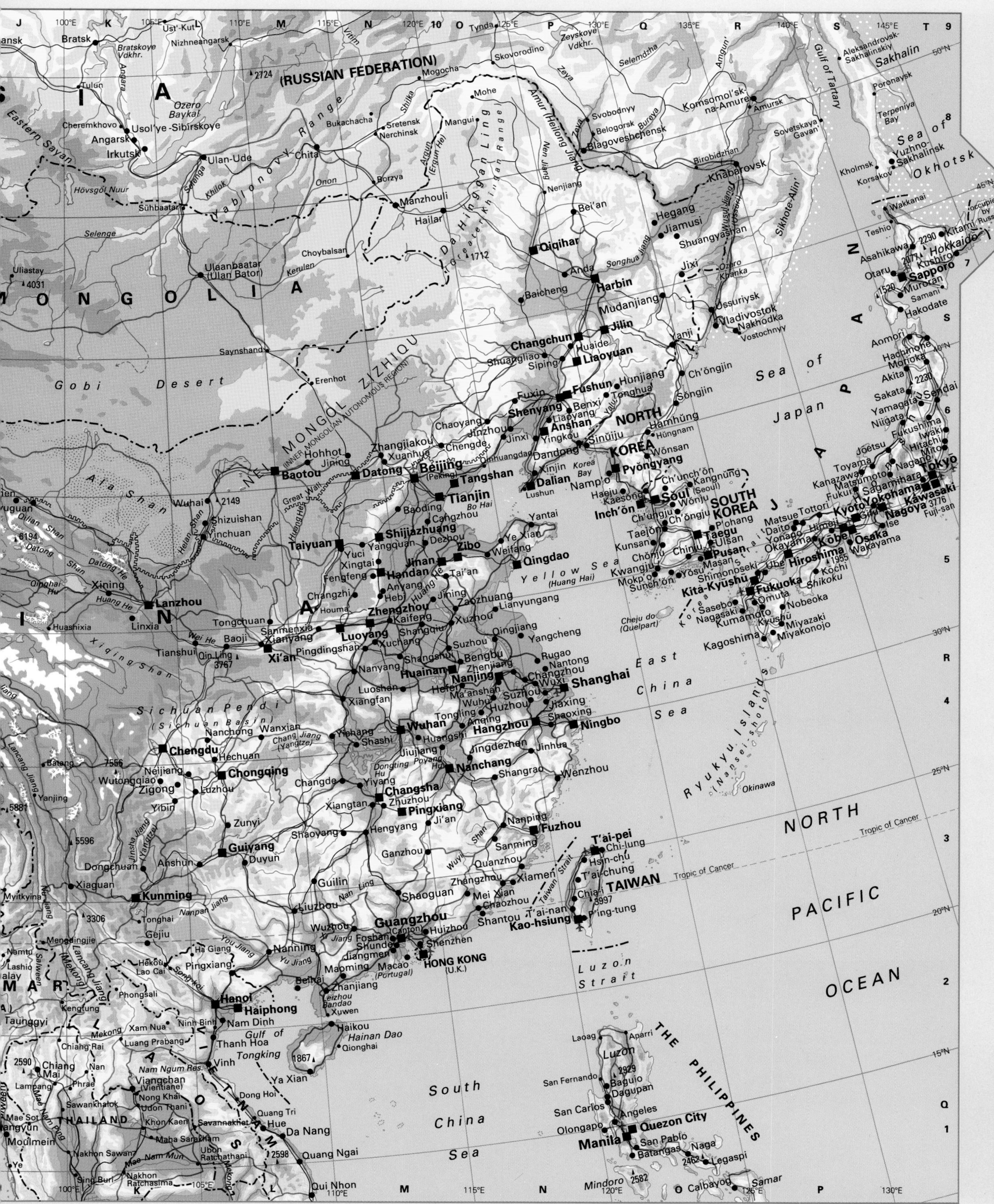
(RUSSIAN FEDERATION)
Bratsk
Bratskoye Vdkhr.
Ust'-Kut
Nizhneangarsk
Tynda
Zeyskoye Vdkhr.
Skovorodino
Mogocha
Ozero Baykal
Eastern Sayan
Cheremkhovo
Usol'ye-Sibirskoye
Angarsk
Irkutsk
Ulan-Ude
Chita
Yablonovy Range
Bukachacha
Sretensk
Nerchinsk
Mohe
Mangui
Da Hinggan Ling
(Greater Khingan Range)
Amur (Heilong Jiang)
Svobodnyy
Belogorsk
Blagoveshchensk
Selemdzha
Amgun'
Gulf of Tartary
Komsomol'sk-na-Amure
Amursk
Aleksandrovsk-Sakhalinskiy
Sakhalin
Poronaysk
Terpeniya Bay
Sovetskaya Gavan'
Birobidzhan
Khabarovsk
Yuzhno-Sakhalinsk
Kholmsk
Korsakov
Sea of Okhotsk
Hövsgöl Nuur
Sühbaatar
Selenge
Onon
Borzya
Manzhouli
Hailar
Nenjiang
Bei'an
Hegang
Jiamusi
Shuangyashan
Sikhote-Alin'
Wakkanai
Occupied by Russia
Teshio
Asahikawa
Kitami
Hokkaido
Kushiro
Otaru
Sapporo
Muroran
Samani
Hakodate
Choybalsan
Kerulen
Qiqihar
Songhua Jiang
Jixi
Ozero Khanka
Uliastay
4031
Ulaanbaatar (Ulan Bator)
MONGOLIA
Anda
Harbin
Baicheng
Mudanjiang
Ussuriysk
Vladivostok
Nakhodka
Vostochnyy
Jilin
Changchun
Huaide
Liaoyuan
Shuangliao
Siping
Yanji
Saynshand
Erenhot
Gobi Desert
NEI MONGOL ZIZHIQU
(INNER MONGOLIAN AUTONOMOUS REGION)
Fuxin
Fushun
Hunjiang
Tonghua
Ch'ŏngjin
Sea of Japan
Aomori
Hachinohe
Morioka
Akita
Sakata
Sendai
Yamagata
Niigata
Fukushima
Iwaki
Hitachi
Mito
Toyama
Joetsu
Nagano
Tokyo
Kanazawa
Matsumoto
Fukui
Sagamihara
Yokohama
Kawasaki
Kyoto
Gifu
Nagoya
Fuji-san
3776
Shenyang
Benxi
Liaoyang
Anshan
Yingkou
Chaoyang
Jinzhou
Jinxi
Chengde
Zhangjiakou
Xuanhua
Hohhot
Jining
Baotou
Datong
Beijing
(Peking)
Qinhuangdao
Dandong
Sinŭiju
Sŏngjin
Hamhŭng
Hŭngnam
NORTH KOREA
Wŏnsan
P'yŏngyang
Korea Bay
Xinjin
Dalian
Lushun
Nampo
Ch'unch'ŏn
Kangnŭng
Haeju
Kaesŏng
Sŏul (Seoul)
Inch'ŏn
Wŏnju
Ch'ŏngju
SOUTH KOREA
P'ohang
Taejŏn
Taegu
Ulsan
Kunsan
Chŏnju
Kwangju
Masan
Pusan
Mokp'o
Sunch'ŏn
Yŏsu
Tangshan
Tianjin
Bo Hai
Great Wall
Baoding
Cangzhou
Yantai
Ala Shan
Wuhai
2149
Shizuishan
Yinchuan
Helan Shan
Huang He
Shijiazhuang
Dezhou
Yangquan
Taiyuan
Yuci
Xingtai
Zibo
Weifang
Qingdao
Jinan
Handan
Tai'an
Yellow Sea
(Huang Hai)
Fengfeng
Anyang
Hebi
Changzhi
Houma
Zhengzhou
Kaifeng
Jining
Zaozhuang
Lianyungang
Xuzhou
Qilian Shan
6194
Datong Shan
Datong He
Qinghai Hu
Xining
Lanzhou
Linxia
Huashixia
Tongchuan
Sanmenxia
Xianyang
Baoji
Wei He
Tianshui
Qin Ling
3767
Xi'an
Luoyang
Pingdingshan
Shangqiu
Xuchang
Qingjiang
Yangcheng
Xiqing Shan
Shangshui
Suzhou
Bengbu
Rugao
Nantong
Nanyang
Huainan
Zhenjiang
Changzhou
Nanjing
Hefei
Wuxi
Shanghai
East China Sea
Luoshan
Xiangfan
Ma'anshan
Wuhu
Suzhou
Huzhou
Jiaxing
Shaoxing
Ningbo
Tongling
Anqing
Hangzhou
Sichuan Pendi
(Sichuan Basin)
Nanchong
Wanxian
Chang Jiang (Yangtze)
Yichang
Shashi
Wuhan
Huangshi
Jinhua
Chengdu
Hechuan
Jiujiang
Jingdezhen
Dongting Hu
Poyang Hu
Nanchang
Shangrao
Wenzhou
Batang
7556
Wutongqiao
Neijiang
Zigong
Luzhou
Chongqing
Changde
Yiyang
Changsha
Zhuzhou
Xiangtan
Pingxiang
Ji'an
Yanjing
5881
Yibin
Zunyi
Jinsha Jiang (Yangtze)
5596
Shaoyang
Hengyang
Nanping
Fuzhou
Sanming
Guiyang
Duyun
Anshun
Dongchuan
Xiaguan
Kunming
Ganzhou
Quanzhou
Wuyi Shan
Xiamen
Zhangzhou
Mei Xian
Chaozhou
Shantou
Taiwan Strait
T'ai-pei
Chi-lung
Hsin-chu
T'ai-chung
Chia-i
TAIWAN
3997
T'ai-nan
P'ing-tung
Kao-hsiung
Tropic of Cancer
Guilin
Nan Ling
Shaoguan
Liuzhou
Wuzhou
Guangzhou
(Canton)
Foshan
Shunde
Huizhou
Shenzhen
Jiangmen
Maoming
Macao
(Portugal)
HONG KONG
(U.K.)
Nanning
Yu Jiang
You Jiang
Beihai
Zhanjiang
Leizhou Bandao
Xuwen
Haikou
Hainan Dao
Qionghai
1867
Luzon Strait
Myitkyina
3306
Tonghai
Gejiu
Nanpan Jiang
Mengdingjie
Namtu
Lashio
Salween
Lancang Jiang
(Mekong)
Hekou
Lao Cai
Pingxiang
Song Koi
Phongsali
Kengtung
Taunggyi
Hanoi
Haiphong
Ninh Binh
Nam Dinh
Thanh Hoa
Gulf of Tongking
Vinh
Ya Xian
Mekong
Xam Nua
Luang Prabang
Chiang Rai
Nan
2590
Chiang Mai
Lampang
Phrae
Nam Ngum Res.
Viangchan
(Vientiane)
Nong Khai
Udon Thani
Sawankhalok
Mae Sot
THAILAND
Khon Kaen
Savannakhet
Hue
Da Nang
Moulmein
Maha Sarakham
Nakhon Sawan
Mae Nam Mun
Ubon Ratchathani
2598
Quang Ngai
Dong Hoi
Quang Tri
Nakhon Ratchasima
Sing Buri
Qui Nhon
South China Sea
Laoag
Aparri
Luzon
2929
Baguio
Dagupan
San Fernando
San Carlos
Angeles
Olongapo
Quezon City
Manila
San Pablo
Batangas
Naga
2462
Legaspi
Mindoro
2582
Calbayog
Samar
THE PHILIPPINES
NORTH PACIFIC OCEAN
Ryukyu Islands
(Nansei-shoto)
Okinawa
Cheju do
(Quelpart)
Korea Strait
Kita-Kyushu
Fukuoka
Shimonoseki
Ube
Hiroshima
Kochi
Shikoku
1955
Okayama
Kobe
Osaka
Wakayama
Ise
Matsue
Tottori
Daito
Yonago
Himeji
Sasebo
Nagasaki
Omuta
Kumamoto
Kyushu
Nobeoka
Miyazaki
Miyakonojo
Kagoshima
100°E
105°E
110°E
115°E
120°E
125°E
130°E
135°E
140°E
145°E
50°N
45°N
40°N
30°N
25°N
20°N
15°N

Taiwan, Hong Kong

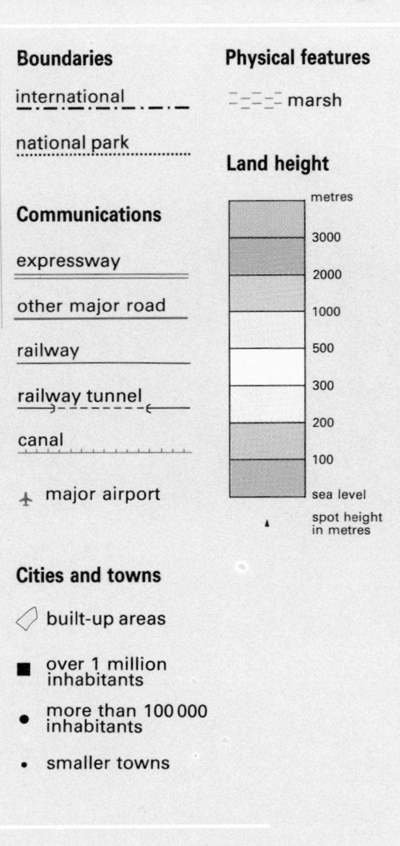

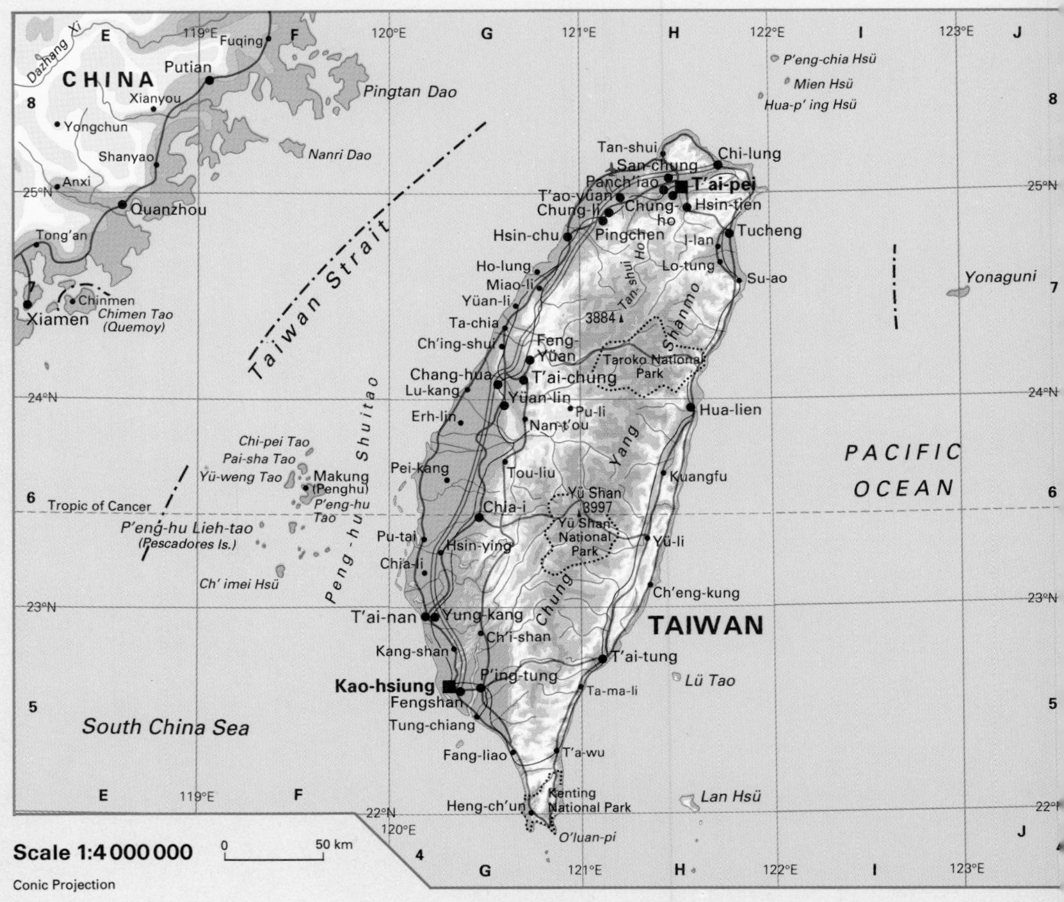

Scale 1:400 000

5 km

Gauss Conformal Projection

CHINA

HONG KONG

NEW TERRITORIES

Deep Bay

Mirs Bay

South China Sea

Sham Chun River

Robin's Nest 492

Man Kam To

Ping Yeung

Sha Tau Kok

Lo Wu

Lai Chi Wo

Crooked I.

Ping Chau

Lok Ma Chau

Sheung Shui

Kwan Tei

Luk Keng

Crescent I.

Kwu Tung

Shek Wu Hui

Nam Chung

Double I.

San Tin

Luen Wo Hui

San Uk Ha

Port I.

Mai Po Lo Wai

Kam Tsin

Fanling

Nam Sha Po

Fairview Park

Ngau Tam Mei

Ling Tong Mei

Kai Kung Leng 572

Ying Pun

Tai Mei Tuk

Plover Cove Reservoir

Grass I.

Hang Hau Tsuen

Hong Lok Yuen

Shuen Wan

Tolo Channel

Hoi Ha

Shui Tau

Tai To Yan 565

Hang Ha Po

Tai Po

Lai Chi Chong

Ping Shan

Yuen Long

Wang Toi Shan

Tolo Harbour

Sham Chung

Tai Tan

Sharp Peak 468

Ha Tsuen

Kat Hing Wai

Wong Chuk Yuen

481

Shek Uk Shan

Tan Kwai Tsuen

Shek Kong

Ma Liu Shui

Ma On Shan

Chek Keng

Nim Wan

Lam Tei

Pak Sha Tsuen

Tai Mo Shan 957

Grassy Hill 645

Kei Ling Ha Lo Wai

Tai Long

Tai Long Wan

Black Point

Kei Lun Wai

Ho Pui

702

Ma On Shan

Pak Tam Chung

Urmston Road

Castle Peak 583

Tuen Mun

507

Jubilee Reservoir

Sha Tin

Tai Mong Tsai

High Island Reservoir

Lung Kwu Chau

Tai Lam Chung Reservoir

Sai Kung

So Kwun Wat Tsuen

Chai Wan Kok

Tai Lam Chung

Sham Tseng

Tsuen Wan

Tai Wai

Tate's Cairn 577

Sharp I.

Kwai Chung

Ho Chung

Kau Sai Chau

High I.

Ma Wan

Cheung Shue Tau

Tsing Yi

Lion Rock 495

Tsz Wan Shan

Ta Ku Ling

Sha Chau

Tsing Chau Tsai

Tsing Yi

Shek Kip Mei

602

Kowloon Peak

Tiu Chung Chau

Fu Tau Fan Chau

The Brothers

Cheung Sha Wan

Ngau Chi Wan

Sham Shui Po

Kowloon City

Tseung Kwan O

Wang Chau

Mong Tong Hang

Mong Kok

Ho Man Tin

Jordan Valley

Shelter I.

Chek Lap Kok

Stonecutters I.

Kowloon

Ngau Tau Kok

Kwun Tong

Hang Hau

Basalt I.

Discovery Bay

Discovery Bay

Yau Ma Tei

Hung Hom

Yau Tong

Tiu Keng Leng

Bluff I.

Ngau Kwu Long

Peng Chau

Kau Yi Chau

Victoria Harbour

Junk Bay

Sham Shek Tsuen

Sha Lo Wan

Ma Wan Chung

Peng Chau

Green I.

Kennedy Town

Sai Ying Pun

Victoria

North Point

Quarry Bay

Tai Wan Tau

Tung Chung

Tai Shui Hang

554

Victoria Peak

Shau Kei Wan

Steep I.

Lantau Island

Mui Wo

Sunshine I.

Pok Fu Lam

Happy Valley

531

Mt. Parker

Chai Wan

Ninepin Group

Tai O

Ngong Ping

869

933

Sunset Peak

Hei Ling Chau

Aberdeen

Wong Chuk Hang

Tai Tam Reservoir

Tung Lung Chau

Lantau Peak

Pui O

West Lamma Channel

East Lamma Channel

Ap Lei Chau

Shek Pik Reservoir

Cheung Sha

Chi Ma Wan Peninsula

Cheung Chau

Yung Shue Wan

Tsin Shui Wan

Shek O

Shek Pik

Tong Fuk

Round I.

Chung Hom Kok

Tai Tam Wan

Cheung Chau

Lamma Island

Sok Kwu Wan

Chek Chue (Stanley)

Fan Lau

Shek Kwu Chau

Sung Kong

Beaufort I.

Waglan I.

Lantau Channel

Soko Is.

Po Toi Island

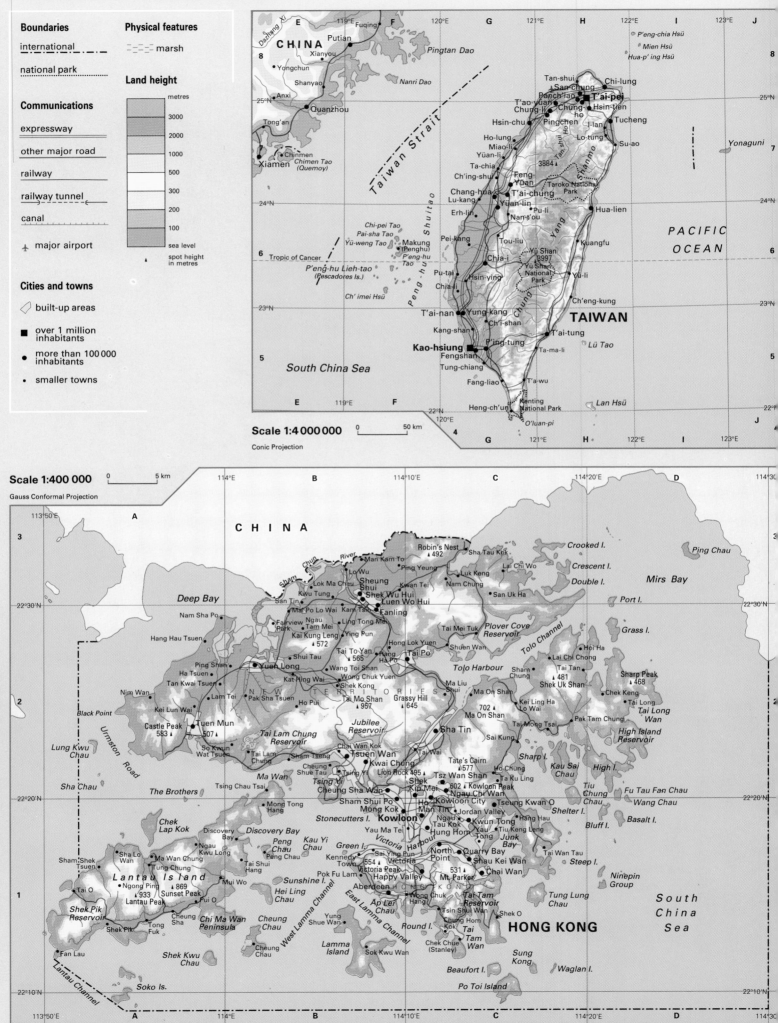

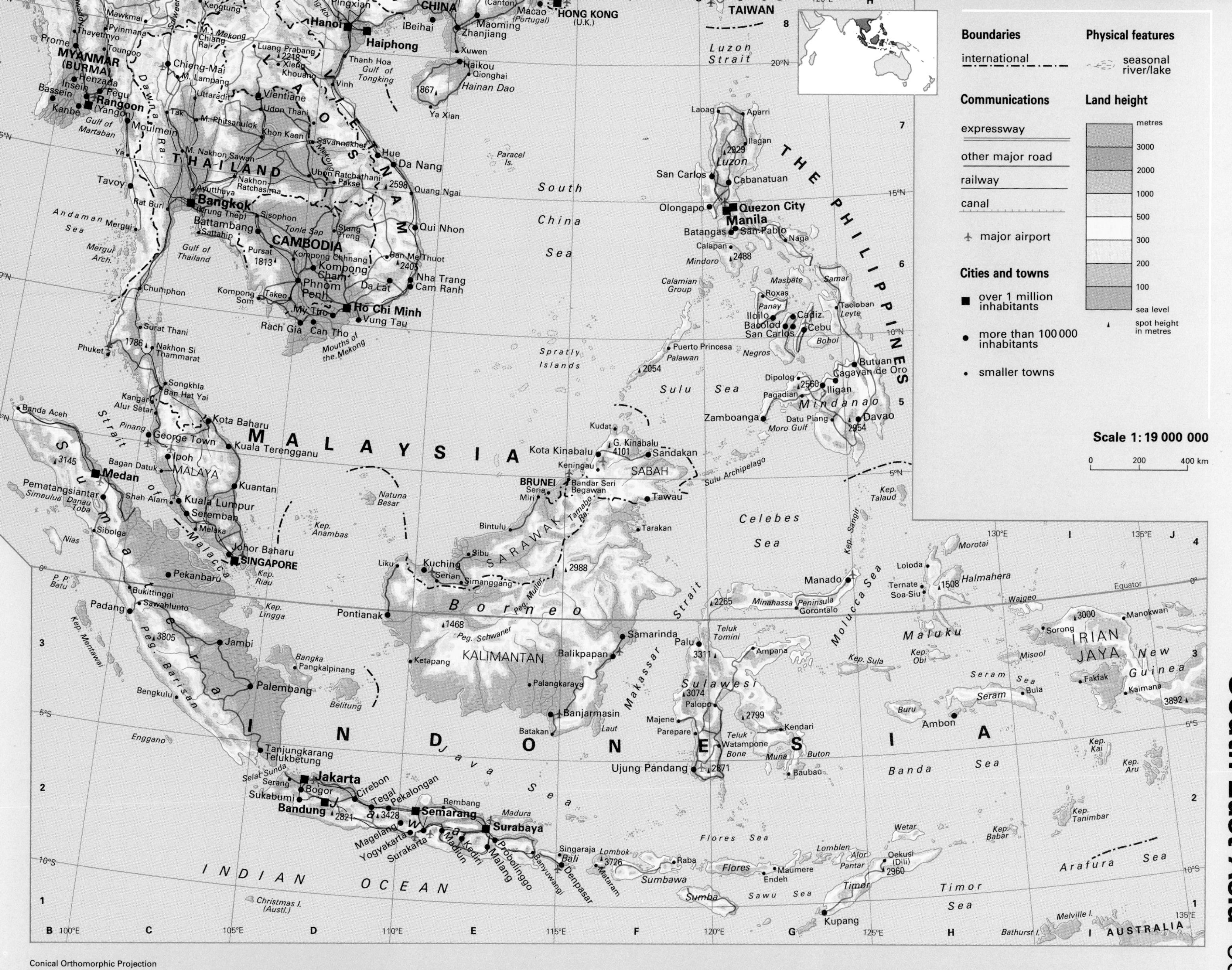

Scale 1:19 000 000

Physical features
seasonal river/lake

Land height
metres	
3000	
2000	
1000	
500	
300	
200	
100	
sea level	

spot height in metres

Boundaries
international

Communications
expressway
other major road
railway
canal
major airport

Cities and towns
■ over 1 million inhabitants
● more than 100 000 inhabitants
• smaller towns

Conical Orthomorphic Projection

© Oxford University Press

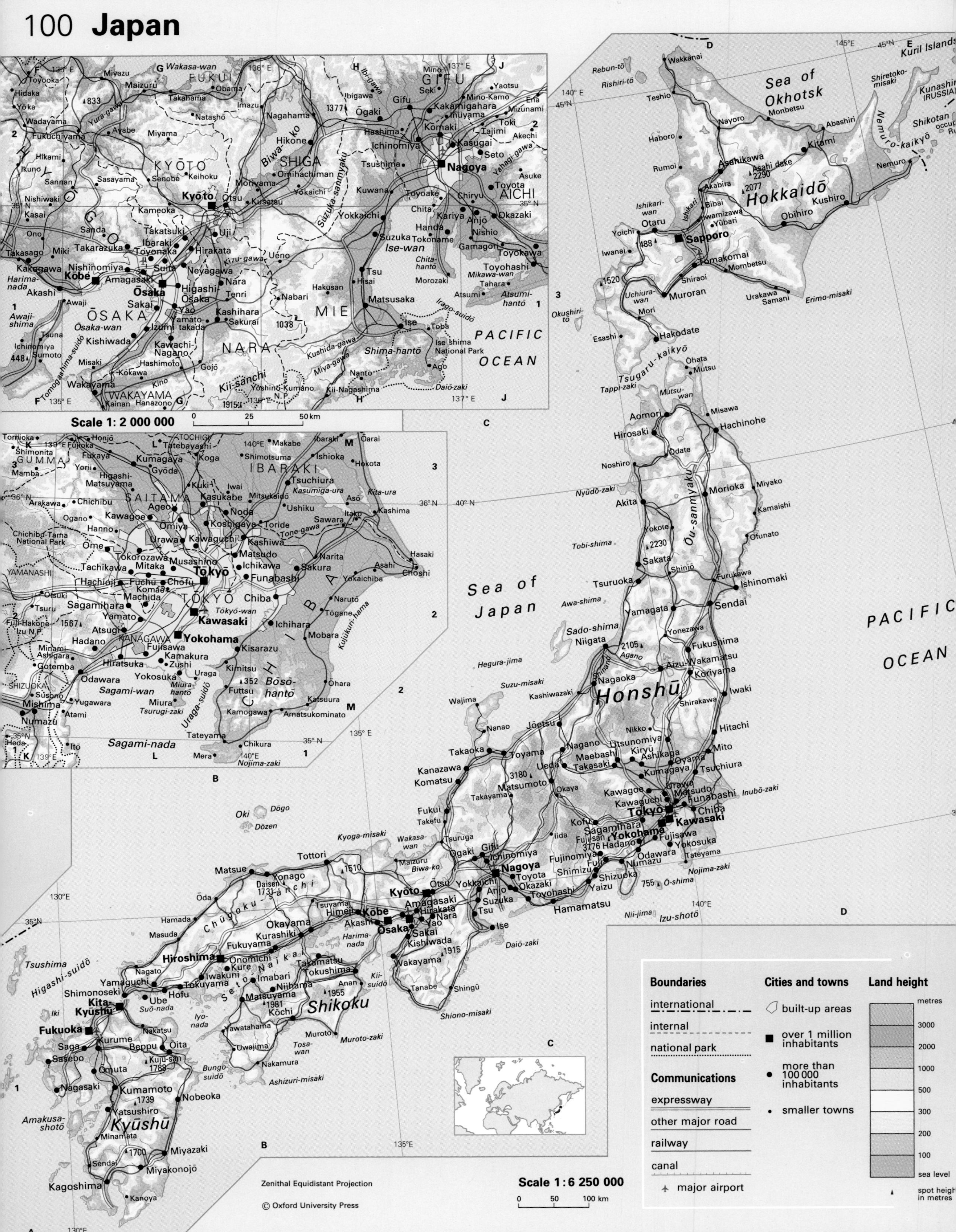
Sea of Okhotsk
Kuril Islands
Kunashir (RUSSIA)
Hokkaidō
Sapporo
Asahikawa
Hakodate
Tsugaru-kaikyō
Sea of Japan
PACIFIC OCEAN
Honshū
Ōu-sanmyaku
Aomori
Sendai
Niigata
Tōkyō
Yokohama
Kawasaki
Nagoya
Kyōto
Ōsaka
Kōbe
Hiroshima
Chūgoku-sanchi
Seto-Naikai
Shikoku
Kyūshū
Kita-Kyūshū
Fukuoka
Kagoshima
Tsushima
Kii-sanchi
Ise-wan
Biwa-ko
Scale 1: 2 000 000
Scale 1 : 6 250 000
Zenithal Equidistant Projection
© Oxford University Press
Boundaries
international
internal
national park
Communications
expressway
other major road
railway
canal
major airport
Cities and towns
built-up areas
over 1 million inhabitants
more than 100 000 inhabitants
smaller towns
Land height
metres
3000
2000
1000
500
300
200
100
sea level
spot height in metres

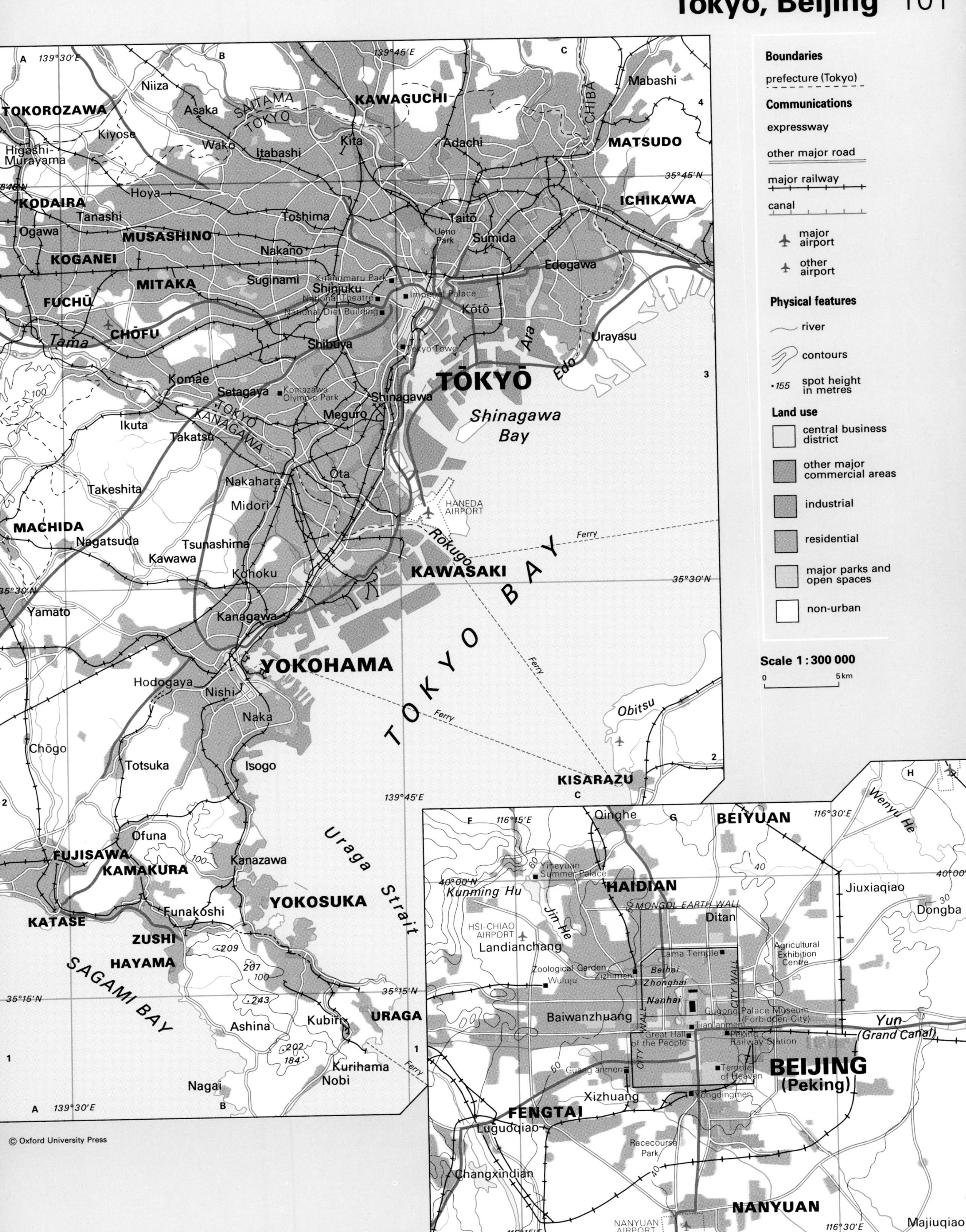

Boundaries
prefecture (Tokyo)

Communications
expressway

other major road

major railway

canal

✈ major airport

✈ other airport

Physical features
～ river

contours

·155 spot height in metres

Land use
central business district

other major commercial areas

industrial

residential

major parks and open spaces

non-urban

Scale 1 : 300 000

0   5km

A 139°30'E   B   139°45'E   C

TOKOROZAWA

Niiza

Higashi-Murayama   Kiyose   Asaka   Wako   SAITAMA / TOKYO   Itabashi   Kita   KAWAGUCHI   Mabashi   CHIBA

KODAIRA   Hoya   Adachi   MATSUDO

Ogawa   Tanashi   Toshima   Taitō   ICHIKAWA

MUSASHINO   Nakano   Ueno Park   Sumida

KOGANEI   Suginami   Kitanomaru Park   Edogawa

MITAKA   Shinjuku   Imperial Palace   35°45'N

FUCHŪ   National Theatre   National Diet Building   Kōtō

Tama   CHŌFU   Shibuya   Tokyo Tower   Urayasu

Komae   Tokyo Tower   TŌKYŌ   Ara   Edo

Setagaya   Komazawa Olympic Park   Shinagawa   Shinagawa Bay

Ikuta   Meguro

Takashita   TOKYO / KANAGAWA   Ōta

Nakahara   HANEDA AIRPORT   Ferry

MACHIDA   Midori   Rokugo   Ferry   35°30'N

Nagatsuda   Tsunashima   KAWASAKI

Kawawa   TOKYO BAY

Yamato   Kohoku   Ferry

Kanagawa   Obitsu

YOKOHAMA   Ferry

Hodogaya   Nishi   KISARAZU

Chōgo   Naka

Totsuka   Isogo   C

Ofuna   Kanazawa   Uraga Strait

FUJISAWA   100   BEIYUAN

KAMAKURA   Kanazawa   Qinghe   116°30'E

KATASE   YOKOSUKA   HAIDIAN   Jiuxiaqiao   Dongba

ZUSHI   Funakoshi   Kunming Hu   Summer Palace   Ditan

HAYAMA   ·209   Yiheyuan   MONGOL EARTH WALL   40°00'

SAGAMI BAY   ·207 100   HSI-CHIAO AIRPORT   Jin He   Agricultural Exhibition Centre

Ashina   Kubiri   ·243   Landianchang   Lama Temple

Nagai   Kurihama Nobi   URAGA   Zoological Garden   Beihai   Yun (Grand Canal)

Wuluju   Zizhimen   Zhonghai

Baiwanzhuang   Nanhai   Gugong Palace Museum (Forbidden City)

Tiananmen   Peking Railway Station

Great Hall of the People   BEIJING (Peking)

Guang'anmen   Temple of Heaven

Xizhuang   Yongdingmen

FENGTAI   116°30'E

Luguoqiao   Racecourse Park

Changxindian   NANYUAN

NANYUAN AIRPORT   Majiuqiao

116°15'E

© Oxford University Press

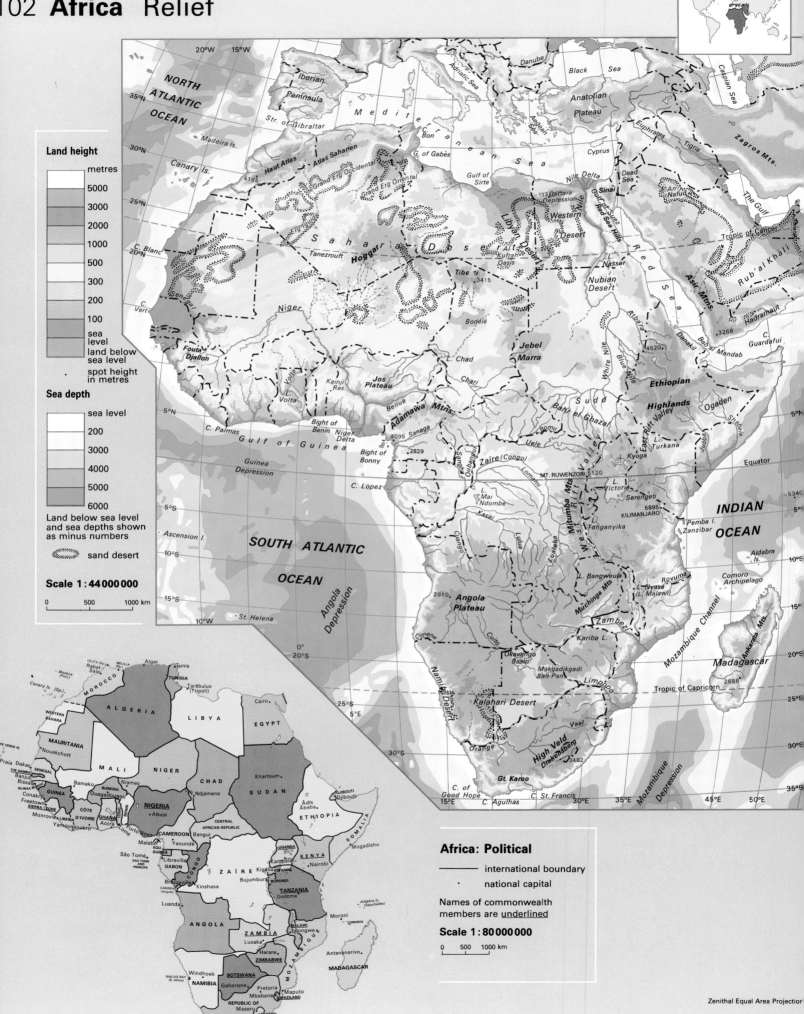

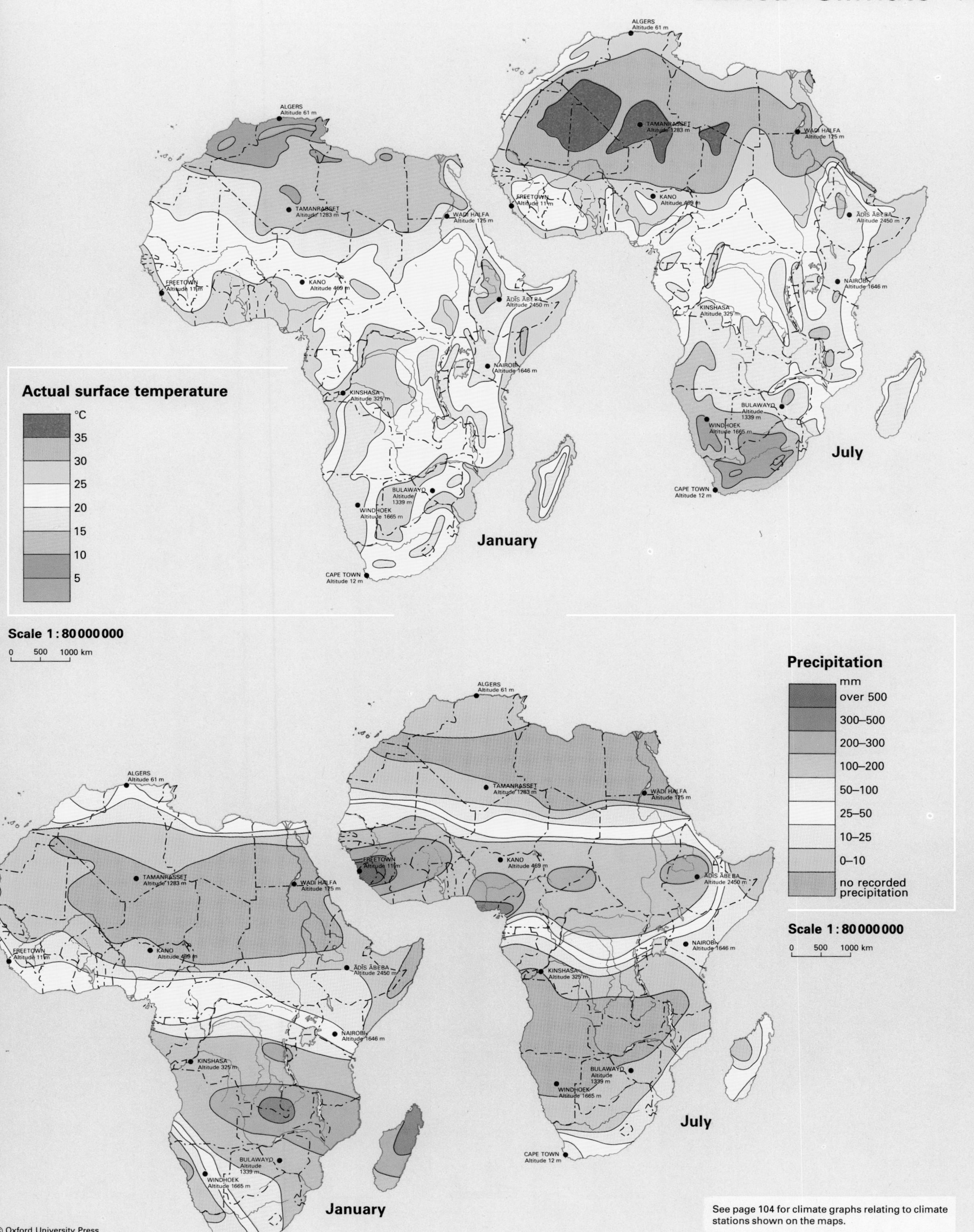

Actual surface temperature

°C
35
30
25
20
15
10
5

Scale 1 : 80 000 000

0   500   1000 km

July

January

Precipitation

mm
over 500
300–500
200–300
100–200
50–100
25–50
10–25
0–10
no recorded precipitation

Scale 1 : 80 000 000

0   500   1000 km

July

January

See page 104 for climate graphs relating to climate stations shown on the maps.

ALGERS
Altitude 61 m

TAMANRASSET
Altitude 1283 m

WADI HALFA
Altitude 125 m

FREETOWN
Altitude 11m

KANO
Altitude 469 m

ĀDĪS ĀBEBA
Altitude 2450 m

NAIROBI
Altitude 1646 m

KINSHASA
Altitude 325 m

BULAWAYO
Altitude 1339 m

WINDHOEK
Altitude 1665 m

CAPE TOWN
Altitude 12 m

arable, predominantly cereals

arable, predominantly paddy

general arable

arable with cash crops

irrigated crops

grazing and dry farming

deciduous forest, farming and grazing

mixed forest, farming and grazing

tropical dry forest and savanna, farming and grazing

tropical rain forest, lumbering, crops,

desert, nomadic herding

marsh or swamp

Scale 1 : 44 000 000

0   500   1000 km

Tsetse fly

infected areas

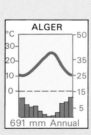

ALGER

691 mm Annual

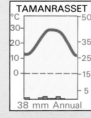

TAMANRASSET

38 mm Annual

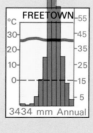

FREETOWN

3434 mm Annual

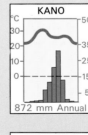

KANO

872 mm Annual

KINSHASA

1371 mm Annual

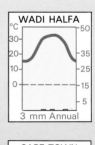

WADI HALFA

3 mm Annual

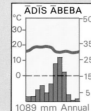

ĀDĪS ĀBEBA

1089 mm Annual

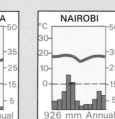

NAIROBI

926 mm Annual

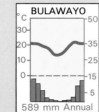

BULAWAYO

589 mm Annual

WINDHOEK

370 mm Annual

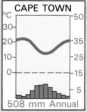

CAPE TOWN

508 mm Annual

Precipitation figures on graphs in tens of millimetres except for annual totals

Zenithal Equal Area Project

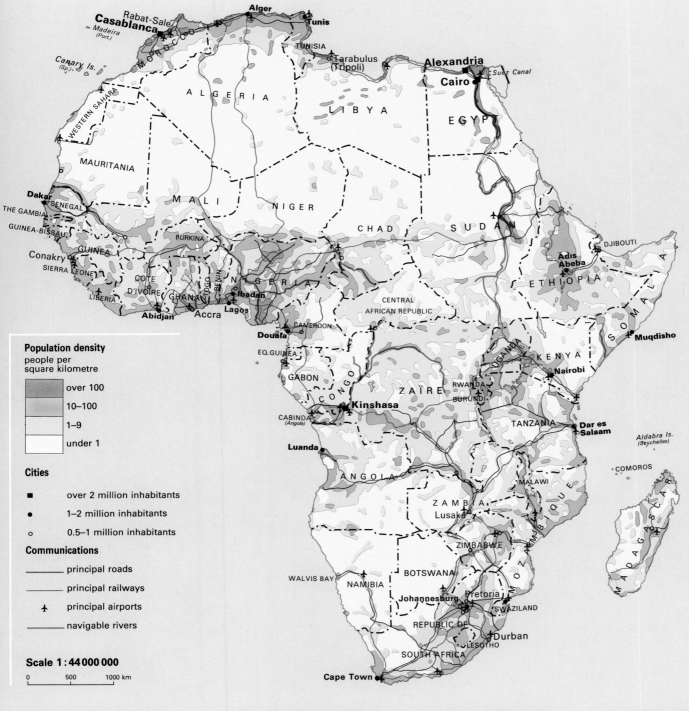

Rabat-Salé
Casablanca
Madeira (Port.)
Canary Is. *(Sp.)*
Alger
Tunis
TUNISIA
Tarabulus (Tripoli)
Alexandria
Suez Canal
Cairo
MOROCCO
WESTERN SAHARA
ALGERIA
LIBYA
EGYPT
MAURITANIA
Dakar
SENEGAL
THE GAMBIA
GUINEA-BISSAU
Conakry
GUINEA
SIERRA LEONE
LIBERIA
COTE D'IVOIRE
GHANA
TOGO
BENIN
MALI
BURKINA
NIGER
NIGERIA
CHAD
SUDAN
DJIBOUTI
Adis Abeba
ETHIOPIA
SOMALIA
Muqdisho
Ibadan
Lagos
Abidjan
Accra
CAMEROON
Douala
EQ.GUINEA
GABON
CONGO
CENTRAL AFRICAN REPUBLIC
ZAÏRE
Kinshasa
CABINDA *(Angola)*
UGANDA
KENYA
Nairobi
RWANDA
BURUNDI
TANZANIA
Dar es Salaam
Aldabra Is. *(Seychelles)*
Luanda
ANGOLA
ZAMBIA
Lusaka
MALAWI
COMOROS
MADAGASCAR
ZIMBABWE
MOZAMBIQUE
BOTSWANA
WALVIS BAY
NAMIBIA
Johannesburg
Pretoria
SWAZILAND
Durban
REPUBLIC OF
LESOTHO
SOUTH AFRICA
Cape Town

Population density
people per
square kilometre

over 100
10–100
1–9
under 1

Cities

■ over 2 million inhabitants
● 1–2 million inhabitants
○ 0.5–1 million inhabitants

Communications

───── principal roads
───── principal railways
✈ principal airports
───── navigable rivers

Scale 1 : 44 000 000

0   500   1000 km

© Oxford University Press

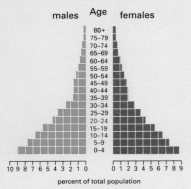

Algeria:Population, 1984

males   Age   females

80+
75–79
70–74
65–69
60–64
55–59
50–54
45–49
40–44
35–39
30–34
25–29
20–24
15–19
10–14
5–9
0–4

10 9 8 7 6 5 4 3 2 1 0   0 1 2 3 4 5 6 7 8 9

percent of total population

Total Population:20.8 million

Crude Birth Rate per thousand:37

Crude Death Rate per thousand:10

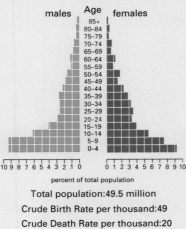

Ethiopia:Population, 1989

males   Age   females

85+
80–84
75–79
70–74
65–69
60–64
55–59
50–54
45–49
40–44
35–39
30–34
25–29
20–24
15–19
10–14
5–9
0–4

10 9 8 7 6 5 4 3 2 1 0   0 1 2 3 4 5 6 7 8 9 10

percent of total population

Total population:49.5 million

Crude Birth Rate per thousand:49

Crude Death Rate per thousand:20

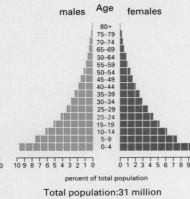

Zaïre:Population, 1985

males   Age   females

80+
75–79
70–74
65–69
60–64
55–59
50–54
45–49
40–44
35–39
30–34
25–29
20–24
15–19
10–14
5–9
0–4

10 9 8 7 6 5 4 3 2 1 0   0 1 2 3 4 5 6 7 8 9 10

percent of total population

Total population:31 million

Crude Birth Rate per thousand:46

Crude Death Rate per thousand:14

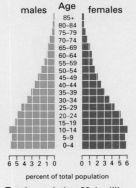

South Africa:Population, 1985

males   Age   females

85+
80–84
75–79
70–74
65–69
60–64
55–59
50–54
45–49
40–44
35–39
30–34
25–29
20–24
15–19
10–14
5–9
0–4

6 5 4 3 2 1 0   0 1 2 3 4 5 6

percent of total population

Total population:23.4 million

Crude Birth Rate per thousand:35

Crude Death Rate per thousand:8

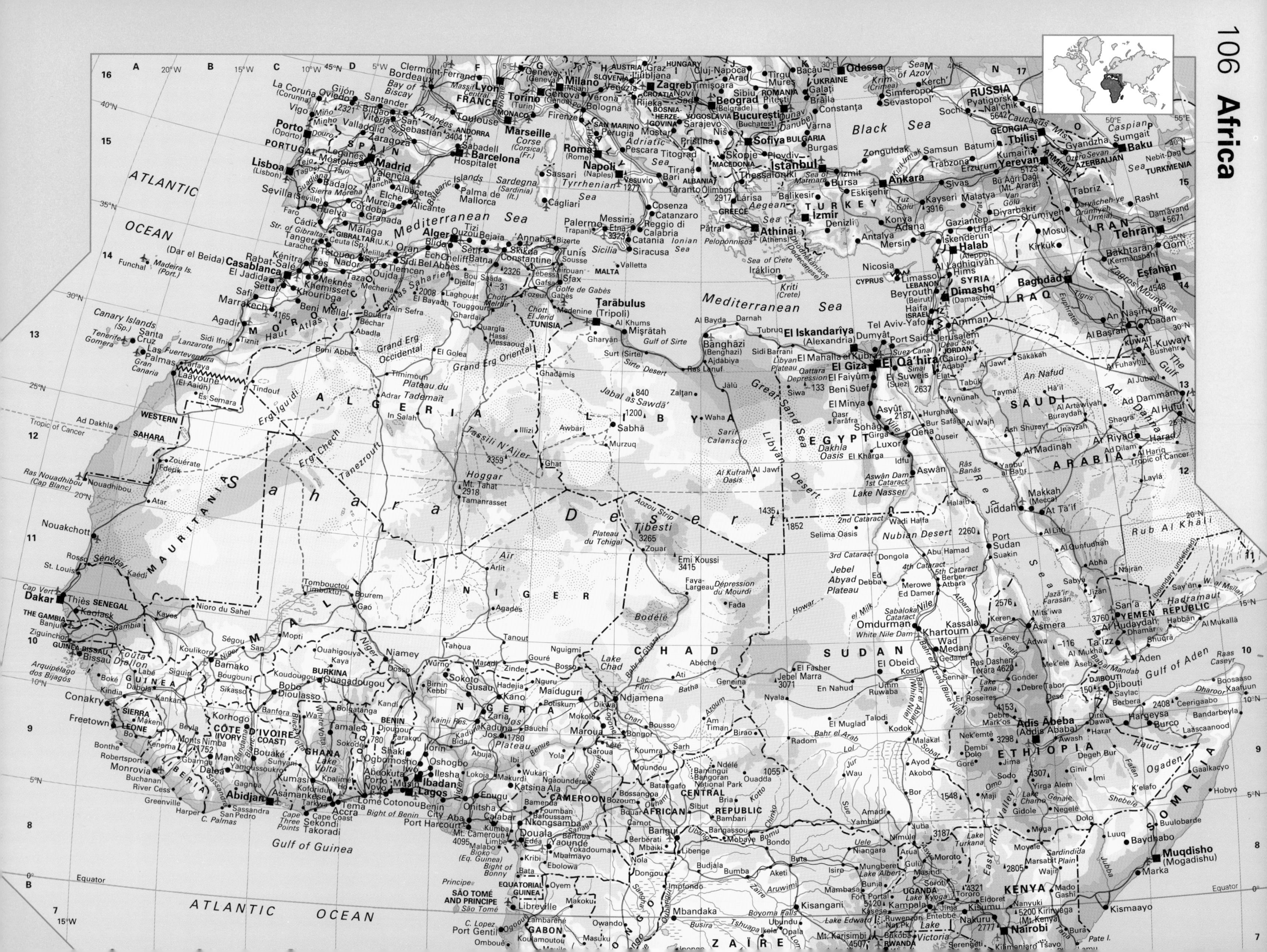

ATLANTIC OCEAN
Mediterranean Sea
Black Sea
Red Sea
Gulf of Guinea
Gulf of Aden
Sahara Desert
Libyan Desert
Nubian Desert
Great Sand Sea
SUDAN
CHAD
NIGER
ALGERIA
LIBYA
EGYPT
MAURITANIA
MALI
NIGERIA
ETHIOPIA
SOMALIA
KENYA
ZAÏRE
SAUDI ARABIA
IRAQ
IRAN
TURKEY
SPAIN
WESTERN SAHARA
CAMEROON
CENTRAL AFRICAN REPUBLIC

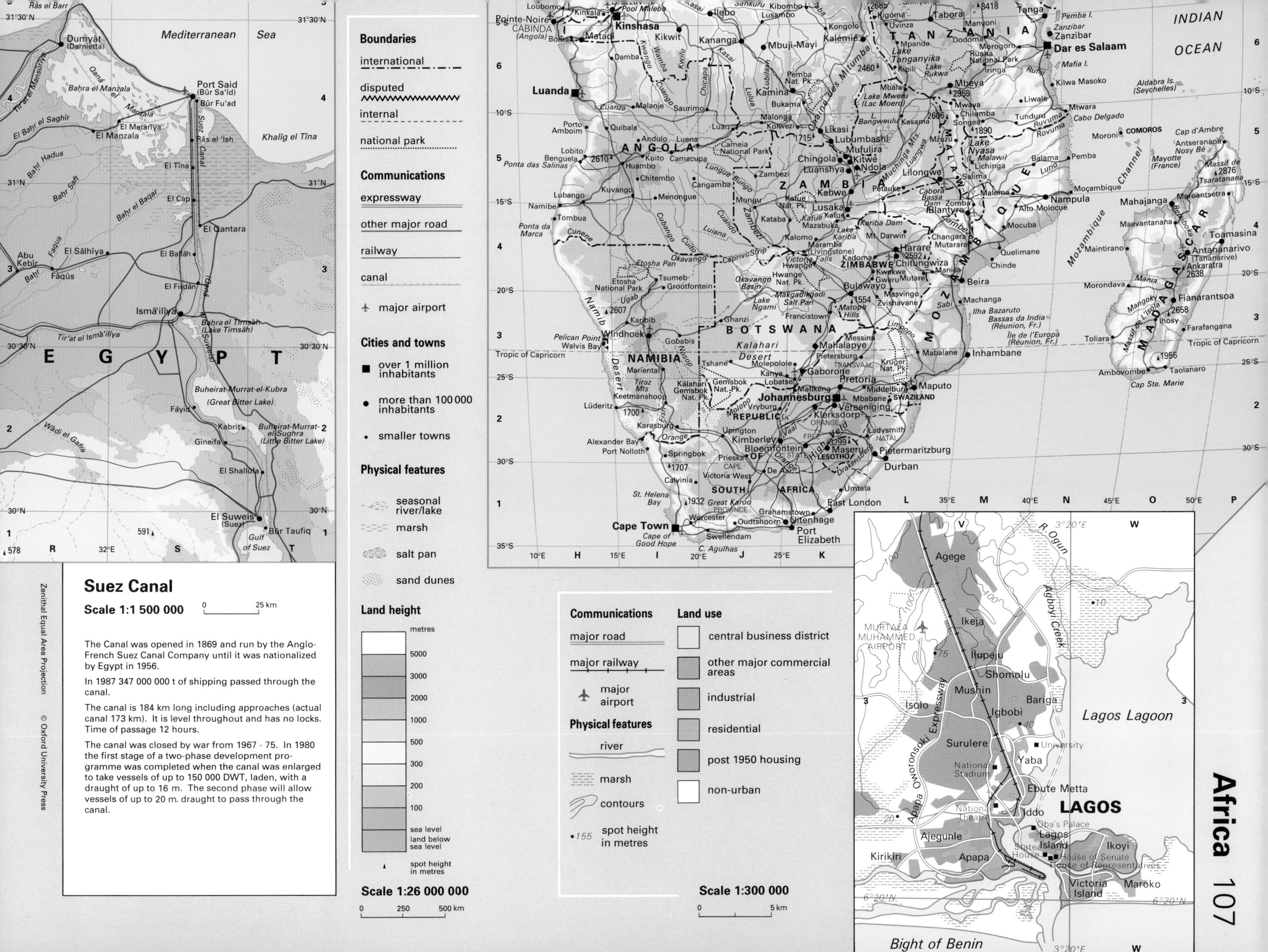

Suez Canal

Scale 1:1 500 000

0 ___ 25 km

The Canal was opened in 1869 and run by the Anglo-French Suez Canal Company until it was nationalized by Egypt in 1956.

In 1987 347 000 000 t of shipping passed through the canal.

The canal is 184 km long including approaches (actual canal 173 km). It is level throughout and has no locks. Time of passage 12 hours.

The canal was closed by war from 1967 - 75. In 1980 the first stage of a two-phase development programme was completed when the canal was enlarged to take vessels of up to 150 000 DWT, laden, with a draught of up to 16 m. The second phase will allow vessels of up to 20 m. draught to pass through the canal.

Zenithal Equal Area Projection   © Oxford University Press

Boundaries
- — · — international
- ⌃⌃⌃⌃⌃⌃ disputed
- — — — internal
- ········· national park

Communications
- ═════ expressway
- ───── other major road
- ───── railway
- ───── canal
- ✈ major airport

Cities and towns
- ■ over 1 million inhabitants
- ● more than 100 000 inhabitants
- · smaller towns

Physical features
- ⌇⌇⌇ seasonal river/lake
- ⌇⌇⌇ marsh
- ░░░ salt pan
- ∴∴∴ sand dunes

Land height

metres
| 5000 |
| 3000 |
| 2000 |
| 1000 |
| 500 |
| 300 |
| 200 |
| 100 |
| sea level |
| land below sea level |
▲ spot height in metres

Scale 1:26 000 000

0 ___ 250 ___ 500 km

Communications
- ───── major road
- ┼┼┼┼┼ major railway
- ✈ major airport

Physical features
- ⌇⌇⌇ river
- ⌇⌇⌇ marsh
- ┈┈┈ contours
- ·155 spot height in metres

Land use
- central business district
- other major commercial areas
- industrial
- residential
- post 1950 housing
- non-urban

Scale 1:300 000

0 ___ 5 km

Key place names (main map)

INDIAN OCEAN

MADAGASCAR

Cap d'Ambre, Nosy Bé, Antseranana, Massif de 2876, Antsiranana, Toamasina, Mahajanga, Antananarivo, Fianarantsoa, Farafangana, Toliara, Taolanaro

Aldabra Is. (Seychelles), COMOROS, Moroni, Mayotte (France), Cap Ste. Marie

TANZANIA, Dar es Salaam, Zanzibar, Pemba I., Mafia I., Tanga, Tabora, Dodoma, Morogoro, Mwanza, Mbeya, Iringa

Lake Victoria, Lake Tanganyika, Lake Nyasa, Lake Malawi

MOZAMBIQUE, Nampula, Beira, Maputo, Inhambane, Quelimane, Mozambique

MALAWI, Lilongwe, Blantyre, Lake Malawi

ZAMBIA, Lusaka, Kitwe, Ndola, Kabwe, Livingstone

ZIMBABWE, Harare, Bulawayo, Gweru, Mutare, Kariba Dam, Victoria Falls

BOTSWANA, Gaborone, Francistown, Kalahari Desert, Okavango Basin

NAMIBIA, Windhoek, Walvis Bay, Lüderitz, Namib Desert, Etosha National Park

ANGOLA, Luanda, Lobito, Benguela, Huambo, Cabinda

Kinshasa, Matadi, Pointe-Noire

SOUTH AFRICA, Pretoria, Johannesburg, Kimberley, Bloemfontein, Durban, Pietermaritzburg, East London, Port Elizabeth, Cape Town, Cape of Good Hope

LESOTHO, Maseru

SWAZILAND, Mbabane

Egypt / Suez map labels

Mediterranean Sea, Port Said (Bûr Sa'îd), Damietta (Dumyât), El Mansûra, Ismâ'ilîya, Lake Timsah (Buheirat-Murrat-el-Kubra), Great Bitter Lake, Little Bitter Lake, El Suweis (Suez), Gulf of Suez, EGYPT

Lagos map labels

LAGOS, Lagos Lagoon, Agboyi Creek, R. Ogun, Agege, Ikeja, Mushin, Yaba, Ebute Metta, Iddo, Apapa, Victoria Island, Ikoyi, Surulere, National Stadium, National Theatre, Murtala Muhammed Airport, Bight of Benin

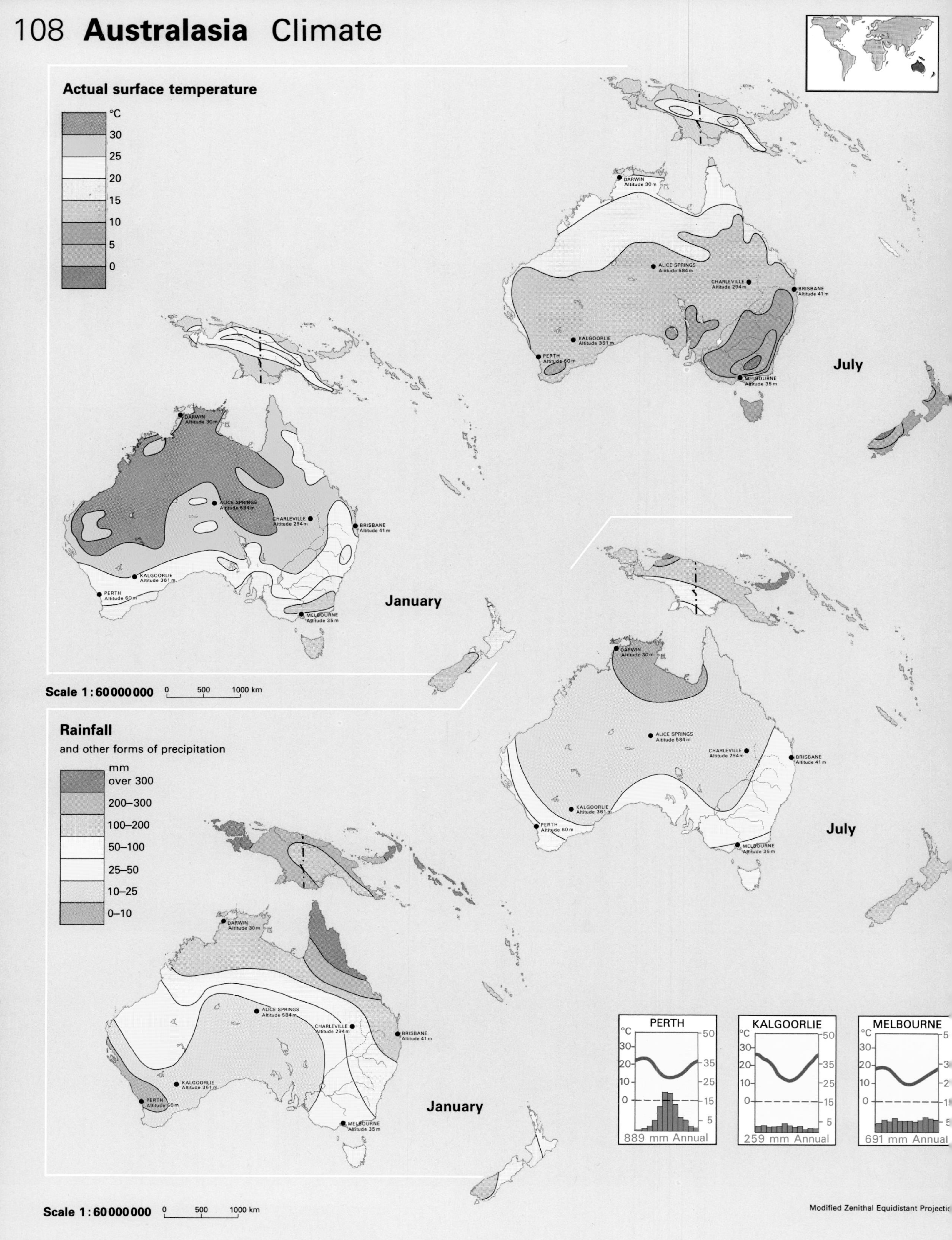

Actual surface temperature

°C
30
25
20
15
10
5
0

July

January

Scale 1 : 60 000 000   0   500   1000 km

Rainfall

and other forms of precipitation

mm
over 300
200–300
100–200
50–100
25–50
10–25
0–10

July

January

Scale 1 : 60 000 000   0   500   1000 km

DARWIN
Altitude 30 m

ALICE SPRINGS
Altitude 584 m

CHARLEVILLE
Altitude 294 m

BRISBANE
Altitude 41 m

KALGOORLIE
Altitude 361 m

PERTH
Altitude 60 m

MELBOURNE
Altitude 35 m

PERTH
°C   50
30   35
20
10   25
0   15
5
889 mm Annual

KALGOORLIE
°C   50
30   35
20
10   25
0   15
5
259 mm Annual

MELBOURNE
°C   5
30
20   3
10
0   1
5
691 mm Annual

Modified Zenithal Equidistant Projection

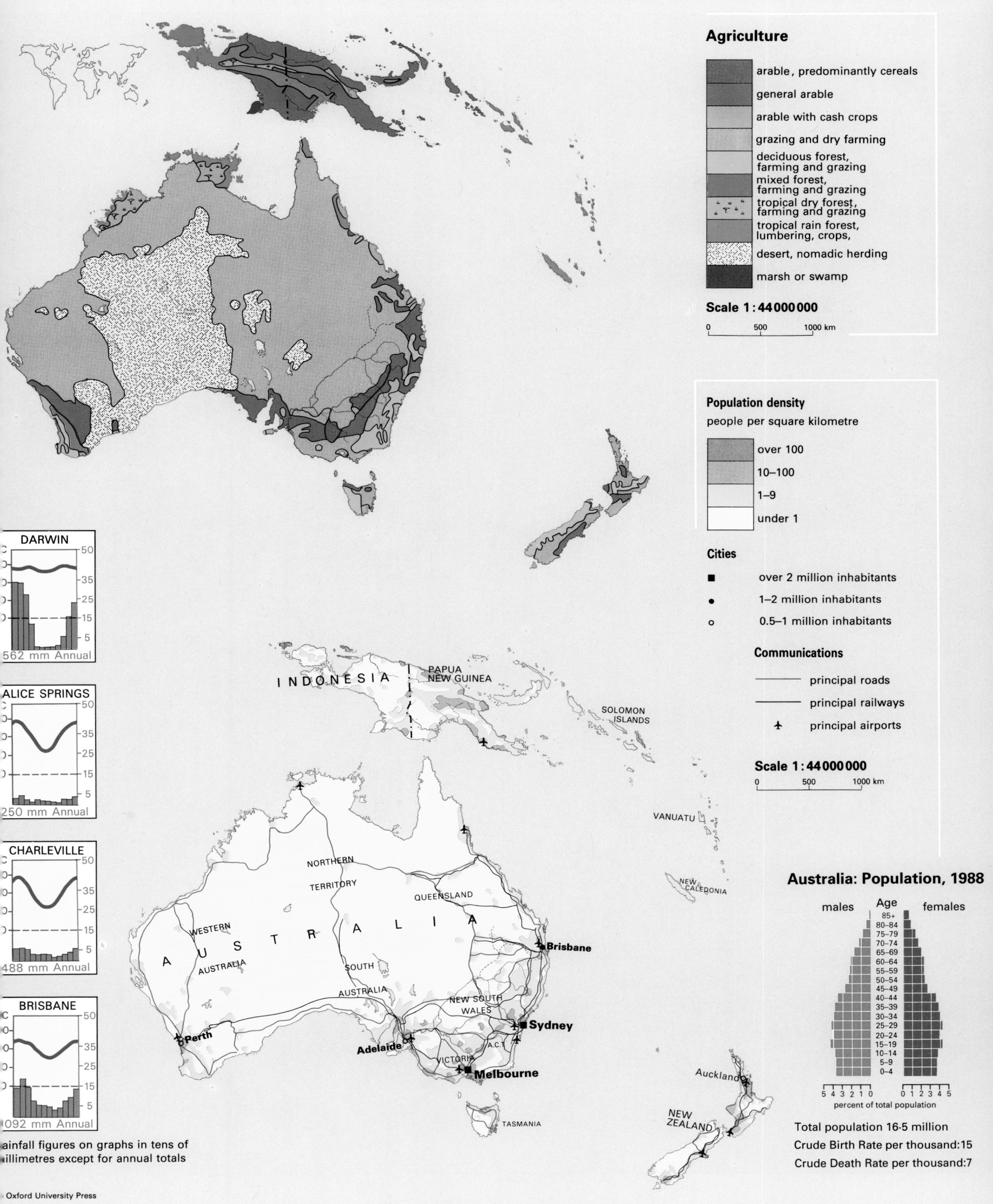

Agriculture

- arable, predominantly cereals
- general arable
- arable with cash crops
- grazing and dry farming
- deciduous forest, farming and grazing
- mixed forest, farming and grazing
- tropical dry forest, farming and grazing
- tropical rain forest, lumbering, crops,
- desert, nomadic herding
- marsh or swamp

Scale 1:44 000 000

0   500   1000 km

Population density

people per square kilometre

- over 100
- 10–100
- 1–9
- under 1

Cities

■ over 2 million inhabitants

● 1–2 million inhabitants

○ 0.5–1 million inhabitants

Communications

— principal roads

— principal railways

✈ principal airports

Scale 1:44 000 000

0   500   1000 km

DARWIN
562 mm Annual

ALICE SPRINGS
250 mm Annual

CHARLEVILLE
488 mm Annual

BRISBANE
1092 mm Annual

rainfall figures on graphs in tens of millimetres except for annual totals

INDONESIA

PAPUA NEW GUINEA

SOLOMON ISLANDS

VANUATU

NEW CALEDONIA

NORTHERN TERRITORY

QUEENSLAND

WESTERN AUSTRALIA

A U S T R A L I A

SOUTH AUSTRALIA

NEW SOUTH WALES

A.C.T.

VICTORIA

TASMANIA

○ Perth

Adelaide ○

■ Sydney

■ Melbourne

■ Brisbane

Auckland ○

NEW ZEALAND

Australia: Population, 1988

males	Age	females
	85+	
	80–84	
	75–79	
	70–74	
	65–69	
	60–64	
	55–59	
	50–54	
	45–49	
	40–44	
	35–39	
	30–34	
	25–29	
	20–24	
	15–19	
	10–14	
	5–9	
	0–4	

5 4 3 2 1 0   0 1 2 3 4 5
percent of total population

Total population 16·5 million

Crude Birth Rate per thousand: 15

Crude Death Rate per thousand: 7

Oxford University Press

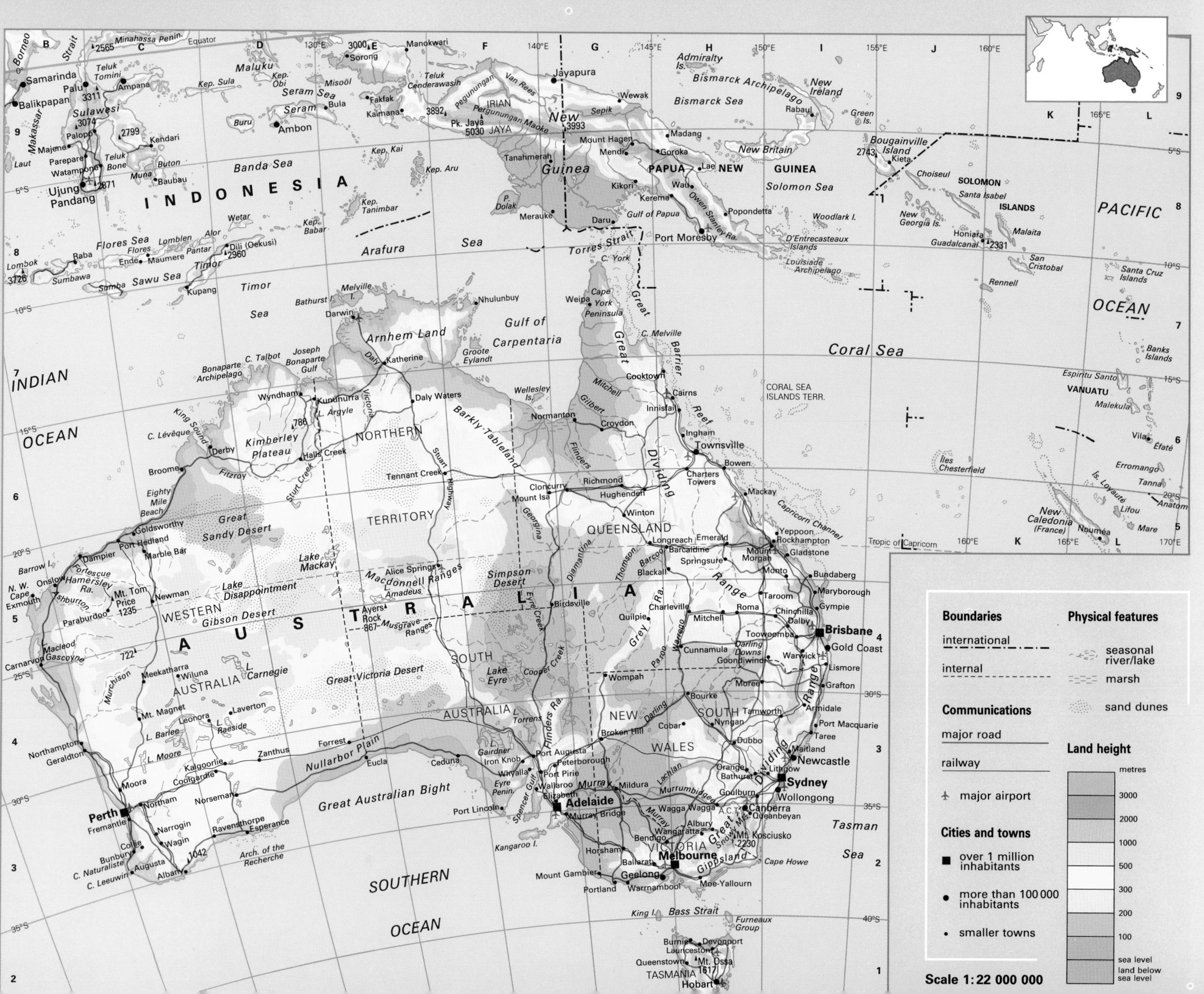

Zenithal Equidistant Project

© Oxford University Press

Boundaries
international
internal
Communications
major road
railway
major airport
Cities and towns
over 1 million inhabitants
more than 100 000 inhabitants
smaller towns
Physical features
seasonal river/lake
marsh
sand dunes
Land height
metres
3000
2000
1000
500
300
200
100
sea level
land below sea level
Scale 1:22 000 000
PACIFIC OCEAN
Coral Sea
Tasman Sea
SOUTHERN OCEAN
INDIAN OCEAN
Great Australian Bight
Gulf of Carpentaria
Arafura Sea
Timor Sea
Banda Sea
Solomon Sea
Bismarck Sea
I N D O N E S I A
A U S T R A L I A
PAPUA NEW GUINEA
SOLOMON ISLANDS
VANUATU
New Caledonia (France)
QUEENSLAND
NEW SOUTH WALES
VICTORIA
SOUTH AUSTRALIA
WESTERN AUSTRALIA
NORTHERN TERRITORY
TASMANIA
Great Dividing Range
Sydney
Melbourne
Brisbane
Adelaide
Perth
Canberra
Hobart
Darwin
Port Moresby

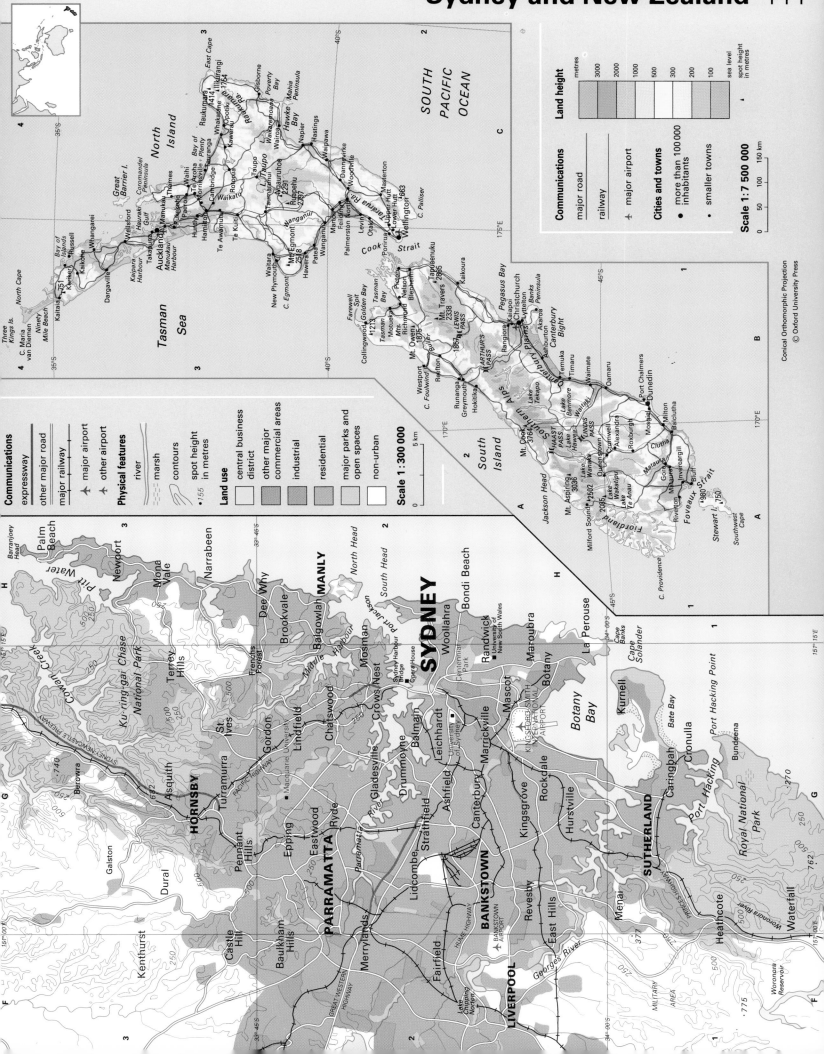

Land height

metres	
	3000
	2000
	1000
	500
	300
	200
	100
sea level	
▲	spot height in metres

Communications
— major road
—— railway
✈ major airport

Cities and towns
● more than 100 000 inhabitants
• smaller towns

Scale 1:7 500 000

0   50   100   150 km

Conical Orthomorphic Projection
© Oxford University Press

Communications
expressway
other major road
major railway
✈ major airport
✈ other airport

Physical features
—— river
=== marsh
contours
•155 spot height in metres

Land use
central business district
other major commercial areas
industrial
residential
major parks and open spaces
non-urban

Scale 1:300 000

0   5 km

North Island

Three Kings Is.
C. Maria van Diemen
North Cape
Ninety Mile Beach
Kaitaia
Kerikeri 351
Bay of Islands
Russell
Kaikohe
Whangarei
Dargaville
Wellsford
Kaipara Harbour
Great Barrier I.
Hauraki Gulf
Coromandel Peninsula
Takapuna
Auckland
Manukau
Manukau Harbour
Waiuku
Pukekohe
Thames
Paeroa
Waihi
Te Aroha
Morrinsville
Cambridge
Hamilton
Waikato
Te Awamutu
Te Kuiti
Waitara
New Plymouth
C. Egmont
Mt Egmont 2518
Hawera
Patea
Wanganui
Waikaremoana
East Cape
Hikurangi 1754
Raukumara 1414
Ruatoria
Opotiki
Whakatane
Tauranga
Bay of Plenty
Rotorua
Tarawera
Te Anga
Taupo
L. Taupo
Tongariro 1968
Ngauruhoe 2291
Ruapehu 2797
Waiouru
Manganui
Gisborne
Poverty Bay
Mahia Peninsula
Wairoa
Napier
Hastings
Waipawa
Dannevirke
Woodville
Masterton
Pahiatua
Palmerston North
Feilding
Marton
Levin
Otaki
Upper Hutt
Lower Hutt 1463
Porirua
Wellington
Cook Strait
C. Palliser

South Island

Farewell Spit
Golden Bay
Collingwood
Tasman Bay
Takaka
Motueka
Tasman Mts.
Mt Owen 1875
Nelson
Richmond
Blenheim
Picton
Tapuaenuku 2885
Kaikoura
Mt Travers 2338
Westport
Runanga
Greymouth
Hokitika
C. Foulwind
Buller
Reefton
ARTHUR'S PASS
LEWIS PASS
Southern Alps
Mt Cook 3764
HAAST PASS
Mt Aspiring 3036
Jackson Head
Milford Sound
Fiordland
Southwest Cape
Stewart I.
Foveaux Strait
Te Anau
Lake Te Anau
Lake Manapouri
Riverton
Invercargill
Bluff
980
750
Gore
Mataura
Balclutha
Clutha
Milton
Mosgiel
Dunedin
Port Chalmers
Oamaru
Waitaki
Lake Benmore
Lake Tekapo
Lake Pukaki
Lindis Pass
Alexandra
Roxburgh
Lumsden
Queenstown
Lake Wakatipu 2502
Lake Wanaka
Lake Hawea
Cromwell
2085
Timaru
Temuka
Ashburton
Rangiora
Kaiapoi
Christchurch
Lyttelton
Akaroa
Banks Peninsula
Canterbury Plains
Canterbury Bight
Pegasus Bay

SOUTH PACIFIC OCEAN
Tasman Sea

Sydney

Barranjoey Head
Palm Beach
Pitt Water
Newport
Mona Vale
Narrabeen
Dee Why
Brookvale
MANLY
Balgowlah
North Head
South Head
Middle Harbour
Mosman
Crows Nest
Port Jackson
Sydney Harbour Bridge
Opera House
SYDNEY
Woollahra
Bondi Beach
Centennial Park
Randwick
University of New South Wales
Maroubra
La Perouse
Cape Banks
Botany
Mascot
KINGSFORD-SMITH INTERNATIONAL AIRPORT
Botany Bay
Cape Solander
Kurnell
Port Hacking
Port Hacking Point
Cronulla
Caringbah
Bundeena
Bate Bay
SUTHERLAND
Menai
Heathcote
Royal National Park
Waterfall
762
Woronora Reservoir
Woronora River
Georges River
PRINCES HIGHWAY
East Hills
Revesby
Kingsgrove
Hurstville
Rockdale
Canterbury
Marrickville
Ashfield
Leichhardt
University of Sydney
Balmain
Drummoyne
Strathfield
Lidcombe
377
BANKSTOWN AIRPORT
BANKSTOWN
Fairfield
Merrylands
HUME HIGHWAY
L. Chipping Norton
LIVERPOOL
GREAT WESTERN HIGHWAY
MILITARY AREA
Gladesville
Ryde
Parramatta River
PARRAMATTA
Eastwood
Epping
PACIFIC HIGHWAY
Lindfield
Chatswood
Gordon
St Ives
Frenchs Forest
Terrey Hills
Ku-ring-gai Chase National Park
Turramurra
Asquith
HORNSBY
632
Pennant Hills
Berowra
Cowan Creek
SYDNEY-NEWCASTLE FREEWAY
Galston
Dural
Kenthurst
Castle Hill
Baulkham Hills
740
775
270
500
250

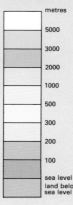
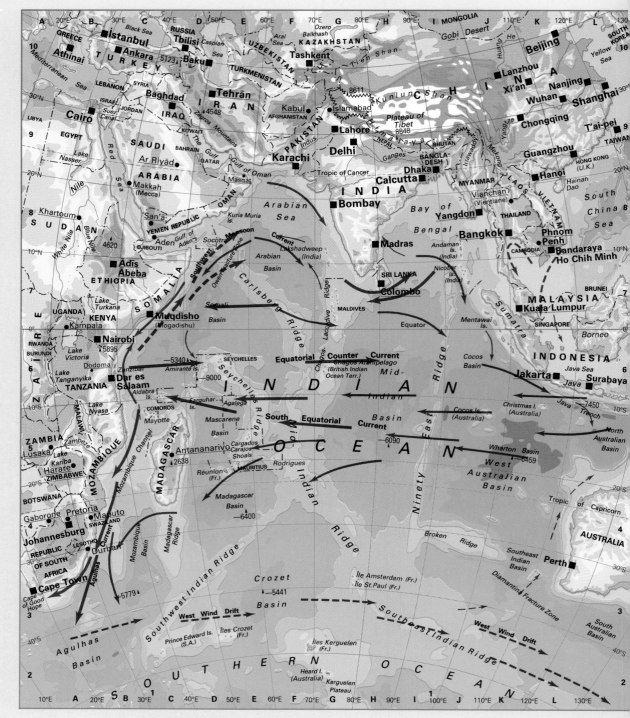
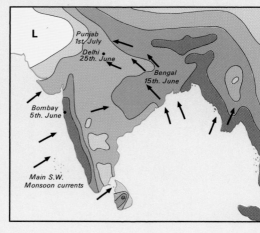
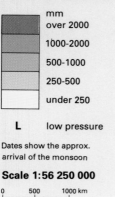

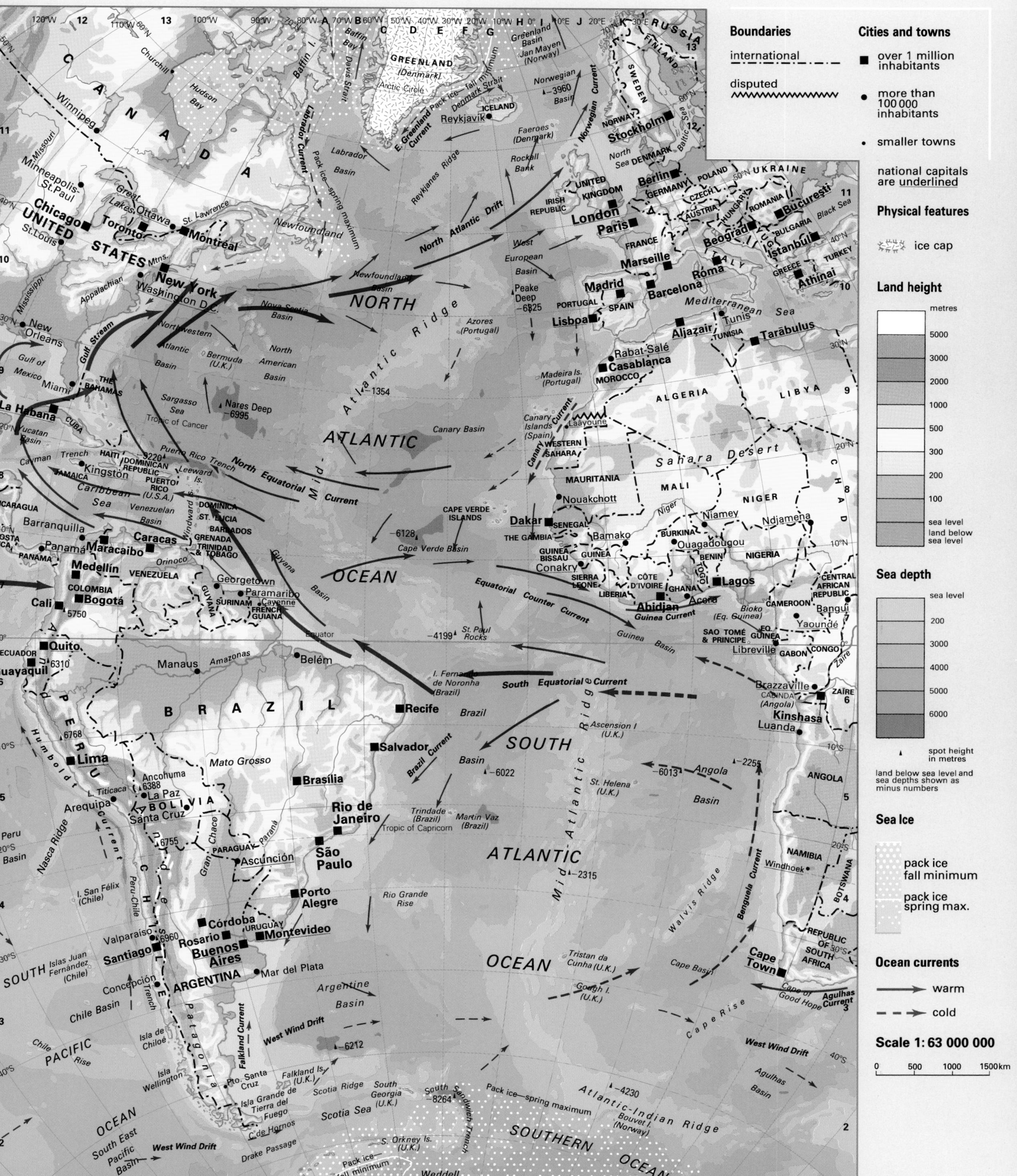

Boundaries

international – · – · – · –

disputed ~~~~~

Cities and towns

■ over 1 million inhabitants

● more than 100 000 inhabitants

• smaller towns

national capitals are <u>underlined</u>

Physical features

ice cap

Land height

	metres
	5000
	3000
	2000
	1000
	500
	300
	200
	100
	sea level
	land below sea level

Sea depth

	sea level
	200
	3000
	4000
	5000
	6000

▲ spot height in metres

land below sea level and sea depths shown as minus numbers

Sea Ice

pack ice fall minimum

pack ice spring max.

Ocean currents

→ warm

⇢ cold

Scale 1 : 63 000 000

0 500 1000 1500km

Modified Zenithal Equidistant Projection

© Oxford University Press

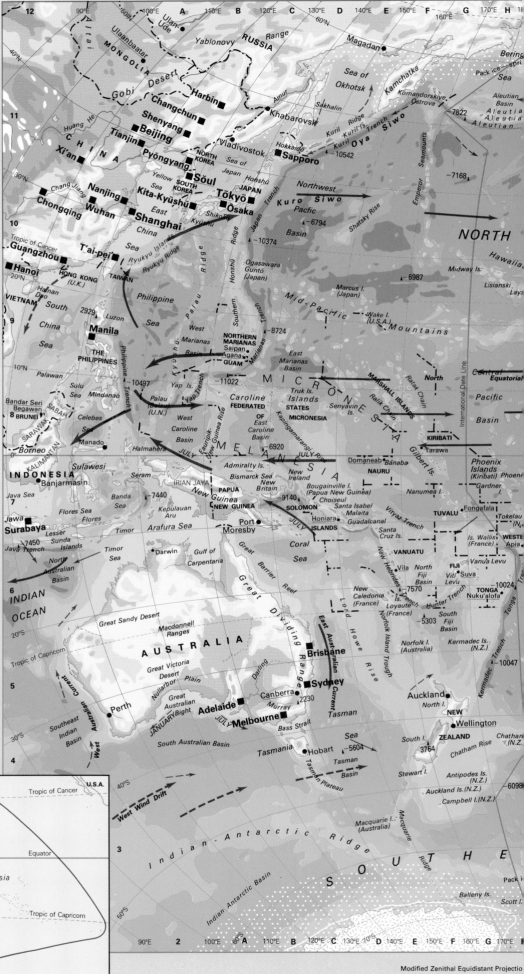

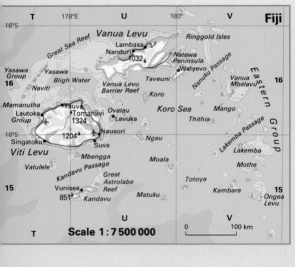

Fiji
Scale 1:7 500 000

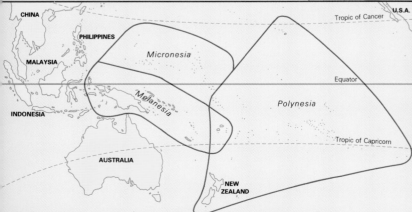

Subregions of Oceania

Modified Zenithal Equidistant Projection

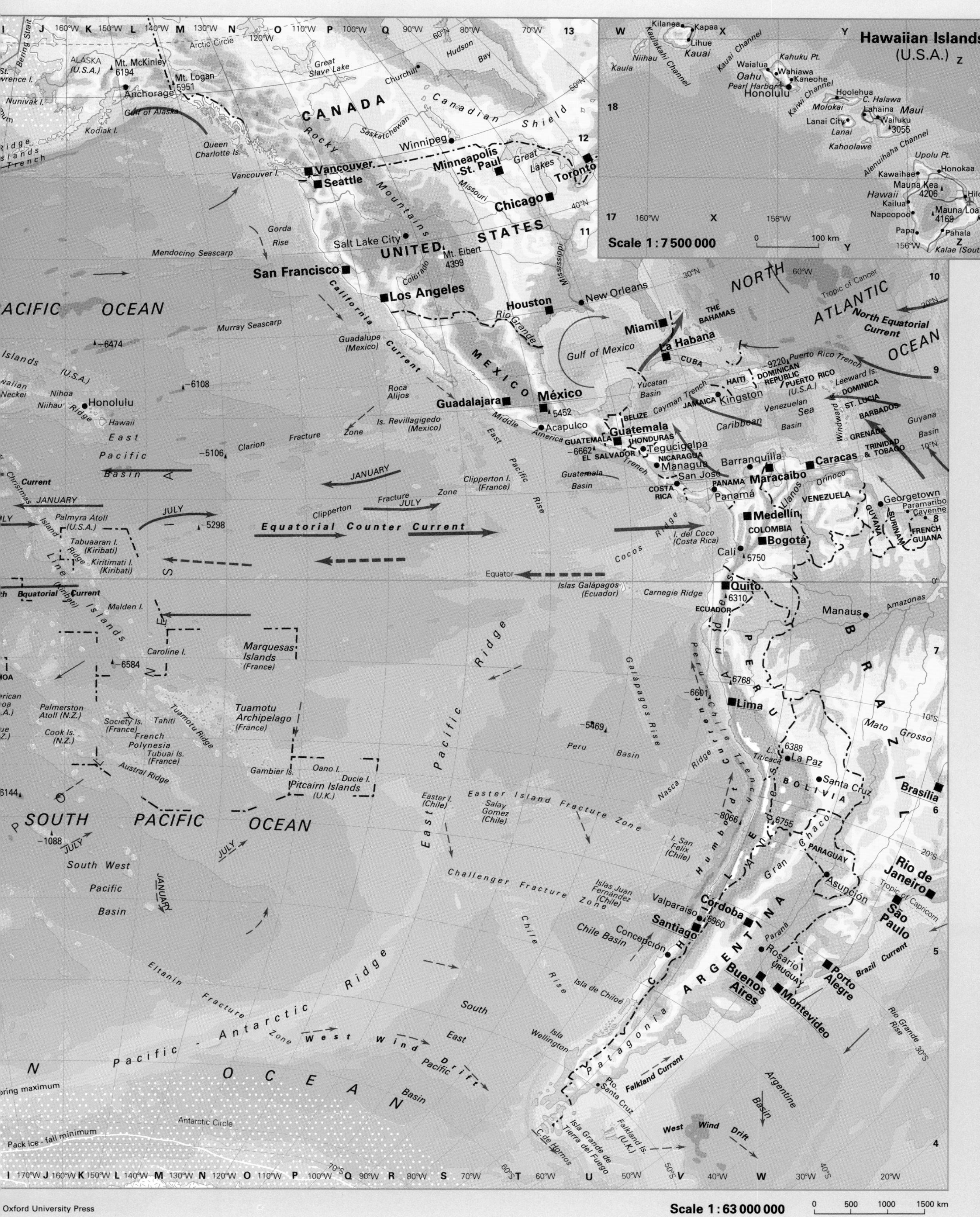

Hawaiian Islands (U.S.A.)

Scale 1 : 7 500 000

0   100 km

Scale 1 : 63 000 000

0   500   1000   1500 km

Oxford University Press

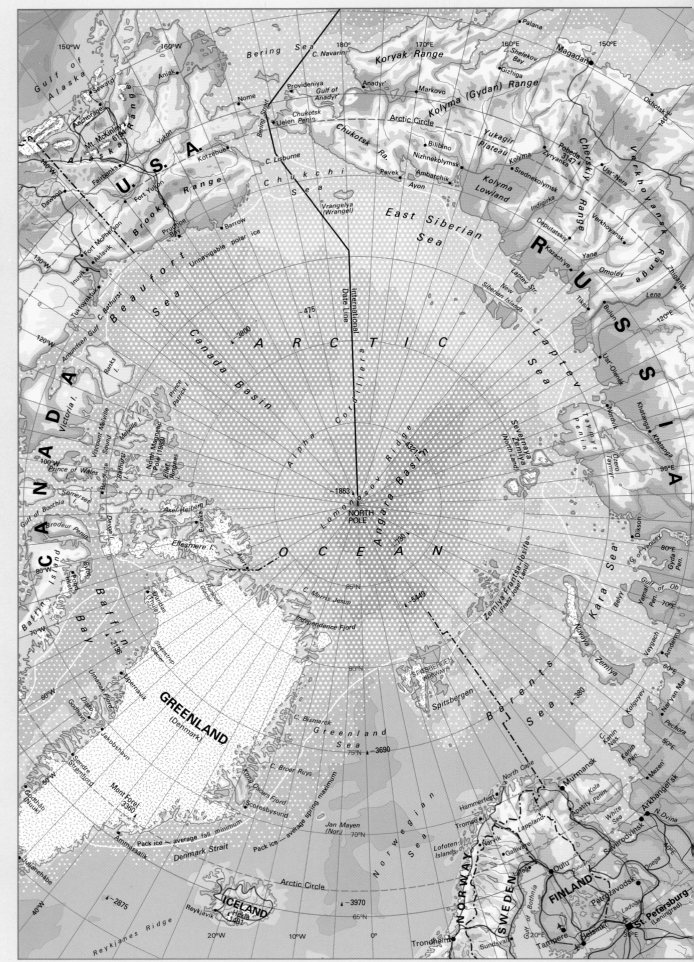

Zenithal Equidistant Projection

© Oxford University Press

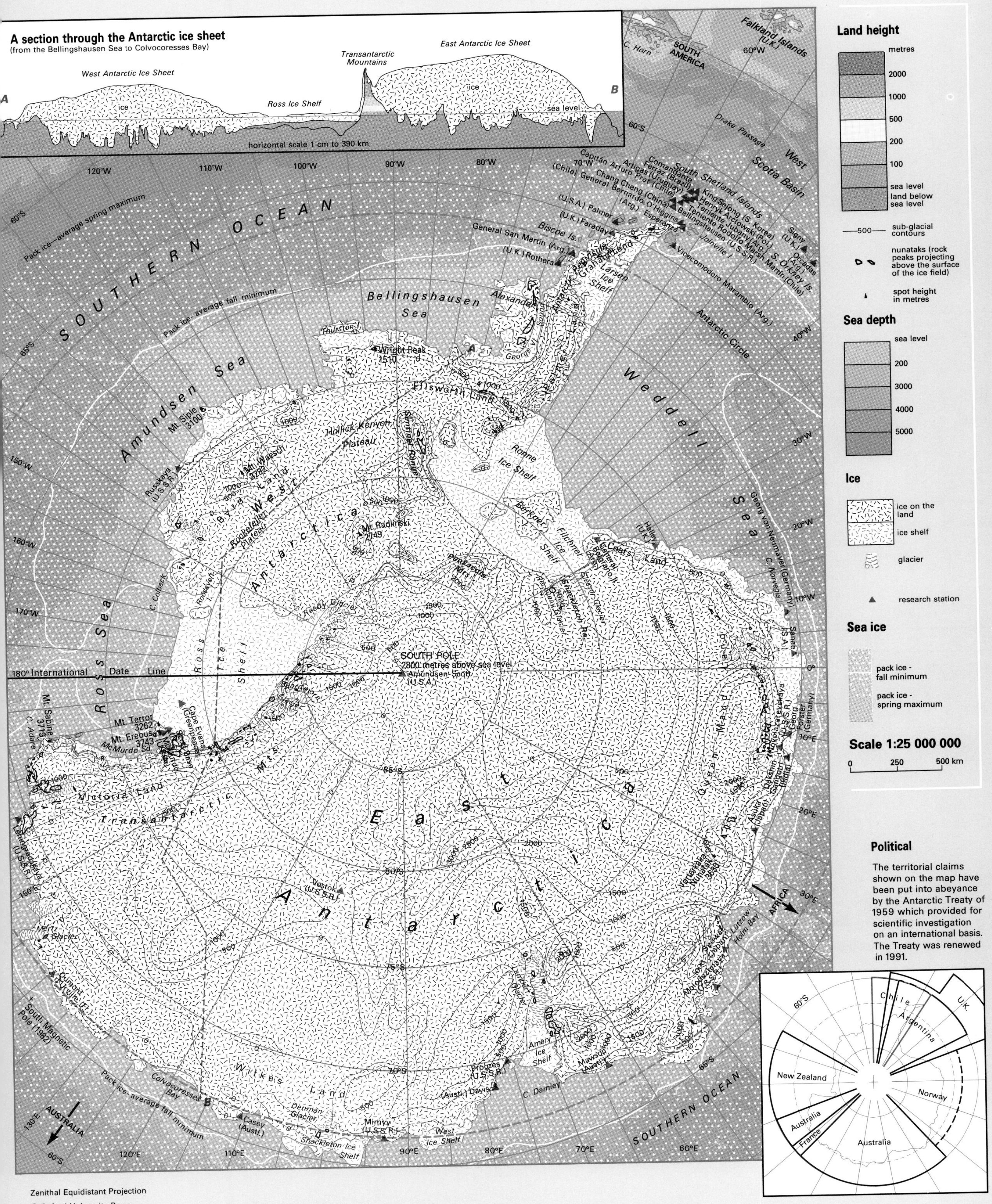
A section through the Antarctic ice sheet
(from the Bellingshausen Sea to Colvocoresses Bay)
West Antarctic Ice Sheet
Transantarctic Mountains
East Antarctic Ice Sheet
Ross Ice Shelf
ice
sea level
A
B
horizontal scale 1 cm to 390 km
Land height
metres
2000
1000
500
200
100
sea level
land below sea level
sub-glacial contours
nunataks (rock peaks projecting above the surface of the ice field)
spot height in metres
Sea depth
sea level
200
3000
4000
5000
Ice
ice on the land
ice shelf
glacier
research station
Sea ice
pack ice - fall minimum
pack ice - spring maximum
Scale 1:25 000 000
0
250
500 km
Political
The territorial claims shown on the map have been put into abeyance by the Antarctic Treaty of 1959 which provided for scientific investigation on an international basis. The Treaty was renewed in 1991.
Chile
U.K.
Argentina
New Zealand
Norway
Australia
France
Australia
SOUTHERN OCEAN
SOUTHERN OCEAN
Amundsen Sea
Bellingshausen Sea
Weddell Sea
Ross Sea
Ross Ice Shelf
Ronne Ice Shelf
Filchner Ice Shelf
Amery Ice Shelf
West Ice Shelf
Shackleton Ice Shelf
Larsen Ice Shelf
Scotia Basin
Drake Passage
Falkland Islands (U.K.)
SOUTH AMERICA
C. Horn
South Shetland Islands
S. Orkney Is.
Antarctic Peninsula
Graham Land
Palmer Land
Alexander I.
Ellsworth Land
Marie Byrd Land
West Antarctica
East Antarctica
Queen Maud Land
Coats Land
Victoria Land
Wilkes Land
Transantarctic Mts.
Hollick-Kenyon Plateau
Rockefeller Plateau
Pensacola Mts.
Shackleton Ra.
SOUTH POLE
2800 metres above sea level
Amundsen-Scott (U.S.A.)
Vostok (U.S.S.R.)
Mirnyy (U.S.S.R.)
Casey (Austl.)
Davis (Austl.)
Mawson (Austl.)
Halley (U.K.)
Rothera (U.K.)
Mt. Siple 3100
Mt. Erebus 3743
Mt. Terror 3262
Mt. Sabine 3719
Mt. Radlinski 2749
Wright Peak 1510
McMurdo Sd.
C. Adare
C. Colbeck
C. Darnley
C. Norvegia
Mertz Glacier
Denman Glacier
Lambert Glacier
Beardmore Glacier
Reedy Glacier
Lützow-Holm Bay
Colvocoresses Bay
South Magnetic Pole (1982)
Antarctic Circle
Pack ice—average spring maximum
Pack ice - average fall minimum
180° International Date Line
AFRICA
AUSTRALIA
60°S
65°S
70°S
75°S
80°S
85°S
60°W
40°W
30°W
20°W
10°W
0°
10°E
20°E
30°E
60°E
70°E
80°E
90°E
110°E
120°E
130°E
150°E
170°W
160°W
150°W
120°W
110°W
100°W
90°W
80°W
70°W

Zenithal Equidistant Projection

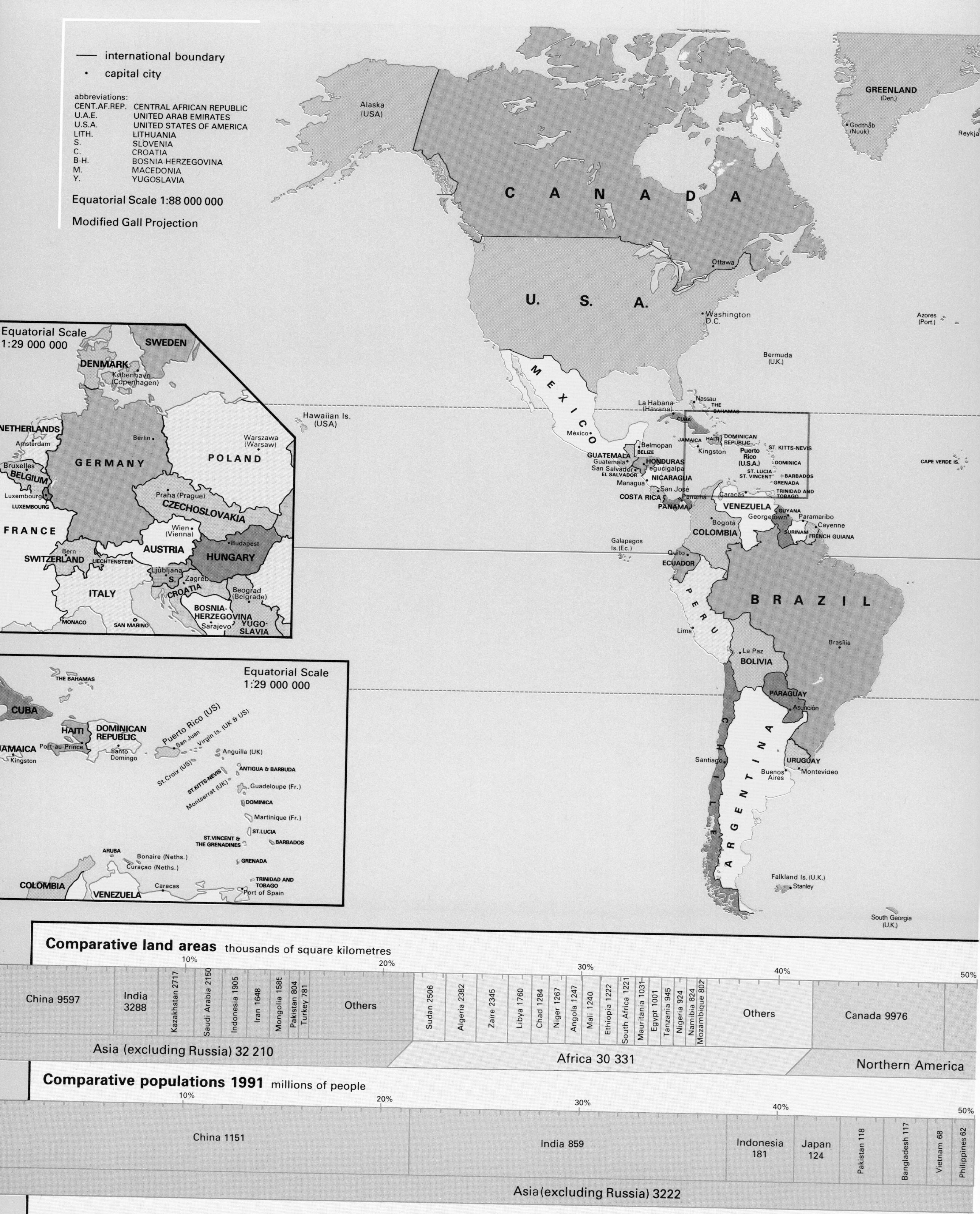

international boundary
capital city
abbreviations:
CENT.AF.REP. CENTRAL AFRICAN REPUBLIC
U.A.E. UNITED ARAB EMIRATES
U.S.A. UNITED STATES OF AMERICA
LITH. LITHUANIA
S. SLOVENIA
C. CROATIA
B-H. BOSNIA-HERZEGOVINA
M. MACEDONIA
Y. YUGOSLAVIA
Equatorial Scale 1:88 000 000
Modified Gall Projection
Alaska (USA)
CANADA
GREENLAND (Den.)
Godthåb (Nuuk)
Ottawa
U.S.A.
Washington D.C.
Azores (Port.)
Bermuda (U.K.)
MEXICO
México
Hawaiian Is. (USA)
La Habana (Havana)
Nassau
THE BAHAMAS
CUBA
JAMAICA
Kingston
HAITI
DOMINICAN REPUBLIC
Puerto Rico (U.S.A.)
ST. KITTS-NEVIS
DOMINICA
ST. LUCIA
ST. VINCENT
BARBADOS
GRENADA
TRINIDAD AND TOBAGO
CAPE VERDE IS.
Belmopan
BELIZE
GUATEMALA
Guatemala
HONDURAS
Tegucigalpa
San Salvador
EL SALVADOR
NICARAGUA
Managua
San José
COSTA RICA
Panamá
PANAMA
Caracas
VENEZUELA
GUYANA
Georgetown
Paramaribo
SURINAM
Cayenne
FRENCH GUIANA
Bogotá
COLOMBIA
Galapagos Is. (Ec.)
Quito
ECUADOR
PERU
Lima
BRAZIL
Brasília
La Paz
BOLIVIA
PARAGUAY
Asunción
CHILE
Santiago
ARGENTINA
URUGUAY
Buenos Aires
Montevideo
Falkland Is. (U.K.)
Stanley
South Georgia (U.K.)
Equatorial Scale 1:29 000 000
SWEDEN
DENMARK
København (Copenhagen)
NETHERLANDS
Amsterdam
Berlin
GERMANY
Warszawa (Warsaw)
POLAND
Bruxelles
BELGIUM
Luxembourg
LUXEMBOURG
Praha (Prague)
CZECHOSLOVAKIA
FRANCE
Wien (Vienna)
AUSTRIA
Budapest
HUNGARY
Bern
SWITZERLAND
LIECHTENSTEIN
Ljubljana
S.
Zagreb
CROATIA
ITALY
Beograd (Belgrade)
BOSNIA-HERZEGOVINA
Sarajevo
YUGOSLAVIA
MONACO
SAN MARINO
Equatorial Scale 1:29 000 000
THE BAHAMAS
CUBA
HAITI
DOMINICAN REPUBLIC
JAMAICA
Port-au-Prince
Kingston
Santo Domingo
Puerto Rico (US)
San Juan
Virgin Is. (UK & US)
Anguilla (UK)
St.Croix (US)
ST.KITTS-NEVIS
ANTIGUA & BARBUDA
Montserrat (UK)
Guadeloupe (Fr.)
DOMINICA
Martinique (Fr.)
ST.LUCIA
ST.VINCENT & THE GRENADINES
BARBADOS
GRENADA
ARUBA
Bonaire (Neths.)
Curaçao (Neths.)
COLOMBIA
VENEZUELA
Caracas
TRINIDAD AND TOBAGO
Port of Spain
Comparative land areas thousands of square kilometres
10%
20%
30%
40%
50%
China 9597
India 3288
Kazakhstan 2717
Saudi Arabia 2150
Indonesia 1905
Iran 1648
Mongolia 1565
Pakistan 804
Turkey 781
Others
Sudan 2506
Algeria 2382
Zaïre 2345
Libya 1760
Chad 1284
Niger 1267
Angola 1247
Mali 1240
Ethiopia 1222
South Africa 1221
Mauritania 1031
Egypt 1001
Tanzania 945
Nigeria 924
Namibia 824
Mozambique 802
Others
Canada 9976
Asia (excluding Russia) 32 210
Africa 30 331
Northern America
Comparative populations 1991 millions of people
10%
20%
30%
40%
50%
China 1151
India 859
Indonesia 181
Japan 124
Pakistan 118
Bangladesh 117
Vietnam 68
Philippines 62
Asia (excluding Russia) 3222

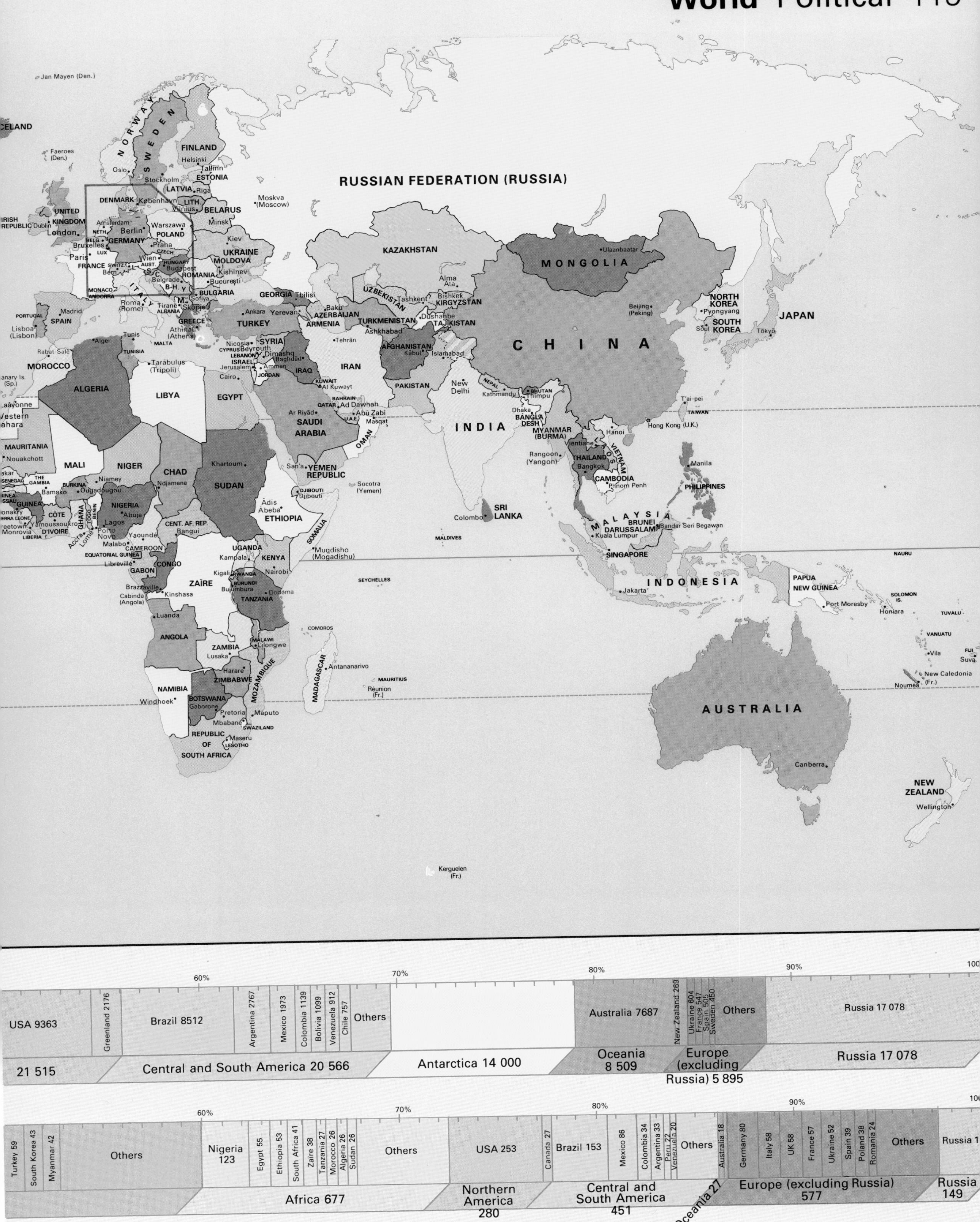

ICELAND

Jan Mayen (Den.)

Faeroes (Den.)

NORWAY
SWEDEN
FINLAND
Oslo
Helsinki
Stockholm
Tallinn
ESTONIA
LATVIA
Riga

DENMARK
København
LITH.
Vilnius

RUSSIAN FEDERATION (RUSSIA)

Moskva (Moscow)

IRISH REPUBLIC
Dublin

UNITED KINGDOM
London

BELARUS
Minsk
Kiev

Amsterdam
Berlin
NETH.
BEL.
Bruxelles
LUX.
Paris
GERMANY
Praha
CZECH
FRANCE SWITZ.
Bern
Warszawa
POLAND

UKRAINE
MOLDOVA

KAZAKHSTAN

MONGOLIA
Ulaanbaatar

AUST.
HUNGARY
Budapest
ROMANIA
Kishinev
Bucureşti

NORTH KOREA
Pyongyang

JAPAN

PORTUGAL
Lisboa (Lisbon)

SPAIN
Madrid

ANDORRA
MONACO
ITALY
Roma (Rome)
M.
B.-H.
Belgrade
BULGARIA
Sofiya
Skopje
ALBANIA
Tirane
GREECE
Athinai (Athens)

GEORGIA
Tbilisi

Beijing (Peking)

SOUTH KOREA
Sŏul
Tōkyō

UZBEKISTAN
Tashkent
Bishkek
KIRGYZSTAN

TURKEY
Ankara
Yerevan
AZERBAIJAN
ARMENIA
Baku
TURKMENISTAN
Ashkhabad
Dushanbe
TAJIKISTAN

CHINA

Rabat-Salé
MOROCCO
Alger
Tunis
TUNISIA
MALTA

Nicosia
CYPRUS
SYRIA
LEBANON
Beyrouth
Dimashq
ISRAEL
Jerusalem
JORDAN
Amman
Baghdād
IRAQ
Tehrān
IRAN

AFGHANISTAN
Kābul
Islamabad

T'ai-pei
TAIWAN

anary Is. (Sp.)

Western Sahara

ALGERIA
LIBYA
EGYPT
Cairo

KUWAIT
Al Kuwayt
BAHRAIN
QATAR
Ad Dawhah
Ar Riyāḍ
U.A.E.
Abu Zabi
Masqat
OMAN

PAKISTAN

New Delhi

NEPAL
Kathmandu
BHUTAN
Thimpu
Dhaka
BANGLA DESH

Hong Kong (U.K.)

MAURITANIA
Nouakchott

MALI
NIGER

SAUDI ARABIA

INDIA

Hanoi

MYANMAR (BURMA)

Vientiane
LAOS
VIETNAM

THE GAMBIA
akar
SENEGAL
BURKINA
Niamey
CHAD
Ndjamena
Khartoum
SUDAN

San'ā
YEMEN REPUBLIC
DJIBOUTI
Djibouti
Socotra (Yemen)

Rangoon (Yangon)
THAILAND
Bangkok
CAMBODIA
Phnom Penh

Manila

PHILIPPINES

INEA
SSAU
onakry
Bamako
Ougadougou

NIGERIA
Abuja
CENT. AF. REP.
Bangui
Ādis Ābeba
ETHIOPIA
SOMALIA

SRI LANKA
Colombo

MALAYSIA

BRUNEI
DARUSSALAM
Bandar Seri Begawan

ERRA LEONE
Freetown
Monrovia
LIBERIA
CÔTE D'IVOIRE
Yamoussoukro
GHANA
TOGO
BENIN
Accra
Lomé
Porto Novo
Lagos
Yaoundé
CAMEROON

Kuala Lumpur

MALDIVES

EQUATORIAL GUINEA
Malabo
Libreville
GABON
CONGO
Brazzaville
Cabinda (Angola)
Kinshasa
ZAÏRE

UGANDA
Kampala
Kigali
RWANDA
BURUNDI
Bujumbura
KENYA
Nairobi
Dodoma
Muqdisho (Mogadishu)

SEYCHELLES

SINGAPORE

INDONESIA
Jakarta

NAURU

PAPUA NEW GUINEA
Port Moresby

SOLOMON IS.
Honiara

TUVALU

Luanda
ANGOLA
TANZANIA

ZAMBIA
Lusaka
MALAWI
Lilongwe

COMOROS

VANUATU

Vila
FIJI
Suva
New Caledonia (Fr.)
Noumea

NAMIBIA
Windhoek
ZIMBABWE
Harare
BOTSWANA
Gaborone
MOZAMBIQUE
MADAGASCAR
Antananarivo

MAURITIUS
Réunion (Fr.)

AUSTRALIA

Pretoria
REPUBLIC OF SOUTH AFRICA
Mbabane
Maseru
LESOTHO
SWAZILAND
Maputo

Canberra

NEW ZEALAND

Wellington

Kerguelen (Fr.)

60%   70%   80%   90%   100

| USA 9363 | Greenland 2176 | Brazil 8512 | Argentina 2767 | Mexico 1973 | Colombia 1139 | Bolivia 1099 | Venezuela 912 | Chile 757 | Others | Australia 7687 | New Zealand 269 | Ukraine 604 | France 547 | Spain 505 | Sweden 450 | Others | Russia 17 078 |

| 21 515 | Central and South America 20 566 | Antarctica 14 000 | Oceania 8 509 | Europe (excluding Russia) 5 895 | Russia 17 078 |

60%   70%   80%   90%   100

| Turkey 59 | South Korea 43 | Myanmar 42 | Others | Nigeria 123 | Egypt 55 | Ethiopia 53 | South Africa 41 | Zaïre 38 | Tanzania 27 | Morocco 26 | Algeria 26 | Sudan 26 | Others | USA 253 | Canada 27 | Brazil 153 | Mexico 86 | Colombia 34 | Argentina 33 | Peru 22 | Venezuela 20 | Others | Australia 18 | Germany 80 | Italy 58 | UK 58 | France 57 | Ukraine 52 | Spain 39 | Poland 38 | Romania 24 | Others | Russia 1 |

| | Africa 677 | Northern America 280 | Central and South America 451 | Oceania 27 | Europe (excluding Russia) 577 | Russia 149 |

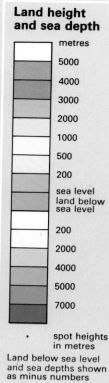

Land height and sea depth

metres

	5000
	4000
	3000
	2000
	1000
	500
	200
	sea level
	land below sea level
	200
	2000
	4000
	5000
	7000

• spot heights in metres

Land below sea level and sea depths shown as minus numbers

Equatorial Scale 1:88 000 000

Modified Gall Projection

Plate tectonics

The present positions of the major tectonic plates are shown with the white areas representing the smaller plates

Plate boundaries

▲▲ subduction zones

═══ ridge zones

─── transform zones

➡ direction of sea-floor spreading

─── major fracture zones

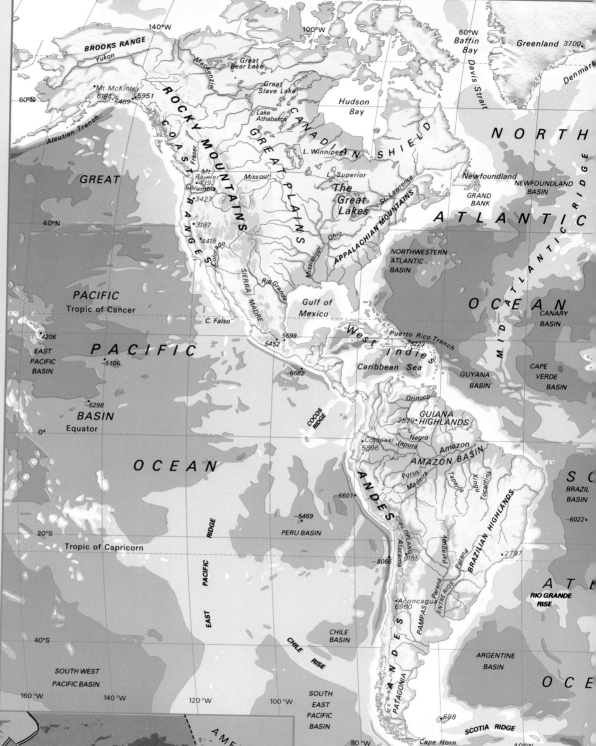

Gall Projection

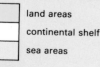

The moving continents

	land areas
	continental shelf
	sea areas
	orogenic belts

.... uncertain coastline

•••••••••• uncertain continental shelf edge

Lines of latitude and longitude indicate position on the globe.

The graticules show how earlier positions of the continents compare with the present

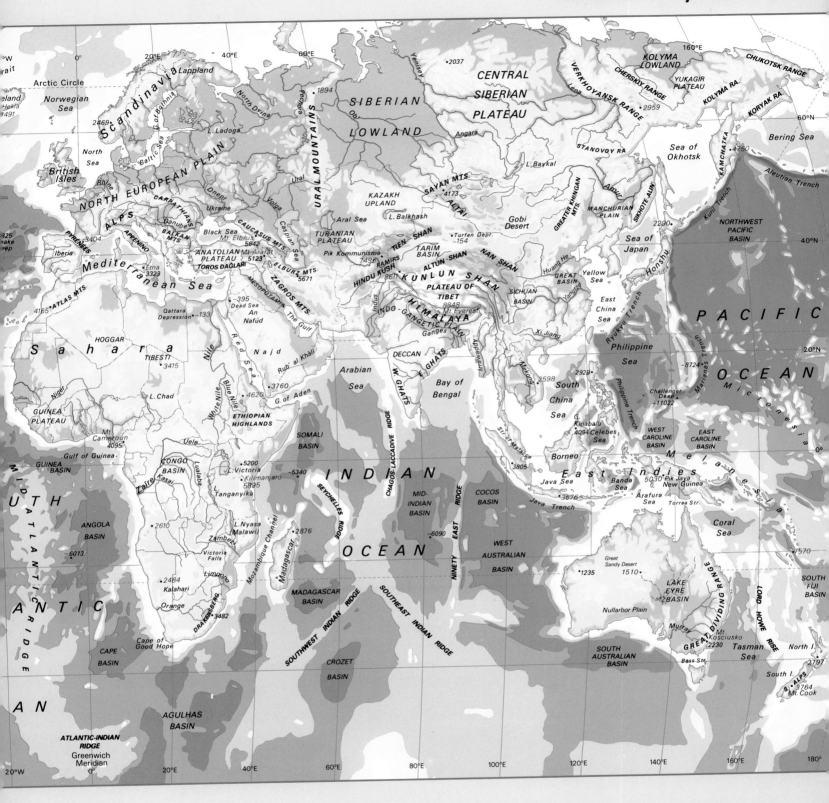

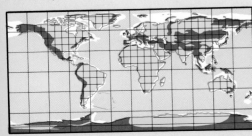

Present day

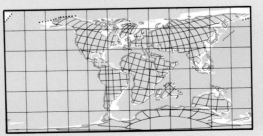

100 million years ago (Cretaceous period)

200 million years ago (Triassic period)

Rainfall
and other forms of precipitation

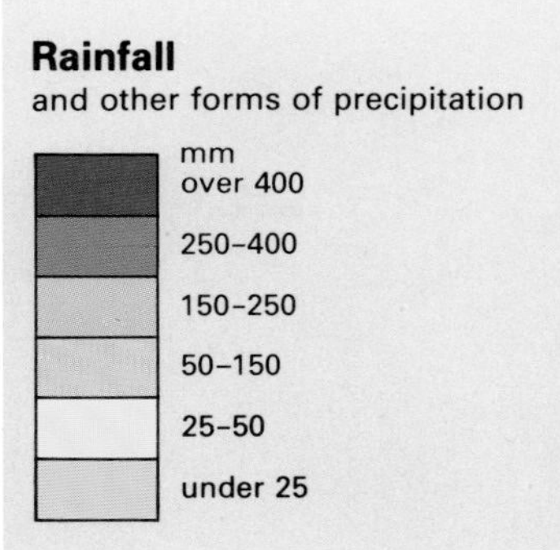

mm
over 400
250–400
150–250
50–150
25–50
under 25

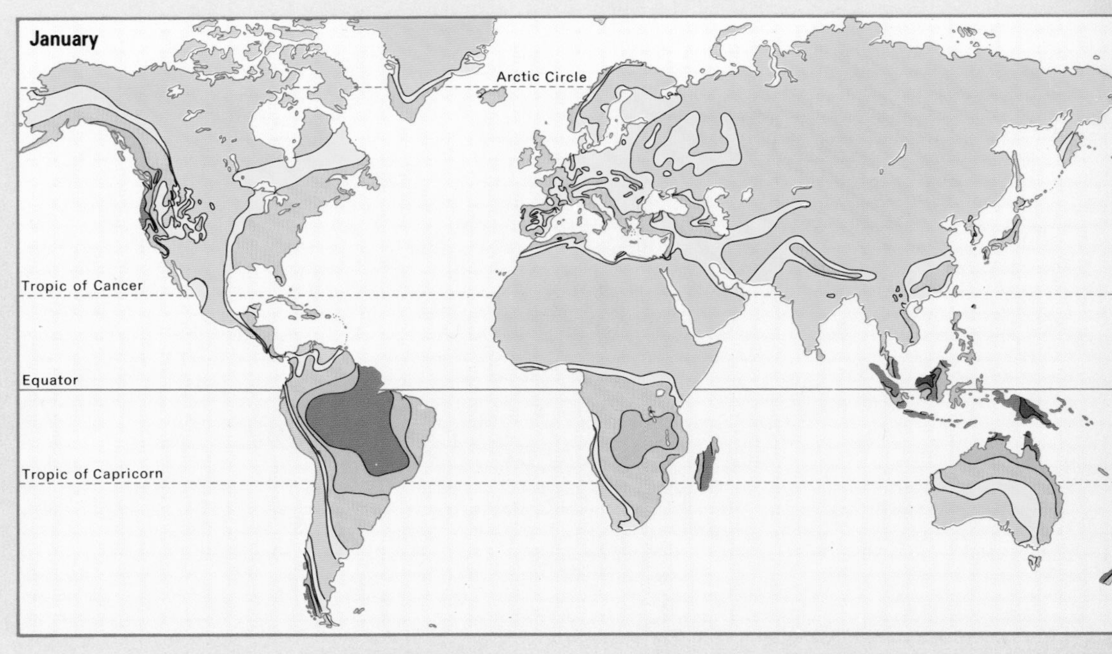

January

Temperature, ocean currents

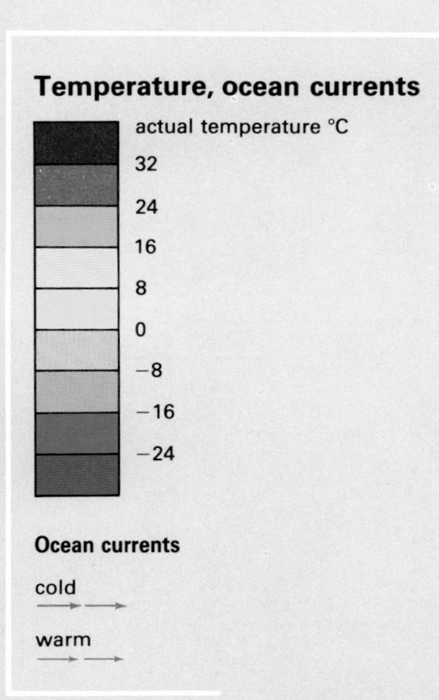

actual temperature °C

32
24
16
8
0
−8
−16
−24

Ocean currents

cold

warm

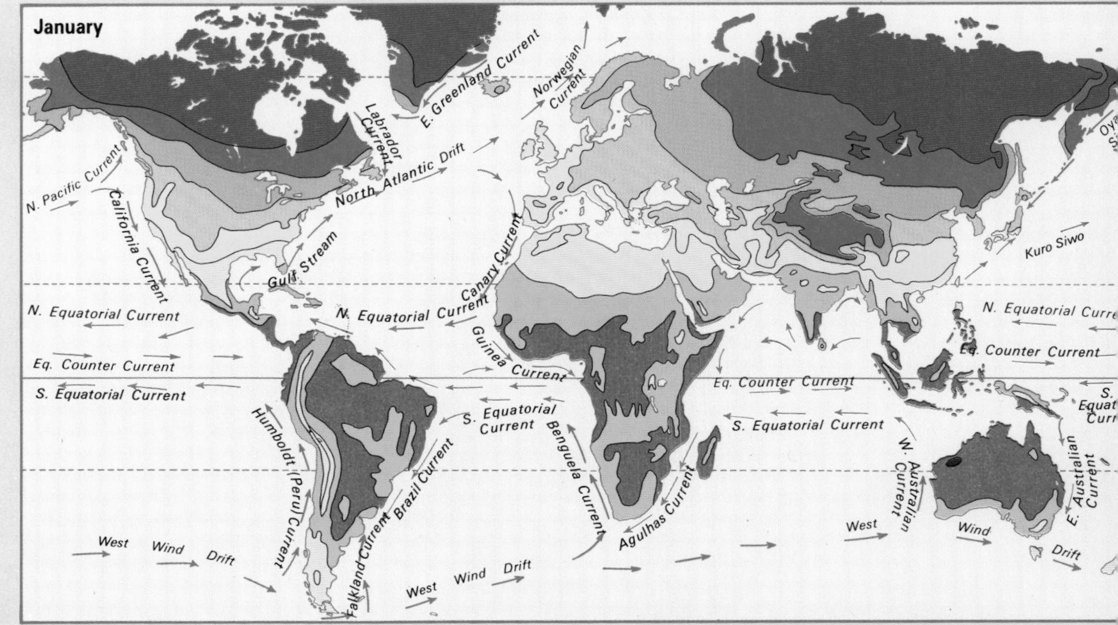

January

Pressure and winds
Pressure reduced to sea level

103.5 kilopascals
103.0
102.5
102.0
101.5
101.0
100.5
100.0
99.5

H high pressure cell

L low pressure cell

Prevailing winds
Arrows fly with the wind:
the heavier the arrow, the
more regular ('constant')
the direction of the wind

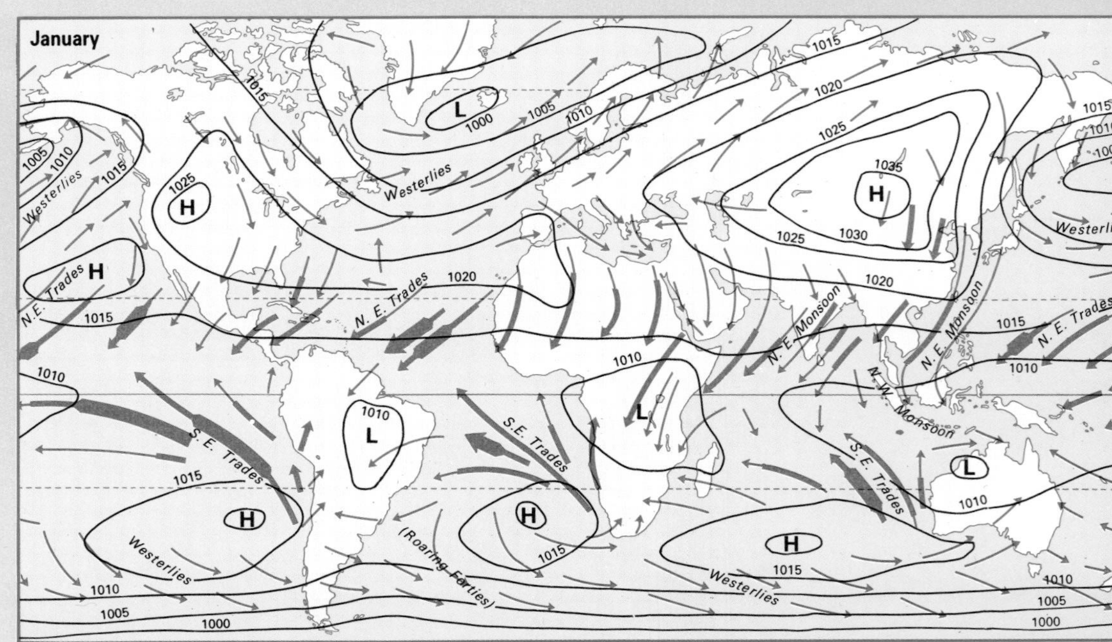

January

Equatorial Scale 1:218 000 000

Modified Gall Projection

Tropical revolving storms

temperature 27°C and over at mean sea level

Northern hemisphere
Maximum frequency August - September

Typhoon   *Hurricane*   *Typhoon*
Cyclone

Southern hemisphere
Maximum frequency January - March

Hurricane   *Cyclone*   *Hurricane*

Air masses

--- fronts

Arctic

Polar

Temperate

Equatorial

January

Pacific Arctic Front   Atlantic Arctic Front

Atlantic Polar Front   Mediterranean Front   Pacific Polar Front

Intertropical   Convergence

Polar Front   Polar Front

July

Atlantic Arctic Front   Pacific Arctic Front

Atlantic Polar Front

Convergence

Intertropical

Polar Front   Polar Front

July (left top map)

Arctic Circle

Tropic of Cancer

Equator

Tropic of Capricorn

July (middle map — ocean currents)

E. Greenland Current
Labrador Current
Norwegian Current
North Atlantic Drift
Oya Siwo
Kuro Siwo
N. Pacific Current
California Current
Gulf Stream
Canary Current
N. Equatorial Current
N. Equatorial Current
Equatorial Counter Current
Guinea Current
Eq. Counter Current
Eq. Counter Current
S. Equatorial Current
S. Equatorial Current
S. Equatorial Current
Humboldt (Peru) Current
Benguela Current
Brazil Current
Falkland Current
Agulhas Current
W. Australian Current
E. Australian Current
West Wind Drift
West Wind Drift
West Wind Drift

July (bottom map — pressure and winds)

1010
1015
L
L
1015
1015
Westerlies
1020
H
1025
N.E. Trades
1010
1015
S.E. Trades
1015
Westerlies
1015
L
N.E. Trades
H
1020
Westerlies
1005
1000
L
S.W. Monsoon
1010
1015
S.E. Trades
S.E. Trades
1020
H
Westerlies
H
Westerlies
N.E. Trades
S.E. Monsoon
S.E. Monsoon
Westerlies
1015
(Roaring Forties)
H
1015
1010
1005
1000

© Oxford University Press

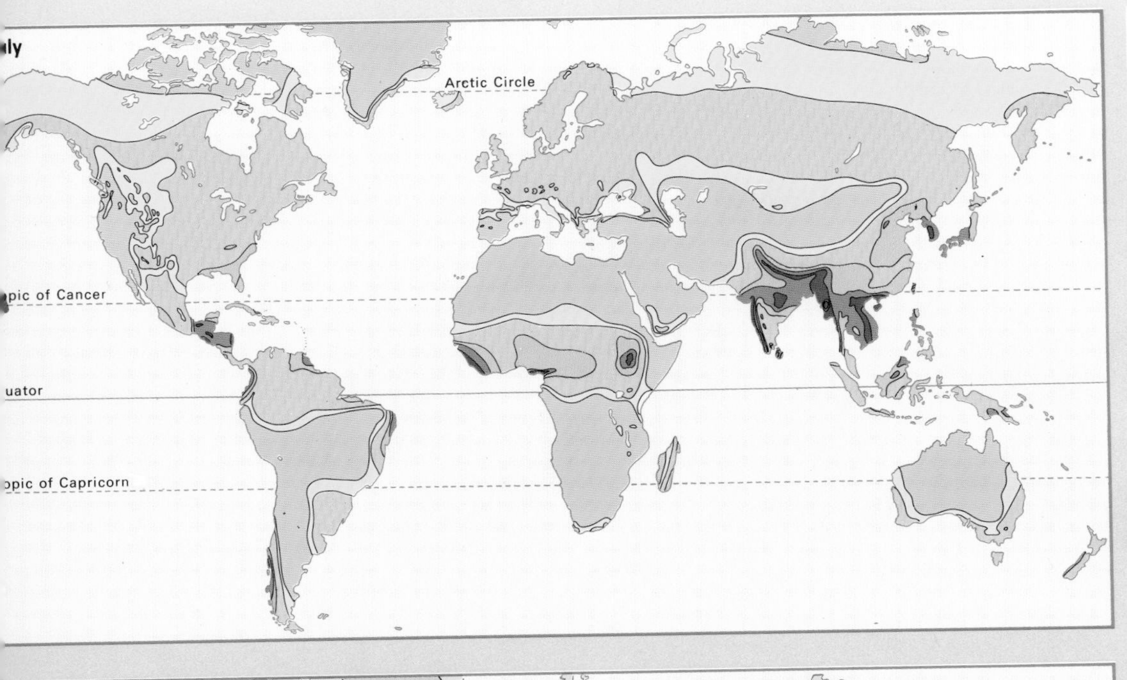

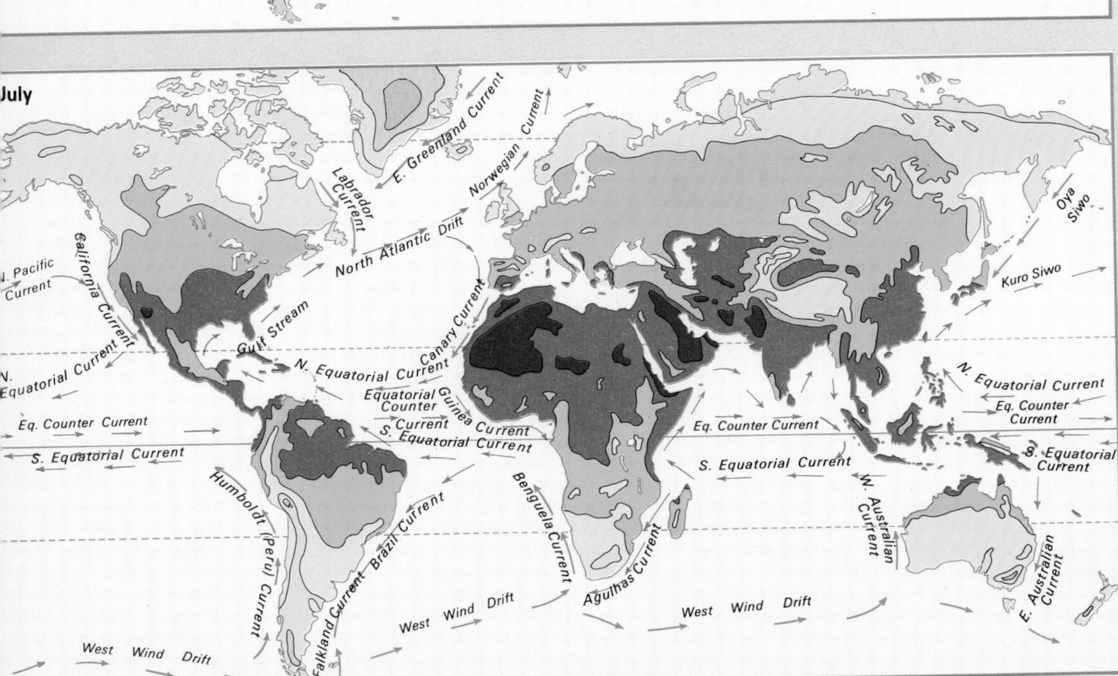

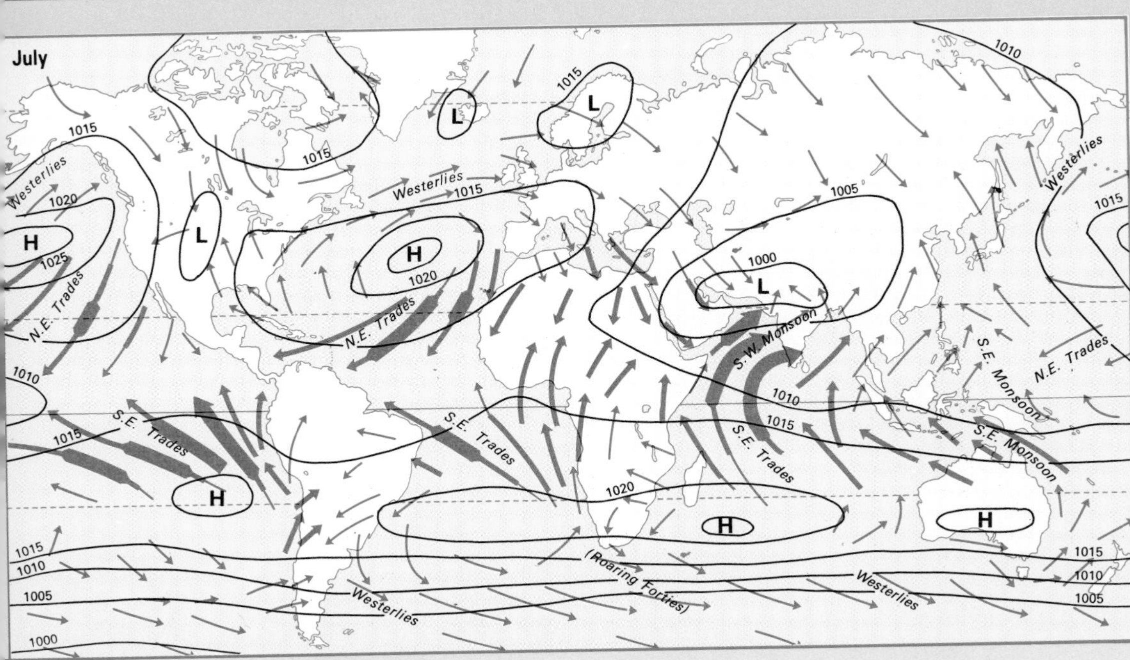

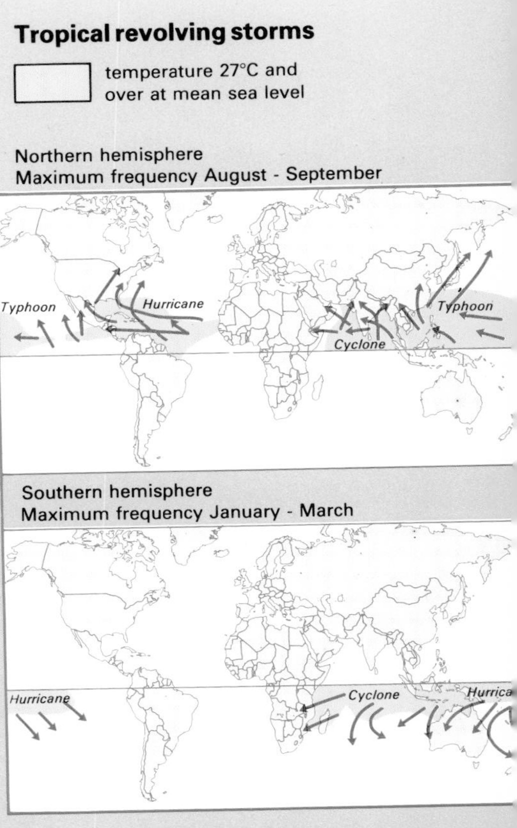

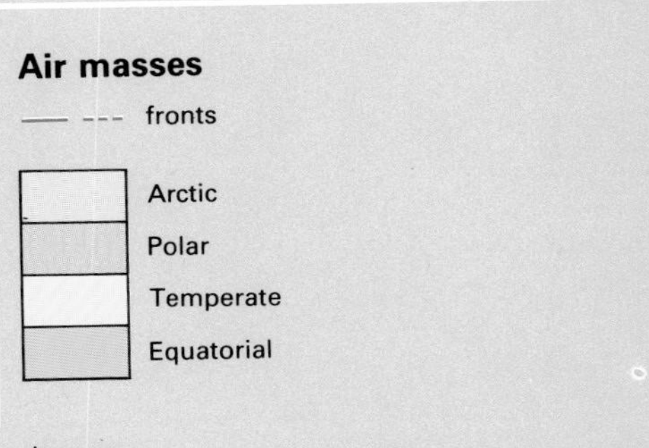

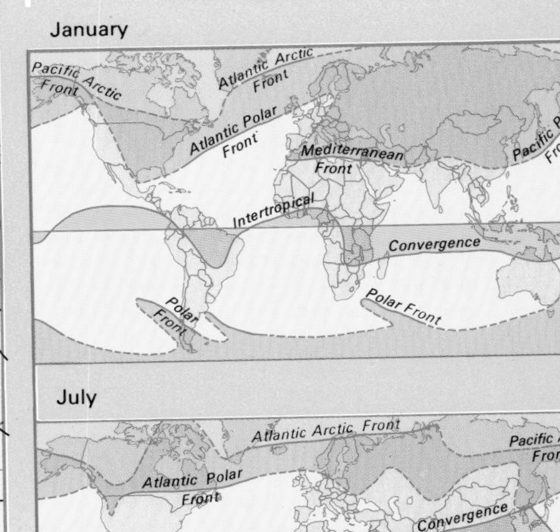

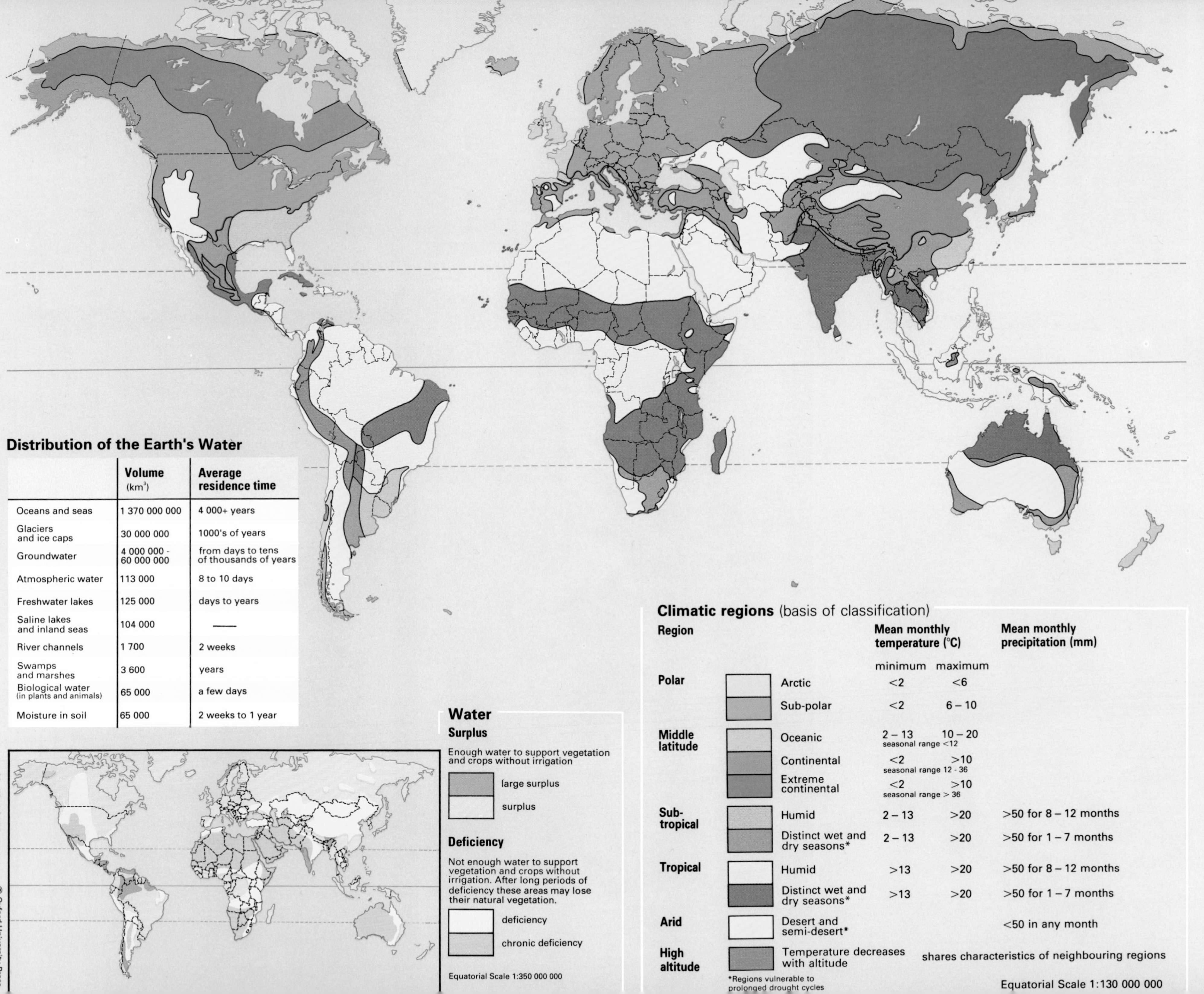

Climatic regions (basis of classification)

Region		Mean monthly temperature (°C)		Mean monthly precipitation (mm)
		minimum	maximum	
Polar	Arctic	<2	<6	
	Sub-polar	<2	6 – 10	
Middle latitude	Oceanic	2 – 13 seasonal range <12	10 – 20	
	Continental	<2 seasonal range 12 - 36	>10	
	Extreme continental	<2 seasonal range > 36	>10	
Sub-tropical	Humid	2 – 13	>20	>50 for 8 – 12 months
	Distinct wet and dry seasons*	2 – 13	>20	>50 for 1 – 7 months
Tropical	Humid	>13	>20	>50 for 8 – 12 months
	Distinct wet and dry seasons*	>13	>20	>50 for 1 – 7 months
Arid	Desert and semi-desert*			<50 in any month
High altitude	Temperature decreases with altitude			shares characteristics of neighbouring regions

*Regions vulnerable to prolonged drought cycles

Equatorial Scale 1:130 000 000

Water

Surplus

Enough water to support vegetation and crops without irrigation

- large surplus
- surplus

Deficiency

Not enough water to support vegetation and crops without irrigation. After long periods of deficiency these areas may lose their natural vegetation.

- deficiency
- chronic deficiency

Equatorial Scale 1:350 000 000

Distribution of the Earth's Water

	Volume (km³)	Average residence time
Oceans and seas	1 370 000 000	4 000+ years
Glaciers and ice caps	30 000 000	1000's of years
Groundwater	4 000 000 - 60 000 000	from days to tens of thousands of years
Atmospheric water	113 000	8 to 10 days
Freshwater lakes	125 000	days to years
Saline lakes and inland seas	104 000	—
River channels	1 700	2 weeks
Swamps and marshes	3 600	years
Biological water (in plants and animals)	65 000	a few days
Moisture in soil	65 000	2 weeks to 1 year

Modified Gall Projection   © Oxford University Press

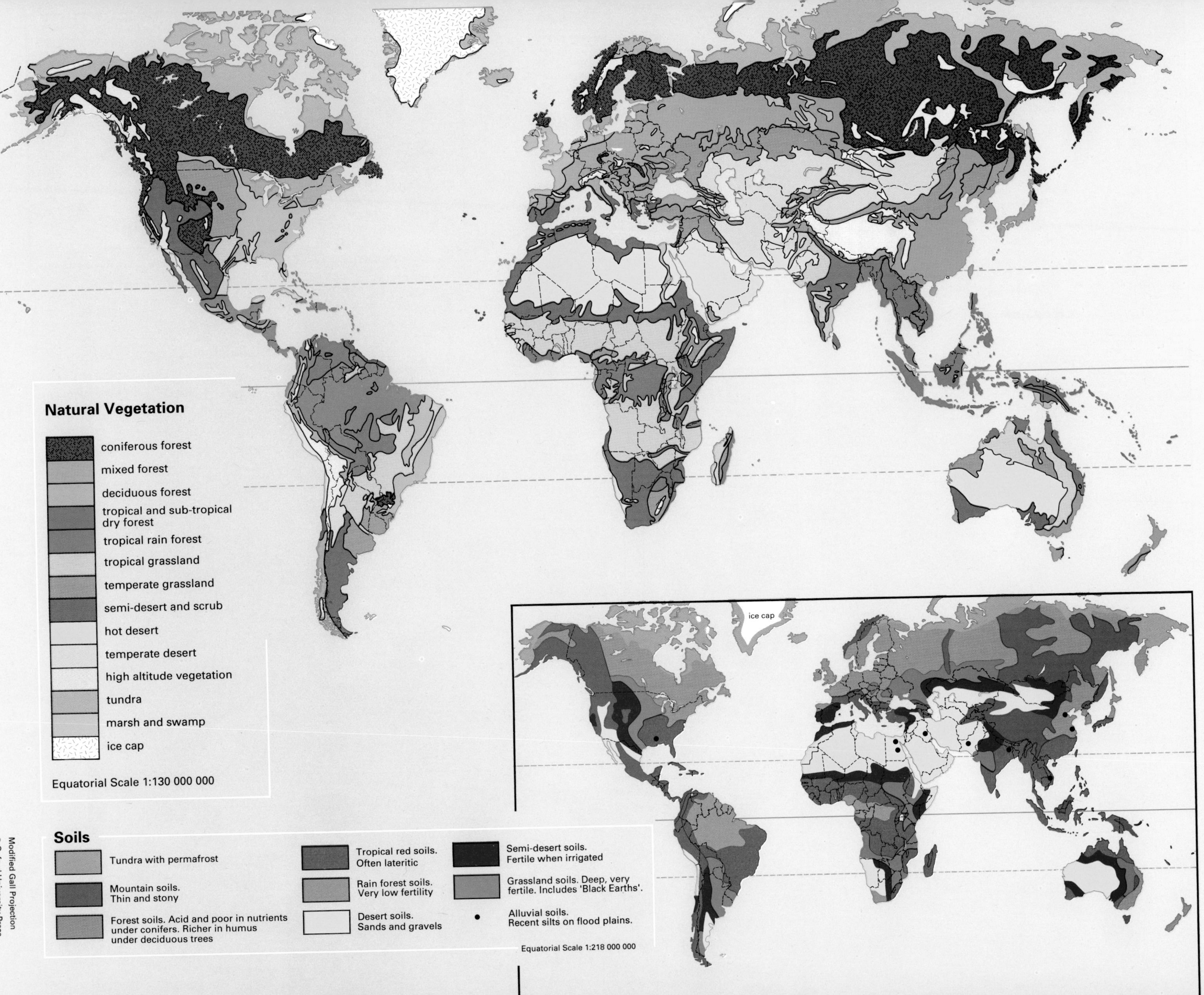

ice cap

Natural Vegetation

- coniferous forest
- mixed forest
- deciduous forest
- tropical and sub-tropical dry forest
- tropical rain forest
- tropical grassland
- temperate grassland
- semi-desert and scrub
- hot desert
- temperate desert
- high altitude vegetation
- tundra
- marsh and swamp
- ice cap

Equatorial Scale 1:130 000 000

Soils

- Tundra with permafrost
- Mountain soils. Thin and stony
- Forest soils. Acid and poor in nutrients under conifers. Richer in humus under deciduous trees
- Tropical red soils. Often lateritic
- Rain forest soils. Very low fertility
- Desert soils. Sands and gravels
- Semi-desert soils. Fertile when irrigated
- Grassland soils. Deep, very fertile. Includes 'Black Earths'.
- Alluvial soils. Recent silts on flood plains.

Equatorial Scale 1:218 000 000

Modified Gall Projection

© Oxford University Press

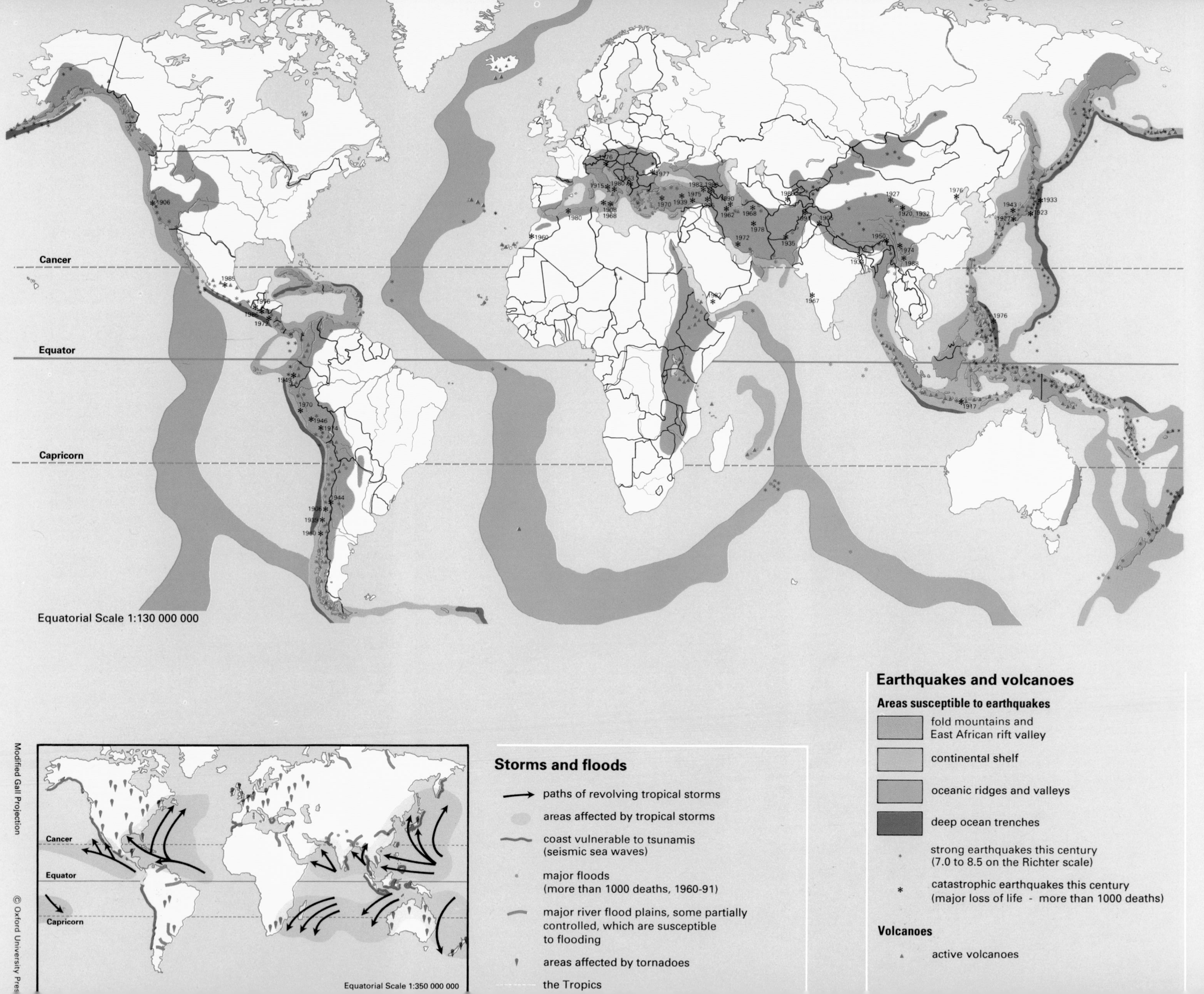

Earthquakes and volcanoes

Areas susceptible to earthquakes

	fold mountains and East African rift valley
	continental shelf
	oceanic ridges and valleys
	deep ocean trenches

* strong earthquakes this century (7.0 to 8.5 on the Richter scale)

* catastrophic earthquakes this century (major loss of life – more than 1000 deaths)

Volcanoes

* active volcanoes

Storms and floods

→ paths of revolving tropical storms

areas affected by tropical storms

coast vulnerable to tsunamis (seismic sea waves)

· major floods (more than 1000 deaths, 1960-91)

major river flood plains, some partially controlled, which are susceptible to flooding

▸ areas affected by tornadoes

––– the Tropics

Equatorial Scale 1:350 000 000

Equatorial Scale 1:130 000 000

Cancer

Equator

Capricorn

Modified Gall Projection   © Oxford University Press

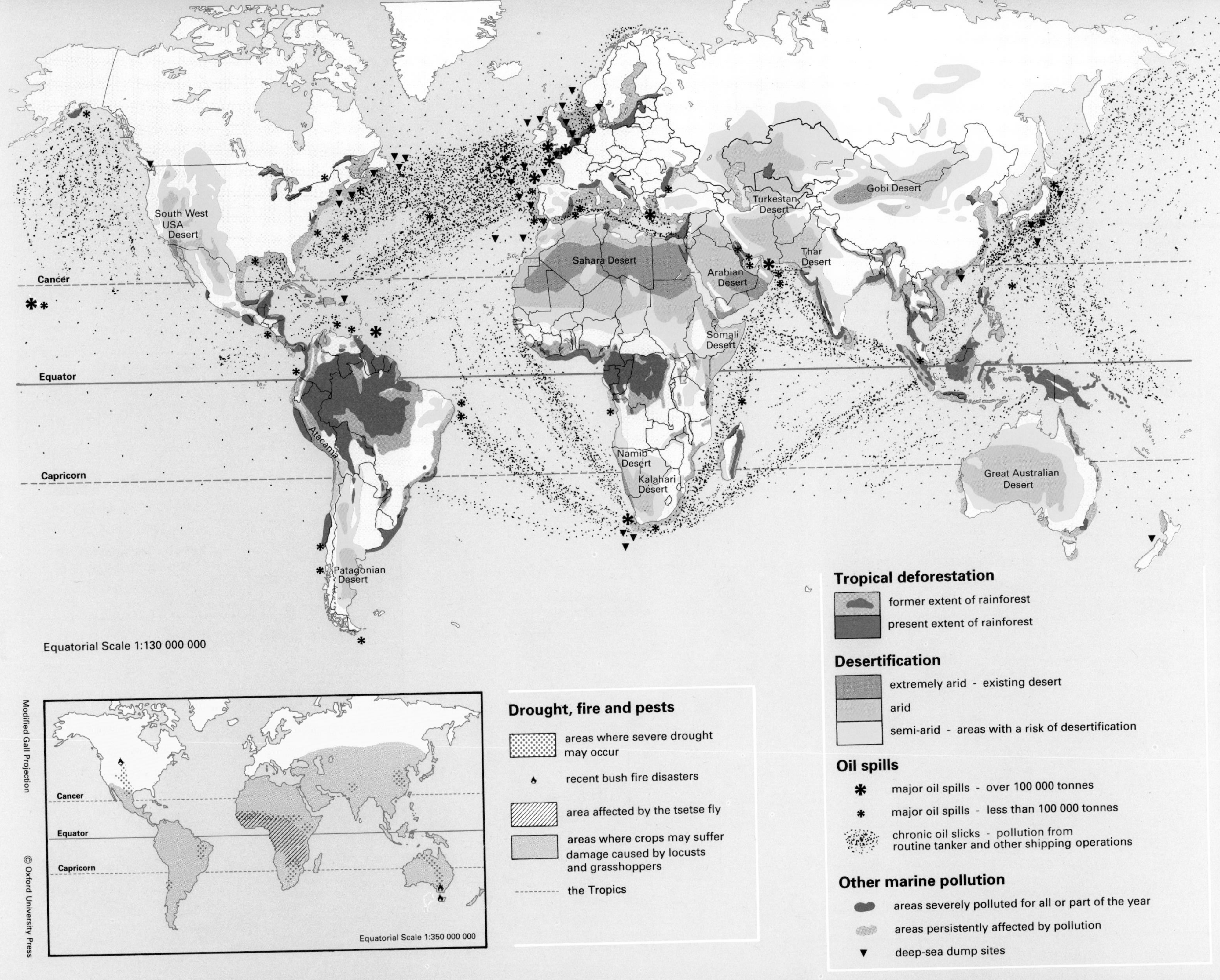

Tropical deforestation

former extent of rainforest

present extent of rainforest

Desertification

extremely arid - existing desert

arid

semi-arid - areas with a risk of desertification

Oil spills

* major oil spills - over 100 000 tonnes

* major oil spills - less than 100 000 tonnes

chronic oil slicks - pollution from routine tanker and other shipping operations

Other marine pollution

areas severely polluted for all or part of the year

areas persistently affected by pollution

▶ deep-sea dump sites

Drought, fire and pests

areas where severe drought may occur

• recent bush fire disasters

area affected by the tsetse fly

areas where crops may suffer damage caused by locusts and grasshoppers

the Tropics

Equatorial Scale 1:130 000 000

Equatorial Scale 1:350 000 000

Gobi Desert

Thar Desert

Turkestan Desert

Arabian Desert

Somali Desert

Sahara Desert

Namib Desert

Kalahari Desert

Great Australian Desert

South West USA Desert

Atacama

Patagonian Desert

Cancer

Equator

Capricorn

Modified Gall Projection

© Oxford University Press

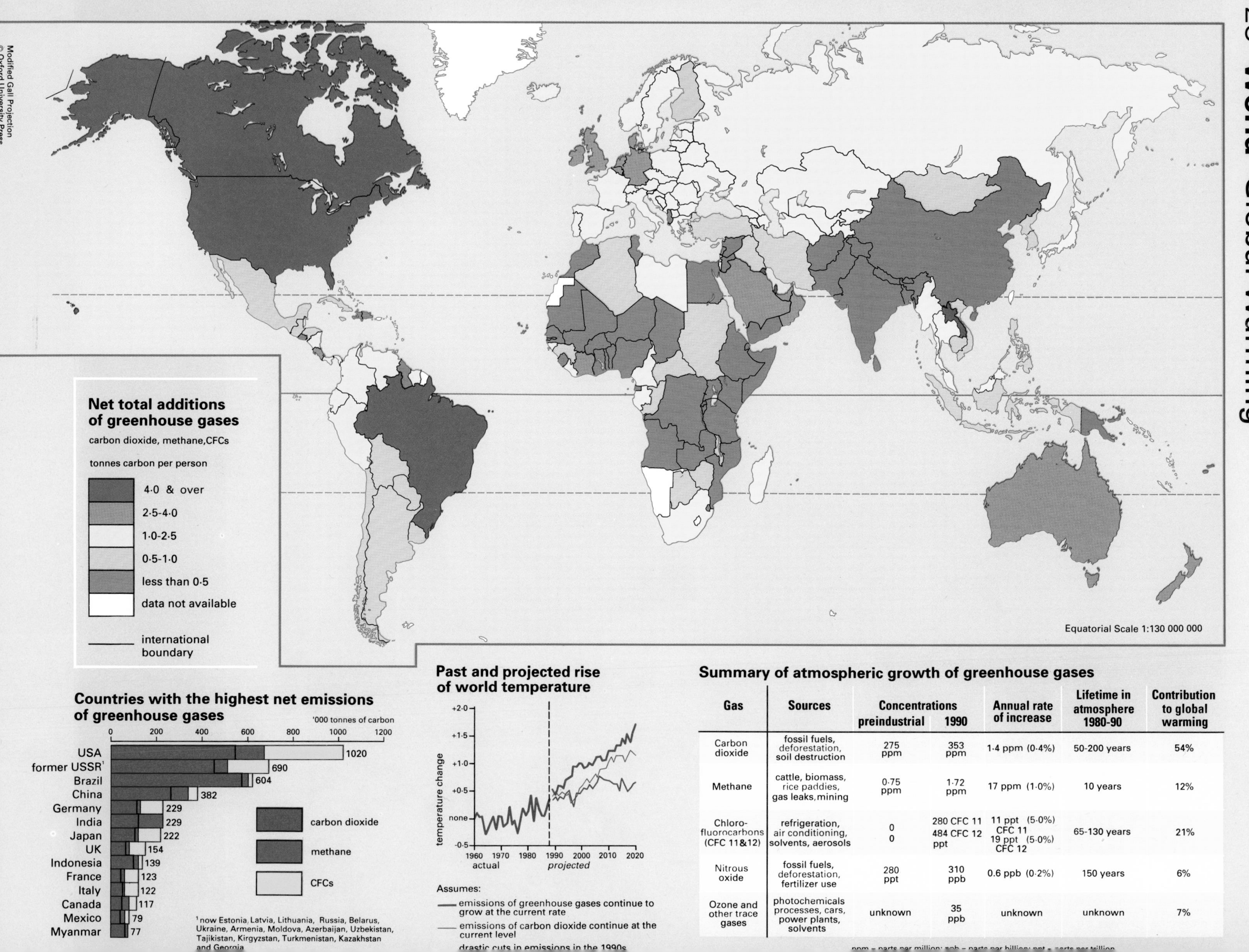

Summary of atmospheric growth of greenhouse gases

Gas	Sources	Concentrations preindustrial	Concentrations 1990	Annual rate of increase	Lifetime in atmosphere 1980-90	Contribution to global warming
Carbon dioxide	fossil fuels, deforestation, soil destruction	275 ppm	353 ppm	1·4 ppm (0·4%)	50-200 years	54%
Methane	cattle, biomass, rice paddies, gas leaks, mining	0·75 ppm	1·72 ppm	17 ppm (1·0%)	10 years	12%
Chloro-fluorocarbons (CFC 11&12)	refrigeration, air conditioning, solvents, aerosols	0 / 0	280 CFC 11 / 484 CFC 12 ppt	11 ppt (5·0%) CFC 11 / 19 ppt (5·0%) CFC 12	65-130 years	21%
Nitrous oxide	fossil fuels, deforestation, fertilizer use	280 ppt	310 ppb	0·6 ppb (0·2%)	150 years	6%
Ozone and other trace gases	photochemicals processes, cars, power plants, solvents	unknown	35 ppb	unknown	unknown	7%

ppm = parts per million; ppb = parts per billion; ppt = parts per trillion

Past and projected rise of world temperature

temperature change: +2·0, +1·5, +1·0, +0·5, none, -0·5
1960 1970 1980 1990 2000 2010 2020
actual projected

Assumes:
— emissions of greenhouse gases continue to grow at the current rate
— emissions of carbon dioxide continue at the current level
— drastic cuts in emissions in the 1990s

Net total additions of greenhouse gases
carbon dioxide, methane, CFCs

tonnes carbon per person
- 4·0 & over
- 2·5-4·0
- 1·0-2·5
- 0·5-1·0
- less than 0·5
- data not available
- international boundary

Equatorial Scale 1:130 000 000

Countries with the highest net emissions of greenhouse gases
'000 tonnes of carbon

carbon dioxide
methane
CFCs

Country	
USA	1020
former USSR¹	690
Brazil	604
China	382
Germany	229
India	229
Japan	222
UK	154
Indonesia	139
France	123
Italy	122
Canada	117
Mexico	79
Myanmar	77

¹ now Estonia, Latvia, Lithuania, Russia, Belarus, Ukraine, Armenia, Moldova, Azerbaijan, Uzbekistan, Tajikistan, Kirgyzstan, Turkmenistan, Kazakhstan and Georgia

Modified Gall Projection
© Oxford University Press

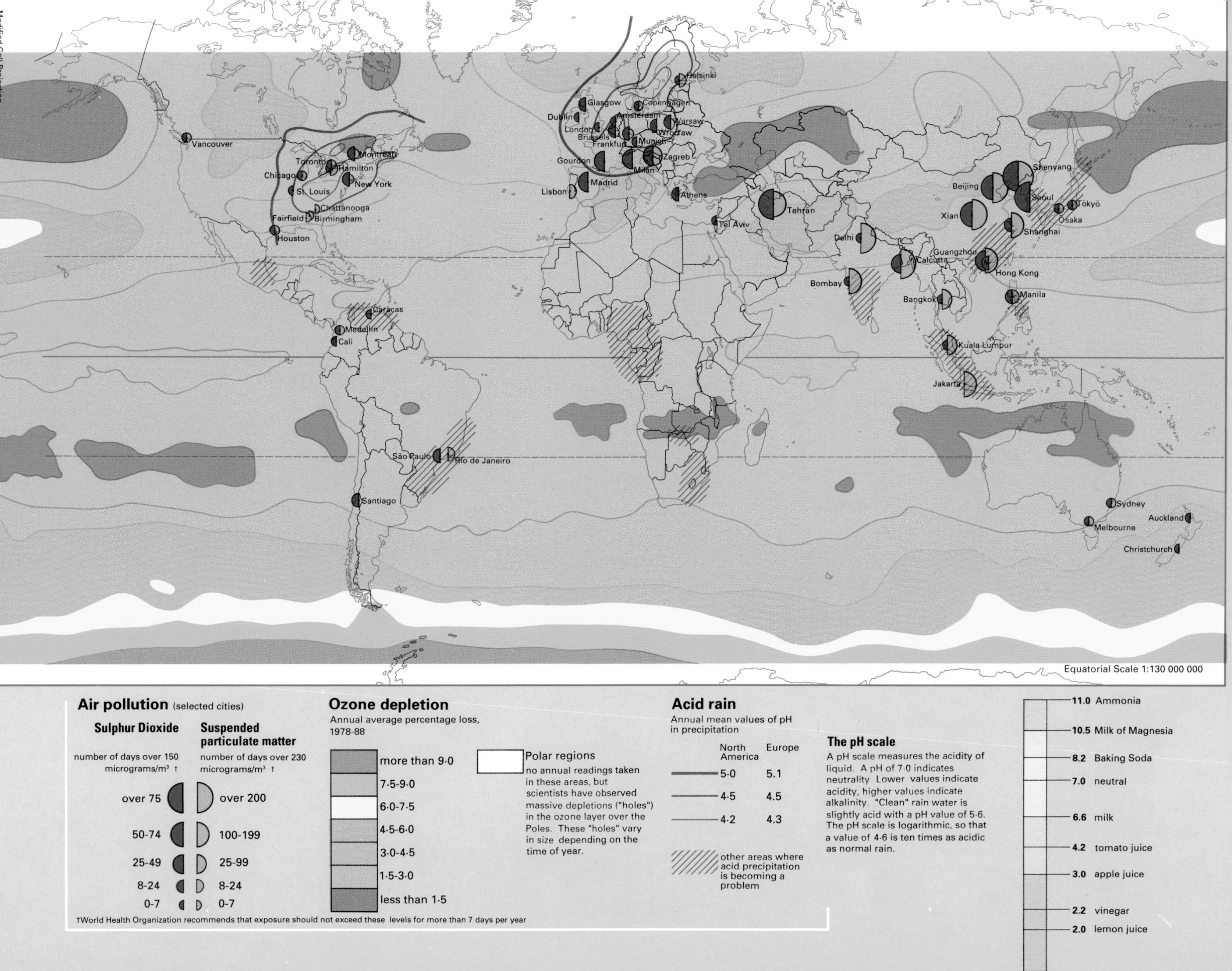

Equatorial Scale 1:130 000 000

Air pollution (selected cities)

Sulphur Dioxide	Suspended particulate matter
number of days over 150 micrograms/m³ †	number of days over 230 micrograms/m³ †

Sulphur Dioxide
- over 75
- 50–74
- 25–49
- 8–24
- 0–7

Suspended particulate matter
- over 200
- 100–199
- 25–99
- 8–24
- 0–7

Ozone depletion

Annual average percentage loss, 1978–88

- more than 9·0
- 7·5–9·0
- 6·0–7·5
- 4·5–6·0
- 3·0–4·5
- 1·5–3·0
- less than 1·5

Polar regions
no annual readings taken in these areas, but scientists have observed massive depletions ("holes") in the ozone layer over the Poles. These "holes" vary in size depending on the time of year.

other areas where acid precipitation is becoming a problem

Acid rain

Annual mean values of pH in precipitation

	North America	Europe
	5·0	5·1
	4·5	4·5
	4·2	4·3

The pH scale

A pH scale measures the acidity of liquid. A pH of 7·0 indicates neutrality. Lower values indicate acidity, higher values indicate alkalinity. "Clean" rain water is slightly acid with a pH value of 5·6. The pH scale is logarithmic, so that a value of 4·6 is ten times as acidic as normal rain.

- 11·0 Ammonia
- 10·5 Milk of Magnesia
- 8·2 Baking Soda
- 7·0 neutral
- 6·6 milk
- 4·2 tomato juice
- 3·0 apple juice
- 2·2 vinegar
- 2·0 lemon juice

†World Health Organization recommends that exposure should not exceed these levels for more than 7 days per year

Modified Gall Projection
© Oxford University Press

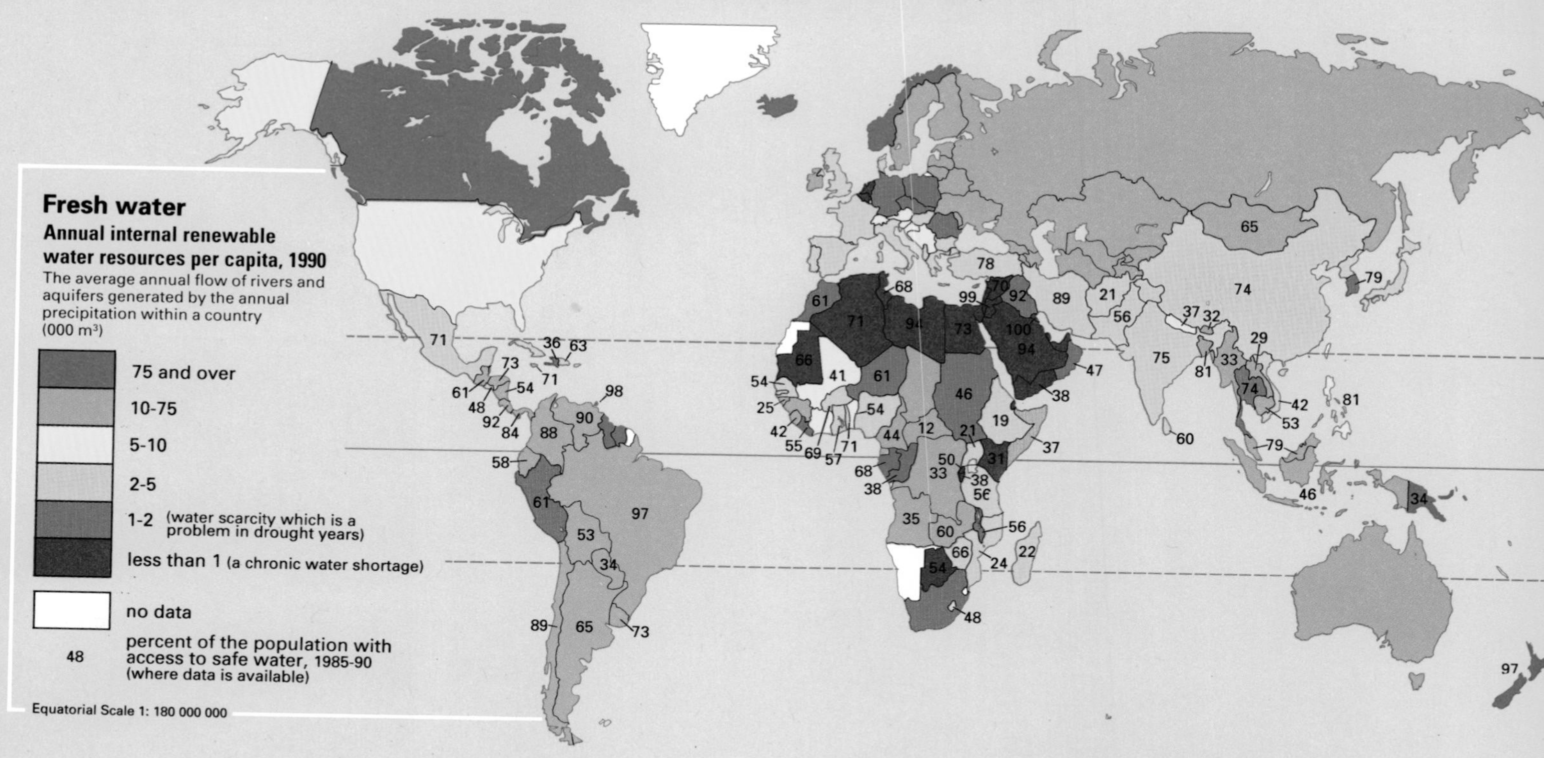

Fresh water

Annual internal renewable water resources per capita, 1990

The average annual flow of rivers and aquifers generated by the annual precipitation within a country (000 m³)

- 75 and over
- 10-75
- 5-10
- 2-5
- 1-2 (water scarcity which is a problem in drought years)
- less than 1 (a chronic water shortage)
- no data

48   percent of the population with access to safe water, 1985-90 (where data is available)

Equatorial Scale 1: 180 000 000

Protected areas

Percent of national land area protected by national protection systems, 1989

Areas of at least 1000 hectares and with partially restricted access, including scientific reserves, strict nature reserves, national parks, provincial parks, natural monuments, natural land marks, managed nature reserves, wildlife sanctuaries, and protected landscapes or seascapes (natural or cultural).

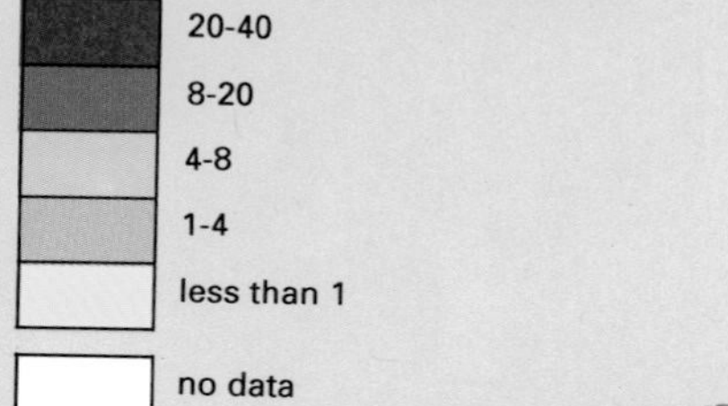

- 20-40
- 8-20
- 4-8
- 1-4
- less than 1
- no data

Estimated number of species worldwide

	Those species already identified	Estimated percentage yet to be identified
invertebrates	1 020 561	73-97
micro-organisms	5760	
plants	322 311	0-33
fish	19 056	0-17
reptiles and amphibians	10 484	5-10
mammals	4 000	
birds	9 040	0-6

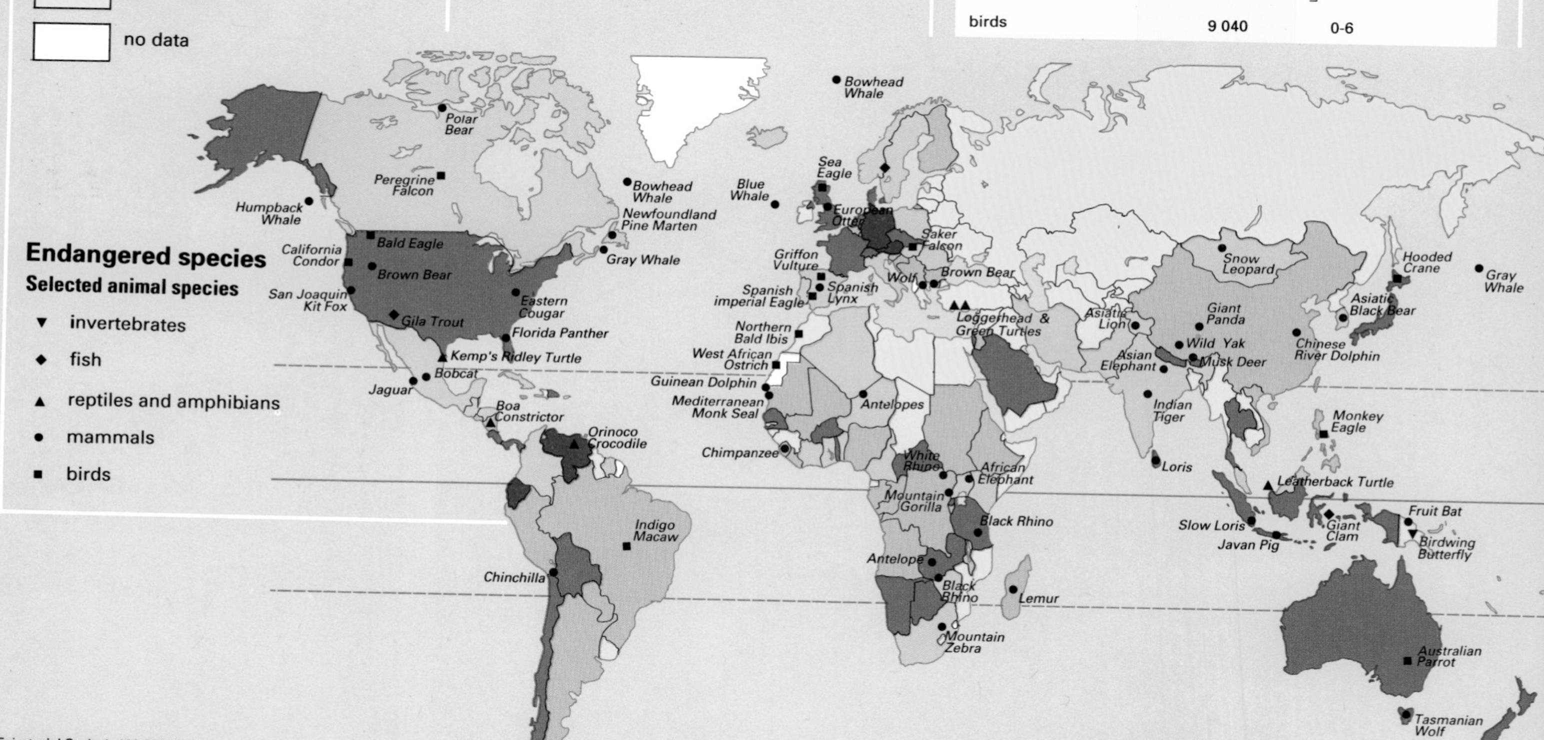

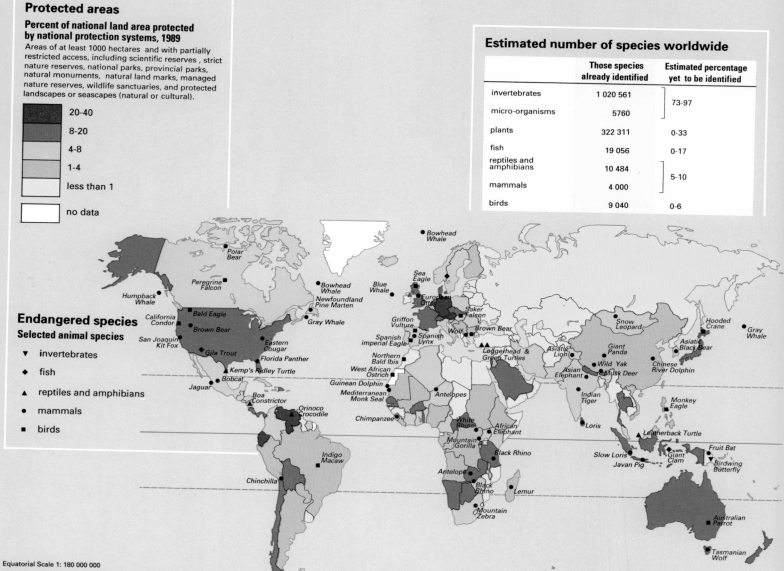

Endangered species
Selected animal species

- ▼ invertebrates
- ◆ fish
- ▲ reptiles and amphibians
- ● mammals
- ■ birds

Equatorial Scale 1: 180 000 000

Modified Gall Projection

© Oxford University Press

Nuclear

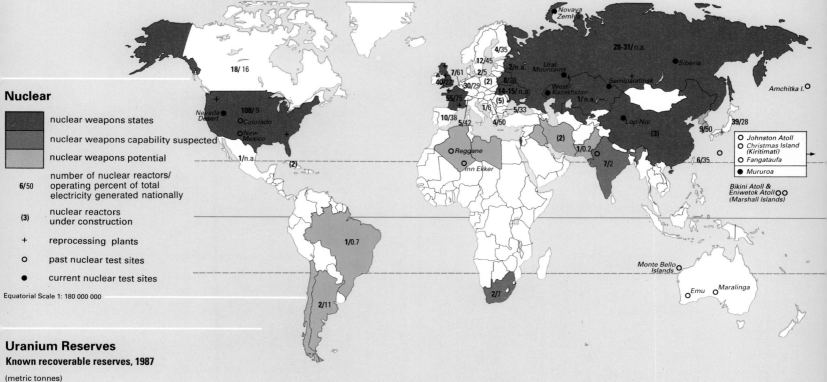

- ⬛ nuclear weapons states
- ⬛ nuclear weapons capability suspected
- ⬛ nuclear weapons potential

6/50 number of nuclear reactors/ operating percent of total electricity generated nationally

(3) nuclear reactors under construction

+ reprocessing plants

○ past nuclear test sites

● current nuclear test sites

Equatorial Scale 1: 180 000 000

Map labels:
- Novaya Zemlya
- 28-31/ n.a.
- Siberia
- 4/35
- 12/45
- 7/61
- 2/5
- 2/n.a.
- Ural Mountains
- Amchitka I.
- 40/38
- 30/29
- 8/28
- West Kazakhstan
- Semipalatinsk
- 1/n.a.
- 55/75
- 14-15/ n.a.
- 10/38
- 1/6
- (5)
- 5/33
- Lop Nur
- 5/42
- 4/50
- (2)
- 9/50
- (3)
- 39/28
- 6/35
- 18/ 16
- Nevada Desert
- 108/ 9
- ○Colorado
- New Mexico
- Reggane
- 1/0.2
- 7/2
- 1/n.a
- (2)
- 1/0.7
- 2/11
- 2/7

Inset:
- ○ Johnston Atoll
- ○ Christmas Island (Kiritimati)
- ○ Fangataufa
- ● Mururoa

- Bikini Atoll & Eniwetok Atoll ○○ (Marshall Islands)
- Monte Bello Islands ○
- ○ Emu ○ Maralinga

Uranium Reserves
Known recoverable reserves, 1987

(metric tonnes)

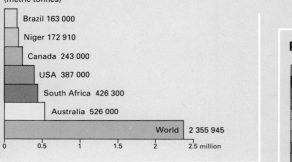

- Brazil 163 000
- Niger 172 910
- Canada 243 000
- USA 387 000
- South Africa 426 300
- Australia 526 000
- World 2 355 945

0   0.5   1   1.5   2   2.5 million

Refugees by country of origin, late 1980s

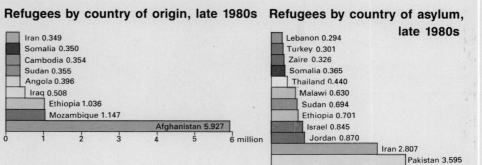

- Iran 0.349
- Somalia 0.350
- Cambodia 0.354
- Sudan 0.355
- Angola 0.396
- Iraq 0.508
- Ethiopia 1.036
- Mozambique 1.147
- Afghanistan 5.927

0   1   2   3   4   5   6 million

Refugees by country of asylum, late 1980s

- Lebanon 0.294
- Turkey 0.301
- Zaire 0.326
- Somalia 0.365
- Thailand 0.440
- Malawi 0.630
- Sudan 0.694
- Ethiopia 0.701
- Israel 0.845
- Jordan 0.870
- Iran 2.807
- Pakistan 3.595

0   1   2   3   4 million

Military expenditure

As a percent of Gross National Product (GNP), 1986

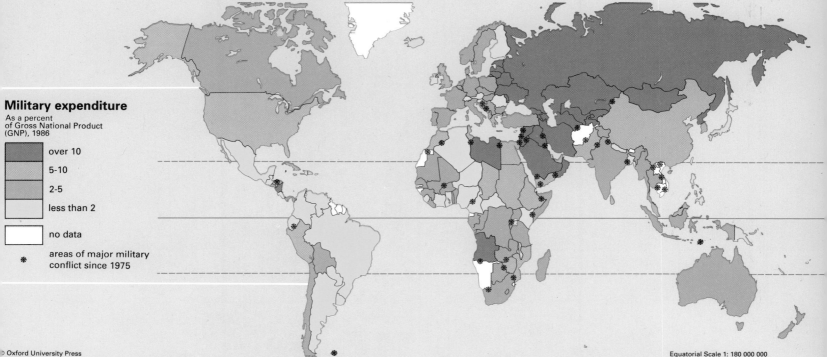

- ⬛ over 10
- ⬛ 5-10
- ⬛ 2-5
- ⬛ less than 2
- ⬜ no data
- ✳ areas of major military conflict since 1975

© Oxford University Press

Equatorial Scale 1: 180 000 000

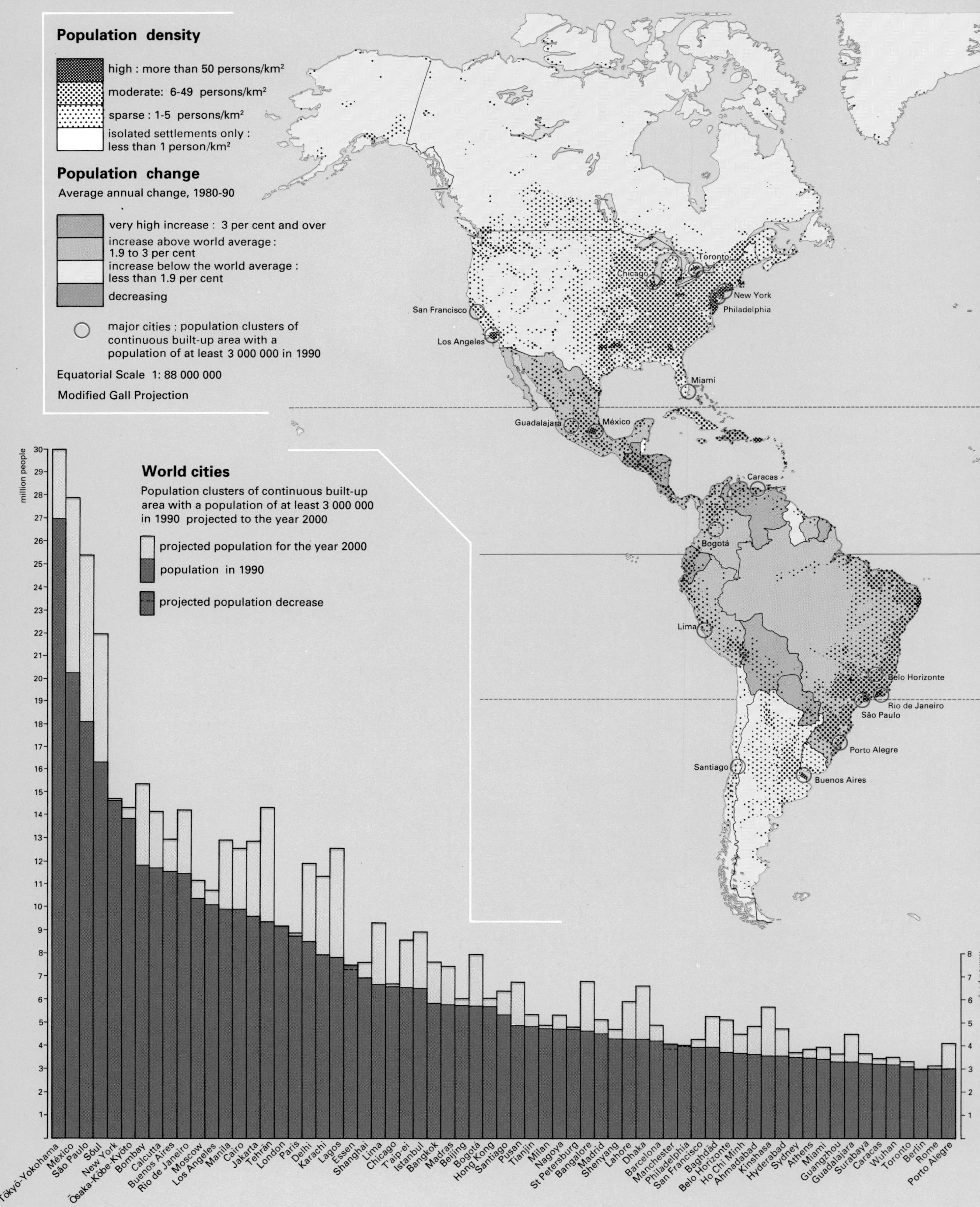

Population density

- high : more than 50 persons/km²
- moderate: 6-49 persons/km²
- sparse : 1-5 persons/km²
- isolated settlements only : less than 1 person/km²

Population change

Average annual change, 1980-90

- very high increase : 3 per cent and over
- increase above world average : 1.9 to 3 per cent
- increase below the world average : less than 1.9 per cent
- decreasing

○ major cities : population clusters of continuous built-up area with a population of at least 3 000 000 in 1990

Equatorial Scale 1: 88 000 000

Modified Gall Projection

World cities

Population clusters of continuous built-up area with a population of at least 3 000 000 in 1990 projected to the year 2000

- projected population for the year 2000
- population in 1990
- projected population decrease

million people

Tōkyō-Yokohama, México, São Paulo, Sŏul, New York, Ōsaka-Kōbe-Kyōto, Bombay, Calcutta, Buenos Aires, Rio de Janeiro, Moscow, Los Angeles, Manila, Cairo, Jakarta, Tehran, London, Paris, Delhi, Karachi, Lagos, Essen, Shanghai, Lima, Chicago, T'ai-pei, Istanbul, Bangkok, Madras, Beijing, Bogotá, Hong Kong, Santiago, Pusan, Tianjin, Milan, Nagoya, St Petersburg, Bangalore, Madrid, Shenyang, Lahore, Dhaka, Barcelona, Manchester, Philadelphia, San Francisco, Baghdad, Belo Horizonte, Ho Chi Minh, Ahmadabad, Kinshasa, Hyderabad, Sydney, Athens, Miami, Guangzhou, Guadalajara, Surabaya, Caracas, Wuhan, Toronto, Berlin, Rome, Porto Alegre

Toronto, Chicago, San Francisco, Los Angeles, New York, Philadelphia, Miami, Guadalajara, México, Caracas, Bogotá, Lima, Santiago, Buenos Aires, Belo Horizonte, Rio de Janeiro, São Paulo, Porto Alegre

Map labels (cities):

St Petersburg · Moscow · Manchester · Berlin · London · Paris · Essen · Milan · Barcelona · Rome · Madrid · Istanbul · Athens · Tehrān · Baghdad · Cairo · Lagos · Kinshasa · Karachi · Lahore · Delhi · Ahmadabad · Bombay · Hyderabad · Bangalore · Madras · Calcutta · Dhaka · Bangkok · Ho Chi Minh · Manila · Jakarta · Surabaya · Shenyang · Beijing · Tianjin · Sŏul · Pusan · Tōkyō-Yokohama · Nagoya · Ōsaka-Kōbe-Kyōto · Wuhan · Shanghai · T'aip-ei · Guangzhou · Hong Kong · Sydney

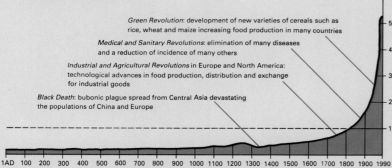

World population growth

Past growth (1AD to 1990)

Green Revolution: development of new varieties of cereals such as rice, wheat and maize increasing food production in many countries

Medical and Sanitary Revolutions: elimination of many diseases and a reduction of incidence of many others

Industrial and Agricultural Revolutions in Europe and North America: technological advances in food production, distribution and exchange for industrial goods

Black Death: bubonic plague spread from Central Asia devastating the populations of China and Europe

thousand million
6 — 5 — 4 — 3 — 2 — 1

1AD 100 200 300 400 500 600 700 800 900 1000 1100 1200 1300 1400 1500 1600 1700 1800 1900 1990

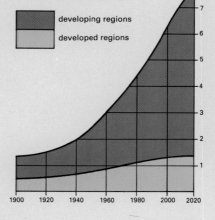

Recent growth (1900 to 1990), projected to the year 2020

- developing regions
- developed regions

8 — thousand million
7 — 6 — 5 — 4 — 3 — 2 — 1

1900 1920 1940 1960 1980 2000 2020

Additional statistical population information for all of the countries of the world is found on pages 185-190 as well as the endpaper.

Age-sex graphs for a number of countries are found on pages 60-61, 73, 94, 105 and 109.

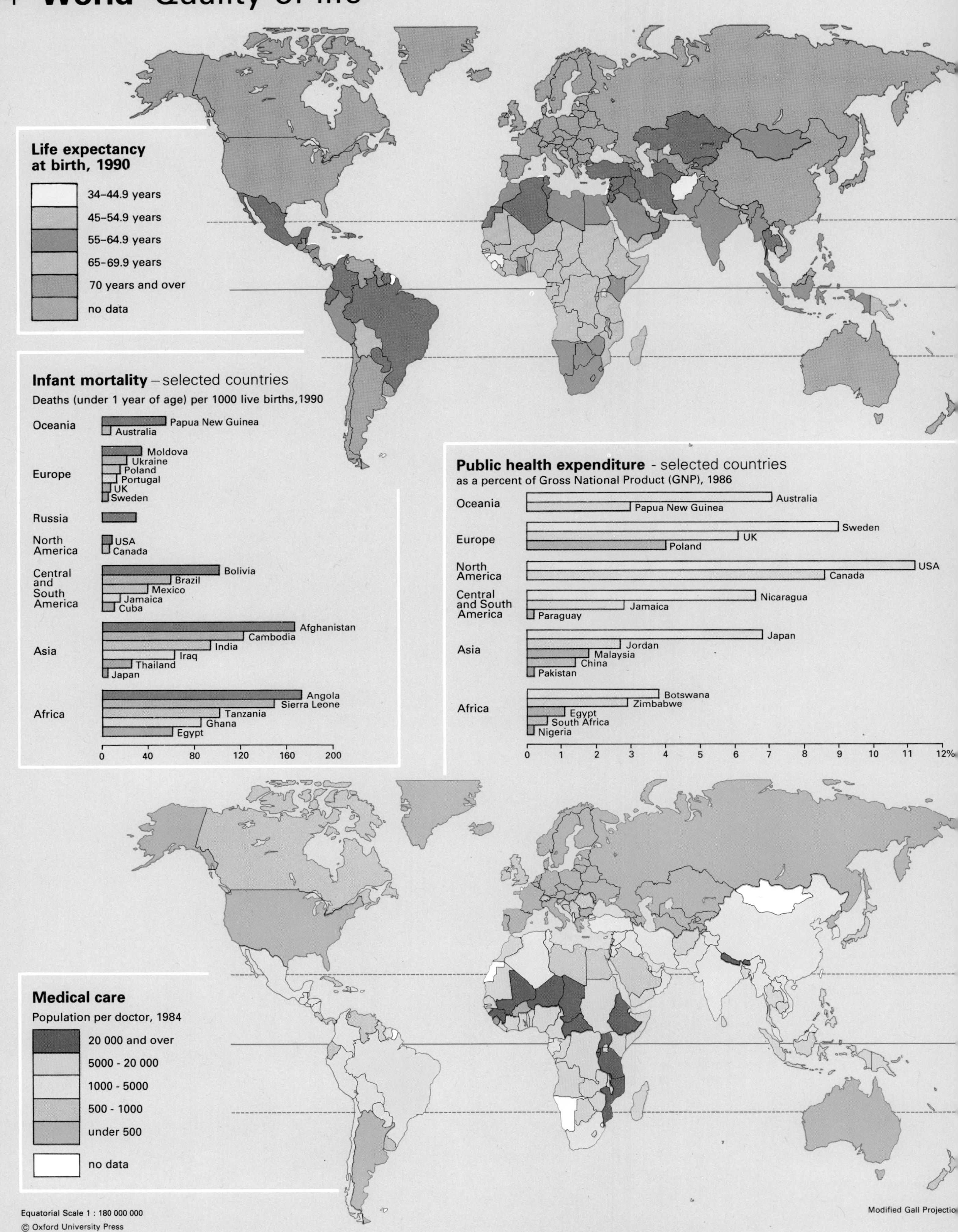

**Life expectancy
at birth, 1990**

- 34–44.9 years
- 45–54.9 years
- 55–64.9 years
- 65–69.9 years
- 70 years and over
- no data

Infant mortality – selected countries

Deaths (under 1 year of age) per 1000 live births, 1990

Oceania
- Papua New Guinea
- Australia

Europe
- Moldova
- Ukraine
- Poland
- Portugal
- UK
- Sweden

Russia

North America
- USA
- Canada

Central and South America
- Bolivia
- Brazil
- Mexico
- Jamaica
- Cuba

Asia
- Afghanistan
- Cambodia
- India
- Iraq
- Thailand
- Japan

Africa
- Angola
- Sierra Leone
- Tanzania
- Ghana
- Egypt

0   40   80   120   160   200

Public health expenditure - selected countries

as a percent of Gross National Product (GNP), 1986

Oceania
- Australia
- Papua New Guinea

Europe
- Sweden
- UK
- Poland

North America
- USA
- Canada

Central and South America
- Nicaragua
- Jamaica
- Paraguay

Asia
- Japan
- Jordan
- Malaysia
- China
- Pakistan

Africa
- Botswana
- Zimbabwe
- Egypt
- South Africa
- Nigeria

0   1   2   3   4   5   6   7   8   9   10   11   12%

Medical care

Population per doctor, 1984

- 20 000 and over
- 5000 - 20 000
- 1000 - 5000
- 500 - 1000
- under 500
- no data

Equatorial Scale 1 : 180 000 000

© Oxford University Press

Modified Gall Projection

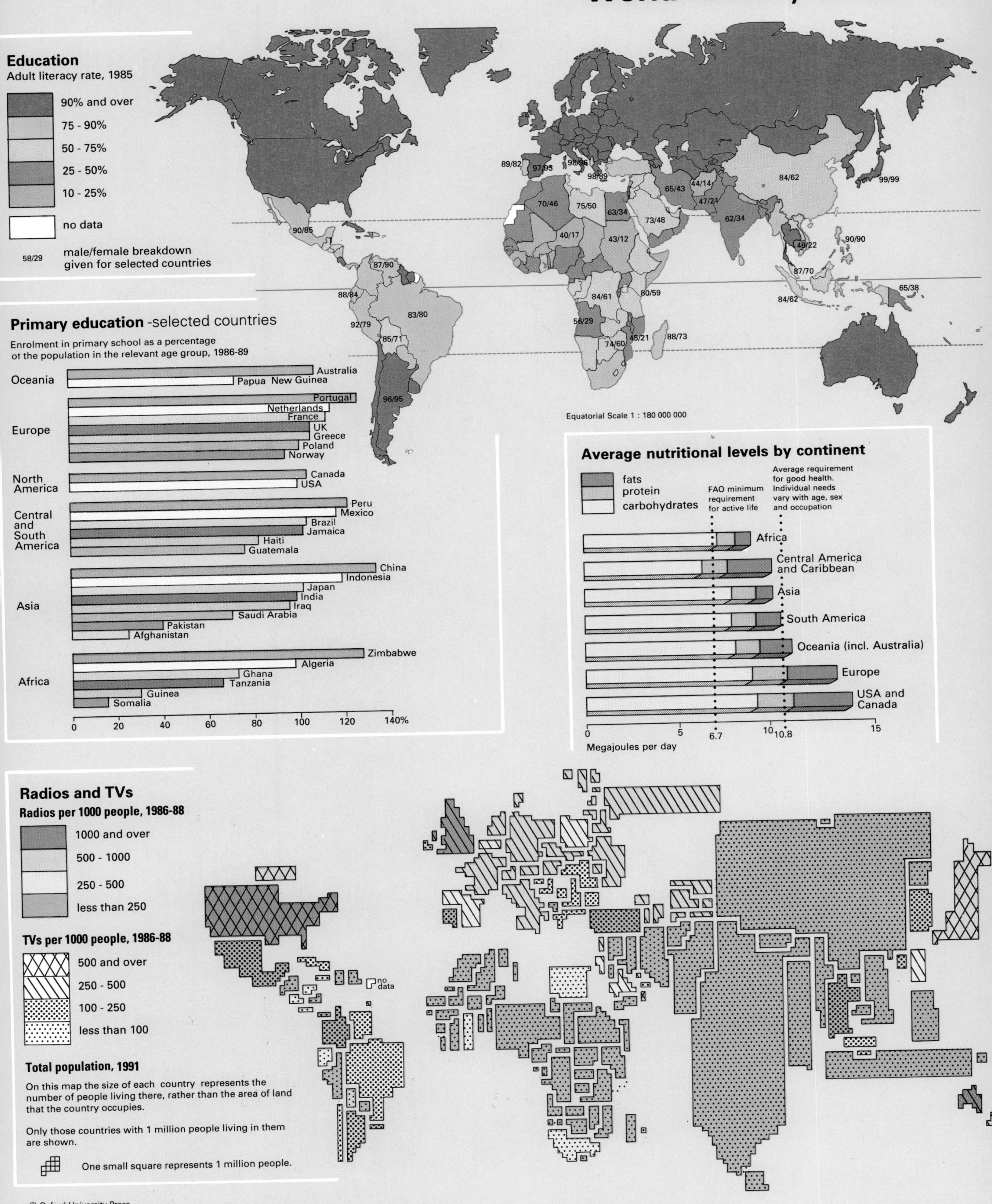

Education
Adult literacy rate, 1985

- 90% and over
- 75 - 90%
- 50 - 75%
- 25 - 50%
- 10 - 25%
- no data

58/29   male/female breakdown given for selected countries

Primary education -selected countries

Enrolment in primary school as a percentage of the population in the relevant age group, 1986-89

Oceania
- Australia
- Papua New Guinea

Europe
- Portugal
- Netherlands
- France
- UK
- Greece
- Poland
- Norway

North America
- Canada
- USA

Central and South America
- Peru
- Mexico
- Brazil
- Jamaica
- Haiti
- Guatemala

Asia
- China
- Indonesia
- Japan
- India
- Iraq
- Saudi Arabia
- Pakistan
- Afghanistan

Africa
- Zimbabwe
- Algeria
- Ghana
- Tanzania
- Guinea
- Somalia

0   20   40   60   80   100   120   140%

Equatorial Scale 1 : 180 000 000

Average nutritional levels by continent

- fats
- protein
- carbohydrates

FAO minimum requirement for active life

Average requirement for good health. Individual needs vary with age, sex and occupation

- Africa
- Central America and Caribbean
- Asia
- South America
- Oceania (incl. Australia)
- Europe
- USA and Canada

0   5   6.7   10   10.8   15

Megajoules per day

Radios and TVs
Radios per 1000 people, 1986-88
- 1000 and over
- 500 - 1000
- 250 - 500
- less than 250

TVs per 1000 people, 1986-88
- 500 and over
- 250 - 500
- 100 - 250
- less than 100

no data

Total population, 1991

On this map the size of each country represents the number of people living there, rather than the area of land that the country occupies.

Only those countries with 1 million people living in them are shown.

One small square represents 1 million people.

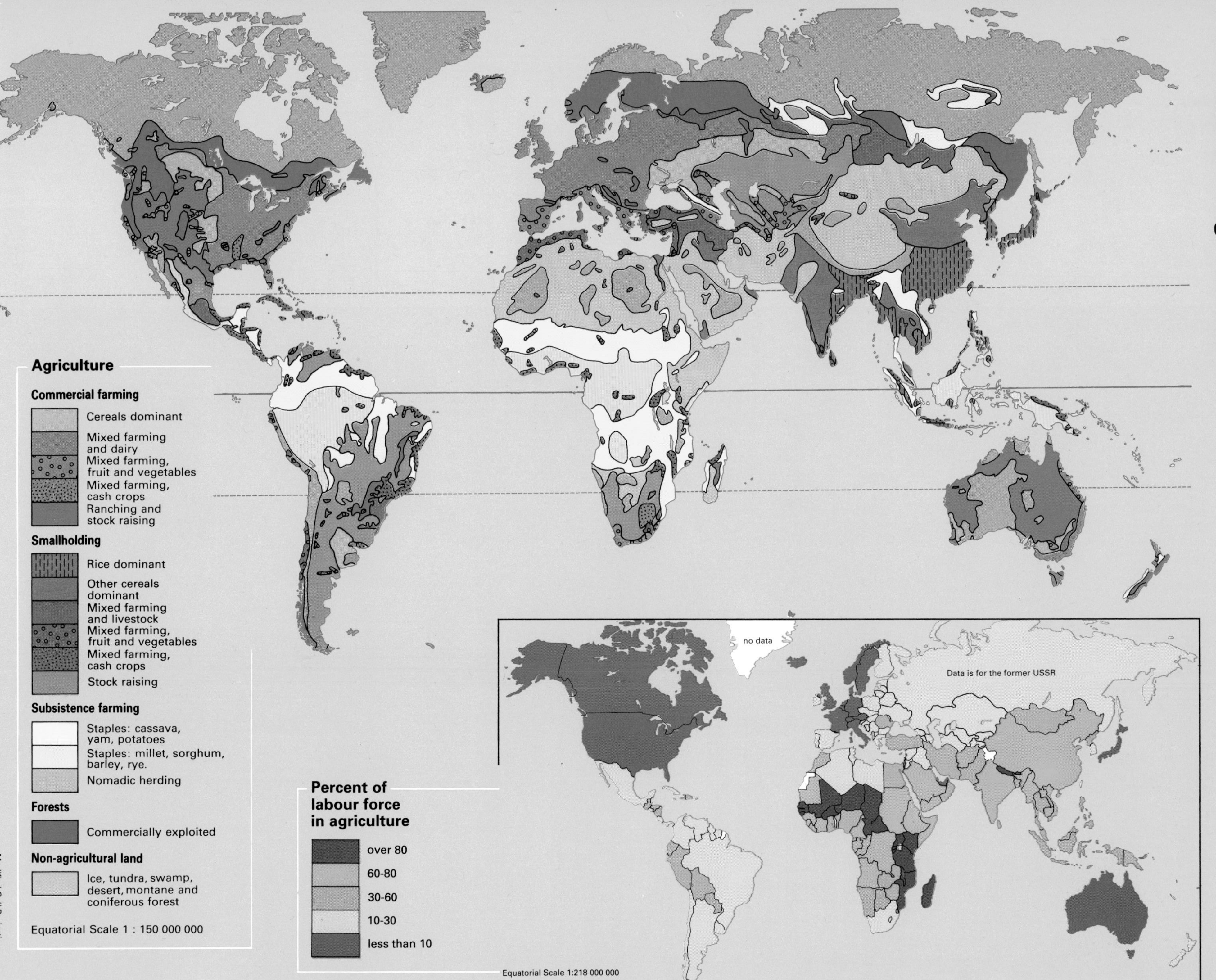

Data is for the former USSR

no data

Equatorial Scale 1:218 000 000

**Percent of
labour force
in agriculture**

- over 80
- 60-80
- 30-60
- 10-30
- less than 10

Agriculture

Commercial farming

- Cereals dominant
- Mixed farming and dairy
- Mixed farming, fruit and vegetables
- Mixed farming, cash crops
- Ranching and stock raising

Smallholding

- Rice dominant
- Other cereals dominant
- Mixed farming and livestock
- Mixed farming, fruit and vegetables
- Mixed farming, cash crops
- Stock raising

Subsistence farming

- Staples: cassava, yam, potatoes
- Staples: millet, sorghum, barley, rye.
- Nomadic herding

Forests

- Commercially exploited

Non-agricultural land

- Ice, tundra, swamp, desert, montane and coniferous forest

Equatorial Scale 1 : 150 000 000

Modified Gall Projection
© Oxford University Press

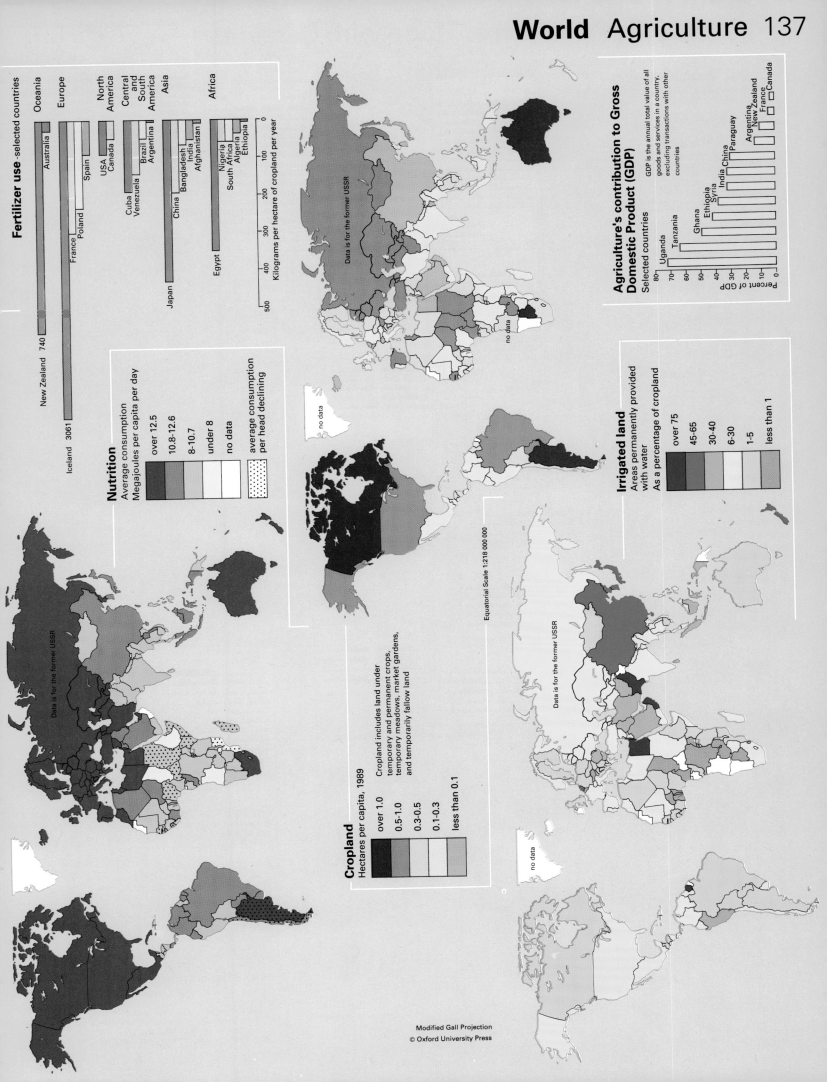

Fertilizer use -selected countries

Oceania — Australia — New Zealand 740

Europe — France, Poland, Spain

North America — USA, Canada

Central and South America — Cuba, Venezuela, Brazil, Argentina

Asia — Japan, China, Bangladesh, India, Afghanistan

Africa — Egypt, Nigeria, South Africa, Algeria, Ethiopia

Iceland 3061

Kilograms per hectare of cropland per year
0 100 200 300 400 500

Agriculture's contribution to Gross Domestic Product (GDP)
Selected countries

GDP is the annual total value of all goods and services in a country, excluding transactions with other countries

Uganda, Tanzania, Ghana, Ethiopia, Syria, India, China, Paraguay, Argentina, New Zealand, France, Canada

Percent of GDP
80 70 60 50 40 30 20 10 0

Nutrition
Average consumption
Megajoules per capita per day

- over 12.5
- 10.8-12.6
- 8-10.7
- under 8
- no data
- average consumption per head declining

Irrigated land
Areas permanently provided with water
As a percentage of cropland

- over 75
- 45-65
- 30-40
- 6-30
- 1-5
- less than 1

Data is for the former USSR

no data

Equatorial Scale 1:218 000 000

Cropland
Hectares per capita, 1989

Cropland includes land under temporary and permanent crops, temporary meadows, market gardens, and temporarily fallow land

- over 1.0
- 0.5-1.0
- 0.3-0.5
- 0.1-0.3
- less than 0.1

no data

Data is for the former USSR

Modified Gall Projection
© Oxford University Press

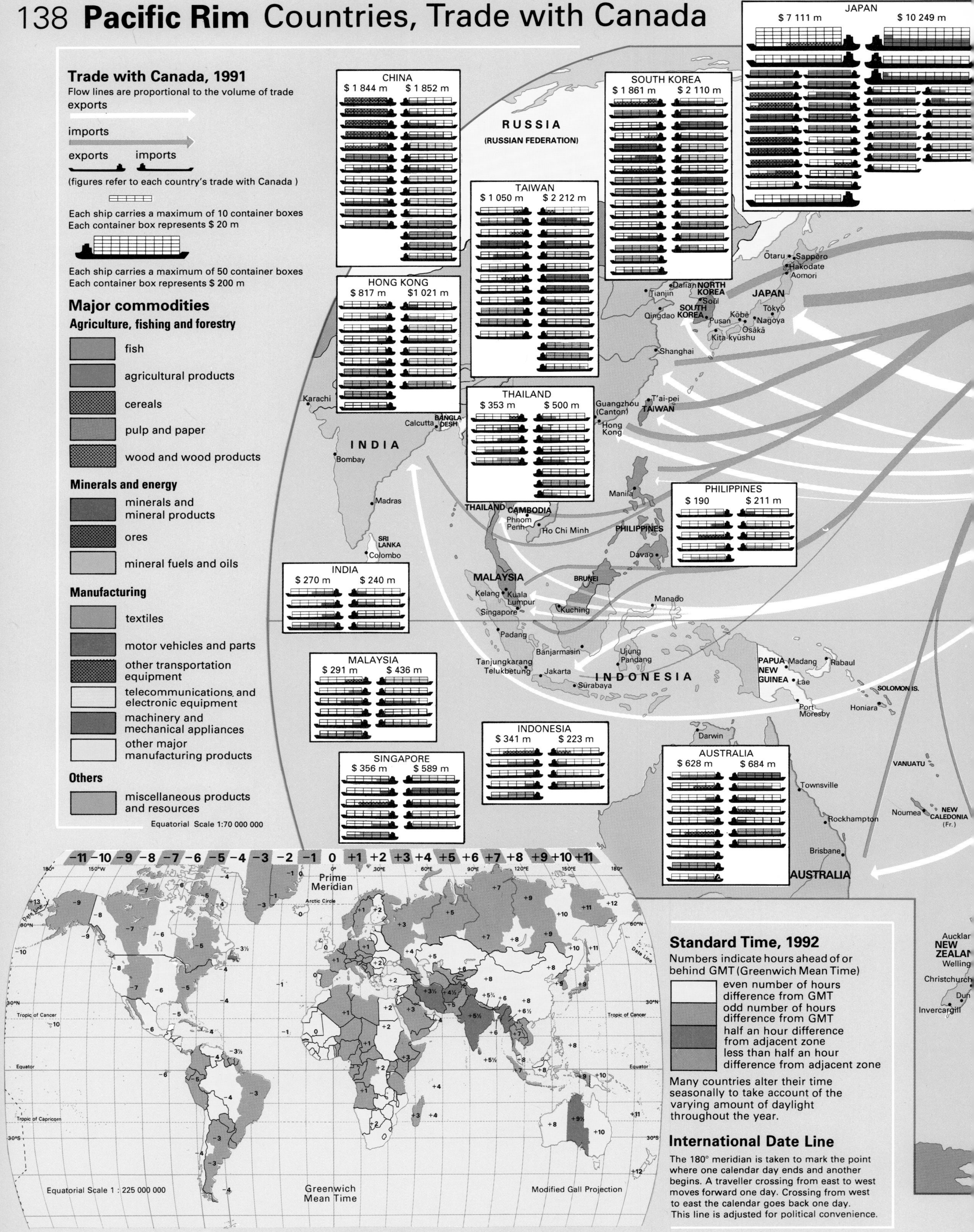

Trade with Canada, 1991

Flow lines are proportional to the volume of trade

exports

imports

exports   imports

(figures refer to each country's trade with Canada)

Each ship carries a maximum of 10 container boxes
Each container box represents $ 20 m

Each ship carries a maximum of 50 container boxes
Each container box represents $ 200 m

Major commodities

Agriculture, fishing and forestry

fish

agricultural products

cereals

pulp and paper

wood and wood products

Minerals and energy

minerals and mineral products

ores

mineral fuels and oils

Manufacturing

textiles

motor vehicles and parts

other transportation equipment

telecommunications and electronic equipment

machinery and mechanical appliances

other major manufacturing products

Others

miscellaneous products and resources

Equatorial Scale 1:70 000 000

JAPAN
$ 7 111 m $ 10 249 m

CHINA
$ 1 844 m $ 1 852 m

SOUTH KOREA
$ 1 861 m $ 2 110 m

RUSSIA
(RUSSIAN FEDERATION)

TAIWAN
$ 1 050 m $ 2 212 m

HONG KONG
$ 817 m $1 021 m

THAILAND
$ 353 m $ 500 m

PHILIPPINES
$ 190 $ 211 m

INDIA
$ 270 m $ 240 m

MALAYSIA
$ 291 m $ 436 m

INDONESIA
$ 341 m $ 223 m

AUSTRALIA
$ 628 m $ 684 m

SINGAPORE
$ 356 m $ 589 m

Karachi

Calcutta BANGLA-DESH

INDIA

Bombay

Madras

SRI LANKA

Colombo

THAILAND CAMBODIA

Phnom Penh

Ho Chi Minh

PHILIPPINES

MALAYSIA BRUNEI

Kelang Kuala Lumpur

Singapore

Kuching

Padang

Tanjungkarang Telukbetung

Banjarmasin

Jakarta

Surabaya

Ujung Pandang

INDONESIA

Manado

Manila

Davao

Tianjin

Dalian NORTH KOREA

Qingdao SOUTH KOREA

Sŏul

Pusan

Shanghai

Guangzhou (Canton)

Hong Kong

T'ai-pei TAIWAN

Ōtaru Sapporo

Hakodate

Aomori

JAPAN

Tōkyō

Kōbe Nagoya

Ōsaka

Kita-kyūshū

Darwin

PAPUA NEW GUINEA

Madang Rabaul

Lae

SOLOMON IS.

Port Moresby

Honiara

VANUATU

Townsville

Rockhampton

Brisbane

AUSTRALIA

NEW CALEDONIA (Fr.)

Noumea

Auckland
NEW ZEALAND
Wellington

Christchurch

Dunedin

Invercargill

Standard Time, 1992

Numbers indicate hours ahead of or behind GMT (Greenwich Mean Time)

even number of hours difference from GMT

odd number of hours difference from GMT

half an hour difference from adjacent zone

less than half an hour difference from adjacent zone

Many countries alter their time seasonally to take account of the varying amount of daylight throughout the year.

International Date Line

The 180° meridian is taken to mark the point where one calendar day ends and another begins. A traveller crossing from east to west moves forward one day. Crossing from west to east the calendar goes back one day. This line is adjusted for political convenience.

-11 -10 -9 -8 -7 -6 -5 -4 -3 -2 -1 0 +1 +2 +3 +4 +5 +6 +7 +8 +9 +10 +11

Prime Meridian

Arctic Circle

Tropic of Cancer

Equator

Tropic of Capricorn

Greenwich Mean Time

Modified Gall Projection

Equatorial Scale 1 : 225 000 000

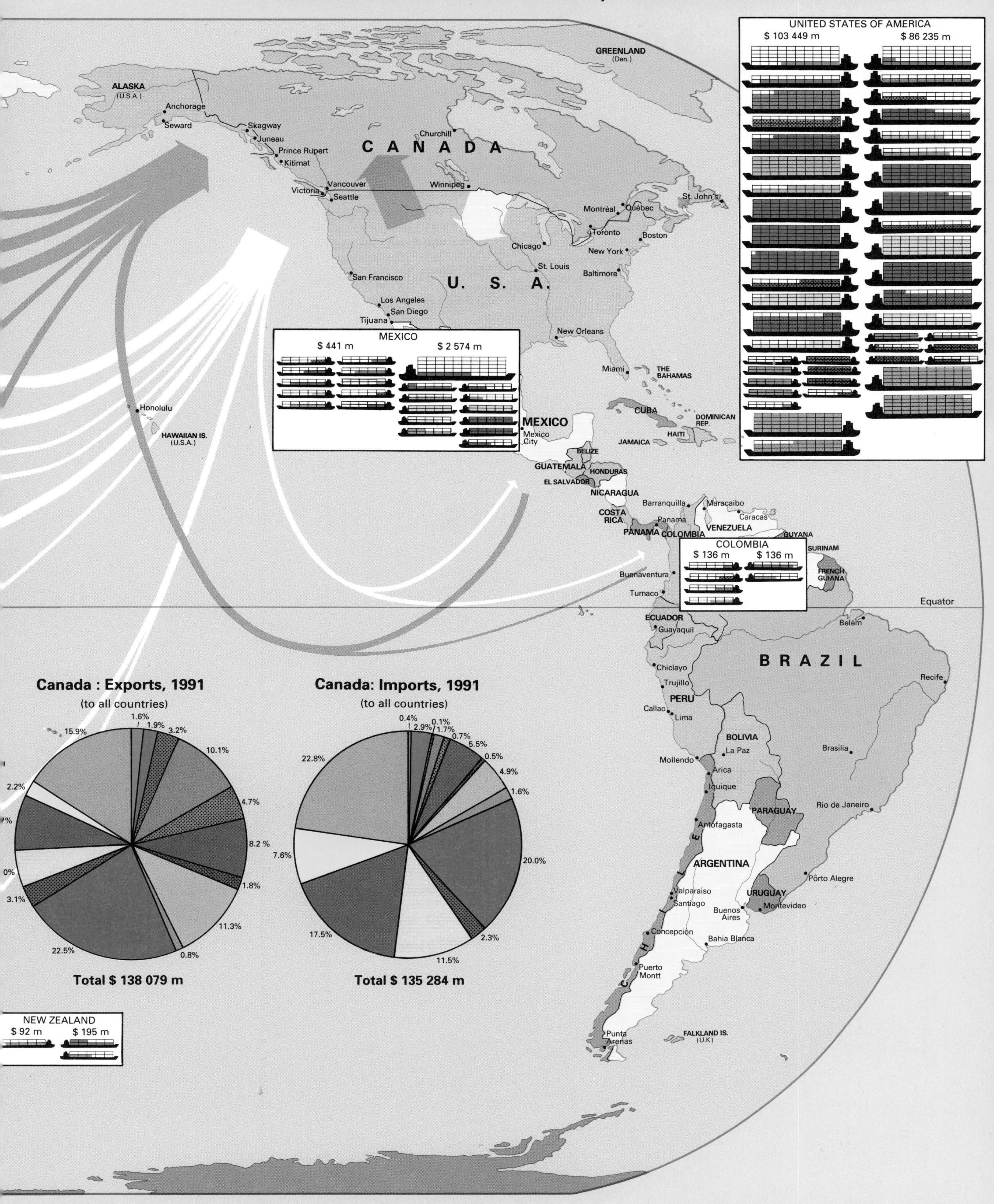

GREENLAND
(Den.)

ALASKA
(U.S.A.)

Anchorage

Seward

Skagway
Juneau
Prince Rupert
Kitimat

C A N A D A

Churchill

Victoria
Vancouver
Seattle

Winnipeg

St. John's

Montréal Québec

Toronto
Chicago
Boston
New York
St. Louis
Baltimore

San Francisco

U. S. A.

Los Angeles
San Diego
Tijuana

New Orleans

Miami
THE
BAHAMAS

CUBA
DOMINICAN
REP.
JAMAICA HAITI

MEXICO
Mexico
City

BELIZE

GUATEMALA
EL SALVADOR

HONDURAS

NICARAGUA

COSTA
RICA
PANAMA

Barranquilla
Panama

COLOMBIA

Maracaibo
Caracas
VENEZUELA

GUYANA

SURINAM

FRENCH
GUIANA

Buenaventura

Tumaco

ECUADOR
Guayaquil

Belém

Equator

B R A Z I L

Recife

Chiclayo
Trujillo
Callao
Lima

PERU

BOLIVIA
La Paz

Brasilia

Mollendo
Arica
Iquique

PARAGUAY

Rio de Janeiro

Antofagasta

ARGENTINA

Pôrto Alegre

URUGUAY
Montevideo

Valparaiso
Santiago

Buenos
Aires

Concepción
Bahia Blanca

Puerto
Montt

Punta
Arenas

FALKLAND IS.
(U.K)

Honolulu

HAWAIIAN IS.
(U.S.A.)

UNITED STATES OF AMERICA
$ 103 449 m $ 86 235 m

MEXICO
$ 441 m $ 2 574 m

COLOMBIA
$ 136 m $ 136 m

Canada : Exports, 1991
(to all countries)

15.9%
1.6%
1.9%
3.2%
10.1%
2.2%
4.7%
8.2 %
1.8%
0%
3.1%
11.3%
22.5%
0.8%

Total $ 138 079 m

Canada: Imports, 1991
(to all countries)

0.4%
0.1%
2.9%
1.7%
0.7%
5.5%
22.8%
0.5%
4.9%
1.6%
7.6%
20.0%
17.5%
11.5%
2.3%

Total $ 135 284 m

NEW ZEALAND
$ 92 m $ 195 m

Modified Eckert IV Projection
Oxford University Press

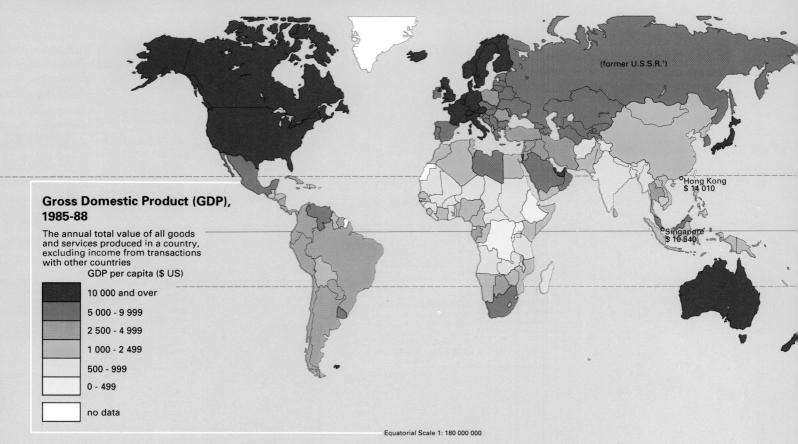

Gross Domestic Product (GDP), 1985-88

The annual total value of all goods and services produced in a country, excluding income from transactions with other countries

GDP per capita ($ US)

- 10 000 and over
- 5 000 - 9 999
- 2 500 - 4 999
- 1 000 - 2 499
- 500 - 999
- 0 - 499
- no data

(former U.S.S.R.¹)

Hong Kong $ 14 010

Singapore $ 10 540

Equatorial Scale 1: 180 000 000

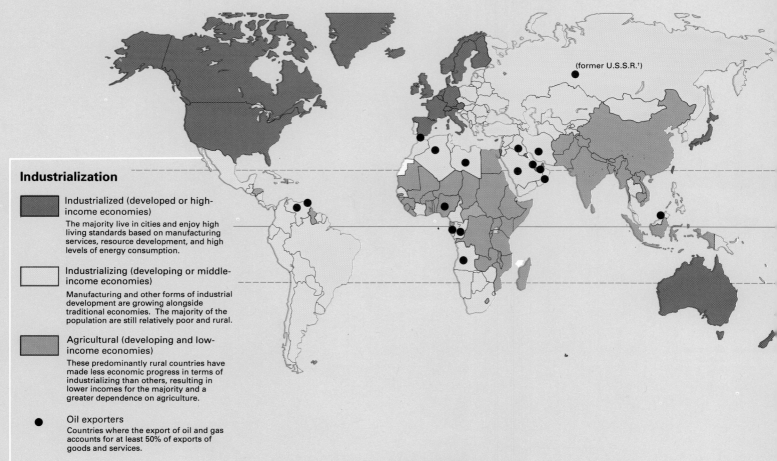

Industrialization

Industrialized (developed or high-income economies)
The majority live in cities and enjoy high living standards based on manufacturing services, resource development, and high levels of energy consumption.

Industrializing (developing or middle-income economies)
Manufacturing and other forms of industrial development are growing alongside traditional economies. The majority of the population are still relatively poor and rural.

Agricultural (developing and low-income economies)
These predominantly rural countries have made less economic progress in terms of industrializing than others, resulting in lower incomes for the majority and a greater dependence on agriculture.

● **Oil exporters**
Countries where the export of oil and gas accounts for at least 50% of exports of goods and services.

(former U.S.S.R.¹)

Equatorial Scale 1: 180 000 000

Modified Gall Projection

© Oxford University Press

Employment, 1985-88
Proportion of labour force in agriculture, industry, and service industries

services   ⊘   agriculture
     industry

Equatorial Scale 1: 180 000 000

(former U.S.S.R.†)

† Now the independent republics of Armenia, Azerbaijan, Belarus, Estonia, Georgia, Kazakhstan, Kirgyzstan, Latvia, Lithuania, Moldova, Russia, Tajikistan, Turkmenistan, Ukraine, and Uzbekistan.

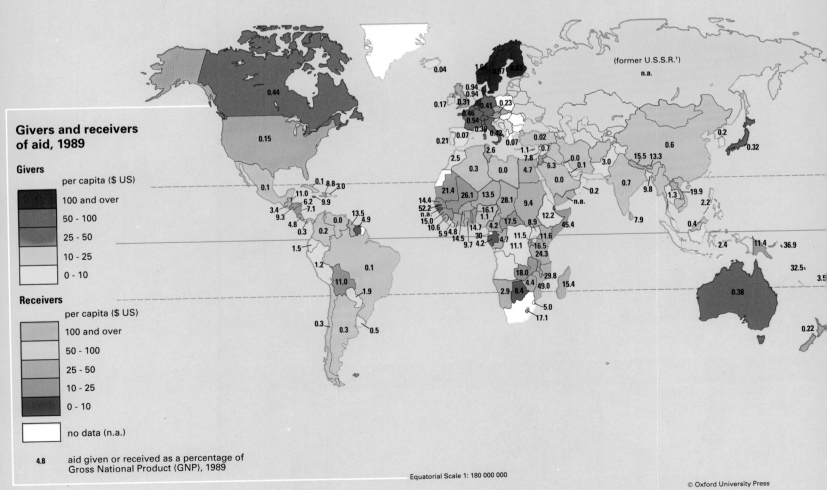

Givers and receivers of aid, 1989

Givers

per capita ($ US)

■	100 and over
■	50 - 100
■	25 - 50
■	10 - 25
□	0 - 10

Receivers

per capita ($ US)

■	100 and over
■	50 - 100
■	25 - 50
■	10 - 25
■	0 - 10
□	no data (n.a.)

4.8   aid given or received as a percentage of Gross National Product (GNP), 1989

Equatorial Scale 1: 180 000 000

Modified Gall Projection

© Oxford University Press

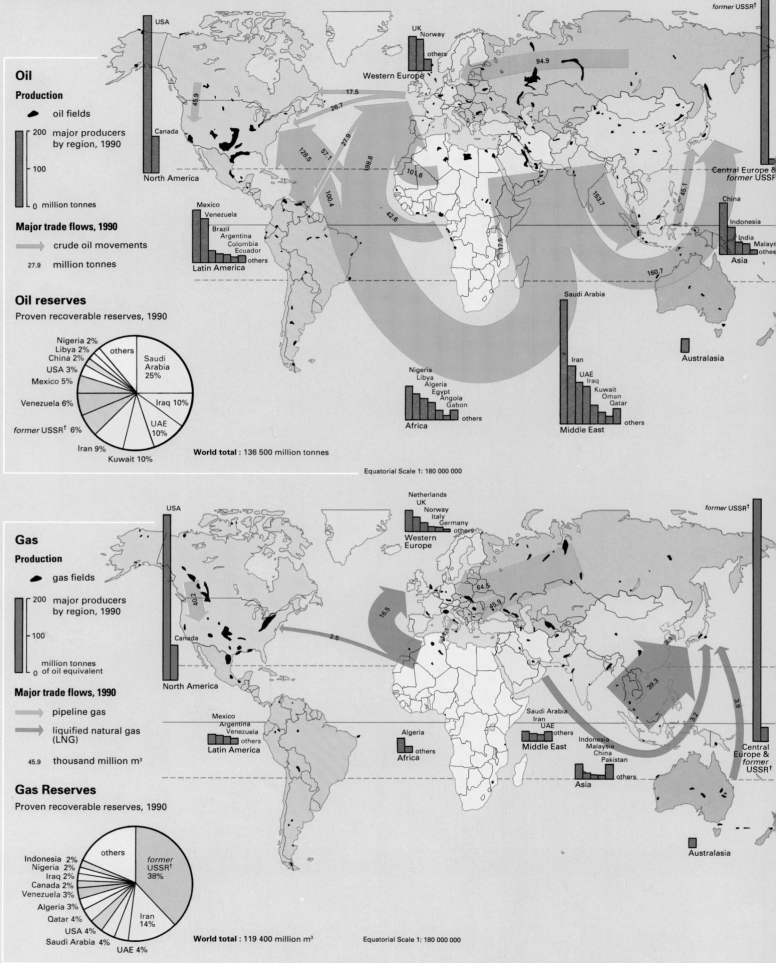

Oil

Production

- oil fields

200 — major producers by region, 1990

100 —

0 — million tonnes

Major trade flows, 1990

→ crude oil movements

27.9 million tonnes

Oil reserves

Proven recoverable reserves, 1990

Nigeria 2%
Libya 2%
China 2%
USA 3%
Mexico 5%
Venezuela 6%
former USSR† 6%
Iran 9%
Kuwait 10%
others
Saudi Arabia 25%
Iraq 10%
UAE 10%

World total : 136 500 million tonnes

USA
Canada
North America

UK
Norway
others
Western Europe

94.9

17.5
26.7
27.9
128.5
57.1
198.8
100.4
42.6
101.6
17.5
153.7
45.1
160.7
former USSR†
Central Europe & former USSR

Mexico
Venezuela
Brazil
Argentina
Colombia
Ecuador
others
Latin America

Nigeria
Libya
Algeria
Egypt
Angola
Gabon
others
Africa

Saudi Arabia
Iran
UAE
Iraq
Kuwait
Oman
Qatar
others
Middle East

China
Indonesia
India
Malaysia
others
Asia

Australasia

Equatorial Scale 1: 180 000 000

Gas

Production

- gas fields

200 — major producers by region, 1990

100 —

0 — million tonnes of oil equivalent

Major trade flows, 1990

→ pipeline gas

→ liquified natural gas (LNG)

45.9 thousand million m³

Gas Reserves

Proven recoverable reserves, 1990

Indonesia 2%
Nigeria 2%
Iraq 2%
Canada 2%
Venezuela 3%
Algeria 3%
Qatar 4%
USA 4%
Saudi Arabia 4%
UAE 4%
Iran 14%
others
former USSR† 38%

World total : 119 400 million m³

USA
Canada
North America

Netherlands
UK
Norway
Italy
Germany
others
Western Europe

former USSR†

40.2
16.5
2.5
64.5
45.9
39.3
3.2
3.9
Central Europe & former USSR†

Mexico
Argentina
Venezuela
others
Latin America

Algeria
others
Africa

Saudi Arabia
Iran
UAE
others
Middle East

Indonesia
Malaysia
China
Pakistan
others
Asia

Australasia

Equatorial Scale 1: 180 000 000

Modified Gall Projection

© Oxford University Press

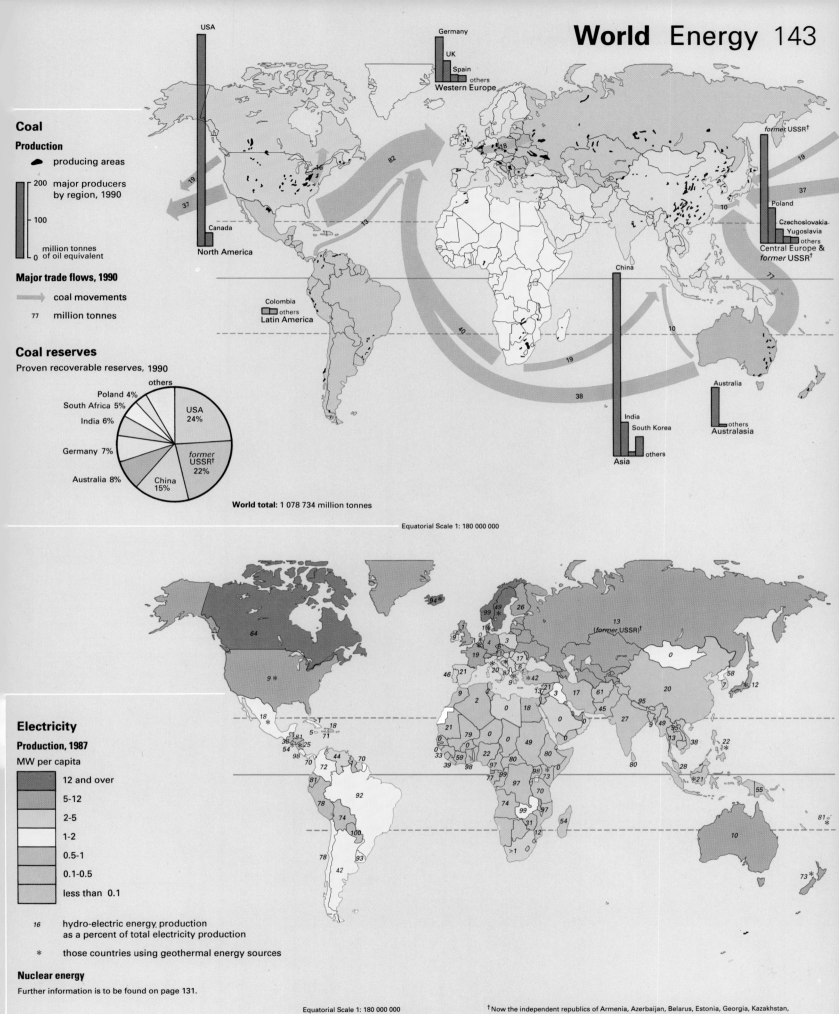

Coal

Production

🖤 producing areas

major producers by region, 1990

200

100

0 — million tonnes of oil equivalent

Major trade flows, 1990

→ coal movements

77 million tonnes

Coal reserves

Proven recoverable reserves, 1990

others
Poland 4%
South Africa 5%
India 6%
Germany 7%
Australia 8%
China 15%
USA 24%
former USSR† 22%

World total: 1 078 734 million tonnes

USA
Germany
UK
Spain
others
Western Europe

former USSR†
19
37
Poland
Czechoslovakia
Yugoslavia
others
Central Europe & *former* USSR†

Canada
North America

Colombia
others
Latin America

China
India
South Korea
others
Asia

Australia
others
Australasia

82
19
37
46
10
13
77
40
19
38
10

Equatorial Scale 1: 180 000 000

Electricity

Production, 1987

MW per capita

12 and over
5-12
2-5
1-2
0.5-1
0.1-0.5
less than 0.1

16 hydro-electric energy production as a percent of total electricity production

* those countries using geothermal energy sources

Nuclear energy

Further information is to be found on page 131.

Equatorial Scale 1: 180 000 000

† Now the independent republics of Armenia, Azerbaijan, Belarus, Estonia, Georgia, Kazakhstan, Kirgyzstan, Latvia, Lithuania, Moldova, Russia, Tajikistan, Turkmenistan, Ukraine, and Uzbekistan.

Modified Gall Projection

© Oxford University Press

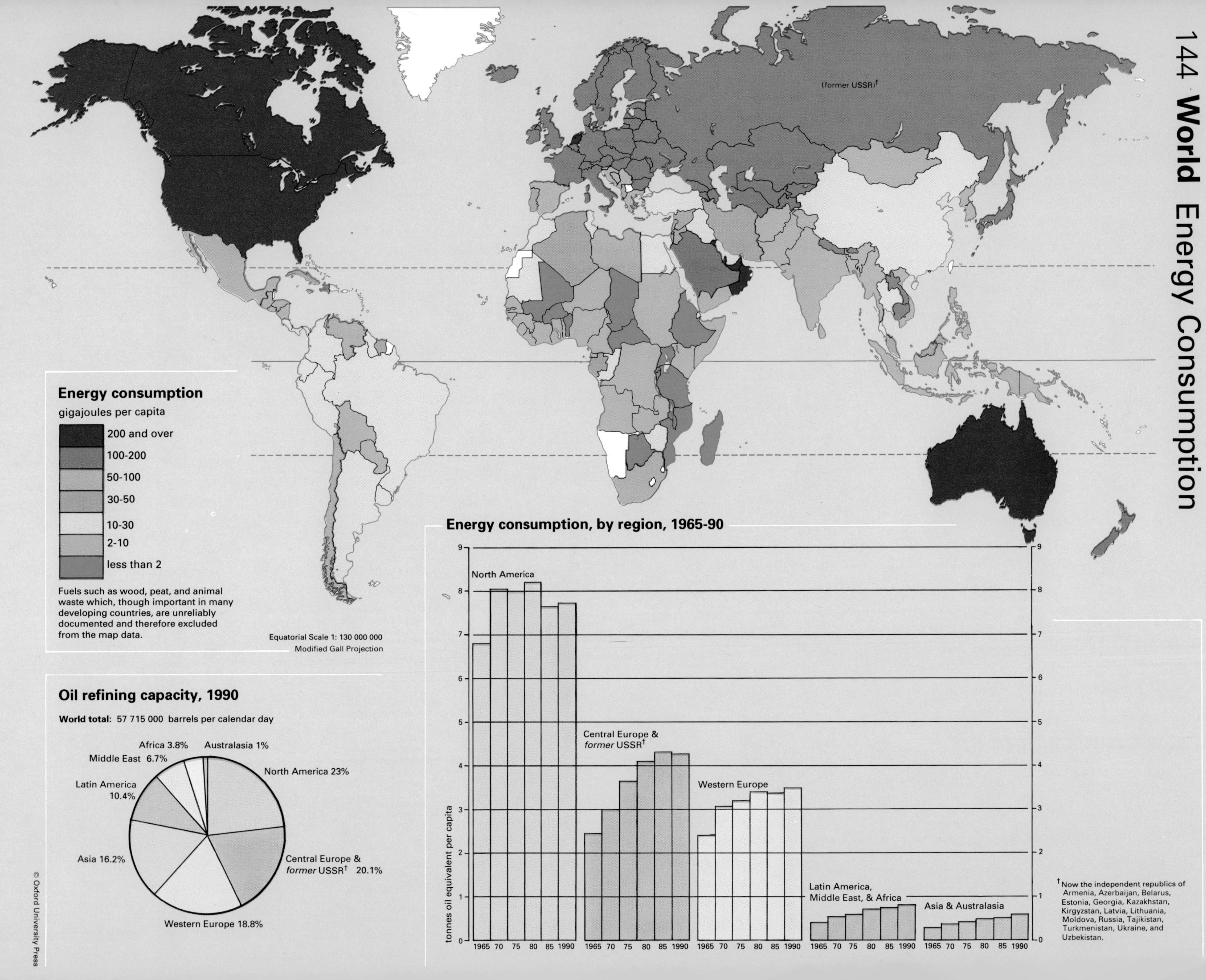

Energy consumption, by region, 1965-90

tonnes oil equivalent per capita

North America

Central Europe & *former* USSR[†]

Western Europe

Latin America, Middle East, & Africa

Asia & Australasia

[†] Now the independent republics of Armenia, Azerbaijan, Belarus, Estonia, Georgia, Kazakhstan, Kirgyzstan, Latvia, Lithuania, Moldova, Russia, Tajikistan, Turkmenistan, Ukraine, and Uzbekistan.

Energy consumption

gigajoules per capita

200 and over
100-200
50-100
30-50
10-30
2-10
less than 2

Fuels such as wood, peat, and animal waste which, though important in many developing countries, are unreliably documented and therefore excluded from the map data.

(former USSR)[†]

Equatorial Scale 1: 130 000 000

Modified Gall Projection

Oil refining capacity, 1990

World total: 57 715 000 barrels per calendar day

Africa 3.8%
Australasia 1%
North America 23%
Central Europe & *former* USSR[†] 20.1%
Western Europe 18.8%
Asia 16.2%
Latin America 10.4%
Middle East 6.7%

© Oxford University Press

Gazetteer

How to use the gazetteer

To find a place on an atlas map use either the grid code or latitude and longitude.

For more information on latitude and longitude look at pages 6 and 7.

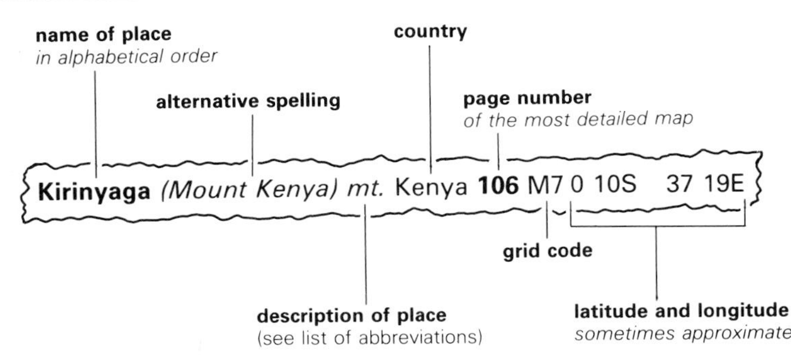

name of place
in alphabetical order

country

alternative spelling

page number
of the most detailed map

Kirinyaga *(Mount Kenya) mt.* Kenya **106** M7 0 10S 37 19E

grid code

description of place
(see list of abbreviations)

latitude and longitude
sometimes approximate

Grid code Kirinyaga is in grid square M7

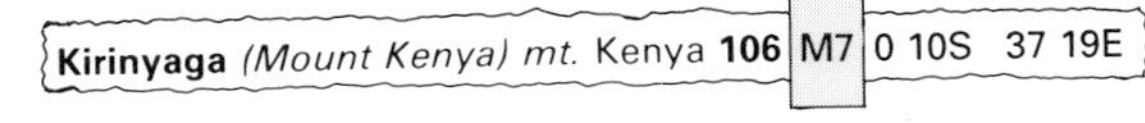

Kirinyaga *(Mount Kenya) mt.* Kenya **106** M7 0 10S 37 19E

Kirinyaga

Latitude and Longitude Kirinyaga is at latitude 0 10S longitude 37 19E

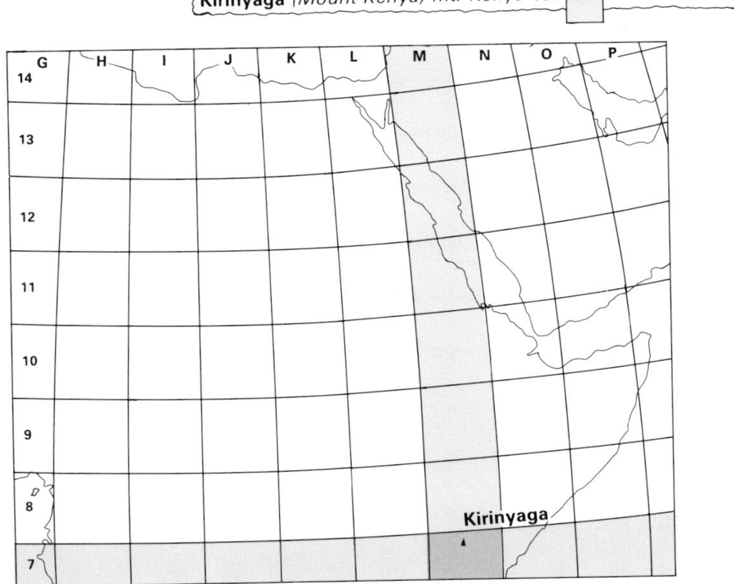

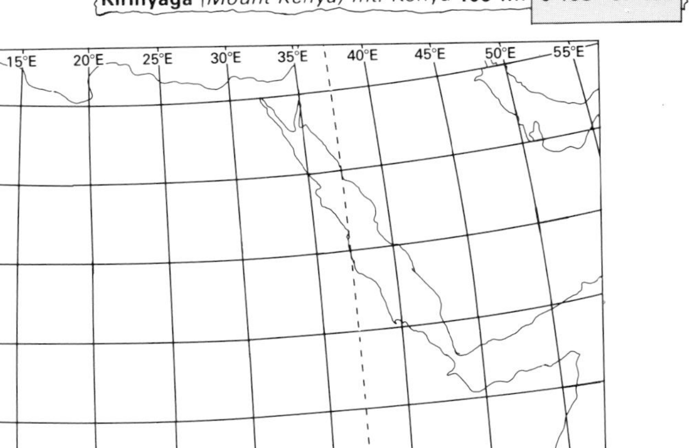

Kirinyaga *(Mount Kenya) mt.* Kenya **106** M7 0 10S 37 19E

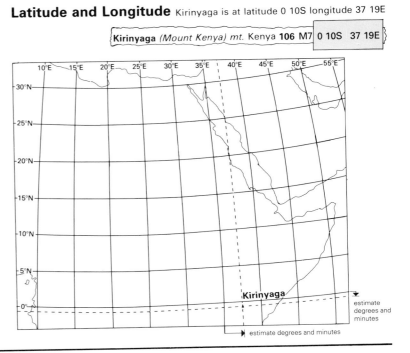

Kirinyaga

estimate
degrees and
minutes

estimate degrees and minutes

Abbreviations used in the gazetteer

admin.	administrative area	*mts.*	mountains
A.C.T.	Australian Capital Territory	*p.*	peninsula
b.	bay or harbour	*pk.*	park
bor.	borough	*plat.*	plateau
c.	cape, point or headland	*pn.*	plain
can.	canal	*pref.*	prefecture
co.	county	*r.*	river
d.	desert	*rd.*	road
dep.	depression	*r.s.*	research station
est.	estuary	*reg.*	region
fj.	fjord	*rep.*	republic
F.R.G.	Federal Republic of Germany	*res.*	reservoir
g.	gulf	*salt l.*	salt lake
G.D.R.	German Democratic Republic	*sd.*	sound, strait or channel
geog. reg.	geographical region	*S.S.R.*	Soviet Socialist Republic
G.R.A.	Government Residential Area	*sum.*	summit
hist. site	historical site	*tn.*	town
i.	island	*U.A.E.*	United Arab Emirates
in.	inlet	*U.K.*	United Kingdom
I.R.	Indian Reservation	*U.S.A.*	United States of America
is.	islands	*U.S.S.R.*	Union of Soviet Socialist Republics
ist.	isthmus	*v.*	valley
l.	lake, lakes, lagoon	*vol.*	volcano
m.	marsh		
m.s.	manned meteorological station		
mt.	mountain		

Abbreviations used on the maps

A.C.T.	Australian Capital Territory	Peg.	Pegunungan
Ákr.	Ákra	Pen.; Penin.	Peninsula
App.	Appennino	Pl.	Planina
Arch.	Archipelago	Port.	Portugal
Arg.	Argentina	P.P.	Provincial Park
Arq.	Arquípelago	proj.	projected
Austl.	Australia	Pt.	Point
C.	Cape; Cabo; Cap	Pta.	Punta
Col.	Colombia	Pte.	Pointe
D.C.	District of Columbia	Pto.	Porto; Puerto
Den.	Denmark	R.	River; Rio
E.	East	Ra.	Range
Ec.	Ecuador	R.A.	Recreation Area
Eq.	Equatorial	Res.	Reservoir
Fj.	Fjord	Résr.	Réservoir
Fr.	France	R.M.	Regional Municipality
F.R.G.	Federal Republic of Germany	S.	South; San
G.	Gunung; Gebel	S.A.	South Africa
G.D.R.	German Democratic Republic	Sa.	Sierra
Hwy.	Highway	Sd.	Sound
I.	Island; Île; Isla; Ilha	Sev.	Severnaya
Is.	Islands; Îles; Islas; Ilhas	Sp.	Spain
J.	Jezioro	St.	Saint
Jez.	Jezero	Ste.	Sainte
Kep.	Kepulauan	Str.	Strait
M.	Muang	Terr.	Territory
Mt.	Mount; Mountain; Mont	U.A.E.	United Arab Emirates
Mte.	Monte	u/c.	under construction
Mts.	Mountains; Monts	U.K.	United Kingdom
N.	North	U.N.	United Nations
Nat. Pk.	National Park	U.S.A.	United States of America
Neths.	Netherlands	U.S.S.R.	Union of Soviet Socialist Republics
N.P.	National Park	W.	West
N.Z.	New Zealand		
Pa.	Passage		

A

Abbotsford British Columbia **42** H4 49 02N 122 18W
Aberdeen Saskatchewan **40** B2 52 20N 106 16W
Aberdeen Lake Northwest Territories **45** L3 64 30N 99 00W
Abitibi, Lake Ontario/Québec **35** E2 48 42N 79 45W
Abitibi River Ontario **35** D2 49 40N 81 20W
Abloviak Fiord Québec **32** C4 59 30N 65 25W
Acadia Alberta **41** A1 50 56N 114 03W
Acton Ontario **38** B2 43 38N 80 04W
Actonvale Québec **37** O6 45 39N 72 34W
Adair, Cape Northwest Territories **45** R5 71 32N 71 24W
Adams Lake British Columbia **43** E2 51 10N 119 30W
Adams River British Columbia **43** E2 51 23N 119 23W
Adelaide Peninsula Northwest Territories **45** M4 68 15N 97 30W
Adlatok River Newfoundland **30** B4 55 40N 62 50W
Adlavik Islands Newfoundland **30** C3 55 00N 58 40W
Admiralty Inlet Northwest Territories **45** O5 72 30N 86 00W
Admiralty Island Northwest Territories **45** M4 69 25N 101 10W
Advocate Harbour *tn.* Nova Scotia **31** F7 45 20N 64 45W
Agassiz British Columbia **42** H4 49 14N 121 52W
Agassiz Ice Cap Northwest Territories **45** Q7 80 15N 76 00W
Agassiz Provincial Forest Manitoba **39** B1 49 50N 96 20W
Aguasaban River Ontario **35** C2 48 50N 87 00W
Ailsa Craig Ontario **38** A2 43 08N 81 34W
Ainslie, Lake Nova Scotia **31** F7 46 10N 61 10W
Airdrie Alberta **41** C2 51 20N 114 00W
Air Force Island Northwest Territories **45** R4 67 58N 74 05W
Ajax Ontario **38** C2 43 48N 79 00W
Akimiski Island Northwest Territories **45** P1 52 30N 81 00W
Akimiski Island Bird Sanctuary Northwest Territories **45** P1 53 00N 81 00W
Akimiski Strait Northwest Territories/Ontario **34** D3 52 40N 82 00W
Aklavik Northwest Territories **44** E4 68 15N 135 02W
Akpatok Island Northwest Territories **32** C5 60 30N 68 00W
Akulivik Québec **32** A5 60 53N 78 15W
Albany Island Ontario **34** D3 52 15N 81 34W
Albany River Ontario **34** D3 51 40N 83 20W
Alberni Inlet *admin.* British Columbia **42** H4 49 05N 124 52W
Albert *admin.* New Brunswick **31** E7 45 40N 65 10W
Alberta *province* **41**
Alberton Prince Edward Island **31** F7 46 50N 64 08W
Albiti *admin.* Québec **37** K7 48 11N 76 48W
Aldershot Ontario **38** C2 43 17N 79 51W
Aldersyde Alberta **41** C2 50 44N 113 53W
Alert *m.s.* Northwest Territories **45** T7 80 31N 60 05W
Alert Bay *tn.* British Columbia **43** C2 50 34N 126 58W
Alexandria Ontario **37** M6 45 19N 74 38W
Alexis Creek *tn.* British Columbia **43** D2 52 05N 123 12W
Alexis River Newfoundland **30** C3 52 50N 57 60W
Alfred Ontario **37** M6 45 34N 74 53W
Alfred, Mount British Columbia **42** H5 50 13N 124 07W
Algoma *admin.* Ontario **36** C7 48 00N 84 00W
Algonquin Park *tn.* Ontario **36** H6 45 33N 78 35W
Algonquin Provincial Park Ontario **36** H6 45 50N 78 30W
Alix Alberta **41** C2 52 25N 113 11W
Allan Saskatchewan **40** B2 51 54N 106 02W
Allan Water *tn.* Ontario **34** B3 50 14N 90 12W
Alliston Ontario **38** C3 44 09N 79 51W
Alma New Brunswick **31** F7 45 36N 64 58W
Alma Québec **33** B2 48 32N 71 41W
Almonte Ontario **37** K6 45 14N 76 12W
Alouette Lake British Columbia **42** H4 49 22N 121 22W
Alsask Saskatchewan **40** B2 51 22N 110 00W
Alsek Ranges *mts.* British Columbia **42** A3 59 30N 137 30W
Altona Manitoba **39** B1 49 06N 97 35W
Alvin British Columbia **42** H4 49 25N 122 34W
Amadjuak Lake Northwest Territories **45** R3 65 00N 71 08W
Amaranthe Manitoba **39** B2 50 36N 98 43W
Amberley Ontario **38** A3 44 02N 81 44W
Amery Manitoba **39** C3 56 45N 94 00W
Amherst Nova Scotia **31** F7 45 50N 64 14W
Amherstburg Ontario **35** E1 42 06N 83 07W
Amherst Island Ontario **37** K5 44 08N 76 43W
Amisk Lake Saskatchewan **40** C2 54 30N 102 15W
Amos Québec **33** A2 48 04N 78 08W
Amund Ringnes Island Northwest Territories **45** M6 78 00N 96 00W
Amundsen Gulf Northwest Territories **44** F5 70 30N 125 00W
Anahim Lake *tn.* British Columbia **43** C2 52 25 125 18W
Ancaster Ontario **38** C2 43 13N 79 58W
Anderson Lake British Columbia **42** H5 50 38N 122 24W
Anderson River Northwest Territories **44** F4 69 42N 129 01W
Anderson River Delta Bird Sanctuary Northwest Territories **44** F4 69 50N 128 00W
Andover New Brunswick **31** A2 46 48N 67 43W
Andrew Alberta **41** C2 53 52N 112 14W
Andrew Gordon Bay Northwest Territories **45** R3 60 27N 75 30W
Angers Québec **47** L3 45 32N 75 29W
Angikuni Lake Northwest Territories **45** M3 62 00N 99 45W
Angling Lake *I.R.* Ontario **34** C3 53 50N 89 30W
Anguille, Cape Newfoundland **31** C2 47 55N 59 24W
Angus Ontario **38** C3 44 19N 79 53W
Anjou Québec **37** N6 45 37N 73 35W
Annacis Island British Columbia **46** G3 49 09N 122 57W
Annapolis *admin* Nova Scotia **31** E6 44 40N 65 20W
Annapolis Royal Nova Scotia **31** E6 44 44N 65 32W
Annieville British Columbia **46** G3 49 10N 122 54W
Anthony Island British Columbia **42** B2 52 05N 131 14W
Antigonish Nova Scotia **31** F7 45 39N 62 00W
Antigonish *admin.* Nova Scotia **31** F7 45 30N 62 10W
Anvil Range Yukon Territory **44** E3 62 25N 133 15W
Apsley Ontario **36** H5 44 45N 78 06W
Arborfield Saskatchewan **40** C2 53 06N 103 39W
Arborg Manitoba **39** B2 50 55N 97 12W
Arcola Saskatchewan **40** C1 49 38N 102 26W
Arctic Bay *tn.* Northwest Territories **45** O5 73 05N 85 20W
Arctic Red River Northwest Territories **44** E4 65 00N 125 00W
Arctic Red River *tn.* Northwest Territories **44** E4 67 27N 133 46W
Ardrossan Alberta **48** H5 53 33N 113 11W
Argenteuil *admin.* Québec **37** M6 45 50N 74 40W
Arichat Nova Scotia **31** F7 45 31N 61 00W
Aristazabal Island British Columbia **42** C2 52 40N 129 40W
Armstrong British Columbia **43** E2 50 27N 119 14W
Armstrong Ontario **34** C3 50 20N 89 02W
Arnold's Cove *tn.* Newfoundland **31** D2 47 45N 54 00W
Arnot Manitoba **39** B3 55 46N 96 42W
Arnprior Ontario **37** K6 45 26N 76 21W
Arnqui Québec **33** C2 48 30N 67 30W
Aroland Ontario **34** C3 50 14N 86 59W
Aroostook New Brunswick **31** A2 46 45N 67 40W
Arran Lake Ontario **38** A3 44 29N 81 16W
Arrowsmith, Mount British Columbia **42** H4 49 00N 124 00W
Arthabaska Québec **37** P7 46 03N 71 55W
Arthabaska *admin.* Québec **37** O6 45 58N 72 11W
Arthur Ontario **38** B2 43 50N 80 32W
Artillery Lake Northwest Territories **44** K3 63 09N 107 52W
Arviat *(Eskimo Point)* Northwest Territories **45** N3 61 10N 94 05W
Ashcroft British Columbia **43** D2 50 41N 121 17W
Ashern Manitoba **39** B2 51 10N 98 20W
Asheweig River Ontario **34** B3 53 50N 87 50W
Ashihik Lake Yukon Territory **44** D3 61 00N 135 05W
Ashnola River British Columbia **42** H4 49 13N 119 58W
Ashuanipi Newfoundland **30** A3 52 46N 66 05W
Ashuanipi Lake Newfoundland **30** A3 52 45N 66 15W
Ashuanipi River Newfoundland **30** A3 53 50N 66 50W
Aspy Bay Nova Scotia **31** F7 46 50N 60 20W
Assiniboia Saskatchewan **40** B1 49 39N 105 59W
Assiniboine Forest Manitoba **48** D2 49 51N 97 15W
Assiniboine River Manitoba/Saskatchewan **39** B1 49 40N 98 50W
Aston, Cape Northwest Territories **45** S4 70 00N 67 15W
Astray Newfoundland **30** A3 54 38N 66 42W
Astray Lake Newfoundland **30** A3 54 36N 66 30W
Athabasca Alberta **41** C2 54 44N 113 15W
Athabasca, Lake Alberta/Saskatchewan **40** B3 59 10N 109 30W
Athabasca River Alberta **41** C3 57 30N 111 40W
Athabasca Sand Dunes Parkland Reserve Saskatchewan **40** B3 59 10N 108 30W
Athens Ontario **37** L5 44 38N 75 57W
Atherley Ontario **38** C3 44 36N 79 21W
Athol Nova Scotia **31** F7 45 40N 64 10W
Atikaki Provincial Park Manitoba **39** B2 51 30N 95 30W
Atik Lake Manitoba **39** B3 55 20N 96 10W
Atikokan Ontario **34** B2 48 45N 91 38W
Atikonak Lake Newfoundland **30** B3 52 40N 64 32W
Atikonak River Newfoundland **30** B3 53 20N 64 50W
Atkinson, Point British Columbia **46** E4 49 20N 123 16W
Atlin British Columbia **42** B3 59 31N 133 41W
Atlin Lake British Columbia **42** B3 59 31N 133 41W
Atlin Provincial Park British Columbia **42** B3 59 10N 133 50W
Atna Peak British Columbia **43** C2 53 53N 128 07W
Attawapiskat Ontario **34** D3 53 00N 82 30W
Attawapiskat Lake Ontario **34** C3 52 18N 87 54W
Attawapiskat River Ontario **34** D3 53 00N 84 00W
Aubry, Lake Northwest Territories **44** F4 67 23N 126 30W
Auden Ontario **34** C3 50 14N 87 54W
Aulac New Brunswick **31** F7 45 50N 64 20W
Aulneau Peninsula Ontario **34** B2 49 23N 94 29W
Aupaluk Québec **32** C4 59 12N 69 35W
Aurora Ontario **38** C3 43 00N 79 28W
Ausable River Ontario **38** A2 43 06N 81 36W
Austin Channel Northwest Territories **45** L6 75 35N 103 25W
Auyuittuq National Park Northwest Territories **45** S4 67 00N 67 00W
Avalon Peninsula Newfoundland **31** D2 47 30N 53 30W
Avalon Wilderness Reserve Newfoundland **31** D2 47 10N 52 40W
Avola British Columbia **43** E2 51 47N 119 19W
Avon River Ontario **38** A2 43 20N 81 10W
Awenda Provincial Park Ontario **38** B2/C3 44 50N 80 00W
Axel Heiberg Island Northwest Territories **45** N7 80 00N 90 00W
Aylmer Ontario **38** B1 42 47N 80 58W
Aylmer Québec **47** J2 45 23N 75 51W
Aylmer Lake Northwest Territories **44** K3 64 05N 108 30W
Ayr Ontario **38** B2 43 17N 80 26W
Azure Lake British Columbia **43** D2 52 22N 120 07W

B

Babine Lake British Columbia **43** C2 54 45N 125 05W
Babine River British Columbia **43** C3 55 44N 127 29W
Bache Peninsula Northwest Territories **45** Q6 79 08N 76 00W
Backbone Ranges *mts.* Northwest Territories **44** F3 64 30N 130 00W
Back River Northwest Territories **45** L4 65 00N 105 00W
Baddeck Nova Scotia **31** F7 46 06N 60 45W
Badger Newfoundland **31** C2 49 00N 56 04W
Baffin *reg.* Northwest Territories **45** O5 71 30N 88 00W
Baffin Bay Northwest Territories **45** S5 72 00N 64 00W
Baffin Island Northwest Territories **45** Q5 70 00N 75 00W
Baie-Comeau *tn.* Québec **33** C2 49 12N 68 10W
Baie des Chaleurs *b.* Québec/New Brunswick **33** C2 47 59N 65 50W
Baie de Valois *b.* Québec **47** M4 45 27N 73 17W
Baie d'Hudson *(Hudson Bay)* Québec/Northwest Territories/Ontario **32** A3 58 00N 79 00W
Baie d'Ungava *(Ungava Bay)* Québec/Northwest Territories **32** C4 59 00N 67 30W
Baie James *(James Bay)* Québec/Northwest Territories Ontario **33** A3 52 00N 79 00W
Baie-St.-Paul *tn.* Québec **37** O8 47 27N 70 30W
Baie-Trinité *tn.* Québec **33** C2 49 25N 67 20W
Baie Verte *b.* Nova Scotia **31** F7 46 00N 64 00W
Baie Verte *tn.* Newfoundland **31** C2 49 55N 56 12W
Baie Verte Peninsula Newfoundland **31** C2 49 45N 56 15W
Bailey Creek Ontario **38** C3 44 01N 79 56W
Baillie Islands Northwest Territories **44** F5 70 35N 128 10W
Baillie River Northwest Territories **44** K3 64 40N 105 50W
Baird Peninsula Northwest Territories **45** Q4 68 55N 76 04W
Baker Lake Northwest Territories **45** M3 64 00N 95 00W
Baker Lake *tn.* Northwest Territories **45** M3 64 20N 96 10W
Balcarres Saskatchewan **40** C2 50 49N 103 32W
Baldock Lake Manitoba **39** B3 56 30N 98 25W
Baldy Mountain Manitoba **39** A2 51 27N 100 45W
Balgonie Saskatchewan **40** C2 50 31N 104 15W
Ballantyre Strait Northwest Territories **44** H6 77 25N 114 20W
Ball Lake Alberta **48** G5 53 31N 113 16W
Balmertown Ontario **34** B3 51 04N 93 41W
Balsam Lake Ontario **38** D3 44 37N 78 51W
Balsam Lake Provincial Park Ontario **38** D3 44 30N 78 50W
Balzac Alberta **41** C2 51 15N 114 00W
Bamaji Lake Ontario **34** B3 51 09N 91 25W
Bancroft Ontario **36** J6 45 03N 77 51W
Banff Alberta **41** B2 51 10N 115 34W
Banff National Park Alberta **41** B2 51 00N 116 00W
Banks Island Northwest Territories **44** G5 73 15N 121 30W
Banks Island No.1 Bird Sanctuary Northwest Territories **44** G5 72 30N 124 50W
Banks Island No.2 Bird Sanctuary Northwest Territories **44** G5 73 30N 124 00W
Baring, Cape Northwest Territories **44** H5 70 02N 117 20W
Barkerville British Columbia **43** D2 53 06N 121 35W
Barkley Sound British Columbia **42** G4 48 58N 125 11W
Barnes Ice Cap Northwest Territories **45** H5 70 00N 74 00W
Barnfield British Columbia **42** G4 48 50N 125 07W
Barnston Island British Columbia **46** H3 49 11N 122 42W
Barrhaven Ontario **47** J2 45 16N 75 47W
Barrhead Alberta **41** C2 54 10N 114 22W
Barrie Ontario **38** C3 44 22N 79 42W
Barrie Island Ontario **36** D6 45 56N 82 39W
Barrière British Columbia **43** D2 51 10N 120 07W
Barrington Nova Scotia **31** E6 43 34N 65 35W
Barrington Lake Manitoba **39** B3 57 00N 99 50W
Barrow Bay Ontario **38** A3 44 58N 81 11W
Barrows Manitoba **39** A2 52 50N 101 26W
Barrow Strait Northwest Territories **45** N5 74 24N 94 10W
Barry's Bay *tn.* Ontario **36** J6 45 27N 77 41W
Bashaw Alberta **41** C2 52 35N 112 58W
Basin Lake Saskatchewan **40** B2 52 40N 105 10W
Bassano Alberta **41** C2 50 47N 112 28W
Bass Lake Ontario **38** C3 44 36N 79 31W
Bass Lake Provincial Park Ontario **38** C3 44 30N 79 40W
Bataga River British Columbia **43** C3 58 30N 126 40W
Batchawana Bay *tn.* Ontario **35** C2 46 53N 84 36W
Batchawana Mountain Ontario **35** D2 47 04N 84 24W
Bath New Brunswick **31** A2 46 30N 67 36W
Bath Ontario **37** K5 44 11N 76 47W
Bathurst New Brunswick **31** A2 47 37N 65 40W
Bathurst, Cape Northwest Territories **44** F5 70 31N 127 53W
Bathurst Inlet Northwest Territories **44** K4 66 49N 108 00W
Bathurst Inlet *tn.* Northwest Territories **44** K4 66 50N 108 01W
Bathurst Island Northwest Territories **45** L6 76 00N 100 00W
Batoche National Historic Site Saskatchewan **40** B2 52 45N 107 00W
Batteau Newfoundland **30** C3 53 24N 55 47W
Battle Creek Saskatchewan **40** B1 49 20N 109 30W
Battleford Saskatchewan **40** B2 52 45N 108 20W
Battle Harbour *tn.* Newfoundland **30** C3 52 16N 55 35W
Battle River Alberta/Saskatchewan **40** B2 52 50N 109 10W
Bauld, Cape Newfoundland **30** C3 51 40N 55 25W
Bay Bulls *tn.* Newfoundland **31** D2 47 19N 52 50W
Bay de Verde *tn.* Newfoundland **31** D2 48 03N 52 54W
Bayers Lake Nova Scotia **47** P6 44 38N 63 39W
Bayfield Ontario **38** A2 43 33N 81 41W
Bayfield River Ontario **38** A2 43 34N 81 38W
Bay of Islands Newfoundland **30** C4 55 09N 59 49W
Bay of Islands Newfoundland **31** C2 49 10N 58 14W
Bay Roberts *tn.* Newfoundland **31** D2 47 36N 53 16W
Beachburg Ontario **37** K6 45 44N 76 51W
Beacon Hill Ontario **47** K2 45 28N 75 35W
Beaconsfield Québec **47** M4 45 26N 73 52W
Beale, Cape British Columbia **42** G4 48 46N 125 10W
Beamsville Ontario **38** C2 43 10N 79 31W
Beardmore Ontario **34** C2 49 36N 87 59W
Bear Island Northwest Territories **34** E3 64 01N 83 13W
Bear Lake Manitoba **39** B3 55 10N 96 30W
Bear River Ontario **47** L2 45 22N 75 29W
Bear River *tn.* Nova Scotia **31** E6 44 34N 65 40W
Bearskin Lake *I.R.* Ontario **34** B3 53 50N 90 55W
Beatton River British Columbia **43** D3 57 18N 121 15W
Beatty Saugeen River Ontario **38** B3 44 08N 80 54W
Beattyville Québec **33** A2 48 53N 77 10W
Beauce *admin.* Québec **37** Q7 46 15N 71 00W
Beauceville Québec **37** Q7 46 12N 70 45W
Beauharnois Québec **37** N6 45 18N 73 52W
Beaufort Sea Arctic Ocean **10** E7 72 00N 140 00W
Beaumaris Lake Alberta **48** F5 53 38N 113 32W
Beaumont Alberta **48** G4 53 20N 113 28W
Beauport Québec **37** P7 46 52N 71 12W
Beaupré Québec **37** Q8 47 03N 70 56W
Beausejour Manitoba **39** B2 50 04N 96 30W
Beauval Saskatchewan **40** B3 55 09N 107 35W
Beaver Creek Ontario **46** C2 43 51N 79 23W
Beaver Creek *tn.* Yukon Territory **44** D3 60 20N 140 45W
Beaverdell British Columbia **43** E1 49 25N 119 09W
Beaverhill Lake Alberta **41** C2 53 27N 112 32W
Beaver Hill Lake Manitoba **39** B2 54 20N 95 20W
Beaverlodge Alberta **41** B3 55 13N 119 26W
Beaver River Ontario **38** B3 44 21N 80 33W
Beaver River Alberta/Saskatchewan **40** B2 52 10N 108 40W
Beaverton Ontario **38** C3 44 25N 79 10W
Beaverton River Ontario **38** C3 44 08N 79 06W
Bécancour Québec **37** O7 46 20N 72 30W
Beckwith Island Ontario **38** B3 44 53N 80 06W
Beddington Creek Alberta **48** A2 51 15N 114 11W
Bedford Nova Scotia **47** P6 44 44N 61 37W
Bedford Basin Nova Scotia **47** P6 44 41N 63 37W
Beechey Head *c.* British Columbia **42** H4 48 19 123 39W
Beechville Nova Scotia **47** P6 44 37N 63 42W
Beeton Ontario **38** C3 44 04N 79 46W
Beiseker Alberta **41** C2 51 23N 113 32W
Belcher Islands Northwest Territories **45** Q2 56 00N 79 30W
Bella Coola British Columbia **43** C2 52 30N 126 50W
Bella Coola River British Columbia **43** C2 52 22N 126 35W
Bellcarra British Columbia **46** G4 49 19N 122 56W
Belle Bay Newfoundland **31** C2 47 37N 55 18W
Bellechasse *admin.* Québec **37** Q7 46 40N 70 50W
Belledune New Brunswick **31** A2 47 50N 65 45W
Belle Isle *i.* Newfoundland **30** C3 51 57N 55 21W
Belleoram Newfoundland **31** C2 47 31N 55 25W
Belle Plaine Saskatchewan **40** B2 50 25N 105 09W
Belle River *tn.* Ontario **36** D3 42 18N 82 43W
Belleville Ontario **37** J5 44 10N 77 23W
Bell-Irving River British Columbia **42** C3 56 42N 129 40W
Bell Island Newfoundland **31** C3 50 80N 55 50W
Belle Isle, Strait of Newfoundland **30** C3 51 30N 56 30W
Bell Peninsula Northwest Territories **45** P3 63 00N 82 00W
Bells Corners Ontario **47** J2 45 19N 75 49W
Belly River Alberta **41** C1 49 10N 113 40W
Belmont Ontario **38** A1 42 52N 81 06W
Belseil Québec **37** N6 45 34N 73 15W
Belwood, Lake Ontario **38** B2 43 46N 80 20W
Benedict Mountains Newfoundland **30** C3 54 45N 58 45W
Bengough Saskatchewan **40** B1 49 25N 105 10W
Benito Manitoba **39** A2 51 55N 101 30W
Bentley Alberta **41** C2 52 28N 114 04W
Berens River Manitoba/Ontario **39** B2 52 10N 96 40W
Berens River *tn.* Manitoba **39** B2 52 22N 97 00W
Beresford New Brunswick **31** A2 47 40N 65 40W
Bergland Ontario **34** B2 48 57N 94 23W
Bernier Bay Northwest Territories **45** O5 71 05N 88 15W
Berthier *admin.* Québec **37** M8 47 40N 75 20W
Berthierville Québec **27** 46 05N 73 11W
Bertrand New Brunswick **31** A2 47 45N 65 05W
Berwick Nova Scotia **31** F7 45 03N 64 44W
Berwyn Alberta **41** B3 56 09N 117 44W
Besnard Lake Saskatchewan **40** B3 55 30N 106 10W
Bethany Ontario **38** D3 44 11N 78 34W
Betsiamites Québec **33** C2 48 56N 68 40W
Bible Hill *tn.* Nova Scotia **31** F7 45 20N 63 10W
Bienfait Saskatchewan **40** C1 49 09N 102 48W
Big Bay *tn.* British Columbia **42** G5 50 24N 125 08W
Big Creek Ontario **38** B1 42 43N 80 33W
Biggar Saskatchewan **40** B2 52 03N 107 59W
Bighead River Ontario **38** B3 44 30N 80 47W
Big Indian Lake Nova Scotia **47** P6 44 35N 63 42W
Big Island Northwest Territories **45** R3 62 43N 70 43W
Big Island Ontario **34** B2 49 10N 94 30W
Big Island Lake Alberta **48** H4 53 28N 113 12W
Big Lake Alberta **48** F5 53 37N 113 40W
Big Muddy Lake Saskatchewan **40** C1 49 10N 104 50W
Big Otter Creek Ontario **38** B1 42 46N 80 51W
Big River Newfoundland **30** C3 54 40N 59 40W
Big River *tn.* Saskatchewan **40** B2 53 50N 107 01W
Big Salmon Range *mts.* Yukon Territory **44** E3 62 40N 134 59W
Big Sand Lake Manitoba **39** B3 57 50N 99 30W
Big Silver Creek British Columbia **42** H4 49 50N 121 50W
Bigstick Lake Saskatchewan **40** B2 50 20N 109 50W
Bigstone Lake Manitoba **39** B2 53 30N 95 50W
Big Trout Lake Ontario **34** C3 53 40N 89 50W
Big Trout Lake *tn.* Ontario **34** C3 53 49N 89 54W
Birch Cove Nova Scotia **47** P6 44 40N 63 39W
Birch Hills *tn.* Saskatchewan **40** B2 53 00N 105 10W
Birch Island Manitoba **39** B2 52 20N 99 50W
Birch Lake Alberta **41** C2 53 19N 111 35W
Birch Lake Ontario **34** B3 51 20N 92 20W
Birch Mountains Alberta **41** C3 57 20N 113 55W
Birch River Alberta **41** C3 58 20N 113 20W
Birds Hill Manitoba **48** E2 49 58N 96 59W
Birken British Columbia **42** H5 50 29N 122 36W
Birkenhead Lake Provincial Park British Columbia **42** H5 50 35N 122 42W
Birtle Manitoba **39** A2 50 26N 101 04W
Biscotasing Ontario **35** D2 47 17N 82 06W
Bishop's Falls *tn.* Newfoundland **31** C2 49 01N 55 30W
Bistcho Lake Alberta **41** B3 59 45N 118 50W
Bjorne Peninsula Northwest Territories **45** M6 77 37N 87 00W
Black Bear Island Lake Saskatchewan **40** B3 55 45N 105 50W
Black Birch Lake Saskatchewan **40** B3 56 55N 107 25W
Blackburn Ontario **47** K2 45 26N 75 33W
Black Diamond Alberta **41** C2 50 45N 114 12W
Blackfalds Alberta **41** C2 52 23N 113 47W
Black Island *tn.* Newfoundland **30** C3 54 30N 58 50W
Black Lake Saskatchewan **40** C3 59 10N 104 30W
Black Lake *tn.* Québec **37** P7 46 03N 71 21W
Black Lake *tn.* Saskatchewan **40** B3 59 05N 105 35W
Blackmud Creek Alberta **48** F4 53 25N 113 33W
Black River Ontario **38** C3 44 48N 79 08W
Blacks Harbour New Brunswick **31** A2 45 03N 66 49W
Blackville New Brunswick **31** A2 46 44N 65 51W
Blackwater Lake Northwest Territories **44** G3 64 00N 123 05W
Blaine Lake *tn.* Saskatchewan **40** B2 52 50N 106 54W
Blainville Québec **47** M5 45 39N 73 52W
Blair Ontario **38** B2 43 23N 80 23W
Blanc Sablon Québec **32** E3 51 26N 57 08W
Blenheim Ontario **36** E3 42 20N 82 00W
Blind River *tn.* Ontario **36** D7 46 10N 82 58W
Bloodvein River Manitoba **39** B2 51 50N 96 40W
Bloomfield Ontario **37** J4 43 59N 77 14W
Blubber Bay *tn.* British Columbia **42** H4 49 48N 124 37W
Bluenose Lake Northwest Territories **44** G4 68 30N 119 35W
Blue Ridge *tn.* Alberta **41** B2 54 08N 115 22W
Blue River *tn.* British Columbia **43** E2 52 05N 119 09W
Blyth Ontario **38** A2 43 43N 81 26W
Blyth Brook Ontario **38** A2 43 45N 81 31W
Boag Lake Alberta **48** H5 53 31N 113 09W
Bobcaygeon Ontario **38** D3 44 32N 78 33W
Boisbriand Québec **47** M5 45 35N 73 51W
Boissevain Manitoba **39** A1 49 14N 100 02W
Bolton Ontario **38** C2 43 53N 79 44W
Bonavista Newfoundland **31** D2 48 39N 53 07W
Bonavista Bay Newfoundland **31** D2 48 45N 53 30W

Canada 147

Bonavista Peninsula Newfoundland **31** D2 48 60N 53 30W
Bon Echo Provincial Park Ontario **37** J5 44 55N 77 15W
Bonnet Plume River Yukon Territory **44** E4 65 25N 135 00W
Bonnyville Alberta **41** C2 54 16N 110 44W
Boothia, Gulf of Northwest Territories **45** O4 69 00N 88 00W
Boothia Peninsula Northwest Territories **45** N5 70 30N 94 30W
Borden Prince Edward Island **31** F7 46 20N 63 40W
Borden Island Northwest Territories **44** J6 78 30N 111 30W
Borden Peninsula Northwest Territories **45** P5 73 00N 82 30W
Boston Bar British Columbia **42** H4 49 52N 121 25W
Botwood Newfoundland **31** C2 49 09N 55 21W
Boucherville Québec **47** O5 45 35N 73 26W
Bouctouche New Brunswick **31** F7 46 30N 64 40W
Boundary Range *mts.* British Columbia **42** B3 58 00N 133 00W
Bourne, Cape Northwest Territories **81** 35N 91 50W
Bowden Alberta **41** C2 51 55N 114 02W
Bowen Island British Columbia **42** H4 49 23N 123 26W
Bow Island *tn.* Alberta **41** C1 49 52N 111 22W
Bowman Bay Wildlife Sanctuary Northwest Territories **45** R4 66 00N 74 00W
Bowmanville Ontario **38** D2 43 55N 78 43W
Bowmanville Creek Ontario **38** D3 44 02N 78 47N
Bowness Alberta **48** A2 51 05N 114 14W
Bow River Alberta **41** C2 50 47N 111 55W
Bowron Lake Provincial Park British Columbia **43** D2 53 00N 121 00W
Bowron River British Columbia **43** D2 53 38N 121 40W
Bowser British Columbia **42** H4 49 26N 124 41W
Boyle Alberta **41** C2 54 35N 112 49W
Boyne River Ontario **38** B3 44 07N 80 07W
Bracebridge Ontario **36** G6 45 02N 79 19W
Bradford *see* Bradford West Gwillimbury
Bradford West Gwillimbury Ontario **38** C3 44 07N 79 34W
Bralorne British Columbia **42** H5 50 46N 122 51W
Bramalea Ontario **46** B1 43 44N 79 44W
Brampton Ontario **46** A1 43 42N 79 46W
Brandon Manitoba **39** B1 49 50N 99 57W
Brant *admin.* Ontario **38** B2 43 03N 80 29W
Brantford Ontario **38** B2 43 09N 80 17W
Bras d'Or Lake Nova Scotia **31** F7 45 50N 60 50W
Brazeau, Mount Alberta **41** B2 52 33N 117 21W
Brazeau River Alberta **41** B2 52 50N 116 20W
Brechin Ontario **38** C3 44 32N 79 11W
Bremner Alberta **48** H5 53 34N 113 13W
Brent Ontario **36** H7 46 02N 78 29W
Bretona Alberta **48** G4 53 26N 113 19W
Breton, Cape Nova Scotia **31** G7 45 50N 59 50W
Breton Cove *tn.* Nova Scotia **31** F7 46 30N 60 30W
Brevoort Island Northwest Territories **45** T3 63 19N 64 08W
Bridgenorth Ontario **38** D3 44 23N 78 23W
Bridgeport Ontario **38** B2 43 29N 80 29W
Bridge River British Columbia **42** H5 50 55N 123 25W
Bridgetown Nova Scotia **31** E6 44 50N 65 20W
Bridgewater Nova Scotia **31** F6 44 23N 64 32W
Brier Island Nova Scotia **31** E6 44 20N 66 20W
Brighouse British Columbia **46** F3 49 09N 123 11W
Brighton Ontario **36** J5 44 07N 77 45W
Bristol New Brunswick **31** A2 46 28N 67 38W
Britannia Beach *tn.* British Columbia **42** H4 49 38N 123 10W
British Columbia *province* **42/43**
British Empire Range *mts.* Northwest Territories **45** P7 82 30N 78 10W
British Mountains Yukon Territory Canada/Alaska U.S.A. **44** D4 69 00N 141 00W
Britt Ontario **36** F6 45 46N 80 33W
Broadview Saskatchewan **40** C2 50 22N 102 31W
Brockville Ontario **37** L5 44 35N 75 41W
Brodeur Peninsula Northwest Territories **45** O5 72 00N 87 30W
Brome *admin.* Québec **37** O6 45 10N 72 10W
Bromont Québec **37** O6 45 18N 72 38W
Bronte Ontario **38** C2 43 23N 79 43W
Brookfield Nova Scotia **31** F7 45 15N 63 18W
Brooklyn Nova Scotia **31** F6 44 04N 64 42W
Brooks Alberta **41** C2 50 35N 111 54W
Brooks Peninsula British Columbia **43** C2 50 05N 127 45W
Brossard Québec **37** N6 45 28N 73 30W
Broughton Island *tn.* Northwest Territories **45** T4 67 40N 63 50W
Brown Lake Northwest Territories **45** M4 65 54N 91 15W
Bruce *admin.* Ontario **38** A3 44 15N 81 24W
Bruce Creek Ontario **46** C2 43 55N 79 20W
Bruce Mines *tn.* Ontario **36** C7 46 18N 83 48W
Bruce Peninsula Ontario **38** A4 45 00N 81 20W
Bruce Peninsula National Park Ontario **38** A4 45 00N 81 20W
Bruderheim Alberta **41** C2 53 47N 112 56W
Brunette Island Newfoundland **31** C2 47 16N 55 55W
Bruno Saskatchewan **40** B2 52 17N 105 31W
Brussels Ontario **38** A2 43 44N 81 15W
Bryan Channel Northwest Territories **45** K5 74 50N 105 00W
Buchan Gulf Northwest Territories **45** R5 71 47N 74 16W
Buchans Newfoundland **31** C2 48 49N 56 53W
Buckhorn Ontario **38** D3 44 33N 78 20W
Buckhorn Lake Ontario **38** D3 44 29N 78 25W
Buckingham Québec **37** L6 45 35N 75 25W
Buffalo Head Hills Alberta **41** B3 57 25N 115 55W
Buffalo Lake Alberta **41** C2 52 27N 112 54W
Buffalo Narrows *tn.* Saskatchewan **40** B3 55 52N 108 28W
Buffalo River Alberta **41** C3 59 25N 114 35W
Buffalo Trail Alberta **41** C2 51 45N 110 35W
Bulkley River British Columbia **43** C2 55 00N 127 10W
Buntzen Lake British Columbia **46** G4 49 20N 124 51W
Burden, Mount British Columbia **43** D3 56 10N 123 09W
Burford Ontario **38** B2 43 46N 80 25W
Burgeo Newfoundland **31** C2 47 37N 57 37W
Burin Newfoundland **31** C2 47 02N 55 10W
Burin Peninsula Newfoundland **31** C2 47 00N 55 40W
Burk's Falls *tn.* Ontario **36** G6 45 37N 79 25W
Burlington Ontario **38** C2 43 19N 79 48W
Burnaby British Columbia **42** H4 49 16N 122 58W
Burnaby Lake British Columbia **46** G3 49 14N 122 57W
Burns Alberta **48** A1 50 59N 114 02W
Burnside Nova Scotia **47** P6 44 41N 63 35W
Burnside River Northwest Territories **44** F4 66 20N 109 30W
Burns Lake *tn.* British Columbia **43** C2 54 14N 125 45W
Burnt Islands *tn.* Newfoundland **31** C2 47 37N 58 50W
Burnt Lake Newfoundland **30** B3 52 20N 63 40W
Burnt Lake Québec **33** D3 52 15N 63 50W
Burnt River Ontario **38** D3 44 41N 78 43W
Burntwood Lake Manitoba **39** A3 55 20N 100 10W
Burntwood River Manitoba **39** B3 55 50N 97 40W
Burquitlam British Columbia **46** G4 49 15N 122 56W
Burrard Inlet British Columbia **46** F4 49 19N 123 14W
Burstall Saskatchewan **40** B2 50 40N 109 56W
Bushell Park *tn.* Saskatchewan **40** B2 50 25N 105 30W
Bute Inlet British Columbia **42** H5 50 31N 124 59W
Buttle Lake British Columbia **42** G4 49 47N 125 30W
Button Bay Manitoba **39** C3 58 50N 94 30W
Button Islands Northwest Territories **32** D5 60 35N 64 40W
Buttonville Ontario **46** C2 43 51N 79 22W
Byam Martin Island Northwest Territories **45** L6 75 15N 104 15W
Bylot Island Northwest Territories **45** Q5 73 30N 79 00W
Bylot Island Bird Sanctuary Northwest Territories **45** Q5 73 20N 79 00W
Byron Bay Newfoundland **30** C3 54 40N 57 40W

C

Cabano Québec **33** C2 47 40N 68 56W
Cabot Head Ontario **38** A4 45 15N 81 17W
Cabot Lake Newfoundland **30** B4 56 09N 62 37W
Cabot Strait Nova Scotia/Newfoundland **31** C2 47 10N 59 30W
Cabri Saskatchewan **40** B2 50 38N 108 28W
Cache Creek *tn.* British Columbia **43** D2 50 46N 121 17W
Calabogie Ontario **37** K6 45 18N 76 43W
Calais New Brunswick **31** A2 45 10N 67 15W
Caledon East Ontario **38** C2 43 52N 79 53W
Caledonia Nova Scotia **31** E6 44 24N 65 02W
Caledonia Ontario **38** C2 43 05N 79 57W
Calgary Alberta **41** C2 51 05N 114 05W
Calgary City *admin.* Alberta **48** A2 51 10N 114 09W
Callander Ontario **36** G7 46 13N 79 22W
Calling Lake Alberta **41** C3 55 15N 113 20W
Calmar Alberta **41** C2 53 16N 113 49W
Calvert Island British Columbia **43** C2 51 30N 128 00W
Cambridge Ontario **38** B2 43 22N 80 20W
Cambridge Bay *tn.* Northwest Territories **44** L4 69 09N 105 00W
Cambridge-Narrows New Brunswick **31** A2 45 50N 65 55W
Cameron Hills Alberta **41** B3 59 48N 118 00W
Campbell Dam Saskatchewan **40** C2 53 40N 103 20W
Campbellford Ontario **36** J5 44 18N 77 48W
Campbell Lake British Columbia **42** G4 49 59N 125 30W
Campbell, Mount Yukon Territory **44** D3 64 23N 138 43W
Campbell River *tn.* British Columbia **42** G5 50 00N 125 18W
Campbellton New Brunswick **31** A2 48 00N 66 41W
Campbellton Newfoundland **31** D2 49 17N 54 56W
Campbellville Ontario **38** C2 43 29N 79 59W
Camperville Manitoba **39** A2 51 00N 100 08W
Campobello Island New Brunswick **31** A1 44 50N 66 50W
Camp Robinson Ontario **34** B3 50 08N 93 12W
Camrose Alberta **41** C2 53 01N 112 50W
Camsell Portage Saskatchewan **40** B3 59 39N 109 12W
Canal Flats *tn.* British Columbia **43** E2 50 09N 115 50W
Canal Lake Ontario **38** C3 44 34N 79 02W
Candiac Québec **47** N4 45 24N 73 31W
Candle Lake Saskatchewan **40** B2 53 55N 105 10W
Candle Lake *tn.* Saskatchewan **40** B2 53 50N 105 10W
Canmore Alberta **41** B2 51 07N 115 18W
Canning Nova Scotia **31** F7 45 10N 64 26W
Canoe Lake Saskatchewan **40** B3 55 10N 108 30W
Canora Saskatchewan **40** C2 51 38N 102 28W
Canso Nova Scotia **31** F7 45 20N 61 00W
Canso, Cape Nova Scotia **31** F7 45 19N 60 59W
Cap-aux-Meules *tn.* Québec **33** D2 47 25N 62 00W
Cap-Chat *tn.* Québec **33** C2 49 06N 66 42W
Cap-de-la-Madeleine *tn.* Québec **37** O7 46 00N 72 00W
Cap Dufferin *c.* Québec **32** A4 58 35N 78 32W
Cape Breton *admin.* Nova Scotia **31** F7 45 50N 60 00W
Cape Breton Highlands National Park Nova Scotia **31** F7 46 45N 60 40W
Cape Breton Island Nova Scotia **31** F7 46 45N 60 00W
Cape Charles *tn.* Newfoundland **30** C3 52 13N 55 38W
Cape Croker *tn.* Ontario **38** B3 44 56N 81 01W
Cape Dorset *tn.* Northwest Territories **45** Q3 64 10N 76 40W
Cape Dorset Sanctuaries Northwest Territories **45** Q3 63 50N 77 00W
Cape Dyer *m.s.* Northwest Territories **45** T4 66 37N 61 16W
Cape Le Havre Island Nova Scotia **31** F6 44 10N 64 20W
Cape North *tn.* Nova Scotia **31** F7 46 55N 60 30W
Cape Parry *m.s.* Northwest Territories **44** F5 70 08N 124 34W
Cape Sable Island Nova Scotia **31** E6 43 30N 65 40W
Cape St. George *tn.* Newfoundland **31** C2 48 28N 59 15W
Cape Scott Provincial Park British Columbia **43** C2 50 42N 128 20W
Cape Tormentine *tn.* New Brunswick **31** F7 46 08N 63 47W
Cap Gaspé *c.* Québec **33** D2 48 46N 64 10W
Cap Hopes Advance *c.* Québec **32** C5 61 00N 69 40W
Capilano Lake British Columbia **46** F4 49 22N 123 06W
Cap Pelé *tn.* New Brunswick **31** F7 46 10N 64 10W
Cap Prince-de-Galles *c.* Québec **32** C5 61 42N 71 30W
Cap Rouge *c.* Québec **37** P7 46 40N 71 32W
Cap-Saint-Ignace *c.* Québec **37** Q8 47 00N 70 29W
Capstick Nova Scotia **31** F7 47 00N 60 31W
Caramat Ontario **35** C2 49 37N 86 09W
Caraquet New Brunswick **31** B2 47 48N 64 59W
Carberry Manitoba **39** B1 49 52N 99 20W
Carbonear Newfoundland **31** D2 47 44N 53 13W
Carcross Yukon Territory **44** E3 60 11N 134 41W
Cardigan Prince Edward Island **31** F7 46 14N 62 37W
Cardinal Ontario **37** L5 44 47N 75 23W
Cardston Alberta **41** C1 49 12N 113 18W
Cariboo Mountains British Columbia **43** D2 53 20N 120 50W
Caribou Manitoba **39** B3 59 20N 97 50W
Caribou Mountains Alberta **41** B3 59 00N 115 30W
Caribou River Manitoba **39** B3 59 30N 95 30W
Carleton Québec **33** C2 48 08N 66 10W
Carleton *admin.* New Brunswick **31** A2 46 10N 67 50W
Carleton, Mount New Brunswick **31** A2 47 24N 66 52W
Carleton Place Ontario **37** K6 45 15N 75 45W
Carling Ontario **38** B4 45 24N 80 09W
Carlsbad Springs Ontario **47** L2 45 22N 75 29W
Carlson Landing Alberta **41** C3 58 59N 111 45W
Carlyle Saskatchewan **40** C1 49 39N 102 18W
Carmacks Yukon Territory **44** D3 62 04N 136 21W
Carman Manitoba **39** B1 49 32N 97 59W
Carmanville Newfoundland **31** D2 49 24N 54 18W
Carnduff Saskatchewan **40** C1 49 11N 101 50W
Carp Lake British Columbia **43** D2 54 48N 123 20W
Carp Lake Provincial Park British Columbia **43** D2 54 08N 123 30W
Carp River Ontario **47** J2 45 18N 75 55W
Carrot River Manitoba **39** B2 54 50N 96 40W
Carrot River Saskatchewan **40** C2 53 05N 104 15W
Carrot River *tn.* Saskatchewan **40** C2 53 18N 103 32W
Carstairs Alberta **41** C2 51 34N 114 06W
Cartierville Québec **47** N5 45 31N 73 43W
Cartmel, Mount British Columbia **42** C3 57 45N 129 12W
Cartwright Newfoundland **30** C3 53 42N 57 01W
Cascade Range *mts.* British Columbia **42** H4 50 48N 121 15W
Cascade Recreation Area British Columbia **42** H4 49 16N 120 56W
Cascumpec Bay Prince Edward Island **31** F7 46 45N 64 00W
Cassiar British Columbia **42** C3 59 15N 129 49W
Cassiar Highway British Columbia **42** B3 57 30N 130 10W
Cassiar Mountains British Columbia **42** B3 59 50N 131 50W
Castlegar British Columbia **43** E1 49 18N 117 41W
Castor Alberta **41** C2 52 13N 111 53W
Catalina Newfoundland **31** D2 48 31N 53 05W
Cat Arm Reservoir Newfoundland **31** C3 50 10N 56 40W
Catchacoma Lake Ontario **38** D3 44 46N 78 16W
Cathedral National Park British Columbia **42** H4 49 05N 120 11W
Cat Lake Ontario **34** B3 51 30N 91 50W
Cat Lake *I.R.* Ontario **34** B3 51 40N 91 50W
Caubvick, Mount *(Mont D'Iberville)* Newfoundland/Québec **30** B4 58 50N 64 40W
Causapscal Québec **33** C2 48 22N 67 14W
Cavendish Prince Edward Island **31** F7 46 30N 63 20W
Cawes Lake Alberta **48** G4 53 22N 113 28W
Cayoosh Creek British Columbia **42** H4 50 00N 122 00W
Cayuga Ontario **38** C1 42 57N 79 50W
Cecil Lake *tn.* British Columbia **43** D3 56 19N 120 40W
Cedar Lake Manitoba **39** A2 53 40N 100 30W
Central Butte Saskatchewan **40** B2 50 50N 106 30W
Central Patricia Ontario **34** B3 51 30N 90 09W
Centreville Newfoundland **31** D2 49 01N 53 53W
Centreville Nova Scotia **31** F7 45 10N 64 30W
Chalk River *tn.* Ontario **37** J7 46 01N 77 27W
Chambly Québec **37** N6 45 27N 73 19W
Champlain *admin.* Québec **37** N8 48 20N 74 20W
Chandler Québec **33** D2 48 21N 64 41W
Channel-Port aux Basques Newfoundland **31** C2 47 34N 59 09W
Chantrey Inlet Northwest Territories **45** M4 67 48N 96 20W
Chapais Québec **33** B2 49 47N 74 54W
Chapleau Ontario **35** D2 47 50N 83 24W
Chaplin Saskatchewan **40** B2 50 29N 106 40W
Chaplin Lake Saskatchewan **40** B2 50 25N 106 30W
Charlesbourg Québec **37** O7 46 53N 71 16W
Charles Island Northwest Territories **45** R3 62 39N 74 15W
Charles Lake Alberta **41** C3 59 50N 110 33W
Charles, Lake Nova Scotia **47** P6 44 43N 63 32W
Charlevoix-Est *admin.* Québec **37** Q8 47 50N 70 20W
Charlevoix-Ouest *admin.* Québec **37** Q8 47 57N 71 05W
Charlo New Brunswick **31** A2 47 55N 66 20W
Charlotte *admin.* New Brunswick **31** A2 45 20N 67 20W
Charlotte Lake British Columbia **43** C2 52 11N 125 19W
Charlottetown Newfoundland **30** C3 52 06N 56 07W
Charlottetown Prince Edward Island **31** F7 46 14N 63 09W
Charlton Island Northwest Territories **34** D3 52 00N 79 30W
Charron Lake Manitoba **39** B2 52 40N 95 40W
Chase British Columbia **43** E2 50 49N 119 41W
Châteauguay Québec **37** N6 45 20N 73 42W
Chatham New Brunswick **31** A2 47 02N 65 30W
Chatham Ontario **36** D3 42 24N 82 11W
Chatham Sound British Columbia **42** B2 54 30N 130 30W
Chatsworth Ontario **38** B3 44 27N 80 54W
Chedabucto Bay Nova Scotia **31** F7 45 20N 61 10W
Cheepay River Ontario **34** D3 50 50N 83 40W
Chelsea Québec **47** J2 45 29N 75 48W
Chelsea Brook Québec **47** J3 45 31N 75 51W
Chemainus British Columbia **42** H4 48 54N 123 42W
Chemainus River British Columbia **42** H4 48 58N 124 09W
Chemong Lake Ontario **38** D3 44 26N 78 22W
Cheslatta Lake British Columbia **43** C2 53 44N 125 20W
Chesley Ontario **38** A3 44 18N 81 07W
Chester Nova Scotia **31** F6 44 33N 64 16W
Chesterfield Inlet Northwest Territories **45** N3 64 00N 93 00W
Chesterfield Inlet *tn.* Northwest Territories **45** N3 63 21N 90 42W
Chesterville Ontario **37** L6 45 06N 75 14W
Cheticamp Nova Scotia **31** F7 46 39N 61 01W
Cheticamp Island Nova Scotia **31** F7 46 40N 61 05W
Chetwynd British Columbia **43** D3 55 38N 121 40W
Chibougamau Québec **33** B2 49 56N 74 24W
Chicoutimi Québec **37** P9 48 26N 71 06W
Chicoutimi *admin.* Québec **37** Q9 48 10N 71 10W
Chidley, Cape Northwest Territories **30** B4 60 23N 64 26W
Chignecto Bay Nova Scotia **31** F7 45 40N 64 40W
Chignecto, Cape Nova Scotia **31** F7 45 20N 64 55W
Chilanko Forks British Columbia **43** D2 52 04N 124 00W
Chilcotin River British Columbia **43** D2 51 54N 123 20W
Chilko Lake British Columbia **43** D2 51 15N 124 59W
Chilko River British Columbia **43** D2 51 59N 124 05W
Chilliwack British Columbia **42** H4 49 06N 121 56W
Chilliwack Lake British Columbia **42** H4 49 04N 121 22W
Chilliwack River British Columbia **42** H4 49 04N 121 52W
Chin, Cape Ontario **38** A4 45 05N 81 17W
Chinchaga River Alberta **41** B3 57 30N 119 00W
Chip Lake Alberta **41** B2 53 40N 115 23W
Chipman New Brunswick **31** A2 46 11N 65 54W
Chippawa Ontario **38** C2 43 03N 79 04W
Chiputneticook Lakes New Brunswick/U.S.A. **33** C2 45 40N 67 45W
Chisasibi *(Fort George)* Québec **32** T3 53 50N 79 01W
Chisel Lake *tn.* Manitoba **39** A2 54 50N 100 20W
Choiceland Saskatchewan **40** C2 53 30N 104 33W
Chomedey Québec **47** M5 45 32N 73 46W
Chorkbak Inlet Northwest Territories **45** R3 64 30N 74 25W
Chown, Mount Alberta **41** B2 53 24N 119 25W
Christian Island Ontario **38** B3 44 50N 80 14W
Christian Island *tn.* Ontario **38** B3 44 49N 80 10W
Christie Bay Northwest Territories **44** J3 62 32N 111 10W
Christina River Alberta **41** C3 55 50N 111 00W
Churchbridge Saskatchewan **40** C2 50 55N 101 38W
Churchill Manitoba **39** C3 58 45N 94 00W
Churchill, Cape Manitoba **39** C3 58 45N 93 00W
Churchill Falls *tn.* Newfoundland **30** A3 53 35N 64 00W
Churchill Lake Saskatchewan **40** B3 56 05N 108 15W
Churchill Peak British Columbia **43** C3 58 20N 125 02W
Churchill River Manitoba/Saskatchewan **45** M3 57 30N 96 00W
Churchill River Newfoundland **30** A3 53 20N 63 40W
Chute-aux-Outardes Québec **33** C2 49 17N 67 57W
Cirque Mountain Newfoundland **30** B4 58 56N 63 33W
City of Edmonton *admin.* Alberta **48** F4 53 23N 113 30W
City of Winnipeg *admin.* Manitoba **48** C2 49 55N 97 23W
City View Ontario **47** K2 45 21N 75 44W
Clarence Head *c.* Northwest Territories **45** Q6 76 47N 77 47W
Clarenville Newfoundland **31** D2 48 10N 53 38W
Claresholm Alberta **41** C2 50 02N 113 35W
Clarke City Québec **33** C3 50 11N 66 39W
Clark's Harbour *tn.* Nova Scotia **31** E6 43 25N 65 38W
Clarkson Ontario **38** C2 43 30N 79 38W
Clayoquot Sound British Columbia **43** C1 49 12N 126 05W
Clear Hills Alberta **41** B3 56 40N 119 30W
Clearwater British Columbia **43** D2 51 37N 120 03W
Clearwater Bay *tn.* Ontario **34** B2 49 93N 94 48W
Clearwater Lake British Columbia **43** D2 52 13N 120 20W
Clearwater Lake Manitoba **39** A2 53 50N 101 40W
Clearwater Lake Provincial Park Manitoba **39** A2 54 00N 101 00W
Clearwater River Alberta **41** B2 51 59N 115 20W
Clearwater River Alberta/Saskatchewan **40** A3 56 45N 110 59W
Clearwater River Provincial Park Saskatchewan **40** B3 57 10N 108 10W
Clifford Ontario **38** B2 43 58N 80 00W
Climax Saskatchewan **40** B1 49 12N 108 22W
Clinton British Columbia **43** D2 51 05N 121 38W
Clinton Ontario **38** A2 43 36N 81 33W
Clinton-Colden Lake Northwest Territories **44** K3 64 58N 107 27W
Close Lake Saskatchewan **40** C3 57 50N 104 40W
Clover Bar Alberta **48** G5 53 35N 113 19W
Cloverdale British Columbia **46** G3 49 05N 122 46W
Cluff Lake *tn.* Saskatchewan **40** B3 58 20N 109 35W
Clyde River *tn.* Northwest Territories **45** S5 70 30N 68 30W
Coaldale Alberta **41** C1 49 43N 112 37W
Coalhurst Alberta **41** C1 49 45N 112 56W
Coal River British Columbia **43** C3 59 56N 127 11W
Coast Mountains British Columbia **42** B3 58 10N 132 40W
Coates Creek Ontario **38** B3 44 22N 80 07W
Coaticook Québec **37** P6 45 08N 71 40W
Coats Island Northwest Territories **45** P3 63 30N 83 00W
Cobalt Ontario **35** E2 47 24N 79 41W
Cobequid Bay Nova Scotia **31** F7 45 20N 63 50W
Cobequid Mountains Nova Scotia **31** F7 45 30N 64 50W
Cobourg Ontario **35** E2 43 58N 78 11W
Cochrane Alberta **41** C2 51 11N 114 28W
Cochrane Ontario **35** D2 49 04N 81 02W
Cochrane River Manitoba/Saskatchewan **40** C3 58 50N 102 20W
Cockburn Island Ontario **36** C6 45 55N 83 22W
Codette Lake Saskatchewan **40** C2 53 15N 104 10W
Cod Island Newfoundland **30** B4 57 47N 61 47W
Colborne Ontario **36** J5 44 00N 77 53W
Colchester *admin.* Nova Scotia **31** F7 45 30N 63 30W
Cold Lake Alberta **41** C2 54 35N 110 00W
Cold Lake *tn.* Alberta **41** C2 54 28N 110 15W
Cold Lake Air Weapons Range Alberta **41** C3 55 10N 110 25W
Coldspring Head *c.* Nova Scotia **31** F7 45 55N 63 50W
Coldstream British Columbia **43** E2 50 10N 119 12W
Coldwater Ontario **38** C3 44 43N 79 39W
Cole Harbour Nova Scotia **47** Q6 44 40N 63 27W
Cole Harbour *tn.* Nova Scotia **47** Q6 44 40N 63 30W
Collingwood Ontario **38** B3 44 30N 80 14W
Collins Ontario **34** C3 50 17N 89 27W
Collins Bay *tn.* Saskatchewan **40** C3 58 10N 103 40W
Colonsay Saskatchewan **40** B2 51 59N 105 52W
Colpoys Bay Ontario **38** A3 44 48N 81 04W
Columbia, Mount British Columbia/Alberta **41** B2 52 09N 117 25W
Columbia Mountains British Columbia **43** D2 53 12N 120 49W
Columbia River British Columbia **43** E2 51 15N 116 58W
Colville Lake Northwest Territories **44** F4 67 10N 126 00W
Colville Lake *tn.* Northwest Territories **44** F4 67 02N 126 07W
Colwood British Columbia **42** H4 48 27N 123 28W
Combermere Ontario **36** J6 45 22N 77 37W
Comfort Bight *tn.* Newfoundland **30** C3 53 09N 55 48W
Comma Island Newfoundland **30** B4 55 20N 60 20W
Committee Bay Northwest Territories **45** O4 68 30N 86 30W
Comox British Columbia **42** H4 49 41N 124 56W
Comox Lake British Columbia **42** G4 49 37N 125 10W
Compton *admin.* Québec **37** P6 45 10N 71 40W
Conception Bay Newfoundland **31** D2 47 45N 53 00W
Conception Bay South *tn.* Newfoundland **31** D2 47 30N 53 00W

Conche Newfoundland 31 C3 50 53N 55 54W
Conestoga Lake Ontario 38 B2 43 47N 80 44W
Conestogo River Ontario 38 B2 43 41N 80 42W
Conklin Alberta 41 C3 55 38N 111 05W
Conne River tn. Newfoundland 31 C2 47 50N 55 20W
Consort Alberta 41 C2 52 01N 110 46W
Contrecoeur Québec 37 N6 45 51N 73 15W
Contwoyto Lake Northwest Territories 44 K4 65 42N 110 50W
Cook's Bay Ontario 38 C3 44 53N 79 31W
Cookshire Québec 27 45 25N 72 09W
Cookstown Ontario 38 C3 44 12N 79 42W
Coppermine Northwest Territories 44 J4 65 00N 110 00W
Coppermine River Northwest Territories 44 J4 67 10N 115 00W
Coquihalla Highway British Columbia 42 H4 49 25N 121 20W
Coquitlam British Columbia 46 G4 49 15N 122 52W
Coquitlam Lake British Columbia 46 G4 49 21N 122 46W
Coquitlam River British Columbia 46 G4 49 17N 122 45W
Coral Harbour tn. Northwest Territories 45 P3 64 10N 83 15W
Cormorant Manitoba 39 A2 54 14N 100 35W
Cormorant Lake Manitoba 39 A2 54 15N 100 45W
Cormorant Provincial Forest Manitoba 39 A2 54 10N 100 50W
Corner Brook tn. Newfoundland 31 C2 48 58N 57 58W
Cornwall Ontario 37 M6 45 02N 74 45W
Cornwall Prince Edward Island 31 F7 46 10N 63 10W
Cornwallis Island Northwest Territories 45 N6 74 40N 97 30W
Cornwall Island Northwest Territories 45 M6/N6 77 25N 95 00W
Coronation Alberta 41 C2 52 05N 111 27W
Coronation Gulf Northwest Territories 44 J4 68 15N 112 30W
Cortes Island British Columbia 42 H5 50 07N 125 01W
Cosselman Ontario 37 L6 45 19N 78 07W
Côte-St-Luc Québec 37 N6 45 28N 73 39W
Couchiching, Lake Ontario 38 C3 44 39N 79 22W
Courtenay British Columbia 42 H4 49 40N 124 58W
Courtright Ontario 36 D3 42 49N 82 28W
Coutts Alberta 41 C1 49 00N 111 57W
Cove Island Ontario 38 A4 45 19N 81 44W
Cowansville Québec 37 O6 45 13N 72 44W
Cow Bay Nova Scotia 47 Q6 44 36N 63 26W
Cow Head tn. Newfoundland 31 C2 49 55N 57 48W
Cowichan Lake British Columbia 42 H4 48 50N 124 04W
Cowichan River British Columbia 42 H4 48 48N 123 58W
Cox's Cove tn. Newfoundland 31 C2 49 07N 58 04W
Craigellachie British Columbia 43 E2 50 59N 118 38W
Craigleith Provincial Park Ontario 38 B3 44 30N 80 15W
Craik Saskatchewan 40 B2 51 03N 105 50W
Cranberry Portage Manitoba 39 A2 54 36N 101 22W
Cranbrook British Columbia 43 E1 49 29N 115 48W
Crane Lake Saskatchewan 40 B2 50 10N 109 20W
Crane River Ontario 38 A4 45 53N 81 31W
Credit River Ontario 38 B3 43 35N 79 43W
Cree Lake Saskatchewan 40 B3 57 30N 106 30W
Creemore Ontario 38 B3 44 20N 80 07W
Cree River Saskatchewan 40 B3 58 00N 106 30W
Creighton Saskatchewan 40 C2 54 46N 101 50W
Cresswell Bay tn. Northwest Territories 45 N5 72 40N 93 30W
Creston British Columbia 43 E1 49 05N 116 32W
Crofton British Columbia 42 H4 48 52N 123 38W
Croker, Cape Ontario 38 B4 44 58N 80 59W
Crossfield Alberta 41 C2 51 26N 114 02W
Cross Lake Manitoba 39 B2 54 50N 97 20W
Cross Lake tn. Manitoba 39 B2 54 38N 97 45W
Crow Lake Ontario 34 B2 49 10N 93 56W
Crowsnest Highway Alberta 41 C1 49 50N 111 55W
Crowsnest Pass Alberta/British Columbia 43 E1 49 40N 114 41W
Crumlin Ontario 38 A2 43 01N 81 08W
Crystal Bay Ontario 47 J2 45 21N 75 51W
Crystal Beach tn. Ontario 38 C1 42 52N 79 03W
Crystal Lake Ontario 38 D3 44 45N 78 30W
Cub Hills, The Saskatchewan 40 C2 54 20N 104 40W
Cudworth Saskatchewan 40 B2 52 31N 105 44W
Cumberland British Columbia 42 H4 49 37N 124 59W
Cumberland Ontario 47 L3 45 31N 75 23W
Cumberland admin. Nova Scotia 31 F7 45 30N 64 10W
Cumberland House tn. Saskatchewan 40 C2 53 57N 102 20W
Cumberland Lake Saskatchewan 40 C2 54 10N 102 30W
Cumberland Peninsula Northwest Territories 45 T4 67 00N 65 00W
Cumberland Sound Northwest Territories 45 S4 65 30N 66 00W
Cupar Saskatchewan 40 C2 50 57N 104 12W
Cushing, Mount British Columbia 43 C3 57 36N 126 51W
Cut Knife Saskatchewan 40 B2 52 45N 109 01W
Cypress Hills Alberta/Saskatchewan 41 C1 49 30N 110 00W
Cypress Hills Provincial Park Alberta/Saskatchewan 41 C1 49 38N 110 00W

D

Dalhousie Alberta 48 A2 51 06N 114 10W
Dalhousie New Brunswick 31 A2 48 03N 66 22W
Dalhousie, Cape Northwest Territories 44 F5 70 14N 129 42W
Dalmeny Saskatchewan 40 B2 52 22N 106 46W
Dalrymple Lake Ontario 38 C3 44 41N 79 07W
Daniel's Harbour tn. Newfoundland 31 C3 50 14N 57 35W
Danville Québec 37 O6 45 48N 72 01W
D'Arcy British Columbia 42 H5 50 33N 122 28W
Darlington Provincial Park Ontario 38 D2 44 00N 78 50W
Darnley Bay Northwest Territories 44 G4 69 30N 123 30W
Dartmouth Nova Scotia 31 F6 44 40N 63 35W
Dauphin Manitoba 39 A2 51 09N 100 05W
Dauphin, Cape Nova Scotia 31 F7 46 20N 60 25W
Dauphin Lake Manitoba 39 B2 51 15N 99 45W
Dauphin River Manitoba 39 B2 51 50N 98 20W
Dauphin River tn. Manitoba 39 B2 51 50N 98 00W
Daveluyville Québec 27 46 12N 72 09W
Davidson Saskatchewan 40 B2 51 15N 105 59W
David Thompson Highway Alberta 41 B2 52 15N 116 35W

Davin Lake Saskatchewan 40 C3 56 45N 103 40W
Davis Inlet tn. Newfoundland 30 A3 55 51N 60 52W
Davis Strait Canada/Greenland 45 T4 65 00N 57 00W
Davy Lake Saskatchewan 40 B3 58 50N 108 10W
Dawson Yukon Territory 44 D3 64 04N 139 24W
Dawson Creek tn. British Columbia 43 D3 55 44N 120 15W
Dawson, Mount British Columbia 43 E2 51 08N 117 26W
Dawson Bay Manitoba 39 A2 52 50N 100 50W
Dawson Range mts. Yukon Territory 44 D3 63 00N 139 30W
Dawsons Landing British Columbia 43 C2 51 28N 127 33W
Daysland Alberta 41 C2 52 52N 112 15W
Dean Channel British Columbia 43 C2 52 18N 127 35W
Dean River British Columbia 43 C2 52 45N 126 40W
Dease Arm b. Northwest Territories 44 G4 66 52N 119 37W
Dease Lake British Columbia 42 B3 58 05N 130 04W
Dease Lake tn. British Columbia 42 B3 58 28N 130 00W
Dease River British Columbia 42 C3 59 05N 129 40W
Dease Strait Northwest Territories 44 K4 68 40N 108 00W
Debah Northwest Territories 44 J3 62 25N 114 30W
Déception Québec 32 B5 62 10N 74 45W
Dee Lake British Columbia 46 G3 49 14N 122 59W
Deep Cove British Columbia 46 G4 49 19N 122 58W
Deep Inlet Newfoundland 30 B4 55 22N 60 14W
Deep River Ontario 37 J7 46 06N 77 30W
Deer Island New Brunswick 31 A1 45 00N 67 00W
Deer Lake Ontario 34 B3 52 38N 94 25W
Deer Lake tn. Newfoundland 31 C2 49 11N 57 27W
Delhi Ontario 38 B1 42 51N 80 30W
Delisle Saskatchewan 40 B2 51 56N 107 10W
Deloraine Manitoba 39 A1 49 11N 100 30W
Delta British Columbia 42 H4 49 06N 123 01W
Dempster Highway Yukon Territory 44 D4 65 30N 138 10W
Denbigh Ontario 37 J6 45 08N 77 15W
Denman Island British Columbia 42 H4 49 32N 124 49W
Deschambault Lake Saskatchewan 40 C2 54 50N 103 50W
Deseronto Ontario 37 J5 44 12N 77 03W
Desmaraisville Québec 33 A2 49 30N 76 18W
Desolation Sound Marine Park British Columbia 42 H5 50 08N 124 45W
Destruction Bay tn. Yukon Territory 44 D3 61 16N 138 50W
Détroit de Jacques-Cartier sd. Québec 33 D3 50 10N 64 10W
Détroit d'Honguedo sd. Québec 33 D2 49 30N 64 20W
Détroit d'Hudson (Hudson Strait) Québec/Northwest Territories 32 B5 62 00N 70 00W
Detroit River Ontario Canada/U.S.A. 52 E2 42 15N 83 00W
Deux-Montagnes Québec 47 M5 45 32N 73 56W
Deux Rivieres Ontario 36 H7 46 15N 78 17W
Devil's Glen Provincial Park Ontario 38 B3 44 20N 80 30W
Devon Alberta 41 C2 53 22N 113 44W
Devon Island Northwest Territories 45 O6 75 47N 88 00W
Dewar Lakes Northwest Territories 45 R4 68 30N 71 20W
Dewey Soper Game Sanctuary Northwest Territories 45 R4 66 20N 68 50W
Diamond Jenness Peninsula Northwest Territories 44 H5 71 20N 117 00W
Dickson Peak British Columbia 42 H5 50 54N 122 59W
Didsbury Alberta 41 C2 51 40N 114 08W
Diefenbaker, Lake Saskatchewan 40 B2 51 10N 107 30W
Dieppe New Brunswick 31 F7 46 10N 64 40W
Digby Nova Scotia 31 E6 44 37N 65 47W
Digby admin. Nova Scotia 31 E7 44 20N 65 40W
Digby Neck p. Nova Scotia 31 E6 44 30N 66 00W
Dillon Saskatchewan 40 B3 55 56N 108 54W
Dingwall Nova Scotia 31 F7 46 50N 60 30W
Dinorwic Ontario 34 B2 49 41N 92 30W
Dinosaur Provincial Park Alberta 22 50 45N 111 30W
Disappointment Lake Newfoundland 30 B3 53 49N 62 31W
Dismal Lakes Northwest Territories 44 H4 67 26N 117 07W
Disraeli Québec 37 P6 45 54N 71 22W
Dixon Entrance sd. British Columbia Canada/Alaska U.S.A. 42 B2 54 28N 132 50W
Doaktown New Brunswick 31 A2 46 34N 66 06W
Dobie River Ontario 34 B3 51 30N 90 50W
Dodge Lake Saskatchewan 40 B3 59 50N 105 25W
Dodsland Saskatchewan 40 B2 51 48N 108 51W
Dog Creek tn. British Columbia 43 D2 51 35N 122 18W
Dog (High) Island Newfoundland 30 B4 56 38N 61 10W
Dog Lake Manitoba 39 B2 51 00N 98 20W
Dog Lake Ontario 35 C2 48 45N 89 33W
Dolbeau Québec 33 B2 48 52N 72 15W
Dollarton British Columbia 46 G4 49 18N 122 58W
Dolphin and Union Strait Northwest Territories 44 H4 69 05N 114 45W
Dominion Nova Scotia 31 F7 46 14N 60 01W
Dominion Lake Newfoundland 30 B3 52 40N 61 43W
Don Mills Ontario 46 C1 43 44N 79 22W
Donnacona Québec 37 P7 46 41N 71 45W
Don River Ontario 46 C2 43 48N 79 24W
Dorcas Bay Ontario 38 A4 45 10N 81 38W
Dorchester New Brunswick 31 F7 45 54N 64 32W
Dorchester admin. Québec 37 Q7 46 20N 70 40W
Dorchester, Cape Northwest Territories 45 Q4 65 27N 77 27W
Doré Lake Saskatchewan 40 B2 54 50N 107 20W
Dorion Ontario 35 C2 48 49N 88 33W
Dorval Québec 47 N4 45 27N 73 44W
Double Mer in. Newfoundland 30 C3 54 04N 59 10W
Douglas Lake British Columbia 46 G3 49 13N 122 46W
Dowling Lake Alberta 41 C2 51 44N 112 00W
Downton Lake British Columbia 42 H5 50 48N 123 10W
Downtown, Mount British Columbia 43 D2 52 45N 124 53W
Dows Lake Ontario 47 K2 45 24N 75 42W
Drayton Ontario 38 B2 43 45N 80 40W
Drayton Valley tn. Alberta 41 B2 53 13N 114 59W
Dresden Ontario 26 42 34N 82 11W
Drowning River Ontario 34 C3 50 30N 86 10W
Drumheller Alberta 41 C2 51 28N 112 40W
Drummond admin. Québec 37 O6 45 55N 72 40W
Drummondville Québec 37 O6 45 52N 72 30W
Dryden Ontario 34 B2 49 48N 92 48W

Drylake tn. Newfoundland 30 A3 52 38N 65 59W
Dubawnt Lake Northwest Territories 45 L3 68 15N 102 00W
Dubreuilville Ontario 35 D2 48 21N 84 32W
Duck Bay tn. Manitoba 39 A2 52 10N 100 10W
Duck Lake tn. Saskatchewan 40 B2 52 52N 106 12W
Duck Mountain Provincial Forest Manitoba 39 A2 51 20N 100 50W
Duck Mountain Provincial Park Manitoba/Saskatchewan 39 A2 51 40N 101 00W
Dufferin admin. Ontario 38 B3 44 00N 80 20W
Duffey Lake British Columbia 42 H5 50 24N 122 23W
Duncan British Columbia 42 H4 48 46N 123 40W
Duncan, Cape Northwest Territories 34 D3 52 40N 80 50W
Duncan Lake British Columbia 43 E2 50 23N 116 57W
Dundalk Ontario 38 B3 44 10N 80 24W
Dundas Ontario 38 C2 43 16N 79 57W
Dundas Island British Columbia 42 B3 54 33N 131 20W
Dundas Peninsula Northwest Territories 44 J5 74 50N 111 30W
Dundurn Saskatchewan 40 B2 51 49N 106 30W
Dunkirk Saskatchewan 40 B2 50 04N 105 41W
Dunnville Ontario 38 C1 42 54N 79 36W
Dunville Newfoundland 31 D2 47 16N 53 54W
Durham Ontario 38 B3 44 11N 80 49W
Durham admin. Ontario 38 C3 44 04N 79 11W
Durrell Newfoundland 31 D2 49 40N 54 44W
Dutton Ontario 38 A1 42 39N 81 30W
Dyer's Bay Ontario 38 A4 45 10N 81 18W
Dyer's Bay tn. Ontario 38 A4 45 09N 81 20W
Dyke Lake Newfoundland 30 A3 54 30N 66 18W

E

Eabamet Lake Ontario 34 C3 51 32N 87 46W
Eagle Plains tn. Yukon Territory 44 D4 66 30N 136 50W
Eagle River Newfoundland 30 C3 53 00N 58 30W
Eagle River Ontario 34 B2 49 50N 93 12W
Eagle River tn. Ontario 34 B2 51 35N 107 40W
Ear Falls tn. Ontario 34 B3 50 38N 93 13W
Earl Rowe Provincial Park Ontario 38 C3 44 15N 79 45W
East Angus Québec 27 45 30N 71 40W
East Bay Bird Sanctuary Northwest Territories 45 P3 66 20N 74 00W
East Chezzetcook Nova Scotia 31 F6 44 34N 63 14W
Eastend Saskatchewan 40 B2 49 32N 108 50W
Eastern Passage tn. Nova Scotia 47 Q6 44 36N 63 29W
Easterville Manitoba 39 B2 53 00N 99 40W
East Lake Nova Scotia 47 Q7 44 46N 63 29W
Eastmain Québec 33 A3 52 10N 78 30W
East Point Prince Edward Island 31 F7 46 27N 61 59W
Eastport Newfoundland 31 D2 48 39N 53 45W
East St. Paul admin. Manitoba 48 D2 47 16N 97 04W
East Thurlow Island British Columbia 42 G5 50 24N 125 26W
East York bor. Metropolitan Toronto Ontario 46 C1 43 43N 79 20W
Eatonia Saskatchewan 40 B2 51 13N 109 22W
Echoing River Ontario 34 B3 54 30N 92 00W
Echo, Lake Nova Scotia 47 Q6 44 44N 63 24W
Eclipse Sound Northwest Territories 45 Q5 72 38N 79 00W
Ecum Secum Nova Scotia 31 F6 44 58N 62 08W
Eddies Cove tn. Newfoundland 30 C3 51 25N 56 27W
Edehon Lake Northwest Territories 45 N3 60 25N 97 15W
Edgewood British Columbia 43 E1 49 47N 118 08W
Edmonton Alberta 41 G4 53 34N 113 25W
Edmund Lake Manitoba 39 C2 54 50N 93 30W
Edmundston New Brunswick 31 A2 47 22N 68 20W
Edson Alberta 41 B2 53 35N 116 26W
Eduni, Mount Northwest Territories 44 F3 64 13N 128 10W
Edwards Ontario 47 L2 45 19N 75 48W
Edziza, Mount British Columbia 42 B3 57 43N 130 42W
Edzo Northwest Territories 44 H3 63 50N 116 00W
Eganville Ontario 37 J6 45 32N 77 06W
Eglington Island Northwest Territories 44 H6 75 48N 118 30W
Egmont British Columbia 42 H4 49 45N 123 55W
Egmont Bay Prince Edward Island 31 F7 46 30N 64 20W
Egmont, Cape Nova Scotia 31 F7 46 50N 60 20W
Eileen Lake Northwest Territories 44 K3 62 16N 107 37W
Ekwan Point Ontario 34 D3 53 20N 82 30W
Ekwan River Ontario 34 D3 53 30N 83 40W
Elaho River British Columbia 42 H5 50 14N 123 33W
Elbow Saskatchewan 40 B2 51 08N 106 36W
Elbow River Alberta 48 A1 50 59N 114 13W
Elgin admin. Ontario 38 A1 42 38N 81 36W
Elkford British Columbia 43 E2 50 02N 114 55W
Elkhorn Manitoba 39 A1 49 58N 101 14W
Elk Island Manitoba 39 B2 50 50N 96 40W
Elk Island National Park Alberta 41 C2 53 36N 112 53W
Elk Lake tn. Ontario 35 D2 47 44N 80 20W
Elk Lakes Provincial Park British Columbia 43 E2 50 00N 115 00W
Elk Point tn. Alberta 41 C2 53 54N 110 54W
Ellef Ringnes Island Northwest Territories 44 L6 78 30N 102 00W
Ellerslie Alberta 48 A4 53 24N 113 28W
Ellesmere Island Northwest Territories 45 P6 77 30N 82 30W
Ellesmere Island National Park Reserve Northwest Territories 45 R7 82 00N 72 30W
Ellice River Northwest Territories 44 L4 66 20N 105 00W
Elliot Lake tn. Ontario 36 D7 46 25N 82 40W
Elmira Ontario 38 B2 43 36N 80 34W
Elmvale Ontario 38 C3 44 35N 79 52W
Elora Ontario 38 B2 43 42N 80 26W
Elrose Saskatchewan 40 B2 51 12N 108 01W
Elsa Yukon Territory 44 D3 63 55N 135 29W
Elvira, Cape Northwest Territories 44 K5 73 16N 107 10W
Embree Newfoundland 31 D2 49 18N 55 02W
Emerald Island Northwest Territories 44 J6 76 48N 114 10W
Emerson Manitoba 39 B1 49 00N 97 11W
Emily Provincial Park Ontario 38 D3 44 20N 78 28W
Endako British Columbia 43 C2 54 05N 125 01W
Enderby British Columbia 43 E2 50 32N 119 10W
Enfield Nova Scotia 31 F6 44 56N 63 34W
Englee Newfoundland 31 C3 50 44N 56 06W
Englehart Ontario 35 D2 47 50N 79 52W
English Bay British Columbia 46 F4 49 17N 123 12W
English River Ontario 38 C3 50 20N 94 50W

Ennadai Lake Northwest Territories 45 L3 60 58N 101 20W
Eramosa River Ontario 38 B2 43 33N 80 11W
Erieau Ontario 36 E3 42 16N 81 56W
Erie Beach tn. Ontario 36 D3 42 16N 82 00W
Erie Beach tn. Ontario 38 D1 42 53N 78 56W
Erie, Lake Canada/USA 36 E2 42 15N 81 00W
Eriksdale Manitoba 39 B2 50 52N 98 07W
Erin Ontario 38 B2 43 45N 80 04W
Escuminac, Point New Brunswick 31 B2 47 04N 64 49W
Esker Newfoundland 30 A3 53 53N 66 25W
Eskimo Lakes Northwest Territories 44 E4 68 30N 132 30W
Eskimo Point see Arviat
Espanola Ontario 36 E7 46 15N 81 46W
Esquimalt British Columbia 42 H4 48 25N 123 29W
Essex Ontario 36 D3 42 10N 82 49W
Essex admin. Ontario 36 D3 42 10N 82 50W
Esterhazy Saskatchewan 40 C2 50 40N 102 02W
Estevan Saskatchewan 40 C1 49 09N 103 00W
Eston Saskatchewan 40 B2 51 09N 108 42W
Etawney Lake Manitoba 39 A2 51 32N 100 25W
Ethelbert Manitoba 39 A2 51 32N 100 25W
Etobicoke bor. Metropolitan Toronto Ontario 46 B1 43 38N 79 30W
Etobicoke Creek Ontario 46 A1 43 43N 79 47W
Eugenia Lake Ontario 38 B3 44 20N 80 30W
Eureka m.s. Northwest Territories 45 O6 79 59N 85 57W
Eureka River tn. Alberta 41 B3 56 25N 118 48W
Eutsuk Lake British Columbia 43 C2 53 12N 126 32W
Evansburg Alberta 41 B2 53 36N 115 01W
Evans, Mount Alberta 41 B2 52 26N 118 07W
Evans Strait Northwest Territories 45 P3 63 15N 82 30W
Exeter Ontario 38 A2 43 21N 81 30W
Exploits River tn. Newfoundland 31 C2 48 40N 56 30W
Eyehill River Saskatchewan 40 B2 52 25N 109 50W

F

Faber Lake Northwest Territories 44 H3 63 56N 117 15W
Fairchild Creek Ontario 38 B2 43 13N 80 11W
Fairview Alberta 41 B3 56 03N 118 28W
Fairweather Mountain British Columbia Canada/Alaska U.S.A. 42 A3 58 50N 137 55W
Falher Alberta 41 B3 56 03N 117 15W
Fallowfield Ontario 47 J2 45 17N 75 51W
Fall River Nova Scotia 47 P7 44 49N 63 36W
False Creek British Columbia 46 F4 49 16N 123 08W
Family Lake Manitoba 39 B2 51 50N 95 40W
Farnham Québec 37 O6 45 17N 72 59W
Farnham, Mount British Columbia 43 E2 50 27N 116 37W
Faro Yukon Territory 44 E3 62 30N 133 00W
Fathom Five National Marine Park Ontario 38 A4 54 20N 81 35W
Fauquier Ontario 35 D2 49 19N 82 02W
Fawn River Ontario 34 C3 55 20N 89 10W
Felix, Cape Northwest Territories 45 M4 69 54N 97 58W
Fenelon Falls tn. Ontario 38 A2 32N 78 45W
Fergus Ontario 38 B2 43 43N 80 24W
Ferland Ontario 34 C2 50 20N 88 00W
Ferme-Neuve Québec 37 L7 46 42N 75 28W
Fermont Québec 33 C3 52 00N 68 00W
Fernie British Columbia 43 E1 49 30N 115 00W
Ferryland Newfoundland 31 D2 47 01N 54 53W
Fife Lake Saskatchewan 40 B1 49 10N 105 45W
Fighting Island Ontario 52 E1 42 13N 83 07W
Finch Ontario 37 L6 45 08N 75 05W
Finlay Ranges mts. British Columbia 43 C3 57 10N 126 00W
Finlay River British Columbia 43 C3 57 20N 125 40W
Fiordland Recreation Area British Columbia 43 C2 52 00N 127 00W
Firebag Hills Saskatchewan 40 B3 57 15N 109 50W
Firebag River British Columbia 41 C3 57 30N 110 40W
Fish Creek Alberta 48 A1 50 55N 114 10W
Fish Creek Provincial Park Alberta 48 A1 50 55N 114 04W
Fisher Bay Manitoba 39 B2 51 30N 97 30W
Fisher Branch tn. Manitoba 39 B2 51 04N 97 38W
Fisher, Mount British Columbia 43 E1 49 55N 114 53W
Fisher Strait Northwest Territories 45 P3 63 00N 84 00W
Fishing Branch Game Reserve Yukon Territory 44 D4 66 30N 139 30W
Fishing Lake Manitoba 39 B2 52 10N 95 40W
Fishing Ships Harbour tn. Newfoundland 30 C3 52 36N 55 47W
Fitzgerald Alberta 41 C3 59 51N 111 36W
Fitzwilliam Island Ontario 38 E6 45 29N 81 45W
Flamborough Ontario 38 C2 43 20N 79 57W
Flathead River British Columbia 43 F1 48 00N 114 00W
Flesherton Ontario 38 B3 44 16N 80 32W
Fletchers Lake Nova Scotia 47 P7 44 51N 63 35W
Fleur de Lys Newfoundland 31 C3 50 07N 56 08W
Fleuve Saint-Laurent (St. Lawrence River) Québec 33 C2 48 20N 69 20W
Flin Flon Manitoba 39 A2 54 50N 102 00W
Florenceville New Brunswick 31 A2 46 20N 67 20W
Flores Island British Columbia 43 C1 49 20N 126 10W
Flour Lake Newfoundland 30 A3 53 44N 64 50W
Foam Lake tn. Saskatchewan 40 C2 51 38N 103 31W
Foch British Columbia 42 H5 50 07N 124 31W
Fogo Newfoundland 31 D2 49 43N 54 17W
Fogo Island Newfoundland 31 D2 49 40N 54 10W
Foley Lake Newfoundland 44 H4 53 24N 113 13W
Foleyet Ontario 35 D2 48 05N 82 26W
Fond du Lac Saskatchewan 40 B3 59 20N 107 09W
Fond du Lac River Saskatchewan 40 C3 59 05N 104 40W
Fontas River British Columbia 43 D3 58 20N 121 25W
Fonthill Ontario 38 C2 43 02N 79 17W
Foothills Municipal District Alberta 48 A1 50 53N 114 08W
Forbes, Mount Alberta 41 B2 51 52N 116 55W
Foremost Alberta 41 C1 49 29N 111 25W
Forest Ontario 36 E4 43 06N 82 00W
Forestburg Alberta 41 C2 52 35N 112 04W
Forest Hill Ontario 46 C1 43 42N 79 25W
Forest Lawn Alberta 48 A2 51 02N 113 58W
Forestville Québec 33 C2 48 45N 69 05W
Forrest Lake Saskatchewan 40 B3 57 35N 109 10W
Fort Albany Ontario 34 C3 52 15N 81 40W
Fort Babine British Columbia 43 C3 55 20N 126 35W
Fort Chipewyan Alberta 41 C3 58 46N 111 09W
Fort Coulonge Québec 37 K6 45 51N 76 46W
Forteau Newfoundland 30 C3 51 28N 56 58W
Fort Erie Ontario 38 D1 42 55N 78 56W
Fort Frances Ontario 34 B2 48 37N 93 23W

Fort Franklin Northwest Territories **44** G4 65 11N 123 26W
Fort Fraser British Columbia **43** D2 54 03N 124 30W
Fort Garry Manitoba **48** D2 49 49N 97 10W
Fort George *see* Chisasibi
Fort Good Hope Northwest Territories **44** F4 66 16N 128 37W
Fort Hope *I.R.* Ontario **34** C3 51 37N 87 55W
Fort Langley British Columbia **42** H4 49 11N 122 38W
Fort Liard Northwest Territories **44** G3 60 14N 123 28W
Fort MacKay Alberta **41** C3 57 11N 111 37W
Fort Macleod Alberta **41** C1 49 44N 113 24W
Fort McMurray Alberta **41** C3 56 45N 111 27W
Fort McPherson Northwest Territories **44** E4 67 29N 134 50W
Fort Nelson British Columbia **43** D3 58 48N 122 44W
Fort Nelson River British Columbia **43** D3 59 20N 124 05W
Fort Norman Northwest Territories **44** F3 64 55N 125 29W
Fort Providence Northwest Territories **44** H3 61 03N 117 40W
Fort Qu'Appelle Saskatchewan **40** C2 50 46N 103 54W
Fort Resolution Northwest Territories **44** J3 61 10N 113 39W
Fort Rouge Manitoba **48** D2 49 52N 97 07W
Fort Rupert *(Waskaganish)* Québec **33** A3 51 30N 79 45W
Fort St. James British Columbia **43** D2 54 26N 124 15W
Fort St. John British Columbia **43** D3 56 14N 120 55W
Fort Saskatchewan Alberta **48** H5 53 42N 113 12W
Fort Severn Ontario **34** C4 56 00N 87 40W
Fort Simpson Northwest Territories **44** G3 61 46N 121 15W
Fort Smith Alberta **41** C3 60 00N 111 51W
Fort Smith Northwest Territories **44** J3 60 01N 111 55W
Fort Smith *reg.* Northwest Territories **44** H3 63 00N 120 00W
Fortune Newfoundland **31** C2 47 04N 55 50W
Fortune Bay Newfoundland **31** C2 47 15N 55 30W
Fort Vermilion Alberta **41** B3 58 22N 115 59W
Fort Ware British Columbia **43** C3 57 30N 125 43W
Fort Whyte Manitoba **48** D2 49 49N 97 12W
Fortymile Yukon Territory **44** C3 64 25N 140 32W
Fosheim Peninsula Northwest Territories **45** P6 80 00N 85 00W
Foster, Mount British Columbia **42** A3 59 49N 135 35W
Foster River Saskatchewan **40** B3 56 20N 105 45W
Fourchu Nova Scotia **31** F7 45 43N 60 17W
Four Mile Lake Ontario **38** D3 44 42N 78 44W
Fox Creek *tn.* Alberta **41** B2 54 24N 116 48W
Foxe Basin *b.* Northwest Territories **44** Q4 66 20N 79 00W
Foxe Channel Northwest Territories **44** Q3 65 00N 81 00W
Foxe Peninsula Northwest Territories **45** Q3 65 00N 76 00W
Fox River Manitoba **39** C3 55 50N 94 10W
Fox Valley *tn.* Saskatchewan **40** B2 50 29N 109 29W
Frances Lake Yukon Territory **44** F3 61 20N 129 30W
François Lake British Columbia **43** C2 54 00N 125 47W
Frankford Ontario **36** J5 44 12N 77 36W
Franklin Bay Northwest Territories **44** F5 69 45N 126 00W
Franklin Island Ontario **38** B4 45 25N 80 20W
Franklin Lake Northwest Territories **45** M4 66 56N 96 03W
Franklin Mountains Northwest Territories **44** G3 61 15N 123 50W
Fraserdale Ontario **35** D2 49 51N 81 37W
Fraser Lake British Columbia **43** D2 54 00N 124 50W
Fraser Lake Newfoundland **30** B3 54 24N 63 40W
Fraser Plateau British Columbia **43** D2 52 32N 124 10W
Fraser River British Columbia **43** D2 51 36N 122 25W
Fraser River Newfoundland **30** B4 56 50N 63 50W
Fredericton New Brunswick **31** A2 45 57N 66 40W
Fredericton Junction New Brunswick **31** A2 45 40N 66 38W
Freels, Cape Newfoundland **31** D2 49 15N 53 29W
Freeport Nova Scotia **31** E6 44 17N 66 19W
Frenchman River Saskatchewan **40** B1 49 30N 108 00W
Frenchman's Cove *tn.* Newfoundland **31** C2 49 04N 58 10W
French River Ontario **36** F7 46 00N 81 00W
French River *tn.* Ontario **36** F7 46 03N 80 34W
Freshwater Newfoundland **31** D2 47 15N 53 59W
Frobisher Bay Northwest Territories **45** S3 62 15N 65 00W
Frobisher Bay *tn. see* Iqaluit
Frobisher Lake Saskatchewan **40** B3 57 00N 108 00W
Frog Lake Alberta **41** C2 53 55N 110 20W
Frontenac *admin.* Ontario **37** K6 44 40N 76 45W
Frontenac *admin.* Québec **37** Q6 45 40N 70 50W
Frontenac Provincial Park Ontario **37** K5 44 32N 76 29W
Frozen Strait Northwest Territories **45** P4 66 08N 85 00W
Fruitvale British Columbia **43** E1 49 08N 117 28W
Fundy, Bay of New Brunswick/Nova Scotia **31** E6 45 00N 66 00W
Fundy National Park New Brunswick **31** E7 45 40N 65 10W
Fury and Hecla Strait Northwest Territories **45** P4 69 56N 84 00W

G

Gabarus Bay Nova Scotia **31** F7 45 50N 60 10W
Gabriola Island British Columbia **42** H4 49 10N 123 51W
Gage, Cape Prince Edward Island **31** F7 46 50N 64 20W
Gagetown New Brunswick **31** A2 45 46N 66 29W
Gagnon Québec **33** C3 51 56N 68 16W
Galiano Island British Columbia **42** H4 48 57N 123 25W
Galt Ontario **38** B2 43 21N 80 19W
Gambier Island British Columbia **42** H4 49 30N 123 25W
Gambo Newfoundland **31** D2 48 46N 54 14W
Gananoque Ontario **37** K5 44 20N 76 10W
Ganaraska River Ontario **38** D3 44 02N 78 34W
Gander Newfoundland **31** D2 48 57N 54 34W
Gander Lake Newfoundland **31** D2 48 55N 54 35W
Ganges British Columbia **42** H4 48 51N 123 31W
Gardiner Dam Saskatchewan **40** B2 51 15N 106 40W
Gardner Canal British Columbia **42** C2 53 30N 128 50W
Garibaldi Lake British Columbia **42** H4 49 55N 122 57W
Garibaldi, Mount British Columbia **42** H4 49 53N 123 00W
Garibaldi Provincial Park British Columbia **42** H4 49 58N 122 45W
Garnish Newfoundland **31** C2 47 14N 55 22W
Garry Lake Northwest Territories **45** F4 66 20N 100 00W
Garry Point British Columbia **46** F3 49 07N 123 14W
Gaspé Québec **33** D2 48 50N 64 30W
Gaspereau Lake Nova Scotia **31** F6 44 50N 64 30W
Gateshead Island Northwest Territories **45** M5 70 36N 100 26W
Gatineau Québec **37** L6 45 29N 75 40W
Gatineau *admin.* Québec **37** K7 45 47N 76 05W
Gauer Lake Manitoba **39** B3 57 10N 97 30W
Gaultois Newfoundland **31** C2 47 36N 55 54W
Geikie River Saskatchewan **40** C3 57 20N 104 40W
George, Cape Nova Scotia **31** F7 45 50N 61 55W
George Island Newfoundland **30** C3 54 16N 57 20W
Georgetown Ontario **38** C2 43 39N 79 56W
Georgetown Prince Edward Island **31** F7 46 12N 62 32W
Georgian Bay Ontario **36** E6 45 00N 81 00W
Georgian Bay Islands National Park Ontario **38** C3 44 53N 79 52W
Georgia, Strait of British Columbia **42** H4 49 39N 124 34W
Georgina Island Ontario **38** C3 44 22N 79 17W
Geraldton Ontario **34** C2 49 44N 86 59W
Germansen Landing *tn.* British Columbia **43** D3 55 47N 124 42W
Giant's Causeway *p.* Northwest Territories **44** G6 75 46N 121 11W
Giants Tomb Island Ontario **38** B3 44 55N 80 00W
Gibsons *tn.* British Columbia **42** H4 49 24N 123 30W
Gilbert, Mount British Columbia **42** H5 50 50N 124 15W
Gilbert Plains *tn.* Manitoba **39** A2 51 09N 100 28W
Gilford Island British Columbia **42** C2 50 45N 126 20W
Gil Island British Columbia **42** C2 53 10N 129 15W
Gillam Manitoba **39** C3 56 25N 94 45W
Gillies Bay *tn.* British Columbia **42** H4 49 42N 124 28W
Gimli Manitoba **39** B2 50 39N 97 00W
Gjoa Haven *tn.* Northwest Territories **45** M4 68 39N 96 09W
Glace Bay *tn.* Nova Scotia **31** F7 46 11N 59 58W
Glacial Mountain British Columbia **42** C3 58 15N 129 25W
Glacier National Park British Columbia **43** E2 51 00N 117 00W
Gladstone Manitoba **39** B2 50 14N 98 56W
Gladys Lake British Columbia **42** B3 59 50N 132 52W
Glaslyn Saskatchewan **40** B2 53 23N 108 22W
Glenboro Manitoba **39** B1 49 35N 99 20W
Glen Cairn Ontario **47** J2 45 15N 75 45W
Glencoe Ontario **38** A1 42 45N 81 44W
Glenmore Reservoir Alberta **48** A1 50 58N 114 08W
Glenwood Newfoundland **31** C2 48 59N 54 53W
Gloucester Ontario **47** K2 45 21N 75 39W
Gloucester *admin.* New Brunswick **31** A2 47 30N 65 50W
Gloucester Glen *tn.* Ontario **47** K2 45 17N 75 41W
Glover Island Newfoundland **31** C2 48 46N 57 43W
Glovertown Newfoundland **31** D2 48 41N 54 02W
Goat Island British Columbia **42** H5 50 03N 124 28W
Goderich Ontario **38** A2 43 43N 81 43W
Gods Lake Manitoba **39** C2 54 40N 94 20W
Gods Lake *tn.* Manitoba **39** C2 54 45N 94 00W
Gods Mercy, Bay of Northwest Territories **45** O3 63 30N 88 10W
Gods River Manitoba **39** C3 56 20N 92 50W
Gogama Ontario **35** D2 47 40N 81 43W
Go Home Lake Ontario **38** C4 45 01N 79 51W
Gold Bridge British Columbia **42** H5 50 51N 122 51W
Golden British Columbia **43** E2 51 19N 116 55W
Golden Ears Provincial Park British Columbia **42** H4 49 28N 122 25W
Golden Hinde *mt.* British Columbia **43** C1 49 35N 125 40W
Gold River British Columbia **43** C1 49 41N 125 59W
Goldsmith Channel Northwest Territories **44** K5 73 00N 106 00W
Golfe du Saint-Laurent *(Gulf of St. Lawrence)* Québec **33** D2 48 40N 62 40W
Goodeve Saskatchewan **40** C2 51 03N 103 11W
Good Hope British Columbia **43** C2 50 59N 124 01W
Good Hope Mountain British Columbia **43** C2 51 08N 124 10W
Goodsoil Saskatchewan **40** B2 54 24N 109 12W
Goose Bay *tn.* Newfoundland **30** A3 53 15N 60 20W
Goose River Newfoundland **30** A3 53 30N 61 50W
Gordon Horne Peak British Columbia **43** E2 51 47N 118 50W
Gordon Lake Alberta **41** C3 56 30N 110 25W
Gordon Pittock Reservoir Ontario **38** B2 43 11N 80 43W
Gordon River British Columbia **42** H4 48 38N 124 25W
Gore Bay *tn.* Ontario **36** D6 45 55N 82 28W
Goshen Nova Scotia **31** F7 45 20N 62 55W
Gott Peak British Columbia **42** H5 50 18N 122 16W
Goulbourne Ontario **47** J2 46 15N 75 54W
Goulds Newfoundland **31** D2 47 29N 52 46W
Gowganda Ontario **35** D2 47 39N 80 46W
Gracefield Québec **37** K7 46 05N 76 05W
Grady Harbour Newfoundland **30** C3 53 48N 56 25W
Graham Island British Columbia **42** B2 53 50N 132 40W
Graham Island Northwest Territories **45** M6 77 25N 90 30W
Granby Québec **37** O6 45 22N 72 43W
Granby River British Columbia **43** E1 49 27N 118 25W
Grand Bank Newfoundland **31** C2 47 06N 55 46W
Grand Bay *tn.* New Brunswick **31** A2 45 19N 66 14W
Grand Bend Ontario **38** A2 43 21N 81 45W
Grand Centre Alberta **41** C2 54 25N 110 13W
Grande-Anse New Brunswick **31** A2 47 50N 65 10W
Grande-Anse Québec **37** O8 47 05N 72 55W
Grande Cache Alberta **41** B2 53 50N 119 08W
Grande Pointe Manitoba **48** D2 49 45N 97 03W
Grande Prairie Alberta **43** E3 55 10N 118 40W
Grande-Rivière *tn.* Québec **33** D2 48 23N 64 31W
Grande rivière de la Baleine *r.* Québec **32** A4 55 08N 76 30W
Grand Étang *tn.* Nova Scotia **31** F7 46 32N 61 02W
Grande-Vallée *tn.* Québec **33** C2 49 15N 65 10W
Grand Falls *tn.* Newfoundland **31** C2 48 56N 55 40W
Grand Falls/Grand-Sault *tn.* New Brunswick **31** A2 47 02N 67 46W
Grand Forks British Columbia **43** E1 49 02N 118 30W
Grand Harbour *tn.* New Brunswick **31** E6 44 41N 66 46W
Grandin, Lake Northwest Territories **44** H3 63 50N 119 50W
Grand Jardin Newfoundland **31** C2 48 28N 59 13W
Grand Lake New Brunswick **31** A2 46 00N 66 40W
Grand Lake Newfoundland **30** A3 53 40N 60 30W
Grand Lake Newfoundland **31** C2 49 00N 57 20W
Grand Manan Island New Brunswick **31** E6 44 45N 66 40W
Grand-Mère Québec **37** O7 46 36N 72 41W
Grand Narrows *tn.* Nova Scotia **31** F7 45 55N 60 50W
Grand Prairie *tn.* Alberta **41** B3 55 10N 118 52W
Grand Rapids *tn.* Manitoba **39** B2 53 12N 99 19W
Grand River Ontario **38** C1 42 51N 79 34W
Grand Valley *tn.* Ontario **38** B2 43 54N 80 18W
Grandview Manitoba **39** A2 51 11N 100 51W
Granisle British Columbia **43** C2 54 56N 126 18W
Granite Bay *tn.* British Columbia **42** G5 50 14N 125 17W
Granite Lake Newfoundland **31** C2 48 11N 57 01W
Granville Falls Manitoba **39** A3 56 10N 100 20W
Granville Lake Manitoba **39** A3 56 00N 101 00W
Grasslands National Park Saskatchewan **40** B1 49 10N 107 30W
Grass River Manitoba **39** B2 54 50N 99 20W
Grass River Provincial Park Manitoba **39** A2 54 40N 101 40W
Grassy Narrows *I.R.* Ontario **34** B3 50 10N 93 55W
Gravelbourg Saskatchewan **40** B1 49 53N 106 33W
Gravenhurst Ontario **36** G5 44 55N 79 22W
Grayling River British Columbia **43** C3 59 43N 125 55W
Greasy Lake Northwest Territories **44** G3 62 55N 122 15W
Great Bear Lake Northwest Territories **45** G4 66 00N 120 00W
Great Central Lake British Columbia **42** G4 49 22N 125 10W
Great Harbour Deep *tn.* Newfoundland **31** C3 50 22N 56 31W
Great Cloche Island Ontario **36** E7 46 01N 81 53W
Great Plain of the Koukdjuak Northwest Territories **45** R4 66 25N 72 50W
Great Pubnico Lake Nova Scotia **31** E6 43 50N 65 30W
Great Sand Hills Saskatchewan **40** B2 50 35N 109 20W
Great Slave Lake Northwest Territories **44** J3 62 00N 114 00W
Great Village Nova Scotia **31** F7 45 25N 63 36W
Greely Ontario **47** K2 45 16N 75 33W
Greely Fiord Northwest Territories **45** P7 80 30N 85 00W
Green Creek Ontario **47** K2 45 25N 75 35W
Green Lake British Columbia **43** D2 51 26N 121 12W
Green Lake *tn.* Saskatchewan **40** B2 54 18N 107 49W
Greenville British Columbia **42** C3 55 05N 129 35W
Greenwater Provincial Park Saskatchewan **40** C2 52 35N 103 25W
Greenwood British Columbia **43** E1 49 08N 118 41W
Grenfell Saskatchewan **40** C2 50 24N 102 56W
Grenville Québec **37** M6 45 40N 74 38W
Grenville, Mount British Columbia **42** H5 50 59N 124 31W
Gretna Manitoba **39** B1 49 01N 97 34W
Grey *admin.* Ontario **38** B3 44 22N 80 33W
Grey Islands Newfoundland **31** C3 50 50N 55 35W
Grey, Point British Columbia **46** E4 49 16N 123 17W
Grey River Newfoundland **31** C2 47 50N 56 50W
Griffith Island Ontario **38** B3 44 50N 80 54W
Grimsby Ontario **38** C2 43 12N 79 35W
Grimshaw Alberta **41** B3 56 11N 117 36W
Grindstone Provincial Recreation Park Manitoba **39** B2 51 10N 96 50W
Grinnell Peninsula Northwest Territories **45** N6 76 40N 95 00W
Grise Fiord *tn.* Northwest Territories **45** P6 76 25N 82 57W
Grizzly Bear Hills Saskatchewan **40** B3 55 50N 109 30W
Groais Island Newfoundland **31** C3 50 57N 55 36W
Gros Morne *mt.* Newfoundland **31** C2 49 36N 57 47W
Gros Morne National Park Newfoundland **31** C2 49 40N 58 40W
Groswater Bay Newfoundland **30** C3 54 20N 57 40W
Groundhog River Ontario **35** D2 49 00N 82 00W
Guelph Ontario **38** B2 43 34N 80 16W
Gull Bay *I.R.* Ontario **34** C2 49 50N 89 00W
Gull Lake Alberta **41** C2 52 34N 114 00W
Gull Lake Ontario **38** D3 44 48N 78 48W
Gull Lake *tn.* Saskatchewan **40** B2 50 05N 108 30W
Gunisao Lake Manitoba **39** B2 53 30N 96 40W
Gunisao River Manitoba **39** B2 53 30N 96 50W
Guysborough Nova Scotia **31** F7 45 23N 61 30W
Guysborough *admin.* Nova Scotia **31** F7 45 20N 61 40W
Gwillim Lake Provincial Park British Columbia **43** D3 55 20N 121 20W
Gypsumville Manitoba **39** B2 51 47N 98 38W
Gyrfalcon Islands Northwest Territories **32** C4 59 05N 69 00W

H

Habay Alberta **41** B3 58 50N 118 44W
Hadley Bay Northwest Territories **44** K5 72 22N 108 30W
Haileybury Ontario **35** E2 47 27N 79 38W
Haines Junction Yukon Territory **44** D3 60 45N 137 21W
Haldimand-Norfolk *admin.* Ontario **38** B1 42 37N 80 39W
Halfway Point *tn.* Newfoundland **31** C2 48 59N 58 06W
Halfway River British Columbia **43** D3 56 42N 122 30W
Haliburton Ontario **36** G6 45 03N 78 31W
Haliburton *admin.* Ontario **38** D3 44 56N 78 42W
Halifax Nova Scotia **31** F6 44 40N 63 41W
Halifax *admin.* Nova Scotia **31** F7 45 00N 63 00W
Halifax Harbour Nova Scotia **47** P6 44 39N 63 33W
Hall Beach *tn.* Northwest Territories **45** P4 68 46N 81 12W
Hall Peninsula Northwest Territories **45** S3 68 40N 66 00W
Halls Harbour Nova Scotia **31** F7 45 12N 64 37W
Halton *admin.* Ontario **38** C2 43 26N 79 57W
Hamilton Ontario **38** C2 43 15N 79 50W
Hamilton Harbour Ontario **38** B2 43 16N 80 50W
Hamilton Inlet Newfoundland **30** C3 54 18N 57 30W
Hamilton Sound Newfoundland **31** D2 49 30N 54 15W
Hamilton-Wentworth *admin.* Ontario **38** B2/C2 43 14N 80 09W
Hamiota Manitoba **39** A2 50 11N 100 38W
Hampden Newfoundland **31** C2 49 33N 56 51W
Hampton New Brunswick **31** E7 45 30N 65 50W
Hanna Alberta **41** C2 51 38N 111 56W
Hannah Bay Ontario **35** D3 51 20N 80 00W
Hanover Ontario **38** A3 44 10N 81 03W
Hanson Lake Road Saskatchewan **40** C2 54 20N 104 35W
Hants *admin.* Nova Scotia **31** F7 45 10N 63 40W
Hantsport Nova Scotia **31** F7 45 04N 64 12W
Happy Valley-Goose Bay Newfoundland **30** A3 53 18N 60 16W
Harbour Breton *tn.* Newfoundland **31** C2 47 29N 55 50W
Harbour Grace *tn.* Newfoundland **31** D2 47 42N 53 13W
Harcourt New Brunswick **31** A2 46 29N 65 18W
Hardisty Alberta **41** C2 52 40N 111 18W
Hardisty Lake Northwest Territories **44** H3 64 30N 117 45W
Hare Bay Newfoundland **31** C3 51 15N 55 45W
Hare Bay *tn.* Newfoundland **31** D2 48 51N 54 00W
Hare Indian River Northwest Territories **44** F4 66 40N 128 00W
Haro Strait British Columbia **42** H4 48 36N 123 17W
Harp Lake Newfoundland **30** B4 55 05N 61 50W
Harrietsfield Nova Scotia **47** P6 44 34N 63 39W
Harrington Harbour *tn.* Québec **33** E3 50 31N 59 30W
Harrison, Cape Newfoundland **30** C3 54 57N 57 57W
Harrison Hot Springs *tn.* British Columbia **42** H4 49 17N 121 47W
Harrison Lake British Columbia **42** H4 49 30N 122 10W
Harriston Ontario **38** B2 43 54N 80 52W
Harrow Ontario **36** D3 42 02N 82 55W
Harrowby Manitoba **39** A2 50 45N 101 28W
Harry Gibbons Bird Sanctuary Northwest Territories **45** O3 63 50N 86 00W
Hartland New Brunswick **31** A2 46 18N 67 31W
Hartney Manitoba **39** A1 49 29N 100 31W
Hart River Yukon Territory **44** D4 65 40N 137 10W
Hastings Ontario **36** J5 44 18N 77 57W
Hastings *admin.* Ontario **36** J5 44 45N 77 40W
Hatchet Lake Saskatchewan **40** C3 58 50N 103 30W
Haultain River Saskatchewan **40** B3 56 20N 106 20W
Havelock Ontario **36** J5 44 26N 77 53W
Havre-Aubert Québec **33** D2 47 15N 61 51W
Havre-Saint-Pierre Québec **33** D3 50 20N 63 38W
Hawke Harbour *tn.* Newfoundland **30** C3 53 03N 55 49W
Hawkes Bay *tn.* Newfoundland **31** C3 50 36N 57 10W
Hawkesbury Ontario **37** M6 45 36N 74 37W
Hay, Cape Northwest Territories **44** J5 74 25N 113 00W
Hayes River Manitoba **39** C3 55 20N 94 10W
Hay Lake Alberta **41** B3 58 52N 119 20W
Hay River Alberta/Northwest Territories **41** B3 58 00N 118 00W
Hay River *tn.* Northwest Territories **44** H3 60 51N 115 42W
Hazeldean Ontario **47** J2 45 18N 75 55W
Hazelton British Columbia **43** C3 55 17N 127 42W
Hazen Strait Northwest Territories **44** K6 77 00N 110 00W
Head Lake Ontario **38** D3 44 45N 78 54W
Head of Bay d'Espoir *tn.* Newfoundland **31** C2 47 56N 55 45W
Head-Smashed-In Bison Jump Alberta **22** 49 43N 113 40W
Hearst Ontario **35** D2 49 42N 83 40W
Heart's Content Newfoundland **31** D2 47 53N 53 22W
Hebron Newfoundland **30** B4 58 12N 62 38W
Hebron Nova Scotia **31** E6 43 57N 66 03W
Hebron Fiord *in.* Newfoundland **30** B4 58 09N 62 45W
Hecate Strait British Columbia **42** B2 53 40N 131 10W
Hecla and Griper Bay Northwest Territories **44** J6 76 25N 113 00W
Hecla Island Manitoba **39** B2 51 00N 96 30W
Hecla Provincial Park Manitoba **39** B2 51 10N 96 30W
Hedley British Columbia **43** D1 49 21N 120 02W
Henley Harbour *tn.* Newfoundland **30** C3 51 59N 55 51W
Henrietta Island Newfoundland **30** C3 54 05N 58 28W
Henrietta Maria, Cape Ontario **34** D4 55 00N 82 30W
Henry Kater Peninsula Northwest Territories **45** S4 69 20N 67 20W
Hensall Ontario **38** A2 43 26N 81 31W
Hepworth Ontario **38** A3 44 37N 81 09W
Herbert Saskatchewan **40** B2 50 26N 107 12W
Heriot Bay *tn.* British Columbia **42** G5 50 06N 125 12W
Hermitage-Sandyville Newfoundland **31** C2 47 33N 55 56W
Heron Bay *I.R.* Ontario **35** C2 48 40N 86 17W
Herring Cove *tn.* Nova Scotia **47** P6 44 34N 63 34W
Herschel Yukon Territory **44** D4 69 34N 139 00W
Herschel Island Yukon Territory **44** D4 69 34N 139 00W
Hespeler Ontario **38** B2 43 26N 80 20W
Hess River Yukon Territory **44** E3 63 25N 133 50W
Hibbard Québec **37** M8 47 53N 74 03W
Hickman, Mount British Columbia **42** B3 57 15N 131 07W
High Level *tn.* Alberta **41** B3 58 10N 117 20W
High Prairie *tn.* Alberta **41** B3 55 26N 116 29W
High River *tn.* Alberta **41** C2 50 35N 113 52W
Highrock Manitoba **39** A3 55 50N 100 22W
Highrock Lake Manitoba **39** A3 55 45N 100 20W
Highrock Lake Saskatchewan **40** B3 57 00N 105 20W
Hillsborough New Brunswick **31** F7 45 56N 64 40W
Hillsborough Bay Prince Edward Island **31** F7 46 10N 63 20W
Hillsburgh Ontario **38** B2 43 46N 80 10W
Hinds Lake Reservoir Newfoundland **31** C2 49 00N 56 00W
Hines Creek *tn.* Alberta **41** B3 56 15N 118 36W
Hinton Alberta **41** B2 53 25N 117 34W
Hoare Bay Northwest Territories **45** T4 65 17N 62 55W
Hodgeville Saskatchewan **40** B2 50 07N 106 58W
Hog Island Prince Edward Island **31** F7 46 35N 63 50W
Holden Alberta **41** C2 53 14N 112 14W
Holdfast Saskatchewan **40** B2 50 58N 105 28W
Holland Landing Ontario **38** C3 44 05N 79 29W
Holland River Ontario **38** C3 44 01N 79 39W
Holman Northwest Territories **44** H5 70 44N 117 44W
Holton Newfoundland **30** C3 54 35N 57 16W
Holyrood Newfoundland **31** D2 47 23N 53 08W
Homathko River British Columbia **43** C2 51 00N 125 05W
Home Bay Northwest Territories **45** S4 69 00N 67 00W
Home Island Newfoundland **30** B5 60 10N 64 14W
Honey Harbour *tn.* Ontario **38** C3 44 51N 79 48W
Hope British Columbia **42** H4 49 21N 121 28W
Hope Bay Ontario **38** A3 44 55N 81 14W
Hopedale Newfoundland **30** B4 55 28N 60 13W
Hope Island British Columbia **43** C2 50 55N 127 55W
Hope Island Ontario **38** B3 44 54N 80 11W
Hopes Advance Bay Québec **32** C4 59 20N 69 40W
Hopewell Nova Scotia **31** F7 45 29N 62 41W
Hornaday River Northwest Territories **44** G4 69 00N 123 00W
Hornby Island British Columbia **42** H4 49 31N 124 40W
Hornepayne Ontario **35** D2 49 13N 84 47W
Horner Creek Ontario **38** B2 43 12N 80 35W

Horn Mountains Northwest Territories **44** H3 62 15N 119 15W
Horsefly Lake British Columbia **43** D2 52 25N 121 00W
Horsehills Creek Alberta **48** G5 53 45N 113 23W
Horse Islands Newfoundland **31** C3 50 13N 55 48W
Horseshoe Bay *tn.* British Columbia **42** H4 49 22N 123 17W
Horton River Northwest Territories **44** G4 68 50N 123 50W
Horwood Lake Ontario **35** D2 48 00N 82 20W
Hottah Lake Northwest Territories **44** H4 65 04N 118 30W
Houston British Columbia **43** C2 54 24N 126 39W
Houston Point Northwest Territories **34** D3 58 20N 81 00W
Howe Sound British Columbia **42** H4 49 30N 123 25W
Howley Newfoundland **31** C2 49 10N 57 07W
Hubbards Nova Scotia **31** F6 44 38N 64 03W
Hubbart Point Manitoba **39** C3 59 21N 94 41W
Hudson Bay *(Baie d'Hudson)* Northwest Territories/Ontario/Québec **11** R5 60 00N 89 00W
Hudson Bay *tn.* Saskatchewan **40** C2 52 45N 102 45W
Hudson's Hope British Columbia **43** D3 56 00N 121 59W
Hudson Strait Northwest Territories **45** R3 62 00N 70 00W
Hugh Keenleyside Dam British Columbia **43** E1 49 33N 118 00W
Hull Québec **39** J2 45 26N 75 45W
Hull *admin.* Québec **37** L6 45 40N 75 40W
Humber Bay Ontario **46** C1 43 36N 79 27W
Humber River Ontario **46** B2 43 48N 79 37W
Humboldt Saskatchewan **40** B2 52 12N 105 07W
Hunter Island British Columbia **43** C2 51 57N 128 05W
Hunter River *tn.* Prince Edward Island **31** F7 46 20N 63 20W
Huntingdon Québec **37** M6 45 05N 74 11W
Huntingdon *admin.* Québec **37** M6 45 00N 74 20W
Huntingdon Island Newfoundland **30** C3 53 47N 56 55W
Hunt River Newfoundland **30** B4 55 20N 61 10W
Huntsville Ontario **36** G6 45 20N 79 13W
Hurd, Cape Ontario **38** A4 45 14N 81 44W
Huron *admin.* Ontario **38** A2 43 27N 81 35W
Huron, Lake Canada/U.S.A. **36** D5 45 00N 83 00W
Hyde Park Ontario **38** A2 43 00N 81 20W
Hythe Alberta **41** B3 55 18N 119 33W

I
Igiusuaktalialuk Island Newfoundland **30** B4 57 20N 61 30W
Igloolik Northwest Territories **45** P4 69 23N 81 46W
Ignace Ontario **34** B2 49 26N 91 40W
Île-à-la-Crosse *tn.* Saskatchewan **40** B3 55 28N 107 53W
Île aux Coudres *i.* Québec **37** Q8 47 23N 70 20W
Île aux Herons *i.* Québec **47** N4 45 26N 73 35W
Île Bizard *i.* Québec **47** M4 45 29N 73 54W
Île D'Anticosti *i.* Québec **33** D2 49 20N 62 30W
Île de Montréal *i.* Québec **47** M4 45 30N 73 43W
Île des Allumettes *i.* Québec **37** J6 45 55N 77 08W
Ile des Chenes Manitoba **48** D2 49 41N 96 58W
Île des Soeurs *(Île des Soeurs ou St. Paul)* Québec **47** N4 45 28N 73 33W
Île des Soeurs ou St. Paul *(Île des Soeurs) i.* Québec **47** N4 45 28N 73 33W
Île d'Orléans *i.* Québec **37** Q7 46 55N 71 00W
Île du Grand Calumet Québec **37** K6 45 30N 76 35W
Île Jésus *i.* Québec **47** N5 45 35N 73 45W
Île Kettle *i.* Québec **47** K2 45 28N 75 39W
Île Lamèque *i.* New Brunswick **31** B2 47 50N 64 40W
Île Lynch *i.* Québec **47** M4 45 25N 73 54W
Île Ste. Hélène *i.* Québec **47** N5 45 31N 73 32W
Île Sainte-Thérèse *i.* Québec **47** O5 45 39N 73 30W
Îles-de-Boucherville *is.* Québec **47** N5 45 36N 73 28W
Îles de la Madeleine *is.* Québec **33** D2 47 40N 61 50W
Ilford Manitoba **39** B3 56 04N 95 40W
Indian Arm *b.* British Columbia **46** G4 49 19N 122 55W
Indian Cabins Alberta **41** B3 59 52N 117 02W
Indian Harbour *tn.* Newfoundland **30** C3 54 27N 57 13W
Indian Head *tn.* Saskatchewan **40** C2 50 35N 103 37W
Indian Tickle Newfoundland **30** C3 53 34N 56 02W
Ingenika River British Columbia **43** C3 56 48N 126 11W
Ingersoll Ontario **38** B2 43 03N 80 53W
Ingonish Nova Scotia **31** F7 46 42N 60 22W
Inklin River British Columbia **42** B3 58 54N 132 50W
Inner Bay Ontario **38** B1 42 35N 80 26W
Innisfail Alberta **41** C2 52 01N 113 59W
Inside Passage British Columbia **42** C2 53 38N 129 40W
Inukjuak Québec **32** A4 58 40N 78 15W
Inuvik Northwest Territories **44** E4 68 16N 133 40W
Inuvik *reg.* Northwest Territories **44** E4 68 21N 133 43W
Inverhuron Provincial Park Ontario **38** A3 44 20N 81 30W
Invermere British Columbia **43** E2 50 30N 116 00W
Inverness Nova Scotia **31** F7 46 14N 61 19W
Inverness *admin.* Nova Scotia **31** F7 46 00N 61 30W
Iqaluit *(Frobisher Bay)* Northwest Territories **45** S3 60 00N 65 00W
Irma Alberta **41** C2 52 55N 111 14W
Iron Bridge *tn.* Ontario **36** C7 46 17N 83 14W
Irondale Ontario **38** D3 44 53N 78 30W
Ironside Québec **47** J2 45 27N 75 46W
Iroquois Ontario **37** L5 44 51N 75 19W
Iroquois Falls *tn.* Ontario **35** D2 48 47N 80 41W
Irvine Creek Alberta **48** G4 53 20N 113 29W
Irvines Landing British Columbia **42** H4 49 37N 124 02W
Isachsen Northwest Territories **45** L6 78 47N 103 30W
Ishpatina Ridge Ontario **35** D2 47 19N 80 44W
Iskut River British Columbia **42** B3 56 45N 131 10W
Island Falls Dam Saskatchewan **40** C3 55 30N 102 20W
Island Lake Manitoba **39** C2 53 50N 94 00W
Island Lake *tn.* Manitoba **39** C2 53 50N 94 00W
Island of Ponds *tn.* Newfoundland **30** C3 53 20N 55 50W
Isle aux Morts *tn.* Newfoundland **31** C2 47 35N 58 59W
Isle Madame *i.* Nova Scotia **31** F7 45 30N 60 50W
Isle Royale Ontario **35** C2 48 10N 88 30W
Isle Royale National Park Ontario **35** C2 48 10N 88 30W
Islington Ontario **46** B1 43 38N 79 32W
Issac Lake Ontario **38** A3 44 46N 81 13W
Itchen Lake Northwest Territories **44** J4 65 33N 112 50W
Ituna Saskatchewan **40** C2 51 09N 103 24W
Ivujivik Québec **32** A5 62 25N 77 54W

J
Jackfish Lake Manitoba **39** B2 50 30N 99 20W
Jackson's Arm *tn.* Newfoundland **31** C2 49 53N 56 47W
Jacksons Point *tn.* Ontario **38** C3 44 18N 79 22W
James Bay *(Baie James)* Ontario/Northwest Territories Québec **34** D3 53 45N 81 00W
James Bay Preserve Ontario/Northwest Territories Québec **45** P1 53 00N 81 00W
James Ross, Cape Northwest Territories **44** G5 74 40N 114 25W
James Ross Strait Northwest Territories **45** M4 69 40N 96 00W
Jarvis Ontario **38** B1 42 52N 80 08W
Jasper Alberta **41** B2 52 55N 118 05W
Jasper National Park Alberta **41** B2 53 00N 118 00W
Jean Marie River *tn.* Northwest Territories **44** G3 61 32N 120 38W
Jellicoe Ontario **34** C2 49 41N 87 31W
Jennings River British Columbia **42** B3 59 33N 131 40W
Jenpeg Manitoba **39** B2 54 30N 98 00W
Jervis Inlet British Columbia **42** H4 49 47N 124 04W
Jock River Ontario **47** J2 45 15N 75 46W
Joggins Nova Scotia **31** F7 45 42N 64 27W
John D'Or Prairie Alberta **41** B3 58 30N 115 08W
John Hart Highway British Columbia **43** D3 55 40N 121 38W
Johnstone Strait British Columbia **43** C2 50 23N 126 30W
Joliette Québec **37** N7 46 02N 73 27W
Joliette *admin.* Québec **37** L8 47 40N 75 40W
Jones Ontario **34** B2 49 59N 94 05W
Jones Sound Northwest Territories **45** P6 76 00N 88 00W
Jonquière Québec **37** P9 48 25N 71 16W
Jordan Lake Nova Scotia **31** E6 44 05N 65 20W
Jordan River *tn.* British Columbia **42** H4 48 26N 123 59W
Joseph, Lake Ontario **38** C4 45 11N 79 44W
Joutel Québec **33** A2 49 28N 78 28W
Juan de Fuca Strait British Columbia **42** H4 48 30N 124 31W
Judique Nova Scotia **31** F7 45 55N 61 30W

K
Kabania Lake Ontario **34** C3 52 12N 88 20W
Kabinakagami, Lake Ontario **35** D2 48 54N 84 25W
Kabinakagami River Ontario **35** D2 49 10N 84 10W
Kagawong Ontario **36** D6 45 54N 82 15W
Kahnawake Québec **47** N4 45 25N 73 42W
Kahshe Lake Ontario **38** C3 44 51N 79 17W
Kaipokok Bay Newfoundland **30** C3 55 00N 59 35W
Kakabeka Falls *tn.* Ontario **35** C2 48 24N 89 40W
Kakisa Northwest Territories **44** H3 60 58N 117 30W
Kakwa River Alberta **41** B2 54 15N 119 45W
Kaladar Ontario **37** J5 44 39N 77 07W
Kamilukuak Lake Northwest Territories **45** L3 62 22N 101 40W
Kaminak Lake Northwest Territories **45** N3 62 10N 95 00W
Kamloops British Columbia **43** D2 50 39N 120 24W
Kamloops Lake British Columbia **43** D2 50 45N 120 40W
Kamouraska Québec **37** R8 47 34N 69 51W
Kamouraska *admin.* Québec **37** R8 47 10N 69 50W
Kamsack Saskatchewan **40** C2 51 34N 101 51W
Kamuchawie Lake Manitoba/Saskatchewan **40** C3 56 20N 102 20W
Kanaaupscow Québec **32** A3 54 00N 76 40W
Kanata Ontario **47** J2 45 20N 75 53W
Kangiqsualujjuaq Québec **32** C4 58 48N 66 08W
Kangiqsujuaq Québec **32** B5 61 40N 71 59W
Kangirsuk Québec **32** B5 60 00N 70 00W
Kapiskau River Ontario **34** D3 52 00N 89 50W
Kapuskasing Ontario **35** D2 49 25N 82 26W
Kapuskasing River Ontario **35** D2 48 40N 82 50W
Kasabonika *I.R.* Ontario **34** C3 53 32N 88 37W
Kasabonika Lake Ontario **34** C3 53 35N 88 35W
Kasba Lake Northwest Territories **45** L3 60 18N 102 07W
Kashechewan *I.R.* Ontario **34** D3 52 18N 81 37W
Kaskattama River Manitoba **39** C3 56 25N 91 10W
Kaslo British Columbia **43** E1 49 54N 116 57W
Kasmere Lake Manitoba **39** A3 59 30N 101 10W
Kates Needle *mt.* British Columbia **42** B3 57 02N 132 05W
Kaumajet Mountains Newfoundland **30** B4 57 48N 61 51W
Kawawachikamach *see* Schefferville
Kayano Québec **32** B3 53 52N 73 30W
Kazabazua Québec **37** K6 45 56N 76 01W
Kearney Ontario **36** G6 45 35N 79 17W
Kechika River British Columbia **43** C3 58 44N 127 25W
Kedgwick New Brunswick **31** A2 47 38N 67 21W
Keefers British Columbia **42** H5 50 03N 121 32W
Keele Peak Yukon Territory **44** E3 63 25N 130 17W
Keele River Northwest Territories **44** F3 64 15N 126 00W
Keewatin Ontario **34** B2 49 47N 94 30W
Keewatin *reg.* Northwest Territories **45** M3 63 30N 98 00W
Keewatin River Manitoba **39** A3 56 59N 100 59W
Keith Arm *b.* Northwest Territories **44** G4 65 20N 122 15W
Kejimkujik National Park Nova Scotia **31** E6 44 20N 65 20W
Keller Lake Northwest Territories **44** G3 64 00N 121 30W
Kellett, Cape Northwest Territories **44** F5 71 59N 126 00W
Kellett Strait Northwest Territories **44** H6 75 45N 117 30W
Kelliher Saskatchewan **40** C2 51 15N 103 41W
Kelowna British Columbia **43** E1 49 50N 119 29W
Kelsey Bay *tn.* British Columbia **43** C2 50 22N 125 29W
Kelvington Saskatchewan **40** C2 52 10N 103 30W
Kemano British Columbia **43** C2 53 39N 127 58W
Kempenfelt Bay Ontario **38** C3 44 22N 79 39W
Kemptville Ontario **37** L6 45 01N 75 38W
Kenamu River Newfoundland **30** B3 52 50N 60 20W
Kenaston Saskatchewan **40** B2 51 30N 106 15W
Kendall Island Bird Sanctuary Northwest Territories **44** D4 69 30N 135 00W
Kennebecasis River New Brunswick **31** E7 45 30N 65 55W
Kennedy Saskatchewan **40** C2 50 01N 102 21W
Kennedy Lake British Columbia **42** G4 49 12N 125 32W
Kennetcook Nova Scotia **31** F7 45 10N 63 43W
Kenney Dam British Columbia **43** D2 53 38N 124 59W
Kenogami River Ontario **34** D3 50 50N 84 30W
Kenogamissi Lake Ontario **35** D2 48 15N 81 33W
Kenora Ontario **34** B2 49 47N 94 26W
Kensington Prince Edward Island **31** F7 46 26N 63 39W
Kent *admin.* New Brunswick **31** A2 46 30N 65 20W
Kent *admin.* Ontario **36** D3 42 25N 82 10W
Kent Peninsula Northwest Territories **44** K4 68 30N 106 00W
Kentville Nova Scotia **31** F7 45 04N 64 30W
Keremeos British Columbia **43** E1 49 12N 119 50W
Kerrobert Saskatchewan **40** B2 51 56N 109 09W
Kesagami Lake Ontario **35** D3 50 00N 80 00W
Kesagami River Ontario **35** D3 50 30N 80 10W
Keswick Ontario **38** C3 44 15N 79 28W
Kettle Creek Ontario **38** A1 42 47N 81 13W
Kettle Rapids *tn.* Manitoba **39** C3 56 25N 94 30W
Kettle River British Columbia **43** E1 49 10N 119 02W
Kettle River Manitoba **39** D3 56 40N 89 50W
Key Lake Mine *tn.* Saskatchewan **40** B3 57 10N 105 30W
Kicking Horse Pass Alberta/British Columbia **43** E2 51 28N 116 23W
Kiglapait, Cape Newfoundland **30** B4 57 06N 61 22W
Kiglapait Mountains Newfoundland **30** B4 57 06N 61 35W
Kikerk Lake Northwest Territories **44** J4 66 55N 113 20W
Kikkertarjote Island Newfoundland **30** B4 57 30N 61 28W
Kikkertavak Island Newfoundland **30** B4 56 22N 61 35W
Kikona Park Manitoba **48** D2 49 56N 97 03W
Kildonan Park Manitoba **48** D2 49 57N 97 07W
Killam Alberta **41** C2 52 47N 111 51W
Killarney Manitoba **39** B1 49 12N 99 40W
Killarney Ontario **36** E6 45 59N 81 30W
Killarney Provincial Park Ontario **36** E7 46 00N 81 00W
Killbear Provincial Park Ontario **35** B4 45 22N 80 13W
Killinek Island Newfoundland/Northwest Territories **30** B4 60 24N 64 31W
Kimberley British Columbia **43** E1 49 40N 115 58W
Kinbasket Lake British Columbia **43** E2 51 57N 118 02W
Kincardine Ontario **38** A3 44 11N 81 38W
Kincolith British Columbia **42** C3 55 00N 129 57W
Kincora Prince Edward Island **31** F7 46 20N 63 40W
Kindersley Saskatchewan **40** B2 51 27N 109 08W
King Christian Island Northwest Territories **45** L6 77 45N 102 00W
Kingcome Inlet *tn.* British Columbia **43** C2 50 58N 125 15W
Kingfisher Lake Ontario **34** C3 53 05N 89 49W
Kingfisher Lake *I.R.* Ontario **34** C3 53 02N 89 50W
King George, Mount British Columbia **43** E2 50 36N 115 26W
King Island British Columbia **43** C2 52 10N 127 35W
Kings *admin.* New Brunswick **31** E7 45 30N 65 40W
Kings *admin.* Nova Scotia **31** F6 44 50N 64 50W
Kings *admin.* Prince Edward Island **31** F7 46 20N 62 40W
Kingsburg Nova Scotia **31** F6 44 20N 64 10W
Kings Landing New Brunswick **31** A2 45 50N 67 00W
Kingsmere Québec **47** J2 45 29N 75 50W
Kingston Ontario **37** K5 44 14N 76 30W
Kingsville Ontario **36** D3 42 02N 82 45W
Kingurutik Lake Newfoundland **30** B4 56 49N 62 20W
King William Island Northwest Territories **45** M4 69 00N 97 30W
Kinistino Saskatchewan **40** B2 52 58N 105 01W
Kinnoosao Saskatchewan **40** B3 57 06N 102 02W
Kinoje River Ontario **34** D3 51 40N 81 50W
Kinsac Nova Scotia **47** P7 44 51N 63 39W
Kinsac Lake Nova Scotia **47** P7 44 50N 63 38W
Kinusheseo River Ontario **34** D3 54 30N 83 50W
Kiosk Ontario **36** H7 46 05N 78 53W
Kipahigan Lake Manitoba **39** A3 55 20N 101 50W
Kipawa Québec **36** G7 46 47N 79 00W
Kipling Saskatchewan **40** C2 50 08N 102 40W
Kirkfield Lift Lock National Park Ontario **38** D3 44 30N 79 00W
Kirkland Québec **47** M4 45 27N 73 53W
Kirkland Lake Ontario **35** D2 48 10N 80 02W
Kirkpatrick Lake Alberta **41** C2 51 52N 111 18W
Kirriemuir Alberta **41** C2 51 56N 110 18W
Kiskittogisa Lake Manitoba **39** B2 54 10N 98 50W
Kiskitto Lake Manitoba **39** B2 54 20N 98 50W
Kispiox British Columbia **43** C3 55 21N 127 41W
Kississing Lake Manitoba **39** A3 55 10N 101 30W
Kistigan Lake Manitoba **39** C2 54 50N 92 40W
Kitchener Ontario **38** B2 43 27N 80 30W
Kitikmeot *reg.* Northwest Territories **44** K4 69 50N 107 30W
Kitimat British Columbia **42** C2 54 05N 128 38W
Klappan River British Columbia **42** C3 57 50N 129 40W
Kleinburg Ontario **46** B2 43 50N 79 36W
Klinaklini River British Columbia **43** C2 51 18N 125 45W
Klondike Highway Yukon Territory **44** D3 62 55N 136 10W
Klondike River Yukon Territory **44** D3 64 20N 138 50W
Kluane Game Sanctuary Yukon Territory **44** D3 61 30N 139 50W
Kluane Lake Yukon Territory **44** D3 62 20N 139 00W
Kluane National Park Yukon Territory **44** D3 60 30N 139 00W
Knee Lake Manitoba **39** C3 55 10N 94 40W
Knight Inlet British Columbia **42** G5 50 45N 125 36W
Knox, Cape British Columbia **42** B2 54 09N 133 05W
Koch Island Northwest Territories **45** Q4 69 38N 78 15W
Kogaluc Bay Québec **32** A4 59 20N 78 00W
Kogaluk River Newfoundland **30** B4 56 10N 63 30W
Kokanee Glacier Park British Columbia **43** E1 49 45N 117 10W
Komoka Ontario **38** A1 42 56N 81 26W
Kootenay Lake British Columbia **43** E1 49 35N 116 30W
Kootenay National Park British Columbia **43** E2 51 15N 116 25W
Kopka River Ontario **34** C3 50 00N 90 00W
Kotcho Lake British Columbia **43** D3 59 05N 121 10W
Kouchibouguac National Park New Brunswick **31** F7 46 45N 64 50W
Koukdjuak Northwest Territories **45** R4 66 50N 72 50W
Kunghit Island British Columbia **42** B2 52 02N 131 02W
Kuujjuaq Québec **32** C4 58 25N 68 55W
Kuujjuarapik *(Poste-de-la-Baleine, Whapmagoostui)* Québec **32** A4 55 15N 77 41W
Kwadacha Wilderness Park British Columbia **43** C3 57 50N 125 00W
Kwataboahegan River Ontario **34** D3 51 10N 82 30W
Kyle Saskatchewan **40** B2 50 50N 108 02W
Kyuquot Sound British Columbia **43** C1 50 02N 127 22W

L
La Baie Québec **37** Q9 48 20N 70 55W
La Barrière Park Manitoba **48** D1 49 43N 97 09W
Labelle Québec **37** M7 46 17N 74 45W
Labelle *admin.* Québec **37** L7 46 30N 75 40W
Laberge, Lake Yukon Territory **44** E3 61 10N 134 59W
Labrador *geog. reg.* Newfoundland **30** B3 54 00N 64 00W
Labrador City Newfoundland **30** A3 52 57N 66 55W
Labrador Sea Canada/Greenland **11** V3 52 54N 66 50W
Lac Abitibi *l.* Québec **33** A2 48 40N 79 40W
Lac Albanel *l.* Québec **33** B3 51 00N 73 20W
Lac à l'Eau Claire *l.* Québec **32** B4 56 20N 74 30W
Lac Anuc *l.* Québec **32** A4 59 15N 75 10W
Lac Assinica *l.* Québec **33** A3 50 20N 75 12W
Lac au Goéland *l.* Québec **33** A2 49 45N 76 55W
Lac Aylmer *l.* Québec **37** P6 45 50N 71 20W
Lac Bacqueville *l.* Québec **32** B4 58 05N 74 00W
Lac Batiscan *l.* Québec **37** P8 47 23N 71 53W
Lac Bécard *l.* Québec **32** B5 60 05N 73 45W
Lac Belot *l.* Northwest Territories **44** F4 66 53N 126 16W
Lac Bérard *l.* Québec **32** B4 58 25N 70 05W
Lac Bermen *l.* Québec **32** C3 53 40N 69 00W
Lac Berté *l.* Québec **33** C3 50 52N 68 35W
Lac Bienville *l.* Québec **32** B4 55 30N 73 00W
Lac Bourdel *l.* Québec **32** B4 56 42N 74 15W
Lac Boyd *l.* Québec **33** A3 52 45N 76 45W
Lac Brochet *l.* Manitoba **39** A3 58 40N 101 20W
Lac Brome *l.* Québec **37** O6 45 15N 72 30W
Lac Brome *tn.* Québec **37** O6 45 13N 72 30W
Lac Burton *l.* Québec **32** A3 54 45N 79 25W
Lac Cambrien *l.* Québec **32** C4 56 30N 69 22W
Lac Cananée *l.* Québec **32** D4 56 05N 64 05W
Lac Chaconipau *l.* Québec **32** C4 56 20N 68 45W
Lac Champdoré *l.* Québec **32** C4 56 50N 66 20W
Lac Champlain *(Lake Champlain) l.* Québec Canada/U.S.A. **37** N6 45 08N 73 08W
Lac Châtelain *l.* Québec **32** B5 60 20N 74 20W
Lac Chavigny *l.* Québec **32** A4 58 10N 75 10W
Lac Chibougamau *l.* Québec **33** B2 49 55N 74 20W
Lac Couture *l.* Québec **32** A5 60 00N 75 20W
Lac de Gras *l.* Northwest Territories **44** K3 64 10N 109 00W
Lac de la Hutte Sauvage *l.* Québec **32** D4 56 18N 65 00W
Lac des Bois *l.* Northwest Territories **44** F4 67 00N 126 00W
Lac Deschênes *(Lake Ontario)* Ontario/Québec **47** J2 45 22N 75 50W
Lac des Commissaires *l.* Québec **37** O9 48 09N 72 13W
Lac des Deux Montagnes *l.* Québec **47** M4 45 30N 73 58W
Lac des Loups Marins *l.* Québec **32** B4 56 30N 73 30W
Lac des Mille Lacs *l.* Ontario **34** B2 48 53N 90 22W
Lac des Quinze *l.* Québec **33** A2 47 45N 79 15W
Lac des Trente et Un Milles *l.* Québec **37** L7 46 18N 75 43W
Lac D'Iberville *l.* Québec **32** B4 55 55N 73 25W
Lac du Bonnet *l.* Manitoba **39** B2 50 30N 95 50W
Lac du Bonnet *tn.* Manitoba **39** B2 50 16N 96 03W
Lac Dumoine *l.* Québec **36** H7 46 07N 78 58W
Lac Duncan *l.* Québec **33** A3 53 25N 78 00W
Lac du Sable *l.* Québec **32** C3 54 25N 67 59W
Lac Édouard *l.* Québec **37** O8 47 40N 72 16W
Lac-Etchemin *tn.* Québec **37** Q7 46 23N 70 32W
Lac Faribault *l.* Québec **32** B4 59 10N 72 00W
Lac Fleur-de-May *l.* Newfoundland **30** B3 52 00N 65 02W
Lac Gaotanaga *l.* Québec **37** J8 47 47N 77 28W
Lac Guillaume-Delisle *l.* Québec **32** A4 56 15N 77 20W
Lachine Québec **47** N4 45 26N 73 42W
Lachute Québec **37** M6 51 00N 71 00W
Lac Île-à-la-Crosse *l.* Saskatchewan **40** B3 55 40N 107 30W
Lac Jeannin *l.* Québec **32** C4 56 25N 66 30W
Lac Joseph *l.* Newfoundland **30** A3 52 45N 65 18W
Lac Kempt *l.* Québec **37** M8 47 28N 74 08W
Lac Kénogami *l.* Québec **33** B2 48 22N 71 25W
Lac Kipawa Québec **36** G7 46 55N 79 06W
Lac Klotz *l.* Québec **32** B5 60 30N 73 30W
Lac la Biche *l.* Alberta **41** C2 54 55N 112 58W
Lac la Biche *tn.* Alberta **41** C2 54 46N 111 58W
Lac la Croix *l.* Ontario **35** B2 48 21N 92 09W
Lac la Loche *l.* Saskatchewan **40** B3 56 30N 109 40W
Lac la Martre *l.* Northwest Territories **44** H3 63 20N 118 30W
Lac la Martre *tn.* Northwest Territories **44** H3 63 00N 117 30W
Lac la Plonge *l.* Saskatchewan **40** B3 55 05N 107 00W
Lac la Ronge *l.* Saskatchewan **40** B3/C3 55 10N 105 00W
Lac la Ronge Provincial Park Saskatchewan **40** C3 55 20N 104 45W
Lac le Moyne *l.* Québec **32** C4 57 10N 68 33W
Lac le Roy *l.* Québec **32** A4 58 35N 75 25W
Lac Lesdiguières *l.* Québec **32** B5 60 00N 74 20W
Lac Magpie *l.* Québec **33** D3 51 00N 64 40W
Lac Maicasagi *l.* Québec **33** A3 50 00N 76 45W
Lac Manitou *l.* Québec **33** C3 50 50N 65 20W
Lac Manouane *l.* Québec **33** B3 50 45N 70 45W
Lac Matagami *l.* Québec **33** A2 49 55N 77 50W
Lac Maunoir *l.* Northwest Territories **44** G4 67 30N 124 55W
Lac-Mégantic *tn.* Québec **37** Q6 45 34N 70 53W
Lac Memphrémagog *l.* Québec **37** O6 45 05N 72 13W
Lac Mesgouez *l.* Québec **33** A3 51 25N 75 00W
Lac Minto *l.* Québec **32** B4 57 35N 75 00W
Lac Mistassini *l.* Québec **33** B3 51 00N 73 20W
Lac Mistinibi *l.* Québec **32** D4 55 50N 64 20W
Lac Mitchinamécus *l.* Québec **37** M8 47 20N 75 00W
Lac Musquaro *l.* Québec **33** D3 50 50N 60 50W
Lac Nantais *l.* Québec **32** B5 61 10N 74 20W
Lac Naococane *l.* Québec **33** B3 52 53N 70 40W
Lac Nichicapau *l.* Québec **32** C4 56 42N 68 28W
Lac Nichicun *l.* Québec **33** B3 53 05N 71 05W
Lacombe Alberta **41** C2 52 28N 113 44W
Lac Opiscotéo *l.* Québec **33** C3 53 15N 68 20W
Lac Otelnuk *l.* Québec **32** C4 56 10N 68 20W
Lac Parent *l.* Québec **37** J9 48 30N 77 08W
Lac Payne *l.* Québec **32** B4 59 25N 74 25W
Lac Pélican *l.* Québec **32** B4 59 57N 73 40W
Lac Péribonca *l.* Québec **33** B3 50 10N 71 23W
Lac Plétipi *l.* Québec **33** B3 51 50N 70 10W
Lac Poncheville *l.* Québec **33** A3 50 12N 77 00W
Lac Potherie *l.* Québec **32** B4 58 50N 72 25W
Lac Qilalugalik *l.* Québec **32** A4 58 35N 76 00W
Lac Ramusio *l.* Québec **32** D4 55 10N 63 59W
Lac Résolution *l.* Québec **32** D4 55 15N 64 40W
Lac Roberts *l.* Québec **32** B5 60 25N 70 25W
Lac Saindon *l.* Québec **32** B4 55 35N 73 30W
Lac Sainte-Anne *l.* Québec **33** C3 50 15N 68 00W
Lac Saint-François *l.* Québec **37** P6 45 56N 71 08W

Lac Saint-Jean *l.* Québec **33** B2 48 35N 72 00W
Lac-St.-Jean-Est *admin.* Québec **37** P9 48 20N 71 40W
Lac-St.-Jean-Ouest *admin.* Québec **37** O9 48 20N 72 20W
Lac St. Joseph *l.* Ontario **34** B3 51 30N 91 40W
Lac Saint-Louis *l.* Québec **47** M4 45 25N 73 49W
Lac Saint-Patrice *l.* Québec **37** J7 46 20N 77 30W
Lac Saint-Pierre *l.* Québec **37** O7 46 12N 72 49W
Lac Sakami *l.* Québec **33** A3 53 20N 76 50W
Lac Seul *l.* Ontario **34** B3 50 20N 92 00W
Lac Seul *I.R.* Ontario **34** B3 50 15N 92 15W
Lac Simard *l.* Québec **33** A2 47 40N 78 50W
Lac Simon *l.* Québec **37** L6 45 55N 75 05W
Lac Soscumica *l.* Québec **33** A3 50 15N 77 35W
Lac Tasiaalujjuak *l.* Québec **32** B4 59 35N 71 59W
Lac Tasiat *l.* Québec **32** A4 59 05N 75 25W
Lac Tasiataq *l.* Québec **32** B4 58 40N 71 40W
Lac Tassialouc *l.* Québec **32** B4 58 59N 74 00W
Lac Témiscamingue (Lake Timiskaming) Québec **33** A2 47 28N 79 30W
Lac Tiblemont *l.* Québec **37** J9 48 17N 77 20W
Lac Tudor *l.* Québec **32** C4 55 58N 65 30W
Lac Wakuach *l.* Québec **32** C4 55 35N 67 40W
Lac Waswanipi *l.* Québec **33** A2 49 35N 76 36W
Lac Wayagamac *l.* Québec **37** O8 47 23N 72 35W
Lac Whitegull *l.* Québec **32** D4 55 25N 65 05W
Lady Evelyn-Smoothwater *provincial park* Ontario **35** D2 47 20N 80 30W
Ladysmith British Columbia **42** H4 48 57N 123 50W
Laflèche Saskatchewan **40** B1 49 44N 106 32W
Lagoon City Ontario **38** C3 44 31N 79 11W
La Grande 2 *dam* Québec **32** A3 53 45N 77 38W
La Grande 3 *dam* Québec **32** A3 53 40N 76 09W
La Grande 4 *dam* Québec **32** B3 53 59N 72 30W
La Grande Rivière *r.* Québec **32** B3 53 34N 74 36W
La Guadeloupe Québec **37** Q8 45 58N 70 57W
Lake Cowichan *tn.* British Columbia **42** H4 48 50N 124 04W
Lakefield Ontario **36** H5 44 26N 78 16W
Lake Harbour *tn.* Northwest Territories **45** S3 62 50N 69 50W
Lakeland Provincial Park Alberta **41** C2 54 45N 112 25W
Lakeland Provincial Recreation Area Alberta **41** C2 54 45N 111 15W
Lake of Bays *l.* Ontario **36** G6 45 00N 79 00W
Lake of the Rivers Saskatchewan **40** B1 49 50N 105 30W
Lakeside Nova Scotia **47** P6 44 38N 63 42W
Lakeview Newfoundland **31** D2 47 20N 54 10W
Lakeview Ontario **47** J2 45 20N 75 48W
La Loche Saskatchewan **40** A3 56 30N 109 27W
La Malbaie Québec **37** Q8 47 39N 70 11W
Lamaline Newfoundland **31** C2 46 52N 55 49W
Lambeth Ontario **38** A1 42 54N 81 20W
Lambton *admin.* Ontario **36** D3 43 00N 82 05W
Lambton, Cape Northwest Territories **44** G5 71 05N 123 09W
Lamèque New Brunswick **31** B2 47 45N 64 40W
Lampman Saskatchewan **40** C1 49 23N 102 48W
Lanark Ontario **37** K6 45 01N 74 30W
Lanark *admin.* Ontario **37** K6 45 05N 76 20W
Lancaster Ontario **37** M6 45 08N 74 40W
Lancaster Park Alberta **48** F5 53 41N 113 33W
Lancaster Sound Northwest Territories **45** O5 74 00N 87 30W
L'Ancienne Lorette Québec **37** P7 46 48N 71 20W
Land's End Northwest Territories **44** G6 76 22N 122 33W
Langenburg Saskatchewan **40** C2 50 50N 101 42W
Langham Saskatchewan **40** B2 52 22N 106 55W
Langley British Columbia **42** H4 49 06N 122 38W
Lanigan Saskatchewan **40** B2 51 50N 105 01W
L'Annonciation Québec **37** M7 46 24N 74 52W
Lansdowne House *tn.* Ontario **34** C3 52 05N 88 00W
L'Anse-au-Loup Newfoundland **30** C3 51 31N 56 45W
L'Anse aux Meadows Newfoundland **30** C3 51 36N 55 32W
L'Anse Pleureuse Québec **33** C2 49 15N 65 40W
Lantzville British Columbia **42** H4 49 15N 124 05W
La Pocatière Québec **37** Q8 47 22N 70 03W
La Poile Newfoundland **31** C2 47 41N 58 24W
La Prairie Québec **47** O4 45 25N 73 29W
Larder Lake Ontario **35** E2 48 05N 79 38W
L'Ardoise Nova Scotia **31** F7 45 37N 60 46W
Lark Harbour *tn.* Newfoundland **31** C2 49 06N 58 23W
La Ronge Saskatchewan **40** B3 55 07N 105 18W
Larrys River *tn.* Nova Scotia **31** F7 45 15N 61 25W
La Salle Manitoba **48** C1 49 41N 97 04W
La Salle Québec **47** N4 45 26N 73 40W
La Salle River Manitoba **48** C1 49 42N 97 16W
La Sarre Québec **33** A2 48 50N 79 20W
La Scie Newfoundland **31** C2 49 57N 55 36W
Lashburn Saskatchewan **40** B2 53 08N 109 36W
Lasqueti Island British Columbia **42** H4 49 28N 124 20W
Last Mountain Lake Saskatchewan **40** B2 51 40N 106 55W
La Tabatière Québec **32** E3 50 50N 58 57W
Latchford Ontario **35** E2 47 20N 79 49W
La Tuque Québec **37** O8 47 26N 72 47W
Laurie River Manitoba **39** A3 56 30N 101 30W
Laurier-Station Québec **27** 46 33N 71 37W
Lauzon Québec **37** P7 46 49N 71 10W
Laval, (Ville de) Québec **37** N6 45 38N 73 45W
Laval-des-Rapides Québec **47** N5 45 33N 73 42W
Lawn Newfoundland **31** C2 46 57N 55 32W
Lawrencetown Nova Scotia **31** E6 44 54N 65 10W
Leader Saskatchewan **40** B2 50 55N 109 31W
Leading Tickles Newfoundland **31** C2 49 30N 55 28W
Leaf Rapids *tn.* Manitoba **39** A3 56 30N 100 00W
Leamington Ontario **36** D3 42 03N 82 36W
Leaside Ontario **46** C1 43 44N 79 15W
Lebel-sur-Quévillon Québec **33** A2 49 05N 77 08W
Leduc Alberta **41** C2 53 17N 113 30W
Leduc County Alberta **48** E3 53 19N 113 32W
Leeds and Grenville *admin.* Ontario **37** L6 44 35N 76 00W
Le Havre River Nova Scotia **31** F6 44 30N 64 30W
Leitrim Ontario **47** K2 45 20N 75 38W
Lemieux Islands Northwest Territories **45** T3 63 40N 64 20W
Lennox and Addington *admin.* Ontario **37** J5 44 30N 77 00W
Lenore Lake Saskatchewan **40** C2 52 30N 105 00W
Leoville Saskatchewan **40** B2 53 39N 107 33W
Leslie Street Spit Ontario **46** C1 43 38N 79 19W
Lesser Slave Lake Alberta **41** B3 55 25N 115 25W
Lethbridge Alberta **41** C1 49 43N 112 48W

Level Mountain British Columbia **42** B3 58 33N 131 25W
Lévis Québec **37** P7 46 47N 71 12W
Lewis Hill *mt.* Newfoundland **31** C2 49 48N 58 30W
Lewisporte Newfoundland **31** C2 49 15N 55 03W
Liard River Northwest Territories **44** G3 60 00N 120 00W
Liard River *tn.* British Columbia **42** B3 59 28N 126 18W
Liddon Gulf Northwest Territories **44** J6 75 00N 113 00W
L'Île Dorval *i.* Québec **47** N4 45 26N 73 44W
L'Île-Perrot *i.* Québec **47** M4 45 24N 73 55W
Lillooet British Columbia **43** D2 50 41N 121 59W
Lillooet Lake British Columbia **42** H5 50 15N 122 38W
Lillooet River British Columbia **42** H4 49 59N 122 25W
Limbour Québec **47** K2 45 29N 75 44W
Lindsay Ontario **38** D3 44 21N 78 44W
Linzee, Cape Nova Scotia **31** F7 46 00N 61 30W
Lions Bay Ontario **38** A3 49 28N 123 13W
Lion's Head *tn.* Ontario **38** A3 44 59N 81 16W
Lipton Saskatchewan **40** C2 50 55N 103 49W
L'Islet *admin.* Québec **37** Q8 47 00N 70 20W
L'Isle-Verte Québec **37** R9 48 00N 69 20W
Lismore Nova Scotia **31** F7 45 42N 62 16W
Listowel Ontario **38** B2 43 44N 80 57W
Little Bow River Alberta **41** C2 50 20N 113 40W
Little Buffalo River Alberta **41** C3 59 45 113 30W
Little Churchill River Manitoba **39** B3 56 40N 96 10W
Little Current *tn.* Ontario **36** E6 45 58N 81 56W
Little Dover Nova Scotia **31** F7 45 20N 61 05W
Little Grand Rapids *tn.* Manitoba **39** B2 52 10N 95 30W
Little Maitland River Ontario **38** A2 43 48N 81 10W
Little Mecatina River (Rivière du Petit Mécatina) Newfoundland **30** B3 52 40N 61 50W
Little Narrows *tn.* Nova Scotia **31** F7 45 59N 61 00W
Little River Ontario **52** F2 42 19N 82 55W
Little Rouge Creek Ontario **46** C2 43 54N 79 15W
Little Sachigo Lake Ontario **34** B3 53 24N 90 50W
Little Smoky River Alberta **41** B2 54 05N 117 45W
Little White River Ontario **36** C7 46 23N 83 20W
Liverpool Nova Scotia **31** F6 44 03N 64 43W
Liverpool Bay Northwest Territories **44** E4 69 45N 130 00W
Livingstone Cove *tn.* Nova Scotia **31** F7 45 52N 61 58W
Lloyd George, Mount British Columbia **43** D3 57 50N 124 58W
Lloyd Lake Alberta **48** A1 50 52N 114 10W
Lloyd Lake Saskatchewan **40** A3 57 20N 108 40W
Lloydminster Alberta/Saskatchewan **40** B2 53 18N 110 00W
Lobstick Lake Newfoundland **30** A3 54 00N 65 00W
Lockport Manitoba **48** C1 50 05N 96 56W
Lodge Creek Canada/U.S.A. **41** C1/D1 49 15N 110 05W
Logan Lake Ontario **38** D3 44 57N 78 59W
Logan Lake British Columbia **43** D2 50 28N 120 50W
Logan, Mount Yukon Territory **44** D3 60 34N 140 25W
Logan Mountains Yukon Territory **44** F3 60 30N 128 30W
London Ontario **38** A1 42 58N 81 15W
Long Beach *tn.* Ontario **38** C1 42 51N 79 23W
Long Cove *tn.* Newfoundland **31** D2 47 34N 53 40W
Long Creek Saskatchewan **40** C1 49 20N 103 55W
Long Harbour *tn.* Newfoundland **31** D2 47 26N 53 48W
Long Island Northwest Territories **45** G1 54 00N 79 00W
Long Island Nova Scotia **31** E6 44 20N 66 15W
Longlac Ontario **34** C2 49 47N 86 34W
Long Lake New Brunswick **31** A2 47 00N 66 50W
Long Lake Nova Scotia **47** P6 44 37N 63 37W
Long Lake Ontario **34** C2 49 45N 86 32W
Long Lake *I.R.* Ontario **34** C2 49 45N 86 32W
Long Point Manitoba **39** B2 52 50N 98 20W
Long Point Ontario **38** B1 42 33N 80 04W
Long Point *tn.* Ontario **38** B1 42 34N 80 15W
Long Point Bay Ontario **38** B1 42 40N 80 14W
Long Point Provincial Park Ontario **38** B1 42 40N 80 15W
Long Pond Newfoundland **31** C2 48 00N 55 52W
Long Range Mountains Newfoundland **31** C2 50 00N 57 00W
Long Sault Ontario **37** M6 45 02N 74 53W
Longueuil Québec **37** N6 45 32N 73 31W
Looking Back Lake Alberta **48** H4 53 18N 113 10W
Lookout, Cape Ontario **34** D4 55 18N 83 56W
Looma Alberta **48** G3 53 20N 113 15W
Loon Lake Nova Scotia **47** P6 44 42N 63 30W
Loon Lake *tn.* Saskatchewan **40** C2 54 00N 109 10W
Loon River Alberta **41** B3 56 40N 115 20W
L'Original Ontario **37** M6 45 37N 74 42W
Loring Ontario **36** F6 45 56N 80 00W
Lorne Park *tn.* Ontario **38** C2 43 31N 79 36W
Lorraine Québec **47** M5 45 38N 73 47W
Lotbinière *admin.* Québec **37** P7 46 20N 71 65W
Loughborough Inlet British Columbia **42** G5 50 35N 125 32W
Lougheed Island Northwest Territories **45** K6 77 26N 105 06W
Louisbourg Nova Scotia **31** G7 45 56N 59 58W
Louise Island British Columbia **42** B2 52 59N 131 50W
Louise, Lake Alberta **41** B2 51 25N 116 14W
Louiseville Québec **37** O7 46 16N 72 56W
Lourdes Newfoundland **31** C2 48 39N 59 00W
Low, Cape Northwest Territories **45** O3 63 07N 85 18W
Lower Arrow Lake British Columbia **43** E1 49 40N 118 09W
Lower Foster Lake Saskatchewan **40** B3 56 30N 105 10W
Lower Manitou Lake Ontario **34** B2 49 15N 93 00W
Lower Post British Columbia **43** C3 59 56N 128 09W
Lower Sackville Nova Scotia **31** F6 44 45N 63 40W
Lubicon Lake Alberta **41** B3 56 23N 115 56W
Lucan Ontario **38** A2 43 11N 81 24W
Lucknow Ontario **38** A2 43 58N 81 31W
Lucky Lake *tn.* Saskatchewan **40** B2 50 59N 107 10W
Lulu Island British Columbia **46** E5 50 15N 118 58W
Lumby British Columbia **43** E2 50 15N 118 58W
Lumsden Saskatchewan **40** C2 50 39N 104 52W
Lund British Columbia **42** H4 50 14N 124 46W
Lundar Manitoba **39** B2 50 41N 98 01W
Lunenburg Nova Scotia **31** F6 44 23N 64 21W
Lunenburg *admin.* Nova Scotia **31** F6 44 35N 64 30W
Luseland Saskatchewan **40** B2 52 06N 109 24W
Luther Lake Ontario **38** B2 43 52N 80 26W
Lyall, Mount Alberta/British Columbia **41** C2 50 05N 114 42W
Lyell Islands British Columbia **42** B2 52 00N 131 00W
Lyndonville Ontario **38** D2 43 30N 78 45W

Lynn Lake *tn.* Manitoba **39** A3 56 51N 101 01W
Lynx Lake Northwest Territories **44** L3 62 25N 106 15W
Lytton British Columbia **43** D2 50 12N 121 34W

M

Maaset British Columbia **42** B2 54 00N 132 01W
Mabel Lake British Columbia **43** E2 50 35N 118 40W
Mabou Nova Scotia **31** F7 46 04N 61 22W
McAdam New Brunswick **31** A2 45 34N 67 20W
MacAlpine Lake Northwest Territories **45** L4 66 45N 130 00W
McArthur Game Sanctuary Yukon Territory **44** D3 62 25N 135 50W
McBride British Columbia **43** D2 53 21N 120 19W
MacBrien Yukon Territory **44** F3 60 00N 130 00W
McCabe Lake Nova Scotia **47** P7 44 47N 63 43W
Maccan Nova Scotia **31** F7 45 41N 64 15W
McClintock Manitoba **39** C3 57 50N 94 10W
M'Clintock Channel Northwest Territories **45** L5 73 00N 104 00W
M'Clure, Cape Northwest Territories **44** G5 74 32N 121 19W
M'Clure Strait Northwest Territories **44** F5 74 59N 120 10W
McConnell River Bird Sanctuary Northwest Territories **45** N3 60 30N 94 00W
McCreary Manitoba **39** B2 50 45N 99 30W
Macdonald *admin.* Manitoba **48** C2 49 48N 97 18W
MacDowell Ontario **34** B3 52 10N 92 40W
MacDowell Lake Ontario **34** B3 52 15N 92 42W
McFarlane River Saskatchewan **40** B3 57 50N 107 55W
McGivney New Brunswick **31** A2 46 22N 66 34W
MacGregor Manitoba **39** B1 49 57N 98 48W
McGregor Lake Alberta **41** C2 50 25N 112 52W
McGregor River British Columbia **43** D2 54 10N 121 20W
McKay Lake Northwest Territories **30** A3 53 44N 65 37W
Mackay Lake Northwest Territories **44** J3 63 55N 110 25W
McKeller Ontario **36** G6 45 30N 79 00W
Mackenzie British Columbia **43** D3 55 18N 123 10W
Mackenzie Bay Yukon Territory **44** D4 69 00N 137 30W
Mackenzie Bison Sanctuary Northwest Territories **44** H3 61 30N 116 30W
McKenzie Creek Ontario **38** B2 43 02N 80 17W
Mackenzie Highway Alberta **41** B3 57 55N 117 40W
Mackenzie King Island Northwest Territories **44** J6 77 45N 111 00W
Mackenzie Mountains Yukon Territory/Northwest Territories **43** B3 66 00N 132 00W
Mackenzie River Northwest Territories **44** F4 66 20N 125 55W
Mackey Ontario **36** J7 46 10N 77 49W
Macklin Saskatchewan **40** B2 52 20N 109 58W
Maclean Strait Northwest Territories **45** L6 77 30N 102 30W
McLennan Alberta **41** B3 55 42N 116 54W
McLeod Lake *tn.* British Columbia **43** D2 55 00N 123 00W
McLeod River Alberta **41** B2 53 40N 116 20W
Macmillan Pass Yukon Territory **44** E3 63 25N 130 00W
Macmillan River Yukon Territory **44** E3 63 00N 134 00W
McNabs Island Nova Scotia **47** P6 44 37N 63 31W
McNutt Island Nova Scotia **31** E6 43 40N 65 20W
Macoun Lake Saskatchewan **40** C3 56 30N 103 40W
Macrae Point Provincial Park Ontario **38** C3 44 30N 79 10W
McTavish Arm *b.* Northwest Territories **44** H4 66 06N 118 04W
MacTier Ontario **36** G6 45 08N 79 47W
McVicar Arm *b.* Northwest Territories **44** G3 65 20N 120 10W
Madawaska Ontario **36** J6 45 30N 77 59W
Madawaska *admin.* New Brunswick **31** A2 47 30N 68 00W
Madawaska River Ontario **35** E2 45 10N 77 30W
Madoc Ontario **37** J5 44 30N 77 29W
Mad River Ontario **38** B3 44 18N 80 02W
Madsen Ontario **34** B3 50 58N 93 55W
Maelpaeg Reservoir Newfoundland **31** C2 48 20N 56 40W
Magnetawan Ontario **36** G6 45 40N 79 39W
Magnetawan River Ontario **36** F6 45 46N 80 37W
Magog Québec **37** O6 45 16N 72 09W
Magpie River Ontario **35** D2 48 00N 84 50W
Magrath Alberta **41** C1 49 27N 112 52W
Maguse Lake Northwest Territories **45** N3 61 40N 95 10W
Mahone Bay Nova Scotia **31** F6 44 25N 64 15W
Mahone Bay *tn.* Nova Scotia **31** F6 44 27N 64 24W
Mahood Creek British Columbia **46** G3 49 09N 122 50W
Maidstone Québec **52** F1 42 12N 82 56W
Maidstone Saskatchewan **40** B2 53 06N 109 18W
Main Brook *tn.* Newfoundland **31** C3 51 11N 56 01W
Main Channel Ontario **36** E6 45 00N 82 00W
Maitland River Ontario **38** A2 43 50N 81 28W
Major, Lake Nova Scotia **47** Q6 44 45N 63 30W
Makkovik Newfoundland **30** C4 55 05N 59 11W
Makkovik, Cape Newfoundland **30** C4 55 14N 59 09W
Makoop Lake Ontario **34** B3 53 24N 90 50W
Malartic Québec **33** A2 48 09N 78 09W
Malaspina Strait British Columbia **42** H4 49 47N 124 30W
Mallet River Ontario **38** B2 43 51N 80 42W
Malpeque Bay Prince Edward Island **31** F7 46 35N 63 50W
Malton Ontario **38** C2 43 42N 79 38W
Manigotagan Manitoba **39** B2 51 06N 96 18W
Manigotagan River Manitoba **39** B2 51 00N 96 10W
Manitoba *province* **39**
Manitoba, Lake Manitoba **39** B2 50 30N 98 15W
Manito Lake Saskatchewan **40** B2 52 40N 109 20W
Manitou Manitoba **39** B1 49 15N 98 32W
Manitou Lake Ontario **36** E6 45 48N 82 00W
Manitoulin *admin.* Ontario **36** E6 45 50N 82 30W
Manitoulin Island Ontario **36** D6 45 50N 82 20W
Manitouwadge Ontario **35** D2 49 08N 85 55W
Maniwaki Québec **37** K7 46 22N 75 58W
Manning Alberta **41** B3 56 55N 117 37W
Manning Provincial Park British Columbia **42** H4 49 00N 120 50W
Manotick Ontario **47** K1 45 14N 75 43W
Mansel Island Northwest Territories **45** Q3 62 00N 80 00W
Manson Creek *tn.* British Columbia **43** D3 55 40N 124 32W
Manyberries Alberta **41** C1 49 24N 110 42W

Maple Ontario **46** B1 43 50N 79 30W
Maple Creek *tn.* Saskatchewan **40** B1 49 55N 109 28W
Maple Grove Park Manitoba **48** D2 49 47N 97 06W
Maple Ridge British Columbia **42** H4 49 13N 122 36W
Mara Provincial Park Ontario **38** C3 44 30N 79 15W
Marathon Ontario **35** C2 48 44N 86 23W
Margaree Forks Nova Scotia **31** F7 46 21N 61 10W
Margaret Lake Alberta **41** B3 58 56N 115 25W
Margaretville Nova Scotia **31** E7 45 05N 65 05W
Marieville Québec **37** N6 45 27N 73 08W
Markdale Ontario **38** B3 44 19N 80 39W
Markham Ontario **38** C2 43 54N 79 16W
Markham Bay Northwest Territories **45** R3 63 02N 72 00W
Marmora Ontario **36** J5 44 29N 77 41W
Marten Falls Ontario **34** C3 51 40N 85 55W
Martensville Saskatchewan **40** B2 52 10N 106 30W
Maryfield Saskatchewan **40** C1 49 50N 101 30W
Mary's Harbour Newfoundland **30** D3 52 19N 55 50W
Marystown Newfoundland **31** C2 47 10N 55 09W
Marysville New Brunswick **31** A2 45 58N 66 35W
Mascouche Québec **37** N6 45 47N 73 49W
Maskinongé Québec **27** 46 14N 73 01W
Maskinongé *admin.* Québec **37** M8 47 40N 74 50W
Masset British Columbia **42** B2 54 00N 132 09W
Massey Ontario **36** C7 46 12N 82 05W
Massey Sound Northwest Territories **45** N6 74 00N 94 59W
Masson Québec **47** L3 45 33N 75 24W
Matachewan Ontario **35** D2 47 56N 80 39W
Matagami Québec **33** A2 49 40N 77 40W
Matane Québec **33** C2 48 50N 67 31W
Matheson Ontario **35** D2 48 32N 80 28W
Matsqui British Columbia **42** H4 49 05N 122 22W
Mattagami Québec **33** A2 49 40N 77 10W
Mattagami Lake Ontario **35** D2 47 54N 81 35W
Mattagami River Ontario **35** D2 50 50N 81 50W
Mattawa Ontario **35** E2 46 19N 78 42W
Mattice Ontario **35** D2 49 36N 83 16W
Maurelle Island British Columbia **42** G5 50 16N 125 11W
Maxwell Ontario **38** B3 44 18N 80 23W
Mayerthorpe Alberta **41** B2 53 57N 115 08W
Mayne Island British Columbia **42** H4 48 50N 123 18W
Maynooth Ontario **36** H6 45 14N 77 57W
Mayo Yukon Territory **44** D3 63 34N 135 52W
Mayo Lake Yukon Territory **44** D3 135 00N 63 30W
Mayson Lake Saskatchewan **40** B3 56 50N 107 30W
Meadow Lake *tn.* Saskatchewan **40** B2 54 09N 108 26W
Meadow Lake Provincial Park Saskatchewan **40** B2 54 30N 108 00W
Meadowvale West Ontario **52** C2 43 35N 79 45W
Meaford Ontario **38** B3 44 36N 80 35W
Meaghers Grant Nova Scotia **31** F6 44 57N 63 15W
Mealy Mountains Newfoundland **30** C3 53 10N 60 00W
Meander River *tn.* Alberta **41** B3 59 02N 117 42W
Meath Park *tn.* Saskatchewan **40** B2 53 27N 105 22W
Medicine Hat Alberta **41** C2 50 03N 110 41W
Medley Alberta **41** C2 54 25N 110 16W
Medway Creek Ontario **38** A2 43 07N 81 18W
Medway River Nova Scotia **31** F6 44 15N 64 50W
Mégantic *admin.* Québec **37** P7 46 10N 71 40W
Meighen Island Northwest Territories **45** M7 80 00N 99 30W
Melbourne Island Northwest Territories **44** K4 68 30N 104 45W
Meldrum Bay *tn.* Ontario **36** C6 45 56N 83 06W
Melfort Saskatchewan **40** C2 52 52N 104 38W
Melita Manitoba **39** A1 49 16N 101 00W
Melville Saskatchewan **40** C2 50 57N 102 49W
Melville Hills Northwest Territories **44** G4 69 00N 121 00W
Melville Island Northwest Territories **44** J6 75 30N 112 00W
Melville, Lake Newfoundland **30** C3 53 45N 59 00W
Melville Peninsula Northwest Territories **45** P4 68 00N 84 00W
Melville Sound Northwest Territories **44** K4 68 05N 107 30W
Melville Sound Ontario **38** A3 43 00N 81 04W
Menihek Newfoundland **30** A3 54 28N 66 36W
Menihek Lakes Newfoundland **30** A3 53 50N 66 50W
Mer Bleue Ontario **47** K2 45 24N 75 31W
Mercy Bay Northwest Territories **44** H5 74 05N 119 00W
Merigomish Nova Scotia **31** F7 45 37N 62 25W
Merivale Ontario **47** K2 45 19N 75 44W
Merrickville Ontario **37** L5 44 55N 75 50W
Merritt British Columbia **43** D1 50 09N 120 49W
Mersey River Nova Scotia **31** E6 44 10N 65 00W
Metabetchouane Québec **37** P9 48 26N 71 52W
Meta Incognita Peninsula Northwest Territories **45** S3 63 30N 70 00W
Metcalfe Ontario **47** K1 45 14N 75 29W
Metchosin British Columbia **42** H4 48 22N 123 32W
Meteghan Nova Scotia **31** E6 44 12N 66 10W
Metropolitan Toronto *admin.* Ontario **46** C2 43 44N 79 16W
Mica Creek *tn.* British Columbia **43** E2 52 00N 118 28W
Mica Dam British Columbia **43** E2 52 04N 118 28W
Michaud Point Nova Scotia **31** F7 45 36N 60 40W
Michel Peak British Columbia **43** C2 53 30N 126 25W
Michikamats Lake Newfoundland **30** B3 54 38N 64 19W
Michikamau Lake Newfoundland **30** B3 54 15N 64 00W
Michipicoten Island Ontario **35** C2 47 45N 85 45W
Micmac, Lake Nova Scotia **47** P6 44 23N 103 21W
Midale Saskatchewan **40** C1 49 23N 103 21W
Middle Arm *tn.* Newfoundland **31** C2 49 42N 56 06W
Middle Maitland River Ontario **38** A2 43 43N 81 11W
Middle Ridge Newfoundland **31** C2 48 20N 55 15W
Middle Sackville Nova Scotia **47** P7 44 47N 63 41W
Middlesex *admin.* Ontario **38** A2 42 46N 81 46W
Middleton Nova Scotia **31** E6 44 56N 65 04W
Midhurst Ontario **38** C3 44 28N 79 44W
Midland Ontario **38** C3 44 45N 79 53W
Midnapore Alberta **48** A1 49 02N 118 45W
Midway British Columbia **43** E1 49 02N 118 45W
Midway Mountains British Columbia **43** E1 49 25N 118 45W
Mikkwa River Alberta **41** C3 57 40N 114 08W
Mildmay Ontario **38** A3 44 03N 81 08W
Milestone Saskatchewan **40** C1 49 59N 104 31W
Milk River Alberta **41** C1 49 09N 112 05W
Milk River *tn.* Alberta **41** C1 49 09N 112 05W
Millbrook Ontario **38** D3 44 09N 78 28W
Mill Creek Alberta **48** G4 53 27N 113 23W
Miller Lake Nova Scotia **47** P7 44 49N 63 35W

Millet Alberta **41** C2 53 06N 113 28W
Mill Island Northwest Territories **45** Q3 64 00N 78 00W
Milltown Newfoundland **31** C2 47 54N 55 46W
Mill Village Nova Scotia **31** F6 44 10N 64 40W
Millville New Brunswick **31** A2 46 08N 67 12W
Milo Alberta **41** C2 50 34N 112 53W
Milton Nova Scotia **31** F6 44 04N 64 44W
Milton Ontario **38** C2 43 31N 79 53W
Milton Prince Edward Island **31** F7 46 20N 63 10W
Milverton Ontario **38** B2 43 34N 80 55W
Minaki Ontario **34** D2 50 00N 94 40W
Minas Basin Nova Scotia **31** F7 45 15N 64 15W
Minas Channel Nova Scotia **31** F7 45 10N 64 50W
Minden Ontario **36** H5 44 56N 78 42W
Minipi Lake Newfoundland **30** B3 52 25N 60 45W
Miniss Lake Ontario **34** B3 50 48N 90 50W
Minitonas Manitoba **39** A2 52 04N 101 02W
Minnedosa Manitoba **39** B1 50 14N 99 50W
Minnitaki Lake Ontario **34** B3 49 58N 92 00W
Minonipi Lake Newfoundland **30** B3 52 50N 60 50W
Minto New Brunswick **31** A2 46 05N 66 05W
Minto Yukon Territory **44** D3 62 34N 136 50W
Minto Inlet Northwest Territories **44** H5 71 20N 117 00W
Mira Bay Nova Scotia **31** G7 46 05N 59 50W
Mirabel Québec **37** M6 45 41N 74 20W
Miramichi Bay New Brunswick **31** A2 47 05N 65 00W
Mira River Nova Scotia **31** F7 46 00N 60 10W
Miscouche Prince Edward Island **31** F7 46 26N 63 52W
Miscou Island New Brunswick **31** B2 47 50N 64 30W
Misery Point Newfoundland **30** C2 52 01N 55 18W
Missanabie Ontario **35** D2 48 19N 84 05W
Missinaibi Lake Ontario **35** D2 48 23N 83 40W
Missinaibi River Ontario **35** D2 49 30N 83 20W
Mission British Columbia **42** H4 49 08N 122 20W
Missisa Lake Ontario **34** D3 52 18N 85 12W
Mississagi River Ontario **36** C7 46 10N 83 01W
Mississauga Ontario **46** B1 43 38N 79 36W
Mississauga Lake Ontario **38** D3 44 43N 78 17W
Missouri Coteau *hills* Saskatchewan **40** B2 50 40N 106 30W
Mistassini Québec **33** B2 48 54N 72 13W
Mistastin Lake Newfoundland **30** B3 55 50N 63 00W
Mitchell Ontario **38** A2 43 27N 81 13W
Mitchells Brook *tn.* Newfoundland **31** D2 47 08N 53 31W
Mobert *I.R.* Ontario **35** C2 48 40N 85 40W
Moisie Québec **33** C3 50 12N 66 06W
Molson Manitoba **39** B2 50 02N 96 19W
Molson Lake Manitoba **39** B2 54 20N 96 50W
Monarch Mountain British Columbia **43** C2 51 55N 125 57W
Monashee Mountains British Columbia **43** E2 51 30N 118 50W
Moncton New Brunswick **31** F7 46 04N 64 50W
Monkman Pass British Columbia **43** D2 54 30N 121 10W
Monkman Provincial Park British Columbia **43** D2 54 00N 121 10W
Mono Mills Ontario **38** C2 43 55N 79 57W
Montague Prince Edward Island **31** F7 46 10N 62 39W
Montcalm *admin.* Québec **37** L8 47 40N 76 15W
Mont D'Iberville (*Mount Caubvick*) Québec/ Newfoundland **30** B4 58 50N 64 40W
Montgomery Québec **37** Q7 46 58N 70 34W
Mont Jacques-Cartier *mt.* Québec **33** C2 49 00N 66 00W
Mont-Joli *tn.* Québec **33** C2 48 36N 68 14W
Mont-Laurier *tn.* Québec **36** L7 46 33N 75 31W
Montmagny Québec **33** B2 46 50N 70 33W
Montmagny *admin.* Québec **37** Q7 46 50N 70 20W
Montmartre Saskatchewan **40** C2 50 14N 103 24W
Montmorency *admin.* Québec **37** P8 47 34N 71 20W
Montréal Québec **37** N6 45 32N 73 36W
Montréal Est Québec **47** N5 45 37N 73 32W
Montreal Lake Saskatchewan **40** B2 54 15N 105 30W
Montreal Lake *tn.* Saskatchewan **40** B2 54 03N 105 49W
Montréal Nord **47** N5 45 35N 73 36W
Montreal River Ontario **35** D2 47 20N 84 20W
Montreal River Saskatchewan **40** B2 54 50N 105 30W
Montreal River *tn.* Ontario **35** D2 47 14N 84 39W
Montrose British Columbia **43** E1 49 06N 117 30W
Mont Royal *mt.* Québec **47** N5 45 31N 73 40W
Monts Chic-Chocs *mts.* Québec **33** C2 49 00N 66 40W
Monts Notre Dame *mts.* Québec **33** C2 47 59N 69 00W
Monts Otish *mts.* Québec **33** B3 52 00N 70 20W
Monts Povungnituk *mts.* Québec **32** A5 61 30N 75 59W
Monts Torngat (*Torngat Mountains*) Québec/ Newfoundland **32** D5 59 00N 64 15W
Moon River Ontario **38** C4 45 05N 79 51W
Moose Factory Ontario **34** D3 51 16N 80 37W
Moose Jaw Saskatchewan **40** B2 50 23N 105 35W
Moosejaw River Saskatchewan **40** B2 50 15N 105 10W
Moose Lake *tn.* Manitoba **39** A2 53 43N 100 20W
Moose Mountain Creek Saskatchewan **40** C2 50 15N 103 25W
Moose Mountain Provincial Park Saskatchewan **40** C1 49 50N 102 20W
Moose River Ontario **34** D3 50 00N 82 00W
Moose River *tn.* Ontario **34** D3 50 48N 81 18W
Moosomin Saskatchewan **40** C2 50 09N 101 41W
Moosonee Ontario **34** D3 51 18N 80 39W
Morden Manitoba **39** B1 49 12N 98 05W
Morell Prince Edward Island **31** F7 46 25N 62 42W
Moresby Island British Columbia **42** B2 53 00N 132 00W
Morice Lake British Columbia **43** C2 53 55N 127 30W
Moricetown British Columbia **43** C3 55 02N 127 20W
Morinville Alberta **41** C2 53 48N 113 39W
Morris Manitoba **39** B1 49 22N 97 21W
Morrisburg Ontario **37** L5 44 54N 75 11W
Morse Saskatchewan **40** B2 50 24N 107 00W
Morson Ontario **34** B2 49 03N 94 19W
Moser River *tn.* Nova Scotia **31** F6 44 58N 62 18W
Mostoos Hills Saskatchewan **40** B3 56 20N 109 50W
Mould Bay *m.s.* Northwest Territories **44** H6 76 14N 119 20W
Mountain Lake Ontario **38** A3 44 42N 81 02W
Mount Albert *tn.* Ontario **38** C3 44 07N 79 18W
Mount Brydges *tn.* Ontario **38** A1 42 54N 81 30W
Mount Burke British Columbia **46** H4 49 18N 122 42W
Mount Carleton Provincial Park New Brunswick **31** A2 47 20N 66 30W
Mount Edziza Provincial Park British Columbia **42** B3 57 40N 131 40W
Mount Forest *tn.* Ontario **38** B2 43 58N 80 44W
Mount Hope *tn.* Ontario **38** C2 43 09N 79 54W
Mount Revelstoke National Park British Columbia **43** E2 50 40N 118 00W
Mount Robson Provincial Park British Columbia **43** E2 52 50N 118 40W

Mount Seymour Provincial Park British Columbia **46** G4 49 22N 122 56W
Mount Stewart *tn.* Prince Edward Island **31** F7 46 22N 62 52W
Mount Uniacke *tn.* Nova Scotia **31** F6 44 54N 63 50W
Mud Bay British Columbia **46** G3 49 04N 122 53W
Mudjatik River Saskatchewan **40** B3 56 40N 107 10W
Mud Lake *tn.* Newfoundland **30** B3 53 19N 60 10W
Mukutawa River Manitoba **39** B2 53 10N 97 10W
Mulgrave Nova Scotia **31** F7 45 36N 61 25W
Muncho Lake British Columbia **43** C3 59 05N 125 47W
Muncho Lake *tn.* British Columbia **43** C3 59 00N 125 46W
Muncho Lake Provincial Park British Columbia **43** C3 58 50N 125 40W
Mundare Alberta **41** C2 53 36N 112 20W
Murdochville Québec **33** C2 48 57N 65 30W
Murray Harbour *tn.* Prince Edward Island **31** F7 46 00N 62 32W
Murray River *tn.* Prince Edward Island **31** F7 46 00N 62 38W
Murtle Lake British Columbia **43** E2 52 09N 119 40W
Musgrave Harbour *tn.* Newfoundland **31** D2 49 27N 53 58W
Musgravetown Newfoundland **31** D2 48 24N 53 53W
Muskawa River British Columbia **43** D3 58 30N 123 20W
Muskoka *admin.* Ontario **38** C3 44 57N 79 53W
Muskoka Falls *tn.* Ontario **36** G5 44 59N 79 16W
Muskrat Dam Lake Ontario **34** B3 53 25N 91 40W
Musquodoboit Harbour *tn.* Nova Scotia **31** F6 44 48N 63 10W
Muzon, Cape British Columbia **42** B2 54 41N 132 40W
Myles Bay Ontario **38** A3 44 56N 81 23W
Myrnam Alberta **41** C2 53 40N 111 14W

N

Nachvak Fiord *in.* Newfoundland **30** B4 59 03N 63 45W
Nackawic New Brunswick **31** A2 46 00N 67 15W
Nagagami Lake Ontario **35** C2 49 25N 85 01W
Nagagami River Ontario **35** D2 49 30N 84 40W
Nahanni Butte *tn.* Northwest Territories **44** G3 61 30N 123 20W
Nahanni National Park Reserve Northwest Territories **44** F3 61 30N 126 00W
Nahatlatch River British Columbia **42** H4 49 55N 121 59W
Nahlin River British Columbia **42** B3 58 58N 131 30W
Naicam Saskatchewan **40** C2 52 26N 104 31W
Naikoon Provincial Park British Columbia **42** B2 53 59N 131 35W
Nain Newfoundland **30** B4 56 32N 61 41W
Nakina Ontario **34** C3 50 11N 86 43W
Nakina River British Columbia **42** B3 59 07N 132 59W
Nakusp British Columbia **43** E2 50 15N 117 45W
Namao Alberta **48** G5 53 41N 113 28W
Nanaimo British Columbia **42** H4 49 08N 123 58W
Nanaimo River British Columbia **42** H4 49 00N 123 54W
Nanisivik Northwest Territories **45** P5 73 00N 79 58W
Nansen Sound Northwest Territories **45** O7 81 00N 90 35W
Nanticoke Ontario **38** B1 42 48N 80 04W
Nanticoke Creek Ontario **38** B1 42 56N 80 16W
Nanton Alberta **41** C2 50 21N 113 46W
Napaktok (Black Duck) Bay Newfoundland **30** B4 58 01N 62 19W
Napaktulik Lake Northwest Territories **44** J4 66 30N 112 50W
Napanee Ontario **37** K5 44 15N 76 57W
Napishish Lake Newfoundland **30** B3 54 10N 60 30W
Nares Strait Canada/Greenland **11** U8 78 30N 72 30W
Narrows, The *sd.* Nova Scotia **47** P6 44 40N 63 35W
Naskaupi River British Columbia **42** C3 50 10N 129 20W
Natashquan Québec **33** D3 50 10N 61 50W
Natashquan River (*Rivière Natashquan*) Newfoundland **30** B3 52 00N 62 50W
Nation Lakes British Columbia **43** C3 55 08N 125 15W
Nation River British Columbia **43** C3 55 11N 124 25W
Nauwigewauk New Brunswick **31** E7 45 28N 65 53W
Nazko British Columbia **43** D2 53 00N 123 37W
Nechako Plateau British Columbia **43** D2 54 40N 124 40W
Nechako River British Columbia **43** D2 53 35N 124 50W
Neeb Saskatchewan **40** B2 54 00N 107 50W
Neepawa Manitoba **39** B2 50 14N 99 29W
Neguac New Brunswick **31** A2 47 14N 65 03W
Nejanilini Lake Manitoba **39** B3 59 30N 98 00W
Nelson British Columbia **43** E1 49 29N 117 17W
Nelson Forks British Columbia **43** D3 59 30N 124 00W
Nelson House *tn.* Manitoba **39** B3 55 49N 98 51W
Nelson Island British Columbia **42** H4 49 43N 124 03W
Nelson-Miramichi New Brunswick **31** A2 46 55N 65 35W
Nelson River Manitoba **39** C3 56 50N 93 40W
Némiscau Québec **33** A3 51 20N 77 10W
Nepean Ontario **37** L6 45 16N 75 48W
Nepewassi Lake Ontario **36** F7 46 22N 80 38W
Nepisiguit River New Brunswick **31** A2 47 20N 66 30W
Nesselrode, Mount British Columbia **42** B3 58 55N 134 20W
Nestor Falls *tn.* Ontario **34** B2 49 06N 93 55W
Nettilling Lake Northwest Territories **45** S4 66 30N 71 10W
Neudorf Saskatchewan **40** C2 50 43N 103 00W
Neustadt Ontario **38** A3 44 04N 81 00W
Newboro' Ontario **37** K5 44 39N 76 19W
New Brunswick *province* **31** A2
Newburgh Ontario **37** K5 44 19N 76 52W
New Carlisle Québec **33** C2 48 00N 65 22W
Newcastle New Brunswick **31** A2 47 01N 65 36W
Newcastle Ontario **38** D2 43 55N 78 35W
New Denver British Columbia **43** E1 49 59N 117 22W
Newell, Lake Alberta **41** C2 50 26N 111 55W
Newfoundland *i.* Newfoundland **31** C2 48 30N 57 56W
Newfoundland *province* **31**
New Germany Nova Scotia **31** F6 44 34N 64 44W
New Glasgow Nova Scotia **31** F7 45 36N 62 38W
New Hazelton British Columbia **43** C3 55 15N 127 30W
New Liskeard Ontario **35** E2 47 31N 79 41W
Newmarket Ontario **38** C3 44 03N 79 27W
New Minas Nova Scotia **31** F7 45 00N 64 30W
New Richmond Québec **33** C2 48 10N 65 50W
New Ross Nova Scotia **31** F6 44 44N 64 27W
Newton British Columbia **46** G3 49 07N 122 50W
Newtown Newfoundland **31** D2 49 12N 53 31W
New Waterford Nova Scotia **31** G7 46 17N 60 05W

New Westminster British Columbia **42** H4 49 10N 122 58W
Niagara *admin.* Ontario **38** C2 43 02N 79 34W
Niagara Escarpment Ontario **38** C2 43 05N 80 10W
Niagara Falls *tn.* Ontario **38** C2 43 05N 79 06W
Niagara-on-the-Lake Ontario **38** C2 43 14N 79 16W
Nicolet Québec **37** O7 46 14N 72 36W
Nicolet *admin.* Québec **37** O7 46 00N 72 30W
Nicomekl River British Columbia **46** H3 49 05N 122 43W
Nictau New Brunswick **31** A2 47 16N 67 11W
Night Hawk Lake Ontario **35** D2 48 28N 80 60W
Nipawin Saskatchewan **40** C2 53 23N 104 01W
Nipawin Provincial Park Saskatchewan **40** C2 54 10N 103 30W
Nipigon Ontario **35** C2 49 02N 88 26W
Nipigon Bay Ontario **35** C2 48 58N 88 10W
Nipigon, Lake Ontario **34** C2 49 50N 88 30W
Nipissing Ontario **36** G7 46 05N 79 31W
Nipissing *admin.* Ontario **36** G7 46 00N 79 00W
Nipissing, Lake Ontario **36** G7 46 17N 80 00W
Nisku Alberta **48** F4 53 18N 113 32W
Nisling Range *mts.* Yukon Territory **44** D3 62 00N 138 40W
Nitchequon Québec **33** B3 53 10N 70 58W
Nith River Ontario **38** B2 43 12N 80 22W
Nitinat Lake British Columbia **42** H4 48 45N 124 42W
Nitinat River British Columbia **42** H4 49 06N 124 35W
Niverville Manitoba **39** B1 49 39N 97 03W
Nobleton Ontario **38** C2 43 53N 79 39W
Nogies Creek Ontario **38** D3 44 19N 78 30W
Nogies Creek *tn.* Ontario **38** D3 44 19N 78 30W
Nokomis Saskatchewan **40** B2 51 30N 105 00W
Nokomis Lake Saskatchewan **40** C3 56 55N 103 00W
Nootka Island British Columbia **43** C1 49 45N 126 50W
Nootka Sound British Columbia **43** C1 49 34N 126 39W
Nopiming Provincial Park Manitoba **39** B2 50 40N 95 10W
Noralee British Columbia **43** C2 53 59N 126 26W
Norman Bay *tn.* Newfoundland **30** C3 52 55N 56 10W
Norman, Cape Newfoundland **30** C3 51 38N 55 54W
Normandale Ontario **38** B1 42 41N 80 19W
Normansland Point Ontario **34** D3 52 00N 81 00W
Norman Wells *tn.* Northwest Territories **44** F4 65 19N 126 46W
Normétal Québec **33** A2 48 59N 79 53W
Norquay Saskatchewan **40** C2 51 52N 102 00W
Norris Arm *tn.* Newfoundland **31** C2 49 05N 55 15W
Norris Point *tn.* Newfoundland **31** C2 49 31N 57 53W
North Arm *b.* Northwest Territories **44** H3 62 05N 114 40W
North Arm *r.* British Columbia **46** F3 49 12N 123 05W
North Aulatsivik Island Newfoundland **30** B4 59 46N 64 05W
North Battleford Saskatchewan **40** B2 52 47N 108 19W
North Bay *tn.* Ontario **36** G7 46 20N 79 28W
North Cape Nova Scotia **31** F7 47 10N 60 00W
North, Cape Prince Edward Island **31** F7 47 10N 64 00W
North Caribou Lake Ontario **34** B3 52 50N 90 40W
North Castor River Ontario **47** K2 45 18N 75 31W
North Channel Ontario **36** C7 46 00N 83 00W
Northern Indian Lake Manitoba **39** B3 57 30N 97 30W
Northern Peninsula Newfoundland **31** C3 50 30N 57 00W
Northern Woods and Water Route Alberta/Manitoba/ Saskatchewan **40** B2 54 10N 107 20W
North French River Ontario **35** D3 50 20N 81 00W
North Head *tn.* New Brunswick **31** E6 44 46N 66 45W
North Kent Island Northwest Territories **45** M6 76 40N 90 14W
North Knife Lake Manitoba **39** B3 58 10N 96 40W
North Knife River Manitoba **39** B3 58 40N 95 50W
North Magnetic Pole (1992) Northwest Territories **45** L6 78 02N 103 07W
North Moose Lake Manitoba **39** A2 54 00N 100 10W
North Pender Island British Columbia **42** H4 48 49N 123 17W
North River Newfoundland **30** B4 57 30N 63 20W
North River Ontario **38** C3 44 47N 79 35W
North River *tn.* Nova Scotia **31** F7 46 08N 60 40W
North River Bridge *tn.* Nova Scotia **31** F7 46 07N 60 39W
North Rustico Prince Edward Island **31** F7 46 26N 63 20W
North Saskatchewan River Alberta/Saskatchewan **40** B2 52 40N 106 40W
North Saugeen River Ontario **38** A3 44 18N 81 10W
North Seal River Manitoba **39** A3 59 00N 100 30W
North Spirit Lake Ontario **34** B3 52 31N 92 55W
North Spirit Lake *tn.* Ontario **34** B3 52 31N 93 01W
North Sydney Nova Scotia **31** F7 46 13N 60 15W
North Thames River Ontario **38** A2 43 02N 81 14W
North Thompson River British Columbia **43** E2 51 32N 120 00W
North Twin Islands Northwest Territories **34** E3 53 20N 80 00W
Northumberland *admin.* New Brunswick **31** A2 47 10N 66 30W
Northumberland Strait Atlantic Provinces **31** F7 46 30N 64 30W
North Vancouver British Columbia **42** H4 49 21N 123 05W
North Wabasca Lake Alberta **41** C3 56 10N 114 40W
Northwest Angle Provincial Forest Manitoba **39** B1 49 20N 95 30W
Northwest Bay *tn.* Ontario **34** B2 48 50N 93 38W
Northwest Gander River Newfoundland **31** C2 48 30N 55 40W
North West River *tn.* Newfoundland **30** A3 53 32N 60 08W
Northwest Territories *territory* **44/45**
North York *bor.* Metropolitan Toronto Ontario **46** C2 43 44N 79 26W
North Yukon National Park Yukon Territory **44** D4 69 20N 139 30W
Norton New Brunswick **31** E7 45 38N 65 43W
Norway House *tn.* Nova Scotia **39** B2 53 59N 97 50W
Norwich Ontario **38** B1 42 59N 80 36W
Nose Creek Alberta **48** A2 51 08N 114 02W
Nose Hill Alberta **48** A2 51 06N 114 07W
Notekwin River Alberta **41** B3 56 55N 118 20W
Notre Dame Bay Newfoundland **31** C2 49 45N 55 00W
Notre-Dame-des-Champs Ontario **47** L2 45 25N 75 28W
Nottawasaga Bay Ontario **38** B3 44 40N 80 30W
Nottawasaga River Ontario **38** C3 44 27N 79 53W
Nottingham Island Northwest Territories **45** Q3 63 05N 78 00W
Nouveau-Comptoir *see* Wemindji

Nova Scotia *province* **31** F7 45 30N 63 00W
Nueltin Lake Manitoba/Northwest Territories **45** L3 60 30N 99 00W
Nunaksaluk Island Newfoundland **30** B4 55 49N 60 20W
Nutak Newfoundland **30** B4 57 28N 61 52W
Nut Mountain Saskatchewan **40** C2 52 20N 102 50W
Nut Mountain *tn.* Saskatchewan **40** C2 52 08N 103 21W

O

Oak Bay British Columbia **42** H4 48 27N 123 18W
Oak Bluff Manitoba **48** C2 49 46N 97 18W
Oak Lake *tn.* Manitoba **39** A1 49 40N 100 45W
Oakville Ontario **38** C2 43 27N 79 41W
Oakwood Ontario **38** D3 44 28N 78 52W
Oban Saskatchewan **40** B2 52 09N 108 09W
Obaska Québec **37** J9 48 12N 77 22W
Observatory Inlet British Columbia **42** C3 55 05N 129 59W
Ocean Falls *tn.* British Columbia **43** C2 52 24N 127 42W
Oder River British Columbia **43** D3 55 50N 98 00W
Ogden Alberta **48** A1 50 59N 114 00W
Ogidaki Mountain Ontario **35** D2 46 57N 83 59W
Ogilvie Mountains Yukon Territory **44** D4 65 05N 139 00W
Ogoki Ontario **34** C3 51 38N 85 57W
Ogoki Lake Ontario **34** C3 50 50N 87 10W
Ogoki Reservoir Ontario **34** C3 50 48N 88 18W
Ogoki River Ontario **34** C3 50 50N 86 50W
Oil Springs *tn.* Ontario **36** D3 42 47N 82 07W
Ojibway Prairie Provincial Park Ontario **52** E1 42 14N 83 03W
Okak Bay Newfoundland **30** B4 57 28N 62 00W
Okak Islands Newfoundland **30** B4 57 30N 61 50W
Okanagan Lake British Columbia **43** E1 49 45N 119 32W
Okotoks Alberta **41** C2 50 44N 113 59W
Olcott Ontario **38** D2 43 20N 78 40W
Old Crow Yukon Territory **44** D4 67 34N 139 43W
Old Crow River Yukon Territory **44** D4 68 00N 140 00W
Oldman River Alberta **41** C1 49 50N 112 05W
Old Perlican Newfoundland **31** D2 48 05N 53 01W
Olds Alberta **41** C2 51 50N 114 06W
Old Wives Lake Saskatchewan **40** B2 50 15N 106 40W
O'Leary Prince Edward Island **31** F7 46 43N 64 15W
Oliphant Ontario **38** A3 44 44N 81 16W
Oliver British Columbia **43** E1 49 10N 119 37W
Omemee Ontario **38** D3 44 19N 78 33W
Omineca Mountains British Columbia **43** C3 57 15N 127 50W
Omineca River British Columbia **43** C3 56 02N 126 00W
Onaman Lake Ontario **35** C2 49 50N 87 26W
Onaping Lake Ontario **35** D2 46 57N 81 30W
100 Mile House British Columbia **43** D2 51 36N 121 18W
Ontario *province* **34/35**
Ontario, Lake Canada/U.S.A. **36** H4 43 45N 78 00W
Ontario, Lake (*Lac Deschênes*) Ontario/Québec **47** J2 45 22N 75 50W
Ootsa Lake British Columbia **43** C2 53 40N 126 30W
Ootsa Lake *tn.* British Columbia **43** C2 53 42N 125 56W
Opasatika Ontario **35** D2 49 32N 82 52W
Opasquia Provincial Park Ontario **34** B3 53 30N 93 10W
Opeongo Lake Ontario **35** E2 45 42N 78 23W
Opinnagau River Ontario **34** D3 53 30N 83 50W
Orangeville Ontario **38** B2 43 55N 80 06W
Orient Bay *tn.* Ontario **34** C2 49 23N 88 08W
Orillia Ontario **38** C3 44 36N 79 26W
Orleans Ontario **47** K2 45 28N 75 34W
Ormstown Québec **37** M6 45 08N 74 02W
Oromocto New Brunswick **31** A2 45 50N 66 28W
Orono Ontario **38** D2 43 59N 78 36W
Oshawa Ontario **38** D2 43 53N 78 51W
Oskélanéo Québec **37** J9 48 07N 75 14W
Osoyoos British Columbia **43** E1 49 00N 119 29W
Ospika River British Columbia **43** D3 56 55N 124 10W
Ossokmanuan Reservoir Newfoundland **30** A3 53 25N 65 00W
Otoskwin River Ontario **34** C3 51 50N 89 40W
Ottawa Ontario **47** K2 45 24N 75 38W
Ottawa-Carleton *admin.* Ontario **37** L6 45 31N 75 22W
Ottawa Islands Northwest Territories **45** P2 59 10N 80 25W
Ottawa River (*Rivière des Outaouais*) Ontario/Québec **37** K6 45 34N 76 30W
Otter Lake Saskatchewan **40** C3 55 35N 104 30W
Otter Rapids *tn.* Ontario **35** D3 50 12N 81 40W
Outlook Saskatchewan **40** B2 51 30N 107 03W
Outremont Québec **47** N5 45 31N 73 36W
Owen Sound Ontario **38** B3 44 34N 80 56W
Owen Sound *tn.* Ontario **38** B3 44 34N 80 56W
Owl River Manitoba **39** C3 57 50N 93 20W
Oxbow Saskatchewan **40** C1 49 16N 102 12W
Oxford Nova Scotia **31** F7 45 43N 63 52W
Oxford *admin.* Ontario **38** B2 43 06N 80 59W
Oxford House *tn.* Manitoba **39** B2 54 58N 95 17W
Oxford Lake Manitoba **39** B2 54 50N 95 50W
Oyen Alberta **41** C2 51 22N 110 28W
Oyster River British Columbia **42** G4 49 50N 125 24W
Ozhiski Lake Ontario **34** C3 52 01N 88 30W

P

Pacific Rim National Park British Columbia **42** G4 48 52N 125 35W
Packs Harbour *tn.* Newfoundland **30** C3 53 51N 56 59W
Pacquet Newfoundland **31** C2 49 59N 55 53W
Paddle Prairie *tn.* Alberta **41** B3 57 57N 117 29W
Paint Lake Provincial Recreation Park Manitoba **39** B3 55 30N 97 00W
Paisley Ontario **38** A3 44 17N 81 16W
Pakashkan Lake Ontario **34** B2 49 21N 90 15W
Pakowki Lake Alberta **41** C1 49 20N 111 50W
Pakwash Lake Ontario **34** B3 50 45N 93 30W
Palmerston Ontario **38** B2 43 50N 80 50W
Panache, Lake Ontario **36** F7 46 15N 81 20W
Pangnirtung Northwest Territories **45** S4 66 05N 65 45W
Panmure Island Prince Edward Island **31** F7 46 10N 62 30W
Papineau *admin.* Québec **37** L6 45 40N 75 30W
Paradise Hill *tn.* Saskatchewan **40** B2 53 32N 109 26W
Paradise River Newfoundland **30** C3 52 50N 57 50W
Paradise River *tn.* Newfoundland **30** C3 53 27N 57 11W
Parc de Conservation d'Aiguebelle Québec **33** A2 48 30N 78 50W
Parc de Conservation de la Gaspésie Québec **33** C2 48 52N 65 57W

Parc de Conservation de la Jacques-Cartier Québec 37 P8 47 23N 71 30W
Parc de Conservation des Grands-Jardins Québec 37 Q8 47 47N 70 59W
Parc de Conservation du Saguenay Québec 37 Q9 48 15N 70 45W
Parc de la Gatineau Québec 47 J3 45 31N 75 53W
Parc de Récréation des Îles-de-Boucherville Québec 47 N5 45 36N 73 27W
Parc de Récréation D'Oka Québec 47 M4 45 24N 73 58W
Parc de Récréation du Mont-Tremblant Québec 37 M7 46 20N 74 43W
Parc National de Forillon Québec 33 D2 49 00N 64 00W
Parc National de la Mauricie Québec 37 N7 46 50N 73 05W
Parent Québec 37 M8 47 55N 74 36W
Paris Ontario 38 B2 43 12N 80 25W
Parke Lake Newfoundland 30 C3 53 10N 58 50W
Parkhill Ontario 38 A2 43 10N 81 41W
Parkland County Alberta 48 F4 53 40N 113 30W
Parksville British Columbia 42 H4 49 20N 124 19W
Parrsboro Nova Scotia 31 F7 45 25N 64 21W
Parry Island Ontario 38 B4 45 17N 80 11W
Parry Islands Northwest Territories 44 J6 75 15N 109 00W
Parry Sound Ontario 38 B4 45 21N 80 08W
Parry Sound *admin.* Ontario 36 G6 45 22N 80 08W
Parry Sound *tn.* Ontario 38 B4 45 21N 80 03W
Parson's Pond *tn.* Newfoundland 31 C3 50 02N 57 43W
Pasadena Newfoundland 31 C2 49 01N 57 36W
Pasfield Lake Saskatchewan 40 B3 58 20N 105 45W
Pasquia Hills Saskatchewan 40 C2 53 10N 103 00W
Pass Lake Ontario 34 C2 48 34N 88 44W
Pattullo, Mount British Columbia 42 C3 56 15N 129 43W
Paudash Ontario 36 J5 44 56N 78 04W
Paulatuk Northwest Territories 44 G4 69 49N 123 59W
Paul Island Newfoundland 30 B4 56 30N 61 25W
Payne Bay Québec 32 C4 60 00N 70 01W
Peace Point *tn.* Alberta 41 C3 59 07N 112 27W
Peace River Alberta 41 B3 58 40N 114 30W
Peace River *tn.* Alberta 41 B3 56 15N 117 18W
Peachland British Columbia 43 E1 49 49N 119 48W
Peary Channel Northwest Territories 45 L6 79 40N 101 30W
Peawanuck Ontario 34 C4 55 00N 85 30W
Peche Island Provincial Park Ontario 52 F2 42 20N 82 55W
Peel *admin.* Ontario 38 C2 43 49N 79 57W
Peel County Ontario 46 B2 43 48N 79 41W
Peel River Yukon Territory 44 D4 66 05N 136 00W
Peel River Game Reserve Northwest Territories 44 E4 66 30N 134 00W
Peel Sound Northwest Territories 45 M5 73 15N 96 30W
Peerless Lake Alberta 41 C3 56 40N 114 35W
Pefferlaw Brook Ontario 38 C3 44 10N 79 15W
Peggys Cove *tn.* Nova Scotia 31 F6 44 30N 63 50W
Pelee Island Ontario 36 D2 41 47N 82 40W
Pelee Point Ontario 36 D2 41 45N 82 39W
Pelham Ontario 38 C2 43 02N 79 19W
Pelican Bay Manitoba 39 A2 52 40N 100 30W
Pelican Lake Manitoba 39 A2 52 30N 100 30W
Pelican Mountains Alberta 41 C3 55 35N 114 00W
Pelican Narrows *tn.* Saskatchewan 40 C3 55 12N 102 55W
Pelly Bay Northwest Territories 45 N4 68 53N 89 51W
Pelly Bay *tn.* Northwest Territories 45 O4 68 32N 89 48W
Pelly Crossing Yukon Territory 44 D3 62 48N 136 30W
Pelly Mountains Yukon Territory 44 E3 62 10N 134 10W
Pelly Point British Columbia 46 F3 49 06N 123 13W
Pelly River Yukon Territory 44 E3 62 50N 134 50W
Pemberton British Columbia 42 H5 50 19N 122 49W
Pembina Alberta 41 B2 53 08N 115 09W
Pembina River Alberta 41 B2 53 15N 116 05W
Pembina River Manitoba 39 B1 49 10N 99 10W
Pembroke Ontario 38 D2 45 49N 77 08W
Penetanguishene Ontario 38 C3 44 47N 79 56W
Penhold Alberta 41 C2 52 08N 113 52W
Péninsule de la Gaspésie *p.* Québec 33 C2 48 30N 65 30W
Péninsule d'Ungava *p.* Québec 32 A5/B5 60 50N 76 00W
Penticton British Columbia 43 E1 49 49N 119 38W
Percé Québec 33 D2 48 32N 64 14W
Percé, Cape Nova Scotia 31 G7 46 10N 59 40W
Perdue Saskatchewan 40 B2 52 05N 107 33W
Perkinsfield Ontario 38 C3 44 41N 79 58W
Perrault Falls *tn.* Ontario 34 B3 50 20N 93 08W
Perry Island *tn.* Northwest Territories 45 L4 67 48N 102 33W
Perth-Andover New Brunswick 31 A2 46 45N 67 42W
Perth Ontario 37 K5 44 54N 76 15W
Perth *admin.* Ontario 38 A2 43 22N 81 10W
Petawana Ontario 35 E2 45 54N 77 18W
Petawawa Ontario 37 J6 45 54N 77 17W
Peterborough Ontario 38 D3 44 19N 78 20W
Peterborough *admin.* Ontario 38 D3 44 14N 78 32W
Peter Pond Lake Saskatchewan 40 B3 55 50N 108 50W
Petitcodiac New Brunswick 31 E7 45 57N 65 11W
Petite Rivière *tn.* Nova Scotia 31 F6 44 15N 64 25W
Petite Rivière de la Baleine *r.* Québec 32 A4 55 05N 76 28W
Petit Étang *tn.* Nova Scotia 31 F7 46 39N 61 00W
Petit lac des Loups Marins *l.* Québec 32 B4 56 30N 73 30W
Petit lac Manicouagan *l.* Québec 33 C3 52 10N 67 40W
Petitot River British Columbia 43 D3 59 55N 122 15W
Petitsikapau Lake Newfoundland 30 A3 54 37N 66 25W
Petre, Point Ontario 35 E1 43 50N 77 09W
Petrolia Ontario 36 D3 42 52N 82 09W
Phelps Lake Saskatchewan 40 C3 59 20N 102 55W
Philpots Island Northwest Territories 45 Q5 74 57N 79 58W
Pickerel Lake Ontario 35 B2 48 37N 91 19W
Pickering Ontario 46 D2 43 48N 79 11W
Pickering Village Ontario 38 C2 43 51N 79 02W
Pickle Lake *tn.* Ontario 34 B3 51 28N 90 12W
Pic River Ontario 35 C2 48 50N 86 20W
Picton Ontario 37 J5 44 00N 77 07W
Pictou Nova Scotia 31 F7 45 41N 62 42W
Pictou *admin.* Nova Scotia 31 F7 45 30N 62 40W
Pictou Island Nova Scotia 31 F7 45 41N 62 42W
Picture Butte *tn.* Alberta 41 C1 49 53N 112 47W
Pie Island Ontario 35 C2 48 15N 89 06W
Pierceland Saskatchewan 40 B2 54 20N 109 40W
Pierrefords Québec 47 M5 45 30N 73 50W
Pigeon Lake Alberta 41 C2 53 01N 114 02W
Pigeon Lake Ontario 38 D3 44 27N 78 30W
Pigeon River Manitoba 39 B2 52 10N 96 50W
Pigeon River Ontario 38 D3 44 13N 78 42W
Pikangikum *I.R.* Ontario 34 B3 51 48N 93 59W
Pikangikum Lake Ontario 34 B3 51 48N 94 00W
Pike Creek Ontario 52 F2 41 15N 82 53W
Pikwitonei Manitoba 39 B3 55 35N 97 11W
Pilot Butte *tn.* Saskatchewan 40 C2 50 29N 104 28W
Pilot Mound *tn.* Manitoba 39 B1 49 13N 98 52W
Pinawa Manitoba 39 B2 50 13N 95 56W
Pincher Creek *tn.* Alberta 41 C1 49 29N 113 57W
Pinchi Lake British Columbia 43 D2 54 36N 124 25W
Pine, Cape Newfoundland 31 D2 46 38N 53 35W
Pine Falls *tn.* Manitoba 39 B2 50 33N 96 14W
Pinehouse Lake Saskatchewan 40 B3 55 35N 106 50W
Pineimuta River Ontario 34 B3 52 10N 90 40W
Pine Pass British Columbia 43 D3 55 30N 122 25W
Pine Point Northwest Territories 44 J3 60 50N 114 28W
Pine River British Columbia 43 D3 55 50N 121 50W
Pine River Ontario 38 B3 44 18N 80 06W
Pinery Provincial Park Ontario 36 D4 43 16N 81 50W
Pinto Butte *mt.* Saskatchewan 40 B1 49 21N 107 25W
Pinware Newfoundland 30 C3 51 37N 56 42W
Pipestone River Ontario 34 B3 52 20N 90 40W
Pistolet Bay Newfoundland 30 C3 51 35N 55 45W
Pit Island British Columbia 42 C2 53 38N 129 59W
Pitman River British Columbia 43 C3 58 00N 128 15W
Pitt Lake British Columbia 42 H4 49 25N 122 33W
Pitt Meadows *tn.* British Columbia 42 H4 49 13N 122 42W
Pitt River British Columbia 42 H4 49 42N 122 40W
Placentia Newfoundland 31 D2 47 14N 53 58W
Placentia Bay Newfoundland 31 D2 47 00N 54 30W
Plantagenet Ontario 37 L6 45 32N 75 00W
Plaster Rock *tn.* New Brunswick 31 A2 46 55N 67 24W
Playgreen Lake Manitoba 39 B2 53 50N 98 10W
Pleasant Bay *tn.* Nova Scotia 31 F7 46 50N 60 48W
Pledger Lake Ontario 34 D3 50 53N 83 42W
Plessisville Québec 37 P7 46 14N 71 46W
Plum Coulee Manitoba 39 B1 49 12N 97 45W
Plum Point *tn.* Newfoundland 31 C3 51 04N 56 53W
Pohénégamook Québec 37 R8 47 28N 69 17W
Pointe au Baril *tn.* Ontario 38 B4 45 36N 80 23W
Pointe au Baril Station *tn.* Ontario 36 F6 45 36N 80 22W
Pointe aux Pins Ontario 36 D3 42 29N 84 28W
Pointe-aux-Pins Creek Alberta 48 G5 53 39N 113 16W
Pointe-Claire *tn.* Québec 37 N6 45 27N 73 50W
Pointe de l'Est *c.* Québec 33 D2 49 00N 64 00W
Pointe-Gatineau *tn.* Québec 47 K2 45 27N 75 42W
Pointe Jacques-Cartier *c.* Québec 33 C3 50 20N 66 00W
Pointe Louis-XIV *c.* Québec 32 A3 54 38N 79 45W
Point Lake Northwest Territories 44 J4 65 15N 113 04W
Point Pelee National Park Ontario 36 D2 41 57N 82 31W
Point Pleasant Park Nova Scotia 47 P6 44 37N 63 33W
Polar Bear Provincial Park Ontario 34 D3 54 50N 83 40W
Pomquet Nova Scotia 31 F7 45 34N 61 50W
Pond Inlet Northwest Territories 45 Q5 72 41N 78 00W
Pond Inlet *tn.* Northwest Territories 45 Q5 42 40N 77 59W
Ponhook Lake Nova Scotia 31 F6 44 50N 64 10W
Ponoka Alberta 41 C2 52 42N 113 33W
Ponteaix Saskatchewan 40 B1 49 45N 107 20W
Pontiac *admin.* Québec 36 J7 46 28N 77 40W
Pont-Rouge Québec 27 46 45N 71 43W
Pont-Viau Québec 47 N5 45 33N 73 41W
Poplar Hills *tn.* Ontario 34 B3 52 05N 94 18W
Poplar River Manitoba 39 B2 52 50N 97 00W
Porcher Island British Columbia 42 B2 54 00N 130 30W
Porcupine, Cape Newfoundland 30 C3 53 56N 57 08W
Porcupine Hills Manitoba/Saskatchewan 40 C2 52 30N 101 40W
Porcupine Plain *tn.* Saskatchewan 40 C2 52 36N 103 15W
Porcupine Provincial Forest Manitoba 39 A2 52 30N 101 20W
Portabello Nova Scotia 47 P6 44 44N 63 32W
Portage la Prairie Manitoba 39 B1 49 58N 98 20W
Port Alberni British Columbia 42 H4 49 11N 124 49W
Port Alice British Columbia 43 C2 50 23N 127 24W
Port au Choix Newfoundland 31 C3 50 43N 57 22W
Port au Port Peninsula Newfoundland 31 C2 48 35N 59 00W
Port Bickerton Nova Scotia 31 F7 45 10N 61 40W
Port Blandford Newfoundland 31 D2 48 21N 54 10W
Port Bruce Ontario 38 A1 42 40N 81 00W
Port Bruce Provincial Park Ontario 38 B1 42 40N 81 00W
Port Burwell Northwest Territories 32 D5 60 30N 64 50W
Port Burwell Ontario 38 B1 42 39N 80 47W
Port Burwell Provincial Park Ontario 38 B1 42 40N 80 45W
Port Carling Ontario 36 G6 45 07N 79 35W
Port-Cartier Québec 33 C3 50 02N 66 58W
Port Clements British Columbia 42 B2 53 41N 132 11W
Port Colborne Ontario 38 C1 42 53N 79 16W
Port Coquitlam British Columbia 42 H4 49 16N 122 45W
Port Credit Ontario 46 B1 43 33N 79 36W
Port Dover Ontario 38 B1 42 47N 80 12W
Port Edward British Columbia 42 B2 54 11N 130 16W
Port Elgin Ontario 38 A3 44 25N 81 23W
Port Elgin New Brunswick 31 F7 46 03N 64 08W
Porter Lake Saskatchewan 40 B3 56 20N 107 10W
Port Essington British Columbia 42 C2 54 08N 130 54W
Port Hammond British Columbia 46 H3 49 12N 122 40W
Port Hardy British Columbia 43 C2 50 37N 127 15W
Port Hawkesbury Nova Scotia 31 F7 45 36N 61 22W
Port Hood Nova Scotia 31 F7 46 00N 61 32W
Port Hope Ontario 35 F1 43 58N 78 18W
Port Hope Simpson Newfoundland 30 C3 52 33N 56 18W
Port Kells British Columbia 46 H3 49 09N 122 43W
Portland Inlet British Columbia 42 B2 54 40N 130 30W
Port Lorne Nova Scotia 31 E6 44 50N 65 20W
Port McNeill British Columbia 43 C2 50 30N 127 01W
Port McNicoll Ontario 38 C3 44 44N 79 49W
Port Maitland Ontario 38 C1 42 51N 79 33W
Port Maitland Nova Scotia 31 E6 43 59N 66 04W
Port Mellon British Columbia 42 H4 49 31N 123 30W
Port-Menier Québec 33 D2 49 50N 64 20W
Port Moody British Columbia 42 H4 49 13N 122 57W
Port Mouton Nova Scotia 31 F6 43 58N 64 50W
Port Nelson Manitoba 39 C3 57 10N 92 35W
Portneuf *admin.* Québec 37 O7 46 50N 72 20W
Port Perry Ontario 38 D3 44 06N 78 58W
Port Renfrew British Columbia 42 H4 48 33N 124 25W
Port Rowan Ontario 38 B1 42 38N 80 27W
Port Royal Nova Scotia 31 E6 44 45N 65 40W
Port Saunders Newfoundland 31 C3 50 39N 57 18W
Port Simpson British Columbia 42 B2 54 32N 130 25W
Port Stanley Ontario 38 A1 42 61 540N 81 14W
Portuniq Québec 32 B5 2N 74 00W
Poste-de-la-Baleine *see* Kuujjuarapik
Postville Newfoundland 30 C3 54 54N 59 47W
Pouce Coupé British Columbia 43 D3 55 40N 120 08W
Pouch Cove *tn.* Newfoundland 31 D2 47 46N 52 46W
Povungnituk Québec 32 A5 59 45N 77 20W
Powassan Ontario 36 G7 46 05N 79 22W
Powell Lake British Columbia 42 H5 50 08N 124 26W
Powell River *tn.* British Columbia 42 H4 49 54N 124 34W
Powerview Manitoba 39 B2 50 30N 96 10W
Preeceville Saskatchewan 40 C2 51 58N 102 40W
Prelate Saskatchewan 40 B2 50 52N 109 22W
Prescott Ontario 37 L5 44 43N 75 33W
Prescott and Russell *admin.* Ontario 37 M6 45 30N 74 45W
Preston Nova Scotia 47 Q6 44 41N 63 26W
Preston Ontario 38 B2 43 23N 80 21W
Price Island British Columbia 42 C2 52 25N 128 40W
Prim, Point *c.* Prince Edward Island 31 F7 46 10N 63 00W
Primrose Lake Saskatchewan 40 B2 54 50N 109 30W
Primrose Lake Air Weapons Range Saskatchewan 40 B3 55 00N 109 00W
Prince *admin.* Prince Edward Island 31 F7 46 30N 64 00W
Prince Albert Saskatchewan 40 B2 53 13N 105 45W
Prince Albert National Park Saskatchewan 40 B2 54 00N 106 00W
Prince Albert Peninsula Northwest Territories 44 J5 72 30N 117 00W
Prince Albert Sound Northwest Territories 44 H5 70 15N 117 30W
Prince Alfred, Cape Northwest Territories 44 F5 74 20N 124 46W
Prince Charles Island Northwest Territories 45 Q4 67 40N 77 00W
Prince Edward Island *province* 31 F7 46 30N 63 00W
Prince Edward National Park Prince Edward Island 31 F7 46 10N 63 10W
Prince George British Columbia 43 D2 53 55N 122 49W
Prince Gustaf Adolf Sea Northwest Territories 45 K6 78 30N 107 00W
Prince of Wales Island Northwest Territories 45 M5 73 00N 98 00W
Prince of Wales Strait Northwest Territories 44 H5 71 00N 119 50W
Prince Patrick Island Northwest Territories 44 H6 77 00N 120 00W
Prince Regent Inlet Northwest Territories 44 H6 72 40N 91 00W
Prince Rupert British Columbia 42 B2 54 09N 130 20W
Princess Margaret Range *mts.* Northwest Territories 45 N7 81 00N 92 30W
Princess Royal Island British Columbia 42 C2 53 04N 129 00W
Princeton British Columbia 43 D1 49 25N 120 35W
Princeville Québec 37 P7 46 10N 71 52W
Prophet River British Columbia 43 D3 58 20N 122 50W
Provost Alberta 41 C2 52 21N 110 16W
Pubnico Nova Scotia 31 E6 43 42N 65 48W
Puce Ontario 52 F2 42 18N 82 46W
Puce River Ontario 52 F2 42 15N 82 47W
Pugwash Nova Scotia 31 F7 45 52N 63 40W
Pukaskwa Ontario 35 C2 48 20N 85 40W
Pukatawagan Manitoba 39 A3 55 46N 101 14W
Pukeashun Mountain British Columbia 43 E2 51 12N 119 14W
Purcell Mountains British Columbia 43 E2 50 58N 116 59W
Purcell's Cove *tn.* Nova Scotia 47 P6 44 35N 63 33W
Purcell Wilderness Conservancy British Columbia 43 E2 50 00N 116 00W

Q

Quadra Island British Columbia 42 G5 50 11N 125 20W
Qualicum Beach *tn.* British Columbia 42 H4 49 21N 124 27W
Qu'Appelle Saskatchewan 40 C2 50 33N 103 54W
Qu'Appelle Dam Saskatchewan 40 B2 50 55N 106 20W
Qu'Appelle River Saskatchewan 40 C2 50 30N 102 20W
Quaqtaq Québec 32 C5 61 00N 69 40W
Quathiaski Cove *tn.* British Columbia 42 G5 50 03N 125 11W
Quatsino Sound British Columbia 43 C2 50 25N 128 55W
Québec Québec 37 P7 46 50N 71 15W
Québec *admin.* Québec 37 O8 47 50N 72 30W
Québec *province* 32/33
Queen Bess, Mount British Columbia 43 D2 51 13N 124 35W
Queen Charlotte British Columbia 42 B2 53 18N 132 04W
Queen Charlotte Islands British Columbia 42 B2 53 30N 131 50W
Queen Charlotte Sound British Columbia 42 C2 51 48N 129 25W
Queen Charlotte Strait British Columbia 43 C2 51 00N 127 55W
Queen Elizabeth Foreland Northwest Territories 45 T3 62 23N 64 28W
Queen Elizabeth Islands Northwest Territories 44 H6 77 30N 105 00W
Queen Maud Bird Sanctuary Northwest Territories 45 L4 67 30N 103 20W
Queen Maud Gulf Northwest Territories 45 L4 68 00N 101 00W
Queens *admin.* New Brunswick 31 A2 45 50N 65 50W
Queens *admin.* Nova Scotia 31 E6 44 10N 65 20W
Queens *admin.* Prince Edward Island 31 F7 46 20N 63 10W
Queenston Ontario 38 C2 43 09N 79 03W
Queenswood Heights Ontario 47 L2 45 28N 75 29W
Quesnel British Columbia 43 D2 53 03N 122 31W
Quesnel Lake British Columbia 43 D2 52 30N 121 20W
Quesnel River British Columbia 43 D2 52 58N 122 29W
Quetico Provincial Park Ontario 35 B2 48 30N 91 30W
Quill Lake *tn.* Saskatchewan 40 C2 52 03N 104 12W
Quill Lakes Saskatchewan 40 C2 52 03N 104 12W
Quince, Bay of Ontario 37 J5 44 07N 77 32W
Quirke Lake Ontario 35 D2 46 28N 82 33W
Quispamsis New Brunswick 31 E7 45 25N 65 55W
Quoich River Northwest Territories 45 N3 64 50N 94 40W

R

Raanes Peninsula Northwest Territories 45 P6 78 30N 85 45W
Rabbit River British Columbia 43 C3 59 20N 127 20W
Radisson Québec 32 A3 53 43N 77 46W
Radisson Saskatchewan 40 B2 52 27N 107 24W
Radville Saskatchewan 40 C1 49 28N 104 19W
Rae Northwest Territories 44 H3 62 50N 116 03W
Rae Lakes *tn.* Northwest Territories 44 H3 64 10N 117 20W
Rae River Northwest Territories 44 H4 68 10N 116 50W
Ragged Lake Nova Scotia 47 P6 44 37N 63 39W
Rainbow Lake Alberta 41 B3 58 17N 119 16W
Rainbow Lake *tn.* Alberta 41 B3 58 30N 119 23W
Rainy Lake Ontario 34 B2 48 00N 93 00W
Rainy River Ontario 34 B2 48 40N 94 10W
Rainy River *tn.* Ontario 34 B2 48 44N 94 33W
Ralston Alberta 41 C2 50 15N 111 10W
Ralz, Mount British Columbia 42 B3 57 24N 132 19W
Ramea Newfoundland 31 C2 47 31N 57 23W
Ramea Islands Newfoundland 31 C2 47 31N 57 22W
Ramsey Lake Ontario 35 D2 47 13N 82 15W
Rankin Inlet Northwest Territories 45 N3 62 45N 92 05W
Rankin Inlet *tn.* Northwest Territories 45 N3 62 49N 92 05W
Rapide-Blanc-Station Québec 37 N8 47 41N 73 03W
Rapides de Lachine *rapids* Québec 47 N4 45 26N 73 39W
Rat Lake Manitoba 39 B3 56 10N 99 40W
Rat River Manitoba 39 B3 56 10N 99 20W
Ray, Cape Newfoundland 31 C2 47 37N 59 19W
Raymond Alberta 41 C1 49 27N 112 39W
Raymore Saskatchewan 40 C2 51 24N 104 32W
Razorback *mt.* British Columbia 43 D2 51 28N 124 35W
Read Island British Columbia 42 G5 50 11N 125 05W
Red Bay *tn.* Newfoundland 30 C3 51 44N 56 25W
Redberry Lake Saskatchewan 40 B2 52 45N 107 20W
Redcliff Alberta 41 C2 50 05N 110 47W
Red Deer Alberta 41 C2 52 15N 113 48W
Red Deer Lake Manitoba 39 A2 52 50N 101 30W
Red Deer River Alberta 41 C2 51 20N 112 35W
Red Deer River Saskatchewan 40 C2 52 50N 103 05W
Red Indian Lake Newfoundland 31 C2 48 40N 57 10W
Red Lake Ontario 34 B3 51 50N 93 40W
Red Lake *tn.* Ontario 34 B3 51 01N 93 50W
Redonda Island British Columbia 42 H5 50 15N 124 50W
Red River British Columbia 43 C3 59 23N 128 14W
Red River Manitoba 39 B1 49 30N 97 20W
Red Rock Ontario 35 C2 48 55N 88 15W
Redstone River Northwest Territories 44 F3 63 47N 128 00W
Red Sucker Lake Manitoba 39 C2 54 10N 94 10W
Redvers Saskatchewan 40 C1 49 34N 101 42W
Redwater Alberta 41 C2 53 57N 113 06W
Red Wine River Newfoundland 30 B3 54 10N 62 10W
Reed Lake Manitoba 39 A2 54 30N 100 10W
Refuge Cove *tn.* British Columbia 42 H5 50 07N 124 51W
Regina Saskatchewan 40 C2 50 30N 104 38W
Reindeer Grazing Reserve Northwest Territories 44 E4 69 00N 132 00W
Reindeer Island Manitoba 39 B2 52 30N 98 20W
Reindeer Lake Saskatchewan/Manitoba 40 C3 57 30N 102 30W
Reindeer River Saskatchewan 40 C3 56 10N 103 10W
Reliance Northwest Territories 44 K3 62 42N 109 08W
Renews Newfoundland 31 D2 46 56N 52 56W
Renfrew Ontario 37 K6 45 28N 76 44W
Renfrew *admin.* Ontario 37 J6 45 28N 76 41W
Rennie Lake Northwest Territories 44 K3 61 32N 105 35W
Repentigny Québec 37 N6 45 29N 73 46W
Repulse Bay *tn.* Northwest Territories 45 O4 66 32N 86 15W
Réserve de la Rivière Matamec *reserve* Québec 33 C3 50 30N 65 30W
Réserve Duchénier *reserve* Québec 33 C2 48 08N 68 40W
Réserve du Parc National de l'Archipel de Mingan *reserve* Québec 33 D3 50 10N 62 30W
Réserve Faunique Ashuapmushuan *reserve* Québec 33 B2 49 00N 73 30W
Réserve Faunique Assinica *reserve* Québec 33 A3 50 48N 75 40W
Réserve Faunique de Baldwin *reserve* Québec 33 C2 48 40N 66 10W
Réserve Faunique de Dunière *reserve* Québec 33 C2 48 30N 66 40W
Réserve Faunique de l'Île D'Anticosti *reserve* Québec 33 D2 49 25N 62 58W
Réserve Faunique de Papineau-Labelle *reserve* Québec 37 L7 46 20N 75 21W
Réserve Faunique de Port-Daniel *reserve* Québec 33 D2 48 13N 65 00W
Réserve Faunique de Portneuf *reserve* Québec 37 O8 47 15N 72 30W
Réserve Faunique de Rimouski *reserve* Québec 33 C2 48 00N 68 20W
Réserve Faunique des Chic-Chocs *reserve* Québec 33 C2 49 10N 65 10W
Réserve Faunique de Sept-Îles-Port-Cartier *reserve* Québec 33 C3 50 30N 67 30W
Réserve Faunique des Lacs-Albanel-Mistassini-et-Waconichi *reserve* Québec 33 B3 50 10N 74 20W
Réserve Faunique des Laurentides *reserve* Québec 37 P8 47 50N 71 47W
Réserve Faunique de Cap-Chat *reserve* Québec 33 C2 48 50N 66 50W
Réserve Faunique du Saint-Maurice *reserve* Québec 37 N8 47 08N 73 18W
Réserve Faunique la Vérendrye *reserve* Québec 37 J8 47 08N 73 18W
Réserve Faunique Mastigouche *reserve* Québec 37 N7 46 35N 73 47W
Réserve Faunique Rouge-Matawin *reserve* Québec 37 M7 46 52N 74 35W
Réserve Frontenac *reserve* Québec 37 P6 45 52N 71 17W
Réservoir Baskatong *res.* Québec 37 L7 47 00N 76 00W
Réservoir Blanc *res.* Québec 37 N8 47 49N 73 06W
Réservoir Cabonga *res.* Québec 37 K8 47 31N 76 45W
Réservoir Caniapiscau *res.* Québec 32 C3 54 10N 69 10W

Réservoir de La Grande 2 *res.* Québec **33** A3 53 38N 78 40W
Réservoir de La Grande 3 *res.* Québec **32** A3 54 10N 72 30W
Réservoir de La Grande 4 *res.* Québec **32** B3 53 59N 72 50W
Réservoir Dozois *res.* Québec **37** J8 47 30N 77 26W
Réservoir du Poisson Blanc *res.* Québec **37** L7 46 05N 75 50W
Réservoir Evans *res.* Québec **33** A3 50 45N 76 50W
Réservoir Gavin *res.* Québec **37** L9 48 35N 75 15W
Réservoir Gouin *res.* Québec **33** B2 48 30N 74 00W
Réservoir Laforge 1 *res.*Québec **32** B3 54 20N 71 50W
Réservoir Laforge 2 *res.* Québec **32** B3 54 30N 71 20W
Réservoir Manic 2 *res.* Québec **33** C2 49 30N 68 25W
Réservoir Manic 3 *res.* Québec **33** C3 51 30N 67 58W
Réservoir Manicouagan *res.* Québec **33** C3 51 00N 58 00W
Réservoir Opinaca *res.* Québec **33** A3 52 30N 75 30W
Réservoir Outardes 4 *res.* Québec **33** C3 50 20N 69 20W
Réservoir Pipmuacan *res.* Québec **33** B2 49 30N 70 10W
Réservoir Soscumica-Matagami *res.* Québec **33** A3 50 10N 77 32W
Réservoir Taureau *res.* Québec **37** N7 46 47N 73 47W
Resolute Northwest Territories **45** N5 74 40N 95 00W
Resolution Island Northwest Territories **45** T3 61 18N 64 53W
Restigouche *admin.* New Brunswick **31** A2 47 40N 67 10W
Restigouche River New Brunswick **31** A2 47 35N 67 30W
Reston Manitoba **39** A1 49 33N 101 05W
Revelstoke British Columbia **43** E2 51 02N 118 12W
Revelstoke, Lake British Columbia **43** E2 51 32N 118 40W
Rexton New Brunswick **31** F7 46 41N 64 56W
Ribstone Creek Alberta **41** C2 52 10N 111 55W
Rice Lake Ontario **36** H5 44 12N 78 10W
Richard Collinson Inlet Northwest Territories **44** J5 72 45N 113 55W
Richards Island Northwest Territories **44** E4 69 20N 134 30W
Richardson Mountains Yukon Territory/Northwest Territories **44** D4 67 50N 137 00W
Richardson River Alberta **41** C3 58 15N 110 W
Rich, Cape Ontario **38** B3 44 43N 80 39W
Richibucto New Brunswick **31** F7 46 42N 64 54W
Richmond British Columbia **42** H4 49 09N 123 09W
Richmond Québec **37** O6 45 40N 72 10W
Richmond *admin.* Nova Scotia **31** F7 45 40N 60 40W
Richmond *admin.* Québec **37** O6 45 30N 72 10W
Richmond Hill *tn.* Ontario **46** C2 43 53N 79 26W
Rideau River Ontario **35** F1 44 50N 76 10W
Rideau River and Canal Ontario **47** K2 45 16N 75 43W
Ridgetown Ontario **36** E3 42 26N 81 54W
Riding Mountain Manitoba **39** A2 50 40N 100 40W
Riding Mountain National Park Manitoba **39** A2 50 50N 100 30W
Rigolet Newfoundland **30** C3 54 11N 58 26W
Rimbey Alberta **41** C2 52 38N 114 14W
Rimouski Québec **33** C2 48 27N 68 32W
Riondel British Columbia **43** E1 49 46N 116 51W
Riou Lake Saskatchewan **40** B3 59 00N 106 30W
Ripley Ontario **38** A3 44 04N 81 34W
Ritchot *admin.* Manitoba **48** D1 49 44N 97 07W
River Herbert *tn.* Nova Scotia **31** F7 45 42N 64 25W
River John *tn.* Nova Scotia **31** F7 45 44N 63 03W
Rivers *tn.* Manitoba **39** A2 50 02N 100 14W
Riverside Ontario **52** F2 42 20N 82 56W
Riverside-Albert New Brunswick **31** F7 45 40N 64 40W
Rivers Inlet British Columbia **43** C2 51 30N 127 30W
Riverton Manitoba **39** B2 51 00N 97 00W
Rivière Aguanus *r.* Québec **33** D3 51 05N 62 02W
Rivière à la Baleine *r.* Québec **32** C4 57 54N 67 40W
Rivière Arnaud *r.* Québec **32** B4 59 37N 72 55W
Rivière Ashuapmushuan *r.* Québec **33** B2 49 22N 73 25W
Rivière aux Feuilles *r.* Québec **32** B4 57 45N 73 00W
Rivière aux Mélèzes *r.* Québec **32** B4 56 50N 72 45W
Rivière aux Outardes *r.* Québec **33** C3 51 38N 69 55W
Rivière-aux-Rats *tn.* Québec **37** O8 47 11N 72 52W
Rivière Bécancour *r.* Québec **37** O7 46 15N 72 20W
Rivière Bell *r.* Québec **33** A2 49 30N 77 30W
Rivière Betsiamites *r.* Québec **33** C2 49 27N 69 30W
Rivière Blanche *r.* Québec **47** K3 45 32N 75 38W
Rivière Broadback *r.* Québec **33** A3 51 15N 77 42W
Rivière Caniapiscau *r.* Québec **32** C4 56 38N 69 15W
Rivière Capitachouane *r.* Québec **37** K8 47 42N 76 49W
Rivière Casapédia *r.* Québec **33** C2 48 45N 66 20Wc
Rivière Chaudière *r.* Québec **37** P7 46 30N 71 10W
Rivière Chicoutimi *r.* Québec **37** P9 48 11N 71 29W
Rivière Chukotat *r.* Québec **32** A5 61 02N 77 15W
Rivière Coats *r.* Québec **32** A4 55 30N 77 10W
Rivière Coulogne *r.* Québec **37** J7 46 44N 77 10W
Rivière d'Argent *r.* Québec **37** L7 46 59N 75 00W
Rivière Delay *r.* Québec **32** B4 56 50N 71 10W
Rivière de Pas *r.* Québec **32** C4 55 12N 65 35W
Rivière de Rupert *r.* Québec **33** A3 51 22N 78 30W
Rivière des Mille Îles *r.* Québec **47** M5 45 37N 73 47W
Rivière des Outaouais *(Ottawa River)* Ontario/Québec **36** K6 45 35N 76 30W
Rivière des Prairies *r.* Québec **47** N5 45 36N 73 37W
Rivière du Chêne *r.* Québec **47** M5 45 34N 73 59W
Rivière du Gué *r.* Québec **32** B4 56 48N 72 05W
Rivière du Lièvre *r.* Québec **37** L6 45 50N 75 39W
Rivière-du-Loup *admin.* Québec **37** R8 47 50N 69 20W
Rivière-du-Loup *tn.* Québec **37** R8 47 49N 69 32W
Rivière Dumoine *r.* Québec **36** H7 46 20N 77 52W
Rivière du Petit Mécatina *(Little Mecatina River)* Québec **36** H7 46 20N 77 52W
Rivière du Sable *r.* Québec **32** C4 55 28N 68 20W
Rivière du Vieux Comptoir *r.* Québec **33** A3 52 33N 78 40W
Rivière Eastmain *r.* Québec **33** B3 52 20N 77 52W
Rivière False *r.* Québec **32** C4 57 40N 68 30W
Rivière Ford *r.* Québec **32** C4 58 40N 58 20W
Rivière Gatineau *r.* Québec **37** L6 45 58N 75 52W
Rivière George *r.* Québec **32** C4 57 50N 65 30W
Rivière Harricana *r.* Québec **33** A3 50 40N 79 20W
Rivière Innuksuac *r.* Québec **32** A4 58 40N 77 50W
Rivière Kanaaupscow *r.* Québec **32** A3 54 20N 76 10W
Rivière Kitchigama *r.* Québec **33** A3 50 50N 78 30W
Rivière Kogaluc *r.* Québec **32** A4 59 33N 77 18W
Rivière Koksoak *r.* Québec **32** C4 57 50N 69 10W
Rivière Koroc *r.* Québec **32** C4 58 50N 65 20W
Rivière Kovik *r.* Québec **32** A5 61 50N 77 20W
Rivière Magpie *r.* Québec **33** D3 50 42N 64 25W
Rivière Malbaie *r.* Québec **37** Q9 48 01N 70 40W
Rivière Manicouagan *r.* Québec **33** C3 50 51N 68 55W
Rivière Manitou *r.* Québec **33** C3 51 08N 65 20W
Rivière Manouane *r.* Québec **33** B2 49 45N 70 59W
Rivière Maquatua *r.* Québec **33** A3 53 05N 78 40W
Rivière Mariet *r.* Québec **32** A4 59 05N 77 30W
Rivière Matapédia *r.* Québec **33** C2 48 30N 67 30W
Rivière Matawin *r.* Québec **37** N7 46 55N 73 39W
Rivière-Matawin *tn.* Québec **37** O7 46 54N 72 55W
Rivière Mégiscane *r.* Québec **33** A2 48 17N 76 50W
Rivière Métabetchouane *r.* Québec **37** O8 47 59N 72 05W
Rivière Mistassibi *r.* Québec **33** B3 50 20N 72 15W
Rivière Mistassibi Nord-Est *r.* Québec **33** B3 50 01N 71 59W
Rivière Mistassini *r.* Québec **33** B2 49 50N 72 40W
Rivière Moisie *r.* Québec **33** C3 50 52N 66 33W
Rivière Montmorency *r.* Québec **37** P8 47 19N 71 12W
Rivière Mucaliq *r.* Québec **32** C4 58 15N 67 30W
Rivière Nabisipi *r.* Québec **33** D3 50 59N 62 32W
Rivière Nastapoca *r.* Québec **32** A4 56 52N 76 10W
Rivière Natashquan *(Natashquan River)* Québec **33** D3 51 12N 61 35W
Rivière Nicolet *r.* Québec **37** O7 46 14N 72 35W
Rivière Nipissis *r.* Québec **33** C3 50 30N 66 05W
Rivière Noire *r.* Québec **37** J7 46 40N 77 23W
Rivière Nottaway *r.* Québec **33** A3 51 05N 77 35W
Rivière Olomane *r.* Québec **33** D3 50 58N 60 35W
Rivière Opinaca *r.* Québec **33** A3 52 20N 78 00W
Rivière Pentecôte *r.* Québec **33** C3 50 18N 67 35W
Rivière Péribonca *r.* Québec **33** B2 48 58N 71 30W
Rivière Pons *r.* Québec **32** C4 55 05N 69 50W
Rivière Pontax *r.* Québec **33** A3 51 35N 78 05W
Rivière Racine de Bouleau *r.* Québec **33** C3 52 00N 68 40W
Rivière Richelieu *r.* Québec **37** N6 45 03N 73 25W
Rivière Romaine *r.* Québec **33** D3 51 40N 63 40W
Rivière Saguenay *r.* Québec **33** B2 48 20N 70 43W
Rivière Saint-Augustin *r.* Québec **32** E3 51 58N 60 10W
Rivière Sainte-Anne *r.* Québec **37** O7 46 40N 72 11W
Rivière Sainte-Anne *r.* Québec **37** Q8 47 05N 70 05W
Rivière Saint-François *r.* Québec **37** O6 45 52N 72 21W
Rivière Saint-Jean *r.* Québec **33** D3 51 08N 64 08W
Rivière Saint-Marguerite *r.* Québec **33** C3 51 20N 56 59W
Rivière Saint-Maurice *r.* Québec **33** B2 47 55N 73 46W
Rivière Saint-Paul *r.* Québec **32** E3 51 55N 57 59W
Rivière Sakami *r.* Québec **33** B3 53 05N 74 05W
Rivière Sérigny *r.* Québec **32** C4 55 30N 69 59W
Rivière Témiscamie *r.* Québec **33** B3 51 15N 72 40W
Rivière Vachon *r.* Québec **32** B5 60 40N 72 25W
Rivière Vermillon *r.* Québec **37** N8 47 19N 73 32W
Rivière-Verte *tn.* New Brunswick **31** A2 47 19N 68 09W
Rivière Wacouna *r.* Québec **33** C3 50 57N 66 05W
Rivière Wheeler *r.* Québec **32** C4 56 25N 67 35W
Rivière Yamaska *r.* Québec **37** N6 45 40N 73 00W
Robert's Arm *tn.* Newfoundland **31** C2 49 29N 55 49W
Roberts Bank Superport British Columbia **42** H4 49 04N 123 28W
Roberts Creek *tn.* British Columbia **42** H4 49 25N 123 37W
Roberval Québec **37** O9 48 31N 72 16W
Roblin Manitoba **39** A2 51 15N 101 20W
Robson, Mount British Columbia **43** E2 53 08N 118 18W
Rock Bay *tn.* British Columbia **42** G5 50 18N 125 31W
Rockcliffe Park Ontario **47** K2 45 27N 75 39W
Rock Forest *tn.* Québec **37** O6 45 22N 72 00W
Rockglen Saskatchewan **40** B1 49 11N 105 57W
Rockland Ontario **37** L6 45 33N 75 18W
Rock Point Provincial Park Ontario **38** C1 42 50N 79 30W
Rockwood Ontario **38** B2 43 37N 80 10W
Rocky Bay *I.R.* Ontario **34** C2 49 26N 88 08W
Rocky Harbour *tn.* Newfoundland **31** C2 49 39N 57 55W
Rocky Island Lake Ontario **35** D2 46 55N 83 04W
Rocky Lake Nova Scotia **47** P7 44 45N 63 36W
Rocky Mountain House Alberta **41** C2 52 24N 114 52W
Rocky Mountains Canada/U.S.A. **10** K4/N1
Rocky Mountains Forest Reserve Alberta **41** B2 52 30N 116 30W
Rocky Mountain Trench British Columbia **43** C3 57 50N 126 00W
Rocky Saugeen River Ontario **38** B3 44 13N 80 52W
Roddickton Newfoundland **31** C3 50 52N 56 08W
Rodney Ontario **36** E3 42 34N 81 41W
Roes Welcome Sound Northwest Territories **45** O3 63 30N 87 30W
Rogers Pass British Columbia **43** E2 51 23N 117 23W
Rogersville New Brunswick **31** A2 46 44N 65 28W
Romaine River Newfoundland **30** B3 52 30N 64 00W
Rondeau Provincial Park Ontario **36** E3 42 17N 81 51W
Root River Ontario **34** B3 50 50N 91 40W
Rorketon Manitoba **39** B2 51 24N 99 35W
Roseau River Manitoba **39** B1 49 10N 96 50W
Rose Blanche Newfoundland **31** C2 47 37N 58 41W
Rosedale Ontario **38** D3 44 34N 78 47W
Rose Point British Columbia **42** B2 54 11N 131 39W
Rosetown Saskatchewan **40** B2 51 34N 107 59W
Rose Valley *tn.* Saskatchewan **40** C2 52 19N 103 49W
Ross Bay Junction *tn.* Newfoundland **30** A3 53 03N 66 12W
Rossburn Manitoba **39** A2 50 40N 100 49W
Rosseau Ontario **36** G6 45 16N 79 39W
Rosseau, Lake Ontario **36** G6 45 10N 79 35W
Rossignol, Lake Nova Scotia **31** E6 44 10N 65 20W
Ross Island Manitoba **39** B2 54 20N 97 50W
Rossland British Columbia **43** E1 49 05N 117 48W
Rossport Ontario **35** C2 48 50N 87 31W
Ross River *tn.* Yukon Territory **44** E3 62 02N 132 28W
Rosswood British Columbia **42** C2 54 49N 128 42W
Rosthern Saskatchewan **40** B2 52 40N 106 20W
Rothesay New Brunswick **31** E7 45 23N 66 00W
Rougemont Québec **27** 45 26N 73 03W
Rouge River Ontario **46** D2 43 52N 79 15W
Rouge Valley Park Ontario **46** D2 43 50N 79 13W
Rouleau Saskatchewan **40** C2 50 12N 104 56W
Round Pond Newfoundland **31** C2 48 10N 55 50W
Rouyn-Noranda Québec **33** A2 48 15N 79 00W
Rowley Island Northwest Territories **45** Q4 69 06N 77 52W
Russell Manitoba **39** A2 50 47N 101 17W
Russell, Cape Northwest Territories **44** H6 75 15N 117 35W
Russell Point *c.* Northwest Territories **44** J5 73 30N 115 00W

S

Saanich British Columbia **42** H4 48 28N 123 22W
Sabine Peninsula Northwest Territories **44** K6 76 20N 109 30W
Sable, Cape Nova Scotia **31** A1 43 23N 65 37W
Sable Island Nova Scotia **11** X1 43 57N 60 00W
Sable River *tn.* Nova Scotia **31** E6 43 50N 65 05W
Sachigo *I.R.* Ontario **34** B3 53 50N 92 10W
Sachigo Lake Ontario **34** B3 53 49N 92 08W
Sachigo River Ontario **34** B3 54 50N 90 50W
Sachs Harbour *tn.* Northwest Territories **44** F5 71 59N 125 13W
Sackville New Brunswick **31** F7 45 54N 64 23W
Sacré-Coeur Québec **37** R9 48 26N 68 35W
Saglek Bay Newfoundland **30** B4 58 30N 63 00W
Saglek Fiord Newfoundland **30** B4 58 29N 63 15W
Saguenay *admin.* Québec **37** R9 48 20N 70 00W
Saint-Agapit Québec **37** P7 46 34N 71 26W
St. Albans Newfoundland **31** C2 47 52N 55 51W
St. Albert Alberta **48** F5 53 38N 113 38W
Saint-Ambroise Québec **33** B2 48 33N 71 20W
St. Andrews New Brunswick **31** A2 45 05N 67 04W
Saint-Anselm Québec **27** 46 37N 70 58W
St. Anthony Newfoundland **30** C3 51 22N 55 35W
Saint-Antoine New Brunswick **31** F7 46 20N 64 50W
St. Antoine Québec **37** M6 45 47N 74 01W
Saint-Apollinaire Québec **27** 46 37N 71 29W
St. Barbe Newfoundland **31** C3 51 13N 56 45 W
St. Bernard's Newfoundland **31** D2 47 32N 54 47W
St. Boniface Manitoba **48** D2 49 53N 97 06W
St. Bride's Newfoundland **31** D2 46 55N 54 10W
St. Catharines Ontario **38** C2 43 10N 79 15W
Saint-Césaire Québec **27** 45 25N 73 01W
St. Charles Manitoba **48** C2 49 53N 97 17W
St. Clair, Lake Ontario Canada/Michigan U.S.A. **36** D3 42 28N 82 40W
St. Croix River New Brunswick **31** A2 45 30N 67 40W
Saint-Donat Québec **37** M7 46 19N 74 15W
Ste. Agathe des Monts Québec **37** M7 46 03N 74 19W
Ste. Anne Manitoba **39** B1 49 40N 96 40W
Ste. Anne de Beaupré Québec **37** O8 47 02N 70 58W
Sainte-Anne-de-Bellevue Québec **47** M4 45 25N 73 56W
Sainte-Anne-des-Monts Québec **33** C2 49 07N 66 29W
Sainte-Anne-du-Lac Québec **37** L7 46 54N 75 20W
Sainte-Catherine Québec **47** N4 45 25N 73 35W
Sainte-Claire Québec **37** Q7 46 37N 70 51W
Sainte-Croix Québec **37** P7 46 38N 71 43W
Sainte-Eustache Québec **47** M5 45 33N 73 54W
Ste.-Foy Québec **37** P7 46 47N 71 18W
Sainte-Geneviève Québec **47** M4 45 28N 73 54W
St. Eleanors Prince Edward Island **31** F7 46 30N 63 50W
Saint Elias Mountains Yukon Territory Canada/Alaska U.S.A. **44** D3 60 12N 140 57W
Sainte-Marie Québec **37** P7 46 26N 71 00W
Sainte-Rose Québec **47** M5 45 36N 73 47W
Ste. Rose du Lac Manitoba **39** B2 51 04N 99 31W
Sainte-Thérèse Québec **47** M5 45 38N 73 50W
St.-Félicien Québec **33** B2 48 38N 72 29W
Saint-Felix-de-Valois Québec **27** 46 10N 73 26W
St. Francis Harbour *tn.* Nova Scotia **31** F7 45 30N 61 20W
St. George New Brunswick **31** A2 45 08N 66 50W
St. George's Newfoundland **31** C2 48 26N 58 29W
Saint-Georges Québec **37** O7 46 38N 72 35W
St.-Georges Québec **37** Q7 46 08N 70 40W
St. Georges Bay Newfoundland **31** C2 48 28N 59 16W
St. Georges Bay Nova Scotia **31** F7 45 40N 61 40W
St. Germain Manitoba **48** D2 49 46N
Saint-Gilles Québec **27** 46 29N 71 23W
Saint-Henri Québec **27** 46 42N 71 04W
Saint-Hubert Québec **47** O5 45 31N 73 25W
Saint-Hyacinthe Québec **37** O6 45 38N 72 57W
St. Ignace Island Ontario **35** C2 48 45N 87 55W
St. Jacobs Ontario **38** B2 43 32N 80 33W
Saint-Jacques New Brunswick **31** A2 47 20N 68 28W
St. James, Cape British Columbia **42** B2 51 58N 131 00W
St. Jean Baptiste Manitoba **39** B1 49 15N 97 20W
Saint-Jean-Port-Joli Québec **37** O8 47 13N 70 16W
Saint-Jean-sur-Richelieu Québec **37** N6 45 18N 73 18W
St.-Jerôme Québec **37** M6 45 47N 74 01W
Saint John New Brunswick **31** E7 45 16N 66 03W
Saint John *admin.* New Brunswick **31** E7 45 20N 65 50W
St. John *r.* New Brunswick **31** A2 47 00N 68 00W
St. John Bay Newfoundland **31** C3 50 55N 57 09W
St. John, Cape Newfoundland **31** C2 50 00N 55 32W
St. John, Lake Ontario **38** C3 44 38N 79 19W
St. John's Newfoundland **31** D2 47 34N 52 43W
St. Joseph New Brunswick **31** F7 45 59N 64 30W
St-Joseph-de-la-Beauce Québec **27** 46 19N 70 52W
St. Joseph Island Ontario **37** C7 46 13N 83 57W
St. Joseph, Lake Ontario **34** B3 51 05N 90 35W
Saint-Jovite Québec **27** 46 07N 74 36W
Saint-Lambert Québec **47** O5 45 30N 73 29W
Saint-Laurent Québec **47** N5 45 30N 73 43W
St. Lawrence, Cape Nova Scotia **31** F7 47 10N 60 40W
St. Lawrence Seaway Canada/U.S.A. **37** L5/M5 44 38N 78 34W
St. Lawrence River *(Fleuve Saint-Laurent)* Québec **31** C2 46 55N 55 24W
St. Léonard New Brunswick **31** A1 47 10N 67 55W
Saint-Léonard Québec **47** N5 45 34N 73 36W
St. Lewis Newfoundland **30** C3 52 22N 55 41W
St. Lewis River Newfoundland **30** C3 52 20N 56 50W
Saint-Louis-de-Kent New Brunswick **31** E7 46 50N 65 00W
St. Lunaire Newfoundland **30** C3 51 30N 55 29W
St. Malo Manitoba **39** B1 49 20N 96 55W
St. Margarets Bay Nova Scotia **31** F6 44 30N 64 50W
St. Martin, Lake Manitoba **39** B2 51 40N 98 20W
St. Martins New Brunswick **31** E7 45 20N 65 30W
St. Marys Ontario **38** A2 43 15N 81 09W
St. Mary, Cape Nova Scotia **31** E6 44 10N 66 10W
St. Mary's Newfoundland **31** D2 46 55N 53 34W
St. Mary's Bay Newfoundland **31** D2 46 50N 53 45W
St. Mary's Bay Nova Scotia **31** E6 44 20N 66 10W
St. Mary's River Nova Scotia **31** F7 45 20N 62 30W
St.-Maurice *admin.* Québec **37** M8 47 40N 74 30W
Saint-Michel-des-Saints Québec **37** N7 46 40N 73 55W
St. Norbert Manitoba **48** D2 49 46N 97 12W
Saint-Pacôme Québec **37** R8 47 24N 69 58W
St.-Pamphile Québec **37** R7 46 58N 69 48W
Saint-Pascal Québec **37** R8 47 32N 69 48W
St. Paul Alberta **41** C2 53 59N 111 17W
St. Paul Junction Alberta **48** G5 53 37N 113 20W
St. Peters Nova Scotia **31** F7 45 40N 60 53W
St. Peters Prince Edward Island **31** F7 46 26N 62 35W
Saint-Pie Québec **27** 45 31N 72 55W
St. Pierre-Jolys Manitoba **39** B1 49 28N 96 58W
Saint-Prosper Québec **37** Q7 46 12N 70 29W
Saint-Quentin New Brunswick **31** A2 47 30N 67 20W
Saint-Raymond Québec **37** P7 46 54N 71 50W
Saint-Rémi Québec **27** 45 15N 73 37W
St.-Romauld Québec **37** P7 46 52N 71 49W
Saint-Siméon Québec **37** R8 47 50N 69 55W
St. Stephen New Brunswick **31** A2 45 12N 67 18W
St. Stephens Newfoundland **31** D2 46 47N 53 37W
St. Theresa Point *tn.* Manitoba **39** C2 53 45N 94 50W
St. Thomas Ontario **38** A1 42 46N 81 12W
Saint-Tite Québec **37** O7 46 44N 72 34W
Saint-Victor Québec **27** 46 09N 70 55W
St. Walburg Saskatchewan **40** B2 53 38N 109 12W
Sakami Québec **33** A3 53 50N 76 10W
Salaberry-de-Valleyfield Québec **37** M6 45 16N 74 11W
Salisbury New Brunswick **31** E7 46 02N 65 03W
Salisbury Island Northwest Territories **45** Q3 63 10N 77 20W
Salluit Québec **32** A5 62 20N 75 40W
Salmo British Columbia **43** E1 49 11N 117 16W
Salmon Arm *tn.* British Columbia **43** E2 50 41N 119 18W
Salmon Inlet British Columbia **42** H4 49 39N 123 47W
Salmon River British Columbia **43** D2 54 27N 123 34W
Salmon River New Brunswick **31** A2 46 10N 65 50W
Salmon River *tn.* Nova Scotia **31** E6 44 10N 66 10W
Saltcoats Saskatchewan **40** C2 51 03N 102 12W
Saltspring Island British Columbia **42** H4 48 50N 123 30W
Sambro, Cape Nova Scotia **31** F6 44 30N 63 30W
Sandilands Provincial Forest Manitoba **39** B1 49 30N 96 00W
Sandspit British Columbia **42** B2 53 14N 131 50W
Sandy Bay *tn.* Saskatchewan **40** C3 55 30N 102 10W
Sandy Lake Newfoundland **31** C2 49 20N 56 50W
Sandy Lake Nova Scotia **47** P6 44 44N 63 40W
Sandy Lake Ontario **34** B3 53 02N 93 00W
Sandy Lake *I.R.* Ontario **34** B3 53 04N 93 20W
Sanikiluaq Northwest Territories **45** Q2 56 32N 79 14W
San Juan River British Columbia **42** H4 48 37N 124 20W
Sardis British Columbia **42** H4 49 07N 121 57W
Sarnia Ontario **36** D3 42 58N 82 23W
Sasaginnigak Lake Manitoba **39** B2 51 30N 95 30W
Sasamat Lake British Columbia **46** G4 49 19N 122 52W
Saskatchewan *province* **40**
Saskatchewan River Manitoba/Saskatchewan **40** C2 53 50N 103 10W
Saskatoon Saskatchewan **40** B2 52 10N 106 40W
Saturna Island British Columbia **42** H4 48 47N 123 07W
Sauble Falls Provincial Park Ontario **38** A3 44 40N 81 15W
Sauble River Ontario **38** A3 44 36N 81 09W
Saugeen River Ontario **38** A3 44 23N 81 18W
Sault Ste. Marie Ontario **36** B7 46 31N 84 20W
Saunders Lake Alberta **48** G4 53 18N 113 29W
Savant Lake Ontario **34** B3 50 30N 90 25W
Savant Lake *tn.* Ontario **34** B3 50 14N 90 43W
Sawbill Newfoundland **30** A3 53 37N 66 21W
Sayward British Columbia **43** C2 50 19N 125 58W
Scarborough *bor.* Metropolitan Toronto Ontario **46** D2 43 44N 79 16W
Scaterie Island Nova Scotia **31** G7 46 00N 59 40W
Schefferville *(Kawawachikamach)* Québec **32** C3 54 50N 67 00W
Schreiber Ontario **35** C2 48 48N 87 17W
Schultz Lake Northwest Territories **45** M3 64 45N 97 30W
Scotsburn Nova Scotia **31** F7 45 40N 62 51W
Scott Island British Columbia **42** C2 50 48N 128 38W
Scott Lake Saskatchewan **40** B3 59 50N 106 30W
Scugog Island Ontario **38** D3 44 10N 78 52W
Scugog, Lake Ontario **38** D3 44 10N 78 51W
Scugog River Ontario **38** D3 44 16N 78 46W
Seaforth Ontario **38** A2 43 03N 81 24W
Sea Island British Columbia **46** F3 49 11N 123 11W
Seal Cove *tn.* Newfoundland **31** C2 47 30N 56 00W
Seal Cove *tn.* Newfoundland **31** C2 49 56N 56 23W
Seal Cove *tn.* Nova Scotia **31** E6 44 38N 66 52W
Seal Harbour *tn.* New Brunswick **31** F7 45 10N 61 30W
Seal Lake Newfoundland **30** B3 54 20N 61 40W
Seal River Manitoba **39** B3 58 50N 97 00W
Sechelt British Columbia **42** H4 49 28N 123 46W
Sechelt Peninsula British Columbia **42** H4 49 45N 123 58W
Seine River Manitoba **48** D2 49 46N 97 02W
Selkirk Manitoba **39** B2 50 10N 96 52W
Selkirk Mountains British Columbia **43** E2 51 40N 118 20W
Selkirk Provincial Park Ontario **38** C1 42 50N 80 00W
Selwyn Lake Northwest Territories **44** L3 60 05N 104 25W
Selwyn Mountains Yukon Territory **44** E3 64 30N 134 50W
Semchuck Trail Saskatchewan **40** B3 57 35N 109 20W
Senneterre Québec **37** J9 48 24N 77 16W
Sentinel Peak British Columbia **43** D2 54 56N 121 59W
Sept-Îles *tn.* Québec **33** C3 50 10N 66 00W
Serpentine British Columbia **46** G3 49 06N 122 46W
Seseganaga Lake Ontario **34** B3 50 00N 90 28W
Setting Lake Manitoba **39** B3 55 10N 98 50W
Seven Islands Bay Newfoundland **30** B4 59 25N 63 45W
70 Mile House British Columbia **43** D2 51 21N 121 25W
Severn Bridge *tn.* Ontario **38** C3 44 46N 79 20W
Severn Lake Ontario **34** B3 53 54N 90 48W
Severn River Ontario **34** C4 55 30N 88 30W
Severn Sound Ontario **38** C3 44 47N 79 51W
Sexsmith Alberta **41** B3 55 21N 118 47W
Seymour Creek British Columbia **46** F4 49 18N 123 01W
Seymour Inlet British Columbia **43** C2 51 03N 127 05W
Shabaqua Ontario **35** C2 48 35N 89 54W
Shabo Newfoundland **30** A3 53 19N 66 12W
Shabogamo Lake Newfoundland **30** A3 53 15N 66 30W
Shag Harbour *tn.* Nova Scotia **31** E6 43 30N 65 40W
Shakespeare Ontario **38** B2 43 22N 80 50W
Shaler Mountains Northwest Territories **44** J5 72 10N 111 00W
Shallow Lake *tn.* Ontario **38** A3 44 38N 81 06W
Shamattawa Manitoba **39** C3 55 51N 92 05W
Shamattawa River Ontario **34** C3 54 05N 85 50W
Shapio Lake Newfoundland **30** B3 55 00N 61 18W
Sharon Ontario **38** C3 44 06N 79 26W
Shaunavon Saskatchewan **40** B1 49 40N 108 25W
Shawanaga Ontario **38** B4 45 32N 81 18W
Shawanaga Inlet Ontario **38** B4 45 26N 80 24W

Shawanaga Island Ontario 38 B4 45 16N 80 33W
Shawinigan Québec 37 O7 46 33N 72 45W
Shawinigan Sud Québec 37 O7 46 33N 72 45W
Shawnigan Lake tn. British Columbia 42 H4 48 38N 123 39W
Shawville Québec 37 K6 45 36N 76 30W
Shebandowan Ontario 35 B2 48 38N 90 04W
Shediac New Brunswick 31 F7 46 13N 64 35W
Sheet Harbour tn. Nova Scotia 31 F6 44 56N 62 31W
Shefford admin. Québec 37 O6 45 30N 72 45W
Shelburne Nova Scotia 31 E6 43 45N 65 20W
Shelburne Ontario 38 B3 44 05N 80 13W
Shelburne admin. Nova Scotia 31 E6 43 50N 65 30W
Sheldon Creek Ontario 38 B4 44 05N 80 06W
Shellbrook Saskatchewan 40 B2 53 14N 106 24W
Shelsey River British Columbia 42 B3 58 33N 132 02W
Shelter Bay tn. British Columbia 43 E2 50 38N 117 59W
Shepherd Bay Northwest Territories 45 N4 65 00N 90 00W
Sherbrooke Nova Scotia 31 F7 45 10N 61 58W
Sherbrooke Québec 37 P6 45 24N 71 54W
Sherbrooke admin. Québec 37 O6 45 20N 72 10W
Sherbrooke Lake British Columbia 43 E1 49 40N 64 40W
Sherridon Manitoba 39 A3 55 07N 101 05W
Sherwood Park tn. Alberta 48 G5 53 31N 113 19W
Sheshatsheits Newfoundland 30 B3 53 30N 60 10W
Shibogama Lake Ontario 34 C3 53 35N 88 15W
Shipiskan Lake Newfoundland 30 B3 54 39N 62 19W
Shippagan New Brunswick 31 B2 47 45N 64 44W
Shirleys Bay Ontario 47 J2 45 22N 75 54W
Shoal Bay tn. Newfoundland 31 D2 49 41N 54 12W
Shoal Harbour tn. Newfoundland 31 D2 48 11N 53 59W
Shoal Lake Ontario/Manitoba 34 D2 49 33N 95 01W
Shoal Lake tn. Manitoba 39 A2 50 28N 100 35W
Shubenacadie Nova Scotia 31 F7 45 05N 63 24W
Shubenacadie Grand Lake Nova Scotia 47 P7 44 53N 63 37W
Shubenacadie River Nova Scotia 31 F7 45 20N 63 30W
Shunacadie Nova Scotia 31 F7 46 00N 60 40W
Shuswap Lake British Columbia 43 E2 51 00N 119 00W
Sibbald Point Provincial Park Ontario 38 C3 44 15N 79 20W
Sibley p.p. Ontario 35 C2 48 10N 88 50W
Sicamous British Columbia 43 E2 50 50N 119 00W
Sidney British Columbia 42 H4 48 39N 123 25W
Sidney Bay Ontario 38 B1 45 24N 81 04W
Sifton Manitoba 39 A2 51 21N 100 09W
Sifton Pass British Columbia 43 C3 57 51N 126 17W
Sikanni Chief British Columbia 43 D3 57 11N 122 43W
Sikanni Chief River British Columbia 43 D3 57 16N 123 25W
Sillery Québec 37 P7 46 46N 71 15W
Silverthrone Mountain British Columbia 43 C2 51 30N 126 03W
Silvertip Mountain British Columbia 42 H4 49 09N 121 12W
Simcoe Ontario 38 B1 42 50N 80 19W
Simcoe admin. Ontario 38 C3 44 32N 79 54W
Simcoe, Lake Ontario 38 C3 44 23N 79 18W
Similkameen River British Columbia 42 H4 48 55N 119 25W
Simonette River Alberta 41 B2 54 25N 118 20W
Simpson Bay Northwest Territories 44 J4 69 00N 113 40W
Simpson Peninsula Northwest Territories 45 O4 68 34N 88 45W
Simpson Strait Northwest Territories 45 M4 68 27N 97 45W
Sioux Lookout Ontario 34 B3 50 07N 91 54W
Sioux Narrows Ontario 34 B2 49 23N 94 08W
Sipiwesk Manitoba 39 B3 55 27N 97 24W
Sipiwesk Lake Manitoba 39 B3 55 10N 98 50W
Sir Alexander, Mount British Columbia 43 D2 53 52N 120 25W
Sir James McBrien, Mount Yukon Territory 44 E3 62 15N 128 01W
Sir Wilfred Laurier, Mount British Columbia 43 E2 52 45N 119 40W
Sisipuk Lake Manitoba 39 A3 55 30N 101 40W
Sistonens Corners tn. Ontario 35 C2 48 35N 89 40W
Six Mile Lake Provincial Park Ontario 38 C3 44 50N 79 50W
Skagit Valley Recreation Area British Columbia 42 H4 49 06N 121 09W
Skeena Mountains British Columbia 42 C3 57 30N 129 59W
Skeena River British Columbia 42 C2 54 15N 129 15W
Skidegate British Columbia 42 B2 53 13N 132 02W
Skihist Mountain British Columbia 42 H5 50 12N 122 53W
Skownan Manitoba 39 B2 51 58N 99 35W
Slave Lake tn. Alberta 41 C3 55 17N 114 43W
Slave River Alberta/Northwest Territories 44 J3 60 30N 112 50W
Slocan British Columbia 43 E1 49 46N 117 28W
Slocan Lake British Columbia 43 E1 49 50N 117 20W
Smallwood Reservoir Alberta/Newfoundland 30 B3 54 10N 63 50W
Smeaton Saskatchewan 40 C2 53 30N 104 50W
Smith Alberta 41 C3 55 10N 114 02W
Smith Arm b. Northwest Territories 44 G4 66 15N 124 00W
Smith Bay Northwest Territories 45 Q6 77 12N 78 50W
Smithers British Columbia 43 C2 54 47N 127 10W
Smith Point Nova Scotia 31 F7 45 52N 63 25W
Smith River British Columbia 43 B3 59 56N 126 28W
Smiths Falls tn. Ontario 37 K5 44 45N 76 01W
Smithville Ontario 38 C2 43 06N 79 32W
Smokey Newfoundland 30 C3 54 28N 57 14W
Smoky, Cape Nova Scotia 31 F7 46 40N 60 20W
Smoky Lake tn. Alberta 41 C2 54 07N 112 28W
Smoky River Alberta 41 B3 55 10N 117 59W
Smooth Rock Falls tn. Ontario 35 D2 49 17N 81 38W
Smoothrock Lake Ontario 34 C3 50 30N 89 30W
Smoothstone Lake Saskatchewan 40 B2 54 40N 106 30W
Snake Creek Ontario 38 A3 44 19N 81 16W
Snake River Yukon Territory 44 E4 65 20N 133 30W
Snare Lakes tn. Northwest Territories 44 J3 64 10N 114 20W
Snegamook Lake Newfoundland 30 B3 54 33N 61 27W
Snowbird Lake Northwest Territories 45 L3 60 41N 102 56W
Snowdrift Northwest Territories 44 J3 62 24N 110 44W
Snow Lake tn. Manitoba 39 A2 54 56N 100 00W
Snug Harbour tn. Newfoundland 30 C3 52 53N 55 52W

Snug Harbour tn. Ontario 38 B4 45 22N 80 17W
Soldier Lake Nova Scotia 47 P7 44 49N 63 33W
Somerset Manitoba 39 B1 49 26N 98 39W
Somerset Island Northwest Territories 45 N5 73 15N 93 30W
Sonora Island British Columbia 42 G5 50 21N 125 13W
Sooke British Columbia 42 H4 48 20N 123 42W
Sorel Québec 37 N7 46 03N 73 06W
Soulanges admin. Québec 37 M6 45 15N 74 20W
Sounding Creek Alberta 41 C2 51 40N 111 05W
Sounding Lake Alberta 41 C2 52 08N 110 29W
Souris Manitoba 39 A1 49 38N 100 17W
Souris Prince Edward Island 31 F7 46 22N 62 16W
Souris River Manitoba/North Dakota U.S.A. 39 A1 49 30N 100 50W
Souris River Saskatchewan 40 C1 49 20N 103 30W
Southampton Ontario 38 A3 44 29N 81 22W
Southampton Island Northwest Territories 45 P3 64 50N 85 00W
South Aulatsivik Island Newfoundland 30 B4 56 46N 61 30W
South Bay tn. Ontario 38 B3 51 03N 92 45W
South Brookfield Nova Scotia 31 E6 44 23N 65 58W
Southend Saskatchewan 40 C3 56 20N 103 14W
Southern Indian Lake Manitoba 39 B3 57 00N 98 00W
Southey Saskatchewan 40 C2 50 57N 104 33W
Southgate River British Columbia 42 H5 50 54N 124 42W
South Gloucester Ontario 47 K2 45 17N 75 34W
South Henik Lake Northwest Territories 45 M3 61 30N 97 30W
South Knife River Manitoba 39 B3 58 20N 96 10W
South Maitland River Ontario 38 A2 43 39N 81 27W
South Moose Lake Manitoba 39 A2 53 40N 100 10W
South Moresby National Park Reserve British Columbia 42 B2 52 30N 130 40W
South Nahanni River Northwest Territories 44 F3 61 30N 123 22W
South Porcupine Ontario 35 D2 48 28N 81 13W
Southport Prince Edward Island 31 F7 46 10N 63 05W
South River tn. Ontario 36 G6 45 50N 79 23W
South Saskatchewan River Saskatchewan 40 A2 50 50N 110 00W
South Saugeen River Ontario 38 B3 44 00N 80 45W
South Seal River Manitoba 39 B3 58 00N 99 10W
South Twin Island Northwest Territories 34 E3 53 10N 79 50W
Southwest Miramichi River New Brunswick 31 A2 46 30N 66 50W
Spanish Ontario 36 D7 46 12N 82 12W
Spanish River Ontario 36 E7 46 32N 81 57W
Sparrow Lake Ontario 38 C3 44 47N 79 23W
Sparwood British Columbia 43 F1 49 55N 114 53W
Spatsizi Plateau Wilderness Park British Columbia 43 C3 57 30N 128 30W
Spear Harbour tn. Newfoundland 30 C3 52 25N 55 42W
Speed River Ontario 38 B2 43 29N 80 17W
Speers Saskatchewan 40 B2 52 43N 107 32W
Spence Bay tn. Northwest Territories 45 N4 69 30N 93 20W
Spicer Islands Northwest Territories 45 Q4 63 19N 71 52W
Spirit River tn. Alberta 41 B3 55 46N 118 51W
Spiritwood Saskatchewan 40 B2 53 24N 107 33W
Split, Cape Nova Scotia 31 F7 45 20N 64 30W
Split Lake Manitoba 39 B3 56 10N 95 50W
Split Lake tn. Manitoba 39 B3 56 16N 96 08W
Spotted Island Newfoundland 30 C3 53 31N 55 47W
Sprague Manitoba 39 B1 49 02N 95 36W
Springdale Newfoundland 31 C2 49 30N 56 04W
Springfield Nova Scotia 31 F6 44 37N 64 52W
Springfield Ontario 38 B1 42 49N 80 57W
Springfield admin. New Brunswick 31 A2 46 48N 96 57W
Springhill Nova Scotia 31 F7 45 40N 64 04W
Spring Water Provincial Park Ontario 38 C3 44 30N 79 45W
Sproat Lake British Columbia 42 G4 49 16N 125 05W
Spruce Grove Alberta 41 C2 53 32N 113 55W
Spruce Woods Provincial Forest Manitoba 39 B1 49 40N 99 40W
Spruce Woods Provincial Park Manitoba 39 B1 49 40N 99 10W
Spry Harbour tn. Nova Scotia 31 F6 44 50N 62 45W
Spuzzum British Columbia 42 H4 49 40N 121 25W
Squamish British Columbia 42 H4 49 42N 123 11W
Squamish River British Columbia 42 H4 49 45N 123 11W
Square Island Newfoundland 30 C3 52 45N 55 52W
Stanley New Brunswick 31 A2 46 17N 66 45W
Stanstead admin. Québec 37 O6 45 10N 72 10W
Star City Saskatchewan 40 C2 52 52N 104 20W
Stave Lake British Columbia 42 H4 49 21N 122 19W
Stayner Ontario 38 B3 44 25N 80 06W
Stefansson Island Northwest Territories 45 L5 73 20N 105 45W
Steinbach Manitoba 39 B1 49 32N 96 40W
Stellarton Nova Scotia 31 F7 45 34N 62 40W
Stephens Lake Manitoba 39 B3 56 30N 95 00W
Stephenville Newfoundland 31 C2 48 33N 57 32W
Stephenville Crossing Newfoundland 31 C2 48 30N 58 26W
Stettler Alberta 41 C2 52 19N 112 43W
Stevenson Lake Manitoba 39 B2 53 50N 95 50W
Stewart British Columbia 42 C3 55 57N 129 58W
Stewart Yukon Territory 44 D3 63 15N 139 15W
Stewart Crossing Yukon Territory 44 D3 63 60 37N 128 37W
Stewart River Yukon Territory 44 D3 63 40N 138 20W
Stewiacke Nova Scotia 31 F7 45 09N 63 22W
Stikine British Columbia 42 B2 57 46N 131 45W
Stikine Ranges mts. British Columbia 42 B3 57 00N 127 20W
Stikine River British Columbia/Alaska U.S.A. 42 C3 57 00N 132 00W
Stikine River Recreation Area British Columbia 42 C3 58 07N 129 35W
Stillwater British Columbia 42 H4 49 46N 124 19W
Stirling Alberta 41 C2 49 34N 112 30W
Stirling Ontario 37 J5 44 18N 77 33W
Stittsville Ontario 47 J2 45 16N 75 54W
Stokes Bay Ontario 38 A3 45 00N 81 23W
Stone Mountain Provincial Park British Columbia 43 D3 58 35N 124 40W
Stonewall Manitoba 39 B2 50 08N 97 20W
Stoney Creek tn. Ontario 38 C2 43 13N 79 46W
Stony Lake Manitoba 39 B3 58 50N 98 30W
Stony Lake Ontario 36 H5 44 33N 78 06W

Stony Mountain tn. Manitoba 39 B2 50 04N 97 14W
Stony Plain tn. Alberta 41 C2 53 32N 114 00W
Stony Rapids tn. Saskatchewan 40 B3 59 14N 105 48W
Storkerson Peninsula Northwest Territories 44 K5 72 30N 106 30W
Stormont, Dundas and Glengarry admin. Ontario 37 M6 45 10N 75 00W
Stormy Lake Ontario 34 B2 49 23N 92 18W
Stouffville Ontario 38 C2 43 59N 79 15W
Stoughton Saskatchewan 40 C1 49 40N 103 00W
Stout Lake Ontario 34 B3 52 08N 94 35W
Strasbourg Saskatchewan 40 C2 51 05N 104 58W
Stratford Ontario 38 B2 43 07N 81 00W
Strathcona Alberta 48 G5 53 31N 113 29W
Strathcona County Alberta 48 G5 53 33N 113 16W
Strathcona Provincial Park British Columbia 42 G4 49 40N 125 30W
Strathmore Alberta 41 C2 51 03N 113 23W
Strathnaver British Columbia 43 D2 53 21N 122 32W
Strathroy Ontario 38 A1 42 57N 81 40W
Streetsville Ontario 38 C2 43 25N 79 44W
Stuart Island tn. British Columbia 42 G5 50 22N 125 09W
Stuart Lake British Columbia 43 D2 54 35N 124 40W
Stuart River British Columbia 43 D2 54 10N 124 05W
Stupart River Manitoba 39 C3 56 00N 93 30W
Sturgeon Bay Manitoba 39 B2 51 50N 98 00W
Sturgeon Creek Manitoba 48 C2 49 56N 97 25W
Sturgeon Falls tn. Ontario 36 G7 46 22N 79 57W
Sturgeon Lake Alberta 41 B3 55 06N 117 32W
Sturgeon Lake Ontario 38 D3 50 00N 91 00W
Sturgeon Landing Saskatchewan 40 C2 54 18N 101 49W
Sturgeon Municipal District Alberta 48 F5 53 38N 113 30W
Sturgeon Point tn. Ontario 38 D3 44 28N 78 42W
Sturgeon River Alberta 48 F5 53 38N 113 38W
Sturgeon River Ontario 35 D2 47 00N 80 30W
Sturgeon River Ontario 36 G4 36N 79 46W
Sturgeon River Saskatchewan 40 B2 53 30N 106 20W
Sturgis Saskatchewan 40 C2 51 58N 102 32W
Styx River Ontario 38 B3 44 15N 80 58W
Sudbury Ontario 36 E7 46 30N 81 01W
Sudbury admin. Ontario 36 E7 47 10N 82 00W
Sudbury, Regional Municipality of Ontario 36 E7 46 32N 81 00W
Suggi Lake Saskatchewan 40 C2 54 20N 103 10W
Sullivan Bay tn. British Columbia 43 C2 50 55N 126 52W
Sullivan Lake Alberta 41 C2 52 00N 112 00W
Sultan Ontario 35 D2 47 36N 82 45W
Summer Beaver Ontario 34 C3 52 50N 88 30W
Summerford Newfoundland 31 D2 49 29N 54 47W
Summerland British Columbia 43 E1 49 35N 119 41W
Summerside Prince Edward Island 31 F7 46 24N 63 46W
Summerville Newfoundland 31 D2 48 27N 53 33W
Sunbury admin. New Brunswick 31 A2 45 50N 66 40W
Sundre Alberta 41 C2 51 48N 114 38W
Sundridge Ontario 36 G6 45 46N 79 24W
Sunnyside Newfoundland 31 D2 47 51N 53 55W
Superb Mountain British Columbia 42 H5 50 48N 124 41W
Superior, Lake Canada/U.S.A. 35 B2 48 00N 88 00W
Surrey British Columbia 42 H4 49 08N 122 50W
Sussex New Brunswick 31 E7 45 43N 65 32W
Sussex Corner New Brunswick 31 E7 45 40N 65 30W
Sutherland Saskatchewan 40 B2 52 10N 106 35W
Sutton Ontario 38 C3 44 18N 79 22W
Sutton Québec 37 O6 45 05N 72 36W
Sutton Lake Ontario 34 D3 54 15N 84 44W
Sutton River Ontario 34 D3 54 50N 84 30W
Svendsen Peninsula Northwest Territories 45 P6 77 45N 84 00W
Sverdrup Islands Northwest Territories 45 M6 79 00N 96 00W
Swan Hills Alberta 41 B2 54 45N 115 45W
Swan Hills tn. Alberta 41 B2 54 43N 115 24W
Swan Lake Manitoba 39 A2 52 20N 100 50W
Swannell Range mts. British Columbia 43 C3 56 38N 126 10W
Swan River tn. Manitoba 39 A2 52 06N 101 17W
Swift Current tn. Saskatchewan 40 B2 50 17N 107 49W
Swift Current Creek Saskatchewan 40 B1 49 40N 108 30W
Swinburne, Cape Northwest Territories 45 M5 71 13N 98 33W
Swindle Island British Columbia 42 C2 52 33N 128 25W
Sydenham River Ontario 38 A2 42 20N 82 00W
Sydney Nova Scotia 31 F7 46 10N 60 10W
Sydney Mines tn. Nova Scotia 31 F7 46 16N 60 15W
Sylvan Lake tn. Alberta 41 C2 52 19N 114 05W

T

Taber Alberta 41 C1 49 48N 112 09W
Table Bay Newfoundland 30 C3 53 40N 56 25W
Tache admin. Manitoba 48 C2 49 47N 96 43W
Tadoussac Québec 37 N9 48 09N 69 43W
Tadule Lake Manitoba 39 B3 58 30N 98 50W
Tagish Lake British Columbia 42 B3 59 50N 134 33W
Tahiryuak Lake Northwest Territories 44 J5 70 56N 112 15W
Tahoe Lake Northwest Territories 44 K5 70 15N 108 45W
Tahsis British Columbia 43 C1 49 50N 126 39W
Tahtsa Lake British Columbia 43 C2 53 41N 127 30W
Takla Lake British Columbia 43 C3 55 12N 125 45W
Takla Landing British Columbia 43 C3 55 27N 125 59W
Taku Arm l. British Columbia 42 B4 60 10N 134 05W
Taku River British Columbia 42 B3 58 43N 133 20W
Talbot Lake Manitoba 39 B2 54 00N 99 40W
Taltson River Northwest Territories 44 J3 60 40N 111 30W
Taseko Mountain British Columbia 43 D2 51 12N 123 07W
Taseko River British Columbia 43 D2 51 35N 123 40W
Tasisuak Lake Newfoundland 30 B4 56 45N 62 46W
Tasiujaq Québec 32 B4 58 40N 70 00W
Tatamagouche Nova Scotia 31 F7 45 45N 63 15W
Tatamagouche Bay Nova Scotia 31 F7 45 45N 63 15W
Tathlina Lake Northwest Territories 44 H3 60 33N 117 39W
Tatla Lake British Columbia 43 D2 51 59N 124 25W
Tatlatui Provincial Park British Columbia 43 C3 57 00N 127 20W
Tatlayoko Lake British Columbia 43 D2 51 39N 124 23W
Tatnam, Cape Manitoba 39 C3 57 25N 91 00W
Tatshenshini River British Columbia 42 A3 59 30N 137 30W

Tavistock Ontario 38 B2 43 19N 80 50W
Taylor British Columbia 43 D3 56 09N 120 40W
Taylor Head c. Nova Scotia 31 F6 44 40N 62 30W
Tazin Lake Saskatchewan 40 B3 59 50N 109 10W
Tazin River Saskatchewan 40 B3 59 50N 109 30W
Tecumseh Ontario 52 F2 42 01N 82 45W
Teeswater Ontario 38 A2 43 59N 81 17W
Teeswater River Ontario 38 A3 44 07N 81 22W
Tehek Lake Northwest Territories 45 N3 64 55N 95 38W
Telegraph Creek tn. British Columbia 42 B3 57 56N 131 11W
Telkwa British Columbia 43 C2 54 44N 127 05W
Temagami Ontario 35 E2 47 04N 79 47W
Temagami, Lake Ontario 36 F7 47 00N 80 05W
Témiscaming Québec 36 G7 46 44N 79 05W
Témiscamingue admin. Québec 36 F7 47 29N 75 36W
Templeton Québec 47 J2 45 29N 75 36W
Terence Bay Nova Scotia 31 F6 44 20N 63 40W
Terrace British Columbia 43 C2 54 31N 128 32W
Terra Cotta Ontario 38 C2 43 42N 79 55W
Terra Nova National Park Newfoundland 31 D2 48 40N 54 20W
Terrebonne Québec 37 N6 45 25N 73 37W
Terrebonne admin. Québec 37 M7 46 00N 74 30W
Terrence Bay tn. Ontario 35 C2 48 47N 87 06W
Terrenceville Newfoundland 31 C2 47 40N 54 44W
Teslin Yukon Territory 44 E3 60 10N 132 42W
Teslin British Columbia/Yukon Territory 44 E3 59 50N 132 25W
Teslin River British Columbia 42 B3 59 20N 131 50W
Tetachuck Lake British Columbia 43 C2 53 20N 126 00W
Teulon Manitoba 39 B2 50 26N 97 18W
Texada Island British Columbia 42 H4 49 30N 124 30W
Thamesford Ontario 38 A2 43 03N 81 00W
Thames River Ontario 36 E2 42 19N 82 27W
Thelon River Northwest Territories 44 L3 64 40N 102 30W
Thelon River Game Sanctuary Northwest Territories 45 L3 64 30N 103 00W
The Pas Manitoba 39 A2 53 49N 101 14W
Thesiger Bay Northwest Territories 44 F5 71 30N 124 05W
Thessalon Ontario 37 C7 46 15N 83 34W
Thetford Mines tn. Québec 37 P7 46 06N 71 18W
Thicket Portage Manitoba 39 B3 55 20N 97 42W
Thirty Thousand Islands Ontario 36 F6 45 56N 80 57W
Thlewiaza River Northwest Territories 45 M3 60 50N 98 00W
Thompson Manitoba 39 B3 55 45N 97 54W
Thompson River British Columbia 43 D2 50 12N 121 30W
Thomsen River Northwest Territories 44 H5 73 00N 119 50W
Thorah Island British Columbia 38 C3 44 27N 79 13W
Thorhild Alberta 41 C2 54 10N 113 07W
Thornbury Ontario 38 B3 44 34N 80 27W
Thornhill tn. Ontario 46 C2 43 49N 79 26W
Thorold Ontario 38 C2 43 08N 79 14W
Thorsby Alberta 41 C2 53 14N 114 03W
Thousand Islands Ontario 37 K5 44 22N 75 55W
Three Hills tn. Alberta 41 C2 51 42N 113 16W
Three Mile Plains tn. Nova Scotia 31 F6 44 55N 64 10W
Thunder Bay tn. Ontario 35 C2 48 27N 89 12W
Thurso Québec 37 L6 45 38N 75 19W
Thutade Lake British Columbia 43 C3 56 59N 126 40W
Tide Head tn. New Brunswick 31 A2 47 58N 66 49W
Tignish Prince Edward Island 31 F7 46 58N 64 03W
Tikkoatokak Bay Newfoundland 30 B4 56 42N 62 12W
Tilbury Ontario 36 D2 42 16N 82 26W
Tilbury Island British Columbia 46 F3 49 08N 123 02W
Tilden Lake Ontario 36 G7 46 39N 79 39W
Tillsonburg Ontario 38 B2 42 53N 80 44W
Timberlea Nova Scotia 31 F6 44 40N 63 45W
Timiskaming, Lake (Lac Témiscamingue) Ontario 35 E2 46 52N 79 15W
Timmins Ontario 35 D2 48 30N 81 20W
Tinniswood, Mount British Columbia 42 H5 50 19N 123 47W
Tip Top Mountain Ontario 35 C2 48 16N 85 59W
Tisdale Saskatchewan 40 C2 52 51N 104 01W
Tiverton Ontario 38 A3 44 15N 81 33W
Toad River tn. British Columbia 43 C3 58 50N 125 12W
Toba Inlet British Columbia 42 H5 50 25N 124 40W
Toba River British Columbia 42 H5 50 31N 124 18W
Tobermory Ontario 38 A4 45 15N 81 39W
Tobin Lake Saskatchewan 40 C2 53 30N 103 30W
Tofield Alberta 41 C2 53 22N 112 40W
Tofino British Columbia 43 C1 49 05N 125 51W
Tomlinson, Mount British Columbia 43 C3 55 30N 127 30W
Torbay Newfoundland 31 D2 47 40N 52 44W
Tor Bay Nova Scotia 31 F7 45 15N 61 15W
Torch River Saskatchewan 40 C2 53 40N 103 50W
Tornado Mountain Alberta/British Columbia 43 F1 49 57N 114 39W
Torngat Mountains (Monts Torngat) Newfoundland/Québec 30 B4 59 00N 63 40W
Toronto Ontario 46 C1 43 42N 79 46W
Toronto Islands Ontario 46 C1 43 48N 79 25W
Tottenham Ontario 38 C3 44 02N 79 48W
Touraine Québec 47 K2 45 29N 75 42W
Tracadie New Brunswick 31 B2 47 32N 64 57W
Tracadie Nova Scotia 31 F7 45 38N 61 40W
Tracy New Brunswick 31 A2 45 41N 66 42W
Tracy Québec 37 N7 45 59N 73 04W
Trail British Columbia 43 E1 49 04N 117 39W
Tramping Lake Saskatchewan 40 B2 52 10N 109 10W
Trans-Canada Highway 10 N3 50 00N 100 00W
Transcona Manitoba 48 D2 49 54N 97 01W
Treherne Manitoba 39 B1 49 39N 98 41W
Trembleur Lake British Columbia 43 D2 54 50N 124 55W
Trent Canal Ontario 38 C3 44 13N 79 23W
Trenton Nova Scotia 31 F7 45 37N 62 38W
Trenton Ontario 36 J5 44 07N 77 34W
Trepassey Newfoundland 31 D2 46 45N 53 20W
Trinity Bay Newfoundland 31 D2 47 50N 53 40W
Trinity East Newfoundland 31 D2 48 23N 53 20W
Triton Newfoundland 31 C2 49 30N 55 30W
Trochu Alberta 41 C2 51 50N 113 13W
Trois-Pistoles Québec 34 P9 48 08N 69 10W
Trois-Rivières Québec 37 O7 46 21N 72 34W
Trout Creek tn. Ontario 36 G6 45 59N 79 22W
Trout Lake Ontario 34 B3 51 20N 93 20W
Trout Lake tn. Alberta 41 B3 56 30N 114 32W
Trout Lake tn. Northwest Territories 44 G3 61 00N 121 30W

Trout River *tn.* Newfoundland **31** C2 49 29N 58 08W
Troy Nova Scotia **31** F7 45 40N 61 30W
Truro Nova Scotia **31** F7 45 24N 63 18W
Tuchitua Yukon Territory **44** F3 61 20N 129 00W
Tuktoyaktuk Northwest Territories **14** E4 69 24N 133 01W
Tulameen River British Columbia **42** H4 49 30N 120 58W
Tulemalu Lake Northwest Territories **45** M3 62 58N 99 25W
Tumbler Ridge *tn.* British Columbia **43** D3 55 10N 121 01W
Tungsten Northwest Territories **44** F3 61 59N 128 09W
Tunungayualok Island Newfoundland **30** B4 56 05N 61 05W
Turkey Point Ontario **38** B1 42 37N 80 20W
Turkey Point *tn.* Ontario **38** B1 43 41N 80 20W
Turkey Point Provincial Park Ontario **38** B1 42 45N 80 20W
Turnagain River British Columbia **42** C3 58 25N 129 08W
Turnavik Island Newfoundland **30** C4 55 18N 59 21W
Turner Valley *tn.* Alberta **41** C2 50 40N 114 17W
Turnor Lake *Saskatchewan* **40** B3 56 35N 109 10W
Turnor Lake *tn.* Saskatchewan **40** B3 56 25N 108 40W
Turtleford Saskatchewan **40** B2 53 25N 108 58W
Turtle Mountain Provincial Park Manitoba **39** A1 49 00N 100 10W
Tusket Nova Scotia **31** E6 43 53N 65 58W
Tuxedo Manitoba **48** D2 49 51N 97 13W
Tuya River British Columbia **42** B3 58 46N 130 50W
Tweed Ontario **37** J5 44 29N 77 19W
Tweedsmuir Provincial Park British Columbia **43** C2 52 50N 126 20W
Twelve Mile Bay Ontario **38** B4 45 05N 80 00W
Twenty Mile Creek Ontario **38** C2 43 09N 79 48W
Twillingate Newfoundland **31** D2 49 39N 54 46W
Twin Falls *tn.* Newfoundland **30** A3 53 30N 64 32W
Twin Islands Northwest Territories **34** E3 53 20N 80 10W
Two Hills *tn.* Alberta **41** C2 53 43N 111 45W
Tyne Valley *tn.* Prince Edward Island **31** F7 46 36N 63 57W

U
Ucluelet British Columbia **42** G4 48 55N 125 34W
Ugjoktok Bay Newfoundland **30** B3 55 08N 60 30W
Uivak, Cape Newfoundland **30** B4 58 29N 62 34W
Ukasiksalik Island Newfoundland **30** B4 55 55N 60 47W
Umingmaktok Northwest Territories **44** K4 67 48N 108 00W
Umiujaq Québec **32** A4 56 00N 76 44W
Ungava Bay *(Baie d'Ungava)* Northwest Territories/ Québec **45** S2 58 00N 72 30W
Unionville Ontario **46** C2 43 51N 79 19W
United States Range *mts.* Northwest Territories **45** R7 82 25N 68 00W
Unity Saskatchewan **40** B2 52 27N 109 10W
Upper Arrow Lake British Columbia **43** E2 50 25N 117 56W
Upper Campbell Lake British Columbia **42** G4 49 57N 125 36W
Upper Foster Lake Saskatchewan **40** B3 56 40N 105 35W
Upper Liard Yukon Territory **44** F3 60 00N 129 20W
Upper Musquodoboit Nova Scotia **31** F7 45 10N 62 58W
Upper Sackville Nova Scotia **47** P7 44 48N 63 42W
Upper Salmon Reservoir Newfoundland **31** C2 48 20N 55 30W
Upper Windigo Lake Ontario **34** B3 52 30N 91 35W
Uranium City Saskatchewan **40** B3 59 32N 108 43W
Utikuma Lake Alberta **41** B3 55 50N 115 25W
Uxbridge Ontario **38** C3 44 07N 79 09W

V
Valdes Island British Columbia **42** H4 49 05N 123 40W
Val-d'Or *tn.* Québec **33** A2 48 07N 77 47W
Valemount British Columbia **43** E2 52 50N 119 15W
Valhalla Provincial Park British Columbia **43** E1 49 00N 118 00W
Valleyview Alberta **41** B3 55 04N 117 17W
Val Marie Saskatchewan **40** B1 49 15N 107 44W
Vancouver British Columbia **42** H4 49 13N 123 06W
Vancouver Island British Columbia **42** G4 48 55N 124 33W
Vanderhoof British Columbia **43** D2 54 00N 124 00W
Vanier Ontario **47** K2 45 27N 75 40W
Vankleek Hill Ontario **37** M6 45 31N 74 39W
Vanscoy Saskatchewan **40** B2 52 01N 106 50W
Vansittart Island Northwest Territories **45** P4 65 50N 84 00W
Varennes Québec **47** O6 45 39N 73 26W
Vaudreuil *admin.* Québec **37** M6 45 20N 74 20W
Vaughan Ontario **38** C2 43 39N 79 25W
Vauxhall Alberta **41** C2 50 04N 112 07W
Vegreville Alberta **41** C2 53 30N 112 03W
Verdun Québec **47** N4 45 28N 73 34W
Vermilion Alberta **41** C2 53 22N 110 51W
Vermilion Bay *tn.* Ontario **34** B2 49 51N 93 21W
Vermilion Pass Alberta/British Columbia **41** B2 51 14N 116 03W
Vermilion River Alberta **41** C2 53 40N 111 25W
Vernon British Columbia **43** E2 50 17N 119 19W
Victoria British Columbia **42** H4 48 26N 123 20W
Victoria Newfoundland **31** D2 47 46N 53 14W
Victoria Prince Edward Island **31** F7 46 10N 63 30W
Victoria *admin.* New Brunswick **31** A2 47 10N 67 30W
Victoria *admin.* Nova Scotia **31** F7 46 30N 60 30W
Victoria *admin.* Ontario **38** C3 44 45N 79 03W
Victoria Bridge Nova Scotia **31** F7 45 56N 60 20W
Victoria Harbour Ontario **38** C3 44 45N 79 45W
Victoria Island Northwest Territories **44** J5 70 45N 115 00W
Victoria Lake Newfoundland **31** C2 48 18N 57 20W
Victoria River Newfoundland **31** C2 48 30N 57 50W
Victoriaville Québec **37** P7 46 04N 71 57W
Vienna Ontario **38** B1 42 39N 80 47W
Vieux-Fort Québec **33** E3 51 59N 57 59W
Viking Alberta **41** C2 53 06N 111 46W
Virden Manitoba **39** A1 49 50N 100 57W
Virgil Ontario **38** C2 43 13N 79 07W
Virginiatown Ontario **35** E2 48 08N 79 35W
Viscount Melville Sound Northwest Territories **44** J5 74 10N 105 00W
Voisey Bay Newfoundland **30** B4 56 15N 61 50W
Vulcan Alberta **41** C2 50 24N 113 15W

W
Wabakimi *provincial park* Ontario **34** B3 50 30N 90 50W
Wabakimi Lake Ontario **34** B3 50 38N 89 45W
Wabana Newfoundland **31** D2 47 38N 52 57W
Wabasca-Desmarais Alberta **41** C3 55 59N 113 50W
Wabasca River Alberta **41** B3 57 45N 115 15W
Wabowden Manitoba **39** B2 54 57N 98 38W
Wabuk Point Ontario **34** C4 55 20N 85 05W
Wabush Newfoundland **30** A3 52 55N 66 52W
Wabush Lake Newfoundland **30** A3 53 05N 66 52W
Wabuskasing Ontario **34** B3 50 20N 93 10W
W.A.C. Bennet Dam British Columbia **43** D3 55 00N 122 11W
Waddington, Mount British Columbia **43** C2 51 22N 125 14W
Wade Lake Newfoundland **30** A3 54 20N 65 38W
Wadena Saskatchewan **40** C2 51 57N 103 58W
Wager Bay Northwest Territories **45** P4 66 00N 89 00W
Waglisla British Columbia **43** C2 52 05N 128 10W
Wainfleet Ontario **38** C1 42 52N 79 22W
Wainwright Alberta **41** C2 52 49N 110 52W
Wakaw Saskatchewan **40** B2 52 40N 105 45W
Wakefield Québec **37** L6 45 38N 75 56W
Waldheim Saskatchewan **40** B2 52 39N 106 40W
Wales Island Northwest Territories **45** O4 68 01N 86 40W
Walker Lake Manitoba **39** B2 54 40N 96 40W
Walkerton Ontario **38** A3 44 08N 81 10W
Wallace Nova Scotia **31** F7 45 48N 63 26W
Wallaceburg Ontario **36** D3 42 34N 82 22W
Walton Nova Scotia **31** F7 45 14N 64 00W
Wanapitei Lake Ontario **36** E7 46 45N 80 45W
Wanham Alberta **41** B3 55 44N 118 24W
Wanless Manitoba **39** A2 54 11N 101 21W
Wapawekka Hills Saskatchewan **40** C2 54 50N 104 30W
Wapawekka Lake Saskatchewan **40** C3 55 00N 104 30W
Wapella Saskatchewan **40** C1 50 16N 101 59W
Wapiti River Alberta **41** B3 54 40N 119 50W
Wardlow Alberta **41** C2 50 54N 111 33W
Wardsville Ontario **36** E3 42 39N 81 45W
Warman Saskatchewan **40** B2 52 19N 104 34W
Warner Alberta **41** C1 49 17N 112 12W
Warrender, Cape Northwest Territories **45** P5 74 28N 81 46W
Warren Landing *tn.* Manitoba **39** B2 53 42N 97 54W
Warwick Québec **27** 45 57N 71 59W
Wasaga Beach *tn.* Ontario **38** B3 44 31N 80 02W
Wasaga Beach Provincial Park Ontario **38** B3 44 30N 80 05W
Wascana Creek Saskatchewan **40** C2 50 20N 104 20W
Wasekamio Lake Saskatchewan **40** B3 56 50N 108 30W
Washago Ontario **38** C3 44 45N 79 20W
Waskaiowaka Lake Manitoba **39** B3 56 40N 96 40W
Waskesiu Lake *tn.* Saskatchewan **40** B2 53 55N 106 00W
Waterbury Lake Saskatchewan **40** C3 58 10N 104 55W
Waterdown Ontario **38** C2 43 20N 79 54W
Waterford Ontario **38** B1 42 55N 80 19W
Waterhen Manitoba **39** B2 51 50N 99 30W
Waterhen Lake Manitoba **39** B2 52 00N 99 20W
Waterhen River Saskatchewan **40** B2 54 25N 108 50W
Waterloo Ontario **38** B2 43 28N 80 32W
Waterloo Québec **27** 45 21N 72 31W
Waterloo *admin.* Ontario **38** B2 43 30N 80 46W
Waterton Lakes National Park Alberta **41** C1 49 00N 114 45W
Watford Ontario **36** E3 42 57N 81 53W
Wathaman Lake Saskatchewan **40** C3 57 00N 104 10W
Wathaman River Saskatchewan **40** C3 56 50N 104 50W
Watrous Saskatchewan **40** B2 51 40N 105 29W
Watson Saskatchewan **40** C2 52 09N 104 31W
Watson Lake *tn.* Yukon Territory **44** F3 60 07N 128 49W
Waubuno Channel Ontario **38** B4 45 11N 80 16W
Waverley Nova Scotia **31** F6 44 48N 63 38W
Waverley Game Sanctuary Nova Scotia **47** P7 44 49N 63 31W
Wawa Ontario **35** D2 48 04N 84 49W
Wawota Saskatchewan **40** C1 49 56N 102 00W
Weagamow Lake *tn.* Ontario **34** B3 52 53N 91 22W
Weaver Lake Manitoba **39** B2 52 40N 96 40W
Webbwood Ontario **36** E7 46 16N 81 53W
Webequie Ontario **34** C3 52 59N 87 21W
Wedge Mountain British Columbia **42** H5 50 07N 122 49W
Wedgeport Nova Scotia **31** E6 43 44N 66 00W
Wekusko Manitoba **39** B2 54 31N 99 45W
Wekusko Lake Manitoba **39** B2 54 30N 99 40W
Weldon Saskatchewan **40** B2 53 00N 105 08W
Welland Ontario **38** C1 42 59N 79 14W
Welland Canal Ontario **38** C2 43 14N 79 13W
Welland River Ontario **38** C2 43 05N 79 46W
Wellesley Ontario **38** B2 43 39N 80 46W
Wellington Nova Scotia **31** F6 44 50N 63 35W
Wellington Ontario **37** J4 43 57N 77 21W
Wellington *admin.* Ontario **38** B2 43 46N 80 41W
Wellington Channel Northwest Territories **45** N6 75 00N 93 00W
Wells British Columbia **43** D2 53 00N 121 30W
Wells Gray Provincial Park British Columbia **43** D2 52 00N 120 00W
Wells Lake Manitoba **39** A3 57 10N 100 30W
Wembley Alberta **41** B3 55 09N 119 08W
Wemindji *(Nouveau-Comptoir)* Québec **33** A3 52 59N 78 50W
Wenebegon Lake Ontario **35** D2 47 23N 83 06W
Wentworth Nova Scotia **31** F7 45 39N 63 35W
Werner Lake Ontario **34** B3 50 27N 94 54W
Wesleyville Newfoundland **31** D2 49 09N 53 34W
West Bay *tn.* Newfoundland **30** C3 54 08N 57 26W
West Bay *tn.* Nova Scotia **31** F7 45 40N 61 10W
West Don River Ontario **46** B2 43 49N 79 31W
West Duffins Creek Ontario **46** D2 43 53N 79 10W
Western River Northwest Territories **44** K4 66 40N 107 00W
Westham Island British Columbia **42** H3 49 05N 123 10W
West Highland Creek Ontario **46** C2 43 46N 79 15W
West Humber River Ontario **46** B2 43 48N 79 43W
Westlock Alberta **41** C2 54 09N 113 52W
West Lorne Ontario **38** A1 42 36N 81 35W
Westmorland *admin.* New Brunswick **31** F7 46 10N 64 50W
Westmount Nova Scotia **31** F7 46 10N 60 10W
Westmount Québec **47** N4 45 29N 73 37W
West Point Prince Edward Island **31** F7 46 38N 64 26W
Westport Nova Scotia **31** E6 44 20N 66 20W
Westport Ontario **37** K5 44 41N 76 24W

West Road River British Columbia **43** D2 53 12N 123 50W
West St. Modeste Newfoundland **30** C3 51 36N 56 42W
West St. Paul *admin.* Manitoba **48** D2 49 59N 97 08W
West Thurlow Island British Columbia **42** G5 50 27N 125 35W
West Vancouver British Columbia **42** H4 49 22N 123 11W
Westville Nova Scotia **31** F7 45 34N 62 44W
Wetaskiwin Alberta **41** C2 52 57N 113 20W
Weyburn Saskatchewan **40** C1 49 39N 103 51W
Weymouth Nova Scotia **31** E6 44 26N 66 00W
Whale Cove *tn.* Northwest Territories **45** N3 62 10N 92 36W
Whaletown British Columbia **42** G5 50 06N 125 02W
Whapmagoostui *see* Kuujjuarapik
Wheatley Ontario **38** A2 42 06N 82 27W
Wheeler River Saskatchewan **40** B3 57 30N 105 10W
Whippoorwill Bay Ontario **38** A4 45 01N 81 15W
Whirl Creek Ontario **38** A2 43 29N 81 07W
Whistler British Columbia **42** H5 50 08N 122 58W
Whitby Ontario **38** D2 43 52N 78 56W
White Bay Newfoundland **31** C3 50 00N 56 32W
White Bear Lake Newfoundland **30** B4 57 54N 61 42W
White Bear Lake Newfoundland **30** C3 54 32N 59 30W
Whitecap Mountain British Columbia **42** H5 50 44N 122 30W
White City Saskatchewan **40** C2 50 35N 104 20W
Whitecourt Alberta **41** B2 54 10N 115 41W
Whitefish Ontario **36** E7 46 23N 81 22W
Whitefish Bay Ontario **35** D2 46 38N 84 33W
Whitefish Lake Northwest Territories **44** K3 62 30N 106 40W
Whitefish Lake Ontario **35** D2 48 05N 84 10W
Whitefox River Saskatchewan **40** C2 53 25N 104 55W
White Handkerchief, Cape Newfoundland **30** B4 59 17N 63 23W
Whitehorse Yukon Territory **44** E3 60 41N 135 08W
White Lake Ontario **35** C2 48 50N 85 30W
Whitemouth Manitoba **39** B1 49 58N 95 59W
Whitemouth Lake Manitoba **39** B1 49 10N 96 00W
Whitemouth River Manitoba **39** B1 49 50N 97 10W
Whitemud Creek Alberta **48** F4 53 18N 113 38W
White Otter Lake Ontario **34** B2 49 07N 91 52W
White Pass British Columbia **42** B3 59 37N 135 07W
White River Ontario **35** C2 48 30N 86 20W
White River *tn.* Ontario **35** C2 48 35N 85 16W
White River Yukon Territory **44** D3 62 25N 140 05W
White Rock British Columbia **42** H4 49 02N 122 50W
Whitesail Lake British Columbia **43** C2 53 25N 127 10W
Whitesand River Alberta **41** B3 59 00N 115 00W
Whiteshell Provincial Forest Manitoba **39** B1 49 50N 95 40W
Whiteshell Provincial Park Manitoba **39** B2 50 00N 95 20W
Whitewater Lake Ontario **34** C3 50 40N 89 30W
Whitewood Saskatchewan **40** C2 50 19N 102 16W
Whitney Ontario **36** H6 45 29N 78 15W
Whitworth Québec **37** R8 47 42N 69 17W
Wholdaia Lake Northwest Territories **44** L3 60 43N 104 10W
Whycocomagh Nova Scotia **31** F7 45 58N 61 08W
Wiarton Ontario **38** A3 44 44N 81 19W
Wickham Québec **27** 45 45N 72 31W
Wildcat Hill Wilderness Area Saskatchewan **40** C2 53 20N 102 20W
Wildwood Alberta **41** B2 53 37N 115 14W
Wilkie Saskatchewan **40** B2 52 27N 108 42W
William, Lake Nova Scotia **47** P7 44 46N 63 34W
William River Saskatchewan **40** B3 58 50N 108 55W
Williams Lake *tn.* British Columbia **43** D2 52 08N 122 07W
Williston Lake British Columbia **43** D3 56 00N 124 00W
Willmore Wilderness Park Alberta **41** B2 53 40N 119 30W
Will, Mount British Columbia **42** C3 57 30N 128 44W
Willowbunch Lake Saskatchewan **40** B1 49 20N 105 50W
Willow Lake Northwest Territories **44** H3 60 00N 115 00W
Wilson Ontario **38** D2 43 15N 78 50W
Winchester Ontario **37** L6 45 06N 75 21W
Windermere Lake Ontario **35** D2 47 58N 83 47W
Windigo Québec **37** N8 47 45N 73 22W
Windigo Lake Ontario **34** B3 52 35N 91 32W
Windsor Newfoundland **31** C2 48 57N 55 40W
Windsor Nova Scotia **38** C2 43 12N 79 38W
Windsor Ontario **36** D3 42 18N 83 00W
Windsor Québec **37** O6 45 35N 72 01W
Windsor Junction Nova Scotia **47** P7 44 48N 63 38W
Winefred Lake Alberta **41** C3 55 30N 110 31W
Wingham Ontario **38** A2 43 54N 81 19W
Winisk Lake Ontario **34** C3 52 55N 87 22W
Winisk River Ontario **34** C3 54 50N 87 00W
Winisk River Provincial Park Ontario **34** C3 52 50N 87 30W
Winkler Manitoba **39** B1 49 12N 97 55W
Winnipeg Manitoba **39** B1 53 49N 97 10W
Winnipeg Beach *tn.* Manitoba **39** B2 50 30N 97 00W
Winnipeg, Lake Manitoba **39** B2 53 00N 97 00W
Winnipegosis Manitoba **39** B2 51 40N 99 59W
Winnipegosis, Lake Manitoba **39** A2 52 10N 100 00W
Winnipeg River Manitoba **39** B2 50 20N 95 30W
Winokapau Lake Newfoundland **30** B3 53 10N 62 52W
Winona Ontario **38** C2 43 12N 79 38W
Winterburn Alberta **48** F5 53 33N 113 41W
Witless Bay *tn.* Newfoundland **31** D2 47 16N 52 50W
Wolfe *admin.* Québec **37** P6 45 40N 71 40W
Wolfe Island Ontario **37** K5 44 31N 75 59W
Wolfville Nova Scotia **31** F7 45 06N 64 22W
Wollaston, Cape Northwest Territories **44** H5 71 06N 118 04W
Wollaston Lake Saskatchewan **40** C3 58 20N 103 00W
Wollaston Lake *tn.* Saskatchewan **40** C3 58 05N 103 38W
Wollaston Peninsula Northwest Territories **44** J4 70 00N 115 00W
Wolseley Saskatchewan **40** C2 50 25N 103 15W
Woodbridge Ontario **46** B2 43 47N 79 36W
Wood Buffalo National Park Alberta/Northwest Territories **42** J2 59 00N 112 30W
Woodfibre British Columbia **42** H4 49 36N 123 00W
Wood Islands *tn.* Prince Edward Island **31** F7 45 50N 62 40W

Woodland Caribou Provincial Park Ontario **34** B3 51 10N 94 20W
Wood Mountain Saskatchewan **40** B1 49 15N 106 20W
Woodside Nova Scotia **47** P6 44 39N 63 31W
Woods Lake Newfoundland **30** B3 54 30N 65 13W
Woods, Lake of the Ontario **34** B2 49 15N 94 45W
Woodstock New Brunswick **31** A2 46 10N 67 36W
Woodstock Ontario **38** B2 43 07N 80 46W
Woodville Ontario **38** D3 44 24N 78 44W
Wright Corners Ontario **38** D2 43 10N 78 45W
Wrigley Northwest Territories **44** G3 63 16N 123 39W
Wrong Lake Manitoba **39** B2 52 40N 96 10W
Wunnummin Lake Ontario **34** C3 52 55N 89 10W
Wyebridge Ontario **38** C3 44 41N 79 53W
Wynniatt Bay Northwest Territories **44** J5 72 45N 110 30W
Wynyard Saskatchewan **40** C2 51 50N 104 10W

Y
Yale British Columbia **42** H4 49 31N 121 29W
Yamachiche Québec **27** 46 17N 72 50W
Yamaska *admin.* Québec **37** O7 46 00N 72 50W
Yarmouth Nova Scotia **31** E6 43 50N 66 05W
Yarmouth *admin.* Nova Scotia **31** E6 44 50N 65 40W
Yates River Alberta **41** B3 59 40N 116 53W
Yathkyed Lake Northwest Territories **45** M3 62 40N 98 00W
Yellow Grass Saskatchewan **40** C1 49 49N 104 11W
Yellowhead Highway **10** N3 54 00N 109 00W
Yellowhead Pass Alberta/British Columbia **41** B2 52 53N 118 28W
Yellowhead River Alberta **41** C2 53 20N 110 45W
Yellowknife Northwest Territories **44** J3 62 30N 114 29W
Yellowknife River Northwest Territories **44** J3 62 35N 114 10W
Yoho National Park British Columbia **43** E2 51 00N 116 00W
York New Brunswick **31** A2 46 10N 66 50W
York *admin.* Ontario **38** C2 43 57N 79 39W
York *bor.* Metropolitan Toronto Ontario **46** C2 43 41N 79 28W
York, Cape Northwest Territories **45** O5 73 48N 87 00W
York Factory Manitoba **39** C3 57 08N 92 25W
Yorkton Saskatchewan **40** C2 51 12N 102 29W
Youbou British Columbia **42** H4 48 52N 124 12W
Young Saskatchewan **40** B2 51 45N 105 45W
Yukon River Yukon Territory Canada/Alaska U.S.A. **44** D3 63 00N 138 50W
Yukon Territory *territory* **44**

Z
Zeballos British Columbia **43** C1 49 57N 126 10W
Zürich Ontario **38** A2 43 25N 81 37W

A

Aachen Germany **76** C5 50 46N 6 06E
Aaper Wald *hills* Germany **76** H2 51 17N 6 50E
Aba Nigeria **106** G9 5 06N 7 21E
Ābādān Iran **93** G5 30 20N 48 15E
Abadla Algeria **106** E14 31 01N 2 45W
Abaetetuba Brazil **68** H12 1 45S 48 54W
Abakan Russia **91** P5 53 43N 91 25E
Abakan *r.* Russia **91** O5 52 00N 88 00E
Abancay Peru **68** C10 13 37S 72 52W
Abashiri Japan **100** D3 44 02N 144 17E
Abbeville France **76** C4 50 06N 1 51E
Abbotstown Pennsylvania U.S.A. **64** C2 39 54N 77 00W
Ābd al Kūrī *i.* Socotra **93** H1 11 55N 52 20E
Abéché Chad **106** J10 13 49N 20 49E
Abeokuta Nigeria **106** E9 7 10N 3 26E
Aberdeen Hong Kong U.K. **98** B1 22 14N 114 09E
Aberdeen Maryland U.S.A. **64** D2 39 31N 76 10W
Aberdeen Scotland **78** I9 57 10N 2 04W
Aberdeen South Dakota U.S.A. **63** G6 45 28N 98 30W
Aberdeen Washington U.S.A. **62** B6 46 58N 123 49W
Aberystwyth Wales **78** G4 52 25N 4 05W
Abhā Saudi Arabia **92** F2 18 14N 42 31E
Abidjan Côte d'Ivoire **106** E9 5 19N 4 01W
Abilene Texas U.S.A. **62** G3 32 27N 99 45W
Absaroka Range *mts.* U.S.A. **62** D6 45 00N 110 00W
Abu Dhabi *see* Abū Zabī
Abu Durba Egypt **92** N9 28 29N 33 20E
Abu Hamed Sudan **92** D2 19 32N 33 20E
Abuja Nigeria **106** G9 9 10N 7 11E
Abu Kamal Syria **92** F5 34 29N 40 56E
Abu Kebir Egypt **107** R3 30 44N 31 48E
Abunã Brazil **68** D11 9 41S 65 20W
Abu Tig Egypt **92** D4 27 06N 31 17E
Abū Zabī *(Abu Dhabi)* United Arab Emirates **93** H3 24 28N 54 25E
Acambaro Mexico **66** D4 20 01N 100 42W
Acaponeta Mexico **66** C4 22 30N 102 25W
Acapulco Mexico **66** E3 16 51N 99 56W
Açari *r.* Brazil **69** P2 22 50S 43 22W
Acarigua Venezuela **68** D14 9 35N 69 12W
Acatlán Mexico **66** E3 18 12N 98 02W
Acayucán Mexico **66** E3 17 59N 94 58W
Accra Ghana **106** E9 5 33N 0 15W
Achacachi Bolivia **68** D9 16 01S 68 44W
Achill Island Irish Republic **78** A5 53 55N 10 05W
Achinsk Russia **91** P6 56 20N 90 33E
Acklins Island The Bahamas **67** J4 22 30N 74 30W
Aconcagua *mt.* Argentina **69** C6 32 40S 70 02W
Acre *admin.* Brazil **68** C11 8 30S 71 30W
Acton England **82** B3 51 31N 0 17W
Ada Oklahoma U.S.A. **63** G3 34 47N 96 41W
Adachi Japan **101** C4 35 46N 139 48E
Adaga *r.* Spain **77** B3 40 45N 4 45W
Adamawa Mountains *mts.* Africa **102** 7 00N 13 00E
Adams Massachusetts U.S.A. **65** G5 42 38N 73 08W
Adam's Bridge India/Sri Lanka **95** D1 9 10N 79 30E
Adana Turkey **92** E6 37 00N 35 19E
Adapazari Turkey **92** D7 40 45N 30 23E
Adare, Cape Antarctica **117** 71 30S 170 24E
Ad Dahna *geog. reg.* Saudi Arabia **106** O13 26 00N 47 00E
Ad Dakhla Western Sahara **106** B12 23 50N 15 58W
Ad Dammām Saudi Arabia **93** H4 26 25N 50 06E
Ad Dawhah *(Doha)* Qatar **93** H4 25 15N 51 36E
Ad Dilam Saudi Arabia **93** G3 23 59N 47 06E
Ad Dir'īyah Saudi Arabia **93** G3 24 45N 46 32E
Addis Ababa *see* Ādīs Ābeba
Addison New York U.S.A. **64** C5 42 07N 77 16W
Ad Dīwānīyah Iraq **92** F5 32 00N 44 57E
Adelaide Australia **110** F3 34 56S 138 36E
Aden Yemen Republic **93** G1 12 50N 45 03E
Aden, Gulf of **93** G1 12 30N 47 30E
Adirondack Mountains New York U.S.A. **65** F6 43 15N 74 40W
Ādīs Ābeba *(Addis Ababa)* Ethiopia **106** M9 9 03N 38 42E
Admiralty Island Alaska U.S.A. **42** B3 52 45N 134 30W
Admiralty Islands Papua New Guinea **110** H9 2 30S 147 00E
Adoni India **95** D3 15 38N 77 16E
Adra Spain **77** B2 36 45N 3 01W
Adrar Algeria **106** E13 27 51N 0 19W
Adrian Michigan U.S.A. **36** B2 41 55N 84 01W
Adriatic Sea Mediterranean Sea **81** B3/C3 43 00N 15 00E
Adwa Ethiopia **92** E1 14 12N 38 56E
Aegean Sea Mediterranean Sea **81** D2 39 00N 24 00E
AFGHANISTAN **93** J5
Afognak Island Alaska U.S.A. **10** E4 58 10N 152 50W
Afyon Turkey **92** D6 38 46N 30 32E
Agadès Niger **106** G11 17 00N 7 56E
Agadir Morocco **106** D14 30 30N 9 40W
Agalega Islands Seychelles **112** E5 10 00S 56 00E
Agana Guam **114** E9 13 28N 144 45E
Agano *r.* Japan **100** C2 37 50N 139 30E
Agartala India **95** G4 23 49N 91 15E
Agboyi Creek *r.* Nigeria **107** V3 6 37N 3 30E
Agege Nigeria **107** V3 6 41N 3 24E
Agen France **77** C3 44 12N 0 38E
Ageo Japan **100** L2 35 57N 139 36E
Ago Japan **100** H1 34 20N 136 50E
Agout *r.* France **77** C3 43 50N 1 50E
Agra India **95** D5 27 09N 78 00E
Agram *see* Zagreb
Agri *r.* Italy **81** C3 40 00N 16 00E
Agrigento Italy **81** B2 37 19N 13 35E
Agrínion Greece **81** D2 38 38N 21 25E
Aguadas Colombia **68** B14 5 36N 75 30W
Aguadilla Puerto Rico **67** K3 18 27N 67 08W
Agua Prieta Mexico **66** C6 31 20N 109 32W
Aguascalientes Mexico **66** D4 21 51N 102 18W
Agueda *r.* Spain **77** A3 40 50N 6 50W
Aguilas Spain **77** B2 37 25N 1 35W
Agulhas Basin Indian Ocean **112** A2 45 00S 20 00E
Agulhas, Cape Republic of South Africa **107** J1 34 50S 20 00E
Ahklun Mountains Alaska U.S.A. **10** C4 60 00N 161 00W
Ahmadabad India **95** C4 23 03N 72 40E
Ahmadnagar India **95** C3 19 08N 74 48E
Ahrensfelde Germany **83** G2 52 35N 13 35E
Ahuachapán El Salvador **66** G2 13 57N 89 49W
Ahvāz Iran **93** G5 31 17N 48 43E
Aichi *pref.* Japan **100** J2 35 00N 137 15E
Ain *r.* France **77** D4 46 30N 5 30E
Aïn Beïda Algeria **77** D2 35 44N 7 22E
Aïn Sefra Algeria **106** E14 32 45N 0 35W
Aïn Témouchent Algeria **77** B2 35 18N 1 09W
Aïr *mts.* Niger **106** G11 19 10N 8 20E
Aire *r.* England **78** J5 53 40N 1 00W
Aiviekste *r.* Latvia **79** F2 57 00N 26 40E
Aix-en-Provence France **77** D3 43 31N 5 27E
Aíyion Greece **81** D2 38 15N 22 05E
Aizu-Wakamatsu Japan **100** C2 37 30N 139 58E
Ajaccio Corsica **77** D3 41 55N 8 43E
Ajdābiyā Libya **106** J14 30 46N 20 14E
Ajegunle Nigeria **107** V3 6 24N 3 24E
Ajlūn Jordan **92** O11 32 20N 35 45E
Ajmer India **95** C5 26 29N 74 40E
Akabira Japan **100** D3 43 40N 141 55E
Akaroa New Zealand **111** B2 43 50S 172 59E
Akashi Japan **100** F1 34 39N 135 00E
Akechi Japan **100** J2 35 19N 137 22E
Aketi Zaïre **106** J8 2 42N 23 51E
Akhelóös *r.* Greece **81** D2 39 00N 21 00E
Akhisar Turkey **68** E2 38 54N 27 50E
Akhtubinsk Russia **90** F4 48 20N 46 10E
Akita Japan **100** D2 39 44N 140 05E
'Akko Israel **92** O11 32 55N 35 04E
Akobo Sudan **106** L9 7 50N 33 05E
Akola India **95** D4 20 40N 77 05E
Ak'ordat Ethiopia **92** E2 15 26N 37 45E
Ákra Akrítas *c.* Greece **81** D2 36 43N 21 52E
Ákra Kafirévs *c.* Greece **81** D2 38 10N 24 35E
Ákra Maléa *c.* Greece **81** D2 36 27N 23 12E
Akranes Iceland **79** H6 64 19N 22 05W
Ákra Taínaron *c.* Greece **81** D2 36 23N 22 29E
Akron New York U.S.A. **64** B6 43 02N 78 30W
Akron Ohio U.S.A. **63** J5 41 04N 81 31W
Akron Pennsylvania U.S.A. **64** D3 40 09N 76 12W
Aksum Ethiopia **92** E1 14 10N 38 45E
Aktyubinsk Kazakhstan **91** H5 50 16N 57 13E
Akureyri Iceland **79** I7 65 41N 18 04W
Alabama *r.* Alabama U.S.A. **63** I3 31 00N 88 00W
Alabama *state.* U.S.A. **63** I3 32 00N 87 00W
Alagoas *admin.* Brazil **68** J11 9 30S 37 00W
Alagoinhas Brazil **68** J10 12 09S 38 21W
Alagón *r.* Spain **77** A3 40 00N 6 30W
Alajuela Costa Rica **67** H2 10 00N 84 12W
Alakanuk Alaska U.S.A. **10** C5 62 39N 164 48W
Al'Amārah Iraq **93** G5 31 51N 47 10E
Alameda California U.S.A. **49** B3 37 44N 122 14W
Alameda County California U.S.A. **49** C2 37 35N 122 11W
Alameda Creek California U.S.A. **49** C2 37 35N 122 03W
Alamo California U.S.A. **49** C3 37 51N 122 03W
Alamosa Colorado U.S.A. **62** E4 37 28N 105 54W
Åland *i.* Finland **79** D3 60 15N 20 00E
Alanya Turkey **92** D6 36 32N 32 02E
Al Artāwī yah Saudi Arabia **93** G4 26 31N 45 21E
Ala Shan *mts.* China **97** K7/K6 40 00N 102 30E
Alaska *state* U.S.A. **10** D5 63 10N 157 30W
Alaska, Gulf of Alaska U.S.A. **44** F4 58 00N 147 00W
Alaska Peninsula Alaska U.S.A. **10** D4 56 30N 159 00W
Alaska Range *mts.* Alaska U.S.A. **44** B3/C3 62 30N 152 30W
Alatna Alaska U.S.A. **10** E6 66 33N 152 49W
Al'Ayn United Arab Emirates **93** I3 24 10N 55 43E
Alay Range *mts.* Kirgyzstan/Tajikistan **91** L2 39 30N 72 00E
Albacete Spain **77** B2 39 00N 1 52W
Alba Iulia Romania **81** D4 46 04N 23 33E
ALBANIA **81** C3
Albany California U.S.A. **49** B3 37 53N 122 17W
Albany Georgia U.S.A. **63** J3 31 37N 84 10W
Albany New York U.S.A. **65** G5 42 40N 73 49W
Albany Oregon U.S.A. **62** B5 44 38N 123 07W
Al Başrah Iraq **93** G5 30 30N 47 50E
Al Bayḍā' Libya **106** J14 32 00N 21 30E
Albert, Lake Uganda/Zaïre **106** L8 2 00N 31 00E
Albert Lea Minnesota U.S.A. **63** H5 43 38N 93 16W
Albi France **77** C3 43 56N 2 08E
Albion Michigan U.S.A. **36** B3 42 14N 84 45W
Albion New York U.S.A. **64** B6 43 14N 78 12W
Al Bi'r Saudi Arabia **92** P9 28 50N 36 16E
Ålborg Denmark **80** A6 57 05N 9 50E
Albuquerque New Mexico U.S.A. **62** E4 35 05N 106 38W
Al Buraymī Oman **93** I3 24 16N 55 48E
Albury Australia **110** H2 36 03S 146 53E
Alcalá de Henares Spain **77** B3 40 28N 3 22W
Alcamo Italy **81** B2 37 58N 12 58E
Alcañiz Spain **77** B3 41 03N 0 09W
Alcatraz Island California U.S.A. **49** B3 37 50N 122 26W
Alcázar de San Juan Spain **77** B2 39 24N 3 12W
Alcira Spain **77** B2 39 10N 0 27W
Alcoy Spain **77** B2 38 42N 0 29W
Alcudia Balearic Islands **77** C2 39 51N 3 06E
Aldabra Islands Indian Ocean **107** O6 9 00S 46 00E
Aldama Mexico **66** E4 22 54N 98 05W
Aldan Russia **89** O7 58 44N 124 22E
Aldan *r.* Russia **89** P7 59 00N 132 30E
Alderney *i.* Channel Islands British Isles **78** I1 49 43N 2 12W
Alegrete Brazil **69** F7 29 45S 55 40W
Aleksandrovsk-Sakhalinskiy Russia **89** Q6 50 55N 142 12E
Alençon France **76** C4 48 25N 0 05E
Alenuihaha Channel Hawaiian Islands **115** Y18 20 20N 156 20W
Aleppo *see* Halab
Alès France **77** C3 44 08N 4 05E
Alessándria Italy **81** A3 44 55N 8 37E
Ålesund Norway **79** B3 62 28N 6 11E
Aleutian Basin Pacific Ocean **114** I13 54 00N 178 00W
Aleutian Range *mts.* Alaska U.S.A. **10** D4 56 30N 159 00W
Aleutian Ridge Pacific Ocean **114/115** I13 53 55N 178 00W
Aleutian Trench Pacific Ocean **114/115** I13 50 55N 178 00W
Alexander Archipelago *is.* Alaska U.S.A. **10** H4 57 00N 137 30W
Alexander Bay *tn.* Republic of South Africa **107** I2 28 40S 16 30E
Alexander Island Antarctica **117** 71 00S 70 00W
Alexandra New Zealand **111** A1 45 14S 169 26E
Alexandria *(El Iskandarîya)* Egypt **92** C5 31 13N 29 55E
Alexandria Louisiana U.S.A. **63** H3 31 19N 92 29W
Alexandria Romania **81** E3 43 59N 25 19E
Alexandroúpolis Greece **81** E3 40 51N 25 53E
Alfambra *r.* Spain **77** B3 40 40N 1 00W
Alfiós *r.* Greece **81** D2 37 00N 22 00E
Al Fuḥayḥīl Kuwait **93** G4 29 07N 47 02E
Algeciras Spain **77** A2 36 08N 5 27W
Alger *(Algiers)* Algeria **106** F15 36 50N 3 00E
ALGERIA **106** E13
Alghero Italy **81** A3 40 34N 8 19E
Algiers *see* Alger
Al Ḥadīthah Iraq **92** F5 34 06N 42 25E
Alhambra California U.S.A. **51** B3 34 05N 118 10W
Al Ḥarīq Saudi Arabia **93** G3 23 34N 46 35E
Al Ḥasakah Syria **92** F6 36 32N 40 44E
Al Ḥillah Iraq **92** F5 32 28N 44 29E
Al Hoceima Morocco **77** B2 35 14N 3 56W
Al Ḥudaydah Yemen Republic **92** F1 14 50N 42 58E
Al Hufūf Saudi Arabia **93** G4 25 20N 49 34E
Aliákmon *r.* Greece **81** D3 40 00N 22 00E
Alicante Spain **77** B2 38 21N 0 29W
Alice Texas U.S.A. **63** G2 27 45N 98 06W
Alice Springs Australia **110** E5 23 42S 133 52E
Aligarh India **95** D5 27 54N 78 04E
Aling Kangri *mt.* China **96** F5 32 51N 81 03E
Alipur India **94** K2 22 32N 88 19E
Alison Park Pennsylvania U.S.A. **53** E3 40 30N 79 45W
Alivérion Greece **81** D2 38 24N 24 02E
Al Jahrah Kuwait **93** G4 29 22N 47 40E
Al Jawf Libya **106** J12 24 12N 23 18E
Al Jawf Saudi Arabia **92** E4 29 49N 39 52E
Al Jubayl Saudi Arabia **93** G4 26 59N 49 40E
Aljustrel Portugal **77** A2 37 52N 8 10W
Al Khums Libya **106** H14 32 39N 14 16E
Alkmaar Netherlands **76** C5 52 38N 4 44E
Al Kufrah Oasis Libya **106** J12 24 10N 23 15E
Al Kuwayt Kuwait **93** G4 29 20N 48 00E
Al Kūt Iraq **93** G5 32 30N 45 51E
Al Lādhiqīyah Syria **92** E6 35 31N 35 47E
Allagash River Maine U.S.A. **37** R7 46 45N 69 20W
Allahabad India **95** E5 25 27N 81 50E
Allantown New York U.S.A. **64** B5 42 05N 78 05W
Allegany New York U.S.A. **64** B5 42 06N 78 30W
Alleghenies *see* Allegheny Mountains
Allegheny Mountains Pennsylvania U.S.A. **64** B3 40 30N 78 30W
Allegheny Reservoir U.S.A. **64** B4 41 00N 79 00W
Allegheny River Pennsylvania U.S.A. **64** B4 41 57N 78 26W
Allegheny County Pennsylvania U.S.A. **53** D1 40 18N 80 06W
Allende Mexico **66** D5 28 22N 100 50W
Allen Park Michigan U.S.A. **52** E2 42 14N 83 11W
Allentown Pennsylvania U.S.A. **64** E3 40 37N 75 30W
Alleppey India **95** D1 9 30N 76 22E
Alliance Nebraska U.S.A. **62** F5 42 08N 102 54W
Alliance Ohio U.S.A. **36** E1 40 56N 81 06W
Allier *r.* France **77** C4 46 40N 3 00E
Al Līth Saudi Arabia **92** F3 20 10N 40 20E
Alloa Scotland **78** H8 56 07N 3 49W
Alma Michigan U.S.A. **36** B4 43 23N 84 40W
Alma-Ata Kazakhstan **91** M3 43 19N 76 55E
Almada Portugal **77** A2 38 40N 9 09W
Almadén Spain **77** B2 38 47N 4 50W
Al Madīnah Saudi Arabia **92** E3 24 30N 39 35E
Almalyk Uzbekistan **91** K3 40 50N 69 40E
Al Manāmah Bahrain **93** H4 26 12N 50 38E
Almansa Spain **77** B2 38 52N 1 06W
Almanzora *r.* Spain **77** B2 37 15N 2 10W
Al Mayādīn Syria **92** F6 35 01N 40 28E
Almería Spain **77** B2 36 50N 2 26W
Al'met'yevsk Russia **90** G5 54 50N 52 22E
Älmhult Sweden **79** C2 56 32N 14 10E
Al Miqdādīyah Iraq **92** F5 33 58N 44 58E
Almodôvar Portugal **77** A2 37 31N 8 03W
Al Mubarraz Saudi Arabia **93** G4 25 26N 49 37E
Al Mukallā Yemen Republic **93** G1 14 34N 49 09E
Al Mukhā Yemen Republic **92** F1 13 20N 43 16E
Alor *i.* Indonesia **99** G2 8 00S 124 30E
Alpena Michigan U.S.A. **36** C6 45 04N 83 27W
Alpes Maritimes *mts.* France/Italy **77** D3 44 15N 6 45E
Alpha New Jersey U.S.A. **64** E3 40 40N 75 11W
Alpha Cordillera *ridge* Arctic Ocean **116** 85 00N 120 00W
Alpi Carniche *mts.* Europe **81** B4 46 00N 13 00E
Alpi Dolomitiche *mts.* Italy **81** B4 46 00N 12 00E
Alpi Lepontine *mts.* Switzerland **77** D4 46 26N 8 30E
Alpine Texas U.S.A. **62** F3 30 22N 103 40W
Alpi Pennine *mts.* Switzerland/Italy **77** D4 45 55N 7 30E
Alpi Retiche *mts.* Switzerland **77** D4/5 46 25N 9 45E
Alps *mts.* Europe **77** D4 46 00N 7 30E
Al Qunfudhah Saudi Arabia **92** F2 19 09N 41 07E
Alstead New Hampshire U.S.A. **65** H6 43 10N 72 24W
Alta Norway **79** E4 69 57N 23 10E
Altadena California U.S.A. **51** B3 34 12N 118 08W
Altaelv *r.* Norway **79** E4 69 50N 23 30E
Alta Gracia Argentina **69** E6 31 42S 64 25W
Altai *mts.* Mongolia **96** H8 47 00N 92 30E
Altamaha *r.* Georgia U.S.A. **63** J3 32 00N 82 00W
Altamura Italy **81** C3 40 49N 16 34E
Altay China **96** G8 47 48N 88 07E
Altay *mts.* Russia **91** O5 51 00N 89 00E
Altenessen Germany **76** J2 51 29N 7 02E
Altiplano *plat.* South America **68** D9 17 00S 67 00W
Altlandsberg Germany **83** G2 52 34N 13 45E
Alto da Boa Vista Brazil **69** P2 22 58S 43 17W
Alto Molocue Mozambique **107** M4 15 38S 37 42E
Altoona Pennsylvania U.S.A. **64** B3 40 32N 78 23W
Altun Shan *mts.* China **96** G6 37 30N 86 00E
Altus Oklahoma U.S.A. **62** G3 34 39N 99 21W
Alur Setar Malaysia **99** C5 6 06N 100 23E
Alva Oklahoma U.S.A. **62** G4 36 48N 98 40W
Alvarado California U.S.A. **49** C2 37 36N 122 05W
Al Wajh Saudi Arabia **92** E4 26 16N 32 28E
Alwar India **95** D5 27 32N 76 35E
Alyat Azerbaijan **90** F2 39 57N 49 25E
Amadeus, Lake Australia **110** E5 24 00S 132 30E
Amadi Sudan **106** L9 5 32N 30 20E
Amagansett New York U.S.A. **65** H3 40 59N 72 09W
Amagasaki Japan **100** G1 34 42N 135 23E
Amakusa-shotō *is.* Japan **100** A1 32 50N 130 05E
Amapá Brazil **68** G13 2 00N 50 50W
Amapá *admin.* Brazil **68** G13 2 00N 52 30W
Amarillo Texas U.S.A. **62** F4 35 14N 101 50W
Amatsukominato Japan **100** M2 35 08N 140 14E
Amazon *see* Rio Amazonas
Amazonas *admin.* Brazil **68** D12/F12 4 30S 65 00W
Amazon, Mouths of the Brazil **68** H13 1 00N 50 00W
Ambala India **95** D6 30 19N 76 49E
Ambarchik Russia **89** S9 69 39N 162 27E
Ambato Ecuador **68** B12 1 18S 78 39W
Ambon Indonesia **99** H3 3 41S 128 10E
Ambovombe Madagascar **107** O2 25 10S 46 06E
Amderma Russia **89** I9 66 44N 61 35E
Amdo China **96** H5 32 22N 91 07E
Ameca Mexico **66** D4 20 34N 104 03W
American Falls *tn.* Idaho U.S.A. **62** D5 42 47N 112 50W
American Samoa Pacific Ocean **115** J6 15 00S 170 00W
Amersham England **82** A3 51 40N 0 38W
Amery Ice Shelf Antarctica **117** 70 00S 70 00E
Amesbury Massachusetts U.S.A. **65** K5 42 50N 70 56W
Amfípolis Greece **81** D3 40 48N 23 52E
Amga Russia **89** P8 61 51N 131 59E
Amga *r.* Russia **89** P8 60 00N 130 00E
Amgun' *r.* Russia **89** P6 52 00N 137 00E
Amherst Massachusetts U.S.A. **65** H5 42 23N 72 31W
Amherst New Hampshire U.S.A. **65** J5 42 52N 71 36W
Amiens France **76** C4 49 54N 2 18E
Amirante Islands Seychelles **112** E6 5 00S 55 00E
Amman Jordan **92** O10 31 57N 35 56E
Amne Machin Shan *mts.* China **84** 35 00N 100 00E
Ampana Indonesia **99** G3 0 54S 121 35E
Amravati India **95** D4 20 58N 77 50E
Amritsar India **95** D6 31 35N 74 56E
Amroha India **95** D5 28 54N 78 29E
Amsterdam Netherlands **76** C5 52 22N 4 54E
Amsterdam New York U.S.A. **65** F5 42 56N 74 12W
Amstetten Austria **81** B4 48 08N 14 52E
Am Timan Chad **106** J10 10 59N 20 18E
Amudar'ya *(Oxus)* *r.* Asia **91** J2 39 00N 64 00E
Amundsen-Scott *r.s.* South Pole Antarctica **117** 90 00S
Amundsen Sea Southern Ocean **117** 72 00S 130 00W
Amungen *l.* Sweden **79** D3 61 10N 15 35E
Amur *(Heilong Jiang)* *r.* Asia **97** P9 52 30N 126 30E
Amursk Russia **89** P6 50 16N 136 55E
Anabar *r.* Russia **89** N10 71 30N 113 00E
Anaconda Montana U.S.A. **62** D6 46 09N 112 56W
Anacortes Washington U.S.A. **42** H4 48 30N 122 42W
Anadyr' Russia **89** T8 64 50N 178 00E
Anadyr' *r.* Russia **89** T9 65 00N 175 00E
Anadyr', Gulf of Russia **89** U8 65 00N 178 00W
Anaheim California U.S.A. **51** C2 33 50N 117 56W
Anai Mudi *mt.* India **95** D2 10 20N 77 15E
Anan Japan **100** B1 33 54N 134 40E
Ananindeua Brazil **68** H12 1 22S 48 20W
Anantapur India **95** D2 14 42N 77 05E
Anápolis Brazil **68** H9 16 19S 48 58W
Anatolian Plateau Turkey **84** 39 00N 39 00E
Anatom *i.* Vanuatu **110** L5 20 10S 169 50E
Anchorage Alaska U.S.A. **10** F5 61 10N 150 00W
Ancona Italy **81** B3 43 37N 13 31E
Anda China **97** P8 46 25N 125 20E
Andalsnes Norway **79** B3 62 33N 7 43E
Andaman Islands India **95** G2 12 00N 94 00E
Andaman Sea Indian Ocean **99** B6 12 30N 97 00E
Anderson Indiana U.S.A. **63** I5 40 05N 85 41W
Anderson South Carolina U.S.A. **63** J3 34 30N 82 39W
Andes *mts.* South America **68/69** B13/C5
Andhra Pradesh *admin.* India **95** D3 16 00N 79 00E
Andizhan Uzbekistan **91** L3 40 40N 72 12E
Andkhvoy Afghanistan **93** K6 36 58N 65 00E
ANDORRA **77** C3
Andorra la Vella Andorra **77** C3 42 30N 1 30E
Andover New Jersey U.S.A. **65** F3 40 58N 74 45W
Andrésy France **83** A2 48 59N 2 03E
Andreyevka Kazakhstan **96** F8 45 50N 80 34E
Andreyevka Ukraine **90** D4 49 34N 36 38E
Andropov *see* Rybinsk
Ándros *i.* Greece **81** D2 37 49N 24 54E
Andros *i.* The Bahamas **67** I4 24 00N 78 00W
Androscoggin River Maine U.S.A. **33** B1 44 00N 71 00W
Androth Island India **95** C2 10 51N 73 41E
Andújar Spain **77** B2 38 02N 4 03W
Andulo Angola **107** I5 11 29S 16 43E
Angara *r.* Russia **89** L7 58 00N 96 00E
Angara Basin Arctic Ocean **116** 80 00N
Angarsk Russia **89** M6 52 31N 103 55E
Angel de la Guarda *i.* Mexico **66** B5 29 00N 113 30W
Angeles National Forest California U.S.A. **51** B4 34 15N 118 10W
Angelholm Sweden **80** B6 56 15N 12 50E
Angelica New York U.S.A. **64** B5 42 18N 78 02W
Angel Island California U.S.A. **49** B3 37 51N 122 26W
Angel Island State Park California U.S.A. **49** B3 37 51N 122 24W
Ångermanälvern *r.* Sweden **79** D3 64 30N 16 15E
Angers France **77** B4 47 29N 0 32W
Anglesey *i.* Wales **78** G5 53 18N 4 25W
ANGOLA **107** I5
Angola Indiana U.S.A. **36** A2 41 38N 85 01W
Angola Basin Atlantic Ocean **113** I5 15 00S 3 00E
Angola Plateau Africa **102** 14 00S 17 00E
Angoon Alaska U.S.A. **42** B3 57 30N 133 35W
Angoulême France **77** C4 45 40N 0 10E
Angren Uzbekistan **91** L3 41 01N 70 10E
Anguilla *i.* Leeward Islands **67** L3 18 14N 63 05W
Anjō Japan **100** J1 34 56N 137 05E
Ankaratra *mt.* Madagascar **107** O4 19 25S 47 12E
'Annaba Algeria **106** G15 36 55N 7 47E
An Nabk Saudi Arabia **92** E5 31 21N 37 20E
An Nabk Syria **92** E5 34 02N 36 43E
An Nafud *d.* Saudi Arabia **92** F4 28 20N 40 30E
An Najaf Iraq **92** F5 31 59N 44 19E
Annam Range *hills* Asia **84** 15 00N 107 00E
Annapolis Maryland U.S.A. **64** D1 38 59N 76 30W
Annapurna *mt.* Nepal **95** E5 28 34N 83 50E
Ann Arbor Michigan U.S.A. **36** C3 42 18N 83 43W
An Nāsirīyah Iraq **93** G5 31 04N 46 17E
Annecy France **77** D4 45 54N 6 07E
Annette Island Alaska U.S.A. **42** B3 55 5N 131 30W
Anniston Alabama U.S.A. **63** I3 33 38N 85 50W
Annotto Bay *tn.* Jamaica **67** R8 18 16N 76 47W
Anqing China **97** N5 30 46N 119 40E
Ansari Nagar India **94** L4 28 33N 77 12E

Ansbach Germany **76** E5 49 18N 10 36E
Anshan China **97** O7 41 05N 122 58E
Anshun China **97** L4 26 15N 105 51E
Ansonia Connecticut U.S.A. **65** G4 41 21N 73 05W
Antonia Pennsylvania U.S.A. **64** C4 41 44N 77 26W
Antakya Turkey **92** E6 36 12N 36 10E
Antalya Turkey **92** D6 36 53N 30 42E
Antananarivo *(Tananarive)* Madagascar **107** O4 18 52S 47 30E
Antarctica 117
Antarctic Peninsula Antarctica **117** 68 00S 65 00W
Antequera Spain **77** B2 37 01N 4 34W
Anthony Chabot Regional Park California U.S.A. **49** C3 37 36N 122 07W
Antibes France **77** D3 43 35N 7 07E
Antigua Guatemala **66** F2 14 33N 90 42W
Antigua *i.* Antigua & Barbuda **67** L3 17 09N 61 49W
ANTIGUA & BARBUDA 67 L3
Antipodes Islands Southern Ocean **114** H3 49 42S 178 50E
Antler North Dakota U.S.A. **40** C1 48 58N 101 18W
Antofagasta Chile **69** C8 23 40S 70 23W
Antrim New Hampshire U.S.A. **65** J6 43 02N 71 57W
Antrim Mountains Northern Ireland **78** E6 55 00N 6 10W
Antseranana Madagascar **107** N5 12 19S 49 17E
Antwerp Ohio U.S.A. **36** B2 41 10N 84 44W
Antwerpen *(Anvers)* Belgium **76** C5 51 13N 4 25E
Anuradhapura Sri Lanka **95** E1 8 20N 80 25E
Anvers *see* Antwerpen
Anxi China **97** J7 40 32N 95 57E
Anxi China **98** E8 25 03N 118 13E
Anyang China **97** M6 36 04N 114 20E
Anzhero-Sudzhensk Russia **91** O6 56 10N 86 01E
Aomori Japan **100** D3 40 50N 140 43E
Aosta Italy **81** A4 45 43N 7 19E
Aozou Strip Chad **106** I12 23 00N 17 00E
Apapa Nigeria **107** V3 6 22N 3 25E
Aparri The Philippines **99** G7 18 22N 121 40E
Apatity Russia **88** F9 67 32N 33 21E
Apatzingán Mexico **66** D3 19 05N 102 20W
Apennines *see* Appennini
Apia Western Samoa **114** I6 13 48S 171 45W
Ap Lei Chau *i.* Hong Kong U.K. **98** B1 22 10N 114 00E
Apostle Islands Wisconsin U.S.A. **35** B2 47 00N 90 00W
Appalachian Mountains U.S.A. **63** J4 37 00N 82 00W
Appennini *(Apennines) mts.* Italy **81** B3
Appennino Abruzzese *mts.* Italy **81** B3 42 00N 14 00E
Appennino Ligure *mts.* Italy **81** A3 44 00N 9 00E
Appennino Lucano *mts.* Italy **81** C3 40 00N 15 00E
Appennino Tosco-Emiliano *mts.* Italy **81** B3 44 00N 12 00E
Appleton Wisconsin U.S.A. **63** I5 44 17N 88 24W
'Aqaba Jordan **92** O9 29 32N 35 00E
'Aqaba, Gulf of Middle East **92** O9 28 40N 34 40E
Aquidauana Brazil **68** F8 20 27S 55 45W
Ara India **95** E5 25 34N 84 40E
Ara *r.* Japan **101** C3 35 39N 139 51E
Arabian Basin Indian Ocean **112** F7/8 10 00N 65 00E
Arabian Sea Indian Ocean **93** J2 17 00N 60 00E
Aracaju Brazil **68** J10 10 54S 37 07W
Arad Romania **81** D4 46 10N 21 19E
Arafura Sea Australia/Indonesia **110** E8/F8 10 00S 135 00E
Aragón *r.* Spain **77** B3 42 15N 1 40W
Araguaina Brazil **68** H11 7 16S 48 18W
Araguari Brazil **68** H9 18 38S 48 13W
Arāk Iran **93** G5 34 05N 49 42E
Arakan Yoma *mts.* Myanmar **96** H3 18 00N 94 00E
Arakawa Japan **100** L2 35 58N 139 03E
Araks *(Aras, Araxes) r.* Armenia/Azerbaijan **90** F2 39 30N 45 00E
Aral Sea Kazakhstan/Uzbekistan **91** J4 45 00N 60 00E
Aral'sk Kazakhstan **91** J4 46 56N 61 43E
Aranda de Duero Spain **77** B3 41 40N 3 41W
Aranjuez Spain **77** B3 40 02N 3 37W
Aran Island Irish Republic **78** C6 55 00N 8 30W
Aran Islands Irish Republic **78** B5 53 10N 9 50W
Arapiraca Brazil **68** J11 9 45S 36 40W
Ar'ar Saudi Arabia **92** F5 30 58N 41 03E
Araraquara Brazil **69** H8 21 46S 48 08W
Ararat, Mount *see* Bü Ağri Daği
Aras *(Araks, Araxes) r.* Turkey **92** F7 40 00N 43 30E
Arauca Colombia **68** C14 7 04N 70 41W
Araure Venezuela **67** K1 9 36N 69 15W
Araxá Brazil **68** H9 19 37S 46 50W
Araxes *(Araks, Aras) r.* Iran **93** G6 38 40N 46 30E
Arbil Iraq **92** F6 36 12N 44 01E
Arbroath Scotland **78** I8 56 34N 2 35W
Arcachon France **77** B3 44 40N 1 11W
Arcade New York U.S.A. **64** B5 42 32N 78 25W
Arcadia California U.S.A. **51** B3 34 09N 118 00W
Arcadia Pennsylvania U.S.A. **64** B3 40 46N 78 50W
Arcati Brazil **68** J12 4 32S 37 45W
Archipelago Dehalak *is.* Ethiopia **92** F2 15 45N 40 12E
Arctic National Wildlife Refuge Alaska U.S.A. **44** C4 68 30N 145 00W
Arctic Ocean 116
Arda *r.* Bulgaria **81** E3 41 30N 26 00E
Ardabīl Iran **88** G6 38 15N 48 18E
Ardennes *mts.* Belgium **76** D5 50 10N 5 45E
Ardila *r.* Spain **77** A2 38 15N 6 50W
Ardmore Oklahoma U.S.A. **63** G3 34 11N 97 08W
Arendal Norway **79** B2 58 27N 8 56E
Arequipa Peru **68** C9 16 25S 71 32W
Arezzo Italy **81** B3 43 28N 11 53E
Argentan France **76** C4 48 45N 0 01W
Argenteuil France **83** A2 48 57N 2 14E
ARGENTINA 69 D5
Argentine Basin Atlantic Ocean **113** D2 42 00S 45 00W
Argeş *r.* Romania **81** E3 44 00N 26 00E
Argonne Forest Illinois U.S.A. **53** A1 41 43N 87 53W
Argun *(Ergun He) r.* Asia **97** N9 52 00N 120 00E
Argyle Minnesota U.S.A. **39** B1 48 10N 96 50W
Argyle, Lake Australia **110** D6 17 00S 128 30E
Århus Denmark **80** B6 56 15N 10 10E
Arica Chile **68** C9 18 30S 70 20W
Arima Trinidad and Tobago **66** T10 10 38N 61 17W
Aripuanã *r.* Brazil **68** E11 7 00S 60 30W
Ariquemes Brazil **68** E11 9 55S 63 06W
Arizona *state* U.S.A. **62** D3 34 00N 112 00W
Arizpe Mexico **66** B6 30 20N 110 11W
Arjeplog Sweden **79** D4 66 04N 18 00E
Arjona Colombia **68** B15 10 14N 75 22W
Arkalyk Kazakhstan **91** K5 50 17N 66 51E
Arkansas *r.* U.S.A. **63** H4 35 00N 93 00W
Arkansas *state* U.S.A. **63** H3 34 00N 93 00W
Arkansas City Kansas U.S.A. **63** G4 37 03N 97 02W
Arkhangel'sk Russia **88** G8 64 32N 40 40E
Arlanza *r.* Spain **77** B3 42 00N 3 30W
Arlanzón *r.* Spain **77** B3 42 00N 4 00W
Arles France **77** C3 43 41N 4 38E
Arlington Massachusetts U.S.A. **52** B2 42 23N 71 09W
Arlington Vermont U.S.A. **65** G6 43 04N 73 09W
Arlington Washington U.S.A. **42** H4 42 12N 122 09W
Arlington Heights Illinois U.S.A. **53** A3 42 06N 87 59W
Arlit Niger **106** G11 18 50N 7 00E
Arlon Belgium **76** D4 49 41N 5 49E
Armagh Northern Ireland **78** E6 54 21N 6 39W
Armavir Russia **90** E3 44 59N 41 10E
ARMENIA 90 E4/F4
Armenia Colombia **68** B13 4 32N 75 40W
Armenia New York U.S.A. **65** G4 41 51N 73 33W
Armidale Australia **110** I3 30 32S 151 40E
Arnhem Netherlands **76** D5 52 00N 5 53E
Arnhem Land *geog. reg.* Australia **110** E7 13 00S 133 00E
Arno *r.* Italy **81** B3 43 00N 10 00E
Arquipélago dos Bijagós *is.* Guinea-Bissau **106** B10 11 20N 16 40W
Ar Ramādī Iraq **92** F5 33 27N 43 19E
Ar Ramlah Jordan **92** O9 29 28N 35 58E
Arran *i.* Scotland **78** F7 55 35N 5 15W
Ar Raqqah Syria **92** E6 35 57N 39 03E
Ar Riyād Saudi Arabia **93** G3 24 39N 46 46E
Arta Greece **81** D2 39 10N 20 59E
Arthur's Pass New Zealand **111** B2 42 55S 171 34E
Artigas Uruguay **69** F6 30 25S 56 28W
Artigas *r.s.* Antarctica **117** 62 11S 58 51W
Arua Uganda **106** L8 3 02N 30 56E
ARUBA 68 D15 12 30N 70 00W
Arun *r.* England **78** K2 51 00N 0 30W
Arunachal Pradesh *admin.* India **95** H5 28 00N 95 00E
Arusha Tanzania **106** M7 3 23S 36 40E
Aruwimi *r.* Zaïre **106** J8 2 00N 25 00E
Arvika Sweden **79** C2 59 41N 12 38E
Arys' Kazakhstan **91** K3 42 26N 68 49E
Arzamas Russia **90** E6 55 24N 43 48E
Arzew Algeria **77** B2 35 50N 0 19W
Asahi Japan **100** M2 35 43N 140 38E
Asahi-dake *mt.* Japan **100** D3 43 42N 142 54E
Asahikawa Japan **100** D3 43 46N 142 23E
Asaka Japan **101** B4 35 47N 139 37E
Asamankese Ghana **106** E9 5 45N 0 45W
Asansol India **95** F4 23 40N 86 59E
Åsarna Sweden **79** C3 62 40N 14 20E
Asbury Park New Jersey U.S.A. **65** F3 40 14N 74 00W
Ascension Island Atlantic Ocean **113** G6 7 57S 14 22W
Ascoli Piceno Italy **81** B3 42 52N 13 35E
Aseb Ethiopia **92** F1 13 01N 42 47E
Asenovgrad Bulgaria **81** D3 42 00N 24 53E
Ashburton New Zealand **111** B2 43 54S 171 46E
Ashburton *r.* Australia **110** B5 22 30S 116 00E
Ashdod Israel **92** O10 31 48N 34 48E
Åshen *l.* Sweden **79** C2 56 45N 14 40E
Asheville North Carolina U.S.A. **63** J4 35 35N 82 35W
Ashfield Australia **111** G2 33 53S 151 07E
Ash Fork Arizona U.S.A. **62** D4 35 13N 112 29W
Ashikaga Japan **100** C2 36 21N 139 26E
Ashina Japan **101** B1 35 13N 139 36E
Ashizuri-misaki *c.* Japan **100** B1 32 42N 133 00E
Ashkhabad Turkmenistan **91** H2 37 58N 58 24E
Ashland Kentucky U.S.A. **63** J4 38 28N 82 40W
Ashland Ohio U.S.A. **36** D1 40 52N 82 19W
Ashland Oregon U.S.A. **62** B5 42 14N 122 44W
Ashland Wisconsin U.S.A. **35** B2 46 34N 90 54W
Ashokan Reservoir New York U.S.A. **65** F4 42 00N 74 15W
Ashok Nagar India **94** L4 28 38N 77 07E
Ashqelon Israel **92** O10 31 40N 34 35E
Ash Shāriqah United Arab Emirates **93** I4 25 20N 55 20E
Ash Shurayf Saudi Arabia **92** E4 25 50N 39 00E
Ashtabula Ohio U.S.A. **36** F2 41 53N 80 47W
Asilah Morocco **77** A2 35 32N 6 04W
Asir Mountains Saudi Arabia **102** 18 00N 44 00E
Askim Norway **80** B6 59 15N 11 10E
Asmera Ethiopia **92** E2 15 20N 38 58E
Asnières France **83** B2 48 55N 2 17E
Asō Japan **100** M3 36 00N 141 29E
Aspiring, Mount New Zealand **111** A2 44 23S 168 46E
Asquith Australia **111** G3 33 41S 151 07E
Assam *admin.* India **95** G5 26 20N 92 00E
As Samawah Iraq **93** G5 31 18N 45 18E
Assis Brazil **69** G8 22 37S 50 25W
Assisi Italy **81** B3 43 04N 12 37E
As Suq Saudi Arabia **92** F3 21 55N 42 02E
As Suwaydā' Syria **92** P11 32 43N 36 33E
Astārā Azerbaijan **93** G6 38 27N 48 53E
Asti Italy **81** A3 44 54N 8 13E
Astipálaia *i.* Greece **81** E2 36 00N 26 00E
Astoria Oregon U.S.A. **62** B6 46 12N 123 50W
Astrakhan' Russia **90** F4 46 22N 48 04E
Asuka *r.s.* Antarctica **117** 71 32S 24 08E
Asuke Japan **100** J2 35 08N 137 19E
Asunción Paraguay **69** F7 25 15S 57 40W
Aswa *r.* Uganda **106** L8 3 30N 32 30E
Aswân Egypt **92** D3 24 05N 32 56E
Aswân Dam Egypt **92** D3 23 40N 31 50E
Asyût Egypt **92** D4 27 14N 31 07E
Atacama Desert *see* Desierto de Atacama
Atami Japan **100** L2 35 07N 139 04E
Atar Mauritania **106** C12 20 32N 13 08W
Atbara Sudan **92** D2 17 42N 34 00E
Atbara *r.* Sudan **92** D2 17 28N 34 30E
Atbasar Kazakhstan **91** K5 51 49N 68 18E
Atchison Kansas U.S.A. **63** G4 39 33N 95 09W
Athambra *r.* California U.S.A. **49** C3 37 57N 122 07W
Athens Georgia U.S.A. **63** J3 33 57N 83 24W
Athens Greece *see* Athínai
Athens Pennsylvania U.S.A. **64** D4 41 57N 76 31W
Atherton California U.S.A. **49** C1 37 28N 122 11W
Athínai *(Athens)* Greece **81** D2 38 00N 23 44E
Athlone Irish Republic **78** E6 53 25N 7 56W
Athol Massachusetts U.S.A. **65** H5 42 36N 72 14W
Athol Springs *tn.* New York U.S.A. **38** D1 42 45N 78 51W
Áthos *mt.* Greece **81** D3 40 10N 24 19E
Ati Chad **106** I10 13 11N 18 20E
Atlanta Georgia U.S.A. **63** J3 33 45N 84 23W
Atlanta Michigan U.S.A. **35** D1 45 00N 84 07W
Atlantic City New Jersey U.S.A. **65** F2 39 23N 74 27W
Atlantic Ocean 113
Atlantic-Indian Range Atlantic Ocean **113** I1 53 00S 3 00E
Atlas Saharien *mts.* Algeria **106** E14 33 30N 1 00E
Atrek *r.* Asia **93** H6 37 00N 54 50E
Atsugi Japan **100** L2 35 28N 139 22E
Atsumi Japan **100** J1 34 37N 137 06E
Atsumi-hantō *p.* Japan **100** J1 34 40N 137 15E
At Tā'if Saudi Arabia **92** F3 21 15N 40 21E
Attica New York U.S.A. **64** B5 42 52N 78 16W
Attleboro Massachusetts U.S.A. **65** J4 41 57N 71 16W
Aubagne France **77** D3 43 17N 5 35E
Aubenas France **76** C3 44 37N 4 24E
Aubervilliers France **83** B2 48 55N 2 22E
Auburn Indiana U.S.A. **36** A2 41 22N 85 02W
Auburn Maine U.S.A. **63** L5 44 04N 70 27W
Auburn Massachusetts U.S.A. **65** J5 42 13N 71 50W
Auburn New York U.S.A. **64** D5 42 57N 76 34W
Auch France **77** C3 43 40N 0 36E
Auckland New Zealand **111** B3 36 55S 174 47E
Auckland Islands Southern Ocean **114** G2 50 35S 116 00E
Au Gres Michigan U.S.A. **36** C5 44 03N 83 40W
Augsburg Germany **76** E4 48 21N 10 54E
Augusta Australia **110** B3 34 19S 115 09E
Augusta Georgia U.S.A. **63** J3 33 29N 82 00W
Augusta Maine U.S.A. **63** M5 44 17N 69 50W
Aulnay-sous-Bois France **83** C2 48 57N 2 31E
Aulne *r.* France **76** B4 48 10N 4 00W
Aurangābād India **95** D3 19 52N 75 22E
Aurillac France **77** C3 44 56N 2 26E
Au Sable Michigan U.S.A. **36** C5 44 25N 83 20W
Au Sable River Michigan U.S.A. **36** B5 44 40N 84 00W
Austin Texas U.S.A. **63** G3 30 18N 97 47W
AUSTRALIA 110
Australian Capital Territory *(A.C.T.) admin.* Australia **110** H2 35 00S 144 00E
Austral Ridge Pacific Ocean **115** K5 24 00S 155 30W
AUSTRIA 81 B4
Autlán Mexico **66** D3 19 48N 104 20W
Autun France **77** C4 46 58N 4 18E
Auxerre France **77** C4 47 48N 3 35E
Avallon France **77** C4 47 30N 3 54E
Avalon New Jersey U.S.A. **65** F2 39 06N 74 43W
Aveiro Portugal **77** A3 40 38N 8 40W
Avellaneda Argentina **69** F6 34 40S 58 20W
Avesta Sweden **79** D3 60 09N 16 10E
Aveyron *r.* France **77** C3 44 30N 2 05E
Avezzano Italy **81** B3 42 02N 13 26E
Avignon France **77** C3 43 56N 4 48E
Avila Spain **77** B3 40 39N 4 42W
Avilés Spain **77** A3 43 33N 5 55W
Avon Connecticut U.S.A. **65** H4 41 47N 72 51W
Avon New York U.S.A. **64** C5 42 55N 77 44W
Avon *r.* England **78** J3 51 27N 1 40W
Avon Lake *tn.* Ohio U.S.A. **36** D2 41 31N 82 01W
Avranches France **76** B4 48 42N 1 21W
Awaji Japan **100** G1 34 35N 135 00E
Awaji-shima *l.* Japan **100** F1 34 30N 135 45E
Awali *r.* Lebanon **92** O11 33 35N 35 32E
Awash Ethiopia **106** N9 9 01N 41 10E
Awbārī Libya **106** H13 26 35N 12 46E
Ayabe Japan **100** G2 35 19N 135 16E
Ayaguz Kazakhstan **91** N4 47 59N 80 27E
Ayamonte Spain **77** A2 37 13N 7 24W
Ayan Russia **89** P7 56 29N 138 07E
Ayaviri Peru **68** C10 14 53S 70 35W
Aydin Turkey **80** E2 37 51N 27 51E
Ayios Nikólaos Greece **81** E2 35 11N 25 43E
Ayod Sudan **106** L9 8 08N 31 24E
Ayon *i.* Russia **89** S9 69 55N 168 10E
'Aynūnah Saudi Arabia **92** O9 28 06N 35 08E
Ayr Scotland **78** G7 55 28N 4 38W
Ayres Rock *mt.* Australia **110** E4 25 18S 131 18E
Ayutthaya Thailand **99** C6 14 20N 100 35E
AZERBAIJAN 90 F3
Aziscohos Lake Maine U.S.A. **37** Q6 45 00N 71 00W
Azogues Ecuador **68** B12 2 46S 78 56W
Azores *is.* Atlantic Ocean **113** F10 38 30N 28 00W
Azoum *r.* Chad **106** J10 12 00N 21 00E
Azuero, Peninsula de Panama **67** H1 7 40N 81 00W
Azul Argentina **69** F5 36 46S 59 50W
Azurduy Bolivia **68** E9 20 00S 64 29W
Azusa California U.S.A. **51** C3 34 08N 117 54W
Az Zabadānī Syria **92** P11 33 42N 36 03E
Az Zahrān *(Dhahran)* Saudi Arabia **93** H4 26 13N 50 02E

B

Baalbek Lebanon **92** P12 34 00N 36 12E
Babahoyo Ecuador **68** B12 1 53S 79 31W
Babar, Kepulauan *is.* Indonesia **99** H2 8 00S 129 30E
Babatang China **97** J5 30 02N 99 01E
Bab el Mandab *sd.* Red Sea **106** N10 12 30N 47 00E
Babelsberg Germany **83** E1 52 23N 13 05E
Babushkin Russia **88** M2 55 55N 37 44E
Babylon New York U.S.A. **65** G3 40 42N 73 20W
Babylon *hist. site* Iraq **92** F5 32 33N 44 25E
Bacabal Brazil **68** I12 4 15S 44 45W
Bacău Romania **81** E4 46 33N 26 58E
Bacolod The Philippines **99** G6 10 38N 122 58E
Badajoz Spain **77** A2 38 53N 6 58W
Badalona Spain **77** C3 41 27N 2 15E
Bad Axe Michigan U.S.A. **36** D4 43 49N 82 59W
Baden Austria **81** C4 48 01N 16 14E
Badli India **94** L4 28 44N 77 09E
Badulla Sri Lanka **95** E1 6 59N 81 03E
Bafoussam Cameroon **106** H9 5 31N 10 25E
Bāfq Iran **93** I5 31 35N 55 21E
Bagé Brazil **69** G6 31 22S 54 06W
Bagenalstown *see* Muinebeag
Baghdād Iraq **92** F5 33 20N 44 26E
Baghlān Afghanistan **93** K6 36 11N 68 44E
Bahamas Bank Atlantic Ocean **54** 24 00N 77 00W
BAHAMAS, THE 67 I4
Baharampur India **95** F4 24 00N 88 30E
Bahawalpur Pakistan **95** C5 29 24N 71 47E
Bahia *admin.* Brazil **68** I10 12 00S 42 30W
Bahia Blanca Argentina **69** E5 38 45S 62 15W
Bahı'a Blanca *b.* Argentina **69** E5 39 00S 61 00W
Bahia de Campeche *b.* Mexico **66** E4/F4 20 00N 95 00W
Bahia, Grande *b.* Argentina **69** D2 51 30S 68 00W
Bahra el Manzala *l.* Egypt **107** R4 31 18N 31 54E
Bahra el Timsâh *(Lake Timsâh)* Egypt **107** S3 30 34N 32 18E
Bahraich India **95** E5 27 35N 81 36E
BAHRAIN 93 H4
Bahrain, Gulf of The Gulf **93** H4 25 55N 50 30E
Bahr el Abiad *(White Nile) r.* Sudan **92** D1 14 00N 32 20E
Bahr el Arab *r.* Sudan **106** K10 10 00N 27 30E
Bahr el Azraq *(Blue Nile) r.* Sudan **92** D1 13 30N 33 45E
Bahr el Baqar *r.* Egypt **107** S3 30 54N 32 02E
Bahr el Ghazal *r.* Chad **106** I10 14 00N 16 00E
Bahr Faqus *r.* Egypt **107** R3 30 42N 31 42E
Bahr Hadus *r.* Egypt **107** R4 31 01N 31 43E
Bahr Saft *r.* Egypt **107** R3 30 57N 31 48E
Baia Mare Romania **81** D4 47 39N 23 36E
Baicheng China **97** O8 45 37N 122 48E
Baidyabati India **94** K3 22 48N 88 20E
Baie de la Seine *b.* France **76** B4 49 40N 0 30W
Baiwanzhuang China **100** G1 39 55N 116 18E
Baja Hungary **81** C4 46 11N 18 58E
Baja California *p.* Mexico **66** B5 27 30N 113 00W
Baj Baj India **94** J1 22 28N 88 10E
Baker Oregon U.S.A. **62** C5 44 46N 117 50W
Baker Island Alaska U.S.A. **42** B3 55 30N 133 30W
Baker, Mount Washington U.S.A. **42** H4 48 48N 121 50W
Baker River Washington U.S.A. **42** H4 48 40N 121 35W
Baku Azerbaijan **90** F3 40 22N 49 53E
Balaghat India **95** E4 21 48N 80 16E
Balaghat Range *mts.* India **95** D3 18 45N 77 00E
Balakovo Russia **90** F5 52 04N 47 46E
Bala, Lake *see* Tegid, Llyn
Balama Mozambique **107** M5 13 19S 38 35E
Bālā Morghāb Afghanistan **93** J6 35 34N 63 20E
Balashikha Russia **90** D6 55 47N 37 59E
Balashov Russia **90** E5 51 31N 43 10E
Balassagyarmat Hungary **81** C4 48 06N 19 17E
Balaton *l.* Hungary **81** C4 47 00N 17 30E
Balboa Panama **67** Y2 8 57N 79 33W
Balclutha New Zealand **111** A1 46 16S 169 46E
Baldeney-see *l.* Germany **76** J2 51 24N 7 02E
Baldwin Park *tn.* California U.S.A. **51** C3 34 05N 117 59W
Balearic Islands Mediterranean Sea **77** E4
Balgowlah Australia **111** H2 33 48S 151 16E
Bali *i.* Indonesia **99** E2/F2 8 00S 115 00E
Balikesir Turkey **92** C6 39 37N 27 51E
Balikpapan Indonesia **99** F3 1 15S 116 50E
Balkham Hills Australia **111** F2 33 46S 150 58E
Balkhash Kazakhstan **91** L4 46 50N 74 57E
Balkhash, Lake *see* Ozero Balkhash
Ballarat Australia **110** G2 37 36S 143 58E
Balleny Islands Southern Ocean **114** H1 66 30S 1 64E
Ballston Spa New York U.S.A. **65** G6 43 00N 73 49W
Bālly India **94** K2 22 38N 88 20E
Ballygunge India **94** K2 22 31N 88 20E
Ballymena Northern Ireland **78** E6 54 52N 6 17W
Balmain Australia **111** G2 33 51S 151 11E
Balsas Mexico **66** E3 18 00N 99 44W
Balta Ukraine **81** E4 47 58N 29 39E
Baltic Sea Europe **79** D2 55 15N 17 00E
Baltimore Maryland U.S.A. **64** D2 39 18N 76 38W
Baluchistan *geog. reg.* Pakistan **94** A5/B5 27 30N 65 00E
Bam Iran **93** I4 29 07N 58 20E
Bamako Mali **106** D10 12 40N 7 59W
Bambari Central African Republic **106** J9 5 40N 20 37E
Bamberg Germany **76** E5 49 54N 10 54E
Bamenda Cameroon **106** H9 5 55N 10 09E
Bamingui Bangoran National Park Central African Republic **106** I9 8 00N 20 00E
Banaba *i.* Nauru **114** G7 1 00S 167 00E
Banas *r.* India **95** D5 26 00N 75 00E
Banbury England **78** J4 52 04N 1 20W
Banda India **95** E5 25 28N 80 20E
Banda Aceh Indonesia **99** B5 5 30N 95 20E
Bandama Blanc *r.* Cote d'Ivoire **106** D9 8 00N 5 45W
Bandar Abbās Iran **93** I4 27 12N 56 15E
Bandar-e Lengeh Iran **93** H4 26 34N 54 52E
Bandar-e Torkeman Iran **93** H6 36 55N 54 01E
Bandar Khomeynī Iran **93** G5 30 40N 49 08E
Bandar Seri Begawan Brunei **99** F4 4 56N 114 58E
Bandarbeyla Somalia **106** P9 9 30N 50 50E
Banda Sea Indonesia **99** H2 6 00S 127 00E
Bandeirantes Beach Brazil **69** P2 23 01S 43 23W
Bandel India **94** K3 22 55N 88 23E
Bandirma Turkey **92** C7 40 21N 27 58E
Bandundu Zaïre **107** I7 3 20S 17 24E
Bandung Indonesia **99** D2 6 57S 107 34E
Banfora Burkina **106** E10 10 36N 4 45W
Bangalore India **95** D2 12 58N 77 35E
Bangassou Central African Republic **106** J8 4 41N 22 48E
Banghāzī *(Benghazi)* Libya **106** J14 32 07N 20 04E
Bangka *i.* Indonesia **99** D3 2 00S 106 30E
Bangkok *(Krung Thep)* Thailand **99** C6 13 44N 100 30E
BANGLADESH 95 F/G4
Bangor Maine U.S.A. **63** M5 44 49N 68 47W
Bangor Northern Ireland **78** F6 54 40N 5 40W
Bangor Wales **78** G5 53 13N 4 08W
Bangui Central African Republic **106** I8 4 23N 18 37E
Bangweulu, Lake Zambia **107** K5 11 15S 29 45E
Ban Hat Yai Thailand **99** C5 7 00N 100 28E
Banja Luka Bosnia-Herzegovina **81** C3 44 47N 17 11E
Banjarmasin Indonesia **99** E3 3 22S 114 33E
Banjul The Gambia **106** B10 13 28N 16 39W
Banka India **94** K2 22 36N 88 17E
Banks, Cape Australia **111** G1 34 00S 151 15E
Banks Islands Vanuatu **110** L7 13 40S 167 30E
Banks Peninsula New Zealand **111** B2 43 50S 173 10E
Bankstown Australia **111** G2 33 55S 151 02E
Ban Me Thuot Vietnam **99** D6 12 41N 108 02E
Bann *r.* Northern Ireland **78** E7 54 20N 6 10W
Bannu Pakistan **93** L5 33 00N 70 40E
Bansberia India **94** K3 22 57N 88 23E
Banská Bystrica Czechoslovakia **80** C4 48 44N 19 10E
Banstead England **82** C2 51 19N 0 12W
Bantry Bay Irish Republic **78** B3 51 35N 9 40W
Banyuwangi Indonesia **99** E2 8 12S 114 22E
Baoding China **97** N6 38 54N 115 26E
Baoji China **97** L5 34 23N 107 16E
Baotou China **97** M7 40 38N 109 59E
Ba'qūbah Iraq **92** F5 33 45N 44 40E
Baracaldo Spain **77** B3 43 17N 2 59W
Barahanagar India **94** K2 22 38N 88 23E

Barahona Dominican Republic **67** J3 18 13N 71 07W
Barajala Canal India **94** J2 22 35N 88 12E
Bārākpur India **94** K3 22 45N 88 22E
Baral India **94** K1 22 27N 88 22E
Baranof Alaska U.S.A. **42** B3 57 05N 134 50W
Baranof Island Alaska U.S.A. **42** A3 57 30N 135 00W
Baranovichi Belarus **90** B5 53 09N 26 00E
Bārāsat India **94** K2 22 43N 88 26E
Barbacena Brazil **69** I8 21 13S 43 47W
BARBADOS **66** V12
Barbastro Spain **77** C3 42 02N 0 07E
Barbuda *i.* Antigua & Barbuda **67** L3 17 41N 61 48W
Barcaldine Australia **110** H5 23 31S 145 15E
Barcellona Italy **81** C2 38 10N 15 15E
Barcelona Spain **77** C3 41 25N 2 10E
Barcelona Venezuela **68** E15 10 08N 64 43W
Barcelonette France **76** D3 44 24N 6 40E
Barcelos Brazil **68** E12 0 59S 62 58W
Barcoo *r.* Australia **110** G5 23 30S 144 00E
Barcs Hungary **81** C4 45 58N 17 30E
Barddhamān India **95** F4 23 20N 88 00E
Barduelv *r.* Norway **79** D4 68 48N 18 22E
Bareilly India **95** D5 28 20N 79 24E
Barents Sea Arctic Ocean **116** 75 00N 40 00E
Barga China **95** E6 30 51N 81 20E
Barge Canal New York U.S.A. **64** C6 43 07N 77 27W
Bari Italy **68** C3 41 07N 16 52E
Bariga Nigeria **107** V3 6 32N 3 28E
Barinas Venezuela **68** C14 8 36N 70 15W
Barisal Bangladesh **95** G4 22 41N 90 20E
Bariti, Lake India **94** K3 22 48N 88 26E
Barking *bor.* Greater London England **82** D3 51 33N 0 06E
Barkly Tableland Australia **110** F6 17 30S 137 00E
Bar-le-Duc France **76** D4 48 46N 5 10E
Barlee, Lake Australia **110** B4 28 30S 120 00E
Barletta Italy **81** C3 41 20N 16 17E
Barnaul Russia **91** N5 53 21N 83 45E
Barnes England **82** C2 51 28N 0 15W
Barnet *bor.* Greater London England **82** C3 51 39N 0 12W
Barnstable Massachusetts U.S.A. **65** K4 41 00N 70 00W
Barnstaple Devon England **78** G3 51 05N 4 04W
Barquisimeto Venezuela **68** D15 10 03N 69 18W
Barra *i.* Scotland **78** D8 57 00N 7 25W
Barra da Tijuca Brazil **69** P1 23 00S 43 20W
Barra do Corda Brazil **68** H11 5 30S 45 12W
Barrancabermeja Colombia **68** C14 7 06N 73 54W
Barrancas Venezuela **68** E14 8 45N 62 13W
Barrancones Point Trinidad and Tobago **66** T10 10 30N 61 28W
Barranjoey Head *c.* Australia **111** H3 33 35S 151 20E
Barranquilla Colombia **68** C15 11 10N 74 50W
Barre Massachusetts U.S.A. **65** H5 42 25N 72 07W
Barre Vermont U.S.A. **63** L5 44 13N 72 31W
Barreiras Brazil **68** I10 12 09S 44 58W
Barreiro Portugal **77** A2 38 40N 9 05W
Barron Wisconsin U.S.A. **35** B2 45 24N 91 50W
Barrow Alaska U.S.A. **10** D7 71 16N 156 50W
Barrow *r.* Irish Republic **78** D4 52 55N 7 00W
Barrow-in-Furness England **78** H6 54 07N 3 14W
Barrow Island Australia **110** B5 21 00S 115 00E
Barrow, Point Alaska U.S.A. **10** D7 71 05N 156 00W
Barry Wales **78** H3 51 24N 3 18W
Bartlesville Oklahoma U.S.A. **63** G4 36 44N 95 59W
Bartolome, Cape Alaska U.S.A. **42** B3 55 15N 133 39W
Basalt Island Hong Kong U.K. **98** D1 22 19N 114 21E
Basdorf Germany **83** F2 52 44N 13 27E
Basel Switzerland **77** D4 47 33N 7 36E
Basildon England **78** L3 51 34N 0 25E
Basingstoke England **78** J3 51 16N 1 05W
Baskunchak Russia **90** F4 48 14N 46 44E
Bassas da India *i.* Mozambique Channel **107** M3 22 00S 40 00E
Bassein Myanmar **96** H2 16 46N 94 45E
Basse Terre Trinidad and Tobago **66** T9 10 07N 61 17W
Basse Terre *i.* Lesser Antilles **67** L3 16 00N 61 20W
Bass Strait Australia **110** H2 40 00S 145 00E
Basswood Lake Canada/U.S.A. **35** B2 48 04N 91 34W
Bastia Corsica France **77** D3 42 14N 9 26E
Bastogne Belgium **76** D4 50 00N 5 43E
Bastrop Louisiana U.S.A. **63** H3 32 49N 91 54W
Bata Equatorial Guinea **106** G8 1 51N 9 49E
Batakan Indonesia **99** E3 4 03S 114 39E
Batala India **95** D6 31 48N 75 17E
Batanagar India **94** K2 22 30N 88 14E
Batan Datuk Malaysia **99** C4 3 58N 100 47E
Batangafo Central African Republic **106** I9 7 27N 18 11E
Batangas The Philippines **99** G6 13 46N 121 01E
Batavia New York U.S.A. **64** B5 43 00N 73 11W
Bate Bay Australia **111** G1 34 03S 151 11E
Bath England **78** I3 51 23N 2 22W
Bath Jamaica **67** R7 17 57N 76 22W
Bath New York U.S.A. **64** C5 42 21N 77 19W
Batha *r.* Chad **106** I10 13 00N 19 00E
Bathsheba Barbados **66** V12 13 12N 59 32W
Bathurst Australia **110** H3 33 27S 149 35E
Bathurst Island Australia **110** E7 12 00S 130 00E
Batna Algeria **106** G15 35 34N 6 10E
Baton Rouge Louisiana U.S.A. **63** G3 30 30N 91 10W
Batroûn Lebanon **92** O12 36 16N 35 40E
Battambang Cambodia **99** C6 13 06N 103 13E
Batticaloa Sri Lanka **95** E1 7 43N 81 42E
Battle Creek *tn.* Michigan U.S.A. **63** J5 42 20N 85 21W
Batumi Georgia **90** E3 41 37N 41 36E
Bat Yam Israel **92** O10 32 01N 34 45E
Baubau Indonesia **99** G2 5 30S 122 37E
Bauchi Nigeria **106** G10 10 16N 9 50E
Baudette Minnesota U.S.A. **39** B1 48 40N 95 40W
Bauriā India **94** J1 22 29N 88 09E
Bauru Brazil **69** H8 22 19S 49 07W
Bautzen Germany **76** E5 51 11N 14 29E
Baxter State Park Maine U.S.A. **33** C2 46 00N 69 00W
Bayamo Cuba **67** I4 20 23N 76 39W
Bayan Ha Shan *mts.* China **84** 34 00N 100 00E
Bay City Michigan U.S.A. **63** J5 43 35N 83 52W
Bay City Texas U.S.A. **63** G2 28 59N 96 00W
Baydhabo Somalia **106** N8 3 08N 43 34E
Bayerische Alpen *mts.* Germany **77** E4 47 00N 11 00E
Bayeux France **76** B4 49 16N 0 42W
Bayfield Barbados **66** W12 13 10N 59 25W
Baykal, Lake *see* Ozero Baykal
Baykonyr Kazakhstan **91** K4 47 50N 66 03E
Bayonne France **77** B3 43 30N 1 28W
Bayonne New Jersey U.S.A. **50** B1 40 39N 74 07W
Bayreuth Germany **76** E5 49 27N 11 35E
Bay Ridge *tn.* New York U.S.A. **50** C1 40 37N 74 02W
Bay Shore New York U.S.A. **65** G3 40 43N 73 15W
Baytown Texas U.S.A. **63** H2 29 43N 94 59W
Baza Spain **77** B2 37 30N 2 45W
Bcharre Lebanon **92** P12 34 15N 36 00E
Beachy Head *c.* England **78** L2 50 44N 0 16E
Beacon New York U.S.A. **65** G4 41 31N 73 59W
Beardmore Glacier Antarctica **117** 84 00S 170 00E
Bear Lake U.S.A. **62** D5 42 00N 111 20W
Bearpaw Mountain Montana U.S.A. **41** D1 48 09N 109 39W
Beatrice Nebraska U.S.A. **63** G5 40 17N 96 45W
Beatty Nevada U.S.A. **62** C4 36 54N 116 45W
Beauchamp France **83** A3 49 00N 2 12E
Beaufort South Carolina U.S.A. **63** J3 32 26N 80 40W
Beaufort Island Hong Kong U.K. **98** C1 22 11N 114 15E
Beaufort Sea Arctic Ocean **116** 72 00N 135 00W
Beaumont Texas U.S.A. **63** H3 30 04N 94 06W
Beaune France **77** C4 47 92N 4 50E
Beauvais France **76** C4 49 26N 2 05E
Beaver Alaska U.S.A. **44** B4 66 22N 147 30W
Beaver Island Michigan U.S.A. **36** A6 45 40N 85 30W
Béchar Algeria **106** E14 31 35N 2 17W
Becharof Lake Alaska U.S.A. **10** D4 58 00N 156 30W
Beckenham England **82** C2 51 24N 0 01W
Beckley West Virginia U.S.A. **63** J4 37 46N 81 12W
Becontree England **82** D3 51 34N 0 10E
Bedford England **78** K4 52 08N 0 29W
Bedford Massachusetts U.S.A. **52** A2 42 28N 71 17W
Bedford Pennsylvania U.S.A. **64** B3 40 02N 78 31W
Beersheba Israel **92** O10 31 15N 34 47E
Beeville Texas U.S.A. **63** G2 28 25N 97 47W
Begna *r.* Norway **79** B3 61 00N 9 00E
Behala *see* South Suburbs
Behbehān Iran **93** H5 30 34N 50 18E
Behm Canal *sd.* Alaska U.S.A. **42** B3 56 00N 131 00W
Beht *r.* Morocco **77** A1 34 30N 5 50W
Bei'an China **97** P8 48 16N 126 36E
Beihai China **97** L3 21 29N 109 10E
Beihai *l.* China **101** G1 39 57N 116 22E
Beijing *(Peking)* China **97** N7 39 55N 116 26E
Beira Mozambique **107** L4 19 49S 34 52E
Beirut *see* Beyrouth
Beiyuan China **101** G2 40 02N 116 25E
Beja Portugal **77** A2 38 01N 7 52W
Bejaïa Algeria **106** G15 36 49N 5 03E
Békes Hungary **81** D4 46 45N 21 09E
Bela Pakistan **94** B5 26 12N 66 20E
BELARUS *(BYELORUSSIA)* **90** B5
Belaya Tserkov Ukraine **90** C4 49 49N 30 10E
Belchertown Massachusetts U.S.A. **65** H5 42 17N 72 25W
Belém Brazil **68** H12 1 27S 48 29W
Belfast Maine U.S.A. **33** C1 44 26N 69 01W
Belfast New York U.S.A. **64** B5 42 21N 78 08W
Belfast Northern Ireland **78** F6 54 35N 5 55W
Belford Roxe Brazil **69** P2 22 45S 43 24W
Belfort France **77** D4 47 38N 6 52E
Belgaum India **95** C3 15 54N 74 36E
Belgharia India **94** K2 22 39N 88 23E
BELGIUM **76** D2
Belgorod Russia **90** D5 50 38N 36 36E
Belgorod Dnestrovskiy Ukraine **90** C4 46 10N 30 19E
Belgrade *see* Beograd
Beliaghata India **94** K2 22 34N 88 23E
Belitung *i.* Indonesia **99** D3 2 30S 108 00E
BELIZE **66** G3
Belize Belize **66** G3 17 29N 88 10W
Bellaire Michigan U.S.A. **36** A5 44 59N 85 12W
Bellary India **95** D3 15 11N 76 54E
Bella Vista Argentina **69** F7 28 31S 59 00W
Belle-Île *i.* France **77** B4 47 20N 3 10W
Belle Island Michigan U.S.A. **52** F2 42 21N 82 59W
Belleplaine Barbados **66** V12 13 14N 59 35W
Bellevue Ohio U.S.A. **36** D2 41 16N 82 51W
Bellevue Pennsylvania U.S.A. **53** D1 40 32N 80 08W
Bellflower California U.S.A. **51** B2 33 53N 118 08W
Bellingham Washington U.S.A. **62** B6 48 45N 122 29W
Bellingshausen *r.s.* Antarctica **117** 62 12S 58 58W
Bellingshausen Sea Southern Ocean **117** 71 00S 85 00W
Bello Colombia **68** B14 6 20N 75 41W
Belluno Italy **81** B4 46 08N 12 13E
Bellwood Illinois U.S.A. **53** A2 41 51N 87 52W
Bellwood Pennsylvania U.S.A. **64** B3 40 36N 78 21W
Belmont California U.S.A. **49** B2 37 34N 122 20W
Belmont Massachusetts U.S.A. **52** B2 42 22N 71 11W
Belmopan Belize **66** G3 17 13N 88 48W
Belogorsk Russia **89** O6 50 55N 128 26E
Belo Horizonte Brazil **68** I9 19 54S 43 54W
Belovo Russia **91** O5 54 27N 86 19E
Bel'tsy Moldova **90** B4 47 44N 27 41E
Belur India **94** K2 22 37N 88 20E
Belvidere New Jersey U.S.A. **64** E3 40 50N 75 05W
Belyy *i.* Russia **89** J10 73 00N 70 00E
Belyy Yar Russia **91** O6 58 28N 85 03E
Bembézar *r.* Spain **77** A2 38 00N 5 15W
Bemidji Minnesota U.S.A. **63** H6 47 29N 94 52W
Benavente Spain **77** A3 42 00N 5 40W
Benbecula *i.* Scotland **78** D9 57 25N 7 20W
Bend Oregon U.S.A. **62** B5 44 04N 121 20W
Bendery Moldova **90** B4 46 50N 29 29E
Bendigo Australia **110** G2 36 48S 144 21E
Benevento Italy **81** B3 41 08N 14 46E
Benfica Brazil **69** P2 22 52S 43 16W
Bengal, Bay of Indian Ocean **95** F3/G3 17 00N 88 00E
Bengbu China **97** N5 32 56N 117 27E
Benghazi *see* Banghāzī
Bengkulu Indonesia **99** C3 3 46S 102 16E
Benguela Angola **107** H5 12 34S 13 24E
Beni Abbès Algeria **106** E14 30 11N 2 14W
Benicarló Spain **77** C3 40 25N 0 25E
Beni Mellal Morocco **106** D14 32 22N 6 29W
BENIN **106** F10
Benin, Bight of W. Africa **106** F9 5 05N 2 30E
Benin City Nigeria **106** G9 6 19N 5 41E
Beni, Rio *r.* Bolivia **68** D10 13 00S 67 30W
Beni Saf Algeria **77** B2 35 28N 1 22W
Beni Suef Egypt **92** D4 29 05N 31 05E
Benjamin Constant Brazil **68** C12 4 23S 69 59W
Ben Macdui *mt.* Scotland **78** H9 57 04N 3 40W
Benmore, Lake New Zealand **111** B2 44 10S 170 20E
Ben Nevis *mt.* Scotland **78** G8 56 40N 5 00W
Bennington Vermont U.S.A. **65** G5 42 54N 73 12W
Bénoué *(Benue) r.* Cameroon **106** H9 8 10N 13 50E
Benson Arizona U.S.A. **62** D3 31 58N 110 19W
Bentham's Barbados **66** V13 13 18N 59 40W
Benton Harbor *tn.* Michigan U.S.A. **63** I5 42 07N 86 27W
Benue *(Bénoué) r.* Nigeria **106** H9 8 00N 7 40E
Ben Wyvis *mt.* Scotland **78** G9 57 40N 4 35W
Benxi China **97** O7 41 21N 123 45E
Beograd *(Belgrade)* Serbia Yugoslavia **81** D3 44 50N 20 30E
Beppu Japan **100** B1 33 18N 131 30E
Berat Albania **81** D3 40 43N 19 46E
Berber Sudan **92** D2 18 01N 34 00E
Berbera Somalia **106** O10 10 28N 45 02E
Berbérati Central African Republic **106** I8 4 19N 15 51E
Berck France **76** C5 50 24N 1 35E
Berdichev Ukraine **90** B4 49 54N 28 39E
Berdyansk Ukraine **90** D4 46 45N 36 47E
Beregovo Ukraine **81** D4 48 13N 22 39E
Berezina *r.* Belarus **90** B5 54 00N 29 00E
Berezniki Russia **91** H6 59 26N 56 49E
Berezovo Russia **89** I8 63 58N 65 00E
Bergama Turkey **80** E2 39 08N 27 10E
Bergamo Italy **81** A4 45 42N 9 40E
Bergen Norway **79** B3 60 23N 5 20E
Bergenfield New Jersey U.S.A. **50** C2 40 56N 74 00W
Bergerac France **77** C3 44 50N 0 29E
Bering Sea Pacific Ocean **114** H13/I13 60 00N 175 00W
Berkåk Norway **79** C3 62 48N 10 03E
Berkakit Russia **89** O7 56 36N 124 49E
Berkeley California U.S.A. **49** B3 37 53N 122 17W
Berkeley Illinois U.S.A. **53** A2 41 53N 87 56W
Berkeley Springs *tn.* West Virginia U.S.A. **64** B2 39 38N 78 14W
Berkley Michigan U.S.A. **52** E2 42 31N 83 12W
Berkner Island Antarctica **117** 80 00S 45 00W
Berkshire *co.* England **82** A2 51 28N 1 00W
Berlevåg Norway **79** F5 70 50N 29 09E
Berlin Germany **76** E5 52 32N 13 25E
Berlin New Hampshire U.S.A. **63** L5 44 27N 71 13W
Berliner Forst *pk.* Germany **83** F2 52 38N 13 16E
Berliner Forst Düppel *pk.* Germany **83** E1 52 24N 13 07E
Berliner Forst Grunewald *pk.* Germany **83** E1 52 28N 13 13E
Berliner Forst Spandau *pk.* Germany **83** E2 52 35N 13 10E
Berliner Stadtforst *pk.* Germany **83** G1 52 28N 13 24E
Berliner Stadtforst Köpenick *pk.* Germany **83** G1 52 24N 13 37E
Berlin Lake *res.* Ohio U.S.A. **36** E1 40 57N 81 06W
Bermuda *i.* Atlantic Ocean **113** B10 32 50N 64 20W
Bern Switzerland **77** D4 46 57N 7 26E
Bernardston Massachusetts U.S.A. **65** H5 42 39N 72 35W
Bernardsville New Jersey U.S.A. **65** F3 40 43N 74 35W
Bernau Germany **83** G2 52 41N 13 36E
Berner Alpen *mts.* Switzerland **77** D4 46 25N 7 30E
Berowra Australia **111** G3 33 37S 151 09E
Berthold North Dakota U.S.A. **40** C1 48 20N 101 44W
Bertoua Cameroon **106** H8 4 34N 13 42E
Berwick Maine U.S.A. **65** K6 43 17N 70 54W
Berwick Pennsylvania U.S.A. **64** D4 41 04N 76 13W
Berwick-upon-Tweed England **78** I7 55 46N 2 00W
Berwyn Illinois U.S.A. **53** A2 41 49N 87 52W
Besançon France **77** D4 47 14N 6 02E
Besenville Illinois U.S.A. **53** A2 41 56N 87 59W
Beskidy Zachodnie *mts.* Poland **80** D4 50 00N 20 00E
Beskudnikovo Russia **88** M2 55 54N 37 38E
Bethal Park Pennsylvania U.S.A. **53** D1 40 19N 80 03W
Bethel Alaska U.S.A. **10** C5 60 49N 161 49W
Bethesda Maryland U.S.A. **64** C1 39 00N 77 05W
Bethlehem Jordan **92** O10 31 42N 35 12E
Bethlehem Pennsylvania U.S.A. **64** E3 40 36N 75 22W
Béthune France **76** C5 50 32N 2 38E
Betsiboka *r.* Madagascar **107** O4 17 00S 46 30E
Beverley Massachusetts U.S.A. **65** K5 42 35N 70 52W
Beverly Hills California U.S.A. **51** A3 34 03N 118 22W
Bexley *bor.* Greater London England **82** D2 51 27N 0 09E
Bexley Heath England **82** D2 51 28N 0 05E
Beyla Guinea **106** D9 8 42N 8 39W
Beyrouth *(Beirut)* Lebanon **92** O11 33 52N 35 30E
Beyşehir Gölü *l.* Turkey **92** D6 37 40N 31 43E
Béziers France **77** C3 43 21N 3 13E
Bhadgaon Nepal **95** F5 27 41N 85 26E
Bhadravati India **95** D2 13 54N 75 38E
Bhadreswar India **94** K3 22 50N 88 20E
Bhagalpur India **95** F5 25 14N 86 59E
Bhandara India **95** D4 21 10N 79 41E
Bharatpur India **95** D5 27 14N 77 29E
Bharuch India **95** C4 21 40N 73 02E
Bhatinda India **95** C6 30 10N 74 58E
Bhātpāra India **94** K3 22 52N 88 25E
Bhavnagar India **95** C4 21 46N 72 14E
Bhilwara India **95** C5 25 23N 74 39E
Bhima *r.* India **95** D3 17 00N 77 00E
Bhiwandi India **95** C3 19 21N 73 08E
Bhopal India **95** D4 23 17N 77 28E
Bhubaneshwar India **95** F4 20 13N 85 50E
Bhuj India **94** B4 23 12N 69 54E
Bhusawal India **95** D4 21 01N 75 50E
BHUTAN **95** F/G5
Biała Podlaska Poland **80** D5 52 03N 23 05E
Białystok Poland **80** D5 53 09N 23 10E
Biarritz France **77** B3 43 29N 1 33W
Bibai Japan **100** D3 43 21N 141 53E
Biche Trinidad and Tobago **66** T9 10 26N 61 07W
Bida Nigeria **106** G9 9 06N 5 59E
Bidar India **95** D3 17 56N 77 35E
Biddeford Maine U.S.A. **63** L5 43 29N 70 27W
Biebrza *r.* Poland **80** D5 53 00N 22 00E
Biel Switzerland **77** D4 46 27N 8 13E
Bielefeld Germany **76** D5 52 02N 8 32E
Biella Italy **81** A4 45 34N 8 04E
Bielsko-Biała Poland **80** C4 49 50N 19 00E
Bielsk Podlaski Poland **80** D5 52 47N 23 11E
Bièvres France **83** A2 48 45N 2 11E
Biferno *r.* Italy **81** B3 41 00N 14 00E
Biğa Turkey **80** E3 40 13N 27 14E
Big Bay De Noc Michigan U.S.A. **35** C2 45 50N 86 30W
Big Black *r.* Mississippi U.S.A. **63** H3 33 00N 90 00W
Bigelow Mountain Maine U.S.A. **37** Q6 45 10N 70 18W
Big Flats New York U.S.A. **64** D5 42 08N 76 57W
Big Fork River Minnesota U.S.A. **35** B2 48 00N 93 45W
Biggin Hill *tn.* England **82** D2 51 18N 0 04E
Bighorn *r.* U.S.A. **62** E6 45 00N 108 00W
Bighorn Mountains U.S.A. **62** E5 44 00N 108 00W
Big Lake Maine U.S.A. **31** A2 45 10N 67 45W
Big Muddy Creek Montana U.S.A. **40** C1 48 40N 104 50W
Big Rapids *tn.* Michigan U.S.A. **36** A4 43 42N 85 31W
Big Santa Anita Reservoir California U.S.A. **51** B3 34 11N 118 01W
Big Sioux *r.* Minnesota/South Dakota U.S.A. **63** G5 44 00N 96 00W
Big Spring *tn.* Texas U.S.A. **62** F3 32 15N 101 30W
Big Tujunga Reservoir California U.S.A. **51** B4 34 19N 118 11W
Bihac Bosnia-Herzegovina **81** C3 44 49N 15 53E
Bihar *admin.* India **95** F4 24 40N 86 00E
Bijapur India **95** D3 16 47N 75 48E
Bījar Iran **93** G6 35 52N 47 39E
Bikaner India **95** C5 28 01N 73 22E
Bilaspur India **95** E4 27 51N 82 00E
Bilbao Spain **77** B3 43 15N 2 56W
Bilibino Russia **89** S9 68 00N 166 15E
Billings Montana U.S.A. **62** E6 45 47N 108 30W
Biloxi Mississippi U.S.A. **63** I3 30 24N 88 55W
Binghamton New York U.S.A. **64** E5 42 06N 75 55W
Bintulu Malaysia **99** E4 3 12N 113 01E
Bioko *i.* Equatorial Guinea **106** G8 3 00N 8 20E
Birao Central African Republic **106** J10 10 11N 22 49E
Biratnagar Nepal **95** F5 26 27N 87 17E
Birch Creek Montana U.S.A. **41** C1 48 20N 112 50W
Birch Lake Minnesota U.S.A. **35** B2 47 45N 91 48W
Birdsville Australia **110** F4 25 50S 139 20E
Bīrjand Iran **93** I5 32 55N 59 10E
Birkenhead England **78** H5 53 24N 3 02W
Birkenwerder Germany **83** F2 52 42N 13 17E
Bîrlad Romania **81** E4 46 14N 27 40E
Birmingham Alabama U.S.A. **63** I3 33 30N 86 55W
Birmingham England **78** J4 52 30N 1 50W
Birnin Kebbi Nigeria **106** F10 12 30N 4 11E
Birobidzhan Russia **89** P5 48 49N 132 54E
Biscay, Bay of Atlantic Ocean **77** B4 45 30N 2 50W
Biscoe Islands Antarctica **117** 66 00S 67 00W
Bishkek *(Frunze)* Kirgyzstan **91** L3 42 53N 74 46E
Bismarck North Dakota U.S.A. **62** F6 46 50N 100 48W
Bismarck Archipelago Papua New Guinea **110** H9/I9 2 30S 149 00E
Bismarck, Cape Greenland **116** 77 00N 18 00W
Bismarck Sea Papua New Guinea **110** H9 4 00S 147 30E
Bissau Guinea-Bissau **106** B10 11 52N 15 39W
Bistrița Romania **81** D4 47 08N 24 30E
Bistrița *r.* Romania **81** E4 47 00N 25 00E
Bitola Macedonia **81** D3 41 01N 21 21E
Bitterroot Range *mts.* U.S.A. **62** D6 46 00N 114 00W
Biwa-ko *l.* Japan **100** H2 35 10N 136 00E
Biya *r.* Russia **91** O5 51 00N 88 00E
Biysk Russia **91** O5 52 35N 85 16E
Bizerte Tunisia **106** G15 37 18N 9 52E
Blackall Australia **110** H5 24 23S 145 27E
Blackburn England **78** I5 53 45N 2 29W
Black Forest *see* Schwarzwald
Black Lake Michigan U.S.A. **36** B6 45 30N 84 20W
Black Mountains Wales **78** H3 51 55N 3 10W
Black Point Hong Kong U.K. **98** A2 22 24N 113 54E
Blackpool England **78** H5 53 50N 3 03W
Black River Michigan U.S.A. **36** D4 43 25N 82 35W
Black River *tn.* Jamaica **67** Q8 18 02N 77 52W
Black Sea Eurasia **90** C3 43 00N 35 00E
Black Volta *r.* Ghana **106** E10 9 00N 2 40W
Blackwater *r.* Irish Republic **78** C4 52 10N 9 05W
Blackwell Oklahoma U.S.A. **63** G4 36 47N 97 18W
Blagoevgrad Bulgaria **81** D3 41 01N 23 05E
Blagoveshchensk Russia **89** O6 50 19N 127 30E
Blaine Washington U.S.A. **42** H4 49 00N 122 44W
Blair Island California U.S.A. **49** C2 37 31N 122 13W
Blanc, Cape *see* Ras Nouadhibou
Blanchisseuse Trinidad and Tobago **66** T10 10 47N 61 20W
Blankenburg Germany **83** F2 52 35N 13 26E
Blankenfelde Germany **83** F1 52 19N 13 24E
Blantyre Malawi **107** L4 15 46S 35 00E
Blenheim New Zealand **111** B2 41 32S 173 58E
Bligh Water *sd.* Fiji **114** T16 17 00S 178 00E
Block Island Rhode Island U.S.A. **65** J4 41 10N 71 34W
Block Island Sound New York U.S.A. **65** H4 41 08N 72 00W
Bloemfontein Republic of South Africa **107** K2 29 07S 26 14E
Bloody Foreland *c.* Irish Republic **78** C7 55 10N 8 15W
Bloomington Illinois U.S.A. **63** I5 40 29N 89 00W
Bloomington Indiana U.S.A. **63** I4 39 10N 86 31W
Bloomfield New Jersey U.S.A. **50** B2 40 49N 74 10W
Bloomfield New York U.S.A. **50** B1 40 37N 74 10W
Bloomsburg Pennsylvania U.S.A. **64** D3 40 59N 76 27W
Bluefield West Virginia U.S.A. **63** J4 37 14N 81 17W
Bluefields Nicaragua **67** H2 12 00N 83 49W
Blue Hills Reservation Massachusetts U.S.A. **52** B1 42 13N 71 05W
Blue Island Illinois U.S.A. **53** B1 41 40N 87 42W
Blue Mountain Pennsylvania U.S.A. **64** C3 40 10N 77 45W
Blue Mountains, The Jamaica **67** R8 18 00N 76 30W
Blue Nile *see* Bahr el Azraq
Bluff New Zealand **111** A1 46 38S 168 21E
Bluff Island Hong Kong U.K. **98** D1 22 19N 114 21E
Bluffton Indiana U.S.A. **35** C1 40 44N 85 11W
Blumberg Germany **83** G2 52 37N 13 28E
Blumenau Brazil **69** H7 26 55N 49 07W
Blyth England **78** J7 55 07N 1 30W
Bo Sierra Leone **106** C9 7 58N 11 45W
Boa Vista Brazil **68** E13 3 23S 55 30W
Bobigny France **83** B2 48 55N 2 28E
Bobo Dioulasso Burkina **106** E10 11 11N 4 18W
Bobruysk Belarus **90** B5 53 08N 29 10E
Bocas del Dragons *(The Dragon's Mouths) sd.* Venezuela **66** S10 10 47N 61 18W
Bocholt Germany **76** D5 51 49N 6 37E
Bochum Germany **76** J2 51 28N 7 11E
Bodélé *dep.* Chad **106** I11 17 00N 17 50E
Boden Sweden **79** E4 65 50N 21 44E
Bodensee *l.* Switzerland **77** D4 47 40N 9 30E
Bodmin Moor England **78** G2 50 35N 4 40W

Bodø Norway 79 C4 67 18N 14 26E
Bogalusa Louisiana U.S.A. 63 I3 30 56N 89 53W
Bogor Indonesia 99 D2 6 34S 106 45E
Bogotá Colombia 68 C13 4 38N 74 05W
Bog Walk Jamaica 67 Q8 18 06N 77 01W
Bo Hai b. China 97 N6 38 30N 118 30E
Bohnsdorf Germany 83 G1 52 23N 13 33E
Bohol i. The Philippines 99 G5 10 00N 124 00E
Bois Blanc Island Michigan U.S.A. 36 B6 45 45N 84 30W
Boise Idaho U.S.A. 62 C5 43 38N 116 12W
Boise City Oklahoma U.S.A. 62 F4 36 44N 102 31W
Bokaro India 95 F4 23 46N 85 55E
Boké Guinea 106 C10 10 57N 14 13W
Boknafjorden fj. Norway 79 B2 59 20N 6 00E
Bolesławiec Poland 80 C5 51 16N 34E
Bolgatanga Ghana 106 E10 10 44N 0 53W
Bolgrad Ukraine 90 B4 45 42N 28 35E
Bolivar, Pico mt. Venezuela 68 C14 8 33N 71 03W
BOLIVIA 68 E9
Bollnäs Sweden 79 D3 61 20N 16 25E
Bolmen l. Sweden 80 B6 57 00N 13 30E
Bologna Italy 81 B3 44 30N 11 20E
Bolton England 78 I5 53 35N 2 26W
Bolzano Italy 81 B4 46 30N 11 22E
Boma Zaïre 107 H6 5 50S 13 03E
Bombay India 95 C3 18 56N 72 51E
Bom Jesus da Lapa Brazil 68 I10 13 16S 43 23W
Bomu r. Central Africa 106 J8 4 50N 24 00E
Bonaire i. Lesser Antilles 67 K2 12 15N 68 27W
Bonaparte Archipelago Australia 110 D7 19 00S 126 00E
Bonasse Trinidad and Tobago 66 S9 10 05N 61 52W
Bondi Beach Australia 111 H2 33 45S 151 17E
Bondo Zaïre 106 J8 1 22S 23 54E
Bongor Chad 106 I10 10 18N 15 20E
Bonifacio Corsica 77 D3 41 23N 9 10E
Bonifacio, Strait of Corsica/Sardinia 77 D3 41 20N 8 45E
Bonita, Point California U.S.A. 49 A3 37 49N 122 32W
Bonn Germany 76 D5 50 44N 7 06E
Bonners Ferry Idaho U.S.A. 43 E1 48 41N 116 20W
Bonny, Bight of b. West Africa 106 G8 2 10N 7 30E
Bonthe Sierra Leone 106 C9 7 32N 12 30W
Boonsboro Maryland U.S.A. 64 C2 39 31N 77 39W
Boonton New Jersey U.S.A. 65 F3 40 55N 74 24W
Boosaasa Somalia 106 O10 11 18N 49 10E
Bor Sudan 106 L9 6 18N 31 34E
Borås Sweden 80 B6 57 44N 12 55E
Bordeaux France 77 B3 44 50N 0 34W
Borehamwood tn. England 82 B3 51 40N 0 16W
Borgholm Sweden 79 D2 56 51N 16 40E
Borgsdorf Germany 83 F2 52 44N 13 17E
Borislav Ukraine 80 D4 49 18N 23 28E
Borisoglebsk Russia 90 E5 51 23N 42 02E
Borisov Belarus 90 B5 54 09N 28 30E
Borlänge Sweden 79 D3 60 29N 15 25E
Borneo i. Asia 99 E4 0 00 114 00E
Bornholm i. Denmark 80 B6 55 02N 15 00E
Borough Green England 82 E2 51 17N 0 19E
Borūjerd Iran 93 G5 33 55N 48 48E
Borzya Russia 89 N6 50 24N 116 35E
Bosna r. Bosnia-Herzegovina 81 C3 45 00N 18 00E
BOSNIA-HERZEGOVINA 81 C3
Bossangoa Central African Republic 106 I9 6 27N 17 21E
Bosso Niger 106 H10 13 43N 13 19E
Boston England 78 K4 52 59N 0 01W
Boston Massachusetts U.S.A. 65 K5 42 20N 71 05W
Boston Harbor Massachusetts U.S.A. 52 C2 42 20N 71 00W
Boston Harbor Island State Park Massachusetts U.S.A. 52 C2 42 16N 70 54W
Boston Mountains Arkansas U.S.A. 63 H4 36 00N 94 00W
Botafogo Brazil 69 Q2 22 57S 43 11W
Botany Australia 111 G1 33 58S 151 12E
Botany Bay Australia 111 G1 34 04S 151 08E
Bothnia, Gulf of Sweden/Finland 79 D3 61 00N 19 10E
Botoşani Romania 81 E4 47 44N 26 41E
BOTSWANA 107 J3
Bottineau North Dakota U.S.A. 39 A1 48 30N 100 28W
Bottrop Germany 76 H3 51 31N 6 55E
Bötzow Germany 83 E2 52 40N 13 07E
Bouaké Côte d'Ivoire 106 D9 7 42N 5 00W
Bouar Central African Republic 106 I9 5 58N 15 35E
Bouârfa Morocco 106 E14 32 30N 1 59W
Boufarik Algeria 77 C2 36 36N 2 54E
Bougainville Island Papua New Guinea 110 J8 6 50S 155 00E
Bougouni Mali 106 D10 11 25N 7 28W
Bougzoul Algeria 77 C2 35 42N 2 51E
Boulder Colarado U.S.A. 62 E5 40 02N 105 16W
Boulogne-Billancourt France 83 B2 48 50N 2 15E
Boulogne-sur-Mer France 76 C5 50 43N 1 37E
Boundary Bald Mountain Maine U.S.A. 37 Q6 45 45N 70 14W
Bourem Mali 106 E11 16 59N 0 20W
Bourges France 77 C4 47 05N 2 23E
Bourke Australia 110 H3 30 09S 145 59E
Bournemouth England 78 J2 50 43N 1 54W
Bou Saâda Algeria 106 F15 35 10N 4 09E
Bousso Chad 106 I10 10 32N 16 45E
Bouvet Island Southern Ocean 113 I1 54 26S 3 24E
Bowbells North Dakota U.S.A. 40 C1 48 48N 102 14W
Bowen Australia 110 H6 20 00S 148 10E
Bowling Green Kentucky U.S.A. 63 I4 37 00N 86 29W
Bowling Green Missouri U.S.A. 63 H4 39 21N 91 11W
Bowling Green Ohio U.S.A. 36 C2 41 22N 83 40W
Bowman North Dakota U.S.A. 62 F6 46 11N 103 26W
Box Hill England 82 B2 51 16N 0 13W
Boyne r. Irish Republic 78 E5 53 40N 6 35W
Boyne City Michigan U.S.A. 36 A6 45 13N 85 00W
Boyoma Falls Zaïre 106 K8 0 18N 25 30E
Bozeman Montana U.S.A. 62 D6 45 40N 111 00W
Bozoum Central African Republic 106 I9 6 16N 16 22E
Bōsō-hantō p. Japan 100 M2 35 15N 140 05E
Brač i. Croatia 81 C3 43 00N 16 00E
Braddock Pennsylvania U.S.A. 53 E1 40 24N 79 53W
Bradford Pennsylvania U.S.A. 64 B4 41 57N 78 39W
Bradford England 78 J5 53 48N 1 45W
Brady Texas U.S.A. 62 G3 31 08N 99 22W
Braga Portugal 77 A3 41 32N 8 26W
Bragança Brazil 68 H12 1 02S 46 46W
Bragança Portugal 77 A3 41 47N 6 46W
Brahmapur India 95 E3 19 21N 84 51E
Brahmaputra r. India 95 G5 26 40N 93 00E
Brăila Romania 81 E4 45 17N 27 58E
Brainerd Minnesota U.S.A. 63 H6 46 20N 94 10W
Braintree Massachusetts U.S.A. 52 B1 42 14N 71 00W
Brandenburg Germany 76 E5 52 25N 12 34E
Branford Connecticut U.S.A. 65 H4 41 17N 72 48W
Brasileia Brazil 68 D10 10 59S 68 45W
Brásilia Brazil 68 H9 15 45S 47 57W
Braşov Romania 81 E4 45 39N 25 35E
Bratislava Czechoslovakia 81 C4 48 10N 17 10E
Bratsk Russia 89 M7 56 20N 101 50E
Bratsk Reservoir Russia 89 M7 56 00N 102 00E
Brattleboro Vermont U.S.A. 65 H5 42 51N 72 36W
Braunschweig Germany 76 E5 52 15N 10 30E
Bray Irish Republic 78 E5 53 12N 6 06W
BRAZIL 68 G10
Brazil Basin Atlantic Ocean 113 F5 10 00S 26 00W
Brazilian Highlands Brazil 55 10 00S 50 00W
Brazil Plateau Brazil 55 20 00S 45 00W
Brazos r. Texas U.S.A. 63 G3 32 00N 97 00W
Brazzaville Congo 107 I7 4 14S 15 14E
Breakheart Reservation Massachusetts U.S.A. 52 B2 42 29N 71 02W
Brea Reservoir California U.S.A. 51 C2 33 54N 117 56W
Brecon Beacons National Park Wales 78 H3 51 53N 3 30W
Breda Netherlands 76 C5 51 35N 4 46E
Bredy Russia 91 J5 52 23N 60 16E
Breidha Fjördur b. Iceland 79 H7 65 15N 23 00W
Brekstad Norway 79 B3 63 50N 9 50E
Bremen Germany 76 D5 53 05N 8 48E
Bremerhaven Germany 76 D5 53 33N 8 35E
Bremerton Washington U.S.A. 62 B6 47 34N 122 40W
Brenham Texas U.S.A. 63 G3 30 09N 96 24W
Brenner Pass Austria/Italy 81 B2 47 02N 11 32E
Brent bor. Greater London England 82 B3 51 34N 0 17W
Brentwood England 82 E3 51 38N 0 18E
Brentwood New York U.S.A. 65 G3 40 47N 73 14W
Brentwood Pennsylvania U.S.A. 53 E1 40 22N 79 59W
Brescia Italy 81 B4 45 33N 10 13E
Brest Belarus 90 A5 52 08N 23 40E
Brest France 76 B4 48 23N 4 30W
Brewer Maine U.S.A. 33 C1 44 52N 68 01W
Brewerton New York U.S.A. 64 D6 43 15N 76 09W
Brewster Massachusetts U.S.A. 65 K4 41 46N 70 05W
Brewster New York U.S.A. 65 G4 41 24N 73 37W
Brewster Washington U.S.A. 42 J4 48 05N 119 50W
Brezhnev see Naberezhnyye Chelny
Bria Central African Republic 106 J9 67 32N 22 00E
Briançon France 77 D3 44 53N 6 39E
Brick New Jersey U.S.A. 65 F3 40 04N 74 08W
Brickfield Trinidad and Tobago 66 T9 10 20N 61 16W
Bridgeport Connecticut U.S.A. 65 G4 41 12N 73 12W
Bridgeton New Jersey U.S.A. 64 E2 39 26N 75 14W
Bridgetown Barbados 66 V12 13 06N 59 37W
Bridgeville Pennsylvania U.S.A. 53 D1 40 20N 80 08W
Bridgewater New York U.S.A. 64 E5 42 52N 75 16W
Bridgwater England 78 H3 51 08N 3 00W
Brie-Comte-Robert France 83 C1 48 41N 2 37E
Brieselang Germany 83 E2 52 36N 13 00E
Briey France 76 D4 49 15N 5 57E
Brigantine New Jersey U.S.A. 65 F2 39 24N 74 22W
Brigham City Utah U.S.A. 62 D5 41 30N 112 02W
Brighton England 78 K2 50 50N 0 10W
Brighton Beach tn. New York U.S.A. 50 C1 40 34N 73 58W
Brindisi Italy 81 C3 40 37N 17 57E
Briones Reservoir California U.S.A. 49 C3 37 55N 122 12W
Brisbane Australia 110 I4 27 30S 153 00E
Brisbane California U.S.A. 49 B2 37 41N 122 24W
Bristol England 78 I3 51 27N 2 35W
Bristol Connecticut U.S.A. 65 H4 41 41N 72 57W
Bristol Rhode Island U.S.A. 65 J4 41 41N 71 12W
Bristol Bay Alaska U.S.A. 10 D4 57 30N 159 00W
Bristol Channel England/Wales 78 H3 51 20N 3 50W
British Isles Atlantic Ocean 54 55 00N 2 00W
British Mountains Canada/U.S.A. 44 D4 69 00N 141 00W
Brno Czechoslovakia 80 C4 49 13N 16 40E
Broadview Illinois U.S.A. 53 A2 41 50N 87 51W
Brockport New York U.S.A. 64 C6 43 13N 77 56W
Brockton Massachusetts U.S.A. 65 J5 42 06N 71 01W
Brockway Pennsylvania U.S.A. 64 B4 41 15N 78 48W
Brody Ukraine 90 B5 50 05N 25 08E
Broer Ruys, Cape Greenland 116 73 30N 20 20W
Broken Hill tn. Australia 110 G3 31 57S 141 30E
Broken Ridge Indian Ocean 112 H3 30 00S 93 00E
Bromley bor. Greater London England 82 D2 51 31N 0 01W
Brønnøysund Norway 79 C4 65 38N 12 15E
Bronx New York U.S.A. 65 G3 40 50N 73 52W
Brookfield Illinois U.S.A. 53 A2 41 48N 87 51W
Brookings South Dakota U.S.A. 63 G5 44 19N 96 47W
Brookline Massachusetts U.S.A. 52 B2 42 20N 71 07W
Brooklyn Connecticut U.S.A. 65 J4 41 47N 71 57W
Brooklyn Maryland U.S.A. 64 D2 39 14N 76 38W
Brooklyn New York U.S.A. 50 C1 40 41N 73 57W
Brooks Island California U.S.A. 49 B3 37 53N 122 21W
Brooks Range mts. Alaska U.S.A. 44 A3/B3 67 55N 155 00W
Brookvale Australia 111 H2 33 46S 151 16E
Broome Australia 110 C6 17 58S 122 15E
Browning Montana U.S.A. 62 D6 48 33N 113 00W
Brown's Town Jamaica 67 Q8 18 28N 77 22W
Brownsville Texas U.S.A. 63 G2 25 54N 97 30W
Browntown New Jersey U.S.A. 65 F3 40 25N 74 20W
Brownwood Texas U.S.A. 62 G3 31 42N 98 59W
Bruay-en-Artois France 76 C5 50 29N 2 33E
Bruges see Brugge
Brugge (Bruges) Belgium 76 C5 51 13N 3 14E
BRUNEI 99 E4
Brunoy France 83 C1 48 40N 2 31E
Brunswick Georgia U.S.A. 63 J3 31 09N 81 30W
Brunswick Maryland U.S.A. 64 C2 39 19N 77 37W
Brussel see Bruxelles
Brussels see Bruxelles
Bruxelles (Brussel, Brussels) Belgium 76 C5 50 50N 4 21E
Bryan Ohio U.S.A. 36 B2 41 30N 84 34W
Bryan Texas U.S.A. 63 G3 30 41N 96 24W
Bryansk Russia 90 C5 53 15N 34 09E
Brzeg Poland 80 C5 50 52N 17 27E
Bū Ağri Daği (Mt. Ararat) Turkey 92 F6 39 44N 44 15E
Bucaramanga Colombia 68 C14 7 08N 73 10W
Buchanan Liberia 106 C9 5 57N 10 02W
Bucharest see Bucureşti
Buchholz Germany 83 F2 52 37N 13 24E
Bucholz Germany 76 H2 51 25N 6 45E
Buckinghamshire co. England 82 B3 51 50N 0 50W
Buckow Germany 83 F1 52 24N 13 24E
Bucureşti (Bucharest) Romania 81 E3 44 25N 26 07E
Budapest Hungary 81 C4 47 30N 19 03E
Budd Lake tn. New Jersey U.S.A. 65 F3 40 52N 74 44W
Büderich Germany 76 G1 51 15N 6 20E
Budjala Zaïre 106 I8 2 38N 19 48E
Buena Park tn. California U.S.A. 51 B2 33 52N 118 02W
Buenaventura Mexico 66 C5 29 50N 107 30W
Buenos Aires Argentina 69 F6 34 40S 58 30W
Buenos Aires, Lake Argentina/Chile 69 C3 47 00S 72 00W
Buer Germany 76 J3 51 35N 7 05E
Buffalo New York U.S.A. 38 D1 42 52N 78 55W
Buffalo Wyoming U.S.A. 62 E5 44 21N 106 40W
Buff Bay tn. Jamaica 67 R8 18 18N 76 40W
Bugul'ma Russia 91 G5 54 32N 52 46E
Buheirat-Murrat-el-Kubra (Great Bitter Lake) Egypt 107 S2 30 22N 32 22E
Buheirat-Murrat-el-Sughra (Little Bitter Lake) Egypt 107 T2 30 14N 32 33E
Bujumbura Burundi 107 K7 3 22S 29 19E
Bukachacha Russia 89 N6 53 00N 116 58E
Bukama Zaïre 107 K6 9 13S 25 52E
Bukavu Zaïre 106 K7 2 30S 28 50E
Bukhara Uzbekistan 91 J2 39 47N 64 26E
Bukittinggi Indonesia 99 C3 0 18S 100 20E
Bukoba Tanzania 106 L7 1 19S 31 49E
Bula Indonesia 99 I3 3 07S 130 27E
Bulandshahr India 95 D5 28 30N 77 49E
Bulawayo Zimbabwe 107 K3 20 10S 28 43E
BULGARIA 81 D3
Buller r. New Zealand 111 B2 41 50S 172 20E
Bull Shoals Lake U.S.A. 63 H4 36 00N 93 00W
Bulun Russia 89 O10 70 45N 127 20E
Bumba Zaïre 106 J8 2 10N 22 30E
Bunbury Australia 110 B3 33 20S 115 34E
Bundaberg Australia 110 I5 24 50S 152 21E
Bundeena Australia 111 G1 34 06S 151 07E
Bungo-suidō sd. Japan 100 B1 33 00N 132 30E
Bunia Zaïre 106 L8 1 33N 30 13E
Bura Kenya 106 M7 1 06S 39 58E
Buraydah Saudi Arabia 92 F4 26 20N 43 59E
Burbank California U.S.A. 51 A3 34 10N 118 25W
Burbank Illinois U.S.A. 53 A2 41 45N 87 48W
Burco Somalia 106 O9 9 31N 45 33E
Burdur Turkey 92 D6 37 44N 30 17E
Bure r. England 78 L4 52 47N 1 20E
Bureya r. Russia 89 P6 52 00N 133 00E
Būr Fu'ad Egypt 107 S4 31 50N 32 19E
Burgas Bulgaria 81 E3 42 30N 27 29E
Burgos Spain 77 B3 42 21N 3 41W
Burgsvik Sweden 80 C6 57 03N 18 19E
Burhanpur India 95 D4 21 18N 76 08E
Buri Khali India 94 J2 22 30N 88 10E
BURKINA 106 E10
Burlingame California U.S.A. 49 B2 37 35N 122 25W
Burlington Colorado U.S.A. 62 F4 39 17N 102 17W
Burlington Iowa U.S.A. 63 H5 40 50N 91 07W
Burlington Massachusetts U.S.A. 65 J5 42 29N 71 12W
Burlington New Jersey U.S.A. 64 F3 40 05N 74 51W
Burlington Vermont U.S.A. 63 L5 44 28N 73 14W
Burlington Washington U.S.A. 42 H4 48 28N 122 20W
BURMA see MYANMAR
Burnham Park Illinois U.S.A. 53 B2 41 49N 87 35W
Burnie Australia 110 H1 41 03S 145 55E
Bursa Turkey 92 C7 40 12N 29 04E
Būr Sa'īd see Port Said
Būr Safāga Egypt 92 D4 25 43N 33 55E
Būr Taufiq Egypt 107 T1 29 57N 32 34E
Burt Lake Michigan U.S.A. 36 B6 45 30N 84 40W
Buru i. Indonesia 99 3 20S 126 30E
BURUNDI 107 L7
Burwell Nebraska U.S.A. 62 G5 41 48N 99 09W
Būshehr Iran 93 H4 28 57N 50 52E
Bushey England 82 B3 51 39N 0 22W
Bushy Park England 82 B2 51 25N 0 11W
Busira r. Zaïre 106 I7 1 00S 20 00E
Busto Arsizio Italy 81 A4 43 37N 8 51E
Buta Zaïre 106 K8 2 49N 24 50E
Butare Rwanda 106 K7 2 35S 29 44E
Bute i. Scotland 78 F7 55 50N 5 05W
Buton i. Indonesia 99 G3 5 00S 122 40E
Butovo Russia 88 M1 55 30N 37 32E
Butte Montana U.S.A. 62 D6 46 00N 112 31W
Butt of Lewis c. Scotland 78 E10 58 30N 6 20W
Butuan The Philippines 99 H5 8 56N 125 31E
Buulobarde Somalia 106 O8 3 50N 45 33E
Buzău Romania 81 E4 45 09N 26 49E
Buzzards Bay Massachusetts U.S.A. 65 K4 41 35N 70 50W
Buzzards Bay tn. Massachusetts U.S.A. 65 K4 41 45N 70 37W
Bydgoszcz Poland 80 C5 53 16N 18 00E
BYELORUSSIA see BELARUS
Byfleet England 82 B2 51 21N 0 29W
Bygland Norway 79 B2 58 50N 7 49E
Byrd Land geog. reg. Antarctica 117 77 00S 130 00W
Byrranga Mountains Russia 89 L10 75 00N 100 00E
Bytom Poland 80 C5 50 21N 18 51E

C

Cabanatuan The Philippines 99 G7 15 30N 120 58E
Cabimas Venezuela 68 C15 10 26N 71 27W
Cabinda admin. Angola 107 H6 5 30S 12 20E
Cabinet Mountains Montana U.S.A. 43 E1 48 15N 115 45W
Cabo Brazil 68 J11 8 16S 35 00W
Cabo Blanco c. Costa Rica 67 G1 9 36N 85 06W
Cabo Catoche c. Mexico 67 G4 21 38N 87 08W
Cabo Corrientes c. Colombia 68 B14 5 29N 77 36W
Cabo Corrientes c. Mexico 66 C4 20 25N 105 42W
Cabo de Creus c. Spain 77 C3 42 19N 3 19E
Cabo de Gata c. Spain 77 B2 36 44N 2 10W
Cabo de Hornos (Cape Horn) Chile 69 D1 56 00S 67 15W
Cabo de la Nao c. Spain 77 C2 38 44N 0 14E
Cabo Delgado c. Mozambique 107 N5 10 45S 40 45E
Cabo de Palos c. Spain 77 B2 37 38N 0 40W
Cabo de Peñas c. Spain 77 A3 43 39N 5 50W
Cabo de São Vicente c. Portugal 77 A2 37 01N 8 59W
Cabo de Tortosa c. Spain 77 C3 40 44N 0 54E
Cabo Dos Bahías c. Argentina 69 D4 45 00S 65 30W
Cabo Espichel c. Portugal 77 A2 38 24N 9 13W
Cabo Falso c. Mexico 66 B4 22 50N 110 00W
Cabo Finisterre c. Spain 77 A3 42 52N 9 16W
Cabo Gracias á Dios c. Nicaragua 67 H3 15 00N 83 10W
Cabo Orange c. Brazil 68 G13 4 25N 51 32W
Cabo Ortegal c. Spain 77 A3 43 46N 7 54W
Cabora Bassa Dam Mozambique 107 L4 16 00S 33 00E
Caborca Mexico 66 B6 30 42N 112 10W
Cabo San Juan c. Argentina 69 E2 54 45S 63 46W
Cabo Santa Elena c. Costa Rica 67 G2 10 54N 85 56W
Cabo Vírgenes c. Argentina 69 D2 52 20S 68 00W
Cabrera i. Balearic Islands 77 C2 39 00N 2 59E
Cabriel r. Spain 77 B2 39 20N 1 15W
Čačak Serbia Yugoslavia 81 D3 43 54N 20 22E
Cáceres Brazil 68 F9 16 05S 57 40W
Cáceres Spain 77 A2 39 29N 6 23W
Cachoeira Brazil 68 J10 12 35S 38 59W
Cachoeira do Sul Brazil 69 G6 30 03S 52 52W
Cachoeiro de Itapemirim Brazil 69 I8 20 51N 41 07W
Cadillac Michigan U.S.A. 36 A5 44 15N 85 23W
Cádiz Spain 77 A2 36 32N 6 18W
Cadiz The Philippines 99 G6 10 57N 123 18E
Cádiz, Gulf of Spain 77 A2 36 30N 7 15W
Caen France 76 B4 49 11N 0 22W
Caernarfon Wales 78 G5 53 08N 4 16W
Cagayan de Oro The Philippines 99 G5 8 29N 124 40E
Cagliari Italy 81 A2 39 13N 9 08E
Caguas Puerto Rico 67 K3 18 41N 66 04W
Caha Mountains Irish Republic 78 B3 51 40N 9 40W
Cahors France 77 C3 44 28N 0 26E
Caicos Passage sd. West Indies 67 J4 22 20N 72 30W
Cairngorms mts. Scotland 78 H9 57 10N 3 30W
Cairns Australia 110 H6 16 51S 145 43E
Cairo (El Qâ'hira) Egypt 92 D5 30 03N 31 15E
Cairo Illinois U.S.A. 63 I4 37 01N 89 09W
Cajamarca Peru 68 B11 7 09S 78 32W
Cajàzeiras Brazil 68 J11 6 52S 38 31W
Caju Brazil 69 Q2 22 53S 43 13W
Cakovec Croatia 81 C4 46 24N 16 26E
Calabar Nigeria 106 G8 4 56N 8 22E
Calabozo Venezuela 67 K1 8 58N 67 28W
Calahorra Spain 77 B3 49 19N 1 58W
Calais France 76 C5 50 57N 1 52E
Calama Chile 69 D8 22 30S 68 55W
Calamar Colombia 68 C15 10 16N 74 55W
Calamian Group is. The Philippines 99 F6 12 00N 120 00E
Calapan The Philippines 99 G6 13 23N 121 10E
Calatayud Spain 77 B3 41 21N 1 39W
Calçoene Brazil 68 G13 2 30N 50 55W
Calcutta India 94 K2 22 30N 88 20E
Caldwell Idaho U.S.A. 62 C5 43 39N 116 40W
Caldwell New Jersey U.S.A. 50 A2 40 49N 74 16W
Cali Colombia 68 B13 3 24N 76 30W
Calicut India 95 D2 11 15N 75 45E
Caliente Nevada U.S.A. 62 D4 37 36N 114 31W
California state U.S.A. 62 C4
California Trinidad and Tobago 66 T9 10 24N 61 28W
Callicoon New York U.S.A. 64 E4 41 46N 75 03W
Calmut Harbor Indiana U.S.A. 53 C1 41 44N 87 30W
Caltanissetta Italy 81 B2 37 29N 14 04E
Calumet City Illinois U.S.A. 53 B1 41 36N 87 32W
Calumet Park Indiana U.S.A. 53 B1 41 43N 87 30W
Calumet River Illinios U.S.A. 53 B1 41 40N 87 33W
Calumet Sag Channel Illinois U.S.A. 53 A1 41 41N 87 52W
Calvi Corsica 77 D3 42 34N 8 44E
Calvinia Republic of South Africa 107 I1 31 25S 19 47E
Camaçari Brazil 68 J10 12 44S 38 16W
Camacupa Angola 107 I5 12 03S 17 50E
Camagüey Cuba 67 I4 21 25N 77 55W
CAMBODIA (KAMPUCHEA) 99 C6
Cambrian Mountains Wales 78 H4 52 15N 3 45W
Cambridge England 78 L4 52 12N 0 07E
Cambridge Jamaica 67 Q8 18 18N 77 54W
Cambridge Maryland U.S.A. 63 K4 38 34N 76 04W
Cambridge Massachusetts U.S.A. 52 B2 42 22N 71 06W
Cambridge New Zealand 111 C3 37 53S 175 29E
Cambridge Reservoir Massachusetts U.S.A. 52 A2 42 25N 71 16W
Camden bor. Greater London England 82 C3 51 33N 0 10W
Camden New Jersey U.S.A. 64 E2 39 57N 75 06W
Camden New York U.S.A. 64 E6 43 21N 75 45W
Cameia National Park Angola 107 I5 12 00S 22 00E
CAMEROON 106 H9
Cametá Brazil 68 H12 2 12S 49 30W
Camiri Bolivia 68 E8 20 08S 63 33W
Camocim Brazil 68 I12 2 55S 40 50W
Camorta i. Nicobar Islands 95 G1 7 30N 93 30E
Campbell New York U.S.A. 64 C5 42 14N 77 11W
Campbell Island Southern Ocean 114 G2 52 30S 169 10E
Campbeltown Scotland 78 F7 55 26N 5 36W
Campeche Mexico 66 F3 19 50N 90 30W
Camp Hill tn. Pennsylvania U.S.A 64 D3 40 14N 76 56W
Campina Grande Brazil 68 J11 7 15S 35 50W
Campinas Brazil 69 H8 22 54S 47 06W
Campine see Kempen Land
Campoalegre Colombia 68 B13 2 49N 75 19W
Campobasso Italy 81 B3 41 33N 14 39E
Campo Grande Brazil 68 G8 20 24S 54 35W
Campo Maior Brazil 68 I12 4 50S 42 12W
Campo Mourão Brazil 69 G8 24 01S 52 24W
Campos Brazil 69 I8 21 46S 41 21W
Campos Elyseos Brazil 69 P3 22 42S 43 16W
Cam Ranh Vietnam 99 C6 11 54N 109 14E
Canaan Connecticut U.S.A. 65 G5 42 02N 73 20W
Canada Basin Arctic Ocean 116 80 00N 140 00W
Canadaigua New York U.S.A. 64 C5 42 00N 77 00W
Canadian r. U.S.A. 62 F4 35 00N 104 00W
Canajoharie New York U.S.A. 65 F5 42 54N 74 37W
Canakkale Turkey 92 C7 40 09N 26 25E
Canal de l'Ourcq France 83 C2 48 55N 2 32E
Canal du Midi France 77 C3 43 20N 2 00E
Canandaigua Lake New York U.S.A. 64 C5 42 50N 77 20W
Cananea Mexico 66 B6 30 59N 110 20W
Canary Basin Atlantic Ocean 113 F9 26 20N 30 00W
Canary Islands Spain 106 B13 28 30N 15 10W

Canastea Pennsylvania U.S.A. **64** C4 41 07N 77 27W
Canastota New York U.S.A. **64** E6 43 04N 75 47W
Canaveral, Cape Florida U.S.A. **63** J2 28 28N 80 28W
Canberra Australia **110** H2 35 18S 149 08E
Candlestick Point California U.S.A. **49** B2 37 42N 122 22W
Candlewood Lake Connecticut U.S.A. **65** G4 41 30N 73 30W
Cando North Dakota U.S.A. **39** B1 48 30N 99 11W
Canfield Ohio U.S.A. **36** F2 41 02N 80 47W
Cangamba Angola **107** I5 13 40S 19 47E
Cangrejos Point Trinidad and Tobago **66** T9 10 25N 61 29W
Cangzhou China **97** N6 38 19N 116 54E
Canisteo River New York U.S.A. **64** C5 42 15N 77 30W
Cannanore India **95** D2 11 53N 75 23E
Cannes France **77** D3 43 33N 7 00E
Cannonsville Reservoir New York U.S.A. **64** E5 42 05N 75 20W
Canõas Brazil **69** G7 28 55S 51 10W
Cantabrian Mountains *see* Cordillera Cantabrica
Cantaro Trinidad and Tobago **66** T10 10 42N 61 28W
Canterbury Australia **111** G2 33 55S 151 07E
Canterbury England **78** M3 51 17N 1 05E
Canterbury Bight *b.* New Zealand **111** B2 44 00S 172 30E
Canterbury Plains New Zealand **111** B2 43 30S 172 00E
Can Tho Vietnam **99** D6 10 03N 105 46E
Canto de Rio Brazil **69** Q2 22 55S 43 06W
Canton *see* Guangzhou
Caparo Trinidad and Tobago **66** T9 10 27N 61 19W
Caparo *r.* Trinidad and Tobago **66** T10 10 31N 61 25W
Cap Blanc *see* Ras Nouâdhibou
Cap Bon *c.* Tunisia **81** B2 37 08N 11 00E
Cap Corse *c.* Corsica **77** D3 43 00N 9 21E
Cap d'Ambre *c.* Madagascar **107** N5 12 00S 49 15E
Cap de la Hague *c.* France **76** B4 49 44N 1 56W
Cap des Trois Fourches *c.* Morocco **77** B2 35 26N 2 57W
Cape Basin Atlantic Ocean **113** I3 36 00S 6 00E
Cape Coast *tn.* Ghana **106** E9 5 10N 1 13W
Cape Cod Bay U.S.A. **65** K4 41 55N 70 20W
Cape Cod Canal Massachusetts U.S.A. **65** K4 41 45N 70 30W
Cape Girardeau *tn.* Missouri U.S.A. **63** I4 37 19N 89 31W
Cape Evans *r.s.* Antarctica **117** 77 38S 166 24E
Cape May *tn.* New Jersey U.S.A. **64** F1 38 56N 74 54W
Cape May Court House *tn.* New Jersey U.S.A. **64** F2 39 05N 74 50W
Cape Province *admin.* Republic of South Africa **107** J1 31 00S 22 00E
Cape Rise Indian Ocean **113** J3 42 00S 11 00E
Cape Town Republic of South Africa **107** I1 33 56S 18 28E
Cape Verde Basin Atlantic Ocean **113** E8 11 00N 35 00W
CAPE VERDE ISLANDS Atlantic Ocean **113** F8 16 00N 24 00W
Cape York Peninsula Australia **110** G7 12 30S 142 30E
Cap-Haïtien Haiti **67** J3 19 47N 72 17W
Capitán Arturo Prat *r.s.* Antarctica **117** 62 30S 59 41W
Capo Carbonara *c.* Italy **81** A2 39 07N 9 33E
Capo Passero *c.* Italy **81** C2 36 42N 15 09E
Capo Santa Maria di Leuca *c.* Italy **81** C2 39 47N 18 22E
Capo San Vito *c.* Italy **81** B2 38 12N 12 43E
Capri *i.* Italy **81** B3 40 33N 14 15E
Capricorn Channel Australia **110** I5 23 00S 152 30E
Caprivi Strip Namibia **107** J4 17 30S 27 50E
Cap Ste. Marie *c.* Madagascar **107** O2 25 34S 45 10E
Cap Vert *c.* Senegal **106** B10 14 43N 17 33W
Caracal Romania **81** D3 44 07N 24 18E
Caracas Venezuela **68** D15 10 35N 66 56W
Caratinga Brazil **68** I9 19 50S 42 06W
Caravelas Brazil **68** J9 17 45S 39 15W
Carbondale Pennsylvania U.S.A. **64** E4 41 35N 75 31W
Carcassonne France **77** C3 43 13N 2 21E
Cardamon Hills India **95** D1 9 50N 77 00E
Cárdenas Mexico **66** E4 22 00N 99 41W
Cardiff Wales **78** H3 51 30N 3 13W
Cardigan Bay Wales **78** G4 52 30N 4 30W
Carei Romania **81** D4 47 40N 22 28E
Cargados Carajos Shoals Indian Ocean **112** E5 16 00S 60 00E
Cariacica Brazil **68** I8 20 15S 40 23W
Caribbean Sea Central America **67** I3 15 00N 75 00W
Caribou Maine U.S.A. **33** C2 46 52N 68 01W
Caringbah Australia **111** G1 34 03S 151 07E
Caripito Venezuela **68** E15 10 07N 63 07W
Carlisle England **78** I6 54 54N 2 55W
Carlisle Pennsylvania U.S.A. **64** C3 40 12N 77 12W
Carlisle Bay Barbados **66** V12 13 05N 59 37W
Carlsbad New Mexico U.S.A. **62** F3 32 25N 104 14W
Carlsberg Ridge Indian Ocean **112** E7/F6 5 00N 65 00E
Carlton Washington U.S.A. **42** H4 48 14N 120 05W
Carmarthen Wales **78** G3 51 51N 4 20W
Carmel New York U.S.A. **65** G4 41 25N 73 40W
Carmen Colombia **68** B14 9 46N 75 06W
Carnarvon Australia **110** A5 24 51S 113 45E
Carnegie Pennsylvania U.S.A. **53** D1 40 24N 80 06W
Carnegie, Lake Australia **110** C4 27 00S 124 00E
Carnegie Ridge Pacific Ocean **115** R7 1 30S 95 00W
Car Nicobar *i.* Nicobar Islands **95** G1 9 00N 93 00E
Carnot Central African Republic **106** I8 4 59N 15 56E
Carnsore Point Irish Republic **78** E4 52 10N 6 22W
Caro Michigan U.S.A. **36** C4 43 29N 83 24W
Carolina Brazil **68** H11 7 20S 47 25W
Caroline Island Pacific Ocean **115** L7 10 00S 150 00W
Caroline Islands Pacific Ocean **114** E8 8 00N 148 00E
Caroni Trinidad and Tobago **66** T10 10 36N 61 22W
Caroni *r.* Trinidad and Tobago **66** T10 10 35N 61 20W
Carpatii Meridionali *mts.* Romania **81** D4 45 00N 24 00E
Carpentaria, Gulf of Australia **110** F7 13 30S 138 00E
Carpentras France **77** D3 44 03N 5 03E
Carpio North Dakota U.S.A. **40** C1 48 25N 101 34W
Carrauntoohill *mt.* Irish Republic **78** B3 52 00N 9 45W
Carrion *r.* Spain **77** B3 42 30N 4 45W
Carson California U.S.A. **51** A2 33 49N 118 16W
Carson City Nevada U.S.A. **62** C4 39 10N 119 46W
Cartagena Colombia **68** B15 10 24N 75 33W
Cartagena Spain **77** B2 37 36N 0 59W
Cartago Costa Rica **67** H1 9 50N 83 52W
Carteret New Jersey U.S.A. **50** B1 40 34N 74 13W
Caruarú Brazil **68** J11 8 15S 35 55W
Carúpano Venezuela **68** E15 10 39N 63 14W
Casablanca *(Dar el Beida)* Morocco **106** D14 33 39N 7 35W
Casa Grande Arizona U.S.A. **62** D3 32 52N 111 46W
Cascade Range *mts.* North America **62** B6 48 00N 121 00W
Cascadura Brazil **69** P2 22 53S 43 21W
Cascais Portugal **77** A2 38 41N 9 25W
Cascavel Brazil **68** J12 4 10S 38 15W
Caserta Italy **81** B3 41 04N 14 20E
Casey *r.s.* Antarctica **117** 66 17S 77 58E
Casper Wyoming U.S.A. **62** E5 42 50N 106 20W
Caspian Lowlands *geog. reg.* Kazakhstan **90** F4 48 00N 50 00E
Caspian Sea Eurasia **90** G3 42 30N 50 00E
Cassino Italy **81** B3 41 29N 13 50E
Cass River Michigan U.S.A. **36** C4 43 30N 83 30W
Castellane France **77** D3 43 50N 6 30E
Castellón de la Plana Spain **77** B2 39 59N 0 03W
Castelo Branco Portugal **77** A2 39 50N 7 30W
Castle Hill Australia **111** F3 33 44S 150 59E
Castlebar Irish Republic **78** B5 53 52N 9 17W
Castle Peak Hong Kong U.K. **98** A2 22 23N 113 57E
Castleton on Hudson New York U.S.A. **65** G5 42 31N 73 45W
Castres France **77** C3 43 36N 2 14E
Castries St. Lucia **67** L2 14 02N 60 59W
Castrop-Rauxel Germany **76** K3 51 33N 7 18E
Castro Valley California U.S.A. **49** C2 37 42N 122 03W
Castrovillari Italy **81** C2 39 48N 16 12E
Catamarca Argentina **69** D7 28 28S 65 46W
Catánia Italy **81** C2 37 31N 15 06E
Catanzaro Italy **81** C2 38 54N 16 36E
Cataract, 1st *(R. Nile)* Egypt **92** D3 24 00N 32 45E
Cataract, 2nd *(R.Nile)* Sudan **92** D3 21 40N 31 12E
Cataract, 3rd *(R.Nile)* Sudan **92** D2 19 45N 30 25E
Cataract, 4th *(R.Nile)* Sudan **92** D2 18 40N 32 10E
Cataract, 5th *(R.Nile)* Sudan **92** D2 18 25N 33 52E
Caterham England **82** C2 51 17N 0 04W
Cat Island The Bahamas **67** I4 24 30N 75 30W
Catskill New York U.S.A. **65** G5 42 14N 73 52W
Catskill Mountains New York U.S.A. **65** F5 42 10N 74 20W
Cattaraugus Creek New York U.S.A. **64** B5 42 30N 78 40W
Caucaia Brazil **68** J12 3 44S 38 45W
Caucasus Mountains Eurasia **90** E3 42 30N 45 00E
Cavalier North Dakota U.S.A. **39** B1 48 48N 97 48W
Caxias Brazil **68** I12 4 53N 43 20W
Caxias do Sul Brazil **69** G7 29 14S 51 10W
Cayenne French Guiana **68** G13 4 55N 52 18W
Cayman Trench Caribbean Sea **115** R9 15 00N 80 00W
Cayuga Lake New York U.S.A. **64** D5 42 40N 76 45W
Cazenovia New York U.S.A. **64** E5 42 54N 75 51W
Ceara *admin.* Brazil **68** I11/J11 5 30S 40 00W
Cebu The Philippines **99** G6 10 17N 123 56E
Cebu *i.* The Philippines **84** 10 30N 123 30E
Cedar *r.* Iowa U.S.A. **63** H5 42 00N 92 00W
Cedar City Utah U.S.A. **62** D4 37 40N 113 04W
Cedar Creek *r.* North Dakota U.S.A. **62** F6 46 00N 102 00W
Cedar Grove New Jersey U.S.A. **50** B2 40 51N 74 14W
Cedar Rapids Iowa U.S.A. **63** H5 41 59N 91 39W
Cedros *i.* Mexico **66** A5 28 00N 115 00W
Cedros Bay Trinidad and Tobago **66** S9 10 08N 61 50W
Cedros Point Trinidad and Tobago **66** S9 10 07N 61 49W
Ceduna Australia **110** E3 32 07S 133 42E
Ceerigaabo Somalia **106** O10 10 40N 47 20E
Cegléd Hungary **81** C4 47 10N 19 47E
Celaya Mexico **66** D4 20 32N 100 48W
Celebes *see* Sulawesi
Celebes Sea Indonesia **99** G4 3 00N 122 30E
Celje Slovenia **81** C4 46 15N 15 16E
Celle Germany **76** E5 52 37N 10 05E
Celtic Sea British Isles **78** E3 51 00N 7 00W
Center Line Michigan U.S.A. **52** E2 42 28N 83 01W
Center Moriches New York U.S.A. **65** H3 40 48N 72 47W
Centerport New York U.S.A. **65** G3 40 54N 73 22W
Centerville Massachusetts U.S.A. **65** K4 41 39N 70 22W
CENTRAL AFRICAN REPUBLIC **106** I9
Central Pacific Basin Pacific Ocean **114** I9 10 00N 177 00W
Central Plain Ireland **70** 53 30N 8 00W
Central Russian Uplands Europe **84** 55 00N 35 00E
Central Siberian Plateau Russia **89** M9/N8 65 00N 110 00E
Centreville Maryland U.S.A. **64** D2 39 02N 76 05W
Centro Brazil **69** Q2 22 53S 43 07W
Cerro de Pasco Peru **68** B10 10 43S 76 15W
České Budějovice Czechoslovakia **80** B4 48 58N 14 29E
Ceuta *territory* Spain **77** A2 35 53N 5 19W
Cévennes *mts.* France **77** C3 44 20N 3 30E
Ceyhan *r.* Turkey **92** E6 37 45N 36 45E
Cèze *r.* France **77** C3 44 30N 4 00E
Chacachacare *i.* Trinidad and Tobago **66** S10 10 41N 61 45W
Chachapoyas Peru **68** B11 6 13S 77 54W
CHAD **106** I10
Chad, Lake West Africa **106** H10 13 50N 14 00E
Chagai Hills Afghanistan/Pakistan **93** J5 29 30N 63 00E
Chaghcharān Afghanistan **93** K5 34 31N 65 15E
Chagos Archipelago *(British Indian Ocean Territory)* Indian Ocean **112** G6 6 00S 73 00E
Chagos-Laccadive Ridge Indian Ocean **112** G6/G7
Chaguanas Trinidad and Tobago **66** T10 10 31N 61 25W
Chaguaramas Trinidad and Tobago **66** S10 10 41N 61 38W
Chāh Bahār Iran **93** J4 25 16N 60 41E
Chaine des Mitumba *(Mitumba Mountains)* Zaïre **107** K5 7 30S 27 30E
Chai Wan Hong Kong U.K. **98** C1 22 15N 114 14E
Chai Wan Kok Hong Kong U.K. **98** B2 22 23N 114 06E
Chalfont St. Peter England **82** A3 51 37N 0 33W
Chalkyitsik Alaska U.S.A. **44** C4 66 38N 143 49W
Challenger Fracture Zone Pacific Ocean **115** Q4 33 30S 100 00W
Chalon-sur-Saône France **77** C4 46 47N 4 51E
Châlons-sur-Marne France **76** C4 48 58N 4 22E
Chaman Pakistan **94** B6 30 55N 66 27N
Chambal India **95** D5 26 00N 77 00E
Chamberlain Lake Maine U.S.A. **37** R7 46 15N 69 20W
Chambersburg Pennsylvania U.S.A. **64** C2 39 57N 77 40W
Chambéry France **77** D4 45 34N 5 55E
Chamo, Lake Ethiopia **106** M9 5 55N 37 35E
Champaign Illinois U.S.A. **63** I5 40 07N 88 14W
Champdani India **94** K3 22 48N 88 21E
Champigny France **83** C2 48 49N 2 32E
Champlain, Lake *(Lac Champlain)* Canada/U.S.A. **33** B1 44 00N 73 00W
Champotón Mexico **66** F3 19 20N 90 43W
Champs-sur-Marne France **83** C2 48 51N 2 35E
Chañaral Chile **69** C7 26 23S 70 40W
Chandalar *r.* Alaska U.S.A. **44** B4 67 00N 149 00W
Chandigarh India **95** D6 30 44N 76 54E
Chandle Park Michigan U.S.A. **52** F2 42 23N 82 58W
Chandnagar India **94** K3 22 52N 88 22E
Chandrapur India **95** D3 19 58N 79 21E
Changara Mozambique **107** L4 16 50S 33 17E
Chang Cheng *r.s.* Antarctica **117** 62 13S 58 58W
Changchun China **97** P7 43 50N 125 20E
Changde China **97** M4 29 03N 111 35E
Chang-hua Taiwan **98** G7 24 06N 120 31E
Chang Jiang *(Yangtze)* *r.* China **97** L5/M5 31 00N 110 00E
Changsha China **97** M4 28 10N 113 00E
Changxindian China **101** F1 39 50N 116 12E
Changzhi China **97** M6 36 05N 113 12E
Changzhou China **97** N5 31 39N 120 45E
Channel Islands British Isles **78** I6 49 30N 2 30W
Chaouèn Morocco **77** A2 35 15N 5 15W
Chaoyang China **97** O7 41 36N 120 25E
Chaozhou China **97** N3 23 42N 116 36E
Chapada Diamantina *mts.* Brazil **68** I10 12 30S 42 30W
Chapecó Brazil **69** G7 27 14S 52 41W
Chapelton Jamaica **67** Q8 18 05N 77 16W
Chardzhou Turkmenistan **91** J2 39 09N 63 34E
Chari *r.* Chad **106** I10 11 00N 16 00E
Chārīkār Afghanistan **93** K5 35 01N 69 11E
Charleroi Belgium **76** C5 50 25N 4 27E
Charles *r.* Massachusetts U.S.A. **52** A2 42 15N 71 16W
Charleston South Carolina U.S.A. **63** K3 32 48N 79 58W
Charleston West Virginia U.S.A. **63** J4 38 23N 81 40W
Charlestown New Hampshire U.S.A. **65** H6 43 14N 72 25W
Charlestown Rhode Island U.S.A. **65** J4 41 24N 71 38W
Charles Town West Virginia U.S.A. **64** C2 39 18N 77 54W
Charleville Australia **110** H4 26 25S 146 13E
Charleville *see* Rath Luirc
Charleville-Mézières France **76** C4 49 46N 4 43E
Charlevoix Michigan U.S.A. **36** A6 45 19N 85 16W
Charlotte Michigan U.S.A. **36** B3 42 33N 84 50W
Charlotte North Carolina U.S.A. **63** J4 35 03N 80 50W
Charlottenburg Germany **83** E2 52 32N 13 18E
Charlottesville Virginia U.S.A. **63** K4 38 02N 78 29W
Charters Towers Australia **110** H5 20 02S 146 20E
Chartiers Creek Pennsylvania U.S.A. **53** D1 40 27N 80 05W
Chartres France **76** C4 48 27N 1 30E
Châteaubriant France **77** B4 47 43N 1 22W
Châteauroux France **77** C4 46 49N 1 41E
Château-Thierry France **76** C4 49 03N 3 24E
Châtellerault France **77** C3 49 49N 0 33E
Chatham Alaska U.S.A. **42** A3 57 30N 135 00W
Chatham Massachusetts U.S.A. **65** K4 41 40N 69 57W
Chatham Islands Pacific Ocean **114** I3 44 00S 176 30W
Chatham Rise Pacific Ocean **114** H3 45 00S 175 00E
Chatham Strait Alaska U.S.A. **42** B3 57 45N 134 50W
Chatou France **83** A2 48 54N 2 10E
Chatswood Australia **111** G2 33 48S 151 11E
Chattanooga Tennessee U.S.A. **63** I4 35 02N 85 18W
Chaumont France **76** D4 48 07N 5 08E
Cheb Czechoslovakia **80** B5 50 08N 12 28E
Cheboksary Russia **90** F6 56 08N 47 12E
Cheboygan Michigan U.S.A. **36** B6 45 40N 84 28W
Cheduba *i.* Myanmar **95** G3 18 52N 93 44E
Cheju do *(Quelpart)* *i.* South Korea **97** P5 33 00N 126 30E
Chek Chue *(Stanley)* Hong Kong U.K. **98** C1 22 12N 114 12E
Chek Keng Hong Kong U.K. **98** D2 22 25N 114 21E
Chek Lap Kok *i.* Hong Kong U.K. **98** A1 22 18N 113 56E
Chelan, Lake Washington U.S.A. **42** H4 48 10N 120 32W
Chelan National Recreation Area Washington U.S.A. **42** H4 48 20N 120 40W
Chélif *r.* Algeria **77** C2 36 00N 0 30E
Chelles France **83** C2 48 53N 2 53E
Chełm Poland **80** D5 51 08N 23 29E
Chelmsford England **78** L3 51 44N 0 28E
Chelsea England **82** C2 51 29N 0 10W
Chelsea Massachusetts U.S.A. **52** B2 42 24N 71 02W
Chelsea Michigan U.S.A. **36** B3 42 19N 84 01W
Cheltenham England **78** I3 51 54N 2 04W
Chelyabinsk Russia **91** J6 55 12N 61 25E
Chemnitz *(Karl-Marx-Stadt)* Germany **76** E5 50 50N 12 55E
Chenab *r.* Pakistan **95** C6 30 30N 71 30E
Chenango River New York U.S.A. **64** E5 42 30N 75 30W
Chengde China **97** N7 40 59N 117 52E
Chengdu China **97** K5 30 37N 104 06E
Ch'eng-kung Taiwan **98** H6 23 06N 121 22E
Cher *r.* France **77** C4 47 17N 0 50E
Cherbourg France **76** B4 49 38N 1 37W
Cherchell Algeria **77** C2 36 36N 2 11E
Cheremkhovo Russia **89** M6 53 08N 103 01E
Cheremushki Russia **88** M1 55 38N 37 38E
Cherepovets Russia **90** D6 59 09N 37 50E
Cherkassy Ukraine **90** C4 49 27N 32 04E
Cherkessk Russia **90** E3 44 14N 42 05E
Cherkizovsky Russia **88** M2 55 50N 37 44E
Chernigov Ukraine **90** C5 51 30N 31 18E
Chernobyl' Ukraine **90** C5 51 17N 30 15E
Chernogorsk Russia **91** P5 53 48N 91 16E
Chernovtsy Ukraine **90** B4 48 19N 25 52E
Chernyakhovsk Russia **80** D5 54 36N 21 48E
Cherokee Iowa U.S.A. **63** G5 42 45N 95 32W
Cherrapunji India **95** G5 25 16N 91 42E
Cherskiy Range *mts.* Russia **89** P9/Q8 66 30N 140 00E
Chertanovo Russia **88** M1 55 34N 37 35E
Chertsey England **82** A2 51 23N 0 30W
Chervonograd Ukraine **80** D5 50 25N 24 10E
Chesaning Michigan U.S.A. **36** B4 43 12N 84 08W
Chesapeake Virginia U.S.A. **63** K4 36 45N 76 15W
Chesapeake Bay U.S.A. **64** D2 39 00N 76 20W
Chesham England **82** A3 51 43N 0 38W
Cheshunt England **82** C3 51 43N 0 02W
Chester England **78** I5 53 12N 2 54W
Chester Connecticut U.S.A. **65** H4 41 24N 72 26W
Chester Maryland U.S.A. **64** D1 38 59N 76 16W
Chester Massachusetts U.S.A. **65** G5 42 17N 72 59W
Chester New Jersey U.S.A. **65** F3 40 47N 74 42W
Chester Pennsylvania U.S.A. **64** E2 39 50N 75 23W
Chester Vermont U.S.A. **65** H6 43 16N 72 38W
Chesterfield England **78** J5 53 15N 1 25W
Chestertown Maryland U.S.A. **64** D2 39 13N 76 04W
Chesuncook Lake Maine U.S.A. **37** R7 46 00N 69 22W
Chetlat Island India **95** C2 11 46N 72 50E
Chetumal Mexico **66** G3 18 30N 88 17W
Cheung Chau *i.* Hong Kong U.K. **98** B1 22 13N 114 01E
Cheung Sha Hong Kong U.K. **98** A1 22 14N 113 57E
Cheung Sha Wan Hong Kong U.K. **98** B2 22 20N 114 08E
Cheung Shue Tau Hong Kong U.K. **98** B2 22 22N 114 05E
Chevak Alaska U.S.A. **10** B5 63 33N 165 36W
Cheviot Hills England **78** I7 55 25N 2 20W
Chevreuse France **83** A1 48 43N 2 05E
Chewack River Washington U.S.A. **42** H4 48 40N 120 10W
Chewelah Washington U.S.A. **43** E1 48 17N 117 44W
Cheyenne Wyoming U.S.A. **62** F5 41 08N 104 50W
Cheyenne *r.* U.S.A. **62** F5 44 00N 102 00W
Chhapra India **95** E5 25 46N 84 44E
Chia-i Taiwan **98** G6 23 38N 120 27E
Chia-li Taiwan **98** H7 23 09N 120 11E
Chiang Rai Thailand **99** B7 19 56N 99 51E
Chiba Japan **100** M2 35 38N 140 07E
Chiba *pref.* Japan **100** M2 35 30N 140 15E
Chicago Illinois U.S.A. **63** I5 41 50N 87 45W
Chicago Harbor Illinois U.S.A. **53** B2 41 53N 87 35W
Chicago Sanitary and Ship Canal Illinois U.S.A. **53** A2 41 45N 87 52W
Chicapa *r.* Angola/Zaïre **107** J6 8 00S 20 30E
Chichagof Island Alaska U.S.A. **42** A3 57 40N 136 00W
Chichibu Japan **100** L2 35 59N 139 08E
Chichibu-Tama National Park Japan **100** K2 35 50N 138 50E
Chickasha Oklahoma U.S.A. **63** G4 35 03N 97 57W
Chicken Alaska U.S.A. **44** C3 64 04N 142 00W
Chiclayo Peru **68** B11 6 47S 79 47W
Chieng-Mai Thailand **99** B7 18 48N 98 59E
Chienti *r.* Italy **81** B3 43 00N 14 00E
Chieti Italy **81** B3 42 21N 14 10E
Chignik Alaska U.S.A. **10** D4 56 18N 158 27W
Chigwell England **82** D3 51 37N 0 05E
Chihuahua Mexico **66** C5 28 40N 106 06W
Chikura Japan **100** L1 34 57N 139 58E
CHILE **69** D6
Chile Basin Pacific Ocean **115** R4 36 00S 84 00W
Chile Chico Chile **69** C3 46 34S 71 44W
Chile Rise Pacific Ocean **115** Q4 40 00S 92 00W
Chillán Chile **69** C5 36 37S 72 10W
Chilpancingo Mexico **66** E3 17 33N 99 30W
Chiltern Hills England **78** K3 51 40N 1 00W
Chilumba Malawi **107** L5 10 25S 34 18E
Chi-lung Taiwan **98** J3 25 10N 121 43E
Chi Ma Wan Peninsula Hong Kong U.K. **98** A1 22 14N 113 58E
Chimborazo *mt.* Ecuador **68** B12 1 29S 78 52W
Chimbote Peru **68** B11 9 04S 78 34W
Ch'imei Hsü *i.* Taiwan **98** F6 23 11N 119 25E
Chimen Tao *(Quemoy)* *i.* Taiwan **98** E8 24 26N 118 24E
Chimkent Kazakhstan **91** K3 42 16N 69 05E
CHINA **96/97** G6/M6
Chinandega Nicaragua **66** G2 12 35N 87 10W
Chincha Alta Peru **68** B10 13 25S 76 07W
Chinchilla Australia **110** I4 26 42S 150 35E
Chinde Mozambique **107** M4 18 35S 36 28E
Chindwin *r.* Myanmar **95** H5 26 00N 95 30E
Chinese Turkestan *geog. reg.* China **96** E7/F7 40 00N 80 00E
Ch'ing-shui Taiwan **98** G7 24 12N 120 33E
Chingola Zambia **107** K5 12 31S 27 53E
Chin Hills Asia **84** 21 00N 94 00E
Chinju South Korea **97** P6 35 10N 128 06E
Chinko *r.* Central African Republic **106** J9 5 00N 24 00E
Chinmen Taiwan **98** E8 24 30N 118 20E
Chinook Montana U.S.A. **41** D1 48 35N 109 14W
Chi-pei Tao *i.* Taiwan **98** F6 23 44N 119 36E
Chippewa Falls Wisconsin U.S.A. **35** B2 44 56N 91 25W
Chippewa River Michigan U.S.A. **36** B4 43 36N 84 45W
Chipping Norton, Lake Australia **111** F2 33 54S 150 56E
Chipping Ongar England **82** E3 51 43N 0 15E
Chiputneticook Lakes U.S.A./Canada **33** C2 45 40N 67 45W
Chiquimula Guatemala **66** G2 14 48N 89 32W
Chiquitos Plateau South America **55** 17 00S 63 00W
Chirchik Uzbekistan **91** K3 41 28N 69 31E
Chiryu Japan **100** J2 35 01N 137 04E
Ch'i-shan Taiwan **98** G5 22 44N 120 31E
Chita Japan **100** H1 35 00N 136 51E
Chita Russia **89** N6 52 03N 113 35E
Chita-hantō *p.* Japan **100** H1 34 45N 136 53E
Chitembo Angola **107** I5 13 33S 16 47E
Chitpur India **94** K2 22 36N 88 23E
Chitral Pakistan **95** C7 35 52N 71 58E
Chittagong Bangladesh **95** G4 22 20N 91 48E
Chittenango New York U.S.A. **64** E6 43 02N 75 52W
Chittoor India **95** D2 13 13N 79 06E
Chitungwiza Zimbabwe **107** L4 18 00S 31 06E
Chōfu Japan **101** B3 35 39N 139 34E
Chōgo Japan **101** A2 35 24N 139 29E
Choiseul *i.* Solomon Islands **110** J8 7 00S 157 00E
Choisy-le-Roi France **83** B2 48 47N 2 29E
Chojnice Poland **80** C5 53 42N 17 32E
Cholet France **77** B4 47 04N 0 53W
Choluteca Honduras **66** G2 13 15N 87 10W
Chone Ecuador **68** A12 0 44S 80 04W
Ch'ŏngjin North Korea **97** P7 41 50N 129 55E
Ch'ŏngju South Korea **97** P6 36 39N 127 27E
Chōshi Japan **100** M2 35 43N 140 51E
Chŏnju South Korea **97** P6 35 50N 127 05E
Chongqing China **97** L4 29 30N 106 35E
Chott el Hodna *salt l.* Algeria **77** C2 35 30N 4 30E
Chott El Jerid *salt l.* Tunisia **106** G14 30 00N 9 00E
Chott Melrhir *salt l.* Algeria **106** G14 33 30N 6 10E
Choybalsan Mongolia **97** M8 48 02N 114 32E
Christchurch New Zealand **111** B2 43 33S 172 40E
Christiana Jamaica **67** Q8 18 13N 77 29W
Christmas Island Indian Ocean **99** D1 10 30S 105 40E
Chu Kazakhstan **91** L3 43 34N 73 44E
Chu *r.* Kazakhstan/Kirgyzstan **91** L3 44 30N 72 00E

Chugach Mountains Alaska U.S.A. **10** G5 61 40N 145 00W
Chūgoku-sanchi *mts.* Japan **100** B2 35 00N 133 00E
Chukchi Sea Arctic Ocean **116** 70 00N 170 00W
Chukotsk Peninsula Russia **89** U9 66 00N 175 00W
Chukotsk Range *mts.* Russia **89** T9 68 00N 175 00E
Chulucanas Peru **68** A11 5 08S 80 10W
Chulym *r.* Russia **91** O6 57 00N 87 00E
Chumphon Thailand **99** B6 10 30N 99 11E
Chuna *r.* Russia **91** Q6 57 30N 95 00E
Ch'unch'ŏn South Korea **97** P6 37 56N 127 40E
Chung-ho Taiwan **98** H7 25 00N 121 00E
Chung Hom Kok Hong Kong U.K. **98** C1 22 13N 114 12E
Chung-li Taiwan **98** H7 24 55N 121 08E
Chung Yang Shanmo *mts.* Taiwan **98** G6/H7 23 00N 120 00E
Chunya *r.* Russia **89** M8 62 00N 101 00E
Chupara Point Trinidad and Tobago **66** T10 10 48N 61 22W
Chur Switzerland **77** D4 46 52N 9 32E
Churu India **95** C5 28 18N 75 00E
Churuguara Venezuela **67** K2 10 52N 69 35W
Chusovaya *r.* Russia **91** H6 58 00N 59 00E
Chu'ungju South Korea **97** P6 36 59N 127 53E
Cicero Illinois U.S.A. **53** A2 41 50N 87 46W
Cidade de Deus Brazil **69** P2 22 58S 43 20W
Cidade Nova Brazil **69** Q2 22 55S 43 12W
Ciego de Avila Cuba **67** I4 21 51N 78 47W
Ciénaga Colombia **68** C15 11 01N 74 15W
Cienfuegos Cuba **67** H4 22 10N 80 27W
Cilician Gates *pass* Turkey **92** D6 37 17N 34 46E
Cimarron *r.* U.S.A. **62** F4 37 00N 103 00W
Cimpina Romania **81** E4 45 08N 25 44E
Cinca *r.* Spain **77** C3 41 45N 0 15E
Cincinnati Ohio U.S.A. **63** J4 39 10N 83 30W
Cincinnatus New York U.S.A. **64** E5 42 33N 75 55W
Cine Turkey **80** E2 37 37N 28 03E
Circle Alaska U.S.A. **44** C4 65 50N 144 11W
Cirebon Indonesia **99** D2 6 46S 108 33E
C.I.S. *see* Commonwealth of Independent States
Cisco Texas U.S.A. **62** G3 32 23N 98 59W
Cisneros Colombia **68** B14 6 32N 75 04W
Citlaltépetl *mt.* Mexico **66** E3 19 00N 97 18W
City Island New York U.S.A. **50** C2 40 51N 73 48W
Ciucea Romania **81** D4 46 58N 22 50E
Ciudad Acuña Mexico **66** D5 29 20N 100 58W
Ciudad Bolívar Venezuela **68** E14 8 06N 63 36W
Ciudad Camargo Mexico **66** C5 27 41N 105 10W
Ciudad del Carmen Mexico **66** F3 18 38N 91 50W
Ciudad del Este *(Presidente Stroessner)* Paraguay **69** G7 25 32S 54 34W
Ciudadela Balearic Islands **77** C2 40 00N 3 50E
Ciudad Guayana Venezuela **68** E14 8 22N 62 37W
Ciudad Juárez Mexico **66** C6 31 42N 106 29W
Ciudad Lerdo Mexico **66** D5 25 34N 103 30W
Ciudad Madero Mexico **66** E4 22 19N 97 50W
Ciudad Manté Mexico **66** E4 22 44N 98 59W
Ciudad Obregón Mexico **66** C5 27 28N 109 59W
Ciudad Real Spain **77** B2 38 59N 3 55W
Ciudad Rodrigo Spain **77** A3 40 36N 6 33W
Ciudad Victoria Mexico **66** E4 23 43N 99 10W
Civil Lines India **94** L4 28 40N 77 13E
Civitavecchia Italy **81** B3 42 05N 11 47E
Cizre Turkey **92** F6 37 21N 42 11E
Clairton Pennsylvania U.S.A. **53** E1 40 17N 79 56W
Clare *r.* Irish Republic **78** C5 53 25N 8 55W
Clare Michigan U.S.A. **36** B4 43 49N 84 47W
Claremont New Hampshire U.S.A. **65** H6 43 23N 72 21W
Clarence New York U.S.A. **64** B5 42 59N 78 36W
Clarence Island South Shetland Islands **69** G0 61 10S 54 00W
Clarence Strait Alaska U.S.A. **42** B3 56 00N 133 30W
Clarendon Pennsylvania U.S.A. **64** A4 41 46N 79 06W
Clarion Fracture Zone Pacific Ocean **115** M9 18 00N 130 00W
Clarion River Pennsylvania U.S.A. **64** A4 41 22N 79 00W
Clark Fork *r.* Montana U.S.A. **43** E1 43 00N 115 55W
Clark Hill Lake U.S.A. **63** J3 33 00N 82 00W
Clarksburg Maryland U.S.A. **64** C2 39 14N 77 15W
Clarksburg West Virginia U.S.A. **63** J4 39 16N 80 22W
Clarks Ferry Pennsylvania U.S.A. **64** D3 40 23N 77 00W
Clarksville Tennessee U.S.A. **63** I4 36 31N 87 21W
Clear, Cape Irish Republic **78** B3 51 30N 9 30W
Clearfield Pennsylvania U.S.A. **64** B4 41 02N 78 27W
Clearwater Florida U.S.A. **63** J2 27 57N 82 48W
Clearwater *r.* Idaho U.S.A. **62** C6 46 00N 116 00W
Clermont-Ferrand France **77** C4 45 47N 3 05E
Cleveland New York U.S.A. **64** D6 43 15N 75 50W
Cleveland Peninsula Alaska U.S.A. **42** B3 55 30N 132 00W
Clichy France **83** B2 48 54N 2 19E
Clifton New Jersey U.S.A. **50** B2 40 52N 74 08W
Clinton Connecticut U.S.A. **65** H4 41 16N 72 32W
Clinton Iowa U.S.A. **63** H5 41 51N 90 12W
Clinton Massachusetts U.S.A. **65** J5 42 25N 71 41W
Clinton Oklahoma U.S.A. **62** G4 35 32N 98 59W
Clipperton Fracture Zone Pacific Ocean **115** N8 10 00N 120 00W
Clipperton Island Pacific Ocean **115** P9 10 20N 109 13W
Cloncurry Australia **110** G5 20 41S 140 30E
Clonmel Irish Republic **78** D4 52 21N 7 42W
Cloppenburg Germany **76** D5 52 52N 8 02E
Cloquet Massachusetts U.S.A. **35** B2 46 39N 92 27W
Clovis New Mexico U.S.A. **62** F3 34 14N 103 13W
Cluj-Napoca Romania **81** D4 46 47N 23 37E
Clutha *r.* New Zealand **111** A1 46 30S 169 20E
Clyde Ohio U.S.A. **36** D2 41 59N 82 18W
Clyde *r.* Scotland **78** G7 55 50N 4 25W
Clydebank Scotland **78** G7 55 54N 4 24W
Coari Brazil **68** E12 4 08S 63 07W
Coast Range *mts.* U.S.A. **62** B5/C3
Coatepec Mexico **66** E3 19 29N 96 59W
Coatesville Pennsylvania U.S.A. **64** E2 39 59N 75 50W
Coats Land *geog. reg.* Antarctica **117** 77 00S 25 00W
Coatzacoalcos *(Puerto Mexico)* Mexico **66** E3 18 10N 94 25W
Cobán Guatemala **66** F3 15 28N 90 20W
Cobar Australia **110** H3 31 32S 145 51E
Cobham England **82** B2 51 20N 0 24W
Cobija Bolivia **68** D10 11 01S 68 45W
Coburg Germany **76** E5 50 15N 10 58E
Cochabamba Bolivia **68** D9 17 26S 66 10W
Cochin India **95** D1 9 56N 76 15E
Cochituate, Lake Massachusetts U.S.A. **52** A2 42 17N 71 22W
Cochrane Chile **69** C3 47 16S 72 33W
Cochranton Pennsylvania U.S.A. **36** F2 41 32N 80 03W
Cocos Basin Indian Ocean **112** I6 5 00S 96 00E
Cocos Bay Trinidad and Tobago **66** T9 10 25N 61 05W
Cocos Island *see* Isla del Coco
Cocos Islands Indian Ocean **112** I5 12 30S 97 00E
Cocos Ridge Pacific Ocean **115** R8 4 00N 90 00W
Cocota Brazil **69** Q2 22 48S 43 11W
Codajás Brazil **68** E12 3 55S 62 00W
Cod, Cape Massachusetts U.S.A. **65** K5 42 05N 70 12W
Codó Brazil **68** I12 4 28S 43 51W
Codrington Antigua & Barbuda **67** L3 17 43N 61 49W
Coelhodo Rocha Brazil **69** P2 22 46S 43 21W
Coeur d'Alene Idaho U.S.A. **62** C6 47 40N 116 46W
Cognac France **77** B4 45 42N 0 19W
Cogswell Reservoir California U.S.A. **51** C3 34 14N 117 59W
Cohocton New York U.S.A. **64** C5 42 30N 77 30W
Cohocton River New York U.S.A. **64** C5 42 20N 77 20W
Coihaique Chile **69** C3 45 35S 72 08W
Coimbatore India **95** D2 11 00N 76 57E
Coimbra Portugal **77** A3 40 12N 8 25W
Colbeck, Cape Antarctica **117** 77 00S 158 00W
Colchester Connecticut U.S.A. **65** H4 41 35N 72 19W
Colchester England **78** L3 51 54N 0 54E
Coldwater Michigan U.S.A. **36** A2 41 57N 85 01W
Coleen *r.* Alaska U.S.A. **44** C4 67 30N 142 30W
Coleraine Northern Ireland **78** E7 55 08N 6 40W
Colima Mexico **66** D3 19 14N 103 41W
Coll *i.* Scotland **78** E8 56 40N 6 35W
College Alaska U.S.A. **44** B3 64 54N 147 55W
Collie Australia **110** B3 33 20S 116 06E
Collingwood New Zealand **111** B2 40 41S 172 41E
Collinsville Connecticut U.S.A. **65** H4 41 49N 72 55W
Colma California U.S.A. **49** B2 37 42N 122 29W
Colmar France **76** D4 48 05N 7 21E
Cologne *see* Köln
Colombes France **83** B2 48 55N 2 15E
COLOMBIA **68** C13
Colombo Sri Lanka **95** D1 6 55N 79 52E
Colón Panama **67** Y2 9 21N 79 54W
Colonsay *i.* Scotland **78** E8 56 05N 6 15W
Colorado *r.* North America **62** D3 33 00N 114 00W
Colorado *state* U.S.A. **62** E4 39 00N 106 00W
Colorado Plateau Arizona U.S.A. **62** D4 36 00N 111 00W
Colorado Springs *tn.* Colorado U.S.A. **62** F4 38 50N 104 50W
Columbia Missouri U.S.A. **63** H4 38 58N 92 20W
Columbia Pennsylvania U.S.A. **64** D3 40 02N 76 30W
Columbia *r.* North America **62** B6 46 00N 120 00W
Columbia South Carolina U.S.A. **63** J3 34 00N 81 00W
Columbia City Indiana U.S.A. **35** C1 41 09N 85 20W
Columbia Falls *tn.* Montana U.S.A. **41** C1 48 24N 114 11W
Columbus Georgia U.S.A. **63** J3 32 28N 84 59W
Columbus Indiana U.S.A. **63** I4 39 12N 85 57W
Columbus Mississippi U.S.A. **63** I3 33 30N 88 27W
Columbus Nebraska U.S.A. **63** G5 41 27N 97 21W
Columbus Ohio U.S.A. **63** J5 39 59N 83 03W
Columbus Channel Trinidad and Tobago/Venezuela **66** S9 10 00N 61 45W
Colville *r.* Alaska U.S.A. **44** A4 69 00N 158 00W
Colville Washington U.S.A. **43** E1 48 33N 117 55W
Colvocorresses Bay Antarctica **117** 66 00S 120 00E
Colwyn Bay *tn.* Wales **78** H5 53 18N 3 43W
Comandante Ferraz *r.s.* Antarctica **117** 62 05S 58 23W
Comilla Bangladesh **95** G4 23 28N 91 10E
Comitán Mexico **66** F3 16 18N 92 09W
Commonwealth of Independent States *see individual member countries:* ARMENIA, AZERBAIJAN BELARUS, KAZAKHSTAN KIRGYZSTAN MOLDOVA, RUSSIA,TAJIKISTAN TURKMENISTAN UKRAINE, UZBEKISTAN
Como Italy **81** A4 45 48N 9 05E
Comodoro Rivadavia Argentina **69** D3 45 50S 67 30W
Comorin, Cape India **95** D1 8 04N 77 35E
Comoro Archipelago *is.* Indian Ocean **102** 12 00S 44 00E
COMOROS **107** N5
Compiègne France **76** C4 49 25N 2 50E
Compton California U.S.A. **51** B2 33 55N 118 14W
Conakry Guinea **106** C9 9 30N 13 43W
Concepción Chile **69** C5 36 50S 73 03W
Concepción Mexico **66** D4 24 38N 101 25W
Concepción Paraguay **69** F8 23 22S 57 26W
Concepción del Uruguay Argentina **69** F6 32 30S 58 15W
Conchos *r.* Mexico **66** C5 27 30N 107 00W
Concord California U.S.A. **49** C3 37 59N 122 04W
Concord Massachusetts U.S.A. **52** A2 42 28N 71 15W
Concord New Hampshire U.S.A. **65** J6 43 13N 71 34W
Concordia Argentina **69** F6 31 25S 58 00W
Concordia Kansas U.S.A. **63** G4 39 35N 97 39W
Concord River Massachusetts U.S.A. **52** A2 42 28N 71 21W
Concrete Washington U.S.A. **42** H4 48 32N 121 46W
Condom France **77** C3 43 58N 0 23E
Conduit *r.* Israel **92** O11 32 25N 35 00E
Conecuh *r.* Alabama U.S.A. **63** I3 31 00N 87 00W
Conesus Lake New York U.S.A. **64** C5 42 46N 77 43W
Coney Island New York U.S.A. **50** C1 40 34N 74 00W
Conflans-Ste. Honorine France **83** A3 49 01N 2 09E
CONGO **106** I7
Congo *(Zaïre) r.* Congo **106** I7 2 00S 17 00E
Conneaut Ohio U.S.A. **36** F2 41 58N 80 34W
Connecticut *state* U.S.A. **65** H4 41 00N 73 00W
Connecticut River U.S.A. **65** H5 42 10N 72 35W
Conset Bay Barbados **66** W12 13 10N 59 25W
Constanța Romania **81** E3 44 12N 28 40E
Constantine Algeria **106** H15 36 22N 6 40E
Constitución Chile **69** C5 31 05S 57 51W
Contanama Peru **68** B11 7 19S 75 04W
Contra Costa Canal California U.S.A. **49** C3 37 58N 122 05W
Contra Costa County California U.S.A. **49** B3 37 58N 122 26W
Conyngham Pennsylvania U.S.A. **64** D3 40 59N 76 04W
Cook County Illinois U.S.A. **53** A1 41 39N 87 59W
Cook Inlet Alaska U.S.A. **10** E5 60 00N 152 30W
Cook Islands Pacific Ocean **115** K6 19 30S 159 50W
Cook, Mount New Zealand **111** B2 43 37S 170 08E
Cook Strait New Zealand **111** B2 41 00S 174 30E
Cooktown Australia **110** H6 15 29S 145 15E
Coolgardie Australia **110** C3 31 01S 121 12E
Cooper Creek *r.* Australia **110** F4 28 00S 138 00E
Cooperstown New York U.S.A. **64** F5 42 43N 74 56W
Coosa *r.* U.S.A. **63** I3 33 00N 86 00W
Coos Bay *tn.* Oregon U.S.A. **62** B5 43 23N 124 12W
Copacabana Brazil **69** Q2 22 58S 43 11W
Copacabana Beach Brazil **69** Q2 22 59S 43 11W
Copenhagen *see* København
Copiapó Chile **69** C7 27 20S 70 23W
Copper *r.* Alaska U.S.A. **10** F5 60 30N 144 50W
Copper Harbor Michigan U.S.A. **63** I6 47 28N 87 54W
Coquet *r.* England **78** J7 55 20N 1 50W
Coquimbo Chile **69** C7 29 57S 71 25W
Coral Sea Islands Territory *admin.* Australia **110** H6/I6 17 00S 150 00E
Coral Sea Pacific Ocean **110** I7 15 00S 154 00E
Corantijn *(Courantyne) r.* Surinam **68** F13 4 30N 57 30W
Cordillera Cantabrica *(Cantabrian Mountains)* Spain **77** A3 43 00N 5 30W
Cordillera de Mérida *mts.* Venezuela **67** J1 8 00N 72 00W
Córdoba Argentina **69** E6 31 25S 64 11W
Córdoba Mexico **66** E3 18 55N 96 55W
Córdoba Spain **77** B2 37 53N 4 46W
Cordova Alaska U.S.A. **10** F5 60 29N 145 52W
Corfu *see* Kérkira
Corinth Mississippi U.S.A. **63** I3 34 58N 88 30W
Cork Irish Republic **78** C3 51 54N 8 28W
Çorlu Turkey **80** E3 41 11N 27 48E
Cormeilles-en-Parisis France **83** A2 48 58N 2 11E
Corning New York U.S.A. **64** C5 42 10N 77 04W
Cornwall Bridge Connecticut U.S.A. **65** G4 41 49N 73 23W
Coro Venezuela **68** D15 11 20N 70 00W
Coroico Bolivia **68** D9 16 19S 67 45W
Coromandel Coast India **95** D2 12 30N 81 30E
Coromandel Peninsula New Zealand **111** C3 36 30S 175 45E
Corona Arena Dam Trinidad and Tobago **66** T10 10 32N 61 12W
Coronation Island Alaska U.S.A. **42** B3 55 50N 134 15W
Coronel Pringles Argentina **69** E5 37 56S 61 25W
Corpus Christi Texas U.S.A. **63** G2 27 47N 97 26W
Corrientes Argentina **69** F7 27 30S 58 48W
Corrieverton Guyana **68** F14 5 53N 57 10W
Corse *(Corsica) i.* France **77** D3 42 00N 9 00E
Corsica *see* Corse
Corte Corsica **77** D3 42 18N 9 08E
Cortland New York U.S.A. **64** D5 42 36N 76 10W
Çoruh *r.* Turkey **92** F7 40 45N 40 45E
Corumbá Brazil **68** F9 19 00S 57 35W
Corunna Michigan U.S.A. **36** B3 42 58N 84 05W
Corunna *see* La Coruña
Corvallis Oregon U.S.A. **62** B5 44 34N 123 16W
Cosenza Italy **81** C2 39 17N 16 16E
Cossipore India **94** K2 22 37N 88 23E
Costa Blanca *geog. reg.* Spain **77** B2 38 15N 0 20W
Costa Brava *geog. reg.* Spain **77** C3 41 40N 3 50E
Costa del Sol *geog. reg.* Spain **77** B2 36 40N 4 40W
COSTA RICA **67** H1/2
Cotagaita Bolivia **68** D8 20 47S 65 40W
Côte D'Azur France **77** D3 43 00N 7 00E
CÔTE D'IVOIRE **106** D9
Cotonou Benin **106** F9 6 24N 2 31E
Cotopaxi *mt.* Ecuador **68** B12 0 40S 78 28W
Cotswold Hills England **78** I3 51 40N 2 10W
Cottbus Germany **76** E5 51 43N 14 21E
Coudersport Pennsylvania U.S.A. **35** E1 41 46N 78 03W
Council Bluffs Iowa U.S.A. **63** G5 41 14N 95 54W
Coupeville Washington U.S.A. **42** H4 48 14N 122 40W
Courtrai *see* Kortrijk
Couva *r.* Trinidad and Tobago **66** T9 10 25N 61 24W
Coventry Rhode Island U.S.A. **65** J4 41 45N 71 38W
Coventry England **78** J4 52 25N 1 30W
Covilhã Portugal **77** A3 40 17N 7 30W
Covina California U.S.A. **51** C3 34 04N 117 53W
Covington Kentucky U.S.A. **63** J4 39 04N 84 30W
Cowan Creek Australia **111** G3 33 36S 151 13E
Cowanesque River Pennsylvania U.S.A. **64** C4 41 55N 77 30W
Cox's Bazar Bangladesh **95** G4 21 25N 91 59E
Coyote Creek *r.* California U.S.A. **51** B2 33 50N 118 05W
Coyote Hills Regional Park California U.S.A. **49** C2 37 34N 122 06W
Craig Alaska U.S.A. **42** B3 55 29N 133 06W
Craiova Romania **81** D3 44 18N 23 47E
Crandon Wisconsin U.S.A. **35** C2 45 34N 88 54W
Cranston Rhode Island U.S.A. **65** J4 41 47N 71 27W
Crawley England **78** K3 51 07N 0 12W
Cremona Italy **81** B4 45 08N 10 01E
Cres *i.* Croatia **81** B3 45 00N 14 00E
Crescent Island Hong Kong U.K. **98** C3 22 32N 114 19E
Creston Iowa U.S.A. **63** H5 41 04N 94 20W
Crete *see* Kriti
Créteil France **83** B2 48 47N 2 28E
Crete, Sea of Mediterranean Sea **81** D2 36 00N 25 00E
Crewe England **78** I5 53 05N 2 27W
Criciúma Brazil **69** H7 28 45S 49 25W
Crimea *see* Krim
CROATIA **81** C4
Cromwell New Zealand **111** A1 45 03S 169 14E
Cronulla Australia **111** G1 34 04S 151 09E
Crooked Island Hong Kong U.K. **98** C3 22 33N 114 18E
Crooked Island The Bahamas **67** J4 22 45N 74 10W
Crookston Minnesota U.S.A. **63** G6 47 47N 96 36W
Crosby North Dakota U.S.A. **40** C1 48 56N 103 20W
Cross Sound Alaska U.S.A. **42** A3 58 00N 137 00W
Crotone Italy **81** C2 39 05N 17 08E
Crow Peak *mt.* Montana U.S.A. **62** D6 46 19N 111 56W
Crows Nest Australia **111** G2 33 50S 151 12E
Croydon Australia **110** G6 18 10S 142 15E
Croydon *bor.* Greater London England **82** C2 51 23N 0 06W
Crozet Basin Indian Ocean **112** E3/F3 40 00S 55 00E
Cruzeiro do Sul Brazil **68** C11 7 40S 72 39W
Cuando *r.* Southern Africa **107** J4 16 00S 21 30E
Cuango *r.* Angola **107** I6 9 00S 18 30E
Cuanza *r.* Angola **107** H6 9 40S 15 00E
CUBA **67** I4
Cuba New York U.S.A. **64** B5 42 13N 78 16W
Cubango *r.* Angola **107** I4 17 00S 18 00E
Cúcuta Colombia **68** C14 7 55N 73 31W
Cuddalore India **95** D2 11 43N 79 46E
Cuddapah India **95** D2 14 30N 78 50E
Cuenca Ecuador **68** B12 2 54S 79 00W
Cuenca Spain **77** B3 40 04N 2 07W
Cuernavaca Mexico **66** E3 18 57N 99 15W
Cuiabá Brazil **68** F9 15 32S 56 05W
Cuito *r.* Angola **107** I4 17 30S 19 30E
Culiacán Mexico **66** C4 24 50N 107 23W
Cull Creek California U.S.A. **49** C3 37 45N 122 04W
Culver City California U.S.A. **51** A3 34 01N 118 24W
Cumaná Venezuela **68** E15 10 29N 64 12W
Cumberland Maryland U.S.A. **64** B2 39 40N 78 47W
Cumbernauld Scotland **78** H7 55 57N 4 00W
Cumbrian Mountains England **78** H6 54 30N 3 00W
Cumuta Trinidad and Tobago **66** T10 10 35N 61 12W
Cunene *r.* Angola/Namibia **107** H4 17 00S 13 30E
Cuneo Italy **81** A3 44 24N 7 33E
Cunnamula Australia **110** H4 28 04S 145 40E
Cunupia Trinidad and Tobago **66** T10 10 32N 61 22W
Cuova Trinidad and Tobago **66** T9 10 25N 61 27W
Curaçao *i.* Lesser Antilles **67** K2 12 20N 68 20W
Curacautin Chile **69** C5 38 28S 71 52W
Curicó Chile **69** C5 35 00S 71 15W
Curitiba Brazil **69** H7 25 25S 49 25W
Curvelo Brazil **68** I9 18 45S 44 27W
Cut Bank Montana U.S.A. **41** C1 48 38N 112 20W
Cut Bank Creek Montana U.S.A. **41** C1 48 38N 112 20W
Cuttack India **95** F4 20 26N 85 56E
Cuxhaven Germany **76** D5 53 52N 8 42E
Cuyahoga Falls *tn.* Ohio U.S.A. **36** E2 41 08N 81 27W
Cuyahoga River Ohio U.S.A. **36** E2 41 20N 81 35W
Cuzcu Peru **68** C10 13 32S 71 57W
Cwmbran Wales **78** H3 51 39N 3 00W
Cyclades *see* Kikládhes
CYPRUS **92** D5
CZECHOSLOVAKIA **80** C4
Czech Republic *admin.* Czechoslovakia **80** C4
Częstochowa Poland **80** C5 50 49N 19 07E

D

Dabola Guinea **106** C10 10 48N 11 02W
Dadra & Nagar Haveli *admin.* India **95** C4 20 00N 73 00E
Dagenham England **82** D3 51 33N 0 08E
Da Hinggan Ling *(Greater Khingan Range) mts.* China **97** O8/O9 50 00N 122 00E
Dahlewitz Germany **83** F1 52 19N 13 27E
Dāhod India **95** C4 22 48N 74 18E
Dahongliutan Kashmir **95** D7 35 55N 79 10E
Dahuk Iraq **94** F6 36 58N 43 01E
Daiō-zaki *c.* Japan **100** H1 34 16N 136 55E
Dairût Egypt **92** D4 27 34N 30 48E
Daisen *mt.* Japan **100** B2 35 23N 133 34E
Dakar Senegal **106** B10 14 38N 17 27W
Dakhla Oasis Egypt **106** K13 26 00N 28 00E
Dakshin Gangotri *r.s.* Antarctica **117** 70 05S 12 00E
Dalälven *r.* Sweden **80** C7 60 30N 17 00E
Da Lat Vietnam **99** D6 11 56N 108 25E
Dalbandin Pakistan **94** A5 28 56N 64 30E
Dalby Australia **110** I4 27 11S 151 12E
Dalhart Texas U.S.A. **62** F4 36 05N 102 32W
Dalian China **97** O6 38 53N 121 37E
Dallas Texas U.S.A. **63** G3 32 47N 96 48W
Dallgow Germany **83** E2 52 32N 13 03E
Dall Island Alaska U.S.A. **42** B2 55 00N 133 00W
Daloa Côte d'Ivoire **106** D9 6 56N 6 28W
Dalton Georgia U.S.A. **63** J3 34 46N 84 59W
Dalton Massachusetts U.S.A. **65** G5 42 28N 73 10W
Daly *r.* Australia **110** E7 14 00S 132 00E
Daly City California U.S.A. **49** B2 37 42N 122 28W
Daly Waters *tn.* Australia **110** E6 16 13S 133 20E
Daman India **95** C4 20 15N 72 58E
Damanhûr Egypt **92** D5 31 03N 30 28E
Damascus *see* Dimashq
Damāvand Iran **93** H6 35 47N 52 04E
Damāvand *mt.* Iran **93** H6 35 56N 52 08E
Damba Angola **107** I6 6 44S 15 20E
Damietta *see* Dumyât
Damoh India **95** D4 23 50N 79 30E
Dampier Australia **110** B5 20 45S 116 48E
Danakil *geog. reg.* Africa **102** 14 00N 40 00E
Da Nang Vietnam **99** D7 16 04N 108 14E
Danau Toba *l.* Indonesia **99** B4 2 40N 98 50E
Danbury Connecticut U.S.A. **65** G4 41 24N 73 26W
Danforth Maine U.S.A. **31** A2 45 42N 67 52W
Dangori India **95** H5 27 40N 95 35E
Danielson Connecticut U.S.A. **65** J4 41 48N 71 53W
Danli Honduras **67** G2 14 02N 86 30W
Dannevirke New Zealand **111** C2 40 12S 176 08E
Dansville New York U.S.A. **64** C5 42 34N 77 41W
Danube *see* Donau, Duna, Dunarea, Dunav
Danvers Massachusetts U.S.A. **65** K5 42 35N 70 58W
Danville Illinois U.S.A. **63** I5 40 09N 87 37W
Danville Pennsylvania U.S.A. **64** D3 40 57N 76 36W
Danville Virginia U.S.A. **63** K4 36 34N 79 25W
Dar'ā Syria **92** P11 32 37N 36 06E
Darbhanga India **95** F5 26 10N 85 54E
Dardanelles *sd.* Turkey **92** C6 40 08N 26 10E
Dar el Beida *see* Casablanca
Dar es Salaam Tanzania **107** M6 6 51S 39 18E
Dargaville New Zealand **111** B3 35 57S 173 53E
Darien Connecticut U.S.A. **65** G4 41 05N 73 28W
Darien Center New York U.S.A. **64** B5 42 53N 78 22W
Darjiling India **95** F5 27 02N 88 20E
Darling *r.* Australia **110** G3 31 30S 144 00E
Darling Downs *mts.* Australia **110** H4 28 00S 148 30E
Darlington England **78** J6 54 31N 1 34W
Darmstadt Germany **76** D5 49 52N 8 39E
Darnah Libya **106** J14 32 46N 22 39E
Darnley, Cape Antarctica **117** 67 16S 69 53E
Daroca Spain **77** B3 41 07N 1 25W
Darrington Washington U.S.A. **42** H4 48 15N 121 37W
Dartford England **82** D2 51 27N 0 13E
Dartmoor National Park England **78** H2 50 35 3 50W
Daru Papua New Guinea **110** G8 9 05S 143 10E
Darwin Australia **110** E7 12 23S 130 44E
Daryācheh-ye Orūmīyeh *(L. Urmia) l.* Iran **93** G6 37 20N 45 55E
Dasht-e-Kavir *geog. reg.* Iran **93** H5 34 30N 54 30E
Dasht-e-Lut *geog. reg.* Iran **93** I5 32 00N 57 00E
Dasht-i-Margo *d.* Afghanistan **93** J5 30 30N 62 30E
Datchet England **82** A2 51 30N 0 35W
Datong China **97** M7 40 02N 113 33E
Datong He *r.* China **97** K6 37 30N 102 00E

Datong Shan *mts.* China 97 J6 38 00N 99 00E
Datu Piang The Philippines 99 G5 7 02N 124 30E
Daugavpils Latvia 79 E7 55 52N 26 31E
Dauphin Pennsylvania U.S.A. 64 D3 40 23N 76 56W
Davangere India 95 D2 14 30N 75 52E
Davao The Philippines 99 H5 7 05N 125 38E
Davenport Iowa U.S.A. 63 H5 41 32N 90 36W
David Panama 67 H1 8 26N 82 26W
Davidson Mountains Alaska U.S.A. 44 C4 68 00N 144 00W
Davis *r.s.* Antarctica 117 68 17S 77 58E
Davison Michigan U.S.A. 36 C4 43 02N 83 30W
Davos Switzerland 77 D4 46 47N 9 50E
Dawna Range *mts.* Thailand 99 B7 17 30N 98 00E
Dax France 77 B3 43 43N 1 03W
Dayr az Zawr Syria 92 F6 35 20N 40 02E
Dayton Ohio U.S.A. 63 J4 39 45N 84 10W
Daytona Beach *tn.* Florida U.S.A. 63 J2 29 11N 81 01W
Dayville Connecticut U.S.A. 65 J4 41 51N 71 54W
Dazhang Xi *r.* China 98 E8 25 00N 118 00E
De Aar Republic of South Africa 107 J1 30 40S 24 01E
Dead Sea Israel/Jordan 92 O10 31 35N 35 30E
Dean Funes Argentina 69 E6 30 25S 64 22W
Dearborn Michigan U.S.A. 52 E2 42 18N 83 14W
Dearborn Heights Michigan U.S.A. 52 D2 42 15N 83 15W
Death Valley National Monument California/Nevada U.S.A. 66 A7 37 30N 117 30W
Débé Trinidad and Tobago 66 T9 10 12N 61 27W
Debrecen Hungary 81 D4 47 30N 21 37E
Debre Mark'os Ethiopia 106 M10 10 19N 37 41E
Debre Tabor Ethiopia 106 M10 11 50N 38 06E
Debreta-Turnu-Severin Romania 81 D3 44 36N 22 39E
Decatur Alabama U.S.A. 63 I3 34 36N 87 00W
Decatur Illinois U.S.A. 63 I4 39 51N 88 57W
Decatur Indiana U.S.A. 36 B1 40 50N 84 57W
Deccan *plat.* India 95 D3 18 00N 78 00E
Dedham Massachusetts U.S.A. 52 B1 42 15N 71 10W
Dee *r.* Scotland 78 G7 54 55N 4 00W
Dee *r.* Scotland 78 I9 57 05N 2 10W
Dee *r.* Wales/England 78 I4 53 16N 3 10W
Deep Bay Hong Kong U.K. 98 A3 22 30N 113 55E
Deerfield Illinois U.S.A. 53 A3 42 09N 87 50W
Dee Why Australia 111 H2 33 45S 151 17E
Defiance Ohio U.S.A. 36 B2 41 17N 84 21W
Degeh Bur Ethiopia 106 N9 8 11N 43 31E
Dehra Dun India 95 D6 30 19N 78 03E
Dej Romania 81 D4 47 08N 23 55E
Dekese Zaïre 107 J7 3 28S 21 24E
Delaware *state* U.S.A. 64 E2 39 00N 75 00W
Delaware Bay U.S.A. 64 E2 39 10N 75 10W
Delaware River U.S.A. 64 E2 39 40N 75 30W
Delhi India 94 L4 28 40N 77 14E
Delhi Cantonment India 94 L4 28 35N 77 08E
Dellen *l.* Sweden 79 D3 61 50N 16 45E
Dellys Algeria 77 C2 36 57N 3 55E
De Long Mountains Alaska U.S.A. 10 C6 68 30N 162 00W
Delphos Ohio U.S.A. 36 B1 40 50N 84 21W
Del Rio Texas U.S.A. 62 F2 29 23N 100 56W
Delta Colorado U.S.A. 62 E4 38 42N 108 04W
Delta Junction Alaska U.S.A. 44 B3 63 30N 146 00W
Delta Lake *res.* New York U.S.A. 64 E6 43 17N 75 26W
Dembī Dolo Ethiopia 106 L9 8 34N 34 50E
Deming New Mexico U.S.A. 62 E3 32 17N 107 46W
Deming Washington U.S.A. 42 H4 48 50N 122 14W
Denain France 76 C5 50 19N 3 24E
Den Haag *(The Hague) see* 's-Gravenhage
Den Helder Netherlands 76 C5 52 58N 4 46E
Denison Texas U.S.A. 63 G3 33 47N 96 34W
Denizli Turkey 92 C6 37 46N 29 05E
Denman Glacier Antarctica 117 67 00S 100 00E
DENMARK 80 A6/B6
Denpasar Indonesia 99 F2 8 40S 115 14E
Denton Texas U.S.A. 63 G3 33 14N 97 18W
D'Entrecasteaux Islands Papua New Guinea 110 I8 9 30S 150 30E
Denver Colorado U.S.A. 62 E4 39 45N 105 00W
Deodora Brazil 69 P2 22 51S 43 22W
Depew New York U.S.A. 64 B5 42 54N 78 00W
Dépression du Mourdi *dep.* Chad 106 J11 17 00N 22 41E
Deputatskiy Russia 89 P9 69 15N 139 59E
Dera Ghazi Khan Pakistan 95 C6 30 05N 70 44E
Dera Ismail Khan Pakistan 95 C6 31 51N 70 56E
Derbent Russia 90 F3 42 03N 48 18E
Derby Australia 110 C6 17 19S 123 38E
Derby Connecticut U.S.A. 65 G4 41 19N 73 05W
Derby England 78 J4 52 55N 1 30W
Derry New Hampshire U.S.A. 65 J5 42 00N 71 00W
De-Ruyter New York U.S.A. 64 E5 42 46N 75 54W
Deseado Argentina 69 D3 47 44S 65 56W
Desē Ethiopia 106 M10 11 05N 39 40E
Desierto de Atacama *(Atacama Desert) d.* Chile **68/69** C8 22 30S 70 00W
Des Moines Iowa U.S.A. 63 H5 41 35N 93 35W
Des Moines *r.* Iowa U.S.A. 63 H5 41 00N 92 00W
Desna *r.* Russia/Ukraine 90 C5 51 00N 30 30E
Des Plaines Illinois U.S.A. 53 A3 42 02N 87 54W
Des Plaines River Illinois U.S.A. 53 A1 41 30N 87 45W
Dessau Germany 76 E5 51 51N 12 15E
Detroit Michigan U.S.A. 63 J5 42 23N 83 05W
Detroit River Canada/U.S.A. 52 E2 42 15N 83 00W
Deva Romania 81 D4 45 53N 22 55E
Deventer Netherlands 76 D5 52 15N 6 10E
Deveron *r.* Scotland 78 I9 57 25N 3 03W
Devils Gate Reservoir California U.S.A. 51 B3 34 11N 118 10W
Devonport Australia 110 H1 41 09S 146 16E
Dexter Maine U.S.A. 33 C2 45 01N 69 19W
Dezfūl Iran 93 G5 32 23N 48 28E
Dezhou China 97 N6 37 29N 116 11E
Dhahran *see* Az Zahrān
Dhaka Bangladesh 95 G4 23 42N 90 22E
Dhamār Yemen Republic 92 F1 14 33N 44 30E
Dhanbad India 95 F4 23 47N 86 32E
Dharoor *r.* Somalia 106 O10 10 00N 54 00E
Dhārwād India 95 D3 15 30N 75 04E
Dhodhekánisos *(Dodecanese) is.* Greece 81 E2 37 00N 26 00E
Dhoraji India 94 C4 21 42N 70 32E
Dhule India 95 C4 20 52N 74 50E
Diablo Lake Washington U.S.A. 42 H4 48 45N 121 05W
Diamantina Brazil 68 I9 18 17S 43 37W
Diamantina *r.* Australia 110 G5 24 00S 142 00E
Diamantina Fracture Zone Indian Ocean 112 J3/K3
Dibrugarh India 95 G5 27 29N 94 56E
Dickinson North Dakota U.S.A. 62 F6 46 54N 102 48W
Diego Martin Trinidad and Tobago 66 S10 10 48N 61 34W
Diepholz Germany 76 D5 52 37N 8 22E
Dieppe France 76 C4 49 55N 1 05E
Digne France 77 D3 44 05N 6 14E
Dijon France 77 D4 47 20N 5 02E
Dikson Russia 89 K10 73 32N 80 39E
Dikwa Nigeria 106 H10 12 01N 13 55E
Dili *see* Oekusi
Dillingham Alaska U.S.A. 10 D4 59 03N 158 30W
Dimashq *(Damascus)* Syria 92 P11 33 30N 36 19E
Dimitrovgrad Bulgaria 81 E3 42 03N 25 34E
Dimitrovgrad Russia 90 F5 54 14N 49 37E
Dinajpur Bangladesh 95 F5 25 38N 88 44E
Dinan France 76 B4 48 27N 2 02W
Dinant Belgium 76 C5 50 16N 4 55E
Dinara Planina *(Dinaric Alps) mts.* Europe 81 C3 44 00N 17 00E
Dinaric Alps *see* Dinara Planina
Dindigul India 95 D2 10 23N 78 00E
Dingle Bay Irish Republic 78 A4 52 05N 10 15W
Dingwall Scotland 78 G9 57 35N 4 29W
Dinslaken Germany 76 G3 51 34N 6 43E
Dipolog The Philippines 99 G5 8 34N 123 23E
Dir Pakistan 95 C7 35 12N 71 54E
Dirē Dawa Ethiopia 106 N9 9 35N 41 50E
Disappointment, Lake Australia 110 C5 23 00S 123 00E
Discovery Bay Hong Kong U.K. 98 B1 22 18N 114 02E
Discovery Bay *tn.* Hong Kong U.K. 98 B1 22 18N 114 01E
Disko Bugt *b.* Greenland 45 V4 69 00N 54 00W
Disko Island Greenland 45 V4 70 00N 54 00W
Distins Barbados 66 V12 13 04N 59 35W
Distins Bay Barbados 66 V12 13 03N 59 34W
Ditan China 101 G1 39 58N 116 24E
Diu India 94 C4 20 41N 71 03E
Divinópolis Brazil 68 I8 20 08S 44 55W
Divriği Turkey 92 E6 39 23N 38 06E
Dixon Entrance *sd.* Canada/U.S.A. 42 B2 54 28N 132 50W
Diyarbakir Turkey 92 F6 37 55N 40 14E
Djambala Congo 106 H7 2 32S 14 43E
Djelfa Algeria 106 F14 34 43N 3 14E
DJIBOUTI 92 F1
Djibouti Djibouti 92 F1 11 35N 43 11E
Djougou Benin 106 F9 9 40N 1 47E
Dnepr *r.* Belarus/Ukraine 90 C4 48 00N 35 00E
Dneprodzerzhinsk Ukraine 90 C4 48 30N 34 37E
Dnepropetrovsk Ukraine 90 C4 48 29N 35 00E
Dnestr *r.* Moldova/Ukraine 90 A4 49 30N 24 30E
Dobrich *(Tolbukhin)* Bulgaria 81 E3 43 34N 27 51E
Dobrogea *geog. reg.* Romania 81 E3 44 00N 29 00E
Dodecanese *see* Dhodhekánisos
Dodge City Kansas U.S.A. 62 F4 37 45N 100 02W
Dodoma Tanzania 107 M6 6 10S 35 40E
Dodson Montana U.S.A. 40 B1 48 25N 108 16W
Dogai Coring *l.* China 95 F6 34 30N 89 00E
Dōgo *i.* Japan 100 B2 36 20N 133 15E
Doha *see* Ad Dawhah
Dolgeville New York U.S.A. 65 F6 43 08N 74 46W
Dolina Ukraine 80 D4 49 00N 23 59E
Dolo Ethiopia 106 N8 4 11N 42 03E
Dolton Illinois U.S.A. 53 B1 41 36N 87 36W
Domaneab Nauru 114 G7 0 35S 166 40E
Dombas Norway 79 B3 62 05N 9 07E
DOMINICA 67 L3
DOMINICAN REPUBLIC 67 K3
Don *r.* England 78 J5 53 37N 1 02W
Don *r.* Russia 90 E4 50 00N 41 00E
Don *r.* Scotland 78 I9 57 15N 2 55W
Donau *(Danube) r.* Germany/Austria 76 E4 48 00N 16 00E
Don Benito Spain 77 A2 38 57N 5 52W
Doncaster England 78 J5 53 32N 1 07W
Donegal Irish Republic 78 C6 54 39N 8 07W
Donegal Bay Irish Republic 78 C6 54 30N 8 30W
Donegal Mountains Irish Republic 78 C6/D7 55 00N 8 05W
Donetsk Ukraine 90 D4 48 00N 37 50E
Dongba China 101 H1 39 58N 116 35E
Dongchuan China 97 K4 26 07N 103 05E
Dong Hoi Vietnam 97 L2 17 32N 106 35E
Dongola Sudan 92 D2 19 10N 30 27E
Dongou Congo 106 I8 2 02N 18 02E
Dønna *i.* Norway 79 C4 66 05N 12 30E
Donting Hu *l.* China 97 M4 29 00N 112 30E
Devils Lake *tn.* North Dakota U.S.A. 62 G6 48 08N 98 50W
Door Peninsula Wisconsin U.S.A. 63 I6 45 00N 87 00W
Dordogne *r.* France 77 C3 44 55N 0 30E
Dordrecht Netherlands 76 C5 51 48N 4 40E
Dori *r.* Afghanistan 93 K5 31 20N 65 00E
Dorking England 82 B1 51 14N 0 20W
Dormont Pennsylvania U.S.A. 53 D1 40 23N 80 03W
Dornbirn Austria 81 A4 47 25N 9 46E
Dornoch Firth *est.* Scotland 78 H9 57 55N 3 55W
Dortmund Germany 76 E5 51 32N 7 27E
Dortmund-Ems-Kanal *can.* Germany 76 K3 51 40N 7 20E
Dosso Niger 106 F10 13 03N 3 10E
Dothan Alabama U.S.A. 63 I3 31 12N 85 25W
Douai France 76 C5 50 22N 3 05E
Douala Cameroon 106 H8 4 04N 9 43E
Douarnenez France 77 B4 48 05N 4 20W
Double Island Hong Kong U.K. 98 C3 22 31N 114 08E
Doubs *r.* France 77 D4 47 20N 6 25E
Douglas Alaska U.S.A. 44 D3 58 15N 134 24W
Douglas Arizona U.S.A. 62 E3 31 21N 109 34W
Douglas Isle of Man British Isles 78 G6 54 09N 4 29W
Douglas Park Illinois U.S.A. 53 B2 41 51N 87 43W
Dourados Brazil 69 G8 22 09S 54 52W
Douro *r.* Portugal 77 A3 41 00N 8 30W
Dover Delaware U.S.A. 64 E2 39 10N 75 32W
Dover England 78 M3 51 08N 1 19E
Dover Massachusetts U.S.A. 52 A1 42 15N 71 17W
Dover New Hampshire U.S.A. 65 K6 43 12N 70 55W
Dover, Strait of English Channel 78 M3 51 00N 1 20E
Dovrefjell *mts.* Norway 79 B3 62 15N 9 10E
Downers Grove Illinois U.S.A. 53 A2 41 47N 87 59W
Downey California U.S.A. 51 B2 33 56N 118 25W
Doylestown Pennsylvania U.S.A. 64 E3 40 18N 75 08W
Dōzen *is.* Japan 100 B2 36 05N 133 00E
Dragan *l.* Sweden 79 D3 64 05N 15 20E
Dragon's Mouths, The *(Bocas del Dragons) sd.* Trinidad and Tobago 66 S10 10 37N 61 50W
Draguignan France 77 D3 43 32N 6 28E
Drakensberg *mts.* Republic of South Africa 107 K1 30 00S 28 00E
Drake Passage *sd.* Southern Ocean 69 C1/E1 58 00S 66 00W
Dráma Greece 81 D3 41 10N 24 11E
Drammen Norway 79 C2 59 45N 10 15E
Drancy France 83 B2 48 55N 2 28E
Drau *r.* Austria 81 B4 46 00N 14 00E
Drayton North Dakota U.S.A. 39 B1 48 35N 97 11W
Dresden Germany 76 E5 51 03N 13 45E
Dreux France 76 C4 48 44N 1 23E
Drewitz Germany 83 E1 52 20N 13 08E
Drin *r.* Albania 81 D3 42 00N 20 00E
Drina *r.* Europe 81 C3 43 30N 15 19E
Drogheda Irish Republic 78 E5 53 43N 6 21W
Drogobyč Ukraine 80 D4 49 22N 23 33E
Drôme *r.* France 77 D3 44 50N 5 00E
Drummond Island Michigan U.S.A. 36 C7 46 00N 83 40W
Drummoyne Australia 111 G2 33 51S 151 09E
Druzhba Kazakhstan 91 N4 45 18N 82 29E
Dryden New York U.S.A. 64 D5 42 29N 76 17W
Dubayy United Arab Emirates 93 I4 25 14N 55 17E
Dubbo Australia 110 H3 32 16S 148 41E
Dublin Georgia U.S.A. 63 J3 32 31N 82 54W
Dublin Irish Republic 78 E5 53 20N 6 15W
Dubno Ukraine 90 B5 50 28N 25 40E
Du Bois Pennsylvania U.S.A. 64 B4 41 06N 78 46W
Dubrovnik Croatia 81 C3 42 40N 18 07E
Dubuque Iowa U.S.A. 63 H5 42 31N 90 41W
Ducie Island Pitcairn Islands 115 N5 24 40S 124 48W
Dudinka Russia 89 K9 69 27N 86 13E
Dudley Massachusetts U.S.A. 65 J5 42 03N 71 55W
Dudley England 78 I4 52 30N 2 05W
Duero *(Douro) r.* Spain/Portugal 77 A3 41 25N 6 30W
Duffy Preserve Illinois U.S.A. 53 A1 41 39N 87 55W
Dugi Otok *i.* Croatia 81 C3 44 00N 15 00E
Duisberg Germany 76 H2 51 26N 6 45E
Duke Island Alaska U.S.A. 42 B2 54 50N 131 30W
Duluth Minnesota U.S.A. 63 H6 46 45N 92 10W
Dum Dum India 94 K2 22 37N 88 24E
Dumfries Scotland 78 H7 55 04N 3 37W
Dumont d'Urville *r.s.* Antarctica 117 66 40S 140 01E
Dümpten Germany 76 H2 51 28N 6 50E
Dumyât *(Damietta)* Egypt 107 R4 31 26N 31 48E
Duna *(Danube) r.* Hungary 81 C4 46 00N 19 00E
Dunarea *(Danube) r.* Romania 81 E3 44 00N 28 00E
Dunaújváros Hungary 81 C4 47 00N 18 55E
Dunav *(Danube) r.* Serbia/Bulgaria 81 D3 45 00N 20 00E
Duncan Oklahoma U.S.A. 63 G3 34 30N 97 57W
Duncan Passage *sd.* Andaman Islands 95 G2 11 00N 93 00E
Duncannon Pennsylvania U.S.A. 64 C3 40 24N 77 03W
Duncansby Head *c.* Scotland 78 H10 58 39N 3 02W
Duncansville Pennsylvania U.S.A. 64 B3 40 27N 78 25W
Dundalk Irish Republic 78 E6 54 01N 6 25W
Dundalk Maryland U.S.A. 64 D2 39 15N 76 31W
Dundas *(Uummannaq)* Greenland 45 S6 76 30N 68 58W
Dundee Scotland 78 I8 56 28N 3 00W
Dunedin New Zealand 111 B1 45 52S 170 30E
Dunfermline Scotland 78 H8 56 04N 3 29W
Dungeness Washington U.S.A. 42 H4 48 08N 123 07W
Dunkerque *(Dunkirk)* France 76 C5 51 02N 2 23E
Dunkirk *see* Dunkerque
Dunkirk New York U.S.A. 63 K5 42 29N 79 21W
Dún Laoghaire Irish Republic 78 E5 53 17N 6 08W
Dunmore Pennsylvania U.S.A. 64 E4 41 25N 75 38W
Du Page County Illinois U.S.A. 53 A2 41 59N 87 59W
Duque de Caxias Brazil 69 P2 22 46S 43 18W
Duquesne Pennsylvania U.S.A. 53 E1 40 23N 79 53W
Dural Australia 111 G3 33 41S 151 02E
Durance *r.* France 77 D3 43 50N 5 15E
Durand Michigan U.S.A. 36 C3 42 55N 83 58W
Durango Colorado U.S.A. 62 E4 37 16N 107 53W
Durango Mexico 66 D4 24 01N 104 40W
Durant Oklahoma U.S.A. 63 G3 33 59N 96 24W
Durazno Uruguay 69 F6 33 22S 56 31W
Durban Republic of South Africa 107 L2 29 53S 31 00E
Durgapur India 95 J1 22 47N 87 44E
Durgāpur India 95 J1 22 27N 88 08E
Durg-Bhilai India 95 E4 21 12N 81 20E
Durham England 78 J6 54 47N 1 34W
Durham New Hampshire U.S.A. 65 K6 43 10N 70 52W
Durham North Carolina U.S.A. 63 K4 36 00N 78 54W
Durrës Albania 81 C3 41 18N 19 28E
Dushanbe Tajikistan 91 K2 38 38N 68 51E
Düssel *r.* Germany 76 H1 51 13N 6 55E
Düsseldorf Germany 76 H1 51 13N 6 47E
Duxbury Massachusetts U.S.A. 65 K5 42 02N 70 40W
Duyun China 97 L4 26 16N 107 29E
Dvina, North *see* Severnaya Dvina
Dzerzhinsk Belarus 90 B5 55 40N 27 01E
Dzhambul Kazakhstan 91 L3 42 50N 71 25E
Dzhetygara Kazakhstan 91 J5 52 14N 61 10E
Dzhezkazgan Kazakhstan 91 K4 47 44N 67 42E
Dzhugdzhur Range *mts.* Russia 89 P7 57 00N 137 00E
Dzungurian Basin *see* Junggar Pendi

E

Eagle Alaska U.S.A. 44 G5 64 46N 141 20W
Eagle Lake Maine U.S.A. 37 R7 46 25N 69 20W
Eagle Mountains Minnesota U.S.A. 35 B2 47 55N 90 30W
Eagle Pass *tn.* Texas U.S.A. 62 F2 28 44N 100 31W
Eagle River *tn.* Wisconsin U.S.A. 35 C2 45 56N 89 15W
Ealing *bor.* Greater London England 82 B3 51 31N 0 18W
East Antarctica *geog. reg.* Antarctica 117
East Aurora New York U.S.A. 64 B5 42 45N 78 36W
East Berlin Pennsylvania U.S.A. 64 C2 39 58N 77 00W
Eastbourne England 78 L2 50 46N 0 17E
East Branch Clarion River Reservoir Pennsylvania U.S.A. 64 B4 41 35N 78 35W
East Branch Delaware River New York U.S.A. 65 F5 42 15N 74 35W
East Cape New Zealand 111 C3 37 42S 178 35E
East Caroline Basin Pacific Ocean 114 E8 4 00N 148 00E
East Chicago Indiana U.S.A. 53 C1 41 38N 87 27W
East China Sea China/Japan 97 P5 32 00N 126 00E
East Detroit Michigan U.S.A. 52 F2 42 29N 82 57W
Easter Island Pacific Ocean 115 P5 27 05S 109 20W
Easter Island Fracture Zone Pacific Ocean 115 Q5 24 00S 100 00W
Eastern Ghats *mts.* India 95 D2/E2 15 00N 80 00E
Eastern Group *is.* Fiji 114 V16 17 40S 178 30W
Eastern Sayan *mts.* Russia 89 L6 53 00N 97 30E
East Falkland *i.* Falkland Islands 69 F2 52 00S 58 50W
East Fishkill New York U.S.A. 65 G4 41 33N 73 47W
East Fork Chandalar *r.* Alaska U.S.A. 44 B4 66 50N 147 00W
East Frisian Islands *see* Ostfriesische Inseln
East Glacier Park *tn.* Montana U.S.A. 41 C1 48 25N 113 35W
East Haddam Connecticut U.S.A. 65 H4 41 27N 72 28W
Easthampton Massachusetts U.S.A. 65 H5 42 16N 72 40W
East Hills Australia 111 G2 33 58S 150 59E
East Horsley England 82 B2 51 16N 0 26W
East Kilbride Scotland 78 G7 55 46N 4 10W
East Lamma Channel Hong Kong U.K. 98 B1 22 14N 114 08E
East London Republic of South Africa 107 K1 33 00S 27 54E
East Los Angeles California U.S.A. 51 B3 34 02N 118 12W
East Marianas Basin Pacific Ocean 114 F9 13 00N 153 00E
Easton Pennsylvania U.S.A. 64 E3 40 41N 75 13W
East Pacific Basin Pacific Ocean 115 K9 16 00N 153 00E
East Pacific Ridge Pacific Ocean 115 O5 20 00S 113 00W
East Pacific Rise Pacific Ocean 115 P9 13 00N 103 00W
Eastport Maine U.S.A. 31 A1 44 55N 67 01W
Eastport New York U.S.A. 65 H3 40 49N 72 44W
East Rift Valley East Africa 106 M8 6 00N 37 00E
East Siberian Sea Arctic Ocean 116 72 00N 165 00E
Eastsound Washington U.S.A. 42 H4 48 41N 122 54W
East Stroudsburg Pennsylvania U.S.A. 64 E4 41 00N 75 00W
Eastwood Australia 111 G2 33 48S 151 05E
Eaton Rapids *tn.* Michigan U.S.A. 36 B3 42 30N 85 40W
Eatontown New Jersey U.S.A. 65 F3 40 18N 74 06W
Eaton Wash Reservoir California U.S.A. 51 B3 34 10N 118 05W
Eau Claire *tn.* Wisconsin U.S.A. 63 H5 44 50N 91 30W
Eauripik-New Guinea Rise Pacific Ocean 114 E8 2 00N 142 00E
Ebensburg Pennsylvania U.S.A. 64 B3 40 28N 78 45W
Eberswalde-Finow Germany 76 E5 52 50N 13 53E
Ebinur Hu *l.* China 96 F7/6 45 00N 83 00E
Ebolowa Cameroon 106 H8 2 56N 11 11E
Ebro *r.* Spain 77 C3 41 00N 0 30E
Ebute Metta Nigeria 107 V3 6 27N 3 28E
Ech Cheliff Algeria 106 F15 36 05N 1 15E
Ecija Spain 77 A2 37 33N 5 04W
Ecorse Michigan U.S.A. 52 E2 42 16N 83 09W
Écouen France 83 B3 49 01N 2 22E
ECUADOR 68 B12
Ed Damer Sudan 92 D2 17 37N 33 59E
Ed Debba Sudan 106 L11 18 02N 30 56E
Edéa Cameroon 106 H8 3 47N 10 13E
Eden New York U.S.A. 64 B5 42 39N 78 56W
Eden North Carolina U.S.A. 63 K4 37 30N 79 46W
Eden *r.* England 78 I6 54 50N 2 45W
Eden, Mount California U.S.A. 49 C2 37 38N 122 09W
Eder *r.* Germany 76 D5 51 00N 9 00E
Edgartown Massachusetts U.S.A. 65 K4 41 24N 70 31W
Edgecombe, Cape Alaska U.S.A. 42 A3 57 00N 135 45W
Edgewood Maryland U.S.A. 64 D2 39 25N 76 18W
Edgware England 82 B3 51 36N 0 16W
Édhessa Greece 81 D3 40 48N 22 03E
Edinboro Pennsylvania U.S.A. 36 F2 41 53N 80 08W
Edinburgh Scotland 78 H7 55 57N 3 13W
Edirne Turkey 80 E3 41 40N 26 34E
Edison New Jersey U.S.A. 65 F3 40 31N 74 24W
Edmonton England 82 C3 51 37N 0 04W
Edo *r.* Japan 101 C3 35 38N 139 53E
Edogawa Japan 101 C3 35 41N 139 51E
Edremit Turkey 80 E2 39 34N 27 01E
Edward, Lake Zaïre/Uganda 106 K7 0 30S 29 00E
Edwards Plateau Texas U.S.A. 62 F3 31 00N 100 00W
Eems *(Ems) est.* Netherlands 76 D5 53 25N 6 55E
Éfaté *i.* Vanuatu 110 L5 17 30S 168 00E
Eger Hungary 81 D4 47 53N 20 28E
Egham England 82 A2 51 26N 0 34W
Egmont, Cape New Zealand 111 B3 39 15S 173 46E
Egmont, Mount New Zealand 111 B3 39 18S 174 05E
Egridir Gölü Turkey 92 D6 37 52N 30 51E
EGYPT 92 D4
Eichwalde Germany 83 G1 52 23N 13 37E
Eifel *plat.* Germany 76 D5 50 00N 7 00E
Eigg *i.* Scotland 78 E8 56 55N 6 10W
Eight Degree Channel Indian Ocean 95 C1 8 00N 73 30E
Eighty Mile Beach Australia 110 C6 19 00S 121 00E
Eindhoven Netherlands 76 D5 51 26N 5 30E
Eisenach Germany 76 E5 50 59N 10 19E
Ekibastuz Kazakhstan 91 M5 51 50N 75 10E
Eksjö Sweden 80 B6 57 40N 15 00E
EL SALVADOR 66 G2
El Aaiún *see* Laayoune
El Arco Mexico 66 B5 28 00N 113 25W
El'Arîsh Egypt 92 N10 31 08N 33 48E
Elat Israel 92 O9 29 33N 34 57E
Elâziğ Turkey 92 E6 38 41N 39 14E
El Bahr el Saghîr Egypt 107 R4 31 38N 31 39E
El Ballâh Egypt 107 S3 30 47N 32 19E
El Banco Colombia 68 C14 9 04N 73 59W
Elbasan Albania 81 D3 41 07N 20 05E
El Bayadh Algeria 77 C2 36 35N 1 18E
El Bayadh Algeria 106 F14 33 40N 1 00E
Elbe *(Labe) r.* Europe 76 D5 53 00N 9 00E
Elbert, Mount Colorado U.S.A. 62 E4 39 05N 106 27W
Elbląg Poland 80 C5 54 10N 19 25E
Elburz Mountains Iran 93 H6 36 15N 51 00E
El Cerro del Aripo *mt.* Trinidad and Tobago 66 T10 10 49N 61 14W
Elche Spain 77 B2 38 16N 0 41W
Elda Spain 77 B2 38 29N 0 47W
Eldoret Kenya 106 M8 0 31N 35 17E
Eldred Pennsylvania U.S.A. 64 B4 41 57N 78 23W

El Dorado Arkansas U.S.A. **63** H3 33 12N 92 40W
El Dorado Kansas U.S.A. **63** G4 37 51N 96 52W
Elektrostal' Russia **90** D6 55 46N 38 30E
Elephant Island South Shetland Islands **69** G0 62 00S 55 00W
El Eulma Algeria **77** D2 36 00N 5 30E
Eleuthera *i.* The Bahamas **67** I5 25 05N 76 30W
El Faiyûm Egypt **92** D4 29 19N 30 50E
El Fasher Sudan **106** K10 13 37N 25 22E
El Ferrol del Caudillo Spain **77** A3 43 29N 8 14W
El Firdân Egypt **107** S3 30 42N 32 20E
El Fuerte Mexico **66** C5 26 28N 108 35W
Elgin Scotland **78** H9 57 39N 3 20W
El Gîza Egypt **92** D5 30 01N 31 12E
El Golea Algeria **106** F14 30 35N 2 51E
El Granada California U.S.A. **49** B2 37 31N 122 28W
El Harrach Algeria **77** C2 36 45N 4 00E
El Iskandarîya *see* Alexandria
Elista Russia **90** E4 46 18N 44 14E
Eliza Howell Park Michigan U.S.A. **52** D2 42 29N 83 57W
Elizabeth Australia **110** F3 34 45S 138 39E
Elizabeth New Jersey U.S.A. **50** B1 40 39N 74 13W
Elizabeth City North Carolina U.S.A. **63** K4 36 18N 76 16W
Elizabeth Islands Massachusetts U.S.A. **65** K4 41 00N 70 00W
Elizabethtown Pennsylvania U.S.A. **64** D3 40 10N 76 38W
El Jafr Jordan **92** P10 30 16N 36 11E
Ełk Poland **80** D5 53 51N 22 20E
Elk City Oklahoma U.S.A. **62** G4 34 25N 99 26W
Elk Grove Village Illinois U.S.A. **53** A3 42 00N 87 58W
El Khârga Egypt **92** D4 25 27N 30 32E
Elkhart Indiana U.S.A. **63** I5 41 52N 85 56W
Elkhorn *r.* Nebraska U.S.A. **63** G5 42 00N 98 00W
Elkland Pennsylvania U.S.A. **64** C4 42 00N 77 20W
Elko Nevada U.S.A. **62** C5 40 50N 115 46W
Ellenville New York U.S.A. **65** F4 41 43N 74 23W
Ellis Island New Jersey U.S.A. **50** B1 40 42N 74 02W
Ellsworth Land *geog. reg.* Antarctica **117** 75 00S 80 00W
Ellsworth Maine U.S.A. **33** C1 44 34N 68 24W
El Mahalla El Kubra Egypt **92** D5 30 59N 31 10E
El Manzala Egypt **107** S4 31 09N 31 57E
El Matariya Egypt **107** S4 31 10N 32 02E
El Médano Mexico **66** B4 24 35N 111 29W
Elmhurst Illinois U.S.A. **53** A2 41 54N 87 56W
Elmhurst Pennsylvania U.S.A. **64** E4 41 20N 75 32W
el Milk *r.* Sudan **106** K11 17 00N 29 00E
El Minya Egypt **92** D4 28 06N 30 45E
Elmira New York U.S.A. **64** D5 42 06N 76 50W
El Monte California U.S.A. **51** B3 34 04N 118 01W
El Muglad Sudan **106** K10 11 01N 27 50E
Elmwood Park Illinois U.S.A. **53** A2 41 54N 87 49W
El Obeid Sudan **106** L10 13 11N 30 10E
El Paso Texas U.S.A. **62** E3 31 45N 106 30W
El Porvenir Mexico **66** C6 31 15N 105 48W
El Puerto de Sta. Maria Spain **77** A2 36 36N 6 14W
El Qantara Egypt **107** S3 30 53N 32 20E
El Qâ'hira *see* Cairo
El Qunaytirah Syria **92** O11 33 08N 35 49E
El Reno Oklahoma U.S.A. **63** G4 35 32N 97 57W
El Sâlhiya Egypt **107** R3 30 47N 31 59E
El Salto Mexico **66** C4 23 47N 105 22W
El Shallûfa Egypt **107** T2 30 06N 32 33E
El Sobrante California U.S.A. **49** B3 37 59N 122 18W
El Sueco Mexico **66** C5 29 54N 106 22W
El Suweis *(Suez)* Egypt **107** T1 29 59N 32 33E
Eltanin Fracture Zone Pacific Ocean **115** M2 52 00S 135 00W
El Tigre Venezuela **68** E14 8 44N 64 18W
El Tîna Egypt **107** S4 31 03N 32 19E
El Tucuche *mt.* Trinidad and Tobago **66** T10 10 44N 61 25W
El Tûr Egypt **92** N9 28 14N 33 37E
Eluru India **95** E3 16 45N 81 10E
Elvas Portugal **77** A2 38 53N 7 10W
Elverum Norway **80** B7 60 54N 11 33E
Elwell, Lake Montana U.S.A. **41** C1 48 25N 111 58W
Ely Nevada U.S.A. **62** D4 39 15N 114 53W
Elyria Ohio U.S.A. **63** J5 41 22N 82 06W
Emāmrūd Iran **93** H6 36 15N 54 59E
Emba Kazakhstan **91** H4 48 47N 58 05E
Emba *r.* Kazakhstan **91** H4 47 30N 56 00E
Embalse de Guri *l.* Venezuela **68** E14 7 30N 62 30W
Emden Germany **76** D5 53 23N 7 13E
Emerald Australia **110** H5 23 30S 148 08E
Emeryville California U.S.A. **49** B3 37 50N 122 19W
Emi Koussi *mt.* Chad **106** I11 19 52N 18 31E
Emmaus Pennsylvania U.S.A. **64** E3 40 32N 75 30W
Empalme Mexico **66** B5 28 00N 110 49W
Emperor Seamounts Pacific Ocean **114** G12 42 00N 169 00E
Ems *r.* Germany **76** D5 53 00N 7 00E
Emscher *r.* Germany **76** K3 51 35N 7 25E
Ena Japan **100** J2 35 28N 137 25E
Encantado Brazil **69** P2 22 54S 43 18W
Encarnación Paraguay **69** F7 27 20S 55 50W
Endeh Indonesia **99** G2 8 51S 121 40E
Endicott New York U.S.A. **64** D5 42 06N 76 03W
Endicott Mountains Alaska U.S.A. **44** A4 67 35N 154 00W
Enfield *bor.* Greater London England **82** C3 51 39N 0 05W
Engel's Russia **90** F5 51 30N 46 07E
Engenno Novo Brazil **69** P2 22 54S 43 16W
Enggano *i.* Indonesia **99** C2 5 10S 102 40E
Enghien France **83** B2 48 58N 2 19E
England United Kingdom **78** I5
Englewood New Jersey U.S.A. **50** C2 40 53N 73 58W
English Channel *(La Manche)* U.K./France **76** B4/5 50 00N 2 30W
Enna Italy **81** B2 37 34N 14 16E
En Nahud Sudan **106** K10 12 41N 28 28E
Enniskillen Northern Ireland **78** D6 54 21N 7 38W
Enns *r.* Austria **81** B4 48 00N 14 00E
Enontekiö Finland **79** E4 68 25N 23 40E
Enosburg Falls *tn.* Vermont U.S.A. **37** O5 44 55N 72 49W
Enschede Netherlands **76** D5 52 13N 6 55E
Ensenada Mexico **66** A6 31 53N 116 38W
Entebbe Uganda **106** L8 0 04N 32 27E
Enugu Nigeria **106** G9 6 20N 7 29E
Épernay France **76** C4 49 02N 3 58E
Épinal France **76** D4 48 10N 6 28E
Epping Australia **111** G2 33 46S 151 05E
Epping England **82** D3 51 42N 0 08E
Epping Forest England **82** D3 51 40N 0 04E
Epsom England **82** B2 51 20N 0 16W
EQUATORIAL GUINEA 106 G8/H8
Erebus, Mount Antarctica **117** 77 40S 167 20E
Erechim Brazil **69** G7 27 35S 52 15W
Erenhot China **97** M7 43 50N 112 00E
Erfurt Germany **76** E5 50 58N 11 02E
Erg Chech *geog. reg.* Algeria **106** E12 24 30N 3 00W
Ergene *r.* Turkey **80** E3 41 00N 27 00E
Erg Iguidi *geog. reg.* Algeria **106** D13 26 00N 6 00W
Ergun He *see* Argun
Erh-lin Taiwan **98** G6 23 52N 120 18E
Erie Pennsylvania U.S.A. **63** J5 42 07N 80 05W
Erie, Lake Canada/U.S.A. **36** E2 42 15N 81 00W
Erimo-misaki *c.* Japan **100** D3 41 55N 143 13E
Erin Point Trinidad and Tobago **66** S9 10 03N 61 39W
Erith England **82** D2 51 29N 0 11E
Erith Marshes England **82** D3 51 30N 0 08E
Eritrea *see* Ertra
Erkner Germany **83** H1 52 25N 13 46E
Erkrath Germany **76** H1 51 13N 6 54E
Erne *r.* Irish Republic **78** D5 53 50N 7 30W
Erode India **95** D2 11 21N 77 43E
Erris Head *c.* Irish Republic **78** A6 54 20N 10 00W
Erromango *i.* Vanuatu **110** L6 19 00S 169 00E
Er Roseires Sudan **106** L10 11 52N 34 23E
Ertra *(Eritrea) admin.* Ethiopia **92** F1 14 40N 40 15E
Erzgebirge *(Krušnéhory) mts.* Europe **76** E5 50 00N 13 00E
Erzincan Turkey **92** E6 39 44N 39 30E
Erzurum Turkey **92** F6 39 57N 41 17E
Esashi Japan **100** D3 41 54N 140 09E
Esbjerg Denmark **80** A6 55 20N 8 20E
Escanaba Michigan U.S.A. **63** I6 45 47N 87 04W
Escobal Panama **67** Y2 9 11N 79 59W
Eşfahān Iran **93** H5 32 41N 51 41E
Esher England **82** B2 51 22N 0 22W
Eskilstuna Sweden **79** D2 59 22N 16 31E
Eskişehir Turkey **92** D6 39 46N 30 30E
Esmeraldas Ecuador **68** B13 0 56N 79 40W
Esperance Australia **110** C3 33 49S 121 52E
Esperanza *r.s.* Antarctica **117** 63 24S 56 59W
Espirito Santo *admin.* Brazil **68** J9 18 40S 40 00W
Espiritu Santo *i.* Vanuatu **110** L6 15 10S 167 00E
Espoo Finland **79** E3 60 10N 24 40E
Esquel Argentina **69** C4 42 55S 71 20W
Es Semara Western Sahara **106** C13 26 25N 11 30W
Essen Germany **76** J2 51 27N 6 57E
Essequibo *r.* Guyana **68** F13 2 30N 58 00W
Essex Connecticut U.S.A. **65** H4 41 21N 72 23W
Essex Maryland U.S.A. **64** D2 39 00N 76 00W
Essex *co.* England **82** D3 51 46N 0 30E
Essex County Massachusetts U.S.A. **52** B2 42 28N 71 04W
Estância Brazil **68** J10 11 15S 37 28W
ESTONIA 79 F2
Estrecho de Magallanes *sd.* Chile **69** C2 53 00S 71 00W
Estrêla *r.* Brazil **69** Q3 22 42S 43 14W
Etawah India **95** D5 26 46N 79 01E
ETHIOPIA 106 M9
Ethiopian Highlands Africa **102** 8 00N 37 00E
Etna Pennsylvania U.S.A. **53** E3 40 31N 79 57W
Etna *mt.* Italy **81** C2 37 45N 15 00E
Etolin Island Alaska U.S.A. **42** B3 56 10N 132 30W
Etosha National Park Namibia **107** I4 18 30S 16 00E
Etosha Pan *salt l.* Namibia **107** I4 18 30S 16 30E
Euboea *see* Evvoia
Eucla Australia **110** D3 31 40S 128 51E
Euclid Ohio U.S.A. **36** E2 41 34N 81 33W
Eugene Oregon U.S.A. **62** B5 44 03N 123 04W
Euphrates *r.* Iraq **93** F5 34 40N 42 00E
Eureka Montana U.S.A. **43** B1 48 52N 115 04W
Evanston Illinois U.S.A. **53** B3 42 02N 87 41W
Evansville Indiana U.S.A. **63** I4 38 00N 87 33W
Eveleth Minnesota U.S.A. **35** B2 47 29N 92 46W
Everest, Mount China/Nepal **95** F5 27 59N 86 56E
Everett Massachusetts U.S.A. **52** B2 42 23N 71 03W
Everett Washington U.S.A. **62** B6 47 59N 122 14W
Everett Lake New Hampshire U.S.A. **65** J6 43 05N 71 40W
Evergreen Park Illinois U.S.A. **53** B1 41 43N 87 43W
Evora Portugal **77** A2 38 46N 7 41W
Evreux France **76** C4 49 03N 1 11E
Evvoia *(Euboea) i.* Greece **81** D2 38 00N 24 00E
Ewarton Jamaica **67** Q8 18 11N 77 06W
Exe *r.* England **78** H2 50 55N 3 32W
Exeter England **78** H2 50 43N 3 31W
Exeter New Hampshire U.S.A. **65** K5 42 59N 70 56W
Exmoor National Park England **78** H3 51 08N 3 40W
Exmouth Australia **110** A5 21 54S 114 10E
Eyasi, Lake Tanzania **107** L7 4 00S 35 00E
Eynsford England **82** D2 51 22N 0 13E
Eyre Creek *r.* Australia **110** F4 26 00S 138 00E
Eyre, Lake Australia **110** F4 28 00S 136 00E
Eyre Peninsula Australia **110** F3 34 00S 136 00E

F

Fada Chad **106** J11 17 14N 21 32E
Faeroe Islands *(Faroes)* Europe **70** 62 00N 7 00W
Faeroes *see* Faeroe Islands
Fafan *r.* Ethiopia **106** N9 7 30N 44 00E
Fagersta Sweden **80** C6 59 59N 15 49E
Fairbanks Alaska U.S.A. **44** B3 64 50N 147 50W
Fairfax Virginia U.S.A. **64** C1 38 51N 77 19W
Fairfield Australia **111** F2 33 52S 150 57E
Fair Isle *i.* Scotland **78** J11 59 32N 1 38W
Fair Lawn New Jersey U.S.A. **50** B2 40 57N 74 06W
Fairmont West Virginia U.S.A. **63** J4 39 28N 80 08W
Fairview Park Hong Kong U.K. **98** B2 22 29N 114 03E
Fairweather Mountain Canada/U.S.A. **42** A3 58 50N 137 55W
Faisalabad Pakistan **95** C6 31 25N 73 09E
Faizabad India **95** E5 26 46N 82 08E
Fakfak Indonesia **99** I3 2 55S 132 17E
Falam Myanmar **96** H3 22 58N 93 45E
Falfurrias Texas U.S.A. **63** G2 27 17N 98 10W
Falkenburg Sweden **80** B6 56 55N 12 30E
Falkensee *l.* Germany **83** E2 52 35N 13 08E
Falkirk Scotland **78** H8 55 59N 3 48W
Falkland Islands South Atlantic Ocean **69** E2/F2 52 30S 60 00W
Falköping Sweden **80** B6 58 10N 13 32E
Fall River Massachusetts U.S.A. **65** J4 41 00N 71 00W
Fall River *tn.* Massachusetts U.S.A. **65** J4 41 42N 71 08W
Falmouth Jamaica **67** Q8 18 29N 77 39W
Falmouth Massachusetts U.S.A. **65** K4 41 33N 70 37W
Falun Sweden **79** D3 60 37N 15 40E
Famagusta Cyprus **92** D6 35 07N 33 57E
Fang-liao Taiwan **98** G5 22 22N 120 36E
Fan Lau Hong Kong U.K. **98** A1 22 12N 113 51E
Fanling Hong Kong U.K. **98** B2 22 29N 114 07E
Fâqûs Egypt **107** R3 30 44N 31 48E
Faraday *r.s.* Antarctica **117** 65 15S 64 16W
Farafangana Madagascar **107** L3 22 50S 47 50E
Farāh Afghanistan **93** J5 32 22N 62 07E
Farah Rud *r.* Afghanistan **93** J5 32 00N 62 00E
Farewell Spit New Zealand **111** B2 40 40S 173 00E
Fargo North Dakota U.S.A. **63** G6 46 52N 96 49W
Faridabad India **95** D5 28 24N 77 18E
Farmington Maine U.S.A. **37** Q5 44 41N 70 11W
Farmington Michigan U.S.A. **52** D2 42 29N 83 22W
Farmington New Hampshire U.S.A. **65** J6 43 23N 71 06W
Farmington New Mexico U.S.A. **62** E4 36 43N 108 12W
Farmington Falls *tn.* Maine U.S.A. **37** Q5 44 36N 70 05W
Farnham New York U.S.A. **38** C1 42 36N 79 06W
Faro Portugal **77** A2 37 01N 7 56W
Fåron *i.* Sweden **79** D2 58 00N 19 10E
Farquhar Islands Seychelles **112** E5 9 00N 50 00E
Fastov Ukraine **80** E5 50 08N 29 59E
Fatehgarh India **95** D5 27 22N 79 38E
Faxaflói *b.* Iceland **79** H6 64 20N 23 00W
Faya-Largeau Chad **106** I11 17 58N 19 06E
Fayetteville Arkansas U.S.A. **63** H4 36 03N 94 10W
Fayetteville New York U.S.A. **64** D6 43 01N 76 02W
Fayetteville North Carolina U.S.A. **63** K4 35 03N 78 53W
Fâyid Egypt **107** S2 30 18N 31 19E
Fderik Mauritania **106** C12 22 30N 12 30W
Fécamp France **76** C4 49 45N 0 23E
FEDERATED STATES OF MICRONESIA 114 E8
Feilding New Zealand **111** C2 40 12S 175 37E
Feira de Santana Brazil **68** J10 12 17S 38 53W
Felixstowe England **78** M3 51 58N 1 20E
Feltham England **82** B2 51 27N 0 25W
Femund *l.* Norway **79** C3 62 30N 11 50E
Fengfeng China **97** M6 37 00N 114 00E
Feng-shan Taiwan **98** G5 22 38N 120 21E
Fengtai China **101** G1 39 51N 116 17E
Feng-Yüan Taiwan **98** G7 24 15N 120 43E
Fens, The *geog. reg.* England **78** K4/L4 52 45N 0 05E
Fenton Michigan U.S.A. **36** C3 42 48N 83 42W
Fergana Uzbekistan **91** L3 40 23N 71 19E
Fergus Falls *tn.* Minnesota U.S.A. **63** G6 46 18N 96 07W
Ferndale Michigan U.S.A. **52** E2 42 26N 83 08W
Ferndale Washington U.S.A. **42** H4 48 51N 122 36W
Ferrara Italy **81** B3 44 50N 11 38E
Ferreñafe Peru **68** B11 6 42S 79 45W
Fès Morocco **106** D14 34 05N 5 00W
Fethiye Turkey **92** C6 36 37N 29 06E
Fetlar *i.* Scotland **78** K12 60 37N 0 52W
Feyzābad Afghanistan **93** L6 37 06N 70 34E
Fianarantsoa Madagascar **107** L3 21 27S 47 05E
Fier Albania **81** C3 40 44N 19 33E
Figeac France **77** C3 44 32N 2 01E
Figueira da Foz Portugal **77** A3 40 09N 8 51W
Figueras Spain **77** C3 42 16N 2 57E
FIJI 114 H6
Filchner Ice Shelf Antarctica **117** 80 00S 37 00W
Finchley England **82** C3 51 36N 0 10W
Findlay Ohio U.S.A. **36** C2 41 02N 83 40W
FINLAND 79 E3
Finland, Gulf of Finland/Russia **79** E2 59 40N 23 30E
Fiordland *geog. reg.* New Zealand **111** A1 45 30S 167 30E
Firat *r.* Turkey **92** E6 37 30N 38 00E
Fire Island New York U.S.A. **65** G3 40 20N 73 00W
Firenze Italy **81** B3 43 47N 11 15E
Firozabad India **95** D5 27 09N 78 24E
Firozpur India **95** C6 30 55N 74 38E
Firth of Clyde *est.* Scotland **78** F7 55 45N 5 00W
Firth of Forth *est.* Scotland **78** I8 56 05N 3 00W
Firth of Lorn *est.* Scotland **78** E8 56 15N 6 00W
Fish *r.* Namibia **107** I2 26 30S 17 30E
Fishers Island New York U.S.A. **65** J4 41 16N 72 00W
Fishguard Wales **78** G3 51 59N 4 59W
Fitchburg Massachusetts U.S.A. **65** J5 42 35N 71 50W
Fitzroy *r.* Australia **110** C6 18 00S 124 00E
Flagstaff Arizona U.S.A. **62** D4 35 12N 111 38W
Flagstaff Lake Maine U.S.A. **37** Q6 45 14N 70 20W
Flambeau River Wisconsin U.S.A. **35** B2 45 30N 91 00W
Flamborough Head England **78** K6 54 06N 0 04W
Flamengo Brazil **69** Q2 22 56S 43 10W
Flatbush New York U.S.A. **50** C1 40 38N 73 56W
Flathead Lake Montana U.S.A. **62** D6 47 55N 114 05W
Flathead River Montana U.S.A. **43** F1 48 55N 114 30W
Flatlands New York U.S.A. **50** C1 40 37N 73 54W
Flattery, Cape Washington U.S.A. **62** B6 48 24N 124 43W
Flekkefjord Norway **79** B2 58 17N 6 40E
Flemington New Jersey U.S.A. **64** F3 40 31N 74 52W
Flensburg Germany **80** A5 54 47N 9 27E
Flers France **76** B4 48 45N 0 34W
Fletcher Pond Michigan U.S.A. **36** C5 45 00N 83 53W
Flinders *r.* Australia **110** G6 19 00S 141 30E
Flinders Range *mts.* Australia **110** F3 32 00S 138 00E
Flint Michigan U.S.A. **63** J5 43 03N 83 40W
Flint *r.* Georgia U.S.A. **63** J3 31 00N 84 00W
Flint River Michigan U.S.A. **36** C4 43 12N 83 50W
Florence Alabama U.S.A. **63** I3 34 48N 87 40W
Florence South Carolina U.S.A. **63** K3 34 12N 79 44W
Florence Wisconsin U.S.A. **35** C2 45 55N 88 14W
Florencia Colombia **68** B13 1 37N 75 37W
Flores Guatemala **66** G3 16 58N 89 50W
Flores *i.* Indonesia **99** G2 8 00S 121 00E
Flores Sea Indonesia **99** G2 7 30S 121 00E
Floriano Brazil **68** I11 6 45S 43 00W
Florianópolis Brazil **69** H7 27 35S 48 31W
Florida Uruguay **69** F6 34 04S 56 14W
Florida *state* U.S.A. **63** J2 28 00N 82 00W
Florida Bay Florida U.S.A. **63** J2 25 00N 81 00W
Florida Keys *is.* Florida U.S.A. **63** J1 25 00N 80 00W
Florida, Straits of U.S.A./Cuba **67** H4 24 00N 81 00W
Flórina Greece **81** D3 40 48N 21 26E
Florissant Missouri U.S.A. **63** H4 38 49N 90 24W
Florø Norway **79** B3 61 36N 5 04E
Flushing New York U.S.A. **50** C2 40 45N 73 49W
Focşani Romania **81** E4 45 41N 27 12E
Fóggia Italy **81** C3 41 28N 15 33E
Fohnsdorf Austria **81** B4 47 13N 14 40E
Foix France **77** C3 42 57N 1 35E
Folda *sd.* Norway **79** C3 64 42N 10 30E
Foligno Italy **81** B3 42 57N 12 43E
Folkestone England **78** M3 51 05N 1 11E
Fonda New York U.S.A. **65** F5 42 57N 74 24W
Fond du Lac Wisconsin U.S.A. **63** I5 43 48N 88 27W
Fongafala Tuvalu **114** H7 8 00S 178 30E
Fontainebleau France **76** C3 48 24N 2 42E
Fonte Boa Brazil **68** D12 2 33S 65 59W
Forest Hills New York U.S.A. **50** C1 40 43N 73 51W
Forêt de Montmorency France **83** B3 49 01N 2 18E
Forlì Italy **81** B3 44 13N 12 02E
Formentera *i.* Balearic Islands **77** C2 38 41N 1 30E
Formosa Argentina **69** F7 26 07S 58 14W
Formosa Brazil **68** H9 15 30S 47 22W
Forrest Australia **110** D3 30 49S 128 03E
Forssa Finland **79** E3 60 49N 23 40E
Fortaleza Brazil **68** J12 3 45S 38 35W
Fort Collins Colorado U.S.A. **62** E5 40 35N 105 05W
Fort-de-France Lesser Antilles **67** L2 14 36N 61 05W
Fort Dodge Iowa U.S.A. **63** H5 42 31N 94 10W
Fort Edward New York U.S.A. **65** G6 43 17N 73 36W
Fortescue *r.* Australia **110** B5 23 00S 117 30E
Forth *r.* Scotland **78** G8 56 00N 3 30W
Fort Kent Maine U.S.A. **33** C2 47 15N 68 35W
Fort Lauderdale Florida U.S.A. **63** J2 26 08N 80 08W
Fort Myers Florida U.S.A. **63** J2 26 39N 81 51W
Fort Peck Lake Montana U.S.A. **62** E6 48 01N 106 28W
Fort Pierce Florida U.S.A. **63** J2 27 28N 80 20W
Fort Plain New York U.S.A. **65** F5 42 56N 74 39W
Fort Portal Uganda **106** L8 0 40N 30 17E
Fort Randall Alaska U.S.A. **10** C4 55 10N 162 47W
Fort Scott Kansas U.S.A. **63** G4 37 52N 94 43W
Fort Smith Arkansas U.S.A. **63** H4 35 22N 94 27W
Fort Stockton Texas U.S.A. **62** F3 30 54N 102 54W
Fort Sumner New Mexico U.S.A. **62** F3 34 27N 104 16W
Fortuna North Dakota U.S.A. **40** C1 48 55N 103 47W
Fort Walton Beach *tn.* Florida U.S.A. **63** I3 30 25N 86 38W
Fort Wayne Indiana U.S.A. **63** I5 41 05N 85 08W
Fort William Scotland **78** F8 56 49N 5 07W
Fort Worth Texas U.S.A. **63** G3 32 45N 97 20W
Fort Yukon Alaska U.S.A. **44** B4 66 35N 145 20W
Foshan China **97** M3 23 03N 113 08E
Fosna *geog. reg.* Norway **79** C3 64 00N 10 30E
Foster City California U.S.A. **49** C2 37 30N 122 15W
Fougères France **76** B4 48 21N 1 12W
Foula *i.* Scotland **78** I12 60 08N 2 05W
Foulwind, Cape New Zealand **111** B2 41 45S 171 26E
Foumban Cameroon **106** H9 5 43N 10 50E
Fountain Valley *tn.* California U.S.A. **51** C1 33 41N 117 58W
Four Roads *tn.* Trinidad and Tobago **66** S10 10 42N 61 33W
Fouta Djallon *geog. reg.* Guinea **106** C10 12 00N 13 10W
Foveaux Strait New Zealand **111** A1 47 00S 148 00E
Foxboro Massachusetts U.S.A. **65** J5 42 05N 71 15W
Foyle Northern Ireland **78** D6 54 40N 7 30W
Foz do Iguaçú Argentina **69** G7 25 33S 54 31W
Framingham Massachusetts U.S.A. **65** J5 42 18N 71 25W
Franca Brazil **68** H8 20 33S 47 27W
FRANCE 76/77
Francis Case, Lake South Dakota U.S.A. **62** G5 43 00N 99 00W
Francistown Botswana **107** K3 21 11S 27 32E
Frankenmuth Michigan U.S.A. **36** C4 43 19N 83 44W
Frankfield Jamaica **67** Q8 18 08N 77 22W
Frankfort Kentucky U.S.A. **63** J4 38 11N 84 53W
Frankfurt *bor.* Germany **83** F2 52 41N 13 25E
Frankfurt am Main Germany **76** D5 50 06N 8 41E
Fränkische Alb *mts.* Germany **76** E4 49 00N 11 00E
Franklin New Jersey U.S.A. **65** F4 41 07N 74 35W
Franklin Pennsylvania U.S.A. **36** G2 41 24N 79 49W
Franklin Canyon Reservoir California U.S.A. **51** A3 34 05N 118 25W
Franklin D. Roosevelt Lake Washington U.S.A. **62** C6 48 05N 118 15W
Franklin Park Illinois U.S.A. **53** A2 41 50N 87 52W
Franklin Park Massachusetts U.S.A. **52** B2 42 18N 71 06W
Franz Josef Land *see* Zemlya Frantsa-Iosifa
Fraserburgh Scotland **78** I9 57 42N 2 00W
Frederick Maryland U.S.A. **64** C2 39 25N 77 25W
Fredericksburg Pennsylvania U.S.A. **64** D3 40 27N 76 26W
Fredericksburg Virginia U.S.A. **63** K4 38 18N 77 30W
Frederikshåb Greenland **11** Z5 62 05N 49 30W
Frederick Sound Alaska U.S.A. **42** B3 57 00N 134 00W
Frederikshavn Denmark **80** B6 57 28N 10 33E
Fredersdorf Germany **83** G2 52 31N 13 44E
Fredrikstad Norway **79** C2 59 20N 10 50E
Freehold New Jersey U.S.A. **65** F3 40 16N 74 16W
Freemantle Australia **110** B3 32 07S 115 44E
Freeport New York U.S.A. **65** G3 40 40N 73 35W
Freeport Texas U.S.A. **63** G2 28 56N 95 20W
Freetown Sierra Leone **106** C9 8 30N 13 17W
Freewood Acres New Jersey U.S.A. **65** F3 40 10N 74 16W
Freiburg im Breisgau Germany **76** D4 48 00N 7 52E
Fréjus France **77** D3 43 26N 6 44E
Fremont Ohio U.S.A. **36** C2 41 21N 83 08W
French Creek Pennsylvania U.S.A. **36** F2 41 40N 80 10W
French Guiana *territory* France **68** G13 5 00N 53 00W
Frenchman Fork *r.* U.S.A. **62** F5 40 00N 103 00W
French Polynesia Pacific Ocean **115** L5 21 00S 150 00W
French's Forest *tn.* Australia **111** G3 33 45S 151 14E
Fresh Pond Massachusetts U.S.A. **52** B2 42 23N 71 09W
Fresnillo Mexico **66** D4 23 10N 102 54W
Fresno Reservoir Montana U.S.A. **41** C1 48 40N 110 00W
Frewsburg New York U.S.A. **64** A5 42 03N 79 11W
Frick Park Pennsylvania U.S.A. **53** E1 40 25N 79 55W
Friday Harbor Washington U.S.A. **42** H4 48 33N 123 04W

Friedrichshagen Germany 83 G1 52 27N 13 38E
Friedrichshain Germany 83 F2 52 32N 13 26E
Frohavet sd. Norway 79 B3 63 55N 9 10E
Frohnau Germany 83 F2 52 38N 13 19E
Frontera Mexico 66 F3 18 32N 92 39W
Front Royal Virginia U.S.A. 64 B1 38 56N 78 13W
Frosinone Italy 81 B3 41 38N 13 22E
Frostburg Maryland U.S.A. 64 B2 39 39N 78 56W
Frøya i. Norway 79 B3 63 45N 8 45E
Frunze see Bishkek
Fuchū Japan 101 A3 35 40N 139 29E
Fuerteventura i. Canary Islands 106 C13 28 25N 14 00W
Fuji Japan 100 C2 35 10N 138 37E
Fuji-Hakone-Izu National Park Japan 100 K2 35 28N 138 47E
Fujinomiya Japan 100 C2 35 16N 138 33E
Fujioka Japan 100 L3 36 15N 139 03E
Fuji-san mt. Japan 100 C2 35 23N 138 42E
Fujisawa Japan 101 A2 35 22N 139 29E
Fukaya Japan 100 L3 36 12N 139 17E
Fukuchiyama Japan 100 G2 35 19N 135 08E
Fukui Japan 100 C2 36 04N 136 12E
Fukui pref. Japan 100 G2 35 30N 135 40E
Fukuoka Japan 100 B1 33 39N 130 21E
Fukushima Japan 100 D2 37 44N 140 28E
Fukuyama Japan 100 B1 34 29N 133 21E
Fulda Germany 76 D5 50 33N 9 41E
Fullarton Trinidad and Tobago 66 S9 10 05N 61 54 W
Fullerton California U.S.A. 51 C2 33 53N 117 55W
Fullerton Reservoir California U.S.A. 51 C2 33 54N 117 54W
Fulton New York U.S.A. 64 D6 43 20N 76 26W
Funabashi Japan 100 L2 35 42N 139 59E
Funakoshi Japan 101 B2 35 18N 139 34E
Funchal Madeira 106 B14 32 40N 16 55W
Fuqing China 98 F8 25 43N 119 21E
Furneaux Group is. Australia 110 H1 45 00S 148 00E
Furukawa Japan 100 D2 38 34N 140 56E
Fushun China 97 O7 41 50N 123 54E
Fustic Barbados 66 V13 13 18N 59 43W
Fu Tau Fan Chau Hong Kong U.K. 98 D2 22 20N 114 21E
Futtsu Japan 100 L2 35 13N 139 53E
Fuxin China 97 O7 42 04N 121 39E
Fuzhou China 97 N4 26 09N 119 17E

G
Gaalkacyo Somalia 106 O9 6 47N 47 21E
Gabès Tunisia 106 H14 33 52N 10 06E
GABON 106 H7
Gaborone Botswana 107 K3 24 45S 25 55E
Gabrovo Bulgaria 81 E3 42 52N 25 19E
Gadag India 95 D3 15 26N 75 42E
Gadsden Alabama U.S.A. 63 I3 34 00N 86 00W
Gaeta Italy 81 B3 41 13N 13 36E
Gafsa Tunisia 106 G14 34 28N 8 43E
Gagarin Russia 88 L1 55 40N 37 27E
Gagnoa Côte d'Ivoire 106 D9 6 04N 5 55W
Gaillard Cut Panama 67 Y2 9 05N 79 47W
Gainesville Florida U.S.A. 63 J2 29 37N 82 21W
Gainesville Texas U.S.A. 63 G3 33 09N 97 38W
Gairdner, Lake Australia 110 F3 32 50S 136 00E
Gaithersburg Maryland U.S.A. 64 C2 39 08N 77 13W
Galana r. Kenya 106 M7 3 30S 34 30E
Galapagos Islands see Islas Galapagos
Galapagos Rise Pacific Ocean 115 R6 12 00S 87 00W
Galashiels Scotland 78 I7 55 37N 2 49W
Galata Montana U.S.A. 41 C1 48 29N 111 20W
Galaţi Romania 81 E4 45 27N 28 02E
Galeão Brazil 69 Q2 22 49S 43 14W
Galeda Point Trinidad and Tobago 66 U9 10 09N 60 00W
Galera Point Trinidad and Tobago 66 U10 10 49N 60 54W
Galesburg Illinois U.S.A. 63 H5 40 58N 90 22W
Galeton Pennsylvania U.S.A. 64 C4 41 43N 77 39W
Galilee, Sea of see Tiberias, Lake
Galina Point Jamaica 67 R8 18 24N 76 58W
Galle Sri Lanka 95 E1 6 01N 80 13E
Gallego r. Spain 77 B3 41 55N 0 56W
Gallipoli Italy 81 C3 40 03N 17 59E
Gallipoli Turkey see Gelibolu
Gallup New Mexico U.S.A. 62 E4 32 32N 108 46W
Galston Australia 111 G3 33 39S 151 03E
Galty Mountains Irish Republic 78 C4 52 20N 8 10W
Galveston Texas U.S.A. 63 H2 29 17N 94 48W
Galway Bay Irish Republic 78 B5 53 15N 9 15W
Galway Irish Republic 78 B5 53 16N 9 03W
Gamagōri Japan 100 J1 34 49N 137 15E
Gambell Alaska U.S.A. 10 A5 63 46N 171 45W
Gambia r. Senegal 106 C10 13 45N 13 15W
GAMBIA, THE 106 B10
Gambier Islands Pitcairn Islands 115 N5 23 10S 135 00W
Gamboa Panama 67 Y2 9 08N 79 42W
Gand see Gent
Gandak r. India 95 E5 26 30N 84 30E
Ganga (Ganges) r. India 95 E4 25 30N 82 00E
Ganga, Mouths of the est. India/Bangladesh 95 F4 21 30N 89 00E
Ganganagar India 95 C5 29 54N 73 56E
Gangdisê Shan mts. China 96 F5 31 00N 82 30E
Ganges see Ganga
Gangtok India 95 F5 27 20N 88 39E
Ganzhou China 97 M4 25 52N 114 51E
Gao Mali 106 E11 16 19N 0 09W
Gap France 77 D3 44 33N 6 05E
Garanhuns Brazil 68 J11 8 53S 36 28W
Gard r. France 77 C3 44 05N 4 20E
Gardena California U.S.A. 51 A2 33 53N 118 19W
Garden City Kansas U.S.A. 62 F4 37 57N 100 54W
Garden City Michigan U.S.A. 52 D2 42 18N 83 20W
Garden City New York U.S.A. 50 D1 40 43N 73 39W
Garden Grove California U.S.A. 51 C2 33 48N 117 52W
Garden Reach India 94 K2 22 32N 88 16E
Gardēz Afghanistan 93 K5 33 37N 69 07E
Gardner Massachusetts U.S.A. 65 J5 42 33N 71 59W
Gardner Island Pacific Ocean 114 I7 4 40S 174 32W
Garfield New Jersey U.S.A. 50 B2 40 52N 74 05W
Garfield Park Illinois U.S.A. 53 B2 41 52N 87 43W
Gariya India 94 K1 22 27N 88 23E
Garland Texas U.S.A. 63 G3 32 55N 96 37W
Garonne r. France 77 C3 44 45N 0 15E
Garoua Cameroon 106 H9 9 17N 13 22E
Garulia India 94 K3 22 49N 88 23E
Gary Indiana U.S.A. 53 C1 41 34 87 20W
Garyarsa China 95 E6 31 46N 80 21E
Garzón Colombia 68 B13 2 14N 75 37W
Gascoyne r. Australia 110 A5 25 00S 114 00E
Gasherbrum mts. Kashmir 95 D7 35 46N 76 38E
Gaspar Grande Trinidad and Tobago 66 S10 10 40N 61 39W
Gastonia North Carolina U.S.A. 63 J4 35 14N 81 12W
Gata, Cape Cyprus 92 N12 34 40N 33 01E
Gateshead England 78 J6 54 58N 1 35W
Gates of the Arctic National Park and Preserve Alaska U.S.A. 44 A4 67 00N 153 00W
Gatún Panama 67 Y2 9 16N 79 55W
Gatún Lake Panama 67 Y2 9 15N 79 50W
Gatún Locks Panama 67 Y2 9 16N 79 55W
Gauhati India 95 G5 26 10N 91 45E
Gaukler Point Michigan U.S.A. 52 F2 42 27N 82 51W
Gávdhos i. Greece 81 D1 34 00N 24 00E
Gävle Sweden 80 C7 60 41N 17 10E
Gaya India 95 F4 24 48N 85 00E
Gaylord Michigan U.S.A. 36 B6 45 02N 84 41W
Gaza Israel 92 O10 31 30N 34 28E
Gaza Strip territory Israel 92 O10 31 28N 34 05E
Gaziantep Turkey 92 E6 37 04N 37 21E
Gbarnga Liberia 106 D9 7 02N 9 26W
Gdańsk Poland 80 C5 54 22N 18 41E
Gdańsk, Gulf of Baltic Sea 80 C5 54 00N 19 00E
Gdynia Poland 80 C5 54 31N 18 30E
Gebel el Tîh p. Egypt 92 N9 29 30N 33 45E
Gebel Katherina hill Egypt 92 O9 28 30N 33 57E
Gebel Mûsa (Mount Sinai) mt. Egypt 92 N9 28 32N 33 59E
Gedaref Sudan 92 E1 14 01N 35 24E
Gediz r. Turkey 92 C6 38 40N 27 30E
Geelong Australia 110 G2 38 10S 144 26E
Geistown Pennsylvania U.S.A. 64 B3 40 17N 78 52W
Gejiu China 97 K3 23 25N 103 05E
Gela Italy 81 B2 37 04N 14 15E
Gelibolu (Gallipoli) Turkey 80 E3 40 25N 26 41E
Gelsenkirchen Germany 76 J3 51 30N 7 05E
Gemsbok National Park Botswana 107 J2 26 00S 21 00E
Genalē r. Ethiopia 106 M9 6 00N 40 00E
Geneina Sudan 106 J10 13 27N 22 30E
General Belgrano II r.s. Antarctica 117 77 52S 34 37W
General Bernardo O'Higgins r.s. Antarctica 117 63 19S 57 54W
General San Martin r.s. Antarctica 117 68 08S 67 04W
Genesee River New York U.S.A. 64 B5 42 40N 78 00W
Geneva New York U.S.A. 64 D5 42 53N 76 59W
Geneva Ohio U.S.A. 36 F2 41 48N 80 57W
Geneva see Genève
Geneva, Lake see Lac Léman
Genève (Geneva) Switzerland 77 D4 46 13N 6 09E
Genil r. Spain 77 B2 37 20N 4 45W
Genk Belgium 76 D5 50 58N 5 30E
Gennevilliers France 83 B2 48 56N 2 17E
Genoa see Genova
Genova (Genoa) Italy 81 A3 44 24N 8 56E
Gent (Gand) Belgium 76 C5 51 02N 3 42E
George VI Sound Antarctica 117 72 00S 67 00W
Georges River Australia 111 F2 33 57S 150 57E
Georgetown Guyana 68 F14 6 46N 58 10W
George Town Malaysia 99 C5 5 30N 100 28E
Georgetown South Carolina U.S.A. 63 K3 33 23N 79 18W
Georg Forster r.s. Antarctica 117 70 46S 11 50E
GEORGIA 90 E3
Georgia state U.S.A. 63 J3 33 00N 83 00W
Georgina r. Australia 110 F5 22 00S 137 00E
Georg von Neumayer r.s. Antarctica 117 70 37S 08 22W
Gera Germany 76 E5 50 51N 12 11E
Geraldton Australia 110 A4 28 49S 114 36E
GERMANY 76
Gerona Spain 77 C3 41 59N 2 49E
Gerrards Cross England 82 A3 51 35N 0 34W
Getafe Spain 77 B3 40 18N 3 44W
Gettysburg Pennsylvania U.S.A. 64 C2 39 50N 77 16W
Gettysburg National Military Park Pennsylvania U.S.A. 64 C2 39 57N 77 15W
Ghadāmis Libya 106 G14 30 08N 9 30E
Ghaghara r. India 95 E4 26 20N 83 30E
GHANA 106 E9
Ghanzi Botswana 107 J3 21 42S 21 39E
Ghardaïa Algeria 106 F14 32 20N 3 40E
Gharyān Libya 106 H14 32 10N 13 01E
Ghāt Libya 106 H12 24 58N 10 11E
Ghaziabad India 95 D5 28 39N 77 26E
Ghazni Afghanistan 93 K5 33 33N 68 26E
Ghent New York U.S.A. 65 G5 42 19N 73 37W
Gheorghe Gheorghiu-Dej Romania 81 E4 46 17N 26 45E
Ghisonaccia Corsica 77 D3 42 01N 9 24E
Gibraltar territory U.K. 77 A2 36 09N 5 21W
Gibraltar, Strait of Spain/Morocco 77 A2 35 58N 5 30W
Gibson Desert Australia 110 C5 25 00S 123 00E
Gīdolē Ethiopia 106 M9 5 38N 37 28E
Gifu Japan 100 H2 35 27N 136 46E
Gifu pref. Japan 100 H2 35 30N 136 50E
Gigüela r. Spain 77 B2 39 40N 3 15W
Gijón Spain 77 A3 43 32N 5 40W
Gila r. U.S.A. 62 D3 33 00N 114 00W
Gila Bend Arizona U.S.A. 62 D3 32 56N 112 42W
Gilbert r. Australia 110 G6 17 00S 142 30E
Gilbert Islands Pacific Ocean 114 H7 0 00 173 00E
Gildford Montana U.S.A. 41 C1 48 35N 110 15W
Gilgit Kashmir 95 C7 35 54N 74 20E
Gillette Wyoming U.S.A. 62 E5 44 18N 105 30W
Gillingham England 78 L3 51 24N 0 33E
Gineifa Egypt 107 S2 30 12N 32 26E
Gīnīr Ethiopia 106 N9 7 06N 40 40E
Gippsland geog. reg. Australia 110 H2 37 30S 147 00E
Girard Pennsylvania U.S.A. 36 F3 42 01N 80 20W
Girardot Colombia 68 C13 4 19N 74 47W
Girga Egypt 92 D4 26 17N 31 58E
Gironde r. France 77 B4 45 30N 0 45W
Gisborne New Zealand 111 C3 38 41S 178 02E
Giurgiu Romania 81 E3 43 53N 25 58E
Gizhiga Russia 89 S8 62 00N 160 34E
Gjirokastër Albania 81 D3 40 05N 20 10E
Gjøvik Norway 80 B7 60 47N 10 41E
Glacier Washington U.S.A. 42 H4 48 53N 121 57W
Glacier Bay Alaska U.S.A. 42 A3 58 50N 136 30W
Glacier Bay National Park Alaska U.S.A. 42 A3 58 45N 136 30W
Glacier National Park Montana U.S.A. 62 D6 48 50N 114 00W
Gladbeck Germany 76 H3 51 34N 6 59E
Gladesville Australia 111 G2 33 50S 151 08E
Gladstone Australia 110 I5 23 52S 151 16E
Glåma r. Norway 79 C3 60 15N 12 00E
Glasgow Scotland 78 G7 55 53N 4 15W
Glassboro New Jersey U.S.A. 64 E2 39 42N 75 07W
Glazov Russia 91 G6 58 09N 52 42E
Glen Burnie Maryland U.S.A. 64 D2 39 10N 76 37W
Glencoe Illinois U.S.A. 53 B3 42 07N 87 45W
Glendale California U.S.A. 51 B3 34 09N 118 20W
Glendale Dam Pennsylvania U.S.A. 64 B3 40 19N 78 37W
Glendora California U.S.A. 51 C3 34 07N 117 53W
Glen Grove tn. New York U.S.A. 50 D2 40 52N 73 38W
Glen Ridge New Jersey U.S.A. 50 B2 40 47N 74 13W
Glens Falls tn. New York U.S.A. 65 G6 43 17N 73 41W
Glenshaw Pennsylvania U.S.A. 53 E2 40 32N 79 57W
Glenview Illinois U.S.A. 53 A3 42 05N 87 49W
Glienicke Germany 83 F2 52 39N 13 19E
Gliwice Poland 80 C5 50 20N 18 40E
Globe Arizona U.S.A. 62 D3 33 23N 110 48W
Głogów Poland 80 C5 51 40N 16 06E
Gloucester England 78 I3 51 53N 2 14W
Gloucester Massachusetts U.S.A. 65 K5 42 37N 70 41W
Gloversville New York U.S.A. 65 F6 43 03N 74 19W
Gniezno Poland 80 C5 52 32N 17 32E
Goa, Damān & Diu admin. India 95 C3 15 00N 74 00E
Goalpara India 95 G5 26 10N 90 38E
Gobabis Namibia 107 I3 22 30S 18 58E
Godāvari r. India 95 D3/E3 19 00N 80 00E
Gobi Desert Mongolia 96/97 J7/L7 48 30N 100 00E
Godhavn see Qeqertarsuaq
Godhra India 95 C4 22 49N 73 40E
Godthåb (Nuuk) Greenland 45 V4 64 10N 51 40W
Godwin Austen see K2
Goiânia Brazil 68 H9 16 43S 49 18W
Goiás Brazil 68 G9 15 57S 50 07W
Goiás admin. Brazil 68 H10 12 30S 48 00W
Goias Massif hills South America 55 15 00S 53 00W
Gojō Japan 100 G1 34 21N 135 42E
Gökçeada i. Turkey 80 E3 40 00N 25 00E
Golan Heights territory Israel 92 O11 33 00N 35 50E
Gold Coast tn. Australia 110 I4 27 59S 153 22E
Golden Bay New Zealand 111 B2 40 40S 173 00E
Golden Gate sd. California U.S.A. 49 A3 37 48N 122 30W
Golden Gate National Recreation Area California U.S.A. 49 A3 37 49N 122 32W
Golden Gate Park California U.S.A. 49 B3 37 46N 122 30W
Goldsboro North Carolina U.S.A. 63 K4 35 23N 78 00W
Goldsworthy Australia 110 B5 20 20S 119 31E
Golfe de Gabès g. Tunisia 106 H14 34 20N 10 30E
Golfe de St-Malo g. France 76 B4 48 55N 2 30W
Golfe du Lion g. France 77 C3 43 10N 4 00E
Golfo de California g. Mexico 66 B5 27 00N 111 00W
Golfo de Guayaquil g. Ecuador 68 A12 3 00S 81 30W
Golfo de Honduras g. Caribbean Sea 66/67 G3 17 00N 87 30W
Golfo del Darién g. Panamá/Colombia 67 I1 9 00N 77 00W
Golfo de Panamá g. Panama 67 I1 8 00N 79 00W
Golfo de San Jorge g. Argentina 69 D3 47 00S 66 00W
Golfo de Tehuantepec g. Mexico 66 E3/F3 15 30N 95 00W
Golfo de Venezuela g. Venezuela 68 C15 12 00N 71 30W
Golfo di Cágliari Italy 81 A2 39 00N 9 00E
Golfo di Catania Italy 81 C2 37 30N 15 20E
Golfo di Gaeta g. Italy 81 B3 41 00N 13 00E
Golfo di Genova g. Italy 81 A3 44 00N 9 00E
Golfo di Squillace g. Italy 81 C2 38 30N 17 00E
Golfo di Táranto g. Italy 81 C3 40 00N 17 00E
Golfo di Venézia Adriatic Sea 81 B4 45 00N 13 00E
Golfo San Matías g. Argentina 69 E4 42 00S 64 00W
Golmud China 96 H6 36 22N 94 55E
Gomel' Belarus 90 C5 52 25N 31 00E
Gomera i. Canary Islands 106 B13 28 08 17 14W
Gómez Palacio Mexico 66 D5 25 39N 103 30W
Gonder Ethiopia 106 M10 12 39N 37 29E
Gondia India 95 E4 21 23N 80 14E
Gonesse France 83 B2 48 59N 2 27E
Good Hope, Cape of Republic of South Africa 107 I1 34 30S 19 00E
Goodland Kansas U.S.A. 62 F4 39 20N 101 43W
Goondiwindi Australia 110 I4 28 30S 150 17E
Gora Kamen' mt. Russia 89 L9 69 06N 94 59E
Gorakhpur India 95 E5 26 45N 83 23E
Gora Narodnaya mt. Russia 89 I9 65 02N 60 01E
Gora Pobeda mt. Russia 89 Q9 65 10N 146 00E
Gorda Rise Pacific Ocean 115 M12 43 00N 130 00W
Gordon Australia 111 G2 33 46S 151 09E
Gorē Ethiopia 106 M9 8 10N 35 29E
Gore New Zealand 111 A1 46 06S 168 58E
Gorgān Iran 93 H6 36 50N 54 29E
Gorizia Italy 81 B4 45 57N 13 37E
Gorki Belarus 90 C5 54 17N 30 59E
Gor'kiy see Nizhniy Novgorod
Görlitz Germany 76 F5 51 09N 15 00E
Gorlovka Ukraine 90 D4 48 17N 38 05E
Gorno-Altaysk Russia 91 O5 51 59N 85 56E
Goroka Papua New Guinea 110 H8 6 02S 145 22E
Gorontalo Indonesia 99 G4 0 33N 123 05E
Goryn' r. Ukraine 80 E5 51 00N 26 00E
Gorzów Wielkopolski Poland 80 C5 52 42N 15 12E
Gostivar Macedonia Yugoslavia 81 D3 41 47N 20 55E
Göta älv r. Sweden 79 C2 58 00N 12 00E
Göta Kanal can. Sweden 80 C6 58 30N 15 00E
Göteborg Sweden 79 C2 57 45N 12 00E
Gotemba Japan 100 K2 35 20N 138 58E
Gotha Germany 76 E5 50 57N 10 43E
Gotland i. Sweden 79 D2 57 30N 18 40E
Göttingen Germany 76 E5 51 32N 9 57E
Gottwaldov see Zlín
Gough Island Atlantic Ocean 113 H2 40 20S 10 00W
Goulburn Australia 110 H3 34 47S 149 43E
Gourde, Point Trinidad and Tobago 66 S10 10 40N 61 36W
Gourdon France 77 C3 44 45N 1 22E
Gouré Niger 106 G10 13 59N 10 15E
Goussainville France 83 B3 49 02N 2 28E
Governador Valadares Brazil 68 I9 18 51S 41 57W
Gowanda New York U.S.A. 64 B5 42 28N 78 57W
Gozo i. Malta 81 B2 35 00N 14 00E
Grafton Australia 110 I4 29 40S 152 56E
Grafton North Dakota U.S.A. 39 B1 48 28N 97 25W
Grafton Pennsylvania U.S.A. 53 D1 40 26N 80 03W
Graham Texas U.S.A. 62 G3 33 07N 98 36W
Graham Land geog. reg. Antarctica 117 67 00S 64 00W
Grahamstown Republic of South Africa 107 K1 33 18S 26 32E
Grampian Pennsylvania U.S.A. 64 B3 40 58N 78 37W
Grampian Mountains Scotland 78 G8/H8 56 45N 4 00W
Granada Nicaragua 67 G2 11 58N 85 59W
Granada Spain 77 B2 37 10N 3 35W
Granby Connecticut U.S.A. 65 H4 41 57N 72 47W
Gran Canaria i. Canary Islands 106 B13 28 00N 15 35W
Gran Chaco geog. reg. Argentina 69 E8 25 00S 62 30W
Gran Couva Trinidad and Tobago 66 T9 10 24N 61 23W
Grand r. South Dakota U.S.A. 62 F6 46 00N 102 00W
Grand Bahama i. The Bahamas 67 I5 27 00N 78 00W
Grand Banks Atlantic Ocean 54 47 00N 47 00W
Grand Canyon U.S.A. 62 D4 36 04N 112 07W
Grand Canyon National Park Arizona/Nevada U.S.A. 62 D4 34 00N 114 00W
Grand Canyon Village Arizona U.S.A. 62 D4 36 02N 112 09W
Grand Cayman i. Caribbean Sea 67 H3 19 20N 81 15W
Grand Coulee Washington U.S.A. 43 E1 47 58N 119 00W
Grand Coulee Dam Washington U.S.A. 62 C6 47 59N 118 58W
Grand Erg Occidental geog. reg. Algeria 106 E14 30 35N 0 30E
Grand Erg Oriental geog. reg. Algeria 106 F13 30 15N 6 45E
Grande Terre i. Lesser Antilles 67 L3 17 00N 61 40W
Grand Forks North Dakota U.S.A. 63 G6 47 57N 97 05W
Grand Gorge tn. New York U.S.A. 65 F5 42 22N 74 30W
Grand Island New York U.S.A. 38 D2 43 02N 79 00W
Grand Island tn. Nebraska U.S.A. 63 G5 40 56N 98 21W
Grand Junction Colorado U.S.A. 62 E4 39 04N 108 33W
Grand Ledge Michigan U.S.A. 36 B3 42 45N 85 44W
Grand Marias Minnesota U.S.A. 35 B2 47 45N 90 20W
Grand Rapids tn. Michigan U.S.A. 63 I5 42 57N 86 40W
Grand Rapids tn. Minnesota U.S.A. 63 H6 47 13N 93 31W
Grand Rapids tn. Ohio U.S.A. 36 C2 41 23N 83 52W
Grand River Michigan U.S.A. 36 A3 42 55N 85 15W
Grand River Ohio U.S.A. 36 F2 41 25N 80 57W
Grand Riviere tn. Trinidad and Tobago 66 T10 10 50N 61 03W
Grand Traverse Bay Michigan U.S.A. 36 A6 45 00N 85 30W
Grand Union Canal England 82 B3 51 37N 0 29W
Grandyle New York U.S.A. 38 D2 43 00N 78 57W
Grane Norway 79 C4 65 35N 13 25E
Grange Hill tn. Jamaica 67 P8 18 19N 78 11W
Granite Peak Montana U.S.A. 62 E6 45 10N 109 50W
Grant Park Illinois U.S.A. 53 B2 41 52N 87 35W
Grants Pass Oregon U.S.A. 62 B5 42 26N 123 20W
Granville New York U.S.A. 65 G6 43 24N 73 16W
Grasonville Maryland U.S.A. 64 D1 38 58N 76 12W
Grasse France 77 D3 43 40N 6 56E
Grass Island Hong Kong U.K. 98 D2 22 29N 114 22E
Grassy Hill Hong Kong U.K. 98 B2 22 25N 114 10E
Gravesend New York U.S.A. 50 C1 40 36N 73 58W
Gravina Island Alaska U.S.A. 42 B3 55 25N 131 45W
Grayling Michigan U.S.A. 36 B5 44 40N 84 43W
Grays Thurrock England 82 E2 51 29N 0 20E
Graz Austria 81 C4 47 05N 15 22E
Great Abaco i. The Bahamas 67 I5 26 40N 77 00W
Great Astrolabe Reef Fiji 114 U15 18 45S 178 50E
Great Australian Bight Australia 110 D3 33 00S 130 00E
Great Barrier Island New Zealand 111 C3 35 00S 175 00E
Great Barrier Reef Australia 110 G7/H6 15 00S 146 00E
Great Barrington Massachusetts U.S.A. 65 G5 42 12N 73 22W
Great Basin Nevada U.S.A. 62 C4 40 00N 117 00W
Great Bay New Hampshire U.S.A. 65 K6 43 05N 70 53W
Great Bay New Jersey U.S.A. 65 F2 39 30N 74 20W
Great Bend Kansas U.S.A. 62 G4 38 22N 98 47W
Great Bend Pennsylvania U.S.A. 64 E4 41 58N 75 45W
Great Bitter Lake see Buheirat-Murrat-el-Kubra
Great Bookham England 82 B2 51 16N 0 21W
Great Britain i. Europe 70
Great Dividing Range mts. Australia 110 G7/H2
Great Egg Harbor River New Jersey U.S.A. 64 F2 39 35N 74 55W
Greater Antilles is. West Indies 67 H4/K3
Greater Khingan Range see Da Hinggan Ling
Greater London admin. England 67 C4 51 30N 0 10W
Greater Exuma i. The Bahamas 67 I4 23 30N 76 00W
Great Falls tn. Montana U.S.A. 62 D6 47 30N 111 16W
Great Inagua i. The Bahamas 67 J4 21 40N 73 00W
Great Karoo mts. Republic of South Africa 107 J1 32 30S 22 30E
Great Lakes North America 54 45 00N 85 00W
Great Meadows National Wildlife Refuge Massachusetts U.S.A. 52 A2 42 24N 71 22W
Great Neck New York U.S.A. 50 D2 40 48N 72 44W
Great Nicobar i. Nicobar Islands 95 G1 6 30N 94 00E
Great Oasis, The geog. reg. Egypt 92 D3 25 00N 30 30E
Great Ouse r. England 78 K4 52 30N 0 20E
Great Peconic Bay New York U.S.A. 65 H3 40 55N 72 30W
Great Pedro Bluff c. Jamaica 67 Q7 17 51N 77 45W
Great Sacandaga Lake res. New York U.S.A. 65 F6 43 10N 74 10W
Great Salt Lake Utah U.S.A. 62 D5 41 10N 112 40W
Great Sand Sea Sahara Desert 106 J13 27 00N 25 00E
Great Sandy Desert Australia 110 C5 21 00S 124 00E
Great Sea Reef Fiji 114 T16 16 30S 178 00E
Great Victoria Desert Australia 110 D4/E4 28 00S 130 00E
Great Wall China 97 M6 40 00N 111 00E
Great Yarmouth England 78 M4 52 37N 1 44E
GREECE 81 D2
Greely Colorado U.S.A. 62 F5 40 26N 104 43W
Green r. U.S.A. 62 D5 42 00N 110 00W
Green r. Utah U.S.A. 62 E4 39 00N 110 10W

Green Bay Wisconsin U.S.A. 63 I6 45 00N 87 00W
Green Bay tn. Wisconsin U.S.A. 63 I5 44 32N 88 00W
Greenbush Minnesota U.S.A. 39 B1 48 42N 96 10W
Green Creek tn. New Jersey U.S.A. 65 F2 39 03N 74 54W
Greenfield Massachusetts U.S.A. 65 H5 42 36N 72 37W
Green Island Hong Kong U.K. 98 B1 22 17N 114 06E
Green Islands Papua New Guinea 110 I9 4 50S 154 50E
GREENLAND 116 Z7
Greenland Basin Arctic Ocean 113 H14 72 00N 0 00
Greenland Sea Arctic Ocean 116 76 00N 5 00W
Green Mountains Vermont U.S.A. 65 H5 43 00N 73 00W
Greenock Scotland 78 G7 55 57N 4 45W
Greensboro Maryland U.S.A. 64 E1 38 58N 75 49W
Greensboro North Carolina U.S.A. 63 K4 36 03N 79 50W
Greenville Liberia 106 D9 5 01N 9 03W
Greenville Maine U.S.A. 37 R6 45 28N 69 36W
Greenville Mississippi U.S.A. 63 H3 33 23N 91 03W
Greenville Rhode Island U.S.A. 65 J4 41 51N 71 34W
Greenville South Carolina U.S.A. 63 J3 34 52N 82 25W
Greenville Texas U.S.A. 63 G3 33 09N 96 07W
Greenwich bor. England 82 C2 51 29N 0 00
Greenwich Connecticut U.S.A. 65 G4 41 00N 73 00W
Greenwood Mississippi U.S.A. 63 H3 33 31N 90 10W
Greenwood Lake New York U.S.A. 65 F4 41 13N 74 17W
Grenå Denmark 80 B6 56 25N 10 53E
GRENADA 67 L2
Grenoble France 77 D4 45 11N 5 43E
Greymouth New Zealand 111 B2 42 28S 171 12E
Grey Range mts. Australia 110 G4 27 00S 144 00E
Griffin Georgia U.S.A. 63 J3 33 15N 84 17W
Grimsby England 78 K5 53 35N 0 05W
Grimsey i. Iceland 79 I7 66 33N 18 00W
Grindstone Lake Wisconsin U.S.A. 35 B2 45 55N 91 23W
Grodno Belarus 90 A5 53 40N 23 50E
Groningen Netherlands 76 D5 53 13N 6 35E
Grønnedal Greenland 11 Z5 61 20N 48 00W
Groote Eylandt i. Australia 110 F7 14 00S 137 00E
Grootfontein Namibia 107 I4 19 32S 18 05E
Grosbeeren Germany 83 F1 52 20N 13 19E
Grosse Pointe Michigan U.S.A. 52 F2 42 23N 82 59W
Grosse Pointe c. Michigan U.S.A. 52 F2 42 23N 82 54W
Grosse Pointe Park Michigan U.S.A. 52 F2 42 23N 82 56W
Grosse Pointe Shores Michigan U.S.A. 52 F2 42 25N 82 08W
Grosser Müggelsee l. Germany 83 G1 52 26N 13 39E
Grosser Zernsee l. Germany 83 D1 52 22N 12 57E
Grosseto Italy 81 B3 42 46N 11 07E
Gross Glockner mt. Austria 81 B4 47 05N 12 44E
Groton Connecticut U.S.A. 65 H4 41 22N 72 05W
Groton New York U.S.A. 64 D5 42 36N 76 23W
Groznyy Russia 90 F3 43 21N 45 42E
Grudziądz Poland 80 C5 53 29N 18 45E
Guadalajara Mexico 66 D4 20 40N 103 20W
Guadalajara Spain 77 B3 40 37N 3 10W
Guadalcanal i. Solomon Islands 110 J8 9 30S 160 00E
Guadalope r. Spain 77 B3 40 50N 0 30W
Guadalquivir r. Spain 77 A2 37 45N 5 30W
Guadalupe Brazil 69 P2 22 50S 43 23W
Guadalupe i. Mexico 66 A5 29 00N 118 24W
Guadeloupe i. Lesser Antilles 67 L3 16 30N 61 30W
Guadiana r. Portugal 77 A2 38 30N 7 30W
Guadix Spain 77 B2 37 19N 3 08W
Guaito Trinidad and Tobago 66 T10 10 35N 61 09W
Guajará Mirim Brazil 68 D10 10 50S 65 21W
GUAM Pacific Ocean 114 E9 13 30N 144 40E
Guamúchil Mexico 66 C5 25 28N 108 10W
Guanabara Bay Brazil 69 Q2 22 45S 43 10W
Guanare Venezuela 67 K1 9 04N 69 45W
Guangzhou (Canton) China 97 M3 23 08N 113 20E
Guantánamo Cuba 67 I4 20 09N 75 14W
Guapo Bay Trinidad and Tobago 66 S9 10 12N 61 40W
Guaqui Bolivia 68 D9 16 38S 68 50W
Guarapuava Brazil 69 G7 25 22S 51 28W
Guarda Portugal 77 A3 40 32N 7 17W
Guardafui, Cape see Raas Caseyr
Guardiana r. Spain 77 B2 39 00N 4 00W
Guasdualito Venezuela 68 C14 7 15N 70 40W
GUATEMALA 66 F3
Guatemala Guatemala 66 F2 14 38N 90 22W
Guatemala Basin Pacific Ocean 115 Q9 12 00N 95 00W
Guatuara Point Trinidad and Tobago 66 U9 10 20N 60 58W
Guayaguayare Trinidad and Tobago 66 T9 10 09N 61 01W
Guayaguayare Bay Trinidad and Tobago 66 T9 10 07N 61 03W
Guayaquil Ecuador 68 A12 2 13S 79 54W
Guaymas Mexico 66 B5 27 59N 110 54W
Gudbrandsdalen v. Norway 79 B3 62 00N 58 50E
Guelma Algeria 77 D2 36 29N 7 25E
Guéret France 77 C4 46 10N 1 52E
Guernsey i. Channel Islands British Isles 78 I6 49 27N 2 35W
Guiana Highlands South America 55 4 00N 60 00W
Guilderland New York U.S.A. 65 G5 42 42N 73 54W
Guildford England 82 A2 51 14N 0 35W
Guilford Connecticut U.S.A. 65 H4 41 16N 72 41W
Guilin China 97 M4 25 21N 110 11E
Guimarães Portugal 77 A3 41 26N 8 19W
GUINEA 106 C10
Guinea Basin Atlantic Ocean 113 H7 1 00N 8 00W
GUINEA-BISSAU 106 B10
Guinea, Gulf of 106 E9 3 50N 3 00W
Güines Cuba 67 H4 22 50N 82 02W
Güiria Venezuela 68 E15 10 37N 62 21W
Guiyand China 97 L4 26 35N 106 40E
Gujarat admin. India 95 C4 23 20N 72 00E
Gujranwala Pakistan 95 C6 32 06N 74 11E
Gujrat Pakistan 95 C6 32 35N 74 06E
Gula de Pacobaiba Brazil 69 Q3 22 42S 43 10W
Gulbarga India 95 D3 17 22N 76 47E
Gulfport Mississippi U.S.A. 63 I3 30 21N 80 08W
Gulf, The Middle East 93 H4 27 20N 51 00E
Gulian see Mohe
Gullivare Sweden 79 E4 67 08N 20 25E
Gulu Uganda 106 L8 2 46N 32 21E
Gumma pref. Japan 100 K3 36 10N 138 27E
Gunnison r. Colorado U.S.A. 62 E4 38 00N 107 00W
Guntersville Lake Alabama U.S.A. 63 I3 34 00N 86 00W
Guntur India 95 E3 16 20N 80 27E
Gunung Kinabalu mt. Malaysia 99 F5 6 03N 116 32E
Gur'yev Kazakhstan 90 G4 47 08N 51 59E
Gusau Nigeria 106 G10 12 12N 6 40E
Gusev Russia 80 D5 54 32N 22 12E
Güstrow Germany 76 E5 53 48N 12 11E
Guthrie Oklahoma U.S.A. 63 G4 35 53N 97 26W
GUYANA 68 F13
Guyana Basin Atlantic Ocean 113 D7 8 00N 50 00W
Gwalior India 95 D5 26 12N 78 09E
Gweru Zimbabwe 107 K4 19 27S 29 49E
Gyandzha (Kirovabad) Azerbaijan 90 F3 40 39N 46 20E
Gyangze China 95 F5 28 53N 89 35E
Gyaring Co l. China 95 F6 31 05N 88 00E
Gydan Range see Kolyma Range
Gyda Peninsula Russia 89 J10 70 00N 77 30E
Gympie Australia 110 I4 26 10S 152 35E
Gyöngyös Hungary 81 C4 47 46N 20 00E
Györ Hungary 81 C4 47 41N 17 40E
Gyōda Japan 100 L3 36 10N 139 27E

H

Haapsalu Estonia 79 E2 58 58N 23 32E
Haarlem Netherlands 76 C5 52 23N 4 39E
Haast Pass New Zealand 111 A2 44 07S 169 22E
Hab r. Pakistan 94 B5 25 00N 67 00E
Habbān Yemen Republic 93 G1 14 21N 47 04E
Haboro Japan 100 D3 44 23N 141 43E
Hachinohe Japan 100 D3 40 30N 141 30E
Hachioji Japan 100 L2 35 40N 139 20E
Hackensack New Jersey U.S.A. 50 B2 40 53N 74 03W
Hackensack River New Jersey U.S.A. 50 B2 40 47N 74 06W
Hackettstown New Jersey U.S.A. 64 F3 40 52N 74 50W
Hackney bor. Greater London England 82 C3 51 33N 0 03W
Hadano Japan 100 L2 35 22N 139 10E
Haddonfield New Jersey U.S.A. 64 E2 39 53N 75 01W
Hadejia Nigeria 106 G10 12 30N 10 03E
Hadera Israel 92 O11 32 26N 34 55E
Haderslev Denmark 80 A6 55 15N 9 30E
Hadhramaut admin. Yemen Republic 93 G2 15 40N 47 30E
Hadiboh Socotra 93 H1 12 36N 53 59E
Haeju North Korea 97 P6 38 04N 125 40E
Hafnafjördur Iceland 79 H6 64 04N 21 58W
Hagerstown Maryland U.S.A. 64 C2 39 39N 77 44W
Ha Giang China 97 L3 23 00N 105 00W
Hague, The (Den Haag) see 's-Gravenhage
Haidian China 101 G1 39 59N 116 21E
Haifa Israel 92 O11 32 49N 34 59E
Haikou China 97 M2 20 05N 110 25E
Ha'il Saudi Arabia 92 F4 27 31N 41 45E
Hailar China 97 N8 49 15N 119 41E
Hailuoto i. Finland 79 E3 65 01N 24 45E
Hainan Dao i. China 97 M2 18 50N 109 50E
Haines Alaska U.S.A. 42 A3 59 11N 135 23W
Haiphong Vietnam 99 L3 20 50N 106 41E
HAITI 67 J3
Hakodate Japan 100 D3 41 46N 140 44E
Hakusan Japan 100 H1 34 38N 136 20E
Halab (Aleppo) Syria 92 E6 36 14N 37 10E
Halaib Sudan 92 E3 22 12N 36 35E
Halawa, Cape Hawaiian Islands 115 Y18 21 09N 157 15W
Halba Lebanon 92 P12 34 33N 36 04E
Halberstadt Germany 76 E5 51 54N 11 04E
Halden Norway 80 B6 59 08N 11 13E
Half Moon Bay California U.S.A. 49 B1 37 35N 122 28W
Half Moon Bay tn. California U.S.A. 49 B1 37 37N 122 29W
Halishahar India 94 K3 22 55N 88 25E
Halle Germany 76 E5 51 28N 11 58E
Halley r.s. Antarctica 117 75 35S 68 07W
Hallock Minnesota U.S.A. 39 B1 48 48N 96 56W
Halls Creek tn. Australia 110 D6 18 17S 127 38E
Hallstead Pennsylvania U.S.A. 64 E4 41 57N 75 45W
Halmahera i. Indonesia 99 H4 2 00N 127 30E
Halmstad Sweden 80 B6 56 41N 12 55E
Hamada Japan 100 B1 34 56N 132 04E
Hamadān Iran 93 G5 34 46N 48 35E
Hamamatsu Japan 100 C1 34 42N 137 42E
Hamar Norway 80 B7 60 57N 10 55E
Hamāh Syria 92 E6 35 10N 36 45E
Hambantota Sri Lanka 95 E1 6 07N 81 07E
Hamborn Germany 76 G2 51 29N 6 45E
Hamburg Germany 76 E5 53 33N 10 00E
Hamburg New York U.S.A. 64 B6 43 44N 78 50W
Hamburg Pennsylvania U.S.A. 64 E3 40 33N 75 59W
Hamden Connecticut U.S.A. 65 H4 41 23N 72 55W
Hämeenlinna Finland 79 E3 61 00N 24 25E
Hamersley Range mts. Australia 110 B5 22 00S 117 00E
Hamhŭng North Korea 97 P7 39 54N 127 35E
Hami (Kumul) China 96 H7 42 37N 93 32E
Hamilton New York U.S.A. 64 E5 42 50N 75 33W
Hamilton New Zealand 111 C3 37 46S 175 18E
Hamilton Ohio U.S.A. 63 J4 39 23N 84 33W
Hamm Germany 76 D5 51 40N 7 49E
Hammerdal Sweden 79 D3 63 35N 15 20E
Hammerfest Norway 79 E5 70 40N 23 44E
Hammersmith bor. Greater London England 82 B2 51 30N 0 14W
Hammond Indiana U.S.A. 53 C1 41 36N 87 30W
Hammondsport New York U.S.A. 64 C5 42 24N 77 15W
Hammonton New Jersey U.S.A. 64 F2 39 38N 74 49W
Hampstead Heath England 82 C3 51 34N 0 10W
Hampton New Hampshire U.S.A. 65 K5 42 56N 70 51W
Hampton Virginia U.S.A. 63 K4 37 02N 76 23W
Hamtramck Michigan U.S.A. 52 E2 42 26N 83 02W
Hanazono Japan 100 G1 34 09N 135 31E
Hancock Maryland U.S.A. 64 B2 39 42N 78 13W
Hancock Michigan U.S.A. 35 C2 47 08N 88 34W
Hancock New York U.S.A. 64 E4 41 58N 75 17W
Handa Japan 100 H1 34 52N 136 57E
Handan China 97 M6 36 35N 114 31E
Hang Ha Po Hong Kong U.K. 98 B2 22 27N 114 08E
Hang Hau Hong Kong U.K. 98 C1 22 18N 114 16E
Hang Hau Tsuen Hong Kong U.K. 98 A2 22 28N 113 59E
Hangö Finland 79 E2 59 50N 22 50E
Hangzhou China 97 N5 30 18N 120 07E
Hannah North Dakota U.S.A. 39 B1 48 59N 98 40W
Hannibal New York U.S.A. 64 D6 43 16N 76 35W
Hannibal Missouri U.S.A. 63 H4 39 41N 91 20W
Hanno Japan 100 L2 35 52N 139 19E
Hannover Germany 76 D5 52 23N 9 44E
Hanöbukten b. Sweden 79 C2 55 50N 14 30E
Hanoi Vietnam 99 D8 21 01N 105 52E
Hanover Massachusetts U.S.A. 65 K5 42 50N 70 54W
Hanover Pennsylvania U.S.A. 64 D2 39 47N 76 59W
Haora India 94 K2 22 35N 88 19E
Happy Valley Hong Kong U.K. 98 C1 22 16N 114 11E
Haql Saudi Arabia 92 O9 29 14N 34 56E
Harad Saudi Arabia 93 G3 24 12N 49 12E
Harare Zimbabwe 107 L4 17 50S 31 03E
Harbin China 97 P8 45 45N 126 41E
Harbor Beach tn. Michigan U.S.A. 36 D4 43 51N 82 40W
Harbor Springs Michigan U.S.A. 36 B6 45 25N 84 59W
Hardangerfjorden fj. Norway 79 B2 59 45N 5 20E
Hardangervidda plat. Norway 79 B3 60 10N 7 00E
Harefield England 82 B3 51 36N 0 28W
Härer Ethiopia 106 N9 9 20N 42 10E
Hargeysa Somalia 106 N9 9 31N 44 02E
Haridwar India 95 D5 29 58N 78 09E
Harima-nada sea Japan 100 B1 34 30N 134 30E
Haringey bor. Greater London England 82 C3 51 35N 0 07W
Hari Rud r. Afghanistan 93 J5 34 00N 64 00E
Harlem Montana U.S.A. 41 D1 48 33N 108 47W
Harlem New York U.S.A. 50 C2 40 48N 73 56W
Harlingen Texas U.S.A. 63 G2 26 12N 97 43W
Härnösand Sweden 79 D3 62 37N 17 55E
Harper Liberia 106 D9 4 25N 7 43W
Harper Woods Michigan U.S.A. 52 F2 42 25N 82 57W
Harriman Reservoir Vermont U.S.A. 65 H5 42 58N 72 42W
Harrington Delaware U.S.A. 64 E1 38 55N 75 35W
Harris i. Scotland 78 D9 57 50N 6 55W
Harrisburg Pennsylvania U.S.A. 64 D3 40 17N 76 54W
Harrison New York U.S.A. 65 G3 40 22N 73 40W
Harrisonburg Virginia U.S.A. 63 K4 38 27N 78 54W
Harrisville Michigan U.S.A. 36 C5 44 41N 83 19W
Harrogate England 78 J6 54 00N 1 33W
Harrow bor. Greater London England 82 B3 51 34N 0 20W
Hartford Connecticut U.S.A. 65 H4 41 00N 72 00W
Hartland Point England 78 G3 51 02N 4 31W
Hartlepool England 78 J6 54 41N 1 13W
Harveys Lake tn. Pennsylvania U.S.A. 64 D4 41 22N 76 04W
Harwich England 78 M3 51 57N 1 17E
Harwood Heights Illinois U.S.A. 53 A2 41 58N 87 48W
Haryana admin. India 95 D5 29 20N 75 30E
Hasaki Japan 100 M2 35 46N 140 50E
Hashima Japan 100 H2 35 19N 136 43E
Hashimoto Japan 100 G1 34 19N 135 33E
Hassan India 95 D2 13 01N 76 03E
Hasselt Belgium 76 C5 50 56N 5 20E
Hassi Messaoud Algeria 106 G14 31 52N 5 43E
Hastings Barbados 66 V12 13 05N 59 36W
Hastings England 78 L2 50 51N 0 36E
Hastings Michigan U.S.A. 36 A3 42 38N 85 17W
Hastings Nebraska U.S.A. 63 G5 40 37N 98 22W
Hastings New Zealand 111 C3 39 39S 176 52E
Ha Tsuen Hong Kong U.K. 98 A2 22 26N 113 59E
Hatteras, Cape North Carolina U.S.A. 63 K4 35 14N 75 31W
Hattiesburg Mississippi U.S.A. 63 I3 31 20N 89 19W
Hattingen Germany 76 J2 51 24N 7 10E
Haud geog. reg. Africa 106 N9 8 00N 50 00E
Haugesund Norway 79 B2 59 25N 5 16E
Haukivesi l. Finland 79 F3 62 10N 28 30E
Hauraki Gulf New Zealand 111 C3 36 40S 175 00E
Haut Atlas mts. Morocco 106 D14 30 45N 6 50W
Hauz Khas India 94 L4 28 34N 77 11E
Havana see La Habana
Havel r. Germany 83 E2 52 35N 13 13E
Havelkanal can. Germany 83 E2 52 38N 13 02E
Haverhill Massachusetts U.S.A. 65 J5 42 47N 71 07W
Havering bor. Greater London England 82 D3 51 34N 0 14E
Havey Illinois U.S.A. 53 B1 41 36N 87 40W
Havre Montana U.S.A. 62 E6 48 34N 109 40W
Havre de Grace Maryland U.S.A. 64 D2 39 33N 76 06W
Hawaii i. Hawaiian Islands 115 Z17 19 50N 157 50W
Hawaiian Islands Pacific Ocean 115 J10 25 00N 166 00W
Hawaiian Ridge Pacific Ocean 115 J10 23 00N 166 00W
Hawea, Lake New Zealand 111 A2 44 20S 169 20E
Hawera New Zealand 111 B3 39 35S 174 19E
Hawick Scotland 78 I7 55 25N 2 47W
Hawke Bay New Zealand 111 C3 39 10S 175 30E
Hawley Pennsylvania U.S.A. 64 E4 41 28N 75 11W
Hawthorne California U.S.A. 51 A2 33 54N 118 21W
Hawthorne New Jersey U.S.A. 50 B2 40 57N 74 10W
Hawthorne New York U.S.A. 65 G4 41 06N 73 47W
Hayama Japan 101 B2 35 16N 139 35E
Hayes England 82 B3 51 31N 0 25W
Hayes Halvø p. Greenland 45 S6 76 00N 67 30W
Hayward California U.S.A. 49 C2 37 40N 122 07W
Hayward Wisconsin U.S.A. 35 B2 46 02N 91 26W
Hazel Park Michigan U.S.A. 52 E2 42 27N 83 05W
Hazleton Pennsylvania U.S.A. 64 E3 40 58N 75 59W
Heard Island Indian Ocean 112 G1 53 07S 73 20E
Heart r. North Dakota U.S.A. 62 F2 47 00N 102 00W
Heathcote Australia 111 G1 34 05S 151 00E
Hebi China 97 M6 35 57N 114 08E
Hebron Jordan 92 O10 31 32N 35 06E
Heceta Island Alaska U.S.A. 42 B3 55 45N 134 30W
Hechuan China 97 L5 30 02N 106 15E
Heda Japan 100 K1 34 58N 138 46E
Hedesundafjärdarna l. Sweden 79 D3 60 20N 17 00E
Heerlen Netherlands 76 D5 50 53N 5 59E
Hefei China 96/97 N5 31 55N 117 18E
Hegang China 97 Q8 47 36N 130 30E
Hegura-jima i. Japan 100 C2 37 52N 136 56E
Heidelberg Germany 76 D5 49 25N 8 42E
Heilbronn Germany 76 D5 49 08N 9 14E
Heiligenhaus Germany 76 H2 52 20N 6 49E
Heilong Jiang see Amur
Hei Ling Chau i. Hong Kong U.K. 98 B1 22 15N 114 02E
Hekla mt. Iceland 79 I6 64 00N 19 41W
Hekou China 97 K3 22 30N 103 54E
Helan Shan mts. China 97 L6 38 00N 106 00E
Helena Montana U.S.A. 62 D6 46 35N 112 00W
Helgeland geog. reg. Norway 79 C4 64 45N 13 00E
Heligoland Bight b. Germany 76 D5 54 00N 8 00E
Hellersdorf Germany 83 G2 52 32N 13 35E
Hellín Spain 77 B2 38 31N 1 43W
Helmand r. Afghanistan 93 J5 30 00N 62 30E
Helsingborg Sweden 79 C2 56 03N 12 43E
Helsingfors see Helsinki
Helsingør Denmark 80 B6 56 03N 12 38E
Helsinki (Helsingfors) Finland 79 E3 60 08N 25 00E
Hemlock Lake New York U.S.A. 64 C5 42 45N 77 37W
Hempstead New York U.S.A. 50 D1 40 41N 73 39W
Henares r. Spain 77 B3 40 45N 3 10W
Henderson Nevada U.S.A. 62 D4 36 01N 115 00W
Hendon England 82 C3 51 35N 0 14W
Heng-ch'un Taiwan 98 G5 22 03N 120 45E
Hengelo Netherlands 76 D5 52 16N 6 46E
Hengyang China 97 M4 26 58N 112 31E
Henniker New Hampshire U.S.A. 65 J6 43 10N 71 50W
Henningsdorf admin. Germany 83 E2 52 39N 13 08E
Henryetta Oklahoma U.S.A. 63 G4 35 27N 96 00W
Henryk Arctowski r.s. Antarctica 117 62 09S 58 28W
Henzada Myanmar 99 B7 17 36N 95 26E
Herāt Afghanistan 93 J5 34 20N 62 12E
Hérault r. France 77 C3 43 50N 3 30E
Hereford England 78 I4 52 04N 2 43W
Herkimer New York U.S.A. 64 F6 43 02N 74 59W
Hermel Lebanon 92 P12 34 25N 36 23E
Hermon, Mount Lebanon/Syria 92 O11 33 24N 35 50E
Hermosillo Mexico 66 B5 29 15N 110 59W
Herndon Virginia U.S.A. 64 C1 38 59N 77 26W
Herne Germany 76 J3 51 32N 7 12E
Herning Denmark 80 A6 56 08N 8 59E
Hernodorf Germany 83 F2 52 38N 13 18E
Herten Germany 76 J3 51 36N 7 08E
Hertfordshire co. England 82 C3 51 50N 0 05W
Hibbing Minnesota U.S.A. 35 B2 47 25N 92 55W
Hickory North Carolina U.S.A. 63 J4 35 44N 81 23W
Hicksville Ohio U.S.A. 36 B2 41 18N 84 45W
Hidaka Japan 100 F2 35 29N 134 44E
Hidalgo Mexico 66 E4 24 16N 99 28W
Hidalgo del Parral Mexico 66 C5 26 58N 105 40W
Higashi-Matsuyama Japan 100 L3 36 02N 139 25E
Higashi-Murayama Japan 101 A4 35 46N 139 28E
Higashi-Ōsaka Japan 100 G1 34 40N 135 35E
Higashi-suidō sd. Japan 100 A1 34 10N 130 00E
Higganum Connecticut U.S.A. 65 H4 41 30N 72 34W
High Bridge New Jersey U.S.A. 64 F3 40 42N 74 53W
Highgate Jamaica 67 R8 18 16N 76 53W
High Island Hong Kong U.K. 98 D2 22 21N 114 21E
High Island Reservoir Hong Kong U.K. 98 D2 22 22N 114 20E
Highland Indiana U.S.A. 53 C1 41 33N 87 27W
Highland Park Illinois U.S.A. 53 A3 42 10N 87 45W
Highland Park Michigan U.S.A. 52 E2 42 23N 83 09W
Highland Park Pennsylvania U.S.A. 53 E1 40 28N 79 55W
High Point tn. North Carolina U.S.A. 63 K4 35 58N 80 00W
Highlands New Jersey U.S.A. 65 F3 40 24N 74 59W
High Veld mts. Republic of South Africa 107 K2 28 00S 28 00E
Hikami Japan 100 F2 35 12N 135 00E
Hikone Japan 100 H2 35 17N 136 13E
Hildesheim Germany 76 E5 52 09N 9 58E
Hillaby, Mount Barbados 66 V12 13 12N 59 35W
Hillingdon bor. Greater London England 82 B3 51 32N 0 27W
Hillsboro New Hampshire U.S.A. 65 J6 43 07N 71 54W
Hillsdale Michigan U.S.A. 36 B2 41 56N 84 37W
Hilo Hawaiian Islands 115 Z17 19 42N 155 04W
Hilversum Netherlands 76 C5 52 14N 5 10E
Himachal Pradesh admin. India 95 D6 32 00N 77 30E
Himalaya mts. Asia 95 D6/G5
Himeji Japan 100 B1 34 50N 134 40E
Ḥimṣ Syria 92 P12 34 42N 36 40E
Hinckley Lake res. New York U.S.A. 64 E6 43 20N 75 05W
Hindu Kush mts. Afghanistan 93 K6 35 00N 70 00E
Hingham Massachusetts U.S.A. 52 C1 42 15N 70 53W
Hingham Bay Massachusetts U.S.A. 52 C2 42 18N 70 55W
Hinnøya i. Norway 79 D4 68 35N 15 50E
Hinsdale Illinois U.S.A. 53 A2 41 48N 87 55W
Hirakata Japan 100 G1 34 49N 135 39E
Hirakud Reservoir India 95 E4 21 40N 83 40E
Hiratsuka Japan 100 L2 35 20N 139 19E
Hirosaki Japan 100 D3 40 34N 140 28E
Hiroshima Japan 100 B1 34 23N 132 27E
Hisai Japan 100 H1 34 42N 136 28E
Hisar India 95 D5 29 10N 75 45E
Hispaniola i. West Indies 67 J3 18 00N 70 00W
Hitachi Japan 100 D2 36 35N 140 40E
Hitra i. Norway 79 B3 63 37N 8 46E
Hjørring Denmark 80 A6 57 28N 9 59E
Ho Ghana 106 E9 6 38N 0 38E
Hobart Australia 110 H1 42 54S 147 18E
Hoboken New Jersey U.S.A. 50 B1 40 44N 74 02W
Hobyo Somalia 106 O9 5 20N 48 30E
Ho Chi Minh Vietnam 99 D6 10 46N 106 43E
Ho Chung Hong Kong U.K. 98 C2 22 22N 114 14E
Hódmezovásárhely Hungary 81 D4 46 26N 20 21E
Hodogaya Japan 101 B2 35 26N 139 36E
Hof Germany 76 E5 50 19N 11 56E
Hoffmeister New York U.S.A. 65 F6 43 22N 74 42W
Höfn Iceland 79 I6 64 16N 15 10W
Hofsjökull ice cap Iceland 79 I6 64 45N 18 45W
Hofu Japan 100 B1 34 02N 131 34E
Hogeland Montana U.S.A. 41 D1 48 51N 108 39W
Hohhot China 97 M7 40 49N 111 37E
Hoi Ha Hong Kong U.K. 98 C2 22 28N 114 20E
Hokitika New Zealand 111 B2 42 42S 170 59E
Hokkaidō i. Japan 100 D3 43 30N 143 00E
Hokota Japan 100 M3 36 10N 141 30E
Holbaek Denmark 80 B6 56 33N 10 19E
Holetown Barbados 66 V12 13 11N 59 38W
Holguín Cuba 67 I4 20 54N 76 15W
Hollick-Kenyon Plateau Antarctica 117 77 00S 100 00W
Hollidaysburg Pennsylvania U.S.A. 64 B3 40 26N 78 24W
Hollis Reservoir Trinidad and Tobago 66 T10 10 42N 61 11W
Holly Michigan U.S.A. 36 C3 42 48N 83 37W
Hollywood California U.S.A. 51 A3 34 05N 118 21W
Hollywood Reservoir California U.S.A. 51 A3 34 07N 118 20W
Holstebro Denmark 80 A6 56 22N 8 38E
Holsteinsborg Greenland 45 V4 66 55N 53 30W

Holston r. U.S.A. 63 J4 37 00N 82 00W
Ho-lung Taiwan 98 G7 24 37N 120 46E
Holy Cross Alaska U.S.A. 10 D5 62 10N 159 53W
Holyhead Wales 78 G5 53 19N 4 38W
Holy Island Wales 78 G5 53 16N 4 39W
Holy Island England 78 J7 55 41N 1 48W
Holyoke Massachusetts U.S.A. 65 H5 42 12N 72 37W
Ho Man Tin Hong Kong U.K. 98 C1 22 19N 114 10E
Homberg Germany 76 G2 51 27N 6 41E
Homer Alaska U.S.A. 10 E4 59 40N 151 37W
Homer New York U.S.A. 64 D5 42 38N 76 12W
Homestead Florida U.S.A. 63 J2 25 29N 80 29W
Homewood Illinois U.S.A. 53 B1 41 42N 87 18W
Honda Colombia 68 C14 5 15N 74 50W
HONDURAS 66/67 G2
Hønefoss Norway 80 B7 60 10N 10 16E
Honesdale Pennsylvania U.S.A. 64 E4 41 34N 75 15W
Hong Kong i. Hong Kong U.K. 98 C1 22 10N 114 10E
Hong Kong territory U.K. 97
Hong Lok Yuen Hong Kong U.K. 98 B2 22 27N 114 09E
Honiara Solomon Islands 110 J8 9 28S 159 57E
Honjō Japan 100 L3 36 16N 139 09E
Honokaa Hawaiian Islands 115 Z18 20 04N 155 27W
Honolulu Hawaiian Islands 115 Y18 21 19N 157 50W
Honshū i. Japan 100 C2 37 15N 139 00E
Hood, Mount Oregon U.S.A. 62 B6 45 24N 121 41W
Hook England 82 B2 51 17N 0 58W
Hooksett New Hampshire U.S.A. 65 J6 43 05N 71 25W
Hoolehua Hawaiian Islands 115 Y18 21 11N 157 06W
Hoonah Alaska U.S.A. 42 A3 58 06N 135 25W
Hooper Bay tn. Alaska U.S.A. 10 B5 61 29N 166 10W
Hoosic River U.S.A. 65 G5 42 50N 73 20W
Hoosick Falls tn. New York U.S.A. 65 G5 42 54N 73 22W
Hope Barbados 66 V13 13 20N 59 36W
Hope Valley tn. Rhode Island U.S.A. 65 J4 41 30N 71 42W
Hopkinsville Kentucky U.S.A. 63 I4 36 50N 87 30W
Hopkinton Lake New Hampshire U.S.A. 65 J6 43 10N 71 45W
Ho Pui Hong Kong U.K. 98 B2 22 24N 114 04E
Hörde Germany 76 K2 51 29N 7 31E
Hormuz, Strait of The Gulf 93 I4 26 35N 56 30E
Hornavan l. Sweden 79 D4 66 15N 17 40E
Horn, Cape see Cabo de Hornos
Hornchurch England 82 D3 51 34N 0 13E
Hornell New York U.S.A. 64 C5 42 19N 77 39W
Hornsby Australia 111 G3 33 42S 151 06E
Horseheads New York U.S.A. 64 D5 42 11N 76 51W
Horsens Denmark 80 A6 55 53N 9 53E
Horsham Australia 110 G2 36 45S 142 15E
Hospet India 95 D3 15 16N 76 20E
Hospitalet Spain 77 C3 41 21N 2 06E
Hotan China 96 E6 37 07N 79 57E
Hotan He r. China 96 F6 37 07N 79 57E
Hoting Sweden 79 D3 64 08N 16 15E
Hot Springs tn. Arkansas U.S.A. 63 H3 34 30N 93 02W
Houghton Michigan U.S.A. 35 C2 47 06N 88 34W
Houghton New York U.S.A. 64 B5 42 27N 78 10W
Houghton Lake Michigan U.S.A. 36 B5 44 20N 84 45W
Houghton Lake tn. Michigan U.S.A. 36 B5 44 17N 84 45W
Houlton Maine U.S.A. 33 C2 46 09N 67 50W
Houma China 97 M6 35 36N 111 15E
Houma Louisiana U.S.A. 63 H2 29 35N 90 44W
Hounslow bor. Greater London England 82 B2 51 28N 0 21W
Housatonic River Connecticut/Massachusetts U.S.A. 65 G4 41 00N 73 00W
Houston Texas U.S.A. 63 G2 29 45N 95 25W
Hovd Mongolia 96 H8 48 00N 91 43E
Hövsgöl Nuur l. Mongolia 97 K9 51 00N 100 00E
Howar r. Sudan 106 K11 17 00N 25 00E
Howe, Cape Australia 110 H2 37 20S 149 59E
Howell Illinois U.S.A. 53 A1 41 39N 87 46W
Hoy i. Scotland 78 H10 58 48N 3 20W
Hoya Japan 101 B3 35 44N 139 34E
Hradec Králové Czechoslovakia 80 C5 50 13N 15 50E
Hron r. Czechoslovakia 81 C4 48 00N 18 00E
Hsin-chu Taiwan 98 G7 24 48N 120 59E
Hsin-tien Taiwan 98 H7 24 57N 121 32E
Hsin-ying Taiwan 98 G6 23 18N 120 18E
Huacho Peru 68 B10 11 05S 77 36W
Huaide China 97 N7 43 30N 124 48E
Huainan China 97 N5 32 41N 117 06E
Huajuápan de León Mexico 66 E3 17 50N 97 48W
Hua-lien Taiwan 98 H6 23 58N 121 35E
Huambo Angola 107 I5 12 44S 15 47E
Huancayo Peru 68 B10 12 05S 75 12W
Huang Hai see Yellow Sea
Huang He r. China 97 K6/M6 38 00N 111 00E
Huangshi China 97 N5 30 13N 115 05E
Huanuco Peru 68 B11 9 55S 76 11W
Hua-p'ing Hsü i. Taiwan 98 H8 25 26N 121 57E
Huaráz Peru 68 B11 9 33S 77 31W
Huascaran mt. Peru 68 B11 9 08S 77 36W
Huashixia China 97 J6 35 13N 99 12E
Hubbard Lake Michigan U.S.A. 36 C5 44 50N 83 30W
Huckarde Germany 76 K3 51 33N 7 25E
Huddart Park California U.S.A. 49 B1 37 26N 122 19W
Huddersfield England 78 J5 53 39N 1 47W
Hudson New Hampshire U.S.A. 65 J5 42 44N 71 26W
Hudson New York U.S.A. 65 G5 42 14N 73 48W
Hudson River New York U.S.A. 65 G5 42 00N 73 55W
Hue Vietnam 99 D7 16 28N 107 35E
Huelva Spain 77 A2 37 15N 6 56W
Huesca Spain 77 B3 42 08N 0 25W
Huevos i. Trinidad and Tobago 66 S10 10 47N 61 11W
Hughenden Australia 110 G5 20 50S 144 10E
Hugli r. India 94 J2 22 30N 88 14E
Hugli-Chinsurah India 94 K3 22 54N 88 23E
Hugo Oklahoma U.S.A. 63 G3 34 01N 95 31W
Huixtla Mexico 66 F3 15 09N 92 30W
Huizhou China 97 M3 23 08N 114 28W
Hull Massachusetts U.S.A. 52 C2 42 19N 70 54W
Humaitá Brazil 68 E11 7 33S 63 01W
Humber r. England 78 K5 53 40N 0 10W
Humboldt r. Nevada U.S.A. 62 C5 41 00N 118 00W
Humboldt Glacier Greenland 116 79 40N 64 00W
Humbolt Park Illinois U.S.A. 53 B2 41 41N 87 51W
HUNGARY 81 C4
Hung Hom Hong Kong U.K. 98 C1 22 18N 114 11E
Hŭngnam North Korea 97 P6 39 49N 127 40E
Hunjiang China 97 P7 41 54N 126 23E
Hunter Trench Pacific Ocean 114 H5 23 00S 175 00E
Hunters Point California U.S.A. 49 B2 37 43N 122 21W
Huntingdon Indiana U.S.A. 35 C1 40 54N 85 30W
Huntingdon Pennsylvania U.S.A. 64 B3 40 31N 78 02W
Huntington Indiana U.S.A. 35 C1 40 54N 85 30W
Huntington Massachusetts U.S.A. 65 H5 42 37N 72 44W
Huntington West Virginia U.S.A. 63 J4 38 24N 82 26W
Huntington Beach tn. California U.S.A. 51 B1 33 40N 118 00W
Huntly New Zealand 87 C3 37 35S 175 10E
Huntsville Alabama U.S.A. 63 I3 34 44N 86 35W
Huntsville Texas U.S.A. 63 G3 30 43N 95 34W
Hurghada Egypt 92 D4 27 17N 33 47E
Hurley New York U.S.A. 65 F4 41 56N 74 03W
Hurley Wisconsin U.S.A. 35 B2 46 25N 90 15W
Huron River Michigan U.S.A. 36 C3 42 10N 83 15W
Huron, Lake Canada/U.S.A. 36 D5 45 00N 83 00W
Hurstville Australia 111 G2 33 58S 151 06E
Húsavík Iceland 79 I7 66 03N 17 17W
Huskvarna Sweden 80 B6 57 47N 14 15E
Husn Jordan 92 O11 32 29N 35 53E
Hutchinson Kansas U.S.A. 63 G4 38 03N 97 56W
Huzhou China 97 N5 30 56N 120 04E
Hvar i. Croatia 81 C3 43 00N 17 00E
Hwange Zimbabwe 107 K4 18 22S 26 29E
Hwange National Park Zimbabwe 107 K4 19 00S 26 00E
Hyde Park Greater London England 82 C3 51 31N 0 10W
Hyder Alaska U.S.A. 42 B3 55 54N 130 10W
Hyderabad India 95 D3 17 22N 78 26E
Hyderabad Pakistan 94 B5 25 23N 68 24E
Hyōgo pref. Japan 100 F2 35 00N 135 00E
Hyvinkää Finland 79 E3 60 37N 24 50E

I

Ialomiţa r. Romania 81 E3 44 00N 27 00E
Iaşi Romania 81 E4 47 09N 27 38E
Ibadan Nigeria 106 F9 7 23N 3 56E
Ibagué Colombia 68 B13 4 25N 75 20W
Ibaraki Japan 100 G1 34 50N 135 34E
Ibaraki Japan 100 M3 36 17N 140 25E
Ibaraki pref. Japan 100 M3 36 10N 140 00E
Ibarra Ecuador 68 B13 0 23N 78 05W
Ibb Yemen Republic 92 F1 14 03N 44 10E
Iberian Peninsula Europe 102 40 00N 15 00W
Ibi Nigeria 106 G9 8 11N 9 44E
Ibigawa Japan 100 H2 35 32N 136 31E
Ibi-gawa r. Japan 100 H2 35 34N 136 30E
Ibiza Balearic Islands 77 C2 38 54N 1 26E
Ibiza i. Balearic Islands 77 C2 39 00N 1 20E
Ibotirama Brazil 68 I10 12 13S 43 12W
Ibrī Oman 93 I3 23 15N 56 35E
Ica Peru 68 B10 14 02S 75 48W
Icacos Trinidad and Tobago 66 S9 10 04N 61 55W
Icacos Point Trinidad and Tobago 66 S9 10 41N 61 42W
ICELAND 79 I6
Ichalkaranji India 95 C3 16 40N 74 33E
Ichāpur India 94 K3 22 48N 88 22E
Ichihara Japan 100 M2 35 32N 140 04E
Ichikawa Japan 100 L2 35 45N 139 55E
Ichinomiya Japan 100 F1 34 25N 134 47E
Ichinomiya Japan 100 H2 35 18N 136 48E
Icy Strait Alaska U.S.A. 42 A3 58 20N 135 45W
Idaho state U.S.A. 62 D5 44 00N 115 00W
Idaho Falls tn. Idaho U.S.A. 62 D5 43 30N 112 01W
Iddo Nigeria 107 V3 6 25N 3 27E
Idfu Egypt 92 D3 24 58N 32 50E
Idre Sweden 79 C3 61 52N 12 45E
Igarka Russia 89 K9 67 31N 86 33E
Igbobi Nigeria 107 V3 6 32N 3 27E
Iglesias Italy 81 A2 39 19N 8 32E
Iguaçu r. Brazil 69 P3 22 44S 43 16W
Iguala Mexico 66 E3 18 21N 99 31W
Iguape Brazil 69 G8 24 37S 47 30W
Iguatu Brazil 68 J11 6 22S 39 20W
Ihosy Madagascar 107 O3 22 23S 46 09E
Iisalmi Finland 79 F3 63 34N 27 08E
IJsselmeer l. Netherlands 76 D5 52 50N 5 15E
Ikaría i. Greece 81 E2 37 00N 26 00E
Ikeja Nigeria 107 V3 6 37N 3 25E
Ikela Zaïre 106 J7 1 06S 23 06E
Iki i. Japan 100 A1 33 50N 129 40E
Ikoyi Nigeria 107 W3 6 23N 3 32E
Ikuno Japan 100 F2 35 12N 134 46E
Ikuta Japan 101 B3 35 36N 139 34E
Ilagan The Philippines 99 G7 17 07N 121 53E
I-lan Taiwan 98 H7 24 45N 121 44E
Île Amsterdam i. Indian Ocean 112 G3 37 56S 77 40E
Ilebo Zaïre 107 J7 4 20S 20 35E
Île de l'Europa i. Mozambique Channel 95 H3 22 20S 40 20E
Île de Ré i. France 77 B4 46 10N 1 26W
Île d'Oléron i. France 77 B4 45 55N 1 16W
Île d'Ouessant i. France 76 A4 48 28N 5 05W
Île d'Yeu i. France 77 B4 46 43N 2 20W
Ilek r. Kazakhstan/Russia 91 H5 51 00N 57 00E
Ilesha Nigeria 106 F9 7 39N 4 38E
Île St. Paul i. Indian Ocean 112 G3 38 44S 77 30E
Îles Chesterfield is. Pacific Ocean 110 J6 19 00S 158 30E
Îles Crozet is. Indian Ocean 112 E2 46 27S 52 00E
Îles d'Hyères is. France 77 D3 43 01N 6 25E
Îles Kerguelen is. Indian Ocean 112 F2 49 30S 69 30E
Îles Kerkenah is. Tunisia 81 B1 34 50N 11 30E
Îles Loyauté is. Pacific Ocean 110 L5/L6 21 00S 167 00E
Îles Wallis is. Pacific Ocean 114 I6 13 16S 176 15W
Ilford England 82 D3 51 33N 0 06E
Ilha Bazaruto i. Mozambique 107 M3 21 40S 35 30E
Ilha de Marajó i. Brazil 68 G12/H12 1 30S 50 00W
Ilha de Paquetá i. Brazil 69 Q2 22 46S 43 07W
Ilha do Fundão i. Brazil 69 Q2 22 52S 43 13W
Ilha do Governador i. Brazil 69 Q2 22 47S 43 13W
Ilha do Pai i. Brazil 69 Q2 22 59S 43 05W
Ilha Fernando de Noronha i. Brazil 68 K12 3 50S 32 25W
Ilhéus Brazil 68 J10 14 50S 39 06W
Ili r. Asia 89 J4 44 00N 78 00E
Iliamna Lake Alaska U.S.A. 10 D4 59 30N 155 30W
Iligan The Philippines 99 G5 8 12N 124 13E
Ilikurangi mt. New Zealand 111 C3 37 57S 178 00E
Ilion New York U.S.A. 64 E6 43 01N 75 04W
Illapel Chile 69 C6 31 40S 71 13W
Illinois state U.S.A. 63 I5 40 00N 89 00W
Illinois and Michigan Canal Illinois U.S.A. 53 A2 41 45N 87 50W
Illizi Algeria 106 G13 26 45N 8 30E
Iloilo The Philippines 99 G6 10 41N 122 33E
Ilorin Nigeria 106 F9 8 32N 4 34E
Ilupeju Nigeria 107 V3 6 35N 3 25E
Imabari Japan 100 B1 34 04N 132 59E
Imatra Finland 79 B7 61 14N 28 50E
Imazu Japan 100 H2 35 25N 136 01E
Īmī Ethiopia 106 N9 6 28N 42 10E
Imperatriz Brazil 68 H11 5 32S 47 28W
Imperia Italy 81 A3 43 53N 8 03E
Impfondo Congo 106 I8 1 36N 18 00E
Imphal India 95 G4 24 47N 93 55E
Inarijärvi l. Finland 79 F4 69 15N 27 30E
In Salah Algeria 106 F13 27 20N 2 03E
Inca Balearic Islands 77 C2 39 43N 2 54E
Inch'ŏn South Korea 97 P6 37 30N 126 38E
Indalsälven r. Sweden 79 D3 63 00N 16 30E
Independence Fjord Greenland 116 82 00N 30 00W
INDIA 94/95 B4/F4
Indiana state U.S.A. 63 I5 40 00N 86 00W
Indian Antarctic Basin Southern Ocean 114 B2 57 00S 113 00E
Indian-Antarctic Ridge Southern Ocean 114 C2 51 00S 124 00E
Indianapolis Indiana U.S.A. 63 I4 39 45N 86 10W
Indian Creek Illinois U.S.A. 53 A3 42 13N 87 59W
Indiana Harbor Indiana U.S.A. 53 C1 41 41N 87 27W
Indian Ocean 112
Indigirka r. Russia 89 Q9 70 00N 147 30E
INDONESIA 99 C3/H3
Indore India 95 D4 22 42N 75 54E
Indravati r. India 95 E3 19 00N 81 30E
Indre r. France 77 C4 46 50N 1 25E
Indus r. Pakistan 94/95 B5/C6 26 00N 68 00E
Indus, Mouths of the est. Pakistan 94 B4 24 00N 67 00E
Ingham Australia 110 H6 18 35S 146 12E
Inglewood California U.S.A. 51 A2 33 58N 118 22W
Ingolstadt Germany 76 E4 48 46N 11 27E
Inhambane Mozambique 107 M3 23 51S 35 29E
Inkster Michigan U.S.A. 52 D2 42 16N 83 18W
Inn r. Europe 81 B4 48 00N 12 00E
Inner Hebrides is. Scotland 78 E8 56 45N 6 45W
Inner Mongolia Autonomous Region see Nei Mongol Zizhiqu
Innherad geog. reg. Norway 79 C3 63 50N 12 00E
Innisfail Australia 110 H6 17 30S 146 00E
Innsbruck Austria 81 B4 47 17N 11 25E
Inongo Zaïre 106 I7 1 55S 18 20E
Inowrocław Poland 80 C5 52 49N 18 12E
Insein Myanmar 97 J2 16 54N 96 08E
Inta Russia 89 I9 66 04N 60 01E
Interlaken New York U.S.A. 64 D5 42 37N 76 44W
International Falls tn. Minnesota U.S.A. 39 C1 48 38N 93 26W
Inubō-zaki c. Japan 100 D2 35 41N 140 52E
Inuyama Japan 100 H2 35 22N 136 56E
Invercargill New Zealand 111 A1 46 26S 168 21E
Inverness Scotland 78 G9 57 27N 4 15W
Ioánnina Greece 81 D2 39 40N 20 51E
Iona i. Scotland 78 E8 56 19N 6 25W
Ione Washington U.S.A. 43 E1 48 45N 117 25W
Ionia Michigan U.S.A. 36 A3 42 58N 85 06W
Ionian Islands see Iónioi Nísoi
Ionian Sea Mediterranean Sea 81 C2 37 00N 18 00E
Iónioi Nísoi (Ionian Islands) is. Greece 81 C2 39 00N 20 00E
Íos i. Greece 81 E2 36 00N 25 00E
Iowa state U.S.A. 63 H5 42 00N 94 00W
Iowa City Iowa U.S.A. 63 H5 41 39N 91 31W
Ipanema Brazil 69 Q2 22 59S 43 13W
Ipanema Beach Brazil 69 Q2 23 00S 43 14W
Ipatinga Brazil 68 I9 19 32S 42 30W
Ipiales Colombia 68 B13 0 52N 77 38W
Ipoh Malaysia 99 C4 4 36N 101 02E
Ipswich Massachusetts U.S.A. 65 K5 42 41N 70 51W
Ipswich England 78 M4 52 04N 1 10E
Ipu Brazil 68 I12 4 23S 40 44W
Iquique Chile 68 C8 20 15S 70 08W
Iquitos Peru 68 C12 3 51S 73 13W
Irago-suidō sd. Japan 100 H1 34 27N 137 00E
Irajá Brazil 69 P2 22 50S 43 19W
Iráklion Greece 81 E2 35 20N 25 08E
IRAN 93 H5
Irapuato Mexico 66 D4 20 40N 101 30W
IRAQ 92 F5
Irecê Brazil 68 I10 11 22S 41 51W
Irian Jaya admin. Indonesia 110 F9 4 00S 137 50E
Iringa Tanzania 107 M6 7 49S 35 39E
Iriri r. Brazil 68 G11 7 00S 53 30W
IRISH REPUBLIC 78
Irish Sea British Isles 78 F5 53 30N 5 30W
Irkutsk Russia 89 M6 52 18N 104 15E
Irois Bay Trinidad and Tobago 66 S9 10 09N 61 45W
Irondequoit New York U.S.A. 64 C6 43 10N 77 38W
Iron Gate see Portile de Fier
Iron Knob Australia 110 F3 32 44S 137 08E
Iron Mountain tn. Michigan U.S.A. 35 C2 45 51N 88 03W
Ironwood Michigan U.S.A. 35 B2 46 25N 90 08W
Irrawaddy r. Myanmar 96 J2 20 00N 95 00E
Irrawaddy, Mouths of the est. Myanmar 95 G3 15 30N 94 30E
Irtysh r. Kazakhstan/Russia 91 L6 57 30N 72 30E
Irún Spain 77 B3 43 20N 1 48W
Irving Texas U.S.A. 63 G3 32 49N 96 57W
Irvington New Jersey U.S.A. 50 B1 40 44N 74 15W
Ísafjördur Iceland 79 H7 66 05N 23 08W
Ise Japan 100 H1 34 29N 136 41E
Isère r. France 77 D4 45 17N 5 47E
Ise shima National Park Japan 100 H1 34 25N 136 50E
Iset' r. Russia 91 K6 56 30N 65 00E
Ise-wan b. Japan 100 H1 34 50N 136 40E
Ishikari r. Japan 100 D3 43 20N 141 45E
Ishikari-wan b. Japan 100 D3 43 30N 141 00E
Ishim Russia 91 K6 56 21N 69 30E
Ishim r. Russia 91 K5 54 00N 68 00E
Ishimskaya Step' geog. reg. Russia 91 L5 54 00N 71 00E
Ishinomaki Japan 100 D2 38 25N 141 18E
Ishioka Japan 100 M3 36 11N 140 16E
Isiro Zaïre 106 J8 2 50N 27 40E
Iskŭr r. Bulgaria 81 D3 43 30N 24 00E
Isla Asinara i. Italy 81 A3 41 00N 8 00E
Isla de Chiloé i. Chile 69 C4 42 30S 74 00W
Isla de Coiba i. Panama 67 H1 7 40N 82 00W
Isla de Cozumel i. Mexico 67 G4 20 30N 87 00W
Isla d'Elba i. Italy 81 B3 42 00N 10 00E
Isla de la Juventud i. Cuba 67 H4 22 00N 82 30W
Isla del Coco (Cocos Island) Costa Rica 115 R8 5 33N 87 00W
Isla de los Estados i. Argentina 69 D2 55 00S 64 00W
Isla de Patos i. Venezuela 66 S10 10 38N 61 51W
Isla Grande de Tierra del Fuego i. Chile/Argentina 69 D2 54 00S 67 30W
Islamabad Pakistan 95 C6 33 40N 73 08E
Isla Margarita i. Venezuela 68 E15 11 30N 64 00W
Island Beach New Jersey U.S.A. 65 F2 39 55N 74 05W
Island Park tn. New York U.S.A. 50 D1 40 36N 73 39W
Isla San Ambrosio i. Chile 69 B7 26 28S 79 53W
Isla San Felix i. Chile 69 A7 26 23S 80 05W
Islas de la Bahia is. Honduras 67 G3 16 40N 86 00W
Islas Galapagos is. Pacific Ocean 115 Q7 0 05S 90 00W
Islas Juan Fernández is. Chile 69 B6 33 30S 78 00W
Islas Marias is. Mexico 66 C4 22 00N 107 00W
Islas Revillagigedo is. Pacific Ocean 115 O9 19 00N 112 30W
Isla Wellington i. Chile 115 S3 48 50S 79 00W
Islay i. Scotland 78 E7 55 48N 6 12W
Isle of Man British Isles 78 G6 54 15N 4 30W
Isle of Wight co. England 78 J2 50 40N 1 20W
Islington bor. Greater London England 82 C3 51 33N 0 06W
Ismâ'ilîya Egypt 107 S3 30 36N 32 16E
Isogo Japan 101 B2 35 23N 139 37E
Isole Lipari is. Italy 81 B2 38 00N 14 00E
Isolo Nigeria 107 V3 6 32N 3 23E
Issyk-Kul' (Rybach'ye) Kirgyzstan 91 M3 42 28N 76 09E
Istmo de Tehuantepec ist. Mexico 66 F3 17 20N 93 10W
Itabaiana Brazil 68 J10 10 42S 37 37W
Itabashi Japan 101 B4 35 46N 139 39E
Itabuna Brazil 68 J10 14 48S 39 18W
Itacoatiara Brazil 68 F12 3 06S 58 22W
Itagüí Colombia 68 B14 6 13N 75 40W
Itaituba Brazil 68 F12 4 15S 55 56W
Itajaí Brazil 69 H7 26 50S 48 39W
Itako Japan 100 M2 35 57N 140 31E
ITALY 81 B3
Itapipoca Brazil 68 J12 3 29S 39 35W
Itaqui Brazil 69 F7 29 10S 56 30W
Itarsi India 95 D4 22 39N 77 48E
Ithaca New York U.S.A. 64 D5 42 26N 76 30W
Itō Japan 100 L2 34 58N 139 04E
Itui r. Brazil 68 C11 5 30S 71 00W
Ivano-Frankovsk Ukraine 90 A4 48 40N 24 40E
Ivanovo Russia 90 E6 57 00N 41 00E
Ivdel' Russia 91 J7 60 45N 60 30E
Ivry-sur-Seine France 83 B2 48 48N 2 24E
Iwai Japan 100 L3 36 02N 139 53E
Iwaki Japan 100 D2 37 03N 140 58E
Iwakuni Japan 100 B1 34 10N 132 09E
Iwamizawa Japan 100 D3 43 12N 141 47E
Iwanai Japan 100 D3 43 01N 140 32E
Iwo Nigeria 106 F9 7 38N 4 11E
Ixtaccihuatl mt. Mexico 66 E3 19 11N 98 38W
Ixtepec Mexico 66 E3 16 32N 95 10W
Iyo-nada b. Japan 100 B1 33 50N 132 00E
Izhevsk Russia 91 G6 56 49N 53 11E
Izhma r. Russia 91 G7 64 00N 54 00E
Izmail Ukraine 81 E4 45 20N 28 48E
Izumi Japan 100 G1 34 29N 135 25E
Izu-shotō is. Japan 100 C1 34 20N 139 20E

J

Jabal Akhdar mts. Oman 93 I3 23 10N 57 25E
Jābal as Sawdā' mts. Libya 106 H13 29 00N 15 00E
Jabalpur India 95 D4 23 10N 79 59E
Jablonec Czechoslovakia 80 C5 50 44N 15 10E
Jaboatão Brazil 68 J11 8 05S 35 00W
Jacarepaguá Brazil 69 P2 22 57S 43 21W
Jackman Maine U.S.A. 37 Q6 45 37N 70 16W
Jack Mountain Washington U.S.A. 42 H4 48 47N 120 58W
Jackson Barbados 66 V12 13 09N 59 40W
Jackson Michigan U.S.A. 36 B3 42 15N 84 24W
Jackson Mississippi U.S.A. 63 H3 32 20N 90 11W
Jackson Tennessee U.S.A. 63 I4 35 37N 88 50W
Jackson Wyoming U.S.A. 62 D5 43 28N 110 45W
Jackson Head New Zealand 111 A2 43 58S 168 38E
Jackson Heights New York U.S.A. 50 C2 40 45N 73 52W
Jackson Park Illinois U.S.A. 53 B2 41 47N 87 34W
Jacksonville Florida U.S.A. 63 J3 30 20N 81 40W
Jacksonville North Carolina U.S.A. 63 K3 34 45N 77 26W
Jacksonville Beach tn. Florida U.S.A. 63 J3 30 18N 81 24W
Jack Wade Alaska U.S.A. 44 C3 64 05N 141 35W
Jacmel Haiti 67 J3 18 18N 72 32W
Jacobabad Pakistan 94 B5 28 16N 68 30E
Jacobina Brazil 68 I10 11 13S 40 30W
Jaén Spain 77 B2 37 46N 3 48W
Jaffna Sri Lanka 95 D1 9 40N 80 01E
Jaffrey New Hampshire U.S.A. 65 H5 42 00N 72 00W
Jagdalpur India 95 E3 19 04N 82 05E
Jahrom Iran 93 H4 28 29N 53 32E
Jaipur India 95 D5 26 53N 75 50E
Jaisalmer India 93 L4 26 52N 70 55E
Jakarta Indonesia 99 D2 6 08S 106 45E
Jakobstad Finland 79 E3 63 40N 22 42E
Jalālābād Afghanistan 93 L5 34 26N 70 28E
Jalapa Enriquez Mexico 66 E3 19 32N 96 56W
Jalgaon India 95 D4 21 01N 75 39E
Jalna India 95 D3 19 50N 75 58E
Jalón r. Spain 77 B3 41 30N 1 35W
Jālū Libya 106 J13 29 02N 21 33E
JAMAICA 67 Q8
Jamaica New York U.S.A. 50 C1 40 42N 73 48W
Jamaica Bay New York U.S.A. 50 C1 40 37N 73 50W
Jamana, Mount Trinidad and Tobago 66 T9 10 27N 61 14W
Jambi Indonesia 99 C3 2 00S 103 30E
James r. U.S.A. 63 G6 47 00N 98 00W
James r. Virginia U.S.A. 63 K4 37 00N 77 00W
Jamestown New York U.S.A. 63 K5 42 05N 79 15W
Jamestown North Dakota U.S.A. 63 G6 46 54N 98 42W
Jamestown Rhode Island U.S.A. 65 J4 41 30N 71 23W
Jamiltepec Mexico 66 E3 16 18N 97 51W
Jammu India 95 D6 32 43N 74 54E
Jammu & Kashmir state Southern Asia 95 D6 29 40N 76 30E
Jamnagar India 95 C4 22 28N 70 06E

Jamshedpur India **95** F4 22 47N 86 12E
Janesville Wisconsin U.S.A. **63** I5 42 42N 89 02W
Jan Mayen *i.* Arctic Ocean **116** 71 00N 9 00W
Januária Brazil **68** H9 15 28S 44 23W
JAPAN 100
Japan Trench Pacific Ocean **114** E11 35 00N 143 00E
Japan, Sea of 100 C2 39 00N 136 00E
Jarú Brazil **68** E10 10 24S 62 45W
Jāsk Iran **93** I4 25 40N 57 46E
Jastrowie Poland **80** C5 53 25N 16 50E
Jasło Poland **80** D4 49 45N 21 28E
Jaunpur India **95** E5 25 44N 82 41E
Java Sea Indonesia **99** E2 6 00S 113 00E
Java Trench Indian Ocean **112** J6 10 00S 110 00E
Jawa *i.* Indonesia **99** D2/E2 2 30S 110 00E
Jayapura Indonesia **110** G9 2 37S 140 39E
Jazā'ir Farasān *is.* Saudi Arabia **92** F2 16 45N 42 10E
Jebel Abyad Plateau Sudan **106** K11 18 00N 28 00E
Jebel Marra *mts.* Sudan **106** J10 13 00N 24 00E
Jefferson Ohio U.S.A. **36** F2 41 44N 80 46W
Jēkabpils Latvia **79** F2 56 22N 25 50E
Jelenia Góra Poland **80** C5 50 55N 15 45E
Jelgava Latvia **79** E2 56 39N 23 40E
Jena Germany **76** E5 50 56N 11 35E
Jenin Jordan **92** O11 32 28N 35 18E
Jequié Brazil **68** I10 13 52S 40 06W
Jérémie Haiti **67** J3 18 40N 74 09W
Jerez de la Frontera Spain **77** A2 36 41N 6 08W
Jerez de los Caballeros Spain **77** A2 38 20N 6 45W
Jericho Jordan **92** O10 31 51N 35 27E
Jersey *i.* Channel Islands British Isles **78** I6 49 13N 2 07W
Jersey City New Jersey U.S.A. **50** B1 40 44N 74 06W
Jerusalem Israel/Jordan **92** O10 31 47N 35 13E
Jessore Bangladesh **95** F4 23 10N 89 12E
Jevisy-sur-Orge France **83** B1 48 42N 2 22E
Jewett City Connecticut U.S.A. **65** J4 41 37N 71 59W
Jezioro Sniardwy *l.* Poland **80** D5 53 00N 21 00E
Jhang Mghiana Pakistan **95** C6 31 19N 72 22E
Jhansi India **95** D5 25 27N 78 34E
Jhelum Pakistan **95** C6 32 58N 73 45E
Jhelum *r.* Pakistan **95** C6 32 30N 72 30E
Ji'an China **97** M4 27 08N 115 00E
Jiangmen China **97** M3 22 40N 113 05E
Jiamusi China **97** Q8 46 59N 130 29E
Jiaxing China **97** O5 30 15N 120 52E
Jiayuguan China **97** J6 39 47N 98 14E
Jiddah Saudi Arabia **92** E3 21 30N 39 10E
Ješjavrre *l.* Norway **79** E4 69 40N 24 10E
Jihlavà Czechoslovakia **80** C4 49 24N 15 34E
Jijel Algeria **77** D2 36 45N 5 45E
Jilin China **97** P7 43 53N 126 35E
Jiloca *r.* Spain **77** B3 41 08N 1 45W
Jīma Ethiopia **106** M9 7 39N 36 47E
Jim Thorpe Pennsylvania U.S.A. **64** E3 40 52N 75 43W
Jinan China **97** N6 36 41N 117 00E
Jingdezhen China **97** N4 29 17N 117 12E
Jin He *r.* China **101** G1 39 58N 116 16E
Jinhua China **97** N4 29 06N 119 40E
Jining China **97** M7 40 58N 113 01E
Jining China **97** N6 35 25N 116 40E
Jinja Uganda **106** L8 0 27N 33 14E
Jinsha Jiang *(Yangtze) r.* China **97** K4 27 30N 103 00E
Jinxi China **97** O7 40 46N 120 47E
Jinzhou China **97** O7 41 07N 121 06E
Jiparaná *r.* Brazil **68** E11 8 00S 62 30W
Jiujiang China **97** N4 29 41N 116 03E
Jiul *r.* Romania **81** D3 44 00N 24 00E
Jiuxiaqiao China **101** H1 39 59N 116 30E
Jixi China **97** Q8 45 17N 131 00E
Jīzān Saudi Arabia **92** F2 16 56N 42 33E
João Pessoa Brazil **68** J11 7 06S 34 53W
Jodhpur India **95** C5 26 18N 73 08E
Joensuu Finland **79** F3 62 35N 29 46E
Johannesburg Republic of South Africa **107** K2 26 10S 28 02E
John Day *r.* Oregon U.S.A. **62** B5 45 00N 120 00W
John H. Kerr Reservoir U.S.A. **63** K4 36 31N 78 18W
Johnsonburg Pennsylvania U.S.A. **64** B4 41 00N 78 00W
Johnson City New York U.S.A. **64** E5 42 06N 75 57W
Johnson City Tennessee U.S.A. **63** J4 36 20N 82 23W
Johnstown New York U.S.A. **65** F6 43 00N 74 00W
Johnstown Pennsylvania U.S.A. **64** B3 40 20N 78 56W
Johor Baharu Malaysia **99** C4 1 29N 103 44E
Joinville Brazil **69** H7 26 20S 48 55W
Joinville Island Antarctica **117** 63 00S 56 00W
Jokkmokk Sweden **79** D4 66 37N 19 50E
Jonesboro Arkansas U.S.A. **63** H4 35 50N 90 41W
Jonesville Michigan U.S.A. **36** B2 41 59N 84 39W
Jönköping Sweden **79** C2 57 45N 14 10E
Jefferson City Missouri U.S.A. **63** H4 38 33N 92 10W
Joplin Missouri U.S.A. **63** H4 37 04N 94 31W
JORDAN 92 E5
Jordan *r.* Middle East **92** O11 32 15N 32 10E
Jordan Valley *tn.* Hong Kong U.K. **98** C1 22 19N 114 13E
Jos Nigeria **106** G9 9 54N 8 53E
Joseph Bonaparte Gulf Australia **110** D7 14 00S 128 30E
Jos Plateau Nigeria **106** G10 9 30N 8 55E
Jostedalsbreen *glacier* Norway **79** B3 61 40N 7 00E
Jotunheimen *mts.* Norway **79** B3 61 40N 8 00E
Jõunié Lebanon **92** O11 33 58N 35 38E
Juan de Fuca Strait North America **62** B6 48 00N 124 00W
Juàzeiro Brazil **68** I11 9 25S 40 30W
Juàzeiro do Norte Brazil **68** J11 7 10S 39 18W
Juba Sudan **106** L8 4 50N 31 35E
Jubba *r.* Somalia **106** N8 3 00N 42 30E
Jubilee Reservoir Hong Kong U.K. **98** B2 22 24N 114 08E
Júcar *r.* Spain **77** B2 39 08N 1 50W
Juchitán Mexico **66** E3 16 27N 95 05W
Juiz de Fora Brazil **69** I8 21 47S 43 23W
Julijske Alpe *mts.* Europe **81** B4 46 00N 13 00E
Jullundur India **95** D6 31 18N 75 40E
Junagadh India **94** C4 21 32N 70 32E
Junction City Kansas U.S.A. **63** G4 39 02N 96 51W
Jundiaí Brazil **69** H8 23 10S 46 54W
Juneau Alaska U.S.A. **42** B3 58 20N 134 20W
Junggar Pendi *(Dzungarian Basin)* China **96** G7 44 00N 87 30E
Juniata River Pennsylvania U.S.A. **64** C3 40 30N 77 20W
Junk Bay Hong Kong U.K. **98** C1 22 18N 114 15E
Junsele Sweden **79** D3 63 40N 16 55E
Jur *r.* Sudan **106** K9 8 00N 28 00E
Jura *mts.* France/Switzerland **77** D4 46 30N 6 00E
Jura Krakowska *mts.* Poland **80** C5 50 00N 20 00E
Jylland *p.* Denmark **80** A6 55 00N 9 00E
Jyväskylä Finland **79** F3 62 16N 25 50E

K
K2 *(Qogir Feng, Godwin Austen) mt.* China/India **96** E6 35 47N 76 30E
Kabrit Egypt **107** S2 30 16N 32 29E
Kābul Afghanistan **93** K5 34 31N 69 12E
Kabul *r.* Afghanistan **93** K5 34 00N 69 30E
Kabwe Zambia **107** K5 14 29S 28 25E
Kachchh, Gulf of India **94** B4 22 40N 69 30E
Kadmat Island India **95** C2 11 08N 72 46E
Kadoma Zimbabwe **107** K4 18 21N 29 55E
Kaduna Nigeria **106** G10 10 28N 7 25E
Kaduna *r.* Nigeria **106** G9 10 00N 6 30E
Kaédi Mauritania **106** C11 16 12N 13 32W
Kaesŏng South Korea **97** P6 37 59N 126 30E
Kafue Zambia **107** K4 15 44S 28 10E
Kafue *r.* Zambia **107** K4 16 00S 27 00E
Kafue National Park Zambia **107** K5 15 00S 25 30E
Kagan Uzbekistan **90** J2 39 45N 64 32E
Kagoshima Japan **100** B1 31 37N 130 32E
Kahoolawe *i.* Hawaiian Islands **115** Y18 20 30N 156 40W
Kahuku Point Hawaiian Islands **115** Y18 21 42N 158 00W
Kaiapoi New Zealand **111** B2 43 24S 172 40E
Kaifeng China **97** M5 34 47N 114 20E
Kaikohe New Zealand **111** B3 35 25S 173 49E
Kaikoura New Zealand **111** B2 42 24S 173 41E
Kai Kung Leng *mt.* Hong Kong U.K. **98** B2 22 27N 114 04E
Kailash India **94** L4 28 33N 77 15E
Kailua Hawaiian Islands **115** Z17 19 43N 155 59W
Kainan Japan **100** G1 34 09N 135 12E
Kainji Reservoir Nigeria **106** F10 10 25N 4 56E
Kaipara Harbour New Zealand **111** B3 36 40S 174 00E
Kairouan Tunisia **106** H15 35 42N 10 01E
Kaiserslautern Germany **76** D4 49 27N 7 47E
Kaitaia New Zealand **111** B3 35 08S 173 18E
Kaiwi Channel Hawaiian Islands **115** Y18 21 20N 157 30W
Kajaani Finland **79** F3 64 14N 27 37E
Kakamigahara Japan **100** H2 35 23N 136 52E
Kakhovskoye Vodokhranilishche *res.* Ukraine **90** C4 47 30N 35 00E
Kākināda India **95** E3 16 59N 82 20E
Kakogawa Japan **100** F1 34 49N 134 52E
Kalachinsk Russia **91** L6 55 02N 74 40E
Kalae *(South Cape)* Hawaiian Islands **115** Z17 18 58N 155 24W
Kalahari Desert Southern Africa **107** J3 23 30S 23 00E
Kalahari Gemsbok National Park Republic of South Africa **107** I2 26 00S 20 30E
Kalámai Greece **81** D2 37 02N 22 07E
Kalamazoo Michigan U.S.A. **35** C1 42 17N 85 36W
Kalat Pakistan **94** B5 29 01N 66 38E
Kalémié Zaïre **107** K6 5 57S 29 10E
Kalevala Russia **79** G4 65 15N 31 08E
Kalgoorlie Australia **110** C3 30 49S 121 29E
Kaliavesi *l.* Finland **79** F3 63 00N 27 20E
Kalimantan *admin.* Indonesia **99** E3 2 00S 112 00E
Kálimnos *i.* Greece **81** E2 37 00N 26 00E
Kalinin *see* Tver'
Kaliningrad *reg.* Russia **80** D5 54 40N 21 00E
Kaliningrad Russia **80** D5 54 40N 20 30E
Kaliningrad Russia **90** D6 55 56N 37 55E
Kalin Kovichi Belarus **90** B5 52 10N 29 13E
Kalispell Montana U.S.A. **62** D6 48 12N 114 19W
Kalisz Poland **80** C5 51 46N 18 02E
Kalix älv *r.* Sweden **79** E4 66 40N 22 30E
Kalkajl India **94** M4 28 32N 77 16E
Kallsjön *l.* Sweden **79** C3 63 30N 13 05E
Kalmar Sweden **80** C6 56 39N 16 20E
Kalomo Zambia **107** K4 17 02S 26 29E
Kalpeni Island India **95** C2 10 05N 73 15E
Kaluga Russia **90** D5 54 31N 36 16E
Kalundborg Denmark **80** B6 55 42N 11 06E
Kalutara Sri Lanka **95** D1 6 35N 79 59E
Kama *r.* Russia **91** H6 57 00N 55 00E
Kamaishi Japan **100** D2 39 18N 141 52E
Kamakura Japan **101** B2 35 19N 139 33E
Kamarān *i.* Yemen Republic **92** F2 15 21N 42 40E
Kamarhati India **94** K2 22 40N 88 22E
Kambara *i.* Fiji **114** V15 18 57S 178 58W
Kamchatka *p.* Russia **89** R7 57 30N 160 00E
Kamchatka Bay Russia **89** S7 55 00N 164 00E
Kamchiya *r.* Bulgaria **81** E3 43 00N 27 00E
Kamenets Podol'skiy Ukraine **90** B4 48 40N 26 36E
Kamensk-Ural'skiy Russia **91** J6 56 29N 61 49E
Kameoka Japan **100** G2 35 02N 135 35E
Kamet *mt.* India **95** D6 30 55N 79 36E
Kamina Zaïre **107** K6 8 46S 25 00E
Kamogawa Japan **100** M2 35 06N 140 09E
Kampala Uganda **106** L8 0 19N 32 35E
KAMPUCHEA *see* CAMBODIA
Kamskoye Vodokhranilishche *res.* Russia **91** H6 58 30N 56 00E
Kam Tsin Hong Kong U.K. **98** B3 22 30N 114 07E
Kamyshin Russia **90** F5 50 05N 45 24E
Kamyshlov Russia **91** J6 56 55N 62 41E
Kan *r.* Russia **91** P6 56 30N 94 00E
Kanagawa Japan **101** B2 35 29N 139 38E
Kanagawa *pref.* Japan **100** L2 35 25N 139 20E
Kananga Zaïre **107** J6 5 53S 22 26E
Kanazawa Japan **100** C2 36 35N 136 38E
Kanazawa Japan **101** B2 35 20W 139 37E
Kanbe Myanmar **99** B7 16 15N 95 40E
Kanchipuram India **95** D2 12 50N 79 44E
Kānchrāpāra India **94** K3 22 56N 88 26E
Kandahār Afghanistan **93** K5 31 35N 65 45E
Kandalaksha Russia **88** F9 67 09N 32 31E
Kandavu *i.* Fiji **114** U15 19 10S 178 30E
Kandavu Passage *sd.* Fiji **114** U15 18 50S 178 00E
Kandi Benin **106** F10 11 05N 2 59E
Kandla India **94** B4 23 03N 70 11E
Kandy Sri Lanka **95** E1 7 17N 80 40E
Kane Pennsylvania U.S.A. **64** B4 41 40N 78 48W
Kaneohe Hawaiian Islands **115** Y18 21 25N 157 48W
Kaneya Japan **100** B1 31 22N 130 50E
Kangan Iran **93** H4 27 51N 52 07E
Kangar Malaysia **99** C5 6 28N 100 10E
Kangaroo Island Australia **110** F2 35 50S 137 50E
Kangerlussuaq *(Søndre Strømfjord)* Greenland **45** V4 67 00N 50 59W
Kangnŭng South Korea **97** P6 37 48N 127 52E
Kang-shan Taiwan **98** G5 22 45N 120 18E
Kanin Peninsula Russia **88** G9 68 00N 45 00E
Kankakee Illinois U.S.A. **63** I5 41 08N 87 52W
Kankan Guinea **106** D10 10 22N 9 11W
Kanker India **95** E4 20 17N 81 30E
Kannapolis North Carolina U.S.A. **63** J4 35 30N 80 36W
Kano Nigeria **106** G10 12 00N 8 31E
Kanpur India **95** E5 26 27N 80 14E
Kansas *state* U.S.A. **62/63** G4 38 00N 98 00W
Kansas City Missouri U.S.A. **63** H4 39 02N 94 33W
Kansk Russia **91** P6 56 11N 95 48E
Kanye Botswana **107** J3 24 59S 25 19E
Kao-hsiung Taiwan **98** G5 22 36N 120 17E
Kaolack Senegal **106** B10 14 09N 16 08W
Kapaa Hawaiian Islands **115** X19 22 04N 159 20W
Kapfenberg Austria **81** C4 47 27N 15 18E
Kapingamarangi Rise Pacific Ocean **114** F8 3 00N 154 00E
Kaposvár Hungary **81** C4 46 21N 17 49E
Kapsukas *see* Marijampole
Karabük Turkey **92** D7 41 12N 32 36E
Karachi Pakistan **94** B4 24 51N 67 02E
Karaganda Kazakhstan **91** L4 49 53N 73 07E
Karaginskiy *i.* Russia **89** S7 58 00N 164 00E
Karaikkudi India **95** D2 10 04N 78 46E
Karaj Iran **93** H6 35 48N 50 58E
Karak Jordan **92** O10 31 11N 35 42E
Karakoram *mts.* Asia **84** 36 00N 76 00E
Karakoram Pass Kashmir/China **95** D7 35 33N 77 51E
Kara Kum *geog. reg.* Turkmenistan **91** H2/E2 40 00N 60 00E
Karakumskiy Kanal *can.* Turkmenistan **91** J2 37 30N 62 30E
Karama Jordan **92** O10 31 58N 35 34E
Karasburg Namibia **107** I2 28 00S 18 43E
Kara Sea Russia **89** I11/J10 75 00N 70 00E
Karasjok Norway **79** F4 69 27N 25 30E
Karatal *r.* Kazakhstan **91** M4 45 00N 78 00E
Karatau *mts.* Kazakhstan **91** K3 43 00N 70 00E
Karaturgay *r.* Kazakhstan **91** J5 50 00N 65 00E
Karbalā' Iraq **92** F5 32 37N 44 03E
Karcag Hungary **81** D4 47 19N 20 53E
Kariba Dam Zambia/Zimbabwe **107** K4 16 31S 28 50E
Kariba, Lake Zambia/Zimbabwe **107** K4 17 00S 28 00E
Karibib Namibia **107** I3 21 59S 15 51E
Karisimbi, Mount Rwanda/Zaïre **106** K7 1 32S 29 27E
Kariya Japan **100** J1 35 00N 137 00E
Karkinitskiy Zaliv *g.* Ukraine **90** C4 46 00N 32 50E
Karl-Marx-Stadt *see* Chemnitz
Karlino Poland **80** C5 54 02N 15 52E
Karlovac Croatia **81** C4 45 30N 15 34E
Karlovy Vary Czechoslovakia **80** B5 50 13N 12 52E
Karlshamn Sweden **80** B6 56 10N 14 50E
Karlshorst Germany **83** G1 52 28N 13 32E
Karlsruhe Germany **76** D4 49 00N 8 24E
Karlstad Minnesota U.S.A. **39** B1 48 35N 96 31W
Karnafuli Reservoir Bangladesh **95** G4 22 30N 92 20E
Karnal India **95** D5 29 41N 76 58E
Karnataka *admin.* India **95** D2 14 40N 75 30E
Karol Bagh India **94** L4 28 39N 77 11E
Karow Germany **83** F2 52 38N 13 28E
Kárpathos *i.* Greece **81** E2 35 30N 27 12E
Karpenísion Greece **81** D2 38 55N 21 47E
Kars Turkey **92** F7 40 35N 43 05E
Karsakpay Kazakhstan **88** I5 47 47N 66 43E
Karshi Uzbekistan **91** K2 38 53N 65 45E
Kartaly Russia **91** J5 53 06N 60 37E
Karwar India **95** C2 14 50N 74 09E
Kasai Japan **100** F1 34 56N 134 50E
Kasai *r.* Angola/Zaïre **107** I7 4 00S 19 00E
Kasama Zambia **107** L5 10 10S 31 11E
Kasaragod India **95** C2 12 30N 74 59E
Kasese Uganda **106** L8 0 10N 30 06E
Kāshān Iran **93** H5 33 59N 51 35E
Kashi China **96** E6 39 29N 76 02E
Kashihara Japan **100** G1 34 28N 135 46E
Kashima Japan **100** M2 35 58N 140 39E
Kashiwa Japan **100** L2 35 51N 139 58E
Kashiwazaki Japan **100** C2 37 22N 138 33E
Kaskö Finland **79** E3 62 23N 21 10E
Kasli Russia **91** J6 55 54N 60 45E
Kásos *i.* Greece **81** E2 35 00N 28 00E
Kassala Sudan **92** E2 15 24N 36 30E
Kassel Germany **76** E5 51 18N 9 30E
Kasserine Tunisia **81** B2 35 13N 8 43E
Kastoria Greece **81** D3 40 33N 21 15E
Kasugai Japan **100** H2 35 15N 136 57E
Kasukabe Japan **100** L2 35 59N 139 45E
Kasumiga-ura *l.* Japan **100** M3 36 03N 140 20E
Kaśur Pakistan **95** C6 31 07N 74 30E
Kataba Zambia **107** K4 16 02S 25 03E
Katase Japan **101** A2 35 18N 139 30E
Katchall *i.* Nicobar Is. **95** G1 7 30N 93 30E
Katerini Greece **81** D3 40 15N 22 30E
Katha Myanmar **96** J3 24 11N 96 20E
Katherine Australia **110** E7 14 29S 132 20E
Kathiawar *p.* India **94/95** C4 21 10N 71 00E
Kat Hing Wai Hong Kong U.K. **98** B2 22 26N 114 03E
Kathmandu Nepal **95** F5 27 42N 85 19E
Katihar India **95** F5 25 33N 87 34E
Katowice Poland **80** C5 50 15N 18 59E
Katrineholm Sweden **79** D2 58 59N 16 15E
Katsina Ala Nigeria **106** G9 7 10N 9 30E
Katsuura Japan **100** M2 35 10N 140 20E
Kattakurgan Uzbekistan **91** K2 39 54N 66 13E
Kattegat *sd.* Denmark/Sweden **79** C2 57 00N 11 00E
Katun' *r.* Russia **91** O5 51 30N 86 00E
Kauai *i.* Hawaiian Islands **115** X18 22 00N 159 30W
Kauai Channel Hawaiian Islands **115** X18 21 45N 158 50W
Kaula *i.* Hawaiian Islands **115** W18 21 35N 160 40W
Kaulakahi Channel Hawaiian Islands **115** X18 21 58N 159 50W
Kaulsdorf Germany **83** G1 52 29N 13 34E
Kaunas Lithuania **80** D5 54 52N 23 55E
Kau Sai Chau *i.* Hong Kong U.K. **98** C2 22 22N 114 19E
Kau Yi Chau *i.* Hong Kong U.K. **98** B1 22 17N 114 04E
Kavajë Albania **81** C3 41 11N 19 33E
Kavála Greece **81** D3 40 56N 24 25E
Kavaratti Island India **95** C2 10 32N 72 43E
Kawachi-Nagano Japan **100** G1 34 24N 135 32E
Kawagoe Japan **100** L2 35 55N 139 30E
Kawaguchi Japan **101** B4 35 47N 139 44E
Kawaihae Hawaiian Islands **115** Z18 20 02N 155 50W
Kawasaki Japan **101** C3 35 30N 139 45E
Kawawa Japan **101** B3 35 31N 139 33E
Kawerau New Zealand **111** C3 38 03S 176 43E
Kaya Burkina **106** E10 13 04N 1 09W
Kayes Mali **106** C10 14 26N 11 28W
Kayseri Turkey **92** E6 38 42N 35 28E
Kazach'ye Russia **89** P10 70 46N 136 15E
KAZAKHSTAN 91 H4/N4
Kazakh Upland Kazakhstan **91** M4 47 00N 75 00E
Kazan' Russia **90** F6 55 45N 49 10E
Kazanlŭk Bulgaria **81** E3 42 37N 25 23E
Kazatin Ukraine **80** E4 49 41N 28 49E
Kāzerūn Iran **93** H4 29 35N 51 40E
Kazym *r.* Russia **91** K7 63 00N 67 30E
Kéa *i.* Greece **81** D2 37 00N 24 00E
Keansburg New Jersey U.S.A. **65** F3 40 27N 74 08W
Kearney Nebraska U.S.A. **62** G5 40 42N 99 04W
Kearny New Jersey U.S.A. **50** B2 40 45N 74 07W
Kecskemét Hungary **81** C4 46 56N 19 43E
Kediri Indonesia **99** E2 7 45S 112 01E
Keene New Hampshire U.S.A. **65** H5 42 55N 72 17W
Keetmanshoop Namibia **107** I2 26 36S 18 08E
Kefallinia *i.* Greece **81** D2 38 00N 20 00E
Keflavik Iceland **79** H6 64 01N 22 35W
Keihoku Japan **100** G2 35 09N 135 37E
Kei Ling Ha Lo Wai Hong Kong U.K. **98** C2 22 25N 114 16E
Kei Lun Wai Hong Kong U.K. **98** A2 22 24N 113 58E
Keitele *l.* Finland **79** F3 63 10N 26 24E
K'elafo Ethiopia **106** N9 5 37N 44 10E
Kelkit *r.* Turkey **92** E7 40 20N 37 40E
Kells Irish Republic **78** E5 53 44N 6 53W
Kemerovo Russia **91** O6 55 25N 86 05E
Kemi Finland **79** E4 65 46N 24 34E
Kemijärvi *l.* Finland **79** F4 66 42N 27 30E
Kemijöki *r.* Finland **79** F4 66 00N 25 00E
Kempten Germany **76** E4 47 44N 10 19E
Kemsing England **82** D2 51 18N 0 14E
Kenai Alaska U.S.A. **10** E5 60 35N 151 19W
Kendal England **78** I6 54 20N 2 45W
Kendari Indonesia **99** G3 3 57S 122 36E
Kenema Sierra Leone **106** C9 7 57N 11 11W
Kengtung Myanmar **97** J3 21 16N 99 39E
Keningau Malaysia **99** F5 5 21N 116 11E
Kénitra Morocco **106** D14 34 20N 6 34W
Kenmare North Dakota U.S.A. **40** C1 48 40N 102 05W
Kennebec River Maine U.S.A. **33** B1 44 00N 69 00W
Kennebunk Maine U.S.A. **65** K6 43 24N 70 33W
Kennedy New York U.S.A. **64** A5 42 10N 79 07W
Kennedy Town Hong Kong U.K. **98** B1 22 17N 114 07E
Kennobec River Maine U.S.A. **37** R6 45 20N 70 00W
Kenosha Wisconsin U.S.A. **63** I5 42 34N 87 50W
Kensington *bor.* Inner London England **82** C3 51 29N 0 10W
Kent Connecticut U.S.A. **65** G4 41 43N 73 28W
Kent *co.* England **82** D2 51 10N 0 00E
Kenthurst Australia **111** F3 33 40S 151 01E
Kenting National Park Taiwan **98** G5 22 00N 120 50E
Kentucky *state* U.S.A. **63** I4 37 00N 85 00W
KENYA 106 M8
Kenya, Mount *see* Kirinyaga
Kepulauan Anambas *is.* Indonesia **99** D4 3 00N 106 40E
Kepulauan Aru *is.* Indonesia **99** I2 7 00S 134 00E
Kepulauan Kai *is.* Indonesia **99** I2 5 30S 133 00E
Kepulauan Lingga *is.* Indonesia **99** C3 0 30S 104 00E
Kepulauan Mentawai *is.* Indonesia **99** B3 2 00S 99 00E
Kepulauan Obi *is.* Indonesia **99** H3 1 40S 127 30E
Kepulauan Riau *is.* Indonesia **99** C4 1 00N 104 20E
Kepulauan Sangir *is.* Indonesia **99** H4 2 30N 125 20E
Kepulauan Sula *is.* Indonesia **99** G3/H3 2 00S 125 00E
Kepulauan Talaud *is.* Indonesia **99** H4 4 00N 126 50E
Kepulauan Tanimbar *is.* Indonesia **99** I2 7 30S 132 00E
Kerala *admin.* India **95** D2 10 10N 76 30E
Kerch' Ukraine **90** D4 45 22N 36 27E
Kerema Papua New Guinea **110** H8 7 59S 145 46E
Keren Ethiopia **92** E2 15 46N 38 30E
Kerguelen Plateau Indian Ocean **112** G1/H1 55 00S 80 00E
Kerikeri New Zealand **111** B3 35 12S 173 59E
Kerki Turkmenistan **91** K2 37 53N 65 10E
Kérkira *(Corfu) i.* Greece **81** C2 39 00N 19 00E
Kérkira Greece **81** C2 39 38N 19 55E
Kermadec Islands Pacific Ocean **114** I5 30 00S 178 30W
Kermadec Trench Pacific Ocean **114** I4 33 00S 177 00W
Kermān Iran **93** I5 30 18N 57 05E
Kermānshāh Iran **93** G5 34 19N 47 04E
Kerme Körfezi *b.* Turkey **80** E2 37 00N 27 00E
Kerrville Texas U.S.A. **62** G3 30 03N 99 09W
Kert *r.* Morocco **77** B2 35 00N 3 30W
Kerulen *r.* Mongolia **97** M8 47 30N 112 30E
Keşan Turkey **80** E3 40 52N 26 37E
Ket' *r.* Russia **91** O6 58 30N 86 30E
Ketapang Indonesia **99** E3 1 50S 109 59E
Ketchikan Alaska U.S.A. **42** B3 55 25N 131 40W
Ketrzyn Poland **80** D5 54 05N 21 24E
Kettwig Germany **76** H2 51 22N 6 55E
Keuka Lake New York U.S.A. **64** C5 42 30N 77 10W
Kevin Montana U.S.A. **41** C1 48 44N 111 58W
Keweenaw Bay Michigan U.S.A. **35** C2 46 50N 88 20W
Keweenaw Peninsula Michigan U.S.A. **63** I6 47 00N 88 00W
Khabarovsk Russia **89** P5 48 32N 135 08E
Khairpur Pakistan **93** K4 27 30N 68 50E
Khalig el Tina Egypt **107** T4 31 08N 32 36E
Khalkidhikí *p.* Greece **81** D3 40 30N 23 00E
Khalkis Greece **81** D2 38 28N 23 36E
Khambhat India **95** C4 22 19N 72 39E
Khambhat, Gulf of India **95** C4 20 30N 72 00E
Khamman India **95** E3 17 16N 80 13E
Khānābad Afghanistan **93** K6 36 42N 69 08E
Khānaqīn Iraq **93** G5 34 22N 45 22E
Khandwa India **95** D4 21 49N 76 23E
Khaniá Greece **81** D2 35 31N 24 01E
Khanty-Mansiysk Russia **89** I8 61 01N 69 00E
Khān Yūnis Israel **92** O10 31 21N 34 18E
Kharagpur India **95** F4 22 23N 87 22E
Kharan Pakistan **94** B5 28 35N 65 26E
Khardah India **94** K2 22 43N 88 23E
Khārg Island Iran **93** H4 29 14N 50 20E

Khar'kov Ukraine **90** D5 50 00N 36 15E
Khartoum Sudan **92** D2 15 33N 32 35E
Khāsh Iran **93** J4 28 14N 61 15E
Khash *r.* Afghanistan **93** J5 31 30N 62 30E
Khashm el Girba Sudan **92** E1 14 59N 35 59E
Khaskovo Bulgaria **81** E3 41 57N 25 32E
Khatanga Russia **89** M10 71 59N 102 31E
Khatanga *r.* Russia **89** M10 72 30N 102 30E
Khemisset Morocco **106** D14 33 50N 6 03W
Khenchela Algeria **77** D2 35 22N 7 09E
Kherson Ukraine **90** C4 46 39N 32 38E
Kheta *r.* Russia **89** L10 71 30N 95 00E
Khilok *r.* Russia **89** M6 51 00N 107 30E
Khimki Russia **88** L2 55 56N 37 26E
Khimki-Khovrino Russia **88** L2 55 56N 37 30E
Khimki Reservoir Russia **88** L2 55 54N 37 28E
Khios Greece **81** E2 38 23N 26 07E
Khios *i.* Greece **81** E2 38 00N 26 00E
Khiva Uzbekistan **91** J3 41 25N 60 49E
Khmel'nitskiy Ukraine **90** B4 49 25N 26 59E
Khodzheyli Uzbekistan **91** H3 42 25N 59 25E
Kholmsk Russia **89** Q5 47 02N 142 03E
Khon Kaen Thailand **99** C7 16 25N 102 50E
Khoper *r.* Russia **90** 50 00N 40 00E
Khorochevo Russia **88** L2 55 47N 37 30E
Khorog Tajikistan **91** L2 37 22N 71 32E
Khorramābād Iran **93** G5 33 29N 48 21E
Khorramshahr Iran **93** G5 30 25N 48 09E
Khotin Ukraine **80** E4 48 30N 26 31E
Khouribga Morocco **106** D14 32 54N 6 57W
Khrebet Kopet-Dag' *can.* Iran/Turkmenistan **91** H2 38 30N 57 00E
Khrishnapur Canal India **94** K2 22 34N 88 27E
Khujand *(Leninabad)* Tadjikistan **91** K3 40 14N 69 40E
Khulna Bangladesh **95** F4 22 49N 89 34E
Khyber Pass Afghanistan/Pakistan **93** L5 34 06N 71 05E
Kiantajärvi *l.* Finland **79** F4 65 02N 29 00E
Kibombo Zaïre **107** K7 3 58S 25 54E
Kiel Germany **76** E5 54 20N 10 08E
Kielce Poland **80** D5 50 51N 20 39E
Kieta Papua New Guinea **110** J8 6 15S 155 37E
Kiev *see* Kiyev
Kigali Rwanda **106** L7 1 56S 30 04E
Kigoma Tanzania **107** K7 4 52S 29 36E
Kii-Nagashima Japan **100** H1 34 11N 136 19E
Kii-sanchi *mts.* Japan **100** G1 34 15N 135 50E
Kii-suidō *sd.* Japan **100** B1 34 00N 134 45E
Kikinda Serbia Yugoslavia **81** D4 45 50N 20 30E
Kikori Papua New Guinea **110** G8 7 25S 144 13E
Kikwit Zaïre **107** I6 5 02S 18 51E
Kilanea Hawaiian Islands **115** X19 22 05N 159 35W
Kilimanjaro *mt.* Tanzania **106** M7 3 04S 37 22E
Kilkenny Kilkenny Irish Republic **78** D4 52 39N 7 15W
Kilkís Greece **81** D3 40 59N 22 52E
Killarney Kerry Irish Republic **78** B4 52 03N 9 30W
Killeen Texas U.S.A. **63** G3 31 08N 97 44W
Kilmarnock Strathclyde Scotland **78** G7 55 36N 4 30W
Kiltan Island India **95** C2 11 30N 73 00E
Kilwa Masoko Tanzania **107** M6 8 55S 39 31E
Kilyos Turkey **80** E3 41 14N 29 02E
Kimberley Republic of South Africa **107** J2 28 45S 24 46E
Kimberley Plateau Australia **110** D6 17 30S 126 00E
Kimitsu Japan **100** L2 35 19N 139 53E
Kindia Guinea **106** C10 10 03N 12 49W
Kindu Zaïre **107** K7 3 00S 25 56E
Kineshma Russia **90** E6 57 28N 42 08E
King George Island South Shetland Islands **69** F0 62 00S 58 00W
King George's Reservoir Essex England **82** C3 51 39N 0 01W
King Island Australia **110** G2 40 00S 144 00E
Kingisepp see Kuressaare
Kingman Arizona U.S.A. **62** D4 35 12N 114 02W
King Sejong *r.s.* Antarctica **117** 62 13S 58 45W
Kingsgrove Australia **111** G2 33 57S 151 06E
Kings Langley Hertfordshire England **82** B3 51 43N 0 28W
King's Lynn Norfolk England **78** L4 52 45N 0 24E
King Sound Australia **110** C6 16 00S 123 00E
Kings Point *tn.* New York U.S.A. **50** C2 40 49N 73 45W
Kingsport Tennessee U.S.A. **63** J4 36 33N 82 34W
Kingston Jamaica **67** R7 17 58N 76 48W
Kingston Massachusetts U.S.A. **65** K4 42 00N 70 44W
Kingston New Hampshire U.S.A. **65** J5 42 55N 71 02W
Kingston New York U.S.A. **65** G4 41 55N 74 00W
Kingston upon Hull Humberside England **78** K5 53 45N 0 20W
Kingstonupon Thames *bor.* Greater London England **82** B2 51 25N 0 18W
Kingstown St. Vincent & The Grenadines **67** L2 13 12N 61 14W
Kingsville Texas U.S.A. **63** G2 27 32N 97 53W
Kinkala Congo **107** H7 4 18S 14 49E
Kino *r.* Japan **100** G1 34 15N 135 30E
Kinshasa Zaïre **107** I7 4 18S 15 18E
Kiparissiakós Kólpos *g.* Greece **81** D2 37 00N 21 00E
Kipili Tanzania **107** L6 7 30S 30 39E
Kirchhörde Germany **76** K2 51 27N 7 27E
Kirensk Russia **89** M7 57 45N 108 02E
KIRGHIZIA *see* KIRGYZSTAN
Kirghiz Step' *geog. reg.* Kazakhstan **90/1** H4 49 00N 55 00E
KIRGYZSTAN *(KIRGHIZIA)* **91** L3/M3
KIRIBATI Pacific Ocean **114** H8
Kirikiri Nigeria **107** V3 6 22N 3 22E
Kirikkale Turkey **92** D6 39 51N 33 32E
Kirinyaga *(Mount Kenya) mt.* Kenya **106** M7 0 10S 37 19E
Kiritimati Island Kiribati **115** K8 2 10N 157 00W
Kirkağaç Turkey **80** E2 39 06N 27 40E
Kirkcaldy Fife Scotland **78** H8 56 07N 3 10W
Kirkcudbright Dumfries and Galloway Scotland **78** G6 54 50N 4 03W
Kirkládhes *(Cyclades) is.* Greece **81** D2 37 00N 25 00E
Kirklareli Turkey **80** E3 41 45N 27 12E
Kirkūk Iraq **92** F6 35 28N 44 26E
Kirkwall Orkney Islands Scotland **78** H10 58 59N 2 58W
Kirov Russia **90** F6 58 00N 49 38E
Kirovabad *see* Gyandzha
Kirovakan Armenia **90** E3 40 49N 44 30E
Kirovo-Chepetsk *r.* Russia **90** G6 58 30N 51 00E
Kirovograd Ukraine **90** C4 48 31N 32 15E
Kirti Nagar India **94** L4 28 39N 77 09E
Kiruna Sweden **79** E4 67 53N 20 15E
Kiryū Japan **100** C2 36 26N 139 18E
Kisangani Zaïre **106** K8 0 33N 25 14E
Kisarazu Japan **101** C2 35 22N 139 55E
Kiselevsk' Russia **91** O5 54 01N 86 41E
Kishinev Moldova **90** B4 47 00N 28 50E
Kishiwada Japan **100** G1 34 28N 135 22E
Kiskunfélegyháza Hungary **81** C4 46 42N 19 52E
Kiskunhalas Hungary **81** C4 46 26N 19 29E
Kislovodsk Russia **90** E3 43 56N 42 44E
Kismaayo Somalia **106** N7 0 25S 42 31E
Kisumu Kenya **106** L7 0 08S 34 47E
Kita Japan **101** B4 35 46N 139 43E
Kita-Kyūshū Japan **100** B1 33 52N 130 49E
Kitami Japan **100** D3 43 51N 143 54E
Kita-ura *l.* Japan **100** M3 36 02N 140 33E
Kithira *i.* Greece **81** D2 36 00N 23 00E
Kithnos *i.* Greece **81** D2 37 00N 24 00E
Kitridge Point Barbados **66** W12 13 08N 59 22W
Kittery Maine U.S.A. **65** K6 43 05N 70 45W
Kitwe Zambia **107** K5 0 08S 30 30E
Kitzbühel Austria **81** B4 47 27N 12 23E
Kivu, Lake Zaïre/Rwanda **106** K7 2 00S 29 00E
Kiyev *(Kiev)* Ukraine **90** C5 50 25N 30 30E
Kiyose Japan **101** B4 35 46N 139 32E
Kızıl Irmak *r.* Turkey **92** D7 40 30N 34 00E
Kizlyar Russia **90** F3 43 51N 46 43E
Kizyl Arvat Turkmenistan **91** H2 39 00N 56 23E
Kladno Czechoslovakia **80** B5 50 10N 14 07E
Kladow Germany **83** E1 52 27N 13 08E
Klagenfurt Austria **81** B4 46 38N 14 20E
Klaipėda Lithuania **80** D8 55 43N 21 07E
Klamath *r.* U.S.A. **62** B5 42 00N 123 00W
Klamath Falls *tn.* Oregon U.S.A. **62** B5 42 14N 121 47W
Klarälven *r.* Sweden **79** C3 60 45N 13 00E
Klatovy Czechoslovakia **80** B4 49 24N 13 17E
Kleine Emscher *can.* Germany **76** G3 51 35N 6 45E
Kleinmachnow Germany **83** E1 52 24N 13 13E
Klerksdorp Republic of South Africa **107** K2 26 52S 26 39E
Klintehamn Sweden **80** C6 57 24N 18 14E
Kłodzko Poland **80** C5 50 28N 16 40E
Klöfta Norway **79** C3 60 04N 11 06E
Klyazma *r.* Russia **90** E6 56 00N 42 00E
Klyuchevskaya Sopka *mt.* Russia **89** S7 56 03N 160 38E
Knokke-Heist Belgium **76** C5 51 21N 3 19E
Knossós *hist. site* Greece **92** C6 35 18N 25 10E
Knoxville Tennessee U.S.A. **63** J4 36 00N 83 57W
Kōbe Japan **100** G1 34 40N 135 12E
København *(Copenhagen)* Denmark **80** B6 55 43N 12 34E
Koblenz Germany **76** D5 50 21N 7 36E
Kobrin Belarus **90** A5 52 16N 24 22E
Kobuk *r.* Alaska U.S.A. **10** D6 67 00N 157 30W
Koca *r.* Turkey **80** E2 39 00N 27 00E
Koch Bihār India **95** F5 26 18N 89 32E
Kōchi Japan **100** B1 33 33N 133 32E
Kochubey Russia **90** F3 44 25N 46 33E
Kodaira Japan **101** A3 35 44N 139 28E
Kodiak Alaska U.S.A. **10** E4 57 49N 152 30W
Kodiak Island Alaska U.S.A. **10** E4 57 20N 153 40W
Kodok Sudan **106** L9 9 51N 32 07E
Koforidua Ghana **106** E9 6 01N 0 12W
Kofu Japan **100** C2 35 42N 138 34E
Koga Japan **100** L3 36 12N 139 42E
Koganei Japan **101** B3 35 42N 139 30E
Kohat Pakistan **95** C6 33 37N 71 30E
Koh-i-Mazar *mt.* Afghanistan **93** K5 32 30N 66 23E
Kohoku Japan **101** B3 35 30N 139 39E
Kohtla-Järve Estonia **79** F2 59 28N 27 20E
Kokand Uzbekistan **91** L3 40 33N 70 55E
Kokawa Japan **100** G1 34 16N 135 24E
Kokchetav Kazakhstan **91** K5 53 18N 69 25E
Kokkola Finland **79** E3 62 45N 30 06E
Kokomo Indiana U.S.A. **63** I5 40 30N 86 09W
Kola Peninsula Russia **88** F9 67 30N 37 30E
Kolar Gold Fields *tn.* India **95** D2 12 54N 78 16E
Kolding Denmark **67** B2 55 29N 9 30E
Kolguyev *i.* Russia **88** G9 69 00N 49 30E
Kolhapur India **95** C3 16 40N 74 20E
Kolin Czechoslovakia **80** C5 50 02N 15 11E
Köln *(Cologne)* Germany **76** D5 50 56N 6 57E
Kołobrzeg Poland **80** C5 54 10N 15 35E
Kolomna Russia **90** D6 55 05N 38 45E
Kolomyya Ukraine **80** E4 48 31N 25 00E
Kolpashevo Russia **91** N6 58 21N 82 59E
Kolpino Russia **90** C6 59 44N 30 39E
Kolvereid Norway **79** C3 64 53N 11 35E
Kolwezi Zaïre **107** K5 10 45S 25 25E
Kolyma *r.* Russia **89** R9 66 30N 152 00E
Kolyma *(Gydan)* **Range** *mts.* Russia **89** R8 63 00N 160 00E
Kolyma Lowland Russia **89** R9 69 00N 155 00E
Komae Japan **101** B3 35 38N 139 36E
Komaki Japan **100** H2 35 18N 136 54E
Komandorskiye Ostrova *is.* Russia **114** G13 55 00N 166 30E
Komárno Czechoslovakia **81** C4 47 46N 18 05E
Komatsu Japan **100** C2 36 25N 136 27E
Kommunarsk Ukraine **90** D4 48 30N 38 47E
Komotini Greece **81** E3 41 06N 25 25E
Kompong Cham Cambodia **99** D6 11 59N 105 26E
Kompong Chhnang Cambodia **99** C6 12 16N 104 39E
Kompong Som Cambodia **99** C6 11 03N 103 41E
Komsomol'sk-na-Amure Russia **89** P6 50 32N 136 59E
Konda *r.* Russia **91** J7 60 00N 65 00E
Kondüz Afghanistan **93** K6 36 45N 68 51E
Kongola Zaïre **107** K6 5 20S 27 00E
Königsheide Germany **83** F1 52 27N 13 28E
Königs Wusterhausen Germany **83** G1 52 18N 13 37E
Konin Poland **80** C5 52 12N 18 12E
Konnagar India **94** K2 22 42N 88 20E
Konosha Russia **90** E7 60 58N 40 08E
Konotop Ukraine **90** C5 51 15N 33 14E
Konstantinovka Ukraine **90** D4 48 33N 37 45E
Konstanz Germany **77** D4 47 40N 9 10E
Konya Turkey **92** D6 37 51N 32 30E
Koocanusa, Lake Montana U.S.A. **43** E1 48 55N 115 10W
Köpenick Germany **83** G1 52 27N 13 36E
Koper Slovenia **81** B4 45 31N 13 44E
Kopeysk Russia **91** J6 55 08N 61 39E
Kopychintsy Ukraine **80** E4 49 10N 25 58E
Korçë Albania **81** D3 40 38N 20 44E
Korčula *i.* Croatia **81** C3 43 00N 17 00E
Korea Bay China/North Korea **97** N6 39 00N 124 00E
Korea Strait South Korea/Japan **97** P5/Q5 33 00N 129 00E
Korhogo Côte d'Ivoire **106** D9 9 22N 5 31W
Korinthiakós Kólpos *g.* Greece **81** D2 38 00N 22 00E
Kórinthos Greece **81** D2 37 56N 22 55E
Kōriyama Japan **100** D2 37 23N 140 22E
Korla China **96** G7 41 48N 86 10E
Koro *i.* Fiji **114** U16 17 20S 179 25E
Koro Sea Fiji **114** U16 17 35S 180 00E
Korosten Ukraine **90** B5 51 00N 28 30E
Korsakov Russia **89** Q5 46 36N 142 50E
Kortrijk *(Courtrai)* Belgium **76** C5 50 50N 3 17E
Koryak Range *mts.* Russia **89** T8 62 00N 170 00E
Kos *i.* Greece **81** E2 36 00N 27 00E
Kosciusko Island Alaska U.S.A. **42** B3 56 00N 133 45W
Kosciusko, Mount Australia **110** H2 36 28S 148 17E
Koshigaya Japan **100** L2 35 54N 139 47E
Kosti Sudan **92** D1 13 11N 32 28E
Kostroma Russia **90** E6 57 46N 40 59E
Kostrzyn Poland **80** B5 52 35N 14 40E
Koszalin Poland **80** C5 54 10N 16 10E
Košice Czechoslovakia **80** D4 48 44N 21 15E
Kota India **95** D5 25 11N 75 58E
Kota Baharu Malaysia **99** C5 6 07N 102 15E
Kota Kinabalu Malaysia **99** F5 5 59N 116 04E
Kotka Finland **79** F3 60 26N 26 55E
Kotlas Russia **90** F7 61 15N 46 35E
Kōtō Japan **101** C3 35 40N 139 49E
Kotri Pakistan **94** B5 25 22N 68 18E
Kotto *r.* Central African Republic **106** J9 7 00N 22 30E
Kotuy *r.* Russia **89** M9 67 30N 102 00E
Kotzebue Alaska U.S.A. **10** C6 66 51N 162 40W
Kotzebue Sound Alaska U.S.A. **10** C6 66 40N 162 20W
Koudougou Burkina **106** E10 12 15N 2 23W
Koulamoutou Gabon **106** H7 1 12S 12 29E
Koulikoro Mali **106** D10 12 55N 7 31W
Koumra Chad **106** I9 8 56N 17 32E
Kounradskiy Kazakhstan **91** L4 46 58N 74 59E
Kourou French Guiana **68** G14 5 08N 52 37W
Kouvola Finland **79** F3 60 54N 26 45E
Kovel' Ukraine **90** A5 51 12N 24 48E
Kovrov Russia **90** E6 56 23N 41 21E
Kovzha *r.* Russia **90** D7 61 00N 37 00E
Kowloon Hong Kong U.K. **98** C1 22 19N 114 11E
Kowloon City Hong Kong U.K. **98** C2 22 20N 114 11E
Kowloon Peak Hong Kong U.K. **98** C2 22 20N 114 13E
Koyukuk *r.* Alaska U.S.A. **44** A4 66 00N 154 00W
Kozáni Greece **81** D3 40 18N 21 48E
Kpalimé Togo **106** E9 6 55N 0 44E
Kragujevac Serbia Yugoslavia **81** D3 44 01N 20 55E
Kra, Isthmus of Asia **84** 10 00N 104 00E
Kraków Poland **80** C5 50 03N 19 55E
Kraljevo Serbia Yugoslavia **81** D3 43 44N 20 41E
Kramatorsk Ukraine **90** D4 48 43N 37 33E
Kranj Slovenia **81** B4 46 15N 14 20E
Krasnodar Russia **90** D4 45 02N 39 00E
Krasnovodsk Turkmenistan **90** G3 40 01N 53 00E
Krasnoyarsk Russia **91** P6 56 05N 92 46E
Krasnoyarskoye Vodokhranilishche *res.* Russia **91** P5 55 00N 91 00E
Krasny Stroitel Russia **88** M1 55 31N 37 08E
Krasnyy Kut Russia **90** F5 50 58N 47 00E
Krasnyy Luch Ukraine **90** D4 48 10N 39 00E
Kremenchug Ukraine **90** C4 49 03N 33 25E
Kremenchugskoye Vodokranilishche *res.* Ukraine **90** C4 49 30N 32 30E
Kremenets Ukraine **80** E5 50 05N 25 48E
Krems Austria **81** C4 48 25N 15 36E
Kreuzberg Germany **83** F2 52 30N 13 24E
Kribi Cameroon **106** H8 2 56N 9 56E
Krim *(Crimea) p.* Ukraine **90** C4 46 00N 34 00E
Krishna *r.* India **95** D3 16 00N 79 00E
Kristiansand Norway **79** B2 58 08N 8 01E
Kristianstad Sweden **79** C2 56 02N 14 10E
Kristiansund Norway **79** B3 63 06N 7 58E
Kristinehamn Sweden **80** B6 59 17N 14 09E
Kriti *(Crete) i.* Greece **81** D1 35 00N 25 00E
Krivoy Rog Ukraine **90** C4 47 55N 33 24E
Krk *i.* Croatia **81** B4 45 00N 14 00E
Krosno Poland **80** D4 49 40N 21 46E
Kruger National Park Republic of South Africa **107** L3 24 00S 32 00E
Krung Thep *see* Bangkok
Kruševac Serbia Yugoslavia **81** D3 43 34N 21 20E
Krušnéhory *see* Erzgebirge
Kruzof Island Alaska U.S.A. **42** A3 57 15N 135 40W
Ksar-el-Kebir Morocco **77** A2 35 04N 5 56W
Kuala Lumpur Malaysia **99** C4 3 08N 101 42E
Kuala Terengganu Malaysia **99** C5 5 30N 103 07E
Kuangfu Taiwan **98** H6 23 40N 121 25E
Kuantan Malaysia **99** C4 3 50N 103 19E
Kuban' *r.* Russia **90** E4 45 00N 41 00E
Kubiri Japan **101** B1 35 13N 139 42E
Kuching Malaysia **99** E4 1 32N 110 20E
Kudat Malaysia **99** F5 6 54N 116 47E
Kuhumo Finland **79** F3 64 04N 29 30E
Kuito Angola **107** I5 12 25S 16 56E
Kuiu Island Alaska U.S.A. **42** B3 56 45N 134 00W
Kujūkuri-hama *beach* Japan **100** M2 35 30N 140 30E
Kujū-san *mt.* Japan **100** B1 33 07N 131 14E
Kukës Albania **81** D3 42 05N 20 24E
Kuki Japan **100** L3 36 03N 139 41E
Kuldiga Latvia **79** E2 56 58N 21 58E
Kulundinskaya Step' *geog. reg.* Russia **91** M5 52 00N 80 00E
Kuma *r.* Russia **90** E4 45 00N 45 00E
Kumagaya Japan **100** C2 36 09N 139 22E
Kumairi *(Leninakan)* Armenia **90** E3 40 47N 43 49E
Kumamoto Japan **100** B1 32 50N 130 42E
Kumanovo Macedonia Yugoslavia **81** D3 42 07N 21 40E
Kumasi Ghana **106** E9 6 45N 1 35W
Kumba Cameroon **106** G8 4 39N 9 26E
Kumbakonam India **95** D2 10 59N 79 24E
Kumukahi, Cape Hawaiian Islands **115** Z17 19 30N 154 50W
Kumul *see* Hami
Kunar *r.* Asia **93** L5 35 30N 71 20E
Kunashir *i.* Russia **100** E3 44 30N 146 20E
Kungrad Uzbekistan **91** H3 43 06N 58 54E
Kunlun Shan *mts.* China **96** F6/G6 36 30N 85 00E
Kunming China **97** K4 25 04N 102 41E
Kunming Hu *l.* China **101** G2 40 00N 116 15E
Kunsan South Korea **97** P6 35 57N 126 42E
Kuntsevo Russia **88** L1 55 43N 37 25E
Kununurra Australia **110** D6 15 42S 128 50E
Kuopio Finland **79** F3 62 54N 27 40E
Kupa *r.* Croatia **81** C4 45 30N 15 00E
Kupang Indonesia **99** G1 10 13S 123 38E
Kupferdreh Germany **76** J2 51 24N 7 06E
Kupreanof Island Alaska U.S.A. **42** B3 56 50N 133 30W
Kura *r.* Azerbaijan **88** G4 41 00N 47 30E
Kurashiki Japan **100** B1 34 36N 133 43E
Kurchum *r.* Kazakhstan **91** N4 49 00N 85 00E
Kure Japan **100** B1 34 14N 132 32E
Kuressaare *(Kingissepp)* Estonia **79** E2 59 22N 28 40E
Kureyka *r.* Russia **89** L9 67 30N 91 00E
Kurgan Russia **91** K6 55 30N 65 20E
Kuria Muria Islands Oman **93** I2 17 30N 56 00E
Kurihama Japan **101** B1 35 12N 139 41E
Kurikka Finland **79** E3 62 36N 22 25E
Kuril Islands Russia **89** R5/R6 50 00N 155 00E
Kuril Ridge Pacific Ocean **114** F12 47 50N 152 00E
Kuril Trench Pacific Ocean **114** F12 45 40N 154 00E
Ku-ring-gai Chase National Park Australia **111** G3 33 40S 151 00E
Kurnell Australia **111** G1 34 01S 151 12E
Kurnool India **95** D3 15 51N 78 01E
Kursk Russia **90** D5 51 45N 36 14E
Kurskiy Zaliv *g.* Russia **80** D6 55 00N 21 00E
Kurume Japan **100** B1 33 20N 130 29E
Kusatsu Japan **100** G2 35 02N 135 59E
Kushida-gawa *r.* Japan **100** H1 34 23N 136 15E
Kushiro Japan **100** D3 42 58N 144 24E
Kushka Afghanistan **93** J6 35 14N 62 15E
Kushva Russia **91** H6 58 20N 59 48E
Kuskokwim *r.* Alaska U.S.A. **10** C5 61 30N 160 45W
Kuskokwim Bay Alaska U.S.A. **10** C4 58 50N 164 00W
Kuskokwim Mountains Alaska U.S.A. **10** D5 62 00N 158 00W
Kustanay Kazakhstan **91** J5 53 15N 63 40E
Kütahya Turkey **92** C6 39 25N 29 56E
Kutaisi Georgia **90** E3 42 15N 42 44E
Kutno Poland **80** C5 52 13N 19 20E
Kutztown Pennsylvania U.S.A. **64** E3 40 32N 74 46W
Kuusamo Finland **79** F4 65 57N 29 15E
Kuvango Angola **107** I5 14 27S 16 20E
KUWAIT **93** G4
Kuwana Japan **100** H2 35 04N 136 40E
Kuybyshev *see* Samara
Kuytun China **96** F7 44 30N 85 00E
Kuzbass *geog. reg.* Russia **91** O5/6 55 00N 87 00E
Kuzey Anadolu Dağlari *mts.* Turkey **92** E7 41 15N 36 20E
Kuz'minki Russia **88** N1 55 41N 37 45E
Kwai Chung Hong Kong U.K. **98** B2 22 22N 114 07E
Kwangju South Korea **96** P6 35 07N 126 52E
Kwango *r.* Zaïre **107** I6 6 00S 17 00E
Kwan Tei Hong Kong U.K. **98** B3 22 31N 114 09E
Kwekwe *(Que Que)* Zimbabwe **107** K4 18 55S 29 49E
Kwethluk Alaska U.S.A. **10** C5 60 46N 161 34W
Kwigillingok Alaska U.S.A. **10** C4 59 50N 163 10W
Kwilu *r.* Zaïre **107** I6 6 00S 19 00E
Kwun Tong Hong Kong U.K. **98** C1 22 18N 114 13E
Kwu Tung Hong Kong U.K. **98** B3 22 30N 114 06E
Kyaukpyu Myanmar **95** G3 19 27N 93 33E
Kyle of Lochalsh Scotland **78** F9 57 17N 5 43W
Kyoga, Lake Uganda **106** L8 2 00N 34 00E
Kyoga-misaki *c.* Japan **100** C2 35 48N 135 12E
Kyōto Japan **100** G2 35 02N 135 45E
Kyronjöki *r.* Finland **79** E3 63 00N 21 30E
Kyūshū *i.* Japan **100** B1 32 20N 131 00E
Kyūshū-Palau Ridge Pacific Ocean **114** D9 15 00N 135 00E
Kyustendil Bulgaria **81** D3 42 16N 22 40E
Kyzyl Russia **89** L6 51 45N 94 28E
Kyzyl Kum *desert* Kazakhstan/Uzbekistan **91** J3 43 00N 65 00E
Kzyl-Orda Kazakhstan **91** K3 44 25N 65 28E

L

Laascaanood Somalia **106** O9 8 35N 46 55E
La Asunción Venezuela **67** L2 11 06 N 63 53W
Laayoune *(El Aaiún)* Western Sahara **106** C13 27 10N 13 11W
la Baule-Escoublac France **77** B4 47 18N 2 22W
Labé Guinea **106** C10 11 17N 12 11W
Labe *see* Elbe
Labrador Basin Atlantic Ocean **113** C12 58 00N 50 00W
Lábrea Brazil **68** E11 7 20S 64 46W
La Brea Trinidad and Tobago **66** S9 10 14N 61 37W
Labytnangi Russia **89** I9 66 43N 66 28E
La Canada California U.S.A. **51** B3 34 12N 118 12W
La Ceiba Honduras **67** G3 15 45N 86 45W
Lac Fitri *l.* Chad **106** I10 13 00N 17 30E
Lachlan *r.* Australia **110** H3 33 30S 145 30E
La Chorrera Panama **67** Y1 8 51N 79 46W
Lackawack New York U.S.A. **65** F4 41 48N 74 25W
Lackawanna New York U.S.A. **64** F4 42 49N 78 49W
Lac Léman *(Lake Geneva) l.* Switzerland **77** D4 46 20N 6 20E
Lac Mai-Ndombe *l.* Zaïre **106** I7 2 00S 18 20E
Lac Moero *see* Mweru
La Coruña *(Corunna)* Spain **77** A3 43 22N 8 24W
La Cresenta California U.S.A. **51** B3 34 13N 118 14W
La Crosse Wisconsin U.S.A. **63** H5 43 48N 91 04W
Lacul Razelm *l.* Romania **81** E3 45 00N 29 00E
Ladakh Range *mts.* Kashmir **95** D6 34 30N 78 30E
la Défense France **83** A2 48 53N 2 14E
Ladozhskoye Ozero *(Lake Ladoga) l.* Russia **90** C7 61 00N 30 00E
Ladysmith Republic of South Africa **107** K2 28 34S 29 47E
Ladysmith Wisconsin U.S.A. **35** B2 45 27N 91 07W
Lae Papua New Guinea **110** H8 6 45S 147 00E
Laedalsøyri Norway **79** B3 61 05N 7 15E
La Esmeralda Venezuela **68** D13 3 11N 65 33W
Lafayette California U.S.A. **49** C3 37 53N 122 08W
Lafayette Indiana U.S.A. **63** I5 40 25N 86 54W
Lafayette Louisiana U.S.A. **63** G3 30 12N 92 18W
Lafayette Reservoir California U.S.A. **49** C3 37 52N 122 08W
La Fé Cuba **67** H4 22 02N 84 15W
Lågen *r.* Norway **79** B3 61 40N 9 45E
Laghouat Algeria **106** F14 33 49N 2 55E
Lago Argentino *l.* Argentina **69** C3 50 10S 72 30W
Lago da Tijuca *l.* Brazil **69** P2 22 59S 43 22W

Lago de Chapala *l.* Mexico **66** D4 20 05N 103 00W
Lago de Maracaibo *l.* Venezuela **68** C14 9 50N 71 30W
Lago de Nicaragua *l.* Nicaragua **67** G2 11 50N 86 00W
Lago de Piratininga *l.* Brazil **69** Q2 22 57S 43 05W
Lago de Poopó *l.* Bolivia **68** D9 18 30S 67 20W
Lago di Bolsena *l.* Italy **81** B3 42 00N 12 00E
Lago di Como *l.* Italy **81** A4 46 00N 9 00E
Lago di Garda *l.* Italy **81** B4 45 00N 10 00E
Lago do Jacarepaguá *l.* Brazil **69** P2 22 58S 43 23W
Lago Maggiore *l.* Italy **81** A4 46 00N 8 00E
Lago Rodrigo de Freitas *l.* Brazil **69** Q2 22 58S 43 13W
Lagos Nigeria **107** V3 6 27N 3 28E
Lagos Portugal **77** A2 37 05N 8 40W
Lagos Island *tn.* Nigeria **107** V3 6 24N 3 28E
Lagos Lagoon Nigeria **107** W3 6 30N 3 33E
Lago Titicaca *l.* Peru/Bolivia **68** C9/D9 16 00S 69 30W
La Grande Oregon U.S.A. **62** C6 45 21N 118 05W
La Grange Georgia U.S.A. **63** I3 33 02N 85 02W
La Grange Illinois U.S.A. **53** A2 41 47N 87 53W
La Guaira Venezuela **68** D15 10 38N 66 55W
Laguna Brazil **69** H7 28 29S 48 45W
Laguna Caratasca *l.* Honduras **67** H3 15 05N 84 00W
Laguna de Perlas *l.* Nicaragua **67** H2 12 30N 83 30W
Laguna Mar Chiquita *l.* Argentina **69** E6 30 30S 62 30W
Lagunillas Venezuela **68** C15 10 07N 71 16W
Lagøy *i.* Norway **79** C4 68 45N 15 00E
La Habana *(Havana)* Cuba **67** H4 23 07N 82 25W
La Habra California U.S.A. **51** C2 33 56N 117 59W
Lahaina Hawaiian Islands **115** Y18 20 23N 156 40W
Lahore Pakistan **95** C6 31 34N 74 22E
Lahti Finland **79** F3 61 00N 25 40E
Lai Chi Chong Hong Kong U.K. **98** C2 22 27N 114 17E
Lai Chi Wo Hong Kong U.K. **98** B3 22 32N 114 15E
Lajes Brazil **69** G7 27 48S 50 20W
Lajpat Nagar India **94** M4 28 34N 77 15E
La Junta Colorado U.S.A. **62** F4 37 59N 103 34W
Lake Calumet Harbor Illinois U.S.A. **53** B1 41 41N 87 35W
Lake Chabot California U.S.A. **49** C2 37 43N 122 06W
Lake Charles *tn.* Louisiana U.S.A. **63** H3 30 13N 93 13W
Lake City Michigan U.S.A. **35** C1 44 22N 85 12W
Lake Forest *tn.* Illinois U.S.A. **53** A4 42 15N 87 50W
Lake Forest Park Massachusetts U.S.A. **52** A2 42 18N 71 22W
Lake George New York U.S.A. **65** G6 43 27N 73 40W
Lakehurst New Jersey U.S.A. **65** F3 40 01N 74 19W
Lakeland Florida U.S.A. **63** J2 28 02N 81 59W
Lake Luzerne *tn.* New York U.S.A. **65** G6 43 19N 73 50W
Lakemba *i.* Fiji **114** V15 18 10S 178 49W
Lakemba Passage *sd.* Fiji **114** V15 18 10S 179 00W
Lake Merced California U.S.A. **49** B2 37 43N 122 29W
Lake Merritt California U.S.A. **49** B3 37 48N 122 15W
Lake Orion *tn.* Michigan U.S.A. **36** C3 42 47N 83 13W
Lakeview Oregon U.S.A. **62** B5 42 13N 120 21W
Lake View *tn.* New York U.S.A. **38** D1 42 42N 78 55W
Lake Wallenpaupack Pennsylvania U.S.A. **64** E4 41 25N 75 15W
Lakewood California U.S.A. **51** B2 33 49N 118 08W
Lakewood New Jersey U.S.A. **65** F3 40 00N 74 00W
Laksefjord *fj.* Norway **79** F5 70 40N 26 30E
Lakselv Norway **79** E5 70 03N 24 55E
Lakshadweep *admin.* India **95** C1 9 30N 73 00E
La Línea de la Concepción Spain **77** A2 36 10N 5 21W
Lalitpur India **95** D4 24 42N 78 24E
La Mancha *admin.* Spain **77** B2 39 10N 2 45W
La Manche *see* English Channel
Lamar Colorado U.S.A. **62** F4 38 04N 102 37W
Lamar Pennsylvania U.S.A. **64** C4 41 01N 77 33W
Lambaréné Gabon **106** H7 0 41S 10 13E
Lambasa Fiji **114** U16 16 25S 179 24E
Lambert Glacier Antarctica **117** 73 00S 70 00E
Lambertville New Jersey U.S.A. **64** F3 40 22N 74 57W
Lambeth *bor.* Greater London England **82** C2 51 30N 0 07W
Lamego Portugal **77** A3 41 05N 7 49W
Lamía Greece **81** D2 38 55N 22 26E
Lamma Island Hong Kong U.K. **98** B1 22 12N 114 08E
Lammermuir Hills Scotland **78** I7 55 50N 2 45W
Lampazos Mexico **66** D5 27 00N 100 30W
Lampedusa *i.* Italy **81** B2 35 00N 12 00E
Lam Tei Hong Kong U.K. **98** A2 22 25N 113 59E
Lamu Kenya **106** N7 2 17S 40 54E
Lanai *i.* Hawaiian Islands **115** Y18 20 50N 156 55W
Lanai City Hawaiian Islands **115** Y18 20 50N 156 56W
Lancang Jiang *r.* China **97** J5/K3 30 00N 98 00E
Lancaster England **78** I6 54 03N 2 48W
Lancaster Ohio U.S.A. **63** J4 39 43N 82 37W
Lancaster Pennsylvania U.S.A. **64** D3 40 01N 76 19W
Landes *geog. reg.* France **77** B3 44 15N 1 00E
Landianchang China **101** G1 39 58N 116 17E
Land's End *c.* England **78** F2 50 03N 5 44W
Landshut Germany **76** E4 48 31N 12 10E
Landskrona Sweden **79** C2 55 53N 12 50E
Langdon North Dakota U.S.A. **39** B1 48 46N 98 21W
Langer See *l.* Germany **83** G1 52 24N 13 36E
Langjökull *ice cap* Iceland **79** H6 64 45N 20 00W
Langon France **77** B3 44 33N 0 14W
Langres France **77** D4 47 53N 5 20E
Lan Hsü Taiwan **98** H5 22 04N 121 32E
Lannion France **76** B4 48 44N 3 27W
Lansdale Pennsylvania U.S.A. **64** E3 40 14N 75 17W
L'Anse Michigan U.S.A. **35** C2 46 45N 88 27W
Lansing Illinois U.S.A. **53** B1 41 33N 87 33W
Lansing Michigan U.S.A. **63** J5 42 44N 85 34W
Lantau Channel Hong Kong U.K. **98** A1 22 11N 113 52E
Lantau Island Hong Kong U.K. **98** A1 22 15N 113 56E
Lantau Peak Hong Kong U.K. **98** A1 22 15N 113 55E
Lanzarote *i.* Canary Islands **106** C13 29 00N 13 38W
Lanzhou China **97** K6 36 01N 103 45E
Laoag The Philippines **99** G7 18 14N 120 36E
Lao Cai Vietnam **97** K3 22 30N 103 57E
Laon France **76** C4 49 34N 3 37E
La Oroya Peru **68** B10 11 36S 75 54W
LAOS **99** C7
La Paz Bolivia **68** D9 16 30S 68 10W
La Paz Mexico **66** B4 24 10N 110 17W
Lapeer Michigan U.S.A. **36** C4 43 03N 83 09W
Laporte Pennsylvania U.S.A. **64** D4 41 25N 76 29W
Lappajärvi *l.* Finland **79** E3 63 13N 23 40E
Lappland *geog. reg.* Sweden/Finland **79** E4 67 30N 20 05E
La Perouse Australia **111** G2 33 59S 151 14E
La Pesca Mexico **66** E4 23 46N 97 47W
La Plata Argentina **69** F5 34 52S 57 55W
Laptev Sea Arctic Ocean **89** O11 76 00N 125 00E
Laptev Strait Russia **89** Q10 73 00N 141 00E
Lapua Finland **79** E3 62 57N 23 00E
La Puente California U.S.A. **51** C3 34 01N 117 58W
L'Aquila Italy **81** B3 42 22N 13 24E
Lār Iran **93** H4 27 42N 54 19E
Larache Morocco **106** D15 35 12N 6 10W
Laramie Wyoming U.S.A. **62** E5 41 20N 105 38W
Lärbro Sweden **80** C6 57 47N 18 50E
Laredo Texas U.S.A. **62** G2 27 32N 99 22W
La Rioja Argentina **69** D7 29 26S 66 50W
Lárisa Greece **81** D2 39 38N 22 25E
Larkana Pakistan **94** B5 27 32N 68 18E
Larnaca Cyprus **92** D5 34 54N 33 29E
Larne Northern Ireland **78** F6 54 51N 5 49W
la Rochelle France **77** B4 46 10N 1 10W
la Roche-sur-Yon France **77** B4 46 40N 1 25W
La Romana Dominican Republic **67** K3 18 27N 68 57W
Larsen Ice Shelf Antarctica **117** 67 00S 62 00W
Las Cruces New Mexico U.S.A. **62** E3 32 18N 106 47W
La Serena Chile **69** C7 29 54S 71 18W
la Seyne-sur-Mer France **77** D3 43 06N 5 53E
Lashio Myanmar **97** J3 22 58N 97 48E
Las Marismas *geog.reg.* Spain **77** A2 36 55N 6 00W
Las Palmas Canary Islands **106** B13 28 08N 15 27W
La Spezia Italy **81** A3 44 07N 9 48E
Las Vegas Nevada U.S.A. **62** C4 36 10N 115 10W
Las Vegas New Mexico U.S.A. **62** E4 35 36N 105 15W
Latacunga Ecuador **68** B12 0 58S 78 36W
Latina Italy **81** B3 41 28N 12 53E
Latur India **95** D3 18 24N 76 34E
LATVIA **79** E2
Launceston Australia **110** H1 41 25S 147 07E
Laurel Maryland U.S.A. **64** D2 39 06N 76 51W
Laurel Mississippi U.S.A. **63** I1 31 41N 89 09W
Laurence Harbor New Jersey U.S.A. **65** F3 40 27N 74 16W
Lausanne Switzerland **77** D4 46 32N 6 39E
Laut *i.* Indonesia **99** F3 4 00S 116 40E
Lautoka Fiji **114** T16 17 36S 177 28E
Laval France **77** B4 48 04N 0 45W
La Vega Dominican Republic **67** J3 19 15N 70 33W
Laverton Australia **110** C4 28 49S 122 25E
La Victoria Venezuela **68** D15 10 16N 67 21W
Lawndale California U.S.A. **51** A2 33 52N 118 21W
Lawrence Kansas U.S.A. **63** G4 38 58N 95 15W
Lawrence Massachusetts U.S.A. **65** J5 42 00N 71 00W
Lawrence Park *tn.* Pennsylvania U.S.A. **36** F3 42 08N 80 02W
Lawton Oklahoma U.S.A. **62** G3 34 36N 98 25W
Laylá Saudi Arabia **93** G3 22 16N 46 45E
Laysan *i.* Hawaiian Islands **114** I10 25 46N 171 44W
Lea *r.* England **78** K3 51 40N 0 20W
Leatherhead England **82** B2 51 18N 0 20W
LEBANON **92** D5
Lebanon Missouri U.S.A. **63** H4 37 40N 92 40W
Lebanon Pennsylvania U.S.A. **64** D3 40 21N 76 25W
Lebanon, Mount Pennsylvania U.S.A. **53** D1 40 21N 80 03W
le Blanc-Mesnil France **83** B2 48 56N 2 28E
Lebu Chile **69** C5 37 38S 73 43W
Lecce Italy **81** C3 40 21N 18 11E
Lee Massachusetts U.S.A. **65** G5 42 19N 73 15W
Lee *r.* Irish Republic **78** C3 51 50N 8 50W
Leeds England **78** J5 53 50N 1 35W
Leesburg Virginia U.S.A. **64** C2 39 00N 77 00W
Leeuwin, Cape Australia **110** B3 34 24S 115 09E
Leeward Islands Lesser Antilles **67** L3 17 30N 64 00W
Legnica Poland **80** C5 51 12N 16 10E
Leh Kashmir **95** D6 34 09N 77 35E
le Havre France **76** C4 49 30N 0 06E
Lehighton Pennsylvania U.S.A. **64** E3 40 50N 75 42W
Leicester England **78** J4 52 38N 1 05W
Leichhardt Australia **111** G2 33 53S 151 09E
Leiden Netherlands **76** C5 52 10N 4 30E
Leipzig Germany **76** E5 51 20N 12 25E
Leiria Portugal **77** A2 39 45N 8 49W
Leizhou Bandao *p.* China **97** M3 21 00N 110 00E
Lekkous *r.* Morocco **77** A1/2 35 00N 5 40W
le Mans France **77** C4 48 00N 0 12E
Lena *r.* Russia **89** O9 70 00N 125 00E
Leninabad *see* Khujand
Leninakan *see* Kumairi
Leningrad *see* St. Petersburg
Leningradskaya *r.s.* Antarctica **117** 69 30S 159 23E
Lenino Russia **88** M1 55 35N 37 10E
Leninogorsk Kazakhstan **91** N5 50 23N 83 32E
Leninsk-Kuznetskiy Russia **91** O5 54 44N 86 13E
Lenkoran' Azerbaijan **90** F2 38 45N 48 50E
Lenkoran' Russia **93** G6 38 45N 48 50E
Lens France **76** C5 50 26N 2 50E
Lensk Russia **89** N8 60 48N 114 55E
Leoben Austria **81** C4 47 23N 15 06E
Leominster Massachusetts U.S.A. **65** J5 42 31N 71 45W
Leon *r.* Texas U.S.A. **63** G3 32 00N 98 00W
León Spain **77** A3 42 35N 5 34W
Leonora Australia **110** C4 28 54S 121 20E
le Puy France **77** C3 45 03N 3 53E
le Raincy France **83** C2 48 54N 2 32E
Léré Chad **106** H9 9 41N 14 17E
Lérida *(Lleida)* Spain **77** C3 41 37N 0 38E
Lerwick Scotland **78** J12 60 09N 1 09W
Les Cayes Haiti **67** J3 18 15N 73 46W
Les Coudreaux France **83** C2 48 54N 2 36E
Leskovac Serbia Yugoslavia **81** D3 43 00N 43 21 57E
LESOTHO **107** K2
Lesser Antilles *is.* West Indies **67** K2/L3
Lesser Sunda Islands Indonesia **85** 8 00S 120 00E
les Sables-d'Olonne France **77** B4 46 30N 1 47W
les Ulis France **83** A1 48 41N 2 11E
Lésvos *i.* Greece **81** E2 39 00N 26 00E
Leszno Poland **80** C5 51 51N 16 35E
Leticia Colombia **68** C12 4 09S 69 57W
le Tréport France **76** C5 50 04N 1 22E
Leuven *(Louvain)* Belgium **76** C5 50 53N 4 42E
Levádhia Greece **81** D2 38 26N 22 53E
Lévêque, Cape Australia **110** C6 16 25S 122 55E
Levice Czechoslovakia **81** C4 48 14N 18 35E
Levin New Zealand **111** C2 40 37S 175 18E
Levkás *i.* Greece **81** D2 38 00N 20 00E
Levuka Fiji **114** U16 17 42N 178 50E
Lewis *i.* Scotland **78** E10 58 15N 6 30W
Lewisburg Pennsylvania U.S.A. **64** D3 40 58N 76 55W
Lewisham *bor.* Greater London England **82** C2 51 27N 0 00
Lewis Pass New Zealand **111** B2 42 22S 172 27E
Lewiston Idaho U.S.A. **62** C6 46 25N 117 00W
Lewiston Maine U.S.A. **63** L5 44 08N 70 14W
Lewiston New York U.S.A. **64** A6 43 11N 79 03W
Lewistown Montana U.S.A. **62** E6 47 04N 109 26W
Lewistown Pennsylvania U.S.A. **64** C3 40 37N 77 36W
Lexington Kentucky U.S.A. **63** J4 38 02N 84 30W
Lexington Massachusetts U.S.A. **52** A2 42 26N 71 58W
Lexington Heights *tn.* Michigan U.S.A. **36** D4 43 15N 82 32W
Leyte *i.* The Philippines **99** G6 11 00N 124 50E
Lezhë Albania **81** C3 41 47N 19 39E
Lhasa China **96** H4 29 41N 91 10E
Lhazê China **96** G4 29 08N 87 43E
Lianyungang China **97** N5 34 37N 119 10E
Liao *r.* China **84** 44 00N 121 00E
Liaoyang China **97** O7 41 16N 123 12E
Liaoyuan China **97** P7 42 53N 125 10E
Libby Montana U.S.A. **43** E1 48 25N 115 33W
Libenge Zaïre **106** I8 3 39N 18 39E
Liberal Kansas U.S.A. **62** F4 37 03N 100 56W
Liberec Czechoslovakia **80** C5 50 48N 15 05E
LIBERIA **106** D9
Liberty New York U.S.A. **65** F4 41 47N 74 46W
Liberty Reservoir Maryland U.S.A. **64** D2 39 25N 76 55W
Libourne France **77** B3 44 55N 0 14W
Libreville Gabon **106** G8 0 30N 9 25E
LIBYA **106** H13
Libyan Desert North Africa **106** J13 25 00N 25 00E
Libyan Plateau Egypt **106** J14 31 00N 26 00E
Lichinga Mozambique **107** M5 13 19S 35 13E
Lichtenberg Germany **83** G2 52 32N 13 30E
Lichtenrade Germany **83** F1 52 23N 13 22E
Lida Belarus **90** B5 53 05N 25 19E
Lidcombe Australia **111** G2 33 52S 151 03E
Lidköping Sweden **80** B6 58 30N 13 10E
LIECHTENSTEIN **81** A4
Liège Belgium **76** D5 50 38N 5 35E
Lienz Austria **81** B4 46 51N 12 50E
Liepāja Latvia **79** E2 56 30N 21 00E
Lifou *i.* Îles Loyauté Pacific Ocean **110** L5 21 00S 167 00E
Ligurian Sea Mediterranean Sea **77** D3 44 00N 9 00E
Lihue Hawaiian Islands **115** X18 21 59N 159 23W
Likasi Zaïre **107** K5 10 58S 26 47E
Liku Indonesia **99** D4 1 47N 109 19E
Lille France **76** C5 50 39N 3 05E
Lillehammer Norway **79** C3 61 06N 10 27E
Lilongwe Malawi **107** L5 13 58S 33 49E
Liluah India **94** K2 22 37N 88 20E
Lim *r.* Europe **81** C3 43 00N 19 00E
Lima Ohio U.S.A. **63** J5 40 43N 84 06W
Lima Peru **68** B10 12 06S 8 40W
Lima *r.* Portugal **77** A3 42 00N 8 30W
Limassol Cyprus **92** D5 34 04N 33 03E
Limay *r.* Argentina **69** D5 39 30S 69 30W
Limbe Cameroon **106** G8 3 58N 9 10E
Limeira Brazil **69** H8 22 34S 47 25W
Limerick Irish Republic **78** C4 52 04N 8 38W
Limestone New York U.S.A. **64** B5 42 02N 78 39W
Limfjorden *sd.* Denmark **80** A6 57 00N 8 50E
Límnos *i.* Greece **81** E2 39 00N 25 00E
Limoges France **77** C4 45 50N 1 15E
Limón Costa Rica **67** H2 10 00N 83 01W
Limoux France **77** C3 43 03N 2 13E
Limpopo *r.* Southern Africa **107** L3 22 30S 32 00E
Linares Mexico **66** E3 24 54N 99 38W
Linares Spain **77** B2 38 05N 3 38W
Lincoln England **78** K5 53 14N 0 33W
Lincoln Massachusetts U.S.A. **52** A2 42 24N 71 18W
Lincoln Nebraska U.S.A. **63** G5 40 49N 96 41W
Lincoln Park California U.S.A. **49** A3 37 47N 122 30W
Lincoln Park Illinois U.S.A. **53** B2 41 56N 87 37W
Lincoln Park Michigan U.S.A. **52** E1 42 13N 83 10W
Lincoln Wolds *hills* England **78** K5 53 25N 0 05W
Lincolnwood Illinois U.S.A. **53** B3 42 01N 87 44W
Linda Mar California U.S.A. **49** B2 37 35N 122 29W
Linden Guyana **68** F14 5 59N 58 19W
Linden New Jersey U.S.A. **50** B1 40 37N 74 13W
Lindenberg Germany **83** G2 52 37N 13 31E
Lindfield Australia **111** G2 33 47S 151 10E
Lindis Pass New Zealand **111** A2 44 33S 169 43E
Line Islands Kiribati **115** K7 0 00 160 00W
Linglestown Pennsylvania U.S.A. **64** D3 40 20N 76 50W
Ling Tong Mei Hong Kong U.K. **98** B2 22 29N 114 06E
Linhares Brazil **68** J9 19 22S 40 04W
Linköping Sweden **79** D2 58 25N 15 35E
Linsell Sweden **79** C3 62 10N 13 50E
Linstead Jamaica **67** Q8 18 08N 77 02W
Linton North Dakota U.S.A. **62** F6 46 17N 100 14W
Linxia China **97** K6 35 31N 103 08E
Linz Austria **81** B4 48 19N 14 18E
Lion Rock *mt.* Hong Kong U.K. **98** C2 22 21N 114 11E
Lipetsk Russia **90** D5 52 37N 39 36E
Lisas, Point Trinidad and Tobago **66** T9 10 22N 61 37W
Lisboa *(Lisbon)* Portugal **77** A2 38 44N 9 08W
Lisbon *see* Lisboa
Lisburn Northern Ireland **78** E6 54 31N 6 03W
Lisburn, Cape Alaska U.S.A. **10** B6 68 54N 166 18W
Lisianski *i.* Hawaiian Islands **114** I10 26 04N 173 58W
Lisichansk Ukraine **90** D4 48 53N 38 25E
Lisieux France **76** C4 49 09N 0 14E
Lismore Australia **110** I4 28 48S 153 17E
Litani *r.* Lebanon **92** O11 33 35N 35 40E
Lithgow Australia **110** I3 33 30S 150 09E
LITHUANIA **80** D6
Little Aden Yemen Republic **93** F1 12 47N 44 55E
Little Andaman *i.* Andaman Islands **95** G2 10 30N 92 40E
Little Bitter Lake *see* Buheirat-Murrat-el-Sughra
Little Calumet River Indiana U.S.A. **53** C1 42 19N 87 26W
Little Colorado *r.* Arizona U.S.A. **62** D4 36 00N 111 00W
Little Falls *tn.* Minnesota U.S.A. **63** H6 45 58N 94 20W
Little Fork River Minnesota U.S.A. **35** B2 48 00N 93 30W
Little Minch *sd.* Scotland **78** E9 57 45N 6 30W
Little Missouri *r.* U.S.A. **62** F6 46 00N 104 00W
Little Nicobar *i.* Nicobar Islands **95** G1 7 00N 94 00E
Little Rock Kansas U.S.A. **63** H3 34 42N 92 17W
Little Sioux *r.* U.S.A. **63** A2 42 00N 96 00W
Little Snake *r.* U.S.A. **62** E5 41 00N 108 00W
Little Traverse Bay Michigan U.S.A. **36** A6 45 25N 85 00W
Little Valley *tn.* New York U.S.A. **64** B5 42 15N 78 47W
Liuzhou China **97** L3 24 17N 109 15E
Liverpool Australia **111** F2 33 56S 150 55E
Liverpool England **78** I5 53 25N 2 55W
Liverpool Pennsylvania U.S.A. **64** C3 40 34N 77 01W
Livingston Montana U.S.A. **62** D6 45 40N 110 33W
Livingstone *see* Maramba
Livingston Island South Shetland Islands **69** E0 62 38S 60 30W
Livonia Michigan U.S.A. **52** D2 42 25N 83 23W
Livorno Italy **81** B3 43 33N 10 18E
Liwale Tanzania **107** M6 9 47S 38 00E
Lizard Point England **78** F1 49 56N 5 13W
Ljubljana Slovenia **81** B4 46 04N 14 30E
Ljungan *r.* Sweden **79** D3 62 35N 16 00E
Ljungby Sweden **80** B6 56 49N 13 55E
Ljus Sweden **79** D3 61 57N 16 05E
Ljusnan *r.* Sweden **79** D3 62 05N 15 10E
Llanelli Wales **78** G3 51 42N 4 10W
Lleida *see* Lérida
Lobatse Botswana **107** K2 25 11S 25 40E
Lobito Angola **107** H5 12 20S 13 34E
Lobos, Point California U.S.A. **49** A3 37 47N 122 31W
Loch Linnhe *b.* Scotland **78** F8 56 35N 5 25W
Loch Lomond *l.* Scotland **78** G8 56 10N 4 35W
Loch Ness *l.* Scotland **78** G9 57 02N 4 30W
Loch Shin *l.* Scotland **78** G10 58 05N 4 30W
Loch Tay *l.* Scotland **78** G8 56 31N 4 10W
Lockhart Texas U.S.A. **63** G2 29 54N 97 41W
Lock Haven Pennsylvania U.S.A. **64** C4 41 00N 77 00W
Lockport New York U.S.A. **64** B6 43 11N 78 39W
Lod Israel **92** O10 31 57N 34 54E
Lodeynoye Pole Russia **90** C7 60 43N 33 30E
Lodge Creek Canada/U.S.A. **41** C1 49 15N 110 05W
Lodi India **94** L4 28 35N 77 13E
Łódź Poland **80** C5 51 49N 19 28E
Lofoten Islands Norway **79** C4 68 30N 15 00E
Logan Utah U.S.A. **62** D5 41 45N 111 50W
Logan, Mount Washington U.S.A. **42** H4 48 33N 120 55W
Logone *r.* Chad **106** H10 11 00N 15 00E
Logroño Spain **77** B3 42 28N 2 26W
Loir *r.* France **77** C4 46 45N 0 35E
Loire *r.* France **77** C4 47 20N 1 20W
Loja Ecuador **68** B12 3 59S 79 16W
Loja Spain **77** B2 37 10N 4 09W
Lokan tekojärvi *l.* Finland **79** F4 68 00N 27 30E
Lok Ma Chau Hong Kong U.K. **98** B3 22 31N 114 05E
Lokoja Nigeria **106** G9 7 49N 6 44E
Lol *r.* Sudan **106** K9 9 00N 28 00E
Lolland *i.* Denmark **80** B5 54 45N 12 20E
Loloda Indonesia **99** H4 1 39N 127 37E
Lomblen *i.* Indonesia **99** G2 8 00S 123 30E
Lombok *i.* Indonesia **99** F2 8 29S 116 40E
Lomé Togo **106** F9 6 10N 1 21E
Lomela Zaïre **106** J7 2 19S 23 15E
Lomela *r.* Zaïre **106** J7 3 00S 23 00E
Lomonosov Ridge Arctic Ocean **116** 87 00N 60 00W
Łomza Poland **80** D5 53 11N 22 04E
London England **78** K3 51 30N 0 10W
London Colney England **82** B3 51 44N 0 18W
Londonderry Northern Ireland **78** D6 54 59N 7 19W
Londrina Brazil **69** G8 23 18S 51 13W
Long Bay Barbados **66** W12 13 05N 59 30W
Long Beach *beach* New Jersey U.S.A. **65** G3 40 35N 73 40W
Long Beach *tn.* California U.S.A. **51** B2 33 47N 118 15W
Long Beach *tn.* New York U.S.A. **50** D1 40 35N 73 40W
Long Beach Island New York U.S.A. **65** F2 39 40N 74 10W
Long Branch New Jersey U.S.A. **65** F3 40 17N 73 59W
Longfellow Mountains Maine U.S.A. **37** Q6 45 10N 70 00W
Longford Irish Republic **78** D5 53 44N 7 47W
Long Island The Bahamas **67** J4 23 20N 75 00W
Long Island Massachusetts U.S.A. **52** C2 42 20N 70 58W
Long Island New York U.S.A. **65** G3 40 50N 73 00W
Long Island City New York U.S.A. **50** C2 40 46N 73 55W
Long Island Sound New York/Connecticut U.S.A **65** G4 41 50N 73 00W
Longreach Australia **110** G5 23 30S 144 15E
Longview Texas U.S.A. **63** H3 32 20N 94 45W
Longwy France **76** D4 49 32N 5 46E
Loop Head *c.* Irish Republic **78** B4 52 30N 9 55W
Lopez, Cape Gabon **106** G7 0 36S 8 45E
Lopez Island Washington U.S.A. **42** H4 48 30N 122 54W
Lop Nur *l.* China **96** H7 40 15N 90 20E
Lopphavet *sd.* Norway **79** E5 70 30N 21 00E
Lorain Ohio U.S.A. **63** J5 41 28N 82 11W
Lorca Spain **77** B2 37 40N 1 41W
Lord Howe Rise Pacific Ocean **114** G5 27 30S 162 00E
Lorica Colombia **67** I1 9 14N 75 50W
Lorient France **77** B4 47 45N 3 21W
Los Alamos Mexico U.S.A. **62** E4 35 52N 106 19W
Los Altos California U.S.A. **49** C1 37 24N 122 07W
Los Angeles California U.S.A. **51** A3 34 00N 118 15W
Los Angeles Chile **69** C5 37 28S 72 23W
Los Angeles River California U.S.A. **51** B2 33 50N 118 13W
Los Mochis Mexico **66** C5 25 48N 109 00W
Los Teques Venezuela **68** D15 10 25N 67 01W
Lost River West Virginia U.S.A. **64** B2 39 10N 78 35W
Lot *r.* France **77** C3 44 35N 1 10E
Lo-tung Taiwan **98** H7 24 00N 121 00E
Loubomo Congo **107** H7 4 09S 12 47E
Loudéac France **76** B4 48 11N 2 45W
Lough Allen *l.* Irish Republic **78** C6 54 15N 8 00W
Lough Conn *l.* Irish Republic **78** B6 54 05N 9 10W
Lough Corrib *l.* Irish Republic **78** B5 53 10N 9 10W
Lough Derg *l.* Irish Republic **78** C4 54 35N 7 55W
Lough Foyle *b.* Irish Republic **78** D7 55 10N 7 10W
Lough Mask *l.* Irish Republic **78** B5 53 40N 9 30W
Lough Neagh *l.* Northern Ireland **78** E6 54 35N 6 30W
Lough Ree *l.* Irish Republic **78** D5 53 35N 8 00W
Loughton England **82** D3 51 39N 0 03E
Louisiade Archipelago *is.* Papua New Guinea **110** I7 12 00S 153 00E
Louisiana *state* U.S.A. **63** H3 32 00N 92 00W
Louisville Kentucky U.S.A. **63** I4 38 13N 85 48W
Lourdes France **77** B3 43 06N 0 02W

Louvain *see* Leuven
Lowell Massachusetts U.S.A. **65** J5 42 38N 71 19W
Lower Bay New York U.S.A. **50** B1 40 32N 74 04W
Lower Crystal Springs Reservoir California U.S.A. **49** B2 37 32N 122 24W
Lower Hutt New Zealand **111** B2 41 12S 174 54E
Lower Lough Erne *l.* Northern Ireland **78** D6 54 25N 7 45W
Lower Red Lake Minnesota U.S.A. **63** H6 48 00N 95 00W
Lower River Rouge Michigan U.S.A. **52** D2 42 17N 83 22W
Lower River Rouge Park Michigan U.S.A. **52** D2 42 17N 83 22W
Lower Tunguska *see* Nizhnyaya Tunguska
Lowestoft England **78** M4 52 29N 1 45E
Łowicz Poland **80** C5 52 06N 19 55E
Lo Wu Hong Kong U.K. **98** B3 22 32N 114 06E
Loyalsock Creek Pennsylvania U.S.A. **64** D4 41 25N 76 50W
Lualaba *r.* Zaïre **107** K7 4 00S 26 30E
Luanda Angola **107** H6 8 50S 13 15E
Luang Prabang Laos **99** C7 19 53N 102 10E
Luangwa *r.* Zambia **107** L5 12 00S 32 30E
Luanshya Zambia **107** K5 13 09S 28 24E
Luarca Spain **77** A3 43 33N 6 31W
Luau Angola **107** J5 10 42S 22 12E
Lubango Angola **107** H5 14 55S 13 30E
Lubbock Texas U.S.A. **62** F3 33 35N 101 53W
Lübeck Germany **76** E5 53 52N 10 40E
Lubilash *r.* Zaïre **107** J6 4 00S 24 00E
Lublin Poland **80** D5 51 18N 22 31E
Lubumbashi Zaïre **107** K5 11 41S 27 29E
Lucea Jamaica **67** P8 18 26N 78 11W
Lucena Spain **77** B2 37 25N 4 29W
Luckenwalde Germany **76** E5 52 05N 13 11E
Lucknow India **95** E5 26 50N 80 54E
Lüderitz Namibia **107** I2 26 38S 15 10E
Ludhiana India **95** D6 30 56N 75 52E
Ludington Michigan U.S.A. **35** C1 43 58N 86 27W
Ludlow Vermont U.S.A. **65** H6 43 22N 72 39W
Ludvika Sweden **79** D3 60 08N 15 14E
Ludwigsfelde Germany **83** F1 52 18N 13 16E
Luena Angola **107** I5 11 47S 19 52E
Luen Wo Hui Hong Kong U.K. **98** B3 22 30N 114 08E
Lufkin Texas U.S.A. **63** H3 31 21N 94 47W
Lugansk *(Voroshilovgrad)* Ukraine **90** D4 48 35N 39 20E
Lugo Spain **77** A3 43 00N 7 33W
Lugoj Romania **81** D4 45 41N 21 57E
Luguoqiao China **101** F1 39 51N 116 13E
Luiana *r.* Angola **107** J4 17 00S 21 00E
Lu-kang Taiwan **98** G7 24 04N 120 23E
Lukens, Mount California U.S.A. **51** B1 34 16N 118 14W
Luk Keng Hong Kong U.K. **98** B3 22 32N 114 13E
Łuków Poland **80** D5 51 57N 22 21E
Luleå Sweden **79** E4 65 35N 22 10E
Lule älv *r.* Sweden **79** E4 66 15N 20 30E
Lüleburgaz Turkey **80** E3 41 25N 27 22E
Lulua *r.* Zaïre **107** J6 9 00S 22 00E
Lumberton North Carolina U.S.A. **63** K3 34 37N 79 03W
Lummi Island Washington U.S.A. **42** H4 48 42N 122 40W
Lund Sweden **79** C2 55 42N 13 10E
Lundy *i.* England **78** G3 51 11N 4 40W
Lune *r.* England **78** I6 54 07N 2 40W
Lüneburg Germany **76** E5 53 15N 10 24E
Lünen Germany **76** K3 51 38N 7 31E
Lunéville France **76** D4 48 35N 6 30E
Lung Kwu Chau *i.* Hong Kong U.K. **98** A2 22 23N 113 53E
Lungue Bungo *r.* Angola/Zambia **107** J5 13 00S 22 00E
Luni *r.* India **95** C5 26 00N 73 00E
Luninets Belarus **80** E5 52 18N 26 50E
Luoshan China **97** M5 31 12N 114 30E
Luoyang China **97** M5 34 47N 112 26E
Lurgan Northern Ireland **78** E6 54 28N 6 20W
Lurio *r.* Mozambique **107** M5 14 00S 39 00E
Lusaka Zambia **107** K4 15 26S 28 20E
Lusambo Zaïre **107** J7 4 59S 23 26E
Lushun China **97** O6 38 46N 121 15E
Lü Tao *i.* Taiwan **98** H5 22 38N 121 30E
Luton England **78** K3 51 53N 0 25W
Lutsk Ukraine **80** E5 50 42N 25 15E
Lützow-Holm Bay Antarctica **117** 69 00S 38 00E
Luuq Somalia **106** M8 2 52N 42 34E
LUXEMBOURG 76 D4
Luxembourg Luxembourg **76** D4 49 37N 6 08E
Luxor Egypt **92** D4 25 41N 32 24E
Luzern Switzerland **77** D4 47 03N 8 17E
Luzhou China **97** L4 28 55N 105 25E
Luziânia Brazil **68** H9 16 16S 47 57W
Luzon *i.* The Philippines **99** G7 16 30N 121 30E
Luzon Strait China/Philippines **99** G8 20 00N 121 30E
L'vov Ukraine **90** A4 49 50N 24 00E
Lycksele Sweden **79** D3 64 34N 18 40E
Lyme Bay England **78** H2 50 40N 2 55W
Łyna *r.* Poland **80** D5 54 00N 20 00E
Lynchburg Virginia U.S.A. **63** K4 37 24N 79 09W
Lynden Washington U.S.A. **42** H4 48 56N 122 28W
Lynn Massachusetts U.S.A. **52** C2 42 29N 70 57W
Lynn Canal *sd.* Alaska U.S.A. **42** A3 58 50N 135 05W
Lynn Woods Reservation Massachusetts U.S.A. **52** C2 42 29N 70 59W
Lyon France **77** C4 45 46N 4 50E
Lyons Illinois U.S.A. **53** A2 41 48N 87 49W
Lyons New York U.S.A. **64** D6 43 04N 76 59W
Lyttelton New Zealand **111** B2 43 36S 172 42E
Lyubertsy Russia **90** D6 55 38N 37 58E
Lyublino Russia **88** M1 55 38N 37 44E

M

Ma'ān Jordan **92** O10 30 11N 35 43E
Maanselka *geog. reg.* Finland **79** F4 68 45N 25 10E
Ma'anshan China **97** N5 31 49N 118 32E
Maastricht Netherlands **76** C5 50 51N 5 42E
Mabalane Mozambique **107** L3 23 51S 32 38E
Mabashi Japan **101** C4 35 48N 139 55E
McAlester Oklahoma U.S.A. **63** G3 34 56N 95 46W
McAllen Texas U.S.A. **63** G2 26 13N 98 15W
Macao *territory* Portugal **97** M3 22 10N 113 40E
Macapá Brazil **68** G13 0 04N 51 04W
McComb Mississippi U.S.A. **63** H3 31 13N 90 29W
McConnellsburg Pennsylvania U.S.A. **64** B2 39 00N 78 00W
McCook Nebraska U.S.A. **62** F5 40 13N 100 35W
McDonald, Lake Montana U.S.A. **41** C1 48 40N 113 50W
Macdonnell Ranges *mts.* Australia **110** E5 24 00S 132 30E
Macedonia Yugoslavia **81** D3
Maceió Brazil **68** J11 9 40S 35 44W
Macerata Italy **81** B3 43 18N 13 27E
McGrath Alaska U.S.A. **10** D5 62 58N 155 40W
Machala Ecuador **68** B12 3 20S 79 57W
Machanga Mozambique **107** L3 20 58N 35 01E
Machias Maine U.S.A. **33** C1 44 00N 67 00W
Machida Japan **101** A3 35 32N 139 27E
Machilipatnam India **95** E3 16 12N 81 11E
Machiques Venezuela **68** C15 10 04N 72 37W
Mackay Australia **110** H5 21 10S 149 10E
Mackay, Lake Australia **110** D5 22 30S 128 00E
McKee City New Jersey U.S.A. **65** F2 39 26N 74 40W
McKeesport Pennsylvania U.S.A. **53** E1 40 21N 79 52W
McKees Rocks Pennsylvania U.S.A. **53** D1 40 29N 80 29W
Mackinac, Straits of Michigan U.S.A. **36** B6 45 48N 84 43W
Mackinaw City Michigan U.S.A. **63** J6 45 47N 84 43W
McKinley, Mount Alaska U.S.A. **10** E5 62 02N 151 01W
McKinney Texas U.S.A. **63** G3 33 14N 96 37W
McLaren Park California U.S.A. **49** B2 37 43N 122 25W
Macleod, Lake Australia **110** A5 24 00S 113 30E
McMurdo *r.s.* Antarctica **117** 77 51S 166 40E
McMurdo Sound Antarctica **117** 75 00S 165 00E
Macomb County Michigan U.S.A. **52** F2 42 27N 82 59W
Mâcon France **77** C4 46 18N 4 50E
Macon Georgia U.S.A. **63** J3 32 49N 83 37W
McPherson Kansas U.S.A. **63** G4 38 22N 97 41W
Macquarie Island Southern Ocean **114** F2 54 29S 158 58E
Macquarie Ridge Southern Ocean **114** F2 55 00S 160 00E
Macuro Venezuela **66** S10 10 38N 61 55W
Mādāba Jordan **92** O10 31 44N 35 48E
MADAGASCAR 107 O3
Madagascar Basin Indian Ocean **112** E4 25 00S 55 00E
Madagascar Ridge Indian Ocean **112** D3/4 30 00S 45 00E
Madang Papua New Guinea **110** H8 5 14S 145 45E
Madden Lake Panama **67** Y2 9 15N 79 35 W
Madeira Islands Atlantic Ocean **106** B14 32 45N 17 00W
Madhya *admin.* India **95** D4 23 00N 78 30E
Madhyamgrām India **94** K2 22 41N 88 27E
Madīnat ash Sha'b Yemen Republic **93** F1 12 50N 44 56E
Madison Maine U.S.A. **37** R5 44 48N 69 53W
Madison Wisconsin U.S.A. **63** I5 43 04N 89 22W
Madison Heights Michigan U.S.A. **52** E2 42 29N 83 05W
Madium Indonesia **99** E2 7 37S 111 33E
Mado Gashi Kenya **106** M8 0 45N 39 11E
Madras India **95** E2 13 05N 80 18E
Madrid Spain **77** B3 40 25N 3 43W
Madura *i.* Indonesia **99** E2 7 10S 113 30E
Madurai India **95** D1 9 55N 78 07E
Madureira Brazil **69** P2 22 52S 43 21W
Maebashi Japan **100** C2 36 24N 139 04E
Mae Nam Mun *r.* Thailand **97** K2 15 10N 102 05E
Mae Nam Ping *r.* Thailand **97** J2 18 00N 104 00E
Mae Sot Thailand **97** J2 16 44N 98 32E
Maevantanana Madagascar **107** O4 16 57S 46 50E
Mafia Island Tanzania **107** M6 7 00S 39 00E
Mafikeng Republic of South Africa **107** K2 25 53S 25 39E
Mafraq Jordan **92** P11 32 20N 36 12E
Magadan Russia **89** R7 59 38N 150 50E
Magangué Colombia **68** C14 9 14N 74 46W
Magdalena Mexico **66** B6 30 38N 110 59W
Magdeburg Germany **76** E5 52 08N 11 37E
Magelang Indonesia **99** E2 7 28S 110 11E
Maghâgha Egypt **92** D4 28 39N 30 50E
Magnitogorsk Russia **91** H5 53 28N 59 06E
Magwe Myanmar **96** J2 20 08N 94 55E
Mahadeo Hills India **95** D4 22 30N 78 30E
Mahajanga Madagascar **107** O4 15 40S 46 20E
Mahalapye Botswana **107** K3 23 05S 26 52E
Mahanadi *r.* India **95** E4 21 00N 84 00E
Maharashtra *admin.* India **95** C3/D3 19 30N 75 00E
Maha Sarakham Thailand **97** K2 16 12N 103 16E
Mahdia Tunisia **81** B2 35 29N 11 03E
Mahia Peninsula New Zealand **111** C3 39 10S 138 00E
Mahlow Germany **83** F1 52 22N 13 24E
Mahón Balearic Islands **77** C2 39 54N 4 15E
Mahoning River Ohio U.S.A. **36** F2 41 05N 80 40W
Mahrauli India **94** L4 28 30N 77 11E
Maidstone England **78** L3 51 17N 0 32E
Maiduguri Nigeria **106** H10 11 53N 13 16E
Maikala Range *mts.* India **95** E4 22 30N 81 30E
Maila The Philippines **99** G6 14 37N 120 58E
Main *r.* Germany **76** E5 50 00N 8 00E
Maine *state* U.S.A. **63** M6 45 00N 70 00W
Mainland *i.* Scotland **78** H11 59 00N 3 15W
Mainland *i.* Scotland **78** J12 60 15N 1 20W
Maintirano Madagascar **107** N4 18 01S 44 03E
Mainz Germany **76** D5 50 00N 8 16E
Mai Po Lo Wai Hong Kong U.K. **98** B2 22 29N 114 03E
Maiquetia Venezuela **68** D15 10 38N 66 59W
Maisons-Laffitte France **83** A2 48 57N 2 09E
Maitland Australia **110** I3 32 33S 151 33E
Maizuru Japan **100** G2 35 30N 135 20E
Majene Indonesia **99** F3 3 33S 118 59E
Maji Ethiopia **106** M9 6 12N 35 32E
Majiuqiao China **101** H1 39 45N 116 33E
Majorca *see* Mallorca
Makabe Japan **100** M3 36 15N 140 05E
Makassar Strait Indonesia **99** F3/F4 2 00S 117 30E
Makat Kazakhstan **91** G4 47 38N 53 16E
Makeni Sierra Leone **106** C9 8 57N 12 02W
Makeyevka Ukraine **90** D4 48 01N 38 00E
Makgadikgadi Salt Pan Botswana **107** K3 21 00S 26 00E
Makhachkala Russia **90** F3 42 59N 47 30E
Makkah *(Mecca)* Saudi Arabia **92** E3 21 26N 39 49E
Makó Hungary **81** D4 46 11N 20 30E
Makoku Gabon **106** H8 0 38N 12 47E
Makran *geog. reg.* Iran/Pakistan **93** J4 25 55N 61 30E
Makung *(Penghu)* Taiwan **98** F6 23 35N 119 33E
Makurdi Nigeria **106** G9 7 44N 8 35E
Malabar Coast India **95** C2/D1 12 00N 74 00E
Malabo Equatorial Guinea **106** G8 3 45N 8 48E
Malacca, Strait of Indonesia/Malaysia **99** B5/C4
Malaga New Jersey U.S.A. **64** E2 39 34N 75 03W
Málaga Spain **77** B2 3 43N 4 25W
Malaita *i.* Solomon Islands **110** K8 9 00S 161 00E
Malakal Sudan **106** L9 9 31N 31 40E
Malang Indonesia **99** E2 7 59S 112 45E
Malanje Angola **107** I6 9 32S 16 20E
Mälar, Lake *see* Mälaren
Mälaren *(Lake Mälar) l.* Sweden **79** D2 59 30N 17 00E
Malatya Turkey **92** E6 38 22N 38 18E
MALAWI 107 L5
Malawi, Lake *see* Nyasa Lake
Malaya *admin.* Malaysia **99** C4 4 00N 102 30E
Malay Peninsula Asia **84** 5 00N 102 00E
MALAYSIA 99 C5/E5
Malbork Poland **80** C5 54 02N 19 01E
Malden Massachusetts U.S.A. **52** B2 42 24N 71 04W
Malden Island Pacific Ocean **115** K7 4 03S 154 59W
Maldive Archipelago *is.* Indian Ocean **84** 5 00N 73 00E
MALDIVES 95 C1
Maldonado Uruguay **69** G6 34 57S 54 59W
Malegaon India **95** C4 20 32N 74 38E
Malekula *i.* Vanuatu **110** L6 16 30S 167 20E
Malema Mozambique **107** M5 14 57S 37 25E
MALI 106 D10
Malines *see* Mechelen
Malin Head *c.* Irish Republic **78** D7 55 30N 7 20W
Ma Liu Shui Hong Kong U.K. **98** C2 22 25N 114 12E
Mallaig Scotland **78** F9 57 00N 5 50W
Mallawi Egypt **92** D4 27 44N 30 50E
Mallorca *(Majorca) i.* Balearic Islands **77** C2 39 50N 2 30E
Malmédy Belgium **76** D5 50 26N 6 02E
Malmö Sweden **79** C2 55 35N 13 00E
Malonga Zaïre **107** J5 10 26S 23 10E
Måløy Norway **79** B3 61 57N 5 06E
Malpelo *i.* Colombia **68** A13 4 00N 81 35W
MALTA 81 B2
Malta Montana U.S.A. **62** E6 48 22N 107 51W
Malta *i.* Mediterranean Sea **81** B2 35 00N 14 00E
Maluku *is.* Indonesia **99** H3 1 00S 127 00E
Malviya Nagar India **94** L4 28 32N 77 12E
Mamanutha Group *is.* Fiji **114** T16 17 40S 177 00E
Mamaroneck New York U.S.A. **50** D2 40 57N 73 43W
Mamba Japan **100** K3 36 07N 138 54E
Mambasa Zaïre **106** K8 1 20N 29 05E
Man Côte d'Ivoire **106** D9 7 31N 7 37W
Manacapuru Brazil **68** E12 3 16S 60 37W
Manacor Balearic Islands **77** C2 39 35N 3 12E
Manado Indonesia **99** G4 1 32N 124 55E
Managua Nicaragua **67** G2 12 06N 86 18W
Manali India **95** D6 32 12N 77 06E
Manasquan New Jersey U.S.A. **65** F3 40 07N 74 02W
Manaus Brazil **68** F12 3 06S 60 00W
Manchester Connecticut U.S.A. **65** H4 41 47N 72 31W
Manchester England **78** I5 53 30N 2 15W
Manchester Massachusetts U.S.A. **65** K5 42 34N 70 46W
Manchester Michigan U.S.A. **36** B3 42 10N 84 01W
Manchester New Hampshire U.S.A. **65** J5 42 59N 71 28W
Manchester Tennessee U.S.A. **63** I4 35 29N 86 04W
Manchester Center Vermont U.S.A. **65** G6 43 11N 73 03W
Mandal Norway **79** B2 58 02N 7 30E
Mandalay Myanmar **96** J3 21 57N 96 04E
Mandeville Jamaica **67** Q8 18 02N 77 31W
Mandvi India **94** B4 22 50N 69 25E
Mandya India **95** D2 12 34N 76 55E
Manfredonia Italy **81** C3 41 37N 15 55E
Mangalore India **95** C2 12 54N 74 51E
Mango *i.* Fiji **114** V16 17 20S 179 20W
Mangoky *r.* Madagascar **107** N3 22 00S 45 00E
Mangui China **97** O9 52 05N 122 17E
Manhasset New York U.S.A. **50** D2 40 48N 73 41W
Manhattan Kansas U.S.A. **63** G4 39 11N 96 35W
Manhattan New York U.S.A. **50** C2 40 48N 73 58W
Manhattan Beach *tn.* California U.S.A. **51** A2 33 53N 118 24W
Mania *r.* Madagascar **107** N4 19 30S 50 30E
Manica Mozambique **107** L4 18 56S 32 52E
Manicoré Brazil **68** E11 5 48S 61 16W
Manikpur India **94** J2 22 32N 88 12E
Manipur *admin.* India **95** G4 24 30N 94 00E
Manipur *r.* Myanmar/India **95** G4 23 30N 93 00E
Manisa Turkey **80** E2 38 36N 27 29E
Manistee Michigan U.S.A. **35** C1 44 14N 86 20W
Manistee River Michigan U.S.A. **35** C1 44 20N 85 50W
Manistique Michigan U.S.A. **35** C2 45 58N 86 17W
Manistique Lake Michigan U.S.A. **36** A7 46 15N 85 50W
Manitowoc Wisconsin U.S.A. **63** I5 44 04N 87 40W
Manizales Colombia **68** B13 5 03N 75 32W
Manjra *r.* India **95** D3 18 30N 76 00E
Man Kam To Hong Kong U.K. **98** B3 22 32N 114 07E
Mankato Minnesota U.S.A. **63** H5 44 10N 94 00W
Manly Australia **111** H2 33 48S 151 17E
Mannar Sri Lanka **95** D1 8 58N 79 54E
Mannar, Gulf of India/Sri Lanka **95** D1 8 30N 79 00E
Mannheim Germany **76** D5 49 30N 8 28E
Manokwari Indonesia **99** I3 0 53S 134 05E
Manresa Spain **77** C3 41 43N 1 50E
Mansfield Massachusetts U.S.A. **65** J5 42 02N 71 12W
Mansfield Ohio U.S.A. **63** J5 40 46N 82 31W
Mansfield Pennsylvania U.S.A. **64** C4 41 47N 77 05W
Manta Ecuador **68** B12 0 59S 80 44W
Mantes-la-Jolie France **76** C4 48 59N 1 43E
Mantova Italy **81** B4 45 10N 10 47E
Manukau Harbour New Zealand **111** B3 37 00S 174 30E
Manyoni Tanzania **107** L6 5 46S 34 50E
Manzanares Spain **77** B2 39 00N 3 23W
Manzanilla Bay Trinidad and Tobago **66** T10 10 40N 61 55W
Manzanilla Point Trinidad and Tobago **66** T10 10 31N 61 01W
Manzanillo Cuba **67** I4 20 21N 77 21W
Manzanillo Mexico **66** D3 19 00N 104 20W
Maoming China **97** M3 21 50N 110 56E
Ma On Shan Hong Kong U.K. **98** C2 22 26N 114 13E
Ma On Shan *mt.* Hong Kong U.K. **98** C2 22 24N 114 16E
Maple Heights *tn.* Ohio U.S.A. **36** E2 41 24N 81 35W
Maputo Mozambique **107** L2 25 58S 32 35E
Marabá Brazil **68** H11 5 23S 49 10W
Maracaibo Venezuela **68** C15 10 44N 71 37W
Maracay Venezuela **68** D15 10 20N 67 28W
Maradi Niger **106** G10 13 29N 7 10E
Maramba *(Livingstone)* Zambia **107** K4 17 50S 25 53E
Maranhão *admin.* Brazil **68** H11 5 20S 46 00W
Marathon New York U.S.A. **64** D5 42 25N 76 04W
Maraval Trinidad and Tobago **66** T10 10 42N 61 31W
Marbella Spain **77** B2 36 31N 4 53W
Marble Bar *tn.* Australia **110** B5 21 16S 119 45E
Marble Canyon *tn.* Arizona U.S.A. **62** D4 36 50N 111 38W
Marblehead Massachusetts U.S.A. **52** C3 42 30N 70 50W
Marburg Germany **76** D5 50 49N 8 36E
Marchfield Barbados **66** W12 13 07N 59 129W
Marcus Island Pacific Ocean **114** F10 24 30N 157 30E
Mardan Pakistan **95** C6 34 14N 72 05E
Mar del Plata Argentina **69** F5 38 00S 57 32W
Mardin Turkey **92** F6 37 19N 40 43E
Mare *i.* Îles Loyauté **110** L5 22 00S 167 30E
Margai Caka *l.* China **95** F7 35 00N 87 00E
Margate England **78** M3 51 24N 1 24E
Margilan Uzbekistan **91** L3 40 30N 71 45E
Maria Elena Chile **69** D8 22 18S 69 40W
Marianas Trench Pacific Ocean **114** E9 16 00N 147 30E
Marias River Montana U.S.A. **41** C1 48 25N 111 50W
Maria van Diemen, Cape New Zealand **111** B4 34 29S 117 39E
Maribor Slovenia **81** C4 46 34N 15 38E
Mariehamn Finland **79** D3 60 05N 19 55E
Mariental Namibia **107** I3 24 36S 17 59E
Mariestad Sweden **80** B6 58 44N 13 50E
Marietta Pennsylvania U.S.A. **64** D3 40 04N 76 33W
Mariinsk Russia **91** O6 56 14N 87 45E
Marijampole *(Kapsukas)* Lithuania **80** D6 54 31N 23 20E
Marilia Brazil **69** G8 22 13S 49 58W
Marina del Rey California U.S.A. **51** A2 33 58N 118 28W
Marin City California U.S.A. **49** A3 37 52N 122 31W
Marin County California U.S.A. **49** B3 37 55N 122 26W
Maringá Brazil **69** G8 23 26S 52 02W
Marin Peninsula California U.S.A. **49** A3 37 52N 122 33W
Marion New York U.S.A. **64** C6 43 09N 77 11W
Marion Ohio U.S.A. **63** J5 40 35N 83 08W
Marion, Lake South Carolina U.S.A. **63** J3 33 00N 80 00W
Mariscal Estigarribia Paraguay **69** E8 22 03S 60 35W
Mariupol' *(Zhdanov)* Ukraine **90** D4 47 05N 37 34E
Marjayoun Lebanon **92** O11 33 22N 35 34E
Marka Somalia **106** N8 1 42N 44 47E
Markha *r.* Russia **89** N8 64 00N 12 30E
Markovo Russia **89** T8 64 40N 170 24E
Marlborough Massachusetts U.S.A. **65** J5 42 21N 71 33W
Marlette Michigan U.S.A. **36** C4 43 20N 83 04W
Marlton New Jersey U.S.A. **64** F2 39 55N 74 55W
Marly-le-Roi France **83** A2 48 52N 2 05E
Marmara, Sea of Turkey **92** C7 15 40N 28 10E
Maroantsetra Madagascar **107** O4 15 23S 49 44E
Maroko Nigeria **107** W3 6 21N 3 32E
Maroni *r.* Surinam **68** G13 4 00N 54 30W
Maroua Cameroon **106** H10 10 35N 14 20E
Maroubra Australia **111** G2 33 57S 151 15E
Marquesas Islands Pacific Ocean **115** M7 10 00S 137 00W
Marquette Michigan U.S.A. **63** I6 46 33N 87 23W
Marquette Park Illinois U.S.A. **53** B2 41 46N 87 43W
Marrakech Morocco **106** D14 31 49N 8 00W
Marrickville Australia **111** G2 33 55S 151 09E
Marsabit Kenya **106** M8 2 20N 37 59E
Marsala Italy **81** B2 37 48N 12 27E
Marseille France **77** D3 43 18N 5 22E
Marshall Michigan U.S.A. **36** B3 42 16N 84 57W
Marshall Virginia U.S.A. **64** C1 38 53N 77 52W
MARSHALL ISLANDS 114 G8
Martaban, Gulf of Myanmar **96/97** J1 16 00N 97 00E
Martha's Vineyard *i.* Massachusetts U.S.A. **65** K4 41 00N 70 00W
Martinique *i.* Lesser Antilles **67** L2 14 30N 61 00W
Martin Lake Alabama U.S.A. **63** I3 33 00N 86 00W
Martinsburg West Virginia U.S.A. **64** C2 39 28N 77 59W
Martinsville Virginia U.S.A. **63** K4 36 43N 79 53W
Martin Vaz *i.* Atlantic Ocean **113** F4 21 00S 27 30W
Marton New Zealand **111** C2 40 04S 175 25E
Marwitz Germany **83** E2 52 44N 13 08E
Mary Turkmenistan **91** J2 37 42N 61 54E
Maryborough Australia **110** I4 25 32S 152 36E
Maryland *state* U.S.A. **63** K4 39 00N 77 00W
Marysville Pennsylvania U.S.A. **64** D3 40 00N 76 00W
Masada *see* Mezada
Masan South Korea **97** P6 35 10N 128 35E
Masaya Nicaragua **67** G2 11 59N 86 03W
Masbate *i.* The Philippines **99** G6 12 21N 123 36E
Mascara Algeria **77** C2 35 20N 0 09E
Mascarene Basin Indian Ocean **112** E5 15 00S 55 00E
Mascot Australia **111** G2 33 56S 151 12E
Maseru Lesotho **107** K2 29 19S 27 29E
Mashhad Iran **93** I6 36 16N 59 34E
Masindi Uganda **106** L8 1 41N 31 45E
Masīrah *i.* Oman **93** I3 20 25N 58 40E
Mason Michigan U.S.A. **36** B3 42 34N 85 27W
Mason City Iowa U.S.A. **63** H5 43 10N 93 10W
Masqaṭ Oman **93** I3 23 37N 58 38E
Massabesic, Lake New Hampshire U.S.A. **65** J5 42 00N 71 00W
Massachusetts *state* U.S.A. **65** H5 42 00N 72 00W
Massachusetts Bay Massachusetts U.S.A. **52** C2 42 26N 70 54W
Massif Central *mts.* France **77** C3/4 45 00N 3 30E
Massif de l'Ouarsenis *mts.* Algeria **77** C2 36 00N 2 00E
Massif de L'Isola *mts.* Madagascar **107** N3 23 00S 45 00E
Massif de Tsaratanana *mts.* Madagascar **107** N5 14 00S 49 00E
Massillon Ohio U.S.A. **36** E1 40 48N 81 32W
Massy France **83** B1 48 44N 2 17E
Masterton New Zealand **111** C2 40 57S 175 39E
Masuda Japan **100** B1 34 42N 131 51E
Masuku Gabon **106** H7 1 40S 13 31E
Masvingo Zimbabwe **107** L3 20 05S 30 50E
Matachel *r.* Spain **77** A2 38 40N 6 00W
Matadi Zaïre **107** H6 5 50S 13 32E
Matagalpa Nicaragua **67** G2 12 52N 85 58W
Matale Sri Lanka **95** E1 7 28N 80 37E
Matamoras Pennsylvania U.S.A. **65** F4 41 23N 74 43W
Matamoros Mexico **66** D5 25 33N 103 15W
Matamoros Mexico **66** E5 25 50N 97 31W
Matanzas Cuba **67** H4 23 04N 81 35W
Matara Sri Lanka **95** E1 5 57N 80 32E
Mataram Indonesia **99** F2 8 36S 116 07E

Mataró Spain 77 C3 41 32N 2 27E
Mataura New Zealand 111 A1 46 10S 168 53E
Mataura r. New Zealand 111 A1 46 40S 168 50E
Matehuala Mexico 66 D4 23 40N 100 40W
Matelot Trinidad and Tobago 66 T10 10 49N 61 07W
Matera Italy 81 C3 40 40N 16 37E
Mateur Tunisia 81 A2 37 03N 9 40E
Mathura India 95 D5 27 30N 77 42E
Mato Grosso admin. Brazil 68 F10 14 00S 56 00W
Mato Grosso tn. Brazil 68 F9 15 05S 59 57W
Mato Grosso do Sul admin. Brazil 68 F8/9 20 00S 55 00W
Matopo Hills Zimbabwe 107 K3 21 00S 28 30E
Matosinhos Portugal 77 A3 41 08N 8 45W
Matrah Oman 93 I3 23 31N 58 18E
Matsudo Japan 101 C4 35 46N 139 54E
Matsue Japan 100 B2 35 29N 133 04E
Matsumoto Japan 100 C2 36 18N 137 58E
Matsusaka Japan 100 H1 34 33N 136 31E
Matsuyama Japan 100 B1 33 50N 132 47E
Matterhorn mt. Switzerland 77 D4 45 59N 7 39E
Matuku i. Fiji 114 V15 19 11S 179 45E
Matura Trinidad and Tobago 66 T10 10 40N 61 04W
Matura Bay Trinidad and Tobago 66 T10 10 40N 61 04W
Maturín Venezuela 68 E14 9 45N 63 10W
Matveyevskoye Russia 88 L1 55 42N 37 30E
Maubeuge France 76 C5 50 17N 3 58E
Maués Brazil 68 F12 3 22S 57 38W
Maui i. Hawaiian Islands U.S.A. 119 Y18 20 55N 156 20W
Maumee River Ohio U.S.A. 36 C2 41 30N 83 50W
Maumere Indonesia 99 G2 8 35S 122 13E
Mauna Kea mt. Hawaiian Islands 115 Z17 19 50N 155 25W
Mauna Loa vol. Hawaiian Islands 115 Z17 19 28N 155 35W
MAURITANIA 106 C11
MAURITIUS 112 E4 20 15S 57 30E
Ma Wan i. Hong Kong U.K. 98 B2 22 21N 114 03E
Ma Wan Chung Hong Kong U.K. 98 A1 22 17N 113 56E
Mawkmai Myanmar 96 B8 20 12N 97 37E
Mawlaik Myanmar 96 H3 23 40N 94 26E
Mawson r.s. Antarctica 117 67 36S 62 52E
Mayaguana i. The Bahamas 67 J4 22 30N 72 40W
Mayagüez Puerto Rico 67 K3 18 13N 67 09W
Mayaro Bay Trinidad and Tobago 66 U9 10 07N 61 00W
Mayenne r. France 77 B4 47 45N 0 50W
Mayfield New York U.S.A. 65 J4 43 07N 74 17W
Maykop Russia 90 E3 44 37N 40 48E
Mayotte i. Indian Ocean 107 N5 13 00S 45 00E
Mays Landing New Jersey U.S.A. 65 F2 39 27N 74 44W
Mayumba Gabon 107 H7 3 23S 10 38E
Maywood Illinois U.S.A. 53 A2 41 51N 87 48W
Mazabuka Zambia 107 K4 15 50S 27 47E
Mazama Washington U.S.A. 42 H4 48 37N 120 25W
Mazatenango Guatemala 66 F2 14 31N 91 30W
Mazār-e Sharif Afghanistan 93 K6 36 42N 67 06E
Mazirbe Latvia 79 E2 57 40N 22 21E
Mbabane Swaziland 107 L2 26 20S 31 08E
Mbaiki Central African Republic 106 I8 3 53N 18 01E
Mbala Zambia 107 L6 8 50S 31 24E
Mbalmayo Cameroon 106 H8 3 30N 11 31E
Mbandaka Zaire 106 I7 0 03N 18 28E
Mbengga i. Fiji 114 U15 18 24S 178 09E
Mbeya Tanzania 107 L6 8 54S 33 29E
Mbuji-Mayi Zaïre 107 J6 6 10S 23 39E
Mead, Lake U.S.A. 62 D4 36 10N 114 25W
Meadville Pennsylvania U.S.A. 63 J5 41 38N 80 10W
Meaux France 76 C4 48 58N 2 54E
Mecca see Makkah
Mechelen (Malines) Belgium 76 C5 51 02N 4 29E
Mecheria Algeria 106 E14 33 31N 0 20W
Mecklenburg Bay Europe 76 E5 54 00N 12 00E
Medan Indonesia 99 B4 3 35N 98 39E
Médéa Algeria 77 C2 36 15N 2 48E
Medellín Colombia 68 B14 6 15N 75 36W
Medenine Tunisia 106 H14 33 24N 10 25E
Medford Massachusetts U.S.A. 52 B2 42 25N 71 05W
Medford New York U.S.A. 65 G3 40 49N 73 00W
Medford Oregon U.S.A. 62 B5 42 20N 122 52W
Medford Wisconsin U.S.A. 35 B2 45 08N 90 22W
Media Pennsylvania U.S.A. 64 E2 39 56N 75 23W
Medicine Lake Montana U.S.A. 40 C1 48 30N 104 10W
Medina New York U.S.A. 64 B4 43 14N 78 23W
Medina Ohio U.S.A. 36 E2 41 07N 81 51W
Medina del Campo Spain 77 B3 41 18N 4 55W
Medinipur India 95 F4 22 25N 87 24E
Mediterranean Sea 74/75
Medvedkovo Russia 88 M2 55 6N 37 08E
Medvezh'yegorsk Russia 88 F8 62 56N 34 28E
Medway r. England 78 L3 51 24N 0 40E
Meekatharra Australia 110 B4 26 30S 118 30E
Meerut India 95 D5 29 00N 77 42E
Mēga Ethiopia 106 M8 4 02N 38 19E
Meghalaya admin. India 95 G5 25 30N 91 00E
Meguro Japan 101 B3 35 36N 139 43E
Mei Xian China 97 N3 24 19N 116 13E
Mejerda r. Tunisia 81 A2 36 30N 9 00E
Mek'elē Ethiopia 106 M10 13 32N 39 33E
Meknès Morocco 106 D14 33 53N 5 37W
Mekong r. South East Asia 99 C7/D6 16 30N 105 00E
Mekong, Mouths of the Vietnam 99 D5 9 00N 107 00E
Melaka Malaysia 99 C4 2 14N 102 14E
Melanesia geog. reg. Pacific Ocean 114 F7
Melbourne Australia 110 H2 37 45S 144 58E
Melbourne Florida U.S.A. 63 J2 28 04N 80 38W
Melilla territory Spain 77 B2 35 17N 2 57W
Melitopol' Ukraine 90 D4 46 51N 35 22E
Mellégue r. Tunisia 77 D2 36 00N 8 00E
Melo Uruguay 69 G6 32 22S 54 10W
Melrose Massachusetts U.S.A. 52 B2 42 26N 71 04W
Melrose Park Illinois U.S.A. 53 A2 41 52N 87 51W
Melun France 76 C4 48 32N 2 40E
Melville Bugt b. Greenland 43 T6 75 30N 62 00W
Melville, Cape Australia 110 G7 14 08S 144 31E
Melville Island Australia 110 E7 11 30S 131 00E
Melvindale Michigan U.S.A. 52 E2 42 16N 83 41W
Memmingen Germany 76 E4 47 59N 10 11E
Memphis Tennessee U.S.A. 63 I3 35 10N 90 00W
Memphis hist. site Egypt 92 D4 29 52N 31 12E
Menai Australia 111 L13 34 01S 151 01E
Mende France 77 C3 44 32N 3 30E
Menderes r. Turkey 92 C6 37 50N 28 10E

Mendi Papua New Guinea 110 G8 6 13S 143 39E
Mendip Hills England 78 I3 51 18N 2 45W
Mendocino Seascarp Pacific Ocean 115 L12 41 00N 145 00W
Mendoza Argentina 69 D6 32 48S 68 52W
Mengdingjie China 97 J3 23 30N 99 03E
Menlo Park California U.S.A. 49 C1 37 26N 122 13W
Menongue Angola 107 I5 14 36S 17 48E
Menorca (Minorca) i. Balearic Islands 77 C2 39 45N 4 15E
Mensk see Minsk
Mentawai Islands Indonesia 112 I7 2 00N 99 00E
Mentor Ohio U.S.A. 63 J5 41 42N 81 22W
Mera Japan 100 L1 34 56N 139 50E
Merauke Indonesia 110 G8 8 30S 140 22E
Mercedes Argentina 69 D6 33 41S 65 28W
Mercedes Uruguay 69 F6 34 15S 58 02W
Mercerville New Jersey U.S.A. 65 F3 40 14N 74 42W
Mergui Myanmar 99 B6 12 26N 98 34E
Mergui Archipelago is. Myanmar 99 B6 12 00N 98 00E
Mérida Mexico 66 G4 20 59N 89 39W
Mérida Spain 77 A2 38 55N 6 20W
Mérida Venezuela 68 C14 8 24N 71 08W
Meriden Connecticut U.S.A. 65 H4 41 32N 72 48W
Meridian Mississippi U.S.A. 63 I3 32 21N 88 42W
Merowe Sudan 92 D2 18 30N 31 49E
Merrimack New Hampshire U.S.A. 65 J5 42 50N 71 30W
Merrimack River U.S.A. 65 J5 42 40N 71 15W
Merrylands Australia 111 F2 33 50S 150 59E
Mersey r. England 78 I5 53 20N 2 53W
Mersin Turkey 92 D6 36 47N 34 37E
Merthyr Tydfil Wales 78 H3 51 46N 3 23W
Merton bor. Greater London England 82 C2 51 25N 0 12W
Mertz Glacier Antarctica 117 68 00S 145 00E
Mesa Arizona U.S.A. 62 D3 33 25N 111 50W
Mesabi Range Minnesota U.S.A. 35 B2 47 30N 93 00W
Mesolóngion Greece 81 D2 38 21N 21 26E
Messina Italy 81 C2 38 13N 15 33E
Messina Republic of South Africa 107 K3 22 23S 30 00E
Methow River Washington U.S.A. 42 H4 48 35N 120 25W
Metlakatla Alaska U.S.A. 42 B3 55 09N 131 35W
Metz France 76 D4 49 07N 6 11E
Meudon France 82 A2 48 48N 2 15E
Meuse r. Belgium/France 76 C5 50 03N 4 40E
MEXICO 66 D4
México Mexico 66 E3 19 25N 99 10W
Mexico, Gulf of Mexico 66/67 F4/G4 25 00N 90 00W
Meymaneh Afghanistan 93 J6 35 55N 64 47E
Mezada (Masada) hist. site Israel 92 O10 31 17N 35 20E
Mezen' Russia 88 G9 65 50N 44 20E
Mezhdurechensk Russia 91 O5 53 43N 88 11E
Miami Florida U.S.A. 63 J2 25 45N 80 15W
Miami Oklahoma U.S.A. 63 H4 36 53N 94 54W
Miāneh Iran 93 G6 37 23N 47 45E
Mianwali Pakistan 95 C6 32 32N 71 33E
Miao-li Taiwan 98 G7 24 37N 120 49E
Miass Russia 91 J6 55 00N 60 08E
Michelson, Mount Alaska U.S.A. 44 C4 69 19N 144 20W
Michigan state U.S.A. 63 I6 45 00N 85 00W
Michurinsk Russia 90 E5 52 54N 40 30E
Micronesia geog. reg. Pacific Ocean 114 G8
Mid-Atlantic Ridge Atlantic Ocean 113 E10/G4
Middle America Trench Pacific Ocean 115 Q9 16 30N 99 00W
Middle Andaman i. Andaman Islands 95 G2 12 30N 93 00E
Middleboro Massachusetts U.S.A. 65 K4 41 54N 70 55W
Middleburg Pennsylvania U.S.A. 64 C3 40 47N 77 03W
Middleburg Republic of South Africa 107 K2 31 28S 25 01E
Middleburg Virginia U.S.A. 64 C1 38 58N 77 46W
Middleburg Heights tn. Ohio U.S.A. 36 E2 41 20N 81 49W
Middle Harbour Australia 111 G2 33 48S 151 14E
Middle Loup r. Nebraska U.S.A. 62 F5 42 00N 101 00W
Middleport New York U.S.A. 64 B4 43 13N 78 28W
Middle River Rouge Michigan U.S.A. 52 D2 42 23N 83 21W
Middle Rouge Park Michigan U.S.A. 52 D2 42 23N 83 21W
Middlesbrough England 78 J6 54 35N 1 14W
Middlesex County Massachusetts U.S.A. 52 A2 42 19N 71 20W
Middlesex Fells Reservation Massachusetts U.S.A. 52 B2 42 26N 71 07W
Middletown Connecticut U.S.A. 65 H4 41 34N 72 39W
Middletown Delaware U.S.A. 64 E2 39 27N 75 44W
Middletown New York U.S.A. 65 F4 41 26N 74 26W
Middletown Pennsylvania U.S.A. 64 D2 40 12N 76 44W
Mid-Indian Basin Indian Ocean 112 H6 10 00S 80 00E
Mid-Indian Ridge Indian Ocean 112 F5/G3
Midland Michigan U.S.A. 36 B4 43 38N 84 14W
Midland Texas U.S.A. 62 F3 32 00N 102 09W
Midland Beach New York U.S.A. 50 B1 40 33N 74 07W
Midori Japan 101 B3 35 33N 139 39E
Mid-Pacific Mountains Pacific Ocean 114 F10 21 00N 160 00E
Midway Islands Pacific Ocean 114 I10 28 15N 177 25W
Mie pref. Japan 100 H1 34 35N 136 20E
Mien Hsü i. Taiwan 98 I8 25 31N 122 07E
Mieres Spain 77 A3 43 15N 5 46W
Mifflintown Pennsylvania U.S.A. 64 C3 40 34N 77 24W
Mijares r. Spain 77 B3 40 03N 0 30W
Mikawa-wan b. Japan 100 J1 34 42N 137 10E
Mikhaylovgrad Bulgaria 81 D3 43 25N 23 11E
Miki Japan 100 F1 34 50N 134 59E
Mikkeli Finland 79 F3 61 44N 27 15E
Milagra Valley California U.S.A. 49 B2 37 28N 122 28W
Milagro Ecuador 68 B12 2 11S 79 36W
Milan see Milano
Milano (Milan) Italy 81 A4 45 28N 9 12E
Milâs Turkey 80 E2 37 19N 27 48E
Mildura Australia 110 G3 34 14S 142 13E
Milesburg Pennsylvania U.S.A. 64 C3 40 57N 77 49W
Miles City Montana U.S.A. 62 E6 46 25N 105 48W
Milford Delaware U.S.A. 64 E1 38 54N 75 25W
Milford Massachusetts U.S.A. 65 J4 42 08N 71 31W
Milford New Hampshire U.S.A. 65 J5 42 50N 71 40W
Milford New Jersey U.S.A. 64 E3 40 34N 75 06W
Milford Pennsylvania U.S.A. 65 F4 41 19N 74 48W
Milford Utah U.S.A. 62 D4 38 22N 113 00W

Milford Haven Wales 78 F3 51 44N 5 02W
Milford Sound New Zealand 111 A2 44 41S 167 56E
Miliana Algeria 77 C2 36 20N 2 15E
Millau France 77 C3 44 06N 3 05E
Mill Creek Michigan U.S.A. 36 C4 43 10N 83 00W
Mille Lacs Lake Minnesota U.S.A. 35 B2 46 00N 94 00W
Millersburg Pennsylvania U.S.A. 64 D3 40 32N 76 57W
Millerstown Pennsylvania U.S.A. 64 C3 40 32N 77 08W
Millerton New York U.S.A. 65 G4 41 57N 73 31W
Millinocket Maine U.S.A. 33 C2 45 42N 68 43W
Mill Valley California U.S.A. 49 B2 37 54N 122 32W
Millville New Jersey U.S.A. 64 E2 39 24N 75 02W
Milos i. Greece 81 D2 36 00N 24 00E
Milroy Pennsylvania U.S.A. 64 C3 40 44N 77 35W
Milton New Zealand 111 A2 46 08S 169 59E
Milton, Lake Ohio U.S.A. 36 E2 41 05N 81 00W
Milton Keynes England 78 K4 52 02N 0 42W
Milton, Lake Ohio U.S.A. 36 E2 41 05N 81 00W
Milwaukee Wisconsin U.S.A. 63 I5 43 03N 87 56W
Mimizan France 77 B3 44 12N 1 14W
Mina r. Algeria 77 C2 35 30N 1 00E
Minahassa Peninsula Indonesia 99 G4 0 30N 122 30E
Minamata Japan 100 B1 32 13N 130 23E
Minami-Ashigara Japan 100 L2 35 20N 139 06E
Minas Uruguay 69 F6 34 20S 55 15W
Minas Gerais admin. Brazil 68 I9 17 30S 45 00W
Minatitlán Mexico 66 F3 17 59N 94 32W
Minch, The sd. 78 F10 58 00N 6 00W
Mindanao i. The Philippines 99 G5/H5 7 30N 124 00E
Minden Germany 76 D5 52 18N 8 54E
Minden Louisiana U.S.A. 63 H3 32 36N 93 17W
Mindoro i. The Philippines 99 G6 13 20N 121 30E
Mingechaur Azerbaijan 90 F3 40 45N 47 03E
Minho see Miño
Minicoy Island India 95 C1 8 29N 73 01E
Minneapolis Minnesota U.S.A. 63 H5 45 00N 93 15W
Minnesota state U.S.A. 63 H6 47 00N 95 00W
Minnesota r. Minnesota U.S.A. 63 G5 44 00N 95 00W
Mino Japan 100 H2 35 34N 136 56E
Mino-Kamo Japan 100 J2 35 29N 137 01E
Minorca see Menorca
Minot North Dakota U.S.A. 62 F6 48 16N 101 19W
Minsk (Mensk) Belarus 90 C5 53 51N 27 30E
Minusinsk Russia 91 P5 53 43N 91 45E
Minute Man National Historical Park Massachusetts U.S.A. 52 A2 42 26N 71 26W
Miño (Minho) r. Spain/Portugal 77 A3 42 00N 8 40W
Mio Michigan U.S.A. 35 D1 44 40N 84 09W
Miraflores Locks Panama 67 Z1 8 59N 79 36W
Miraj India 95 C3 16 51N 74 42E
Miram Shah Pakistan 95 L3 33 00N 70 05E
Miranda de Ebro Spain 77 B3 42 41N 2 57W
Miri Malaysia 99 E4 4 28N 114 00E
Mirnyy Russia 91 N8 62 30N 113 58E
Mirnyy r.s. Antarctica 117 66 33S 93 01E
Mirpur Khas Pakistan 94 A6 25 33N 69 05E
Mirs Bay Hong Kong U.K. 98 B2 22 33N 114 24E
Mirtoan Sea Greece 81 D2 37 00N 23 00E
Mirzapur India 95 E5 25 09N 82 34E
Misaki Japan 100 G1 34 19N 135 09E
Misawa Japan 100 D3 40 42N 141 26E
Misfaq Egypt 92 N19 31 01N 31 54E
Mishima Japan 100 L2 35 08N 138 54E
Miskolc Hungary 81 D4 48 06N 20 47E
Misool i. Indonesia 99 I3 2 00S 130 00E
Mişrātah Libya 106 H14 32 23N 15 06E
Mississippi r. U.S.A. 63 H3 35 00N 90 00W
Mississippi state U.S.A. 63 H3 32 00N 90 00W
Mississippi Delta Louisiana U.S.A. 63 H3 30 00N 90 00W
Missoula Montana U.S.A. 62 D6 46 52N 114 00W
Missouri r. U.S.A. 63 H4 39 00N 93 00W
Missouri state U.S.A. 63 H4 38 00N 93 00W
Mitaka Japan 101 B3 35 41N 139 35E
Mitcham England 82 C2 51 24N 0 09W
Mitchell Indiana U.S.A. 63 I4 26 30S 147 56E
Mitchell South Dakota U.S.A. 63 G5 43 40N 98 01W
Mitchell r. Australia 110 G6 17 00S 142 30E
Mitilini Greece 81 E2 39 06N 26 34E
Mitino Russia 88 L2 55 53N 37 24E
Mitkof Island Alaska U.S.A. 42 B3 56 40N 132 45W
Mito Japan 100 D2 36 22N 140 29E
Mitry-Mory France 83 C2 48 58N 2 38E
Mits'iwa Ethiopia 92 E2 15 42N 39 25E
Mitsukaidō Japan 100 L3 36 03N 139 59E
Mitú Colombia 68 C13 1 07N 70 05W
Mitumba Mountains see Chaine des Mitumba
Miura Japan 100 L2 35 14N 139 40E
Miura-hantō p. Japan 100 L2 35 14N 139 40E
Miya-gawa r. Japan 100 H1 34 20N 136 16E
Miyako Japan 100 D3 39 38N 141 59E
Miyakonojō Japan 100 B1 31 43N 131 02E
Miyama Japan 100 G2 35 17N 135 32E
Miyazaki Japan 100 B1 31 56N 131 27E
Miyazu Japan 100 G2 35 33N 135 12E
Mizen Head c. Irish Republic 78 B3 51 30N 9 50W
Mizunami Japan 100 J2 35 25N 137 16E
Mjölby Sweden 80 C6 58 19N 15 10E
Mjøsa l. Norway 79 C3 60 40N 10 40E
Mladá Boleslav Czechoslovakia 80 B5 50 26N 14 55E
Mława Poland 80 D5 53 08N 20 20E
Mnevniki Russia 88 N6 53 44N 37 29E
Moala i. Fiji 114 U15 18 34S 179 56E
Mobara Japan 100 M2 35 26N 140 20E
Mobaye Central African Republic 106 J8 4 19N 21 11E
Mobile Alabama U.S.A. 63 I3 30 40N 88 05W
Moçambique Mozambique 107 N5 15 03S 40 45E
Mocuba Mozambique 107 M4 16 52S 36 57E
Módena Italy 81 B3 44 39N 10 55E
Moe-Yallourn Australia 110 H2 38 09S 146 22E
Mogadishu see Muqdisho
Mogilev Belarus 90 C5 53 54N 30 20E
Mogil'ev Podol'skiy Ukraine 90 B4 48 29N 27 49E
Mogocha Russia 89 N6 53 44N 119 45E
Mogollon Rim plat. Arizona U.S.A. 62 D3 34 00N 111 00W
Mohall North Dakota U.S.A. 40 C1 48 47N 101 31W
Mohammadia Algeria 77 C2 35 35N 0 05E
Mohawk New York U.S.A. 64 E6 43 00N 75 00W
Mohawk River New York U.S.A. 65 F6 43 00N 74 40W
Mohe (Gulian) China 97 N9 52 55N 122 20E
Mo-i-Rana Norway 79 C4 66 18N 14 00E
Mokolo Cameroon 106 H10 10 49N 13 54E
Mokp'o South Korea 97 P5 34 50N 126 25E
Moksha r. Russia 90 E5 50 00N 43 00E

Molango Mexico 66 E4 20 48N 98 44W
MOLDAVIA see MOLDOVA
MOLDOVA (MOLDAVIA) 90 B4
Moldova r. Romania 81 E4 47 00N 26 00E
Mole r. England 82 B2 51 15N 0 20W
Molepolole Botswana 107 K3 24 25S 25 30E
Mollendo Peru 68 C9 17 00S 72 00W
Mölndal Sweden 79 C2 57 40N 12 00E
Molodechno Belarus 80 F5 54 16N 26 50E
Molodezhnaya r.s. Antarctica 117 67 40S 45 50E
Molokai i. Hawaiian Islands 115 Y18 21 40N 155 55W
Molopo r. Southern Africa 107 J2 26 30S 22 30E
Molucca Sea Indonesia 99 G3/H4 0 00 125 00E
Mombasa Kenya 107 L7 4 04S 39 40E
Monacacy River Maryland U.S.A. 64 C2 39 30N 77 20W
MONACO 77 D3
Monadhliath Mountains Scotland 78 G9 57 10N 4 00W
Monahans Texas U.S.A. 62 F3 31 35N 102 54W
Monastir Tunisia 81 B2 35 46N 10 59E
Mona Vale Australia 111 G3 33 41S 151 18E
Monbetsu Japan 100 D3 44 23N 143 22E
Monção Brazil 68 H12 3 30S 45 15W
Mönchengladbach Germany 76 D5 51 12N 6 25E
Monclova Mexico 66 D5 26 55N 101 25W
Mondego r. Portugal 77 A3 40 30N 8 15W
Mondovi Italy 81 A3 44 23N 7 49E
Monemvasia Greece 81 D2 36 41N 23 03E
Mong Kok Hong Kong U.K. 98 B1 22 09N 114 09E
MONGOLIA 96/97 J7/M7
Mong Tong Hang Hong Kong U.K. 98 B1 22 20N 114 02E
Mongu Zambia 107 J4 15 13S 23 09E
Monomoy Island Massachusetts U.S.A. 65 K4 41 35N 70 00W
Monongahela River Pennsylvania U.S.A. 53 E1 40 19N 79 54W
Monopoli Italy 81 C3 40 57N 17 18E
Monos i. Trinidad and Tobago 66 S10 10 42N 61 42W
Monroe Louisiana U.S.A. 63 H3 32 31N 92 06W
Monroe Michigan U.S.A. 36 C2 41 56N 83 21W
Monroe New York U.S.A. 65 F4 41 20N 74 11W
Monroeville Pennsylvania U.S.A. 53 E1 40 25N 79 47W
Monrovia Liberia 106 C9 6 20N 10 46W
Montana state U.S.A. 62 D6 47 00N 111 00W
Montañas de León mts. Spain 77 A3 42 30N 6 15E
Montara California U.S.A. 49 B2 37 32N 122 29W
Montara Mountain California U.S.A. 49 B2 37 34N 122 29W
Montara Point California U.S.A. 49 A2 37 32N 122 33W
Montargis France 77 C4 48 00N 2 44E
Montauban France 77 B3 44 01N 1 20E
Montauk New York U.S.A. 65 J4 41 02N 71 57W
Montauk Point New York U.S.A. 65 J4 41 04N 71 51W
Montbéliard France 77 D4 47 31N 6 48E
Mont Blanc mt. France/Italy 77 D4 45 50N 6 52E
Mont Cameroun mt. Cameroon 106 G8 4 13N 9 10E
Montclair New Jersey U.S.A. 50 B2 40 48N 74 12W
Mont-de-Marsan France 77 B3 43 54N 0 30W
Montebello California U.S.A. 51 B3 34 01N 118 07W
Monte Cinto mt. Corsica 77 D3 42 23N 8 57E
Montego Bay tn. Jamaica 67 Q8 18 27N 77 56W
Montélimar France 77 C3 44 34N 4 45E
Montenegro admin. Yugoslavia 81 C3
Monterey Park tn. California U.S.A. 51 B3 34 03N 118 08W
Monteria Colombia 68 B14 8 45N 75 54W
Montero Bolivia 68 E9 17 20S 63 15W
Monte Roraima mt. South America 68 E14 5 14N 60 44W
Monterrey Mexico 66 D5 25 40N 100 20W
Montes Claros tn. Brazil 68 I9 16 45S 43 52W
Montes de Toledo mts. Spain 77 B2 39 35N 4 30W
Montevideo Uruguay 69 F6 34 55S 56 10W
Montgeron France 83 B1 48 42N 2 27E
Montgomery Alabama U.S.A. 63 I3 32 22N 86 20W
Montgomery Pennsylvania U.S.A. 64 D4 41 09N 76 54W
Monticello New York U.S.A. 65 F4 41 39N 74 41W
Monti del Gennargentu mts. Sardinia Italy 81 A2 40 00N 9 30E
Monti Nebrodi mts. Italy 81 B2 37 00N 14 00E
Montluçon France 77 C4 46 20N 2 36E
Montmorency France 83 B2 48 59N 2 19E
Monto Australia 110 I5 24 53N 151 06E
Montpelier Ohio U.S.A. 36 C3 41 35N 84 35W
Montpellier France 77 C3 43 36N 3 53E
Montreux Switzerland 77 D4 46 27N 6 55E
Montrose Colorado U.S.A. 62 E4 38 29N 107 53W
Montrose Pennsylvania U.S.A. 64 E4 41 49N 75 53W
Montrouge France 83 B2 48 49N 2 19E
Monts d'Auvergne mts. France 77 C4 45 30N 2 50E
Monts de Medjerda mts. Algeria/Tunisia 77 D2 36 50N 8 00E
Monts de Tébessa mts. Algeria/Tunisia 77 D2 35 00N 8 00E
Monts du Hodna mts. Algeria 77 C2 36 00N 4 00E
Montserrat i. Lesser Antilles 67 L3 16 45N 62 14W
Monts Nimba mts. Guinea/Liberia 106 D9 7 39N 8 30W
Monywa Myanmar 96 J3 22 05N 95 12E
Monza Italy 81 A4 45 35N 9 16E
Moora Australia 110 B3 30 40S 116 01E
Moorhead Minnesota U.S.A. 63 G6 46 51N 96 44W
Moore, Lake Australia 110 B4 30 00S 117 30E
Moorestown New Jersey U.S.A. 64 E2 39 58N 74 54W
Moosehead Lake Maine U.S.A. 37 R6 45 40N 69 40W
Moosup Connecticut U.S.A. 65 J4 41 43N 71 53W
Mopti Mali 106 E10 14 29N 4 10W
Mora Sweden 79 C3 61 00N 14 30E
Moradabad India 95 D5 28 50N 78 45E
Moraga California U.S.A. 49 C3 37 49N 122 08W
Morant Bay tn. Jamaica 67 R7 17 53N 76 25W
Morant Point c. Jamaica 67 R7 17 55N 76 12W
Moratuwa Sri Lanka 95 D1 6 47N 79 53E
Morava r. Europe 80 C4 48 00N 17 00E
Morava r. Yugoslavia 81 D3 43 00N 21 00E
Moravia New York U.S.A. 64 D5 42 43N 76 26W
Moray Firth est. Scotland 78 H9 57 45N 3 45W
Morbi India 95 L2 22 50N 70 52E
Moreau r. South Dakota U.S.A. 62 F6 45 00N 102 00W
Moree Australia 110 H4 29 29S 149 53E
Morenci Arizona U.S.A. 62 E3 33 05N 109 22W
Morgantown West Virginia U.S.A. 63 K4 39 38N 79 57W
Mori Japan 100 D3 42 07N 140 33E
Morioka Japan 100 D2 39 43N 141 08E

Moriyama Japan 100 G2 35 05N 135 59E
Morlaix France 76 B4 48 35N 3 50W
MOROCCO 106 D14
Morogoro Tanzania 107 M6 6 49S 37 40E
Moro Gulf The Philippines 99 G5 7 00N 122 40E
Morón Cuba 67 I4 22 08N 78 39W
Morondava Madagascar 107 N3 20 19S 44 17E
Moroni Comoros 107 N5 11 40S 43 16E
Morotai i. Indonesia 99 H4 2 30N 128 00E
Moroto Uganda 106 L8 2 32N 34 41E
Morozaki Japan 100 H1 34 41N 136 58E
Morrinsville New Zealand 111 C3 37 40S 175 33E
Morris Jesup, Cape Greenland 116 83 20N 33 00W
Morris Reservoir California U.S.A. 51 C3 33 11N 117 53W
Morristown New Jersey U.S.A. 65 F3 40 48N 74 29W
Morrisville New York U.S.A. 64 E5 42 54N 75 40W
Morton Grove Illinois U.S.A. 53 A3 42 02N 87 46W
Moruga Trinidad and Tobago 66 T9 10 06N 61 17W
Moruga r. Trinidad and Tobago 66 T9 10 06N 61 15 W
Moscow Idaho U.S.A. 62 C6 46 44N 117 00W
Moscow see Moskva
Mosel r. Germany 76 D5 50 00N 7 00E
Moses Lake tn. Washington U.S.A. 62 C6 47 09N 119 20W
Mosgiel New Zealand 111 B1 45 54S 170 21E
Moshi Tanzania 106 M7 3 21S 37 19E
Mosjøen Norway 79 C4 65 50N 13 10E
Moskva (Moscow) Russia 90 D6 55 45N 37 42E
Moskva r. Russia 88 M1 55 36N 37 45E
Mosman Australia 111 G2 33 50S 151 14E
Mosquito Creek Lake res. Ohio U.S.A. 36 F2 41 20N 80 45W
Moss Norway 79 C2 59 26N 10 41E
Moss Beach California U.S.A. 49 B2 37 36N 122 30W
Mossoró Brazil 68 J11 5 10S 37 18W
Most Czechoslovakia 80 B5 50 31N 13 39E
Mostaganem Algeria 77 C2 35 45N 0 05E
Mostar Bosnia-Herzegovina 81 C3 43 20N 17 50E
Móstoles Spain 77 B3 40 19N 3 53W
Mosul Iraq 92 F6 36 21N 43 08E
Motala Sweden 80 C6 58 34N 15 05E
Mothe i. Fiji 114 V15 18 39S 178 32W
Motherwell Scotland 78 G7 55 48N 3 59W
Motril Spain 77 B2 36 45N 3 31W
Motueka New Zealand 111 B2 41 08S 173 01E
Mouila Gabon 106 H7 1 50S 11 02E
Moulins France 77 C4 47 00N 3 48E
Moulmein Myanmar 97 J2 16 30N 97 39E
Moulouya r. Morocco 77 B1 34 50N 3 00W
Moundou Chad 106 I9 8 35N 16 01E
Mountain View California U.S.A. 49 C1 37 23N 122 25W
Mountain Village Alaska U.S.A. 10 C5 62 09N 163 49W
Mount Carmel tn. Pennsylvania U.S.A. 64 D3 40 48N 76 25W
Mount Cobb tn. Pennsylvania U.S.A. 64 E4 41 24N 75 32W
Mount Darwin tn. Zimbabwe 107 L4 16 45S 31 39E
Mount Gambier tn. Australia 110 G2 37 51S 140 50E
Mount Hagen tn. Papua New Guinea 110 G8 5 54S 144 13E
Mount Holly tn. New Jersey U.S.A. 65 F2 40 00N 74 47W
Mount Isa tn. Australia 110 F5 20 50 S 139 29E
Mount Jewell tn. Pennsylvania U.S.A. 64 B4 41 44N 78 38W
Mount Magnet tn. Australia 110 B4 28 06S 117 50E
Mount Morgan tn. Australia 110 I5 23 40S 150 25E
Mount Morris tn. New York U.S.A. 64 C5 42 44N 77 51W
Mount Pleasant tn. Michigan U.S.A. 36 B4 43 36N 84 46W
Mount Prospect tn. Illinois U.S.A. 53 A3 42 01N 87 47W
Mount Union tn. Pennsylvania U.S.A. 64 C3 40 23N 77 54W
Mount Vernon tn. New York U.S.A. 50 C2 40 55N 73 51W
Mount Vernon tn. Illinois U.S.A. 63 I4 38 19N 88 52W
Mount Vernon tn. Washington U.S.A. 42 H4 48 25N 122 20W
Mourne Mountains Northern Ireland 78 E6 54 05N 6 05W
Moy r. Irish Republic 78 C5 53 55N 8 55W
Moyale Kenya 106 M8 3 31N 39 04E
Moyobamba Peru 68 B11 6 04S 76 56W
MOZAMBIQUE 107 L4
Mozambique Channel Mozambique/Madagascar 107 N4 18 00S 42 00E
Mozambique Depression Indian Ocean 102 35 00S 40 00E
Mozyr' Belarus 80 E5 52 02N 29 10E
Mpanda Tanzania 107 L6 6 21S 31 01E
M'Sila Algeria 77 C2 35 40N 4 31E
Mtwara Tanzania 107 N5 10 17S 40 11E
Muang Lampang Thailand 99 B7 18 16N 99 30E
Muang Nakhon Sawan Thailand 99 C7 15 42N 100 04E
Muang Phitsanulok Thailand 99 C7 16 50N 100 15E
Muchinga Mountains Zambia 107 L5 12 30S 32 30E
Mudanjiang China 97 P7 44 36N 129 42E
Mud Lake Minnesota U.S.A. 39 B1 48 20N 95 50W
Mufulira Zamiba 107 K5 12 30S 28 12E
Müggelheim Germany 83 G1 52 24N 13 40E
Muğla Turkey 92 C6 37 13N 28 22E
Muhammad Qol Sudan 92 E3 20 53N 37 09E
Mui Wo Hong Kong U.K. 98 A1 22 16N 113 59E
Mukachevo Ukraine 81 D4 48 26N 22 45E
Mulegé Mexico 66 B5 26 54N 112 00W
Mulhacén mt. Spain 77 B2 37 04N 3 19W
Mülheim an der Ruhr Germany 76 H2 51 25N 6 50E
Mulhouse France 77 D4 47 45N 7 21E
Mull i. Scotland 78 F8 56 25N 6 00W
Mullet Lake Michigan U.S.A. 36 B6 45 30N 84 30W
Mullingar Irish Republic 78 D5 53 32N 7 20W
Mull of Galloway c. Scotland 78 G6 54 38N 4 50W
Mull of Kintyre c. Scotland 78 F7 55 17N 5 55W
Multan Pakistan 95 C6 30 10N 71 36E
Mumford New York U.S.A. 64 C6 42 57N 77 50W
Muna i. Indonesia 99 G3 5 00S 122 30E
München (Munich) Germany 76 E4 48 08N 11 35E
Muncie Indiana U.S.A. 63 I5 40 11N 85 22W
Muncy Pennsylvania U.S.A. 64 D4 41 12N 76 47W
Mundo r. Spain 77 B2 38 30N 2 00W
Mungbere Zaïre 106 K8 2 40N 28 25E
Munger India 95 F5 25 24N 86 29E
Munhall Pennsylvania U.S.A. 53 E1 40 24N 79 54W
Munich see München
Municipal Colony Dehli India 94 L4 28 42N 77 12E
Munising Michigan U.S.A. 35 C2 46 24N 86 40W
Münster Germany 76 D5 51 58N 7 37E
Muojärvi l. Finland 79 F4 65 52N 29 30E
Muonio älv r. Sweden/Finland 79 E4 68 20N 22 00E
Muqdisho (Mogadishu) Somalia 106 O8 2 02N 45 21E
Mur r. Europe 81 B4 47 00N 14 00E
Murat r. Turkey 92 F6 38 50N 40 20E
Murchison r. Australia 110 B4 26 00S 117 00E
Murcia Spain 77 B2 37 59N 1 08W
Mureș r. Romania 81 D4 46 00N 22 00E
Murfreesboro Tennessee U.S.A. 63 I4 35 50N 86 25W
Murgab r. Asia 93 J6 37 00N 62 30E
Müritz l. Germany 76 E5 53 00N 12 00E
Murmansk Russia 88 F9 68 59N 33 08E
Murom Russia 90 E6 55 34N 42 04E
Muroran Japan 100 D3 42 21N 140 59E
Muroto-zaki c. Japan 100 B1 33 13N 134 11E
Murray r. Australia 110 G2/G3 34 00S 142 00E
Murray Bridge tn. Australia 110 F2 35 10S 139 17E
Murray Seascarp Pacific Ocean 115 M11 32 00N 138 00W
Murrumbidgee r. Australia 110 H3 34 30S 146 30E
Murwara India 95 E4 23 49N 80 28E
Murzuq Libya 106 H13 25 55N 13 55E
Muș Turkey 92 F6 38 45N 41 30E
Musashino Japan 101 B3 35 43N 139 35E
Musgrave Ranges mts. Australia 110 E4 26 00S 132 00E
Mushin Nigeria 107 V3 6 33N 3 25E
Musin Nigeria 106 F9 6 30N 3 15E
Muskeget Channel Massachusetts U.S.A. 65 K4 41 20N 70 25W
Muskegon Michigan U.S.A. 35 C1 43 13N 86 15W
Muskegon River Michigan U.S.A. 36 A4 44 00N 85 05W
Muskogee Oklahoma U.S.A. 63 G4 35 45N 95 21W
Musselshell r. Montana U.S.A. 62 E6 47 00N 108 00W
Mustafa Kemalpașa Turkey 68 E2 40 03N 28 52E
Mutarara Mozambique 107 M4 17 30S 35 06E
Mutare Zimbabwe 107 L4 18 58N 32 40E
Mutsu Japan 100 D3 41 18N 141 15E
Mutsu-wan b. Japan 100 D3 41 05N 140 40E
Muyun Kum d. Kazakhstan 91 L3 44 00N 70 00E
Muzaffarnagar India 95 D5 29 28N 77 42E
Muzaffarpur India 95 F5 26 07N 85 23E
Muzon, Cape Alaska U.S.A. 42 B2 54 41N 132 40W
Mwanza Tanzania 106 L7 2 31S 32 56E
Mwaya Tanzania 107 L6 9 33S 33 56E
Mweru, Lake (Lac Moero) Zaïre/Zambia 107 K6 8 30S 28 30E
Myanaung Myanmar 95 H3 18 17N 95 19E
MYANMAR (BURMA) 96/97 H3
Myaungmya Myanmar 95 G3 16 33N 94 55E
Myerstown Pennsylvania U.S.A. 64 D3 40 23N 76 18W
Myingyan Myanmar 96 E2 21 25N 95 20E
Myitkyina Myanmar 97 J4 25 24N 97 25E
Mymensingh Bangladesh 95 G4 24 45N 90 23E
Mýrdalsjökull ice cap Iceland 79 I6 63 40N 19 00W
Mys Chelyuskin c. Russia 89 M11 77 44N 103 55E
Mys Kanin Nos c. Russia 88 G9 68 38N 43 20E
Mys Navarin c. Russia 89 T8 62 17N 179 13E
Mys Olyutorskiy c. Russia 89 T7 59 58N 170 25E
Mysore India 95 D2 12 18N 76 37E
Mystic Connecticut U.S.A. 65 J4 41 21N 71 58W
Mystic Lakes Massachusetts U.S.A. 52 B2 42 26N 71 09W
Mystic River Massachusetts U.S.A. 52 B2 42 25N 71 08W
Mys Tolstoy c. Russia 89 R7 59 00N 155 00E
My Tho Vietnam 99 D6 10 21N 106 21E
Mytishchi Russia 90 D6 55 54N 37 47E
Mzuzu Malawi 107 L5 11 31S 34 00E

N

9 de Julio (Nueve de Julio) tn. Argentina 69 E5 35 28S 60 58W
Naas Irish Republic 78 E5 53 13N 6 39W
Nabari Japan 100 H1 34 37N 136 05E
Naberezhnyye Chelny (Brezhnev) Russia 91 G6 55 42N 52 19E
Nabeul Tunisia 81 B2 36 30N 10 44E
Nablus Jordan 92 O11 32 13N 35 16E
Nabq Egypt 92 O9 28 04N 34 26E
Nacogdoches Texas U.S.A. 63 H3 31 36N 94 40W
Nadiad India 95 C4 22 42N 72 55E
Nador Morocco 106 E14 35 10N 3 00W
Nadym Russia 89 J9 65 25N 72 40E
Naestved Denmark 80 B6 55 14N 11 47E
Naga The Philippines 99 G6 13 36N 123 12E
Naga Hills India 95 G5/H5 26 00N 95 00E
Nagahama Japan 100 H2 35 25N 136 16E
Nagai Japan 101 B1 35 11N 139 37E
Nagaland admin. India 95 G5 26 00N 94 30E
Nagano Japan 100 C2 36 39N 138 10E
Nagaoka Japan 100 C2 37 27N 138 50E
Nagasaki Japan 100 A1 32 45N 129 52E
Nagato Japan 100 B1 34 22N 131 11E
Nagatsuda Japan 101 B3 35 31N 139 30E
Nagercoil India 95 D1 8 11N 77 30E
Nagornyy Russia 89 O7 55 57N 124 54E
Nagoya Japan 100 H2 35 08N 136 53E
Nagpur India 95 D4 21 10N 79 12E
Nagqu China 95 G6 31 30N 91 57E
Nagykanizsa Hungary 81 C4 46 27N 17 00E
Nahant Massachusetts U.S.A. 52 C2 42 24N 70 55W
Nahant Bay Massachusetts U.S.A. 52 C2 42 26N 70 56W
Nahariya Israel 92 O11 33 01N 35 05E
Naihati India 94 K3 22 53N 88 27E
Nairobi Kenya 106 L7 1 17S 36 50E
Najd geog. reg. Saudi Arabia 92 F4 25 40N 42 30E
Najrān Saudi Arabia 92 F2 17 37N 44 40E
Naka Japan 101 B2 35 25N 139 38E
Nakahara Japan 101 B3 35 34N 139 39E
Nakamura Japan 100 B1 33 02N 132 58E
Nakano Japan 101 B3 35 42N 139 40E
Nakatsu Japan 100 B1 33 37N 131 11E
Nakhichevan' Azerbaijan 90 F2 39 12N 45 24E
Nakhodka Russia 89 P4 42 53N 132 54E
Nakhon Ratchasima Thailand 99 C6 15 00N 102 06E
Nakhon Si Thammarat Thailand 99 B5 8 24N 99 58E
Nakuru Kenya 106 M7 0 16S 36 05E
Nal r. Pakistan 94 B5 26 10N 65 30E
Nal'chik Russia 90 E3 43 31N 43 38E
Namangan Uzbekistan 91 L3 40 59N 71 41E
Nam Chung Hong Kong U.K. 98 B3 22 31N 114 12E
Nam Co l. China 95 G6 30 50N 90 30E
Namdalen geog. reg. Norway 79 C3 64 40N 12 00E
Nam Dinh Vietnam 97 L3 20 14N 106 00E
Namib Desert Namibia 107 H3 22 00S 14 00E
Namibe Angola 107 H5 15 10S 12 09E
NAMIBIA 107 I3
Nampa Idaho U.S.A. 62 C5 43 35N 116 34W
Nampula Mozambique 107 M4 15 09S 39 14E
Nam Sha Po Hong Kong U.K. 98 A2 22 29N 113 59E
Namsos Norway 79 C3 64 28N 11 30E
Namtu Myanmar 97 J3 23 04N 97 26E
Namur Belgium 76 C5 50 28N 4 52E
Nan Thailand 97 K2 18 50N 100 50E
Nanao Japan 100 C2 37 03N 136 58E
Nanchang China 97 N4 28 33N 115 58E
Nanchong China 97 L5 30 54N 106 06E
Nancy France 76 D4 48 42N 6 12E
Nanda Devi mt. India 95 E6 30 21N 79 58E
Nānded India 95 D3 19 11N 77 21E
Nanduri Fiji 114 U16 16 26S 179 08E
Nangi India 94 J1 22 30N 88 13E
Nanhai l. China 101 G1 39 55N 116 22E
Nanjing China 97 N5 32 03N 118 47E
Nan Ling mts. China 97 M3/M4 25 00N 112 00E
Nanning China 97 L3 22 50N 108 19E
Nanpan Jiang r. China 97 L3 25 00N 106 00E
Nanping China 97 N4 26 40N 118 07E
Nanri Dao i. Taiwan 98 F8 25 13N 119 29E
Nansei-shoto see Ryukyu Islands
Nan Shan mts. China 84 38 00N 103 00E
Nantasket Beach Massachusetts U.S.A. 52 C2 42 17N 70 52W
Nanterre France 83 A2 48 53N 2 12E
Nantes France 77 B4 47 14N 1 35W
Nanticoke Pennsylvania U.S.A. 64 D4 41 13N 76 00W
Nantong China 97 O5 32 06N 121 04E
Nantō Japan 100 H1 34 17N 136 30E
Nan-t'ou Taiwan 98 G6 23 54N 120 42E
Nantucket Massachusetts U.S.A. 65 K4 41 17N 70 05W
Nantucket Island Massachusetts U.S.A. 65 K4 41 15N 70 05W
Nantucket Sound Massachusetts U.S.A. 65 K4 41 20N 70 15W
Nanuku Passage sd. Fiji 114 V16 16 40S 179 25W
Nanumea Island Pacific Ocean 114 H7 5 30S 175 40E
Nanyang China 97 M5 33 06N 112 31E
Nanyuan China 101 G1 39 48N 116 23E
Nanyuki Kenya 106 M8 0 01N 37 05E
Napier New Zealand 111 C3 39 29S 176 58E
Naples Florida U.S.A. 63 J2 26 09N 81 48W
Naples New York U.S.A. 64 C5 42 36N 77 25W
Naples see Napoli
Napoleon Ohio U.S.A. 35 D1 41 24N 84 09W
Napoli (Naples) Italy 81 B3 40 50N 14 15E
Napoopoo Hawaiian Islands 115 Z17 19 29N 155 55W
Nara Japan 100 G1 34 41N 135 49E
Nara pref. Japan 100 G1 34 25N 135 50E
Narayanganj Bangladesh 95 G4 23 36N 90 28E
Narbonne France 77 C3 43 11N 3 00E
Nares Deep Atlantic Ocean 113 C9 26 00N 61 10W
Narew r. Europe 81 D5 53 00N 21 00E
Narita Japan 100 M2 35 46N 140 20E
Narmada r. India 95 C4/D4 22 00N 75 00E
Narrabeen Australia 111 H3 33 43S 151 18E
Narragansett Pier tn. Rhode Island U.S.A. 65 J4 41 26N 71 27W
Narrogin Australia 110 B3 32 57S 117 07E
Narutō Japan 100 M2 35 37N 140 20E
Narva Estonia 79 F2 59 22N 28 17E
Narvik Norway 79 D4 68 26N 17 25E
Nar'yan Mar Russia 88 H9 67 37N 53 02E
Nasca Ridge Pacific Ocean 115 R5 20 00S 81 00W
Nashua New Hampshire U.S.A. 65 J5 42 44N 71 28W
Nashua River Massachusetts U.S.A. 65 J5 42 40N 71 35W
Nashville Tennessee U.S.A. 63 I4 36 10N 86 50W
Näsijärvi l. Finland 79 E3 61 45N 24 00E
Nasik India 95 C3 20 00N 73 52E
Nassau The Bahamas 67 I5 25 05N 77 20W
Nasser, Lake Egypt 92 D3 22 35N 31 40E
Nässjö Sweden 79 C2 57 40N 14 40E
Natal Brazil 68 J11 5 46S 35 15W
Natal province Republic of South Africa 107 L2 29 00S 31 00E
Natashō Japan 100 G2 35 23N 135 39E
Natchez Mississippi U.S.A. 63 H3 31 32N 91 24W
Natewa Peninsula Fiji 114 V16 16 40S 180 00
Natick Massachusetts U.S.A. 52 A2 42 17N 71 21W
Natron, Lake Tanzania 106 M7 2 00S 36 00E
Natuna Besar i. Indonesia 99 D4 4 00N 108 00E
Naturaliste, Cape Australia 110 B3 33 32S 115 01E
Naugatuck Connecticut U.S.A. 65 G4 41 30N 73 04W
NAURU 114 G7
Nausori Fiji 114 U15 18 01S 178 31E
Navadwīp India 95 F4 23 24N 88 23E
Navet Trinidad and Tobago 66 T9 10 15N 61 10W
Navet r. Trinidad and Tobago 66 T9 10 16N 61 10W
Navet Dam Trinidad and Tobago 66 T9 10 26N 61 12W
Navia r. Spain 77 A3 43 10N 7 05W
Naviti i. Fiji 114 T16 17 08S 177 15E
Navoi Uzbekistan 91 K3 40 04N 65 20E
Navojoa Mexico 66 C5 7 04N 109 28W
Návplion Greece 81 D2 37 34N 22 48E
Navsari India 95 C4 20 58N 73 01E
Náxos i. Greece 81 E2 37 00N 25 00E
Nayoro Japan 100 D3 44 21N 142 30E
Nazareth Israel 92 O11 32 41N 35 16E
Nazareth Pennsylvania U.S.A. 64 E3 40 44N 75 18W
Nazca Peru 68 C9 14 53S 74 54W
Nazilli Turkey 80 E2 37 55N 28 20E
Nazwá Oman 93 I3 22 56N 57 33E
Ndélé Central African Republic 106 J9 8 25N 20 38E
Ndjamena Chad 106 I10 12 10N 14 59E
Ndola Zambia 107 K5 13 00S 28 39E
Neah Bay tn. Washington U.S.A. 42 H4 48 22N 124 36W
Néapolis Greece 81 D2 36 31N 23 03E
Neath Wales 78 H3 51 40N 3 48W
Nebit-Dag Turkmenistan 91 G2 39 31N 54 24E
Nebraska state U.S.A. 62 F5 42 00N 102 00W
Neche North Dakota U.S.A. 39 B1 48 59N 97 34W
Neckei i. Hawaiian Islands 115 J10 23 25N 164 42W
Necochea Argentina 69 F5 38 31S 58 46W
Nedrow New York U.S.A. 64 D5 42 57N 76 11W
Needham Massachusetts U.S.A. 52 B2 42 17N 71 14W
Negelē Ethiopia 106 M9 5 20N 39 35E
Negev d. Israel 92 O10 30 50N 30 45E
Negombo Sri Lanka 95 D1 7 13N 79 51E
Negritos Peru 68 A2 4 42S 81 18W
Negros i. The Philippines 99 G5 10 00N 123 00E
Neijiang China 97 L4 29 32N 105 03E
Nei Mongol Zizhiqu (Inner Mongolia Autonomous Region) admin. China 97 L7/N2 42 30N 112 30E
Neisse (Nysa) r. Germany 80 B5 52 00N 14 00E
Neiva Colombia 68 B13 2 58N 75 15W
Nek'emtē Ethiopia 106 M9 9 04N 36 30E
Nellore India 95 D2 14 29N 80 00E
Nelson New Zealand 111 B2 41 18S 173 17E
Nelson Reservoir Montana U.S.A. 40 B1 48 30N 107 40W
Neman r. Lithuania/Russia 80 D5/6 55 00N 22 00E
Nemuro Japan 100 E3 43 22N 145 36E
Nemuro-kaikyō sd. Japan 100 E3 44 00N 146 00E
Nenana Alaska U.S.A. 10 F5 64 35N 149 20W
Nene r. England 78 K4 52 25N 0 05E
Nenjiang China 97 P8 49 10N 125 15E
Nen Jiang r. China 97 P9 50 00N 125 00E
NEPAL 95 E5
Neponset River Massachusetts U.S.A. 52 B2 42 16N 71 06W
Nerchinsk Russia 89 N6 52 02N 116 38E
Neretva r. Bosnia-Herzegovina 81 C3 43 30N 15 18E
Nerva Spain 77 A2 37 41N 6 33W
Neryungri Russia 89 O7 56 39N 124 38E
Neskaupstadur Iceland 79 J7 65 10N 13 43W
Nestor Trinidad and Tobago 66 T10 10 31N 61 09W
Netanya Israel 92 O11 32 20N 34 51E
Netcong New Jersey U.S.A. 65 F3 40 54N 74 43W
NETHERLANDS 76 C5/D5
Neubrandenburg Germany 76 E5 53 33N 13 16E
Neuchâtel Switzerland 77 D4 46 55N 6 56E
Neuenhagen Germany 83 G2 52 32N 13 41E
Neufchâtel-en-Bray France 76 C4 49 44N 1 26E
Neuilly France 83 B2 48 53N 2 17E
Neuilly Plaisance France 83 C2 48 51N 2 31E
Neukölln Germany 83 F1 52 29N 13 28E
Neumünster Germany 76 D5 54 05N 9 59E
Neuquén Argentina 69 D5 38 55N 68 05W
Neuruppin Germany 76 E5 52 56N 12 49E
Neusiedler See l. Austria 81 C4 48 00N 16 00E
Neuss Germany 76 G1 51 12N 6 42E
Neustrelitz Germany 76 E5 53 22N 13 05E
Nevada state U.S.A. 62 C4 39 00N 118 00W
Nevers France 77 C4 47 00N 3 09E
Neversink Reservoir New York U.S.A. 65 F4 41 50N 74 40W
Neves Brazil 69 Q2 22 51S 43 05W
Nevinnomyssk Russia 90 E3 44 38N 41 59E
Neviot Egypt 92 O9 28 58N 34 38E
New r. U.S.A. 63 J4 37 00N 81 00W
New Addington England 82 C2 51 21N 0 01E
New Albany Indiana U.S.A. 63 I4 38 17N 85 50W
New Amsterdam Guyana 68 F14 6 18N 57 30W
Newark California U.S.A. 49 C2 37 31N 122 03W
Newark Delaware U.S.A. 64 E2 39 42N 75 45W
Newark New Jersey U.S.A. 65 F3 40 44N 74 12W
Newark New York U.S.A. 64 C6 43 03N 77 06W
Newark Ohio U.S.A. 63 J5 40 03N 82 25W
Newark Bay New Jersey U.S.A. 50 B1 40 40N 74 08W
New Bedford Massachusetts U.S.A. 65 K4 41 38N 70 55W
New Bern North Carolina U.S.A. 63 K4 35 05N 77 04W
Newberry Michigan U.S.A. 35 C2 46 22N 85 30W
New Bloomfield Pennsylvania U.S.A. 64 D3 40 25N 76 13W
New Braunfels Texas U.S.A. 63 G2 29 43N 98 09W
New Britain Connecticut U.S.A. 65 H4 41 40N 72 47W
New Britain i. Papua New Guinea 110 I8 6 10S 150 00E
New Brunswick New Jersey U.S.A. 65 F3 40 29N 74 27W
Newburgh New York U.S.A. 65 F4 41 30N 74 00W
Newburyport Massachusetts U.S.A. 65 K5 42 47N 70 53W
New Caledonia i. Pacific Ocean 110 K5/L5 22 00S 165 00E
New Canaan Connecticut U.S.A. 65 G4 41 09N 73 30W
Newcastle Australia 110 I3 32 55S 151 46E
New Castle Delaware U.S.A. 64 E2 39 40N 75 34W
Newcastle upon Tyne England 78 J7 54 59N 1 35W
New City New York U.S.A. 65 F4 41 08N 74 00W
New Croton Reservoir New York U.S.A. 65 G4 41 15N 73 45W
New Delhi India 94 M4 28 37N 77 14E
New Dorp New York U.S.A. 50 B1 40 34N 74 06W
Newfane New York U.S.A. 64 B6 43 17N 78 42W
Newfane Vermont U.S.A. 65 H5 42 59N 72 40W
Newfield New York U.S.A. 64 D5 42 22N 76 36W
Newfoundland Basin Atlantic Ocean 113 D11 44 00N 40 00W
New Georgia Islands Solomon Islands 110 J8 8 00S 157 00E
New Grant Trinidad and Tobago 66 T9 10 17N 61 19W
New Guinea i. Pacific Ocean 110 G8 6 00S 142 00E
Newhalem Washington U.S.A. 42 H4 48 41N 121 15W
Newham bor. Greater London England 82 D3 51 30N 0 02E
New Hampshire state U.S.A. 65 H4 43 00N 72 00W
New Hartford Connecticut U.S.A. 65 H4 41 52N 72 58W
New Haven Connecticut U.S.A. 65 H4 41 18N 72 55W
New Hebrides Trench Pacific Ocean 114 G6 15 00S 169 00E
New Hope Pennsylvania U.S.A. 64 E3 40 22N 74 56W
New Hyde Park New York U.S.A. 50 D1 40 44N 73 42W
New Iberia Louisiana U.S.A. 63 H2 30 00N 91 51W
New Ireland i. Papua New Guinea 110 I9 3 00S 152 00E
New Jersey state U.S.A 64/65 E2/F2 40 00N 75 00W
New Kensington Pennsylvania U.S.A. 53 E2 40 34N 79 46W
New Lebanon New York U.S.A. 65 G5 42 27N 73 24W
New London Connecticut U.S.A. 65 H4 41 21N 72 06W
New London New Hampshire U.S.A. 65 J6 43 25N 71 58W
New London Ohio U.S.A. 36 D2 41 05N 82 24W
Newman Australia 110 B5 23 20S 119 34E
New Mexico state U.S.A. 62 E3 35 00N 107 00W
New Milford Connecticut U.S.A. 65 G4 41 35N 73 25W
New Milford Pennsylvania U.S.A. 64 E4 41 52N 75 44W
New Orleans Louisiana U.S.A. 63 H2 30 00N 90 03W
New Paltz New York U.S.A. 65 F4 41 45N 74 05W
New Plymouth New Zealand 111 B3 39 03S 174 04E

Newport Australia **111** H3 33 39S 151 19E
Newport Wales **78** H3 51 35N 3 00W
Newport New Hampshire U.S.A. **65** H6 43 22N 72 11W
Newport Rhode Island U.S.A. **65** J4 41 30N 71 19W
Newport Vermont U.S.A. **33** B1 44 56N 72 13W
Newport News Virginia U.S.A. **63** K4 36 59N 76 26W
New Providence *i.* The Bahamas **67** I5 25 00N 77 30W
New Rochelle New York U.S.A. **50** C2 40 55N 73 46W
Newry Northern Ireland **78** E6 54 11N 6 20W
New Siberian Islands Russia **89** Q10 75 00N 145 00E
New South Wales *state* Australia **110** G3/G4 32 00S 145 00E
New Springville New York U.S.A. **50** B1 40 35N 74 10W
New Territories *admin.* Hong Kong U.K. **98** B2 22 20N 114 00E
Newton Massachusetts U.S.A. **52** B2 42 20N 71 13W
Newton New Jersey U.S.A. **65** E4 41 03N 74 45W
Newtown Connecticut U.S.A. **65** G4 41 25N 73 19W
Newtownabbey Northern Ireland **78** F6 54 40N 5 54W
New Ulm Minnesota U.S.A. **63** H5 44 19N 94 28W
New York New York U.S.A. **65** G3 40 40N 73 50W
New York *state* U.S.A. **63** K5 43 00N 76 00W
NEW ZEALAND 111
Neyagawa Japan **100** G1 34 45N 135 36E
Neyrīz Iran **93** H4 29 14N 54 18E
Neyshābūr Iran **93** I6 36 13N 58 49E
Ngami, Lake Botswana **107** J3 21 00S 23 00E
Ngangla Ringco *l.* China **95** E6 31 40N 83 00E
Nganze Co *l.* China **95** F6 31 00N 87 00E
Ngaoundéré Cameroon **106** H9 7 20N 13 35E
Ngau *i.* Fiji **114** U15 18 00S 179 16E
Ngau Chi Wan Hong Kong U.K. **98** C2 22 25N 114 10E
Ngau Kwu Long Hong Kong U.K. **98** A1 22 18N 113 58E
Ngauruhoe *mt.* New Zealand **111** C3 39 10S 175 40E
Ngau Tam Mei Hong Kong U.K. **98** B2 22 28N 114 04E
Ngau Tau Kok Hong Kong U.K. **98** C1 22 19N 114 13E
Ngong Ping Hong Kong U.K. **98** A1 22 15N 113 54E
Nguigmi Niger **106** H10 14 19N 13 06E
Nguru Nigeria **106** H10 12 53N 10 30E
Nha Trang Vietnam **99** C6 12 15N 109 10E
Nhulunbuy Australia **110** F7 12 30S 136 56E
Niagara Falls *tn.* New York U.S.A. **64** A6 43 06N 79 04W
Niagara River New York U.S.A. **65** C2 43 15N 79 04W
Niamey Niger **106** F10 13 32N 2 05E
Niangara Zaïre **106** K8 3 45N 27 54E
Niantic Connecticut U.S.A. **65** H4 41 20N 72 12W
Nias *i.* Indonesia **99** B4 1 30N 97 30E
Nibra India **94** K2 22 35N 88 15E
NICARAGUA 67 G2
Nice France **77** D3 43 42N 7 16E
Nicobar Islands India **95** G1 8 30N 94 00E
Nicosia Cyprus **92** D6 35 11N 33 23E
Nidd *r.* England **78** J6 54 02N 1 30W
Niedere Tauern *mts.* Austria **81** B4 47 00N 14 00E
Nienburg Germany **76** D5 52 38N 9 13E
Nieuw Nickerie Surinam **68** F14 5 52N 57 00W
NIGER 106 G11
Niger *r.* Nigeria **106** G9 5 30N 6 15E
Niger Delta Nigeria **102** 5 00N 7 00E
NIGERIA 106 G10
Niigata Japan **100** C2 37 58N 139 02E
Niihama Japan **100** B1 33 57N 133 15E
Niihau *i.* Hawaiian Islands **115** W18 21 50N 160 11W
Nii-jima *i.* Japan **100** C1 34 20N 139 15E
Niiza Japan **101** B4 35 48N 139 35E
Nijmegen Netherlands **76** D5 51 50N 5 52E
Nikko Japan **100** C2 36 45N 139 37E
Nikolayev Ukraine **90** C4 46 57N 32 00E
Nikolayevsk-na-Amure Russia **89** Q6 53 10N 140 44E
Nikol'skiy *see* Satlayev
Nikopol Ukraine **90** C4 45 34N 34 25E
Nikšić Montenegro Yugoslavia **81** C3 42 48N 18 56E
Nile *r.* Egypt **92** D4 28 30N 30 40E
Nile Delta Egypt **102** 31 00N 31 00E
Niles Illinois U.S.A. **53** A3 42 00N 87 48W
Nilgri Hills India **95** D2 11 00N 76 30E
Nîmes France **77** C3 43 50N 4 21E
Nimule Sudan **106** L8 3 35N 32 03E
Nim Wan Hong Kong U.K. **98** A2 22 25N 113 56E
Ninepin Group *is.* Hong Kong U.K. **98** D1 22 15N 114 20E
Ninety East Ridge Indian Ocean **112** H4/H6
Ninety Mile Beach New Zealand **111** B4 34 50S 173 00E
Nineveh *hist. site* Iraq **92** F6 36 24N 43 08E
Ningbo China **97** O4 29 54N 121 33E
Ninh Binh Vietnam **97** L3 20 14N 106 00E
Niobrara *r.* U.S.A. **62** F5 42 00N 102 00W
Nioro du Sahel Mali **106** D11 15 12N 9 35W
Niort France **77** B4 46 19N 0 27W
Niš Serbia Yugoslavia **81** D3 43 20N 21 54E
Nishi Japan **101** B2 35 26N 139 37E
Nishinomiya Japan **100** G1 34 44N 135 22E
Nishio Japan **100** J1 34 52N 137 02E
Nishiwaki Japan **100** F2 35 00N 134 58E
Nitra Czechoslovakia **80** C4 48 19N 18 04E
Niue *i.* Pacific Ocean **115** J6 19 02S 169 55W
Nizamabad India **95** D3 18 40N 78 05E
Nizhiy Tagil Russia **91** H6 58 00N 59 58E
Nizhneangarsk Russia **89** M7 55 48N 109 35E
Nizhnekamsk Russia **90** G6 55 38N 51 49E
Nizhnekamskoye Vodokhranilishche *res.* Russia **91** G6 56 00N 53 30E
Nizhnenkolymsk Russia **89** S9 68 34N 160 58E
Nizhnevartovsk Russia **91** M7 60 57N 76 40E
Nizhniy Novgorod *(Gor'kiy)* Russia **90** E6 56 20N 44 00E
Nizhniy Novgorod *(Gor'kovskoye)* **Vodokhranilishche** *res.* Russia **90** E6 57 00N 43 30E
Nizhnyaya *(Lower)* **Tunguska** *r.* Russia **89** L8/M8 64 00N 94 00E
Nizké Tatry *mts.* Czechoslovakia **80** C4 49 00N 19 00E
Nkongsamba Cameroon **106** G9 4 59N 9 53E
Noatak Alaska U.S.A. **10** C6 67 33N 163 10W
Noatak *r.* Alaska U.S.A. **10** C6 67 33N 163 10W
Nobeoka Japan **100** B1 32 36N 131 40E
Nobi Japan **101** B1 35 11N 139 41E
Noda Japan **100** L2 35 57N 139 52E
Nogales Arizona U.S.A. **62** D3 31 20N 110 56W
Nogales Mexico **66** B6 31 20N 111 00W
Nogent France **83** C2 48 50N 2 30E
Noisy-le-Sec France **83** B2 48 53N 2 27E
Nojima-zaki *c.* Japan **100** L1 34 54N 139 54E
Nola Central African Republic **106** I8 3 28N 16 08E
Nome Alaska U.S.A. **10** B5 64 30N 165 30W
Nong Khai Laos **97** K2 18 00N 102 40E
Noorvik Alaska U.S.A. **10** C6 66 50N 161 14W
Nordfjord *fj.* Norway **79** B3 62 00N 5 15E
Nordfold Norway **79** D4 67 48N 15 20E
Nordfriesische Inseln *(North Frisian Islands) is.* Germany **80** A5 54 00N 8 00E
Nordhausen Germany **76** E5 51 31N 10 48E
Nordkapp *(North Cape) c.* Norway **79** E5 71 11N 25 40E
Nordvik Russia **89** N10 74 01N 111 30E
Nore *r.* Irish Republic **78** D4 52 25N 7 02W
Norfolk Nebraska U.S.A. **63** G5 42 01N 97 25W
Norfolk Virginia U.S.A. **63** K4 36 54N 76 18W
Norfolk County Massachusetts U.S.A. **52** A2 42 20N 71 08W
Norfolk Island Pacific Ocean **114** G5 29 05S 167 59E
Norfolk Island Trough Pacific Ocean **114** G5 27 30S 166 00E
Norfolk Lake Arkansas U.S.A. **63** H4 36 00N 92 00W
Noril'sk Russia **89** K9 69 21N 88 02E
Normanton Australia **110** G6 17 40S 141 05E
Norridgewock Maine U.S.A. **37** R5 44 43N 69 48W
Norris Lake Tennessee U.S.A. **63** J4 36 00N 84 00W
Norristown Pennsylvania U.S.A. **64** E3 40 07N 75 20W
Norrköping Sweden **79** D2 58 35N 16 10E
Norrtälje Sweden **80** C6 59 46N 18 43E
Norseman Australia **110** C3 32 15S 121 47E
North Adams Massachusetts U.S.A. **65** G5 42 42N 73 07W
Northam Australia **110** B3 31 40S 116 40E
North American Basin Atlantic Ocean **113** C10 34 00N 55 00W
Northampton Australia **110** A4 28 27S 114 37E
Northampton England **78** K4 52 14N 0 54W
Northampton Massachusetts U.S.A. **65** H2 42 19N 72 38W
North Andaman *i.* Andaman Islands **95** G2 13 00N 93 00E
North Australian Basin Indian Ocean **112** K5 14 00S 115 00E
North Baltimore Ohio U.S.A. **36** C2 41 12N 83 43W
North Barrackpore India **94** K3 22 46N 88 21E
North Bergen New Jersey U.S.A. **50** B2 40 46N 74 02W
North Branch New Hampshire U.S.A. **65** J6 43 05N 71 59W
North Branch Chicago River Illinois U.S.A. **53** A3 42 09N 87 50W
Northbrook Illinois U.S.A. **53** A3 42 07N 87 49W
North Canadian *r.* U.S.A. **62** F4 36 00N 100 00W
North Cape New Zealand **111** B4 34 23S 173 04E
North Cape *see* Nordkapp
North Carolina *state* U.S.A. **63** K4 36 00N 80 00W
North Cascades National Park Washington U.S.A. **42** H4 48 45N 121 20W
North Channel British Isles **78** F7 55 20N 5 50W
North Chili New York U.S.A. **64** C6 43 06N 77 52W
North Collins New York U.S.A. **38** D1 42 36N 78 57W
North Dakota *state* U.S.A. **62** F6 47 00N 102 00W
North Dartmouth Massachusetts U.S.A. **65** K4 41 37N 70 59W
North Downs *hills* England **82** D2 51 13N 0 30W
North East Pennsylvania U.S.A. **36** G3 42 13N 79 15W
Northern Cyprus *admin.* Cyprus **92** D6 35 15N 33 00E
Northern Ireland United Kingdom **78** D6
NORTHERN MARIANAS 114 E9
Northern Range *mts.* Trinidad and Tobago **66** T10 10 47N 61 27W
Northern Territory *territory* Australia **110** E5/E6 19 00S 132 00E
North Esk *r.* Scotland **78** I8 56 50N 2 50W
North European Plain Europe **70** 54 00N 20 00E
North Fiji Basin Pacific Ocean **114** H6 18 00S 173 00E
North Fork *r.* Alaska U.S.A. **44** A4 67 30N 152 00W
North Frisian Islands *see* Nordfriesische Inseln
North Haven Connecticut U.S.A. **65** H4 41 00N 72 00W
North Head Australia **111** H2 33 49S 151 18E
North Hollywood California U.S.A. **51** A3 34 10N 118 22W
North Island New Zealand **111** C3 36 40S 177 00E
NORTH KOREA 97 P6/7
Northlake Illinois U.S.A. **53** A2 41 52N 87 56W
North Land *see* Severnaya Zemlya
North Little Rock Arkansas U.S.A. **63** H3 34 46N 92 16W
North Loup *r.* Nebraska U.S.A. **62** F5 42 00N 100 00W
North Platte Nebraska U.S.A. **62** F5 41 09N 100 45W
North Platte *r.* U.S.A. **62** F5 42 00N 103 00W
North Point Barbados **66** V13 13 20N 59 37W
North Point *tn.* Hong Kong U.K. **98** C1 22 18N 114 12E
North Pole Arctic Ocean **116** 90 00N
Northport New York U.S.A. **65** G3 40 55N 73 21W
North Reading Massachusetts U.S.A. **65** J5 42 35N 71 06W
North Scituate Rhode Island U.S.A. **65** J4 41 49N 71 35W
North Sea Europe **70** 55 00N 3 00E
North Stratford New Hampshire U.S.A. **37** P5 44 46N 71 36W
North Tonawanda New York U.S.A. **64** B6 43 02N 78 54W
North Uist *i.* Scotland **78** D9 57 04N 7 15W
Northumberland Pennsylvania U.S.A. **64** D3 40 54N 76 49W
Northville New York U.S.A. **65** F6 43 14N 74 12W
North West Cape Australia **110** A5 21 48S 114 10E
North West Christmas Island Ridge Pacific Ocean **115** J8 9 30N 170 00W
Northwestern Atlantic Basin Atlantic Ocean **113** B10 33 00N 70 00W
Northwest Highlands Scotland **78** F8/G10
Northwest Pacific Basin Pacific Ocean **114** F11 35 00N 150 00E
Northwood England **82** B3 51 36N 0 25W
North York Moors National Park England **78** K6 55 22N 0 45W
Norton Kansas U.S.A. **62** G4 39 51N 99 53W
Norton Sound Alaska U.S.A. **10** C5 64 00N 162 30W
Norvegia, Cape Antarctica **117** 71 28S 122 25W
Norwalk California U.S.A. **51** B2 33 56N 118 04W
Norwalk Connecticut U.S.A. **65** G4 41 07N 73 25W
Norwalk Ohio U.S.A. **36** D2 41 14N 82 37W
NORWAY 79 B3
Norwegian Basin Arctic Ocean **113** H13 67 00N 0 00
Norwegian Sea Arctic Ocean **116** 70 00N 5 00E
Norwich Connecticut U.S.A. **65** H4 41 32N 72 05W
Norwich England **78** M4 52 38N 1 18E
Norwich New York U.S.A. **64** E5 42 32N 75 32W
Norwood Massachusetts U.S.A. **52** B1 42 12N 71 13W
Noshiro Japan **100** D3 40 13N 140 00E
Nosop *r.* Southern Africa **107** I3 25 00S 20 30E
Nosy Bé *i.* Madagascar **107** N5 13 00S 47 00E
Notéc *r.* Poland **80** C5 53 00N 17 00E
Nottingham England **78** J4 52 58N 1 10W
Nouadhibou Mauritania **106** B12 20 54N 17 01W
Nouakchott Mauritania **106** A11 18 09N 15 58W
Nouméa New Caledonia **110** L5 22 16S 166 26E
Nova Friburgo Brazil **69** I8 22 16S 42 34W
Nova Iguaçu Brazil **69** P2 22 46S 43 23W
Novara Italy **81** A4 45 27N 8 37E
Nova Scotia Basin Atlantic Ocean **113** C19 39 00N 55 00W
Novaya Zemlya *is.* Russia **89** H10 74 00N 55 00E
Novgorod Russia **90** C6 58 30N 31 20E
Novi Pazar Serbia Yugoslavia **81** D3 43 09N 20 29E
Novi Sad SerbiaYugoslavia **81** C4 45 15N 19 51E
Novocheboksarsk Russia **90** F6 56 05N 47 27E
Novocherkassk Russia **90** E4 47 25N 40 05E
Novo Hamburgo Brazil **69** G7 29 37S 51 07W
Novokazalinsk Kazakhstan **91** J4 45 48N 62 06E
Novokuybyshevsk Russia **90** F5 53 05N 49 59E
Novokuznetsk Russia **91** O5 53 45N 87 12E
Novolazarevskaya *r.s.* Antarctica **117** 70 46S 11 50E
Novomoskovsk Russia **90** D5 54 06N 38 15E
Novorossiysk Russia **90** D3 44 44N 37 46E
Novoshakhtinsk Russia **90** D4 47 46N 39 55E
Novosibirsk Russia **91** N6 55 04N 83 05E
Novotroitsk Russia **91** H5 51 11N 58 16E
Novyy Port Russia **89** J9 67 38N 72 33E
Novyy Urengoy Russia **89** J9 66 00N 77 20E
Nowai *r.* India **94** K2 22 39N 88 28E
Nowa Sól Poland **80** C5 51 49N 15 41E
Nowgong India **95** G5 26 20N 92 41E
Nowy Dwor Poland **80** D5 52 27N 20 41E
Nowy Sącz Poland **80** D4 49 39N 20 40E
Noyes Island Alaska U.S.A. **42** B3 56 30N 133 45W
Nubian Desert Sudan **92** D3 21 00N 33 00E
Nueces *r.* Texas U.S.A. **62** G2 28 00N 99 00W
Nueva Rosita Mexico **66** D5 27 58N 101 11W
Nueva San Salvador El Salvador **66** G2 13 40N 89 18W
Nuevitas Cuba **67** I4 21 34N 77 18W
Nuevo Casa Grandes Mexico **66** C6 30 22N 107 53W
Nuevo Laredo Mexico **66** E5 27 39N 99 30W
Nu Jiang *(Salween) r.* China **95** G6 31 30N 94 00E
Nuku'alofa Tonga **114** I5 21 09S 175 14W
Nukus Uzbekistan **91** H3 42 28N 59 07E
Nullarbor Plain Australia **110** D3 32 00S 128 00E
Numazu Japan **100** K2 35 08N 138 50E
Numedal *geog. reg.* Norway **79** B3 60 40N 9 00E
Nunivak Island Alaska U.S.A. **10** B5 60 00N 166 00W
Nura *r.* Kazakhstan **91** L5 51 00N 71 00E
Nuremberg *see* Nürnberg
Nürnberg *(Nuremberg)* Germany **76** E4 49 27N 11 05E
Nuseybin Turkey **92** F6 37 05N 41 11E
Nushki Pakistan **94** B5 29 33N 66 01E
Nuthe *r.* Germany **83** E1 52 21N 13 07E
Nuussuaq *p.* Greenland **11** Y7 70 50N 53 00W
Nyainqêntanglha Shan *mts.* China **96** G4/J5 30 00N 90 00E
Nyala Sudan **106** J10 12 01N 24 50E
Nyasa, Lake *(Lake Malawi)* Southern Africa **107** L5 12 00S 35 00E
Nyíregyháza Hungary **81** D4 47 57N 21 43E
Nykøbing Denmark **80** B5 54 47N 11 53E
Nyköping Sweden **79** D2 58 45N 17 03E
Nyngan Australia **110** H3 31 34S 147 14E
Nyons France **77** D3 44 22N 5 08E
Nysa Poland **80** C5 50 30N 17 20E
Nysa *(Neisse) r.* Poland **80** B5 52 00N 14 00E
Nyū dō-zaki *c.* Japan **100** C2 40 00N 139 42E

O

Oahe, Lake U.S.A. **62** F6 45 00N 100 00W
Oahu *i.* Hawaiian Islands **115** X18 21 30N 158 10W
Oak Bluffs Massachusetts U.S.A. **65** K4 41 28N 70 33W
Oak Brook Illinois U.S.A. **53** A2 41 50N 87 59W
Oak Harbor Ohio U.S.A. **36** C2 41 31N 83 10W
Oak Harbor Washington U.S.A. **42** H4 48 17N 122 38W
Oakland California U.S.A. **49** B3 37 50N 122 15W
Oakland County Michigan U.S.A. **52** D2 42 26N 83 27W
Oakland Inner Harbor California U.S.A. **49** B3 37 47N 122 19W
Oak Lawn Illinois U.S.A. **53** A1 41 42N 87 45W
Oak Park Illinois U.S.A. **53** A2 41 52N 87 47W
Oak Park Michigan U.S.A. **52** E2 42 26N 83 09W
Oak Ridge *tn.* Tennessee U.S.A. **63** J4 36 02N 84 12W
Oak Street Beach Illinois U.S.A. **53** B2 41 54N 87 36W
Oamaru New Zealand **111** B1 45 07S 170 58E
Oano Island Pitcairn Islands **115** N5 23 32S 125 00W
Ōarai Japan **100** M3 36 18N 140 35E
Oaxaca Mexico **66** E3 17 05N 96 41W
Ob' *r.* Russia **91** K7 65 30N 66 00E
Ob', Gulf of Russia **89** J9 68 00N 74 00E
Obama Japan **100** G2 35 25N 135 45E
Oban Scotland **78** F8 56 25N 5 29W
Oberhausen Germany **76** H2 51 27N 6 50E
Oberlin Ohio U.S.A. **36** D2 41 17N 82 14W
Obidos Brazil **68** F12 1 52S 55 30W
Obihiro Japan **100** D3 42 56N 143 10E
Obitsu *r.* Japan **101** C2 35 25N 139 53E
Ocala Florida U.S.A. **63** J2 29 11N 82 09W
Ocaña Colombia **68** C14 8 16N 73 21W
Ocatlán Mexico **66** D4 20 21N 102 42W
Ocean City New Jersey U.S.A. **65** F2 39 16N 74 35W
Ochakovo Russia **88** L1 55 39N 37 30E
Ocho Rios Jamaica **67** Q8 18 24N 77 06W
Ōda Japan **100** B2 35 10N 132 29E
Ōdate Japan **100** D3 40 18N 140 32E
Odawara Japan **100** L2 35 15N 139 08E
Odda Norway **79** B3 60 03N 6 34E
Ödemiş Turkey **80** E2 38 11N 27 58E
Odense Denmark **80** B6 55 24N 10 25E
Odenwald *mts.* Germany **76** D4 49 00N 9 00E
Oder *(Odra) r,* Europe **80** C5 E2 39 27N 75 40W
Odessa New York U.S.A. **64** D5 42 21N 76 46W
Odessa Texas U.S.A. **62** F3 31 50N 102 23W
Odessa Ukraine **90** C4 46 30N 30 46E
Odiel *r.* Spain **77** A2 37 32N 7 00W
Odra *(Oder) r.* Europe **80** C5 52 00N 15 00E
Oekusi *(Dili)* Indonesia **99** H2 8 35S 125 35E
Ofanto *r.* Italy **81** C3 41 00N 15 00E
Ofuna Japan **101** B2 53 21N 139 32E
Ofunato Japan **100** D2 39 04N 141 43E
Ogaden *geog. reg* Africa **106** O9 7 00N 51 00E
Ōgaki Japan **100** H2 35 22N 136 36E
Ogano Japan **100** L2 35 55N 139 11E
Ogasawara Guntō *i.* Pacific Ocean **114** E10 27 30N 43 00E
Ogawa Japan **101** A3 35 43N 135 29E
Ogbomosho Nigeria **106** F9 8 05N 4 11E
Ogden Utah U.S.A. **62** D5 41 14N 111 59W
Ogooué *r.* Gabon **106** G7 0 50S 9 50E
Ogun *r.* Nigeria **107** V3 6 42N 3 29E
Ogunquit Maine U.S.A. **65** K6 43 16N 70 37W
Ōhara Japan **100** M2 35 16N 140 22E
Ōhata Japan **100** D3 41 22N 141 11E
Ohio *state* U.S.A. **63** J5 40 00N 83 00W
Ohio River Pennsylvania U.S.A. **53** D1 40 30N 80 05W
Ohridsko ezero *l.* Europe **81** D3 41 00N 21 00E
Oil City Pennsylvania U.S.A. **36** G2 41 26N 79 44W
Oise *r.* France **76** C4 49 10N 2 10E
Ōita Japan **100** B1 33 15N 131 36E
Ojinaga Mexico **66** D5 29 35N 104 26W
Oka *r.* Russia **90** E6 55 00N 42 00E
Okanogan Washington U.S.A. **42** J4 48 22N 119 35W
Okanogan River Washington U.S.A. **42** J4 48 40N 119 30W
Okara Pakistan **95** C6 30 49N 73 31E
Okavango *r.* Southern Africa **107** I4 17 50S 20 00E
Okavango Basin Botswana **107** J4 19 00S 23 00E
Okaya Japan **100** C2 36 03N 138 00E
Okayama Japan **100** B1 34 40N 133 54E
Okazaki Japan **100** J1 34 58N 137 10E
Okeechobee, Lake Florida U.S.A. **63** J2 27 00N 81 00W
Okha Russia **89** Q6 53 35N 143 01E
Okhla India **94** M4 28 33N 77 16E
Okhotsk Russia **89** Q7 59 20N 143 15E
Okhotsk, Sea of Russia **89** Q7 55 00N 148 00E
Oki *is.* Japan **100** B2 36 05N 133 00E
Okinawa *i.* Japan **97** P4 26 30N 128 00E
Oklahoma *state* U.S.A. **63** G4 36 00N 98 00W
Oklahoma City Oklahoma U.S.A. **63** G4 35 28N 97 33W
Oktyabr'skiy Russia **89** R6 52 43N 156 14E
Okushiri-tō *i.* Japan **100** C3 42 15N 139 30E
Öland *i.* Sweden **79** D2 56 45N 51 50E
Olbia Italy **81** A3 40 56N 9 30E
Old Bridge New Jersey U.S.A. **65** F3 40 27N 74 23W
Oldenburg Germany **76** D5 53 08N 8 13E
Oldham England **78** I5 53 33N 2 07W
Old Harbor Massachusetts U.S.A. **52** B2 42 19N 71 02W
Old Harbour Jamaica **67** Q7 17 56N 77 07W
Old Harbour Bay *tn.* Jamaica **67** Q7 17 54N 77 06W
Old Head of Kinsale *c.* Irish Republic **78** C3 51 40N 8 30W
Old Saybrook Connecticut U.S.A. **65** H4 41 18N 72 22W
Old Town Maine U.S.A. **33** C1 44 55N 68 41W
Olean New York U.S.A. **64** B5 42 05N 78 26W
Olekma *r.* Russia **89** O7 59 00N 121 00E
Olekminsk Russia **89** O8 60 25N 120 25E
Olenëk Russia **89** N9 68 28N 112 18E
Olenëk *r.* Russia **89** O10 72 00N 122 00E
Olga Washington U.S.A. **42** H4 48 36N 122 50W
Olhão Portugal **77** A2 37 01N 7 50W
Ólimbos *(Olympus) mt.* Greece **81** D3 40 05N 22 21E
Olinda Brazil **68** J11 8 00S 34 51W
Olomouc Czechoslovakia **80** C4 49 38N 17 15E
Olongapo The Philippines **99** G6 14 49N 120 17E
Olsztyn Poland **80** D5 53 48N 20 29E
Olt *r.* Romania **81** D3 44 00N 24 00E
O'luan-pi *c.* Taiwan **98** G4 21 54N 120 53E
Olympia Washington U.S.A. **62** B6 47 03N 122 53W
Olympus *see* Ólimbos
Olympus, Mount Washington U.S.A. **62** B6 47 49N 123 42W
Olympus Mountain Cyprus **92** D5 34 55N 32 52E
Om' *r.* Russia **91** M6 55 00N 79 00E
Omaha Nebraska U.S.A. **63** G5 41 15N 96 00W
Omagh Northern Ireland **78** D6 54 36N 7 18W
Omak Washington U.S.A. **43** E1 48 25N 119 30W
OMAN 93 I2
Oman, Gulf of Iran/Oman **93** I3 24 30N 58 30E
Omboué Gabon **106** G7 1 38S 9 20E
Omdurman Sudan **92** D2 15 37N 32 29E
Ome Japan **100** L2 35 48N 139 17E
Omihachiman Japan **100** H2 35 08N 136 04E
Ōmiya Japan **100** L2 35 54N 139 39E
Ommaney, Cape Alaska U.S.A. **42** B3 56 10N 134 40W
Omo *r.* Ethiopia **106** M9 7 00N 37 00E
Omolon *r.* Russia **89** R9 65 00N 160 00E
Omoloy *r.* Russia **89** P9 69 00N 132 00E
Omsk Russia **91** L6 55 00N 73 22E
Ōmuta Japan **100** B1 33 02N 130 26E
Omutinskiy Russia **91** K6 56 30N 67 40E
Onaway Michigan U.S.A. **36** B6 45 23N 84 14W
Oneida New York U.S.A. **64** E6 43 04N 75 40W
Oneida Lake New York U.S.A. **64** E6 43 10N 75 55W
Oneonta New York U.S.A. **64** E5 42 56N 75 04W
Ongea Levu *i.* Fiji **114** V15 19 11S 178 28W
Onitsha Nigeria **106** G9 6 10N 6 47E
Ono Japan **100** F1 34 52N 134 55E
Onomichi Japan **100** B1 34 25N 33 11E
Onon *r.* Mongolia/Russia **97** M9 51 00N 114 00E
Onslow Australia **110** B5 21 41S 115 12E
Ontario, Lake Canada/U.S.A. **36** H4 43 45N 78 00W
Ontonagon Michigan U.S.A. **63** I6 46 52N 89 18W
Oostende Belgium **76** C5 51 13N 2 55E
Opala Zaïre **106** J7 0 40S 24 20E
Opava Czechoslovakia **80** C4 49 58N 17 55E
Opheim Montana U.S.A. **40** B1 48 54N 106 25W
Opole Poland **80** C5 50 40N 17 56E
Oporto *see* Porto
Opotiki New Zealand **87** C3 38 00S 117 18E
Oradea Romania **81** D4 47 03N 21 55E
Oradell Reservoir New Jersey U.S.A. **50** B2 40 58N 74 00W
Oran Algeria **106** E15 35 45N 0 38W
Orán Argentina **69** E8 23 07S 64 16W
Orange Australia **110** H3 33 19S 149 10E
Orange California U.S.A. **51** C2 33 43N 117 54W
Orange France **77** C3 44 08N 4 48E
Orange Massachusetts U.S.A. **65** H5 42 35N 72 20W
Orange New Jersey U.S.A. **50** B2 40 45N 74 14W
Orange Texas U.S.A. **63** H3 30 05N 93 43W
Orange *r.* Southern Africa **107** I2 28 30S 17 30E
Orangeburg South Carolina U.S.A. **63** J3 33 28N 80 53W

Orange Free State *admin.* Republic of South Africa 107 K2 27 30S 27 30E
Oravița Romania 81 D4 45 02N 21 43E
Orbigo *r.* Spain 77 A3 42 15N 5 45W
Orbisonia Pennsylvania U.S.A. 64 C3 40 15N 77 55W
Orcadas *r.s.* Antarctica 117 60 40S 44 44W
Orcas Island Washington U.S.A. 42 H4 48 40N 122 55W
Orchard Park New York U.S.A. 64 B5 42 46N 78 45W
Orcia *r.* Italy 81 B3 42 00N 11 00E
Ordzhonikidze *see* Vladikavkaz
Örebro Sweden 79 D2 59 17N 15 13E
Oregon *state* U.S.A. 62 B5 44 00N 120 00W
Oregon City Oregon U.S.A. 62 B6 45 21N 122 36W
Orekhovo Zuyevo Russia 90 D6 55 47N 39 00E
Orël Russia 90 D5 52 58N 36 04E
Orem Utah U.S.A. 62 D5 40 20N 111 45W
Orenburg Russia 91 H5 51 50N 55 00E
Orense Spain 77 A3 42 20N 7 52W
Orient New York U.S.A. 65 H4 41 09N 72 18W
Orient Point New York U.S.A. 65 H4 41 10N 72 13W
Orihuela Spain 77 B2 38 05N 0 56W
Orinda California U.S.A. 49 C3 37 42N 122 10W
Oriskany New York U.S.A. 64 E6 43 08N 75 19W
Orissa *admin.* India 95 E4 20 20N 83 00E
Oristano Italy 81 A2 39 54N 8 36E
Orizaba Mexico 66 E3 18 51N 97 08W
Orkney Islands *is.* Scotland 78 H11 59 00N 3 00W
Orlando Florida U.S.A. 63 J2 28 33N 81 21W
Orléans France 77 C4 47 54N 1 54E
Orleans Massachusetts U.S.A. 65 K4 41 47N 70 00W
Orly France 83 B1 48 44N 2 24E
Örnsköldsvik Sweden 79 D3 63 19N 18 45E
Oropuche *r.* Trinidad and Tobago 66 T10 10 36N 61 05W
Oroville Washington U.S.A. 43 E1 48 57N 119 27W
Orpington England 82 D2 51 23N 0 05E
Orsay France 83 A1 48 42N 2 11E
Orsha Belarus 90 C5 54 30N 30 23E
Orsk Russia 91 H5 51 13N 58 35E
Ortigueira Spain 77 A3 43 43N 8 13W
Orūmīyeh Iran 92 F6 37 40N 45 00E
Oruro Bolivia 68 D9 17 59S 67 08W
Ōsaka Japan 100 G1 34 40N 135 30E
Ōsaka *pref.* Japan 100 G1 34 30N 135 10E
Ōsaka-wan *b.* Japan 100 G1 34 30N 135 10E
Osh Kirgyzstan 91 L3 40 37N 72 49E
Ō-shima *i.* Japan 100 C1 34 45N 139 25E
Oshkosh Wisconsin U.S.A. 63 I5 44 01N 88 32W
Oshogbo Nigeria 106 F9 7 50N 4 35E
Osijek Croatia 81 C4 45 33N 18 41E
Oskarshamn Sweden 80 C6 57 16N 16 25E
Oslo Norway 79 C2 59 56N 10 45E
Oslofjorden *fj.* Norway 79 C2 59 20N 10 37E
Osmaniye Turkey 92 E6 37 04N 36 15E
Osnabrück Germany 76 D5 52 17N 8 03E
Osorno Chile 69 C4 40 35S 73 14W
Ossa, Mount Australia 110 H1 41 52S 146 04E
Ossining New York U.S.A. 65 G4 41 10N 73 52W
Ostankino Russia 88 M2 55 50N 37 37E
Österdalälven *r.* Sweden 79 C3 61 40N 13 30E
Østerdalen *geog. reg.* Norway 79 C3 62 00N 10 30E
Östersund Sweden 79 C3 63 10N 14 40E
Östervall Sweden 79 D3 62 20N 15 20E
Ostfriesische Inseln *(East Frisian Islands) is.* Germany 76 D5 53 00N 7 00E
Ostowiec Swietokrzyski Poland 80 D5 50 58N 21 22E
Ostrava Czechoslovakia 80 C4 49 50N 18 15E
Ostróda Poland 80 D5 53 42N 19 59E
Ostrołeka Poland 80 D5 53 05N 21 32E
Ostrów Mazowiecki Poland 80 D5 52 50N 21 51E
Ostrów Wielkopolski Poland 80 C5 51 39N 17 50E
Oswego River New York U.S.A. 64 D6 43 20N 76 25W
Ōta Japan 101 B3 35 34N 139 42E
Otaheite Bay Trinidad and Tobago 66 S9 10 15N 61 30W
Otaki New Zealand 111 C2 40 45S 175 09E
Otaru Japan 100 D3 43 14N 140 59E
Otavalo Ecuador 68 B13 0 13N 78 15W
Otra *r.* Norway 79 B2 56 17N 7 30E
Otranto Italy 81 C3 40 08N 18 30E
Otranto, Strait of Adriatic Sea 81 C3 40 00N 19 00E
Otsego Michigan U.S.A. 35 C1 42 26N 85 42W
Otsego Lake New York U.S.A. 64 F5 42 45N 74 55W
Ōtsu Japan 100 G2 35 00N 135 50E
Otsuki Japan 100 K2 35 38N 138 53E
Ottawa Kansas U.S.A. 63 G4 38 35N 95 16W
Ottawa Ohio U.S.A. 36 B2 41 02N 84 03W
Ottumwa Iowa U.S.A. 63 H5 41 02N 92 26W
Ouachita *r.* U.S.A. 63 H3 34 00N 93 00W
Ouachita Mountains U.S.A. 63 G3 34 00N 95 00W
Ouadda Central African Republic 106 J9 8 09N 22 20E
Ouagadougou Burkina 106 E10 12 20N 1 40W
Ouahigouya Burkina 106 E10 13 31N 2 20W
Ouargla Algeria 106 G14 32 00N 5 16E
Ouassel *r.* Algeria 77 C2 35 30N 2 00E
Oudtshoorn Republic of South Africa 107 J1 33 35S 22 12E
Ouerrha *r.* Morocco 77 A1 34 00N 6 00W
Ouezzane Morocco 77 A1 34 25N 5 35W
Ouham *r.* Central African Republic 106 I9 7 00N 17 30E
Oujda Morocco 106 E14 34 41N 1 45W
Oulu Finland 79 F3 65 02N 25 27E
Oulujärvi *l.* Finland 79 F3 64 20N 27 00E
Oulujoki *r.* Finland 79 F3 64 50N 26 00E
Oum El Bouaghi Algeria 77 D2 35 45N 7 00E
Ounasjoki *r.* Finland 79 F4 67 00N 25 00E
Ou-sanmyaku *mts.* Japan 100 D2 39 20N 141 00E
Ouse *r.* England 78 J5 53 40N 1 00W
Oust *r.* France 77 B4 47 50N 2 30W
Outer Hebrides *is.* Scotland 78 D9 58 00N 7 00W
Ovalau *i.* Fiji 114 U16 17 40S 178 47E
Ovalle Chile 69 C6 30 33S 71 16W
Övertorneå Sweden 79 E4 66 22N 23 40E
Ovid New York U.S.A. 64 D5 42 40N 76 49W
Oviedo Spain 77 A3 43 21N 5 50W
Owando Congo 106 I7 0 27S 15 44E
Owasco Lake New York U.S.A. 64 D5 42 50N 76 30W
Owego New York U.S.A. 64 D5 42 06N 76 16W
Owen Fracture Zone Indian Ocean 112 E7/8 10 00N 55 00E
Owen, Mount New Zealand 111 B2 41 33S 172 33E
Owensboro Kentucky U.S.A. 63 I4 37 45N 87 05W
Owen Stanley Range *mts.* Papua New Guinea 110 H8 8 00S 147 30E
Owosso Michigan U.S.A. 36 B4 43 00N 84 11W
Owyhee *r.* U.S.A. 62 C5 43 00N 117 00W
Oxford England 78 J3 51 46N 1 15W
Oxford Massachusetts U.S.A. 65 J5 42 08N 71 52W
Oxford New York U.S.A. 64 E5 42 26N 75 36W
Oxted England 82 C1 51 15N 0 01W
Oxus *see* Amudar'ya
Oyama Japan 100 C2 36 18N 139 48E
Oyapock *r.* Brazil 68 G13 3 00N 52 30W
Oyem Gabon 106 H8 1 34N 11 31E
Oyster Point California U.S.A. 49 B2 37 39N 122 22W
Ozarks, Lake of the Missouri U.S.A. 63 H4 38 00N 93 00W
Ozark Plateau Missouri U.S.A. 63 H4 37 00N 93 00W
Ozero Alakol' *salt l.* Kazakhstan 91 N4 46 00N 82 00E
Ozero Aydarkul' *l.* Kazakhstan 91 K3 41 00N 68 00E
Ozero Balkhash *(Lake Balkhash) salt l.* Kazakhstan 91 M4 46 00N 75 00E
Ozero Baykal *(Lake Baykal)* Russia 89 M6 54 00N 109 00E
Ozero Chany *salt l.* Russia 91 M5 55 00N 77 30E
Ozero Chudskoye *(Lake Peipus) l.* Estonia/Russia 79 F2 58 40N 27 30E
Ozero Il'men' *l.* Russia 90 C6 58 00N 31 30E
Ozero Issyk-Kul' *salt l.* Kirgyzstan 91 M3 42 30N 77 30E
Ozero Khanka *l.* Asia 89 P5 45 00N 132 30E
Ozero Kulundinskoye *l.* Russia 91 M5 53 00N 80 00E
Ozero Manych Gudilo *l.* Russia 90 E4 46 30N 43 00E
Ozero Onezhskoye *(Lake Onega) l.* Russia 90 D7 62 00N 40 00E
Ozero Pskovskoye *l.* Estonia/Russia 79 F2 58 00N 28 00E
Ozero Seletyteniz *l.* Russia 91 L5 53 30N 73 00E
Ozero Sevan *l.* Armenia 90 F3 40 35N 45 00E
Ozero Taymyr Russia 89 M10 74 00N 102 30E
Ozero Teletskoye *l.* Russia 91 O5 52 00N 88 00E
Ozero Tengiz *salt l.* Russia 91 K5 51 00N 69 00E
Ozero Zaysan *l.* Kazakhstan 91 N4 48 00N 84 00E

P

Pabjanice Poland 80 C5 51 40N 19 20E
Pabna Bangladesh 95 F4 24 00N 89 15E
Pacasmayo Peru 68 B11 7 27S 79 33W
Pachuca Mexico 66 E4 20 10N 98 44W
Pacifica California U.S.A. 49 B2 37 37N 122 29W
Pacific-Antarctic Ridge Pacific Ocean 115 M2 55 00S 135 00W
Pacific Ocean 114/115
Padang Indonesia 99 C3 1 00S 100 21E
Paderborn Germany 76 D5 51 43N 8 44E
Padilla Bolivia 68 E9 19 18S 64 20W
Padova Italy 81 B4 45 24N 11 53E
Paducah Kentucky U.S.A. 63 I4 37 03N 88 36W
Paeroa New Zealand 111 C3 37 21S 175 41E
Pag *i.* Croatia 81 B3 44 00N 15 00E
Pagadian The Philippines 99 G5 7 50N 123 30E
Pahala Hawaiian Islands 115 Z17 19 12N 155 28W
Paharganj India 94 L4 28 38N 77 12E
Päijänne *l.* Finland 79 F3 61 30N 25 25E
Painesville Ohio U.S.A. 35 E2 41 43N 81 15W
Pai-sha Tao *i.* Taiwan 98 F6 23 40N 119 33E
Paisley Scotland 78 G7 55 50N 4 26W
Paita Peru 68 A11 5 11S 81 09W
PAKISTAN 94/95 A5/C5
Pakokku Myanmar 96 J3 21 20E 95 05E
Pakse Laos 99 D6 14 09N 105 50E
Pak Sha Tsuen Hong Kong U.K. 98 B2 22 25N 114 01E
Pak Tam Chung Hong Kong U.K. 98 C2 22 24N 114 19E
Palaiseau France 83 A1 48 43N 2 15E
Palana Russia 89 R7 59 05N 159 59E
Palangkaraya Indonesia 99 E3 2 06S 113 55E
Palatine Bridge New York U.S.A. 65 F5 42 55N 74 36W
Palau *(Belau) i.* Pacific Ocean 114 D8 7 30N 134 30E
Palawan *i.* The Philippines 99 F5/F6 9 00N 114 00E
Palayankottai India 95 D1 8 42N 77 46E
Palembang Indonesia 99 C3 2 59S 104 45E
Palencia Spain 77 B3 41 01N 4 32W
Palermo Italy 81 B2 38 08N 13 23E
Palestine Texas U.S.A. 63 G3 31 45N 95 39W
Palghat India 95 D2 10 46N 76 42E
Palk Strait India 95 D2 10 00N 80 00E
Palliser, Cape New Zealand 111 C2 41 37S 175 16E
Palma de Mallorca Balearic Islands 77 C2 39 35N 2 39E
Palmar Sur Costa Rica 67 H1 8 57N 83 28W
Palmas Bellas Panama 67 X2 9 16N 80 05W
Palmas, Cape Liberia 106 D9 4 25N 7 50W
Palm Beach Australia 111 H3 33 36S 151 19E
Palmer Alaska U.S.A. 10 F5 61 35N 149 10W
Palmer Massachusetts U.S.A. 65 H5 42 10N 72 19W
Palmer *r.s.* Antarctica 117 64 46S 83 55W
Palmer Land *geog. reg.* Antarctica 117 72 00S 62 00W
Palmer Park Michigan U.S.A. 52 E2 42 25N 83 08W
Palmerston Atoll *i.* Pacific Ocean 115 J6 18 04S 163 10W
Palmerston North New Zealand 111 C2 40 20S 175 39E
Palmerton Pennsylvania U.S.A. 64 E3 40 46N 75 32W
Palmira Colombia 68 B13 3 33N 76 17W
Palmyra New Jersey U.S.A. 64 E3 40 00N 75 01W
Palmyra New York U.S.A. 64 C6 43 03N 77 14W
Palmyra Atoll *ii.* Pacific Ocean 115 K8 5 52N 162 05W
Palo Alto California U.S.A. 49 C1 37 26N 122 10W
Palo Seco Trinidad and Tobago 66 S9 10 06N 61 36W
Palomares Mexico 66 E3 17 10N 95 04W
Palopo Indonesia 99 G3 3 01S 120 12E
Palos Verdes Hills California U.S.A. 51 A2 33 46N 118 23W
Palu Indonesia 99 F3 0 54S 119 52E
Pamiers France 77 C3 43 07N 1 36E
Pamirs *mts.* Tajikistan 91 L2 38 00N 74 00E
Pamlico Sound North Carolina U.S.A. 63 K4 35 00N 76 00W
Pampas *geog. reg.* Argentina 69 E5 36 00S 63 00W
Pamplona Colombia 68 C14 7 24N 72 38W
Pamplona Spain 77 B3 42 49N 1 39W
PANAMA 67 H1
Panamá Panama 67 Y1 8 57N 79 30W
Panama Canal Panama 67 Y2 9 00N 80 00W
Panama City Florida U.S.A. 63 I3 30 10N 85 41W
Panama Isthmus Central America 55 9 00N 80 00W
Panay *i.* The Philippines 99 G6 11 20N 122 30E
Pančevo Serbia Yugoslavia 81 D3 44 52N 20 40E
Panch'iao Taiwan 98 H8 25 01N 121 27E
Panchla India 94 J2 22 32N 88 08E
Panchur India 94 K2 22 31N 88 15E
Panevežys Lithuania 80 D6 55 44N 24 24E
Pangkalpinang Indonesia 99 D3 2 05S 106 09E
Pānihāti India 94 K2 22 41N 88 23E
Panipat India 95 D5 29 24N 76 58E
Panke *r.* Germany 83 F2 52 38N 13 27E
Pankow Germany 83 F2 52 35N 13 25E
Pantar *i.* Indonesia 99 G2 8 00S 124 00E
Pantelleria *i.* Italy 81 B2 36 00N 12 00E
Pao de Açúcar *(Sugar Loaf) mt.* Brazil 69 Q2 22 57S 43 09W
Papa Hawaiian Islands 115 Z17 19 12N 155 53W
Pápa Hungary 81 C4 47 20N 17 29E
Papantla Mexico 66 E4 20 30N 97 21W
Papua, Gulf of Papua New Guinea 110 H8 8 30S 145 00E
PAPUA NEW GUINEA 110 H8
Pará *admin.* Brazil 68 G12 4 30S 52 30W
Paraburdoo Australia 110 B5 23 15S 117 45E
Paracel Islands South China Sea 99 E7 16 40N 112 00E
PARAGUAY 68/69 F8
Paraíba *admin.* Brazil 68 J11 7 20S 37 10W
Parakou Benin 106 F9 9 23N 2 40E
Paramaribo Surinam 68 F14 5 52N 55 14W
Paramonga Peru 68 B10 10 42S 77 50W
Paramus New Jersey U.S.A. 50 B2 40 55N 74 03W
Paraná Argentina 69 E6 31 45S 60 30W
Parana *admin.* Brazil 69 G8 24 30S 53 00W
Paraná Plateau Brazil 55 25 00S 50 00W
Paranguá Brazil 69 H7 25 32S 48 36W
Parbhani India 95 D3 19 16N 76 51E
Pardubice Czechoslovakia 80 C4 50 03N 15 45E
Parepare Indonesia 99 F3 4 00S 119 40E
Parkersburg West Virginia U.S.A. 63 J4 39 17N 81 33W
Paria, Gulf of Trinidad and Tobago/Venezuela 66 S9 10 30N 61 45W
Parintins Brazil 68 F12 2 38S 56 45W
Paris France 77 C4 48 52N 2 20E
Paris Texas U.S.A. 63 G3 33 41N 95 33W
Paris Basin France 70 48 00N 2 30E
Parish New York U.S.A. 35 E1 43 24N 76 07W
Parkano Finland 79 E3 62 03N 23 00E
Parker, Mount Hong Kong U.K. 98 C1 22 16N 114 13E
Parkertown New Jersey U.S.A. 65 F2 39 37N 74 19W
Park Ridge Illinois U.S.A. 53 A3 42 01N 87 50W
Park River North Dakota U.S.A. 39 B1 48 30N 97 50W
Park Royal England 82 B3 51 32N 0 17W
Parma Italy 81 B3 44 48N 10 19E
Parma Ohio U.S.A. 36 E2 41 24N 81 44W
Parnaíba Brazil 68 I12 2 58S 41 46W
Parnassós *mt.* Greece 81 D2 38 30N 22 37E
Pärnu Estonia 79 E2 58 28N 24 30E
Paroo *r.* Australia 110 G4 27 00S 144 00E
Páros *i.* Greece 81 E2 37 00N 25 00E
Parramatta Australia 111 G2 33 50S 151 00E
Parramatta River Australia 111 G2 33 49S 151 05E
Parras Mexico 66 D5 25 30N 102 11W
Parsippany New Jersey U.S.A. 65 F3 40 50N 74 26W
Pasadena California U.S.A. 51 B3 34 10N 118 09W
Pasadena Texas U.S.A. 63 G2 29 42N 95 14W
Pascagoula Mississippi U.S.A. 63 I3 30 21N 88 32W
Pasco Washington U.S.A. 63 C6 46 15N 119 07W
Pascoag Rhode Island U.S.A. 65 J4 41 57N 71 42W
Passaic New Jersey U.S.A. 50 B2 40 50N 74 08W
Passaic River New Jersey U.S.A. 50 B2 40 46N 74 09W
Passau Germany 76 E4 48 35N 13 28E
Passo Fundo Brazil 69 G7 28 16S 52 20W
Pasto Colombia 68 B13 1 12N 77 17W
Patagonia *geog. reg.* Argentina 69 C2/D4 48 00S 70 00W
Patan India 95 C4 23 51N 72 11E
Patan Nepal 95 F5 27 40N 85 20E
Patchogue New York U.S.A. 65 G3 40 46N 73 01W
Patea New Zealand 111 C3 39 45S 174 29E
Pate Island Kenya 106 N7 2 05S 41 05E
Paterson New Jersey U.S.A. 50 B2 40 55N 74 08W
Pathankot India 95 D6 32 16N 75 43E
Patiala India 95 D6 30 21N 76 27E
Pātipukur India 94 K2 22 36N 88 24E
Patna India 95 F5 25 37N 85 12E
Patos Brazil 68 J11 6 55S 37 15W
Pátrai Greece 81 D2 38 14N 21 44E
Patton Pennsylvania U.S.A. 64 B3 40 38N 78 38W
Patton Park Michigan U.S.A. 52 E2 42 19N 83 07W
Pau France 77 B3 43 18N 0 22W
Paulding Ohio U.S.A. 36 B2 41 10N 84 37W
Paungde Myanmar 95 H3 18 30N 95 30E
Pausin Germany 83 E2 52 39N 13 04E
Pavia Italy 81 A4 45 12N 9 09E
Pavlodar Kazakhstan 91 M5 52 21N 76 59E
Pavlograd Ukraine 90 D4 48 34N 35 50E
Paw Paw Michigan U.S.A. 35 C1 42 13N 85 55W
Pawtucket Massachusetts U.S.A. 65 J4 41 53N 71 23W
Paysandú Uruguay 69 F6 32 21S 58 05W
Pazardzhik Bulgaria 81 D3 42 10N 24 20E
Peake Deep Atlantic Ocean 113 F11 43 00N 20 05W
Pearl *r.* Mississippi U.S.A. 63 H3 32 00N 90 00W
Pearl Harbour Hawaiian Islands 115 X18 21 22N 158 00W
Pearl River *tn.* New York U.S.A. 65 F4 41 03N 74 02W
Peč Serbia Yugoslavia 81 D3 42 40N 20 19E
Pechora Russia 88 H9 65 14N 57 18E
Pechora *r.* Russia 91 H7 60 00N 55 00E
Pecos Texas U.S.A. 62 F3 31 25N 103 30W
Pecos *r.* U.S.A. 62 F3 30 00N 102 00W
Pécs Hungary 81 C4 46 04N 18 15E
Peddocks Island Massachusetts U.S.A. 52 C2 42 17N 70 55W
Pedreiras Brazil 68 I11 4 32S 44 40W
Pedro Juan Caballero Paraguay 69 F8 22 30S 55 44W
Pedro Miguel Locks Panama 67 Y2 9 01N 79 36W
Peekskill New York U.S.A. 65 G4 41 18N 73 56W
Pegasus Bay New Zealand 111 B2 43 00S 173 00E
Pegu Myanmar 97 J2 17 18N 96 31E
Pegu Yoma *mts.* Myanmar 96 J2 19 00N 96 00E
Pegunungan Van Rees *mts.* Indonesia 110 F9 2 30S 138 00E
Pei-kang Taiwan 98 G6 23 38N 120 18E
Peipus, Lake *see* Ozero Chudskoye
Peking *see* Beijing
Pelican Point Namibia 107 H3 22 54S 14 25E
Pelješac *i.* Croatia 81 C3 43 00N 17 00E
Peloponnese *see* Pelopónnisos
Pelopónnisos *(Peloponnese) geog. reg.* Greece 81 D2 37 00N 22 00E
Pelotas Brazil 69 G6 31 45S 52 20W
Pematangsiantar Indonesia 99 B4 2 59N 99 01E
Pemba Mozambique 107 N5 13 00S 40 30E
Pemba Island Tanzania 107 M6 5 30S 39 50E
Pemba National Park Zaïre 107 K6 9 00S 26 30E
Pembina North Dakota U.S.A. 39 B1 48 59N 97 16W
Penal Trinidad and Tobago 66 T9 10 10N 61 28W
Pen Argyl Pennsylvania U.S.A. 64 E3 40 52N 75 25W
Peñarroya-Pueblonuevo Spain 77 A2 38 19N 5 16W
Pendleton Oregon U.S.A. 62 C6 45 40N 118 46W
Pend Oreille Lake Idaho U.S.A. 43 E1 48 10N 116 20W
Pend Oreille River Washington U.S.A. 43 E1 48 50N 117 25W
Penfield Pennsylvania U.S.A. 64 B4 41 13N 78 36W
Peng Chau Hong Kong U.K. 98 B1 22 17N 114 02E
Peng Chau *i.* Hong Kong U.K. 98 B1 22 17N 114 02E
P'eng-chia Hsü *i.* Taiwan 98 I8 25 38N 122 02E
P'eng-hu Lieh-tao *(Pescadores Islands) is.* Taiwan 98 F6 23 30N 119 30E
Peng-hu Shuitao *sd.* Taiwan 98 F6 23 30N 119 30E
P'eng-hu Tao *i.* Taiwan 98 F6 23 34N 119 35E
Penha Brazil 69 P2 22 49S 43 17W
Peninsula de Paria *p.* Venezuela 66 S10 10 44N 61 52W
Peninsula de Taitao *p.* Chile 69 C3 46 30S 75 00W
Pennant Hills Australia 111 G3 33 44S 151 04E
Penner *r.* India 95 D2 14 30N 77 30E
Penn Hills Pennsylvania U.S.A. 53 E1 40 28N 79 49W
Pennines *hills* England 78 I6
Pennsauken New Jersey U.S.A. 64 E2 39 58N 75 03W
Pennsylvania *state* U.S.A. 63 K5 41 00N 78 00W
Penn Yan New York U.S.A. 64 C5 42 41N 77 03W
Penobscot River Maine U.S.A. 33 C2 45 00N 68 40W
Penonomé Panama 67 H1 8 30N 80 20W
Penrith England 78 I6 54 40N 2 44W
Pensacola Florida U.S.A. 63 I3 30 26N 87 12W
Pensacola Mountains Antarctica 117 84 00S 60 00W
Pentland Firth *sd.* Scotland 78 H10 58 45N 3 10W
Penza Russia 90 F5 53 11N 45 00E
Penzance England 78 F2 50 07N 5 33W
Peoria Illinois U.S.A. 63 I5 40 43N 89 38W
Pepacton Reservoir New York U.S.A. 64 F5 42 05N 74 55W
Pereira Colombia 68 B13 4 47N 75 46W
Pergunungan Maoke *mts.* Indonesia 110 F9 4 00S 137 30E
Pergunungan Van Rees *mts.* Indonesia 110 F9 2 30S 137 30E
Perhojöki *r.* Finland 79 E3 63 30N 24 00E
Périgueux France 77 C4 45 12N 0 44E
Perm' Russia 91 H6 58 01N 56 10E
Pernambuco *admin.* Brazil 68 J11 8 00S 37 30W
Pernik Bulgaria 81 D3 42 36N 23 03E
Perovo Russia 88 N1 55 44N 37 46E
Perpignan France 77 C3 42 42N 2 54E
Perrysburg Ohio U.S.A. 36 C2 41 33N 83 39W
Perth Australia 110 B3 31 58N 115 49E
Perth Scotland 78 H8 56 42N 3 28W
Perth Amboy New Jersey U.S.A. 50 A1 40 31N 74 17W
PERU 68 B10
Peru Basin Pacific Ocean 115 Q6 18 00S 95 00W
Peru-Chile Trench Pacific Ocean 115 S6 13 00S 87 00W
Perugia Italy 81 B3 43 07N 12 23E
Pervoural'sk Russia 91 H6 56 59N 59 58E
Pesaro Italy 81 B3 43 54N 12 54E
Pescara Italy 81 B3 42 27N 14 13E
Peshawar Pakistan 95 C6 34 01N 71 40E
Petah Tiqwa Israel 92 O11 32 05N 34 53E
Petare Venezuela 68 D15 10 31N 66 50W
Petauke Zambia 107 L5 14 15S 31 20E
Peterborough Australia 110 F3 33 00S 138 51E
Peterborough England 78 K4 52 35N 0 15W
Peterborough New Hampshire U.S.A. 65 J5 42 53N 71 57W
Peterhead Scotland 78 J9 57 30N 1 46W
Petersburg Alaska U.S.A. 42 B3 56 49N 132 58W
Petosky Michigan U.S.A. 36 B6 45 22N 84 59W
Petra *hist. site* Jordan 92 O10 30 19N 35 26E
Petrolina Brazil 68 I11 9 22S 40 30W
Petropavlovsk Kazakhstan 91 K5 54 53N 69 13E
Petropavlovsk-Kamchatskiy Russia 89 R6 53 03N 158 43E
Petrópolis Brazil 69 I8 22 30S 43 06W
Petroșeni Romania 81 D4 45 25N 23 22E
Petrozavodsk Russia 90 C7 61 46N 34 19E
Petukhovo Russia 91 K6 55 05N 67 55E
Peubla Mexico 66 E3 19 03N 98 10W
Pevek Russia 89 T9 64 41N 170 19E
Pfälzer Wald *mts.* Germany 76 D4 49 00N 8 00E
Phelps New York U.S.A. 64 C5 42 57N 77 03W
Phenix City Alabama U.S.A. 63 I3 32 8N 85 01W
Philadelphia Pennsylvania U.S.A. 64 E3 40 00N 75 10W
Philippine Sea Pacific Ocean 114 C10 21 00N 130 00E
PHILIPPINES, THE 99 G7/H5
Philippine Trench Pacific Ocean 114 C9 12 00N 127 00E
Philipsburg Pennsylvania U.S.A. 64 B3 40 54N 78 14W
Philip Smith Mountains Alaska U.S.A. 44 B4 68 00N 148 00W
Phillipsburg New Jersey U.S.A. 64 E3 40 41N 75 12W
Phnom Penh Cambodia 99 C6 11 35N 104 55E
Phoenix Arizona U.S.A. 62 D3 33 30N 112 03W
Phoenix Island Pacific Ocean 114 I7 3 30S 174 30W
Phoenix Islands Kiribati 114 I7 4 40S 177 30W
Phoenixville Pennsylvania U.S.A. 64 E3 40 07N 75 31W
Phongsali Laos 97 K3 21 40N 102 06E
Phrae Thailand 97 K2 18 07N 100 09E
Phuket Thailand 99 F5 7 52N 98 22E
Piacenza Italy 81 A3 45 03N 9 41E
Piatra Neamt Romania 81 E4 46 53N 26 23E
Piauí *admin.* Brazil 68 I11 7 30S 43 00W
Pico Cristóbal *mt.* Colombia 68 C15 10 53N 73 48W
Pico de Itambé *mt.* Brazil 68 I9 18 23S 43 21W
Pico-Rivera California U.S.A. 51 B2 33 59N 118 06W
Picos Brazil 68 I11 7 05S 41 24W
Picton New Zealand 111 B2 14 17S 174 02E
Picture Rocks Pennsylvania U.S.A. 64 D4 41 17N 76 40W
Pidurutalagala *mt.* Sri Lanka 95 E1 7 01N 80 45E
Piedade Brazil 69 P2 22 53N 43 19W
Piedmont California U.S.A. 49 C3 37 49N 122 13W
Piedras Negras Mexico 66 D5 28 40N 100 32W
Pielinen *l.* Finland 79 F3 63 20N 29 40E
Pierre South Dakota U.S.A. 62 F5 44 23N 100 20W
Pierreville Trinidad and Tobago 66 T9 10 17N 61 01W

Pietermaritzburg Republic of South Africa 107 L2 29 36S 30 24E
Pietersburg Republic of South Africa 107 K3 23 54N 29 23E
Pigeon Michigan U.S.A. 36 C4 43 50N 83 15W
Pijijiapan Mexico 66 F3 15 42N 93 12W
Pikes Peak Colorado U.S.A. 62 E4 38 50N 105 03W
Pikesville Maryland U.S.A. 64 D2 39 23N 76 44W
Pik Kommunizma *mt.* Tajikistan 88 J3 38 59N 72 01E
Pik Pobedy *mt.* Kirgyzstan 89 J4 42 25N 80 15E
Piła Poland 80 C5 53 09N 16 44E
Pilar Paraguay 69 F7 26 51S 58 20W
Pilarcitos Creek California U.S.A. 49 B1 37 28N 122 25W
Pilarcitos Lake California U.S.A. 49 B2 37 33N 122 25W
Pilica *r.* Poland 80 D5 52 00N 21 00E
Pillar Point California U.S.A. 49 B2 37 30N 122 30W
Pimenta Bueno Brazil 68 E10 11 40S 61 14W
Pinang *i.* Malaysia 99 C5 5 30N 100 20E
Pinar del Rio Cuba 67 H4 22 24N 83 42W
Pindhos *mts.* Greece 81 D2 40 00N 21 00E
Pine Bluff Arkansas U.S.A. 63 H3 34 13N 92 00W
Pine City Minnesota U.S.A. 35 B2 45 59N 92 59W
Pine Creek Pennsylvania U.S.A. 64 C4 41 20N 77 30W
Pine River Michigan U.S.A. 36 B4 43 23N 84 40W
Ping Chau *i.* Hong Kong U.K. 98 D3 22 33N 114 26E
Pingchen Taiwan 98 H7 24 57N 121 12E
Pingdingshan China 97 M5 33 50N 113 20E
Ping Shan Hong Kong U.K. 98 B2 22 27N 114 00E
Pingtan Dao *i.* China 98 F8 25 00N 119 00E
P'ing-tung Taiwan 98 G5 22 40N 120 30E
Pingxiang China 96 M4 27 35N 113 46E
Ping Yeung Hong Kong U.K. 98 B3 22 32N 114 09E
Piniós *r.* Greece 81 D2 39 00N 22 00E
Pinsk Belarus 90 B5 52 08N 26 01E
Piombino Italy 81 B3 42 56N 10 32E
Pioneer Ohio U.S.A. 36 B2 41 42N 84 33W
Piotrków Trybunalski Poland 80 C5 51 27N 19 40E
Piraiévs Greece 81 D2 37 57N 23 42E
Pirapora Brazil 68 I9 17 20S 44 54W
Pírgos Greece 81 D2 37 40N 21 27E
Pírgos Greece 81 E2 35 00N 25 10E
Pirineos *(Pyrénées) mts.* Spain/France 77 B3 C3 42 50N 0 30E
Pirin Planina *mts.* Bulgaria 81 D3 41 00N 23 00E
Pisa Italy 81 B3 43 43N 10 24E
Piscataway New Jersey U.S.A. 65 F3 40 33N 74 30W
Pisco Peru 68 B10 13 46S 76 12W
Písek Czechoslovakia 80 B4 49 18N 14 10E
Pistoia Italy 81 B3 43 56N 10 55E
Pitanga Brazil 69 G8 24 45S 51 43W
Pitcairn Islands Pacific Ocean 115 N5 25 04S 130 06W
Pitch Point Trinidad and Tobago 66 S9 10 15N 61 37W
Piteå Sweden 79 E4 65 19N 21 30E
Pite älv *r.* Sweden 79 D4 66 45N 17 20E
Pitești Romania 81 D3 44 51N 24 51E
Pitt Island India 95 C2 11 00N 73 00E
Pittsburgh Pennsylvania U.S.A. 63 K5 40 26N 80 00W
Pittsfield Massachusetts U.S.A. 65 G5 42 27N 73 15W
Pittsfield New Hampshire U.S.A. 65 J6 43 18N 71 20W
Pitt Water Australia 111 H3 33 37S 151 19E
Piura Peru 68 A11 5 15S 80 38W
Pjórsá *r.* Iceland 79 I6 64 15N 19 00W
Plainfield Connecticut U.S.A. 65 J4 41 42N 71 55W
Plainfield New Jersey U.S.A. 65 F3 40 37N 74 25W
Plainview Texas U.S.A. 62 F3 34 12N 101 43W
Planalto de Mato Grosso *geog. reg.* Brazil 68 F10 13 00S 56 00W
Plasencia Spain 77 A3 40 02N 6 05W
Plateau de Langres *hills* France 77 C4 47 40N 4 55E
Plateau du Tademaït *plat.* Algeria 106 F13 8 45N 2 00E
Plateau du Tchigaï *plat.* Chad/Niger 106 H12 21 30N 15 00E
Plateaux du Limousin *hills* France 77 C4 45 45N 1 15E
Platte *r.* U.S.A. 62 F5 41 00N 100 00W
Plattsburgh New York U.S.A. 63 L5 44 42N 73 29W
Plauen Germany 76 E5 50 29N 12 08E
Playa Azul Mexico 66 D3 18 00N 102 24W
Pleasant Hill California U.S.A. 49 C3 37 58N 122 04W
Pleasant Hills Pennsylvania U.S.A. 53 E1 40 19N 79 57W
Pleasantville New Jersey U.S.A. 65 F2 39 23N 74 32W
Plenty, Bay of New Zealand 111 C3 37 30S 117 00E
Plentywood Montana U.S.A. 40 C1 48 46N 104 32W
Pleven Bulgaria 81 D3 43 25N 24 40E
Płock Poland 80 C5 52 32N 19 40E
Ploiești Romania 81 E3 44 57N 26 01E
Plover Cove Reservoir Hong Kong U.K. 98 C2 22 28N 114 15E
Plovdiv Bulgaria 81 D3 42 08N 24 45E
Plunge Lithuania 80 D6 55 52N 21 49E
Plymouth England 78 G2 50 23N 4 10W
Plymouth Massachusetts U.S.A. 65 K4 41 58N 70 40W
Plymouth County Massachusetts U.S.A. 52 C2 42 18N 70 55W
Plzeň Czechoslovakia 80 B4 49 45N 13 25E
Po *r.* Italy 81 B4 45 00N 11 00E
Pocatello Idaho U.S.A. 62 D5 42 35N 112 26W
Pochutla Mexico 66 E3 15 45N 96 30W
Pocono Summit Pennsylvania U.S.A. 64 E4 41 06N 75 25W
Podara India 94 K2 22 34N 88 17E
Podkamennaya *(Stony)* **Tunguska** *r.* Russia 89 L8/M8 62 00N 95 00E
Podol'sk Russia 90 D6 55 23N 37 32E
P'ohang South Korea 97 P6 36 00N 129 26E
Point-à-Pitre Guadeloupe Lesser Antilles 67 L3 16 14N 61 32W
Pointe-à-Pierre *tn.* Trinidad and Tobago 66 T9 10 20N 61 26W
Point Fortin *tn.* Trinidad and Tobago 66 S9 10 21N 61 41W
Point Hope *tn.* Alaska U.S.A. 10 B6 68 20N 166 50W
Pointe-Noire *tn.* Congo 107 H7 4 46S 11 53E
Point Pedro *c.* Sri Lanka 95 E1 9 49N 80 14E
Point Pleasant *tn.* New Jersey U.S.A. 65 F3 40 06N 74 02W
Point San Pedro California U.S.A. 49 A2 37 33N 122 33W
Poissy France 83 A2 48 56N 2 03E
Poitiers France 77 C4 46 35N 0 20E
Pok Fu Lam Hong Kong U.K. 98 B1 22 15N 114 08E
Pokhara Nepal 95 E5 28 14N 83 58E
POLAND 80 C5
Poland New York U.S.A. 64 E6 43 13N 75 05W
Poles'ye Pripyat' *(Pripet Marshes) marsh* Belarus 90 B5 52 00N 27 00E
Políyiros Greece 81 D3 40 23N 23 25E
Pollachi India 95 D2 10 38N 77 00E
Poltava Ukraine 90 C4 49 35N 34 35E
Polynesia *geog. reg.* Pacific Ocean 115 J/L9
Pomeranian Bay Baltic Sea 80 B5 54 00N 14 00E
Ponca City Oklahoma U.S.A. 63 G4 36 41N 97 04W
Ponce Puerto Rico 67 K3 18 01N 66 36W
Pondicherry India 95 D2 11 59N 79 50E
Ponferrada Spain 77 A3 42 33N 6 35W
Ponta da Marca *c.* Angola 107 H4 16 33S 11 43E
Ponta Grossa Brazil 69 G7 25 07S 50 09W
Ponta Porã Brazil 69 F8 22 27S 55 39W
Pontas das Salinas *c.* Angola 107 H5 12 50S 12 54E
Pontchartrain, Lake Louisiana U.S.A. 63 H3 30 00N 90 00W
Pontevedra Spain 77 A3 42 25N 8 39W
Pontiac Michigan U.S.A. 36 C3 42 39N 83 18W
Pontianak Indonesia 99 D3 0 05S 109 16E
Pontivy France 77 B4 48 04N 2 58W
Poole England 78 I2 50 43N 1 59W
Poole *r.* Trinidad and Tobago 66 T9 10 02N 61 11W
Pool Malebo *l.* Zaïre 107 I7 5 00S 17 00E
Popocatepetl *mt.* Mexico 66 E3 19 02N 98 38W
Popayán Colombia 68 B13 2 27N 76 32W
Poplar Bluff *tn.* Missouri U.S.A. 63 H4 36 16N 90 25W
Poplar River Montana U.S.A. 40 B1 48 50N 105 30W
Popondetta Papua New Guinea 110 H8 8 45S 148 15E
Poquetanuck Connecticut U.S.A. 65 H4 41 29N 72 02W
Porbandar India 94 B4 21 04N 69 40E
Porcupine *r.* Alaska U.S.A. 44 C4 67 00N 143 30W
Porcupine Creek Montana U.S.A. 40 B1 48 50N 106 30W
Pordenone Italy 81 B4 45 58N 12 39E
Pori Finland 79 E3 61 28N 21 45E
Porirua New Zealand 111 B2 41 08S 174 52E
Porlamar Venezuela 67 L2 11 01N 63 54W
Poronaysk Russia 89 Q5 49 13N 143 05E
Porsangen *fj.* Norway 79 F5 70 40N 25 30E
Porsgrunn Norway 79 B2 59 10N 9 40E
Portadown Northern Ireland 78 E6 54 26N 6 27W
Portal North Dakota U.S.A. 40 C1 48 00N 102 32W
Portalegre Portugal 77 A2 39 17N 7 25W
Portales New Mexico U.S.A. 62 F3 34 12N 103 20W
Port Alexander Alaska U.S.A. 42 B3 56 13N 134 40W
Port Allegany *tn.* Pennsylvania U.S.A. 64 B4 41 48N 78 18W
Port Angeles Washington U.S.A. 62 B6 48 06N 123 26W
Port Antonio Jamaica 67 R8 18 10N 76 27W
Port Arthur Texas U.S.A. 63 H2 29 55N 93 56W
Port Augusta Australia 110 F3 32 30S 137 27E
Port-au-Prince Haiti 67 J3 18 33N 72 20W
Port Austin Michigan U.S.A. 36 C5 44 04N 82 59W
Port Blair Andaman Islands 95 G2 11 40N 92 44E
Port Byron New York U.S.A. 64 D6 43 03N 76 38W
Port Chalmers New Zealand 111 B1 45 48S 170 38E
Port Clinton Ohio U.S.A. 36 D2 41 30N 82 58W
Port-de-Paix Haiti 67 J3 19 56N 72 52W
Port Elizabeth New Jersey U.S.A. 64 F2 39 19N 74 59W
Port Elizabeth Republic of South Africa 107 K1 33 58S 25 36E
Port Gentil Gabon 106 G7 0 40S 8 50E
Port Hacking *b.* Australia 111 G1 34 04S 151 07E
Port Hacking Point Australia 111 G1 34 05S 151 10E
Port Harcourt Nigeria 106 G8 4 43N 7 05E
Port Hedland Australia 110 B5 20 24S 118 36E
Port Huron Michigan U.S.A. 63 J5 42 59N 82 28W
Portile de Fier *(Iron Gate) gorge* Europe 81 D2 44 00N 22 00E
Portimaõ Portugal 77 A2 37 08N 8 32W
Port Island Hong Kong U.K. 98 D3 22 30N 114 21E
Port Jackson *b.* Australia 111 H2 33 51S 151 15E
Port Jervis *tn.* New York U.S.A. 65 F4 41 22N 74 40W
Port Kaituma Guyana 68 F14 7 44N 59 53W
Portland Australia 110 G2 38 21S 141 38E
Portland Maine U.S.A. 63 L5 43 41N 70 18W
Portland Michigan U.S.A. 36 B3 42 52N 84 53W
Portland Oregon U.S.A. 62 B6 45 32N 122 40W
Portland Canal *sd.* Alaska U.S.A. 42 B3 55 00N 130 10W
Portland Point Jamaica 67 Q7 17 42N 77 11W
Portlaoise Irish Republic 78 D5 53 02N 7 17W
Port Lincoln Australia 110 F3 34 43S 135 49E
Port Macquarie Australia 110 I3 31 28S 152 25E
Port Maria Jamaica 67 R8 18 22N 76 54W
Port Matilda *tn.* Pennsylvania U.S.A. 64 B3 40 47N 78 04W
Port Morant Jamaica 67 R7 17 53N 76 20W
Port Moresby Papua New Guinea 110 H8 9 30S 147 07E
Port Nolloth Republic of South Africa 107 I2 29 17S 16 51E
Port Norris *tn.* New Jersey U.S.A. 64 E2 39 15N 75 02W
Porto *(Oporto)* Portugal 77 A3 41 09N 8 37W
Pôrto Alegre Brazil 69 G6 30 03S 51 10W
Porto Amboim Angola 107 H5 10 47S 13 43E
Portobelo Panama 67 Y2 9 33N 79 37W
Port of Spain Trinidad and Tobago 66 S10 10 38N 61 31W
Pôrto Grande Brazil 68 G13 0 43N 51 23W
Porto Novo Benin 106 F9 6 30N 2 47E
Porto-Vecchio Corsica 77 D3 41 35N 9 16E
Pôrto Velho Brazil 68 E11 8 45S 63 54W
Portoviejo Ecuador 68 A12 1 07S 80 28W
Port Pirie Australia 110 F3 33 11S 138 01E
Port Royal Jamaica 67 R7 17 55N 76 52W
Port Said *(Bûr Sa'îd)* Egypt 107 S4 31 17N 32 18E
Port Sudan Sudan 92 E2 19 38N 37 07E
Portsmouth England 78 J2 50 48N 1 05W
Portsmouth New Hampshire U.S.A. 65 K6 43 03N 70 47W
Portsmouth Rhode Island U.S.A. 65 J4 41 00N 71 00W
Portsmouth Virginia U.S.A. 63 K4 36 50N 76 20W
Porttipahdan tekojärvi *l.* Finland 79 F4 68 15N 26 00E
PORTUGAL 77 A3
Port Washington New York U.S.A. 50 D2 40 50N 73 41W
Porus Jamaica 67 Q8 18 02N 77 25W
Posadas Argentina 69 F7 27 27S 55 50W
Potenza Italy 81 C3 40 38N 15 48E
Poti Georgia 90 E3 42 11N 41 41E
Potiskum Nigeria 106 H10 11 40N 11 03E
Po Toi Island Hong Kong U.K. 98 C1 22 10N 114 10E
Potomac River Maryland U.S.A. 64 C2 39 10N 77 30W
Potosí Bolivia 68 D9 19 34S 65 45W
Potsdam Germany 83 D2 52 24N 13 04E
Potsdam *bor.* Germany 83 F2 52 41N 13 25E
Potter's Bar England 82 C3 51 42N 0 11W
Pottstown Pennsylvania U.S.A. 64 E3 40 15N 75 38W
Pottsville Pennsylvania U.S.A. 64 D3 40 41N 76 1W
Poughkeepsie New York U.S.A. 65 G4 41 43N 73 56W
Poverty Bay New Zealand 111 C3 38 40S 178 00E
Powell, Lake U.S.A. 62 D4 37 00N 110 00W
Powers Lake *tn.* North Dakota U.S.A. 40 C1 48 35N 102 39W
Poza Rica Mexico 66 E4 20 34N 97 26W
Poznań Poland 80 C5 52 25N 16 53E
Pradesh *admin.* India 95 E5 26 00N 81 00E
Prague *see* Praha
Praha *(Prague)* Czechoslovakia 80 B5 50 06N 14 26E
Prairie Dog Town Fork *r.* U.S.A. 62 F3 34 00N 101 00W
Prato Italy 81 B3 43 53N 11 06E
Pratt Kansas U.S.A. 62 G4 37 40N 98 45W
Pñeau Trinidad and Tobago 66 T9 10 12N 61 19W
Prenzlauer Berg Germany 83 F2 52 33N 13 25E
Prerov Czechoslovakia 80 C4 49 28N 17 30E
Prescott Arizona U.S.A. 62 D3 34 34N 112 28W
Presidencia Roque Sáenz Peña Argentina 69 E7 6 45S 60 30W
Presidente Prudente Brazil 69 G8 22 09S 51 24W
Presidio California U.S.A. 49 B3 37 47N 122 28W
Prešov Czechoslovakia 80 D4 49 00N 21 10E
Presque Isle Maine U.S.A. 33 C2 46 42N 68 01W
Preston England 78 I5 53 46N 2 42W
Pretoria Republic of South Africa 107 K2 25 45E 28 12E
Prettyboy Reservoir Maryland U.S.A. 64 D2 39 38N 76 45W
Préveza Greece 81 D2 38 59N 20 45E
Příbham Czechoslovakia 80 B4 49 42N 14 01E
Price Utah U.S.A. 62 D4 39 35N 110 49W
Price *r.* Utah U.S.A. 62 D4 39 00N 110 00W
Prieska Republic of South Africa 107 J2 29 40S 22 45E
Priest Lake Idaho U.S.A. 43 E1 49 45N 116 50W
Priestly Mountain Maine U.S.A. 37 R7 46 34N 69 23W
Priest River *tn.* Idaho U.S.A. 43 E1 48 11N 116 55W
Prijedor Bosnia-Herzegovina 81 C3 45 00N 16 41E
Prilep Yugoslavia 81 D3 41 20N 21 32E
Prince Edward Island Indian Ocean 112 C2 46 30S 37 20E
Prince of Wales Island Alaska U.S.A. 42 B3 56 00N 132 00W
Princes Town Trinidad and Tobago 66 T9 10 16N 61 23W
Princeton New Jersey U.S.A. 65 F3 40 21N 74 40W
Prince William Sound Alaska U.S.A. 10 F5 61 00N 147 30W
Príncipe *i.* Gulf of Guinea 106 G8 1 37N 7 27E
Prinzapolca Nicaragua 67 H2 13 19N 83 35W
Pripet Marshes *see* Poles'ye Pripyat'
Pripyat' *r.* Belarus/Ukraine 90 B5 52 00N 30 00E
Prispansko ezero *l.* Europe 81 D3 41 00N 21 00E
Priština Serbia Yugoslavia 81 D3 42 39N 21 20E
Prizren Serbia Yugoslavia 81 D3 42 12N 20 43E
Probolinggo Indonesia 99 E2 7 45S 113 09E
Proddatur India 95 D2 14 45N 78 34E
Progres *r.s.* Antarctica 117 69 24S 76 24E
Progreso Honduras 66 G3 15 20N 87 50W
Progreso Mexico 66 G4 21 20N 89 40W
Prokhladnyy Russia 90 E3 43 46N 44 03E
Prokop'yevsk Russia 91 O5 53 55N 86 45E
Prome Myanmar 96 J2 18 50N 95 14E
Propriá Brazil 68 J10 10 15S 36 51W
Prospect Heights Illinois U.S.A. 53 A3 42 04N 87 55W
Providence Rhode Island U.S.A. 65 J4 41 50N 71 28W
Providence, Cape New Zealand 111 A1 46 01S 166 28E
Provideniya Russia 89 U8 64 30N 73 11W
Provincetown Massachusetts U.S.A. 65 K5 42 04N 70 11W
Provo Utah U.S.A. 62 D5 40 15N 111 40W
Prudhoe Bay *tn.* Alaska U.S.A. 44 B4 70 05N 148 20W
Prutul *(Prut) r.* Romania 81 E4 47 00N 28 00E
Pruzków Poland 80 D5 52 10N 20 47E
Prýdek-Místek Czechoslovakia 80 C4 49 42N 18 20E
Przemyśl Poland 80 D4 49 48N 22 48E
Przheval'sk Kirgyzstan 91 M3 42 31N 78 22E
Pskov Russia 90 B6 57 48N 28 26E
Ptich' Belarus 90 B5 52 15N 28 49E
Ptich' *r.* Belarus 90 B5 53 00N 28 00E
Pucallpa Peru 68 C11 8 21S 74 33W
Pudasjärvi Finland 79 F4 65 25N 26 50E
Pueblo Colorado U.S.A. 62 F4 38 17N 104 38W
Puerta Eugenia *c.* Mexico 66 A5 27 50N 115 05W
Puerto Aisén Chile 69 C3 45 27S 72 58W
Puerto Armuelles Panama 67 H1 8 19N 82 51W
Puerto Ayacucho Venezuela 68 D14 5 39N 67 32W
Puerto Barrios Guatemala 66 G3 15 41N 88 32W
Puerto Berrio Colombia 68 C14 6 28N 74 28W
Puerto Cabello Venezuela 68 D15 10 29N 68 02W
Puerto Cabezas Nicaragua 67 H2 14 0N 83 24W
Puerto Carreño Colombia 68 D14 6 08N 69 27W
Puerto Cortés Honduras 66 G3 15 50N 87 55W
Puerto Cumarebo Venezuela 67 K2 11 31N 69 30W
Puerto de Morelos Mexico 67 G4 20 49N 86 52W
Puerto La Cruz Venezuela 68 E15 10 14N 64 40W
Puertollano Spain 77 B2 38 41N 4 07W
Puerto Maldonado Peru 68 D10 12 37S 69 11W
Puerto Mexico *see* Coatzacoalcos
Puerto Montt Chile 69 C4 41 28S 73 00W
Puerto Natales Chile 69 C2 51 41S 72 15W
Puerto Peñasco Mexico 66 B6 31 20N 113 35W
Puerto Pilón Panama 67 Y2 9 21N 79 48W
Puerto Princesa The Philippines 99 F5 9 46N 118 45E
PUERTO RICO 67 K3
Puerto Rico Trench Atlantic Ocean 113 B9 21 00N 65 00W
Puerto Santa Cruz Argentina 69 D2 50 03S 68 35W
Puerto Vallarta Mexico 66 C4 20 36N 105 15W
Pui O Hong Kong U.K. 98 A1 22 15N 113 58E
Pukekohe New Zealand 111 B3 37 12S 174 56E
Pula Croatia 81 B3 44 52N 13 52E
Pulacoyo Bolivia 68 D8 20 25S 66 41W
Pulau Dolak *i.* Indonesia 110 F8 8 00S 138 00E
Pulau Pulau Batu *is.* Indonesia 99 B3 0 20S 98 00E
Pu-li Taiwan 98 G6 23 58N 120 55E
Pulkkila Finland 79 F3 64 16N 25 50E
Pullman Washington U.S.A. 62 C6 46 46N 117 09W
Puncak Jaya *mt.* Indonesia 110 F9 4 05S 137 09E
Pune India 95 C3 18 34N 73 58E
Punjab *admin.* India 95 D6 30 40N 75 30E
Puno Peru 68 C9 15 53S 70 03W
Punta Alta Argentina 69 E5 38 50S 62 00W
Punta Arenas Chile 69 C2 53 10S 70 56W
Punta del Mono *c.* Nicaragua 67 H2 11 36N 83 37W
Punta Galera *c.* Ecuador 68 A13 0 49N 80 03W
Punta Gallinas *c.* Colombia 68 C15 12 27N 71 44W
Punta Gorda Belize 66 G3 16 10N 88 45W
Punta Manzanillo *c.* Panama 67 Y2 9 37N 79 36W
Punta Negra *c.* Peru 68 A11 6 06S 81 09W
Punta Peñas *c.* Venezuela 66 S10 10 45N 61 51W
Puntarenas Costa Rica 67 H2 10 00N 84 50W
Punto Fijo Venezuela 68 C15 11 50N 70 16W
Punxsutawney Pennsylvania U.S.A. 64 B3 40 57N 78 59W
Puquio Peru 68 C10 14 44S 74 07W
Pur *r.* Russia 89 J9 66 30N 77 30E
Puri India 95 F3 19 49N 85 54E
Purisma Creek California U.S.A. 49 B1 37 24N 122 24W
Purley England 82 C2 51 21N 0 07W
Purnia India 95 F5 25 47N 87 28E
Pursat Cambodia 99 C6 12 27N 103 40E
Purus *r.* Brazil 68 E11 7 00S 65 00W
Puruvesi *l.* Finland 79 F3 61 50N 29 30E
Pusa India 94 L4 28 38N 77 10E
Pusan South Korea 96 P6 35 05N 129 02E
Pushkin Russia 90 C6 59 43N 30 22E
Pu-tai Taiwan 98 G6 23 21N 120 11E
Putao Myanmar 95 H5 27 22N 97 27E
Putian China 98 E8 25 32N 119 02E
Putnam Connecticut U.S.A. 65 J4 41 55N 71 54W
Putney Vermont U.S.A. 65 H5 42 58N 72 35W
Putoran Mountains Russia 89 L9 68 00N 95 00E
Puttalam Sri Lanka 95 D1 8 02N 79 50E
Putumayo *r.* Colombia/Peru 68 C12 2 30S 72 30W
Puulavesi *l.* Finland 79 F3 61 50N 26 40E
Pyasina *r.* Russia 89 K10 71 00N 90 00E
Pyatigorsk Russia 90 E3 44 04N 43 06E
Pyhäjärvi Finland 79 F3 63 41N 26 00E
Pyhäjärvi *l.* Finland 79 E3 61 00N 22 20E
Pyhäjärvi *l.* Finland/Russia 79 F3 61 50N 30 00E
Pyinmana Myanmar 99 B7 19 45N 96 12E
Pymatuning Lake *res.* Ohio/Pennsylvania U.S.A. 36 F2 41 35N 80 30W
Pyŏngyang North Korea 97 P6 39 00N 125 47E
Pyramid Lake Nevada U.S.A. 62 C5 40 00N 119 00W
Pyramids *hist. site* Egypt 92 D4 29 50N 30 50E
Pyrénées *(Pirineos) mts.* France/Spain 77 B3/C3 42 50N 0 30E
Pysht Washington U.S.A. 42 H4 48 10N 124 08W
Pytäselkä *l.* Finland 79 F3 62 0N 29 30E

Q

Qaidam Basin *see* Qaidam Pendi
Qaidam Pendi (Qaidam Basin) China 96 H6/J6 37 30N 94 00E
Qamdo China 95 H6 31 11N 97 18E
Qanâ el Manzala *can.* Egypt 107 R4 31 21N 31 56E
Qasr-e-Shīrīn Iraq 93 G5 34 32N 45 35E
Qasr Farâfra Egypt 106 K13 27 03N 28 00E
QATAR 93 H4
Qatar Peninsula Middle East 84 25 00N 53 00E
Qatrāna Jordan 92 P10 31 14N 36 03E
Qattara Depression Egypt 106 K13 24 00N 27 30E
Qazvīn Iran 93 G6 36 16N 50 00E
Qena Egypt 92 D4 26 08N 32 42E
Qeqertarsuaq (Godhavn) Greenland 45 V4 69 18N 53 40W
Qezi'ot Israel 92 O10 30 53N 34 28E
Qiemo China 96 G6 38 08N 85 33E
Qila Saifullah Pakistan 94 B6 30 42N 68 30E
Qilian Shan *mts.* China 97 J6 39 00N 98 00E
Qingdao China 97 O6 36 04N 120 22E
Qinghai Hu *l.* China 97 J6 37 00N 100 00E
Qinghe China 101 G2 40 01N 116 20E
Qingjiang China 97 N5 33 35N 119 02E
Qinhuangdao China 97 N6 39 55N 119 37E
Qin Ling *mts.* China 97 J6 34 00N 107 30E
Qionghai China 97 M2 19 17N 110 30E
Qiqihar China 97 O8 47 23N 124 00E
Qogir Feng *see* K2
Qom Iran 93 H5 34 39N 50 57E
Qomishēh Iran 93 H5 32 01N 51 55E
Quabbin Reservoir Massachusetts U.S.A. 65 H5 42 20N 72 20W
Quakertown Pennsylvania U.S.A. 64 E3 40 27N 75 20W
Quang Ngai Vietnam 99 L2 15 09N 108 50E
Quang Tri Vietnam 97 L2 16 46N 107 11E
Quantock Hills England 78 H3 51 05N 3 15W
Quanzhou China 97 N3 24 53N 118 36E
Quarry Bay *tn.* Hong Kong U.K. 98 C1 22 17N 114 13E
Queanbeyan Australia 110 H2 35 24N 149 17E
Queen Mary Reservoir England 82 B2 51 25N 0 27W
Queen Maud Land *geog. reg.* Antarctica 117 73 00S 10 00E
Queens New York U.S.A. 50 C1 40 44N 73 54W
Queensland *state* Australia 110 G5 23 00S 143 00E
Queenstown Australia 110 H1 42 07S 145 33E
Queenstown New Zealand 111 A2 45 03S 168 41E
Quelimane Mozambique 107 M4 17 53S 36 51E
Quelpart *see* Cheju do
Quemahoning Reservoir Pennsylvania U.S.A. 64 B3 40 10N 79 00W
Que Que *see* Kwekwe
Querétaro Mexico 66 D4 20 38N 100 23W
Quetta Pakistan 94 B6 30 15N 67 00E
Quezaltenango Guatemala 66 F2 14 50N 91 30W
Quezon City The Philippines 99 G6 14 39N 121 02E
Quibala Angola 107 H5 10 48S 14 59E
Quibdó Colombia 68 B14 5 40N 76 38W
Quiberon France 77 B4 47 29N 3 07W
Quilá Mexico 66 C4 24 26N 107 11W
Quillacollo Bolivia 68 D9 17 26S 66 16W
Quilon India 95 D1 8 53N 76 38E
Quilpie Australia 110 G4 26 35S 144 14E
Quimper France 77 B4 48 00N 4 06W
Quincy Illinois U.S.A. 63 H4 39 55N 91 22W
Quincy Massachusetts U.S.A. 52 B2 42 17N 71 00W
Quinebaug River Connecticut U.S.A. 65 H4 41 30N 72 00W
Qui Nhon Vietnam 99 D6 13 47N 109 11E
Quito Ecuador 68 B12 0 14S 78 30W
Quixadá Brazil 68 J12 4 57S 39 04W
Qus Egypt 92 D4 25 53N 32 48E
Quseir Egypt 92 D4 26 04N 34 15E

R
Raahe Finland **79** E3 64 42N 24 30E
Raas Caseyr (Guardafui, Cape) Somalia **106** P10 11 50N 51 16E
Raba Indonesia **99** F2 8 27S 118 45E
Rabat-Salé Morocco **106** D14 34 02N 6 51W
Rabaul Papua New Guinea **110** I9 4 13S 152 11E
Rach Gia Vietnam **99** D5 9 55N 105 05E
Racibórz Poland **80** C5 50 05N 18 10E
Radford Virginia U.S.A. **63** J4 37 07N 80 34W
Radlett England **82** B3 51 41N 0 19W
Radlinski, Mount Antarctica **117** 82 30S 105 00W
Radom Poland **80** D5 51 26N 21 10E
Radom Sudan **106** J9 9 58N 24 53E
Radomsko Poland **80** C5 51 04N 19 25E
Raeside, Lake Australia **110** C4 29 00S 122 00E
Rafah Egypt **92** O10 31 18N 34 15E
Rafsanjān Iran **93** I5 30 25N 56 00E
Ragusa Italy **81** B2 36 56N 14 44E
Rahimyar Khan Pakistan **94** B5 28 22N 70 20E
Rahnsdorf Germany **83** G1 52 26N 13 42E
Raichur India **95** D3 16 15N 77 20E
Raigarh India **95** E4 21 53N 83 28E
Rainbow Park Illinois U.S.A. **53** B2 41 45N 87 32W
Rainham England **82** D3 51 31N 0 12E
Rainier, Mount Washington U.S.A. **62** B6 46 52N 121 45W
Raipur India **95** E4 21 16N 81 42E
Raisin, River Michigan U.S.A. **36** C2 41 55N 83 40W
Rajahmundry India **95** E3 17 01N 81 52E
Rajapalaiyam India **95** D1 9 26N 77 36E
Rājasthan admin. India **95** C5 26 30N 73 00E
Rajkot India **95** C4 21 18N 70 53E
Rajpur India **94** K1 22 25N 88 25E
Rajshahi Bangladesh **95** F4 24 24N 88 40E
Raleigh North Carolina U.S.A. **63** K4 35 46N 78 39W
Ralik Chain is. Pacific Ocean **114** G8 7 30N 167 30E
Ramat Gan Israel **92** O11 32 04N 34 48E
Ramos Brazil **69** P2 22 51S 43 16W
Rampur India **95** D5 28 50N 79 05E
Rampur India **95** D6 31 26N 77 37E
Ramree i. Myanmar **96** H2 9 00N 93 30E
Ramtha Jordan **92** O11 32 34N 36 00E
Rancagua Chile **69** C6 34 10S 70 45W
Ranchi India **95** F4 23 22N 85 20E
Randers Denmark **80** B6 56 28N 10 03E
Randolph New York U.S.A. **64** B5 42 10N 78 59W
Randwick Australia **111** G2 33 50S 151 14E
Rangeley Maine U.S.A. **37** Q5 44 58N 70 40W
Rangiora New Zealand **111** B2 43 18S 172 38E
Rangoon (Yangon) Myanmar **96** J2 16 47N 96 10E
Rangpur Bangladesh **95** F5 25 45N 89 21E
Rangsdorf Germany **83** F1 52 16N 13 26E
Rani Bagh India **94** L4 28 41N 77 06E
Raniganj India **95** F4 23 35N 87 07E
Rann of Kachchh geog. reg. India/Pakistan **94** B4/C4 24 00N 69 00E
Rapid City South Dakota U.S.A. **62** F5 44 06N 103 14W
Ras al Hadd c. Oman **93** I3 22 31N 59 45E
Râs Banâs c. Egypt **92** E3 23 58N 35 50E
Ras Dashen Terara mt. Ethiopia **92** E1 13 15N 38 27E
Râs el Barr Egypt **107** R5 31 32N 31 42E
Râs el 'Ish Egypt **107** S4 31 07N 32 18E
Ras Fartak c. Yemen Republic **93** H2 15 20N 52 12E
Râs Ghârib Egypt **92** N9 28 22N 33 04E
Rasht Iran **93** G6 37 18N 49 38E
Raşiţa Romania **81** D4 45 16N 21 55E
Râs Kasar c. Sudan **92** E2 18 02N 38 33E
Ras Lanuf Libya **106** I14 30 31N 18 34E
Ra's Madrakah c. Oman **93** I2 18 58N 57 50E
Râs Muhammad c. Egypt **92** O8 27 44N 34 15E
Ras Nouadhibou (Cap Blanc) c. Mauritania **106** B12 20 53N 17 01W
Rasto geog. reg. Sweden **79** E4 68 40N 21 00E
Ratak Chain is. Pacific Ocean **114** H9 10 00N 172 30E
Rat Buri Thailand **99** B6 13 30N 99 50E
Rathlin Island Northern Ireland **78** E7 55 20N 6 10W
Ratingen Germany **76** H2 51 18N 6 50E
Ratlam India **95** D4 23 18N 75 06E
Ratnapura Sri Lanka **95** E1 6 41N 80 25E
Ratno Ukraine **80** D5 51 40N 24 32E
Raton New Mexico U.S.A. **62** F4 36 54N 104 27W
Raukumara mt. New Zealand **111** C3 37 45N 178 09E
Raukumara Range mts. New Zealand **111** C3 39 00S 178 00E
Rauma Finland **79** E3 61 09N 21 30E
Raurkela India **95** E4 22 16N 85 01E
Ravenna Italy **81** B3 44 25N 12 12E
Ravensburg Germany **77** D4 47 47N 9 37E
Ravensthorpe Australia **110** C3 33 34S 120 01E
Ravi r. Pakistan **95** C6 31 00N 73 00E
Rawalpindi Pakistan **95** C6 33 40N 73 08E
Rawlins Wyoming U.S.A. **62** E5 41 46N 107 16W
Rawson Argentina **69** E4 43 15S 65 06W
Ray North Dakota U.S.A. **40** C1 48 22N 103 11W
Raymondville Texas U.S.A. **63** G2 26 30N 97 48W
Raystown Lake Pennsylvania U.S.A. **64** B3 40 20N 78 15W
Razgrad Bulgaria **81** E3 43 31N 26 33E
Reading England **78** K3 51 28N 0 59W
Reading Pennsylvania U.S.A. **64** E3 40 20N 75 55W
Rebun-tō i. Japan **100** D4 45 25N 141 04E
Recherche, Archipelago is. Australia **110** C2 35 00S 122 50E
Recife Brazil **68** J11 8 06S 34 53W
Recklinghausen Germany **76** J3 51 37N 7 11E
Reconquista Argentina **69** F7 29 08S 59 38W
Recovery Glacier Antarctica **117** 81 00S 25 00W
Red Bank New Jersey U.S.A. **65** F3 40 21N 74 04W
Redbridge bor. Greater London England **82** D3 51 34N 0 05E
Redhead Trinidad and Tobago **66** U10 10 44N 60 58W
Redhill England **82** C1 51 14N 0 11W
Redon France **77** B4 47 39N 2 05W
Redondo Beach tn. California U.S.A. **51** A2 33 51N 118 24W
Red River U.S.A. **63** H3 32 00N 93 00W
Red Sea Middle East **92** D4/F1 27 00N 35 00E
Red Sea Hills Africa **102** 27 00N 33 00E
Red Wing Minnesota U.S.A. **63** H5 44 33N 92 31W
Redwood City California U.S.A. **49** B1 37 28N 122 15W
Redwood Regional Park California U.S.A. **49** C3 37 49N 122 10W
Reed City Michigan U.S.A. **36** A4 43 54N 85 31W
Reedsport Oregon U.S.A. **62** B5 43 42N 124 05W
Reedy Glacier Antarctica **117** 85 00S 140 00W
Reefton New Zealand **111** B2 42 05S 171 51E
Regensburg Germany **76** E4 49 01N 12 07E
Reggio di Calabria Italy **81** C2 38 06N 15 39E
Reggio nell'Emilia Italy **81** B3 44 42N 10 37E
Registan geog. reg. Afghanistan **93** J5 30 30N 65 00E
Rehovot Israel **92** O10 31 54N 34 46E
Reigate England **82** C1 51 14N 0 13W
Reims France **76** C4 49 15N 4 02E
Reinickendorf Germany **83** F2 52 35N 13 22E
Reinosa Spain **77** B3 43 01N 4 09W
Reisa r. Norway **79** E4 69 40N 21 30E
Reisterstown Maryland U.S.A. **64** D2 39 27N 76 51W
Relizane Algeria **77** C2 35 44N 0 35E
Rembang Indonesia **99** E2 6 45S 111 22E
Rennell i. Solomon Islands **110** K7 11 45S 160 15E
Rennes France **77** B4 48 06N 1 40W
Renovo Pennsylvania U.S.A. **64** C4 41 20N 77 45W
Rensselaer New York U.S.A. **65** G5 42 37N 73 44W
Republic Washington U.S.A. **43** E1 48 39N 118 45W
REPUBLIC OF SOUTH AFRICA **107** J2
Resistencia Argentina **69** F7 27 28S 59 00W
Réthimnon Greece **81** D2 35 23N 24 28E
Réunion i. Indian Ocean **112** E4 21 00S 55 30E
Reus Spain **77** C3 41 10N 1 06E
Reutlingen Germany **76** E4 48 30N 9 13E
Reutov Russia **88** N2 55 46N 37 47E
Revere Massachusetts U.S.A. **52** B2 42 25N 71 02W
Revere Beach Massachusetts U.S.A. **52** C2 42 24N 70 59W
Revesby Australia **111** G2 33 57S 151 01E
Revillagigedo Island Alaska U.S.A. **42** B3 55 30N 131 30W
Rewa India **95** E4 24 32N 81 18E
Reykjanes Ridge Atlantic Ocean **113** E12 57 00N 33 00W
Reykjavík Iceland **79** H6 64 09N 21 58W
Reynosa Mexico **66** E5 26 05N 98 18W
Rēzekne Latvia **79** F2 56 30N 27 22E
Rhein (Rijn, Rhine) r.Germany **76** D5 50 30N 7 00E
Rheine Germany **76** D5 52 17N 7 26E
Rhein-Herne-Kanal can. Germany **76** H3 51 30N 7 00E
Rhienhausen Germany **76** G2 51 23N 6 41E
Rhine see Rhein, Rijn
Rhinelander Wisconsin U.S.A. **35** C2 45 39N 89 23W
Rhode Island state U.S.A. **65** J4 41 00N 71 00W
Rhode Island Sound Rhode Island U.S.A. **65** J4 41 00N 71 00W
Rhodes see Ródhos
Rhondda Wales **78** H3 51 40N 3 30W
Rhône r. France **77** C4 45 00N 4 50E
Rhum i. Scotland **78** E9 57 00N 6 20W
Ribble r. England **78** I5 53 44N 2 56W
Ribe Denmark **80** A6 55 20N 8 47E
Ribeirão Prêto Brazil **68** H8 21 09S 47 48W
Riberalta Bolivia **68** D10 10 59S 66 06W
Richfield Springs tn. New York U.S.A. **64** F5 42 53N 75 00W
Richland Washington U.S.A. **62** C6 46 17N 119 17W
Richmond Australia **110** G5 20 45S 143 05E
Richmond California U.S.A. **49** B3 37 56N 122 20W
Richmond Indiana U.S.A. **63** J4 39 50N 84 51W
Richmond New York U.S.A. **50** B1 40 36N 74 10W
Richmond New Zealand **111** B2 41 20S 173 10E
Richmond Virginia U.S.A. **63** K4 37 34N 77 27W
Richmond Park England **82** B2 51 27N 0 16W
Richmond upon Thames bor. Greater London England **82** B2 51 28N 0 19W
Richmond Valley New York U.S.A. **50** B1 40 31N 74 13W
Richmondville New York U.S.A. **65** F5 42 00N 74 00W
Rickmansworth England **82** A3 51 38N 0 29W
Ridgefield Connecticut U.S.A. **65** G4 41 17N 73 30W
Ridgewood New Jersey U.S.A. **50** B2 40 58N 74 08W
Ridgway Pennsylvania U.S.A. **64** B4 41 25N 78 45W
Riesa Germany **76** E5 51 18N 13 18E
Rieti Italy **81** B3 42 24N 12 51E
Rif Mountains Morocco **77** A2 35 00N 5 00W
Riga Latvia **79** E2 56 53N 24 08E
Riga, Gulf of Latvia/Estonia **79** E2 57 30N 23 30E
Rijeka Croatia **81** B4 45 20N 14 27E
Rijn (Rhein, Rhine) r. Netherlands **76** D5 52 00N 51 15E
Rimini Italy **81** B3 44 03N 12 34E
Rimnicu Vilcea Romania **81** D4 45 06N 24 21E
Ringgold Isles Fiji **114** V16 16 10S 179 50W
Ringkøbing Denmark **80** A6 56 06N 8 15E
Ringkøbing Fjord Denmark **80** A6 56 00N 8 00E
Ringvassøy i. Norway **79** D4 69 55N 19 10E
Rio Alto Purus Peru **68** C10 10 30S 72 00W
Rio Amazonas (Amazon) r. Brazil **68** G12 2 00S 53 00W
Río Apaporis r. Colombia **68** C13 1 00N 72 30W
Río Apure r. Venezuela **68** D14 7 40N 68 00W
Rio Aquidauana r. Brazil **68** F9 20 00S 56 00W
Rio Araguaia r. Brazil **68** H11 7 20S 49 00W
Río Arauca r. Venezuela **68** D14 7 10N 68 30W
Riobamba Ecuador **68** B12 1 44S 78 40W
Río Bermejo Argentina **69** E7 25 00S 61 00W
Rio Branco r. Brazil **68** E13 0 00 62 00W
Rio Branco tn. Brazil **68** D11 9 59S 67 49W
Río Caqueta r. Colombia **68** C12 0 05S 72 30W
Río Caroni r. Venezuela **68** E14 7 00N 62 30W
Río Caura r. Venezuela **68** E14 6 00N 64 00W
Río Chico r. Argentina **69** D3 49 00S 70 00W
Río Chico r. Argentina **69** D4 45 00S 67 30W
Río Chubut r. Argentina **69** D4 43 30S 67 30W
Rio Claro Trinidad and Tobago **66** T9 10 33N 61 11W
Río Colorado r. Argentina **69** D5 37 30S 69 00W
Río Corrientes r. Peru **68** B12 2 30S 76 30W
Río Cuarto tn. Argentina **69** E6 33 08S 64 20W
Rio de Janeiro admin. Brazil **69** I8 22 00S 42 30W
Rio de Janeiro tn. Brazil **69** Q2 22 53S 43 17W
Río de la Plata r. Uruguay/Argentina **69** F5 35 00S 57 00W
Rio de Para r. Brazil **68** H12 1 00S 48 00W
Río Deseado r. Argentina **69** D3 47 00S 68 00W
Río Dulce r. Argentina **69** E7 29 00S 63 00W
Río Gallegos tn. Argentina **69** D2 51 35S 68 10W
Rio Grande r. Bolivia **68** E9 18 00S 65 00W
Rio Grande r. Brazil **68** G8 20 00S 50 00W
Rio Grande r. Mexico/U.S.A. **66** D5/D6 30 00N 104 00W
Río Grande tn. Argentina **69** D2 53 45N 67 46W
Rio Grande tn. Brazil **69** G6 32 03S 52 08W
Río Grande tn. Mexico **66** D4 23 50N 103 02W
Rio Grande do Norte admin. Brazil **68** J11 6 00S 37 00W
Rio Grande do Sul admin. Brazil **69** G7 28 00N 52 30W
Rio Grande Rise Atlantic Ocean **113** E3 32 00S 36 00W
Río Guainia r. Colombia/Venezuela **68** D13 2 30N 67 30W
Rio Guaporé r. Brazil/Bolivia **68** E10 13 00S 62 00W
Río Guarico r. Venezuela **67** K1 8 00N 67 30W
Río Guaviare r. Colombia **68** C13 3 00N 70 00W
Rio Gurgueia r. Brazil **68** I11 9 00S 44 00W
Rio Gurupi r. Brazil **68** H12 4 00S 47 00W
Ríohacha Colombia **68** C15 11 34N 72 58W
Río Hondo r. California U.S.A. **51** B3 34 00N 118 07W
Rio Iguaçu r. Brazil **69** G7 26 00S 51 00W
Río Inirida r. Colombia **68** C13/D13 2 30N 70 00W
Río Japurá r. Brazil **68** D12 2 00S 67 30W
Rio Jari r. Brazil **68** G13 2 00N 54 00W
Rio Jequitinhonha r. Brazil **68** I9 16 00S 41 00W
Rio Juruá r. Brazil **68** D12 4 30S 67 00W
Rio Juruena r. Brazil **68** F11 10 00S 57 40W
Rio Madeira r. Brazil **68** E11 6 00S 61 30W
Río Madre de Dios r. Bolivia **68** D10 12 00S 68 00W
Río Magdalena r. Colombia **68** C14 8 00N 73 30W
Río Mamoré r. Bolivia **68** E9 15 00S 65 00W
Río Marañón r. Peru **68** B12 4 50S 77 30W
Río Meta r. Colombia **68** C14 6 00N 71 00W
Río Napo r. Peru **68** C12 2 30S 73 30W
Río Negro r. Argentina **69** E5 40 00S 65 00W
Rio Negro r. Brazil **68** D12 0 05S 67 00W
Río Negro r. Uruguay **69** F6 33 00S 57 30W
Río Orinoco r. Venezuela **68** E14 8 00N 64 00W
Río Paragua r. Venezuela **68** E14 6 00N 63 30W
Río Paraguá r. Bolivia **68** E10 14 00S 61 30W
Río Paraguay r. Paraguay/Argentina **69** F7 26 30S 58 00W
Río Paraná r. Paraguay/Argentina **69** F7 27 00S 56 00W
Rio Paranaíba r. Brazil **68** H9 18 00S 49 00W
Rio Parana Panema r. Brazil **69** G8 22 30S 52 00W
Rio Pardo r. Brazil **68** J9 15 10S 40 00W
Rio Parnaíba r. Brazil **68** I11 7 30S 45 00W
Río Pastaza r. Peru **68** B12 2 30S 77 00W
Río Pilcomayo r. Paraguay/Argentina **69** F8 24 00S 60 00W
Río Salado r. Argentina **69** E7 28 30S 62 30W
Río Salado r. Argentina **69** D6 35 00S 66 30W
Rio São Francisco r. Brazil **68** J11 8 30S 39 00W
Río San Miguel r. Bolivia **68** E9 15 00S 63 30W
Rio Solimões r. Brazil **68** D12 3 30S 69 00W
Rio Tapajós r. Brazil **68** F11 6 30S 57 00W
Rio Taquari r. Brazil **68** F8 18 00S 57 00W
Rio Tefé r. Brazil **68** D12 4 30S 65 30W
Rio Teles Pires r. Brazil **68** F11 8 00S 57 00W
Rio Tocantins r. Brazil **68** H12 3 00S 49 00W
Rio Trombetas r. Brazil **68** F13 1 30N 57 00W
Río Ucayali r. Peru **68** C11 6 00S 74 00W
Rio Uraricuera r. Brazil **68** E13 3 00N 62 30W
Río Uruguay r. Uruguay/Argentina **69** F6 32 00S 57 40W
Río Verde r. Paraguay **69** F8 23 20S 60 00W
Rio Verde tn. Brazil **68** G9 17 50S 50 55W
Río Verde tn. Mexico **66** D4 21 58N 100 00W
Río Vuapés r. Colombia **68** C13 1 30N 72 00W
Rio Xingu r. Brazil **68** G12 2 30S 52 30W
Rio Yavari r. Peru/Brazil **68** C12 5 00S 72 30W
Rishiri-tō i. Japan **100** D4 45 10N 141 20E
Rishra India **94** K2 22 43N 88 19E
Rivera Uruguay **69** F6 30 52S 55 30W
River Cess tn. Liberia **106** D9 5 28N 9 32W
River Forest tn. Illinois U.S.A. **53** A2 41 54N 87 49W
Riverhead New York U.S.A. **65** H3 40 55N 72 40W
River Rouge tn. Michigan U.S.A. **52** E2 42 17N 83 08W
River Rouge Park Michigan U.S.A. **52** E2 42 21N 83 14W
Riverside Illinois U.S.A. **53** A2 41 49N 87 49W
Riverside New Jersey U.S.A. **64** F3 40 02N 74 58W
Riverton New Zealand **111** A1 46 21S 168 02E
Roanne France **77** C4 46 02N 4 05E
Roanoke Virginia U.S.A. **63** K4 37 15N 79 58W
Robbinsville New Jersey U.S.A. **65** F3 40 13N 74 38W
Robert Sibley Regional Park California U.S.A. **49** C3 37 51N 122 11W
Roberts, Point Washington U.S.A. **42** H4 49 00N 123 05W
Robertsport Liberia **106** C9 6 45N 11 22W
Robin's Nest mt. Hong Kong U.K. **98** B3 22 33N 114 11E
Roca Alijos is. Mexico **115** O10 24 59N 115 49W
Rocas Island Atlantic Ocean **55** 3 50S 33 50W
Roche Harbor Washington U.S.A. **42** H4 48 36N 123 10W
Rochefort France **77** B4 45 57N 0 58W
Rochester Minnesota U.S.A. **63** H5 84 01N 92 27W
Rochester New Hampshire U.S.A. **65** K6 43 18N 70 59W
Rochester New York U.S.A. **64** C6 43 12N 77 37W
Rockall Bank Atlantic Ocean **113** G12 58 00N 15 00W
Rockaway Beach New York U.S.A. **50** C1 40 33N 73 55W
Rockaway Inlet New York U.S.A. **50** C1 40 34N 73 56W
Rockdale Australia **111** G2 33 57S 151 08E
Rockefeller Plateau Antarctica **117** 79 00S 140 00W
Rockford Illinois U.S.A. **63** I5 42 16N 89 06W
Rockford Ohio U.S.A. **36** B1 40 42N 84 40W
Rock Hall Maryland U.S.A. **64** D2 39 08N 76 14W
Rockhampton Australia **110** I5 23 22S 150 32E
Rock Hill tn. South Carolina U.S.A. **63** J3 34 55N 81 01W
Rock Island tn. Illinois U.S.A. **63** H5 41 30N 90 34W
Rock Lake tn. North Dakota U.S.A. **39** B1 48 49N 99 16W
Rockland Massachusetts U.S.A. **65** K5 42 08N 70 55W
Rockport Washington U.S.A. **42** H4 48 30N 121 38W
Rock Springs tn. Wyoming U.S.A. **62** E5 41 35N 109 13W
Rockville Maryland U.S.A. **64** C2 39 05N 77 10W
Rockville Center New York U.S.A. **50** D1 40 40N 73 38W
Rocky Mount tn. North Carolina U.S.A. **63** K4 35 56N 77 48W
Rocky Mountains Canada/U.S.A. **10** K4/N1
Rocky Point New York U.S.A. **65** H3 40 57N 72 55W
Rocky Woods Reservation Massachusetts U.S.A. **52** A1 42 13N 71 16W
Rodez France **77** C3 44 21N 2 34E
Ródhos Greece **81** E2 36 26N 28 14E
Ródhos (Rhodes) i. Greece **81** E2 36 00N 28 00E
Roding r. England **82** D3 51 45N 0 15E
Rodopi Planina mts. Bulgaria **81** D3 41 00N 25 00E
Rodrigues i. Indian Ocean **112** F5 19 43S 63 26E
Rogers City Michigan U.S.A. **36** C6 45 24N 83 50W
Rokugo r. Japan **101** C3 35 31N 139 46E
Rolette North Dakota U.S.A. **39** B1 48 41N 99 50W
Rolla Missouri U.S.A. **63** H4 37 56N 91 55W
Rolla North Dakota U.S.A. **39** B1 48 52N 99 36W
Roma (Rome) Italy **81** B3 41 53N 12 30E
Roma Australia **110** H4 26 32S 148 46E
Roman Romania **81** E4 46 56N 26 56E
ROMANIA **81** D4
Rome Georgia U.S.A. **63** I3 34 01N 85 02W
Rome New York U.S.A. **64** E6 43 13N 75 28W
Rome see Roma
Romford England **82** D3 51 35N 0 11E
Romney West Virginia U.S.A. **64** B2 39 21N 78 44W
Romulus Michigan U.S.A. **52** D1 42 14N 83 23W
Rona i. Scotland **78** F11 59 10N 5 50W
Ronda Spain **77** A2 36 45N 5 10W
Rondônia admin. Brazil **68** E10 11 30S 63 00W
Rondonópolis Brazil **68** G9 16 29S 54 37W
Rondout Reservoir New York U.S.A. **65** F4 41 50N 74 30W
Ronne Ice Shelf Antarctica **117** 77 00S 60 00W
Roosevelt Minnesota U.S.A. **39** B1 48 49N 95 06W
Roosevelt Island Antarctica **117** 79 00S 160 00W
Roraima admin. Brazil **68** E13 2 30N 62 30W
Rosario Argentina **69** E6 33 00S 60 40W
Rosário Brazil **68** I12 3 00S 44 15W
Rosario Mexico **66** A6 30 02N 115 46W
Rosario Mexico **66** C4 23 00N 105 51W
Rosario Strait Washington U.S.A. **42** H4 48 30N 122 50W
Rosarito Mexico **66** B5 28 38N 114 02W
Roscoff France **76** B4 48 43N 3 59W
Roscommon Michigan U.S.A. **36** B5 44 31N 84 37W
Roseau Dominica **67** L3 15 18N 61 23W
Roseau Minnesota U.S.A. **39** B1 48 51N 95 46W
Roseburg Oregon U.S.A. **62** B5 43 13N 123 21W
Roselle New Jersey U.S.A. **50** A1 40 40N 74 16W
Rosemead California U.S.A. **51** B3 34 03N 118 07W
Rosenheim Germany **76** E4 47 51N 12 09E
Roseville Michigan U.S.A. **52** F2 42 29N 82 05W
Rossano Italy **81** C2 39 35N 16 38E
Ross Ice Shelf Antarctica **117** 80 00S 180 00
Ross Lake Washington U.S.A. **42** H4 48 50N 121 05W
Ross Lake National Recreation Area Washington U.S.A. **42** H4 48 50N 121 00W
Rosslare Irish Republic **78** E4 52 15N 6 22W
Rosso Mauritania **106** A11 16 29N 15 53W
Ross Sea Southern Ocean **117** 75 00S 180 00
Røssvatnet mt. Sweden **79** D4 66 00N 15 10E
Rostock Germany **76** E5 54 06N 12 09E
Rostov Russia **90** D6 57 11N 39 23E
Rostov-na-Donu Russia **90** D4 47 15N 39 45E
Roswell New Mexico U.S.A. **62** F3 33 24N 104 33W
Rothera r.s. Antarctica **117** 67 34S 68 07W
Rotorua New Zealand **111** C3 38 07S 176 17E
Rotterdam Netherlands **76** C5 51 54N 4 28E
Rotterdam New York U.S.A. **65** G5 42 00N 73 00W
Roubaix France **76** C5 50 42N 3 10E
Rouen France **76** C5 49 26N 1 05E
Rouge, Point Trinidad and Tobago **66** S9 10 09N 61 47W
Rouge, River Michigan U.S.A. **52** E2 42 17N 83 26W
Roulette Pennsylvania U.S.A. **64** B4 41 45N 78 10W
Round Island Hong Kong U.K. **98** C1 22 12N 114 10E
Rovaniemi Finland **79** F4 66 29N 25 40E
Rovigo Italy **81** B4 45 04N 11 47E
Rovno Ukraine **90** B5 50 39N 26 10E
Rovuma (Ruvuma) r. Mozambique **107** M5 11 30S 38 00E
Roxas The Philippines **99** G6 11 36N 122 45E
Roxburgh New Zealand **111** A1 45 34N 169 21E
Roxbury Massachusetts U.S.A. **52** B2 42 19N 71 03W
Royal Botanic Gardens England **82** B2 51 28N 0 18W
Royal National Park Australia **111** G1 34 06S 151 06E
Royal Oak Michigan U.S.A. **36** C3 42 31N 83 08W
Royan France **77** B4 45 38N 1 02W
Rtishchevo Russia **90** E5 52 16N 43 45E
Ruaha National Park Tanzania **107** M6 7 00S 35 00E
Ruapeha mt. New Zealand **111** C3 39 18S 176 36E
Rub'Al Khālī d. Saudi Arabia **93** G2 19 30N 48 00E
Rubtsovsk Russia **90** N5 51 43N 81 11E
Ruby Alaska U.S.A. **10** D5 64 41N 155 35W
Rudnya Russia **90** E5 50 49N 44 35E
Rudnyy Kazakhstan **91** J5 53 00N 63 05E
Rudow Germany **83** F1 52 24N 13 29E
Rudyard Montana U.S.A. **41** C1 48 34N 110 33W
Rueil-Malmaison France **83** A2 48 52N 2 12E
Rufiji r. Tanzania **107** M6 7 30S 38 40E
Rugby England **78** J4 52 23N 1 15W
Ruhrort Germany **76** G2 51 27N 6 44E
Ruislip England **82** B3 51 35N 0 25W
Rukwa, Lake Tanzania **107** L6 8 00S 33 00E
Rumoi Japan **100** D3 43 57N 141 40E
Runanga New Zealand **111** B2 42 24S 171 12E
Rungis France **83** B2 48 45N 2 22E
Ruse Bulgaria **81** E3 43 50N 25 59E
Rusk Texas U.S.A. **63** G3 31 49N 95 11W
Russas Brazil **68** J12 4 56N 38 02W
Russell Kansas U.S.A. **62** G4 38 54N 98 51W
Russell New Zealand **111** B3 35 16S 174 10E
RUSSIA (RUSSIAN FEDERATION) **90/91** E6/K6
RUSSIAN FEDERATION see RUSSIA
Russkaya r.s. Antartica **117** 74 46S 136 51W
Rustavi Georgia **90** F3 41 34N 45 03E
Ruston Louisiana U.S.A. **63** H3 32 32N 92 39W
Ruth Nevada U.S.A. **62** D4 39 16N 114 59W
Rutland Vermont U.S.A. **63** L5 43 37N 72 59W
Rutog China **96** E5 33 27N 79 43E
Ruvuma (Rovuma) r. Tanzania **107** M5 11 30S 38 00E
Ruwenzori, Mount mt. Uganda/Zaïre **102** 0 23N 29 54E
Ruwenzori National Park Rwanda **106** L7 0 30S 29 30E
Ružomberok Czechoslovakia **80** C4 49 04N 19 15E
RWANDA **106** L7
Ryazan' Russia **90** D5 54 37N 39 43E
Rybach'ye Kazakhstan **91** N4 46 27N 81 30E
Rybach'ye see Issyk-Kul'
Rybinsk (Andropov) Russia **90** D6 58 03N 38 50E
Rybinskoye Vodokhranilishche (Rybinsk Reservoir) Russia **90** D6 59 00N 38 00E
Rybinsk Reservoir see Rybinskoye Vodokhranilishche
Rybnik Poland **80** C5 50 07N 18 30E
Ryde Australia **111** G2 33 49S 151 06E
Rye New York U.S.A. **50** D2 40 58N 73 41W
Ryukyu Islands (Nansei-shoto) Japan **97** P4 27 30N 127 30E
Ryukyu Ridge Pacific Ocean **114** C10 25 50N 128 00E
Ryukyu Trench Pacific Ocean **84** 25 00N 128 00E
Rzeszów Poland **80** D5 50 04N 22 00E
Rzhev Russia **90** C6 56 15N 34 18E

S

Saalfeld Germany **76** E5 50 39N 11 22E
Saarbrücken Germany **76** D4 49 15N 6 58E
Saaremaa *i.* Estonia **79** E2 58 20N 22 00E
Sabadell Spain **77** C3 41 33N 2 07E
Šabac Serbia Yugoslavia **81** C3 44 45N 19 41E
Šabah *state* Malaysia **99** F5 5 00N 117 30E
Sabaloka Cataract *(River Nile)* Sudan **92** D2 16 19N 32 40E
Sabanalarga Colombia **67** J2 10 38N 74 55W
Sabhā Libya **106** H13 27 02N 14 26E
Sabi *r.* Zimbabwe/Mozambique **107** L3 20 30S 33 00E
Sabinas Mexico **66** D5 27 50N 101 09W
Sabinas Hidalgo Mexico **66** D5 26 33N 100 10W
Sabine *r.* U.S.A. **63** H3 30 00N 94 00W
Sabine, Mount Antarctica **117** 72 00S 169 00W
Sabkhet el Bardawîl *l.* Egypt **92** N10 31 10N 33 35E
Sable, Cape Florida U.S.A. **63** J2 25 08N 80 07W
Sabor *r.* Portugal **77** A3 41 22N 6 50W
Sabyā Saudi Arabia **92** F2 17 07N 42 39E
Sabzevār Iran **93** I6 36 15N 57 38E
Saclay France **83** A1 48 43N 2 09E
Saco Montana U.S.A. **40** B1 48 27N 107 21W
Sacramento Mountains U.S.A. **62** E3 33 00N 105 00W
Sadar Bazar India **94** L4 28 39N 77 12E
Sadiya India **95** H5 27 49N 95 38E
Sado *r.* Portugal **77** A2 38 15N 8 30W
Sado-shima *i.* Japan **100** C2 38 20N 138 30E
Säffle Sweden **80** B6 59 08N 12 55E
Safi Morocco **106** D14 32 20N 9 17W
Saga Japan **100** B1 33 16N 130 18E
Sagaing Myanmar **95** H4 21 55N 95 56E
Sagami Bay Japan **101** B2 35 15N 139 32E
Sagamihara Japan **100** L2 35 34N 139 22E
Sagami-nada *sea* Japan **100** L1 35 00N 139 30E
Sagami-wan *b.* Japan **100** L2 35 12N 139 20E
Sagar India **95** D4 23 50N 78 44E
Sagavanirktok *r.* Alaska U.S.A. **44** B4 68 00N 149 00W
Sage Creek Montana U.S.A. **41** C1 48 50N 110 50W
Saginaw Michigan U.S.A. **63** J5 43 25N 83 54W
Saginaw Bay Michigan U.S.A. **63** J5 44 00N 84 00W
Sagua la Grande Cuba **67** H4 22 48N 80 06W
Sagunto Spain **77** B2 39 40N 0 17W
Sahara Desert North Africa **106** D12
Saharanpur India **95** D5 29 58N 77 33E
Sahiwal Pakistan **95** C6 30 41N 73 11E
Sahuaripa Mexico **66** C5 29 00N 109 13W
Sahuayo Mexico **66** D4 20 05N 102 42W
Saïda Algeria **77** C1 34 50N 0 10E
Saïda *(Sidon)* Lebanon **92** O11 33 32N 35 22E
Saidpur Bangladesh **95** F5 25 48N 89 00E
Saikhoa Ghat India **95** H5 27 46N 95 38E
Sai Kung Hong Kong U.K. **98** C2 22 23N 114 16E
Saimaa *l.* Finland **79** F3 61 15N 27 45E
St. Abb's Head *c.* Scotland **78** I7 55 55N 2 09W
St. Albans England **78** K3 51 46N 0 21W
St. Albans Vermont U.S.A. **33** B1 44 49N 73 07W
St. Andrews Scotland **78** I8 56 20N 2 48W
St. Ann's Bay *tn.* Jamaica **67** Q8 18 26N 77 12W
St. Augustine Florida U.S.A. **63** J2 29 54N 81 19W
St. Bees Head *c.* England **78** H6 54 31N 3 39W
St-Brieuc France **76** B4 48 31N 2 45W
St. Clair, Lake Canada/U.S.A. **36** D3 42 30N 82 40W
St. Clair Shores Michigan U.S.A. **52** F2 42 29N 82 53W
St-Cloud France **83** A2 48 51N 2 11E
St.Cloud Minnesota U.S.A. **63** H6 45 34N 94 10W
St. Croix *i.* West Indies **67** L3 22 45N 65 00W
St. Croix *r.* North America **63** H6 46 00N 93 00W
St. Croix Falls *tn.* Wisconsin U.S.A. **35** B2 45 25N 92 38W
St. Cyr-l'École France **83** A2 48 47N 2 03E
St. David's Head *c.* Wales **78** F3 51 55N 5 19W
St-Denis France **83** B2 48 57N 2 22E
St.-Dié France **76** D4 48 17N 6 57E
St.-Dizier France **76** C4 48 38N 4 58E
Saint Elias, Mount Canada/U.S.A. **44** C3 60 14N 140 50W
Saint Elias Mountains Canada/U.S.A. **44** D3 60 30N 140 00W
Saintes France **77** B4 45 44N 0 38W
St.-Étienne France **77** C4 45 26N 4 23E
St. Francis *r.* U.S.A. **63** H4 35 00N 90 00W
St. Francis, Cape Republic of South Africa **102** 34 13S 24 51E
St. Gallen Switzerland **77** D4 47 25N 9 23E
St.-Gaudens France **77** C3 43 07N 0 44E
St.-Germain-en-Laye France **83** A2 48 54N 2 04E
St. George New York U.S.A. **50** B1 40 48N 74 06W
St. George's Grenada **67** L2 12 04N 61 44W
St. George's Channel British Isles **78** E3 52 00N 6 00W
St. Helena *i.* Atlantic Ocean **113** H5 15 58S 5 43W
St. Helena Bay Republic of South Africa **107** I1 32 00S 17 30E
St. Helens England **78** I5 53 28N 2 44W
St. Helier Jersey Channel Islands **78** I6 49 12N 2 07W
St. Ignace Michigan U.S.A. **63** J6 45 53N 84 44W
St. Ives Australia **111** G3 33 44S 151 10E
St. John North Dakota U.S.A. **39** B1 48 58N 99 41W
Saint John *r.* North America **63** M6 46 00N 69 00W
St. John's Antigua & Barbuda **67** L3 17 08N 61 50W
St. Johns Michigan U.S.A. **36** B4 43 01N 84 31W
St. Joseph Missouri U.S.A. **63** B1 39 45N 94 51W
St Joseph Trinidad and Tobago **66** T10 10 39N 61 25W
St Joseph Trinidad and Tobago **66** U9 10 17N 60 25W
St. Joseph River U.S.A. **36** B2 41 12N 85 00W
St. Kilda *i.* Scotland **78** C9 57 49N 8 34W
ST. KITTS-NEVIS 67 L3
St. Laurent French Guiana **68** G14 5 29N 54 03W
St. Lawrence Island Alaska U.S.A. **10** B5 63 15N 169 50W
St. Lawrence Seaway Canada/U.S.A. **37** L/M5 44 38N 48 34W
St-Lô France **76** B4 49 07N 1 05W
St. Louis Missouri U.S.A. **63** H4 38 40N 90 15W
St. Louis Senegal **106** A11 16 01N 16 30W
St. Louis River Minnesota U.S.A. **35** B2 47 00N 92 45W
ST. LUCIA 67 L2
St.-Malo France **76** B4 48 39N 2 00W
St-Mandé France **83** B2 48 50N 2 26E
St. Mary Montana U.S.A. **41** C1 48 44N 113 25W
St. Marys Pennsylvania U.S.A. **64** B4 41 27N 78 35W
St. Marys River U.S.A. **36** B1 40 50N 84 55W
St. Maur France **83** B2 48 48N 2 30E
St. Moritz Switzerland **77** D4 46 30N 9 51E
St.-Nazaire France **77** B4 47 17N 2 12W
St.-Omer France **76** C5 50 45N 2 15E
St. Ouen France **83** A3 49 03N 2 07E
St. Paul Rocks Atlantic Ocean **113** F7 0 23N 29 23W
St. Peter Port Guernsey Channel Islands **78** I6 49 27N 3 32W
Saint Petersburg Florida U.S.A. **63** J2 27 45N 82 40W
St. Petersburg *(Leningrad, Sankt-Peterburg)* Russia **90** C6 59 55N 30 25E
Saint-Pierre & Miquelon *is.* Atlantic Ocean **11** X2 47 00N 56 20W
St. Pölten Austria **81** C4 48 13N 15 37E
St.-Quentin France **76** C4 49 51N 3 17E
St. Remy France **83** A1 48 42N 2 04E
St. Thomas *i.* West Indies **67** K3 18 00N 65 30W
St.-Tropez France **77** D3 43 16N 6 39E
St. Vincent *i.* St. Vincent and The Grenadines **67** L2 13 15N 61 12W
ST. VINCENT AND THE GRENADINES 67 L2
Saipan Northern Marianas **114** E9 15 12N 145 43E
Saitama *pref.* Japan **100** L3 36 00N 139 30E
Sai Ying Pun Hong Kong U.K. **98** B1 22 17N 114 08E
Sakai Japan **100** C1 34 35N 135 28E
Sākākah Saudi Arabia **92** F4 29 59N 40 12E
Sakakawea, Lake North Dakota U.S.A. **62** F6 48 00N 103 00W
Sakarya *r.* Turkey **92** D6 40 05N 30 15E
Sakata Japan **100** C2 38 55N 139 51E
Sakhalin *i.* Russia **89** Q6 50 00N 143 00E
Sakhalin Bay Russia **89** Q6 54 00N 141 00E
Sakura Japan **100** M2 35 43N 140 13E
Sakurai Japan **100** G1 34 54N 135 12E
Sala Sweden **80** C6 59 55N 16 38E
Salālah Oman **93** H2 17 00N 54 04E
Salamanca Mexico **66** D4 20 34N 101 12W
Salamanca New York U.S.A. **64** B5 42 11N 78 43W
Salamanca Spain **77** A3 40 58N 5 40W
Salavat Russia **91** H5 53 22N 55 50E
Sala y Gomez *i.* Pacific Ocean **115** P5 26 28S 105 28W
Saldus Latvia **79** E2 56 38N 22 30E
Salekhard Russia **89** I9 66 33N 66 35E
Salem India **95** D2 11 38N 78 08E
Salem Massachusetts U.S.A. **52** C3 42 32N 70 53W
Salem New Jersey U.S.A. **64** E2 39 35N 75 28W
Salem Oregon U.S.A. **62** B5 44 57N 123 01W
Salerno Italy **81** B3 40 40N 14 46E
Salgótarján Hungary **81** C4 49 05N 19 47E
Salgueiro Brazil **68** J11 8 04S 39 05W
Salihli Turkey **80** E2 38 29N 28 08E
Salima Malawi **107** L5 13 45S 34 29E
Salina Kansas U.S.A. **63** G4 38 53N 97 36W
Salinas Ecuador **68** A12 2 15S 80 58W
Salinas Grandes *l.* Argentina **69** D6/E7 30 00S 65 00W
Saline Michigan U.S.A. **36** C3 42 12N 83 46W
Salisbury England **78** J3 51 05N 1 48W
Salisbury Maryland U.S.A. **63** K4 38 22N 75 37W
Salisbury North Carolina U.S.A. **63** J4 35 20N 80 30W
Salisbury Plain England **78** J3 51 10N 1 55W
Salmon Idaho U.S.A. **62** D6 45 11N 113 55W
Salmon *r.* Idaho U.S.A. **62** C6 45 00N 116 00W
Salmon River Mountains Idaho U.S.A. **62** C6 45 00N 115 00W
Salo Finland **79** E3 60 23N 23 10E
Salonta Romania **81** D4 46 49N 21 40E
Salpausselka *geog. reg.* Finland **79** F3 61 40N 26 00E
Salt Jordan **92** O11 32 03N 35 44E
Salt *r.* Arizona U.S.A. **62** D3 34 00N 110 00W
Salta Argentina **69** D8 24 46S 65 28W
Salt Creek Illinois U.S.A. **53** A2 41 52N 87 57W
Saltdal Norway **79** D4 67 06N 15 25E
Salten *geog. reg.* Norway **79** D4 67 05N 15 00E
Salt Fork *r.* Texas U.S.A. **62** F3 33 00N 101 00W
Salt Fork *r.* Texas/Oklahoma U.S.A. **62** F4 35 00N 100 00W
Saltillo Mexico **66** D5 25 30N 101 00W
Salt Lake *tn.* India **94** K2 22 35N 88 23E
Salt Lake City Utah U.S.A. **62** D5 40 45N 111 55W
Salto Uruguay **69** F6 31 27S 57 50W
Salvador Brazil **68** J10 12 58S 38 29W
Salween *(Nu Jiang)* *r.* Myanmar **97** J3 21 00N 98 30E
Salybia Trinidad and Tobago **66** T10 10 42N 61 02W
Salzburg Austria **81** B4 47 48N 13 03E
Salzgitter Germany **76** E5 52 13N 10 20E
Samani Japan **100** D3 42 07N 142 57E
Samar *i.* The Philippines **99** G6 12 30N 125 00E
Samara *r.* Russia **90** G5 52 30N 53 00E
Samara *(Kuybyshev)* Russia **90** G5 53 10N 50 10E
Samara *(Kuybyshevskoye)* **Vodokhranilishche** *res.* Russia **90** F5/6 55 00N 45 00E
Samarinda Indonesia **99** F3 0 30S 117 09E
Samarkand Uzbekistan **91** K2 39 40N 66 57E
Sāmarrā' Iraq **92** F5 34 13N 43 52E
Sambalpur India **95** E4 21 28N 84 04E
Sambor Ukraine **80** D4 49 31N 23 10E
Sámos *i.* Greece **81** E2 37 00N 26 00E
Samothráki *i.* Greece **81** E3 40 00N 25 00E
Samsun Turkey **92** E7 41 17N 36 22E
San Mali **106** D10 13 21N 4 57W
San'ā Yemen Republic **92** F2 15 23N 44 14E
Sanae *r.s.* Antarctica **117** 70 18S 02 25E
Sanaga *r.* Cameroon **106** H8 4 30N 12 20E
Sanak Islands Alaska U.S.A. **10** C3 54 26N 162 40W
Sanandaj Iran **93** G6 35 18N 47 01E
San Andreas Fault California U.S.A. **49** B1 37 28N 122 18W
San Andreas Lake California U.S.A. **49** B2 37 36N 122 25W
San Andrés Tuxtla Mexico **66** E3 18 28N 95 15W
San Angelo Texas U.S.A. **62** F3 31 28N 100 28W
San Antonio Chile **69** C6 33 35S 71 39W
San Antonio Texas U.S.A. **62** G2 29 25N 98 30W
San Antonio *r.* Texas U.S.A. **63** G2 29 00N 97 00W
San Antonio Oeste Argentina **69** E4 40 45S 64 58W
San Bernado Chile **69** C6 33 37S 70 45W
San Bruno California U.S.A. **49** B2 37 33N 122 24W
San Bruno Mountain California U.S.A. **49** B2 37 41N 122 26W
San Carlos California U.S.A. **49** B2 37 30N 122 16W
San Carlos The Philippines **99** G6 10 30N 123 29E
San Carlos The Philippines **99** G7 15 59N 120 22E
San Carlos Venezuela **68** D14 9 39N 68 35W
San Carlos de Bariloche Argentina **69** C4 41 11S 71 23W
San Carlos del Zulia Venezuela **68** C14 9 01N 71 58W
San-chung Taiwan **98** H8 25 04N 121 29E
San Clemente Island U.S.A. **62** C3 32 55N 118 30W
San Cristóbal Argentina **69** E6 30 20S 61 14W
San Cristóbal Mexico **66** F3 16 45N 92 40W
San Cristobal Venezuela **68** C14 7 46N 72 15W
San Cristobal *i.* Solomon Islands **110** K7 11 00S 162 00E
Sanda Japan **100** G1 34 54N 135 12E
Sandakan Malaysia **99** F5 5 52N 118 04E
Sanday *i.* Scotland **78** I11 59 15N 2 30W
Sandefjord Norway **80** B6 59 00N 10 15E
Sandoway Myanmar **95** G3 18 28N 94 20E
Sandpoint Idaho U.S.A. **43** E1 48 17N 116 34W
Sandpoint *tn.* Idaho U.S.A. **62** C6 48 17N 116 34W
Sandusky Michigan U.S.A. **36** D4 43 56N 82 50W
Sandusky Ohio U.S.A. **36** D2 41 27N 85 42W
Sandusky Bay Ohio U.S.A. **36** D2 41 30N 82 50W
Sandusky River Ohio U.S.A. **36** C1 41 00N 83 15W
Sandviken Sweden **80** C7 60 38N 16 50E
Sandy River Maine U.S.A. **37** Q5 44 45N 70 12W
San Felipe Mexico **66** B6 31 03N 114 52W
San Felipe Venezuela **68** D15 10 25N 68 40W
San Feliú de Guixols Spain **77** C3 41 47N 3 02E
San Fernando California U.S.A. **51** A1 34 17N 118 27W
San Fernando Mexico **66** A5 29 59N 115 10W
San Fernando Spain **77** A2 36 28N 6 12W
San Fernando Trinidad and Tobago **66** T10 10 16N 61 28W
San Fernando de Apure Venezuela **68** D14 7 53N 67 15W
Sanford Florida U.S.A. **63** J2 28 49N 81 17W
San Francique Trinidad and Tobago **66** S9 10 05N 61 39W
San Francisco Argentina **69** E6 31 29S 62 06W
San Francisco Dominican Republic **67** J3 19 19N 70 15W
San Francisco Bay California U.S.A. **49** B2 37 40N 122 18W
San Francisco Bay National Wildlife Refuge California U.S.A. **49** C2 37 31N 122 05W
San Francisco County California U.S.A. **49** B3 37 55N 122 25W
San Francisco del Oro Mexico **66** C5 26 52N 105 50W
San Francisco State Fish and Game Refuge California U.S.A. **49** B2 37 34N 122 26W
San Gabriel California U.S.A. **51** B3 34 06N 118 06W
San Gabriel Mountains California U.S.A. **51** B4 34 18N 118 05W
San Gabriel Reservoir California U.S.A. **51** C3 34 12N 117 52W
San Gabriel River California U.S.A. **51** B2 33 58N 118 06W
Sangar Russia **89** O8 64 02N 127 30E
Sangha *r.* Africa **106** I8 2 00N 17 00E
Sangli India **95** C3 16 55N 74 37E
Sangre de Cristo Mountains New Mexico U.S.A. **62** E4 37 00N 105 00W
Sangre Grande Trinidad and Tobago **66** T10 10 35N 61 08W
San Javier Bolivia **68** E9 16 22S 62 38W
San José Costa Rica **67** H1 9 59N 84 04W
San José Uruguay **69** F6 34 27S 56 40W
San José del Cabo Mexico **66** C4 23 01N 109 40W
San Juan Argentina **69** D6 31 33S 68 31W
San Juán Peru **68** B9 15 22S 75 07W
San Juan Puerto Rico **67** K3 18 29N 66 08W
San Juan Trinidad and Tobago **66** T10 10 39N 61 27W
San Juan *r.* U.S.A. **62** D4 37 00N 110 00W
San Juan de los Morros Venezuela **67** K1 9 53N 67 23W
San Juan Islands Washington U.S.A. **42** H4 48 30N 123 00W
San Juan Mountains Colorado U.S.A. **62** E4 37 50N 107 50W
San Julián Argentina **69** D3 49 17S 67 45W
Sānkrāil India **94** J2 22 33N 88 14E
Sankt-Peterburg *see* St. Petersburg
Sankuru *r.* Zaïre **107** J7 4 00S 23 30E
San Leandro California U.S.A. **49** C2 37 43N 122 10W
San Lorenzo California U.S.A. **49** C2 37 41N 122 08W
Sanlúcar de Barrameda Spain **77** A2 36 46N 6 21W
San Lucas Mexico **66** C4 22 50N 109 52W
San Luis Argentina **69** D6 33 20S 66 23W
San Luis Potosí Mexico **66** D4 22 10N 101 00W
San Marcos Texas U.S.A. **63** G2 29 54N 97 57W
San Mateo California U.S.A. **49** B2 37 33N 122 22W
San Mateo County California U.S.A. **49** C2 37 35N 122 12W
Sanmenxia China **97** M5 34 46N 111 17E
San Miguel El Salvador **66** G2 13 28N 88 10W
San Miguel de Tucumán Argentina **69** D7 26 47S 65 15W
Sanming China **97** N4 26 16N 117 35E
Sannan Japan **100** G2 35 05N 135 03E
San Pablo California U.S.A. **49** B3 37 58N 122 21W
San Pablo The Philippines **99** G6 14 03N 121 19E
San Pablo Creek California U.S.A. **49** B3 37 58N 122 20W
San Pablo Reservoir California U.S.A. **49** C3 37 56N 122 14W
San Pedro Argentina **69** E8 24 12S 64 55W
San Pedro California U.S.A. **51** A2 33 45N 118 19W
San Pedro Côte d'Ivoire **106** D9 4 45N 6 37W
San Pedro Dominican Republic **67** K3 18 30N 69 18W
San Pedro Bay California U.S.A. **51** B1 33 43N 118 12W
San Pedro Channel California U.S.A. **51** A1 33 43N 118 22W
San Pedro de las Colonias Mexico **66** D5 25 50N 102 59W
San Pedro Sula Honduras **66** G3 15 26N 88 01W
San Quentin California U.S.A. **49** A3 37 56N 122 30W
San Rafael Argentina **69** D6 34 35S 68 24W
San Rafael California U.S.A. **49** B3 37 58N 122 30W
San Rafael Bay California U.S.A. **49** B3 37 56N 122 29W
San Remo Italy **81** A3 43 48N 7 46E
San Salvador El Salvador **66** G2 13 40N 89 10W
San Salvador *i.* The Bahamas **67** J4 24 00N 74 32W
San Salvador de Jujuy Argentina **69** D8 24 10S 65 48W
San Sebastián Spain **77** B3 43 19N 1 59W
San Severo Italy **81** C3 41 41N 15 23E
Santa Ana Bolivia **68** D10 13 46S 65 37W
Santa Ana California U.S.A. **51** C2 33 44N 117 54W
Santa Ana El Salvador **66** G2 14 00N 89 31W
Santa Ana River California U.S.A. **51** C2 33 46N 117 54W
Santa Barbara Mexico **66** C5 26 48N 105 50W
Santa Catarina *admin.* Brazil **69** G7 27 00S 51 00W
Santa Clara Cuba **67** I4 22 25S 79 58W
Santa Clara County California U.S.A. **49** C1 37 23N 122 11W
Santa Cruz Bolivia **68** E9 17 50S 63 10W
Santa Cruz Canary Islands **106** B13 28 28N 16 15W
Santa Cruz Jamaica **67** Q8 18 03N 77 43W
Santa Cruz *r.* Argentina **69** D2 50 00S 70 00W
Santa Cruz Islands Solomon Islands **110** L7 11 00S 167 00E
Santa Cruz Mountains California U.S.A. **49** B1 37 28N 122 23W
Santa Fé Argentina **69** E6 31 35S 60 50W
Santa Fe New Mexico U.S.A. **62** E4 35 41N 105 57W
Santa Isabel *i.* Solomon Islands **110** J8 7 30S 158 30E
Santa Maria Brazil **69** G7 29 45S 53 40W
Santa Marta Colombia **68** C15 11 18N 74 10W
Santa Monica California U.S.A. **51** A3 34 00N 118 25W
Santa Monica Mountains California U.S.A. **51** A3 33 07N 118 27W
Santana do Livramento Brazil **69** F6 30 52S 55 30W
Santander Colombia **68** B13 3 00N 76 25W
Santander Spain **77** B3 43 28N 3 48W
Sant'Antioco Italy **81** A2 39 04N 8 27E
Santarém Brazil **68** G12 2 26S 54 41W
Santarém Portugal **77** A2 39 14N 8 40W
Santa Rosa Argentina **69** E5 36 37S 64 17W
Santa Rosa Honduras **66** G2 14 48N 88 45W
Santa Rosa New Mexico U.S.A. **62** F3 34 56N 104 42W
Santa Rosalia Mexico **66** B5 27 20N 112 20W
Santa Teresa Brazil **69** Q2 22 57S 43 12W
Santiago Chile **69** C6 33 30S 70 40W
Santiago Dominican Republic **67** J3 19 30N 70 42W
Santiago Panama **67** H1 8 08N 80 59W
Santiago de Compostela Spain **77** A3 42 52N 8 33W
Santiago de Cuba Cuba **67** I4 20 00N 75 49W
Santiago del Estero Argentina **69** E7 27 47S 64 15W
Santiago Ixcuintla Mexico **66** C4 21 50N 105 11W
San Tin Hong Kong U.K. **98** B3 22 30N 114 04E
Santi Nagar India **94** L4 28 40N 77 10E
Santo Andre Brazil **69** H8 23 39S 46 29W
Santo Domingo Dominican Republic **67** K3 18 30N 69 57W
Santos Brazil **69** H8 23 56S 46 22W
San Uk Ha Hong Kong U.K. **98** C3 22 30N 114 14E
San Vicente El Salvador **66** G2 13 38N 88 42W
São Bernardo do Campo Brazil **69** H8 23 45S 46 34W
São Borja Brazil **69** F7 28 35S 56 01W
São Cristovão Brazil **69** Q2 22 54S 43 14W
São Gonçalo Brazil **69** Q2 22 49S 43 03W
São João de Meriti Brazil **69** P2 22 47S 43 22W
São João de Meriti *r.* Brazil **69** P2 22 48S 43 20W
São José Brazil **69** H7 27 35S 48 40W
São José do Rio Prêto Brazil **68** H8 20 50S 49 20W
São José dos Campos Brazil **69** H8 23 07S 45 52W
São Luís Brazil **68** I12 2 34S 44 16W
Saône *r.* France **77** C4 46 28N 4 55E
São Paulo *admin.* Brazil **68** G8/H8 21 30S 50 00W
São Paulo Brazil **69** H8 23 33S 46 39W
São Paulo de Olivença Brazil **68** D12 3 34S 68 55W
São Tomé *i.* Gulf of Guinea **106** G8 0 25N 6 35E
SÃO TOMÉ AND PRINCIPE 106 G8
São Vicente Brazil **69** H8 23 57S 46 23W
Sapporo Japan **100** D3 43 05N 141 21E
Saqqez Iran **93** G6 36 14N 46 15E
Sarajevo Bosnia-Herzegovina **81** C3 43 52N 18 26E
Sarakhs Iran **93** J6 36 32N 61 07E
Saransk Russia **90** F5 54 12N 45 10E
Sarapui *r.* Brazil **69** P3 22 44S 43 17W
Sarapul Russia **91** G6 56 30N 53 49E
Sarasota Florida U.S.A. **63** J2 27 20N 82 32W
Sarata Ukraine **81** E4 46 00N 29 40E
Saratoga Springs *tn.* New York U.S.A. **65** G6 43 04N 73 47W
Saratov Russia **90** F5 51 30N 45 55E
Saravan Iran **93** J4 27 25N 62 17E
Sarawak *state* Malaysia **99** E4 2 30N 112 30E
Sarcelles France **83** B2 48 59N 2 22E
Sardegna *(Sardinia)* *i.* Italy **81** A3 40 00N 9 00E
Sardindida Plain Kenya **106** M8/N8 2 00N 40 00E
Sardinia *see* Sardegna
Sar-e Pol Afghanistan **93** K6 36 13N 65 55E
Sargasso Sea Atlantic Ocean **113** B9 27 00N 66 00W
Sargeant Barbados **66** V12 13 05N 59 35W
Sargodha Pakistan **95** C6 32 01N 72 40E
Sarh Chad **106** I9 9 08N 18 22E
Sarīr Calanscio *d.* Libya **106** J13 26 00N 22 00E
Sark *i.* Channel Islands British Isles **78** I6 49 26N 2 22W
Sarles North Dakota U.S.A. **39** B1 48 58N 99 00W
Sarmiento Argentina **69** D3 45 38S 69 08W
Sarny Ukraine **80** E5 51 21N 26 31E
Saronikós Kólpos *g.* Greece **81** D2 38 00N 23 00E
Sarpsborg Norway **79** C2 59 17N 11 06E
Sarrebourg France **76** D4 48 43N 7 03E
Sarreguemines France **76** D4 49 06N 6 55E
Sartène Corsica **77** D3 41 37N 8 58E
Sartrouville France **83** A2 48 56N 2 11E
Sary-Ishikotrau *d.* Kazakhstan **91** M4 45 00N 77 00E
Sarysu *r.* Kazakhstan **91** K4 47 00N 67 30E
Sasayama Japan **100** G2 35 03N 135 12E
Sasebo Japan **100** A1 33 10N 129 42E
Sassandra Côte d'Ivoire **106** D9 4 58N 6 08W
Sassandra *r.* Côte d'Ivoire **106** D9 5 50N 6 55W
Sassari Italy **81** A3 40 43N 8 34E
Sassnitz Germany **76** E5 54 32N 13 40E
Satlayev *(Nikol'skiy)* Kazakhstan **91** K4 47 54N 67 25E
Satna India **95** E4 24 33N 80 50E
Satpura Range *mts.* India **95** C4/D4 21 40N 75 00E
Sattahip Thailand **99** C6 12 36N 100 56E
Satu Mare Romania **81** D4 47 48N 22 52E
SAUDI ARABIA 92 F3
Saugus Massachusetts U.S.A. **52** B2 42 27N 71 00W
Saurimo Angola **107** J6 9 39S 20 24E
Sausalito California U.S.A. **49** B3 37 51N 122 30W
Savannah Georgia U.S.A. **63** J3 32 04N 81 07W
Savannah *r.* U.S.A. **63** J3 33 00N 82 00W
Savannakhet Laos **97** L2 16 34N 104 45E
Savanna la Mar Jamaica **67** P8 18 13N 78 08W
Savona Italy **81** A3 44 18N 8 28E
Sawahlunto Indonesia **99** C3 0 41S 100 52E
Sawankhalok Thailand **97** J2 17 19N 99 50E
Sawara Japan **100** M2 35 52N 140 31E
Sawpit Canyon Reservoir California U.S.A. **51** B3 34 10N 117 59W
Sawu Sea Indonesia **99** G2 9 30S 122 00E
Sayanogorsk Russia **91** P5 53 00N 91 26E

Sayano-Shushenskoye Vodokhranilishche *res.* Russia 91 P5 52 00N 92 00E
Saylac Somalia 106 N9 11 21N 43 30E
Saynshand Mongolia 97 L8 44 58N 111 10E
Sayre Pennsylvania U.S.A. 64 D4 41 58N 76 03W
Say'ūn Yemen Republic 93 G2 15 59N 48 44E
Scafell Pike *mt.* England 78 H6 54 27N 3 14W
Scandinavia *geog. reg.* Europe 70 65 00N 15 00E
Scarborough England 78 K6 54 17N 0 24W
Scarsdale New York U.S.A. 50 C2 40 59N 73 49W
Sceaux France 83 B2 48 46N 2 18E
Scheldt Estuary Europe 70 51 30N 3 30E
Schenectady New York U.S.A. 65 G5 42 48N 73 57W
Schildow Germany 83 F2 52 40N 13 21E
Schoharie New York U.S.A. 65 F5 42 40N 74 20W
Schoharie Creek New York U.S.A. 65 F5 42 40N 74 20W
Schöneberg Germany 83 F1 52 24N 13 22E
Schöneiche Germany 83 G1 52 28N 13 43E
Schönwalde Germany 83 E2 52 41N 13 27E
Schönwalde Germany 83 F2 52 43N 13 26E
Schulzendorf Germany 83 G1 52 20N 13 34E
Schuykill River Pennsylvania U.S.A. 64 D3 40 40N 76 00W
Schwäbisch Alb *mts.* Germany 76 D4 48 00N 9 00E
Schwanebeck Germany 83 F2 52 40N 13 27E
Schwarzwald *(Black Forest) mts.* Germany 76 D4 47 00N 8 00E
Schweinfurt Germany 76 E5 50 03N 10 16E
Schwerin Germany 76 E5 53 38N 11 25E
Schwielowsee *l.* Germany 83 D1 52 19N 1257E
Scilly, Isles of England 78 E1 49 56N 6 20W
Scituate Reservoir Rhode Island U.S.A. 65 J4 41 00N 71 00W
Scobey Montana U.S.A. 40 B1 48 48N 105 28W
Scoresbysund *tn.* Greenland 116 70 30N 22 00W
Scotia Ridge Antarctica 113 C1 53 00S 50 00W
Scotia Sea Antarctica 113 C1 56 30N 50 00W
Scotland Pennsylvania U.S.A. 64 C3 40 03N 77 35W
Scotland United Kingdom 78
Scott Base *r.s.* Antarctica 117 77 51S 166 45E
Scott Island Southern Ocean 114 H1 66 35S 180 00
Scottsbluff Nebraska U.S.A. 62 F5 41 52N 103 40W
Scranton Pennsylvania U.S.A. 64 E4 41 25N 75 40W
Scunthorpe England 78 K5 53 35N 0 39W
Sealdah India 94 K2 22 32N 88 22E
Sea of Azov Russia/Ukraine 90 D4 46 00N 37 00E
Searsville Lake California U.S.A. 49 C1 37 24N 122 14W
Seattle Washington U.S.A. 62 B6 47 35N 122 20W
Sebewaing Michigan U.S.A. 36 C4 43 44N 83 26W
Sebisseb *r.* Algeria 77 C2 35 30N 4 00E
Seboomook Lake Maine U.S.A. 37 R6 45 55N 69 50W
Sebkra Sidi El Hani *salt l.* Tunisia 81 B2 35 30N 10 00E
Sedalia Missouri U.S.A. 63 H4 38 42N 93 15W
Sedan France 76 C4 49 42N 4 57E
Seddinsee *l.* Germany 83 G1 52 23N 13 42E
Sedro Woolley Washington U.S.A. 42 H4 48 30N 122 15W
Ségou Mali 106 D10 13 28N 6 18W
Segovia Spain 77 B3 40 57N 4 07W
Segre *r.* Spain 77 C3 42 00N 1 10E
Segura *r.* Spain 77 B2 38 00N 1 00W
Seine *r.* France 76 C4 49 15N 1 15E
Seki Japan 100 H2 35 30N 136 54E
Sekiu Washington U.S.A. 42 H4 48 15N 124 19W
Sekondi Takoradi Ghana 106 E9 4 59N 1 43W
Selat Sunda *sd.* Indonesia 99 D2 6 00S 106 00E
Seldovia Alaska U.S.A. 10 E4 59 29N 151 45W
Selemdzha *r.* Russia 89 P6 52 30N 132 00E
Selenga *(Selenge) r.* Russia/Mongolia 97 L9 51 00N 106 00E
Selenge *(Selenga) r.* Mongolia/Russia 97 K8 49 00N 102 00E
Selety *r.* Russia 91 L5 52 50N 73 00E
Selima Oasis Sudan 106 K12 21 22N 29 19E
Selma Alabama U.S.A. 63 I3 32 24N 87 01W
Selinsgrove Pennsylvania U.S.A. 64 D3 40 48N 76 53W
Selvas *geog. reg.* South America 55 7 00S 65 00W
Semarang Indonesia 99 E2 6 58S 110 29E
Semenovskoye Russia 88 M1 55 39N 37 32E
Seminoe Reservoir Wyoming U.S.A. 62 E5 42 00N 106 00W
Seminole Oklahoma U.S.A. 63 G4 35 15N 96 40W
Semiozernoye Kazakhstan 91 J5 52 22N 64 06E
Semipalatinsk Kazakhstan 91 N5 50 26N 80 16E
Semnān Iran 93 H6 35 30N 53 25E
Sendai Japan 100 B1 31 50N 130 17E
Sendai Japan 100 D2 38 16N 140 52E
Seneca Falls tn. New York U.S.A. 64 D5 42 57N 76 47W
Seneca Lake New York U.S.A. 64 D5 42 30N 76 55W
SENEGAL 106 C10
Sénégal *r.* Senegal/Mauritania 106 A11 16 45N 14 45W
Senhor do Bonfim Brazil 68 I10 10 28S 40 11W
Senja *i.* Norway 79 D4 69 15N 17 20E
Sennar Sudan 92 D1 13 31N 33 38E
Sennar Dam Sudan 92 D1 13 20N 33 45E
Senobe Japan 100 G2 35 09N 135 25E
Sens France 76 C4 48 12N 3 18E
Sentinel Range *mts.* Antarctica 117 78 00S 87 00W
Senyavin Islands Pacific Ocean 114 G8 7 00N 161 30E
Seoul *see* Sŏul
Sepik *r.* Papua New Guinea 110 G9 4 00S 142 30E
Sequoia National Park California U.S.A. 66 A7 36 30N 118 30W
Seram *i.* Indonesia 99 H3 2 50S 129 00E
Seram Sea Indonesia 99 H3/I3 2 30S 130 00E
Serang Indonesia 99 D2 6 07S 106 09E
Serbia *admin.* Yugoslavia 81
Serdan Mexico 66 C5 28 40N 105 57W
Seremban Malaysia 99 C4 2 42N 101 54E
Serengeti National Park Tanzania 106 L7 2 30S 35 00E
Sergiev Posad *(Zagorsk)* Russia 90 D6 56 20N 38 10E
Sergino Russia 91 K7 62 30N 65 40E
Sergipe *admin.* Brazil 68 J10 11 00S 38 00W
Seria Brunei 99 E4 4 39N 114 23E
Serian Malaysia 99 E4 1 10N 110 35E
Serov Russia 91 J6 59 42N 60 32E
Serpukhov Russia 90 D5 54 53N 37 25E
Serra Brazil 68 I9 20 06S 40 16W
Serra do Mar *mts.* Brazil 69 H7 27 30S 49 00W
Serra do Navio Brazil 68 G13 1 00N 52 05W
Sérrai Greece 81 D3 41 03N 2 33E
Serrania de Cuenca *mts.* Spain 77 B3 40 30N 2 15W
Serra Tumucumaque *mts.* Brazil 68 F13/G13 2 00N 55 00W
Setagaya Japan 101 B3 35 37N 139 38E
Sete Lagoas Brazil 68 I9 19 29S 44 15W
Sete Pontes Brazil 69 Q2 22 51S 43 04W
Setesdal *geog. reg.* Norway 79 B2 59 30N 7 10E
Sétif Algeria 106 G15 36 11N 5 24E
Setit *r.* Sudan 92 E1 14 20N 36 15E
Seto Japan 100 J2 35 14N 137 06E
Seto-Naikai *sd.* Japan 100 B1 34 00N 132 30E
Settat Morocco 106 D14 33 04N 7 37W
Setúbal Portugal 77 A2 38 31N 8 54W
Sevastopol' Ukraine 90 C3 44 36N 33 31E
Sevenoaks England 82 D2 51 16N 0 12E
Severn *r.* England/Wales 78 I4 52 30N 2 30 W
Severna Park Maryland U.S.A. 64 D2 39 00N 76 00W
Severnaya *(North)* **Donets** *r.* Russia/Ukraine 88 F5 49 00N 37 00E
Severnaya *(North)* **Dvina** *r.* Russia 88 G8 63 00N 43 00E
Severnaya Sos'va *r.* Russia 91 J7 62 30N 62 00E
Severnaya Zemlya *(North Land) is.* Russia 89 L12 80 00N 95 00E
Severodonetsk Ukraine 90 D4 48 58N 38 29E
Severodvinsk Russia 88 F8 64 35N 39 50E
Sevier *r.* Utah U.S.A. 62 D4 39 00N 113 00W
Sevilla *(Seville)* Spain 77 A2 37 24N 5 59W
Seville *see* Sevilla
Sèvres France 83 A2 48 49N 2 13E
Seward Alaska U.S.A. 10 F5 60 05N 149 34W
Seward Peninsula Alaska U.S.A. 10 B6 65 20N 165 00W
SEYCHELLES 112 4 30S 55 30E
Seychelles Ridge Indian Ocean 112 E6/F5
Seym *r.* Russia/Ukraine 90 C5 51 00N 34 00E
Seymchan Russia 89 R8 62 54N 152 26E
Sfax Tunisia 106 H14 34 45N 10 43E
Sfîntu Gheorghe Romania 81 E4 45 51N 25 48E
's-Gravenhage *(Den Haag, The Hague)* Netherlands 76 C5 52 05N 4 16E
Sha Chau *i.* Hong Kong U.K. 98 A2 22 21N 113 53E
Shache China 96 E6 38 27N 77 16E
Shackleton Ice Shelf Antarctica 117 66 00S 100 00E
Shackleton Range *mts.* Antarctica 117 81 00S 20 00W
Shaftesbury Vermont U.S.A. 65 G5 42 59N 73 13W
Shah Alam Malaysia 99 C4 3 02N 101 31E
Shahdara India 94 M4 28 40N 77 17E
Shahdol India 95 E4 23 19N 81 26E
Shahjahanpur India 95 D5 27 53N 79 55E
Shakhty Russia 90 E4 47 43N 40 16E
Shaki Nigeria 106 F9 8 39N 3 25E
Sha Lo Wan Hong Kong U.K. 98 A1 22 17N 113 54E
Sham Chung Hong Kong U.K. 98 C2 22 26N 114 17E
Sham Chun River Hong Kong U.K. 98 B3 22 30N 114 00E
Shamokin Pennsylvania U.S.A. 64 D3 40 46N 76 35W
Sham Shek Tsuen Hong Kong U.K. 98 A1 22 17N 113 53E
Sham Shui Po Hong Kong U.K. 98 B1 22 20N 114 09E
Sham Tseng Hong Kong U.K. 98 B2 22 22N 114 03E
Shandong Bandao *p.* China 84 37 30N 120 00E
Shanghai China 97 O5 31 06N 121 22E
Shangqiu China 97 N5 34 27N 115 07E
Shangrao China 97 N4 28 28N 117 54E
Shangshui China 97 M5 33 36N 114 38E
Shannon *r.* Irish Republic 78 C4 53 30N 9 00W
Shannon, Lake Washington U.S.A. 42 H4 48 35N 121 45W
Shantou China 97 N3 23 23N 116 39E
Shanyao China 98 E8 25 07N 118 44E
Shaoguan China 97 M3 24 54N 113 33E
Shaoxing China 97 O5 30 02N 120 35E
Shaoyang China 97 M4 27 10N 111 25E
Shaqrā' Saudi Arabia 93 G4 25 18N 45 15E
Sharon Massachusetts U.S.A. 65 J5 42 08N 71 11W
Sharon Pennsylvania U.S.A. 63 J5 41 16N 80 30W
Sharp Island Hong Kong U.K. 98 C2 22 22N 114 17E
Sharp Park California U.S.A. 49 B2 37 40N 122 30W
Sharp Peak Hong Kong U.K. 98 D2 22 26N 114 22E
Shashi China 97 M5 30 16N 112 20E
Sha Tau Kok Hong Kong U.K. 98 B3 22 33N 114 13E
Sha Tin Hong Kong U.K. 98 C2 22 22N 114 10E
Shatsky Rise Pacific Ocean 114 G11 34 00N 160 00E
Shau Kei Wan Hong Kong U.K. 98 C1 22 16N 114 13E
Shebelē *r.* Ethiopia/Somalia 106 N9 6 00N 44 00E
Sheberghān Afghanistan 93 K6 36 41N 65 45E
Sheboygan Wisconsin U.S.A. 63 I5 43 46N 87 44W
Sheenjek *r.* Alaska U.S.A. 44 C4 67 30N 149 30W
Sheffield England 78 J5 53 23N 1 30W
Sheffield Massachusetts U.S.A. 65 G5 42 00N 73 00W
Sheffield Pennsylvania U.S.A. 64 A4 41 43N 79 03W
Shek Kip Mei Hong Kong U.K. 98 C2 22 20N 114 10E
Shek Kong Hong Kong U.K. 98 B2 22 26N 114 06E
Shek Kwu Chau *i.* Hong Kong U.K. 98 A1 22 12N 113 59E
Shek O Hong Kong U.K. 98 C1 22 14N 114 15E
Shek Pik Hong Kong U.K. 98 A1 22 13N 113 53E
Shek Pik Reservoir Hong Kong U.K. 98 A1 22 14N 113 54E
Shek Uk Shan *mt.* Hong Kong U.K. 98 C2 22 26N 114 18E
Shek Wu Hui Hong Kong U.K. 98 B3 22 30N 114 07E
Shelby Montana U.S.A. 62 D6 48 30N 111 52W
Shelekhov Bay Russia 89 R8 60 00N 157 00E
Shelikof Strait Alaska U.S.A. 10 E4 57 30N 155 00W
Shell Lake *tn.* Wisconsin U.S.A. 35 B2 45 44N 91 56W
Shelter Island Hong Kong U.K. 98 C1 22 19N 114 19E
Shelton Connecticut U.S.A. 65 G4 41 19N 73 06W
Shenandoah Iowa U.S.A. 63 G5 40 48N 95 22W
Shenandoah Pennsylvania U.S.A. 64 D3 40 49N 76 11W
Shenandoah Mountains U.S.A. 64 B2 39 15N 78 45W
Shenandoah National Park Virginia U.S.A. 64 B1 38 50N 78 15W
Shenyang China 97 N7 41 50N 123 26E
Shenzhen China 97 M3 22 31N 114 08E
Sheoraphuli India 94 K3 22 46N 88 20E
Shepetovka Ukraine 80 E5 50 12N 27 01E
Sherburne New York U.S.A. 64 E5 42 41N 75 30W
Sheridan Wyoming U.S.A. 62 E5 44 48N 106 57W
's-Hertogenbosch Netherlands 76 D5 51 41N 5 19E
Sherwood North Dakota U.S.A. 40 C1 48 58N 101 38W
Shetland Islands Scotland 78 J12 60 00N 1 15W
Sheung Shui Hong Kong U.K. 98 B3 22 31N 114 07E
Shevchenko Kazakhstan 90 G3 43 37N 51 11E
Shiawassee River Michigan U.S.A. 36 B4 43 05N 84 12W
Shibuya Japan 101 B3 35 39N 139 42E
Shickshinny Pennsylvania U.S.A. 64 D4 41 30N 76 00W
Shiderty *r.* Russia 91 L5 51 30N 75 00E
Shiga *pref.* Japan 100 H2 35 10N 136 07E
Shihezi China 96 G7 44 19N 86 10E
Shijiazhuang China 97 M6 38 04N 114 28E
Shikarpur Pakistan 94 B5 27 58N 68 42E
Shikoku *i.* Japan 100 B1 33 40N 134 00E
Shikotan *i.* Japan 100 E3 43 47N 148 45E
Shiliguri India 95 F5 26 42N 88 30E
Shilka *r.* Russia 89 N6 52 30N 117 30E
Shillong India 95 G5 25 34N 91 53E
Shiloh New Jersey U.S.A. 64 E2 39 28N 75 18W
Shima-hantō *p.* Japan 100 H1 34 25N 136 30E
Shimizu Japan 100 C2 35 01N 138 29E
Shimoga India 95 D2 13 56N 75 31E
Shimonita Japan 100 K3 36 12N 138 47E
Shimonoseki Japan 100 B1 33 59N 130 58E
Shimotsuma Japan 100 L3 36 10N 139 58E
Shinagawa Japan 101 B3 35 37N 139 44E
Shinagawa Bay Japan 101 C3 35 56N 139 50E
Shinano *r.* Japan 100 C2 37 40N 139 00E
Shīndand Afghanistan 93 J5 33 16N 62 05E
Shinglehouse Pennsylvania U.S.A. 64 B4 41 58N 78 11W
Shingū Japan 100 C1 33 42N 136 00E
Shinjō Japan 100 D2 38 45N 140 18E
Shinjuku Japan 101 B3 35 41N 139 42E
Shinyanga Tanzania 107 L7 3 40S 33 25E
Shiono-misaki *c.* Japan 100 C1 33 28N 135 47E
Shipki Pass India 95 D6 31 50N 78 50E
Shirakawa Japan 100 D2 37 07N 140 11E
Shiraoi Japan 100 D3 42 34N 141 19E
Shīrāz Iran 93 H4 29 38N 52 34E
Shiretoko-misaki *c.* Japan 100 E3 44 24N 145 20E
Shishmaref Alaska U.S.A. 10 B6 66 15N 166 11W
Shivaji Park *tn.* India 94 L4 28 40N 77 07E
Shizuishan China 97 L6 39 04N 106 22E
Shizuoka Japan 100 C1 34 59N 138 24E
Shizuoka *pref.* Japan 100 K2 35 10N 138 50E
Shkodër Albania 81 C3 42 03N 19 01E
Shomolu Nigeria 107 V3 6 34N 3 26E
Shreveport Louisiana U.S.A. 63 H3 32 30N 93 46W
Shrewsbury England 78 I4 52 43N 2 45W
Shrewsbury Massachusetts U.S.A. 65 J5 42 18N 71 43W
Shrirampur India 94 K3 22 45N 88 21E
Shuangliao China 97 N7 43 30N 123 29E
Shuangyashan China 97 Q8 46 42N 131 20E
Shuen Wan Hong Kong U.K. 98 C2 22 28N 114 12E
Shui Tau Hong Kong U.K. 98 B2 22 27N 114 04E
Shuksan, Mount Washington U.S.A. 42 H4 48 50N 121 36W
Shumagin Islands Alaska U.S.A. 10 D4 55 00N 159 00W
Shumen Bulgaria 81 E3 43 17N 26 55E
Shunde China 97 M3 22 50N 113 16E
Shuqrā Yemen Republic 93 G1 13 23N 45 44E
Shwebo Myanmar 96 J3 24 26N 97 05E
Shyamnagar India 94 K3 22 50N 88 24E
Sialkot Pakistan 95 C6 32 29N 74 35E
Siauliai Lithuania 80 D8 55 51N 23 20E
Šibenik Croatia 81 C3 43 45N 15 55E
Sibi Pakistan 94 B5 29 31N 67 54E
Sibiti Congo 107 H7 3 40S 13 24E
Sibiu Romania 81 D4 45 46N 24 09E
Sibolga Indonesia 99 B4 1 42N 98 48E
Sibpur India 94 K2 22 34N 88 19E
Sibu Malaysia 99 E4 2 18N 111 49E
Sibut Central African Republic 106 I9 5 46N 19 06E
Sichuan Basin *see* Sichuan Pendi
Sichuan Pendi *(Sichuan Basin)* China 97 K5/L5 32 00N 107 00E
Sicilian Channel Mediterranean Sea 81 B2 37 00N 12 00E
Sicily *i.* Italy 81 B2 37 00N 14 00E
Sicuani Peru 68 C10 14 21S 71 13W
Sidcup England 82 D2 51 26N 0 07E
Sidi Barrani Egypt 106 K14 31 38N 25 58E
Sidi Bel Abbès Algeria 106 E15 35 15N 0 39W
Sidi Ifni Morocco 106 C13 29 24N 10 12W
Sidlaw Hills Scotland 78 H8 56 30N 3 10W
Sidney New York U.S.A. 64 E5 42 19N 75 24W
Sidney Lanier, Lake Georgia U.S.A. 63 J3 34 00N 84 00W
Sidon *see* Saïda
Siedlce Poland 80 D5 52 10N 22 18E
Siemensstadt Germany 83 E2 52 33N 13 14E
Siena Italy 81 B3 43 19N 11 19E
SIERRA LEONE 106 C9
Sierra Blanca *tn.* Texas U.S.A. 62 E3 31 10N 105 22W
Sierra de Maracaju *mts.* Brazil 68 F8/G9 20 00S 55 00W
Sierra de Perija *mts.* Colombia/Venezuela 67 I1/2 10 00N 73 00W
Sierra dos Parecis *hills* Brazil 55 7 00S 60 00W
Sierra Madre del Sur *mts.* Mexico 66 D3/E3 17 30N 100 00W
Sierra Madre Occidental *mts.* Mexico 66 C5/D4 26 00N 107 00W
Sierra Madre Oriental *mts.* Mexico 66 D5 E4 23 30N 100 00W
Sierra Morena *mts.* Spain 77 A2/B2 38 05N 5 50W
Sierra Nevada *mts.* Spain 77 B2 37 00N 3 20W
Sierra Nevada *mts.* U.S.A. 62 C4 37 00N 119 00W
Sierras de Córdoba *mts.* Argentina 69 D6/E6 32 30S 65 00W
Sighetu Marmaţiei Romania 81 D4 47 56N 23 53E
Sighişoara Romania 81 D4 46 12N 24 48E
Siglufjördur Iceland 79 I7 66 09N 18 55W
Signy *r.s.* South Orkney Islands 117 60 43S 45 36W
Sigüenza Spain 77 B3 41 04N 2 38W
Siguiri Guinea 106 D10 11 28N 9 07W
Sikar India 95 D5 27 33N 75 12E
Sikasso Mali 106 D10 11 18N 5 38W
Sikhote-Alin' *mts.* Russia 89 P5 45 00N 137 00E
Sikkim *admin.* India 95 F5 27 30N 88 30E
Sil *r.* Spain 77 A3 42 25N 7 05W
Silchar India 95 G4 24 49N 92 47E
Silifke Turkey 92 D6 36 22N 33 57E
Siling Co *l.* China 95 F6 31 45N 88 50E
Silistra Bulgaria 81 E3 44 06N 27 17E
Siljan *l.* Sweden 79 D3 60 55N 14 50E
Silkeborg Denmark 80 A6 56 10N 9 39E
Šilute Lithuania 80 D6 55 18N 21 30E
Silver Bay *tn.* Minnesota U.S.A. 35 B2 47 15N 91 17W
Silver City New Mexico U.S.A. 62 E3 32 47N 108 16W
Silver Creek New York U.S.A. 38 C1 42 32N 79 10W
Silver Lake Reservoir California U.S.A. 51 A3 34 05N 118 16W
Silver Spring *tn.* Maryland U.S.A. 64 C2 39 00N 77 01W
Silves Portugal 77 A2 37 11N 8 26W
Simanggang Malaysia 99 E4 1 10N 111 32E
Simeuluë *i.* Indonesia 99 B4 2 40N 96 00E
Simferopol' Ukraine 90 C3 44 57N 34 05E
Simla India 95 D6 31 07N 77 09E
Simpson Desert Australia 110 F5 24 30S 137 30E
Simsbury Connecticut U.S.A. 65 H4 41 53N 72 48W
Sinai *p.* Egypt 92 N9 29 15N 34 00E
Sinai, Mount *see* Gebel Mûsa
Sincelejo Colombia 68 B14 9 17N 75 23W
Sind *geog. reg.* Pakistan 94 A6 26 20N 68 40E
Sines Portugal 77 A2 37 58N 8 52W
SINGAPORE 99 C4
Singaraja Indonesia 99 F2 8 06S 115 07E
Singatoko Fiji 114 T15 18 10S 177 30E
Sing Bori Thailand 97 K1 14 56N 100 21E
Sinkiang Uighur Autonomous Region *see* Xinjiang Uygur Zizhiqu
Sinop Turkey 92 E7 42 02N 35 09E
Sintra Portugal 77 A2 38 48N 9 22W
Sinŭiju North Korea 97 O7 40 04N 124 25E
Sioux City Iowa U.S.A. 63 G5 42 30N 96 28W
Sioux Falls *tn.* South Dakota U.S.A. 63 G5 43 34N 96 42W
Siparia Trinidad and Tobago 66 S9 10 08N 61 31W
Siping China 97 O7 43 15N 124 25E
Siple, Mount Antarctica 117 73 25S 122 50W
Sira *r.* Norway 79 B2 59 00N 6 40E
Siracusa Italy 81 C2 37 04N 15 18E
Siret *r.* Romania 81 E4 47 00N 26 00E
Sirte *see* Surt
Sirte Desert Libya 106 I14 30 00N 16 00E
Sirte, Gulf of Libya 106 I14 31 00N 17 00E
Sisak Croatia 81 C4 45 30N 16 22E
Sisophon Cambodia 99 C6 13 37N 102 58E
Sisteron France 77 D3 44 16N 5 56E
Sitka Alaska U.S.A. 42 A3 57 05N 135 20W
Sitka Sound Alaska U.S.A. 42 A3 57 00N 135 50W
Sittwe Myanmar 96 H3 20 09N 92 55E
Sivas Turkey 92 E6 39 44N 37 01E
Siwa Egypt 106 K13 29 11N 25 31E
Sjaelland *i.* Denmark 80 B6 55 15N 11 30E
Skadarsko ezero *l.* Europe 81 C3 42 00N 19 00E
Skagen Denmark 80 B6 57 44N 10 37E
Skagerrak *sd.* Norway/Denmark 79 B2 57 30N 8 00E
Skagit River Washington U.S.A. 42 H4 48 40N 121 15W
Skagway Alaska U.S.A. 42 A3 59 23N 135 20W
Skåne *geog. reg.* Sweden 70 56 00N 14 00E
Skaneateles New York U.S.A. 64 D5 42 57N 76 27W
Skaneateles Lake New York U.S.A. 64 D5 42 00N 76 00W
Skegness England 78 L5 53 10N 0 21E
Skelleftea Sweden 79 E3 64 45N 21 00E
Skellefte älv *r.* Sweden 79 D4 65 30N 19 00E
Skien Norway 79 B2 59 14N 9 37E
Skierniewice Poland 80 D5 51 58N 20 10E
Skikda Algeria 106 G15 36 53N 6 54E
Skiros *i.* Greece 81 D2 39 00N 24 00E
Skive Denmark 80 A6 56 34N 9 02E
Skokie Illinois U.S.A. 53 B3 42 02N 87 44W
Skokie River Illinois U.S.A. 53 A3 42 15N 87 51W
Skopje Macedonia Yugoslavia 81 D3 42 00N 21 28E
Skövde Sweden 79 C2 58 24N 13 52E
Skovorodino Russia 89 O6 54 00N 123 53E
Skowhegan Maine U.S.A. 37 R5 44 46N 69 44W
Skye *i.* Scotland 78 E9 57 20N 6 15W
Slaney *r.* Irish Republic 78 E4 52 30N 6 35W
Slatina Romania 81 D3 44 26N 24 22E
Slavonski Brod Croatia 81 C4 45 09N 18 02E
Slavyansk Ukraine 90 D4 48 51N 37 36E
Slessor Glacier Antarctica 117 79 00S 22 00W
Slieve Donard *mt.* Northern Ireland 78 E6 54 11N 5 55W
Sligo Irish Republic 78 C6 54 17N 8 28W
Sliven Bulgaria 81 E3 42 40N 26 19E
Slonim Belarus 80 E5 53 05N 25 21E
Slough England 82 A2 51 31N 0 36W
Slovakia *admin.* Czechoslovakia 80 C4/D4
SLOVENIA 81 B4/C4
Słubice Poland 63 B2 52 20N 14 35E
Sluch' *r.* Ukraine 90 B5 50 00N 27 00E
Słupsk Poland 80 C5 54 28N 17 00E
Slutsk Belarus 80 E5 53 02N 27 31E
Slyne Head *c.* Irish Republic 78 A5 53 25N 10 10W
Smederevo Serbia Yugoslavia 81 D3 44 40N 20 56E
Smethport Pennsylvania U.S.A. 64 B4 41 48N 78 26W
Smoky Hills Kansas U.S.A. 62 G4 39 00N 100 00W
Smøla *i.* Norway 79 B3 63 25N 8 00E
Smolensk Russia 90 C5 54 49N 32 04E
Smolyan Bulgaria 81 D3 41 34N 24 42E
Smyrna Delaware U.S.A. 64 E2 39 18N 75 37W
Snaefell *mt.* Isle of Man British Isles 78 G6 54 16N 4 28W
Snake *r.* U.S.A. 62 C6 47 00N 118 00W
Snake River Plain U.S.A. 62 D5 43 00N 114 00W
Snowdon *mt.* Wales 78 G5 53 04N 4 05W
Snowy Mountains Australia 110 H2 36 50S 147 00E
Snyder Texas U.S.A. 62 F3 32 43N 100 54W
Soar *r.* England 78 J4 52 40N 1 20W
Soa-Siu Indonesia 99 H4 0 40N 127 30E
Sobat *r.* Sudan 106 L9 8 00N 33 00E
Sobral Brazil 68 I12 3 45S 40 20W
Sochi Russia 90 D3 43 35N 39 46E
Society Islands Pacific Ocean 115 K6 16 30S 153 00W
Socotra *i.* Yemen Republic 93 H1 12 05N 54 10E
Sodankylä Finland 79 F4 67 26N 26 35E
Söderhamn Sweden 79 D3 61 19N 17 10E
Södertälje Sweden 79 D2 59 11N 17 39E
Sodo Ethiopia 106 M9 6 49N 37 41E
Sodus New York U.S.A. 64 C6 43 14N 77 04W
Sofiya Bulgaria 81 D3 42 40N 23 18E
Sogamoso Colombia 68 C14 5 43N 72 56W
Sognefjorden *fj.* Norway 79 B3 61 05N 5 30E
Sohâg Egypt 92 D4 26 33N 31 42E
Soissons France 76 C4 49 23N 3 20E
Sok Kwu Wan Hong Kong U.K. 98 B1 22 13N 114 08E
Sokodé Togo 106 F9 8 59N 1 11E
Soko Islands Hong Kong U.K. 98 A1 22 10N 113 54E
Sokoto Nigeria 106 G10 13 02N 5 15E
So Kwun Wat Tsuen Hong Kong U.K. 98 B2 22 23N 114 00E

Solander, Cape Australia **111** G1 34 01S 151 14E
Solāpur India **95** D3 17 43N 75 56E
Soligorsk Belarus **80** E5 52 50N 27 32E
Solihull England **78** J4 52 25N 1 45W
Solikamsk Russia **91** H6 59 40N 56 45E
Sol'-Iletsk Russia **91** G5 51 09N 55 00E
Sollefteå Sweden **79** D3 63 09N 17 15E
Sóller Balearic Islands **77** C2 39 46N 2 42E
Solntsevo Russia **88** L1 55 36N 37 25E
Sologne *geog. reg.* France **77** C4 47 35N 1 47E
SOLOMON ISLANDS 110 J/K8
Solomon Sea Papua New Guinea **110** I8 7 30S 152 00E
Solothurn Switzerland **77** D4 47 13N 7 32E
Soltau Germany **76** D5 52 59N 9 50E
Solway Firth *est.* Scotland/England **78** H6 54 40N 3 40W
SOMALIA 106 O8/9
Somali Basin Indian Ocean **112** E7 5 00N 55 00E
Sombor Serbia Yugoslavia **81** D4 45 46N 19 09E
Sombrerete Mexico **66** D4 23 38N 103 40W
Somerset Massachusetts U.S.A. **65** J4 41 47N 71 08W
Somerset Reservoir Vermont U.S.A. **65** G6 43 00N 72 57W
Somerville Massachusetts U.S.A. **52** B2 42 24N 71 07W
Somerville New Jersey U.S.A. **65** F3 40 34N 74 36W
Somme *r.* France **76** C5 50 00N 1 45E
Sommen *l.* Sweden **79** D2 58 05N 15 15E
Somoto Nicaragua **67** G2 13 29N 86 36W
Son *r.* India **95** E4 24 00N 81 00E
Sonarpur India **94** K1 22 26N 88 26E
Sønderborg Denmark **80** A5 54 55N 9 48E
Søndre Strømfjord *see* Kangerlussuaq
Songea Tanzania **107** M5 10 42S 35 39E
Songhua Jiang *r.* China **97** P8 46 30N 128 00E
Sŏngjin North Korea **97** P7 40 41N 129 12E
Songkhla Thailand **99** C5 7 12N 100 35E
Song-koi *r.* Vietnam **99** C8 22 00N 105 00E
Sonoita Mexico **66** B6 31 53N 112 52W
Sonsonate El Salvador **66** G2 13 43N 89 44W
Sopot Poland **80** C5 54 27N 18 31E
Sopron Hungary **81** C4 47 40N 16 35E
Soria Spain **77** B3 41 46N 2 28W
Sorocaba Brazil **69** H8 23 30S 47 32W
Sorong Indonesia **99** I3 0 50S 131 17E
Soroti Uganda **106** L8 1 42N 33 37E
Sørøya *i.* Norway **79** E5 70 35N 22 30E
Sorraia *r.* Portugal **77** A2 38 55N 9 30W
Sosnowiec Poland **80** C5 50 16N 19 07E
Souillac France **77** C3 44 53N 1 29E
Souk Ahras Algeria **77** D2 36 14N 8 00E
Sŏul *(Seoul)* South Korea **97** P6 37 32N 127 00E
Soûr *(Tyre)* Lebanon **92** O11 33 16N 35 12E
Souris River Canada/U.S.A. **39** A1 49 30N 100 50W
Sousse Tunisia **106** H15 35 50N 10 38E
Southall England **82** B3 51 31N 0 23W
Southampton England **78** J2 50 55N 1 25W
Southampton New York U.S.A. **65** H3 40 54N 72 24W
South Andaman *i.* Andaman Islands **95** G2 11 30N 93 00E
South Australia *state* Australia **110** E4/F4
South Australian Basin Indian Ocean **112** L3 38 00S 125 00E
South Bend Indiana U.S.A. **63** I5 41 40N 86 15W
South Branch Potomac River Maryland/West Virginia U.S.A. **64** B2 39 30N 78 30W
Southbridge Massachusetts U.S.A. **65** H5 42 05N 72 02W
Southbury Connecticut U.S.A. **65** G4 41 28N 73 13W
South Carolina *state* U.S.A. **63** J3 34 00N 81 00W
South China Sea South East Asia **99** E6/E7 15 00N 115 00E
South Dakota *state* U.S.A. **62** F5 45 00N 102 00W
South Downs *hills* England **78** K2 50 50N 0 30W
Southeast Indian Basin Indian Ocean **112** J3 32 00S 108 00E
Southeast Indian Ridge Indian Ocean **112** H2/J2
South East Pacific Basin Pacific Ocean **115** Q2 53 00S 95 00W
Southend-on-Sea England **78** L3 51 33N 0 43E
Southern Alps *mts.* New Zealand **111** B2 43 30S 170 00E
Southern Honshu Ridge Pacific Ocean **114** E10 25 50N 142 30E
Southern Ocean 114/115
Southern Uplands Scotland **78** G7/I7
South Esk *r.* Scotland **78** I8 56 40N 2 55W
Southfield Michigan U.S.A. **52** D2 42 28N 83 16W
South Fiji Basin Pacific Ocean **114** H5 25 00S 176 50E
South Fork Shenandoah River Maryland/Virgina U.S.A. **64** C2 39 00N 78 05W
South Gate California U.S.A. **51** B2 33 56N 118 11W
Southgate Michigan U.S.A. **52** E1 42 11N 83 11W
South Georgia *i.* South Atlantic Ocean **113** E1 54 00S 36 30W
South Head Australia **111** H2 33 50S 151 17E
South Island New Zealand **111** A2 43 00S 169 00E
SOUTH KOREA 97 P6
South Loup *r.* Nebraska U.S.A. **62** G5 42 00N 99 00W
South Negril Point *c.* Jamaica **67** P8 18 16N 78 22W
South Ockenden England **82** E3 51 32N 0 18E
South Orkney Islands Southern Ocean **117** 60 00S 45 00W
South Park Pennsylvania U.S.A. **53** D1 40 19N 80 00W
South Platte *r.* U.S.A. **62** F5 41 00N 103 00W
South Point Barbados **66** V12 13 02N 59 32W
South Pole Antarctica **117** 90 00S
Southport England **78** H5 53 39N 3 01W
South River *tn.* New Jersey U.S.A. **65** F3 40 26N 74 23W
South Sandwich Trench Southern Ocean **113** F1 55 00S 30 00W
South San Francisco California U.S.A. **49** B2 37 30N 122 15W
South Shetland Islands Southern Ocean **69** E0 62 00S 60 00W
South Sioux City Nebraska U.S.A. **63** G5 42 28N 96 24W
South Suburbs *(Behala)* India **94** K1 22 28N 88 18E
South Uist *i.* Scotland **78** D9 57 20N 7 15W
Southwark *bor.* England **82** C3 51 30N 0 06W
Southwest Cape New Zealand **111** A1 47 17S 167 29E
Southwest Indian Ridge Indian Ocean **112** D2/E3 40 00S 50 00E
South West Pacific Basin Pacific Ocean **115** K4 35 00S 155 00W
Southwick Massachusetts U.S.A. **65** H5 42 03N 72 46W
South Yarmouth Massachusetts U.S.A. **65** K4 41 40N 70 12W
Sovetsk Russia **90** A6 55 02N 21 50E
Sovetskaya Gavan' Russia **89** Q5 48 57N 140 16E
Sozh *r.* Belarus **90** C5 53 00N 30 00E
SPAIN 77 A2
Spandau Germany **83** E2 52 32N 13 13E
Spanish Town Jamaica **67** R7 17 59N 76 58W
Sparks Nevada U.S.A. **62** C4 39 34N 119 46W
Spartanburg South Carolina U.S.A. **63** J3 34 56N 81 57W
Spárti Greece **81** D2 37 05N 22 25E
Spassk-Dal'niy Russia **89** P4 44 37N 132 37E
Spasskoye Kazakhstan **91** K5 52 07N 68 32E
Speightstown Barbados **66** V12 13 15N 59 39W
Spencer Iowa U.S.A. **63** G5 43 08N 95 08W
Spencer Gulf Australia **110** F3 34 00S 137 00E
Spencerport New York U.S.A. **64** C6 43 12N 77 46W
Spey *r.* Scotland **78** H9 57 00N 4 30W
Spitsbergen *i.* Arctic Ocean **88** D1 79 00N 15 00E
Spittal an der Drau Austria **81** B4 46 48N 13 30E
Split Croatia **81** C3 43 31N 16 28E
Spokane Washington U.S.A. **62** C6 47 40N 117 25W
Spoleto Italy **81** B3 42 44N 12 44E
Spot Pond Massachusetts U.S.A. **52** B2 42 27N 71 06W
Spratly Islands South China Sea **99** E6 F5 10 00N 115 00E
Spree *r.* Germany **83** G1 52 27N 13 32E
Springbok Republic of South Africa **107** I2 29 44S 17 56E
Springfield Illinois U.S.A. **63** J4 39 49N 89 39W
Springfield Massachusetts U.S.A. **64** H5 42 07N 72 35W
Springfield Missouri U.S.A. **63** H4 37 11N 93 19W
Springfield Ohio U.S.A. **63** J5 39 55N 83 48W
Springfield Oregon U.S.A. **62** B5 44 03N 123 01W
Springfield Vermont U.S.A. **65** H6 43 18N 72 29W
Springfield West Virginia U.S.A. **64** B2 39 26N 78 43W
Springsure Australia **110** H5 24 09S 148 04E
Springville New York U.S.A. **64** B5 42 31N 78 41W
Spurn Head *c.* England **78** L5 53 36N 0 07E
Spy Pond Massachusetts U.S.A. **52** B2 42 24N 71 09W
Sredinnyy Range *mts.* Russia **89** R7 57 00N 158 00E
Srednekolymsk Russia **89** R9 67 27N 153 35E
Sretensk Russia **89** N6 52 15N 117 52E
Srikakulam India **95** E3 18 19N 84 00E
SRI LANKA 95 E1
Srinagar Kashmir **95** C6 34 08N 74 50E
Staaken Germany **83** E2 52 32N 13 06E
Stafford England **78** I4 52 48N 2 07W
Stafford Springs Connecticut U.S.A. **65** H4 41 57N 72 17W
Stahnsdorf Germany **83** E1 52 23N 13 13E
Staines England **82** B2 51 26N 0 30W
Stakhanov Ukraine **90** D4 48 34N 38 40E
Stamford Connecticut U.S.A. **65** G4 41 03N 73 32W
Standish Michigan U.S.A. **36** C4 43 59N 83 58W
Stanhope New Jersey U.S.A. **65** F3 40 55N 74 43W
Stanley Falkland Islands **69** F2 51 45S 57 56W
Stanley North Dakota U.S.A. **40** C1 48 21N 102 23W
Stanovoy Range *mts.* Russia **89** O7 56 00N 122 30E
Stara Planina *mts.* Europe **81** D3 43 00N 23 00E
Stara Zagora Bulgaria **81** E3 42 25N 25 37E
Stargard Szczeciński Poland **80** C5 53 21N 15 01E
Starogard Gdański Poland **80** C5 53 58N 18 30E
Start Point *c.* England **78** H2 50 13N 3 38W
Staryy Oskol Russia **90** D5 51 20N 37 50E
State College Pennsylvania U.S.A. **64** C3 40 48N 77 52W
Staten Island New York U.S.A. **50** B1 40 35N 74 10W
Staunton Virginia U.S.A. **63** K4 38 10N 79 05W
Stavanger Norway **79** B2 58 58N 5 45E
Stavropol' Russia **90** E4 45 03N 41 59E
Stebbins Alaska U.S.A. **10** C5 63 32N 162 20W
Steenstrup Glacier Greenland **11** X8 75 00N 56 00W
Steep Island Hong Kong U.K. **98** C1 22 16N 114 18E
Steglitz Germany **83** F1 52 27N 13 19E
Stehekin Washington U.S.A. **42** H4 48 20N 120 40W
Stendal Germany **76** E5 52 36N 11 52E
Stephen Minnesota U.S.A. **39** B1 48 28N 96 52W
Stephens Passage Alaska U.S.A. **42** B3 58 00N 134 00W
Stepney England **82** C3 51 31N 0 04W
Step' Shaidara *geog. reg.* Kazakhstan **91** K3 40 00N 65 00E
Sterkrade Germany **76** H3 51 31N 6 52E
Sterling Colorada U.S.A. **62** F5 40 37N 103 13W
Sterlitamak Russia **91** H5 53 40N 55 59E
Steubenville Ohio U.S.A. **63** J5 40 22N 80 39W
Stewart Island New Zealand **111** A1 47 30S 168 00E
Steyr Austria **81** B4 48 04N 14 25E
Stickney Illinois U.S.A. **53** A2 41 49N 87 46W
Stikine River Canada/U.S.A. **42** C3 57 00N 132 00W
Stillaguamish River Washington U.S.A. **42** H4 48 17N 121 55W
Stirling Scotland **78** H8 56 07N 3 57W
Štip Macedonia Yugoslavia **81** D3 41 44N 22 12E
Stockbridge Massachusetts U.S.A. **65** G5 42 17N 73 20W
Stockholm Sweden **79** D2 59 20N 18 05E
Stockport England **78** I5 53 25N 2 10W
Stockton-on-Tees England **78** J6 54 34N 1 19W
Stoke-on-Trent England **78** I5 53 00N 2 10W
Stokhod *r.* Ukraine **90** B5 51 30N 25 00E
Stone Canyon Reservoir California U.S.A. **51** A3 34 07N 118 27W
Stonecutters Island Hong Kong U.K. **98** B1 22 18N 114 08E
Stoneham Massachusetts U.S.A. **52** B2 42 27N 71 06W
Stony Brook New York U.S.A. **65** G3 40 56N 73 08W
Stony Brook Reservation Massachusetts U.S.A. **52** B2 42 16N 71 08W
Stony Creek Illinois U.S.A. **53** B1 41 41N 87 44W
Stony Tunguska *see* Podkamennaya Tunguska
Stora Lulevattern *l.* Sweden **79** D4 67 20N 19 00E
Størdal Norway **79** C3 63 18N 11 48E
Støren Norway **79** C3 63 03N 10 16E
Stornoway Scotland **78** E10 58 12N 6 23W
Storsjön *l.* Sweden **79** C3 63 10N 14 10E
Storuman Sweden **79** D4 65 05N 17 10E
Stoughton Massachusetts U.S.A. **65** J5 42 8N 71 05W
Stour *r.* England **78** L4 51 10N 1 10E
Straits of Florida *sd.* Florida U.S.A. **63** J1 25 00N 80 00W
StranraerScotland **78** F6 54 55N 5 02W
Strasbourg France **76** D4 48 35N 7 45E
Stratford Connecticut U.S.A. **65** G4 41 12N 73 08W
Strathfield Australia **111** G2 33 52S 151 06E
Strathmere New Jersey U.S.A. **65** F2 39 12N 74 39W
Straubing Germany **76** E4 48 53N 12 35E
Streatham England **82** C2 51 26N 0 07W
Stretto di Messina *sd.* Italy **81** C2 38 00N 15 00E
Strimón *r.* Greece **81** D3 41 00N 23 00E
Strogino Russia **88** L2 55 49N 37 26E
Stromboli *mt.* Italy **81** C2 38 48N 15 15E
Stronsay *i.* Scotland **78** I11 59 07N 2 37W
Stroudsburg Pennsylvania U.S.A. **64** E3 41 00N 75 11W
Struma *r.* Bulgaria **81** D3 42 00N 23 00E
Stryy Ukraine **80** D4 49 16N 23 51E
Stuart Highway *rd.* Australia **110** E5/E6 20 00S 135 00E
Stung Treng Cambodia **99** D6 13 31N 105 59E
Sturt Creek *r.* Australia **110** D6 18 00S 127 30E
Stuttgart Germany **76** D4 48 47N 9 12E
Stykkishólmur Iceland **79** H7 65 05N 22 44W
Styr' *r.* Ukraine **80** E5 51 00N 25 00E
Su-ao Taiwan **98** H7 24 33N 121 48E
Suakin Sudan **92** E2 19 08N 37 17E
Subotica Serbia Yugoslavia **81** C4 46 04N 19 41E
Suceava Romania **81** E4 47 37N 26 18E
Suck *r.* Irish Republic **78** C5 53 40N 8 30W
Sucre Bolivia **68** D9 19 05S 65 15W
Sucy-en-Brie France **83** C2 48 46N 2 31E
SUDAN 106 K10
Sudd *swamp* Africa **102** 7 00N 30 00E
Sudety Reseniky *mts.* Czechoslovakia/Poland **80** C5 50 40N 16 00E
Sudr Egypt **92** N9 29 40N 32 42E
Sue *r.* Sudan **106** K9 7 00N 28 00E
Suez *see* El Suweis
Suez Canal *(Qanâ el Suweis)* Egypt **107** S4 31 30N 32 20E
Suez, Gulf of Egypt **107** T1 29 56N 32 32E
Suffolk County Massachusetts U.S.A. **52** B2 42 20N 71 09W
Sugar Loaf *see* Pao de Açúcar
Sugarloaf Mountain Maine U.S.A. **37** Q6 45 02N 70 18W
Sugar Notch Pennsylvania U.S.A. **64** E4 41 12N 75 55W
Suginami Japan **101** B3 35 41N 139 40E
Sühbaatar Mongolia **97** L9 50 10N 106 14E
Suiattle River Washington U.S.A. **42** H4 48 17N 121 15W
Suir *r.* Irish Republic **78** D4 52 15N 7 05W
Suita Japan **100** G1 34 46N 135 30E
Sukabumi Indonesia **99** D2 6 55S 106 50E
Sukhona *r.* Russia **90** E7 60 00N 40 00E
Sukhumi Georgia **90** E3 43 01N 41 01E
Sukkertoppen Greenland **45** V4 65 25N 53 00W
Sukkur Pakistan **94** B5 27 42N 68 54E
Sulaiman Range *mts.* Pakistan **94** B5/C6 30 00N 70 00E
Sulawesi *(Celebes) i.* Indonesia **99** F3/G3 2 30S 120 30E
Sulaymānīyah Iraq **93** G6 35 32N 45 27E
Sullana Peru **68** A12 4 52S 80 39W
Sultanpur India **95** E5 26 15N 82 04E
Sulu Archipelago *is.* The Philippines **99** G5 5 30N 121 00E
Sulu Sea Malaysia/The Philippines **99** F5/G5 8 00N 120 00E
Sumas Washington U.S.A. **42** H4 49 00N 122 16W
Sumatera *i.* Indonesia **99** B4/C3 1 00N 101 00E
Sumba *i.* Indonesia **99** F2/G2 10 00S 120 00E
Sumbawa *i.* Indonesia **99** F2 8 00S 117 30E
Sumburgh Head *c.* Scotland **78** J12 59 51N 1 16W
Sumgait Azerbaijan **90** F3 40 35N 49 38E
Sumida Japan **101** C3 35 42N 139 49E
Summit Illinois U.S.A. **53** A2 41 46N 87 49W
Sumner Strait Alaska U.S.A. **42** B3 56 30N 133 30W
Sumoto Japan **100** F1 34 20N 134 53E
Sumy Ukraine **90** C5 50 55N 34 49E
Sunapee New Hampshire U.S.A. **65** H6 43 22N 72 05W
Sunapee Lake New Hampshire U.S.A. **65** H6 43 20N 72 03W
Sunburst Montana U.S.A. **41** C1 48 54N 111 55W
Sunbury England **82** B2 51 24N 0 25W
Sunbury Pennsylvania U.S.A. **64** D3 40 52N 76 47W
Sunch'ŏn South Korea **97** P5 34 56N 127 28E
Suncook New Hampshire U.S.A. **65** J6 43 07N 71 27W
Sundarbans *geog. reg.* Southern Asia **84** 23 00N 90 00E
Sunderland England **78** J6 54 55N 1 23W
Sunderland Massachusetts U.S.A. **65** H5 42 28N 72 35W
Sundsvall Sweden **79** D3 62 22N 17 20E
Sung Kong *i.* Hong Kong U.K. **98** C1 22 11N 114 17E
Sunland California U.S.A. **51** A4 34 15N 118 17W
Sunset Beach *tn.* California U.S.A. **51** B1 33 43N 118 04W
Sunset Peak Hong Kong U.K. **98** A1 22 15N 113 57E
Sunshine Island Hong Kong U.K. **98** B1 22 16N 114 03E
Suntar Russia **88** N8 62 10N 117 35E
Sunyani Ghana **106** E9 7 22N 2 18W
Suō-nada *b.* Japan **100** B1 33 50N 131 30E
Superior Wisconsin U.S.A. **63** H6 46 42N 92 05W
Superior, Lake Canada/U.S.A. **35** B2 48 00N 88 00W
Sūr Oman **93** I3 22 34N 59 32E
Sura *r.* Russia **90** F6 55 00N 46 30E
Surabaya Indonesia **99** E2 7 14S 112 45E
Surakarta Indonesia **99** E2 7 32S 110 50E
Surat India **95** C4 21 10N 72 54E
Surat Thani Thailand **99** B5 9 09N 99 20E
Surendranagar India **95** C4 22 44N 71 43E
Surgut Russia **91** L7 61 13N 73 20E
SURINAM 68 F13
Surrey *co.* England **82** D2 51 15N 0 00E
Surt *(Sirte)* Libya **106** I14 31 13N 16 35E
Surui *r.* Brazil **69** Q3 22 40S 43 08W
Surulere Nigeria **107** V3 6 30N 3 25E
Susitna *r.* Alaska U.S.A. **10** E5 62 10N 150 15W
Susono Japan **100** K2 35 11N 138 50E
Susquehanna Pennsylvania U.S.A. **64** E4 41 56N 75 38W
Susquehanna River U.S.A. **64** D2 40 00N 76 30W
Sussex New Jersey U.S.A. **65** F4 41 12N 74 36W
Susuman Russia **89** Q8 62 46N 148 08E
Sutherland Australia **111** G1 34 02S 151 03E
Sutlej *r.* Pakistan **95** C6 30 00N 73 00E
Sutton *bor.* Greater London England **82** C2 51 22N 0 12W
Suva Fiji **114** U15 18 08S 178 25E
Suvasvesi *l.* Finland **79** F3 62 40N 28 10E
Suzhou China **97** O5 31 21N 120 40E
Suzuka Japan **100** F1 34 52N 136 37E
Suzuka-sanmyaku *mts.* Japan **100** H2 35 00N 136 20E
Suzu-misaki *c.* Japan **100** C2 37 30N 137 21E
Sverdlovsk Ukraine **90** D4 48 05N 39 37E
Svobodnyy Russia **89** O6 51 24N 128 05E
Swale *r.* England **78** J6 54 15N 1 30W
Swampscott Massachusetts U.S.A. **52** C2 42 28N 70 55W
Swanley England **82** D2 51 24N 0 12E
Swansea Wales **78** H3 51 38N 3 57W
Swanton Ohio U.S.A. **36** C2 41 36N 83 54W
Swanton Vermont U.S.A. **37** N5 44 56N 73 08W
SWAZILAND 107 L2
SWEDEN 79 C2
Swedesboro New Jersey U.S.A. **64** E2 39 45N 75 18W
Sweetgrass Montana U.S.A. **41** C1 48 59N 111 58W
Sweetwater *tn.* Texas U.S.A. **62** F3 32 27N 100 25W
Swellendam Republic of South Africa **107** J1 34 01S 20 26E
Świebodzin Poland **80** C5 52 15N 15 31E
Swindon England **78** J3 51 34N 1 47W
Świnoujście Poland **80** B5 53 55N 14 18E
SWITZERLAND 77 D4
Sydney Australia **110** I3 33 55S 151 10E
Syktyvkar Russia **90** G7 61 42N 50 45E
Sylhet Bangladesh **95** G4 24 53N 91 51E
Syowa *r.s.* Antarctica **117** 69 00S 39 35E
Syracuse New York U.S.A. **64** D6 43 03N 76 10W
Syr-Dar'ya *r.* Asia **91** L3 42 00N 72 30E
SYRIA 92 E6
Syrian Desert Middle East **92** E5 32 30N 39 20E
Syzran' Russia **90** F5 53 10N 48 29E
Szczecin Poland **80** B5 53 25N 14 32E
Szczecinek Poland **80** C5 53 42N 16 41E
Szeged Hungary **81** D4 46 15N 20 09E
Székesfehérvár Hungary **81** C4 47 11N 18 22E
Szolnok Hungary **81** D4 47 10N 20 10E
Szombathely Hungary **81** C4 47 14N 16 38E

T

Tabaquite Trinidad and Tobago **66** T9 10 23N 61 18W
Tabas Iran **93** I5 33 37N 56 54E
Table Rock Lake Missouri U.S.A. **63** H4 36 38N 93 17W
Tábor Czechoslovakia **80** B4 49 25N 14 39E
Tabora Tanzania **107** L7 5 01S 32 48E
Tabrīz Iran **93** G5 38 05N 46 18E
Tabuaaran Island Kiribati **115** K8 4 00N 158 10W
Tabūk Saudi Arabia **92** E4 28 33N 36 36E
Ta-chia Taiwan **98** G7 24 20N 120 34E
Tachikawa Japan **100** L2 35 42N 139 28E
Tacloban The Philippines **99** G6 11 15N 125 01E
Tacna Peru **69** C9 18 00S 70 15W
Tacoma Washington U.S.A. **62** B6 47 16N 122 30W
Tadmur Syria **92** E5 34 40N 38 10E
Taegu South Korea **97** P6 35 52N 128 36E
Taejŏn South Korea **97** P6 36 20N 127 26E
Tafila Jordan **92** O10 30 52N 35 36E
Tafna *r.* Algeria **77** B2 35 00N 2 00W
Taganrog Russia **90** D4 47 14N 38 55E
Tagus *see* Tejo
Tahara Japan **100** J1 34 40N 137 18E
Tahat, Mount Algeria **106** G12 23 18N 5 33E
Tahiti *i.* French Polynesia **115** L6 17 30S 148 30W
Tahoe, Lake U.S.A. **62** C4 39 00N 120 00W
Tahoua Niger **106** G10 14 57N 5 19E
Tahta Egypt **92** D4 26 47N 31 31E
Tai'an China **97** N6 36 15N 117 10E
T'ai-chung Taiwan **98** G7 24 09N 124 40E
Tai Lam Chung Hong Kong U.K. **98** B2 22 22N 114 01E
Tai Lam Chung Reservoir Hong Kong U.K. **98** B2 22 23N 114 01E
Tai Long Hong Kong U.K. **98** D2 22 25N 114 22E
Tai Long Wan *b.* Hong Kong U.K. **98** D2 22 20N 114 20E
Tai Mei Tuk Hong Kong U.K. **98** C2 22 28N 114 14E
Tai Mo Shan *mt.* Hong Kong U.K. **98** B2 22 25N 114 07E
Tai Mong Tsai Hong Kong U.K. **98** C2 22 23N 114 18E
T'ai-nan Taiwan **98** G5 23 01N 120 14E
Tai O Hong Kong U.K. **98** A1 22 15N 113 52E
T'ai-pei Taiwan **98** H8 25 05N 121 32E
Tai Po Hong Kong U.K. **98** C2 22 27N 114 10E
Tai Shui Hang Hong Kong U.K. **98** B1 22 17N 114 01E
Tai Tam Reservoir Hong Kong U.K. **98** C1 22 15N 114 12E
Tai Tam Wan *b.* Hong Kong U.K. **98** C1 22 13N 114 13E
Tai Tan Hong Kong U.K. **98** C2 22 26N 114 19E
Taitō Japan **101** C3 35 43N 139 48E
Tai To Yan *mt.* Hong Kong U.K. **98** B2 22 25N 114 07E
T'ai-tung Taiwan **98** H5 22 43N 121 10E
Tai Wai Hong Kong U.K. **98** C2 22 23N 114 10E
TAIWAN 98 H5
Taiwan Strait Taiwan/China **98** F7 24 00N 119 30E
Tai Wan Tau Hong Kong U.K. **98** C1 22 17N 114 17E
Taiyuan China **97** M6 37 50N 112 30E
Ta'izz Yemen Republic **92** F1 13 35N 44 02E
TAJIKISTAN 91 K2/L2
Tajimi Japan **100** J2 35 22N 137 10E
Tajo *(Tejo) r.* Spain/Portugal **77** A2 40 30N 2 00W
Tajo *r.* Spain **77** B3 40 45N 2 00W
Tak Thailand **99** B7 16 51N 99 08E
Takahama Japan **100** G2 35 30N 135 32E
Takamatsu Japan **100** B1 34 20N 134 01E
Takaoka Japan **100** C2 36 47N 137 00E
Takapuna New Zealand **111** B3 36 48S 174 47E
Takarazuka Japan **100** G1 34 49N 135 19E
Takasago Japan **100** F1 34 45N 134 46E
Takasaki Japan **100** C2 36 20N 139 00E
Takatsu Japan **101** B3 35 35N 139 37E
Takatsuki Japan **100** G1 34 52N 135 36E
Takayama Japan **100** C2 36 09N 137 16E
Takefu Japan **100** C2 35 54N 136 10E
Takeo Cambodia **99** C6 11 00N 104 46E
Takeshita Japan **101** B3 35 33N 139 32E
Taku Inlet Alaska U.S.A. **42** B3 58 30N 134 00W
Ta Ku Ling Hong Kong U.K. **98** C2 22 21N 114 15E
Talara Peru **68** A12 4 38S 81 18W
Talavera del la Reina Spain **77** B2 39 58N 4 50W
Talbot, Cape Australia **110** D7 13 49S 126 42E
Talca Chile **69** C5 35 28S 71 40W

Talcahuano Chile **69** C5 36 40S 73 10W
Taldy-Kurgan Kazakhstan **91** M4 45 02N 78 23E
Tallahassee Florida U.S.A. **63** J3 30 26N 84 19W
Tallinn Estonia **79** E2 59 22N 24 48E
Tall Kalakh Syria **92** P12 34 45N 36 17E
Tal'menka Russia **91** N5 53 50N 83 36E
Talodi Sudan **106** L10 10 40N 30 25E
Talparo Trinidad and Tobago **66** T10 10 30N 61 16W
Taltal Chile **69** C7 25 26S 70 33W
Tama *r.* Japan **101** B3 35 40N 139 30E
Tamabo Range *mts.* Malaysia **99** F4 4 00N 115 30E
Tamale Ghana **106** E9 9 26N 0 49W
Ta-ma-li Taiwan **98** H5 22 37N 121 00E
Tamanrasset Algeria **106** G12 22 50N 5 28E
Tamaqua Pennsylvania U.S.A. **64** E3 40 47 75 58W
Tamar *r.* England **78** G2 50 35N 4 15W
Tambov Russia **90** E5 52 44N 41 28E
Tambre *r.* Spain **77** A3 42 55N 8 50W
Tâmega *r.* Portugal **77** A3 41 40N 7 45W
Tamil Nadu *admin.* India **95** D2 12 00N 78 30E
Tampa Florida U.S.A. **63** J2 27 58N 82 38W
Tampere Finland **79** E3 61 32N 23 45E
Tampico Mexico **66** E4 22 18N 97 52W
Tamworth Australia **110** I3 31 07S 150 57E
Tana *r.* Kenya **106** M7 1 00S 39 50E
Tanabe Japan **100** C1 33 43N 135 22E
Tanafjord *fj.* Norway **79** F5 71 00N 28 15E
Tanahmerah Indonesia **110** G8 6 08N 140 18E
Tana, Lake Ethiopia **106** M10 12 20N 37 20E
Tanana Alaska U.S.A. **10** E6 65 11N 152 10W
Tanana *r.* Alaska U.S.A. **10** G5 63 00N 143 00W
Tananarive *see* Antananarivo
Tanashi Japan **101** B3 35 43N 139 31E
Tandil Argentina **69** F5 37 18S 59 10W
Tanezrouft *geog. reg.* Algeria **106** E12 24 00N 0 30W
Tanga Tanzania **107** M6 5 07S 39 05E
Tanganyika, Lake East Africa **107** L6 7 00S 30 00E
Tanger *(Tangiers)* Morocco **106** D15 35 48N 5 45W
Tanggula Shan *mts.* China **96** H5 32 30N 92 30E
Tangra Yumco *l.* China **95** F6 31 00N 86 15E
Tangshan China **97** N6 39 37N 118 05E
Tanjungkarang Telukbetung Indonesia **99** D2 5 22S 105 18E
Tan Kwai Tsuen Hong Kong U.K. **98** A2 22 25N 113 59E
Tanna *i.* Vanuatu **110** L6 19 30S 169 00E
Tanna Ola *mts.* Russia **91** P5 51 00N 92 30E
Tanout Niger **106** G10 15 05N 8 50E
Tan-shui Taiwan **98** H8 25 13N 121 29E
Tan-shui Ho *r.* Taiwan **98** H7 24 40N 121 20E
Tanta Egypt **92** D5 30 48N 31 00E
TANZANIA **107** L6
Taolañaro Madagascar **107** O2 25 01S 47 00E
T'ao-yüan Taiwan **98** H8 25 00N 121 15E
Tapa Estonia **79** F2 59 16N 25 50E
Tapachula Mexico **66** F2 14 54N 92 15W
Tāpi *r.* India **95** D4 21 30N 76 30E
Tappi-zaki *c.* Japan **100** D3 41 14N 140 21E
Tapti *r.* India **95** C4 21 30N 74 30E
Tapuaenuku *mt.* New Zealand **111** B2 42 00S 173 39E
Taquara Brazil **69** P2 22 55S 43 22W
Tara *r.* Russia **91** M6 56 30N 76 00E
Tarābulus *(Tripoli)* Libya **106** H14 32 54N 13 11E
Tarakan Indonesia **99** F4 3 20N 117 38E
Táranto Italy **81** C3 40 28N 17 15E
Tarapoto Peru **68** B11 6 31S 76 23W
Tararua Range *mts.* New Zealand **111** C2 41 00S 175 30E
Tarauacá Brazil **68** C11 8 06SW 70 45W
Tarawa Kiribati **114** H8 1 30N 173 00E
Tarazona Spain **77** B3 41 54N 1 44W
Tarbes France **77** C3 43 14N 0 05E
Taree Australia **110** I3 31 45S 152 26E
Tarfaya Morocco **106** C13 27 58N 12 55W
Tarija Bolivia **68** E8 21 33S 64 45W
Tarim Basin *see* Tarim Pendi
Tarim He *r.* China **96** F7 41 00N 82 00E
Tarim Pendi *(Tarim Basin)* China **96** F6/G6 39 00N 84 00E
Tarko-Sale Russia **89** J8 64 55N 77 50E
Tarkwa Ghana **106** E9 5 16N 1 59W
Tarn *r.* France **77** C3 44 05N 1 40E
Tarnobrzeg Poland **80** D5 50 35N 21 40E
Tarnów Poland **80** D4 50 01N 20 59E
Taroko National Park Taiwan **98** H7 24 15N 121 30E
Taroom Australia **110** H4 25 39S 149 50E
Tarragona Spain **77** C3 41 07N 1 15E
Tarrasa Spain **77** C3 41 34N 2 00E
Tarrytown Connecticut U.S.A. **65** G4 41 00N 73 00W
Tarsus Turkey **92** D6 36 25N 34 52E
Tartary, Gulf of Russia **89** Q5/Q6 50 00N 141 00E
Tartu Estonia **79** F2 58 20N 26 44E
Tartus Syria **92** E5 34 55N 35 52E
Tashkent Uzbekistan **91** K3 41 16N 69 13E
Tashuaz Turkmenistan **91** H3 41 49N 59 58E
Tasman Basin Pacific Ocean **114** F3 46 00S 154 00E
Tasman Bay New Zealand **111** B2 41 00S 173 20E
Tasmania *state* Australia **110** H1 43 00S 147 00E
Tasman Mountains New Zealand **111** B2 41 20S 172 30E
Tasman Plateau Southern Ocean **114** E3 48 00S 147 00E
Tasman Sea Pacific Ocean **114** F4 40 00S 155 00E
Tassili N'Ajjer *mts.* Algeria **106** G13 26 00N 6 20W
Tatabánya Hungary **81** C4 47 31N 18 25E
Tatarsk Russia **90** C5 54 15N 31 34E
Tatarsk Russia **91** M6 55 14N 76 00E
Tatebayashi Japan **100** L3 36 14N 139 30E
Tate's Cairn *mt.* Hong Kong U.K. **98** C2 22 21N 114 13E
Tateyama Japan **100** L1 34 59N 139 50E
Tatry *mts.* Poland **80** C4 49 00N 20 00E
Tauern *mts.* Europe **70** 47 30N 12 00E
Taumarunui New Zealand **111** C3 38 53S 175 16E
Taunton Massachusetts U.S.A. **65** J4 41 54N 71 06W
Taunton England **78** H3 51 01N 3 06W
Taupo New Zealand **111** C3 38 42S 176 06E
Taupo, Lake New Zealand **111** C3 38 50S 175 55E
Tauranga New Zealand **111** C3 37 42S 176 11E
Tauva Fiji **114** T16 17 31S 177 53E
Tavda *r.* Russia **91** J6 58 00N 64 00E
Taverny France **83** A3 49 01N 2 13E
Taveuni *i.* Fiji **114** U16 16 40S 180 00
Tavira Portugal **77** A2 37 07N 7 39W
Tavoy Myanmar **99** B6 14 02N 98 12E
Taw *r.* England **78** H2 50 58N 3 55W
Tawas City Michigan U.S.A. **36** C5 44 16N 83 33W
Tawau Malaysia **99** F4 4 16N 117 54E
T'a-wu Taiwan **98** G5 22 17N 120 54E
Tay *r.* Scotland **78** H8 56 30N 3 25W
Taylor Michigan U.S.A. **52** D1 42 14N 83 16W
Taymā' Saudi Arabia **92** E4 27 37N 38 30E
Taymyr Peninsula Russia **89** L11/M10 75 00N 100 00E
Tayshet Russia **89** L7 55 56N 98 01E
Taz *r.* Russia **89** K9 67 00N 82 00E
Taza Morocco **106** E14 34 16N 4 01W
Tbilisi Georgia **90** E3 41 43N 44 48E
Tchibanga Gabon **106** H7 2 49S 11 00E
Tczew Poland **80** C5 54 05N 18 46E
Te Anua, Lake New Zealand **111** A1 45 30S 168 00E
Te Aroha New Zealand **111** C3 37 32S 175 43E
Te Awamutu New Zealand **111** C3 38 00S 175 20E
Tébessa Algeria **106** G15 35 21N 8 06E
Tecuci Romania **81** E4 45 50N 27 27E
Tecumseh Michigan U.S.A. **36** C3 42 01N 83 56W
Tedzhen *r.* Turkmenistan/Iran **91** J2 37 00N 61 00E
Tees *r.* England **78** J6 54 30N 1 25W
Tefé Brazil **68** E12 3 24S 64 45W
Tegal Indonesia **99** D2 6 52S 109 07E
Tegel Germany **83** E2 52 36N 13 17E
Tegeler See *l.* Germany **83** E2 52 35N 13 00E
Tegucigalpa Honduras **66** G2 14 05N 87 14W
Tehrān Iran **93** H6 35 40N 51 26E
Tehuacán Mexico **66** E3 18 30N 97 26W
Tehuantepec Mexico **66** E3 16 21N 95 13W
Teifi *r.* Wales **78** G4 52 03N 4 15W
Tejo *(Tagus, Tajo)* *r.* Portugal **77** A2 39 30N 8 15W
Tekapo, Lake New Zealand **111** B2 43 30S 170 30E
Tekezē *r.* Ethiopia **92** E1 13 48N 38 05E
Tekirdağ Turkey **80** E3 40 59N 27 31E
Te Kuiti New Zealand **111** C3 38 20S 175 10E
Tel *r.* India **95** E4 20 30N 83 30E
Tela Honduras **66** G3 15 46N 87 25W
Tel Aviv-Yafo Israel **92** O11 32 05N 34 46E
Telemark *geog. reg.* Norway **79** B2 59 42N 8 00E
Telford England **78** I4 52 42N 2 28W
Teller Alaska U.S.A. **10** B6 65 12N 166 23W
Teltow Germany **83** F1 52 24N 13 16E
Teltowkanal *can.* Germany **83** E1 52 23N 13 10E
Teluk Bone *b.* Indonesia **99** G3 4 00S 121 00E
Teluk Cenderawisih *b.* Indonesia **110** F9 2 30S 135 30E
Teluk Tomini *b.* Indonesia **99** G3 1 00S 121 00E
Tema Ghana **106** E9 5 41N 0 00
Teme *r.* England **78** I4 52 15N 2 25W
Temirtau Kazakhstan **91** L5 50 05N 72 55E
Tempelhof Germany **83** F1 52 28N 13 23E
Tempio Pausania Italy **81** A3 40 54N 9 07E
Temple Texas U.S.A. **63** G3 31 06N 97 22W
Temple City California U.S.A. **51** B3 34 06N 118 02W
Temuco Chile **69** C5 38 45S 72 40W
Temuka New Zealand **111** B2 44 12S 171 16E
Tenali India **95** E3 16 13N 80 36E
Ten Degree Channel Andaman Islands/Nicobar Islands **95** G1 10 00N 93 00E
Tenerife *i.* Canary Islands **106** B13 28 15N 16 35W
Tennant Creek *tn.* Australia **110** E6 19 31S 134 15E
Tennessee *r.* U.S.A. **63** I4 35 00N 88 00W
Tennessee *state* U.S.A. **63** I4 35 00N 87 00W
Tenojoki *r.* Finland/Norway **79** F4 69 50N 26 10E
Tenri Japan **100** G1 34 36N 135 49E
Teófilo Otôni Brazil **68** I9 17 52S 41 31W
Tepatitlán Mexico **66** D4 20 50N 102 46W
Tépeji Mexico **66** E3 19 55N 99 21W
Tepic Mexico **66** D4 21 30N 104 51W
Ter *r.* Spain **77** C3 41 55N 2 30E
Teramo Italy **81** B3 42 40N 13 43E
Teresina Brazil **68** I11 5 09S 42 46W
Termez Uzbekistan **91** K2 37 15N 67 15E
Termini Imerese Italy **81** B2 27 59N 13 42E
Ternate Indonesia **99** H4 0 48N 127 23E
Terni Italy **81** B3 42 34N 12 39E
Ternopol' Ukraine **90** B4 49 35N 25 39E
Terpeniya Bay Russia **89** Q5 48 00N 144 00E
Terracina Italy **81** B3 41 17N 13 15E
Terre Haute Indiana U.S.A. **63** I4 39 27N 87 24W
Terrey Hills Australia **111** G3 33 41S 151 14E
Teruel Spain **77** B3 40 21N 1 06W
Teseney Ethiopia **92** E2 15 10N 36 48E
Teshio Japan **100** D3 44 53N 141 46E
Test *r.* England **78** J3 51 05N 1 30W
Testa del Gargano *c.* Italy **81** C3 41 00N 16 00E
Teterev *r.* Ukraine **80** E5 50 00N 29 00E
Tétouan Morocco **106** D15 35 34N 5 22W
Tetovo Macedonia Yugoslavia **81** D3 42 00N 20 59E
Texarkana Arkansas U.S.A. **63** H3 33 28N 94 02W
Texas *state* U.S.A. **62** F3 31 00N 100 00W
Texoma, Lake U.S.A. **63** G3 34 00N 97 00W
THAILAND **99** C7
Thailand, Gulf of South East Asia **99** C6 12 00N 101 30E
Thakhek Laos **99** C7 17 22N 104 50E
Thames New Zealand **111** C3 37 08S 175 35E
Thames *r.* England **78** K3 51 30N 0 20W
Thane India **95** C3 19 14N 73 02E
Thanh Hoa Vietnam **99** D7 19 49N 105 48E
Thanjavur India **95** D2 10 46N 79 09E
Thar Desert India **95** C5 27 30N 72 00E
Thásos *i.* Greece **81** D3 40 00N 24 00E
Thayetmyo Myanmar **99** B7 19 20N 95 10E
Thebes *hist. site* Egypt **92** D4 25 41N 32 40E
The Bronx New York U.S.A. **50** C2 40 50N 73 55W
The Brothers *is.* Hong Kong U.K. **98** A2 22 20N 113 58E
The Crane Barbados **66** W12 13 06N 59 25W
The Dalles Oregon U.S.A. **62** B6 45 36N 121 10W
The Everglades *swamp* Florida U.S.A. **63** J2 26 00N 81 00W
The Loop Illinois U.S.A. **53** B2 41 53N 87 36W
Thermaïkós Kólpos *g.* Greece **81** D3 40 00N 22 50E
Thermopolis Wyoming U.S.A. **62** E5 43 39N 108 12W
Thessaloníki Greece **81** D3 40 38N 22 58E
Thiais France **83** B2 48 45N 2 24E
Thief Lake Minnesota U.S.A. **39** B1 48 30N 95 40W
Thief River Falls *tn.* Minnesota U.S.A. **63** G6 48 12N 96 48W
Thiers France **77** C4 45 51N 3 33E
Thiès Senegal **106** B10 14 49N 16 52W
Thimphu Bhutan **95** F5 27 32N 89 43E
Thingangyun Myanmar **96** J2 16 10N 96 10W
Thionville France **76** D4 49 22N 6 11E
Thira *i.* Greece **81** E2 36 00N 25 00E
Thisted Denmark **80** A6 56 58N 8 42E
Thithia *i.* Fiji **114** V16 17 45S 179 20W
Thívai Greece **81** D2 38 19N 23 19E
Thomasville Georgia U.S.A. **63** J3 30 50N 83 59W
Thompson Island Massachusetts U.S.A. **52** B2 42 20N 71 01W
Thompsonville Connecticut U.S.A. **65** H4 42 00N 72 36W
Thomson *r.* Australia **110** G5 24 00S 143 30E
Thornapple River Michigan U.S.A. **36** A3 42 38N 85 15W
Thousand Islands Canada/U.S.A. **35** E1 44 20N 76 10W
Three Kings Island New Zealand **111** B4 34 00S 172 30E
Three Mile Bay *tn.* New York U.S.A. **35** E1 44 04N 76 12W
Three Points, Cape Ghana **106** E9 4 43N 2 06W
Three Rivers Massachusetts U.S.A. **65** H5 42 11N 72 22W
Thule Greenland **45** S6 77 30N 69 00W
Thun Switzerland **77** D4 46 46N 7 38E
Thunder Bay Michigan U.S.A. **36** C5 45 00N 83 25W
Thüringer Wald *hills* Germany **76** E5 50 00N 10 00E
Thurmont Maryland U.S.A. **64** C2 39 00N 77 00W
Thurso Scotland **78** H10 58 35N 3 32W
Thurso *r.* Scotland **78** H10 58 15N 3 35W
Tianjin China **97** N6 39 08N 117 12E
Tianshui China **97** L5 34 25N 105 58E
Tiaret Algeria **77** C2 35 20N 1 20E
Tiber *r.* Italy **81** B3 42 00N 12 00E
Tiberias Israel **92** O11 32 48N 35 32E
Tiberias, Lake *(Sea of Galilee)* *l.* Israel **92** O11 32 45N 35 30E
Tibesti *mts.* Chad **106** I12 21 00N 17 00E
Tibet Autonomous Region *see* Xizang Zizhiqu
Tibet, Plateau of Asia **84** 33 00N 90 00E
Tiburon California U.S.A. **49** B3 37 53N 122 27W
Tiburón *i.* Mexico **66** B5 28 30N 112 30W
Ticul Mexico **66** G4 20 22N 89 31W
Tien Shan *(Tyan-Shan')* *mts.* China/Kirgyzstan **89** J4 41 00N 76 00E
Tierra Blanca Mexico **66** E3 18 28N 96 21W
Tierra del Fuego *see* Isla Grande de Tierra del Fuego
Tietar *r.* Spain **77** A3 40 07N 5 15W
Tiffany Mountain Washington U.S.A. **42** J4 48 41N 119 56W
Tiffin Ohio U.S.A. **36** C2 41 07N 83 11W
Tigris *r.* Iraq **93** G5 32 00N 46 00E
Tijuana Mexico **66** A6 32 29N 117 10W
Tijuca Brazil **69** P2 22 56S 43 16W
Tikhoretsk Russia **90** E4 45 52N 40 07E
Tikrīt Iraq **92** F5 34 36N 43 42E
Tiksi Russia **89** O10 71 40N 128 45E
Tilak Nagar India **94** L4 28 38N 77 07E
Tilburg Netherlands **76** D5 51 34N 5 05E
Tilden National Park California U.S.A. **49** B3 37 55N 122 15W
Timaru New Zealand **111** B2 44 23S 171 14E
Timbira *r.* Brazil **69** Q3 22 40S 43 12W
Timişoara Romania **81** D4 45 45N 21 15E
Timişul *r.* Romania/Yugoslavia **81** D4 45 00N 21 00E
Timor *i.* Indonesia **99** G2/H2 9 00S 125 00E
Timor Sea Australia/Indonesia **99** H1/H2 10 00S 128 00E
Timsâh, Lake *see* Bahra el Timsâh
Tindouf Algeria **106** D13 27 42N 8 10W
Tinos *i.* Greece **81** E2 37 00N 25 00E
Tioga North Dakota U.S.A. **40** C1 48 26N 102 57W
Tionesta Pennsylvania U.S.A. **36** G2 41 31N 79 30W
Tionesta Lake Pennsylvania U.S.A. **36** G2 41 30N 79 30W
Tioughnioga River New York U.S.A. **64** D5 42 00N 76 00W
Tiranë Albania **81** C3 41 20N 19 49E
Tiraspol' Moldova **90** B4 46 50N 29 38E
Tir'at el Ismâ'iliya *can.* Egypt **107** R3 30 32N 31 48E
Tir'at el Mansûriya Egypt **107** R4 31 12N 31 38E
Tiraz Mountains Namibia **107** I2 25 30S 16 30E
Tiree *i.* Scotland **78** E8 56 30N 6 55W
Tîrgoviste Romania **81** E3 44 56N 25 27E
Tîrgu Jiu Romania **81** D4 45 03N 23 18E
Tîrgu Mures Romania **81** D4 46 33N 24 34E
Tirso *r.* Italy **81** A2 40 00N 9 00E
Tiruchchirāppalli India **95** D2 10 50N 78 41E
Tirunelveli India **95** D1 8 45N 77 43E
Tirupati India **95** D2 13 39N 79 25E
Tiruppur India **95** D2 11 05N 77 20E
Tisza *r.* Hungary/Yugoslavia **81** D4 46 00N 20 00E
Titāgarh India **94** K2 22 44N 88 22E
Titograd Montenegro Yugoslavia **81** C3 42 28N 19 17E
Titova Mitrovica Serbia Yugoslavia **81** D3 42 54N 20 52E
Titovo Uzice Serbia Yugoslavia **81** C3 43 52N 19 50E
Titov Veles Macedonia Yugoslavia **81** D3 41 43N 21 49E
Tittabawassee River Michigan U.S.A. **36** B4 43 50N 84 25W
Titusville Pennsylvania U.S.A. **36** G2 41 37N 79 42W
Tiu Chung Chau *i.* Hong Kong U.K. **98** C2 22 20N 114 19E
Tiu Keng Leng Hong Kong U.K. **98** C1 22 18N 114 15E
Tiverton Rhode Island U.S.A. **65** J4 41 38N 71 13W
Tivoli Italy **81** B3 41 58N 12 48E
Tizimím Mexico **66** G4 21 10N 88 09W
Tizi Ouzou Algeria **106** F15 36 44N 4 05E
Tiznit Morocco **106** D13 29 43N 9 44W
Tlemcen Algeria **106** E14 34 53N 1 21W
Toamasina Madagascar **107** O4 18 10S 49 23E
Toba Japan **100** H1 34 29N 136 51E
Tobago *i.* Trinidad and Tobago **67** L2 11 15N 60 40W
Tobi-shima *i.* Japan **100** C2 39 12N 139 32E
Tobol *r.* Russia **91** J5 54 00N 64 00E
Tobol'sk Russia **91** K6 58 15N 68 12E
Tobyhanna Pennsylvania U.S.A. **64** E4 41 11N 75 25W
Tochigi *pref.* Japan **100** L3 36 20N 139 40E
Toco Trinidad and Tobago **66** U10 10 49N 60 57W
Tocopilla Chile **69** C8 22 05S 70 10W
Togane Japan **100** M2 35 34N 140 22E
TOGO **106** F9
Tok Alaska U.S.A. **44** C3 63 00N 143 00W
Tokelua Islands Pacific Ocean **114** I7 9 00S 168 00W
Toki Japan **100** J2 35 25N 137 12E
Tokoname Japan **100** H1 34 50N 136 50E
Tokorozawa Japan **101** A4 35 47N 139 28E
Tokrau *r.* Kazakhstan **91** M4 48 00N 75 00E
Tokushima Japan **100** B1 34 03N 134 34E
Tokuyama Japan **100** B1 34 03N 131 48E
Tōkyō Japan **100** L2 35 40N 139 45E
Tōkyō *pref.* Japan **100** L2 35 35N 139 40E
Tokyo Bay *(Tōkyō-wan)* Japan **101** C2 35 25N 139 45E
Tōkyō-wan *(Tokyo Bay)* *b.* Japan **100** L2 35 30N 139 50E
Tolbukhin *see* Dobrich
Toledo Ohio U.S.A. **63** J5 41 40N 83 35W
Toledo Spain **77** B2 39 52N 4 02W
Toliara Madagascar **107** N3 23 20S 43 41E
Tollygunge India **94** K2 22 30N 88 19E
Tolo Channel Hong Kong U.K. **98** C2 22 28N 114 17E
Tolo Harbour Hong Kong U.K. **98** C2 22 26N 114 14E
Tolosa Spain **77** B3 43 09N 2 04W
Toluca Mexico **66** E3 19 20N 99 40W
Tol'yatti Russia **90** F5 53 32N 49 24E
Tom' *r.* Russia **91** O6 55 00N 86 30E
Tomaniivi *mt.* Fiji **114** U16 17 37S 178 01E
Tomar Portugal **77** A2 39 36N 8 25W
Tomaszów Mazowiecka Poland **80** C5 51 33N 20 00E
Tomatlán Mexico **66** C3 19 54N 105 18W
Tombigbee *r.* U.S.A. **63** I3 32 00N 88 00W
Tombouctou *(Timbuktu)* Mali **106** E11 16 49N 2 59W
Tombua Angola **107** H4 15 49S 11 53E
Tomioka Japan **100** K3 36 14N 138 45E
Tomogashima-suido *sd.* Japan **100** F1 34 15N 134 00E
Tomokomai Japan **100** D3 42 39N 141 33E
Tom Price, Mount Australia **110** B5 22 49S 117 51E
Tomsk Russia **91** O6 56 30N 85 05E
Toms River *r.* New Jersey U.S.A. **65** F2 39 00N 74 00W
Tonala Mexico **66** F3 16 08N 93 41W
Tonasket Washington U.S.A. **43** E1 48 42N 119 28W
Tonawanda New York U.S.A. **64** B6 43 00N 78 00W
Tonawanda Channel New York U.S.A. **38** D2 43 04N 78 56W
Tonawanda Creek New York U.S.A. **64** B6 43 00N 78 00W
Tone-gawa *r.* Japan **100** M2 35 51N 140 09E
TONGA **114** I5
Tong'an China **98** E7 24 43N 118 07E
Tonga Trench Pacific Ocean **114** I5 20 00S 173 00W
Tongchuan China **97** L6 35 05N 109 02E
Tong Fuk Hong Kong U.K. **98** A1 22 14N 113 56E
Tonghai China **97** K3 24 07N 104 45E
Tonghua China **97** P7 41 42N 125 45E
Tongking, Gulf of Vietnam/China **97** L2 19 00N 107 00E
Tongling China **97** N5 30 58N 117 48E
Tonle Sap *l.* Cambodia **99** C6 13 00N 104 00E
Tonpah Nevada U.S.A. **62** C4 38 05N 117 15W
Tønsberg Norway **79** C2 59 16N 10 25E
Tooele Utah U.S.A. **62** D5 40 32N 112 18W
Toowoomba Australia **110** I4 27 35S 151 54E
Topeka Kansas U.S.A. **63** G4 39 02N 95 41W
Torbali Turkey **80** E2 38 07N 27 08E
Torbay England **78** H2 50 27N 3 30W
Tordesillas Spain **77** A3 41 30N 5 00W
Toride Japan **100** M2 35 54N 140 07E
Torino *(Turin)* Italy **81** A4 45 04N 7 40E
Tormes *r.* Spain **77** A3 41 03N 5 58W
Torne älv *r.* Sweden **79** E4 67 03N 23 02E
Torne-träsk *l.* Sweden **79** D4 68 14N 19 40E
Tornio Finland **79** E4 65 50N 24 10E
Tororo Uganda **106** L8 0 42N 34 12E
Toros Dağlari *mts.* Turkey **92** D6 37 10N 33 10E
Torrance California U.S.A. **51** A2 33 50N 118 20W
Torre del Greco Italy **81** B3 40 46N 14 22E
Torrelavega Spain **77** B3 43 21N 4 03W
Torrens, Lake Australia **110** F3 31 00S 137 50E
Torreón Mexico **66** D5 25 34N 103 25W
Torres Strait Australia **110** G7/G8 10 00S 142 30E
Torrington Connecticut U.S.A. **65** G4 41 48N 73 08W
Tortosa Spain **77** C3 40 49N 0 31E
Toruń Poland **80** C5 53 01N 18 35E
Tosa-wan *b.* Japan **100** B1 33 20N 133 40E
Toshima Japan **101** B3 35 43N 139 41E
Totoya *i.* Fiji **114** V15 18 56S 179 50W
Totsuka Japan **101** B2 35 23N 139 32E
Tottori Japan **100** B2 35 32N 134 12E
Touggourt Algeria **106** G14 33 08N 6 04E
Tou-liu Taiwan **98** G6 23 42N 120 32E
Toulon France **77** D3 43 07N 5 55E
Toulouse France **77** C3 43 33N 1 24E
Toungoo Myanmar **99** B7 18 57N 96 26E
Tournai Belgium **76** C5 50 36N 3 24E
Tours France **77** C4 47 23N 0 42E
Towanda Pennsylvania U.S.A. **64** D4 41 46N 76 27W
Tower Hamlets *bor.* Greater London England **82** C3 51 30N 0 02W
Towner North Dakota U.S.A. **39** A1 48 20N 100 24W
Townsville Australia **110** H6 19 13S 146 48E
Towson Maryland U.S.A. **64** D2 39 25N 76 36W
Toyama Japan **100** C2 36 42N 137 14E
Toyoake Japan **100** H2 35 02N 136 55E
Toyohashi Japan **100** J1 34 46N 137 22E
Toyokawa Japan **100** J1 34 47N 137 24E
Toyonaka Japan **100** G1 34 48N 135 35E
Toyooka Japan **100** F2 35 35N 134 48E
Toyota Japan **100** J2 35 05N 137 09E
Tozeur Tunisia **106** G14 33 55N 8 07E
Trabzona Turkey **92** E7 41 00N 39 43E
Tralee Irish Republic **78** B4 52 16N 9 42W
Tranås Sweden **80** B6 58 03N 15 00E
Transvaal *province* Republic of South Africa **107** K3 24 30S 28 00E
Trāpani Italy **81** B2 38 02N 12 32E
Traverse City Michigan U.S.A. **63** I5 44 46N 85 38W
Travers, Mount New Zealand **111** B2 42 01S 172 47E

Treinta-y-Tres Uruguay 69 G6 33 16S 54 17W
Trelew Chile 69 D4 43 13S 65 15W
Trelleborg Sweden 80 B6 55 22N 13 10E
Tremplinersee *l.* Germany 83 E1 52 21N 13 02E
Trencín Czechoslovakia 80 C4 48 53N 18 00E
Trenque Lauquen Argentina 69 E5 35 56S 62 43W
Trent *r.* England 78 K5 53 10N 0 50W
Trento Italy 81 B4 46 04N 11 08E
Trenton New Jersey U.S.A. 65 F3 40 15N 74 43W
Treptow Germany 83 F1 52 29N 13 27E
Tres Arroyos Argentina 69 E5 38 26S 60 17W
Três Lagoas Brazil 68 G8 20 46S 51 43W
Treviso Italy 81 B4 45 40N 12 15E
Trichu India 95 D2 10 32N 76 14E
Trieste Italy 81 B4 45 39N 13 47E
Tríkkala Greece 81 D2 39 33N 21 46E
Trincomalee Sri Lanka 95 E1 8 34N 81 13E
Trindade *i.* Atlantic Ocean 113 F4 20 30S 29 20W
Trinidad Bolivia 68 E10 14 46S 64 50W
Trinidad Colorado U.S.A. 62 F4 37 11N 104 31W
Trinidad Cuba 67 H4 21 48N 80 00W
Trinidad *i.* Trinidad and Tobago 66 T9 11 00N 61 30W
TRINIDAD AND TOBAGO 67 L2
Trinity *r.* U.S.A. 63 G3 32 00N 96 00W
Trinity Hills Trinidad and Tobago 66 T9 10 07N 61 07W
Trinity Islands Alaska U.S.A. 10 E4 56 45N 154 15W
Trípoli *see* Tarābulus
Trípolis Greece 81 D2 37 31N 22 22E
Tripura Mizoram *admin.* India 95 G4 23 40N 92 30E
Tristan da Cunha *i.* Atlantic Ocean 113 G3 37 15S 12 30W
Trivandrum India 95 D1 8 30N 76 57E
Trnava Czechoslovakia 81 C4 48 23N 17 35E
Troitsk Russia 91 J5 54 08N 61 33E
Troitsko Pechorsk Russia 91 H7 62 40N 56 08E
Trollhättan Sweden 79 C2 58 17N 12 20E
Trollheimen *mts.* Norway 79 B3 63 00N 9 00E
Tromsø Norway 79 D4 69 42N 19 00E
Trondheim Norway 79 C3 63 36N 10 23E
Trondheimsfjorden *fj.* Norway 79 C3 63 40N 10 30E
Trouville France 76 C4 49 22N 0 05E
Troy Alabama U.S.A. 63 I3 31 49N 86 00W
Troy Montana U.S.A. 43 E1 48 28N 115 55W
Troy New York U.S.A. 65 G5 42 43N 73 43W
Troy *hist. site* Turkey 92 C6 39 55N 26 17E
Troyes France 76 C4 48 18N 4 05E
Trujillo Peru 68 B11 8 06S 79 00W
Trujillo Spain 77 A2 39 28N 5 53W
Trujillo Venezuela 68 C14 9 20N 70 38W
Truk Islands Caroline Islands 114 F8 7 30N 152 30E
Trumansburg New York U.S.A. 64 D5 42 32N 76 40W
Truro England 78 F2 50 16N 5 03W
Tsavo National Park Kenya 106 M7 3 30S 38 00E
Tselinograd Kazakhstan 91 L5 51 10N 71 28E
Tseung Kwan O Hong Kong U.K. 98 C1 22 19N 114 14E
Tshane Botswana 107 J3 24 05S 21 54E
Tshuapa *r.* Zaïre 106 J7 1 00S 23 00E
Tsimlyanskoye Vodokhranilishche *res.* Russia 90 E4 47 30N 43 00E
Tsin Shui Wan Hong Kong U.K. 98 C1 22 14N 114 12E
Tsing Chau Tsai Hong Kong U.K. 98 B2 22 20N 114 02E
Tsing Yi Hong Kong U.K. 98 B2 22 21N 114 06E
Tsing Yi *i.* Hong Kong U.K. 98 B2 22 10N 114 00E
Tsu Japan 100 H1 34 41N 136 30E
Tsuchiura Japan 100 M3 36 05N 140 11E
Tsuen Wan Hong Kong U.K. 98 B2 22 22N 114 06E
Tsugaru-kaikyō *sd.* Japan 100 D3 41 30N 140 30E
Tsumeb Namibia 107 I4 19 13S 17 42E
Tsuna Japan 100 F1 34 26N 134 53E
Tsunashima Japan 101 B3 35 13N 139 38E
Tsuruga Japan 100 C2 35 40N 136 05E
Tsurugi-zaki Japan 100 L2 35 08N 139 37E
Tsuruoka Japan 100 C2 38 42N 139 50E
Tsushima Japan 100 H2 35 11N 136 45E
Tsushima *i.* Japan 100 A1 34 30N 129 20E
Tsuyama Japan 100 B2 35 04N 134 01E
Tsz Wan Shan Hong Kong U.K. 98 C2 22 21N 114 12E
Tua *r.* Portugal 77 A3 41 20N 7 30W
Tuamotu Archipelago *is.* Pacific Ocean 115 M6 15 00S 145 00W
Tuamotu Ridge Pacific Ocean 115 L6 19 00S 144 00W
Tuapse Russia 90 D3 44 06N 39 50E
Tuba *r.* Russia 91 P5 54 00N 94 00E
Tübingen Germany 76 D4 48 32N 9 04E
Tubruq Libya 106 J14 32 05N 23 59E
Tubuai Islands Pacific Ocean 115 L5 23 23S 149 27W
Tucheng Taiwan 98 H7 24 52N 121 49E
Tuckerton New Jersey U.S.A. 65 F2 39 36N 74 20W
Tucson Arizona U.S.A. 62 D3 32 15N 110 57W
Tucumcari New Mexico U.S.A. 62 F4 35 11N 103 44W
Tucupita Venezuela 68 E14 9 02N 62 04W
Tucuruí Brazil 68 H12 3 42S 49 44W
Tudela Spain 77 B3 42 04N 1 37W
Tuen Mun Hong Kong U.K. 98 A2 22 23N 113 57E
Tujunga California U.S.A. 51 A3 34 14N 118 16W
Tukums Latvia 79 E2 56 58N 23 10E
Tula Mexico 66 E4 20 01N 99 21W
Tula Mexico 66 E4 23 00N 99 41W
Tula Russia 90 D5 54 11N 37 38E
Tulcán Ecuador 68 B3 0 50N 77 48W
Tulcea Romania 81 E4 45 10N 28 50E
Tulkarm Jordan 92 O11 32 19N 35 02E
Tulle France 77 C4 45 16N 1 46E
Tulsa Oklahoma U.S.A. 63 G4 36 07N 95 58W
Tuluá Colombia 68 B13 4 05N 76 12W
Tulun Russia 89 M6 54 32N 100 35E
Tumaco Colombia 68 B13 1 51N 78 46W
Tumbes Peru 68 A12 3 37S 80 27W
Tumkur India 95 D2 13 20N 77 06E
Tunapuna Trinidad and Tobago 66 T10 10 38N 61 23W
Tunduru Tanzania 107 M5 11 08S 27 21E
Tundzha *r.* Bulgaria 81 E3 42 00N 25 00E
Tungabhadra *r.* India 95 D3 16 00N 77 00E
Tung-chiang Taiwan 98 G5 22 26N 120 30E
Tung Chung Hong Kong U.K. 98 A1 22 17N 113 56E
Tung Lung Chau *i.* Hong Kong U.K. 98 C1 22 15N 114 17E
Tunis Tunisia 106 H15 36 50N 10 13E
TUNISIA 106 G14
Tunja Colombia 68 C14 5 33N 73 23W
Tunkhannock Pennsylvania U.S.A. 64 E4 41 00N 75 00W
Tunnsjøen *l.* Norway 79 C3 64 45N 13 25E
Tupelo Mississippi U.S.A. 63 I3 34 15N 88 43W
Tupiza Bolivia 68 D8 21 27S 65 45W
Túquerres Colombia 68 B13 1 06N 77 37W
Tura Russia 89 M8 64 20N 100 17E
Tura *r.* Russia 91 J6 58 00N 63 00E
Turbotville Pennsylvania U.S.A. 64 D4 41 00N 76 00W
Turda Romania 81 D4 46 35N 23 50E
Turfan Depression *see* Turpan
Turgay *r.* Kazakhstan 91 J4 49 00N 63 00E
Turgutlu Turkey 80 E2 38 30N 27 43E
Turia *r.* Spain 77 B2 39 45N 0 55W
Turin *see* Torino
Turkana, Lake Ethiopia/Kenya 106 M8 4 00N 36 00E
Turkestan Kazakhstan 91 K3 43 17N 68 16E
TURKEY 92 D6
Turkish Republic of Northern Cyprus Cyprus 92 D6 35 20N 33 30E
TURKMENIA *see* TURKMENISTAN
TURKMENISTAN 91 H3/J3
Turks and Caicos Islands West Indies 67 J4 21 30N 72 00W
Turks Island Passage *sd.* West Indies 67 J4 21 30N 71 30W
Turku Finland 79 E3 60 27N 22 15E
Turner Montana U.S.A. 41 D1 48 50N 108 26W
Turnu Măgurele Romania 81 D3 43 44N 24 53E
Turpan *(Turfan Depression)* China 96 G7 42 55N 89 06E
Turramurra Australia 111 G3 33 44S 151 07E
Turukhansk Russia 89 K9 65 49N 88 00E
Tuscaloosa Alabama U.S.A. 63 I3 33 12N 87 33W
Tushino Russia 88 L2 55 52N 37 26E
Tuticorin India 95 D1 8 48N 78 10E
Tuttlingen Germany 76 D4 47 59N 8 49E
TUVALU 114 H7
Tuxpan Mexico 66 C4 21 58N 105 20W
Tuxpan Mexico 66 E4 20 58N 97 23W
Tuxtla Gutierrez Mexico 66 F3 16 45N 93 09W
Túy Spain 77 A3 42 03N 8 39W
Tuz Gölü *l.* Turkey 92 D6 38 40N 33 35E
Tuzla Bosnia-Herzegovina 81 C3 44 33N 18 41E
Tver' *(Kalinin)* Russia 90 D6 56 49N 35 57E
Tweed *r.* Scotland/England 78 I7 55 45N 2 10W
Twin Falls *tn.* Idaho U.S.A. 62 D5 42 34N 114 30W
Twin Peaks California U.S.A. 49 B3 37 45N 122 26W
Twin Rivers *tn.* New Jersey U.S.A. 65 F3 40 17N 74 31W
Twisp Washington U.S.A. 42 H4 48 22N 120 08W
Twisp River Washington U.S.A. 42 H4 48 25N 120 30W
Two Harbors Minnesota U.S.A. 35 B2 47 02N 91 40W
Two Medicine River Montana U.S.A. 41 C1 48 30N 113 05W
Tyan-Shan' *(Tien Shan) mts.* Kirgyzstan/China 89 J4 41 00N 76 00E
Tyler Texas U.S.A. 63 G3 32 22N 95 18W
Tym *r.* Russia 91 N7 60 00N 84 00E
Tynda Russia 89 O7 55 10N 124 35E
Tyne *r.* England 78 J7 55 00N 1 50W
Tynset Norway 79 C3 62 17N 10 47E
Tyre *see* Soûr
Tyrone New York U.S.A. 64 C5 42 22N 77 05W
Tyrone Pennsylvania U.S.A. 64 B3 40 41N 78 15W
Tyrrhenian Sea Europe 81 B3 40 00N 12 00E
Tyumen' Russia 91 K6 57 11N 65 29E
Tyung *r.* Russia 89 N8 65 00N 119 00E
Tywi *r.* Wales 78 H3 51 53N 3 35W

U

Uaupés Brazil 68 D12 0 07S 67 05W
Ubagan *r.* Russia 91 K5 54 00N 65 00E
Ubangi *r.* Central African Republic/Zaïre 106 I8 4 00N 18 00E
Ube Japan 100 B1 33 57N 131 16E
Uberaba Brazil 68 H9 19 47S 47 57W
Uberlândia Brazil 68 H9 18 57S 48 17W
Ubly Michigan U.S.A. 36 D4 43 44N 82 58W
Ubon Ratchathani Thailand 99 D7 15 15N 104 50E
Ubundu Zaïre 106 K7 0 24S 25 30E
Uchiura-wan *b.* Japan 100 D3 42 30N 140 40E
Uda *r.* Russia 89 P6 54 00N 134 00E
Udaipur India 95 C4 24 36N 73 47E
Uddevalla Sweden 80 B6 58 20N 11 56E
Uddjaur *l.* Sweden 79 D4 65 55N 17 50E
Udgir India 95 D3 18 26N 77 11E
Udine Italy 81 B4 46 04N 13 14E
Udon Thani Thailand 99 C7 17 25N 102 45E
Ueda Japan 100 C2 36 27N 138 13E
Uele *r.* Zaïre 106 K8 4 00N 27 00E
Uelen Russia 89 U9 66 13N 169 48W
Uelzen Germany 76 E5 52 58N 10 34E
Ueno Japan 100 H1 34 45N 136 08E
Ufa Russia 91 H5 54 45N 55 58E
Ufa *r.* Russia 91 H6 55 30N 56 30E
Ugab *r.* Namibia 107 I3 21 00S 15 00E
UGANDA 106 L8
Ugra *r.* Russia 90 C5 54 30N 34 00E
Uinta Mountains Utah U.S.A. 62 D5 40 00N 111 00W
Uitenhage Republic of South Africa 107 K1 33 46S 25 25E
Uji Japan 100 G1 34 54N 135 48E
Ujjain India 95 D4 23 11N 75 50E
Ujung Pandang Indonesia 99 F2 5 09S 119 28E
Ukhta Russia 91 G7 63 33N 53 44E
Ukmerge Lithuania 80 D6 55 14N 24 49E
UKRAINE 90 A5/D5
Ulaanbaatar *(Ulan Bator)* Mongolia 97 L8 47 54N 106 52E
Ulaangom Mongolia 96 H8 49 59N 92 00E
Ulan Bator *see* Ulaanbaatar
Ulan-Ude Russia 89 M6 51 55N 107 40E
Ulhasnagar India 95 C3 19 15N 73 08E
Uliastay Mongolia 96 J8 47 42N 96 52E
Ullapool Scotland 78 F9 57 54N 5 10W
Ulm Germany 76 E4 48 24N 10 00E
Uluberiya India 94 J1 22 28N 88 07E
Ulungur Hu *l.* China 96 G8 47 10N 87 10E
Ulutau *mts.* Kazakhstan 91 K4 49 00N 67 00E
Ul'yanovsk Russia 90 F5 54 19N 48 22E
Uman' Ukraine 90 C4 48 45N 30 10E
Umanak Fjord Greenland 11 Y7 71 00N 52 00W
Umbagog Lake Maine/New Hampshire U.S.A. 37 P5 44 45N 71 00W
Umeå Sweden 79 E3 63 50N 20 15E
Ume älv *r.* Sweden 79 D3 64 45N 18 20E
Umiat Alaska U.S.A. 44 A4 69 25N 152 20W
Umm as Samīm *geog. reg.* Oman 93 I3 22 10N 56 00E
Umm Ruwaba Sudan 106 L10 12 50N 31 20E
Umtata Republic of South Africa 107 K1 31 35S 28 47E
Umuarama Brazil 69 G8 23 43S 52 57W
Una *r.* Bosnia-Herzegovina/Croatia 81 C4 45 15N 16 15E
Unalakleet Alaska U.S.A. 10 C5 63 52N 160 50W
'Unayzah Saudi Arabia 92 F4 26 06N 43 58E
UN Buffer Zone Cyprus 92 D6 35 00N 33 30E
Union New Jersey U.S.A. 50 B1 40 42N 74 14W
Union City California U.S.A. 49 C2 37 36N 122 02W
Union City New Jersey U.S.A. 50 B2 40 45N 74 01W
Union City Pennsylvania U.S.A. 36 G2 41 56N 79 51W
Union City Reservoir Pennsylvania U.S.A. 36 G2 42 00N 79 50W
Union of Soviet Socialist Republics *now* ARMENIA, AZERBAIJAN, BELARUS, ESTONIA, GEORGIA, KAZAKHSTAN, KIRGYZSTAN, LATVIA, LITHUANIA, MOLDOVA, RUSSIA, TAJIKISTAN, TURKMENISTAN, UKRAINE,UZBEKISTAN,
Uniontown Pennsylvania U.S.A. 63 K4 39 54N 79 44W
Unionville Michigan U.S.A. 36 C4 43 41N 83 29W
UNITED ARAB EMIRATES *(U.A.E.)* 93 H3
UNITED KINGDOM *(U.K.)* 78
UNITED STATES OF AMERICA *(U.S.A.)* 62/63
Unst *i.* Scotland 78 K12 60 45N 0 55W
Unuk *r.* Alaska U.S.A. 42 B3 56 00N 131 00W
Unzha *r.* Russia 90 E6 58 00N 44 00E
Uparnavik Greenland 11 X7 72 40N 56 05W
Upata Venezuela 68 E14 8 02N 62 25W
Upham North Dakota U.S.A. 39 A1 48 36N 100 44W
Upington Republic of South Africa 107 J2 28 28S 21 14E
Upolu Point Hawaiian Islands 115 Z18 20 16N 155 52W
Upper Bay New Jersey/New York U.S.A. 50 B1 40 40N 74 03W
Upper Crystal Springs Reservoir California U.S.A. 49 B1 37 30N 122 20W
Upper Hutt New Zealand 111 C2 41 06S 175 06E
Upper Lough Erne *l.* Ireland 78 D6 54 15N 7 30W
Upper Manzanilla Trinidad and Tobago 66 T10 10 32N 61 03W
Upper Red Lake Minnesota U.S.A. 63 H6 48 04N 94 48W
Upper Rouge Creek Michigan U.S.A. 52 D2 42 11N 83 18W
Upper Sandusky Ohio U.S.A. 36 C1 40 48N 83 17W
Upper San Leandro Reservoir California U.S.A. 49 C3 37 46N 122 06W
Uppland Sweden 80 C6 59 30N 18 15E
Uppsala Sweden 79 D2 59 55N 17 38E
Ur *hist. site* Iraq 93 G5 30 56N 46 08E
Uraga Japan 101 B1 35 14N 139 43E
Uraga-suidō *sd.* Japan 100 L2 35 10N 139 45E
Urakawa Japan 100 D3 42 10N 142 46E
Ural *r.* Russia 90 G4 50 00N 52 00E
Ural Mountains Russia 91 H4 H7
Ural'sk Kazakhstan 90 G5 51 19N 51 20E
Urawa Japan 100 L2 35 52N 139 40E
Ure *r.* England 78 J5 54 20N 1 40W
Urengoy Russia 89 J9 65 59N 78 30E
Urfa Turkey 92 E6 37 08N 38 45E
Urgench Uzbekistan 91 J3 41 35N 60 41E
Urmia, Lake *see* Daryacheh-ye Orumiyeh
Urmston Road *sd.* Hong Kong U.K. 98 A2 22 22N 113 54E
Uroševac Yugoslavia 81 D3 42 21N 21 09E
Urubamba Peru 68 C10 13 20S 72 07W
Uruguaiana Brazil 69 F7 29 45S 57 05W
URUGUAY 69 F6
Ürümqi China 96 G7 43 43N 87 38E
Uryasu Japan 101 C3 35 39N 139 54E
Urziceni Romania 81 E3 44 43N 26 39E
U.S.A. *see* UNITED STATES OF AMERICA
Usa *r.* Russia 89 H9 66 00N 57 00E
Usan South Korea 97 P6 35 32N 129 21E
Ushiku Japan 100 M2 35 59N 140 10E
Ushuaia Argentina 69 D2 54 48S 68 19W
Usinsk Russia 88 H9 65 57N 57 27E
Usküdar Turkey 92 C7 41 02N 29 02E
Usol'ye-Sibirskoye Russia 89 M6 52 48N 103 40E
Uspenskiy Kazakhstan 91 L4 48 41N 72 43E
Ussuri *(Wusul Jiang) r.* Russia 89 P5 47 00N 134 00E
Ussuriysk Russia 89 P4 43 48N 131 59E
U.S.S.R. *see* Union of Soviet Socialist Republics
Ustica *i.* Italy 81 B2 38 00N 13 00E
Ustinov *see* Izhevsk
Ust'-Kamchatsk Russia 89 S7 56 14N 162 28E
Ust'-Kamenogorsk Kazakhstan 91 N5 50 00N 82 40E
Ust'-Kut Russia 89 M7 56 48N 105 42E
Ústí nad Labem Czechoslovakia 80 B5 50 40N 14 02E
Ust'-Ilimsk Russia 89 M7 58 03N 102 39E
Ust'-Nera Russia 89 Q8 64 35N 143 14E
Ust'Maya Russia 89 P8 60 25N 134 28E
Ust'Olenëk Russia 89 N10 72 59N 119 57E
Ust-Urt Plateau Kazakhstan/Uzbekistan 91 H3 44 00N 57 00E
Usulután El Salvador 66 G2 13 20N 88 25W
Utah *state* U.S.A. 62 D4 39 00N 112 00W
Utah Lake Utah U.S.A. 62 D5 40 10N 111 50W
Utica New York U.S.A. 64 E6 43 06N 75 15W
Utrecht Netherlands 76 D5 52 05N 5 07E
Utrera Spain 77 A2 37 10N 5 47W
Utsunomiya Japan 100 C2 36 33N 139 52E
Uttar *admin.* India 95 E4 27 00N 80 00E
Uttaradit Thailand 99 C7 17 38N 100 05E
Uttarpāra-Kotrung India 94 K2 22 39N 88 20E
Uummannaq *see* Dundas
Uvalde Texas U.S.A. 62 G2 29 14N 99 49W
Uvinza Tanzania 107 L6 5 08S 30 23E
Uvs Nuur *l.* Mongolia 96 H9 50 10N 92 30E
Uwajima Japan 100 B1 33 13N 132 32E
Uxbridge England 82 B3 51 33N 0 30W
Uyuni Bolivia 68 D8 20 28S 66 47W
Uza *r.* Russia 90 F5 52 30N 45 30E
UZBEKISTAN 91 J3
Uzhgorod Ukraine 90 A4 48 39N 22 15E

V

Vaal *r.* Republic of South Africa 107 K2 27 30S 25 30E
Vaasa Finland 79 E3 63 06N 21 36E
Vác Hungary 81 C4 47 46N 19 08E
Vadodara India 95 C4 22 19N 73 14E
Vaga *r.* Russia 90 E7 62 00N 43 00E
Váh *r.* Czechoslovakia 81 C4 48 00N 18 00E
Vail New Jersey U.S.A. 64 F3 40 59N 75 01W
Vakh *r.* Russia 91 N7 61 30N 80 00E
Vakhsh *r.* Tajikistan 91 K2 37 30N 68 30E
Valdai Hills Russia 90 C6 57 00N 32 30E
Valdepeñas Spain 77 B2 38 46N 3 24W
Valdés, Peninsula Argentina 69 E4 42 30S 63 00W
Valdivia Chile 69 C5 39 46S 73 15W
Valdosta Georgia U.S.A. 63 J3 30 51N 83 51W
Valdres *geog. reg.* Norway 79 B3 60 55N 8 40E
Valença Brazil 68 J10 13 22S 39 06W
Valence France 77 C3 44 56N 4 54E
Valencia Spain 77 B2 39 29N 0 24W
Valencia Trinidad and Tobago 66 T10 10 39N 61 12W
Valencia Venezuela 68 D15 10 14N 67 59W
Valencia, Gulf of Spain 77 C2 39 30N 0 20E
Valenciennes France 76 C5 50 22N 3 32E
Valera Venezuela 68 C14 9 21N 70 38W
Valga Estonia 79 F2 57 44N 26 00E
Valier Montana U.S.A. 41 C1 48 19N 112 14W
Valjevo Yugoslavia 81 C3 44 16N 19 56E
Valladolid Mexico 66 G4 20 40N 88 11W
Valladolid Spain 77 B3 41 39N 4 45W
Valle de la Pascua Venezuela 68 D14 9 15N 66 00W
Valledupar Colombia 68 C15 10 31N 73 16W
Valle Grande Bolivia 68 E9 18 30S 64 06W
Vallenar Chile 69 C7 28 36S 70 45W
Valletta Malta 81 B2 35 54N 14 32E
Valley *tn.* Barbados 66 V12 13 07N 59 35W
Valley Stream *tn.* New York U.S.A. 50 D1 40 39N 73 42W
Valmiera Latvia 79 F2 57 32N 25 29E
Valparaíso Chile 69 C6 33 05S 71 40W
Van Turkey 92 F6 38 28N 43 20E
Van Buren Maine U.S.A. 31 A2 47 10N 67 59W
Vancouver Washington U.S.A. 62 B6 45 38N 122 40W
Vänern *l.* Sweden 79 C2 59 00N 13 30E
Vänersborg Sweden 80 B6 58 23N 12 19E
Van Etten New York U.S.A. 64 D5 42 13N 76 33W
Van Gölü *l.* Turkey 92 F6 38 33N 42 46E
Vanna *i.* Norway 79 D5 70 05N 19 50E
Vännäs Sweden 79 D3 63 56N 19 50E
Vannes France 77 B4 47 40N 2 44W
Van Norman Lake California U.S.A. 51 A4 34 17N 118 28W
Vantaa Finland 79 E3 60 20N 24 50E
Vanua Levu *i.* Fiji 114 U16 16 20S 179 00E
Vanua Levu Barrier Reef Fiji 114 U16 17 10S 179 00E
Vanua Mbalavu *i.* Fiji 114 V16 17 15S 178 55W
VANUATU 110 L6
Vanves France 83 B2 48 49N 2 17E
Van Wert Ohio U.S.A. 36 B1 40 53N 84 36W
Var *r.* France 77 D3 43 55N 6 55E
Varanasi India 95 E5 25 20N 83 00E
Varangerfjorden *fj.* Norway 79 G4 70 00N 30 00E
Varangerhalvøya *p.* Norway 79 F5 70 22N 29 40E
Varaždin Croatia 81 C4 46 18N 16 21E
Varberg Sweden 80 B6 57 06N 12 15E
Vardar *r.* Greece 81 D3 41 30N 20 15E
Vardø Norway 79 G5 70 22N 31 06E
Varkhaus Finland 79 F3 62 20N 27 50E
Varna Bulgaria 81 E3 43 12N 27 57E
Värnamo Sweden 80 B6 57 11N 14 03E
Várzea Grande Brazil 68 I11 6 32S 42 05W
Väsby Sweden 80 C6 56 13N 12 37E
Vaslui Romania 81 E4 46 37N 27 46E
Vassar Michigan U.S.A. 36 C4 43 23N 83 33W
Västerås Sweden 79 D2 59 36N 16 32E
Västerdalälven *r.* Sweden 79 C3 61 15N 18 10E
Västervik Sweden 79 D2 57 45N 16 40E
Vasyugan *r.* Russia 89 J7 59 00N 77 00E
Vatnajökull *ice cap* Iceland 79 I6 64 30N 17 00W
Vättern *l.* Sweden 79 C2 58 20N 14 20E
Vatulele *i.* Fiji 114 T15 18 30S 177 38E
Vaucresson France 83 A2 48 51N 2 08E
Växjö Sweden 79 C2 56 52N 14 50E
Vaygach *i.* Russia 89 H10 70 00N 59 00E
Vega *i.* Norway 79 C4 65 38N 11 52E
Vejle Denmark 80 A6 55 43N 9 33E
Velbert Germany 76 J2 51 22N 7 03E
Velebit *mts.* Croatia 81 C3 44 00N 15 00E
Velikaya *r.* Russia 90 B6 57 00N 28 45E
Velikiye-Luki Russia 90 C6 56 19N 30 31E
Veliko Tŭrnovo Bulgaria 81 E3 43 04N 25 39E
Vellore India 95 D2 12 56N 79 09E
Velten Germany 83 E2 52 42N 13 12E
Venézia Italy 81 B4 45 26N 12 20E
VENEZUELA 68 D14
Venezuelan Basin Caribbean Sea 113 B8 15 00N 65 00W
Venta *r.* Latvia/Lithuania 79 E2 56 05N 21 50E
Ventspils Latvia 79 E2 57 22N 21 31E
Ver *r.* England 82 B3 51 43N 0 21W
Veracruz Mexico 66 E3 19 11N 96 10W
Veraval India 94 C4 20 53N 70 28E
Vercelli Italy 81 A4 45 19N 8 26E
Verde *r.* Arizona U.S.A. 62 D3 34 00N 112 00W
Verdun-sur-Meuse France 76 D4 49 10N 5 24E
Vereeniging Republic of South Africa 107 K2 26 41S 27 56E
Verin Spain 77 A3 41 55N 7 26W
Verkhoyansk Russia 89 P9 67 35N 133 25E
Verkhoyansk Range *mts.* Russia 89 O9-P8 65 00N 130 00E
Vermilion Ohio U.S.A. 36 D2 41 24N 82 21W
Vermillion Lake Minnesota U.S.A. 35 B2 42 48N 96 55W
Vermillion Range Minnesota U.S.A. 35 B2 48 00N 91 30W
Vermont *state* U.S.A 63 L5
Vernon Texas U.S.A. 62 G3 34 10N 99 19W
Véroia Greece 81 D3 40 32N 22 11E
Verona Italy 81 B4 45 26N 11 00E
Verrières France 83 B1 48 44N 2 16E

Versailles France **83** A2 48 48N 2 07E
Verviers Belgium **76** D5 50 36N 5 52E
Vestfjorden *fj.* Norway **79** C4 68 00N 14 50E
Vestmannaeyjar *is.* Iceland **79** H6 63 28N 20 30W
Vesuvio *mt.* Italy **81** B3 40 49N 14 26E
Vesuvius *see* Vesuvio
Vetlanda Sweden **79** D2 57 26N 15 05E
Viangchan *(Vientiane)* Laos **97** K2 17 59N 102 38E
Viano do Castelo Portugal **77** A3 41 41N 8 50W
Viar *r.* Spain **77** A2 37 45N 5 50W
Viborg Denmark **80** A6 56 28N 9 25E
Vicecomodoro Marambio *r.s.* Antarctica **117** 64 14S 56 38W
Vicente Guerrero Mexico **66** A6 30 48N 116 00W
Vicenza Italy **81** B4 45 33N 11 32E
Vichy France **77** C4 46 07N 3 25E
Vicksburg Mississippi U.S.A. **63** H3 32 21N 90 51W
Victoria Chile **69** C5 38 20S 72 30W
Victoria Hong Kong U.K. **98** B1 22 16N 114 03E
Victoria Texas U.S.A. **63** G2 28 49N 97 01W
Victoria *r.* Australia **110** E6 131 30S 17 00S
Victoria *state* Australia **110** G2/H2
Victoria Falls Zambia/Zimbabwe **107** K4 17 55S 25 51E
Victoria Harbour Hong Kong U.K. **98** C1 22 21N 114 00E
Victoria Island *tn.* Nigeria **107** W3 6 21N 3 31E
Victoria, Lake East Africa **106** L7 2 00S 33 00E
Victoria Land *geog. reg.* Antarctica **117** 75 00S 157 00E
Victoria Peak Hong Kong U.K. **98** B1 22 17N 114 10E
Victoria West Republic of South Africa **107** J1 31 25S 23 08E
Vidin Bulgaria **81** D3 44 00N 22 50E
Viedma Argentina **69** E4 40 45S 63 00W
Vienna Virginia U.S.A. **64** C1 38 56N 77 17W
Vienna *see* Wien
Vienne France **77** C4 45 32N 4 54E
Vientiane *(Viangchan)* Laos **97** K2 17 59N 102 38E
Vierzon France **77** C4 47 14N 2 03E
VIETNAM **99** D6/8
Vigia Brazil **68** H12 0 50S 48 07W
Vigo Spain **77** A3 42 15N 8 44W
Vijayawada India **95** E3 16 34N 80 40E
Vijosë *r.* Albania **81** D3 40 30N 20 00E
Vikna *l.* Norway **79** C3 64 55N 10 55E
Vila Vanuatu **110** L6 17 45S 168 18E
Vila Nova de Gaia Portugal **77** A3 41 08N 8 37W
Vila Pedro Brazil **69** P2 22 49S 43 20W
Vila Real Portugal **77** A3 41 17N 7 45W
Vila Velha Brazil **68** I8 20 23S 40 18W
Vilhelmina Sweden **79** D3 64 38N 16 40E
Vilhena Brazil **68** J10 12 40S 60 08W
Villa Constitución Mexico **66** B5 25 05N 111 45W
Villahermosa Mexico **66** F3 18 00N 92 53W
Villa María Argentina **69** E6 32 25S 63 15W
Villa Montes Bolivia **68** E8 21 15S 63 30W
Villanueva Mexico **66** D4 22 24N 102 53W
Villaricca Chile **69** C5 39 15S 72 15W
Villarrobledo Spain **77** B2 39 16N 2 36W
Villa Unión Argentina **69** D7 29 27S 62 46W
Villa Unión Mexico **66** C4 23 10N 106 12W
Villavicencio Colombia **68** C13 4 09N 73 38W
Villefranche-sur-Saône France **77** C4 46 00N 4 43E
Villejuif France **83** B2 48 47N 2 23E
Villeneuve St. Georges France **83** B1 48 43N 2 27E
Villeneuve-sur-Lot France **77** C3 44 25N 0 43E
Villeparisis France **83** C2 48 56N 2 37E
Villeurbanne France **77** D4 45 46N 4 54E
Vilnius Lithuania **80** E5 54 40N 25 19E
Vilnya *r.* Lithuania **80** D5 54 00N 25 00E
Vilyuy *r.* Russia **89** O8 64 00N 123 00E
Vilyuysk Russia **89** O8 63 46N 121 35E
Viña del Mar Chile **69** C6 33 02S 71 35W
Vinaroz Spain **77** C3 40 29N 0 28E
Vincennes France **83** B2 48 51N 2 27E
Vincennes Indiana U.S.A. **63** I4 38 42N 87 30W
Vindelälven *r.* Sweden **79** D4 65 15N 18 15E
Vindhya Range *mts.* India **95** C4 23 00N 75 00E
Vineland New Jersey U.S.A. **64** E2 39 29N 75 02W
Vineyard Sound Massachusetts U.S.A. **65** K4 41 30N 70 40W
Vinh Vietnam **99** D7 18 42N 105 41E
Vinkovci Croatia **81** C4 45 16N 18 49E
Vinnitsa Ukraine **90** B4 49 11N 28 30E
Vipiteno Italy **81** B4 46 54N 11 27E
Virgin *r.* U.S.A. **62** D4 37 00N 114 00W
Virginia Minnesota U.S.A. **63** H6 47 30N 92 28W
Virginia *state* U.S.A. **63** K4 38 00N 77 00W
Virginia Beach *tn.* Virginia U.S.A. **63** K4 36 51N 75 59W
Virgin Islands West Indies **67** L3 18 00N 64 30W
Virovitica Croatia **81** C4 45 50N 17 25E
Vis *i.* Croatia **68** C3 43 00N 16 00E
Visby Sweden **79** D2 57 32N 18 15E
Viseu Portugal **77** A3 40 40N 7 55W
Vishakhapatnam India **95** E3 17 42N 83 24E
Vitebsk Belarus **90** C6 55 10N 30 14E
Viterbo Italy **81** B3 42 24N 12 06E
Vitichi Bolivia **68** D8 20 14S 65 22W
Viti Levu *i.* Fiji **114** T15 18 10S 177 55E
Vitim Russia **89** N7 59 28N 112 35E
Vitim *r.* Russia **89** N7 58 00N 113 00E
Vitória Brazil **68** I8 20 20S 40 18W
Vitoria Spain **77** B3 42 51N 2 40W
Vitória da Conquista Brazil **68** I10 14 53S 40 52W
Vitry-le-François France **76** C4 48 44N 4 36E
Vitry-sur-Seine France **83** B2 48 47N 2 24E
Vityaz Trench Pacific Ocean **114** G7 9 30S 170 00E
Vivi *r.* Russia **89** L9 61 00N 96 00E
Vize *i.* Russia **89** J11 79 30N 77 00E
Vizianagaram India **95** E3 18 07N 83 30E
Vladikavkaz *(Ordzhonikidze)* Russia **90** F3 43 02N 44 43E
Vladimir Russia **90** E6 56 08N 40 25E
Vladimir Volynskiy Ukraine **80** D5 50 51N 24 19E
Vladivostok Russia **89** P4 43 09N 131 53E
Vlissingen Netherlands **76** C5 51 27N 3 35E
Vlorë Albania **81** C3 40 29N 19 29E
Vltava *r.* Czechoslovakia **80** B4 49 00N 14 00E
Vokhma *r.* Russia **90** F6 58 00N 45 30E
Volga *r.* Russia **90** F4 47 30N 46 30E
Volgodonsk Russia **90** E4 47 35N 42 08E
Volgograd Russia **90** E4 48 45N 44 30E
Volgogradskoye Vodokhranilishche *res.* Russia **90** F4 50 00N 45 30E
Volkhov *r.* Russia **90** C6 59 00N 31 30E
Vologda Russia **90** D6 59 10N 39 55E
Vólos Greece **81** D2 39 22N 22 57E
Vol'sk Russia **90** F5 52 04N 47 22E
Volta Redonda Brazil **69** I8 22 31S 44 05W
Volta, Lake Ghana **106** E9 7 30N 0 30W
Volturno *r.* Italy **81** B3 41 00N 14 00E
Volzhskiy Russia **90** E4 48 48N 44 45E
Vopnafjördur Iceland **79** J7 65 46N 14 50W
Voríai Sporadhes *is.* Greece **81** D2 39 00N 24 00E
Vorkuta Russia **89** I9 67 27N 64 00E
Vorna *r.* Russia **90** E5 52 00N 42 30E
Voronezh Russia **90** D5 51 40N 39 13E
Voroshilovgrad *see* Lugansk
Vørterkaka Nunatak *mt.* Antarctica **117** 71 45S 32 00E
Võrtsjärv *l.* Estonia **79** F2 58 15N 26 10E
Võru Estonia **79** F2 57 46N 26 52E
Vosges *mts.* France **76-77** C4 48 10N 6 50E
Voss Norway **79** B3 60 38N 6 25E
Vostochnyy Russia **89** P4 42 52N 132 56E
Vostok *r.s.* Antarctica **117** 78 27S 106 51E
Votkinsk Russia **91** G6 57 00N 54 00E
Votkinskoye Vodokhranilishche *res.* Russia **91** H6 57 00N 55 30E
Vouga *r.* Portugal **77** A3 40 45N 8 15W
Voxnan Sweden **79** D3 61 22N 15 39E
Vrangelya *(Wrangel) i.* Russia **89** T10 61 30N 180 00
Vranje Yugoslavia **81** D3 42 33N 21 54E
Vratsa Bulgaria **81** D3 43 12N 23 32E
Vrbas *r.* Bosnia-Herzegovina **81** C3 44 00N 17 00E
Vršac Yugoslavia **81** D4 45 07N 21 19E
Vryburg Republic of South Africa **107** J2 26 57S 24 44E
Vukovar Croatia **81** C4 45 19N 19 01E
Vunisea Fiji **114** U15 19 04S 178 09E
Vung Tau Vietnam **99** D6 10 21N 107 04E
Vyatka *r.* Russia **90** F6 58 00N 49 00E
Vyaz'ma Russia **90** C6 55 12N 34 17E
Vyborg Russia **90** B7 60 45N 28 41E
Vychegda *r.* Russia **90** F7 62 00N 48 00E
Vyshniy-Volochek Russia **90** C6 57 34N 34 23E

W

Wabash *r.* North America **63** I4 38 00N 87 30W
Wachusett Reservoir Massachusetts U.S.A. **65** J5 42 23 71 45W
Waco Texas U.S.A. **63** G3 31 33N 97 10W
Wadayama Japan **100** F2 35 22N 134 49E
W.D. Boyce Regional Park Pennsylvania U.S.A. **53** E1 40 27N 79 28W
Waddeneilanden *(West Frisian Islands)* Netherlands **76** C5 53 25N 5 15E
Waddenzee *sea* Netherlands **76** C5 53 15N 5 15E
Wadī al Masī lah *r.* Yemen Republic **93** H2 16 00N 50 00E
Wadi Araba *r.* Israel **92** O10 30 30N 35 10E
Wadi el'Arîsh *r.* Egypt **92** N10 30 05N 33 50E
Wâdi el Gafra Egypt **107** R2 30 16N 31 46E
Wadi Halfa Sudan **92** D3 21 55N 31 20E
Wad Medani Sudan **92** D1 14 24N 33 30E
Waesch, Mount Antarctica **117** 77 00S 127 30W
Wagga Wagga Australia **110** H2 35 07S 147 24E
Wagin Australia **110** B3 33 20S 117 15E
Waglan Island Hong Kong U.K. **98** C1 22 10N 114 18E
Wah Pakistan **95** C6 33 50N 72 44E
Waha Libya **106** J13 28 10N 19 57E
Wahiawa Hawaiian Islands **115** X18 21 35N 158 05W
Wahpeton North Dakota U.S.A. **63** G6 46 16N 96 36W
Waialua Hawaiian Islands **115** X18 21 35N 158 08W
Waigeo *i.* Indonesia **99** I3 0 00 131 00E
Waihi New Zealand **111** C3 37 22S 175 51E
Waikaremoana, Lake New Zealand **111** C3 38 50S 178 40E
Waikato New Zealand **111** C3 38 00S 175 30E
Wailuku Hawaiian Islands **115** Y18 20 54N 156 30W
Waimate New Zealand **111** B2 44 45S 171 03E
Wainwright Alaska U.S.A. **10** D7 70 39N 160 10W
Waipawa New Zealand **111** C3 39 48S 176 36E
Wairoa New Zealand **111** C3 39 03S 177 25E
Waitaki *r.* New Zealand **111** B2 44 30S 170 30E
Waitara New Zealand **111** B3 38 59S 174 13E
Wajima Japan **100** C2 37 23N 136 53E
Wajir Kenya **106** N8 1 46N 40 05E
Wakasa-wan *b.* Japan **100** C2 35 40N 135 30E
Wakatipu, Lake New Zealand **111** A1 45 00S 168 50E
Wakayama Japan **100** G1 34 12N 135 10E
Wakayama *pref.* Japan **100** G1 34 13N 135 20E
Wake Island Pacific Ocean **114** G10 19 18N 166 36E
Wakefield Massachusetts U.S.A. **52** B3 42 29N 71 04W
Wakefield Rhode Island U.S.A. **65** J4 41 26N 71 30W
Wakkanai Japan **100** D4 45 26N 141 43E
Wako Japan **101** B4 35 46N 139 37E
Wałbrzych Poland **80** C5 50 48N 16 19E
Walden Pond Massachusetts U.S.A. **52** C3 42 30N 70 45W
Walden Pond Reservation Massachusetts U.S.A. **52** A2 42 26N 71 26W
Wales Alaska U.S.A. **100** B6 65 38N 168 09W
Wales United Kingdom **78**
Walhalla North Dakota U.S.A. **39** B1 48 57N 97 54W
Walker Lake Nevada U.S.A. **62** C4 38 40N 118 43W
Wallaroo Australia **110** F3 33 57S 137 36E
Walla Walla Washington U.S.A. **62** C6 46 05N 118 18W
Wallingford Connecticut U.S.A. **65** H4 41 28N 72 49W
Walnut Creek California U.S.A. **49** C3 37 53N 122 03W
Walnut Creek *tn.* California U.S.A. **49** C3 37 55N 122 03W
Walsall England **78** J4 52 35N 1 58W
Walsenburg Colorado U.S.A. **62** F4 37 36N 104 48W
Walsum Germany **76** G3 51 32N 6 41E
Waltham Massachusetts U.S.A. **52** B2 42 23N 71 14W
Waltham Forest *bor.* Greater London England **82** C3 51 36N 0 00
Walthamstow England **82** C3 51 34N 0 01W
Walton-on-Thames England **82** B2 51 24N 0 25W
Waltrop Germany **76** K3 51 37N 7 25E
Walvis Bay *tn.* Namibia **107** H3 22 59S 14 31E
Walvis Ridge Atlantic Ocean **113** I4 30 00S 3 00E
Walyevo Fiji **114** V16 17 35S 179 58W
Wamba *r.* Zaïre **107** I6 6 30S 17 30E
Wanaka, Lake New Zealand **111** A2 44 30S 169 00E
Wandsworth *bor.* Greater London England **82** C2 51 27N 0 11W
Wanganui New Zealand **111** C3 39 56S 175 02E
Wanganui *r.* New Zealand **111** C3 39 30S 175 00E
Wangaratta Australia **110** H2 36 22S 146 20E
Wang Chau *i.* Hong Kong U.K. **98** D1 22 20N 114 22E
Wang Toi Shan Hong Kong U.K. **98** B2 22 26N 114 05E
Wanheim Germany **76** H2 51 23N 6 45E
Wanne-Eickel Germany **76** J3 51 31N 7 09E
Wannsee Germany **83** E1 52 24N 13 09E
Wanstead England **82** D3 51 34N 0 02E
Wanxian China **97** L5 30 54N 108 20E
Wappingers Falls *tn.* New York U.S.A. **65** G4 41 36N 73 55W
Warangal India **95** D3 18 00N 79 35E
Ware River Massachusetts U.S.A. **65** H5 42 15N 72 20W
Warnow *r.* Germany **63** B2 53 00N 12 00E
Warrego *r.* Australia **110** H4 27 30S 146 00E
Warren Michigan U.S.A. **52** E2 42 30N 83 02W
Warren Ohio U.S.A. **36** F2 41 15N 80 49W
Warren Pennsylvania U.S.A. **64** A4 41 52N 79 09W
Warrnambool Australia **110** G2 38 23S 142 03E
Warroad Minnesota U.S.A. **39** B1 48 54N 95 20W
Warsaw *see* Warszawa
Warszawa *(Warsaw)* Poland **80** D5 52 15N 21 00E
Warta *r.* Poland **80** C5 52 00N 17 00E
Waruha *r.* India **95** D4 20 30N 79 00E
Warwick Australia **110** I4 28 12S 152 00E
Warwick New York U.S.A. **65** F4 41 15N 74 21W
Warwick Rhode Island U.S.A. **65** J4 41 42N 71 23W
Washburn Wisconsin U.S.A. **35** B2 46 41N 90 53W
Washington *state* U.S.A. **62** B6 47 00N 120 00W
Washington County Pennsylvania U.S.A. **53** D1 40 18N 80 06W
Washington Crossing Pennsylvania U.S.A. **64** F3 40 17N 74 53W
Washington D.C. District of Columbia U.S.A. **64** C1 38 55N 77 00W
Washington Park Illinois U.S.A. **53** B2 41 48N 87 37W
Wash, The *b.* England **78** L4 52 55N 0 10E
Watampone Indonesia **99** G3 4 33S 120 20E
Waterbury Connecticut U.S.A. **65** G4 41 33NB 73 03W
Waterfall Australia **111** G1 34 08S 151 00E
Waterford Irish Republic **78** D4 52 15N 7 06W
Waterford New York U.S.A. **65** G5 42 46N 73 42W
Waterloo Iowa U.S.A. **63** H5 42 30N 92 20W
Waterloo New York U.S.A. **64** D5 42 55N 76 53W
Waterloo Trinidad and Tobago **66** T9 10 28N 61 28W
Watersmeet Michigan U.S.A. **35** C2 46 28N 89 10W
Watertown Connecticut U.S.A. **65** G4 41 32N 73 08W
Watertown Massachusetts U.S.A. **52** B2 42 21N 71 11W
Watertown New York U.S.A. **63** K5 43 57N 75 56W
Watertown South Dakota U.S.A. **63** G5 44 54N 97 08W
Waterville Maine U.S.A. **63** M5 44 34N 69 41W
Waterville New York U.S.A. **64** E5 42 55N 75 24W
Waterville Ohio U.S.A. **36** C2 41 29N 83 44W
Watford Hertfordshire England **82** B3 51 39N 0 24W
Watkins Glen New York U.S.A. **64** D5 42 23N 76 53W
Wattenscheid Germany **76** J2 51 27N 7 07E
Wau Papua New Guinea **110** H8 7 22S 146 40E
Wau Sudan **106** K9 7 40N 28 04E
Waukegan Illinois U.S.A. **63** I5 42 21N 87 52W
Waukesha Wisconsin U.S.A. **63** I5 43 01N 88 14W
Wausau Wisconsin U.S.A. **63** I5 44 58N 89 40W
Waveney *r.* England **78** M4 52 30N 1 30E
Waverly New York U.S.A. **64** D5 42 01N 76 33W
Waycross Georgia U.S.A. **63** J3 31 12N 82 22W
Wayland Massachusetts U.S.A. **52** A2 42 22N 71 22W
Wayland New York U.S.A. **64** C5 42 33N 77 36W
Wayne Michigan U.S.A. **52** D2 42 16N 83 26W
Wayne New Jersey U.S.A. **50** A2 40 55N 74 15W
Wayne County Michigan U.S.A. **52** F2 42 11N 82 26W
Waynesboro Pennsylvania U.S.A. **64** C2 39 45N 77 36W
Weald, The *geog. reg.* England **78** L3 51 05N 0 25E
Wear *r.* Durham England **78** J6 54 40N 1 50W
Webster Massachusetts U.S.A. **65** J5 42 04N 71 53W
Webster New York U.S.A. **64** C6 43 13N 77 27W
Weddell Sea Southern Ocean **117** 71 00S 40 00W
Wedding Germany **83** F2 52 33N 13 21E
Weedville Pennsylvania U.S.A. **64** B4 41 17N 78 30W
Weiden Germany **76** E4 49 40N 12 10E
Weifang China **97** N6 36 44N 119 10E
Weigelstown Pennsylvania U.S.A. **64** D2 39 59N 76 47W
Wei He *r.* China **97** L5 34 00N 106 00E
Weimar Germany **76** E5 50 59N 11 20E
Weipa Australia **110** G7 12 35S 141 56E
Weirton West Virginia U.S.A. **63** J5 40 24N 80 37W
Weissenfels Germany **76** E5 51 12N 11 58E
Wejherowo Poland **80** C5 54 36N 18 12E
Welland *r.* England **78** K4 52 50N 0 00
Wellesly Massachusetts U.S.A. **52** A2 42 18N 71 18W
Wellesley Islands Australia **110** F6 16 30S 139 00E
Wellfleet Massachusetts U.S.A. **65** K4 41 56N 70 01W
Wellington Kansas U.S.A. **63** G4 37 17N 97 25W
Wellington New Zealand **111** B2 41 17S 174 47E
Wellington Ohio U.S.A. **36** D2 41 11N 82 13W
Wells Maine U.S.A. **65** K6 43 20N 70 35W
Wellsboro Pennsylvania U.S.A. **64** C4 41 45N 77 18W
Wellsford New Zealand **111** B3 36 16S 174 32E
Wellsville New York U.S.A. **64** C5 42 07N 77 56W
Wels Austria **81** B4 48 10N 14 02E
Wembley England **82** B3 51 33N 0 18W
Wensum *r.* England **78** M4 52 45N 1 10E
Wenyu He *r.* China **101** H2 40 20N 116 32E
Wenzhou China **97** N4 28 02N 120 40E
Werder Germany **83** D1 52 23N 12 56E
Wernersville Pennsylvania U.S.A. **64** D3 40 19N 76 06W
Wertach *r.* Germany **76** H1 48 00N 10 00E
Weser *r.* Germany **76** D5 53 00N 8 00E
West Antarctica *geog. reg.* Antarctica **117** 80 00S 120 00W
West Australian Basin Indian Ocean **112** I4 J5 20 00S 100 00E
West Bank *territory* Israel **92** O11 32 00N 35 00E
West Bengal *admin.* India **95** F4 22 00N 88 00E
West Branch Michigan U.S.A. **36** B5 44 16N 84 14W
West Branch Delaware River *r.* New York U.S.A. **64** E5 42 15N 75 00W
West Branch Susquehanna River Pennsylvania U.S.A. **64** B4 41 00N 78 00W
Westby Montana U.S.A. **40** C1 48 32N 104 06W
West Caroline Basin Pacific Ocean **114** D8 3 00N 136 00E
Westchester Illinois U.S.A. **53** A2 41 50N 87 53W
West Chester Pennsylvania U.S.A. **64** E2 39 58N 75 37W
West Covina California U.S.A. **51** C3 34 04N 117 56W
West Dvina *see* Zap Dvina
Westerly Rhode Island U.S.A. **65** J4 41 22N 71 50W
Western Australia *state* Australia **110** C4/C5 25 00S 117 00E
Western Desert Egypt **102** 30 00N 30 00E
Western Ghats *mts.* India **95** C3/C2 15 30N 74 00E
WESTERN SAHARA **106** C12
WESTERN SAMOA **114/115** I6
Western Sayan *mts.* Russia **91** O5 52 30N 92 30E
Western Springs Illinois U.S.A. **53** A2 41 48N 87 54W
Western Yamuna Canal India **94** L4 28 40N 77 08E
Westerwald *geog. reg.* Germany **76** D5 50 00N 8 00E
West European Basin Atlantic Ocean **113** G11 47 00N 18 00W
West Falkland *i.* Falkland Islands **69** E2/F2 51 00S 60 40W
Westfield Massachusetts U.S.A. **65** H5 42 07N 72 45W
West Frisian Islands *see* Waddeneilanden
West Grand Lake Maine U.S.A. **31** A2 45 15N 68 00W
West Ham England **82** D3 51 32N 0 01E
Westhope North Dakota U.S.A. **39** A1 48 56N 101 02W
West Hurley New York U.S.A. **65** F4 41 59N 74 06W
West Ice Shelf Antarctica **117** 66 00S 85 00E
West Indies *is.* Caribbean Sea **67** J4/K4 22 00N 69 00W
West Kingsdown Kent England **82** D2 51 20N 0 16E
Westlake Ohio U.S.A. **36** E2 41 25N 81 54W
West Lamma Channel Hong Kong U.K. **98** B1 22 10N 114 00E
Westland Michigan U.S.A. **52** D2 42 18N 83 25W
West Los Angeles California U.S.A. **51** A3 34 02N 118 25W
West Marianas Basin Pacific Ocean **114** D9 16 00N 137 30E
West Memphis Arkansas U.S.A. **63** A4 35 09N 90 11W
Westminster California U.S.A. **51** C2 33 45N 117 59W
Westminster Maryland U.S.A. **64** C2 39 35N 77 00W
Westminster *bor.* England **82** C2 51 30N 0 09W
Westmoreland County Pennsylvania U.S.A. **53** E1 40 18N 79 48W
Weston Massachusetts U.S.A. **52** A2 42 21N 71 18W
West Palm Beach *tn.* Florida U.S.A. **63** J2 26 42N 80 05W
West Plains *tn.* Missouri U.S.A. **63** H4 36 44N 91 51W
West Point *tn.* New York U.S.A. **65** G4 41 23N 73 58W
Westport Connecticut U.S.A. **65** G4 41 09N 73 22W
Westport Irish Republic **78** B5 53 48N 9 32W
Westray *i.* Scotland **78** I11 59 18N 3 00W
West Rift Valley Africa **102** 0 00 30 00E
West Scotia Basin Southern Ocean **117** 58 00S 52 00W
West Siberian Lowland Russia **91** L7 M6 60 00N 75 00E
West Springfield Massachusetts U.S.A. **65** H5 42 06N 72 38W
West View Pennsylvania U.S.A. **53** D2 40 32N 80 03W
West Virginia *state* U.S.A. **63** J4 39 00N 81 00W
West Winfield New York U.S.A. **64** E5 42 53N 75 16W
Wetar *i.* Indonesia **99** H2 7 30S 126 30E
Wewak Papua New Guinea **110** G9 3 35S 143 35E
Wexford Irish Republic **78** E4 52 20N 6 27W
Wey *r.* England **82** B2 51 18N 0 30W
Weybridge England **82** B2 51 22N 0 28W
Weymouth England **78** I2 50 37N 2 25W
Weymouth Massachusetts U.S.A. **52** C1 42 14N 71 58W
Whakatane New Zealand **111** C3 37 56S 177 00E
Whangarei New Zealand **111** B3 35 43S 174 20E
Wharfe *r.* England **78** 53 50N 1 50W
Wharton Basin Indian Ocean **112** I5 J5 15 00S 100 00E
Whatcom, Lake Washington U.S.A. **42** H4 48 40N 122 20W
Wheeler Lake Alabama U.S.A. **63** I3 34 00N 87 00W
Wheeling West Virginia U.S.A. **63** J5 40 05N 80 43W
Whidbey Island Washington U.S.A. **42** H4 48 20N 122 40W
White *r.* U.S.A. **63** H4 35 00N 92 00W
Whitefish Montana U.S.A. **43** F1 48 25N 114 21W
Whitefish Bay Michigan U.S.A./Ontario Canada **36** B7 46 40N 84 45W
Whitehaven England **78** H6 54 33N 3 35W
White Nile *see* Bahr el Abiad
White Nile *see* Bahr el Jebel
White Nile Dam Sudan **92** D2 14 18N 32 30E
White Oak Park Pennsylvania U.S.A. **53** E1 40 20N 79 48W
White Plains New York U.S.A. **65** G4 41 02N 73 46W
White Sea Russia **88** F9 66 00N 37 30E
White Volta *r.* Ghana **106** E10 9 30N 1 30W
Whitewater *tn.* Montana U.S.A. **40** B1 48 46N 107 38W
Whitewater Creek Montana U.S.A./Canada **40** B1 48 50N 107 40W
Whiting Illinois U.S.A. **53** C1 41 41N 87 32W
Whitmans Ponds Massachusetts U.S.A. **52** C1 42 05N 70 55W
Whitney Point *tn.* New York U.S.A. **64** E5 42 20N 75 58W
Whitney Point Lake New York U.S.A. **64** E5 42 20N 76 00W
Whitney Woods Reservoir Massachusetts U.S.A. **52** C1 42 14N 70 52W
Whittier California U.S.A. **51** B2 33 58N 118 02W
Whyalla Australia **110** F3 33 04S 137 34E
Wichita Kansas U.S.A. **63** G4 37 43N 97 20W
Wichita *r.* Texas U.S.A. **62** F3 33 00N 100 00W
Wichita Falls *tn.* Texas U.S.A. **62** G3 33 55N 98 30W
Wick Higland Scotland **78** H10 58 26N 3 06W
Wickliffe Ohio U.S.A. **36** E2 41 38N 81 25W
Wicklow Mountains Irish Republic **78** E5 53 00N 6 20W
Wien *(Vienna)* Austria **81** C4 48 13N 16 22E
Wiener Neustadt Austria **81** C4 47 49N 16 15E
Wieprz *r.* Poland **80** D5 51 00N 23 00E
Wiesbaden Germany **76** D5 50 05N 8 15E
Wiessensee *l.* Germany **83** F2 52 35N 13 28E
Wigan England **78** I5 53 33N 2 38W
Wilcox Pennsylvania U.S.A. **64** B4 41 36N 78 40W
Wildau Germany **83** G1 52 18N 13 38E
Wildcat Canyon Regional Park California U.S.A. **49** B3 37 57N 122 17W
Wildcat Creek California U.S.A. **49** B3 37 57N 122 19W
Wildrose North Dakota U.S.A. **40** C1 48 39N 103 11W
Wildwood New Jersey U.S.A. **65** F1 38 59N 74 49W
Wilhelmshaven Germany **76** D5 53 32N 8 07E
Wilkes-Barre Pennsylvania U.S.A. **64** E4 41 15N 75 50W
Wilkes Land *geog. reg.* Antarctica **117** 68 00S 105 00E
Wilkinsburg Pennsylvania U.S.A. **53** E1 40 27N 79 53W
Willard New York U.S.A. **64** D5 42 38N 76 50W
Will County Illinois U.S.A. **53** A1 41 38N 87 59W

Willemstad Curaçao 67 K2 12 12N 68 56W
Willesden England 82 C3 51 33N 0 14W
Williams Minnesota U.S.A. 39 C1 48 47N 94 56W
Williamsport Pennsylvania U.S.A. 64 C4 41 16N 77 03W
Williamstown New Jersey U.S.A. 64 F2 39 41N 74 59W
Willimantic Connecticut U.S.A. 65 H4 41 43N 72 12W
Williston North Dakota U.S.A. 62 F6 48 09N 103 39W
Willoughby Hills Ohio U.S.A. 36 E2 41 35N 81 29W
Willow Creek Montana U.S.A. 41 C1 48 55N 111 30W
Willow Grove Pennsylvania U.S.A. 64 E3 40 08N 75 7W
Willow River Michigan U.S.A. 36 D4 43 50N 82 58W
Willow Springs tn. Missouri U.S.A. 63 H4 36 59N 91 59W
Willmar Minnesota U.S.A. 63 G6 45 06N 95 03W
Wilmersdorf Germany 83 F1 52 28N 13 16E
Wilmette Illinois U.S.A. 53 A3 42 04N 87 43W
Wilmington Delaware U.S.A. 64 E2 39 46N 75 31W
Wilmington North Carolina U.S.A. 63 K3 34 14N 77 55W
Wilmington Vermont U.S.A. 65 H5 42 52N 72 53W
Wilson North Carolina U.S.A. 63 K4 35 43N 77 56W
Wiluna Australia 110 C4 26 37S 120 12E
Wimbledon England 82 C2 51 25N 0 13W
Winchendon Massachusetts U.S.A. 65 H5 42 41N 72 04W
Winchester England 78 J3 51 04N 1 19W
Winchester Massachusetts U.S.A. 52 B2 42 26N 71 08W
Winchester New Hampshire U.S.A. 65 H5 42 46N 72 24W
Winchester Virginia U.S.A. 64 B2 39 11N 78 12W
Windber Pennsylvania U.S.A. 64 B3 40 16N 78 51W
Windhoek Namibia 107 I3 22 34S 17 06E
Wind River Ranges mts. Wyoming U.S.A. 62 E5 43 00N 109 00W
Windsor England 82 A2 51 29N 0 38W
Windsor Connecticut U.S.A. 65 H4 41 52N 72 38W
Windsor Locks Connecticut U.S.A. 65 H4 41 56N 72 37W
Windward Islands Lesser Antilles 67 L2 12 30N 62 00W
Windward Passage sd. Cuba/Haiti 67 J3/J4 20 00N 73 00W
Winnemucca Nevada U.S.A. 62 C5 40 58N 117 45W
Winnetka Illinois U.S.A. 53 B3 42 06N 87 46W
Winona Minnesota U.S.A. 63 H5 44 02N 91 37W
Winslow Arizona U.S.A. 62 D4 35 01N 110 43W
Winsted Connecticut U.S.A. 65 G4 41 55N 73 04W
Winston-Salem North Carolina U.S.A. 63 J4 36 05N 80 18W
Winterthur Switzerland 77 D4 47 30N 8 45E
Winthrop Massachusetts U.S.A. 52 C2 42 23N 70 59W
Winthrop Washington U.S.A. 42 H4 48 29N 120 11W
Winton Australia 110 G5 22 22S 143 00E
Wisconsin state U.S.A. 63 H6 45 00N 90 00W
Wisconsin River Wisconsin U.S.A. 63 H6 4500N 90 00W
Wisła r. Poland 80 C5 53 00N 19 00E
Wisłok r. Poland 80 D5 50 00N 22 00E
Wismar Germany 76 E5 53 54N 11 28E
Witham r. England 78 K5 53 05N 0 10W
Witten Germany 76 K2 51 25N 7 19E
Wittenberg Germany 76 E5 51 53N 12 39E
Wittenberge Germany 76 E5 52 59N 11 45E
Włocławek Poland 80 C5 52 39N 19 01E
Woburn Massachusetts U.S.A. 52 B2 42 27N 71 09W
Woking England 82 A2 51 20N 0 34W
Wolcott New York U.S.A. 64 D6 43 14N 76 51W
Wolf Lake State Park and Conservation Indiana U.S.A. 53 C1 41 40N 87 30W
Wolfsberg Austria 81 B4 46 50N 14 50E
Wolfsburg Germany 76 E5 52 27N 10 49E
Wollongong Australia 110 I3 34 25S 150 52E
Wolverton England 78 I4 52 04N 0 50W
Wompah Australia 110 G4 29 04S 142 05E
Wompatuck State Park Massachusetts U.S.A. 52 C1 42 12N 70 52W
Wong Chuk Hang Hong Kong U.K. 98 C1 22 15N 114 10E
Wong Chuk Yuen Hong Kong U.K. 98 B2 22 26N 114 06E
Wŏnju South Korea 97 P6 37 24N 127 52E
Wŏnsan North Korea 97 P6 39 07N 127 26E
Woodbine New Jersey U.S.A. 64 F2 39 14N 74 49W
Woodbridge New Jersey U.S.A. 50 A1 40 33N 74 16W
Woodbury Connecticut U.S.A. 65 G4 41 32N 73 12W
Woodbury New Jersey U.S.A. 64 E2 39 50N 75 09W
Woodford England 82 D3 51 37N 0 02E
Woodlark Island Papua New Guinea 110 I8 9 00S 152 30E
Woodport New Jersey U.S.A. 65 F3 40 59N 74 37W
Woodside California U.S.A. 49 B1 37 26N 122 15W
Woods, Lake of the Canada/USA 34 B2 49 00N 94 00W
Woodstock Virginia U.S.A. 64 B1 38 55N 78 31W
Woodstown New Jersey U.S.A. 64 E2 39 39N 75 19W
Woodville New Zealand 111 C2 40 20S 175 54E
Woodward Oklahoma U.S.A. 62 G4 36 26N 99 25W
Woollahra Australia 111 H2 33 53S 151 15E
Woolwich England 82 D2 51 29N 0 04E
Woonsocket Rhode Island U.S.A. 65 J5 42 00N 71 30W
Wooster Ohio U.S.A. 36 E1 40 46N 81 57W
Worcester England 78 I4 52 11N 2 13W
Worcester Massachusetts U.S.A. 65 J5 42 17N 71 48W
Worcester New York U.S.A. 65 F5 42 36N 74 44W
Worcester Republic of South Africa 107 I1 33 39S 19 26E
Workington England 78 H6 54 39N 3 33W
Worland Wyoming U.S.A. 62 E5 44 01N 107 58W
Woronora Reservoir Australia 111 F1 34 07S 150 56E
Woronora River Australia 111 G1 34 07S 151 00E
Worth Illinois U.S.A. 53 A1 41 40N 87 48W
Worthing Barbados 66 V12 13 05N 59 35W
Worthing England 78 K2 50 48N 0 23W
Worthington Minnesota U.S.A. 63 G5 43 37N 95 36W
Wrangell Alaska U.S.A. 42 B3 56 28N 132 23W
Wrangell Island Alaska U.S.A. 42 B3 56 25N 132 05W
Wrangell Mountains Alaska U.S.A. 44 C3 62 00N 143 00W
Wrangell St. Elias National Park Alaska U.S.A. 44 C3 63 00N 143 00W
Wrath, Cape Scotland 78 G10 58 37N 5 01W
Wrexham Wales 78 H5 53 03N 3 00W
Wright Peak Antarctica 117 73 15S 94 00W
Wrights Corners New York U.S.A. 64 B6 43 12N 78 40W
Wrightsville Pennsylvania U.S.A. 64 D3 40 02N 76 3W
Wrocław Poland 80 C5 51 05N 17 00E
Wuhai China 97 L6 39 40N 106 40E
Wuhan China 97 M5 30 35N 114 19E
Wuhu China 97 N5 31 23N 118 25E
Wukari Nigeria 106 G9 7 49N 9 49E
Wuppertal Germany 76 D5 51 15N 7 10E
Wurtsboro New York U.S.A. 65 F4 41 33N 74 29W
Würzburg Germany 76 E4 49 48N 9 57E
Wusul Jiang (Ussuri) r. China 97 Q8 47 00N 134 00E
Wutongqiao China 97 K4 29 21N 103 48E
Wuxi China 97 N5 31 35N 120 19E
Wuyi Shan mts. China 97 N4 26 00N 116 30E
Wuzhou China 97 M3 23 30N 111 21E
Wyandotte Michigan U.S.A. 52 E1 42 11N 83 10W
Wye r. England 78 H4 1 58N 2 35W
Wyndham Australia 110 D6 15 30S 128 09E
Wyoming state U.S.A. 62 E5 43 00N 108 00W

X

Xaafuun Somalia 106 P10 10 27N 51 15E
Xaidulla China 95 D7 36 27N 77 46E
Xam Nua Laos 97 K3 20 25N 103 50W
Xánthi Greece 81 D3 41 07N 24 56E
Xiaguan China 97 K4 25 33N 100 09E
Xiamen China 97 N3 24 28N 118 05E
Xi'an China 97 L5 34 16N 108 54E
Xiangfan China 97 M5 32 05N 112 03E
Xiangtan China 97 M4 27 48N 112 55E
Xianyang China 97 L5 34 22N 108 42E
Xianyou China 98 E8 25 23N 118 40E
Xieng Khouang Laos 99 C7 19 21N 103 23E
Xigaze China 96 G4 29 18N 88 50E
Xi Jiang r. China 97 M3 23 30N 111 00E
Xingtai China 96 M6 37 08N 114 29E
Xining China 97 K6 36 35N 101 55E
Xinjiang Uygur Zizhiqu (Sinkiang Uighur Autonomous Region) admin. China 96 F6/G7 41 00N 85 00E
Xinjin China 97 O6 39 25N 121 58E
Xiqing Shan mts. China 97 K5 34 00N 102 30E
Xizang Zizhiqu (Tibet Autonomous Region) admin. China 96 F5/G5 33 30N 85 00E
Xizhuang China 101 G1 39 51N 116 20E
Xochimiko Mexico 66 E3 19 08N 99 09W
Xuanhua China 97 N7 40 36N 115 01E
Xuchang China 97 M5 34 03N 113 48E
Xuwen China 97 M3 20 25N 110 08E
Xuzhou China 97 N5 34 17N 117 18E

Y

Yaba Nigeria 107 V3 6 29N 3 27E
Yablonovy Range mts. Russia 89 M6/N6 51 30N 110 00E
Yakima r. Washington U.S.A. 62 B6 47 00N 120 00W
Yakutat Alaska U.S.A. 42 A3 59 29N 139 49W
Yakutat Bay Alaska U.S.A. 42 A3 59 50N 140 00W
Yakutsk Russia 89 O8 62 10N 129 50E
Yalu r. China/North Korea 97 P7 42 00N 127 00E
Yamagata Japan 100 D2 38 16N 140 19E
Yamaguchi Japan 100 B1 34 10N 131 28E
Yamal Peninsula Russia 89 I10/J10 72 00N 70 00E
Yamanashi pref. Japan 100 K2 35 40N 138 48E
Yamato Japan 101 A2 35 29N 139 27E
Yamato-takada Japan 100 G1 34 31N 135 43E
Yambol Bulgaria 81 E3 42 28N 26 30E
Yamburg Russia 89 68 19N 77 09E
Yamoussoukro Côte d'Ivoire 106 D9 6 50N 5 20W
Yamuna r. India 94 L4 28 43N 17 13E
Yamunanagar India 95 D6 30 07N 77 17E
Yana r. Russia 89 P9 69 00N 135 00E
Yanbu'al Baçr Saudi Arabia 92 E3 24 07N 38 04E
Yancheng China 97 O5 33 23N 120 10E
Yangon see Rangoon
Yangquan China 97 M6 37 52N 113 29E
Yangtse see Jinsha Jiang or Chang Jiang
Yanji China 97 P7 42 52N 129 32E
Yanjing China 97 J4 29 01N 98 38E
Yankton South Dakota U.S.A. 63 G5 42 53N 97 24W
Yantai China 97 O6 37 30N 121 22E
Yao Japan 100 C1 34 36N 135 37E
Yaotsu Japan 100 J2 35 29N 137 10E
Yaoundé Cameroon 106 H8 3 51N 11 31E
Yap Islands Pacific Ocean 114 D8 9 30N 138 09E
Yap Trench Pacific Ocean 114 D8 10 00N 139 00E
Yaqui r. Mexico 66 C5 28 00N 109 50W
Yaritagua Venezuela 67 K2 10 05N 69 07W
Yarkant He r. China 89 J3 36 00N 76 00E
Yarlung Zangbo Jiang (Tsangpo) r. China 96 H4 29 00N 92 30E
Yaroslavl' Russia 89 F7 57 34N 39 52E
Yarumal Colombia 68 B14 6 59N 75 25W
Yasawa i. Fiji 114 T16 16 50S 117 30E
Yasawa Group is. Fiji 114 T16 17 00S 177 40E
Yatsushiro Japan 100 B1 32 32N 130 35E
Yau Ma Tei Hong Kong U.K. 98 C1 22 18N 114 10E
Yau Tong Hong Kong U.K. 98 C1 22 18N 114 14E
Yawatahama Japan 100 B1 33 27N 132 24E
Ya Xian China 97 L2 37 10N 119 55E
Yazd Iran 93 H5 31 54N 54 22E
Yazoo r. Mississippi U.S.A. 63 H3 33 00N 90 00W
Ye Myanmar 97 J2 15 15N 97 50E
Yekaterinburg (Sverdlovsk) Russia 91 J6 56 52N 60 35E
Yelets Russia 90 D5 52 35N 38 30E
Yell i. Shetland Islands Scotland 78 J12 60 35N 1 10W
Yellow Sea (Huang Hai) China 97 O6 35 30N 122 30E
Yellowstone r. U.S.A. 62 E6 46 00N 108 00W
Yellowstone Lake Wyoming U.S.A. 62 D5 44 30N 110 20W
Yellowstone National Park Wyoming U.S.A. 62 D5 44 00N 11 30W
YEMEN REPUBLIC 92 F2
Yenakiyevo Ukraine 90 D4 48 14N 38 15E
Yenisey r. Russia 89 K8 65 00N 85 00E
Yenisey, Gulf of Russia 89 J10/K10 72 30N 80 00E
Yeniseysk Russia 91 P6 58 27N 92 13E
Yeppoon Australia 110 I5 23 05S 150 42E
Yerba Buena Island California U.S.A. 49 B3 37 48N 122 21W
Yerevan Armenia 90 E3 40 10N 44 31E
Yermolayevo Russia 91 H5 52 46N 55 54E
Yerres r. France 83 C1 48 40N 2 36E
Yesil r. Turkey 92 E7 41 00N 36 25E
Yeu Myanmar 95 H4 22 49N 95 26E
Yevpatoriya Ukraine 90 C4 45 12N 33 20E
Ye Xian China 97 N6 37 10N 119 55E
Yiannitsá Greece 81 D3 40 46N 22 24E
Yibin China 97 K4 28 42N 104 30E
Yichang China 97 M5 30 46N 111 20E
Yinchuan China 97 L6 38 30N 106 19E
Yingkou China 97 O7 40 40N 122 17E
Ying Pun Hong Kong U.K. 98 B2 22 28N 114 06E
Yining China 96 F7 43 50N 81 28E
Yirga 'Alem Ethiopia 106 M9 6 48N 38 22E
Yiyang China 97 M4 28 39N 112 10E
Yoakum Texas U.S.A. 63 G2 29 18N 97 20W
Yogyakarta Indonesia 99 E2 7 48S 110 24E
Yoichi Japan 100 D3 43 14N 140 47E
Yōka Japan 100 F2 35 25N 134 40E
Yokadouma Cameroon 106 I8 3 26N 15 06E
Yōkaichi Japan 100 H2 35 05N 136 11E
Yōkaichiba Japan 100 M2 35 40N 140 30E
Yokkaichi Japan 100 H1 34 58N 136 38E
Yokohama Japan 101 B2 35 27N 139 38E
Yokosuka Japan 100 L2 35 18N 139 39E
Yokote Japan 100 D2 39 20N 140 31E
Yola Nigeria 106 H9 9 14N 12 32E
Yonago Japan 100 B2 35 27N 133 20E
Yonaguni i. Japan 98 J7 24 29N 123 00E
Yongchun China 98 E8 25 18N 118 13E
Yonkers New York U.S.A. 50 C2 40 56N 73 52W
Yonne r. France 77 C4 48 00N 3 15E
Yorii Japan 100 L3 36 07N 139 12E
York England 78 J5 53 58N 1 05W
York Maine U.S.A. 65 K6 43 00N 70 00W
York Pennsylvania U.S.A. 63 K4 39 57N 76 44W
York, Cape Australia 110 G7 10 42S 142 32E
Yorkshire Wolds hills England 78 K6 54 00N 0 45W
Yoshino-Kumano National Park Japan 100 H1 34 15N 136 00E
Yoshkar-Ola Russia 90 F6 56 38N 47 52E
Yŏsu South Korea 97 P5 34 50N 127 30E
Youghal Irish Republic 78 D3 51 51N 7 50W
You Jiang r. China 97 L3 23 30N 107 00E
Younghiogheny River Pennsylvania U.S.A. 53 E1 40 19N 79 51W
Youngstown New York U.S.A. 38 C2 43 14N 79 01W
Youngstown Ohio U.S.A. 63 J5 41 05N 80 40W
Youngsville Pennsylvania U.S.A. 36 G2 41 52N 79 22W
Ypsilanti Michigan U.S.A. 36 C3 42 15N 83 36W
Yser see Ijzer
Ystad Sweden 80 B6 55 25N 13 50E
Ytterhogdal Sweden 79 C3 623 10N 14 55E
Yuan Jiang r. Asia 84 30 00N 112 00E
Yüan-li Taiwan 98 G7 24 29N 120 40E
Yüan-lin Taiwan 98 G6 23 57N 120 33E
Yūbari Japan 100 D3 43 04N 141 59E
Yucatan p. Mexico 66 G3 19 00N 89 00W
Yucatan Basin Caribbean Sea 115 R9 20 00N 85 00W
Yuci China 97 M6 37 40N 112 44E
Yuen Long Hong Kong U.K. 98 B2 22 26N 114 02E
Yugawara Japan 100 L2 35 09N 139 06E
YUGOSLAVIA 81 C3
Yukagir Plateau Russia 89 R9 66 30N 156 00E
Yü-kitka l. Finland 79 F4 66 15N 28 30E
Yukon Delta Alaska U.S.A. 10 C5 62 45N 164 00W
Yukon Flats National Wildlife Refuge Alaska USA. 44 B4 66 30N 147 30W
Yukon River Canada/U.S.A. 44 D3 63 00N 138 50W
Yü-li Taiwan 98 H6 23 22N 121 20E
Yuma Arizona U.S.A. 62 D3 32 40N 114 39W
Yumen China 96 J6 39 54N 97 43E
Yun (Grand Canal) China 101 H1 39 54N 116 33E
Yung Shue Wan Hong Kong U.K. 98 B1 22 13N 114 06E
Yung-kang Taiwan 98 G5 23 00N 120 15E
Yura-gawa r. Japan 100 G2 35 20N 135 08E
Yurimaguas Peru 68 B11 5 54S 76 07W
Yü Shan mt. Taiwan 98 G6 23 25N 120 52E
Yü Shan National Park Taiwan 98 H6 23 15N 121 00E
Yushu China 95 H6 33 06N 96 48E
Yü-weng Tao i. Taiwan 98 F6 23 36N 119 30E
Yuzhno-Sakhalinsk Russia 89 Q5 46 58N 142 45E
Yuzhnyy Bug r. Ukraine 90 C4 48 00N 30 00E
Yverdon Switzerland 77 D4 46 47N 6 38E
Yvetot France 76 C4 49 37N 0 45E

Z

Zaanstad Netherlands 76 C5 52 27N 4 49E
Zābol Iran 93 J5 31 00N 61 32E
Zabrze Poland 80 C5 50 18N 18 47E
Zacapa Guatemala 66 G3 15 00N 89 30E
Zacatecas Mexico 66 D4 22 48N 102 33W
Zacatecoluca El Salvador 66 G2 13 29N 88 51W
Zadar Croatia 81 C3 44 07N 15 14E
Zafra Spain 77 A2 38 25N 6 25W
Żagań Poland 80 C5 51 37N 15 20E
Zagazig Egypt 92 D5 30 36N 31 30E
Zagorsk see Sergiev Posad
Zagreb (Agram) Croatia 81 C4 45 48N 15 58E
Zagros Mountains Iran 93 G5 32 45N 48 50E
Zāhedān Iran 93 J4 29 32N 60 54E
Zahlé Lebanon 92 O11 33 50N 35 55E
ZAÏRE 106 J7
Zaïre (Congo) r. Zaïre 106 I7 2 00S 17 00E
Zákinthos i. Greece 81 D2 38 00N 20 00E
Zakopane Poland 80 C5 49 17N 19 54E
Zalaegerszeg Hungary 81 C4 46 53N 16 51E
Zal'u Romania 81 D4 47 10N 23 04E
Zaliv Kara Bogaz Gol b. Turkmenistan 90/1 H4 41 30N 53 30E
Zaltan Libya 106 I13 28 15N 19 52E
Zambeze (Zambesi) r. Mozambique 107 L4 16 00S 34 00E
Zambezi (Zambeze) r. Zambia/Zimbabwe 107 J4 16 00S 23 00E
Zambezi Zambia 107 J5 13 33S 23 08E
ZAMBIA 107 K5
Zamboanga The Philippines 99 G5 6 55N 122 05E
Zamora Spain 77 A3 41 30N 5 45W
Zamość Poland 80 D5 50 43N 23 15E
Zanderij Surinam 68 F14 5 26N 55 14W
Zanesville Ohio U.S.A. 63 J4 39 55N 82 02W
Zanjan Iran 93 G6 36 40N 48 30E
Zanthus Australia 110 C3 31 01S 123 32E
Zanzibar Tanzania 107 M6 6 10S 39 12E
Zanzibar i. Tanzania 107 M6 6 10S 39 13E
Zaozhuang China 97 N5 34 53N 117 38E
Zapadnaya (West) Dvina r. Latvia 79 E2 56 45N 24 30E
Zaporozh'ye Ukraine 90 D4 47 50N 35 10E
Zaporozhye Ukraine 90 D4 47 50N 35 10E
Zaragoza Spain 77 B3 41 39N 0 54W
Zarand Iran 93 I5 30 50N 56 35E
Zaraza Venezuela 68 D14 9 23N 65 20W
Zarembo Island Alaska U.S.A. 42 B3 56 30N 132 50W
Zargun mt. Pakistan 94 B6 30 15N 67 11E
Zaria Nigeria 106 G10 11 01N 7 44E
Zarqa Jordan 92 P11 32 04N 36 05E
Zaysan Kazakhstan 91 N4 47 30N 84 57E
Zefat Israel 92 O11 32 57N 35 27E
Zehlendorf Germany 83 F1 52 26N 13 15E
Zell-am-See tn. Austria 81 B4 47 19N 12 47E
Zemlya Frantsa-Iosifa (Franz Josef Land) is. Russia 89 G12-I12 80 00N 50 00E
Zenica Bosnia-Herzegovina 81 C3 44 11N 17 53E
Zepernick Germany 83 G2 52 41N 13 31E
Zernsdorf Germany 83 G1 52 17N 13 42E
Zeya Russia 89 O6 53 48N 127 14E
Zeya r. Russia 89 O6 53 00N 127 30E
Zêzere r. Portugal 77 A2 39 50N 8 05W
Zgierz Poland 80 C5 51 52N 19 25E
Zgorzelec Poland 80 C5 51 10N 15 00E
Zhandov see Mariupol
Zhangjiakou China 97 M7 40 51N 114 59E
Zhangzhou China 97 N2 24 31N 117 40E
Zhanjiang China 97 M3 21 10N 110 20E
Zharma Kazakhstan 91 N4 48 50N 80 50E
Zhdanov see Mariupol
Zhengzhou China 97 M5 34 45N 113 38E
Zhenjiang China 97 N5 32 08N 119 30E
Zhigansk Russia 89 O9 66 48N 123 27E
Zhitomir Ukraine 90 B5 50 18N 28 40E
Zhlobin Belarus 90 B5 52 50N 30 00E
Zhmerinka Ukraine 90 B4 49 00N 28 02E
Zhob Pakistan 94 B6 31 30N 69 30E
Zhonghai l. China 101 G1 39 56N 116 22E
Zhuzhou China 97 M4 27 53N 113 07E
Zibo China 97 N6 36 51N 118 01E
Zielona Góra Poland 80 C5 51 57N 15 30E
Zigong China 97 K4 29 25N 104 47E
Ziguinchor Senegal 106 B10 12 35N 16 20W
ZIMBABWE 107 K4
Zinder Nigeria 106 G10 13 46N 8 58E
Ziqudukou China 96 J5 33 03N 95 51E
Zlatoust Russia 91 H6 55 10N 59 38E
Zlúi (Gottwaldov) Czechoslovakia 80 C4 49 14N 17 40E
Znojmo Czechoslovakia 80 C4 48 52N 16 04E
Zolochev Ukraine 80 D4 49 49N 24 53E
Zomba Malawi 107 M4 15 22S 35 22E
Zouar Chad 106 I12 20 30N 16 30E
Zouérate Mauritania 106 C12 22 44N 12 21W
Zrenjanin Yugoslavia 81 D4 45 22N 20 23E
Zuethener See l. Germany 83 G1 52 20N 13 40E
Zújar r. Spain 77 A2 38 35N 5 30W
Zunyi China 97 L4 27 35N 106 48E
Zürich Switzerland 77 D4 47 23N 8 33E
Zushi Japan 101 B2 35 17N 139 35E
Zvishavane Zimbabwe 107 L3 20 20S 30 02E
Zwickau Germany 76 E5 50 43N 12 30E
Zwolle Netherlands 76 D5 52 31N 6 06E
Zyardów Poland 80 D5 52 02N 20 28E
Zyryanka Russia 89 R9 65 42N 150 49E
Zyryanovsk Kazakhstan 91 N4 49 45N 84 16E

Land

1. Land and Freshwater Area

PROVINCE OR TERRITORY	LAND (km²)	FRESHWATER (km²)	TOTAL (km²)
Newfoundland	371 690	34 030	405 720
Prince Edward Island	5 660	–	5 660
Nova Scotia	52 840	2 650	55 490
New Brunswick	72 090	1 350	73 440
Quebec	1 356 790	183 890	1 540 680
Ontario	891 190	177 390	1 068 580
Manitoba	548 360	101 590	649 950
Saskatchewan	570 700	81 630	652 330
Alberta	644 390	16 800	661 190
British Columbia	929 730	18 070	947 800
Yukon	478 970	4 480	483 450
Northwest Territories	3 293 020	133 300	3 426 320
Canada	**9 215 430**	**755 180**	**9 970 610**

SOURCE: *Canada Year Book 1992*.

2. Primary Land Cover in Canada

LAND COVER CLASS	PREDOMINANT COVER IN THE CLASS	AREA[a] (km², 000s)	% CANADA TOTAL[b]
Forest and taiga	Closed canopy forest and/or open stands of trees with secondary occurrences of wetland, barren land, or others	4 456	45
Tundra/sparse vegetation	Well-vegetated to sparsely vegetated or barren land, mostly in arctic or alpine environments	2 303	23
Wetland	Treed and non-treed fens, bogs, swamps, marshes, shallow open water, and coastal and shore marshes	1 244	12
Freshwater	Lakes, rivers, streams, and reservoirs	755	8
Cropland	Fenced land (including cropland and pasture land), hedge rows, farms, and orchards	658	6
Rangeland	Generally nonfenced pasture land, grazing land; includes natural grassland that is not necessarily used for agriculture	203	2
Ice/snow	Permanent ice and snow fields (glaciers, ice caps)	272	3
Built-up	Urban and industrial land	79	1
Total		**9 970**	**100**

[a]Includes the area of all land and freshwater. [b]Rounded to the nearest percent. NOTE: Data for this table are derived from satellite imagery and may deviate slightly from other sources of data. SOURCE: Energy, Mines and Resources Canada (1989). From *The State of Canada's Environment*, published by the authority of the Minister of the Environment and the Minister of Supply and Services Canada, 1991.

3. Land Activity in Canada

LAND ACTIVITY CLASS	PREDOMINANT ACTIVITY IN THE CLASS	AREA (km², 000s)[a]	% CANADA TOTAL[b]
Forestry	Active forest harvesting or potential for future harvesting	2 440	24
Recreation and conservation	Recreation and conservation within national, provincial, and territorial parks, wildlife reserves, sanctuaries, etc.	708	7
Agriculture	Agriculture on improved farmland (cropland, improved pasture, summerfallow) and unimproved farmland	678	7
Urban/industrial	Residential and industrial activities of urban environments	72[c]	1
Other activities	Includes hunting and trapping, mining, energy developments, and transportation	6 072	61
Total		**9 970**	**100**

[a] Includes the area of land and freshwater. [b]Rounded to the nearest percent. [c] Includes only the 25 major metropolitan areas. SOURCE: Environment Canada (1985). From *The State of Canada's Environment*, published by the authority of the Minister of the Environment and the Minister of Supply and Services Canada, 1991.

Population

4. Total Population Growth, 1851 to 1991

CENSUS YEAR	POPULATION (000)	AVERAGE ANNUAL RATE OF POPULATION GROWTH (%)
1851	2 436.3	—
1861	3 229.6	2.9
1871	3 689.3	1.3
1881	4 324.8	1.6
1891	4 833.2	1.1
1901	5 371.3	1.1
1911	7 206.6	3.0
1921	8 787.9	2.0
1931	10 376.8	1.7
1941	11 506.7	1.0
1951[1]	14 009.4	1.7
1961	18 238.2	2.5
1971	21 568.3	1.5
1981	24 343.2	1.1
1991[2]	27 296.9	1.5

[1]Newfoundland included for the first time. [2]1991 Census SOURCE: *Canada Year Book 1992*. and 1991 Census

186

5. Population Growth, 1961 to 1991, and Population Density, 1991

PROVINCE OR TERRITORY	1961	1971	1981	1991[1]	POPULATION DENSITY/KM² 1991
Newfoundland	457 853	522 104	567 181	568 474	1.4
Prince Edward Island	104 629	111 641	122 506	129 765	22.9
Nova Scotia	737 007	788 960	847 882	899 942	16.2
New Brunswick	597 936	634 557	696 403	723 900	9.9
Quebec	5 259 211	6 027 764	6 438 403	6 895 963	4.5
Ontario	6 236 092	7 703 106	8 625 107	10 084 885	9.4
Manitoba	921 686	988 247	1 026 241	1 091 942	1.7
Saskatchewan	925 181	926 242	968 313	988 928	1.5
Alberta	1 331 944	1 627 874	2 237 724	2 545 553	3.8
British Columbia	1 629 082	2 184 021	2 744 467	3 282 061	3.5
Yukon	14 628	18 388	23 153	27 797	0.06
Northwest Territories	22 998	34 807	45 741	57 649	0.02
Canada	**18 238 247**	**21 568 310**	**24 343 181**	**27 296 859**	**2.7**

SOURCE: *Canada Year Book*, various years; 1991 Census, *A National Overview*, Statistics Canada, April 1992.

6. Births, Deaths, and Migration Rates, 1990, and Infant Mortality and Life Expectancy, 1989

DEMOGRAPHIC CATEGORY	NFLD	PEI	NS	NB	QUE	ONT	MAN	SASK	ALTA	BC	YUKON	NWT	**CANADA**
BirthRate/1000	12.8	14.4	14.1	13.6	14.1	15.2	16.0	16.6	17.5	14.2	19.4	27.6	**15.0**
Death Rate/1000	6.5	8.5	8.5	7.6	7.2	7.4	8.3	8.2	5.6	7.4	4.6	3.9	**7.3**
Immigration Rate/1000	1.0	1.3	1.7	1.1	5.9	11.5	6.1	2.4	7.6	9.1	3.2	1.5	**8.0**
Emigration Rate/1000	0.4	0.4	0.4	1.0	0.7	1.9	1.6	0.8	2.3	1.6	1.4	0.9	**1.4**
Interprovincial In-migration/1000	17.2	23.7	24.2	22.9	4.9	9.6	18.3	20.3	31.4	28.3	99.8	72.7	**14.7**
Interprovincial Out-migration/1000	25.2	35.3	24.6	23.5	6.3	10.5	26.4	35.7	27.9	15.3	94.3	82.1	**14.7**
Infant Mortality/1000	8.2	6.2	5.8	7.1	6.8	6.8	6.6	8.0	7.5	8.2	4.2	16.2	**7.1**
Life Expectancy at birth (in years) M	73.3	72.9	72.6	73.3	72.7	74.0	73.6	74.3	74.3	74.4	n.a.	n.a.	**73.6**
F	79.4	81.1	79.7	80.3	80.3	80.2	80.5	81.3	80.7	80.8	n.a.	n.a.	**80.3**

n.a.—not available
SOURCE: *Quarterly Demographic Statistics*, Oct.–Dec. 1990, April 1991, Statistics Canada, and *Report on the Demographic Situation in Canada 1991*, Statistics Canada, Dec. 1991.

7. Population by First Language, 1981 and 1986

OFFICIAL LANGUAGE	1981[1] NUMBER	%	1986 NUMBER	%
English	14 684 365	60.3	15 334 085	60.6
French	6 127 530	25.2	6 159 740	24.3
NON-OFFICIAL LANGUAGE				
Aboriginal	150 235	0.6	138 060	0.5
Italian	499 920	2.1	455 820	1.8
Portuguese	159 295	0.7	153 985	0.6
Spanish	64 575	0.3	83 130	0.3
German[2]	485 375	2.0	438 680	1.7
Yiddish	27 945	0.1	22 665	0.1
Dutch	136 500	0.6	123 670	0.5
Ukrainian	258 575	1.1	208 415	0.8
Russian	28 525	0.1	24 860	0.1
Polish	116 095	0.5	123 120	0.5
Finnish	31 130	0.1	25 770	0.1
Hungarian	77 630	0.3	69 000	0.3
Greek	116 835	0.5	110 350	0.4
Arabic[3]	44 425	0.2	40 665	0.2
Punjabi	49 670	0.2	63 640	0.3
Chinese	212 785	0.9	266 560	1.1
Vietnamese	28 325	0.1	41 560	0.2
Tagalog (Filipino)	36 195	0.1	42 420	0.2
Other Languages	409 270	1.7	428 205	1.7
Sub-total Single Response	23 745 200	97.5	24 354 390	96.2
Multiple Response	597 980	2.5	954 940	3.8
Canada[4]	**24 343 180**	**100.0**	**25 309 330**	**100.0**

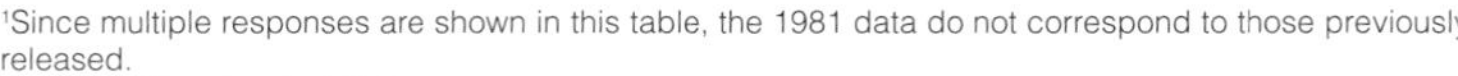

[1]Since multiple responses are shown in this table, the 1981 data do not correspond to those previously released.
[2]Includes Alsacians in 1986.
[3]Includes Maltese in 1981.
[4]The figures for 1986 exclude the population on 136 incompletely enumerated Native reserves and settlements. The total population on these reserves was estimated to be about 45 000 in 1986.
SOURCE: *Canada Year Book 1988*.

8. Components of Population Growth, 1960 to 1990

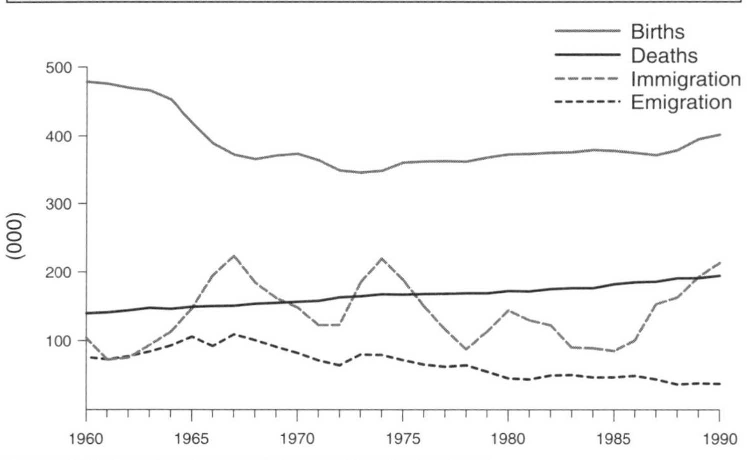

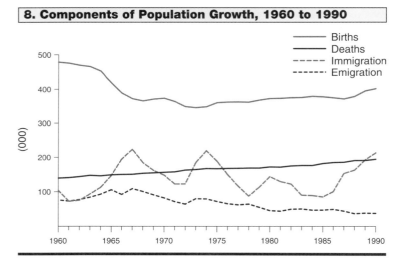

SOURCE: Statistics Canada, Demography Division.

9. Percentage of People Who Are Bilingual (English and French), 1971 and 1986

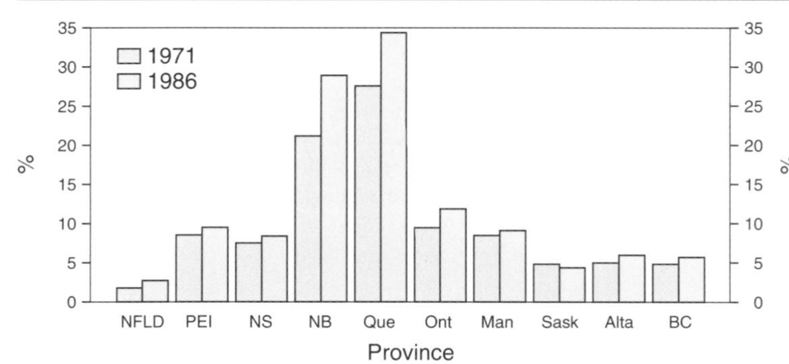

SOURCE: Statistics Canada, *Market Research Handbook*, 1991

10. Population of Census Metropolitan Areas, 1961 to 1991

CENSUS METROPOLITAN AREA	km²	1961	1971	1981[1,2]	1991[3]
Calgary	5 056	279 062	403 319	625 966	754 033
Chicoutimi-Jonquière	1 723	127 616	133 703	158 229	160 928
Edmonton	11 397	359 821	495 702	740 882	839 924
Halifax	2 508	193 353	222 637	277 727	320 501
Hamilton	1 358	401 071	498 523	542 095	599 760
Kitchener	824	154 864	226 846	287 801	356 421
London	2 105	226 669	286 011	326 817	381 522
Montreal	3 509	2 215 627	2 743 208	2 862 286	3 127 242
Oshawa	894	—	120 318[1]	186 446	240 104
Ottawa-Hull	5 138	457 038	602 510	743 821	920 857
Quebec	3 150	379 067	480 502	583 820	645 550
Regina	3 422	113 749	140 734	173 226	191 692
Saint John	2 905	98 083	106 744	121 012	124 981
St. Catharines-Niagara	1 400	257 796	303 429	342 645	364 552
St. John's	1 130	106 666	131 814	154 835	171 859
Saskatoon	4 749	95 564	126 449	175 058	210 023
Sherbrooke	916	—	—	125 183	139 194
Sudbury	2 612	127 446	155 424	156 121	157 613
Thunder Bay	2 203	102 085	112 093	121 948	124 427
Toronto	5 614	1 919 409	2 628 043	3 130 392	3 893 046
Trois-Rivières	872	—	—	125 343	136 303
Vancouver	2 786	826 798	1 082 352	1 268 183	1 602 502
Victoria	1 951	155 763	195 800	241 450	287 897
Windsor	862	217 215	258 643	250 885	262 075
Winnipeg	3 295	476 543	540 262	592 061	652 354

—not applicable
[1] Adjusted due to boundary changes
[2] Based on 1986 Census Metropolitan Area
[3] 1991 Census.
SOURCE: Canada Year Book 1988 and 1992; Statistics Canada, Canada's Population From Ocean to Ocean, Cat. No. 98-120.

11. Population by Ethnic Origin, 1986

PROVINCE OR TERRITORY	BRITISH	FRENCH	DUTCH	GERMAN	ITALIAN	ABORIGINAL PEOPLES	POLISH	SCANDINAVIAN	UKRAINIAN	OTHER SINGLE ORIGINS	MULTIPLE ORIGINS	TOTAL
Newfoundland	449 760	11 315	400	1 155	235	3 825	200	265	105	96 745	93 725	564 005
Total % Distribution	79.7	2.0	0.1	0.2	—	0.7	—	—	—	17.2	16.6	100.0
Prince Edward Island	59 275	11 135	1 275	540	75	415	100	135	65	52 075	50 980	125 090
Total % Distribution	47.4	8.9	1.0	0.4	0.1	0.3	0.1	0.1	0.1	41.6	40.8	100.0
Nova Scotia	417 685	52 905	9 320	21 205	2 260	5 960	1 845	1 230	1 435	350 305	328 245	864 150
Total % Distribution	48.3	6.1	1.1	2.5	0.3	0.7	0.2	0.1	0.2	40.5	38.0	100.0
New Brunswick	251 315	232 575	2 895	3 755	865	3 880	380	1 215	490	204 485	197 505	701 855
Total % Distribution	35.8	33.1	0.4	0.5	0.1	0.6	0.1	0.2	0.1	29.1	28.1	100.0
Quebec	319 550	5 015 565	6 365	26 785	163 875	49 320	18 835	2 540	12 220	839 430	444 480	6 454 485
Total % Distribution	5.0	77.7	0.1	0.4	2.5	0.8	0.3	—	0.2	13.0	6.9	100.0
Ontario	2 912 830	531 575	171 155	285 155	461 375	55 560	117 580	26 755	109 705	4 329 480	3 049 065	9 001 170
Total % Distribution	32.4	5.9	1.9	3.2	5.1	0.6	1.3	0.3	1.2	48.1	33.9	100.0
Manitoba	224 375	55 725	27 875	96 165	8 225	55 415	22 015	14 835	79 940	464 750	367 740	1 049 320
Total % Distribution	21.4	5.3	2.7	9.2	0.8	5.3	2.1	1.4	7.6	44.3	35.0	100.0
Saskatchewan	222 120	33 540	13 020	128 850	1 950	55 645	13 325	24 895	60 550	442 805	391 950	996 700
Total % Distribution	22.3	3.4	1.3	12.9	0.2	5.6	1.3	2.5	6.1	44.4	39.3	100.0
Alberta	592 345	77 585	55 920	182 865	23 635	51 665	28 505	46 525	106 760	1 174 460	950 330	2 340 265
Total % Distribution	25.3	3.3	2.4	7.8	1.0	2.2	1.2	2.0	4.6	50.2	40.6	100.0
British Columbia	871 075	68 965	62 945	148 280	46 755	61 125	19 305	52 565	48 195	1 470 375	1 089 775	2 849 585
Total % Distribution	30.6	2.4	2.2	5.2	1.6	2.1	0.7	1.8	1.7	51.6	38.2	100.0
Yukon	5 370	775	350	880	75	3 275	80	445	345	11 765	10 505	23 360
Total % Distribution	23.0	3.3	1.5	3.8	0.3	14.0	0.3	1.9	1.5	50.4	45.0	100.0
Northwest Territories	7 015	1 510	240	1 085	255	27 175	100	305	395	13 940	12 045	52 020
Total % Distribution	13.5	2.9	0.5	2.1	0.5	52.2	0.2	0.6	0.8	26.8	23.2	100.0
Canada	**6 332 725**	**6 093 165**	**351 765**	**896 715**	**709 590**	**373 265**	**222 260**	**171 715**	**420 210**	**9 450 595**	**6 986 345**	**25 022 005**
Total % Distribution	**25.3**	**24.4**	**1.4**	**3.6**	**2.8**	**1.5**	**0.9**	**0.7**	**1.7**	**37.8**	**27.9**	**100.0**

SOURCE: Statistics Canada, Ethnicity, Immigration and Citizenship, Cat. No. 93-109, 1986 Census of Canada.

12. Percentage of Population in Urban Areas, 1851 to 1991

PROVINCE	1851	1871	1891	1911	1931	1951	1971	1991
Newfoundland	—	—	—	—	—	43.3	57.2	53.6
Prince Edward Island	—	9.4	13.1	16.0	19.5	25.1	38.3	39.9
Nova Scotia	7.5	8.3	19.4	36.7	46.6	54.5	56.7	53.5
New Brunswick	14.0	17.6	19.9	26.7	35.4	42.8	56.9	47.7
Quebec	14.9	19.9	28.6	44.5	59.5	66.8	80.6	77.6
Ontario	14.0	20.6	35.0	49.5	63.1	72.5	82.4	81.8
Manitoba	—	—	23.3	39.3	45.2	56.0	69.5	72.1
Saskatchewan	—	—	—	16.1	20.3	30.4	53.0	63.0
Alberta	—	—	—	29.4	31.8	47.6	73.5	79.8
British Columbia	—	9.0	42.6	50.9	62.3	68.6	75.7	80.4
Canada	**13.1**	**18.3**	**29.8**	**41.8**	**52.5**	**62.4**	**76.1**	**76.6**

SOURCE: *Urban Development in Canada* by Leroy O. Stone, *1961 Census Monograph*; 1971 Census of Canada; 1991 Census of Canada.

13. Native Population, 1986

PROVINCE OR TERRITORY	POPULATION (000s)			
	NATIVE INDIAN	MÉTIS	INUIT	TOTAL[1]
Newfoundland	4.7	1.4	4.1	9.6
Prince Edward Island	1.1	0.2	0.03	1.3
Nova Scotia	13.1	1.1	0.3	14.2
New Brunswick	8.7	0.8	0.2	9.4
Quebec	68.6	11.4	7.4	80.9
Ontario	150.7	18.3	3.0	167.4
Manitoba	56.0	33.3	0.7	85.2
Saskatchewan	55.2	25.7	0.2	77.7
Alberta	69.0	40.1	1.1	103.9
British Columbia	112.8	15.3	1.0	126.6
Yukon	4.8	0.2	0.07	5.0
Northwest Territories	9.4	3.8	18.4	30.5
Canada	**554.1**	**151.6**	**36.5**	**711.7**

[1]Totals do not add up because some individuals are identified as having more than one Native origin.
SOURCE: 1986 Census of Canada.

14. Registered Indian Population On and Off Reserve, 1991

PROVINCE OR TERRITORY	ON RESERVE	% CHANGE 1986-1991	OFF RESERVE	% CHANGE 1986-1991
Atlantic Provinces	12 752	14.6	7 337	62.9
Quebec	35 693	15.0	14 320	80.8
Ontario	65 537	18.5	52 903	69.3
Manitoba	48 979	18.8	27 229	67.2
Saskatchewan	47 972	23.8	32 750	50.2
Alberta	42 032	20.0	25 209	84.3
British Columbia	49 530	21.2	40 098	55.9
Yukon	3 500	42.1	3 124	74.9
Northwest Territories	10 278	22.4	2 218	218.7
Canada	**316 273**	**19.7**	**205 188**	**66.0**

SOURCE: *1966-1988: Indian Register; 1991-2001: Population Projections of Registered Indians, 1987 to 2011, Preliminary Report*, Department of Indian Affairs and Northern Development, 1989.

15. Numbers of Immigrants and Immigration Rates, Canada, 1944-1990

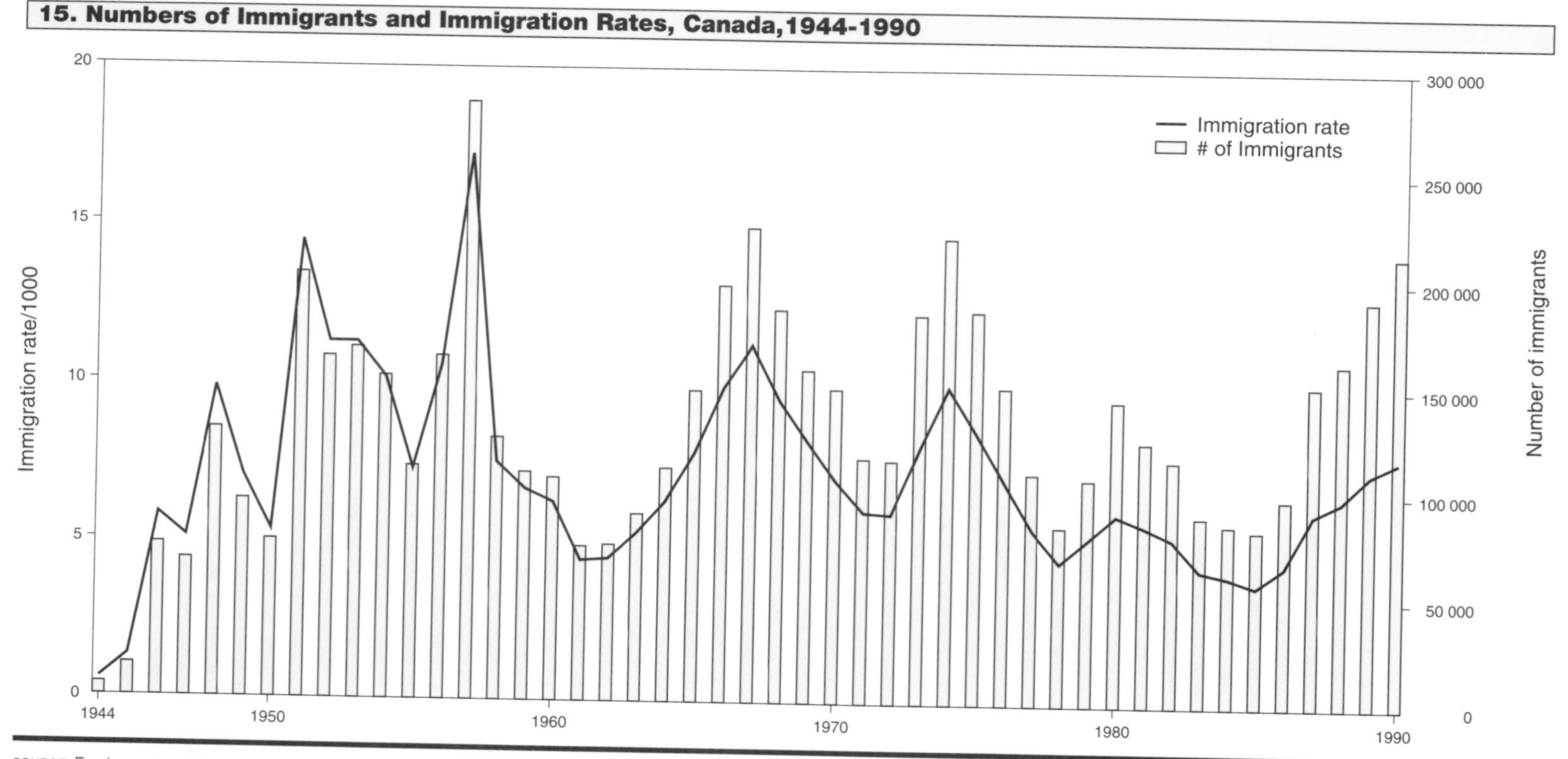

SOURCE: Employment and Immigration Canada, 1990.

16. Population, by Sex and Age Group, 1990

SEX AND AGE	CANADA	NFLD	PEI	NS	NB	QUE	ONT	MAN	SASK	ALTA	BC	YUKON	NWT
						(000)							
Male	**13 104.2**	**285.7**	**64.4**	**437.8**	**357.1**	**3 312.6**	**4 785.0**	**537.4**	**498.0**	**1 237.2**	**1 547.6**	**13.6**	**27.9**
0-4	961.7	19.8	5.0	31.1	25.1	221.7	351.9	43.0	42.5	107.1	109.9	1.3	3.4
5-9	949.1	22.7	5.0	30.8	26.0	231.2	336.4	40.7	41.3	100.6	110.3	1.2	2.9
10-14	938.0	25.7	5.2	31.8	27.9	243.7	325.0	39.3	39.9	91.5	104.5	1.0	2.5
15-19	953.8	27.6	5.3	34.8	29.8	228.8	347.0	41.3	37.4	92.4	105.9	1.0	2.4
20-24	1 016.6	26.3	5.1	36.0	29.4	251.2	376.1	42.3	36.5	98.3	111.8	0.9	2.7
25-29	1 190.4	23.5	5.6	40.3	31.2	306.9	444.8	48.4	41.7	116.0	127.9	1.4	2.8
30-34	1 182.2	23.1	5.3	37.9	30.6	310.4	426.8	46.4	41.6	122.6	133.6	1.5	2.6
35-39	1 082.7	22.9	4.8	34.6	28.9	284.0	386.0	41.5	37.7	108.5	130.2	1.2	2.2
40-44	988.4	21.1	4.6	32.6	27.0	259.2	361.3	36.7	31.0	90.1	121.5	1.2	2.0
45-49	775.9	15.3	3.4	25.0	20.2	212.2	284.2	28.4	24.2	67.2	93.8	0.9	1.3
50-54	636.2	12.3	3.0	20.5	16.2	167.2	238.9	23.9	21.4	54.2	77.2	0.6	0.9
55-59	599.5	11.1	2.7	18.9	14.6	156.3	226.3	23.0	21.4	49.9	74.1	0.5	0.7
60-64	555.3	10.0	2.5	17.1	13.8	142.2	211.5	22.3	20.9	43.5	70.5	0.4	0.5
65-69	475.6	8.6	2.3	15.9	12.8	116.9	180.7	20.4	19.2	34.8	63.5	0.2	0.4
70-74	339.2	7.0	1.9	13.0	9.9	80.3	122.4	15.9	16.1	25.4	47.0	0.1	0.2
75 +	459.6	8.7	2.8	17.5	13.7	100.5	165.7	23.8	25.2	35.2	66.0	0.1	0.2
Female	**13 479.8**	**287.3**	**65.9**	**453.8**	**366.8**	**3 449.7**	**4 946.2**	**552.6**	**502.3**	**1 232.6**	**1 584.1**	**12.3**	**26.2**
0-4	917.9	18.9	4.9	29.9	23.5	211.3	334.6	41.0	40.7	103.1	105.3	1.2	3.5
5-9	902.8	22.1	4.8	29.8	24.9	219.3	320.1	38.4	39.7	95.0	104.8	1.0	2.8
10-14	890.4	24.2	4.9	30.4	26.5	230.0	309.7	37.7	38.0	86.4	99.2	0.9	2.4
15-19	906.6	26.2	4.8	33.0	28.6	217.6	329.2	39.1	35.7	88.3	100.9	1.0	2.4
20-24	981.6	25.7	5.0	34.3	28.2	242.6	362.9	40.2	34.7	95.7	108.8	0.9	2.5
25-29	1 190.8	24.2	5.5	40.1	31.3	304.7	444.7	47.7	41.5	117.1	129.8	1.3	2.8
30-34	1 197.4	24.2	5.4	38.8	31.3	314.7	433.7	45.5	41.0	120.0	139.2	1.4	2.5
35-39	1 101.3	23.6	4.9	35.7	29.8	289.2	399.6	42.1	36.3	104.9	131.9	1.3	2.0
40-44	993.2	21.0	4.7	32.8	26.8	263.1	367.1	36.9	30.5	87.6	120.1	1.1	1.6
45-49	772.9	14.8	3.3	25.1	19.6	214.9	284.1	28.4	24.2	64.7	92.1	0.6	1.0
50-54	639.3	11.9	2.9	20.6	16.2	172.5	240.8	24.2	21.2	52.6	75.2	0.4	0.8
55-59	610.1	10.6	2.6	19.6	15.3	167.0	229.8	23.5	21.2	48.1	71.3	0.4	0.7
60-64	597.8	10.3	2.6	19.1	15.2	161.2	226.8	23.9	21.7	43.9	72.4	0.3	0.5
65-69	566.7	8.9	2.6	19.0	15.0	144.1	217.0	24.8	21.4	39.7	73.7	0.2	0.3
70-74	442.1	8.0	2.4	16.8	12.5	111.2	159.7	20.3	19.4	31.7	59.9	0.1	0.2
75 +	768.5	12.8	4.5	28.9	22.1	186.3	286.3	38.7	35.2	53.8	99.4	0.1	0.2

SOURCE: *Post-censal Annual Estimates of Population by Marital Status, Age, Sex, and Components of Growth for Canada and the Provinces.* 1 June Cat. No. 91-210, Annual. *Market Research Handbook, Statistics Canada,* 1991, Cat. No. 63-224.

17. Immigrant Population by Place of Birth, 1970 to 1990

COUNTRY OR REGION	1970	1975	1980	1985	1990
Great Britain	23 688	29 454	16 445	3 998	6 701
Portugal	8 594	9 158	4 222	917	5 396
Italy	8 659	4 919	1 873	733	1 058
Poland	1 403	1 191	1 395	3 642	16 446
Total Europe	**75 006**	**68 733**	**40 210**	**18 530**	**50 059**
Philippines	3 305	7 688	6 147	3 183	12 492
India	7 089	13 401	9 531	4 517	12 513
Hong Kong	2 250	6 438	3 874	5 121	22 789
China	3 397	6 235	8 965	5 166	13 971
Total Asia	**23 682**	**52 024**	**73 026**	**39 438**	**112 854**
United States	20 859	16 729	8 098	5 614	4 995
Caribbean	13 371	18 790	7 515	6 240	11 721
Africa	4 017	11 715	5 383	3 912	13 691
Australasia	3 462	1 574	1 215	399	714
South America	4 506	13 102	5 381	4 273	8 544
Oceania	—	2 675	944	612	1 671
Total	**147 713**	**187 881**	**143 117**	**84 302**	**212 166**

SOURCE: Statistics Canada, *Report on the Demographic Situation in Canada 1990: Current Demographic Analysis,* Dec. 1991, Cat. No. 91-209E.

18. Employment, Unemployment, and Participation Rates[1], 1989

PROVINCE	POPULATION (000)	LABOUR FORCE (000)	EMPLOYED (000)	UNEMPLOYED (000)	PARTICIPATION RATE (%)
Newfoundland	571	239	201	38	55.7
Prince Edward Island	130	65	54	11	65.0
Nova Scotia	898	414	373	41	61.2
New Brunswick	726	325	284	41	59.5
Quebec	6 812	3 342	3 031	311	64.0
Ontario	9 840	5 213	4 949	264	69.8
Manitoba	1 093	539	498	41	67.0
Saskatchewan	995	482	446	36	66.2
Alberta	2 501	1 308	1 214	94	72.4
British Columbia	3 186	1 579	1 435	144	66.8
Canada	**26 833**	**13 504**	**12 486**	**1 018**	**67.0**

[1]The participation rate is the percentage of the population (over 15 years of age) in the labour force and includes both employed and unemployed.   SOURCE: Statistics Canada.

19. Employees by Industry, 1989

PROVINCE OR TERRITORY	INDUSTRY (000)									
	FORESTRY	MINING	MANUFACTURING	TRANSPORTATION AND COMMUNICATION	CONSTRUCTION	TRADE	FINANCE, INSURANCE AND REAL ESTATE	SERVICES	PUBLIC ADMINISTRATION	TOTAL
Newfoundland	1.4	3.4	17.8	14.5	6.3	29.5	5.4	51.3	18.1	**147.7**
Prince Edward Island	—	—	3.7	3.1	2.1	6.7	1.5	14.3	5.2	**36.6**
Nova Scotia	2.2	4.1	40.1	24.3	16.3	57.0	15.9	108.5	29.3	**297.6**
New Brunswick	3.8	3.2	35.5	21.5	12.2	42.7	9.7	76.6	19.4	**224.6**
Quebec	14.6	17.5	530.4	204.5	118.3	457.9	145.0	888.7	167.7	**2 544.5**
Ontario	9.5	28.9	978.9	307.7	224.1	749.5	292.3	1424.8	253.2	**4 268.9**
Manitoba	0.9	4.4	56.7	44.6	13.2	68.9	25.3	145.1	29.1	**388.3**
Saskatchewan	0.9	8.2	22.6	29.2	12.4	61.1	19.6	121.0	26.5	**301.4**
Alberta	2.4	63.9	85.8	90.2	53.3	181.5	54.9	366.2	72.2	**970.5**
British Columbia, Yukon, and Northwest Territories	23.6	14.5	164.2	111.2	57.5	208.1	75.7	424.9	73.9	**1 159.2**

SOURCE: Statistics Canada, *Market Research Handbook, 1991*, Ottawa, 1990.

20. Geographic Distribution of the Population, 1986

SELECTED PARALLELS OF LATITUDE	POPULATION	%
South of 49°	17 827 382	70.4
Between 49° and 54°	6 898 501	27.3
Between 54° and 60°	505 222	2.0
North of 60°	78 226	0.3
SELECTED DISTANCES NORTH OF CANADA-USA BORDER		
0 - 150 km	18 218 596	72.0
151 - 300 km	3 394 247	13.4
301 - 600 km	2 630 864	10.4
Over 600 km	1 065 624	4.2
Total Canadian Population	**25 354 064**	**100.0**

SOURCE: 1986 Census of Canada, *Canada's Population From Ocean to Ocean*, Minister of Supply and Services Canada, 1989.

Agriculture

21. Net Income and Cash Receipts from Farming

PROVINCE	CASH RECEIPTS ($000 000)		NET INCOME[1] ($000 000)	
	1983	1989	1983	1989
Newfoundland	34.8	57.9	4.5	11.3
Prince Edward Island	172.3	256.1	25.4	77.8
Nova Scotia	236.0	315.1	26.4	71.5
New Brunswick	199.8	272.1	30.8	65.6
Quebec	2 710.1	3 648.9	484.9	917.6
Ontario	4 989.9	5 662.5	810.7	941.2
Manitoba	1 797.6	2 101.7	215.2	295.3
Saskatchewan	4 026.1	4 474.8	702.9	760.1
Alberta	3 750.8	4 509.4	412.4	782.6
British Columbia	914.9	1 163.9	38.1	175.7
Canada	**18 832.3**	**22 462.4**	**2 751.4**	**4 099.0**

[1]Income excludes the value of inventory change.
SOURCE: Statistics Canada, *Agriculture Economic Statistics*, June 1990.

22. Number of Farms and Average Size, 1901 to 1991

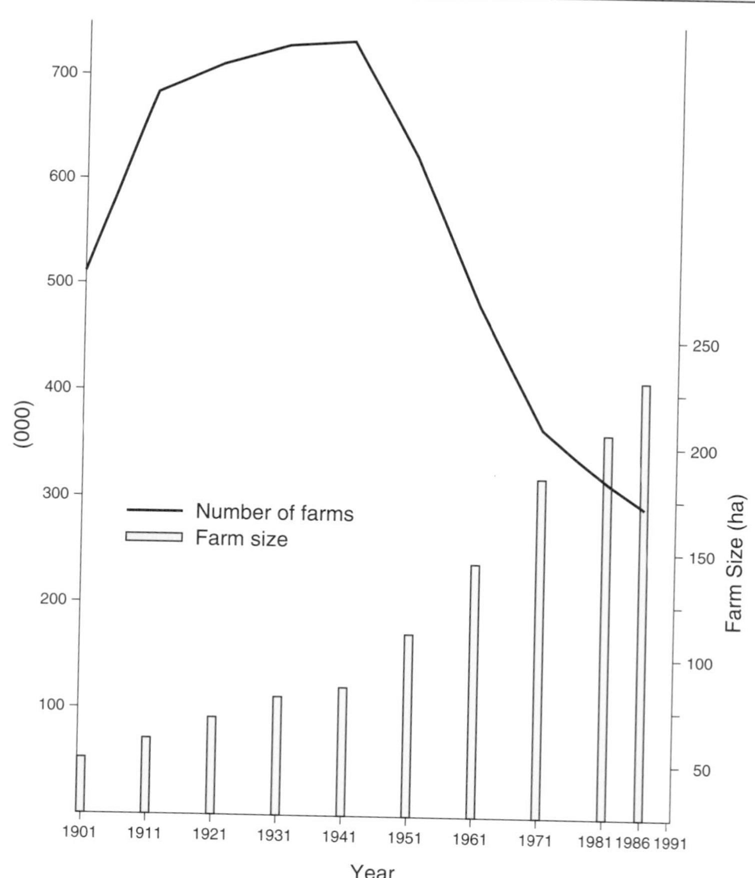

SOURCE: Statistics Canada

23. Agricultural Land Use, 1986

PROVINCE	FARMLAND AREA (000 ha)	% CHANGE 1971–1986	% CLASSED AS CLASS 1, 2, or 3	NUMBER OF FARMS	AVERAGE FARM SIZE (CHANGE 1971–1986)	CROPLAND AREA (000 ha)	SUMMER FALLOW AREA (000 ha)	WOODLAND AREA (000 ha)
Newfoundland	36.6	44.1	0.005	652	56 (+131 %)	4.9	0.4	5.2
Prince Edward Island	272.4	–13.1	71.2	2 838	96 (+39 %)	156.5	2.7	61.2
Nova Scotia	416.5	–22.6	20.7	4 284	97 (+9 %)	109.5	3.9	200.8
New Brunswick	409.0	–24.5	17.9	3 556	115 (+16 %)	129.5	4.3	184.4
Quebec	3 638.8	–16.8	1.4	41 350	88 (+23 %)	1 744.4	31.8	1 029.6
Ontario	5 646.6	–12.6	6.8	72 392	76 (+13.9 %)	3 458.0	80.3	587.5
Manitoba	7 740.2	0.6	8.0	27 350	283 (+29 %)	4 519.3	509.2	124.2
Saskatchewan	26 599.4	1.0	25.0	63 483	419 (+23 %)	13 325.8	5 661.6	152.7
Alberta	20 655.3	3.1	16.2	57 697	358 (+12 %)	9 162.5	2 123.7	288.8
British Columbia	2 411.1	2.2	1.0	19 135	126 (–1.2 %)	570.8	81.2	154.5
Canada	**67 825.8**	**–1.2**	**4.6**	**293 618**	**231 (23 %)**	**33 181.2**	**8 499.0**	**2 789.0**

NOTE: Information about the territories is excluded because of the small number of farms. SOURCE: Statistics Canada, *Human Activity and the Environment, 1991*.

24. Census Farms with Sales of $2500 or More, by Product Type, 1986

PROVINCE	PRODUCT TYPE									MIXED FARMS		TOTAL
	DAIRY	CATTLE	HOGS	POULTRY	WHEAT	SMALL GRAINS (EXCLUDING WHEAT FARMS)	FIELD CROPS, OTHER THAN SMALL GRAINS	FRUITS AND VEGETABLES	MISCELLANEOUS SPECIALTY	LIVESTOCK COMBINATION	OTHER COMBINATIONS[1]	
Newfoundland	68	45	17	54	—	—	13	94	75	12	37	**415**
Prince Edward Island	584	652	221	28	4	90	474	60	149	127	69	**2 458**
Nova Scotia	698	979	132	127	1	62	45	457	481	42	146	**3 170**
New Brunswick	631	739	125	96	7	62	384	252	313	45	122	**2 776**
Quebec	15 906	5 763	2 749	893	217	2 922	771	2 250	4 051	382	1 256	**37 160**
Ontario	11 028	17 160	4 840	1 643	733	13 693	1 988	4 089	4 203	1 653	2 223	**63 253**
Manitoba	1 412	4 682	1 111	356	6 272	8 758	415	100	731	615	810	**25 262**
Saskatchewan	881	7 866	906	166	30 968	16 942	285	36	609	1 064	1 086	**60 809**
Alberta	1 828	17 110	1 635	533	8 504	15 403	1 187	119	1 944	1 399	2 081	**51 743**
British Columbia	1 150	4 266	290	752	151	663	356	2 920	1 893	238	1 020	**13 699**
Canada	**34 186**	**59 262**	**12 026**	**4 648**	**46 857**	**58 595**	**5 918**	**10 377**	**14 449**	**5 577**	**8 850**	**260 745**

[1] In 1986, "field crops combination". SOURCE: *Canada Year Book 1992*.

25. Livestock Facts

PROVINCE	NUMBER OF CATTLE (000 head) JULY 1990	NUMBER OF PIGS (000 head) JULY 1990	NUMBER OF SHEEP AND LAMBS (000 head) JULY 1990	POULTRY PRODUCTION (tonnes) JULY 1989	TURKEY PRODUCTION (tonnes) JULY 1989	EGG PRODUCTION (000 doz.) 1989	MILK AND CREAM PRODUCTION (000 kL) 1989
Newfoundland	9	16	7	6 927	—	8 136	—
Prince Edward Island	97	117	5	1 471	24	2 862	99
Nova Scotia	128	135	34	19 421	3 132	19 185	175
New Brunswick	105	84	10	15 016	2 047	10 675	134
Quebec	1 413	2 975	118	169 909	27 407	82 499	2 873
Ontario	2 250	3 181	215	195 041	52 238	181 409	2 454
Manitoba	1 075	1 240	24	25 659	9 002	54 956	302
Saskatoon	2 160	790	56	17 358	4 734	19 682	225
Alberta	4 310	1 760	233	47 985	9 850	38 248	585
British Columbia	740	234	58	66 477	11 998	59 298	494
TOTAL	**12 287**	**10 532**	**759**	**565 264**	**120 432**	**476 950**	**7 341**[1]

[1] As of October 1988, Nfld data are excluded from Canada total for reasons of confidentiality. SOURCE: *Canada Year Book 1992*.

26. Wheat Statistics, 1983 to 1991

	1983[1]	1984	1985	1986	1987	1988	1989	1990	1991
Carryover from Previous Crop Year (000 t)	9 983	9 190	7 598	8 569	12 731	7 305	5 032	6 442	10 472
Production (000 t)	26 505	21 199	24 252	31 378	25 992	15 996	24 334	32 709	31 904
Total Supply (000 t)	36 448	30 389	31 850	39 947	38 723	23 301	29 366	39 151	42 191
Exports (000 t)	21 765	17 542	17 683	20 783	23 519	12 413	17 418	21 913	n.a.
Domestic Use (000 t)	5 534	5 250	5 598	6 433	7 899	5 856	5 581	6 766	n.a.
Carryover at the End of the Crop Year (000 t)	9 189	7 598	8 569	12 731	7 305	5 032	6 442	10 472	n.a.
Final Price ($/t)	194	186	160	130	134	197	172	135	n.a.

[1] The crop year begins 1 July 1983 and ends 30 June 1984. n.a.—not available SOURCE: *Canada Year Book*, various years; The Canadian Wheat Board *Annual Reports*.

192

27. World Wheat Production, 1981 and 1990

COUNTRY	1981	1990
		(000 000 t)
Argentina	8.3	11.4
Australia	16.4	15.1
Canada	24.8	32.7
China	59.6	98.2
European Community	58.0	84.6
India	36.3	49.7
Soviet Union[1]	81.1	108.0
Turkey	17.0	20.0
United States	75.8	74.5

[1]The Soviet Union was dissolved in 1991. Data for Russia and the other independent countries that were formed after dissolution are not available for the years prior to 1992.
SOURCE: *The Canadian Wheat Board Annual Report, 1990–1991.*

28. World Wheat Imports and Exports, 1981 and 1990

	IMPORTS (000 000 t)	
COUNTRY	1981	1990
Soviet Union[1]	19.6	14.5
China	13.2	9.6
Egypt	6.0	6.0
Japan	5.6	5.5
Iran	1.4	4.1
Brazil	4.6	2.8
Republic of Korea	1.9	4.1
Algeria	2.3	3.5
Iraq	1.6	0.2
Poland	3.8	0.3
Indonesia	1.5	2.0
Bangladesh	1.2	1.4
World Total	**100.7**	**90.6**

	EXPORTS (000 000 t)	
COUNTRY	1981	1990
Argentina	4.3	5.1
Australia	11.4	11.9
Canada	28.5	21.9
European Community	13.9	18.5
United States	48.8	28.3
World Total	**100.7**	**90.6**

[1]The Soviet Union was dissolved in 1991. Data for Russia and the other independent countries that were formed after dissolution are not available for the years prior to 1992.
SOURCE: *The Canadian Wheat Board Annual Report, 1990–1991.*

29. Canadian Wheat Exports, 1980, 1985, and 1990

COUNTRY OR REGION	1980[1]	1985	1990
		(000 t)	
Western Europe	**2 347**	**1 298**	**935**
Great Britain	1 409	633	281
Italy	765	240	320
Eastern Europe	**5 129**	**6 285**	**7 228**
Soviet Union[2]	3 971	6 019	7 228
Africa	**901**	**934**	**2 047**
South Africa	n.a.	55	554
Middle East	**674**	**1 608**	**1 556**
Iran	96	41	1 419
Asia	**4 467**	**4 672**	**7 328**
China	2 879	2 780	2 923
Japan	1 381	1 323	1 393
South Korea	n.a.	n.a.	1 258
North and South America	**2 049**	**2 275**	**2 818**
United States	n.a.	159	660
Total	**15 569**	**17 114**	**21 913**

[1]The crop year extends from 1 July 1980 to 30 June 1981.
[2]The Soviet Union was dissolved in 1991. Data for Russia and the other independent countries that were formed after dissolution are not available for the years prior to 1992.
n.a.—not available
SOURCE: *The Canadian Wheat Board Annual Report, 1990–1991.*

30. Farm Cash Receipts, 1990 ($000 000)

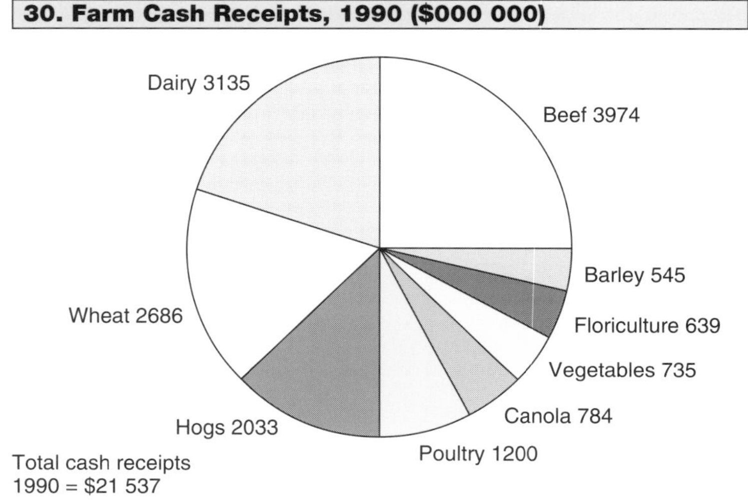

Dairy 3135
Beef 3974
Barley 545
Floriculture 639
Vegetables 735
Canola 784
Poultry 1200
Hogs 2033
Wheat 2686

Total cash receipts
1990 = $21 537

SOURCE: Statistics Canada, *Canadian Economic Observer*, June 1991.

31. Area and Production of Major Field Crops, Various Years

FIELD CROP AND PROVINCE[1]	AREA (000 ha)				TOTAL PRODUCTION (000 t)			
	AVERAGE 1945–49	AVERAGE 1963–67	1974	1990	AVERAGE 1945–49	AVERAGE 1963–67	1974	1990
Wheat	**9 823**	**11 630**	**9 391**	**14 063**	**9 873**	**18 473**	**14 220**	**31 009**
Quebec	5	9	24	55	6	16	42	170
Ontario								
Winter	248	159	168	304	493	433	519	1 301
Spring	16	8	4	20	22	14	8	54
Manitoba	968	1 324	1 200	2 198	1 306	2 145	1 715	5 851
Saskatchewan	5 775	7 575	6 160	8 288	5 035	11 523	8 872	16 847
Alberta	2 766	2 509	1 800	3 136	2 939	4 262	2 994	6 614
British Columbia	42	44	28	51	71	74	52	136
Oats	**4 605**	**3 284**	**2 442**	**1 517**	**5 034**	**5 773**	**3 929**	**3 546**
Prince Edward Island	44	35	20	10	63	67	43	24
New Brunswick	71	32	20	12	95	53	35	25
Quebec	550	430	250	115	508	654	367	315
Ontario	601	547	198	117	876	1 118	361	287

FIELD CROP AND PROVINCE[1]	AREA (000 ha)				TOTAL PRODUCTION (000 t)			
	AVERAGE 1945–49	AVERAGE 1963–67	1974	1990	AVERAGE 1945–49	AVERAGE 1963–67	1974	1990
Manitoba	584	633	480	182	756	1 046	663	432
Saskatchewan	1 634	718	760	405	1 481	1 258	1 157	833
Alberta	1 058	849	680	627	1 157	1 505	1 234	1 511
British Columbia	37	28	26	41	70	51	54	102
Barley	**2 628**	**2 670**	**4 600**	**4 590**	**3 074**	**5 042**	**8 585**	**13 232**
Prince Edward Island	2	5	8	29	4	12	23	78
New Brunswick	4	2	4	13	7	4	10	39
Quebec	34	6	21	162	41	13	36	530
Ontario	94	79	136	198	163	195	337	638
Manitoba	706	282	720	627	914	501	1 154	1 981
Saskatchewan	942	775	1 600	1 416	936	1 463	2 787	3 701
Alberta	835	1 462	2 040	2 084	980	2 761	4 093	6 096
British Columbia	8	57	68	55	16	91	139	150
Soybeans	**29**	**103**	**178**	**504**	**41**	**202**	**300**	**1 259**
Ontario	29	103	178	486	41	202	300	1 211
Quebec	—	—	—	18	—	—	—	48
Mixed Grains	**490**	**646**	**724**	**391**	**999**	**1 726**	**1 831**	**1 051**
Prince Edward Island	19	19	30	21	43	56	99	59
Quebec	76	40	50	30	112	90	106	90
Ontario	366	320	328	190	804	998	993	541
Manitoba	7	61	80	32	11	129	136	78
Saskatchewan	5	49	80	32	6	103	145	67
Alberta	13	148	148	81	17	328	331	204
Flaxseed	**466**	**713**	**600**	**721**	**241**	**518**	**363**	**899**
Manitoba	180	397	300	324	108	263	180	419
Saskatchewan	210	177	220	344	85	136	119	406
Alberta	58	122	80	53	35	102	64	74
Canola/Rapeseed	**16**	**468**	**1 304**	**2 630**	**673**	**430**	**1 200**	**3 257**
Ontario	—	—	—	20	—	—	—	43
Manitoba	—	47	200	384	—	41	193	499
Saskatchewan	16	192	600	1 133	673	195	544	1 406
Alberta	—	229	480	1 052	—	194	442	1 270
British Columbia	—	—	—	41	—	—	—	39
Shelled Corn	**98**	**291**	**584**	**1 003**	**280**	**1 468**	**2 589**	**6 846**
Quebec	—	—	66	260	—	—	293	1 730
Ontario	92	286	516	704	273	1 450	2 291	4 953
Manitoba	5	2	2	34	8	4	5	142
Potatoes	**167**	**118**	**112**	**117**	**1 801**	**2 183**	**2 427**	**2 929**
Prince Edward Island	18	18	18	30	272	403	467	850
New Brunswick	24	23	23	20	396	551	608	567
Quebec	47	29	21	18	406	389	382	385
Ontario	37	20	17	13	363	427	368	365
Manitoba	8	9	14	19	64	119	222	352
Alberta	—	—	—	10	—	—	—	278
Tame Hay	**4 214**	**5 121**	**5 355**	**5 976**	**15 176**	**21 368**	**23 604**	**33 112**
Prince Edward Island	88	72	51	56	302	296	204	290
Nova Scotia	161	90	60	69	634	429	288	435
New Brunswick	214	100	64	71	678	430	251	417
Quebec	1 584	1 345	1 070	991	5 013	5 495	4 518	7 000
Ontario	1 348	1 354	1 080	1 032	5 559	6 701	5 733	7 439
Manitoba	130	407	500	668	504	1 571	2 177	3 084
Saskatchewan	192	467	800	850	617	1 579	2 903	2 722
Alberta	376	1 114	1 480	1 882	1 243	3 949	6 078	9 525
British Columbia	121	174	250	352	624	917	1 451	2 177
Fodder Corn	**162**	**212**	**419**	**233**	**3 183**	**5 594**	**10 043**	**7 734**
Quebec	28	26	64	53	549	705	1 855	1 800
Ontario	123	166	336	150	2 531	4 579	7 697	5 080
Manitoba	6	15	11	12	53	213	190	272
British Columbia	2	2	7	11	38	77	299	354

[1] Only provinces with over 10 000 ha in 1990 in a particular crop are listed. —means not applicable. SOURCE: *Canada Year Book 1961, 1970–71, 1975*, and *1992*.

Forestry and Fishing

32. Areas of Land, Forest Land, and Productive Forest Land

PROVINCE OR TERRITORY	TOTAL AREA (000 000 ha)	AREA OF FOREST LAND (000 000 ha)	AREA OF PRODUCTIVE FOREST LAND (000 000 ha)	WOOD VOLUME (000 000 m)	FOREST FIRE LOSSES AS A % OF PRODUCTIVE FOREST LAND (AVG. ANNUAL %, LATE 1980s)
Newfoundland	40.6	22.5	11.2	525	0.3
Prince Edward Island	0.6	0.3	0.3	26	0.04
Nova Scotia	5.5	4.0	3.9	244	0.01
New Brunswick	7.3	6.3	6.1	571	1.9
Quebec	154.1	94.0	54.8	4 225	1.2
Ontario	106.9	80.7	38.3	3 529	0.7
Manitoba	65.0	34.9	14.9	680	8.8
Saskatchewan	65.2	23.7	15.9	905	1.6
Alberta	66.1	37.7	25.4	2 656	0.03
British Columbia	94.8	60.3	51.1	8 867	0.05
Yukon	48.3	27.4	7.6	480	1.9
Northwest Territories	342.6	61.4	14.3	446	2.4
Canada	**997.1**	**453.3**	**243.7**	**23 154**	**1.2**

SOURCE: Statistics Canada, *Canadian Forestry Statistics*, 1987.

33. Volume of Wood, by Age Class

PROVINCE OR TERRITORY	REGENERATION	IMMATURE	MATURE	OVERMATURE	UNEVEN-AGED	UNDETERMINED	TOTAL	VOLUME OF WOOD CUT 1986
				(000 000 m³)				
Newfoundland	—	—	123	122	—	280	525	2.4
Prince Edward Island	—	—	—	—	—	26	26	0.5
Nova Scotia	1	147	79	3	15	—	244	3.9
New Brunswick	—	210	344	17	1	—	571	8.7
Quebec	119	734	2 167	—	18	1 187	4 225	38.1
Ontario	1	930	1 465	1 132	1	—	3 529	30.2
Manitoba	—	390	246	43	—	—	680	1.7
Saskatchewan	9	443	165	163	—	125	905	3.5
Alberta	1	716	1 330	608	—	—	2 656	10.4
British Columbia	9	1 604	7 226	28	—	—	8 867	77.5
Yukon	—	308	172	—	—	—	480	} 0.2
Northwest Territories	—	144	301	1	—	—	446	}
Total	**140**	**5 625**	**13 619**	**2 117**	**34**	**1 618**	**23 154**	**177.1**

SOURCE: Statistics Canada, *Canadian Forestry Statistics*, 1987.

34. Wood Industries Manufacturing Activity, 1986

PROVINCE	SAWMILLS	OTHER WOOD	PULP AND PAPER	OTHER PAPER	TOTAL
			($000 000)		
Newfoundland	4.6	3.2	141.7	6.3	155.8
Prince Edward Island	0.8	6.6	—	—	7.4
Nova Scotia	40.5	29.3	232.7	26.5	329.0
New Brunswick	91.7	63.9	426.6	13.6	595.8
Quebec	652.1	632.0	2 547.3	551.6	4 383.0
Ontario	323.2	767.9	1 680.2	1 109.6	3 880.9
Manitoba	8.7	78.8	80.3	43.5	211.3
Saskatchewan	21.4	36.7	62.3	10.3	130.7
Alberta	145.2	168.3	108.2	77.7	499.4
British Columbia	1 927.5	520.7	1 694.4	104.7	4 247.3
Total	**3 215.7**	**2 307.4**	**6 973.7**	**1 943.8**	**14 440.6**

SOURCE: *Canada Year Book 1990*.

35. Quantity and Value of Sea and Inland Fish Landed and Persons Employed in Fishing, 1972 and 1986

PROVINCE OR TERRITORY	QUANTITY (t)		VALUE ($000)		PERSONS EMPLOYED FISHING	
	1972	1986	1972	1986	1972	1986
Newfoundland	295 135	515 464	35 723	209 603	14 452	27 075
Prince Edward Island	25 780	45 802	9 540	62 154	3 210	4 462
Nova Scotia	286 856	450 720	66 375	422 738	11 735	14 859
New Brunswick	162 144	143 033	19 923	88 167	5 161	7 784
Quebec	83 210	91 190	11 138	100 163	5 843	6 528
Ontario	19 589	25 180	8 119	46 317	2 097	1 837
Manitoba	11 101	12 143	4 523	20 564	1 827	} 5 850
Saskatchewan	4 864	3 789	1 634	3 968	1 800	
Alberta	2 202	1 613	727	1 891	1 547	
British Columbia	153 060	225 738	75 128	401 959	9 902	20 033
Yukon and Northwest Territories	1 625	1 530	866	1 406	201	n.a.
Totals	**1 045 566**	**1 516 202**	**233 696**	**1 358 930**	**57 775**	**88 428**

n.a.—not available.   SOURCE: *Canada Year Book 1992.*

36. Landings of Chief Commercial Fish, 1990[1]

SPECIES	ATLANTIC COAST		PACIFIC COAST		CANADA	
	Quantity (t)	Value ($000)	Quantity (t)	Value ($000)	Quantity (t)	Value ($000)
Total groundfish	**634 061**	**375 782**	**130 991**	**73 009**	**765 052**	**448 791**
Cod	381 819	239 398	5 502	2 902	387 321	242 300
Haddock	21 346	23 094	—	—	21 346	23 094
Redfish	80 326	22 006	23 380	14 343	103 706	36 349
Halibut	2 135	9 769	4 715	19 688	6 850	29 457
Flatfishes	71 515	37 184	5 926	4 364	77 441	41 548
Turbot	18 888	13 000	1 948	447	20 836	13 447
Pollock	36 819	19 381	545	143	37 364	19 524
Hake	13 087	6 981	79 890	10 982	92 977	17 963
Cusk	3 481	2 183	—	—	3 481	2 183
Catfish	1 516	397	—	—	1 516	397
Other	3 129	2 389	9 085	20 140	12 214	22 529
Total pelagic and other finfish	**370 474**	**77 367**	**139 068**	**299 955**	**509 542**	**377 322**
Herring	255 187	37 508	40 228	74 400	295 415	111 908
Mackerel	14 680	4 081	—	—	14 680	4 081
Tuna	466	6 715	272	837	738	7 552
Alewife	6 331	1 501	—	—	6 331	1 501
Eel	284	1 240	—	—	284	1 240
Salmon	515	2 286	95 271	223 470	95 786	225 756
Skate	98	6	132	23	230	29
Smelt	695	511	—	—	695	511
Capelin	89 787	17 546	—	—	89 787	17 546
Other	2 431	5 973	3 165	1 225	5 596	7 198
Total shellfish	**208 838**	**447 705**	**15 068**	**34 898**	**223 906**	**482 603**
Clams	18 914	14 089	6 227	14 405	25 141	28 494
Oyster	3 200	7 300	3 856	3 200	7 056	10 500
Scallop	80 029	96 264	68	315	80 097	96 579
Squid	3 851	1 003	47	51	3 898	1 054
Lobster	44 963	222 303	—	—	44 963	222 303
Shrimp	27 819	53 120	2 422	7 767	30 241	60 887
Crab	26 062	49 326	2 060	8 441	28 122	57 767
Other	4 000	4 300	388	719	4 388	5 019
Miscellaneous items	—	**6 082**	—	**4 089**	—	**10 171**
Total seafisheries	**1 213 373**	**906 936**	**285 127**	**411 951**	**1 498 500**	**1 318 887**
Inland fisheries					45 000[2]	82 000
Grand total—Canada					**1 543 500**	**1 400 887**

[1]Preliminary estimates (data underestimate the final catch).   [2]Main species by value include smelt, yellow pickerel, perch, and whitefish.
SOURCE: Department of Fisheries and Oceans

Mining

37. Production of Leading Minerals, 1991ₚ ($000)

MINERAL	NFLD	PEI	NOVA SCOTIA	NEW BRUNSWICK	QUEBEC	ONTARIO	MANITOBA	SASKAT-CHEWAN	ALBERTA	BRITISH COLUMBIA	YUKON	NWT	TOTAL CANADA
Petroleum, crude	—	—	—	—	—	36 437	92 104	1 259 208	8 783 753	261 685	—	196 276	10 629 463
Natural gas	—	—	—	—	—	45 506	—	307 031	4 306 480	519 276	—	12 692	5 190 985
Gold	x	—	—	x	692 376	1 025 635	33 289	38 458	453	248 694	67 097	220 742	2 355 325
Natural gas by-products	—	—	—	—	—	—	830	12 272	2 044 095	65 205	—	3 055	2 125 457
Copper	—	—	x	27 535	299 268	723 187	154 598	x	—	895 110	—	—	2 101 168
Coal	—	—	238 000	34 200	—	—	—	95 300	541 100	997 300	—	—	1 905 900
Nickel	—	—	—	—	—	1 237 668	590 567	—	—	—	—	—	1 828 235
Zinc	—	—	x	212 529	143 727	276 536	98 364	x	—	154 205	178 340	279 002	1 350 970
Iron ore	737 704	—	—	—	x	x	—	—	—	3 095	—	—	1 307 888
Potash (K₂O)	—	—	—	x	—	—	—	x	—	—	—	—	918 994
Cement	x	—	x	—	142 330	388 543	x	x	x	x	—	—	816 802
Sand and gravel	11 701	2 453	15 045	14 387	83 022	209 649	35 203	17 597	106 584	120 708	6 883	8 160	631 391
Stone	5 015	—	23 576	18 398	206 173	222 374	7 948	—	2 892	22 725	—	3 735	512 837
Uranium (U)	—	—	—	—	—	165 000	—	307 074	—	—	—	—	472 074
Asbestos	4 023	—	—	—	223 150	—	—	—	—	47 362	—	—	274 535
Salt	—	—	x	x	x	142 614	—	26 759	15 410	—	—	—	258 585
Sulphur, elemental	—	—	—	—	—	153	—	3 032	200 269	40 650	—	—	244 104
Lead	—	—	x	50 225	—	x	2 096	—	—	42 191	81 036	26 724	203 864
Lime	—	—	—	x	x	103 550	7 199	—	20 488	x	—	—	186 287
Silver	x	—	x	22 869	22 159	44 070	7 022	x	—	73 240	12 856	2 876	185 261
Platinum group	—	—	—	—	—	x	x	—	—	—	—	—	141 790
Clay products	x	—	x	x	x	85 279	x	x	x	14 015	—	—	139 411
Peat	69	—	x	26 934	38 892	—	x	x	14 237	—	—	—	91 675
Sulphur in smelter gas	566	—	144	6 547	16 756	44 115	345	—	—	4 924	—	3 195	76 592
Gypsum	x	—	52 342	—	—	13 900	x	—	—	x	—	—	74 315
Total all minerals	793 306	2 453	444 627	617 008	2 934 229	5 062 151	1 107 794	2 852 043	16 147 718	3 749 999	346 215	756 705	34 814 247

ₚ Preliminary;–Nil; x Confidential.
Note: Certain minerals are not included in the leading minerals due to confidentiality constraints. Confidential values are included in totals. Numbers may not add to totals due to rounding.
SOURCE: Energy, Mines and Resources Canada; Statistics Canada.

38. Canada's World Role as a Producer of Certain Important Minerals, 1990[1]

MINERAL	RANK OF FIVE LEADING COUNTRIES (% of World Total)				
	1	2	3	4	5
Uranium (U concentrates)	**Canada 27.7**	Australia 11.2	United States 10.8	Namibia 10.1	France 8.9
Zinc (mine production)	**Canada 16.4**	Australia 12.7	Soviet Union[2] 11.9	China 8.5	Peru 8.0
Gypsum	United States 15.2	**Canada 9.0**	Iran 8.2	China 8.2	Japan 6.5
Potash (K₂O equivalent)	Soviet Union 33.1	**Canada 25.5**	East Germany[3] 9.7	West Germany 8.0	United States 6.0
Nickel (mine production)	Soviet Union 30.0	**Canada 21.0**	New Caledonia 9.1	Australia 7.2	Indonesia 5.8
Asbestos	Soviet Union 61.1	**Canada 17.2**	Brazil 4.8	Zimbabwe 4.5	China 3.9
Molybdenum (Mo content)	United States 55.8	Chile 12.5	**Canada 11.0**	Soviet Union 10.0	Mexico 3.6
Platinum group metals (mine production)	South Africa 48.3	Soviet Union 43.6	**Canada 3.9**	United States 2.7	Japan 0.8
Sulphur, elemental	United States 26.3	Soviet Union 16.3	**Canada 15.1**	Poland 11.4	Mexico 5.5
Aluminum (primary metal)	United States 22.3	Soviet Union 12.1	**Canada 8.6**	Australia 6.8	Brazil 5.1
Cobalt (mine production)	Zaire 40.6	Zambia 19.6	Soviet Union 9.7	**Canada 8.8**	Cuba 6.5
Titanium concentrates (ilmenite)	Australia 30.8	Norway 15.0	South Africa 13.1	**Canada 12.7**	Malaysia 8.4
Copper (mine production)	Chile 17.6	United States 17.6	Soviet Union 10.0	**Canada 8.8**	Zambia 5.5
Silver (mine production)	Mexico 16.3	United States 13.9	Peru 11.4	**Canada 9.6**	Soviet Union 8.8
Lead (mine production)	Australia 16.9	United States 14.9	Soviet Union 14.7	China 9.5	**Canada 7.2**
Cadmium (refined production)	Japan 12.3	Soviet Union 12.0	Belgium 9.8	United States 8.4	**Canada 7.4**
Gold (refined production)	South Africa 29.7	United States 14.3	Soviet Union 12.3	Australia 12.0	**Canada 8.3**

[1]Preliminary data.
[2]The Soviet Union was dissolved in 1991. Data for Russia and the other independent countries that were formed after dissolution are not available for the years prior to 1992.
[3]East and West Germany were reunited in October 1990.
SOURCE: Energy, Mines and Resources Canada, *1992 Canadian Minerals Yearbook.*

Energy

39. Coal, Supply and Demand

	1960	1970	1980	1991
		(10⁶ t)		
Supply				
Production	10.0	15.1	36.7	71.1
Imports	11.5	18.0	15.6	12.4
Total Supply	**21.5**	**33.1**	**52.3**	**83.5**
Demand				
Domestic	20.4	25.7	37.3	49.4
Exports	0.9	4.3	15.3	34.1
Total Demand	**21.3**	**30.0**	**52.6**	**83.5**

Inc. bituminous, sub-bituminous, and lignite.
SOURCE: Statistics Canada, *Coal and Coke Statistics*, Cat. No. 45-002.

40. Electricity Consumption by Sector, 1960 to 1990

	1960	1970	1980	1990*
SECTOR		(GW.h)		
Residential	20 397 (19)	43 431 (21)	92 440 (27)	133 327 (29)
Commercial	12 632 (12)	44 068 (22)	75 912 (21)	107 092 (23)
Industrial	66 353 (60)	98 450 (49)	142 247 (42)	190 903 (41)
Line Losses**	9 920 (9)	16 388 (8)	32 469 (10)	34 295 (7)
Total	**109 304 (100)**	**202 337 (100)**	**340 068 (100)**	**465 617 (100)**

¹Preliminary data.
²Losses during transmission, distribution, and unallocated energy.
Figures in parentheses are percentage shares.
SOURCE: Statistics Canada, *Electric Power Statistics, Volume II*, Cat. No. 57-202.

41. Electricity, Supply and Demand

(10⁹ kW/h)	1960	1970	1980	1991
Supply				
Production	114.0	204.7	367.3	489.2
Imports	1.0	3.2	2.9	6.2
Total Supply	**115.0**	**207.9**	**370.2**	**495.4**
Demand				
Domestic	109.0	202.3	239.9	470.8
Exports	6.0	5.6	30.3	24.6
Total Demand	**115.0**	**207.9**	**370.2**	**495.4**

SOURCE: Statistics Canada, *Electric Power Statistics*, Cat. No. 57-202.

42. Marketable Natural Gas, Supply and Demand

(10⁹ m³)	1960	1970	1980	1991
Supply				
Production	12.5	52.9	69.8	105.2
Imports	0.2	0.3	5.6	0.3
Total Supply	**12.7**	**53.2**	**75.4**	**105.5**
Demand				
Domestic	9.4	29.5	43.3	54.8
Exports	3.1	22.1	22.6	47.6
Total Demand	**12.5**	**51.6**	**75.4**	**102.4**

SOURCE: Statistics Canada, *Crude Petroleum and Natural Gas Production*, Cat. No. 26-006.

43. Petroleum, Supply and Demand

(10⁶ m³)	1960	1970	1980	1991
Supply				
Production	36.5	80.2	89.5	96.7
Imports	21.2	33.1	32.2	31.5
Total Supply	**57.7**	**113.3**	**121.7**	**128.2**
Demand				
Domestic	46.8	74.3	109.8	84.4
Exports	10.7	38.9	11.9	44.2
Total Demand	**57.5**	**113.2**	**121.7**	**128.6**

SOURCE:: Statistics Canada, *Refined Petroleum Products*, Cat. No. 45-004.

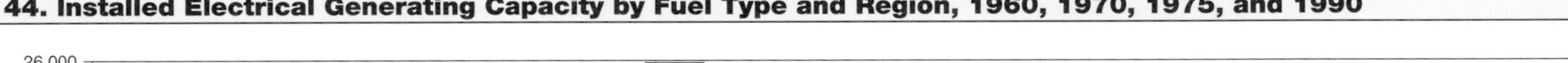

44. Installed Electrical Generating Capacity by Fuel Type and Region, 1960, 1970, 1975, and 1990

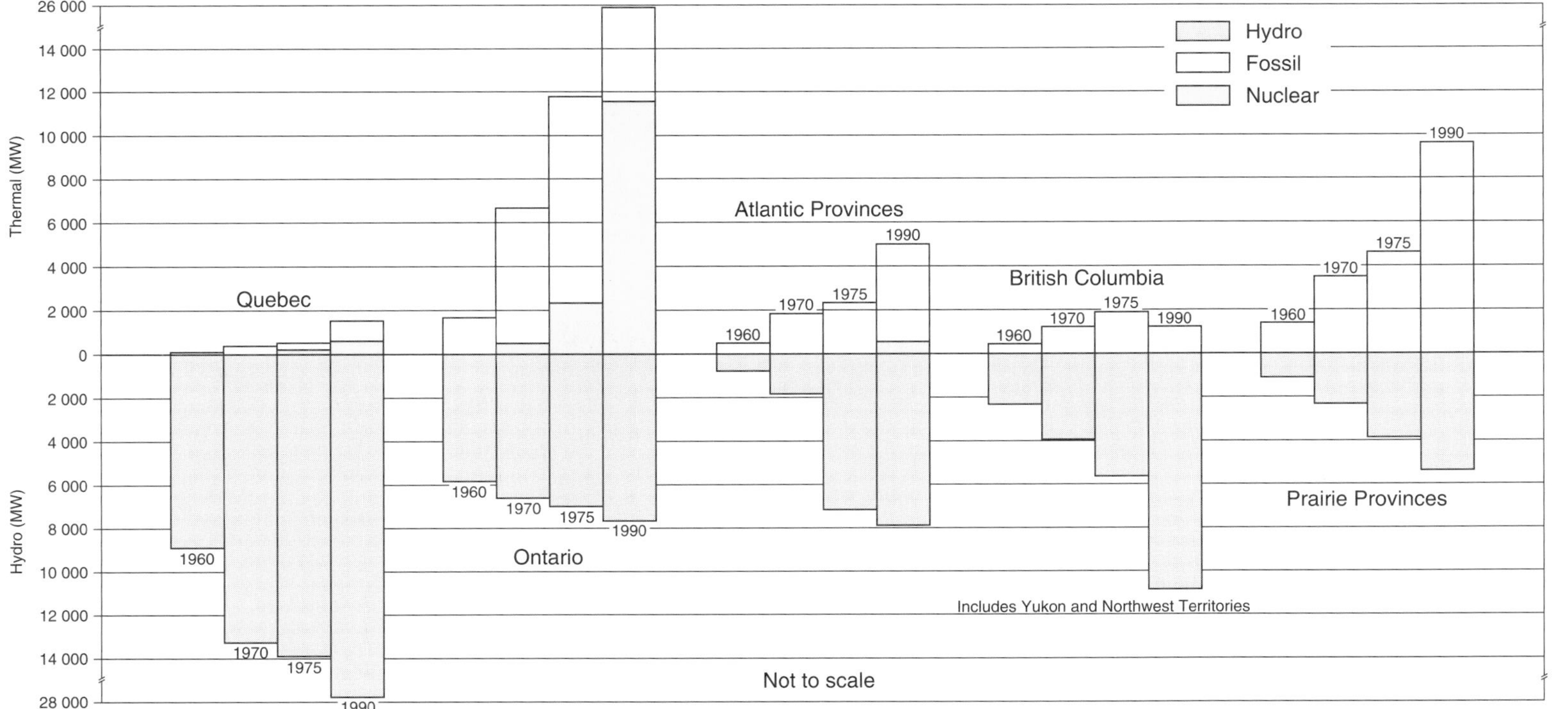

Electrical capacity in the Yukon and Northwest Territories (MW): Fossil 189, Hydro 135, Nuclear 0

SOURCE: Department of Energy, Mines and Resources Canada, *Electrical Power in Canada*, 1975, 1990

45. Crude Oil and Equivalent Remaining Established Reserves, 1990

PROVINCE OR REGION

	BRITISH COLUMBIA	ALBERTA	SASKATCHEWAN	MANITOBA	ONTARIO	EASTERN CANADA	MAINLAND TERRITORIES[2]	MACKENZIE DELTA-BEAUFORT SEA[1]	ARCTIC ISLANDS[1]	EASTCOAST OFFSHORE[2]	CANADA
			(000 m³)								
CRUDE OIL											
Remaining reserves as at 12-31-1989	18 490	582 531	111 909	8 349	1 324	5	22 734	53 950	101	138 600	937 993
Gross additions	1 034	65	16 186	726	339	—	—	—	—	—	18 350
Total crude oil	**19 524**	**582 596**	**128 095**	**9 075**	**1 663**	**5**	**22 734**	**53 950**	**101**	**138 600**	**956 343**
1990 net production[3]	1 958	52 391	11 199	724	249	—	1 841	—	24	—	68 386
Remaining reserves as at 12-31-1990	17 566	530 205	116 896	8 351	1 414	5	20 893	53 950	77	136 600	887 957
Net change in reserves during 1990	−924	−52 326	4 987	2	90	—	−1 841	—	−24	—	−50 036
PENTANES PLUS											
Remaining reserves[1] as at 12-31-1989	4 260	114 157	498	26	—	—	357	11 671	6 617	—	137 586
Gross additions	−13	1 747	31	—	—	—	−9	—	—	—	1 756
Total pentanes plus	**4 247**	**115 904**	**529**	**26**	**—**	**—**	**348**	**11 671**	**6 617**	**—**	**139 342**
1990 net production[3]	223	6 268	26	2	—	—	21	—	—	—	6 540
Remaining reserves as at 12-31-1990	4 024	109 636	503	24	—	—	327	11 671	6 617	—	132 802
Net change in reserves during 1990	−236	−4 521	5	−2	—	—	−30	—	—	—	−4 784
Total crude oil and equivalent	**21 590**	**639 841**	**117 399**	**8 375**	**1 414**	**5**	**21 220**	**65 621**	**6 694**	**138 600**	**1 020 759**

[1]As with all other areas, reserves for frontier areas are carried in accordance with the definition of established reserves. However, reserves for frontier areas are only shown when a threshold volume has been determined to exist.
[2]Crude oil reserves were booked for the eastcoast offshore for the first time in year-end 1981 reserves.
[3]Preliminary estimate.
SOURCE: Canadian Petroleum Association. (excludes oil sands reserves).

46. Marketable Natural Gas Remaining Established Reserves, 1990

PROVINCE OR REGION

	BRITISH COLUMBIA	ALBERTA	SASKATCHEWAN	MANITOBA	ONTARIO	EASTERN CANADA	MAINLAND TERRITORIES[1]	ARCTIC ISLANDS[1]	EASTCOAST OFFSHORE[2]	CANADA
					(000 000 m³)					
Remaining reserves as at 12-31-1989	218 393	1 705 559	74 791	—	17 529	90	10 987	298 730	406 370	2 732 449
Gross additions	16 857	74 069	8 539	—	172	—	—	—	—	99 637
Total natural gas	**235 250**	**1 779 628**	**83 330**	**—**	**17 701**	**90**	**10 987**	**298 730**	**406 370**	**2 832 086**
Net change in underground storage	—	—	—	—	—	—	—	—	—	—
1990 net production[3]	11 612	89 744	4 450	—	798	18	74	—	—	106 696
Remaining reserves at 12-31-1990	223 638	1 689 884	78 880	—	16 903	72	10 913	298 730	406 370	2 725 390
Non-associated	214 484	1 411 564	76 236	—	16 903	67	10 802	274 430	377 040	2 381 526
Associated	9 154	278 320	2 644	—	—	5	111	24 300	29 330	343 864
Dissolved	—	—	—	—	—	—	—	—	—	—
Underground storage	—	—	—	—	—	—	—	—	—	—
Net change in reserves during 1990	5 245	−15 675	4 089	—	−626	−18	−74	—	—	−7 059

[1]As with all other areas, reserves for frontier areas are carried in accordance with the definition of established reserves. However, reserves for frontier areas are only shown when a threshold volume has been determined to exist.
[2]Crude oil reserves were booked for the eastcoast offshore for the first time in year-end 1981 reserves.
[3]Preliminary estimate.
SOURCE: Canadian Petroleum Association.

47. Electricity Production and Consumption, 1960 to 1990

PROVINCE OR TERRITORY	1960 PRODUCTION (GW.h)	1960 CONSUMPTION (GW.h)	1970 PRODUCTION (GW.h)	1970 CONSUMPTION (GW.h)	1980 PRODUCTION (GW.h)	1980 CONSUMPTION (GW.h)	1990 PRODUCTION (GW.h)	1990 CONSUMPTION (GW.h)
Newfoundland	1 512	1 427	4 854	4 770	46 374	8 545	36 813	10 650
Prince Edward Island	79	79	250	250	127	518	81	752
Nova Scotia	1 814	1 733	3 511	3 706	6 868	6 814	9 430	9 678
New Brunswick	1 738	1 684	5 142	4 221	9 323	8 838	16 665	13 173
Quebec	50 433	44 002	75 877	69 730	97 917	118 254	135 458	157 308
Ontario	35 815	37 157	63 857	69 488	110 283	106 509	129 343	142 818
Manitoba	3 742	4 021	8 449	8 601	19 468	13 927	20 149	17 450
Saskatchewan	2 204	2 124	6 011	5 402	9 204	9 827	13 540	13 589
Alberta	3 443	3 472	10 035	9 880	23 451	23 172	42 874	42 041
British Columbia	13 409	13 413	26 209	25 761	43 416	42 789	60 662	57 206
Yukon	89	89	224	220	381	381	480	480
Northwest Territories	100	100	304	308	494	494	472	472
Canada	**114 378**	**109 304**	**204 723**	**202 337**	**367 306**	**340 068**	**465 967**	**465 617**

SOURCE: Statistics Canada, *Electrical Power Statistics, Vol. II*, Cat. No. 57-202.

48. Electrical Energy Production by Fuel Type, 1990

PROVINCE OR TERRITORY	FUEL TYPE COAL	OIL	NATURAL GAS	NUCLEAR	HYDRO	OTHER	TOTAL
				(GW.h)			
Newfoundland	0	1 881	0	0	34 932	0	36 813
Prince Edward Island	107	81	0	0	0	0	188
Nova Scotia	5 680	2 470	0	0	1 150	130	9 430
New Brunswick	1 140	6 293	0	5 338	3 484	303	16 558
Quebec	0	1 908	0	4 146	129 404	0	135 458
Ontario	26 352	1 087	2 000	59 353	40 225	326	129 343
Manitoba	345	5	8	0	19 747	44	20 149
Saskatchewan	8 623	14	507	0	4 220	176	13 540
Alberta	35 195	0	5 123	0	2 060	496	42 874
British Columbia	0	688	1 569	0	57 245	1 160	60 662
Yukon	0	57	0	0	423	0	480
Northwest Territories	0	215	0	0	257	0	472
Canada	**77 442**	**14 699**	**9 207**	**68 837**	**293 147**	**2 635**	**465 967**

SOURCE: Statistics Canada, *Electric Power Statistics, Vol. II*, Cat. No. 57-202.

Manufacturing

49. Summary Statistics, Annual Census of Manufacturers, 1965–1988

YEAR	NUMBER OF ESTABLISHMENTS[1]	PRODUCTION AND RELATED WORKERS NUMBER	WORK HOURS PAID (000)	WAGES ($000)	COST OF FUEL AND ELECTRICITY ($000)	COST OF MATERIALS AND SUPPLIES USED ($000)	VALUE OF SHIPMENTS OF GOODS OF OWN MANUFACTURE ($000)	VALUE ADDED ($000)
1965	33 310	1 115 892	2 384 002	5 012 345	675 641	18 622 213	33 889 425	14 927 764
1970	31 928	1 167 063	2 450 058	7 232 256	903 264	25 699 999	46 380 935	20 047 801
1975	30 100	1 271 786	2 613 062	12 699 228	1 805 398	51 177 942	88 427 031	36 105 457
1980	35 495	1 346 187	2 780 203	22 162 309	4 448 859	99 897 576	168 058 662	65 851 774
1984	36 464	1 240 816	2 583 486	28 294 553	7 306 383	136 133 629	230 070 091	88 667 660
1988	40 262	1 474 738	3 089 681	38 890 576	7 362 810	166 534 406	298 210 479	125 175 167

[1]The increase in the number of establishments between 1975 and 1980 was largely a result of the addition of 4 962 small establishments by improved coverage.
SOURCE: *Canada Year Book 1976-77, 1992.*

50. Value of Shipments of Goods of Own Manufacture, by Industry Group, 1988 ($000 000)

INDUSTRY GROUP	PROVINCE OR TERRITORY NFLD	PEI	NS	NB	QUE	ONT	MAN	SASK	ALTA	BC	YUKON AND NWT	CANADA
Food	799.7	266.0	1 265.1	1 127.8	9 027.0	14 826.1	1 640.3	985.8	4 113.1	2 928.6	—	37 159.5
Beverage	[1]	[1]	144.8	173.0	1 527.6	2 708.1	174.4	117.9	417.5	471.5	—	5 865.4
Tobacco Products	—	—	—	—	[1]	[1]	—	—	—	—	—	1 778.6
Rubber Products	—	—	[1]	[1]	[1]	1 454.9	[1]	[1]	[1]	[1]	—	2 694.7
Plastic Products	[1]	[1]	64.2	64.0	1 469.5	3 390.0	184.9	47.4	289.6	371.4	—	5 893.1
Leather and Allied Products	[1]	—	0.5	[1]	533.9	641.4	40.9	6.0	23.3	[1]	—	1 293.3
Primary Textile	—	[1]	[1]	[1]	1 687.5	1338.5	[1]	—	[1]	20.3	—	3 173.3
Textile Products	[1]	[1]	100.1	[1]	1 629.1	1 460.0	53.0	12.5	65.6	82.5	—	3 411.0
Clothing	[1]	[1]	49.9	15.7	4 062.1	1 812.3	338.2	15.0	140.0	221.6	—	6 656.7
Wood	29.2	14.1	159.8	497.6	3 613.5	2 906.0	220.5	151.9	797.7	6 931.9	—	15 322.2
Furniture and Fixture	0.9	—	18.8	20.7	1 438.4	2 571.4	153.8	10.6	217.4	187.8	—	4 619.7
Paper and Allied Products	[1]	[1]	661.8	1 643.5	8 122.6	7 906.4	322.9	[1]	631.0	5 728.1	—	25 661.1
Printing, Publishing, and Allied	45.1	16.5	146.1	96.3	3 315.0	6 638.0	452.2	203.4	733.9	879.4	—	12 525.7
Primary Metal	[1]	—	[1]	[1]	7465.6	11 903.4	512.4	[1]	1 089.7	1 241.9	—	22 715.4
Fabricated Metal Products	25.0	13.5	113.2	183.5	4 085.7	10 948.1	428.9	145.9	954.9	1 156.8	—	18 055.8
Machinery	1.7	11.5	39.4	69.8	1 667.6	6 162.4	430.7	175.7	761.4	692.3	—	10 012.3
Transportation Equipment	[1]	18.5	368.4	[1]	6 302.5	42 304.7	652.7	98.8	227.5	972.1	—	51 718.1
Electrical and Electronic Products	[1]	[1]	119.0	50.7	4 843.4	11 707.7	514.7	184.6	344.3	407.3	—	18 191.7
Non-metallic Mineral Products	51.6	4.4	105.2	108.5	1 837.5	4 159.2	199.4	99.5	629.7	608.5	—	7 803.6
Petroleum and Coal Products	[1]	—	[1]	[1]	2 700.2	5 376.2	[1]	[1]	2 876.4	1 473.5	[1]	14 938.9
Chemical and Chemical Products	90.5	22.4	58.3	103.1	5 132.6	12 571.0	229.1	164.0	3 442.6	814.6	—	22 628.0
Other Manufacturing	4.1	6.1	[1]	[1]	[1]	[1]	76.9	28.0	229.9	259.1	[1]	6 092.3
All Manufacturing Industries	**1 726.0**	**391.7**	**5 455.7**	**5 627.7**	**73 750.6**	**157 540.2**	**6 671.0**	**3 380.1**	**18 100.5**	**25 510.1**	**57.0**	**298 210.5**

—not applicable [1]Confidential. SOURCE: *Canada Year Book, 1992.*

51. Principal Statistics on Manufacturing Industries, 1987

PROVINCE OR TERRITORY	NUMBER OF ESTABLISHMENTS	NUMBER OF EMPLOYEES	SALARIES AND WAGES	COST OF FUEL AND ELECTRICITY	COST OF MATERIALS, SUPPLIES, AND GOODS FOR RESALE	VALUE OF SHIPMENTS AND OTHER REVENUE	VALUE ADDED
				($000)			
Newfoundland	318	18 627	397 423	97 528	1 181 306	2 056 117	786 407
Prince Edward Island	135	3 530	60 698	7 579	276 838	416 915	137 727
Nova Scotia	761	37 715	904 984	155 234	3 528 073	5 629 641	1 977 995
New Brunswick	691	32 424	838 345	253 059	3 715 621	6 018 550	2 092 485
Quebec	11 183	520 459	13 443 485	2 067 000	40 411 645	72 608 303	30 287 556
Ontario	15 109	956 400	27 488 737	3 007 220	109 362 283	174 700 261	62 452 655
Manitoba	1 186	54 031	1 284 561	165 220	3 904 361	6 992 457	2 910 052
Saskatchewan	810	19 772	516 865	110 302	2 050 042	3 522 989	1 371 214
Alberta	2 590	78 220	2 278 685	438 604	11 275 650	17 242 833	5 538 627
British Columbia	3 969	142 512	4 610 679	751 600	13 450 792	24 805 204	10 708 896
Yukon and Northwest Territories	38	328	7 785	795	30 233	56 249	25 959
Canada	**36 790**	**1 864 018**	**51 832 248**	**7 054 140**	**189 186 844**	**314 049 518**	**118 289 573**

SOURCE: Statistics Canada, *Market Research Handbook*, 1991.

Transportation

52. St. Lawrence Seaway Traffic by Classification and Direction, 1990

MONTREAL-LAKE ONTARIO SECTION

COMMODITIES	UPBOUND (000 t)	SOURCES AND DESTINATIONS OF UPBOUND COMMODITIES (%)	DOWNBOUND (000 t)	SOURCES AND DESTINATIONS OF DOWNBOUND COMMODITIES (%)
Wheat	—	—	9 276.2	Can→Can 76 US→Can 10 US→For 10
Corn	—	—	1 206.0	US→Can 48 US→For 37 Can→Can 13
Barley	2.4	Can→Can 100	1 122.9	US→Can 54 Can→Can 25 US→For 21
Soybeans	—		272.9	US→For 86 Can→For 14
Flaxseed	—	—	165.7	Can→For 100
Total Agricultural Products	**6.5**		**12 426.9**	
Bituminous Coal	—		489.4	US→Can 91 Can→Can 5 US→For 4
Coke			946.2	US→Can 54 US→For 33 Can→Can 10
Iron Ore	11 518.6	Can→US 53 Can→Can 47	9.2	US→Can 100
Aluminium Ore and Concentrates	178.3	For→Can 87 For→US 8 Can→Can 5	—	
Clay and Bentonite	5.9	For→US 100	223.7	US→Can 63 US→For 37
Stone and Gravel	—	—	715.5	Can→Can 73 US→Can 27
Salt	368.7	Can→Can 100	815.1	Can→Can 77 US→Can 23
Total Mine Products	**13 072.9**		**3 470.2**	
Gasoline	37.7	Can→Can 51 For→Can 42 US→Can 5	109.6	Can→Can 78 Can→For 22
Fuel Oil	262.8	Can→Can 39 Can→US 41 For→Can 10	627.8	Can→Can 93 Can→US 6
Chemicals	370.2	For→Can 52 US→Can 30 Can→US 5	446.8	Can→For 59 Can→Can 30 Can→US 11
Sodium Production	13.1	US→Can 91	92.2	Can→Can 100
Iron and Steel Production	2 683.4	For→Can 14 For→US 86	924.1	Can→For 67 US→For 31
Sugar	266.1	For→Can 100	—	
Scrap Iron and Steel	0.8	For→US 97	232.8	US→For 58 Can→For 29 Can→Can 13
Total Manufactures[1]	**4 567.9**		**3 047.0**	
Grand Total (000 t)	**17 647.2**		**19 008.7**	
($000)	**21 286.2**		**15 683.6**	

WELLAND CANAL SECTION

COMMODITIES	UPBOUND (000 t)	SOURCES AND DESTINATIONS OF UPBOUND COMMODITIES (%)	DOWNBOUND (000 t)	SOURCES AND DESTINATIONS OF DOWNBOUND COMMODITIES (%)
Wheat	—	—	9 366.4	Can→Can 77 US→Can 10 US→For 10
Corn	—	—	1 392.7	US→Can 53 US→For 32 Can→Can 13
Barley	—	—	1 125.3	US→Can 54 Can→Can 25 US→For 21
Soybeans	—	—	364.8	US→For 64 US→Can 23 Can→For 10
Flaxseed	—	—	165.7	Can→For 100
Total Agricultural Products	**0.2**		**12 801.2**	
Bituminous Coal	—	—	6 266.0	US→Can 99
Coke	106.2	Can→US 100	930.8	US→Can 57 US→For 33 Can→Can 8
Iron Ore	6 448.9	Can→US 95 Can→Can 4	1 034.1	US→Can 100
Aluminium Ore and Concentrates	178.3	For→Can 87 For→US 8 Can→Can 5	—	
Clay and Bentonite	5.9	For→US 100	223.7	US→Can 63 US→For 37
Stone, Gravel, and Sand	820.4	Can→US 98	1 175.5	Can→Can 65 US→Can 35
Salt	—	—	1 513.2	Can→Can 50 US→Can 47 Can→US 3
Total Mine Products	**7 866.5**		**11 724.0**	

WELLAND CANAL SECTION (Continued)

Gasoline	25.4	Can→Can 63 Can→US 37		198.6	US→Can 99 US→For 1	
Fuel Oils	106.2	Can→Can 39 Can→US 47 For→Can 14		832.5	US→Can 57 US→For 33 Can→Can 8	
Chemicals	144.2	For→Can 47 For→US 34 Can→US 12		540.6	Can→For 47 Can→Can 38 Can→US 14	
Sodium Products	—			87.5	Can→Can 100	
Iron and Steel Production	2 390.0	For→US 97 For→Can 3		440.6	US→For 64 Can→For 34	
Cement	399.0	Can→US 86 Can→Can 14		8.3	Can→US 59	
Scrap Iron and Steel	217.5	Can→Can 54 Can→US 46		151.6	US→For 89 Can→For 11	
Total Manufactures[1]	**4 094.8**			**2 842.8**		
Grand Total (000 t)	**11 961.5**			**27 436.4**		
($000)	**12 190.2**			**19 561.2**		

[1]Includes unclassified cargoes.
SOURCE: *The St. Lawrence Seaway Traffic Report—1990 Navigation Season*, St. Lawrence Seaway Authority (Ottawa) and the Saint Lawrence Seaway Development Corporation (Washington).

53. Canadian Travel Balance of Trade ($000 000)

YEAR	RECEIPTS	PAYMENTS	BALANCE
1930	180	92	88
1935	117	64	53
1940	105	43	62
1945	166	83	83
1950	275	226	49
1955	328	449	−121
1960	420	627	−207
1965	747	796	−49
1970	1 234	1 460	−226
1975	1 815	2 542	−727
1980	3 349	4 577	−1 228
1981	3 760	4 876	−1 116
1982	3 724	5 008	−1 284
1983	3 841	6 045	−2 204
1984	4 416	6 542	−2 126
1985	5 006	7 110	−2 104
1986	6 333	7 499	−1 166
1987	6 299	8 828	−2 529
1988	6 894	9 631	−2 737
1989	7 232	10 708	−3 476
1990[1]	7 437	11 961	−4 524

[1]Preliminary.
SOURCE: Statistics Canada

54. Vessels and Tonnage Handled by Canada Ports Corporation, 1989

PORT	NUMBER OF VESSEL ARRIVALS	CARGO HANDLED (000 t)	GRAIN ELEVATOR SHIPMENTS (000 t)
St. John's	979	977	—
Halifax	2 163	16 784	457
Saint John	1 518	14 702	90
Belledune	39	393	—
Sept-Îles	696	23 302	—
Chicoutimi	94	484	—
Baie-des-Ha! Ha!	206	3 857	—
Quebec	952	15 668	1 813
Trois-Rivières	488	1 584	428
Montreal	2 431	20 423	1 209
Prescott	23	289	239
Port Colborne	—	45	108
Churchill	26	320	292
Vancouver	9 409	64 025	9 624
Prince Rupert	1 705	11 332	3 475
Total	**20 729**	**174 185**	**17 735**

SOURCE: *Canada Year Book, 1992*.

55. Where Canadians Travel (000)[1]

COUNTRY OR REGION	1980	1985	1989
Total Visits	**27 402**	**28 118**	**39 006**
United States	**24 594**	**23 886**	**33 969**
California	826	763	1 047
Florida	1 482	1 536	2 234
Maine	1 098	974	1 333
Michigan	2 099	2 052	2 549
New Hampshire	778	708	942
New York	3 623	3 700	5 299
Ohio	815	757	1 067
Pennsylvania	873	867	1 331
Vermont	1 273	1 189	1 506
Washington	1 833	1 642	2 388
Europe	**1 591**	**2 578**	**2 764**
Austria	75	130	122
Belgium	74	107	129
Denmark	28	29	51
France	205	377	380
West Germany	169	259	293
Greece	38	72	61
Ireland	29	53	58
Italy	105	190	169
Netherlands	120	187	231
Portugal	35	62	82
Spain	39	98	87
Switzerland	117	200	175
United Kingdom	446	644	667
Yugoslavia	13	25	41
Caribbean	**621**	**776**	**929**
Bahamas	125	100	103
Barbados	110	87	64
Bermuda	42	40	62
Cuba	33	60	68
Dominican Republic	n.a.	n.a.	186
Jamaica	70	77	96
Central America	**236**	**290**	**514**
Mexico	220	264	475
Asia	**159**	**274**	**382**
Hong Kong	24	53	75
Japan	27	47	52
Australasia[2]	**66**	**108**	**131**
Africa	**66**	**86**	**100**
South America	**56**	**108**	**204**

[1]Includes visits which lasted less than one day.
[2]Includes islands in the Pacific, Indian, and Atlantic Oceans.
n.a.—not available.
SOURCE: Statistics Canada.

56. Principal Seaway Ports[1], 1990

CANADA

(000 t)[2]	UP	DOWN
Hamilton	10 621.1	1 165.4
Port Cartier	2 948.6	3 014.9
Montreal	2 727.2	276.8
Baie Comeau	2 761.8	3.6
Quebec City	2 143.3	1 210.7
Toronto	1 275.4	83.1
Pointe Noire	258.7	5 082.2
Sarnia	118.1	1 259.6
Sept Îles	616.1	2 211.1
Thunder Bay	9.0	7 991.2
	31 352.1	28 779.0

UNITED STATES

(000 t)	UP	DOWN
Indiana-Burns Harbor	2 682.7	514.0
Cleveland	2 402.8	547.8
Detroit	1 763.5	489.5
Chicago	1 014.9	444.8
Ashtabula	832.4	1 643.7
Conneaut	48.2	1 288.4
Duluth-Superior	131.3	3 730.0
Sandusky	—	1 955.2
Toledo	279.2	2 378.7
	11 746.5	15 245.3

[1]Includes all ports or installations within 20 km radius of the main harbour.
[2]Figures are limited to cargo volumes moved through the seaway lock structures.
SOURCE: *The St. Lawrence Seaway Traffic Report—1990 Navigation Season*, St. Lawrence Seaway Authority (Ottawa) and the Saint Lawrence Seaway Development Corporation (Washington).

Trade

57. Principal Commodities, Imported, 1991

	($000 000)
Food, Feed, Beverages, and Tobacco	**8 268.3**
Fruits and vegetables	1 965.2
Crude Materials, Inedible	**7 709.8**
Crude petroleum	4 416.4
Fabricated Materials, Inedible	**24 888.6**
Plastics and Chemicals	8 284.4
End Products, Inedible	**90 423.9**
Passenger autos	11 660.4
Trucks and other motor vehicles	3 687.0
Motor vehicle parts	15 792.8
Industrial and agricultural machinery	11 123.1
Apparel and footwear	3 460.9
Total	**134 323.2**

SOURCE: Statistics Canada, *Summary of Canadian International Trade*, Cat. No. 65-001.

58. Principal Commodities, Exported, 1991

	($000 000)
Food, Feed, Beverages, and Tobacco	**11 336.4**
Wheat and wheat flour	4 021.1
Fish and fish products	2 447.4
Crude Materials, Inedible	**18 495.2**
Crude petroleum	5 880.9
Natural gas	3 421.3
Metal ores (iron, copper, zinc)	4 443.3
Coal	1 582.7
Fabricated Materials, Inedible	**44 882.6**
Forestry products	18 995.7
Metals and alloys	12 738.3
End Products, Inedible	**64 032.3**
Passenger autos	16 287.4
Trucks and other vehicles	7 778.6
Motor vehicle parts	7 985.1
Aircraft and other transport equipment	6 708.1
Total	**141 701.2**

SOURCE: Statistics Canada, *Summary of Canadian International Trade*, Cat. No. 65-001.

59. Imports To Canada, Principal Nations, 1987, 1989, and 1991

COUNTRY	1987	1989	1991
		($000 000)	
United States	76 716	88 017	86 235
Japan	8 351	9 571	10 249
Great Britain	4 276	4 562	4 182
Germany	3 649	3 709	3 734
South Korea	1 912	2 441	2 110
Taiwan	2 166	2 351	2 212
France	1 590	2 019	2 670
Italy	1 793	2 015	1 792
Mexico	1 165	1 704	2 574
China	812	1 182	1 852
Hong Kong	1 097	1 160	1 021
Brazil	858	1 129	706
All countries	**116 238**	**135 033**	**135 284**

[1]Figures for 1987 and 1989 do not include the former East Germany.
SOURCE: Statistics Canada, *Imports by Countries*, Cat. No. 65-006.

60. Exports From Canada, Principal Nations, 1987, 1989, and 1991

COUNTRY	1987	1989	1991
		($000 000)	
United States	91 756	98 548	103 449
Japan	7 036	8 803	7 111
Great Britain	2 850	3 441	2 920
Germany[1]	1 515	1 801	2 125
South Korea	1 167	1 645	1 861
Netherlands	1 021	1 534	1 655
Belgium	1 123	1 398	1 073
France	1 037	1 268	1 350
China	1 432	1 120	1 849
Italy	843	1 099	1 017
Hong Kong	480	1 050	817
Australia	689	1 031	628
All countries	**121 462**	**134 511**	**138 079**

[1]Figures for 1987 and 1989 do not include the former East Germany.
SOURCE: Statistics Canada, *Exports by Countries*, Cat. No. 65-003.

The Economy

61. Gross Domestic Product at Factor Cost, by Industry[1], 1970 to 1989

INDUSTRY	1970	1980	1989
Agricultural and Related Services	2.9	2.1	1.6
Fishing	0.3	0.2	0.2
Forestry	0.8	0.6	0.6
Mining	6.4	4.1	3.5
Manufacturing	19.7	17.7	16.8
Construction	6.2	5.7	5.8
Trade	10.5	9.6	10.6
Finance, Insurance, and Real Estate	12.3	13.4	14.1
Transportation, Communications, and Utilities	9.1	10.1	10.5
Community, Business, and Personal Services	20.2	20.2	20.0
Public Administration	7.5	6.7	5.8

[1]Based on per cent of Canada's GDP.
SOURCE: *Canada Year Book 1992.*

64. Gross Domestic Product at Market Prices[1], 1970 to 1989

PROVINCE OR TERRITORY	1970	1980	1989
Newfoundland	1.4	1.3	1.3
Prince Edward Island	0.3	0.3	0.3
Nova Scotia	2.5	2.0	2.5
New Brunswick	1.9	1.6	1.9
Quebec	25.5	23.3	23.6
Ontario	42.0	37.1	41.5
Manitoba	4.2	3.6	3.5
Saskatchewan	3.4	4.0	3.1
Alberta	8.0	13.9	10.3
British Columbia	10.6	12.4	11.5
Yukon and Northwest Territories	0.3	0.4	0.4

[1]Based on per cent of Canada's GDP.
SOURCE: *Canada Year Book 1992.*

62. National Finances, 1970 to 1991

YEAR	REVENUE	EXPENDITURE ($ 000 000)	SURPLUS/ DEFICIT	GROSS DEBT
1970-1971	15 364	16 002	(638)[1]	35 250
1975-1976	32 354	37 464	(5 110)	55 889
1980-1981	53 796	67 829	(14 033)	113 170
1985-1986	83 060	116 911	(33 851)	249 452
1990-1991	127 067	155 502	(28 435)	408 483

[1]( ) indicates a negative value.
SOURCE: Statistics Canada, *Canadian Economic Observer*, June 1991.

65. Canadian Balance of International Payments, All Countries, Current Account, 1987 to 1989

ITEM	1987	1988	1989	% CHANGE 1989/1988
	($000 000)			
Current Receipts				
Merchandise Exports	126 120	137 294	138 934	1.2
Non-merchandise Services				
Total Services	18 316	19 982	20 470	2.4
Travel	6 299	6 894	7 091	2.9
Freight and Shipping	4 740	5 065	5 365	5.9
Business Services	6 126	6 678	6 852	2.6
Government Transactions	680	636	669	5.2
Other Services	471	708	493	−30.4
Investment Income	7 061	10 867	7 661	−29.5
Transfers	5 429	7 935	8 722	9.9
Total Non-merchandise Receipts	30 806	38 784	36 853	−5.0
Total Receipts	**156 926**	**176 078**	**175 788**	**−0.2**
Current Payments				
Merchandise Imports	114 767	127 486	134 255	5.3
Non-merchandise Services				
Total Services	24 586	25 964	27 528	6.0
Travel	8 828	9 631	10 589	9.9
Freight and Shipping	4 817	4 614	4 708	2.0
Business Services	9 397	10 111	10 543	4.3
Government Transactions	1 185	1 232	1 293	5.0
Other Services	358	376	395	5.1
Investment Income	23 580	29 279	30 023	2.5
Transfers	3 353	3 665	3 640	−0.7
Total Non-merchandise Payments	51 519	58 908	61 191	3.9
Total Payments	**166 286**	**186 394**	**195 446**	**4.9**
Balances				
Merchandise	+11 353	+9 808	+4 679	−52.3
Non-merchandise	−20 713	−20 124	−24 338	—
Total Current	**−9 360**	**−10 316**	**−19 659**	**—**

SOURCE: Statistics Canada, *Quarterly Estimates of the Canadian Balance of International Payments, Fourth Quarter*, Cat. No. 67-001.

63. Inflation Rates, 1915 to 1990

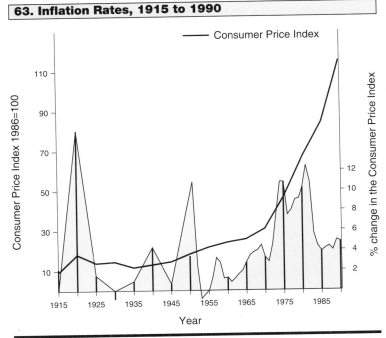

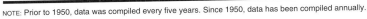

NOTE: Prior to 1950, data was compiled every five years. Since 1950, data has been compiled annually.

Conservation and Pollution

66. Ecozone Biophysical Characteristics[1]

ECOZONE	LANDFORMS	VEGETATION	SOILS AND SURFACE MATERIALS	CLIMATE
Atlantic Maritime	Hills and coastal plains	Mixed broadleaf and conifer stands	Acid and well-weathered soils (podzols) and soils with clay-rich sublayers (luvisols), moraine, marine bottom soils, and rock debris	Cool to cold winters, mild summers, moderate to heavy precipitation
Mixed-Wood Plain	Plains, some interior hills	Mixed broadleaf and conifer stands	Temperate region soils with clay-rich sublayers (luvisols), marine bottom soils, moraine, rock	Cool to cold winters, warm to hot summers, moderate precipitation
Boreal Shield	Plains, uplands, interior hills, many lakes and streams	Conifer and broadleaf boreal stands	Acid and well-weathered soils (podzols), lake bottom soils, moraine, rock	Cold winters, warm to hot summers, moderate precipitation
Prairie	Plains, some foothills	Short and mixed grasslands, aspen parkland	Organically rich, relatively fertile grassland soils (chernozems), moraine, and lake bottom materials	Cold winters, hot summers minimal precipitation
Boreal Plain	Plains, some foothills	Conifer and broadleaf boreal stands	Temperate region soils with clay-rich sublayers (luvisols), moraine and lake bottom materials	Cold winters, warm summers, moderate precipitation
Montane Cordillera	Mountainous highlands, interior plains	Mixed vegetation, conifer stands to sage brush	Temperate region soils with clay-rich sublayers (luvisols), soils with minimal weathering (brunisols), moraine, rock, rock debris	Cool to cold winters, warm to hot summers, and in lee areas, moist in montane areas
Pacific Maritime	Mountainous highlands, some coastal plains	Coastal western and mountain hemlock	Acid and well-weathered soils (podzols), moraine, rock, rock debris	Mild winters, mild summers, heavy precipitation, especially in fall and winter
Boreal Cordillera	Mountainous highlands, some hills and plains	Boreal, some alpine tundra and open woodland	Soils with minimal weathering (brunisols), moraine, rock	Cold winters, mild summers, minimal precipitation in lee areas, moist in montane areas
Tundra Cordillera	Mountainous highlands	Alpine and arctic tundra	Soils with minimal weathering (brunisols), frozen soils (cryosols), moraine, rock	Very cold winters, cool summers, minimal precipitation
Taiga Plain	Plains, some foothills	Open woodland, shrublands, and wetlands	Soils with minimal weathering (brunisols), some frozen soils (cryosols), organic materials, moraine	Cold winters, mild to warm summers, moderate precipitation
Taiga Shield	Plains, uplands, some interior hills, many lakes and streams	Open woodlands, some arctic tundra and lichen heath	Soils with minimal weathering (brunisols), acid and well-weathered soils (podzols), some frozen soils (cryosols), moraine, rock	Cold winters, warm summers, moderate precipitation
Hudson Bay Plain	Plains	Wetland, arctic tundra, and some conifer stands	Organic soils, sea bottom and beach materials	Cold winters, mild summers, minimal precipitation
Southern Arctic	Plains, some interior hills	Shrub/herb/heath arctic tundra	Frozen soils (cryosols), moraine rock, marine bottom sediments	Cold winters, cool summers, minimal precipitation
Northern Arctic	Plains and hills	Herb-lichen arctic tundra	Frozen soils (cryosols), moraine, rock, marine bottom sediments	Very cold winters, cool summers, minimal precipitation
Arctic Cordillera	Mountainous highlands	Largely non-vegetated, some shrub/herb arctic tundra	Frozen soils (cryosols), rock, rock debris, ice	Very cold winters, cool to cold summers, minimal precipitation

This list is meant to be illustrative only and is not a comprehensive presentation of the characteristics of these areas.
SOURCE: Environment Canada, Lands Directorate. *Terrestrial Ecozones of Canada*, by E. Wiken, unpublished working paper, August, 1983.

67. Conservation Lands and Waters, Area and Number of Reserves

PROVINCE OR TERRITORY	NATIONAL PARKS	NATIONAL WILDLIFE AREAS, MIGRATORY BIRD SANCTUARIES	PROVINCIAL/ TERRITORIAL PARKS	PROVINCIAL/ TERRITORIAL WILDLIFE AREAS	PROVINCIAL/ TERRITORIAL WILDERNESS AREAS	PROVINCIAL/ TERRITORIAL ECOLOGICAL RESERVES	OTHER PROVINCIAL/ TERRITORIAL RESERVES	AREA OF PROVINCE/ TERRITORY	% OF PROVINCE/ TERRITORY RESERVED	TOTAL AREA OF RESERVES WITH NO LOGGING, MINING, OR SPORT HUNTING[1]	% OF PROVINCE/ TERRITORY RESERVED WITH NO LOGGING, MINING, OR SPORT HUNTING
					TOTAL AREA IN KM[2] / NUMBER OF RESERVES						
British Columbia	6 302 / 6	54 / 15	52 337 / 387	177 / 6	1 315 / 1	1 558 / 120	—	948 596	6.5	22 685	2.4
Alberta	54 085 / 4.8	145 / 7	1 365 / 106	680 / 8	5 607 / 4	185 / 10	309 / 114	661 185	9.4	56 420	8.5[2]
Saskatchewan	4 781 / 2	827 / 23	9 081 / 31	18 848 / 1 662	—	8 / 1	769 / 298	651 900	5.1	6 289	1.0
Manitoba	2 976 / 1	1 / 2	14 314 / 60	30 658 / 74	—	178 / 9	15 666 / 5	650 087	9.8	3 189	0.5
Ontario	2 171 / 5	443 / 23	56 273 / 217	9 240 / 45	618 / 37	—	539 / 323	1 068 582	6.5	24 249	2.2
Quebec	935 / 3	661 / 42	4 000 / 16	67 000 / 16	—	484 / 21	537 / 1	1 540 680	4.8	5 956	0.4
New Brunswick	445 / 2	62 / 7	217 / 49	3 219 / 19	—	—	1 / 3	73 436	5.4	663	0.9
Nova Scotia	1 332 / 2	66 / 15	131 / 107	1 396 / 25	—	1 / 2	3 / 4	55 491	5.3	1 387	2.5
Prince Edward Island	26 / 1	1 / 1	42 / 67	29 / 5	—	—	—	5 657	1.7	97	1.7
Newfoundland	2 338 / 2	9 / 1	235 / 75	—	1 070 / 1	23 / 6	—	404 517	0.9	2 597	0.6

PROVINCE OR TERRITORY	NATIONAL PARKS	NATIONAL WILDLIFE AREAS, MIGRATORY BIRD SANCTUARIES	PROVINCIAL/ TERRITORIAL PARKS	PROVINCIAL/ TERRITORIAL WILDLIFE AREAS	PROVINCIAL/ TERRITORIAL WILDERNESS AREAS	PROVINCIAL/ TERRITORIAL ECOLOGICAL RESERVES	OTHER PROVINCIAL/ TERRITORIAL RESERVES	AREA OF PROVINCE/ TERRITORY	% OF PROVINCE/ TERRITORY RESERVED	TOTAL AREA OF RESERVES WITH NO LOGGING, MINING, OR SPORT HUNTING[1]	% OF PROVINCE/ TERRITORY RESERVED WITH NO LOGGING, MINING, OR SPORT HUNTING
Yukon	32 183 / 2		114 / 1	5 918 / 2	—	—	—	482 515	7.9	32 273	6.7
Northwest Territories	74 698 / 3.2	113 405 / 15	130 / 44	26 464 / 3	—	—	—	3 379 684	6.4	98 658	2.9
Canada	**182 272 / 34**	**115 674 / 151**	**138 239 / 1 160**	**163 629 / 1 865**	**8 680 / 43**	**2 437 / 169**	**17 824 / 748**	**9 922 330**	**6.3**	**254 463**	**2.6**

[1]Not including hunting by aboriginal people under treaty or land claim settlements.
[2]Two-thirds of this area is accounted for by the Alberta portion of Wood Buffalo National Park.
SOURCE: Reprinted with permission from *Endangered Spaces: The Future for Canada's Wilderness*, Monte Hummel, ed., published by Key Porter Books Limited, Toronto, Ontario. Copyright © 1989 Monte Hummel.

68. Major Air Pollutants for Selected Canadian Cities

CITY	SULPHUR DIOXIDE (PPB)	NITROGEN DIOXIDE (PPB)	OZONE (PPB, 1 HOUR)	CARBON MONOXIDE (PPB, 1 HOUR)	TOTAL SUSPENDED PARTICLES (UG/M)
MAXIMUM ACCEPTABLE CONCENTRATION	23	53	82	13	70
MAXIMUM DESIRABLE CONCENTRATION	11	23	50	5	60
Toronto	5.1	26	100	3	65
Montreal	7.1	27	85	3	40
Vancouver	6	25	58	4.8	36
Ottawa	4.5	28	45	2.5	43
Edmonton	3	24	60	3.6	46
Calgary	3	28	55	4.0	54
Winnipeg	1.5	17	80	2	46
Quebec City	5	31	70	3	*
Hamilton	12	25	110	2	83
St. Catharines-Niagara Falls	6	21	60	2	55
London	6	22	100	2	57
Kitchener	3	25	80	3	60
Halifax	11	12	65	2	35
Victoria	nm	nm	nm	nm	33
Windsor	8	28	100	2	54
Oshawa	6	24	110	3	55
Saskatoon	0.0	15	60	1	31
Regina	*	14	60	3	39
St. John's, Nfld.	8	nm	90	3	31
Chicoutimi-Jonquière	nm	nm	nm	nm	nm
Sudbury	8	11	80	1	36
Sherbrooke	nm	nm	nm	nm	46
Trois-Rivières	8	nm	nm		46
Kingston	nm	nm	nm	nm	
Thunder Bay	0.0	12	70	nm	37
				2	
Saint John, N.B.	10	*	70	2	32
Sydney, N.S.	2	nm	nm	nm	41
Fredericton	nm	nm	nm	nm	30
Charlottetown	2	nm	nm	nm	22
Whitehorse	nm	nm	nm	nm	32
Yellowknife	nm	nm	nm	nm	63
Dorset	2	19	138*m		19

* insufficient data collected nm – not measured *M – based on absolute maximum ozone peak (other measurements use 99.9 percentile, but this was not available for Dorset) *Based on city average.
SOURCE: T. Furmancyk, Environment Canada, Regulatory Affairs and Program Integration Branch, in *The State of Canada's Environment*, published by the Minister of the Environment and the Minister of Supply and Services Canada, 1991.

Climate

69. Average Daily Temperature (°C)

STATION	JAN	FEB	MAR	APR	MAY	JUNE	JULY	AUG	SEPT	OCT	NOV	DEC	ANNUAL
Goose Bay	−17.3	−15.5	−9.2	−1.8	5.1	10.9	15.5	14.2	9.0	2.5	−4.0	−13.4	−0.3
St. John's West	−4.0	−4.6	−2.0	1.8	6.4	11.3	15.8	15.6	11.8	7.3	3.3	−1.4	5.1
Charlottetown	−7.2	−7.5	−3.0	2.7	9.2	14.8	18.8	18.4	14.0	8.6	3.1	−3.6	5.7
Halifax	−5.8	−6.0	−1.7	3.6	9.4	14.7	18.3	18.1	13.8	8.5	3.2	−3.0	6.1
Saint John	−8.2	−7.7	−2.6	3.2	9.1	13.8	16.9	16.7	12.7	7.5	2.1	−5.0	4.9
Kuujjuarapik	−22.8	−23.1	−17.5	−7.1	1.2	6.3	10.2	10.6	7.2	2.1	−5.0	−16.6	−4.5
Quebec	−12.4	−11.0	−4.6	3.3	10.8	16.3	19.1	17.6	12.5	6.5	−0.5	−9.1	4.0
Sept-Îles	−14.6	−13.0	−6.8	0.0	5.9	11.6	15.2	14.2	9.2	3.4	−2.7	−11.0	0.9
Montreal	−10.3	−8.8	−2.4	5.7	12.9	18.0	20.8	19.4	14.5	8.3	1.6	−6.9	6.1
Ottawa	−10.7	−9.2	−2.6	5.9	13.0	18.1	20.8	19.4	14.7	8.3	1.5	−7.2	6.0
Thunder Bay	−15.0	−12.8	−5.6	2.7	9.0	13.9	17.7	16.4	11.2	5.4	−2.6	−11.3	2.4
Toronto	−4.5	−3.8	1.0	7.5	13.8	18.9	22.1	21.1	16.9	10.7	4.9	−1.5	8.9
Windsor	−5.0	−3.9	1.7	8.1	14.4	19.7	22.4	21.3	17.4	10.9	4.7	−1.9	9.1
The Pas	−21.4	−17.5	−10.0	0.5	8.7	14.8	17.7	16.4	9.9	3.5	−7.7	−18.0	−0.3
Winnipeg	−18.3	−15.1	−7.0	3.8	11.6	16.9	19.8	18.3	12.4	5.7	−4.7	−14.6	2.4
Churchill	−26.9	−25.4	−20.2	−10.0	−1.1	6.1	11.8	11.3	5.5	−1.4	−12.5	−22.7	−7.1
Regina	−16.5	−12.9	−6.0	4.1	11.4	16.4	19.1	18.1	11.6	5.1	−5.1	−13.6	2.6
Saskatoon	−17.5	−13.9	−7.0	3.9	11.5	16.2	18.6	17.4	11.2	4.8	−6.0	−14.7	2.0
Calgary	−9.6	−6.3	−2.5	4.1	9.7	14.0	16.4	15.7	10.6	5.7	−3.0	−8.3	3.9
Edmonton	−14.2	−10.8	−5.4	3.7	10.3	14.2	16.0	15.0	9.9	4.6	−5.7	−12.2	2.1
Penticton	−2.0	0.7	4.5	8.7	13.3	17.6	20.3	19.9	14.7	8.7	3.2	−1.1	9.0
Vancouver	3.0	4.7	6.3	8.8	12.1	15.2	17.2	17.4	14.3	10.0	6.0	3.5	9.9
Prince Rupert	0.8	2.5	3.7	5.5	8.4	10.9	12.9	13.3	11.3	8.0	3.8	1.7	6.9
Alert	−31.9	−33.6	−33.1	−25.1	−11.6	−1.0	3.4	1.0	−9.7	−19.5	−27.0	−29.5	−18.1
Inuvik	−28.8	−28.5	−24.1	−14.1	−0.7	10.6	13.8	10.5	3.3	−8.2	−21.5	−26.1	−9.5
Yellowknife	−27.9	−24.5	−18.5	−6.2	5.0	13.1	16.5	14.1	6.7	−1.4	−14.8	−24.1	−5.2
Whitehorse	−18.7	−13.1	−7.2	0.3	6.6	11.6	14.0	12.3	7.3	0.7	−10.0	−15.9	−1.0
Resolute	−32.0	−33.0	−31.2	−23.5	−11.0	−0.6	4.0	1.9	−5.0	−15.2	−24.3	−29.0	−16.6

70. Average Monthly Precipitation (mm)

STATION	JAN	FEB	MAR	APR	MAY	JUNE	JULY	AUG	SEPT	OCT	NOV	DEC	ANNUAL
Goose Bay	64.9	57.0	68.6	57.1	66.4	100.9	119.4	98.3	90.6	78.8	79.9	77.6	959.5
St. John's West	179.4	154.9	146.3	124.5	107.0	93.5	77.8	113.8	117.0	149.0	152.8	163.5	1579.5
Charlottetown	97.1	82.3	83.1	88.3	94.2	87.5	78.5	90.1	91.9	112.4	115.0	116.7	1137.1
Halifax	146.9	119.1	122.6	124.4	110.5	98.4	96.8	109.6	94.9	128.9	154.4	167.0	1473.5
Saint John	128.3	102.6	109.9	109.7	123.1	104.8	103.7	103.0	111.3	122.5	146.2	167.6	1432.8
Kuujjuarapik	28.1	21.1	21.1	25.1	36.4	57.3	72.7	89.0	93.6	73.3	62.1	35.1	614.9
Quebec	90.0	74.4	85.0	75.5	99.9	110.2	118.5	119.6	123.7	96.0	106.1	108.9	1207.7
Sept-Îles	86.8	68.9	80.9	93.4	96.3	92.4	90.8	99.6	111.5	100.8	99.6	107.0	1127.9
Montreal	63.3	56.4	67.6	74.8	68.3	82.5	85.6	100.3	86.5	75.4	93.4	85.6	939.7
Ottawa	50.8	49.7	56.6	64.8	76.8	84.3	86.5	87.8	83.6	74.7	81.0	72.9	869.5
Thunder Bay	32.4	25.6	40.9	47.1	69.3	84.0	79.9	88.5	86.4	60.9	49.4	39.3	703.5
Toronto	55.2	52.6	65.2	65.4	68.0	67.0	71.0	82.5	76.2	63.3	76.1	76.5	818.9
Windsor	50.3	53.7	72.0	80.3	75.7	97.0	85.3	85.7	86.7	57.9	75.4	81.6	901.6
The Pas	16.6	15.1	21.0	26.2	33.6	63.1	69.1	65.0	58.3	37.5	26.6	19.8	451.9
Winnipeg	19.3	14.8	23.1	35.9	59.8	83.8	72.0	75.3	51.3	29.5	21.2	18.6	504.4
Churchill	17.3	12.8	18.3	22.6	30.5	44.5	50.7	60.5	52.6	46.5	35.5	19.7	411.6
Regina	14.7	13.0	16.5	20.4	50.8	67.3	58.9	40.0	34.4	20.3	11.7	15.9	364.0
Saskatoon	15.9	12.9	16.0	19.7	44.2	63.4	58.0	36.8	32.1	16.9	14.1	17.2	347.2
Calgary	12.2	9.9	14.7	25.1	52.9	76.9	69.9	48.7	48.1	15.5	11.6	13.2	398.8
Edmonton	22.9	15.5	15.9	21.8	42.8	76.1	101.0	69.5	47.5	17.7	16.0	19.2	465.8
Penticton	27.3	20.6	20.4	25.8	33.0	34.4	23.3	28.4	23.0	15.7	24.3	32.1	308.5
Vancouver	149.8	123.6	108.8	75.4	61.7	45.7	36.1	38.1	64.4	115.3	169.9	178.5	1167.4
Prince Rupert	250.8	216.5	188.2	181.0	142.0	119.5	112.9	162.8	244.7	378.9	284.4	269.8	2551.6
Alert	7.8	5.2	6.8	9.4	9.9	12.7	25.0	23.8	24.3	13.2	8.8	7.4	154.2
Inuvik	15.6	11.1	10.8	12.6	19.1	22.2	34.1	43.9	24.2	29.6	17.5	16.8	257.4
Yellowknife	14.9	12.6	10.6	10.3	16.6	23.3	35.2	41.7	28.8	34.8	23.9	14.7	267.3
Whitehorse	16.9	11.9	12.1	8.3	14.4	31.2	38.5	39.3	35.2	23.0	18.9	18.9	268.8
Resolute	3.5	3.2	4.7	6.2	8.3	12.7	23.4	31.5	22.8	13.1	5.7	4.6	139.6

SOURCE: Average Daily Temperature and Average Monthly Precipitation statistics are from Environment Canada, Atmospheric Environment Service. These statistics for the 1961-1990 period are from a preliminary draft.

71. Annual Average "Number of Days with" and Bright Sunshine Hours for Selected Weather Stations

STATION	WINDS (>63 km/h)	HAIL[4]	THUNDER[5]	FOG[6]	FREEZING TEMPER-ATURES[7]	FREEZING PRECIP-ITATION[8]	RAIN[9]	SNOW[10]	BRIGHT SUNSHINE[3] (HOURS)
Goose Bay	1	*	9	14	215	13	102	97	1 564.9
St. John's	23	*	3	124	176	38	156	88	1 497.4
Charlottetown	6	*	9	47	169	17	124	68	1 818.4
Halifax	3	*	9	122	163	19	125	64	1 885.0
Saint John	6	*	11	106	173	12	124	59	1 865.3
Kuujjuarapik	3	*	6	45	243	10	83	100	1 497.8
Quebec	*	*	24	35	180	15	115	73	1 851.7
Sept-Îles	9	*	7	51	206	8	93	72	1 990.6
Montreal	1	*	25	20	155	13	114	62	2 054.0
Ottawa	*	*	24	35	165	16	107	62	2 008.5
Thunder Bay	*	*	26	38	204	8	88	61	2 202.8
Toronto	*	*	27	35	155	10	99	47	2 045.4
Windsor	2	*	33	37	136	9	105	45	n/a
The Pas	*	*	23	15	209	12	65	73	2 167.5
Winnipeg	1	3	27	20	195	12	72	57	2 321.4
Churchill	11	*	7	48	258	19	58	100	1 827.9
Regina	9	1	23	29	204	14	59	58	2 331.1
Saskatoon	*	*	19	25	202	9	57	59	2 449.7
Calgary	6	3	25	22	201	5	58	62	2 314.4
Edmonton	*	3	22	17	185	8	70	59	2 263.7
Penticton	*	*	12	1	129	1	78	29	2 032.2
Vancouver	*	*	6	45	55	1	156	15	1 919.6
Prince Rupert	4	8	2	37	107	0	218	35	1 224.1
Alert	10	0	0	46	338	5	10	93	1 767.4
Inuvik	*	*	1	24	267	6	36	99	1 898.8
Yellowknife	*	*	5	21	226	13	46	82	2 276.6
Whitehorse	*	*	6	16	224	1	52	120	1 843.8
Resolute	25	0	*	62	324	13	20	82	1 505.1

*denotes a value less than 0.5 (but no zero).

[1]Average, mean, or normal refer to the value of the particular element averaged over the period from 1951-1980.

[2]A "day with" is counted once per day regardless of the number of individual occurrences of that phenomenon that day.

[3]Bright sunshine is reported in hours and tenths.

[4]Hail is a piece of ice with a diameter of 5 mm or more.

[5]Thunder is reported when thunder is heard or lightning or hail is seen.

[6]Fog is a suspension of small water droplets in air that reduces the horizontal visibility at eye level to less than 1 km.

[7]Freezing temperature is a temperature below 0°C.

[8]Freezing precipitation is rain or drizzle of any quantity that freezes on impact.

[9]Rain is a measurable amount of liquid water (rain, showers, or drizzle) equal to or greater than 0.2 mm.

[10]Snow is a measurable amount of solid precipitation (snow, snow grains, ice crystals, or ice and snow pellets) equal to or greater than 0.2 cm.

SOURCE: Environment Canada. *The Climates of Canada*. David Phillips. Supply and Services Canada. Ottawa, 1990; Environment Canada, Atmospheric Environment Service. *Canadian Climate Normals*; Environment Canada, Atmospheric Environment Service. *Principal Station Data*.

Trade

72. World Trade Total Imports and Exports by Regions, Countries, and Areas, 1970 and 1989

($000 000)

COUNTRY, REGION, OR AREA	IMPORTS 1970	IMPORTS 1989	EXPORTS 1970	EXPORTS 1989
Canada	13 360	114 004	16 119	116 037
USA	42 833	493 195	43 246	363 812
Central and South America	18 380	102 005	16 633	121 315
Europe	148 448	1 360 253	136 127	1 318 800
Eastern Europe (including former USSR)	31 704	202 076	30 969	195 560
Africa	15 166	77 048	14 897	70 801
Asia	48 900	719 899	47 872	786 380
Oceania	7 096	55 703	6 312	46 819
Total Developing Economies	61 992	681 827	59 359	697 983
Total Developed Economies	237 772	2 248 556	223 130	2 126 653
World[1]	331 468	3 132 459	313 457	3 020 295

[1]World total equals the sum of "Developed economies," "Developing economies," and "Eastern Europe," including the former USSR.
SOURCE: United Nations, *1989 International Trade Statistics Yearbook*, Vol. 1, New York, 1991.

73. Imports and Exports by Economic Category and Industrial Origin, 1989

COUNTRY	% IMPORTS BY COMMODITY FOOD PRODUCTS	UNPROCESSED RESOURCES	ENERGY RESOURCES	MACHINERY	TRANSPORT EQUIPMENT	CONSUMER GOODS	OTHERS	% EXPORTS BY COMMODITY AGRICULTURAL PRODUCTS	MINERALS	FOOD BEVERAGES TOBACCO	TEXTILES	WOOD PAPER	CHEMICALS	PROCESSED METALS	OTHER MANUFACTURING
USA	5.4	20.0	11.3	21.2	19.8	19.5	2.7	8.6	2.5	4.9	2.1	4.2	13.5	54.5	9.8
Germany (West)	9.3	31.7	7.2	17.6	12.5	17.0	2.5	1.1	0.8	4.2	5.6	3.5	14.8	65.7	2.5
Japan	13.6	36.9	20.6	10.2	4.2	13.3	1.2	0.3	0.2	0.5	2.3	0.7	8.5	84.5	2.9
UK	8.8	29.6	5.1	22.5	14.6	14.0	1.6	2.0	6.8	5.7	3.8	2.7	17.3	54.9	4.0
France	8.9	32.9	8.7	20.3	13.4	15.7	0.1	6.7	0.6	10.5	6.4	3.5	18.1	51.3	2.8
Italy	11.4	37.0	11.7	17.3	12.7	9.6	0.3	2.2	0.4	4.5	18.2	2.5	12.5	55.9	3.8
USSR (former)	Not available														
Canada	5.3	21.9	4.6	25.0	28.2	12.4	2.6	6.0	10.7	2.9	0.9	17.2	8.3	51.2	2.9
Netherlands	10.8	32.2	9.9	19.6	10.8	15.8	0.9	8.0	3.0	16.1	4.2	3.6	25.3	35.1	4.7
Belgium/Luxembourg	8.6	41.3	7.6	13.2	11.5	12.0	5.7	2.7	8.1	7.9	7.1	3.6	20.0	45.5	5.0
Spain	8.8	30.6	11.6	21.9	16.8	10.2	0.0	10.0	1.0	6.7	7.5	4.0	17.0	52.0	1.7
Hong Kong	6.5	38.6	2.4	19.0	2.8	30.3	0.5	2.3	1.4	2.8	34.1	1.9	8.6	38.1	10.7
South Korea	3.9	43.8	12.4	30.8	5.3	3.6	0.3	2.9	0.2	1.4	30.9	1.0	7.5	52.1	4.0
China	Not available														
Switzerland	5.6	34.6	3.9	20.8	11.4	22.9	0.7	0.5	5.0	2.7	5.6	2.7	23.1	53.3	7.0
Singapore	5.4	25.1	13.8	32.6	8.3	13.3	1.5	4.7	0.4	3.9	5.1	2.7	23.4	57.5	2.4
Sweden	5.3	27.9	7.5	25.0	15.8	17.3	1.1	0.8	1.5	1.7	2.0	19.4	11.2	61.7	1.5
Australia	4.1	24.8	4.9	27.3	18.2	16.0	4.7	21.5	20.4	11.7	2.9	0.7	5.1	18.5	19.2
Austria	4.8	32.5	5.6	23.4	14.0	19.7	0.1	1.4	0.5	2.7	9.3	11.8	13.3	57.8	3.2
Denmark	9.5	35.5	7.0	19.4	10.8	15.2	2.7	9.8	1.4	21.5	5.0	3.7	12.8	39.8	6.1
Thailand (1987)	4.2	41.9	13.3	25.0	7.4	3.8	4.4	22.6	4.8	22.3	21.5	2.1	4.1	17.0	5.5
Finland	4.6	29.9	9.8	25.6	15.0	14.4	0.8	1.5	0.5	1.8	3.7	39.8	8.8	43.3	0.7
Mexico	13.2	37.1	3.8	27.3	6.3	11.4	0.7	9.8	34.6	3.3	2.6	1.8	9.8	37.2	0.9
Malaysia	9.0	33.0	5.3	39.2	6.2	7.0	0.3	20.2	15.3	12.6	5.6	6.3	4.6	34.0	1.4
Saudi Arabia	14.2	22.4	0.3	14.7	16.4	25.2	6.9	1.3	84.9	—	—	—	—	9.1	4.7
India (1987)	8.2	40.8	19.1	18.7	3.5	1.6	8.1	17.0	21.0	5.3	34.0	0.3	9.6	9.9	2.9
OTHER PACIFIC RIM COUNTRIES															
Indonesia	6.0	45.2	7.3	30.3	8.4	2.3	0.4	13.2	38.0	3.9	10.3	16.7	7.4	10.0	0.7
Philippines	7.3	35.9	13.1	15.0	5.1	2.6	20.9	11.2	5.8	12.2	8.0	5.1	6.2	18.7	32.8
New Zealand	6.7	29.7	5.7	21.8	19.2	16.2	0.7	17.4	1.4	37.5	10.6	7.7	6.9	16.7	1.9
Pakistan (1988)	14.8	35.0	14.1	24.6	7.6	3.5	0.3	22.1	0.5	9.9	61.4	0.1	1.1	2.8	2.2
Chile (1988)	4.0	32.1	12.1	27.0	14.0	8.6	2.1	15.2	12.8	11.3	0.8	8.9	3.7	46.6	0.8
Colombia	7.0	45.8	3.6	24.4	13.4	3.6	2.1	45.0	22.3	3.6	8.4	2.3	9.9	6.8	1.6
Bangladesh (1987)	29.4	36.0	13.6	11.7	5.5	3.3	0.4	24.1	0.0	1.1	70.8	0.2	1.6	1.9	0.4
Ecuador	8.0	44.8	4.1	23.6	12.3	6.6	0.6	42.0	44.0	6.0	0.5	0.9	5.3	1.1	0.2
Peru (1987)	16.6	38.8	4.0	25.8	9.4	5.3	0.1	10.2	25.0	14.4	10.7	0.2	17.3	20.1	2.1
Papua New Guinea (1987)	14.2	23.1	10.8	23.8	15.3	11.3	1.6	35.6	57.2	4.8	0.0	0.3	0.4	0.9	0.7
Panama	14.3	33.3	16.5	9.1	8.6	18.2	0.1	63.9	0.0	14.3	10.1	2.1	6.0	3.0	0.6
New Caledonia (1983)	20.8	16.5	22.9	9.2	11.0	19.6	0.1	0.7	15.7	0.9	0.1	0.2	0.5	70.9	11.0

SOURCE: United Nations, *1989 International Trade Statistics Yearbook*, Vol. 1, New York, 1991.

74. Imports and Exports, Principal Nations and Pacific Rim 1989

COUNTRY	($000 000 000) IMPORTS/EXPORTS	OCEANIA	AFRICA	CANADA	EUROPE (EX. USSR)	LATIN AMERICA	ASIA (EX. USSR)	USA	USSR (FORMER)
USA	493.2/363.2	1.2/2.7	3.1/2.1	18.0/12.3	21.5/27.1	10.6/10.7	43.9/31.6	—	0.2/1.2
Germany (West)	269.9/342.4	0.7/0.8	3.0/2.7	0.8/0.8	67.9/74.7	2.7/1.5	15.1/9.9	7.5/7.3	1.7/1.8
Japan	210.8/275.2	6.5/3.6	2.0/1.9	4.0/2.5	16.3/20.7	3.8/1.9	42.3/32.9	23.4/34.1	1.3/1.1
UK	197.7/152.5	1.2/2.3	2.1/3.6	1.8/2.3	65.7/59.6	1.4/1.0	15.4/15.6	10.8/13.1	0.7/0.7
France	192.5/178.9	0.8/1.0	4.9/7.4	0.7/0.9	68.7/70.3	2.0/1.4	11.9/9.7	7.6/6.6	1.4/1.0
Italy	152.9/138.5	0.8/1.0	6.9/4.8	0.7/1.1	70.0/69.0	2.6/1.7	10.5/11.1	5.6/8.6	2.4/1.8
USSR (former)	114.6/109.2	1.0/0.0	1.2/1.4	0.6/—	72.9/70.0	1.5/0.2	13.2/13.6	4.0/0.8	—
Canada	114.0/116.0	0.6/1.0	0.9/0.8	—	13.8/10.0	2.9/1.3	14.6/11.7	65.4/74.2	0.1/0.5
Netherlands	104.3/107.9	0.4/0.5	2.6/2.3	0.8/0.6	70.3/77.9	2.2/0.6	12.5/5.0	8.3/4.1	1.3/0.5
Belgium/Luxembourg	99.7/101.3	0.7/0.4	4.6/2.5	0.6/0.4	78.1/80.6	1.6/0.6	8.3/9.0	4.6/4.8	1.2/0.5
Spain	71.4/44.5	0.6/0.5	6.4/4.6	0.5/0.9	63.6/72.4	4.5/2.7	13.0/7.6	9.1/7.4	1.8/0.9
Hong Kong	72.2/73.1	1.2/2.2	0.8/1.5	0.5/2.1	12.5/18.3	1.0/0.6	75.4/48.7	8.3/25.3	0.1/0.1
South Korea	61.5/62.4	4.4/2.1	0.8/2.0	2.7/3.0	12.4/14.0	2.3/1.5	45.1/40.4	25.9/33.2	—
China	58.6/51.6	3.0/0.9	0.7/1.4	1.8/0.8	21.3/13.2	3.7/0.5	47.9/69.7	13.3/8.4	3.6/3.5
Switzerland	58.2/51.6	0.2/1.0	1.8/2.1	0.4/0.9	79.1/66.0	0.8/2.2	9.5/17.2	6.4/8.9	0.4/1.1
Singapore	52.2/44.7	1.9/4.2	0.9/1.9	0.5/0.9	15.1/15.3	1.0/0.6	62.9/52.5	17.1/23.4	0.3/0.4
Sweden	48.9/51.5	0.5/1.5	0.4/1.8	0.8/1.6	74.1/74.3	1.6/1.4	12.0/8.7	8.2/9.3	1.6/0.7
Australia	40.0/36.7	4.5/7.5	0.4/1.7	2.4/1.4	26.9/16.9	1.5/0.9	41.3/56.5	22.7/11.2	0.1/2.4
Austria	38.9/32.4	0.1/0.5	2.2/1.8	0.5/1.0	80.6/83.0	1.0/0.6	10.0/6.9	3.6/3.5	1.7/2.7
Denmark	26.7/28.1	0.2/0.7	0.9/1.8	0.4/0.6	74.5/73.0	1.6/0.7	11.2/9.5	6.3/5.0	0.8/0.9
Thailand	25.8/20.1	2.1/2.1	1.5/3.5	1.3/1.8	20.1/23.4	1.9/0.1	58.7/47.6	13.6/20.1	0.3/0.4
Finland	24.6/23.3	0.4/1.3	0.5/1.6	0.9/1.4	66.0/64.5	1.5/0.9	11.9/7.3	6.3/6.4	11.1/14.4
Mexico	23.6/22.8	0.5/0.2	0.3/0.4	1.6/1.2	15.5/12.2	3.0/3.2	6.6/8.0	70.4/70.0	0.0/0.2
Malaysia	22.5/25.1	5.3/2.7	0.5/0.7	1.3/0.8	15.1/15.6	1.7/0.8	57.8/61.4	17.9/17.4	0.3/0.6
Saudi Arabia	21.2/28.4	1.2/1.5	1.3/0.7	0.1/—	41.0/45.9	1.5/2.3	35.2/45.9	18.2/26.0	0.1/—
India	19.9/15.7	2.5/1.3	3.0/2.4	1.3/1.0	39.1/31.5	2.2/0.1	33.1/28.2	9.0/18.6	5.2/12.5
OTHER PACIFIC RIM COUNTRIES									
Indonesia	16.4/22.2	6.3/2.1	1.2/1.0	1.9/0.5	19.5/11.4	2.6/0.2	53.7/68.3	13.6/16.0	0.3/0.5
Philippines	10.7/7.7	5.1/2.4	1.1/0.3	1.0/1.5	14.6/18.4	2.0/1.0	54.6/40.7	21.2/35.7	0.4/0.3
New Zealand	9.0/9.0	21.6/22.0	0.4/0.8	2.0/1.7	22.8/19.5	1.3/2.0	34.5/36.5	16.8/13.2	0.2/2.0
Pakistan	7.1/4.6	2.2/1.9	1.1/4.3	1.5/1.6	31.8/34.9	1.2/0.1	48.7/44.1	13.0/11.2	0.4/2.0
Chile	6.7/8.2	0.5/0.5	4.5/0.7	2.3/0.6	27.1/42.4	28.7/13.0	14.6/23.1	21.2/18.3	0.3/—
Colombia	5.0/5.7	0.3/0.1	0.0/1.3	3.6/1.2	26.0/34.2	18.7/11.1	12.1/7.0	36.2/39.3	0.2/0.3
Bangladesh	3.5/1.3	1.7/1.6	1.6/5.7	5.7/2.1	18.7/30.0	0.8/0.9	61.2/24.7	9.1/31.9	1.2/3.1
Ecuador	1.9/2.4	0.7/0.4	1.9/0.5	2.3/0.2	26.3/9.8	20.7/13.3	11.7/5.4	33.9/60.6	0.3/0.2
Peru	1.8/3.6	2.4/0.2	1.3/0.6	2.2/0.7	28.6/14.7	31.5/7.3	7.4/12.3	25.9/16.1	0.1/0.9
Papua New Guinea	1.3/1.3	46.4/7.4	0.1/0.0	2.1/0.0	8.9/33.4	0.5/0.0	33.5/56.2	8.0/2.7	0.0/0.0
Panama	1.0/0.3	0.7/0.0	0.2/0.1	0.6/1.2	10.8/28.0	17.4/4.1	9.6/1.1	38.4/46.1	0.0/0.0
New Caledonia	0.8/0.7	10.3/5.2	0.0/0.0	0.0/0.0	64.6/65.6	0.0/0.0	12.9/22.3	4.9/6.6	0.0/0.0

SOURCE: United Nations, *1989 International Trade Statistics Yearbook*, Vol. 1, New York, 1991.

Demographics

REGION OR COUNTRY	POPULATION ESTIMATE MID-1992 (MILLIONS)	BIRTH RATE (PER 1 000 POP.)	DEATH RATE (PER 1 000 POP.)	NATURAL INCREASE (ANNUAL, %)	POPULATION "DOUBLING TIME" IN YEARS (AT CURRENT RATE)	POPULATION PROJECTED TO 2025 (MILLIONS)	INFANT MORTALITY RATE[a]	TOTAL FERTILITY RATE[b]	% POPULATION UNDER AGE 15/65 +	LIFE EXPECTANCY AT BIRTH MALE/FEMALE (YEARS)	URBAN POPULATION (%)	ADULT LITERACY MALE/FEMALE OR COMBINED 1985-1990	PER CAPITA GNP, 1990 (US$)	HUMAN DEVELOPMENT INDEX (HDI), 1992
WORLD	5 420	26	9	1.7	41	8 545	68	3.3	33/ 6	63/67	43	—	3 790	—
MORE DEVELOPED	1 224	14	9	0.5	148	1 392	18	1.9	21/12	71/78	73	—	17 900	—
LESS DEVELOPED	4 196	30	9	2.0	34	7 153	75	3.8	36/ 4	61/64	34	—	810	—
LESS DEVELOPED (EXCL. CHINA)	3 031	33	10	2.3	30	5 562	84	4.4	39/ 4	58/61	37	—	1 000	—
AFRICA	654	43	14	3.0	23	1 540	99	6.1	45/ 3	52/55	30	—	630	—
Northern Africa	147	35	8	2.6	27	274	72	4.8	42/ 4	59/62	43	—	1 070	—
Algeria	26.0	35	7	2.4	28	47.1	61	4.9	44/ 4	65/67	50	70/46	2 060	0.533
Egypt	55.7	32	7	2.4	28	103.1	73	4.4	41/ 4	58/61	45	63/34	600	0.385
Libya	4.5	37	7	3.0	23	9.3	64	5.2	50/ 2	65/70	76	75/50	—	0.659
Morocco	26.2	33	8	2.4	29	43.9	73	4.2	41/ 4	62/65	46	61/38	950	0.429
Sudan	26.5	45	14	3.1	22	57.3	87	6.5	46/ 2	52/53	20	43/12	—	0.157
Tunisia	8.4	27	6	2.1	33	13.4	44	3.4	38/ 5	65/66	53	62	1 420	0.582
Western Africa	182	47	17	3.0	23	449	111	6.7	46/ 3	48/50	23	—	410	—
Benin	5.0	49	19	3.1	23	12.8	88	7.1	46/ 3	45/49	39	32/16	360	0.111
Burkina Faso	9.6	50	17	3.3	21	26.0	121	7.2	48/ 4	51/52	18	28/ 9	330	0.074
Cape Verde	0.4	41	8	3.3	21	0.9	41	5.4	45/ 5	59/63	33	48	890	0.437
Côte d'Ivoire	13.0	50	14	3.6	19	39.3	92	7.4	48/ 3	52/55	43	67/40	730	0.289
Gambia	0.9	46	21	2.6	27	2.4	138	6.3	44/ 3	42/46	22	25	260	0.083
Ghana	16.0	44	13	3.2	22	35.4	86	6.4	45/ 3	52/56	32	70/51	390	0.310
Guinea	7.8	47	22	2.5	28	16.1	148	6.1	44/ 3	40/44	22	35/13	480	0.052
Guinea-Bissau	1.0	43	23	2.0	35	1.9	151	5.8	41/ 4	40/43	27	50/24	180	0.088
Liberia	2.8	47	15	3.2	22	8.3	144	6.8	46/ 4	53/56	44	50/29	—	0.227
Mali	8.5	52	22	3.0	23	21.7	113	7.3	47/ 4	43/46	22	41/24	270	0.081
Mauritania	2.1	46	18	2.8	25	5.0	122	6.5	44/ 3	46/49	41	47/21	500	0.141
Niger	8.3	52	20	3.2	22	24.3	124	7.1	49/ 3	43/46	15	40/17	310	0.078
Nigeria	90.1	46	16	3.0	23	216.2	114	6.5	45/ 2	48/49	16	62/40	370	0.241
Senegal	7.9	45	17	2.8	25	17.4	84	6.3	46/ 3	47/49	37	52/25	710	0.178
Sierra Leone	4.4	48	23	2.6	27	10.2	147	6.5	44/ 3	41/44	30	31/11	240	0.062
Togo	3.8	50	13	3.7	19	11.3	99	7.2	49/ 2	53/57	24	56/31	410	0.218
Eastern Africa	206	47	15	3.2	22	528	110	7.0	47/ 3	50/53	19	—	230	—
Burundi	5.8	47	15	3.2	21	14.9	111	7.0	46/ 3	50/54	5	61/40	210	0.165
Comoros	0.5	48	12	3.5	20	1.4	89	7.1	48/ 3	54/58	26	15	480	0.269
Djibouti	0.4	46	17	2.9	24	1.1	117	6.6	45/ 3	46/49	79	20	—	0.084
Ethiopia	54.3	47	20	2.8	25	140.2	139	7.5	46/ 3	46/48	12	—	120	0.173
Kenya	26.2	45	9	3.7	19	62.3	62	6.7	49/ 2	59/63	22	80/59	370	0.366
Madagascar	11.9	45	13	3.2	22	31.7	115	6.6	47/ 3	53/56	23	88/73	230	0.325
Malawi	8.7	53	18	3.5	20	23.1	137	7.7	48/ 3	48/50	15	41	200	0.166
Mauritius	1.1	21	7	1.5	48	1.4	20.4	2.2	30/ 5	65/72	41	83	2 250	0.793
Mozambique	16.6	45	18	2.7	26	35.6	136	6.3	44/ 3	46/49	23	45/21	80	0.153
Reunion	0.6	24	6	1.8	38	0.9	13	2.3	33/ 5	67/75	62	—	—	—
Rwanda	7.7	51	16	3.4	20	23.2	117	8.0	48/ 3	48/51	7	64/37	310	0.186
Somalia	8.3	49	19	2.9	24	17.8	127	6.6	46/ 3	44/48	24	27/ 9	150	0.088
Tanzania	27.4	50	15	3.5	20	77.9	105	7.1	48/ 3	49/54	21	93/88	120	0.268
Uganda	17.5	52	15	3.7	19	49.6	96	7.4	49/ 2	50/52	10	62/35	220	0.192
Zambia	8.4	51	13	3.8	18	24.2	76	7.2	49/ 2	51/54	49	81/65	420	0.315
Zimbabwe	10.3	41	10	3.1	22	22.6	61	5.6	45/ 3	58/61	26	74/60	640	0.397
Middle Africa	72	45	15	3.0	23	182	97	6.1	44/ 3	49/53	38	—	460	—
Angola	8.9	47	19	2.8	25	21.6	132	6.4	45/ 3	42/46	26	56/29	—	0.169
Cameroon	12.7	44	12	3.2	22	36.3	85	6.4	46/ 3	54/59	42	66/43	940	0.313

REGION OR COUNTRY	POPULATION ESTIMATE MID-1992 (MILLIONS)	BIRTH RATE (PER 1 000 POP.)	DEATH RATE (PER 1 000 POP.)	NATURAL INCREASE (ANNUAL, %)	POPULATION "DOUBLING TIME" IN YEARS (AT CURRENT RATE)	POPULATION PROJECTED TO 2025 (MILLIONS)	INFANT MORTALITY RATE[a]	TOTAL FERTILITY RATE[b]	% POPULATION UNDER AGE 15/65+	LIFE EXPECTANCY AT BIRTH MALE/FEMALE (YEARS)	URBAN POPULATION (%)	ADULT LITERACY MALE/FEMALE OR COMBINED 1985-1990	PER CAPITA GNP, 1990 (US$)	HUMAN DEVELOPMENT INDEX (HDI), 1992
Central African Republic	3.2	44	18	2.6	27	6.9	141	5.6	42/ 3	45/48	43	52/25	390	0.159
Chad	5.2	44	19	2.5	28	10.3	127	5.8	43/ 4	45/47	30	42/18	190	0.088
Congo	2.4	43	14	2.9	24	5.5	114	5.8	45/ 3	52/55	41	70/44	1 010	0.372
Equatorial Guinea	0.4	43	16	2.6	26	0.8	112	5.5	43/ 4	48/52	28	40	330	0.163
Gabon	1.1	41	16	2.5	28	1.8	99	5.2	33/ 6	51/54	43	74/49	3 220	0.545
Zaïre	37.9	46	14	3.1	22	98.2	83	6.1	43/ 4	50/54	40	84/61	230	0.262
Southern Africa	**47**	**35**	**8**	**2.7**	**26**	**106**	**57**	**4.6**	**40/ 4**	**60/66**	**52**	—	**2 390**	—
Botswana	1.4	40	9	3.1	23	3.3	45	4.8	45/ 3	55/62	24	84/65	2 040	0.534
Lesotho	1.9	41	12	2.9	24	4.4	95	5.8	43/ 4	53/62	19	—	470	0.423
Namibia	1.5	43	11	3.1	22	4.1	102	5.9	46/ 3	59/61	27	—	—	0.295
South Africa	41.7	34	8	2.6	26	92.0	52	4.5	40/ 4	61/67	56	—	2 520	0.674
Swaziland	0.8	44	12	3.2	22	2.2	101	6.2	46/ 3	51/59	23	—	820	0.458
ASIA	**3 207**	**26**	**9**	**1.8**	**39**	**4 998**	**68**	**3.2**	**33/ 5**	**63/66**	**31**	—	**1 680**	—
ASIA (EXCL. CHINA)	**2 042**	**30**	**10**	**2.0**	**34**	**3 407**	**81**	**3.9**	**36/ 4**	**60/63**	**34**	—	**2 520**	—
Western Asia	**139**	**36**	**8**	**2.8**	**24**	**313**	**63**	**4.7**	**41/ 4**	**64/68**	**62**	—	—	—
Bahrain	0.5	27	3	2.4	29	1.0	20	3.9	35/ 2	70/74	81	79/63	—	0.790
Cyprus	0.7	19	9	1.1	66	0.9	11	2.4	26/10	74/78	62	93/85	8 040	0.912
Iraq	18.2	45	8	3.7	19	51.9	67	7.0	45/ 3	66/68	73	70/49	—	0.589
Israel	5.2	21	6	1.5	45	8.0	8.7	2.9	31/ 9	75/78	91	79	10 970	0.939
Jordan	3.6	39	5	3.4	20	9.2	39	5.6	48/ 3	69/73	70	89/70	1 240	0.586
Kuwait	1.4	32	2	3.0	23	4.6	16	4.4	45/ 1	72/76	—	77/67	—	0.815
Lebanon	3.4	28	7	2.1	33	6.1	46	3.7	40/ 5	66/70	84	88/73	—	0.561
Oman	1.6	42	7	3.5	20	4.9	44	6.7	47/ 3	64/68	11	—	—	0.598
Qatar	0.5	27	2	2.5	28	0.9	26	4.5	28/ 1	69/74	90	40	15 860	0.802
Saudi Arabia	16.1	42	7	3.5	20	47.1	65	7.1	45/ 3	63/66	77	52	—	0.687
Syria	13.7	45	7	3.8	18	38.7	48	7.1	49/ 4	64/66	50	78/51	990	0.665
Turkey	59.2	29	7	2.2	32	98.1	59	3.6	35/ 4	64/69	59	90/71	1 630	0.671
United Arab Emirates	2.5	31	3	2.8	25	6.6	25	4.9	35/ 1	69/73	78	58/38	19 860	0.740
Yemen	10.4	51	17	3.5	20	29.9	124	7.5	49/ 3	48/51	25	47/21	—	0.232
Southern Asia	**1 231**	**33**	**11**	**2.2**	**31**	**2 151**	**95**	**4.3**	**38/ 4**	**58/58**	**26**	—	**440**	—
Afghanistan	16.9	48	22	2.6	27	48.5	172	6.9	46/ 4	41/42	18	44/14	—	0.065
Bangladesh	111.4	37	13	2.4	29	211.6	120	4.9	44/ 3	54/53	14	47/22	200	0.185
Bhutan	0.7	39	19	2.0	35	1.4	142	5.9	39/ 4	46/49	13	51/25	190	0.146
India	882.6	30	10	2.0	34	1 383.1	91	3.9	36/ 4	58/59	26	62/34	350	0.297
Iran	59.7	41	8	3.3	21	159.2	43	6.1	46/ 3	63/66	54	65/43	2 450	0.547
Nepal	19.9	42	17	2.5	28	40.8	112	6.1	42/ 3	50/50	8	38/13	170	0.168
Pakistan	121.7	44	13	3.1	23	281.4	109	6.1	44/ 4	56/57	28	47/21	380	0.305
Sri Lanka	17.6	21	6	1.5	46	24.0	19.4	2.4	35/ 4	68/73	22	93/84	470	0.651
Southeast Asia	**451**	**28**	**8**	**1.9**	**36**	**696**	**61**	**3.4**	**37/ 4**	**60/64**	**29**	—	—	—
Cambodia	9.1	38	16	2.2	32	13.4	127	4.5	36/ 3	47/50	13	48/22	—	0.178
Indonesia	184.5	26	8	1.7	40	278.2	70	3.0	37/ 4	58/63	31	84/62	560	0.491
Laos	4.4	46	17	2.9	24	9.8	112	6.8	44/ 4	48/51	16	—	200	0.240
Malaysia	18.7	30	5	2.5	27	34.9	29	3.6	37/ 4	69/73	35	87/70	2 340	0.789
Myanmar (Burma)	42.5	30	11	1.9	36	69.9	72	3.9	37/ 4	58/60	24	89/72	—	0.385
Philippines	63.7	32	7	2.4	28	100.8	54	4.1	39/ 4	63/66	43	90/90	730	0.600
Singapore	2.8	19	5	1.4	51	3.3	6.7	1.8	23/ 6	72/77	100	87	12 310	0.848
Thailand	56.3	20	6	1.4	48	76.4	39	2.4	34/ 4	64/69	18	96/90	1 420	0.685
Viet Nam	69.2	30	8	2.2	31	108.2	45	4.0	39/ 5	62/66	20	92/84	—	0.464
East Asia	**1 386**	**19**	**7**	**1.2**	**57**	**1 839**	**32**	**2.1**	**27/ 6**	**69/73**	**34**	—	**2 910**	—

REGION OR COUNTRY	POPULATION ESTIMATE MID-1992 (MILLIONS)	BIRTH RATE (PER 1 000 POP.)	DEATH RATE (PER 1 000 POP.)	NATURAL INCREASE (ANNUAL, %)	POPULATION "DOUBLING TIME" IN YEARS (AT CURRENT RATE)	POPULATION PROJECTED TO 2025 (MILLIONS)	INFANT MORTALITY RATE[a]	TOTAL FERTILITY RATE[b]	% POPULATION UNDER AGE 15/65 +	LIFE EXPECTANCY AT BIRTH MALE/FEMALE (YEARS)	URBAN POPULATION (%)	ADULT LITERACY MALE/FEMALE OR COMBINED 1985-1990	PER CAPITA GNP, 1990 (US$)	HUMAN DEVELOPMENT INDEX (HDI), 1992
China	1 165.8	20	7	1.3	53	1 590.8	34	2.2	28/ 6	68/71	26	84/62	370	0.612
Hong Kong	5.7	12	5	0.7	99	6.2	6.7	1.2	21/ 9	75/80	—	75	11 540	0.913
Japan	124.4	10	7	0.3	217	124.1	4.6	1.5	18/13	76/82	77	99/99	25 430	0.981
Korea, North	22.2	24	6	1.9	37	32.1	31	2.5	29/ 4	66/72	64	95	—	0.654
Korea, South	44.3	16	6	1.1	65	54.8	15	1.6	26/ 5	67/75	74	99/94	5 400	0.871
Mongolia	2.3	36	8	2.8	25	4.6	64	4.6	44/ 4	62/67	42	—	—	0.574
NORTH AMERICA	**283**	**16**	**8**	**0.8**	**89**	**363**	**9**	**2.0**	**21/12**	**72/79**	**75**	**—**	**21 580**	**—**
Canada	27.4	15	7	0.8	89	35.0	7.1	1.8	21/11	73/80	78	99	20 450	0.982
United States	255.6	16	9	0.8	89	327.5	9.0	2.0	22/13	72/79	75	99	21 700	0.976
LATIN AMERICA	**453**	**28**	**7**	**2.1**	**34**	**729**	**54**	**3.4**	**36/ 5**	**64/70**	**70**	**—**	**2 170**	**—**
Central America	**118**	**31**	**6**	**2.5**	**28**	**204**	**50**	**4.1**	**40/ 4**	**65/71**	**64**	**—**	**2 170**	**—**
Costa Rica	3.2	27	4	2.4	29	5.6	15.3	3.3	36/ 5	75/79	45	93/93	1 910	0.842
El Salvador	5.6	36	8	2.9	24	9.6	55	4.6	44/ 4	61/68	48	76/70	1 100	0.498
Guatemala	9.7	39	7	3.1	22	21.6	61	5.2	45/ 3	60/65	39	63/47	900	0.485
Honduras	5.5	40	8	3.2	22	11.5	69	5.6	46/ 3	62/66	44	76/71	590	0.473
Mexico	87.7	29	6	2.3	30	143.3	47	3.8	38/ 4	66/72	71	90/85	2 490	0.804
Nicaragua	4.1	38	8	3.1	23	8.2	61	5.0	47/ 4	59/65	57	78/78	—	0.496
Panama	2.4	24	5	1.9	37	3.7	21	2.9	35/ 5	71/75	53	88/88	1 830	0.731
Caribbean	**35**	**26**	**8**	**1.8**	**38**	**49**	**54**	**3.1**	**33/ 7**	**67/71**	**58**	**—**	**—**	**—**
Barbados	0.3	16	9	0.7	102	0.3	9.0	1.8	25/11	70/76	32	99/99	6 540	—
Cuba	10.8	18	6	1.1	62	12.9	11.1	1.9	23/ 9	74/78	73	95/93	—	0.732
Dominican Republic	7.5	30	7	2.3	30	11.4	61	3.6	39/ 3	66/69	58	85/82	820	0.595
Haiti	6.4	45	16	2.9	24	12.3	106	6.0	45/ 4	53/56	29	—	370	0.276
Jamaica	2.5	25	5	2.0	35	3.6	17	2.6	34/ 8	71/75	51	98/99	1 510	0.722
Martinique	0.4	18	6	1.2	59	0.5	9	2.0	22/ 9	74/81	82	—	—	—
Trinidad and Tobago	1.3	21	7	1.4	50	1.7	10.2	2.5	34/ 5	67/73	64	96/94	3 470	0.876
South America	**300**	**26**	**7**	**1.9**	**36**	**476**	**56**	**3.2**	**35/ 5**	**64/70**	**74**	**—**	**2 180**	**—**
Argentina	33.1	21	8	1.2	56	45.5	25.7	2.7	30/ 9	66/73	86	96/95	2 370	0.833
Bolivia	7.8	36	10	2.7	26	14.2	89	4.9	41/ 4	58/64	51	63	620	0.394
Brazil	150.8	26	7	1.9	37	237.2	69	3.1	35/ 5	62/68	74	83/80	2 680	0.739
Chile	13.6	23	6	1.8	39	19.8	17.1	2.7	31/ 6	71/76	85	94/93	1 940	0.863
Colombia	34.3	26	6	2.0	35	54.2	37	2.9	36/ 4	68/73	68	88/86	1 240	0.758
Ecuador	10.0	31	7	2.4	29	17.9	57	3.8	41/ 4	65/69	55	88/84	960	0.641
Guyana	0.8	25	7	1.8	39	1.2	52	2.6	33/ 4	61/67	35	97/94	370	0.539
Paraguay	4.5	34	7	2.7	25	9.2	34	4.7	40/ 4	65/69	43	92/88	1 110	0.637
Peru	22.5	31	9	2.2	32	37.4	76	4.0	39/ 4	60/63	70	92/79	1 160	0.600
Suriname	0.4	26	6	2.0	34	0.7	31	2.8	34/ 4	67/72	48	93/92	3 050	0.749
Uruguay	3.1	18	10	0.8	83	3.7	20.4	2.4	26/12	68/75	89	97/96	2 560	0.880
Venezuela	18.9	30	5	2.5	27	34.6	24.2	3.6	38/ 4	67/73	84	87/90	2 560	0.824
EUROPE	**511**	**12**	**10**	**0.2**	**338**	**516**	**11**	**1.6**	**20/14**	**71/78**	**75**	**—**	**12 990**	**—**
Northern Europe	**93**	**14**	**11**	**0.3**	**242**	**97**	**9**	**1.9**	**19/15**	**72/79**	**83**	**—**	**17 930**	**—**
Denmark	5.2	13	12	0.1	753	4.8	7.5	1.7	17/16	72/78	85	99	22 090	0.953
Estonia	1.6	14	12	0.2	365	1.8	25	2.0	22/11	66/75	71	—	—	—
Finland	5.0	13	10	0.3	224	4.8	5.8	1.8	19/13	71/79	62	100	26 070	0.953
Iceland	0.3	19	7	1.2	58	0.3	5.9	2.3	26/11	75/80	90	99	21 150	0.958
Ireland	3.5	15	9	0.6	122	3.3	8.0	2.2	27/11	71/77	56	99	9 550	0.921
Latvia	2.7	14	13	0.1	630	3.0	19	2.0	21/12	65/75	71	—	—	—
Lithuania	3.7	15	11	0.4	158	4.4	18	2.0	23/11	67/76	69	—	—	—
Norway	4.3	14	11	0.4	193	4.7	6.9	1.9	19/16	73/80	71	100	23 120	0.978

REGION OR COUNTRY	POPULATION ESTIMATE MID-1992 (MILLIONS)	BIRTH RATE (PER 1 000 POP.)	DEATH RATE (PER 1 000 POP.)	NATURAL INCREASE (ANNUAL, %)	POPULATION "DOUBLING TIME" IN YEARS (AT CURRENT RATE)	POPULATION PROJECTED TO 2025 (MILLIONS)	INFANT MORTALITY RATE[a]	TOTAL FERTILITY RATE[b]	% POPULATION UNDER AGE 15/65 +	LIFE EXPECTANCY AT BIRTH MALE/FEMALE (YEARS)	URBAN POPULATION (%)	ADULT LITERACY MALE/FEMALE OR COMBINED 1985-1990	PER CAPITA GNP, 1990 (US$)	HUMAN DEVELOPMENT INDEX (HDI), 1992
Sweden	8.7	14	11	0.3	210	9.0	6.0	2.1	18/18	75/80	83	99	23 860	0.976
United Kingdom	57.8	14	11	0.3	257	61.0	7.9	1.8	19/16	73/79	90	99	16 070	0.962
Western Europe	**178**	**12**	**10**	**0.2**	**398**	**174**	**7**	**1.6**	**18/14**	**73/79**	**82**	—	—	—
Austria	7.9	12	11	0.1	495	8.2	7.4	1.5	17/15	73/79	55	98	19 240	0.950
Belgium	10.0	13	11	0.2	347	9.3	7.9	1.6	18/15	72/79	95	98	15 440	0.950
France	56.9	13	9	0.4	169	58.6	7.3	1.8	20/14	73/81	73	99	19 480	0.969
Germany	80.6	11	11	−0.1	(—)	73.7	7.5	1.4	16/15	72/78	90	99	—	0.955
Luxembourg	0.4	13	10	0.3	239	0.4	7.4	1.6	17/13	71/78	78	100	28 770	0.929
Netherlands	15.2	13	9	0.5	147	16.7	6.8	1.6	18/13	74/80	89	99	17 330	0.968
Switzerland	6.9	13	10	0.3	231	6.9	6.8	1.6	16/15	74/81	60	99	32 790	0.977
Eastern Europe	**96**	**13**	**11**	**0.2**	**369**	**103**	**17**	**1.9**	**23/11**	**67/75**	**63**	—	**2 080**	—
Bulgaria	8.9	12	12	−0.0	(—)	8.6	14.8	1.7	20/13	68/75	68	95	2 210	0.865
Czechoslovakia	15.7	14	12	0.2	347	17.2	11.3	2.0	23/12	68/75	76	99	3 140	0.897
Hungary	10.3	12	14	−0.2	(—)	10.4	15.4	1.8	20/14	65/74	63	99	2 780	0.893
Poland	38.4	14	11	0.4	187	42.7	15.9	2.0	25/10	67/76	61	98	1 700	0.874
Romania	23.2	12	11	0.1	578	24.4	25.7	1.6	23/11	67/73	54	98	1 640	0.733
Southern Europe	**144**	**11**	**9**	**0.2**	**344**	**141**	**12**	**1.5**	**20/13**	**72/79**	**68**	—	**12 860**	—
Albania	3.3	25	6	1.9	36	4.5	30.8	3.0	33/ 5	70/76	36	75	—	0.791
Bosnia-Hercegovina[e]	4.2	14	6	0.8	90	4.3	15.2	1.7	28/ 6	69/75	36	—	—	—
Croatia[e]	4.6	12	11	0.1	1 386	4.8	10.0	1.7	21/12	68/76	51	—	—	—
Greece	10.3	10	9	0.1	990	10.0	10.0	1.5	19/14	73/78	58	98/99	6 000	0.791
Italy	58.0	10	9	0.1	1 386	51.9	8.6	1.3	17/14	73/80	72	98/96	16 850	0.901
Macedonia[e]	1.9	17	7	1.0	70	2.3	35.3	2.1	29/ 7	70/74	54	—	—	—
Malta	0.4	15	8	0.7	92	0.4	11.3	2.0	23/11	74/78	85	83	6 630	0.922
Portugal	10.5	11	10	0.1	533	10.5	11.0	1.4	21/13	71/78	30	89/82	4 890	0.854
Slovenia[e]	1.9	13	10	0.3	267	2.2	8.9	1.6	23/11	69/77	49	—	—	—
Spain	38.6	10	9	0.2	433	39.3	7.6	1.3	20/13	73/80	91	97/93	10 920	0.916
Yugoslavia[f]	10.0	15	9	0.5	131	11.0	24.4	2.1	24/ 9	69/74	47	97/88	—	0.857
FORMER USSR[d]	**284**	**17**	**10**	**0.7**	**104**	**362**	**39**	**2.2**	**26/ 9**	**65/74**	**66**	**99**	—	—
Armenia	3.5	24	7	1.8	40	5.0	35	2.9	30/ 5	69/75	68	—	—	—
Azerbaijan	7.1	26	6	2.0	36	11.4	45	2.7	33/ 5	67/74	53	—	—	—
Belarus	10.3	14	11	0.3	217	11.5	20	1.9	23/10	67/76	67	—	—	—
Georgia	5.5	17	9	0.9	80	6.5	33	2.2	25/ 9	68/76	56	—	—	—
Kazakhstan	16.9	22	8	1.4	50	26.8	44	2.7	32/ 6	64/73	58	—	—	—
Kyrgyzstan	4.5	29	7	2.2	31	8.7	35	3.7	37/ 5	64/72	38	—	—	—
Moldova	4.4	18	10	0.8	88	5.8	35	2.3	28/ 8	66/72	48	—	—	—
Russia	149.3	14	11	0.2	301	170.7	30	1.9	23/10	64/75	74	—	—	—
Tajikistan	5.5	38	6	3.2	22	12.2	73	5.0	43/ 4	67/72	31	—	—	—
Turkmenistan	3.9	34	7	2.7	26	6.8	93	4.2	41/ 4	62/68	45	—	—	—
Ukraine	52.1	13	12	0.1	1 155	52.9	22	1.9	22/12	66/75	68	—	—	—
Uzbekistan	21.3	33	6	2.7	25	43.1	64	4.0	41/ 4	66/72	40	—	—	—
OCEANIA	**28**	**20**	**8**	**1.2**	**57**	**39**	**33**	**2.6**	**26/ 9**	**69/75**	**71**	—	**13 190**	—
Australia	17.8	15	7	0.8	83	23.9	8.0	1.9	22/11	73/80	85	99	17 080	0.971
Fiji	0.8	27	7	2.0	35	1.1	20	3.1	38/ 3	62/60	39	80	1 770	0.713
New Zealand	3.4	18	8	1.0	71	4.0	7.6	2.1	23/11	72/78	84	99	12 680	0.947
Papua-New Guinea	3.9	34	11	2.3	31	7.3	99	5.4	40/ 3	53/55	13	32	860	0.321
Solomon Islands	0.4	41	5	3.6	20	0.8	32	6.3	47/ 3	60/61	9	60	580	—

[a] Infant deaths per 1000 live births.
[b] Average number of children born to a woman during her lifetime.
[c] The Human Development Index (HDI) is a measure of human development calculated using life expectancy, educational attainment, and per capita income. The scale ranges from 0 (low) to 1 (high).
[d] Estonia, Latvia, and Lithuania are shown under Northern Europe.
[e] Former republics of Yugoslavia.
[f] On 27 April 1992, Serbia and Montenegro formed a new state, the Federal Republic of Yugoslavia.
— indicates data unavailable or inapplicable.
(—) indicates countries where the natural increase is negative.

214

Definitions

Mid-1992 Population: Estimates are based on a recent census or on official national data or on UN, US Census Bureau, or World Bank projections. The effects of refugee movements, large numbers of foreign workers, and population shifts due to contemporary political events are taken into account to the extent possible.

Birth and Death Rates: These rates are often referred to as "crude rates" since they do not take a population's age structure into account. Thus, crude death rates in more developed countries, with a relatively large proportion of older persons, are often higher than those in less developed countries.

Rate of Natural Increase (RNI): Birth rate minus the death rate, implying the annual rate of population growth without regard for migration. Expressed as a percentage.

Population "Doubling Time": The number of years until the population will double assuming a *constant* rate of natural increase (RNI). Based upon the *unrounded* RNI, this column provides an indication of potential growth associated with a given RNI. It is not intended to forecast the actual doubling of any population.

Population in 2025: Population projections are based on reasonable assumptions on the future course of fertility, mortality, and migration. Projections are based on official country projections, or on series issued by the UN, the US Bureau of the Census, World Bank, or PRB projections.

Infant Mortality Rate: The annual number of deaths of infants under age one year per 1000 live births. Rates shown with decimals are completely registered national statistics, while those without are estimates from sources cited above. Rates shown in italics are based upon less than 50 annual infant deaths and, as a result, are subject to considerable yearly variability.

Total Fertility Rate (TFR): The average number of children a woman will have assuming that current age-specific birth rates will remain constant throughout her childbearing years (usually considered to be ages 15-49).

Population Under Age 15/Age 65+: The percentage of the total population in those age groups, often considered the "dependent ages."

Note

This table lists all geopolitical entities with populations of 150 000 or more and all members of the UN. These include sovereign states, dependencies, overseas departments, and some territories whose status or boundaries may be undetermined or in dispute. *More developed countries*, following the UN classification, comprise all of Europe and North America, plus Australia, Japan, New Zealand, and the former USSR. All other regions are classified as *less developed*.

Sources: The Human Development Index was compiled by the United Nations Development Program, *Human Development Report 1992*, (New York: Oxford University Press, 1992); Adult Literacy data are from the United Nations Development Program, *Human Development Report 1991* (New York: Oxford University Press, 1991); all other data is from the *1992 World Population Data Sheet*, Population Reference Bureau, 1875 Connecticut Avenue NW, Suite 520, Washington, DC 20009.